Administrative Law
—∞—
Cases and Materials

Administrative Law

—∞—

Cases and Materials

J. BEATSON
Fellow of Merton College, Oxford

M. H. MATTHEWS
Fellow of University College, Oxford

CLARENDON PRESS · OXFORD
1983

Oxford University Press, Walton Street, Oxford OX2 6DP

London Glasgow New York Toronto
Delhi Bombay Calcutta Madras Karachi
Kuala Lumpur Singapore Hong Kong Tokyo
Nairobi Dar es Salaam Cape Town
Melbourne Auckland

and associated companies in
Beirut Berlin Ibadan Mexico City Nicosia

Oxford is a trade mark of Oxford University Press

Published in the United States
by Oxford University Press, New York

Introductory Material, Selection, and Notes © J. Beatson and M. H. Matthews 1983

British Library Cataloguing in Publication Data

Beatson, J.
Administrative law.
1. Administrative law – England
– Cases
I. Title II. Matthews, M. H.
344.202'6'0264   KD4878
ISBN 0-19-825340-0
ISBN 0-19-825341-9 Pbk

Library of Congress Cataloguing in Publication Data
Beatson, J.
Administrative Law.
Includes index.
1. Administrative law – Great Britain – Cases.
I. Matthews, M. H. (Martin Hubie) II. Title.
KD4878.B43   1983   342.41'06   83-4012
ISBN 0-19-825340-0   344.1026
ISBN 0-19-825341-9 (pbk.)

Typeset by Oxford Verbatim Limited
Printed in Great Britain by
Thomson Litho Ltd. (East Kilbride)

PREFACE

Our aim in preparing these materials has been to cater for Administrative Law courses in which judicial control of the administration forms a central part while, at the same time, introducing the student to the way administrative bodies work in practice – the 'administrative process' approach to the subject. Both the nature of the subject-matter and constraints on the length of the book have meant that we have not been able to include as much material on the administrative process as we would have liked. The main problem is that dealing with such material tends to a greater involvement with the substantive law of a particular context than is possible or even desirable in a collection of materials on the general principles of Administrative Law. The choice is either to concentrate on one area – with obvious dangers of distorting the general picture – or to court the greater danger of a *pot pourri* of points divorced from their context. The wealth of material in the area of social security has meant that, to some extent, we have concentrated on that in dealing with the administrative process. But in view of our wish to illustrate the general principles of Administrative Law, we have selected material which we think will be helpful in evaluating (*a*) the doctrines imposed by the courts, for instance the requirement that discretion should not be fettered by rules, (*b*) suggestions for reforms, for instance that legal aid be available in tribunals, and (*c*) the relative utility of judicial review and other methods of control, such as parliamentary supervision in the case of delegated legislation.

Although we have included Notes to the extracts, this book is meant to be used together with a textbook. We hope that it can be used with any of the Administrative Law textbooks. We have, however, broadly adopted the structure and arrangement used in Professor H. W. R. Wade's *Administrative Law* in the hope that it will be particularly useful to students who use that book. Not all the topics that are covered in the textbooks are directly transferrable to the casebook format, and we have taken the view that introductory material and descriptions of the types of administrative authority and variety of administrative functions are most appropriately dealt with in a textbook. Much of the material in Parts I and II of Professor Wade's book is of this nature and is not dealt with by us, although we do refer to it in the Notes. We have, however, included material on the Crown and Crown service in Ch. 14, material on land use planning in Ch. 17, and a separate chapter on the Parliamentary Commissioner for Administration (Ch. 18) will be found in the section on Legislative and Adjudicative Procedures. Restrictions of space have meant that material on the local ombudsman has been omitted. While this is a loss, we feel that the chapter on the Parliamentary Commissioner suffices to show the way ombudsmen work and the advantages and disadvantages of the institution for dealing with maladministration. It

will also be noted that we have not included a specific section on the classification of functions, but deal with this in the General Introduction where we
refer the reader to cases extracted which deal with the question.

The fact that this is a casebook rather than a textbook has led to some
rearrangement. In the section on Discretionary Power we have departed from
Professor Wade's arrangement to a greater extent than elsewhere because we
thought it would be useful to have a general introductory chapter to the topic
(Ch. 4). We thought that in a casebook the detailed discussion of the judicial
review of discretionary power in Chs. 5 and 6 (Retention and Abuse of
Discretion) would be clarified by extracts containing a statement of basic
principles of the sort found at pp. 347–59 of Professor Wade's book. Some
other changes in the order of the material will be found in the chapter on
abuse of discretion. More generally, note also that the material on 'acting
fairly' is dealt with at the end of Ch. 8 (The Right to a Fair Hearing), the
material on estoppel is all in Ch. 5 (Retention of Discretion), that on failure to
state reasons is concentrated in Ch. 1 (The Legal Nature of Powers) and
discussion of the distinction between law and fact is in Ch. 2 (Jurisdiction
over Law and Fact) rather than in Ch. 17 (Statutory Tribunals). In these cases
and indeed quite generally we have used headings and the titles of extracts as
cross-references to indicate the various contexts in which a particular extract
is relevant.

In the area of remedies the particularly fluid state of the law since the recent
reforms has caused problems. After the manuscript had been submitted, the
decision of the House of Lords in *O'Reilly* v. *Mackman* was reported. We
were able to retrieve the manuscript and, under pressure of time, to insert
extracts from Lord Diplock's speech in Ch. 10 and to take some account of
the implications of this important decision in other parts of the book. At that
stage, it was, however, not possible to deal in the body of the book with the
distinction between 'public' law and 'private' law which that case has made
particularly important; but the publishers kindly allowed us to do this in a
short Appendix. As will be seen, there are some difficulties with the distinction and although it had appeared in the case law before *O'Reilly* v. *Mackman*,
for instance, in *Anns* v. *Merton L.B.C.*, it was less important. For those
reasons, we referred to 'Administrative Law' rather than 'Public Law' in the
body of the book. Moreover, in respect of some topics, such as the availability
of 'ordinary' remedies (Ch. 9), we have taken the view that it is too early to
predict the precise effect of *O'Reilly's* case with confidence and have kept
material that may in the event turn out to be no longer apposite in a book on
Administrative Law, although, as mentioned above, some changes have been
made. For example, we did decide to delete the extracts from *Punton (No. 2)*.
Before the decision in *O'Reilly* v. *Mackman*, we had taken the view that
despite the introduction of the application for judicial review, enabling an
applicant to seek either a prerogative remedy or declaratory relief by one
procedural form, and the fact that errors of law were more likely to be found
to be jurisdictional (see p. 53 *infra*), it was not altogether clear that the
controversy about the availability of declaratory relief for non-jurisdictional

errors of law on the face of the record – the *Punton (No. 2)* problem – was no longer a live issue: see for instance the reasoning in *Re Tillmire Common, Heslington* [1982] 2 All E.R. 615 at p. 622. However, the fact that the application for judicial review is now for most purposes the exclusive procedure in 'public' law cases made it clear to us that we could no longer justify an extract from *Punton (No. 2)*. We have therefore only dealt with it in a Note.

Many friends and colleagues have helped us in the preparation of these materials. We owe particular debts to Tony Honoré for suggesting the idea, to Professor Wade for his encouragement and for kindly letting us see the proofs of the 5th edition of his book, to David Williams for reading the entire manuscript and for his valuable comments, to Eric Barendt, Peter Cane, Paul Craig, David Pannick and Adrian Zuckerman for help and suggestions on specific points and to Jane Macdonald for preparing the Tables and the Index. We, of course, remain responsible for our mistakes and misjudgments. We also owe debts of a different kind to Adam Hodgkin and the Oxford University Press for forbearance and almost limitless patience, and to our families for their cheerful tolerance of us during the preparation of the book.

We have endeavoured to take account of cases reported and material available before July 1982 although, as well as the House of Lords decision in *O'Reilly* v. *Mackman*, we managed to take some account of *Chief Constable of the North Wales Police* v. *Evans*. We were also able to include some cases at the proofs stage. The Appendix contains short notes on *R*. v. *B.B.C.*, *ex p. Lavelle*; *Davy* v. *Spelthorne B.C.*; *R*. v. *Secretary of State for the Home Department, ex p. Khawaja*; *R*. v. *Knightsbridge Crown Court, ex p. The Aspinall Curzon Ltd.*; *R*. v. *Boundary Commission, ex p. Foot*; *R*. v. *I.R.C., ex p. Preston*; *R*. v. *Rochdale M.B.C., ex p. Cromer Ring Mill Ltd.*; *Attorney General for Hong Kong* v. *Ng Yuen Shiu*; *Cheall* v. *A.P.E.X.* and *Air Canada* v. *Secretary of State for Trade* (No 2). Unfortunately it did not prove possible to take into account the Health and Social Services and Social Security Adjudications Act 1983 which received the Royal Assent on 13 May 1983. When in force, this Act will, *inter alia*, provide for adjudication officers who will perform the functions of insurance officers appointed under the Social Security Act 1975, benefit officers appointed under the Supplementary Benefits Act 1976, and supplement officers appointed under the Family Income Supplements Act 1970. (See p. 546 n. 9.) Of particular importance to this book, since it contains many references to supplementary benefits appeal tribunals, is the provision to be found in para. 2 of Sch. 8 to the Act. This establishes social security appeal tribunals which will take over the functions of local tribunals under the Social Security Act 1975 and of appeal tribunals under the Supplementary Benefits Act 1976. References to supplementary benefits appeal tribunals will in particular be found in Chs. 4, 5, and 16.

Oxford   J.B.
1 June 1983   M.H.M.

Acknowledgements

We wish to express our gratitude to the following for permission to reproduce copyright material:

the Controller of Her Majesty's Stationary Office for permission to include extracts from official publications; the Incorporated Council of Law Reporting for England and Wales for extracts from the *Law Reports* and the *Weekly Law Reports*; Butterworth & Co. Ltd. for extracts from the *All England Law Reports*; Butterworth Pty Ltd. for an extract from the *Australian Law Reports*; the Canadian Bar Review for an extract from "Delegatus non potest delegare" by Professor John Willis; the Cornell International Law Journal; George Allen & Unwin for extracts from *Administrative Tribunals* by R. E. Wraith and P. G. Hutchesson; Charles Knight & Co. Ltd. for extracts from the *Local Government Reports*; the Law Book Co. Ltd. for extracts from the *Commonwealth Law Reports* and *Liability of the Crown* by P. W. Hogg; the Modern Law Review for an extract from "Appeals, Principles and Pragmatism in Natural Justice" by M. J. Elliott; Professor David Donnison and New Society for an extract from "Against Discretion" by Professor David Donnison; the New Zealand Council of Law Reporting for an extract from the *New Zealand Law Reports*; Routledge & Kegan Paul Ltd. for an extract from *Representation and Administrative Tribunals* by Anne Frost and Coral Howard; Sweet & Maxwell Ltd. for extracts from the *Law Quarterly Review* ("Representations by Public Bodies" by P. P. Craig), *Public Law* ("The New Face of Judicial Review" by L. Blom-Cooper, "Natural Justice: Substance & Shadow" by D. H. Clark and "Comment" by P. Cane), the *Property & Compensation Reports* and S. A. de Smith, *Judicial Review of Administrative Action*; the University of Toronto Law Journal for an extract from "Fairness: The New Natural Justice" by D. J. Mullan.

CONTENTS

Part IV. Remedies and Liability

9. ORDINARY REMEDIES   289

10. PREROGATIVE REMEDIES   307

TABLE OF STATUTES

(References in bold type denote reproduction of the text of the Act)

TABLE OF CASES

(References in bold type denote reproduction of a report)

PART I
Powers and Jurisdiction

1

THE LEGAL NATURE OF POWERS

GENERAL INTRODUCTION

Historically the judicial control of administrative action has been based on the doctrine of ultra vires. As administrative power is derived power (usually, but not always, from statute), it is limited to a defined area and action outside that is void and of no effect. The role of the courts is to keep administrative bodies within their allocated authority or jurisdiction and the constitutional justification for so doing is Parliamentary intent. No express authority is needed for the court to exercise its inherent power to supervise the legality of administrative action. On the other hand the ultra vires doctrine, or jurisdictional principle as it is sometimes called, does mean that as a general rule administrative action within the defined limits will not be interfered with by the court. The merits of a particular decision will not concern the court provided the decision is within the administrative body's jurisdiction. The court is not a court of appeal which considers the correctness of a decision but a supervisory court reviewing legality.

There are good policy reasons for supporting a cautious approach to judicial review. These include the need to encourage and recognize administrative expertise within a particular area, the non-adjudicative nature of many administrative decisions, and the need to ensure that decision-making be informal, cheap, and relatively speedy. Whenever there is judicial review the decision of a relatively expert body may be invalidated by the decision of a generalist court. For this reason, as a broad rule, it is suggested that judicial review will be appropriate where there is a danger that administrative specialization has meant that the administrators have neglected general values of the legal system: see Hogg, (1974) 20 McGill L.J. 157; Arthurs, (1979) 17 Osgoode H.L.J. 1. Limits on administrative power may be express (e.g. *R.* v. *Fulham, Hammersmith & Kensington Rent Tribunal, ex p. Zerek*, p. 47 *infra*) or implied by general principles of statutory construction (e.g. *Padfield's* case, p. 164 *infra*). The court may consider findings of fact or law, the exercise of discretion or procedural issues (such as the right to a hearing), but all these are analysed in terms of vires or jurisdiction. The important thing to remember is that however wide a power may seem it will be limited at some point. On the constitutional foundations of the powers of the courts, see Wade, *Administrative Law*, 5th edn., Ch. 2 (hereafter Wade) and p. 47 *infra*. Cf. Galligan, (1982) 2 Ox. J. Leg. Stud. 257 at pp. 263 and 266.

This, then, is the general theory upon which judicial control is based, but it must be qualified. First, no satisfactory test has been formulated to determine whether a particular issue is jurisdictional or merely goes to the merits. This means that the jurisdictional principle is an elastic one and the distinction between 'review' and 'appeal' is wafer-thin at times: see *Anisminic Ltd.* v. *Foreign Compensation Commission*, p. 38 *infra*, and *Pearlman* v. *Harrow School*, p. 53 *infra*.

Secondly, the variety of bodies and functions within the administrative system must be considered. Not all bodies are treated in the same way: contrast the treatment of a taxing power in *Commissioner of Customs and Excise* v. *Cure & Deeley Ltd.*, p. 511 *infra*, and *Congreve* v. *Home Office* [1976] Q.B. 629 with the courts' attitude to the administration of supplementary benefits, p. 79 *infra*. The general theory must, therefore, take account of the relevant statutory and factual context and of the fact that different interests will not be seen as needing exactly the same type of protection by the courts.

This has, however, not always been the case and at times the courts have appeared to apply distinctions based on the classification of the bureaucratic function in question as 'judicial', 'quasi-judicial', 'legislative', or 'administrative' in a somewhat rigid manner. Thus, until the decision in *Ridge* v. *Baldwin*, p. 214 *infra*, in 1964 the development of the principles of natural justice (the right to be heard by an unbiased tribunal) was hampered by the requirement that, if the principles were to apply, the decision-making body had to be exercising a 'judicial' or 'quasi-judicial' function coupled with a restrictive interpretation of what constituted a 'quasi-judicial' function. This has now changed and a similar process may well be taking place in respect of the distinction between 'legislative' and 'administrative' functions: see for instance *Re Toohey*; *ex. p. Northern Land Council*, p. 505 *infra*, and Note 1, p. 518 *infra*. Although it is undoubtedly true that distinctions based on the classification of functions are of less practical importance today, *R.* v. *Secretary of State for the Environment, ex p. Ostler*, p. 385 *infra*, *Re Racal Communications Ltd.*, p. 57 *infra*, *Barnard* v. *National Dock Labour Board*, p. 131 *infra*, and some of the modern natural justice cases show that the distinctions should not be neglected.

It should be remembered, however, that the classification of a function is not made in the abstract but for a particular purpose. One example of this is provided by comments on the nature of the Foreign Compensation Commission, the body considered in the leading case of *Anisminic Ltd.* v. *Foreign Compensation Commission*, pp. 38 and 374 *infra*. Thus, in the context of a statutory provision purporting to restrict judicial review of a Minister's decision to acquire land compulsorily, the decision in *Anisminic* was distinguished *inter alia* because the Foreign Compensation Commission was said to be 'a truly judicial body' (*R.* v. *Secretary of State for the Environment, ex p. Ostler*, p. 388 *infra*). However, when considering the scope of review over subordinate courts *Anisminic* was said to be 'concerned only with decisions of administrative tribunals' (*Re Racal Communications Ltd.*, p. 58 *infra*). It will be seen that the courts have classified functions for a wide variety of purposes. Apart from the scope of the principles of natural justice, some remedies (certiorari and prohibition) have been said to lie only to bodies exercising 'judicial' or 'quasi-judicial' functions (p. 308 *infra*), certain acts are subject to a statutory requirement of publication if they are 'legislative' but not if they are 'administrative' (p. 490 *infra*), and the rule prohibiting the subdelegation of powers is more strictly applied to 'legislative' and 'judicial' powers than to 'administrative' ones (p. 132 and 494 *infra*).

Most confusion has been caused by the term 'judicial'. Rubinstein (*Jurisdiction and Illegality*, p. 14), states that '[t]he truth of the matter is that "judicial" has no definite uniform meaning. It is indeed chameleon hued and changes its meaning according to the various circumstances in which it is being employed. As long as the various meanings are distinctly kept apart, misunderstandings (but not inconvenience) may be averted.' Subject to this caveat, the general conclusion in de Smith's *Judicial Review of Administrative Action*, 4th. edn., p. 89 (hereafter de Smith) is a useful summary of those acts that are likely to be classified as 'judicial':

Judicial acts may be identified by reference to their formal, procedural, or substantive characteristics, or by a combination of any of them. An act may be judicial because it declares and interprets pre-existing rights, or because it changes those rights provided that the power to change them is not unfettered. A duty to act judicially in conformity with natural justice may be inferred from the impact of an administrative act or decision on individual rights. Although sometimes used in a narrow sense, the term 'judicial' in cases involving review by certiorari and prohibition has generally been used in a very wide sense and now seems to have been dropped altogether as a requirement for the availability of those remedies. In natural justice cases, variations in linguistic usage have been particularly spectacular and frequently puzzling; but it is generally more profitable to concentrate on what the court has done than on what it has said.

In 1932, the *Report of the Committee on Ministers' Powers*, Cmd. 4060, attempted to define judicial and quasi-judicial decisions and to distinguish them from administrative decisions, but for a critical appraisal of the Committee's endeavours see Griffith and Street, *Principles of Administrative Law*, 5th edn., p. 141. Guidance as to what the courts have *in a particular context* regarded as a judicial or administrative function can be found in the extracts in this and later chapters and in particular from the cases cited at p. 4 *supra*. For further discussion of the classification of functions, see de Smith, Ch. 2; Wade, pp. 449–52, 463–4 and 551–5; Franks Report, paras. 262–74, p. 585 *infra*.

The third qualification to the general theory of judicial control is that, whereas it states that there must be a limit to all powers, some powers are so broad that, in practice, they are unreviewable whatever the theoretical position might be. Subjectively-worded powers which have sometimes been held reviewable only for bad faith (p. 190 *infra*) and powers held unreviewable because the issue is not justiciable (p. 122 *infra*) are two examples of this.

Finally, the autonomy of administrative bodies acting within jurisdiction is subject to two exceptions. These are errors of law 'on the face of the record' (p. 64 *infra*) and cases in which there is a statutory right of appeal, such as that conferred by s. 13 of the Tribunals and Inquiries Act 1971, p. 64 *infra*. The number of bodies from which such an appeal lies is now sufficiently large (see p. 558 *infra* and for a complete list see the table in Wade, p. 824) to have led some commentators to treat 'error of law' rather than jurisdictional review as the core of administrative law (see, for instance, the approach of Evans, Janisch, Mullan and Risk, *Administrative Law: Cases, Text and Materials*, pp. ii and 335–6, but cf. Wade, p. 36).

This part of the book considers in detail the principles utilized by courts in interpreting statutory powers. The intellectual need for such organizing principles is clear. However, when reading what follows it is worth asking whether the broadening scope of judicial review has meant that the principles are now so open-textured that they are dangerously uncertain and open to instrumental manipulation by courts: see e.g. Galligan, (1982) 2 Ox. J. Leg. Stud. 257. See also the Appendix for discussion of the important new distinction between public law and private law which, while primarily operating at the remedial level, may also affect substantive law.

One of the features of Administrative Law is the variety and intricacy of the remedies which are available to control administrative action. With the exception of habeas corpus these will be considered in detail in Chs. 9–14 *infra*, but, as the student will encounter references to them throughout the book, the main ones are listed here.

(a) *Prerogative Orders*
    (i) *Certiorari*. This remedy quashes the decisions of subordinate bodies for excess or want of jurisdiction or error of law on the face of the record (on which see p. 64 *infra*).

(ii) *Prohibition.* Broadly speaking, this remedy is invoked at an earlier stage than certiorari (though on similar grounds) when there is some future act which it is wished to prohibit.

(iii) *Mandamus.* This lies to compel the performance of a public duty.

(b) *Habeas corpus.* The prerogative writ of habeas corpus enables the courts to review the legality of a detention. Although in a sense it is part of Administrative Law and has been of importance in, for instance, immigration cases, it is traditionally treated in the context of Constitutional Law and will not be considered in this book. On habeas corpus, see Wade, p. 540; de Smith, Appendix 1; Wade and Phillips, *Constitutional and Administrative Law*, 9th edn., p. 455. See further Sharpe, *The Law of Habeas Corpus.*

(c) *Other non-statutory remedies.*

(i) *Injunctions.* These may be prohibitory (restraining unlawful action) or mandatory (compelling the performance of a duty). Many applications are for 'interlocutory' or 'interim' injunctions. These are temporary measures which continue, in the case of the former, until the trial of the action or further order by the court or, in the case of the latter, until a fixed date or further order. In a case of urgency an injunction may be granted *ex parte* (i.e. without hearing the defendant). Injunctions, however, have a limited role in Administrative Law because of s. 21 of the Crown Proceedings Act 1947, p. 290 *infra.*

(ii) *Declarations.* These are very flexible. The plaintiff must assert a personal right or interest which is recognized by law and a declaration may, for instance, state that an administrative act is invalid, set out the true construction of a statute, or simply state the parties' rights.

(d) *Statutory remedies.* These may take the form of rights of appeal (pp. 64 and 558 *infra*), statutory applications to quash, for instance, compulsory purchase orders (p. 393 *infra*) or statutory default powers to compel the performance of public duties, particularly those imposed on local authorities (p. 395 *infra*).

(e) *Collateral challenge.* The above remedies are all available to a plaintiff who wishes to challenge the validity of an administrative act directly. The validity of an administrative act may, however, also arise incidentally (or collaterally) in other proceedings, for example as a defence to a criminal charge (p. 87 *infra*) or in actions for damages (p. 211 *infra*).

The following extract is concerned with the fundamental distinction between review and appeal which was stated *supra.* (On this issue see also *Chief Constable of the North Wales Police* v. *Evans* [1982] 1 W.L.R. 1055, noted at p. 283 *infra.*)

Healey v. Minister of Health

[1955] 1 Q.B. 221   Court of Appeal

The plaintiff was employed as a shoemaker in the shoemaker's shop of a mental hospital. It was necessary to determine whether he was a mental health officer for superannuation purposes. The relevant statute and regulations empowered the Minister of Health to determine all questions arising under the regulations as to the rights and liabilities of mental health officers or of persons claiming to be treated as such. The Minister determined that the plaintiff was not a mental health officer and the plaintiff brought an action for a declaration that he was one. The Minister contended that his determination was final and not subject to review or appeal in the courts.

MORRIS L.J.: . . . Had it been desired to provide some machinery or procedure for an appeal from the decision of the Minister, it could have been done. And such prescribed appeal might or might not have been an appeal to the courts. Questions as to which methods for determining rights are the most desirable raise issues of policy which are for Parliament to decide. But the courts cannot invent a right of appeal where none is given. The courts will not usurp an appellate jurisdiction where none is created . . .

PARKER L.J.: . . . The matter comes before this court on an appeal from the decision of the judge on a preliminary issue which was ordered to be tried.

. . . The issue to be tried is whether, the Minister having made a determination, this court has jurisdiction, by declaration, not to declare that his determination is null and void or that it should be quashed, but to make another determination and one in the opposite sense to that made by the Minister.

In my opinion the court has no such jurisdiction. To hold otherwise would be to invest the court with an appellate jurisdiction, as opposed to a supervisory jurisdiction, which it certainly has not got. A right of appeal is the creature of statute, and the regulations give no right of appeal. Further, the absence of such words as 'whose determination is final' or 'whose determination shall not be called in question in any court of law' cannot preserve a jurisdiction which, apart from such words, did not exist.

The judgments of the Court of Appeal in *Rex v. Northumberland Compensation Appeal Tribunal, Ex parte Shaw,*[1] point the distinction between an appellate jurisdiction and a supervisory jurisdiction. In that case the court were considering the scope of the remedy by way of certiorari under the court's supervisory jurisdiction, and Singleton L.J. expressed his view in these words:[2] 'The decision of the tribunal was a "speaking order" in the sense in which that term has been used. The court is entitled to examine it, and if there be an error on the face of it, to quash it – "not to substitute another order in its place, but to remove that order out of the way, as one which should not be used to the detriment of any of the subjects of Her Majesty," as Lord Cairns said in *Walsall Overseers v. London and North Western Railway Co.*'[3] Further, Denning L.J. said: 'The control is exercised by means of a power to quash any determination by the tribunal which, on the face of it, offends against the law. The King's Bench does not substitute its own views for those of the tribunal, as a Court of Appeal would do. It leaves it to the tribunal to hear the case again, and in a proper case may command it to do so.' And Morris L.J. said:[5] 'It is plain that certiorari will not issue as the cloak of an appeal in disguise. It does not lie in order to bring up an order or decision for rehearing of the issue raised in the proceedings.'

[1] [1952] 1 K.B. 338.
[2] Ibid. 344.   [3] (1878) 4 App. Cas. 30, 39.
[4] [1952] 1 K.B. 338, 347.   [5] Ibid. 357.

In the present case the court, if it were to allow the proceedings to continue, would, in my view, be usurping a jurisdiction, namely, an appellate jurisdiction, which it does not possess. On this ground I would dismiss the appeal.

[DENNING L.J. delivered a judgment in favour of dismissing the appeal.]

Appeal dismissed.

Question

Should a right of appeal on a question of law be classified as 'appeal' or 'review'? See p. 62 *infra*.

NATURE AND SCOPE OF POWERS

Trustees of the Harbour of Dundee v. D. & J. Nicol

[1915] A.C. 550   House of Lords

The franchise of a ferry was vested in the Harbour Trustees by statute. When the vessels were not required for ferry traffic, the Trustees let them out on hire for excursion trips beyond the ferry limits. An action was brought by a firm of shipowners to restrain the Trustees from so doing on the ground that this was ultra vires. Both the Lord Ordinary and the Second Division of the Court of Session found for the plaintiffs. The Trustees appealed.

LORD PARMOOR: . . . It is settled law that a body such as the appellants, constituted by statute, have no authority except such as Parliament has conferred on them, and that they must find a sanction for any powers which they claim to possess in their incorporating statute or statutes. These powers may be expressly authorised or implied as fairly incidental to what is expressly authorised.

[He went on to hold that the activity in question was not reasonably incidental to the power to run a ferry and was accordingly ultra vires.]

[VISCOUNT HALDANE L.C. and LORD DUNEDIN delivered speeches in favour of dismissing the appeal. LORD ATKINSON concurred in LORD DUNEDIN's speech.]

Appeal dismissed.

Notes

1. *The Reasonably Incidental rule.* The courts have taken a fairly wide view on the question of what can fairly be seen as incidental to a power, and do consider the public nature of statutory activities (*Ski Enterprises* v. *Tangariro National Park Board* [1964] N.Z.L.R. 884 at p. 888) recognizing, for example, that certain obligations comprehend a welfare element (*Attorney-General* v. *Crayford U.D.C.* [1962] Ch. 575). Although much will depend on the wording and context of a particular power, *Loweth* v. *Minister of Housing and Local Government* (1971) 22 P. & C.R. 125 provides a good example of the courts' approach. The question was whether a local authority's power 'to acquire or provide and furnish halls, offices and other buildings' and to purchase land compulsorily for this purpose permitted the compulsory acquisition of land for an access road to a county hall. Bridge J. said (at p. 131):

The starting point, in my judgment, for the consideration of any such argument must be in the classic statements of principle with regard to the implication of terms in legislation of this character, which are conveniently collected in a relatively recent decision of the Court of Appeal. *Att.- Gen.* v. *Crayford Urban District Council*, in a passage from the judgment of Lord Evershed M.R. where he said this:

> The principle of law to be applied I take from the speech of Lord Selborne L.C. in *Att.-Gen.* v. *Great Eastern Railway Co.* [(1880) 5 App. Cas. 473] The noble Lord there states after reference to *Ashbury Railway Carriage and Iron Co.* v. *Richie*: 'I agree with James L.J. that this doctrine ought to be reasonably, and not unreasonably, understood and applied, and that whatever may fairly be regarded as incidental to, or consequential upon, those things which the legislature has authorised, ought not (unless expressly prohibited) to be held, by judicial construction, to be *ultra vires*.' That statement of principle was expressly adopted and approved by this Court in 1907 in *Peel* v. *London and North Western Railway Co.* [[1907] 1 Ch. 5] Vaughan Williams L.J. stated [at p. 11]: 'Sir Edward Carson obviously felt a difficulty in contending that the company, as a company, could only do those acts which are expressly authorised by the special Act of the company, or by the Acts that have to be read with it, and had to admit that the company not only has a right to do those acts which are expressly authorised, but also all such acts as may fairly and reasonably be considered as incidental to or consequential upon the works which are so authorised.'

The first question, then, which has to be asked is this: there being no express authorisation in section 125 of the Local Government Act 1933 of the acquisition of land for the purpose of providing access to halls, offices or other buildings for transacting the business of the local authority, is acquisition for such a purpose an act which may fairly and reasonably be considered as incidental to or consequential upon the acquisition or the holding of land for the purpose of providing such halls, offices or other buildings?

To my mind, the answer to this question incontrovertibly must be 'yes'. It is inconceivable that a local authority should be authorised to acquire a site for a county hall in, let us say, the middle of a park and not be authorised to acquire the land around it for all the incidental purposes for which the curtilage is required, including the vital incidental purpose of obtaining an access way from the building to the nearest highway.

2. *Presumptions of Legislative Intent.* For a detailed examination of the common law presumptions, see *Maxwell on Interpretation of Statutes*, 12th edn., Ch. 7. A good example of their operation in Administrative Law is provided by *Mixnam's Properties Ltd.* v. *Chertsey U.D.C.* [1965] A.C. 735. The Caravan Sites and Control of Development Act 1960 required the licensing of caravan sites, and s. 5(1) stated that 'a site licence issued by a local authority in respect of any land may be so issued subject to such conditions as the authority may think it necessary or desirable to impose on the occupier of land in the interests of persons dwelling thereon in caravans, or of any other class of persons, or of the public at large; and in particular, but without prejudice to the generality of the foregoing, a site licence may be issued subject to conditions – (a) for restricting the occasions on which caravans are stationed on the land for the purposes of human habitation, or the total number of caravans which are so stationed at any one time; (b) for controlling . . . the types of caravan which are stationed on the land; (c) for regulating the positions in which caravans are stationed . . . (d) for securing . . . the amenity of the land . . . (e) for securing that . . . proper measures are taken for preventing and detecting the outbreak of fire and adequate means of fighting fire are provided and maintained; (f) for securing that adequate sanitary facilities . . . are provided . . .'. Mixnam's applied for a site licence and the Council imposed a large number of conditions which, *inter alia*, sought to provide site hirers with protection equivalent to that enjoyed by statutory tenants under the Rent Acts. Mixnam's contended that the Council was only allowed to impose conditions relating to the use of the site and that these conditions were therefore ultra vires. Lord Reid, with Lord Donovan concurring, accepted this argument because of the presumption that general

words in a statute are not to be construed as to effect a fundamental alteration of the general law relating to the rights of the persons to whom they apply unless the power to effect such an alteration is expressed in the clearest possible terms (pp. 750–2; see also Willmer L.J. in the Court of Appeal, [1964] 1 Q.B. 214 at p. 226). It was extremely improbable that Parliament intended to introduce a completely new and indeterminate type of security of tenure and rent control for caravan dwellers by such general provisions. Viscount Radcliffe, on the other hand, did not think that this approach was useful because the whole purpose of the statute was to interfere with *some* common law rights. He said that '[if] . . . one is to discover limitations upon the condition-making power, they must be found in the words of the Act itself and by fair deduction from those words' (p. 755).

It will be readily seen that the approach used by Lord Reid will tend to narrow the scope of the administrative body's power only where that power affects common law rights. Where it does not affect such rights – and few welfare-oriented powers will – this approach would give more power to the administrative body and consequently weaken the ability of those affected by its exercise to seek redress in the courts. For further discussion and criticism of the use of presumptions in this way see Ganz, (1967) 27 M.L.R. 611; Robertshaw, [1975] P.L. 113.

Other important presumptions are those against

(*a*) ousting the jurisdiction of the courts (see Ch. 11 *infra*; *Commissioners of Customs and Excise* v. *Cure & Deeley Ltd.* [1962] 1 Q.B. 340, noted at p. 511 *infra*);

(*b*) recognizing a taxing power without express words (*Congreve* v. *Home Office* [1976] Q.B. 629; *Commissioners of Customs and Excise* v. *Cure & Deeley Ltd.*);

(*c*) deprivation of rights, at least without compensation (*Mixnam's Properties Ltd.* v. *Chertsey U.D.C.* [1965] A.C. 735, noted *supra*; *Hall & Co. Ltd.* v. *Shoreham-by-Sea U.D.C.* [1964] 1 W.L.R. 240);

(*d*) deprivation of personal liberty in peacetime (*R.* v. *Halliday* [1917] A.C. 260; and

(*e*) the Crown being bound by statute (*B.B.C.* v. *Johns* [1965] Ch. 32 at p. 78; but see *Town Investments Ltd.* v. *Department of the Environment* [1978] A.C. 359, noted at p. 435 *infra*, and Maxwell, op. cit., pp. 166–8 for cases in which this is not so).

For a critical approach to these presumptions see Twining and Miers, *How to do things with Rules*, Ch. 10. They point out that for every presumption it is possible to find another that points in precisely the opposite direction, see the examples at pp. 210–1.

Statutory and prerogative powers

Note

The nature and extent of a particular statutory power is to be found, expressly or by implication, in the relevant statute. Historically, however, an important non-statutory source of power was the royal prerogative and, though much restricted by statute, the prerogative is still of use in the administrative process, especially in the areas of foreign relations and matters connected with military affairs. (For a detailed examination of the royal prerogative see de Smith, *Constitutional and Administrative Law*, 4th edn., Ch. 4; Wade, pp. 213 and 350; Markesinis, [1973] C.L.J. 287.) Prerogative powers traditionally have four characteristics, though two of them have been put into question by recent decisions. These are that

(*a*) they are derived from custom;

(*b*) they are recognized and enforced by the courts which can determine their ambit (*Case of Proclamations* (1611) 12 Co. Rep. 74) but not the propriety or adequacy of a particular exercise of prerogative power;

(*c*) they are unique in the sense that they can only be applied to those rights which the Crown enjoys alone (Blackstone, *Commentaries*, i, pp. 238–9);

(*d*) they are residual in the sense that they can be abrogated by statute but cannot be enlarged by either the Crown or the courts (*B.B.C.* v. *Johns* [1965] Ch. 32 at p. 79).

The second and third characteristics have been put into question by cases such as *R.* v. *Criminal Injuries Compensation Board, ex p. Lain infra* and the *Laker Airways* case, p. 14 *infra*.

R. v. Criminal Injuries Compensation Board, ex parte Lain

[1967] 2 Q.B. 864   Divisional Court of the Queen's Bench

The widow of a police officer who was shot by a suspect and later died applied to the Criminal Injuries Compensation Board for compensation for herself and her children. A single member of the Board awarded her £300 but on appeal by her to three members the award was reduced to nil. She applied for certiorari to quash the decision on the ground of error of law on the face of the record. The Board, a non-statutory body, had been established in 1964 for the purpose of compensating victims of crimes of violence and a scheme had been drawn up accordingly by the Home Secretary. For further extracts, see p. 312 *infra*.

LORD PARKER C.J. [after finding that the decision disclosed no error of law on its face]: I come back now to the question whether the board is a body of persons amenable to the supervisory jurisdiction of this court. Mr. Bridge for the board submits that it is not and bases his submission on the well-known words of Atkin L.J. in *Rex.* v. *Electricity Commissioners, Ex parte London Electricity Joint Committee Co. (1920) Ltd.*[6] . . . He contends that in the present case [the] conditions are not fulfilled in that (1) the board is not a body of persons having 'legal authority' in the sense of having statutory authority; and (2) the board is not a body of persons having authority 'to determine questions affecting the rights of subjects' in that a determination of the board gives rise to no enforceable rights but only gives the applicant an opportunity to receive the bounty of the Crown.

In invoking Atkin L.J.'s definition, however, it must be remembered that the words used were in relation to a case of a statutory tribunal and where the question was, inter alia, whether a statutory tribunal as opposed to an inferior court was amenable to the jurisdiction. The definition was no wider than was necessary for the purposes of that case and was not in my judgment intended to be an exhaustive definition.

I can see no reason either in principle or in authority why a board set up as this board was set up is not a body of persons amenable to the jurisdiction of this court. True it is not set up by statute but the fact that it is set up by executive government, i.e., under the prerogative, does not render its acts any

[6] [1924] 1 K.B. 171, 205. [The passage is quoted at p. 308 *infra*.]

the less lawful. Indeed, the writ of certiorari has issued not only to courts set up by statute but to courts whose authority is derived, inter alia, from the prerogative. Once the jurisdiction is extended, as it clearly has been, to tribunals as opposed to courts, there is no reason why the remedy by way of certiorari cannot be invoked to a body of persons set up under the prerogative. . . .

With regard to Mr. Bridge's second point I cannot think that Atkin L.J. intended to confine his principle to cases in which the determination affected rights in the sense of enforceable rights. Indeed, in the *Electricity Commissioners* case,[7] the rights determined were at any rate not immediately enforceable rights since the scheme laid down by the commissioners had to be approved by the Minister of Transport and by resolutions of Parliament. The commissioners nevertheless were held amenable to the jurisdiction of this court. . . .

The position as I see it is that the exact limits of the ancient remedy by way of certiorari have never been and ought not to be specifically defined. They have varied from time to time being extended to meet changing conditions. At one time the writ only went to an inferior court. Later its ambit was extended to statutory tribunals determining a lis inter partes. Later again it extended to cases where there was no lis in the strict sense of the word but where immediate or subsequent rights of a citizen were affected. The only constant limits throughout were that it was performing a public duty. Private or domestic tribunals have always been outside the scope of certiorari since their authority is derived solely from contract, that is, from the agreement of the parties concerned. . . .

We have as it seems to me reached the position when the ambit of certiorari can be said to cover every case in which a body of persons of a public as opposed to a purely private or domestic character has to determine matters affecting subjects provided always that it has a duty to act judicially. Looked at in this way the board in my judgment comes fairly and squarely within the jurisdiction of this court. It is, as Mr. Bridge said, 'a servant of the Crown charged by the Crown, by executive instruction, with the duty of distributing the bounty of the Crown.' It is clearly, therefore, performing public duties.

Moreover, it is quite clearly under a duty to act judicially and indeed no argument to the contrary has been presented. It is to consist of a chairman of wide legal experience and five other members who are legally qualified. . . . It is charged with assessing compensation on the basis of common law damages save as varied by the scheme. . . . Its procedure involves the examination and cross-examination of witnesses and it is provided that the burden is on the applicant to make out his case and that the decision shall be arrived at solely in the light of the evidence brought out at the hearing. . . .

Finally, I cannot think that the position created by the setting up of the board is any different from what the position would have been if the Home Secretary had provided that he himself, after a judicial process, should decide

[7] [1924] 1 K.B. 171.

whether, and if so what, compensation should be paid in any particular case. He would then, as it seems to me, have been himself amenable to certiorari in relation to the judicial process.

DIPLOCK L.J.: . . . The jurisdiction of the High Court as successor of the Court of Queen's Bench to supervise the exercise of their jurisdiction by inferior tribunals has not in the past been dependent upon the source of the tribunal's authority to decide issues submitted to its determination, except where such authority is derived solely from agreement of parties to the determination. The latter case falls within the field of private contract and thus within the ordinary civil jurisdiction of the High Court supplemented where appropriate by its statutory jurisdiction under the Arbitration Acts. The earlier history of the writ of certiorari shows that it was issued to courts whose authority was derived from the prerogative, from Royal Charter, from franchise or custom as well as from Act of Parliament. Its recent history shows that as new kinds of tribunals have been created, orders of certiorari have been extended to them too and all persons who under authority of the Government have exercised quasi-judicial functions. True, since the victory of Parliament in the constitutional struggles of the 17th century, authority has been, generally if not invariably, conferred upon new kinds of tribunals by or under Act of Parliament and there has been no recent occasion for the High Court to exercise supervisory jurisdiction over persons whose ultimate authority to decide matters is derived from any other source. But I see no reason for holding that the ancient jurisdiction of the Court of Queen's Bench has been narrowed merely because there has been no occasion to exercise it. If new tribunals are established by acts of government, the supervisory jurisdiction of the High Court extends to them if they possess the essential characteristics upon which the subjection of inferior tribunals to the supervisory control of the High Court is based.

[He went on to find that the Board did possess these characteristics but that as there was no error of law on the face of the record he dismissed the application.]

[ASHWORTH J. delivered a judgment in favour of dismissing the application.]

Application dismissed.

Notes

1. The student will have noted the references to the prerogative remedy of certiorari, on which the case is an important authority: see p. 312 *infra*. Part of it has been set out at this stage because of its importance in relation to prerogative powers.

2. This case was concerned with a governmental body which the court said was established by prerogative (but cf. Wade, p. 214). Is the reasoning of Lord Parker C.J. (favouring judicial control) only applicable to such bodies or to such powers? If not, what should be the limits of the ability of the court to review the activities of other non-statutory bodies? See *Breen* v. *A.E.U.* [1971] 2 Q.B. 175 at pp. 189–90, 195 and 200. The question of judicial control over the decisions of contractual bodies and, if so,

what the appropriate remedy would be, has arisen particularly in the context of natural justice: see pp. 275, 297, and 313 *infra*.

3. On the difference between the judicial control of prerogative powers and the review of statutory powers, see p. 17 *infra*.

Chandler v. Director of Public Prosecutions, p. 123 *infra*

Gouriet v. Union of Post Office Workers, p. 127 *infra*

Laker Airways Ltd. v. Department of Trade

[1977] Q.B. 643   Court of Appeal

The Civil Aviation Authority (C.A.A.), established by statute in 1971, was required to perform its functions so as to secure certain statutory objectives. One of these was to secure participation in the provision of air transportation by a non-nationalized airline. The Secretary of State for Trade had power to intervene in the C.A.A.'s work in two ways. First, the statutory objectives were subject to current 'guidance' by him after Parliamentary approval by resolution and, secondly, he had powers to 'give directions' to the C.A.A. in certain circumstances. 'Directions' were not subject to Parliamentary approval and the statute (the Civil Aviation Act 1971) provided that they were to prevail in the event of conflict with its requirements.

Laker Airways sought a licence to operate a transatlantic passenger service (Skytrain) and in October 1972 the C.A.A. granted a licence. Subsequently the government 'designated' Laker for operations on the specified route, a step which, under the Bermuda Agreement of 1946, obliged the United States government to give Laker landing rights. With the encouragement of the authorities Laker prepared for Skytrain to start and bought the necessary aircraft.

In 1975 the Secretary of State under a new government announced a change of policy stating that the C.A.A. should not licence more than one U.K. carrier on any long-haul route. He used his statutory power to give 'guidance' directing the C.A.A. not to licence competing airlines and to review existing licences accordingly. Parliamentary approval was obtained. The government also removed Laker's Bermuda Agreement designation.

Laker sought declarations that the 'guidance' was ultra vires and that the Department was not entitled to cancel the designation. The Department contested this, but also claimed a prerogative discretion to withdraw the designation which could not be questioned in legal proceedings. Mocatta J. granted the declarations asked for and the Department appealed.

The Court of Appeal unanimously held that the 'guidance' was ultra vires as it was in direct conflict with the express objectives of the 1971 Act, mainly on the basis of the dichotomy between 'guidance' and 'directions', only the latter of which could override the Act. On the defence based on a prerogative discretion:

LORD DENNING M.R.: . . . The Attorney-General contended that the power of the Secretary of State 'to withdraw' the designation was a prerogative power which could not be examined in the courts. It was a power arising under a treaty which, he said, was outside the cognizance of the courts. The Attorney-General recognised that by withdrawing the designation, the Secretary of State would put a stop to Skytrain, but he said that he could do it all the same. No matter that Laker Airways had expended £6 million to £7 million on the faith of the designation, the Secretary of State could withdraw it without paying a penny compensation.

. . . The prerogative is a discretionary power exercisable by the executive government for the public good, in certain spheres of governmental activity for which the law has made no provision, such as the war prerogative (of requisitioning property for the defence of the realm), or the treaty prerogative (of making treaties with foreign powers). The law does not interfere with the proper exercise of the discretion by the executive in those situations: but it can set limits by defining the bounds of the activity: and it can intervene if the discretion is exercised improperly or mistakenly. That is a fundamental principle of our constitution. It derives from two of the most respected of our authorities. In 1611 when the King, as the executive government, sought to govern by making proclamations, Sir Edward Coke declared that: 'the King had no prerogative, but that which the law of the land allows him': see the *Proclamations Case* (1611) 12 Co. Rep. 74, 76. In 1765 Sir William Blackstone added his authority, *Commentaries*, vol. I, p. 252:

> 'For prerogative consisting (as Mr. Locke has well defined it) in the discretionary power of acting for the public good, where the positive laws are silent, if that discretionary power be abused to the public detriment, such prerogative is exerted in an unconstitutional manner.'

Quite recently the House of Lords set a limit to the war prerogative when it declared that, even in time of war, the property of a British subject cannot be requisitioned or demolished without making compensation to the owner of it: see the *Burmah Oil* case [1965] A.C. 75. It has also circumscribed the treaty prerogative by holding that it cannot be used to violate the legal rights of a British subject, except on being liable for any damage he suffered: see *Nissan* v. *Attorney-General* [1970] A.C. 179, 211, by Lord Reid.

Seeing that the prerogative is a discretionary power to be exercised for the public good, it follows that its exercise can be examined by the courts just as any other discretionary power which is vested in the executive. At several times in our history, the executive have claimed that a discretion given by the prerogative is unfettered: just as they have claimed that a discretion given by statute or by regulation is unfettered. On some occasions the judges have upheld these claims of the executive – notably in the *Ship Money* case, *Rex* v. *Hampden* (1637) 3 State Tr. 826 and in one or two cases during the Second World War, and soon after it – but the judges have not done so of late. The two outstanding cases are *Padfield* v. *Minister of Agriculture, Fisheries and Food* [1968] A.C. 997, and *Secretary of State for Education and Science* v. *Tameside Metropolitan Borough Council* [1976] 3 W.L.R. 641, where the

House of Lords have shown that when discretionary powers are entrusted to the executive by statute, the courts can examine the exercise of those powers to see that they are used properly, and not improperly or mistakenly. By 'mistakenly' I mean under the influence of a misdirection in fact or in law. Likewise it seems to me that when discretionary powers are entrusted to the executive by the prerogative – in pursuance of the treaty-making power – the courts can examine the exercise of them so as to see that they are not used improperly or mistakenly. . . .

ROSKILL L.J.: . . . I now turn to consider the prerogative question. The argument for the Crown runs thus. The Bermuda Agreement 1946 is a bilateral treaty between the Government of the United Kingdom and the Government of the United States of America. Treaty-making powers are among the prerogative powers of the Crown. When the Crown in the exercise of those prerogative powers concludes a treaty, the subject gains no personal rights under that treaty enforceable in our courts, unless the treaty becomes part of the municipal law of this country and provides for the subject to acquire certain specified rights thereunder. Some treaties do become part of the municipal law of this country. The Bermuda Agreement did not and has at no time become part of our municipal law. Neither the plaintiffs nor any other airline has any right thereunder enforceable in our courts. They could not, even if they possess valid air transport licences under our municipal law such as the plaintiffs possess, have obliged the Crown to designate them as a 'designated air carrier' so as to attract reciprocal rights from the United States Government under the Bermuda Agreement. Any such act of designation is a prerogative act into the doing or refraining from doing of which neither this court nor any other court in this country has jurisdiction to inquire, still less to interfere with. If therefore the Crown decides to withdraw the plaintiffs' designation under the Bermuda Agreement, it is free so to do. The plaintiffs have no right to object and this court has neither the right nor the power nor indeed the duty to inquire into or to interfere with such withdrawal of designation. The Crown's prerogative in this respect is unfettered by any legislation such as the Act of 1971 and can be used as the Crown pleases. . . .

With much – indeed with most – of the Attorney-General's argument as to the basic constitutional principles applicable to the use of the prerogative by the Crown, as to the incapacity of the courts of this country to control that use of the prerogative in relation to treaty-making powers and the consequences so far as the subject is concerned of treaties concluded in furtherance of prerogative powers, I unhesitatingly agree. . . .

The sole question is whether the relevant prerogative power has been fettered so as to prevent the Crown seeking by use of the prerogative to withdraw the plaintiffs' designation under the Bermuda Agreement and thus in effect achieve what it is unable lawfully to achieve by securing the revocation by the authority of the plaintiffs' air transport licence. . . .

The strength of the Attorney-General's argument undoubtedly lies in the fact that nowhere in the Act of 1971 does one find any express fetter upon the relevant prerogative power of the Crown. . . .

The relevant principles upon which the courts have to determine whether prerogative power has been fettered by statute were exhaustively considered by the House of Lords in *Attorney-General* v. *De Keyser's Royal Hotel Ltd.* [1920] A.C. 508.

[After considering this decision and the statutory provisions involved in the case before him, he concluded:] I think Parliament must be taken to have intended to fetter the prerogative of the Crown in this relevant respect. I would therefore dismiss this appeal.

[LAWTON L.J. delivered a judgment in favour of dismissing the appeal.]

Appeal dismissed.

Note

The courts have not often been prepared to review exercises of discretion where the discretionary power derives from the royal prerogative. *Laker*'s case (per Lord Denning) and *R.* v. *Criminal Injuries Compensation Board, ex p. Lain*, p. 11 *supra*, should be compared with *Chandler* v. *D.P.P.*, p. 123 *infra*; *Gouriet* v. *U.P.O.W.*; p. 127 *infra*; *Rederiaktiebolaget Amphitrite* v. *The King*, p. 446 *infra*; and see further *Blackburn* v. *Attorney-General* [1971] 1 W.L.R. 1307. Other examples of judicial unwillingness to interfere include *Hanratty* v. *Lord Butler of Saffron Walden*, The Times, 13 May 1971 (prerogative of mercy) and *Secretary of State for the Home Department* v. *Lakdawalla* [1972] Imm. A.R. 26 (issue of passport). Lord Denning was a member of the Court of Appeal in *Hanratty*'s case but, despite his views in *Laker*, it should not be assumed that he would now decide the earlier case any differently. Commentators have suggested that the non-reviewability of most exercises of prerogative power is based on their non-justiciability and argue that where this is not so there will be review; see Williams, [1971] C.L.J. 178; Markesinis, [1973] C.L.J. 287 at pp. 293–9. This is supported by the decision of the High Court of Australia in *Re Toohey; ex p. Northern Land Council* (1981) 38 A.L.R. 439, in which the court considered the English authorities. For the facts of this case see p. 505 *infra*.

EXPRESS REQUIREMENTS AND CONDITIONS

Mandatory or directory conditions

Howard v. Bodington

(1877) 2 P.D. 203   Court of Arches

Section 9 of the Public Worship Act 1874 states that where a bishop, who has been sent a complaint about an incumbent within his diocese, intends to proceed on the complaint '. . . he shall within twenty-one days after receiving the representation transmit a copy thereof to the person complained of'. Section 16 of the Act provides that where the bishop is patron of the benefice held by the incumbent who is the subject of a complaint the archbishop of the province shall act in place of such bishop. In both cases the archbishop was to require the Dean of Arches (Lord Penzance) to deal with the matter. The question was whether the provisions of s. 9 were imperative or directory, and whether the Court of Arches could proceed in a case in which some seven weeks had passed before notice of a complaint was served on the incumbent (the respondent).

LORD PENZANCE: . . . It was contended that, although it is a positive provision of the Act that a copy of the representation shall be transmitted to the respondent within twenty-one days from the time the bishop received it, yet that that provision is only what has been called in the law courts 'directory'. Now the distinction between matters that are directory and matters that are imperative is well known to us all in the common language of the courts at Westminster. I am not sure that it is the most fortunate language that could have been adopted to express the idea that it is intended to convey; but still that is the recognised language, and I propose to adhere to it. The real question in all these cases is this: A thing has been ordered by the legislature to be done. What is the consequence if it is not done? In the case of statutes that are said to be imperative, the Courts have decided that if it is not done the whole thing fails, and the proceedings that follow upon it are all void. On the other hand, when the Courts hold a provision to be mandatory or directory, they say that, although such provision may not have been complied with, the subsequent proceedings do not fail. Still, whatever the language, the idea is a perfectly distinct one. There may be many provisions in Acts of Parliament which, although they are not strictly obeyed, yet do not appear to the Court to be of that material importance to the subject-matter to which they refer, as that the legislature could have intended that the non-observance of them should be followed by a total failure of the whole proceedings. On the other hand, there are some provisions in respect of which the Court would take an opposite view, and would feel that they are matters which must be strictly obeyed, otherwise the whole proceedings that subsequently follow must come to an end. Now the question is, to which category does the provision in question in this case belong? . . . It is very difficult to group [the authorities] together, and the tendency of my mind, after reading them, is to come to the conclusion which was expressed by Lord Campbell in the case of the *Liverpool Borough Bank* v. *Turner.*[8] . . .

'No universal rule can be laid down for the construction of statutes, as to whether mandatory enactments shall be considered directory only or obligatory, with an implied nullification for disobedience. It is the duty of courts of justice to try to get at the real intention of the legislature by carefully attending to the whole scope of the statute to be construed.'

I believe, as far as any rule is concerned, you cannot safely go further than that in each case you must look to the subject-matter; consider the importance of the provision that has been disregarded, and the relation of that provision to the general object intended to be secured by the Act; and upon a review of the case in that aspect decide whether the matter is what is called imperative or only directory.

[8] 29 L.J. (Ch.) 827.

But amongst the cases to which attention was called is a case of *Vaux* v. *Vollans*,[9] to which I will call attention, because I think it more nearly resembles the matter we have in hand that any other that I have met with. . . .

In that case the failure was in not serving the notice in a proper form. Here the failure is not serving the notice in a proper time, which, to my mind, is of very much more importance than the form or way in which it was served, provided it got to its ultimate destination. That case is no doubt a strong one to shew that where the legislature chooses to provide for these minute matters with apparent intention that they should be adhered to, no supplemental or different mode which even attains the same end is allowable or permissible, but the proceedings are void. . . .

Then the Court has to consider what is the scope of this enactment. I think nobody can doubt that of all the important steps in the suit there is no step so important as that which regards the service of the first proceedings on the respondent. That which is to give the respondent notice that he is to be made the subject of a suit is the most important step in the whole cause, whatever Court the suit is brought in, or whatever the nature of the proceedings . . . there is not a more important step in the cause than that which provides for the service upon the respondent. . . . But in this statute that we are considering, we must bear in mind that really the whole scope of the statute is to provide a new form of proceedings; it is a new form of suit. . . . The legislature chose to point out in these various sections the particular steps which should be taken, and minutely to tie the parties down to a particular time, and when they came to provide for the machinery of the Act being carried out by rules and orders, they expressly, in the 19th section, excepted those matters that were expressly regulated by the Act. Therefore, the question that we are inquiring into was really, as far as one can see, one treated by the legislature as one of considerable importance. The service upon the respondent is practically the beginning of the suit, because the bishop after he received the representation may say that the proceedings should not go on at all, and the very first step that really gives life and vigour to the suit is the service upon the respondent.

Now, as I said just now, if twenty-one days is not to be adhered to, what limit is there to the time within which it would be lawful to serve this notice upon the respondent? That is a matter that has pressed more upon my mind than any other. It seems to me that there is no limit. . . .

On the other side, in opposition to those views, it has been argued, first of all, that no harm is done to the respondent. I think that everybody will admit that the continuation of a suit and its hanging over a man's head beyond the time that the legislature provided, is a harm, and the extent of that harm it is perhaps not so easy to measure exactly, but I think it is a harm; at any rate, in neither of the two cases to which I have called attention was there any harm done, because the notice really got to the right place, but what was done was not done in the form provided by the statute, and therefore it was held that the proceedings were void. . . .

[9] 4 B. & A. 525.

Then, again it is said that this is a provision intended only for the benefit of the complainants, and it is no doubt considerably for the benefit of the complainants, because they file their representation, and of course they wish to go forward with their suit.

If the bishop holds it back, he is doing them a wrong, but I am unable to see that it is not also a provision intended for the benefit of the respondent, and I do not think the Court is at liberty to speculate too narrowly as to what the motives of the legislature were. They have chosen to provide a definite time within which the representation is to be served, and the question is whether, the matter being one of essential importance, the Court is at liberty to throw what the legislature have provided aside, upon some speculation that they intended it for the benefit of the complainaints and not for the benefit of the respondent. . . .

Upon a review, therefore, of these matters, and after full attention to the excellent argument that I heard upon the subject, I have come to the conclusion that these proceedings cannot go forward. I think the statute has prescribed a particular form to be followed, and that the Court is not at liberty to cast the time mentioned aside, upon any speculation as to the possible reasons why that particular provision was adopted. . . .

Notes

1. Lord Penzance contrasted 'imperative' and 'mandatory or directory' requirements (p. 18 *supra*). In modern usage, however, 'mandatory' is used as a synonym for imperative and the contrast is therefore between 'imperative or mandatory' requirements and 'directory' requirements. 'Directory' requirements are sometimes also called 'procedural': see for example *London & Clydeside Estates Ltd. v. Aberdeen D.C.* [1980] 1 W.L.R. 182 at p. 201 (Lord Keith). See Wade, p. 218; de Smith, p. 142.

2. Lord Penzance's approach, that a distinction be drawn between requirements the breach of which nullifies an administrative act and those the breach of which does not, needs re-examination in the light of *London & Clydeside Estates Ltd.* v. *Aberdeen D.C.*, p. 104 *infra*. There, the House of Lords confirmed that a requirement that notice be given of a right of appeal imposed a mandatory duty upon a planning authority and held that breach of this rendered a certificate (governing the amount of compensation payable for the compulsory acquisition of land) sent without the notice invalid. The requirement was plainly designed to inform the subject of his legal rights. The effect of allowing the authority to ignore it could be to deprive him of those rights with no opportunity to rectify the situation ([1980] 1 W.L.R. 182 at pp. 188 and 202). However, doubt was cast on Lord Penzance's basic approach to the consequences of non-compliance with statutory requirements. Lord Hailsham L.C. (at pp. 188–90) rejected the notion that courts are bound to fit the facts of such cases into rigid legal categories by, for instance, stating that breach of a mandatory requirement always renders an administrative act 'void'. See p. 106 *infra* for the relevant section of his speech with which Lord Wilberforce concurred. See also Lord Keith [1980] 1 W.L.R. at pp. 201–2. See further Note 3 *infra*. Additional support for this approach is to be found in *Brayhead (Ascot) Ltd.* v. *Berkshire C.C.* [1964] 2 Q.B. 303 where the breach of a mandatory requirement to give reasons did not render a notice void (but cf. Wade, p. 219) and see *R.* v. *Dacorum Gaming Licencing Committee, ex p. E.M.I. Cinemas*

and Leisure Ltd. [1971] 3 All E.R. 666. However, it may be too soon to dismiss Lord Penzance's approach. In *Inverclyde D.C.* v. *Lord Advocate* [1982] J.P.L. 313 at p. 314 Lord Keith, with whom the other members of the House of Lords agreed, said of a requirement that it was 'directory in nature and not mandatory in the sense that if it were not complied with, the proceedings were invalid'. See also *O'Reilly* v. *Mackman*, p. 326, *infra*.

3. The question of the need for 'substantial prejudice' to the person complaining of the breach is a matter of some difficulty, both in relation to its effect on the consequences of a breach of an express statutory requirement and in relation to the initial categorization of the statutory requirement. Indeed, the cases have not always kept the two issues separate.

On the question of categorization, a requirement might be regarded as directory if the probability of prejudice is low (*R.* v. *Inspector of Taxes, ex p. Clarke* [1974] Q.B. 220 at pp. 228–9; *Coney* v. *Choyce* [1975] 1 W.L.R. 422 at pp. 433–4) or if the defect can be remedied (*Howard* v. *Secretary of State for the Environment* [1975] Q.B. 235); but this might not be the case where the statutory wording is sufficiently clear or if the context so requires (*R.* v. *Pontypool Gaming Licensing Committee, ex p. Risca Cinemas Ltd.* [1970] 1 W.L.R. 1299; *R.* v. *Leicester Gaming Licensing Committee, ex p. Shine* [1970] 1 W.L.R. 1299, affirmed [1971] 1 W.L.R. 1648). *London & Clydeside Estates Ltd.* v. *Aberdeen D.C.*, p. 104 *infra*, should perhaps be seen as an example of this latter type of case, lack of prejudice being expressly said not to affect the classification of the requirement as mandatory. Lord Fraser said ([1981] 1 W.L.R. at p. 195): '[t]he validity of the certificate is not in my opinion dependent on whether the appellants were actually prejudiced by it or not'.

It would appear from the speech of Lord Hailsham (on which see Note 2 *supra*) and possibly the speech of Lord Keith in the *London & Clydeside* case ([1980] 1 W.L.R. at pp. 201–2) that substantiality of prejudice might be relevant in determining the consequences of breach of a statutory requirement, whether that requirement has been classified as mandatory or directory. This follows from Lord Hailsham's rejection of the notion that the consequences of such a breach are solely determined by the categorization of the statutory requirement. Although not expressly referred to, substantiality of prejudice is surely a relevant consideration in the exercise of the broad discretion as to consequences asserted by Lord Hailsham, although, on the facts of the case, lack of prejudice did not affect the matter. If this is so, cases such as *Patchett* v. *Leatham* (1949) 65 T.L.R. 69, where a notice that a house was to be requisitioned which was served on the owner's husband was held ineffective even though the owner knew of the notice, might now require consideration in the light of the *London & Clydeside* case.

Another role for 'substantial prejudice' is to be found in several statutes which give a remedy to a person who has been substantially prejudiced by breach of a statutory requirement: see s. 24 of the Acquisition of Land Act 1981 re-enacting para. 15 of Schedule 1 to the Acquisition of Land (Authorisation Procedure) Act 1946, which is set out at p. 381 *infra*; ss. 88 (4) (*b*), 243 (2) (*c*), 244 (2) (*b*) and 245 (4) (*b*) of the Town and Country Planning Act 1971 for instances of this.

4. Examples of mandatory requirements, apart from the duty to give notice of rights of appeal, include a duty to consult those affected by a proposed piece of delegated legislation (see p. 519 *infra*), rules governing the composition of a tribunal (*R.* v. *Inner London Quarter Sessions, ex p. D'Souza* [1970] 1 W.L.R. 376), and the obligation to give reasons for decisions (see p. 24 *infra*).

Failure to state reasons

Report of the Committee on Administrative Tribunals and Enquiries (The Franks Report), Cmnd. 218 (1957)

98. 'We are convinced that if tribunal proceedings are to be fair to the citizen reasons should be given to the fullest practicable extent. A decision is apt to be better if the reasons for it have to be set out in writing because the reasons are then more likely to have been properly thought out. Further, a reasoned decision is essential in order that where there is a right of appeal, the applicant can assess whether he has good grounds of appeal and know the case he will have to meet if he decides to appeal.'

Tribunals and Inquiries Act 1971

12. – (1) Subject to the provisions of this section, where –

(*a*) any such tribunal as is specified in Schedule 1 [10] to this Act gives any decision; or

(*b*) any Minister notifies any decision taken by him after the holding by him or on his behalf of a statutory inquiry, or taken by him in a case in which a person concerned could (whether by objecting or otherwise) have required the holding as aforesaid of a statutory inquiry,

it shall be the duty of the tribunal or Minister to furnish a statement, either written or oral, of the reasons for the decision if requested, on or before the giving or notification of the decision, to state the reasons.

(2) The said statement may be refused, or the specification of the reasons restricted, on grounds of national security, and the tribunal or Minister may refuse to furnish the statement to a person not primarily concerned with the decision if of opinion that to furnish it would be contrary to the interests of any person primarily concerned.

(3) Subsection (1) of this section shall not apply to any decision taken by a Minister after the holding by him or on his behalf of any inquiry or hearing which is a statutory inquiry by virtue only of an order made under section 19(2) [11] of this Act unless the order contains a direction that this section is to apply in relation to any inquiry or hearing to which the order applies.

(4) Subsection (1) of this section shall not apply to decisions in respect of which any statutory provision has effect, apart from this section, as to the giving of reasons, or to decisions of a Minister in connection with the preparation, making, approval, confirmation, or concurrence in regulations, rules, or byelaws, or orders or schemes of a legislative and not executive character.

[10] [This is set out by Wade, p. 824.]

[11] [This section simply empowers the designation of certain discretionary inquiries as 'statutory inquiries' for the purposes of the Act. See S.I. 1967 No. 451; S.I. 1975 No. 1379; cf. S.I. 1976 No. 293.]

(5) Any statement of the reasons for such a decision as is mentioned in paragraph (*a*) or (*b*) of subsection (1) of this section, whether given in pursuance of that subsection or of any other statutory provision, shall be taken to form part of the decision and accordingly to be incorporated in the record.

(6) If, after consultation with the Council, it appears to the Lord Chancellor and the Secretary of State that it is expedient that decisions of any particular tribunal or any description of such decisions, or any description of decisions of a Minister, should be excluded from the operation of subsection (1) of this section on the ground that the subject-matter of such decisions, or the circumstances in which they are made, make the giving of reasons unnecessary or impracticable, the Lord Chancellor and the Secretary of State may by order direct that subsection (1) of this section shall not apply to such decisions.[12]

In Re Poyser and Mills' Arbitration

[1964] 2 Q.B. 467   Queen's Bench Division

In October 1961 the landlord of an agricultural holding served on the tenant a notice under the Agriculture Holdings Act 1948 requiring him to remedy certain breaches of the tenancy agreement. In February 1962 the landlord served on the tenant a notice to quit on the ground that the tenant had failed to comply with the notice to remedy the alleged breaches. Both notices were dispatched to the tenant by postal recorded delivery service. The tenant requested a statutory arbitration, and an arbitrator was duly appointed to determine all questions arising out of the reasons stated in the notice to quit. The arbitrator decided that the notice to quit was a good notice. The tenant, pursuant to s. 12 (1) of the Tribunals and Inquiries Act 1958 (re-enacted as s. 12 of the 1971 Act, p. 22 *supra.*) requested the arbitrator to state his reasons. The arbitrator stated that he had arrived at his decision because (1) it was not disputed that the notice to quit had been delivered, (2) he accepted the landlord's evidence as to what work had or had not been done at the relevant date, and (3) he found as a fact that there was sufficient work required to be done by the notice to remedy which ought to have been done and was not done to justify the notice to quit.

On an application by the tenant to set aside the award:

MEGAW J.: . . . The tenant in this case asserted that there is an error of law on the face of the award and what I have to decide . . . is whether or not there was such an error of law. So far as the award itself is concerned, there is no question of any error appearing on its face. The award is in perfectly proper form, clear and unambiguous, and Mr. Bagnall, for the tenant, conceded that if the award stood alone, he could not attack it on that ground. But here again legislation intervenes, because section 12 of the Tribunals and Inquiries Act, 1958, has laid it down in relation to a large number of tribunals, including

[12] [See S.I. 1959 No. 452 (excluding certain Tax Tribunals) and *Annual Report of the Council on Tribunals for 1959*, paras. 58–69.]

arbitrations under Schedule 6 to the Agricultural Holdings Act, 1948, that where any such tribunal gives any decision, it shall be the duty of the tribunal to furnish a statement, either written or oral, of the reasons for the decision if requested. It is not disputed that the reasons for the award were properly asked for by the tenant. Section 12 (3) provides: 'Any statement of the reasons for such a decision as is mentioned in paragraph (a) or (b) of subsection (1) of this section . . . shall be taken to form part of the decision and accordingly to be incorporated in the record.' The question then is: Is the award which incorporates that letter containing those reasons shown to contain an error of law on the face of it? It is said on behalf of the tenant that there is an error of law in relation to paragraph 1 of the letter, and also in relation to paragraph 3.[13] So far as paragraph 3 is concerned, there being seven items in the notice to remedy, the arbitrator has not said which of those items he found to be good, and which he found to be bad. He has not dealt with them individually; he has merely said that he 'found as a fact that there was sufficient work required in the notice which ought to have been done and was not done on the relevant date to justify the notice to quit.'

I am bound to say this, and again I do not think it was disputed by Mr. Langdon-Davies,[14] that a reason which is as jejune as that reason is not satisfactory, but in my view it goes further than that. The whole purpose of section 12 of the Tribunals and Inquiries Act, 1958, was to enable persons whose property, or whose interests, were being affected by some administrative decision or some statutory arbitration to know, if the decision was against them, what the reasons for it were. Up to then, people's property and other interests might be gravely affected by a decision of some official. The decision might be perfectly right, but the person against whom it was made was left with the real grievance that he was not told why the decision had been made. The purpose of section 12 was to remedy that, and to remedy it in relation to arbitrations under this Act. Parliament provided that reasons shall be given, and in my view that must be read as meaning that proper, adequate reasons must be given. The reasons that are set out must be reasons which will not only be intelligible, but which deal with the substantial points that have been raised. In my view, it is right to consider that statutory provision as being a provision as to the form which the arbitration award shall take. If those reasons do not fairly comply with that which Parliament intended, then that is an error on the face of the award. It is a material error of form. Here, having regard to paragraph 3,[15] this award, including the reasons, does not comply with the proper form, and that is, in my view, an error of law on the face of the award and is properly so to be described rather than as technical misconduct. No one here suggests for a moment actual misconduct on the part of the arbitrator, but it may well be that what has gone wrong here is something which is capable properly of being described as both misconduct and error of

[13] [The relevant part of this letter, including paragraphs 1 and 3, are set out in the statement of facts *supra*.]
[14] [Counsel for the landlord.]
[15] [of the arbitrator's letter, set out in the statement of facts *supra*.]

law on the face of the award. If so, the fact that it is the latter brings it within the jurisdiction of this court. I do not say that any minor or trivial error, or failure to give reasons in relation to every particular point that has been raised at the hearing, would be sufficient ground for invoking the jurisdiction of this court. I think there must be something substantially wrong or inadequate in the reasons that are given in order to enable the jurisdiction of this court to be invoked. In my view, in the present case paragraph 3 gives insufficient and incomplete information as to the grounds of the decision; and, accordingly, I hold that there is an error of law on the face of the award, that the motion succeeds and the award must be set aside.

Award set aside.

Question

What would the position have been if the arbitrator had declined to give reasons?

Note

Section 1 (1) of the Arbitration Act 1979 abolished the jurisdiction to set aside an arbitrator's award on the ground of error of law on the face of the award. In its place the statute has created (s. 1 (2)) a new but restricted right of appeal on a point of law. See further *Chitty on Contracts*, 25th edn., §§ 975 and 1004. However, although the precise issue in *Re Poyser and Mills' Arbitration* could not occur now, Megaw J.'s judgment on the requirements of s. 12 of the Tribunals and Inquiries Act 1971 is still authoritative. On the effect of a breach of s. 12, see further the next case.

Crake v. Supplementary Benefits Commission

[1982] 1 All E.R. 498   Queen's Bench Division

The applicant had left her husband and was residing with another man. She claimed that she was acting as his housekeeper and applied for a supplementary allowance. The Commission decided that the two were 'living together as husband and wife' within para. 3 (1) (*b*) of Sch. 1 to the Supplementary Benefits Act 1976, aggregated her requirements and resources with his, and decided that she was not entitled to a supplementary allowance. An appeal tribunal affirmed the decision. The reasons given for the decision were:

The Tribunal considered on the matters before them by oral and written means, that the decision had been reached by the Commission in accordance with up to date criteria. They found that most of these had been satisfied and that accordingly Mrs Crake was to be regarded as living with Mr Watts as husband and wife. There were no exceptional circumstances to justify not aggregating requirements and resources.

The applicant appealed *inter alia* on the ground that the tribunal had not complied with its statutory duty to give reasons.

WOOLF J.: . . . It has got to be borne in mind, particularly with tribunals of this sort, that they cannot be expected to give long and precise accounts of their reasoning; but a short and concise statement in clear language should normally be possible which fairly indicates to the recipient why his appeal was allowed or dismissed; and it seems to me quite clear that when one looks at the findings[16] of this tribunal together with the reasons for its decision, it falls far short of the standard which the Act requires.

... It is next necessary to consider what the consequences of that are. I am afraid that here one enters into a position where the law is somewhat confused. The latest edition, which has just recently come out, of *de Smith's Judicial Review of Administrative Action* (4th edn, 1980) p. 151 deals with what are the consequences of the reasons not being in accordance with a statutory requirement in these terms:

> 'Unfortunately it is still far from clear what are the legal effects of non-compliance with a statutory duty to give reasons for decisions. There is authority for the proposition that failure to give reasons, or to give adequate reasons, is not in itself an error of law entitling the court to set the decision aside.'

And then there is a reference to two cases in particular. One is *Re Allen and Matthew's Arbitration* . . . [1971] 2 QB 518 and the other is *Mountview Court Properties Ltd.* v. *Devlin* (1970) 21 P & CR 689 to which I will have to come back in a moment. The editor continues:

> '. . . if good and bad reasons for a decision are given, the decision should stand provided that the reasons are independent and severable. There is also authority (which it is submitted, is to be preferred) for treating material omissions as errors of law or as a failure to comply with the requirements of the legislation in question, and for regarding the adduction of legally irrelevant reasons as an excess of jurisdiction.'

In support of the alternative way of approaching the matter the editor relies in particular on *Re Poyser and Mills's Arbitration* . . . [1964] 2 QB 467, *Givaudan & Co Ltd* v. *Minister of Housing and Local Government* . . . [1967] 1 W.LR 250 and *United Kingdom Association of Professional Engineers* v. *Advisory, Conciliation and Arbitration Service* . . . [1979] 1 WLR 570.

Those authorities have been cited to me together with a number of other authorities, and it seems to me that in approaching this question one must pay particular regard first of all to the *Mountview* decision. The facts of that case do not matter because it is a case involving a failure of the rent assessment committee to give reasons. In the course of his judgment Lord Parker CJ said (21 P & CR 689 at 695):

> 'For my part, I find it impossible to say that a failure to provide sufficient reasons of itself gives rise to the right of this court on an appeal to quash the decision of the committee. Secondly, it is to be observed that, quite apart from that, *Re Poyser and Mills's Arbitration* was really a case where, on the reasons stated, the proper inference was that there had been an error of law and that the arbitrator had misdirected himself. Of course, if the very insufficiency of the reason gives rise to a proper inference that there has

---

[16] [The findings of fact are omitted from this extract.]

been an error of law in arriving at the decision, then clearly it would be a case for quashing the decision.'

Cooke J agreed with that judgment. Bridge J said (at 695–696):

'It seems to me that there was here a lack of adequate reason for the decision, but I fully agree with my Lord and I add a word on this point because it seems to me to be a point of some importance: that a failure to give reasons pursuant to the duty imposed by section 12 of the Tribunals and Inquiries Act 1958[17] is not *per se* a ground on which the court could properly allow an appeal under section 9,[18] the right of appeal being conferred upon a person who is dissatisfied in point of law with a decision. That language, and, indeed, any analogous language found in the statutes giving a right of appeal on a point of law, to my mind connotes that a successful appellant must demonstrate that the decision with which he is dissatisfied is itself vitiated by reason of the fact that it has been reached by an erroneous process of legal reasoning. Mr. Slynn [as amicus curiae] concedes that there may in theory be cases where from a failure to give reasons one may legitimately infer, on a balance of probabilities, that the tribunal's process of legal reasoning must have been defective.'

And the judge goes on to say that at one stage in the argument he thought that was a case falling within that concession.

That decision of the Divisional Court has never been overruled and, in my view, it is binding on me. There are a number of cases where decisions have been set aside, among those being the decisions referred to by the editor of *de Smith* in the passage to which I have made reference, but when one looks at those cases they are in no way inconsistent with the *Mountview* case because they either turn on the particular statutory provision which gave the grounds for bringing the matter before the High Court in that case, or they turned on a statutory provision which was very different from the statutory provision which is under consideration here. . . .

I would therefore still regard the *Mountview* case as being the main authority to be applied. However, it has to be applied in the light of the ten years which have elapsed since that case was decided. Over that period of ten years the approach of the courts with regard to the giving of reasons has been much more definite than they were at that time and courts are now much more ready to infer that because of inadequate reasons there has been an error of law, than perhaps they were prepared to at the time that the *Mountview* case was decided.

. . . [I]n practice I think that there will be few cases where it will not be possible, where the reasons are inadequate, to say one way or another whether the tribunal has gone wrong in law. In some cases the absence of any reasons would indicate that the tribunal had never properly considered the matter (and it must be part of the obligation in law to consider the matter properly) and that the proper thought processes have not been gone through.

[17] [Re-enacted as s. 12 of the 1971 Act, p. 22 *supra*.]
[18] [Re-enacted as s. 13 of the 1971 Act, p. 64 *infra*.]

In other cases it will be seen from the reasons given that there has been a failure to take into account something which should have been taken into account or that something which should not have been taken into account has in fact been taken into account. Again, in that situation, there will be an error of law which will justify this court interfering on an appeal on a point of law.

In the rare case where it is not possible to decide either way whether or not there is an error of law, then, in my view, this court has got a jurisdiction, as was indicated in the *Mountview* case, to remit the matter to the tribunal for reconsideration. That power arises because of the very wide terms of s 13 of the Tribunals and Inquiries Act 1971, which is the Act which brings the matter before this court; and also because of the wording of RSC Ord 55, r 7. There are great practical disdvantages in that course, as was stressed in argument before me, in relation to tribunals of this nature, because tribunals of this nature are informal bodies which cannot readily be reconvened and, indeed, if they are reconvened, may well have no recollection of the case which they heard; and so obviously the situations where it will be necessary to remit the matter will be limited. . . .

[He then considered the tribunal's reasons together with its findings of fact and the notes of the chairman which were taken at the hearing, and continued:]

Having approached the matter with the notes in mind I have come to the conclusion that notwithstanding the inadequacy of the reasoning of the tribunal, it would be wrong to allow this appeal on the grounds that the tribunal were approaching the matter in the wrong way.

Appeal dismissed.

Question

Would you classify the duty to give reasons imposed by s. 12 of the Tribunals and Inquiries Act 1971 as mandatory or directory? See, in addition to the cases *supra*, p. 567 *infra* (concern of the Council on Tribunals on non-observation of this obligation); *Brayhead (Ascot) Ltd.* v. *Berkshire C.C.* [1964] 2 Q.B. at p. 313; Wade, pp. 223 and 812.

Notes

1. *Crake's* case concerned an appeal and was not an application for judicial review. On statutory appeals, see pp. 64 and 558 *infra*.

2. Although this section is concerned with express statutory requirements, it will perhaps be convenient at this point to consider the question of the effect of a failure to state reasons where there is, in fact, no express requirement. No general rule of English law requires that reasons must be given for administrative or judicial decisions: *R.* v. *Gaming Board of Great Britain, ex p. Benaim and Khaida*, p. 244 *infra*; *McInnes* v. *Onslow-Fane*, p. 266, *infra*. Compare § 8 (*b*) of the United States Administrative Procedure Act 1946 (5 U.S.C. § 557 (*c*)), which states that all decisions shall include a statement of findings and conclusions, and the reasons or basis therefor and Article 190 of the E.E.C. Treaty, which provides that regulations, directives, and decisions shall state the reasons on which they are based (Schermers, *Judicial Protection in the European Communities*, 2nd edn., §§ 273–86). The latter is, by virtue of s. 2 of the

European Communities Act 1972, incorporated into British law and its existence may influence the development of a common law duty to give reasons. For the potential of the common law to do this, see the next two extracts and see further Akehurst, (1970) 33 M.L.R. 154; Flick, [1978] P.L. 16; Wade, pp. 373–4. On the position of professional judges, see the suggestion in R. v. *Knightsbridge Crown Court, ex p. International Sporting Club (London) Ltd.*, p. 75 *infra*.

Padfield v. Minister of Agriculture, Fisheries, and Food

[1968] A.C. 997   House of Lords

For the facts and further extracts see p. 164 *infra*.

LORD REID: . . . It was argued that the Minister is not bound to give any reasons for refusing to refer a complaint to the committee, that if he gives no reasons his decision cannot be questioned, and that it would be very unfortunate if giving reasons were to put him in a worse position. But I do not agree that a decision cannot be questioned if no reasons are given. If it is the Minister's duty not to act so as to frustrate the policy and objects of the Act, and if it were to appear from all the circumstances of the case that that has been the effect of the Minister's refusal, then it appears to me that the court must be entitled to act. . . .

LORD HODSON: . . . The reasons disclosed are not, in my opinion, good reasons for refusing to refer the complaint seeing that they leave out of account altogether the merits of the complaint itself. The complaint is, as the Lord Chief Justice pointed out, made by persons affected by the scheme and is not one for the consumer committee as opposed to the committee of investigation and it was eligible for reference to the latter. It has never been suggested that the complaint was not a genuine one. It is no objection to the exercise of the discretion to refer that wide issues will be raised and the interests of other regions and the regional price structure as a whole would be affected. It is likely that the removal of a grievance will, in any event, have a wide effect and the Minister cannot lawfully say in advance that he will not refer the matter to the committee to ascertain the facts because, as he says in effect, although not in so many words, 'I would not regard it as right to give effect to the report if it were favourable to the appellants.'

It has been suggested that the reasons given by the Minister need not and should not be examined closely for he need give no reason at all in the exercise of his discretion. True it is that the Minister is not bound to give his reasons for refusing to exercise his discretion in a particular manner, but when, as here, the circumstances indicate a genuine complaint for which the appropriate remedy is provided, if the Minister in the case in question so directs, he would not escape from the possibility of control by mandamus through adopting a negative attitude without explanation. As the guardian of the public interest he has a duty to protect the interests of those who claim to have been treated contrary to the public interest. . . .

LORD PEARCE: . . . I do not regard a Minister's failure or refusal to give any reasons as a sufficient exclusion of the court's surveillance. If all the prima

facie reasons seem to point in favour of his taking a certain course to carry out
the intentions of Parliament in respect of a power which it has given him in
that regard, and he gives no reason whatever for taking a contrary course, the
court may infer that he has no good reason and that he is not using the power
given by Parliament to carry out its intentions. In the present case, however,
the Minister has given reasons which show that he was not exercising his
discretion in accordance with the intentions of the Act. . . .

LORD UPJOHN: . . . [A Minister] is a public officer charged by Parliament
with the discharge of a public discretion affecting Her Majesty's subjects; if
he does not give any reason for his decision it may be, if circumstances
warrant it, that a court may be at liberty to come to the conclusion that he had
no good reason for reaching that conclusion and order a prerogative writ to
issue accordingly. . . .

Secretary of State for Employment v. A.S.L.E.F. (No. 2)

[1972] 2 Q.B. 455   Court of Appeal

The Industrial Relations Act 1971 provided emergency procedures
whereby the Secretary of State could order a compulsory ballot if he believed
a strike to be against the wishes of the workers involved. During a railway
strike the Secretary of State ordered a ballot without giving any reasons.

LORD DENNING M.R.: . . . It is said that it must 'appear' to the Minister that
there are 'reasons' for doubting whether the workers are behind their leaders:
and that the Minister has given no reasons. We have been referred to several
recent cases, of which Padfield v. Minister of Agriculture, Fisheries and Food
[1968] A.C.997 is the best example, in which the courts have stressed that in
the ordinary way a Minister should give reasons, and if he gives none the
court may infer that he had no good reasons. Whilst I would apply that
proposition completely in most cases, and particularly in cases which affect
life, liberty or property, I do not think that it applies in all cases. Here we are
concerned with a ballot to ascertain the wishes of 170,000 men. The executive committees of the unions consist, we are told, of 60 men. These 60 are, no
doubt, fully convinced that the whole 170,000 will support them. It is the
honourable tradition of the men to support their leaders. There are many
messages and telegrams which have told of support from the branches. Yet
there are times when even their leaders, in touch as they are, may be mistaken.

The Solicitor-General suggested to us some reasons for doubting whether
the wishes of the individual men were behind this. The Minister, he suggested,
might think that, as the dispute had been discussed and debated, before a
chairman agreed by both sides, many of the workers would wish to accept his
award rather than take part in industrial action. The Minister also had asked
the leaders of the unions earnestly to consider holding a ballot of the workers
so as to ascertain their wishes. The leaders were quite sure, and are quite sure,
that the men are wholly in support of this industrial action. If so, there would
seem to be no good reason why they should in any way not be content for a
ballot to be held. I do not say that those reasons are right, but they are such as

a reasonable Minister might entertain; and, if they are such – if the Minister could on reasonable grounds from the view and opinion that he did – as I read the law and the statute this court has no jurisdiction or power to interfere with his decision.

So, having examined the whole matter, in my opinion the requisites for an order for a ballot were satisfied, and there is no ground on which this court can interfere with the decision. . . .

Notes

1. See also *Gouriet* v. *U.P.O.W.* [1978] A.C. 435 at pp. 489 and 496. A case in which reasons for a decision were implied from the factual context was *Municipal Council of Sydney* v. *Campbell*, p. 176 *infra*.

2. For an example of a statutory exclusion of a duty to give reasons, see s. 44 (2) of the British Nationality Act 1981. Will the existence of such provisions strengthen the position of those who wish to argue that there is a nascent common law duty to give reasons?

3. There may also be considerations of public policy that will justify a refusal by a public officer to give reasons for a particular decision. See, for instance, in the context of public interest immunity, *I.R.C.* v. *Rossminster Ltd.*, p. 92 *infra*, per Lord Diplock. On public interest immunity in general see p. 461 *infra*.

CONCLUSIVENESS AND MISTAKE

Revocable and irrevocable action

In Re 56 Denton Road, Twickenham

[1953] Ch. 51   Chancery Division

The plaintiff's house was badly damaged by enemy action. The War Damage Commission informed her on 12 November 1945 that the preliminary classification of the property for compensation purposes as a total loss had been reviewed, that it was now classified 'not a total loss', and that the Commission would make a 'cost of works' payment. In July 1946 the Commission informed her that it had been decided to revert to the total loss classification under which she would get less compensation. The plaintiff sought a declaration that the letter of 12 November 1945 constituted a final and irrevocable determination of her rights under the War Damage Act 1943.

VAISEY J.: . . . [W]here Parliament confers upon a body such as the War Damage Commission the duty of deciding or determining any question, the deciding or determining of which affects the rights of the subject, such decision or determination made and communicated in terms which are not expressly preliminary or provisional is final and conclusive, and cannot in the absence of express statutory power or the consent of the person or persons affected be altered or withdrawn by that body. I accept that proposition as well-founded, and applicable to the present case. . . .

I think that the letter of November 12, 1945, was one upon which the plaintiff was invited to rely and was and is entitled to rely. It is, I think, admitted that if she had altered her position in reliance upon it, a case of estoppel would have been raised against the defendants. But I really cannot see that it ought to be denied its proper force and effect, quite apart from such a case.

I think that the contrary view would introduce a lamentable measure of uncertainty, and so much disturbance in the minds of those unfortunate persons who have suffered war damage that the Act cannot have contemplated the possibility of such vacillations as are claimed to be permissible in such a case as the present. . . .

The next thing that apparently happened was that the owner of the adjoining house, No. 58 Denton Road, heard of the defendants' decision and claimed to be entitled to be treated in a similar manner. That seems to have shown to the defendants that they had created an awkward precedent, and to meet that predicament they called in someone whom they describe as 'a superior officer' to reconsider the matter. He (the superior officer) appears to have differed from the opinion of the first officer and to have advised the defendants that the conditions of the Treasury direction had not been fulfilled, with the result that they recanted and reversed their previous decision, and wrote the letter of July 15, 1946. . . .

Where, it may be asked, is this process to stop? Is the matter to be referred to a sequence of officers, each one superior to the one immediately before him? If an officer (superior or not) gives advice to the defendants which, having been reported to the person affected, turns out to be embarrassing, can the defendants, without any notice to such person, go on from officer to officer, until they obtain advice which is more to their liking? I cannot think that this is what the War Damage Commission ought to do. I think they should at least refrain from buoying up the hopes and expectations of those with whom they deal by reporting 'determinations' in terms which make them appear to be, although they are not in fact, final, fixed and conclusive.

The judgment can do no harm to the defendants. Let them mark every intimation of a 'determination' of theirs as 'provisional,' 'subject to alteration,' 'not to be relied upon' or words to that effect.

Declaration accordingly.

Questions

1. Would the court in *Re 56 Denton Road* have permitted reconsideration if the letter of 12 November 1945 had not conferred a benefit on the plaintiff? See Rubinstein, *Jurisdiction and Illegality*, p. 30; Ganz, [1965] P.L. 237; de Smith, pp. 107–8.

2. What dangers are there in insisting that an authority is only free to vary a decision if it states that it is 'provisional', 'subject to alteration', or that it is 'not to be relied upon'? See p. 161 *infra*.

Notes

1. In *Rootkin* v. *Kent C.C.* [1981] 1 W.L.R. 1186 Lawton L.J. said (at p. 1195) that the principle in *Re 56 Denton Road* does not apply to 'a case where the citizen has no right to a determination on certain facts being established, but only to the benefit of the exercise of a discretion' by the administrative body. In that case a local authority had determined that the plaintiff's home was over three miles away from her daughter's school, and had accordingly exercised a discretionary power to pay the daughter's bus fares to and from school. When the distance was re-measured and found to be under three miles the authority refused to continue to pay the fares and asked that the unexpired portion of the season ticket issued to the child be returned. This was upheld by the Court of Appeal. Would Lawton L.J.'s reasoning have justified a claim by the authority for reimbursement of the cost of fares paid by it between the date of the original determination and the date on which it changed its mind?

2. The principle in *Re 56 Denton Road* would appear to differ from the estoppel principle discussed at p. 148 *infra* in that it does not depend on a finding of detrimental reliance. Thus, in *Rootkin* v. *Kent C.C.* the two principles were considered separately by the court. Neither was found to be applicable. See further Williams, [1981] C.L.J. 198; Bradley, (1981) 34 C.L.P. 1 at pp. 15–16.

POWER OR DUTY – WORDS PERMISSIVE OR OBLIGATORY

Padfield v. Minister of Agriculture, Fisheries, and Food p. 164 *infra*

Note

See further the Note at p. 111 *infra*; Note 2, p. 169 *infra*; Wade, p. 228 (and note *Julius* v. *Lord Bishop of Oxford* (1880) L.R. 5 App. Cas. 214 which he contrasts with *Padfield*).

ESTOPPEL

Note

This topic is dealt with at p. 148 *infra*. See also Wade, pp. 231 and 341.

WAIVER AND CONSENT

Essex County Council v. Essex Incorporated Congregational Church Union

[1963] A.C. 808   House of Lords

The owners of a church and hall which were affected by certain planning proposals served a notice on the Council under s. 39 of the Town and Country Planning Act 1959 requiring them, as compensating authority, to purchase the property. The Council objected and served a counter-notice under s. 40 of the Act on the ground that two of the conditions specified in s. 39 (that reasonable endeavours had been made to sell the property and that no sale was possible except at a price substantially below that reasonably obtainable if the property had not been affected by planning proposals) were not fulfilled. Section 40 provided that counter-notices may be served 'at any time before the end of the period of two months' after the service of a s. 39 notice. Section 40 (3) provided that a counter-notice 'shall specify the grounds . . . on which the appropriate authority object to the notice'. Where a counter-notice was served the owners could require the matter to be referred to the Lands Tribunal which, by s. 41, was to consider the matters in the notice and counter-notice and determine whether or not the notice was valid. The case was referred to the Tribunal but the Council now put forward a new reason for objecting to the notice. It was argued that, since the property was exempt from rates, it did not qualify for protection under the Act. This was considered as a preliminary point of law and rejected by the Tribunal.

A case was stated on this point and, in the Court of Appeal ([1961] 2 Q.B. 613), it was unsuccessfully argued by the owners that the Tribunal only had jurisdiction to consider objections in the counter-notice. The court did, however, affirm the decision of the Tribunal. On appeal by the Council:

LORD REID: . . .I am of opinion that the Lands Tribunal had no jurisdiction to entertain or decide this preliminary point of law, and that accordingly this case should never have been stated and the question in it should not have been answered by the Court of Appeal, and should not now be answered by your Lordships.

[He then considered the relevant provisions of the Town and Country Planning Act 1959 and concluded:] [I]t appears to me to follow inevitably [from the statutory provisions] that the tribunal had no jurisdiction to do anything more in this case than to determine whether the objection in the appellants' counter-notice should or should not be upheld.

. . . But the appellants say that the respondents cannot be allowed to maintain this point now because they consented to the matter being dealt with by the tribunal. What in fact happened was that the appellants requested the tribunal to deal with this point as a preliminary point of law; this request was intimated to the respondents and they did not object; then the respondents appeared before the tribunal and argued the point but, not being then alive to their rights, they did not protest. I need not consider whether this amounted to a consent to widening the reference to the tribunal, because, in my judgment, it is a fundamental principle that no consent can confer on a court or tribunal with limited statutory jurisdiction any power to act beyond that jurisdiction, or can estop the consenting party from subsequently maintaining that such court or tribunal has acted without jurisdiction.

If the High Court, having general jurisdiction, proceeds in an unauthorised manner by consent there may well be estoppel. And an arbitrator, or other tribunal deriving its jurisdiction from the consent of parties, may well have his jurisdiction extended by consent of parties. But there is no analogy between such cases and the present case. The tribunal in the present case had no power to state a case except with regard to some matter arising out of the exercise of its limited statutory jurisdiction, and this stated case does not deal with any such matter. I am, therefore, of opinion that the stated case was not properly before the Court of Appeal and is not properly before your Lordships. Accordingly this House ought to refuse to answer the question set out in the case stated.

[His Lordship, nevertheless, went on to consider the question and, treating the matter as a pure question of construction, concluded that the property in this case did not qualify for protection.]

LORD DEVLIN: ... I dismiss the notion that by inquiring into the validity of the notice, as the point of law plainly demands that it should do, the tribunal was necessarily exceeding its power. It has power to do so under certain conditions. What are these conditions?

Before answering this question it is convenient to consider what it is that a superior court has to be satisfied about when it is questioning the jurisdiction of an inferior tribunal. It has to be satisfied that the tribunal has general jurisdiction, that is, jurisdiction to enter upon the inquiry. A statute, besides laying down conditions precedent to the entry upon the inquiry, often lays down conditions which have to be satisfied before the tribunal takes some step in the course of the inquiry or makes interim or final orders. If these conditions are not satisfied, it is then sometimes said that the tribunal had no power to take the step or make the order. That is not what is meant by general jurisdiction. If the tribunal makes an order it ought not to have made, it may thereby fall into an error of law which can be corrected, but the error does not derive it of jurisdiction. This distinction is made clear in the opinion of the Judicial Committee in the well known case of *Colonial Bank of Australasia* v. *Willan*[19] where it is said: '... the question is, whether the inferior court had jurisdiction to enter upon the inquiry, and not whether there has been miscarriage in the course of the inquiry.' Lord Sumner spoke to the same effect in *Rex* v. *Nat Bell Liquors Ltd.*[20] The case of *Andrews* v. *Elliott*,[21] which was cited in argument, is an illustration of the same point. It illustrates also the rule that if there is no general jurisdiction, no consent or acquiescence can confer it. But if there is general jurisdiction, consent or lack of objection such as is alleged here might prevent the respondents from relying upon any irregularity in the proceedings.

The scope of the inquiry which the court must make in order to satisfy itself whether there was general jurisdiction is described by Sir James Colville in *Colonial Bank of Australasia* v. *Willan.*[22] The two subjects that are relevant here are 'the nature of the subject-matter of the inquiry' and whether there are 'certain proceedings which have been made essential preliminaries to the inquiry.'

I do not think it can be disputed that service of a counter-notice is an essential preliminary to the inquiry. But there was here a counter-notice, and

[19] (1874) L.R. 5 P.C. 417, P.C.
[20] [1922] 2 A.C. 128, 151.
[21] (1855) 5 E. & B. 502; (1856) 6 E. & B. 338.
[22] L.R. 5 P.C. 417, 442–443.

if that is all that is needed, the court can inquire into the validity of the purchase notice. I do not think, with respect, that it can be right on any view to declare on a preliminary point of law the purchase notice to be valid before the grounds of objection in the counter-notice have been considered, but that is a matter which could be put right in the form of answer to the question if it is to be answered. Of course, it does not follow from the fact that the tribunal can inquire into the validity of the notice that it can properly invalidate it on a ground not stated in the counter-notice. It may well be, and I should, if necessary, so hold, that on the true construction of the Act the notice is conclusively presumed to be valid in all respects which are not covered by grounds of objection. If it were otherwise, there would never be any need to specify more than one ground of objection, which would be directly contrary to section 40 (3). But to construe the Act otherwise would on this hypothesis be an error of law committed in the course of the inquiry. There would be jurisdiction to state a case on the point; and, if it were held that there was an error in going beyond the counter-notice as served, it would be necessary to consider whether the respondents impliedly consented, as the appellants contend, to the extension of the counter-notice to cover the point.

But if the service of the counter-notice is not only 'an essential preliminary to the inquiry' but further by its contents it confines 'the nature of the subject-matter of the inquiry,' the result would be different. I do not find this an easy point because of the rather evasive language of the Act.

But on the whole I have reached the conclusion that the inquiry is limited to the grounds set out in the objection.

. . . I conclude, therefore, that the jurisdiction given to the tribunal to determine the validity of the purchase notice is confined within the grounds set out in the counter-notice; and accordingly that, if the tribunal goes beyond those grounds, it is not merely taking a step which is contrary to the provisions of the Act but is exceeding its jurisdiction.

[LORD JENKINS concurred with LORD REID and LORD HODSON and LORD MORRIS OF BORTH-Y-GEST delivered speeches in favour of dismissing the appeal.]

Appeal dismissed.

Notes

1. The courts have developed the concept of jurisdiction since this case and Lord Devlin's view must be treated with caution. See *Anisminic Ltd.* v. *Foreign Compensation Commission*, p. 38 *infra*, and especially Note 2, p. 45 *infra*.

2. See further Note 2, p. 101 *infra* (problems of invalidity); Wade, p. 234; de Smith, p. 153. See also p. 148 *infra* (restriction of discretion by estoppel). Consider also the fact that most public law remedies are discretionary (pp. 239 and 364 *infra*). What effect, if any, does the discretionary nature of remedies have on the rule that want of jurisdiction cannot be cured by waiver or consent?

RES JUDICATA

Notes

1. For the application of this principle, which prevents a party to a judicial determination from reopening the litigation, to the decisions of administrative bodies, see Wade, p. 239. See also *Re 56 Denton Road, Twickenham*, p. 31 *supra*.

2. On the inapplicability of issue estoppel to applications for judicial review, see *R. v. Secretary of State for the Environment, ex p. Hackney L.B.C.* [1983] 1 W.L.R. 524.

2

JURISDICTION OVER FACT AND LAW

ERROR OUTSIDE JURISDICTION

Jurisdictional error: jurisdictional law

Anisminic Ltd. v. Foreign Compensation Commission

[1969] 2 A.C. 147   House of Lords

The plaintiff, an English company, had owned property in Egypt worth about £4.4 m which the Egyptian authorities sequestrated in 1956. In 1957 the plaintiff sold the property to T.E.D.O., an Egyptian organization, for £0.5 m. By a treaty between the United Arab Republic and the United Kingdom, £27.5 m was paid over to the latter as compensation for property confiscated in 1956 and the plaintiff sought to participate in this fund by applying to the Foreign Compensation Commission. The Commission's provisional determination was that the plaintiff had failed to establish a claim under the Foreign Compensation (Egypt) (Determination and Registration of Claims) Order 1962 on the ground that its successor in title was a non-British national and consequently it did not comply with the terms of Article 4 (1) (*b*) (ii) of the Order. (This is set out at p. 39 *infra*.)

The plaintiff sought a declaration that the provisional determination was a nullity contending that the Commission had misconstrued the Order. The Commission denied this and also contended that the court was precluded from considering whether the determination was a nullity because of the presence of an ouster clause in the Foreign Compensation Act 1950. This aspect of the case is considered at p. 374 *infra*.

Browne J. granted the declaration (see [1962] 2 A.C. at p. 223 for a report of his judgment) but the Court of Appeal reversed his decision ([1968] 2 Q.B. 862) The plaintiff appealed to the House of Lords which, by a majority, reversed the decision of the Court of Appeal.

LORD REID: . . . It has sometimes been said that it is only where a tribunal acts without jurisdiction that its decision is a nullity. But in such cases the word 'jurisdiction' has been used in a very wide sense, and I have come to the conclusion that it is better not to use the term except in the narrow and original sense of the tribunal being entitled to enter on the inquiry in question. But there are many cases where, although the tribunal had jurisdiction to enter on the inquiry, it has done or failed to do something in the course of the inquiry which is of such a nature that its decision is a nullity. It may have given its decision in bad faith. It may have made a decision which it had no power to make. It may have failed in the course of the inquiry to comply with the requirements of natural justice. It may in perfect good faith have misconstrued the provisions giving it power to act so that it failed to deal with the question remitted to it and decided some question which was not remitted to it. It may have refused to take into account something which it was required to take into account. Or it may have based its decision on some matter which, under the provisions setting it up, it had no right to take into account. I do not intend this list to be exhaustive. But if it decides a question remitted to it for decision without committing any of these errors it is as much entitled to decide that question wrongly as it is to decide it rightly. I understand that some confusion has been caused by my having said in *Reg.* v. *Governor of Brixton Prison, Ex parte Armah* [1968] A.C. 192, 234 that if a tribunal has jurisdiction to go right it has jurisdiction to go wrong. So it has, if one uses 'jurisdiction' in the narrow original sense. If it is entitled to enter on the inquiry and does not do any of those things which I have mentioned in the course of the proceedings, then its decision is equally valid whether it is right or wrong subject only to the power of the court in certain circumstances to correct an error of law. I think that, if these views are correct, the only case cited which was plainly wrongly decided is *Davies* v. *Price* [1958] 1 W.L.R. 434. But in a number of other cases some of the grounds of judgment are questionable.

I can now turn to the provisions of the Order under which the commission acted, and to the way in which the commission reached their decision. It was said in the Court of Appeal that publication of their reasons was unnecessary and perhaps undesirable. Whether or not they could have been required to publish their reasons, I dissent emphatically from the view that publication may have been undesirable. In my view, the commission acted with complete propriety, as one would expect looking to its membership.

The meaning of the important parts of this Order is extremely difficult to discover, and, in my view, a main cause of this is the deplorable modern drafting practice of compressing to the point of obscurity provisions which would not be difficult to understand if written out at rather greater length.

The effect of the Order was to confer legal rights on persons who might previously have hoped or expected that in allocating any sums available discretion would be exercised in their favour. We are concerned in this case with article 4 of the Order and more particularly with paragraph (1) (*b*) (ii) of that article. Article 4 is as follows:

'(1) The Commission shall treat a claim under this Part of the Order as established if the applicant satisfies them of the following matters:– (*a*) that his application relates to property in Egypt which is referred to in Annex E; (*b*) if the property is referred to in paragraph (1) (*a*) or paragraph (2) of Annex E – (i) that the applicant is the person referred to in paragraph (1) (*a*) or in paragraph (2), as the case may be, as the owner of the property or is the successor in title of such person; and (ii) that the person referred to as aforesaid and any person who became successor in title of such person on or before February 28, 1959, were British nationals on October 31, 1956, and February 28, 1959; (c) if the property is referred to in paragraph (1) (b) of Annex E – (i) that the applicant was the owner on October 31, 1956, or, at the option of the applicant, on the date of the sale of the property at any time before February 28, 1959, by the Government of the United Arab Republic under the provisions of Egyptian Proclamation No. 5 of November 1, 1956, or is the successor in title of such owner; and (ii) that the owner on October 31, 1956, or on the date of such sale, as the case may be, and any person who became successor in title of such owner on or before February 28, 1959, were British nationals on October 31, 1956, and February 28, 1959 . . .'

The task of the commission was to receive claims and to determine the rights of each applicant. It is enacted that they shall treat a claim as established if the applicant satisfies them of certain matters. About the first there is no difficulty: the appellants' application does relate to property in Egypt referred to in Annex E. But then the difficulty begins.

Annex E originally only included properties which had been sold during the sequestration, so the person mentioned in Annex E as the owner is the person who owned the property before that sale, and his claim is a claim for compensation for having been deprived of that property. Normally he will be the applicant. But there is also provision for an application by a 'successor in title.' The first difficulty is to determine what is meant by 'successor in title.' Before the Order was made the position was that former owners whose property had been sold during the sequestration had no title to anything. They had no title to the property because it had been sold. And they had no title to compensation. All they had was a hope or expectation that they might receive some compensation. They had no legal rights at all. It is now common ground that 'successor in title' cannot mean the person who obtained a title to the property which formerly belonged to the applicant. The person who acquired the property from the sequestrator was generally an Egyptian and he could have no ground for claiming compensation. So 'successor in title' must refer to some person who somehow succeeded to the original owner as the person now having the original owner's hope or expectation of receiving compensation. The obvious case would be where the original owner had died. But for the moment I shall leave that problem.

The main difficulty in this case springs from the fact that the draftsman did not state separately what conditions have to be satisfied (1) where the applicant is the original owner and (2) where the applicant claims as the successor in title of the original owner. It is clear that where the applicant is the original owner he must prove that he was a British national on the dates stated. And it is equally clear that where the applicant claims as being the original owner's successor in title he must prove that both he and the original owner were British nationals on those dates, subject to later provisions in the article about persons who had died or had been born within the relevant period. What is left in obscurity is whether the provisions with regard to successors in title have any application at all in cases where the applicant is himself the original owner. If this provision had been split up as it should have been, and the conditions, to be satisfied where the original owner is the applicant had been set out, there could have been no such obscurity.

This is the crucial question in this case. It appears from the commission's reasons that they construed this provision as requiring them to inquire, when the applicant is himself the original owner, whether he had a successor in title. So they made that inquiry in this case and held that T.E.D.O. was the applicant's successor in title. As T.E.D.O. was not a British national they rejected the appellants' claim. But if, on a true construction of the Order, a claimant who is an original owner does not have to prove anything about successors in title, then the commission made an inquiry which the Order did not empower them to make, and they based their decision on a matter which they had no right to take into account. If one uses the word 'jurisdiction' in its wider sense, they went beyond their jurisdiction in considering this matter. It was argued that the whole matter of construing the Order was something remitted to the commission for their decision. I cannot accept that argument. I find nothing in the Order to support it. The Order requires the commission to consider whether they are satisfied with regard to the prescribed matters. That is all they have to do. It cannot be for the commission to determine the limits of its powers. Of course if one party submits to a tribunal that its powers are wider than in fact they are, then the tribunal must deal with that submission. But if they reach a wrong conclusion as to the width of their powers, the court must be able to correct that – not because the tribunal has made an error of law, but because as a result of making an error of law they have dealt with and based their decision on a matter with which, on a true construction of their powers, they had no right to deal. If they base their decision on some matter which is not prescribed for their adjudication, they are doing something which they have no right to do and, if the view which I expressed earlier is right, their decision is a nullity. So the question is whether on a true construction of the Order the applicants did or did not have to prove anything with regard to successors in title. If the commission were entitled to enter on the inquiry whether the applicants had a successor in title, then their decision as to whether T.E.D.O. was their successor in title would I think be unassailable whether it was right or wrong: it would be a decision on a matter remitted to them for their decision. The question I have to consider is not whether they made a wrong decision but whether they inquired into and decided a matter which they had no right to consider.

. . . In themselves the words 'successor in title' are, in my opinion, inappropriate in the circumstances of this Order to denote any person while the original owner is still in existence, and I think it most improbable that they were ever intended to denote any such person. There is no necessity to stretch them to cover any such person. I would therefore hold that the words 'and any person who became successor in title to such person' in article 4 (1) (b) (ii) have no application to a case where the applicant is the original owner. It follows that the commission rejected the appellants' claim on a ground which they had no right to take into account and that their decision was a nullity. I would allow this appeal.

LORD PEARCE: . . . Lack of jurisdiction may arise in various ways. There may be an absence of those formalities or things which are conditions precedent to the tribunal having any jurisdiction to embark on an inquiry. Or the tribunal may at the end make an order that it has no jurisdiction to make. Or in the intervening stage, while engaged on a proper inquiry, the tribunal may depart from the rules of natural justice; or it may ask itself the wrong questions; or it may take into account matters which it was not directed to take into account. Thereby it would step outside its jurisdiction. It would turn its inquiry into something not directed by Parliament and fail to make the inquiry which Parliament did direct. Any of these things would cause its purported decision to be a nullity. . . .

LORD WILBERFORCE: . . . I must first say something as to the legal framework of this appeal: for though, in my opinion, the solution of this case is to be looked for in the thickets of subsidiary legislation, it is useful to be clear as to the general character of the argument. I do not think that it is difficult to describe this and I shall endeavour to do so, initially at least, in non-technical terms, avoiding for the moment such words as 'jurisdiction,' 'error' and 'nullity' which create many problems.

The Foreign Compensation Commission is one of many tribunals set up to deal with matters of a specialised character, in the interest of economy, speed, and expertise. It has acquired a unique status, since it alone has been excepted from the provisions of section 11 of the Tribunals and Inquiries Act, 1958.[1] It is now well established that specialised tribunals may, depending on their nature and on the subject-matter, have the power to decide questions of law, and the position may be reached, as the result of statutory provision, that even if they make what the courts might regard as decisions wrong in law, these are to stand. The Foreign Compensation Commission is certainly within this category; its functions are predominantly judicial; it is a permanent body, composed of lawyers, with a learned chairman, and there is every ground, having regard to the number and the complexity of the cases with which it must deal, for giving a wide measure of finality to its decisions. . . .

In every case, whatever the character of a tribunal, however wide the range of questions remitted to it, however great the permissible margin of mistake, the essential point remains that the tribunal has a derived authority, derived, that is, from statute: at some point, and to be found from a consideration of the legislation, the field within which it operates is marked out and limited. There is always an area, narrow or wide, which is the tribunal's area; a residual area, wide or narrow, in which the legislature has previously expressed its will and into which the tribunal may not enter. Equally, though this is not something that arises in the present case, there are certain funda-

---

[1] Substantially re-enacted as s. 14 of the Tribunals and Inquiries Act 1971, p. 379 *infra*. This provision restricts the effectiveness of clauses in certain statutes which seek to oust the supervisory jurisdiction of the court but the exception of the Commission is no longer there. On the Commission see now p. 378 *infra*.

mental assumptions, which without explicit restatement in every case, necessarily underlie the remission of power to decide such as (I do not attempt more than a general reference, since the strength and shade of these matters will depend upon the nature of the tribunal and the kind of question it has to decide) the requirement that a decision must be made in accordance with principles of natural justice and good faith. The principle that failure to fulfil these assumptions may be equivalent to a departure from the remitted area must be taken to follow from the decision of this House in *Ridge* v. *Baldwin* [1964] A.C. 40. Although, in theory perhaps, it may be possible for Parliament to set up a tribunal which has full and autonomous powers to fix its own area of operation, that has, so far, not been done in this country. The question, what is the tribunal's proper area, is one which it has always been permissible to ask and to answer, and it must follow that examination of its extent is not precluded by a clause conferring conclusiveness, finality, or unquestionability upon its decisions. . . .

The separate but complementary responsibilities of court and tribunal were very clearly stated by Lord Esher M.R. in *Reg.* v. *Commissioners for Special Purposes of the Income Tax* (1888) 21 Q.B.D. 313, 319, in these words:

'When an inferior court or tribunal or body, which has to exercise the power of deciding facts, is first established by Act of Parliament, the legislature has to consider what powers it will give that tribunal or body. It may in effect say that, if a certain state of facts exists and is shown to such tribunal or body before it proceeds to do certain things, it shall have jurisdiction to do such things, but not otherwise. There it is not for them conclusively to decide whether that state of facts exists, and, if they exercise the jurisdiction without its existence, what they do may be questioned, and it will be held that they have acted without jurisdiction.'

That the ascertainment of the proper limits of the tribunal's power of decision is a task for the court was stated by Farwell L.J. in *Rex* v. *Shoreditch Assessment Committee, Ex parte Morgan* [1910] 2 K.B. 859, 880 in language which, though perhaps vulnerable to logical analysis, has proved its value as guidance to the courts:

'Subjection in this respect to the High Court is a necessary and inseparable incident for all tribunals of limited jurisdiction; for the existence of the limit necessitates an authority to determine and enforce it: it is a contradiction in terms to create a tribunal with limited jurisdiction and unlimited power to determine such limit at its own will and pleasure – such a tribunal would be autocratic, not limited – and it is immaterial whether the decision of the inferior tribunal on the question of the existence or non-existence of its own jurisdiction is founded on law or fact.'[2]

[2] [This passage is immediately preceded by the following:

'No tribunal of inferior jurisdiction can by its own decision finally decide on the question of the existence or extent of such jurisdiction: such question is always subject to review by the High Court, which does not permit the inferior tribunal either to usurp a jurisdiction which it does not possess, whether at all or to the extent claimed, or to refuse to exercise a jurisdiction which it has and ought to exercise.]

Denning L.J. added his authority to this in *Rex* v. *Northumberland Compensation Appeal Tribunal, Ex parte Shaw* [1952] 1 K.B. 338, 346 in the words:

'No one has ever doubted that the Court of King's Bench can intervene to prevent a statutory tribunal from exceeding the jurisdiction which Parliament has conferred on it, but it is quite another thing to say that the King's Bench can intervene when a tribunal makes a mistake of law. A tribunal may often decide a point of law wrongly whilst keeping well within its jurisdiction.'

These passages at least answer one of the respondents' main arguments, to some extent accepted by the members of the Court of Appeal, which is that *because* the commission has (admittedly) been given power, indeed required, to decide some questions of law, arising out of the construction of the relevant Order in Council, it must necessarily have power to decide those questions which relate to the delimitation of its powers; or conversely that if the court has power to review the latter, it must also have power to review the former. But the one does not follow from the other: there is no reason why the Order in Council should not (as a matter of construction to be decided by the court) limit the tribunal's power and at the same time (by the same process of construction) confer upon the tribunal power, in the exercise of its permitted task, to decide other questions of law, including questions of construction of the Order. I shall endeavour to show that this is what the Order has done.

The extent of the interpretatory power conferred upon the tribunal may sometimes be difficult to ascertain and argument may be possible whether this or that question of construction has been left to the tribunal, that is, is within the tribunal's field, or whether, because it pertains to the delimitation of the tribunal's area by the legislature, it is reserved for decision by the courts. Sometimes it will be possible to form a conclusion from the form and subject-matter of the legislation. In one case it may be seen that the legislature, while stating general objectives, is prepared to concede a wide area to the authority it establishes: this will often be the case where the decision involves a degree of policy-making rather than fact-finding, especially if the authority is a department of government or the Minister at its head. I think that we have reached a stage in our administrative law when we can view this question quite objectively, without any necessary predisposition towards one that questions of law, or questions of construction, are necessarily for the courts. In the kind of case I have mentioned there is no need to make this assumption. In another type of case it may be apparent that Parliament is itself directly and closely concerned with the definition and delimitation of certain matters of comparative detail and has marked by its language the intention that these shall accurately be observed. . . . The present case, . . . as examination of the relevant Order in Council will show, is clearly of the latter category.

I do not think it desirable to discuss further in detail the many decisions in the reports in this field. But two points may perhaps be made. First, the cases in which a tribunal has been held to have passed outside its proper limits are not limited to those in which it had no power to enter upon its inquiry or its jurisdiction, or has not satisfied a condition precedent. Certainly such cases exist (for example *Ex parte Bradlaugh* (1878) 3 Q.B.D. 509) but they do not exhaust the principle. A tribunal may quite properly validly enter upon its task and in the course of carrying it out may make a decision which is invalid – not merely erroneous. This may be described as 'asking the wrong question' or 'applying the wrong test' – expressions not wholly satisfactory since they do not, in themselves, distinguish between doing something which is not in the tribunal's area and doing something wrong within that area – a crucial distinction which the court has to make. Cases held to be of the former kind (whether, on their facts, correctly or not does not affect the principle) are *Estate and Trust Agencies (1927) Ltd.* v. *Singapore Improvement Trust* [1937] A.C. 898, 915–917; *Seereelall Jhuggroo* v. *Central Arbitration and Control Board* [1953] A.C. 151, 161

('whether [the board] took into consideration matters outside the ambit of its jurisdiction and beyond the matters which it was entitled to consider');

Reg. v. *Fulham, Hammersmith and Kensington Rent Tribunal, Ex parte Hieroswki* [1953] 2 Q.B. 147. The present case, in my opinion, and it is at this point that I respectfully differ from the Court of Appeal, is of this kind.

[LORD WILBERFORCE went on to agree with LORD REID's analysis of the statutory provisions and was in favour of allowing the appeal.]

[LORD MORRIS OF BORTH-Y-GEST and LORD PEARSON delivered speeches in favour of dismissing the appeal.]

Appeal allowed.

Question

The passage from R. v. *Commissioners for Special Purposes of the Income Tax*, cited by Lord Wilberforce in *Anisminic*, p. 43 *supra*, is slightly misleading as it stands because Lord Esher went on to qualify it: see p. 51 *infra*. So qualified, is Lord Esher's statement consistent with Lord Wilberforce's approach?

Notes

1. Lord Pearson agreed with the majority view of the general nature of the court's supervisory function but dissented on the ground that the Foreign Compensation Commission had not misconstrued the order or made any error affecting its jurisdiction.

2. *Theory versus reality: the 'theory of jurisdiction'.* Lord Wilberforce's reference to 'logical analysis' (p. 43 *supra*) is to the pure or general theory of jurisdiction, the most persistent exponent of which is Gordon: see (1929) 45 L.Q.R. 459; (1931) 47 L.Q.R. 386 and 557; (1960) 1 U.B.C.L.R. 185; (1966) 82 L.Q.R. 263 and 515. This theory, which is almost the direct opposite of the approach of the House of Lords in *Anisminic*, is that jurisdiction means authority to decide or capacity conclusively to determine questions of a particular type, that it is to be determined at the commencement and not at the conclusion of an inquiry and that questions of jurisdiction depend on the nature of the facts into which a tribunal has to inquire and not on the truth or

falsity of those facts (*R. v. Bolton* (1841) 1 Q.B. 66 and Lord Devlin in *Essex C.C. v. Essex Incorporated Congregational Church Union*, p. 35 *supra*). For instance, on this view, if the jurisdiction of a tribunal 'is confined to the City of London it cannot validly find that Piccadilly Circus is in the Ward of Chepe; but it has power to find that something was done in the Ward of Chepe although actually it was done in Piccadilly Circus' ((1929) 45 L.Q.R. 459 at p. 474), even if this finding is entirely without evidential support (see further p. 80 *infra*). This would make the reviewing power of the High Court very narrow indeed. Gordon criticizes the alternative, possibly impure, view of jurisdiction represented *inter alia* by the dictum of Farwell L.J. in *R. v. Shoreditch Assessment Committee, ex p. Morgan* [1920] 2 K.B. 859 at p. 880 (reproduced at p. 43 *supra*) as inconsistent with the undoubted intention of the legislature to give subordinate tribunals some measure of autonomy. He argues that as there is no logical way of distinguishing questions (whether of law or of fact) going to the jurisdiction of a tribunal from non-jurisdictional questions, it is not possible to treat any question upon which a tribunal must make findings as jurisdictional without asserting that a subordinate tribunal has jurisdiction if it is 'right' (in the sense that the superior tribunal agrees with its findings) but not if it is 'wrong'. (See p. 50 *infra* for discussion of jurisdictional fact.) He also argues that it is incorrect to characterize a question as jurisdictional if it is one into which the tribunal must necessarily inquire because where a tribunal *must* make findings in the first instance on a question then the legislature must have given it power to decide the question. Where a tribunal finds wrongly when considering such a question it is still exercising the powers given to it by the legislature although it is exercising those powers badly (1929) 45 L.Q.R. at pp. 470–2; (1969) 1 U.B.C.L.R. at p. 204; (1966) 82 L.Q.R. at pp. 266 and 521). If such a question is characterized as jurisdictional, any conclusion reached by the tribunal can be no more than a working conclusion with no legal force until another tribunal (a reviewing tribunal) makes a finding on it. The autonomy of the first tribunal is thus dramatically reduced. The policy considerations that favour a narrow role for judicial review have been set out at p. 3 *supra*. One attraction of Gordon's theory is that it seeks to provide an analytical basis for this policy.

However, the theory has been criticized on both logical and functional grounds (Bentley, [1962] P.L. 358; Wade, pp. 267–71; de Smith, pp. 111–12) which can be summarized as follows. If correct, the theory reduces jurisdictional review almost to vanishing point and provides too strong a temptation for a tribunal to usurp functions not remitted to it. Further, although it is clear that the power to err cannot cover all questions with which a tribunal may have to deal, no adequate criteria have been provided which can 'logically' distinguish the jurisdictional from the non-jurisdictional. There is certainly no logical reason for the legislature to adopt a temporal concept of jurisdiction, defining the area remitted to a tribunal by reference to factors determinable at the commencement of the inquiry. On this score, then, this theory suffers from the same defects as the 'impure' view of jurisdiction.

The pure theory also fails to recognize that the concept of jurisdiction can denote something other than power in some absolute sense. Because of this it tests the jurisdictional character of a question in isolation from the circumstances surrounding that question (including other questions with which the tribunal has to deal). The theory also appears to allow for the existence of only one jurisdictional question and cannot comfortably distinguish between the multiple findings a tribunal may need to make to arrive at its decision. It seems reasonably clear that more than one such finding may be jurisdictional. An example is provided by the requirements under the Rent Acts that for certain lettings to be controlled it is necessary to find (*a*) that the tenant is entitled to occupy all or part of a house as a residence; (*b*) that the rent includes a payment for the use of furniture or services; (*c*) that the rateable value of the premises is within certain limits; and (*d*) that the terms of letting do not exclude it from the Acts (e.g. where the rent is less than two-thirds of the relevant rateable value). Finally, the theory tends to undervalue the utility of the constitutional principle of validity (p. 3 *supra*; Wade, Ch. 2).

The truth of the matter is that neither solution is entirely "logical', but a possible *via media* may be found in Jaffe's functional approach (see (1957) 70 Harv. L. Rev. 953; *Judicial Control of Administrative Action*, pp. 631–3; or Rubinstein's 'wide definition of jurisdictional subject-matter' (*Jurisdiction and Illegality*, pp. 218–19)). Jaffe's approach was developed in the context of the doctrine of 'jurisdictional fact', on which see p. 50 *infra,* but is equally applicable to questions of law (cf. Wade, p. 253). It recognizes that typically a statutory grant of power is focused and made explicit at some points but blurred at others. The former, but not the latter, are termed jurisdictional. The line between the two cannot be drawn in the abstract but depends on the construction of the statute granting the particular power which, in turn, will depend on the context in which the issue arises and the purpose for which judicial review is sought. Jaffe concludes that the concept of jurisdiction is almost entirely functional – by which he means instrumental – and that 'it is used to validate review when review is felt to be necessary' (opp. citt., pp. 963 and 633 respectively). In what circumstances are courts likely to feel that review is 'necessary'? See *Pearlman* v. *Harrow School*, p. 55 *infra*; *Anisminic Ltd.* v. *F.C.C.*, p. 374 *infra* (ouster clauses). In what circumstances would a court be reluctant to intervene? See *R.* v. *Preston S.B.A.T., ex p. Moore*, p. 79 *infra*; *Gouriet* v. *U.P.O.W.*, p. 127 *infra*; *R.* v. *Secretary of State for the Environment, ex p. Ostler*, p. 385 *infra*; see also pp. 122 ff. *infra*. Rubinstein's 'wide definition of jurisdictional subject-matter' is based on the approach of certain Australian courts to statutory ouster clauses, on which see further Note 2, p. 377*infra*. This would give autonomy to administrative action which, though not strictly in conformity with the statutory requirements, is a *bona fide* attempt to exercise power, relates to the subject-matter of the legislation, and is reasonably capable of reference to the power given to the administrative body. Reasonableness rather than correctness is thus made the criterion. This is, however, unsupported by *Anisminic*. But compare *Secretary of State for Education and Science* v. *Tameside M.B.C.*, p. 182 *infra* which suggests that this may be the approach where the issue can be classified as one of 'discretion' rather than one of 'law' or 'fact'.

3. On the grounds and scope of judicial review the approach of the majority in *Anisminic* should be contrasted with that in *R.* v. *Nat Bell Liquors Ltd.*, p. 80 *infra*.

Jurisdictional error: jurisdictional fact

R v. Fulham, Hammersmith, and Kensington Rent Tribunal, ex parte Zerek

[1951] 2 K.B. 1   Divisional Court of the Queen's Bench Division

A letting was referred to a rent tribunal under the Landlord and Tenant (Rent Control) Act 1949 which governed unfurnished lettings. The landlord contended that the letting was a furnished one and that the reference should have been under the Furnished Houses (Rent Control) Act 1946. He relied on a document referring to the letting as furnished which the tenant had signed.

The tenant stated that the rooms had been let unfurnished by an earlier oral agreement but that the landlord refused to allow him to take possession unless he agreed to hire his furniture to the landlord and to sign the document relied on by the landlord. The tribunal decided that the written agreement was not valid, that as the rooms had been let unfurnished they had jurisdiction to hear the reference and that the rent should be reduced. The landlord sought certiorari on the ground that the tribunal had no jurisdiction:

LORD GODDARD C.J.: . . . The law to be gathered, especially from *Reg.* v. *Income Tax Special Commissioners*[3] and *Rex* v. *Lincolnshire justices; Ex parte Brett*[4] is that if a certain state of facts has to exist before an inferior tribunal have jurisdiction, they can inquire into the facts in order to decide whether or not they have jurisdiction, but cannot give themselves jurisdiction by a wrong decision upon them; and this court may, by means of proceedings for certiorari, inquire into the correctness of the decision. The decision as to these facts is regarded as collateral because, though the existence of jurisdiction depends on it, it is not the main question which the tribunal have to decide.

DEVLIN, J.: . . . It is not disputed that proof of the fact that this is an unfurnished tenancy is a pre-requisite to the exercise by the tribunal of their jurisdiction under s. 1 to fix a reasonable rent. Likewise it is agreed that since the tribunal's jurisdiction depends upon the existence of an unfurnished tenancy, it cannot, in the pithy phrase that was used in *Reg.* v. *Bolton*,[5] and before, give itself jurisdiction merely by its affirmation of the fact: see also *per* Coleridge, J., in *Bunbury* v. *Fuller*.[6] This has been qualified in the terms laid down by Lord Esher, M.R., in *Reg.* v. *Income Tax Special Commissioners*,[7] but it is not suggested, and, indeed, the contrary has been settled by this court, that that qualification applies here.

It is therefore agreed that the finding of the tribunal that the tenancy was unfurnished cannot be conclusive. Mr. Ashworth, on behalf of the tribunal, submits that it had a right, and, indeed, a duty, to make a finding about the nature of the tenancy, subject to review by this court. Mr. Finer, for the applicant, agrees that in a proper case there may be such a right, but argues that it must be limited. It cannot extend to require or permit the tribunal to investigate questions for the determination of which they are by their constitution wholly unsuited, such as whether an agreement is a forgery or has been obtained by fraud or is a sham, which last is what they purported to decide in this case. I do not think that he was able to suggest any principle which would show where the line was to be drawn, except the rather vague one that there must be excluded from the investigation questions which it was inconvenient and undesirable that such a tribunal should investigate. . . .

In my opinion the argument on behalf of the applicant is based on a misconception of what it is that a tribunal in cases such as this is doing. When,

[3] (1888) 21 Q.B.D. 313.   [4] [1926] 2 K.B. 192.
[5] (1841) 1 Q.B. 66.   [6] (1853) 9 Ex. 111, 140.
[7] 21 Q.B.D. 313, 319.

at the inception of an inquiry by a tribunal of limited jurisdiction, a challenge is made to their jurisdiction, the tribunal have to make up their minds whether they will act or not, and for that purpose to arrive at some decision on whether they have jurisdiction or not. If their jurisdiction depends upon the existence of a state of facts, they must inform themselves about them, and if the facts are in dispute reach some conclusion on the merits of the dispute. If they reach a wrong conclusion, the rights of the parties against each other are not affected. For, if the tribunal wrongly assume jurisdiction, the party who apparently obtains an order from it in reality takes nothing. The whole proceeding is, in the phrase used in the old reports, coram non judice. If, for example, the applicant in this case wishes, he can sue for his 35s. rent. He will be met with the defence that by the order of the tribunal it has been reduced to 15s. He can reply that that order is bad for want of jurisdiction, and the defendant will have to justify the order on which he relies and so prove the facts which give the tribunal jurisdiction. This seems to me to be what is laid down by the decision in *Briscoe* v. *Stephens*,[8] and to be in accordance with the opinion of Willes, J., in *London Corporation* v. *Cox*.[9] In such an action, I apprehend, the findings of the tribunal would be irrelevant and inadmissible. They are findings in a preliminary inquiry whose only object is to enable the tribunal to decide for themselves how to act. They are findings, therefore, that cannot ultimately prejudice either party. In these circumstances, I am unable to see why the tribunal should, in making their preliminary inquiry, be restricted to any particular class of case, or how they can be restrained from investigating for their own purposes any point which they think it necessary to determine so that they can decide upon their course of action. . . .

Although tribunals may in my view and in default of any alternative have to determine for themselves in the first instance the extent of their jurisdiction, nothing that I have said means that they should take upon themselves unnecessarily the examination of questions such as those . . . in cases where charges of fraud or forgery and the like are raised. Their own good sense will tell them that. While they will not allow every empty threat to their jurisdiction to deter them from their proper business of fixing reasonable rents, they will likewise appreciate that they are not by their nature equipped for the trial of matters which in the ordinary civil courts would be determined after pleading and discovery had been given and evidence on oath tested by cross-examination, and possibly, also, after trial by jury. The tribunal cannot be required to determine summarily such an issue if it involves a point of substance and if one or other of the parties is willing to have it determined in the ordinary civil courts; an adjournment can always be granted to allow that to be done. This will avoid an inconclusive inquiry by the tribunal and safeguard the tenant against the danger of being presented with an order which may afterwards turn out to be illusory. It may well be that if the tribunal itself insist, notwithstanding that there is a practicable alternative offered to them, in going into points of the sort which they purported to

---

[8] (1824) 2 Bing. 213.
[9] (1867) L.R. 2 H.L. 239, 262.

determine in *Rex* v. *Hackney, etc., Rent Tribunal; Ex parte Keats*[10] there is power in this court to prevent them from doing so. It is quite unnecessary that I should even consider that in relation to the present case, for this tribunal were quite willing that the validity of the alleged agreement should be determined by the ordinary courts, and I think that would be the attitude of most tribunals.

I need say little upon the facts of the present case, which have been fully dealt with by my Lords. Had there been a conflict of evidence, this court would probably not have interfered. But in fact the evidence was all one way and ample to justify the tribunal's conclusion that the document was not intended by the parties as a reduction into writing of their oral agreement, but as a bogus document which the landlord had brought into existence for his own purposes. Having regard to the receipt for the hire of the furniture, about which the landlord offered no explanation, the matter was in my view so clear as not to raise any serious issue. The tribunal's decision to assume jurisdiction cannot, therefore, be questioned in these proceedings.

[HUMPHREYS J. delivered a judgment refusing the application.]

Application refused.

Notes

1. It has been seen (p. 46 *supra*) that many problems of jurisdiction have been discussed in the context of factual issues and what follows is therefore of more general significance. As with the determination of which questions of law go to an administrative body's jurisdiction, the doctrine of 'jurisdictional', 'preliminary', or 'collateral' facts is easier to state than to apply. Apart from problems in determining whether an issue is one of law or of fact (see p. 60 *supra* and p. 71 *infra*), the difficulty of formulating coherent criteria for distinguishing such facts from those which only go to the merits has led some to assert that the concept is a fiction. The best exposition of this view is that of Gordon, who advances it as part of his pure theory of jurisdiction discussed at p. 45 *supra*; see further (1929) 45 L.Q.R. 459 at pp. 476–82; (1966) 82 L.Q.R. 263 and 515. Even those who support it as providing a basis for review concede that 'there is no acid test for recognising collateral or jurisdictional facts' (Wade, (1966) 82 L.Q.R. 226 at p. 231) and that the concept is almost entirely a functional one 'used to validate review when review is felt to be necessary' (Jaffe, 1957) 70 Harv. L.R. 953 at p. 963). It has been abandoned in the United States in favour of a requirement of substantial evidence: see p. 86 *infra*; Schwartz and Wade, *Legal Control of Government*, pp. 228–34; Wade, pp. 287–88.

Where, however, there is an express limitation upon the area of competence allotted to a subordinate body, the determination whether the facts fall within that limitation will probably go to jurisdiction. In *White and Collins* v. *Minister of Health* [1939] 2 K.B. 838 the Court of Appeal considered a power to acquire land compulsorily provided that it did not form 'part of any park, garden or pleasure ground or [was] otherwise required for the amenity or convenience of any house' (s. 75 of the Housing Act, 1936), Luxmore L.J. said (at pp. 855–6):

> The first and most important matter to bear in mind is that the jurisdiction to make the order is dependent on a finding of fact; for, unless the land can be held not to be part of a park or not to be required for amenity or convenience, there is no jurisdiction in the borough council to make, or in

10 [1951] 2 K.B. 15.

the Minister to confirm, the order. In such a case it seems almost self-evident that the Court which has to consider whether there is jurisdiction to make or confirm the order must be entitled to review the vital finding on which the existence of the jurisdiction relied upon depends.

2. The qualification made by Lord Esher M.R. in R. v. *Commissioners for Special Purposes of the Income Tax* (1888) 21 Q.B.D. 313 at pp. 319–20, referred to by Devlin J. in the principal case (p. 48 *supra*), was that in certain cases:

> The legislature may intrust the tribunal or body with a jurisdiction, which includes the jurisdiction to determine whether the preliminary state of facts exist as well as the jurisdiction, of finding that it does exist, to proceed further or do something more. . . . It is an erroneous application of the formula to say that the tribunal cannot give themselves jurisdiction by wrongly deciding certain facts to exist, because the legislature gave them jurisdiction to determine all the facts on which the further exercise of their jurisdiction depends; and if they were given jurisdiction so to decide, without any appeal being given, there is no appeal from such exercise of their jurisdiction.

(See p. 43 *supra* for the passage immediately preceding this and the Question at p. 45 *supra*.) It seems that this is more likely to be the case where the jurisdiction of the subordinate body is defined subjectively as in R. v. *Ludlow, ex p. Barnsley Corporation* [1947] K.B. 634 (a power 'where the committee are satisfied that default has been made by the former employer' included power to determine who the former employer was), though this is not always the case (*Estates and Trust Agencies Ltd.* v. *Singapore Improvement Trust* [1937] A.C. 898; *Secretary of State for Education and Science* v. *Tameside M.B.C.*, p. 182 *infra*) and arguably will not be so if the result is to give full autonomy to the subordinate body (*Anisminic Ltd.* v. *Foreign Compensation Commission*, p. 38 *supra* and p. 374 *infra*) or the liberty of the subject is involved (see Appendix).

Another situation in which it is probable that the subordinate body will be held to have power conclusively to determine whether a fact exists is where the court considers that the determination of the fact is not justiciable. Thus, in *Dowty Boulton Paul Ltd.* v. *Wolverhampton Corp. (No. 2)* [1976] Ch. 13 s. 163 (1) of the Local Government Act, 1933 gave a local authority power to use land belonging to it which was 'not required for the purposes for which [the land] was acquired' for any other purposes for which the authority was authorized to acquire land. This was held to give the authority jurisdiction to decide the issue of 'non-requirement'. The court considered that it was bound to reach this result because of authority interpreting a similar statutory formula, but Russell L.J. (at pp. 26–7) made it clear that the question whether the court will inquire into and decide on the existence of a factual precondition to an administrative step depends on what sort of factual precondition is in issue. Where it involved 'matters both of degree and of comparative needs, as to which there can be no question but that the local authority is better qualified than the Court to judge', it was appropriate for the authority to be made the sole judge of that fact (cf. Buckley L.J. at p. 30).

Disputed questions of fact

R. v. Fulham, Hammersmith & Kensington Rent Tribunal, ex parte Zerek

[1951] 2 K.B. 1   Divisional Court of the Queen's Bench Division

For the facts and further extracts, see p. 47 *supra*.

DEVLIN J.: . . . Orders of certiorari and prohibition are concerned principally with public order, it being part of the duty of the High Court to see that inferior courts confine themselves to their own limited sphere. They also afford speedy and effective remedy to a person aggrieved by a clear excess of jurisdiction by an inferior tribunal. But they are not designed to raise issues of fact for the High Court to determine de novo. Accordingly, it has never been the practice to put the party who asserts that the inferior court has jurisdiction to proof of the facts upon which he relies. It is recognized that the inferior court will have made a preliminary inquiry itself and the superior court is generally content to act upon the materials disclosed at that inquiry and to review in the light of them the decision to assume jurisdiction. This is possible only because the court is not, as I conceive it, finally determining the validity of the tribunal's order as between the parties themselves . . . but is merely deciding whether there has been a plain excess of jurisdiction or not. Where the question of jurisdiction turns solely on a disputed point of law, it is obviously convenient that the court should determine it then and there. But where the dispute turns on a question of fact, about which there is a conflict of evidence, the court will generally decline to interfere. . . .

Notes

1. The basic distinction is between facts which must exist objectively before a tribunal has jurisdiction and facts which it has jurisdiction to determine. As has been seen, only errors, as to facts of the first type give the courts automatic jurisdiction to interfere. Where they have such jurisdiction they *can* admit additional evidence and are not restricted to the evidence before the inferior tribunal: R. v. *Farmer* [1892) 1 Q.B. 637; *Secretary of State for Education and Science* v. *Tameside M.B.C.,* pp. 184 and 188 *infra*; *Ashbridge Investments Ltd.* v. *Minister of Housing and Local Government* [1965] 1 W.L.R. 1320 at p. 1327. Facts of the second type may, however, be reviewable on the grounds of 'no evidence', on which see p. 000 *infra*. Note further the reference to *Edwards* v. *Bairstow* [1956] A.C. 14 in *O'Reilly* v. *Mackman*, p. 331 *infra*.

2. Cross-examination on affidavits was, according to the Law Commission's *Report on Remedies in Administrative Law,* Law Com. No. 73, Cmnd. 6407, para. 15, always available in theory, although only one example of its use could be found this century. Since 1977 express provision has been made for full interlocutory proceedings in applications for judicial review (R.S.C. Ord. 53, r. 8) and potentially cross-examination on affidavits could become more frequent. However, in *I.R.C.* v. *Rossminister Ltd.* [1980] A.C. 952 at p. 1027, Lord Scarman stated that the powers to grant interlocutory process are 'to be sparingly used if the new procedure is to be a success'. See further Note 8, p. 319 *infra*. Why should this be so? In *O'Reilly* v. *Mackman*, p. 331 *infra*, it was said that cross-examination would not normally be necessary in an application for judicial review because of the limited scope of review. It was, however, also said that cross-examination on affidavits and other interlocutory process would be available in an application for judicial review whenever the justice of the case required it. Devlin J's judgment must be viewed in the light of this since it could be argued that in cases in which jurisdictional facts are in dispute the justice of the case might require cross-examination.

3. As well as certiorari and prohibition, other remedies are now available by an application for judicial review: see p. 315 *infra*.

All errors of law to be jurisdictional?

Pearlman v. Keepers and Governors of Harrow School

[1979] Q.B. 56   Court of Appeal

The Leasehold Reform Act 1967 gave certain tenants who resided in houses held on long leases the right to acquire the freehold on very advantageous terms. The Act applied to houses in the London area provided their rateable value was not more than £1,500. The Housing Act 1974 provided that tenants who had improved leasehold property by a 'structural alteration' could have the rateable value of the property reduced for the purposes of the 1967 Act.

Paragraph 2 (2) of Sch. 8 to the 1974 Act provided that where the parties could not agree 'the county court may on the application of the tenant determine that matter, and any determination shall be final and conclusive'. Section 107 of the County Courts Act 1959 provided that 'no judgment or order of any judge of county courts . . . shall be removed by appeal, motion or certiorari or otherwise into any other court' except in accordance with the provisions of that Act. The issue was whether installation of a central heating system was a 'structural alteration'. The county court judge, differing from a previous county court decision, decided that it was not. The tenant sought leave from the Divisional Court to apply for an order of certiorari to quash the judge's order, and, when this was refused, appealed to the Court of Appeal.

LORD DENNING M.R.: . . . In order to qualify for a reduction, the improvement must be an improvement made by the execution of works amounting to structural alteration, extension or addition.' Those are the words of the Housing Act 1974, Schedule 8, paragraph 1 (2). They are simple English words, but they have been interpreted by different judges differently. At any rate, when the judges have had to apply them to the installation of a full central heating system. In each house the primary facts have been exactly the same, or near enough the same, but one judge has found one way. Another the other way. One judge has held that the installation is a 'structural alteration.' Another has found that it is not. It is said, nevertheless, that, being simple English words, we should not interfere. Neither decision can be said to be unreasonable. So let each decision stand. Reliance is placed for this purpose on the speech of Lord Reid in *Cozens* v. *Brutus* [1973] A.C. 854, 861.

I cannot accept this argument. As I pointed out in *Dyson Holdings Ltd.* v. *Fox* [1976] Q.B. 503, 510, when an ordinary word comes to be applied to similar facts, in one case after another, it would be intolerable if half of the judges gave one answer and the other half another. No one would know where he stood. No lawyer could advise his client what to do. In such circumstances, it is the duty of the Court of Appeal to give a definite ruling one way or the other. However simple the words, their interpretation is a matter of law. They have to be applied, in case after case, by lawyers: and it is necessary, in the interests of certainty, that they should always be given the same interpretation, and always applied in the same way. . . .

Applying the words of Schedule 8 to the house here, I am of opinion that the installation of full central heating to this house was an 'improvement made by the execution of works amounting to structural alteration . . . or addition.' . . .

[He then considered s. 107 of the County Courts Act 1959 and found that it did not apply. He continued:]

Jurisdictional error

But even if section 107 [of the County Courts Act 1959] does apply to this case, it only excludes certiorari for error of law on the face of the record.[11] It does not exclude the power of the High Court to issue certiorari for absence of jurisdiction. It has been held that certiorari will issue to a county court judge if he acts without jurisdiction in the matter: see *Reg.* v. *Hurst, Ex parte Smith* [1960] 2 Q.B. 133. If he makes a wrong finding on a matter on which his jurisdiction depends, he makes a jurisdictional error; and certiorari will lie to quash his decision: see *Anisminic Ltd.* v. *Foreign Compensation Commission* [1969] 2 A.C. 147, 208, *per* Lord Wilberforce. But the distinction between an error which entails absence of jurisdiction – and an error made within the jurisdiction – is very fine. So fine indeed that it is rapidly being eroded. Take this very case. When the judge held that the installation of a full central heating system was not a 'structural alteration . . . or addition' we all think – all three of us – that he went wrong in point of law. He misconstrued those words. That error can be described on the one hand as an error which went to his jurisdiction. In this way: if he had held that it was a 'structural alteration . . . or addition' he would have had jurisdiction to go on and determine the various matters set out in paragraph 2 (2) (*b*) (*c*) and (*d*) of Schedule 8. By holding that it was not a 'structural alteration . . . or addition' he deprived himself of jurisdiction to determine those matters. On the other hand, his error can equally well be described as an error made by him within his jurisdiction. It can plausibly be said that he had jurisdiction to inquire into the meaning of the words 'structural alteration . . . or addition'; and that his wrong interpretation of them was only an error within his jurisdiction, and not an error taking him outside it.

That illustration could be repeated in nearly all these cases. So fine is the distinction that in truth the High Court has a choice before it whether to interfere with an inferior court on a point of law. If it chooses to interfere, it can formulate its decision in the words: 'The court below had no jurisdiction to decide this point wrongly as it did.' If it does not choose to interfere, it can say: 'The court had jurisdiction to decide it wrongly, and did so.' Softly be it stated, but that is the reason for the difference between the decision of the Court of Appeal in *Anisminic Ltd.* v. *Foreign Compensation Commission* [1968] 2 Q.B. 862 and the House of Lords [1969] 2 A.C. 147.

---

[11] [On such clauses see p. 370 *infra*.]

I would suggest that this distinction should now be discarded. The High Court has, and should have, jurisdiction to control the proceedings of inferior courts and tribunals by way of judicial review. When they go wrong in law, the High Court should have power to put them right. Not only in the instant case to do justice to the complainant. But also so as to secure that all courts and tribunals, when faced with the same point of law, should decide it in the same way. It is intolerable that a citizen's rights in point of law should depend on which judge tries his case, or in which court it is heard. The way to get things right is to hold thus: no court or tribunal has any jurisdiction to make an error of law on which the decision of the case depends. If it makes such an error, it goes outside its jurisdiction and certiorari will lie to correct it. In this case the finding – that the installation of a central heating system was not a 'structural alteration' – was an error on which the jurisdiction of the county court depended: and, because of that error, the judge was quite wrong to dismiss the application outright. . . .

On these grounds I am of opinion that certiorari lies to quash the determination of the judge, even though it was made by statute 'final and conclusive.'

GEOFFREY LANE L.J.: . . . [What the County Courts Act 1959] has done is to abolish certiorari for error of law on the face of the record as a method of attacking a judgment or order of the county court. . . .

Mr Dawson on behalf of the landlord has conceded however that the Act of 1959 has not affected the power of the High Court in a proper case to remove and quash a decision of the county court which was made in excess of that court's jurisdiction. It must follow that the only basis for an order of certiorari would be if the judge had acted in excess of his jurisdiction.

. . . In order to determine the ambit of the words 'excess of jurisdiction' one must turn to the decision of the House of Lords in *Anisminic Ltd.* v. *Foreign Compensation Commission* [1969] 2 A.C. 147. The effect of the majority speeches in that case may perhaps be expressed as follows: where words in a statute purport to oust the jurisdiction of the High Court to review the decision of an inferior tribunal they must be construed strictly. That is to say, if there is more than one way in which they can reasonably be construed the construction which impairs the power of the High Court the least should be selected. A provision to the effect that the determination of a tribunal 'shall not be called in question in any court of law' does not exclude the power of the High Court to quash a decision which has been reached by the tribunal acting in excess of its jurisdiction. Jurisdiction in this sense has a wide meaning. It includes any case where the apparent determination of the tribunal turns out on examination to be a nullity, because it cannot properly be called a determination at all. . . .

[After citing the passages from Lord Reid and Lord Wilberforce's speeches in the *Anisminic* case, set out at pp. 38–9 and 45 *supra*, he continued:] It is plain that this decision makes the ambit of excess of jurisdiction very wide, but does it embrace what the judge did in the present case?

For my part I am unable to see what the judge did which went outside the proper area of his inquiry. He seems to have taken the view that the word 'structural' qualifies the following words, 'alteration, extension or addition' and does not qualify the part of the house to which the alterations etc. are made. That is to say the words do not mean 'non-structural alterations' or 'additions to a structure'. Assuming he was wrong in that method of interpreting the words of the Schedule, it does not seem to me to be going outside his terms of reference in any way at all, nor does it contravene any of the precepts suggested by Lord Reid and Lord Wilberforce which I have already cited. The question is not whether he made a wrong decision, but whether he inquired into and decided a matter which he had no right to consider: see Lord Reid at p. 174E.

The judge summarised matters in the final passage of his judgment as follows:

'I think in the final analysis it is a matter of first impression tested by argument, analogy and illustration and finally it is a question of fact. There can be little doubt. I do not intend to give any definition at all.'

In short what he is saying is that in his view the works executed by Mr. Pearlman did not amount to structural alteration or addition, within the ordinary meaning of those words. I am, I fear, unable to see how that determination, assuming it to be an erroneous determination, can properly be said to be a determination which he was not entitled to make. The judge is considering the words in the Schedule which he ought to consider. He is not embarking on some unauthorised or extraneous or irrelevant exercise. All he has done is to come to what appears to this court to be a wrong conclusion upon a difficult question. It seems to me that, if this judge is acting outside his jurisdiction, so then is every judge who comes to a wrong decision on a point of law. Accordingly, I take the view that no form of certiorari is available to the tenant. . . .

I would accordingly dismiss the appeal.

[EVELEIGH L.J. delivered a judgment in favour of allowing the appeal.]

Appeal allowed.

Questions

1. Is it satisfactory to say that jurisdiction is lost by 'asking the wrong question'? See *Anisminic* per Lord Pearce at p. 42 *supra* and Lord Wilberforce at p. 45 *supra*; *Pearlman* v. *Harrow School* per Geoffrey Lane L.J. *supra*. Is it more satisfactory to say that a tribunal loses jurisdiction by 'taking into account matters which it was not directed to take into account'? Cf. p. 180 *infra*; *R. v. Barnet and Camden Rent Tribunal, ex p. Frey Investments Ltd.* [1972] 2 Q.B. 342 at pp. 367–9; *Secretary of State for Education and Science* v. *Tameside M.B.C.*, p. 182 *infra* (both in the context of discretionary powers); *R. v. Southampton JJ., ex p. Green* [1976] Q.B. 11 at pp. 21–22 per Browne L.J.

2. Is the approach of the majority in *Anisminic* consistent with the existence of errors of law within jurisdiction? Lord Denning's comments in *Pearlman* v. *Harrow School* must now be read in the light of the next case, *Re Racal Communications Ltd.,*

infra. See also *Interim Report of Committee on Administrative Law*, JUSTICE, paras. 36 and 37; Gould, [1970] P.L. 358 at pp. 364–7. But cf. *R. v. Preston S.B.A.T., ex p. Moore*, p. 77 *infra*; *R. v. Small Claims Tribunal, ex p. Barwiner Nominees Ltd.* [1975] V.R. 831.

    3. Why was the error in *Pearlman* v. *Harrow School* treated as an error of law? This issue is discussed at Note 2 p. 60 and p. 71 *infra*.

Note

    Eveleigh L.J., unlike Lord Denning, applied *Anisminic* and held that the error was jurisdictional because the meaning of 'structural alteration' was a collateral matter upon which the county court's jurisdiction depended. In view of the divisions in the Court of Appeal, the authority of this case was not strong even before the decision in *Re Racal Communications Ltd., infra*. However, Lord Denning's judgment received much attention (see e.g. Griffiths, [1979] C.L.J. 11; Rawlings, [1979] P.L. 404; Wade, pp. 264–7; (1979) 95 L.Q.R. 163) because the application of Occam's razor to the artificialities of the jurisdictional principle was attractive. But, quite apart from the difficulties of precedent, there are disadvantages in it. It would make statutory rights of appeal, such as those given by the Tribunals and Inquiries Act 1971, p. 64 *infra*, redundant and outflank the exemption of certain bodies, from the Tribunals and Inquiries Act structure (see e.g. s. 14 (3) of the 1971 Act p. 379 *infra*). Moreover, the only limit in Lord Denning's formulation – an error *upon which the decision depends* – could conceivably bring consideration of the merits of a case into the formula.

In Re Racal Communications Ltd.

[1981] A.C. 374   House of Lords

    The Director of Public Prosecutions applied for an order to inspect the company's records and papers under s. 441 of the Companies Act 1948, which provides for such an order if there is reasonable cause to believe that any officer of the company committed 'an offence in connection with the management of the company's affairs'. The grounds for this application were that a departmental manager sent fraudulent statements to the company's customers claiming more money than the company was owed. Vinelott J. dismissed the application on the ground that s. 441 only applied to offences committed in the course of the internal management of a company. Nevertheless, despite the provision in s. 441 (3) that the decision of a High Court judge on an application under the section 'shall not be appealable', he gave leave to appeal. The Court of Appeal ([1980] Ch. 138), relying on *Pearlman* v. *Harrow School*, allowed the appeal on the ground that the judge had misconstrued s. 441 and, in refusing jurisdiction as a result of this misconstruction, he had made an error of law going to his jurisdiction. An appeal by the company to the House of Lords was allowed on the ground that the jurisdiction of the Court of Appeal is wholly statutory and appellate, that it did not have jurisdiction to entertain any original application for judicial review, and that an appeal was barred by s. 441 (3). This extract is solely concerned with the scope of judicial review.

LORD DIPLOCK: ... Parliament can, of course, if it so desires, confer upon administrative tribunals or authorities power to decide questions of law as well as questions of fact or of administrative policy; but this requires clear words, for the presumption is that where a decision-making power is conferred on a tribunal or authority that is not a court of law, Parliament did not intend to do so. The break-through made by *Anisminic* [1969] 2 A.C. 147 was that, as respects administrative tribunals and authorities, the old distinction between errors of law that went to jurisdiction and errors of law that did not, was for practical purposes abolished. Any error of law that could be shown to have been made by them in the course of reaching their decision on matters of fact or of administrative policy would result in their having asked themselves the wrong question with the result that the decision they reached would be a nullity. The Tribunals and Inquiries Act 1971, which requires most administrative tribunals from which there is not a statutory right of appeal to the Supreme Court on questions of law, to give written reasons for their decisions, now supplemented by the provisions for discovery in applications for judicial review under Ord. 53 of the Rules of the Supreme Court,[12] facilitates the detection of errors of law by those tribunals and by administrative authorities, generally.

But there is no similar presumption that where a decision-making power is conferred by statute upon a court of law, Parliament did not intend to confer upon it power to decide questions of law as well as questions of fact. Whether it did or not and, in the case of inferior courts, what limits are imposed on the kinds of questions of law they are empowered to decide, depends upon the construction of the statute unencumbered by any such presumption. In the case of inferior courts where the decision of the court is made final and conclusive by the statute, this may involve the survival of those subtle distinctions formerly drawn between errors of law which go to jurisdiction and errors of law which do not that did so much to confuse English administrative law before *Anisminic* [1969] 2 A.C. 147; but upon any application for judicial review of a decision of an inferior court in a matter which involves, as so many do, interrelated questions of law, fact and degree the superior court conducting the review should not be astute to hold that Parliament did not intend the inferior court to have jurisdiction to decide for itself the meaning of ordinary words used in the statute to define the question which it has to decide. This, in my view, is the error into which the majority of the Court of Appeal fell in *Pearlman* [1979] Q.B. 56. The question for decision by the county court judge under paragraph 1 (2) of Schedule 8 to the Housing Act 1974 was whether the installation of central heating in a particular dwelling house amounted to 'structural alteration, extension or addition.' If the meaning of ordinary words when used in a statute becomes a question of law, here was a typical question of mixed law, fact and degree which only a scholiast would think it appropriate to dissect into two separate questions, one for decision by the superior court, viz. the meaning of those words – a question which must entail considerations of degree; and the other

12 [See, p. 318 *infra*.]

for decision by the county court, viz. the application of the words to the particular installation – a question which also entails considerations of degree. The county court judge had not ventured upon any definition of the words 'structural alteration, extension or addition.' So there was really no material on which to hold that he had got the meaning wrong rather than its application to the facts. Nevertheless the majority of the Court of Appeal in *Pearlman* [1979] Q.B. 56 held that Parliament had indeed intended that such a dissection should be made and since they would not have come to the same conclusion themselves on the facts of the case they inferred that the judge's error was one of interpretation of the words 'structural alteration, extension or addition.' This was in the face of a powerful dissent by Geoffrey Lane L.J. Notwithstanding that on the facts of the case he too would have reached a different conclusion from that of the county court judge, he was of opinion that the statute conferred upon the judge jurisdiction to decide finally and conclusively a question which did involve interrelated questions of law, fact and degree, and that the Supreme Court had no jurisdiction to interfere with his decision by way of judicial review. For my part, I find the reasoning in his minority judgment conclusive.

There is in my view, however, also an obvious distinction between jurisdiction conferred by a statute on a court of law of limited jurisdiction to decide a defined question finally and conclusively or unappealably, and a similar jurisdiction conferred on the High Court or a judge of the High Court acting in his judicial capacity. . . . There is simply no room for error going to his jurisdiction, nor . . . is there any room for judicial review. Judicial review is available as a remedy for mistakes of law made by inferior courts and tribunals only. Mistakes of law made by judges of the High Court acting in their capacity as such can be corrected only by means of appeal to an appellate court; and if, as in the instant case, the statute provides that the judge's decision shall not be appealable, they cannot be corrected at all. . . .

LORD EDMUND-DAVIES: . . . My Lords, like the judicial Committee of the Privy Council in a recent decision to which I was a party (*South East Asia Fire Bricks Sdn. Bdh.* v. *Non-Metallic Mineral Products Manufacturing Employees Union* [1981] A.C. 363), I have to say respectfully that the existing law is, in my judgment, to be found in the dissenting judgment of Geoffrey Lane L.J. in *Pearlman* and that the majority view was erroneous.

[LORD KEITH OF KINKEL agreed with LORD DIPLOCK. LORD SALMON and LORD SCARMAN delivered speeches in favour of allowing the appeal.]

Appeal allowed.

Question

To what extent did the fact that, in *Anisminic*, the functions of the Foreign Compensation Commission were 'predominantly judicial' (Lord Wilberforce, p. 42 *supra*) affect the approach of the court to the question whether the error went to jurisdiction? See *R.* v. *Secretary of State for the Environment, ex p. Ostler* [1977] Q.B. 122 at pp. 135 and 138, discussed at p. 392 *infra*; cf. Lord Diplock in *Re Racal Communications Ltd.*, p. 58 *supra*. What other factors affected its approach? In

Pearlman v. *Harrow School* was the need for consistency important? See p. 55 *supra.* Cf. *R.* v. *Preston S.B.A.T., ex p. Moore,* p. 79 *infra; R.* v. *Chief Immigration Officer, Gatwick Airport, ex p. Kharrazi* [1980] 1 W.L.R. 1396. Was the fact that, in *Pearlman* v. *Harrow School,* the court was not dealing with a specialist tribunal important in determining its willingness to intervene? See further Note 5, p. 61 *infra.*

Notes

1. The distinction between inferior courts of law and administrative tribunals, novel in this context, has the advantage of salvaging the virtues in Lord Denning's approach in *Pearlman* v. *Harrow School* (although in a narrower area) and giving some indication of why different bodies are subject to different amounts of judicial review. However, quite apart from the probability that a distinction developed in one context will not be entirely appropriate in another context, Wade points out (p. 266; (1980) 96 L.Q.R. 492) that is has several disadvantages. First, as *Attorney-General* v. *B.B.C.* [1981] A.C. 303 shows, where it has been used the distinction has proved notoriously difficult to operate. Secondly, in so far as the distinction has been said to depend upon whether the power exercised is essentially judicial ([1981] A.C. at p. 360), adoption of the distinction for determining the scope of judicial review may lead to confusion with the 'duty to act judicially' that is discussed in natural justice and in connection with the remedies of certiorari and prohibition: see p. 4 *supra* and pp. 224 and 310 *infra.* Finally, as Lord Salmon's speech in *Attorney-General* v. *B.B.C.* shows (p. 342) the distinction may turn into a test of pedigree, i.e. if the body has been in existence for a long time it will be a court but if it is a newer body, the product of modern (Parliamentary) government, it is more likely to be an administrative body: see e.g. *R.* v. *Surrey Coroner, ex p. Campbell* [1982] 2 W.L.R. 626 at pp. 636–7.

2. In *R.* v. *Chief Immigration Officer, Gatwick Airport, ex p. Kharrazi* [1980] 1 W.L.R. 1396 Lord Denning considered the effect of Lord Diplock's observations in *Re Racal Communications Ltd.* He said (at p. 1403):

These do away with long-standing distinctions between errors within the jurisdiction and errors without it. They do it by the simple device which was adumbrated in *Pearlman* v. *Keepers and Governors of Harrow School.* No administrative tribunal or administrative authority has jurisdiction to make an error of law on which the decision of the case depends. The House of Lords said in *Racal* that we were wrong to apply that concept to the High Court; but left it intact with regard to administrative tribunals and other administrative authorities.

Is this a fair reflection of the ratio in *Pearlman* v. *Harrow School?* In the context of administrative authorities other than the regular courts of law, is there in fact agreement between Lord Denning and Lord Diplock as to the scope of review? One difference is that Lord Denning's formulation is couched in terms of a rule of law whereas Lord Diplock's is stated as a presumption. Another is that the limits of Lord Diplock's formula appear unconnected with the merits of the case (p. 58 *supra*). The most important one, however, is hidden beneath the formulations and stems from their radically different approaches to the classification of a question as one of 'fact' or of 'law'. Whether one accepts Lord Diplock's formulation or that of Lord Denning, perhaps the most important factor in determining the scope of review is whether a question is classified as one of 'fact' or of 'law'. The greater the willingness of the courts to classify questions as 'law' the greater the scope of review. The way in which this has been done will be discussed at p. 71 *infra.* At this stage it is sufficient to note that whereas Lord Denning has consistently classified all inferences from primary facts as questions of law, Lord Diplock appears willing to classify such inferences as fact if they involve 'interrelated' or 'mixed' questions of law, fact, and degree. It is reasonable to suppose that Lord Diplock's method of classification would be used by him to classify questions before administrative authorities, although, in *Re Racal Communications Ltd.* itself, it was used to classify a question before an inferior court of law (the county court in *Pearlman*). Thus, despite the superficial similarity between the two formulations of the scope of judicial review they differ radically. Lord Diplock's more restrictive view of what constitutes an error of law necessarily involves a narrower scope of review. The question of classification did not arise in *R. v. Chief Immigration Officer, Gatwick Airport, ex p. Kharrazi* and it was therefore relatively easy for Lord Denning to use Lord Diplock's approach. However, when it did, in *A.C.T. Construction Ltd. v. Customs and Excise Commissioners* [1981] 1 W.L.R. 49 at p. 54 Lord Denning rejected Lord Diplock's approach to characterization. He said that once the primary facts were established the question is one of law for the court to decide. Is it consistent to accept Lord Diplock's analysis of the effect of an error of law but not his views on the initial question of classification upon which that analysis rests?

3. Lord Edmund-Davies referred to the *South East Asia Fire Bricks* case [1981] A.C. 363 in which a company sought certiorari to have an order of the Malaysian Industrial Court quashed for error of law on the face of the record. The Industrial Court had ruled that a 'lockout' by the company was illegal and ordered it to reinstate the employees concerned. The Privy Council held that the remedy was barred by a very wide statutory ouster clause (on such clauses see p. 374 *infra*). It said that however widely drawn such a clause was it would not prevent judicial review if the error goes to jurisdiction but that it would prevent review for non-jurisdictional errors such as the one in the case before it. It was in this context that the Privy Council rejected Lord Denning's view in *Pearlman v. Harrow School.*

One reason for the Privy Council's view that the particular clause ousted review for non-jurisdictional error was the fact that the functions of the Industrial Court were not purely judicial because of the broad nature of the issues it was required to consider (e.g. 'the financial implications . . . of an award on the economy') and because the ultimate power of decision on any question of law before that Court lay with the Attorney-General, a politician. This is surely as much a factor in the determination of whether an error is jurisdictional as in the determination of the scope of an ouster clause (see Lord Wilberforce in *Anisminic,* p. 44 *supra*; see also p. 51 *supra* (jurisdictional fact)). However, the case provides us with a clear example of the survival of non-jurisdictional error of law. Are there any differences between the approaches of the Privy Council and that of Lord Diplock in *Re Racal Communications Ltd.*? Was the Industrial Court an 'inferior court of law'?

4. A further possible restriction of the *Anisminic* principle was stated in *R. v. Surrey Coroner, ex p. Campbell* [1982] 2 W.L.R. 626 at p. 637, where it was said that the principle is limited to tribunals established by statute, and probably to those tribunals from whose decisions, under the relevant statute, there is no, or only a limited, right of appeal. *Re Racal Communications Ltd.* was relied on but does Lord Diplock's speech in fact support such a limit? How would appeals on a point of law under s. 13 of the Tribunals and Inquiries Act 1971, p. 64, *infra* affect the scope of review on this approach? Cf., in the context of ouster clauses, *R. v. Secretary of State for the Environment, ex p. Ostler,* p. 385 *infra*.

5. In *Re Energy Conversion Devices Incorporated*, The Times, 2 July 1982 Lord Diplock (obiter), with whom the other members of the House of Lords agreed, reaffirmed his view that there is an 'important constitutional principle that questions of construction of all legislation primary or secondary are questions of law to be

determined authoritatively by courts of law; that errors in construing primary or secondary legislation made by inferior tribunals that are not courts of law, however specialised and prestigious they may be, are subject to correction by judicial review . . .'. Does Lord Diplock's approach take any or sufficient account of the specialist nature of the inferior tribunal as a factor in determining the scope of judicial review?

6. Lord Diplock has repeated his view of the effect of *Anisminic* in *O'Reilly* v. *Mackman*, p. 328 *infra*, in a speech with which all the members of the House of Lords agreed. However, the main point in *O'Reilly's* case concerned the method of seeking a remedy in an Administrative Law case and it is probable that the agreement of their Lordships was confined to that. Note, for example, that one of them, Lord Fraser, had delivered the opinion of the Privy Council in the *South East Asia Fire Bricks* case [1981] A.C. 363, noted at p. 61 *supra*, in which it seems to be accepted that there can be non-jurisdictional errors of law in a wider area than that envisaged by Lord Diplock. For another recent case, see the Appendix.

ERROR WITHIN JURISDICTION:
ERROR ON THE FACE OF THE RECORD

Error within jurisdiction

Report of the Committee on Administrative Tribunals and Inquiries (The Franks Report), Cmnd. 218 (1957)

An appeal structure for tribunals

105. The first question is the extent to which appeals should lie to the courts or to further appellate tribunals. An appeal to the courts on matters of fact would not, we think, be desirable since it would constitute an appeal from a body expert in the particular subject to a relatively inexpert body. In the absence of special considerations we consider that the ideal appeal structure for tribunals should take the form of a general appeal from a tribunal of first instance to a second or appellate tribunal. By a general appeal we mean an appeal on fact, law or merits. . . .

106. It is not essential to set up an appellate tribunal when the tribunal of first instance is so exceptionally strong and well qualified that an appellate tribunal would be no better qualified to review its decisions. . . .

Appeals to the courts on points of law

107. We are firmly of the opinion that all decisions of tribunals should be subject to review by the courts on points of law. This review could be obtained either by proceedings for certiorari or by appeal. If, as we recommend, tribunals are compelled to give full reasons for their decisions any error of law in such a decision would subject the decision to quashing by order of certiorari in England, and it is now clear that the fact that the decision of the tribunal may be expressed in the statute as 'final' does not oust this jurisdiction. The courts in Scotland do not, however, exercise this jurisdiction to quash a decision for error of law on the face of the record. Moreover, an application to quash a decision on this ground is quite different from an

appeal on a point of law. In the former case the court can only quash the decision, while in the latter case the court may substitute, or in effect substitute, its own decision.[13] Again, in the former case, the court must find the error, if it can, on the face of the record . . . it cannot look at anything else. In the latter case the court can in addition look at the notes of the evidence given before the tribunal if the point of law is whether there was evidence on which the tribunal could in law have arrived at its decision. An appeal on a point of law is therefore wider in scope. For all these reasons we recommend that review by the courts of decisions of tribunals should in general be provided by making the decisions subject to appeal on points of law. We think, however, that special considerations arise in connection with the National Insurance Commissioner, the Industrial Injuries Commissioner and National Assistance Appeal Tribunals.

108. It is no doubt true that the Commissioners often have to adjudicate on points of law of considerable complexity which could be said to warrant appeals to the courts. Parliament, however, has taken care to provide that each Commissioner and his deputies should be barristers or advocates of considerable experience, appointed by Royal Warrant, and their salaries are in excess of those of County Court judges. Moreover, in difficult cases a Commissioner sits with two deputies, thus constituting a tribunal of exceptional experience and standing. Further, it has always been recognised that the nature of the services with which the Commissioners are concerned makes it essential that final decisions should be reached with the minimum of delay. Finally, there has been little demand for a right of appeal to the courts in these cases. Indeed witnesses on behalf of the Trades Union Congress, which speaks for the great majority of applicants, expressed themselves as completely satisfied with the present position. These considerations lead us to think that it would be right to make an exception and to leave any review by the courts in these cases to be exercised by certiorari.

109. The reasons which lead us to think that appeals on merits from National Assistance Appeal Tribunals are unnecessary (see paragraph 182 [task more like an assessment committee than an adjudicating body and need for speed]) apply equally to appeals on points of law from these Tribunals. Accordingly we think that an exception to the general rule should also be made in the case of these Tribunals, leaving any review by the courts to be exercised by certiorari.

Note

There can now be an appeal on a point of law from Supplementary Benefits Appeal Tribunals (the successors of the National Assistance Appeal Tribunals) to one of the Social Security Commissioners (who replaced the National Insurance Commissioners) and thence to the Court of Appeal: s. 14 (4) of the Social Security Act 1980. See further p. 558 *infra* on rights of appeal more generally.

---

[13] [But see now R.S.C. Ord. 53, r. 9 (3) and s. 31 (5) of the Supreme Court Act 1981, p. 315 *infra*.]

Tribunals and Inquiries Act 1971

13. – (1) If any party to proceedings before any such tribunal as is specified in paragraph 2(*b*), 4, 6, 10, 16, 17(*b*), 18(*a*), 21, 26, 28(*a*) or (*b*) or 32 of Schedule 1 to this Act is dissatisfied in point of law with a decision of the tribunal he may, according as rules of court may provide, either appeal therefrom to the High Court or require the tribunal to state and sign a case for the opinion of the High Court.

(2) Rules of court made with respect to all or any of the said tribunals may provide for authorising or requiring a tribunal, in the course of proceedings before it, to state, in the form of a special case for the decision of the High Court, any question of law arising in the proceedings. . . .

(9) In this section 'decision' includes any direction or order, and references to the giving of a decision shall be construed accordingly. . . .

Notes

1. The tribunals specified in Sch. 1 to the Act are listed by Wade, pp. 824–8, together with a useful table of the relevant rights of appeal.

2. As has been stated at p. 7 *supra*, there is no automatic right of appeal from an inferior tribunal and the only inherent method of controlling such bodies is by reviewing the legality of their acts. Nevertheless, apart from s. 13 of the Tribunals and Inquiries Act, various statutes do grant rights of appeal although there are no hard and fast rules as to when this will be granted, to which court it will lie, or to the grounds on which such an appeal may be brought (see *Halsbury's Laws of England*, 4th edn., i, para. 50; Garner, *Administrative Law*, 5th edn., pp. 98–100; Wraith and Hutchesson, *Administrative Tribunals*, pp. 157–61). Finally, certiorari will be granted for non-jurisdictional error provided that the error is of law and it appears on the face of the record. In practice this is confined to those tribunals from which no right of appeal is provided by statute because of the limitation that the error must appear on 'the face of the record'. (Cf. *R.* v. *Hillingdon L.B.C., ex p. Royco Homes Ltd.*, p. 364 *infra*.) These factors mean that non-jurisdictional control of administrative bodies and tribunals has increased in recent years and the characterization of an issue as one of law or fact has become as important as the question whether or not it goes to jurisdiction. It should, however, be noted that the increased willingness of courts to characterize a question of law as jurisdictional may tend to reduce the importance of non-jurisdictional review and appeal. The approach of Lord Denning in recent cases, e.g. *Pearlman* v. *Harrow School*, p. 53 *supra*, makes non-jurisdictional review redundant and outflanks the elaborate system of appeal and exemption from control established by the Tribunals and Inquiries Act (see e.g. s. 14 (3) of the 1971 Act), but cf. *R.* v. *Surrey Coroner, ex p. Campbell* [1892] 2 W.L.R. 626, noted at p. 61 *supra*.

Error of law on the face of the record

R. v. Northumberland Compensation Appeal Tribunal, ex parte Shaw

[1952] 1 K.B. 338   Court of Appeal

By the passing of the National Health Service Act 1946 the applicant lost his employment as clerk to the West Northumberland Joint Hospital Board.

Aggrieved by the amount of compensation awarded to him by the compensating authority (Gosforth U.D.C.) he referred the matter to the tribunal designated by the National Health Service (Transfer of Offices and Compensation) Regulations, 1948. Regulation 12 imposed a duty on the tribunal to consider the matter 'in accordance with the provisions' of the regulations and 'to determine accordingly whether any and, if so, what compensation ought to be awarded to the claimant'.

The order of the tribunal set out the period of the applicant's service with the hospital board as being from 7 October 1936 to 31 March 1949. It set out the contention of the compensating authority that compensation should be based on this period of service alone. The order did not set out the contention of the applicant that the whole of his local government service should be taken into account and the tribunal dismissed his appeal. The applicant now sought certiorari. In the Divisional Court counsel for the tribunal admitted that there was an error of law on the face of the decision given by the tribunal, and an order of certiorari was made ([1951] 1 K.B. 711). The tribunal appealed.

DENNING L.J.: The question in this case is whether the Court of King's Bench can intervene to correct the decision of a statutory tribunal which is erroneous in point of law. No one has ever doubted that the Court of King's Bench can intervene to prevent a statutory tribunal from exceeding the jurisdiction when Parliament has conferred on it; but it is quite another thing to say that the King's Bench can intervene when a tribunal makes a mistake of law. A tribunal may often decide a point of law wrongly whilst keeping well within its jurisdiction. If it does so, can the King's Bench intervene?

There is a formidable argument against any intervention on the part of the King's Bench at all. The statutory tribunals, like this one here, are often made the judges both of fact and law, with no appeal to the High Court. If, then, the King's Bench should interfere when a tribunal makes a mistake of law, the King's Bench may well be said to be exceeding its own jurisdiction. It would be usurping to itself an appellate jurisdiction which has not been given to it. The answer to this argument, however, is that the Court of King's Bench has an inherent jurisdiction to control all inferior tribunals, not in an appellate capacity, but in a supervisory capacity. This control extends not only to seeing that the inferior tribunals keep within their jurisdiction, but also to seeing that they observe the law. The control is exercised by means of a power to quash any determination by the tribunal which, on the face of it, offends against the law. The King's Bench does not substitute its own views for those of the tribunal, as a Court of Appeal would do. It leaves it to the tribunal to hear the case again, and in a proper case may command it to do so. . . .

Of recent years the scope of certiorari seems to have been somewhat forgotten. It has been supposed to be confined to the correction of excess of jurisdiction, and not to extend to the correction of errors of law; and several judges have said as much. But the Lord Chief Justice has, in the present case, restored certiorari to its rightful position and shown that it can be used to correct errors of law which appear on the face of the record, even though they do not go to jurisdiction. I have looked into the history of the matter, and find that the old cases fully support all that the Lord Chief Justice said. Until about 100 years ago, certiorari was regularly used to correct errors of law on the face of the record. It is only within the last century that it has fallen into disuse, and that is only because there has, until recently, been little occasion for its exercise. Now, with the advent of many new tribunals, and the plain need for supervision over them, recourse must once again be had to this well-tried means of control. I will endeavour to show how the writ of certiorari was used in former times, so that we can take advantage of the experience of the past to help us in the problems of the present.

Let me start with convictions by magistrates in summary proceedings under Acts of Parliament. Ever since the days of Holt C.J. the Court of King's Bench has been extremely strict to see that all was in order. Everything necessary to support the conviction had to appear on the face of the record. The conviction had to recite the information in its precise terms. It had to set out the evidence of each witness as nearly as possible in his actual words. It had to state the adjudication with complete certainty. It had to show that the case was brought within the terms of the Act of Parliament creating the offence. If there was any defect in point of form, or any error in point of law, appearing on the face of the record, the conviction would be moved into the King's Bench by certiorari and quashed. Nothing could be supplied by argument or intendment. . . .

The result of all this strictness, however, was that many convictions were quashed for defects of form and not of substance. The legislature therefore intervened in 1848 to make the record of a conviction much more simple. Instead of a detailed speaking record, there was provided an unspeaking common form, which rarely disclosed any error. Thenceforward there was not so much room for certiorari in the case of convictions, but the fundamental principles remained untouched: see *Rex* v. *Nat Bell Liquors Ld.,*[14] *per* Lord Sumner.

Next I will turn to the orders of justices in civil matters. The Court of King's Bench was never so strict about these as it was about convictions. It did not require a detailed speaking record to be sent up to them. The record had to contain everything necessary to show that the justices had jurisdiction to deal with the matter, and it had to set out their adjudication; but it was not necessary to set out either the evidence or the reasons. If a point of law arose, however, on which either party desired the ruling of the King's Bench, he could ask the justices to make a speaking order, that is, to make a special entry upon the record of the reasons for their judgement. The justices were not bound to do this, but they usually did so if they entertained a doubt about the point. When their reasons thus appeared on the record, the Court of King's Bench would on certiorari inquire into their correctness, and, if the reasons were wrong, would quash the decision. . . .

So far I have considered only the convictions or orders of justices, which were by far the most numerous cases in which certiorari was used. I now come

[14] [1922] 2 A.C. 128, 159.

to the orders of statutory tribunals. The Court of King's Bench has from very early times exercised control over the orders of statutory tribunals, just as it has done over the orders of justices. The earliest instances that I have found are the orders of the Commissioners of Sewers, who were set up by statute in 1532 to see to the repairs of sea walls and so forth. The Court of King's Bench used on certiorari to quash the orders of the commissioners for errors on the face of them, such as when they failed to set out the facts necessary to show that they had jurisdiction in the matter, or when they contained some error in point of law. It is recorded that on one celebrated occasion the commissioners refused to obey a certiorari issued out of the King's Bench, and for this the whole body of them were 'laid by the heels.' The control thus exercised over the Commissioners of Sewers was used by Holt C.J. as a precedent to control by certiorari the orders of any tribunal set up by Parliament, such as the College of Physicians and the Commissioners for the repair of Cardiff Bridge. Since that time it has never been doubted that certiorari will lie to any statutory tribunal. It was suggested before us on behalf of the Crown that, in the case of these statutory tribunals, the Court of King's Bench only interfered by certiorari to keep them within their jurisdiction, and not to correct their errors of law. There are, however, many cases in the books where certiorari was used to correct errors of law on the face of the record. A striking instance was where the Commissioners of Sewers imposed an excessive fine, and it was quashed by the Court of King's Bench on the ground that in law their fines ought to be reasonable. Other instances are the numerous cases where certiorari was used to determine the validity of a sewer's rate imposd by the Commissioners of Sewers. There are several cases where an auditor's certificate has been quashed for error of law on the face of it. And I have no doubt that many more instances could be found throughout the books. The principles on which the court acted in the case of the Commissioners of Sewers will be found set out in *Cummins* v. *Massam.*[15] The decisions of Holt C.J. are *Groenwelt* v. *Burwell*[16] and the case of *Cardiff Bridge.*[17] The case of an auditor's certificate is *Reg.* v. *White.*[18]

. . . What, then, is the record? It has been said to consist of all those documents which are kept by the tribunal for a permanent memorial and testimony of their proceedings: see Blackstone's Commentaries, Vol. III, at p. 24. But it must be noted that, whenever there was any question as to what should, or should not be, included in the record of any tribunal, the Court of King's Bench used to determine it. It did it in this way: When the tribunal sent their record to the King's Bench in answer to the writ of certiorari, this return was examined, and if it was defective or incomplete it was quashed: see *Apsley's* case,[19] *Rex* v. *Levermore,*[20] and *Ashley's* case,[21] or, alternatively, the

[15] (1643) March 196 (ed. 1675), 202 (ed. 1685). See Callis on Sewers (4th ed., 1823), pp. 203–4, 342–4; and Chitty's Practice, Vol. II, at p. 370.
[16] (1700) 1 Salk. 144; 1 Ld. Raym. 454–469.
[17] (1699) 1 Salk. 146; 1 Ld. Raym. 580.
[18] (1883–4) 11 Q.B.D. 309; 14 Q.B.D. 358.
[19] (1648) Style 85.   [20] (1701) 1 Salk. 146.
[21] (1698) 2 Salk. 479.

tribunal might be ordered to complete it: *Williams* v. *Bagot*[22] and *Rex* v. *Warnford*.[23] It appears that the Court of King's Bench always insisted that the record should contain, or recite, the document or information which initiated the proceedings and thus gave the tribunal its jurisdiction; and also the document which contained their adjudication. Thus in the old days the record sent up by the justices had, in the case of a conviction, to recite the information in its precise terms; and in the case of an order which had been decided by quarter sessions by way of appeal, the record had to set out the order appealed from: see *Anon*.[24] The record had also set out the adjudication, but it was never necessary to set out the reasons (see *South Cadbury (Inhabitants)* v. *Braddon, Somerset (Inhabitants)*[25]), nor the evidence, save in the case of convictions. Following these cases, I think the record must contain at least the document which initiates the proceedings; the pleadings, if any; and the adjudication; but not the evidence, nor the reasons, unless the tribunal chooses to incorporate them. If the tribunal does state its reasons, and those reasons are wrong in law, certiorari lies to quash the decision.

The next question which arises is whether affidavit evidence is admissible on an application for certiorari. When certiorari is granted on the ground of want of jurisdiction, or bias, or fraud, affidavit evidence is not only admissible, but it is, as a rule, necessary. When it is granted on the ground of error of law on the face of the record, affidavit evidence is not, as a rule, admissible, for the simple reason that the error must appear on the record itself: see *Rex* v. *Nat Bell Liquors Ld*.[26] Affidavits were, however, always admissible to show that the record was incomplete, as, for instance, that a conviction omitted the evidence of one of the witnesses (see Chitty's Practice, Vol. 2, at p. 222, note (d), or did not set out the fact that the justices had refused to hear a competent witness for the defence (see *Rex* v. *Anon*.[27]), whereupon the court would either order the record to be completed, or it might quash the conviction at once.

Notwithstanding the strictness of the rule that the error of law must appear on the face of the record, the parties could always by agreement overcome this difficulty. If they both desired a ruling of the Court of King's Bench on a point of law which had been decided by the tribunal, but which had not been entered on the record, the parties could agree that the question should be argued and determined as if it were expressed in the order. The first case I have found in which this was done was in 1792, *Rex* v. *Essex*,[28] but thereafter it was quite common. It became a regular practice for parties to supplement the record by affidavits disclosing the points of law that had been decided by the tribunal. This course was only taken if no one objected. It seems to have been adopted by litigants as a convenient alternative to asking the tribunal to make a speaking order. . . . Recent cases such as *Rex* v. *West Riding of*

---

[22] 4 D. & R. 315.　　　　　　　　　[23] (1825) 5 D. & R. 489.
[24] (1697) 2 Salk. 479.　　　　　　　[25] (1710) 2 Salk. 607.
[26] [1922] A.C. 123, 156.　　　　　　[27] (1816) 2 Chit. 137.
[28] (1792) 4 T.R. 591.

Yorkshire Justices[29] and *General Medical Council* v. *Spackman*[30] show that the practice continues today. The explanation of all these cases is, I think, that the affidavits are treated by consent as if they were part of the record and make it into a speaking order.

Apart from these consent cases, it is often a very nice question whether an error which does not appear on the record is one which goes to jurisdiction or is only an error of law within the jurisdiction. If it goes to jurisdiction, affidavits are admissible, but otherwise not. . . . I do not venture on a discussion of what does, or does not, go to jurisdiction, because it does not arise in this case. . . .

We have here a simple case of error of law by a tribunal, an error which they frankly acknowledge. It is an error which deprives Mr. Shaw of the compensation to which he is by law entitled. So long as the erroneous decision stands, the compensating authority dare not pay Mr. Shaw the money to which he is entitled lest the auditor should surcharge them. It would be quite intolerable if in such case there were no means of correcting the error. The authorities to which I have referred amply show that the King's Bench can correct it by certiorari. It is true that the record which has been sent up to the court does not distinctly disclose the error, but that is only because the record itself is incomplete. The tribunal has sent up its decision, but it has not sent up the claim lodged with the compensating authority or the order made by them on it or the notice of appeal to the tribunal. Those documents would, I think, properly be part of the record. They would, I understand, have disclosed the error. If it had been necessary, the court could have ordered the record to be completed. But that is unnecessary, having regard to the fact that it was admitted in open court by all concerned that the decision was erroneous. I am clearly of opinion that an error admitted openly in the face of the court can be corrected by certiorari as well as an error that appears on the face of the record. The decision must be quashed, and the tribunal will then be able to hear the case again and give the correct decision.

In my opinion the appeal should be dismissed.

[SINGLETON and MORRIS L.JJ. delivered judgments in favour of dismissing the appeal.]

Appeal dismissed.

Questions

1. In what sense is it accurate to say, as Lord Denning does at p. 65 *supra*, that this control over inferior tribunals is supervisory and not appellate? See Rubinstein, *Jurisdiction and Illegality*, pp. 90–4 and 190–2; Wade, p. 279; de Smith, pp. 403–4; *R.* v. *Industrial Court, ex p. Aeronautical Engineers Association* [1953] 1 Lloyd's Rep. 597; *R.* v. *Agricultural Land Tribunal for the South Eastern Area, ex p. Bracey* [1960] 1 W.L.R. 911 at p. 914; *R.* v. *Chertsey JJ., ex p. Franks* [1961] 2 Q.B. 152.

2. Does the doctrine of error of law on the face of the record lead to a blurring of the distinction between jurisdictional and non-jurisdictional error? See Rubinstein, op

[29] [1910] 2 K.B. 192.
[30] [1942] 2 K.B. 261; [1943] A.C. 627.

cit., pp. 93, 185–6 and 188–93, but see *R. v. Northumberland Compensation Appeal Tribunal, ex p. Shaw* (and see also the decision of the Divisional Court, [1951] 1 K.B. 711 at pp. 715–16); *R. v. Medical Appeal Tribunal, ex p. Gilmore* [1957] 1 Q.B. 574 at pp. 588–593 per Parker L.J.

Notes

1. Although in *R. v. Northumberland Compensation Appeal Tribunal, ex p. Shaw* both Singleton and Morris L.JJ. thought that it was not open to the tribunal to argue that the error was not on the face of the record as this had been conceded by it in the Divisional Court, only Singleton L.J. thought that the error was in fact on the face of the record ([1952] 1 K.B. 338 at p. 345). Morris L.J. was more doubtful (p. 355). To what extent should consent turn a latent error into a patent one? See de Smith, pp. 406–7; (1952) 15 M.L.R. 217; *R. v. Southampton JJ., ex p. Corker*, The Times, 12 February 1976.

2. For criticism of the doctrine on both historical and policy grounds see Sawer, (1954) 3 U. of W. Austr. Ann. L. Rev. 24.

3. The remedy granted in this case was certiorari. On the position of the declaration, see the Note at p. 398 *infra*.

R. v. Medical Appeal Tribunal, ex parte Gilmore

[1957] 1 Q.B. 574   Court of Appeal

The applicant, who injured his left eye at work, claimed disablement benefit under the National Insurance (Industrial Injuries) Act 1946. At the time of his accident he was, as a result of an earlier industrial accident, already injured in his left eye and almost blind in his right eye. The further injury so aggravated the condition of his left eye that he was almost totally blind. Regulations (S.I. 1948 No. 1372) made under the Act stated *inter alia* that, in cases of injury to one of two similar organs, assessments of the extent of disablement should treat 'any disability in respect of the organ . . . by reason of . . . an injury or disease received . . . before the relevant accident' (reg. 2 (5)) as having been incurred as a result of the loss of faculty caused by the relevant accident. A medical appeal tribunal assessed the aggravation at 20 per cent. The tribunal had before it a specialist's report setting out the facts and this was referred to in its award. The applicant applied for leave to seek certiorari to quash the award on the ground that there was a manifest error of law on the face of the record in so far as the tribunal had not taken into account the disability in the right eye. The application was refused by the Divisional Court. There was an appeal and it was conceded that the tribunal's decision was erroneous in law. For another aspect of this decision, concerning the statutory restriction of remedies, see pp. 370 and 373 *infra*.

DENNING L.J.: . . . The first point is whether the error of the tribunal appears on the face of the record. It does not appear on the face of their written adjudication of June 13, 1956. There is not a word there about the right eye, or even the left eye for that matter. But the tribunal gave an extract from the specialist's report and thereby, I think, they made that report a part of the record. Just as a pleading is taken to incorporate every document referred to in it, so also does an adjudication. Once the specialist's report is read with the record, we have before us the full facts about the previous injury to the right eye and the subsequent injury to the left. These facts are sufficient to disclose the error in law: for it is then apparent that the award of 20 per cent. must be wrong. No reasonable person, who had proper regard to regulation 2 (5) could have come to such a conclusion. It is now settled that when a tribunal come to a conclusion which could not reasonably be entertained by them if they properly understood the relevant enactment, then they fall into error in point of law: see *Edwards (Inspector of Taxes)* v. *Bairstow*.[31] When the primary facts appear on the record, an error of this kind is sufficiently apparent for it to be regarded as an error on the face of the record such as to warrant the intervention of this court by certiorari.

I may add that, even if we had not been able to have recourse to the specialist's report, we would have been able to get the facts by ordering the tribunal to complete the record by finding the facts, as the regulations require them to. By regulation 13 of the National Insurance (Industrial Injuries) (Determination of Claims and Questions) Regulations, 1948, it is enacted that 'A tribunal shall in each case record their decision in writing . . . and shall include in such record, . . . a statement of the reasons for their decision, including their findings on all questions of fact material to the decision.' It seems to me that the tribunal cannot, by failing to find the material facts, defeat an application for certiorari. The court has always had power to order an inferior tribunal to complete the record. Abbott C.J. long ago gave very good reasons in this behalf. He said: 'If an inferior court . . . send up an incomplete record, we may order them to complete it . . . If we are not to order, or allow the officers of the court below to make a perfect record, which unquestionably they are at liberty to do, it will be in their power, by making an imperfect record, to defeat a writ of error whenever it shall be brought. The power of doing that lies in their hands, unless we prevent it': see *Williams* v. *Lord Bagot*.[32] Likewise a tribunal could defeat a writ of certiorari unless the courts could order them to complete or correct an imperfect record. So the courts have power to give such an order: see *Rex* v. *Warnford*.[33] . . .

[ROMER and PARKER L.JJ delivered judgments in favour of allowing the appeal.]

Order of certiorari issued.

Note

Law and fact. The important distinction between errors of law and of fact can be very fine and, as has been seen (p. 60 *supra*), the cases do not adopt a consistent position on the correct method of making it. The approach taken in *Edwards (Inspector of Taxes)* v. *Bairstow* [1956] A.C. 14, albeit in the context of an appeal, has been influential. There Lord Radcliffe said (at p. 33):

My Lords, I think that it is question of law what meaning is to be given to the words of the Income Tax Act 'trade,' 'manufacture, adventure or concern in the nature of trade' and for that

[31] [1956] A.C. 14. [32] (1824) 4 Dow. & Ry. 315.
[33] (1825) 5 Dow. & Ry. 489.

matter what constitute 'profits or gains' arising from it. Here we have a statutory phrase involving a charge of tax, and it is for the courts to interpret its meaning, having regard to the context in which it occurs and to the principles which they bring to bear upon the meaning of income. But, that being said, the law does not supply a precise definition of the word 'trade': much less does it prescribe a detailed or exhaustive set of rules for application to any particular set of circumstances. In effect it lays down the limits within which it would be permissible to say that a 'trade' as interpreted by section 237 of the Act does or does not exist.

But the field so marked out is a wide one and there are many combinations of circumstances in which it could not be said to be wrong to arrive at a conclusion one way or the other. If the facts of any particular case are fairly capable of being so described, it seems to me that it necessarily follows that the determination of the Commissioners, Special or General, to the effect that a trade does or does not exist is not 'erroneous in point of law'; and, if a determination cannot be shown to be erroneous in point of law, the statute does not admit of its being upset by the court on appeal. I except the occasions when the commissioners, although dealing with a set of facts which would warrant a decision either way, show by some reason they give or statement they make in the body of the case that they have misunderstood the law in some relevant particular.

All these cases in which the facts warrant a determination either way can be described as questions of degree and therefore as questions of fact.

On this approach a broad range of questions will be classified as factual even where they involve the application of statutory criteria to primary facts (see e.g. Lord Diplock in *Re Racal Communications Ltd.*, p. 57 *supra*). A narrower approach has, however, been adopted in some cases which classify all applications of statutory criteria to primary facts as questions of law. See, for example, *Birmingham Corporation* v. *Habib Ullah* [1964] 1 Q.B. 178, noted by Wade, (1969), 85 L.Q.R. 18; *Gould* v. *Wily* [1960] N.Z.L.R. 960; *Pearlman* v. *Harrow School*, p. 53 *supra* and Note 2, p. 60 *supra*; *R.* v. *National Insurance Commissioner, ex p. Michael* [1977] 1 W.L.R. 109 at p. 112, but see p. 116 quoted at p. 372 *infra*; *A.C.T. Ltd.* v. *Customs and Excise Commissioners* [1981] 1 W.L.R. 49, noted at p. 61 *supra*. In general see Wade, pp. 816–19; de Smith, pp. 112–20; Wilson, (1963) 26 M.L.R. 609 and (1969) 32 M.L.R. 361; *Lord Luke of Pavenham* v. *Ministry of Housing and Local Government*, p. 615 *infra*; *Ashbridge Investments Ltd.* v. *Minister of Housing and Local Government* [1965] 1 W.L.R. 1320 at p. 1328, and p. 81 *infra* ('no evidence').

Despite the difficulties, a basic distinction can be drawn between primary facts and inferences made from such facts (sometimes known as secondary facts). The former are assertions that a 'phenomenon has happened or is or will be happening independent or anterior to any assertion as to its legal effect' (Jaffe, *Judical Control of Administrative Action*, pp. 546–8). 'They are observed by witnesses and proved by oral testimony or facts proved by the production of a thing itself, such as original documents. Their determination is essentially a question of fact for the tribunal of fact, and the only question of law that can arise on them is whether there was any evidence to support the finding' (*British Launderers' Association* v. *Borough of Hendon Rating Authority* [1949] 1 K.B. 462 at p. 471 per Denning L.J.). Taking *ex p. Gilmore*, p. 70 *supra*, as an example, findings that the applicant's left eye was injured and that his right eye had been injured earlier are primary facts. In the *British Launderers'* case, Denning L.J. continued:

The conclusions drawn from primary facts are, however, inferences deduced by a process of reasoning from them. If, and in so far as, those conclusions can as well be drawn by a layman (properly instructed on the law) as by a lawyer, they are conclusions of fact for the tribunal of fact: and the only questions of law which can arise on them are whether there was a proper direction in point of law; and whether the conclusion is one which could reasonably be drawn from the primary facts. ... If, and in so far, however, as the correct conclusion to be drawn from primary facts requires, for its correctness, determination by a trained lawyer – as, for instance because it involves the interpretation of documents or because the law and the facts cannot be separated, or because the law on the point cannot properly be understood or applied except by a trained lawyer – the conclusion is a conclusion of law on which an appellate tribunal is as competent to form an opinion as the tribunal of first instances.

Thus, in *ex p. Gilmore* the conclusion that the injury aggravated the applicant's existing disability by 20 per cent was prima facie one of fact, but was reviewable because it was one to which the tribunal could not reasonably come on a proper interpretation of the statute and see further Note 3, p. 372 *infra*.

The fluidity of the distinction was well described by Dickinson who, as long ago as 1927, said that questions of fact and questions of law are not 'two mutually exclusive *kinds* of questions based upon a difference of subject matter. Matters of law grow downward into roots of fact, and matters of fact reach upward without a break, into matters of law. The knife of policy alone effects an artificial cleavage where the court chooses to draw the line between public interest and private right' (*Administrative Justice and the Supremacy of the Law in the United States*, p. 55). The requirements of policy will differ in different contexts. And it is the variety of contexts in which it is necessary to draw the line between law and fact that has prevented the development of a coherent general test. However, as has been seen at p. 000 *supra*, the precise place in which the line is drawn will have a profound effect on the scope of judicial review.

What is 'the record'?

R. v. Northumberland Compensation Appeal Tribunal, ex parte Shaw, p. 64 *supra*

R. v. Medical Appeal Tribunal, ex parte Gilmore, p. 70 *supra*

Tribunals and Inquiries Act 1971, Section 12 (5), p. 23 *supra*

R. v. Knightsbridge Crown Court, ex parte International Sporting Club (London) Ltd.

[1982] Q.B. 304   Divisional Court of the Queen's Bench Division

Companies, whose gaming licences had been cancelled by the licensing justices after serious contraventions of the gaming laws, appealed to the Crown Court. Such an appeal takes the form of a rehearing before a circuit judge and magistrates to determine whether the companies were fit and proper persons to hold gaming licences. Before the appeal was heard there was a change of ownership and management of the companies. The new owners contended that this 'restructuring' of the companies meant that, despite their past conduct, the companies were fit and proper persons to hold licences. The court dismissed the appeals. The judge (Judge Friend) delivered an oral judgment in which he said that fitness can only be judged by past conduct. The companies sought orders of certiorari to quash the Crown Court's decision on the ground that it had erred in law in disregarding the corporate restructuring, that this error was disclosed on the face of the judgment, or alternatively that the Crown Court had exceeded its jurisdiction.

GRIFFITHS L.J. read the judgment of the court (GRIFFITHS L.J. and MAY J.): . . . At the end of the hearing the judge gave a judgment in which he gave the reasons why the appeals were dismissed. He ended his judgment by saying:

> 'For those reasons, I think it is right that I should express our reasons and the appeal is dismissed. I could have said simply, "The appeals are dismissed," but I thought it right and proper that you should all know precisely why they are dismissed.'. . .

Mr. Tuckey on behalf of the Gaming Board . . . has submitted that the judgment forms no part of the 'record' and that this court is entitled to look only at the formal order of the court and not at the reasons that the court gave for making the order.

If this submission is well founded, the supervisory power of this court to review the decisions of inferior courts for errors of law will be drastically curtailed. The 'order' of the court rarely, if ever, contains the reasons that led to the making of the order. The order merely recites the decision of the court, not its reasons. . . .

[After noting the decline and revival of the jurisdiction to quash for error of law on the face of the record, he continued:]

Once reborn, the jurisdiction has proved to be a most valuable development in our system of administrative law. In the ever increasing complexity of a modern society there has inevitably been a great increase in the number of tribunals required to regulate its affairs. Trained lawyers play their part in manning these bodies but it is neither possible because there are not enough lawyers, nor desirable because lawyers may lack the special expertise of people from other walks of life, that they should all be in the hands of the lawyers. Laymen play their part and will often outnumber and be able to outvote the lawyers among them when it comes to making a decision. The citizen affected by these decisions is entitled to expect that they will be given in accordance with the law and, if the rule of law is to mean anything, a court manned by trained lawyers is required to speak with authority to correct the decision where it appears that it is founded upon error of law. This function is now performed in many cases by the Divisional Court of the Queen's Bench Division by the use of an order of certiorari to quash an erroneous decision; in other cases Parliament may often give a right of appeal to the High Court.

But before the Divisional Court can exercise its supervisory jurisdiction it must be able to see what the error of law is said to be. The document to which anyone would naturally expect it to look must surely be that which records the reasons given by the court or tribunal for its decision – in this case the transcript of Judge Friend's judgment.

In the collective experience of the members of this court and the very experienced counsel appearing before us it has been the practice of the Divisional Court under the presidency of successive Lord Chief Justices over the last four decades to receive the reasons given by a court or tribunal for its decision and if they show error of law to allow certiorari to go to quash the decision. The court has regarded the reasons as part of the record. They are sometimes referred to as a 'speaking order.' Many of the cases are, of course, unreported but examples of the court acting upon such reasons are to be found in *Reg.* v. *Chertsey Justices, Ex parte Franks* [1961] 2 Q.B. 152 (an oral judgment of justices); *Reg.* v. *Justices for Court of Quarter Sessions for the County of Leicester, Ex parte Gilks* [1966] Crim. L.R. 613 (an oral judgment of quarter sessions) and *Reg.* v. *Leeds Crown Court, Ex parte Bradford Chief Constable* [1975] Q.B. 314 (an oral judgment of the Crown Court in a liquor licensing appeal). . . .

In order to do justice the court has, in addition to regarding the reasons for a decision as part of the record, been prepared to regard other documents as part of the 'record' where if read with the decision they will show that the tribunal has erred in law. In *Baldwin & Francis Ltd.* v. *Patents Appeal Tribunal* [1959] A.C. 663 Lord Denning held that the decision of the super-intending examiner and two patent specifications formed part of the record of the proceedings before a patents appeal tribunal. In *Reg.* v. *Medical Appeal Tribunal, Ex parte Gilmore* [1957] 1 Q.B. 574 the Court of Appeal held that the report of a medical specialist constituted part of the record. As Lord Denning M.R. said in *Reg.* v. *Preston Supplementary Benefits Appeal Tribunal, Ex parte Moore* [1975] 1 W.L.R. 624, 628: 'The "record" is generously interpreted so as to cover all the documents in the case.'

Parliament has set its seal of approval on this practice of the court in the case of all those bodies to which the Tribunals and Inquiries Acts 1958 and 1971 apply. They are required to state their reasons and it is provided that the reasons constitute part of the record, and that certiorari will lie: see sections 12 and 14 of the Act of 1971.

We can see no sensible reason why the court should adopt a different approach to a decision of an inferior court or other quasi-administrative body such as licensing justices from that which it is required to adopt in the cases to which the Act applies. . . .

The argument for the Gaming Board is that it is only if the inferior court chooses to embody its reasons in its order that it becomes part of the record, for only then does it exist as a document for which the Court of Queen's Bench can call and examine. So if at the end of the judgment giving the reasons the judge or chairman adds the words 'and I direct that this judgment be made part of the order,' the court may look at it but not otherwise. It seems to us that it would be a scandalous state of affairs that, if having given a manifestly erroneous judgment, a judge could defeat any review by this court by the simple expedient of refusing a request to make his judgment part of the order. That would indeed be formalism triumphant.

It may be said that the same end can be achieved by the court refusing to give any reasons, as Judge Friend said he was entitled to do in this case. However, it is the function of professional judges to give reasons for their decisions and the decisions to which they are a party. This court would look askance at the refusal by a judge to give his reasons for a decision particularly if requested to do so by one of the parties. It does not fall for decision in this case, but it may well be that if such a case should arise this court would find that it had power to order the judge to give his reasons for his decision.

. . . In the last century the facilities available for recording spoken reasons were not comparable to those which exist today. Shorthand had only recently been invented and there was no electronic recording apparatus with which many courts are now equipped. This court can now rely with confidence upon a transcript of the oral judgment given by a lower court or tribunal as accurately setting out its reasons which may not have been the case 100 years ago. . . .

Although the old authorities do show a stricter approach to what constituted the 'record,' the modern authorities show that the judges have relaxed the strictness of that rule and taken a broader view of the 'record' in order that certiorari may give relief to those against whom a decision has been given which is based upon a manifest error of law. We, therefore, hold that the reasons contained in the transcript of the oral judgment of the Crown Court constitute part of the record for the purposes of certiorari and we are entitled to look at it to see if they contain errors of law.

[He then examined the judgment of the Crown Court and decided that it disclosed an error of law in that it showed that the court had not taken the restructuring into account in reaching its decision that the companies were not fit and proper persons to hold a gaming licence. He concluded:]

As we are of the view that the judgment forms part of the record and discloses error of law, it is not necessary for us to express our opinion on the alternative ground that the court exceeded its jurisdiction. To some extent the two points are inter-related because if the judgment is part of the record it is not necessary for this court to seek by subtle reasoning to find excess or abuse of jurisdiction in order to enable it to do justice by quashing a decision founded on error of law. Upon this difficult question of jurisdiction we are at the moment divided. But as the point is not necessary to our decision we shall not set out on the necessary lengthy analysis to defend our respective positions. It is sufficient to say that if our decision on the scope of the record is challenged it will be open to the applicant companies to seek to uphold the decision of this court on the ground that the Crown Court exceeded their jurisdiction.

Applications granted.

Question

Does the reasoning in this case, that an oral reason forms part of the record at common law, extend beyond the decisions of relatively formal tribunals where a transcript has been made? Would it apply to a Supplementary Benefit Appeal Tribunal? On these tribunals see p. 546 *infra* and *Crake* v. *Supplementary Benefits Commission*, p. 23 *supra*.

Notes

1. The view of the court in the *International Sporting Club* case on the position of oral reasons at common law should be contrasted with the views of de Smith, p. 580;

Megarry, (1961) 77 L.Q.R. 157; and Gordon, (1961) 77 L.Q.R. 322. It would also appear that the ratio of *R. v. Chertsey JJ., ex p. Franks* [1961] 2 Q.B. 152 was in fact that the tribunal there had no jurisdiction: see Wade, pp. 281–2.

2. The judgment in the *International Sporting Club* case considered the question of what documents form part of the record and adopted the approach used by Lord Denning in several cases, including *ex p. Gilmore*, p. 71 *supra*. It should, however, be noted that in one of these, *Baldwin & Francis Ltd. v. Patents Appeal Tribunal* [1959] A.C. 663, all the members of the House of Lords apart from Lord Denning expressly refused to decide the question whether the record included documents apart from the tribunals actual order or decision. Furthermore, Lord Denning's opinion that the record covers all the documents in a case (*R. v. Preston S.B.A.T., ex p. Moore, infra*) needs qualification. The mere fact that a document is referred to in the decision is not enough to incorporate it as part of the record; for this it must be the basis of the decision or the decision must be meaningless unless it is incorporated: *R. v. Patents Appeal Tribunal, ex p. Swift & Co.* [1962] 2 Q.B. 647 at p. 654, following Lord Denning himself in *Baldwin & Francis Ltd. v. Patents Appeal Tribunal* at pp. 688–9.

3. The court's ability to detect error was undoubtedly enhanced by s. 12 of the Tribunals and Inquiries Act 1971. The overall effect of this must, however, be judged in the light of the consequences of non-compliance with the duty to give reasons. On this point, see p. 26 *supra*. For more recent developments, see Appendix.

Allowable margin of error

R. v. Preston Supplementary Benefits Appeal Tribunal, ex parte Moore

R. v. Sheffield Supplementary Benefits Appeal Tribunal, ex parte Shine

[1975] 1 W.L.R. 624   Court of Appeal

LORD DENNING M.R. read the following judgment of the court: These are the first cases we have had under the Supplementary Benefit Act 1966 [formerly Ministry of Social Security Act 1966]. In each case it is a student who makes a claim. Each was in receipt of a grant from the local education authority. Each seeks to supplement the grant on the ground that, during the vacation, he is unemployed and entitled to supplementary benefits.

. . . There is an important provision [in the Supplementary Benefit Act 1966] which says that any determination of the 'tribunal shall be conclusive for all purposes': see sections 18 (3) and 26 (2). The tribunals are under a duty to provide a statement of the reasons for the decision: see section 12 (1) [and] Schedule 1 para. 20 to the Tribunal and Inquiries Act 1971. But their proceedings may be removed into the High Court by order of certiorari: see section 14 (1) of that Act.[34]

The two cases before us arise out of applications for an order of certiorari.[35] They are brought under the established power of the High Court to supervise

[34] [For comment on this sentence see p. 380 *infra*.]
[35] [To quash the decision of the tribunal for error of law on the face of the record.]

inferior tribunals. The High Court can quash any decision of an inferior tribunal for error of law which appears on the face of the record. The 'record' is generously interpreted so as to cover all the documents in the case. An 'error of law' is also interpreted generously so as to include a wrong interpretation of a statute, or a wrong application of it to the facts of the case. But certiorari is a discretionary remedy. And the important question in these cases is how far the High Court should interfere with the decisions of the tribunals on supplementary benefits.

[The Court dismissed Moore's appeal from the Divisional Court on the ground that there had been no error of law by the tribunal.]

Shine's case

Malcolm Shine was a student at the University of Sheffield. He was a single man. His parents had such means that he did not qualify for any educational grant save for the minimum of £50. The local education authority seem to have regarded the parents as liable for all the expenses of the student during term time. They looked upon the £50 as a grant paid by them to help the student in his expenses during vacation. When they made a full grant to a student, they included £46 as a vacation allowance. So they regarded £46 (out of the £50) as a vacation allowance for Mr. Shine. On this account the commission treated £46 as his resources for the 22 weeks of the vacation, i.e. £2.05 a week. This was challenged before us but the challenge was not pressed.

There is this other point. Malcolm Shine shared a flat with three other students. They were four joint tenants. Each of the four bore one-quarter of the rent and expenses. Each paid his one-quarter of the rent separately to the landlord every month. The gas and electricity bills were for convenience sent to one of them – Mr. Fairbairn – but each contributed his quarter share.

In assessing the 'requirements' Mr. Shine claimed that he should be regarded as a householder within paragraph 9 (b) of Schedule 2. There is a special provision which gives a higher benefit for a 'person living alone or householder . . . who is directly responsible for household necessities and rent (if any).'

The Supplementary Benefits Commission rejected Mr. Shine's Claim that he was a 'householder.' On appeal the tribunal also rejected it. Their written reasons said:

'Mr. Fairbairn receives gas and electricity accounts and therefore the others are in the same position as non-dependants contributing towards a householder's commitments.'

Mr. Shine applied to the High Court for an order of certiorari. He said that, being a joint tenant, he was directly responsible for household necessities and rent: and was, therefore, a 'householder.'

If this were to be regarded as a strict point of law, there is much to be said for Mr. Shine's contention. Under the Interpretation Act 1889,[36] singular

---

[36] [See now the Interpretation Act 1978.]

includes plural. So 'householder who is' includes 'householders who are.' And these four students, being *jointly* responsible for household necessities and rent, are all four students, being jointly responsible for household necessities and rent, are all four householders. It makes no difference in law that gas and electricity bills were sent in the name of one of them only. That was a mere matter of convenience which did not affect the responsibility of all four of them.

This seems to me a good instance where the High Court should not interfere with the tribunal's decision, even though it may be said to be erroneous in point of law. It cannot be supposed that each one of these four should each have the full allowance as if he was responsible for the whole. Nor even that one of them – Mr. Fairbairn – should have the full allowance. The better way of administering the Act is to hold that none of the four gets the allowance as being the householder: but that each should be regarded as a lodger contributing towards a householder's commitments. Each should get an allowance in respect of his contribution to the rent: see paragraph 13; and each may be granted a special addition under paragraph 4 (1) (*a*) to take account of the exceptional circumstances. That is what the tribunal allowed to Mr. Shine. It was a reasonable way of administering the Act on a point which was not covered by the Schedule.

Principles on which the Court should interfere

It is plain that Parliament intended that the Supplementary Benefit Act 1966 should be administered with as little technicality as possible. It should not become the happy hunting ground for lawyers. The courts should hesitate long before interfering by certiorari with the decisions of the appeal tribunals. Otherwise the courts would become engulfed with streams of cases just as they did under the old Workmen's Compensation Acts: see *Reg.* v. *Industrial Injuries Commissioners, Ex parte Amalgamated Engineering Union (No. 2)* [1966] 2 Q.B. 31, 45. The courts should not enter into a meticulous discussion of the meaning of this or that word in the Act. They should leave the tribunals to interpret the Act in a broad reasonable way, according to the spirit and not to the letter: especially as Parliament has given them a way of alleviating any hardship. The courts should only interfere when the decision of the tribunal is unreasonable in the sense that no tribunal acquainted with the ordinary use of language could reasonably reach that decision: see *Cozens* v. *Brutus* [1973] A.C. 854, 861. Nevertheless, it must be realised that the Act has to be applied daily by thousands of officers of the commission: and by 120 appeal tribunals. It is most important that cases raising the same points should be decided in the same way. There should be uniformity of decision. Otherwise grievances are bound to arise. In order to ensure this, the courts should be ready to consider points of law of general application. Take these two cases: In Moore's case, Mr. Blom-Cooper raised an important point on the meaning of the word 'resources.' Did it mean actual resources, or notional resources? It applied to all students seeking educational grants. It was very right for the High Court to give a ruling upon it. In Shine's case, Mr. Langan raised an important point on the meaning of 'householder' when there were two or more joint tenants. It applied to all students sharing a flat when all were directly responsible for expenses. Were all entitled to the householder's allowance? Or only one? Or none? It is very desirable for this point to be authoritatively decided. So we have decided it. But so far as Mr. Shine's £50 grant is concerned, that is of small importance, though of general application. So the High Court should not be troubled with it. And Mr. Langan did not press it before us.

In short, the court should be ready to lay down the broad guide lines for tribunals. But no further. The courts should not be used as if there was an appeal to them. Individual cases of particular application must be left to the tribunals.

And, of course, the courts will always be ready to interfere if the tribunals have exceeded their jurisdiction or acted contrary to natural justice. That goes without saying. I would dismiss this appeal.

[STEPHENSON and GEOFFREY LANE L.JJ. agreed.]

Appeals dismissed.

Question

On what principles did the court base its refusal to intervene in *Shine's* case? See further *Baldwin & Francis Ltd.* v. *Patents Appeal Tribunal* [1959] A.C. 663 at pp. 696–7; *R.* v. *Industrial Injuries Commissioner, ex p. A.E.U.* (*No. 2*) [1966] 2 Q.B. 31 at pp. 45 and 48–9; *R.* v. *National Insurance Commissioner, ex p. Stratton* [1979] Q.B. 361; Rubinstein, op cit., pp. 173–5 and 188–91.

Note

On the need for consistency see also *Pearlman* v. *Harrow School*, p. 53 *supra*; *H.T.V. Ltd.* v. *Price Commission* [1976] I.C.R. 170, noted at p. 162 *infra*.

FINDINGS, EVIDENCE, AND JURISDICTION

'No evidence'

R. v. Nat Bell Liquors Ltd.

[1922] 2 A.C. 128   Judicial Committee of the Privy Council

The issue was whether magistrates, who had convicted a firm of unlawfully selling liquor on the uncorroborated evidence of an *agent provocateur,* had acted ultra vires because they had no evidence before them.

LORD SUMNER (delivering the judgment of their Lordships]: ... It has been said that the matter may be regarded as a question of jurisdiction, and that a justice who convicts without evidence is acting without jurisdiction to do so. Accordingly, want of essential evidence, if ascertained somehow, is on the same footing as want of qualification in the magistrate, and goes to the question of his right to enter on the case at all. Want of evidence on which to convict is the same as want of jurisdiction to take evidence at all. This, clearly, is erroneous. A justice who convicts without evidence is doing something that he ought not to do, but he is doing it as a judge, and if his jurisdiction to entertain the charge is not open to impeachment, his subsequent error, however grave, is a wrong exercise of a jurisdiction which he has, and not a usurpation of a jurisdiction which he has not. How a magistrate, who has acted within his jurisdiction up to the point at which the missing evidence should have been, but was not, given, can, thereafter, be said by a kind of relation back to have no jurisdiction over the charge at all, is hard to see. It cannot be said that his conviction is void, and may be disregarded as a nullity, or that the whole proceeding was coram non judice. To say that there is no jurisdiction to convict without evidence is the same thing as saying that there is jurisdiction if the decision is right, and none if it is wrong; or that jurisdiction at the outset of a case continues so long as the decision stands, but that, if it is set aside, the real conclusion is that there never was any jurisdiction at all . . . .

Note

On disputed questions of fact, see p. 51 *supra*.

Coleen Properties Ltd. v. Minister of Housing and Local Government

[1971] 1 W.L.R. 433   Court of Appeal

The owners of a building, which a local authority wished to acquire as part of a redevelopment scheme, applied for a statutory order to quash the Minister's decision that the building was land 'the acquisition of which is reasonably necessary for the satisfactory development or use' of a clearance area (s. 43 (2) of the Housing Act 1957). Lyell J. dismissed the application and the owners appealed.

LORD DENNING M.R.: On May 7, 1968, the inspector held a public local inquiry and inspected the properties. The council called witnesses to show that the old houses in the clearance areas in Sidney Street and Clark Street were in terribly bad condition. They called the medical officer of health, the housing officer, and the public health housing inspector. But they did not call any witnesses as to the planning merits. They did not call an architect or a planning officer. They called no one to show that it was necessary to acquire Clark House. They merely asserted, through the mouth of their advocate, the deputy town clerk, that

'the acquisition of such properties (i.e. the added lands including Clark House) is reasonably necessary for the purpose of the satisfactory development or use of the clearance areas (i.e. the old houses).

In short, the council relied on their own ipse dixt that Clark House fell within the section. The objectors, however, called a qualified surveyor and architect, Mr. Mallett, F.I.A.S., F.A.L.P.A., who could and did give evidence on planning merits.

On May 22, 1968, the inspector made his report to the Minister. He said, as to Clark House: 'This is a first class property and I am of the opinion that its acquisition by the council is not reasonably necessary for the satisfactory development or use of the cleared area.'

So the inspector recommended that it be excluded altogether from the compulsory purchase order. On October 25, 1968, the Minister gave his letter of decision. He rejected the inspector's recommendation in these three sentences:

'The Minister disagrees with the inspector's recommendation with regard to reference no. 13 (i.e., Clark House). It appears to him that by the very nature of its position, the exclusion of this property must seriously inhibit the future redevelopment of the rectangular block of land between Sidney Street and Damien Street in which it stands. He has decided, therefore, that the acquisition of reference 13 (Clark House) is reasonably necessary for the satisfactory development or use of the cleared area. . . .'

So the Minister said that Clark House was to be included in the compulsory purchase order.

The owners appealed to the High Court in accordance with paragraph 2 of Schedule 4 to the Housing Act 1957, which enables an order to be questioned if 'it is not within the powers of this Act or that any requirement of this Act has not been complied with.' Under that provision, it has been held in *Ashbridge Investments Ltd.* v. *Minister of Housing and Local Government* [1965] 1 W.L.R. 1320, 1326 that:

'. . . the court can interfere with the Minister's decision if he has acted on no evidence; or if he has come to a conclusion to which on the evidence he could not reasonably come; or if he has given a wrong interpretation to the words of the statute; or if he has taken into consideration matters which he ought not to have taken into account, or vice versa; or has otherwise gone wrong in law. It is identical with the position when the court has power to interfere with the decision of a lower tribunal which has erred in point of law.'

Lyell J. affirmed the Minister's decision, but I must say that he seems to have proceeded on grounds which were not warranted by the evidence, particularly as to the school. The owners appeal to this court.

In my opinion the Minister was in error in reversing the inspector's recommendation. The Minister had before him only the report of the inspector. He did not see the premises himself. To my mind there was no material on which the Minister could properly overrule the inspector's recommendation. Clark House is a first class new property. It has shops with flats over. In order to acquire it compulsorily, the local authority must show that the acquisition 'is reasonably necessary for the satisfactory development or use of the cleared area.' In order to show it, the local authority ought to have produced some evidence to the inspector as to what kind of development would be a 'satisfactory development' of the area, and to show how the acquisition of Clark House is 'reasonably necessary.' I do not say that they ought to have produced a detailed plan of the proposed development. I realise well enough that in many cases that may not be practicable. For instance, when an area is to be developed for industrial purposes, you cannot go into details until you have the businessmen wanting the factories. But, when an area is to be developed for residential purposes – for the council's own housing plans – it ought to be possible to give an outline plan of the proposed development. I cannot myself see that the council could get any more dwellings on to the site of Clark House than the 6 flats which are already there. The council may desire to make a neat and tidy development of these two streets, including Clark House, but this may well be possible whilst leaving Clark House standing. At any rate, I am quite clear that the mere ipse dixit of the local council is not sufficient. There must be some evidence to support their assertion. And here there was none.

Then there is the report of the inspector. He was clearly of opinion that the acquisition of Clark House was not reasonably necessary. I can see no possible justification for the Minister in overruling the inspector. There was no material whatever on which he could do so. I know that on matters of planning policy the Minister can overrule the inspector, and need not send it back to him, as happened in *Luke* v. *Minister of Housing and Local Government* [1968] 1 Q.B. 172. But the question of what is 'reasonably necessary' is not planning policy. It is an inference of fact on which the Minister should not overrule the inspector's recommendation unless there is material sufficient for the purpose. There was none here. In my judgment the Minister was wrong and this court should intervene and overrule him. . . .

SACHS L.J.: . . . The need for evidence to be available to a Minister before he can act has been the subject of earlier decisions. The question before him was not, to my mind, one of policy: it was in essence a question of fact that had to be established as a condition precedent to the exercise of the powers to take away the subject's property. It was no less a question of fact because it involved forming a judgment on matters on which expert opinion can and indeed ought to be given. (I rather doubt whether there is much material difference between the view I have just expressed and that of Mr. Slynn who has argued that the question was simply a matter of planning judgment which had to be based on evidence.) As long ago as the *Sheffield* case, 52 T.L.R. 171, 173, Swift J. said:

> '. . . it is for the court, if the matter is brought before it, to say whether there is any material on which the Minister could have come to the conclusion that it was reasonably necessary. If the court comes to the conclusion that there is no such material, then it will not hesitate to quash the Minister's order.'

That passage coincides with those passages in the judgment of Lord Denning M.R. in the *Ashbridge* case [1965] 1 W.L.R. 1320 to which he has referred.

The Minister, therefore, cannot come to a conclusion of fact contrary to that which the inspector found in this case unless there was evidence before the latter on which he (the Minister) could form that contrary conclusion. Upon the inquiry, an inspector is, of course, entitled to use the evidence of his own eyes, evidence which he as an expert, in this case he was an architect, can accept. The Minister, on the other hand, can only look at what is on the record. He cannot, as against the subject, avail himself of other expert evidence from within the Ministry – at any rate, without informing the subject and giving him an opportunity to deal with that evidence on the lines which are set out in regard to a parallel matter in the Compulsory Purchase by Local Authorities (Inquiries Procedure) Rules 1962. Whilst the inspector, even if not an architect, may well be looked on as an expert for the purpose of forming an opinion of fact, the Minister is in a different position. It is by no means intended as a criticism to say with all respect that no Minister can personally be an expert on all matters of professional opinion with which his officers deal from day to day.

Before turning to the report and examining the evidence, there is a further observation to be made. When seeking to deprive a subject of his property and cause him to move himself, his belongings and perhaps his business to another area, the onus lies squarely on the local authority to show by clear and unambiguous evidence that the order sought for should be granted. . . .

BUCKLEY L.J.: . . . Mr. Slynn, appearing before us on behalf of the Minister, has submitted that that decision is a matter of planning judgment; but he concedes that the judgment must be based upon some evidence. That evidence must be, I take it, evidence of a kind which would justify a reasonable man in reaching the conclusion which the Minister reached. . . .

Appeal allowed.

Compulsory purchase order quashed
so far as it relates to Clark House.

Question

1. How, if at all, can the decision in *Coleen* be reconciled with that in *Nat Bell Liquors*?

2. To what extent is this ground of review distinct from other grounds? Compare the approach in *Coleen* with that in *White and Collins* v. *Minister of Health* [1939] 2 K.B. 838, noted at p. 50 *supra*. See the discussion of *White and Collins* in *Ashbridge Investments Ltd.* v. *Ministry of Housing and Local Government* [1965] 1 W.L.R. 1320 at pp. 1327–8. Note the difference between Lord Diplock on the one hand (p. 188 *infra*) and Lord Wilberforce and Lord Salmon on the other (pp. 184 and 189 *infra*) in the *Tameside* case.

Notes

1. In *R.* v. *Brixton Prison Governor, ex p. Armah* [1968] A.C. 192 at p. 234 Lord Reid stated that 'whether or not there is evidence to support a particular decision is always a question of law but it is not a question of jurisdiction' so that certiorari will only issue if the lack of evidence appears on the face of the record (see also *R.* v. *Birmingham Compensation Appeal Tribunal of Ministry of Labour and National Service, ex p. Road Haulage Executive* [1952] 2 All E.R. 100 n). Findings based on no evidence can, however, be appealed against where a statutory right of appeal on a point of law has been granted. There is also a body of dicta supporting the proposition that a finding made without evidence constitutes a jurisdictional error. The origins of this lie in habeas corpus cases (see *R.* v. *Board of Control, ex p. Rutty* [1956] 2 Q.B.

109 at p. 124 and Sharpe, *The Law of Habeas Corpus*, pp. 74–80), but since *Coleen*'s case it may well be true of Administrative Law in general. See also *R. v. Deputy Industrial Injuries Commissioner, ex p. Moore* [1965] 1 Q.B. 456 at p. 488 (stating that natural justice requires that a decision be based on evidence of some probative value); *G.E.C. Ltd. v. Price Commission* [1974] I.C.R. 609 at p. 617, approved on appeal [1975] I.C.R. 1 at pp. 12 and 18. However, *Coleen's* case concerned a public inquiry and it has been said to be confined to decisions made after such formal procedures: *R. v. Secretary of State for the Environment, ex p. Powis* [1981] 1 W.L.R. 584. On public inquiries, see ch. 17 *infra*. For a comprehensive discussion of the decision in *Coleen*, see Evans, (1971), 34 M.L.R. 561.

2. Although Lord Denning's dicta in *Ashbridge Investments Ltd. v. Minister of Housing and Local Government* were cited in *Coleen*, it should be noted that Harman and Winn L.JJ. in *Ashbridge* did not go so far: [1965] 1 W.L.R. 1320 at pp. 1328–9. See also *R. v. Secretary of State for the Environment, ex p. Powis* [1981] 1 W.L.R. 584 (*Coleen* principle not applicable where statute permitted written representations only). Consider more generally *Khawaja's* case (see Appendix).

3. The question of what constitutes 'evidence' has not received much attention in the books (de Smith, pp. 208 and 211; Garner, *Administrative Law*, 5th edn., p. 240), It is clear that administrative bodies and tribunals are not bound by the rules of evidence used in courts of law but may consider all material which is logically relevant to the issue: see Wade, p. 805; Elliott, (1972) 32 Sask. L. Rev. 48 at pp. 67–80; pp 560 and 563 *infra*. It is also clear that they are freer than courts in their ability to base decisions upon information within their own knowledge, of which they are said to have 'official notice'. Such information may either be facts used 'to *supplement*, or as a *substitute for*, evidence properly and openly presented' or the '*accumulated background* of special knowledge, understanding and experience [used] to *evaluate and assess* the evidence properly presented' (Smillie, [1975] P.L. 64 at p. 69). See also de Smith, pp. 204–7.

The reasons for the relaxation of the rules which restrict courts are sound and reflect the reasons for creating administrative bodies (see pp. 537 *infra*): the need for speed, informality, and the relative expertise of the administrative body. But the consequence is that only in an exceptional case will the administrative procedures and 'official notice' fail to generate some evidence in support of the decision to be made. Furthermore, the need for 'no evidence' as a ground of review will depend on whether courts characterize issues as factual. *Coleen's* case involved the application of a statutory standard to primary facts, something which several recent Court of Appeal decisions have characterized as a question of law (e.g. *H.T.V. Ltd. v. Price Commission* [1976] I.C.R. 170, noted at p. 162 *infra* and *Pearlman* v. *Harrow School*, p. 53 *supra*). What consequences does this have for the scope of review? Although generalization about the classification of an issue as law or fact is dangerous (see p. 71 *supra*), these decisions do suggest that there may be relatively few occasions in which review on the ground of 'no evidence' will be possible. Finally, there may be issues which are classified as policy despite an apparent similarity to factual issues. In such cases the relevant ground of review is probably 'abuse of discretion' rather than 'no evidence'. An example of this sort of case is *Bushell* v. *Secretary of State for the Environment*, p. 601 *infra*, in which a department's method of predicting the growth of traffic was said to be a non-factual issue of policy. This appears to be what Davis has termed a 'legislative fact', which is normally general and which does not concern the immediate parties. Such facts are contrasted with 'adjudicative facts' which relate to the parties

(*Administrative Law Text*, 3rd. edn., para. 15.03). One difference between the two is that findings of adjudicative facts must be supported by evidence but findings of legislative facts need not be and sometimes cannot be supported by evidence.

4. The decisions in *Coleen* and *Secretary of State for Education and Science v. Tameside M.B.C.*, p. 182 *infra*, raise the question whether English law now permits the review of a decision on the ground that it was reached on *inadequate* evidence (see Austin, (1975) 28 C.L.P. 150). If this is a ground for review the experience of the United States 'substantial evidence' ground of review could prove instructive: see Schwartz and Wade, *Legal Control of Government*, pp. 228–34 and 238–9. 'Substantial evidence is more than a mere scintilla. It means such relevant evidence as a reasonable mind might accept as adequate to support a conclusion'. (*Consolidated Edison Co. v. National Labor Relations Board* 305 U.S. 197 at p. 229 (1938)). Furthermore, the 'substantiality of evidence must take into account whatever in the record fairly detracts from its weight' (*Universal Camera Corporation v. National Labor Relations Board* 340 U.S. 474 at p. 487 (1951)). Thus, although in theory the reviewing court is not to weigh evidence or choose between various reasonable inferences or between conflicting testimony, it is difficult to see how the test can be applied without these things being done (Kramer, (1959) 28 Ford. L. Rev. 1 at p. 84; McGowan, (1967) 20 Admin. L. Rev. 147 at p. 180; McGowan, (1974) 74 Col. L. Rev. 1015 at p. 1021 n. 14). The test has, moreover, been criticized. 'At best concepts such as "substantial evidence" tend to be little more than convenient labels attached to results reached without their aid . . .' (Gellhorn and Robinson, 75 Col. L. Rev. 771 at p. 780 (1975)). Again, 'there is often greater difficulty in applying the test than in formulating it' (*Stork Restaurant Inc. v. Boland* 26 N.E. 2d 247 (1940)). Apart from the merits of the substantial evidence rule itself, it should be remembered that the context in which it is used in the United States is for formal, almost trial-type, decisionmaking and that it may be inappropriate for the far less formal system used by most English administrative bodies and tribunals. See for instance, *R. v. Secretary of State for the Environment, ex p. Powis* [1981] 1 W.L.R. 584, noted at p. 85 *supra*. Furthermore, many of the questions reviewed on this ground (e.g. *National Labor Relations Board v. Hearst Publications* 322 U.S. 111, 131 (1944)) are inferences from primary facts which, in England, would tend to be classified as questions of law rather than as questions of fact or of mixed law and fact (pp. 60, 72–3 *supra*).

Error of material fact

Secretary of State for Education and Science v. Tameside Metropolitan Borough Council, p. 182 *infra*

Note

For comment on Lord Wilberforce's approach on this point see Wade, p. 295.

3

PROBLEMS OF INVALIDITY

COLLATERAL PROCEEDINGS

Director of Public Prosecutions v. Head

[1959] A.C. 83   House of Lords

Under s. 9 of the Mental Deficiency Act 1913, if satisfied from the certificate of two duly qualified medical practitioners that a person in an approved school was a defective, the Secretary of State could order that person's transfer to an institution for defectives. Relying on this section, the Secretary of State made an order on 2 July 1947 transferring Miss Henderson to a particular institution, but neither certificate which he received fully complied with the relevant statutory provisions. Miss Henderson was later transferred to other institutions and continuation orders were made in respect of her.

The respondent was convicted on an indictment charging him with having carnal knowledge of a mental defective (Miss Henderson) contrary to s. 56 (1) (a) of the Mental Deficiency Act 1913. At the time of the alleged offence, Miss Henderson was out on licence from an institution. At the trial the Secretary of State's order and the orders for her transfer were put in evidence, it being necessary to establish that she was a mental defective. Hinchcliffe J. directed the jury that in the light of the documents produced Miss Henderson was properly certified as a defective, and he did not allow the defence to go behind the Secretary of State's order. The Court of Criminal Appeal ([1958] 1 Q.B. 132) quashed the conviction on the basis that Miss Henderson was never lawfully made subject to the Mental Deficiency Act 1913. There was an unsuccessful appeal to the House of Lords by the D.P.P.

LORD SOMERVELL OF HARROW: . . . I have had the advantage of reading the opinion about to be given by my noble and learned friend, Lord Denning, and would like briefly to make my reservations. My noble friend thinks that the Secretary of State's order of July 2, 1947, was voidable and not void.

I am not satisfied that the order was not void. On the wording of section 9 of the Mental Deficiency Act, 1913, I think the certificates may well be for this purpose part of the order to be looked at in order to see whether it is good on its face. If they are not part of the order it might, I think, be maintained that they afford no evidence on which the order made could validly have been based. In either case I would wish to reserve the question whether the order would not be void rather than voidable.

It is conceded that the court had material before it which would have led to the order being quashed on certiorari or other appropriate proceedings. The next question, as it appears to me, can be stated in this way. Is a man to be sent to prison on the basis that an order is a good order when the court knows it would be set aside if proper proceedings were taken? I doubt it. The case was never argued on these lines before the Court of Criminal Appeal.

The distinction between void and voidable is by no means a clear one, as a glance at the entry under 'void' in Stroud's Judicial Dictionary shows. I am not satisfied that the question whether a man should go or not go to prison should depend upon the distinction. . . .

LORD DENNING: . . . Mr. Guthrie Jones[1] said that the original order was bad and that therefore the continuation orders were bad. They depended on the original order which was itself void. Nothing could save the continuation orders, he said, if the original order was bad.

This contention seems to me to raise the whole question of *void* or *voidable*: for if the original order was void, it would in law be a nullity. There would be no need for an order to quash it. It would be automatically null and void without more ado. The continuation orders would be nullities too, because you cannot continue a nullity. The licence to Miss Henderson would be a nullity. So would all the dealings with her property under section 64 of the Act of 1913. None of the orders would be admissible in evidence. The Secretary of State would, I fancy, be liable in damages for all of the 10 years during which she was unlawfully detained, since it could all be said to flow from his negligent act; see section 16 of the Mental Treatment Act, 1930.

But if the original order was only voidable, then it would not be automatically void. Something would have to be done to avoid it. There would have to be an application to the High Court for certiorari to quash it. The application would have to be made by the person aggrieved — Miss Henderson — and not by a stranger: and she would have to make it within six months[2] unless the court extended the time. And being only voidable, the court would have a discretion whether to quash it or not. It would do so if justice demanded it, but not otherwise. Meanwhile the order would remain good and a support for all that had been done under it. See the principles discussed in *Dimes* v. *Grand Junction Canal*,[3] *McPherson* v. *McPherson*.[4] In this case, therefore if the original order was only voidable, the continuation orders would be good. So would the licence. All dealings with her property would be valid. All the orders would be admissible in evidence (see *Leighton* v. *Leighton*,[5] Hubback on Evidence, pp. 590–591) and the Secretary of State would not be liable in damages; see *Everett* v. *Griffiths*.[6]

The vital question to my mind is therefore: Was the original order abso-

---

[1] [Counsel for the respondent.]
[2] [The time limit for certiorari is different now: see p. 317 *infra*.]
[3] (1852) 3 H.L.C. 759, 786.
[4] [1936] A.C. 177, 203–205.
[5] (1720) 1 Str. 308.
[6] [1921] 1 A.C. 631.

lutely void or was it only voidable? If the order had been outside the jurisdiction of the Secretary of State altogether it would have been a nullity and void; see *The Case of the Marshalsea*.[7] But that is not this case. The most that appears here is that the Secretary of State – acting within his jurisdiction – exercised that jurisdiction erroneously. That makes his order voidable and not void. It is said that he made the order on no evidence or on insufficient materials. So be it. His error is a wrong exercise of a jurisdiction which he has, and not a usurpation of a jurisdiction which he has not; see *Rex* v. *Nat Bell Liquors Ltd.*[8] by Lord Sumner. If that error appears on the face of the record – as it is said to do here – it renders the order liable to be quashed on certiorari, but it does not make it a nullity; see *Reg.* v. *Medical Appeal Tribunal, Ex parte Gilmore*[9] by Parker L.J. Unless and until it is so quashed, it is to be regarded as good. It is, moreover, sufficient to support all the continuation orders made on the faith of it. Even if the original order should be set aside, the continuation orders would remain good: for it is a general rule that when a voidable transaction is avoided, it does not invalidate intermediate transactions which were made on the basis that it was good; see *De Reneville* v. *De Reneville*[10] by Lord Greene M.R., and *Reg.* v. *Algar*[11] by Lord Goddard C.J. I would uphold therefore the contention of the Attorney-General that, whatever the position of the original order, the continuation orders were good. . . .

[LORD DENNING concluded that the Court of Criminal Appeal had acted on a mistaken ground in quashing the conviction, but he went on to decide that it would be wrong to restore the conviction.]

[LORD TUCKER delivered a speech in favour of dismissing the appeal. LORD REID and LORD SOMERVELL OF HARROW agreed with LORD TUCKER's speech and LORD REID and LORD TUCKER concurred in the reservations expressed by LORD SOMERVELL OF HARROW. VISCOUNT SIMONDS delivered a speech in favour of allowing the appeal, but he did concur with LORD SOMERVELL OF HARROW's reservations.]

Cooper v. The Board of Works for the Wandsworth District, p. 211 *infra*

Notes

1. On the question of review for 'no evidence', which is referred to in the extracts from *D.P.P.* v. *Head*, see p. 80 *supra*.

2. The two cases *supra* provide examples of proceedings in which the validity of a decision was successfully raised indirectly or collaterally. For general discussion, see Rubinstein, *Jurisdiction and Illegality*, Chs. 3 and 6. One important feature of collateral challenge via, for example, an action for damages or a defence in criminal proceedings is the absence of the discretion to refuse relief which is to be found with the normal Administrative Law remedies (see Chs. 9–12 *infra*).

---

[7] (1612) 10 Co. Rep. 68b, 76a.
[8] [1922] 2 A.C. 128, 151.
[9] [1957] 1 Q.B. 574, 588.
[10] [1948] P. 100, 111–112.
[11] [1954] 1 Q.B. 279, 287.

3. As a matter of principle it would seem that a decision which is marred by an error of law on the face of the record, as opposed to a jurisdictional defect, cannot be questioned in collateral proceedings (although note the developments in relation to jurisdictional errors of law (see p. 53 *supra*) on the question of the difference between these concepts).

The case law is not, however, consistent as to the scope of review in collateral proceedings. *D.P.P.* v. *Head*, for example, can be seen to cause some difficulty. Writers have come to different conclusions as to the majority's opinion of the status of the order (Wade, p. 298–void; cf. Rubinstein, op. cit., p. 186 – 'nowhere in the majority's decision is the detention order treated as a nullity'). But whatever the answer to this question, Viscount Simonds, Lord Reid, and Lord Tucker did concur in Lord Somervell's 'reservations' on the question whether the Secretary of State's order was void or voidable. The fact that it was not thought necessary finally to decide that the order was void, and the doubts Lord Somervell expressed whether a man should be imprisoned on the basis of an order which would be set aside in proper proceedings, suggest that the majority of the House of Lords would have allowed collateral challenge, even if the defect in the order was a non-jurisdictional error of law on the face of the record. One way around this clash with the principle stated at the beginning of this Note is to regard *D.P.P.* v. *Head* as turning on the particular statutory provisions involved: Rubinstein, op. cit., p. 186 and see *Hinton Demolitions Pty. Ltd.* v. *Lower* (No. 2) (1971) 1 S.A.S.R. 512 at p. 547 (per Wells J. – but Bray C.J. (p. 523) was not convinced).

4. The availability of collateral challenge based on a breach of natural justice (see Chs. 7–8 *infra*) also merits consideration. Akehurst, (1968) 31 M.L.R. 2 and 138 concludes (at p. 151) that 'more often than not' collateral attack on the grounds of breach of natural justice has been permitted. Wade, p. 299, suggests that, in addition to the requirement that the complainant be the victim of the breach of natural justice, challenge on this ground might be limited to direct proceedings *against the relevant authority* which would cover not just an action for certiorari or a declaration, but also 'an action for damages based on the nullity of the order'. Thus *Cooper* v. *Wandsworth Board of Works*, p. 211 *infra*, is catered for. Bray C.J. in *Hinton Demolitions Pty. Ltd.* v. *Lower* (No. 2) (1971) 1 S.A.S.R. at pp. 522–3 supports this approach, though note his reliance, following *Durayappah* v. *Fernando*, p. 226 *infra*, on the view that a decision in breach of natural justice is (normally) voidable, on which see pp. 209 and 229 *infra*; cf. Wells J. at p. 549, whose restrictive approach to collateral challenge applies beyond questions of natural justice to other forms of jurisdictional error. (For another restrictive approach in relation to challenge in collateral proceedings, see *Reid* v. *Rowley* [1977] 2 N.Z.L.R. 472 at p. 483.) Contrast with Wade's suggestion a case such as *Bonaker* v. *Evans* (1850) 16 Q.B. 162; in this case the Court of Exchequer Chamber stated the plaintiff should have recovered in an action for money had and received brought against the sequestrator of the profits of the plaintiff's benefice where the sequestration, which was ordered by a bishop, was held void for breach of natural justice.

5. For collateral challenge to the acts of what are termed *de facto* officers or judges, see Rubinstein, op. cit., pp. 205–8.

PARTIAL INVALIDITY

London & Clydeside Estates Ltd. v. Aberdeen District Council,
p. 104 *infra*

Dunkley v. Evans, p. 507 *infra*

Note

See further Wade, p. 302; *Thames Water Auth.* v. *Elmbridge B.C.* [1983] 2 W.L.R. 743.

BURDEN OF PROOF

R. v. Fulham etc. Rent Tribunal, ex parte Zerek, p. 47 *supra*

Associated Provincial Picture Houses Ltd. v. Wednesbury Corporation, p. 118 *infra*

Note

Lord Greene's comments in the last-mentioned case were approved and applied recently in *Cannock Chase D.C.* v. *Kelly* [1978] 1 W.L.R. 1.

Inland Revenue Commissioners v. Rossminster Ltd.

[1980] A.C. 952   House of Lords

Four search warrants, each authorizing the search of particular premises by certain officers of the Inland Revenue, were issued by a circuit judge under s. 20C of the Taxes Management Act 1970 (as amended). By s. 20C (3) the Act provides that when premises are entered under such a warrant the officer may seize 'any things whatsoever found there which he has reasonable cause to believe may be required as evidence for the purposes of proceedings in respect of [an offence involving any form of tax fraud]'. Certain material was taken from all the premises searched. An action in tort based on an allegation of wrongful interference with goods was instituted against the Inland Revenue Commissioners and one of the Revenue's officers. There was also an application to the Divisional Court for, *inter alia,* (*a*) certiorari to quash the search warrants; and (*b*) a declaration that the officers were not entitled to take and were bound to return things taken from the premises in question. This application failed, but an appeal to the Court of Appeal was successful. However, in turn, an appeal from the decision of the Court of Appeal was allowed by the House of Lords. This extract merely covers the question of the burden of proof.

VISCOUNT DILHORNE: . . . The respondents[12] satisfied the Court of Appeal that the seizure and removal were unlawful. When taking so many documents as were taken in this case, mistakes may occur and some documents be taken

---

[12] [The applicants in the Divisional Court.]

that should not have been. But the fact that they should not have been does not, in my opinion, justify the conclusion that the other documents taken were not taken after adequate examination and in the belief that they might be required in evidence. Omnia praesumuntur rite esse acta. If the respondents claimed the entry into their premises was a trespass, they would be met with the answer that the warrants made the entry legal. If they assert that following a lawful entry, documents and things were seized and removed when there was no right to take them, the onus, in my opinion, lies on them to establish a prima facie case of that and that, in my opinion, they have not done. . . .

LORD DIPLOCK: . . .

The onus of proof on an application for judicial review

With the issue of the warrant the functions and responsibilities of the circuit judge come to an end. The power of the officer of the board to seize and remove things that he finds upon the premises which the warrant authorises him to enter and search, is conferred directly upon him by subsection (3) which limits his powers of seizure and removal to things 'which he has reasonable cause to believe may be required as evidence for the purposes of proceedings' for an offence involving a tax fraud. These words appearing in a statute do not make conclusive the officer's own honest opinion, that he has reasonable cause for the prescribed belief. The grounds on which the officer acted must be sufficient to induce in a reasonable person the required belief before he can validly seize and remove anything under the subsection. . . .

I would also accept that since the act of handling a man's goods without his permission is prima facie tortious, at the trial of a civil action for trespass to goods based on the seizure and removal of things by an officer of the board in purported exercise of his powers under the subsection, the onus would be upon the officer to satisfy the court that there did in fact exist reasonable grounds that were known to him for believing that the documents he removed might be required as evidence in proceedings for some offence involving a tax fraud – not that they *would* be so required, for that the seizing officer could not know, but that they *might* be required if sufficient admissible evidence were ultimately forthcoming to support a prosecution for the offence and it were decided to prosecute. . . .

[Having decided that on the basis of public interest immunity (see p. 461 *infra*) the grounds of the officers' belief need not be disclosed at this stage, he continued:]

Seizure of documents by an officer of the board under section 20C (3) involves a decision by the officer as to what documents he may seize. The subsection prescribes what the state of mind of the officer must be in order to make it lawful for him to decide to seize a document: he must believe that the document may be required as evidence in criminal proceedings for some form of tax fraud and that belief must be based on reasonable grounds. The decision-making power is conferred by the statute upon the officer of the board. He is not required to give any reasons for his decision and the public interest immunity provides justification for any refusal to do so. Since he does not disclose his reasons there can be no question of setting aside his decision for error of law on the face of the record and the only ground upon which it can be attacked upon judicial review is that it was ultra vires because a condition precedent to his forming the belief which the statute prescribes, viz. that it should be based upon reasonable grounds, was not satisfied. Where Parliament has designated a public officer as decision-maker for a particular class of decisions the High Court, acting as a reviewing court under Order 53, is not a court of appeal. It must proceed on the presumption omnia praesumuntur rite esse acta until that presumption can be displaced by the applicant for review – upon whom the onus lies of doing so. Since no reasons have been given by the decision-maker and no unfavourable inference can be drawn for this fact because there is obvious justification for his failure to do so, the presumption that he acted intra vires can only be displaced by evidence of facts which cannot be reconciled with there having been reasonable cause for his belief that the documents might be required as evidence or alternatively which cannot be reconciled with his having held such belief at all.

I agree with my noble and learned friend, Viscount Dilhorne, that the evidence filed on behalf of the applicants in the instant case would have fallen short of that even if there had been no affidavits in answer filed on behalf of the board to throw a different light upon the matter. So I would hold, as the Divisional Court did, that the respondents have failed to establish upon their application for judicial review that the officers of the board acted ultra vires or otherwise unlawfully in seizing any of the documents that they seized....

LORD SCARMAN: [having referred to the 'suggestion that the burden of proving the legality of the seizure was upon the Revenue']... The suggestion rests on a misunderstanding. An applicant for judicial review has to satisfy the court that he has a case. If he proves that his house has been entered or his documents seized without his consent, he establishes a prima facie case. But as soon as the respondent pleads justification, e.g. in this case the statute, and leads evidence to show that he has acted within the power conferred on him by law, issue is joined and the prima facie case has to be judged against the strength of the matters urged in defence. Unless the court on judicial review can safely say that the defence will surely fail, it cannot be just to grant final relief, and it must be convenient to allow the issue to go to trial....

Notes

1. A limitation upon the maxim *omnia praesumuntur rite esse acta*, which is referred to in the *Rossminster* case, should be borne in mind. It will not apparently apply when the jurisdiction of an inferior tribunal is questioned in collateral proceedings, though note Wade's point (pp. 307–8) that this limitation 'is concerned not so much with the initial burden of proof as with the matters that may be put in issue'.

2. The question of the burden of proof in habeas corpus cases has been a particular problem in recent years. This cannot be explored here, but see Sharpe, *The Law of Habeas Corpus*, pp. 80–8; Wade, p. 306.

INTERIM EFFECT OF INVALID ORDERS

Effectiveness pending determination

F. Hoffmann-La Roche & Co. A.G. v. Secretary of State for Trade and Industry

[1975] A.C. 295   House of Lords

The appellants marketed the drugs librium and valium. The Department of Health and Social Security, which had to meet a large part of the cost of the drugs, thought that their price was much too high. The matter was referred by the respondent to the Monopolies Commission which in February 1973 recommended, *inter alia*, that the prices charged by the appellants for librium and valium be reduced. A few months later the Regulation of Prices (Tranquillising Drugs) (No. 3) Order 1973 (S.I. 1973 No. 1093), which effected a compulsory price reduction by limiting the prices the appellants could charge, was made under the authority of s. 10 (3) of the Monopolies and Restrictive Practices (Inquiry and Control) Act 1948 and s. 3 (3) (*a*) and (*d*) and (4) (*c*) of the Monopolies and Mergers Act 1965. The order came into effect on 25 June 1973 and was later approved by both Houses of Parliament, as was required by the relevant legislation if it was to remain in force for more than twenty-eight days.

LORD REID: . . . On June 25, 1973, the appellants brought [an] action against the respondent claiming declarations that the Monopolies Commission had proceeded unfairly and in a way contrary to natural justice, that the findings, conclusions and recommendations in their report were invalid and of no effect and that the order . . . was ultra vires, invalid and of no effect.

On June 28, 1973, the respondent sought an injunction restraining the appellants from charging prices in excess of those specified in the No. 3 Order and also sought an interim injunction. Walton J. on an undertaking given by the appellants refused to grant an interim injunction but the Court of Appeal allowed an appeal by the respondent.[13]

Section 11 of the Act of 1948 provides for the enforcement of orders made under this legislation:

'(1) No criminal proceedings shall lie against any person by virtue of the making of any order under the last preceding section on the ground that he has committed, or aided, abetted, counselled or procured the commission of, or conspired or attempted to commit, or incited others to commit, any contravention of the order. (2) Nothing in subsection (1) of this section shall limit any right of any person to bring civil proceedings in respect of any contravention or apprehended contravention of any such order, and, without prejudice to the generality of the preceding words, compliance with any such order shall be enforceable by civil proceedings by the Crown for an injunction or for any other appropriate relief. . . .'

[13] [For these judgments, see [1975] A.C. 295 at pp. 299 and 314.]

It will be seen that there is no reference in this section to interim injunction, but it is not disputed that the court has power to grant interim injunctions. The question in this appeal is in what terms such an injunction should be granted.

An interim injunction against a party to a litigation may cause him great loss if in the end he is successful. In the present case it is common ground that a long time – it may be years – will elapse before a decision can be given. During that period if an interim injunction is granted the appellants will only be able to make the charges permitted by the order. So if in the end the order is annulled that loss will be the difference between those charges and those which they could have made if the order had never been made. And they may not be able to recover any part of that loss from anyone. It is said that the loss might amount to £8m. The appellant's case is that justice requires that such an injunction should not be granted without an undertaking by the respondent to make good that loss to them if they are ultimately successful.

The respondent's first answer is that when an interim injunction is granted to the Crown no undertaking can be required as a condition of granting it. It is not in doubt that in an ordinary litigation the general rule has long been that no interim injunction likely to cause loss to a party will be granted unless the party seeking the injunction undertakes to make good that loss if in the end it appears that the injunction was unwarranted. He cannot be compelled to give an undertaking but if he will not give it he will not get the injunction.

But there is much authority to show that the Crown was in a different position. In general no undertaking was required of it. But whatever justification there may have been for that before 1947 I agree with your Lordships that the old rule or practice cannot be justified since the passing of the Crown Proceedings Act of that year. So if this had been a case where the Crown were asserting a proprietary right I would hold that the ordinary rule should apply and there should be no interlocutory injunction unless the Crown chose to give the usual undertaking.

But this is a case in a different and novel field. No doubt it was thought that criminal penalties were inappropriate as a means of enforcing orders of this kind, and the only method of enforcement is by injunction. Dealing with alleged breaches of the law is a function of the Crown (or of a department of the executive) entirely different in character from its function in protecting its proprietary right. It has more resemblance to the function of prosecuting those who are alleged to have committed an offence. A person who is prosecuted and found not guilty may have suffered serious loss by reason of the prosecution but in general he has no legal claim against the prosecutor. In the absence of special circumstances I see no reason why the Crown in seeking to enforce orders of this kind should have to incur legal liability to the person alleged to be in breach of the order.

It must be borne in mind that an order made under statutory authority is as much the law of the land as an Act of Parliament unless and until it has been found to be ultra vires. No doubt procedure by way of injunction is more flexible than procedure by prosecution and there may well be cases when a court ought to refuse an interim injunction or only to grant it on terms. But I think that it is for the person against whom the interim injunction is sought to show special reason why justice requires that the injunction should not be granted or should only be granted on terms.

The present case has a special feature which requires anxious considera-tion. As I have already indicated, the Crown has a very large financial interest in obtaining an interim injunction. The Department of Health will reap a large immediate benefit from the lower prices set out in the order at the expense of the appellants. If in the end it were decided that the order was ultra vires those prices ought never to have been enforced, the department ought never to have had that benefit and the appellants would have suffered a large loss. So why should the respondent not be required to give the undertaking which the appellants seek as a condition of getting the interim injunction?

But, on the other hand, the order which the appellants seek to annul is the law at present and if an interim injunction is refused that means that the law is not to be enforced and the appellants are to be at liberty to disregard it by charging forbidden prices. And the matter does not stop there. Doctors will continue to prescribe these drugs. Chemists will have to pay the forbidden prices if the public are to be provided with drugs which doctors think they ought to have. And chemists cannot be expected to pay the appellants' prices unless the department is willing to reimburse them. So the department will have to acquiesce in and indeed aid and abet the appellants' breaches of the law if the medical profession and the public are to get what they are entitled to.

It is true that the appellants have proposed an ingenious scheme which they would undertake to operate if an interim injunction is refused. The effect of it would be that they would continue to charge the forbidden prices but that if the order were ultimately held to be intra vires they would repay the dif-ference between the forbidden charges which they had made and the lower charges which they ought to have made. The scheme would involve consider-able practical difficulties and would probably not be fully effective, but I shall not discuss those difficulties because the serious objection would remain that the law laid down in the order is to be disregarded until the case is decided.

My Lords, if I thought that the appellants had a strong case on the merits I would try to stretch a point in their favour to protect them from obvious injustice though I would find difficulty in doing so. It is true that although we heard a good deal of argument on the merits we are not in a position to express any firm opinion as to the appellants' prospects of success. But if it is for them to show us at this stage that their case is so strong that they are entitled to some special consideration, I can say that they have completely failed to convince me that they have a strong prima facie case.

I would therefore dismiss this appeal.

LORD WILBERFORCE: . . It does not, of course, follow that because there is power to impose the condition[14] it ought to be imposed in this case, or similar

---

[14] [i.e. to give an undertaking in damages.]

cases. Regard must be had to the nature of the dispute and the position of the disputants. In a case such as the present, the fact that the effective plaintiff is a government department, acting in the public interest and responsible for public money, is important. The real issue is how far this difference is to be carried. The main argument relied on for preserving, in the present case, a special right for the Crown to obtain injunctions without offering an undertaking is that the Crown is 'enforcing the law,' and – so, I understood the argument – should not be hampered by being put on terms. Or, putting it another way, the company, being in breach of the law, is not in a position to ask for protective terms. My Lords, I am afraid that I regard this argument as fallacious. To say that the Crown is enforcing the law is a petitio principii, since the very issue in the action is whether what is alleged to be law (and denied to be law by the appellants) is law or not. The answer given to this is, I understand, that there is a presumption of validity until the contrary is shown. The consequence drawn from this is that unconditional obedience must be required by the court: 'obey first and argue afterwards' in Lord Denning M.R.'s graphic phrase [1973] 3 W.L.R. 805, 821. I think that there is a confusion here. It is true enough that a piece of subordinate legislation is presumed to be valid against persons who have no locus standi[15] to challenge it – the puzzling case of *Durayappah* v. *Fernando* [1967] 2 A.C. 337 can be understood as exemplifying this. But it is quite another matter to say, and I know of no supporting authority, that such a presumption exists when the validity of the subordinate legislation is legitimately in question before a court and is challenged by a person who has locus standi to challenge it. Certainly no support for any such proposition is to be found in the passage, so often partially quoted, from the speech of Lord Radcliffe in *Smith* v. *East Elloe Rural District Council* [1956] A.C. 736. One has only to read what he said, at pp. 769–770:

'At one time the argument was shaped into the form of saying that an order made in bad faith was in law a nullity and that, consequently, all references to compulsory purchase orders in paragraphs 15 and 16 must be treated as references to such orders only as had been made in good faith. But this argument is in reality a play on the meaning of the word nullity. An order, even if not made in good faith, is still an act capable of legal consequences. It bears no brand of invalidity upon its forehead. Unless the necessary proceedings are taken at law to establish the cause of invalidity and to get it quashed or otherwise upset, it will remain as effective for its ostensible purpose as the most impeccable of orders.'

How this can be said to support an argument that when proceedings *are* taken at law the impugned order must be given full legal effect against the challenger before the proceedings are decided I am unable to comprehend.

In any event the argument proves too much, for if it were right, the court would have no discretion to refuse an injunction whatever the consequences, however irreparably disastrous, to the subject. Such rigidity of power seems

---

[15] [i.e. sufficient interest: see p. 346 *infra*.]

to be contrary to section 45 of the Supreme Court of Judicature (Consolidation) Act 1925.[16] Further, if one considers some of the orders which, under this same Act,[17] can be made under section 3 the injustice of this can be easily perceived. And as an example in practice there is the case of *Post Office* v. *Estuary Radio Ltd.* [1967] 1 W.L.R. 847; [1968] 2 Q.B. 740 which I discuss below, a case where an interim injunction was refused – no doubt just because to grant it would cause irreparable damage. If, then, it is said that there must always remain a residual discretion the argument vanishes: we are back on discretion.

It is said that no understanding should be insisted on unless the effect of the appellants' eventual success were to make the order 'void ab initio' – the argument being that otherwise no injustice would result. Buckley L.J. ([1973] 3 W.L.R. 805, 827–828) made this the conclusion of a judgment with the rest of which I respectfully concur. This phrase 'void ab initio' has engendered many learned distinctions and much confused thinking – unnecessarily, in my opinion. There can be no doubt in the first place that an ultra vires act is simply void – see in confirmation *Ridge* v. *Baldwin* [1964] A.C. 40. In truth when the court says that an act of administration is voidable or void but not ab initio this is simply a reflection of a conclusion, already reached on unexpressed grounds, that the court is not willing in casu to give compensation or other redress to the person who establishes the nullity. Underlying the use of the phrase in the present case, and I suspect underlying most of the reasoning in the Court of Appeal, is an unwillingness to accept that a subject should be indemnified for loss sustained by invalid administrative action. It is this which requires examination rather than some supposed visible quality of the order itself.

In more developed legal systems this particular difficulty does not arise. Such systems give indemnity to persons injured by illegal acts of the administration. Consequently, where the prospective loss which may be caused by an order is pecuniary, there is no need to suspend the impugned administrative act: it can take effect (in our language an injunction can be given) and at the end of the day the subject can, if necessary, be compensated. On the other hand, if the prospective loss is not pecuniary (in our language 'irreparable') the act may be suspended pending decision – in our language, interim enforcement may be refused.

There is clearly an important principle here which has not been elucidated by English law, or even brought into the open. But there are traces of it in some areas. I have referred to *Post Office* v. *Estuary Radio Ltd.* [1967] 1 W.L.R. 847; [1968] 2 Q.B. 740, which arose upon a section in the Wireless Telegraphy Act 1949, similar to section 11 of the Act of 19[4]8.[18] In that case the Post Office applied for an injunction and also moved for interim relief; this was refused, no doubt partly for the reason that to grant it at the interim

---

[16] [This section contained the power to issue injunctions: see now s. 37 of the Supreme Court Acts 1981.]

[17] [The Monopolies and Mergers Act 1965.]

[18] [The Monopolies and Restrictive Practices (Inquiry and Control) Act 1948.]

stage would cause the defendant irreparable damage. We are not bound by the decision, but I suggest that it is based on sound principle.

Secondly, there are instances of statutes which themselves provide for the interim suspension of impugned orders. One such is the Acquisition of Land (Authorisation Procedure) Act 1946, Schedule 1, Part IV.[19] This provides that if any person desires to question the validity of a compulsory purchase order the court may ad interim suspend the effect of the order. These are examples of at least a partial recognition in our law that the subject requires protection against action taken against him or his property under administrative orders which may turn out to be invalid. How far this principle goes need not, and cannot, be decided in the present case. But what can be said is that the combination of section 11 of the Act of 1948 with section 45 of the Supreme Court of Judicature (Consolidation) Act 1925 gives to the court a practical instrument by which injustice to private individuals, faced with possibly invalid action, may be avoided. If this is not possible in every case, it should not be rejected in a case, however special, where justice to both sides can be done.

In the present case there is the feature, special and possibly unique, that the executive, seeking to enforce the order, has itself a pecuniary interest; it is a monopoly buyer confronting a monopoly seller. It stands to make a large profit at the appellants' expense if they are right. So even if one thinks that in general there is no right of compensation for illegal action, that is not a belief which need, or should, influence the present decision. The potentiality of large loss on one side and large profit on the other are factors which are relevant to the court's discretion. . . .

LORD DIPLOCK: . . . Under our legal system . . . the courts as the judicial arm of government do not act on their own initiative. Their jurisdiction to determine that a statutory instrument is ultra vires does not arise until its validity is challenged in proceedings inter partes either brought by one party to enforce the law declared by the instrument against another party or brought by a party whose interests are affected by the law so declared sufficiently directly to give him locus standi to initiate proceedings to challenge the validity of the instrument. Unless there is such challenge and, if there is, until it has been upheld by a judgment of the court, the validity of the statutory instrument and the legality of acts done pursuant to the law declared by it are presumed. It would, however, be inconsistent with the doctrine of ultra vires as it has been developed in English law as a means of controlling abuse of power by the executive arm of government if the judgment of a court in proceedings properly constituted that a statutory instrument was ultra vires were to have any lesser consequence in law than to render the instrument incapable of ever having had any legal effect upon the rights or duties of the parties to the proceedings (cf. *Ridge* v. *Baldwin* [1964] A.C. 40). Although such a decision is directly binding only as between the parties to the proceedings in which it was made, the application of the

---

[19] [See now s. 24 (1) of the Acquisition of Land Act 1981.]

doctrine of precedent has the consequence of enabling the benefit of it to accrue to all other persons whose legal rights have been interfered with in reliance on the law which the statutory instrument purported to declare.

The presumption of validity of the order

My Lords, I think it leads to confusion to use such terms as 'voidable,' 'voidable ab initio,' 'void' or 'a nullity' as descriptive of the legal status of subordinate legislation alleged to be ultra vires for patent or for latent defects, before its validity has been pronounced on by a court of competent jurisdiction. These are concepts developed in the private law of contract which are ill-adapted to the field of public law. All that can usefully be said is that the presumption that subordinate legislation is intra vires prevails in the absence of rebuttal, and that it cannot be rebutted except by a party to legal proceedings in a court of competent jurisdiction who has locus standi to challenge the validity of the subordinate legislation in question.

All locus standi on the part of anyone to rebut the presumption of validity may be taken away completely or may be limited in point of time or otherwise by the express terms of the Act of Parliament which conferred the subordinate legislative power, though the courts lean heavily against a construction of the Act which would have this effect (cf. *Anisminic Ltd.* v. *Foreign Compensation Commission* [1969] 2 A.C. 147). Such was the case, however, in the view of the majority of this House in *Smith* v. *East Elloe Rural District Council* [1956] A.C. 736, at any rate as respects invalidity on the ground of latent defects, so the compulsory purchase order sought to be challenged in the action had legal effect notwithstanding its potential invalidity. Furthermore, apart from express provision in the governing statute, locus standi to challenge the validity of subordinate legislation may be restricted, under the court's inherent power to control its own procedure, to a particular category of persons affected by the subordinate legislation, and if none of these persons chooses to challenge it the presumption of validity prevails. Such was the case in *Durayappah* v. *Fernando* [1967] 2 A.C. 337 where on an appeal from Ceylon, although the Privy Council was of opinion that an order of the Minister was ultra vires owing to a latent defect in the procedure prior to its being made, they nevertheless treated it has having legal effect because the party who sought to challenge it had, in their view, no locus standi to do so.

The legal status of the Regulation of Prices (Tranquillising Drugs) (No. 3) Order 1973 which the appellants seek to challenge in the instant case is aptly stated in the words of Lord Radcliffe in *Smith* v. *East Elloe Rural District Council* [1956] A.C. 736, 769–770:

'An order, . . ., is still an act capable of legal consequences. It bears no brand of invalidity upon its forehead. Unless the necessary proceedings are taken at law to establish the cause of invalidity and to get it quashed or otherwise upset, it will remain as effective for its ostensible purpose as the most impeccable of orders.'

The instant case is not one where the appellants contend that what they are threatening to do would not be a contravention of the order – as was the case in *Post Office* v. *Estuary Radio Ltd.* [1967] 1 W.L.R. 847; [1968] 2 Q.B. 740. Different considerations would apply to that. Their only answer to the application for an interim injunction to enforce the order against them is that they intend to challenge its validity. It is not disputed that they have locus standi to do so, but this does not absolve them from their obligation to obey the order while the presumption in favour of its validity prevails — as it must so long as there has been no final judgment in the action to the contrary.

So in this type of law enforcement action if the only defence is an attack on the validity of the statutory instrument sought to be enforced the ordinary position of the parties as respects the grant of interim injunctions is reversed. The duty of the Crown to see that the law declared by the statutory instrument is obeyed is not suspended by the commencement of proceedings in which the validity of the instrument is challenged. Prima facie the Crown is entitled as of right to an interim injunction to enforce obedience to it. To displace this right or to fetter it by the imposition of conditions it is for the defendant to show a strong prima facie case that the statutory instrument is ultra vires.

Even where a strong prima facie case of invalidity has been shown upon the application for an interim injunction it may still be inappropriate for the court to impose as a condition of the grant of the injunction a requirement that the Crown should enter into the usual undertaking as to damages. For if the undertaking falls to be implemented, the cost of implementing it will be met from public funds raised by taxation and the interests of members of the public who are not parties to the action may be affected by it. . . .

. . . I agree with the majority of your Lordships that the Secretary of State is entitled to the interim injunction that he claimed without giving any undertaking as to damages unless the appellants have succeeded in showing a strong prima facie case that the order sought to be enforced by the injunction is ultra vires. It is not for the Secretary of State to show that the appellant's case cannot possibly succeed as Walton J. thought it was. It is for the appellants to show that their defence of ultra vires is likely to be successful.

I agree with the majority of your Lordships that they have signally failed to do this. . . .

[LORD MORRIS OF BORTH-Y-GEST and LORD CROSS OF CHELSEA delivered speeches in favour of dismissing the appeal.]

Appeal dismissed

Notes

1. Contrast the approach in *Dunlop* v. *Woollahra M.C.,* p. 421 *infra*: see Wade, pp. 309–10. See further the references in Note 2, p. 423 *infra*.

2. Compare with the *Hoffmann-La Roche* case *Lovelock* v. *Minister of Transport* (1980) 40 P. & C.R. 336 in which one ground of attack on two compulsory puchase orders made by a Minister was that a particular consent he had had to obtain from the Secretary of State for the Environment (under the Green Belt (London and Home Counties) Act 1938) was invalid. The Court of Appeal did not think that the Secretary of State had committed any reviewable error, but even if he had, was not prepared to

allow it to be challenged in an application to quash the orders. Lord Denning referred to Lord Radcliffe's words in *Smith* v. *E. Elloe R.D.C.* [1956] A.C. 736 at pp. 769–70, quoted at p. 97 *supra*, and stated (at p. 345) that the 'consent remained valid and effective for all purposes, and for people to act on it, unless and until steps were taken to call it in question'. The consent had not in fact been challenged until the appeal to the Court of Appeal. The difficulty is that the consent was now being challenged in legal proceedings, and yet Lord Denning regarded it as impossible at this stage to question the consent and the orders in the light of all that had been done on the faith of the consent being valid (i.e. the carrying out of the statutory procedure culminating in the making of the orders): see Comment, [1980] J.P.L. 821 at p. 822. In any event, Lord Denning thought the consent should have been challenged earlier by an application for judicial review (see p. 315 *infra*) rather than by an application to quash (see p. 393 *infra*) at this later stage. See further the judgment of Waller L.J., who applied a presumption of validity to the consent, but again see the Comment, op. cit.

3. See *London & Clydeside Estates Ltd.* v. *Aberdeen D.C.*, p. 104 *infra*, and *Calvin* v. *Carr* [1980] A.C. 574, noted at p. 230 *infra*, for the proposition that an appeal can properly be taken from a decision the validity of which is later challenged.

4. On the question of recovery of money paid by virtue of an unlawful act before it was challenged, see p. 431 *infra*.

5. On the question of damages, which is mentioned by Lord Wilberforce, see Ch. 13 *infra*.

VOID OR VOIDABLE?

Director of Public Prosecutions v. Head, p. 87 *supra*

R. v. Paddington Valuation Officer, ex parte Peachey Property Corporation Ltd.

[1966] 1 Q.B. 380   Court of Appeal

The applicant challenged a new rating valuation list prepared by the Paddington Valuation Officer. Mandamus or certiorari were sought, the ground for seeking the latter remedy being an allegation of excess of jurisdiction. The challenge was unsuccessful in the Court of Appeal, as it had been in the Divisional Court ([1964] 1 W.L.R. 1186), but Lord Denning's judgment in particular (in a part with which Danckwerts L.J. agreed) contains a passage which it is instructive to compare with his speech in *D.P.P.* v. *Head*.

LORD DENNING M.R.: . . . It is necessary to distinguish between two kinds of invalidity. The one kind is where the invalidity is so grave that the list is a nullity altogether. In which case there is no need for an order to quash it. It is automatically null and void without more ado. The other kind is when the invalidity does not make the list void altogether, but only voidable. In that case it stands unless and until it is set aside. In the present case the valuation list is not, and never has been, a nullity. At most the valuation officer – acting within his jurisdiction – exercised that jurisdiction erroneously. That makes the list voidable and not void. It remains good until it is set aside. 'It bears no brand of invalidity upon its forehead. Unless the necessary proceedings are taken at law to establish the cause of invalidity and to get it quashed or otherwise upset, it will remain as effective for its ostensible purpose as the most impeccable of orders': see *Smith* v. *East Elloe Rural District Council*[20] by Lord Radcliffe. No doubt if the list is in due course avoided, certiorari must eventually go to quash it. But I see no reason why a mandamus should not issue in advance of the certiorari: compare *Reg.* v. *Cotham etc. JJ. & Webb, ex parte Williams*.[21] If the existing list has been compiled on the wrong footing the court can order the valuation officer to make a new list on the right footing. . . . Once the new list is made and is ready to take effect, the court can quash the old list. In that case everything done under the old list will remain good. The rates that have been demanded and paid cannot be recovered back. For it is a general rule that where a voidable transaction is avoided, it does not invalidate intermediate transactions which were made on the basis that it was good: see the cases collected in *Director of Public Prosecutions* v. *Head*.[22] By this solution, all chaos is avoided. The existing list will remain good until it is replaced by a new list: and then it will be quashed by certiorari. But I think that it must then be quashed. You cannot have two lists in being at the same time. The Divisional Court took the view that certiorari was a necessary pre-requisite to mandamus. I do not think it is a pre-requisite. Certiorari will be necessary some time, but only when the new list is ready to take effect. . . .

SALMON L.J.: . . . I am not altogether satisfied that there would be any power to grant mandamus and keep the 1963 valuation list in force by the simple expedient of postponing certiorari until after a new list had been prepared. No doubt it would be convenient, if possible, to follow this course, were the appeal to be allowed; indeed grave inconvenience, if not chaos, would follow if the 1956 valuation list were to be revived – which both the appellants and respondents at first agreed would be the inevitable result of allowing the appeal. It may be that mandamus can be granted without certiorari, but mandamus cannot be granted if there is a valid valuation list in being. It is not enough that the valuation officer should have prepared the list badly or even very badly. In such a case, he could not be ordered by mandamus to correct his mistakes or make a new list. In order for mandamus to lie, it must be established that he has prepared the list illegally or in bad faith, so that in effect he had not exercised his statutory function at all and that accordingly there is in reality no valid list in existence: *Reg.* v. *Cotham, etc., JJ. and Webb; Ex parte Williams*.[23] Accordingly, it seems to me that a finding that the list is null and void is necessarily implicit in an order of mandamus. . . .

Questions

1. If there was no error on the face of the record (and this was not alleged in the case) on what ground might certiorari have issued if the Valuation Officer was, as Lord

[20] [1956] A.C. 736, 769, 770.
[22] [1959] A.C. 83, 111–113.
[21] [1898] 1 Q.B. 802.
[23] [1898] 1 Q.B. 802.

Denning stated, acting within his jurisdiction? (See generally Wade, (1967) 83 L.Q.R. 499 at pp. 522–4; (1968) 84 L.Q.R. at pp. 113–14.)

2. How far should a court be concerned to avoid administrative chaos? Consider *R. v. Secretary of State for the Environment, ex. p. Ostler*, p. 385 *infra*. Cf. *Bradbury v. Enfield L.B.C.*, p. 289 *infra*, but see s. 31 (6) of the Supreme Court Act 1981, p. 316 *infra*.

Notes

1. Salmon L.J.'s approach, rather than that of Lord Denning, is, it is submitted, the correct approach today, though for difficulties in the case law see Rubinstein, op. cit., pp. 100–5. See further p. 403 *infra*.

2. For the later views of Lord Denning, see Note 2, p. 107 *infra* and Note 1, p. 209 *infra*.

Anismic Ltd. v. Foreign Compensation Commission,
p. 38 *supra* and p. 374 *infra*

London & Clydeside Estates Ltd. v. Aberdeen District Council

[1980] 1 W.L.R. 182   House of Lords

London & Clydeside Estates Ltd. (the appellants) were granted a certificate of alternative development under s. 25 of the Land Compensation (Scotland) Act 1963 by the respondents' precdecessors as the local planning authority. However, this certificate contravened a provision of the Town and Country Planning (General Development) (Scotland) Order 1959 (S.I. No. 1361) in that it did not state in writing the rights of appeal to the Secretary of State, and the Secretary of State later refused to hear an appeal from the appellants on the ground that it was out of time. Both the Lord Ordinary and the Second Division of the Court of Session granted a decree of reduction of the certificate, although the Second Division also refused another claim by the appellants (against which there was a successful appeal to the House of Lords). This extract concerns the cross-appeal against the decree of reduction, in which the House of Lords held that the requirement that had been breached was a mandatory one: see further Note 2, p. 20 *supra*.

LORD HAILSHAM OF ST. MARYLEBONE L.C.: . . . If the requirement that the subject should be informed of his legal rights was mandatory, what follows? The respondents attempted, as I thought, at one time, to argue that it thereupon became a nullity, and that therefore a decree of reduction was inappropriate because there was nothing upon which it could operate. But I do not accept this argument. The certificate was effective until it was struck down by a competent authority (cf. *Brayhead (Ascot) Ltd. v. Berkshire County Council* [1962] 1 Q.B. 229; *James v. Minister of Housing and Local Government* [1968] A.C. 409. . . . The certificate was vitiated in the sense that it failed to comply with a mandatory requirement. But the subject could not safely disregard it as not having been issued. Had he done so, he might well have fallen into the very trap of losing his right to complain of the vitiating factor which has caught other subjects in the reported decisions, and, in my view, he was not only wise but bound to seek a decree of reduction or some other appropriate remedy striking down the offending certificate.

A similar line of reasoning disposes of the next contention of the respondents, also rejected in the Second Division, to the effect that, if the certificate is vitiated, the position is the same as if no certificate had been issued and that section 26 (4) of the Land Compensation (Scotland) Act 1963 then operates in such a way that, no certificate having been issued under section 25, the preceding provisions of the section as to appeals should apply at the expiry of the prescribed period 'as if' the local planning authority had issued a certificate 'containing such a statement as is mentioned in' section 25 (4) (*b*) of the Act. The effect of this read with articles 3 and 4 of the Order would have put the appellants out of time for appeal on the expiry of one month after the expiry of the prescribed (2 months) for the due issue of the certificate by the respondents. The fallacy in this argument lies in the assumption (for it is no more) that the issue by an authority of a certificate vitiated by failure to comply with a mandatory requirement is the same thing as the failure by that authority to issue any purported certificate at all.

. . . In this appeal we are in the field of the rapidly developing jurisprudence of administrative law, and we are considering the effect of non-compliance by a statutory authority with the statutory requirements affecting the discharge of one of its functions. In the reported decisions there is much language presupposing the existence of stark categories such as 'mandatory' and 'directory,' 'void' and 'voidable,' a 'nullity,' and 'purely regulatory.'

Such language is useful; indeed, in the course of this opinion I have used some of it myself. But I wish to say that I am not at all clear that the language itself may not be misleading in so far as it may be supposed to present a court with the necessity of fitting a particular case into one or other of mutually exclusive and starkly contrasted compartments, compartments which in some cases (e.g. 'void' and 'voidable') are borrowed from the language of contract or status, and are not easily fitted to the requirements of administrative law.

When Parliament lays down a statutory requirement for the exercise of legal authority it expects its authority to be obeyed down to the minutest detail. But what the courts have to decide in a particular case is the legal consequence of non-compliance on the rights of the subject viewed in the light of a concrete state of facts and a continuing chain of events. It may be that what the courts are faced with is not so much a stark choice of alternatives but a spectrum of possibilities in which one compartment or description fades gradually into another. At one end of this spectrum there may be cases in which a fundamental obligation may have been so outrageously and flagrantly ignored or defied that the subject may safely ignore what has been done and treat it as having no legal consequences upon himself. In such a case if the defaulting authority seeks to rely on its action it may be that the subject is entitled to use the defect in procedure simply as a shield or defence without having taken any positive action of his own. At the other end of the spectrum the defect in procedure may be so nugatory or trivial that the authority can safely proceed without remedial action, confident that, if the subject is so misguided as to rely on the fault, the courts will decline to listen to his complaint. But in a very great number of cases, it may be in a majority of them, it may be necessary for a subject, in order to safeguard himself, to go to the court for declaration of his rights, the grant of which may well be discretionary, and by the like token it may be wise for an authority (as it certainly would have been here) to do everything in its power to remedy the fault in its procedure so as not to deprive the subject of his due or themselves of their power to act. In such cases, though language like 'mandatory,' 'directory,' 'void,' 'voidable,' 'nullity' and so forth may be helpful in argument, it may be misleading in effect if relied on to show that the courts, in deciding the consequences of a defect in the exercise of power, are necessarily bound to fit the facts of a particular case and a developing chain of events into rigid legal categories or to stretch or cramp them on a bed of Procrustes invented by lawyers for the purposes of convenient exposition. As I have said, the case does not really arise here, since we are in the presence of total non-compliance with a requirement which I have held to be mandatory. Nevertheless I do not wish to be understood in the field of administrative law and in the domain where the courts apply a supervisory jurisdiction over the acts of subordinate authority purporting to exercise statutory powers, to encourage the use of rigid legal classifications. The jurisdiction is inherently discretionary and the court is frequently in the presence of differences of degree which merge almost imperceptibly into differences of kind.

There was only one other argument for the respondents on their cross-appeal that I need notice. This was that the requirement not complied with was separable from the rest of the requirements as to the certificate. I do not read it as such. It was an integral part of the requirement that the certificate should 'include' a written notification of the rights of appeal. . . .

LORD FRASER OF TULLYBELTON: . . . I have no doubt that the effect of the omission in this case was to make the certificate invalid in the sense that it cannot stand, if challenged by the appellants. It is not a complete nullity – for example it could have been appealed against by an appeal taken timeously – and it exists until it is reduced, or set aside in some way. . . .

LORD KEITH OF KINKEL: . . . Here a certificate was issued which, though defective, was not a complete nullity. In this context use of the expressions 'void' and 'voidable,' which have a recognised significance and importance in certain fields of the law of contract, is to be avoided as inappropriate and apt to confuse. A decision or other act of a more or less formal character may be invalid and subject to being so declared in court of law and yet have some legal effect or existence prior to such declaration. In particular, it may be capable of being submitted to an appeal (cf. *Calvin* v. *Carr* [1979] 2 W.L.R. 755, 763, *per* Lord Wilberforce). In my opinion the certificate issued in the present case was of that character. It had some legal effect unless and until reduced, and in particular it might, in my view, have been the proper subject of a timeous appeal to the Secretary of State. . . .

[LORD WILBERFORCE agreed with LORD HAILSHAM OF ST. MARYLEBONE and LORD KEITH OF KINKEL. LORD RUSSELL OF KILLOWEN agreed with LORD KEITH OF KINKEL.]

Cross-appeal dismissed.

Question

Is the citizen (or indeed the public authority involved) entitled to clearer guidance as to the effects of a breach of a statutory provision? (For a similar approach rejecting rigid legal classification in a different context, see *Calvin v. Carr*, p. 254 *infra*.)

Note

The argument (mentioned by Lord Hailsham) that if the certificate was a nullity then a decree of reduction was inappropriate, is reminiscent of the idea, once current, that certiorari will not lie to quash a nullity, on which see Rubinstein, op. cit., pp. 83–5. At p. 85, he concludes:

> As far as contemporary law is concerned, it would probably be right to limit the rule to acts of usurpers, i.e. persons not authorized to exercise authority, or exercising it with regard to a matter so divorced from their authorized functions as to render their acts extra-judicial.

Cf. the judgment of Lord Denning in *R. v. Paddington Valuation Officer, ex p. Peachey Property Corporation Ltd.*, p. 102 *supra*, but see Wade, p. 563.

F. Hoffmann-La Roche & Co. A.G. v. Secretary of State for Trade and Industry, p. 94 *supra*

Notes

1. Lord Diplock's speech in the *Hoffmann-La Roche* case (and see *O'Reilly v. Mackman*, p. 332 *infra*) in particular backs up a point which is well made by Wade, (1967) 83 L.Q.R. 499 at p. 512, in the following passage:

> . . . [T]here is no such thing as voidness in an absolute sense, for the whole question is, void against whom? It makes no sense to speak of an act being void unless there is some person to whom the law gives a remedy. If and when that remedy is taken away, what was void must be treated as valid, being now by law unchallengeable. It is fallacious to suppose that an act can be effective in law only if it has always had some element of validity from the beginning. However destitute of legitimacy at its birth, it is legitimated when the law refuses to assist anyone who wants to bastardise it. What cannot be disputed has to be accepted.

2. Although the use of the term 'void' was recently espoused by Lord Denning (*Co-operative Retail Services Ltd. v. Taff-Ely B.C.* (1980) 39 P & C.R. 223 and see Note 1, p. 209 *infra*), more recently he has grown tired of the discussion of 'void' and 'voidable', since he thinks it is all a question of semantics: *Lovelock v. Minister of Transport* (1980) 40 P. & C.R. 336, noted at p. 101 *supra*. The use in this area of the law of these two terms has also come in for criticism from other judges: see Lord Diplock in the *Hoffmann-La Roche* case (though cf. *O'Reilly v. Mackman*, p. 326 *infra*) and see *London & Clydeside Estates Ltd. v. Aberdeen D.C.*, p. 104 *supra*; *Chief Constable of the North Wales Police v. Evans* [1982] 1 W.L.R. 1155 at p. 1163; cf.

Calvin v. *Carr* [1980] A.C. 574, noted at p. 102 *supra*. For further discussion, see Oliver, (1981) 34 C.L.P. 43.

The word 'voidable' in particular has more than one meaning. One use of the term, which has found some support, is as a description of the status of a decision flawed by an error of law on the face of the record. As such a decision is made within jurisdiction, the quashing of the decision by certiorari does not retroactively invalidate anything done up to that time, but merely has present and prospective effects. The use of 'voidable' in this sense is mentioned by Cane, (1980) 43 M.L.R. 266, but he also identifies 'at least three other ideas which it could be used to convey:

(a) "presumed valid until quashed by a court";

(b) "challengeable only by a person with sufficient interest, *i.e. locus standi*";

(c) "will cease to be challengeable and will become valid if proceedings are not begun within any statutory time limit".'

This article goes on to argue, relying on the presumption of validity in the *Hoffmann-La Roche* case, that an ultra vires decision is not a nullity which has never had any legal existence, but rather that it must be quashed if it is to lose its legal effect. The remedy on this view performs a constitutive as opposed to a declaratory role. *London & Clysdeside Estates Ltd.* v. *Aberdeen D.C.* and the other cases cited in Note 2 and Note 3, pp. 101–2 *supra*, might be thought to lend some support to this argument; cf. Alder, (1980) 43 M.L.R. 670 at pp. 674–5. Cane's view could have had consequences for the declaration as a remedy in relation to errors of law on the face of the record, but in the current state of the case law it seems now to be unimportant: see the Note at p. 298 *infra*.

3. The motive perceived by Wade (p. 315) for the courts holding certain ultra vires administrative acts to be voidable is 'a desire to extend the discretionary power of the court', in relation to which he makes the following criticism:

There are grave objections to giving the courts discretion to decide whether governmental action is lawful or unlawful: the citizen is entitled to resist unlawful action as a matter of right, and to live under the rule of law, not the rule of discretion. . . . The true scope for discretion is in the law of remedies, where it operates within narrow and recognised limits and is far less objectionable.

This, however, should be contrasted with the approach adopted by Lord Hailsham in *London & Clydeside Estates Ltd.* v. *Aberdeen D.C.* These differences in approach, at least in part, reflect the age-old dispute concerning the merits of flexibility as opposed to those of certainty.

4. The 'void/voidable' controversy has been particularly apparent in cases concerning the rules of natural justice, and we will therefore return to this issue in that context: see pp. 208 and 225 *infra*.

PART II
Discretionary Powers

4

DISCRETIONARY POWER:
AN INTRODUCTION

THE NATURE OF DISCRETION

Padfield v. Minister of Agriculture, Fisheries and Food,
p. 164 *infra*

Note

The essence of discretion is the power, usually given by statute, to make a choice between competing solutions. This is contrasted with duty where there is no power of choice as there is only one authorized course of action (see Wade, p. 228; de Smith, pp. 278–9 and 283–5). In fact this bald distinction over-simplifies the problem. Most powers contain both discretion and duty. For instance a soldier who is ordered to deliver a letter to headquarters is undoubtedly under a duty to deliver the letter but he well may have discretion as to timing, route or mode of transport. The same is true of administrative powers. Nearly all of these involve some degree of choice and the study of discretionary power and its control is a central part of Administrative Law. On the relationship between powers and duties see further Note 2 p. 169 *infra*.

There is an initial problem of definition. Does discretion simply signify that there is a power of choice or does it mean that the power of choice is uncontrollable. The *Oxford English Dictionary* does not help. It defines discretion as (*a*) '[the] liberty or power of deciding or, of acting according to one's own judgement or as one thinks fit; [i.e. with an] uncontrolled power of disposal', but also as (*b*) 'the power of a ... person acting in a judicial capacity, to decide, within the limits allowed by positive rules of law. . .'. This dual attitude to discretion also exists in the case-law. Although the development of judicial review of discretionary power has, in the past, been hampered by the adoption of the first meaning (*a*) on occasions (e.g. *Liversidge v. Anderson* [1942] A.C. 206), the majority of cases now adopt the second (see Wade, pp. 353–9). Note in particular that *Liversidge v. Anderson* has now been discredited: *Nakkuda Ali v. Jayaratne* [1951] A.C. 66, noted at p. 000 *infra*; *I.R.C. v. Rossminster Ltd.* [1980] A.C. 952 at pp. 1011 and 1025.

On this view, discretion gives the administrator a power to choose between a limited number of alternatives. The number of alternatives in any given case will depend on the source of the discretionary power but, however large, it is finite. If the administrator's choice falls within the permitted area, his action is not reviewable but, if it does not, the action is ultra vires: see Ch. 6 *infra* and see further Wade, pp. 348–53). The boundaries of discretionary power are typically defined by reference to the process of decision-making (for instance the motives of the administrator, the considerations taken into account and whether an issue has been prejudged), but attention may also be paid to the quality of the decision (see pp.121-2and 174 *infra*). This is simply another indication of the fact that judicial review is not primarily concerned with the rightness or wrongness of a decision. The detailed application of the ultra vires doctrine to discretionary power will be considered in Chs. 5 and 6 *infra*. It is true that the willingness of the courts to intervene does vary and that sometimes the result appears to be the creation of an unreviewable discretion. The reason for this (discussed at p. 122 *infra*) has nothing to do with the *discretionary* nature of the power (i.e. the fact that the administrator has been given a power of choice), although the consequence of stating that the power is not reviewable is effectively to confer an unlimited range of choice. Many of the cases which appear to state that a discretionary power is unreviewable are, in fact, stating that the particular exercise of choice fell within the permitted area (*Liversidge* v. *Anderson* can in fact be explained in this way: [1942] A.C. 206 at p. 267 per Lord Wright).

The vast literature on this subject includes philosophical work and empirical work by political scientists, as well as studies by public lawyers. Although reviewability is the issue which primarily interests the lawyers, it is not the only one. In some areas the merits of discretionary decisions may be reconsidered by a superior administrative body: see e.g. Williams in *Crime, Criminology and Public Policy* (ed. Hood), pp. 189–95; Coleman, *Supplementary Benefits and the Administrative Review of Administrative Action*, C.P.A.G. Poverty Pamphlet No. 7, noted at p. 558 *infra*. Another major issue is the extent to which it is both possible and desirable to establish precise rules against which official decisions may be measured to ensure accountability and uniformity of application, and to enable citizens to plan their conduct accordingly. For analysis of the theoretical issues, see Dworkin in *Essays in Legal Philosophy* (ed. Summers), pp. 26–60; Dworkin, *Taking Rights Seriously*, Chs. 2 and 3; Raz, 81 Yale L.J. 823 at pp. 843–8 (1972); Greenawalt, 75 Col. L.Rev. 359 at pp. 359–86 (1975). On other questions see Davis, *Discretionary Justice: A Preliminary Inquiry*; Titmuss, (1971) 42 Political Quarterly 113; Bell, *Research Study on Supplementary Benefit Appeal Tribunals*, p. 546 *infra*; Jowell, *Law and Bureaucracy: Administrative Discretion and the Limits of Legal Action; Justice, Discretion and Poverty* (eds. Adler and Bradley); *Discretion and Welfare* (eds. Adler and Asquith).

The *Report of the Franks Committee*, Cmnd. 218, stated at p. 6 that 'the rule of law stands for the view that decisions should be made by the application of known principles or laws. . . . On the other hand there is what is arbitrary. A decision may be made without principle, without any rules. It is therefore unpredictable, the antithesis of a decision taken in accordance with the rule of law.' But the rigorous application of the rule of law is impossible in any modern constitution (Wade and Phillips, *Constitutional and Administrative Law*, 9th edn., Ch. 6; Wade, pp. 22–3 and pp. 347–8) because governments will continue to operate in areas in which it is impossible to formulate rules in advance, or where, if it is possible, the desire for individualized justice will mean that discretionary powers are created. The important question then becomes how far the courts can control the exercise of discretion by administrative bodies and tribunals, and this is the concern of this and the next two chapters.

Against Discretion

David Donnison, New Society, 15 September 1977, p. 534

Reliance on the discretion and judgment of administrators, and suspicion of lawyers, litigation, detailed specification procedures and rights, are among the hallmarks of British social policy. Richard Titmuss was one of the most cogent advocates of this philosophy when he was deputy chairman of the

Supplementary Benefits Commission, contrasting the SBC's approach with the 'pathology of legalism' which he saw in American welfare administration. So why is the SBC, which is still led by people who worked with Timuss and revere him, now calling for a reduction in its own discretionary benefits?[1]

The SBC is making constantly increasing use of discretionary additions to its basic rates of benefit. Our attempts to guide staff in using these powers, have created a set of rules which have grown increasingly complicated, incomprehensible and unpublishable. We deplore this trend because it erodes confidence in the scheme – the confidence of claimants that they have clearly defined rights, the confidence of staff that they are getting extra money to those who really need it most, and the confidence of the public that we are being fair to claimants and non-claimants alike. Claimants, we believe, are no better satisfied than before: there has been a massive increase in appeals to tribunals, often against discretionary decisions; and most claimants would prefer to live on pensions and insurance benefits which have no means tests and virtually no discretion. The constant 'flak' provoked by discretion distracts public attention from the more important question of the adequacy of the basic scale rates – and to pathetically little purpose, for discretionary payments do not get a lot of money into claimants' pockets. They account in total for less than 6 per cent of the funds distributed in supplementary benefit.

So what should be done? We must make two distinctions: first, between judgment and discretion. The law, for example, precludes the SBC from giving benefit to anyone who has a full-time job. Deciding what constitutes full-time work is an act of judgment. It can be simplified by laying down rules, but no bureaucracy can avoid making thousands of such judgments every day.

Deciding whether or not to add a regular 'exceptional circumstances addition' (ECA) for fuel to a claimant's weekly benefit, or whether to give him an 'exceptional needs payment' (ENP) for a pair of shoes, is an act of discretion. Discretionary decisions, like administrative judgments, may be appealed against. The tribunals then exercise discretion over again in the light of the evidence before them, but their decisions do not bind those who deal with similar cases in future. They do not constitute precedents. Discretion can be reduced by making rules restricting its scope, or eliminated entirely by depriving the SBC of discretionary powers.

Now to the second distinction to be made: discretion may be mainly the responsibility of the commission (as when we publish rules specifying three standard rates of ECAs for heating and the circumstances to which each rate applies); or it may be mainly the responsibility of an individual official (as when he decides whether to give a claimant an ENP for a pair of shoes). The former consists of general rules which can be published and publicly debated. The latter has to be an individual, private and personal decision.

All these procedures pose problems, but we believe it is discretion rather than judgment, and officer discretion rather than the commission's discretion, which present the main problems. ENPs (one-off grants) call for more

[1] [Annual Report for 1976, Cmnd. 6910.]

officer discretion than ECAs (continuing weekly additions to benefit) and they are most costly and contentious to administer. Thus we believe it is ENPs which should be examined particularly critically.

We should, in future, distinguish more clearly between things (like the costs of moving house, furnishing a home) which the supplementary benefit scale rates are not expected to cover, and things (like food, clothing and the ordinary expenses of housekeeping) which the scale rates are supposed to cover. ENPs should, in future, be available on simpler terms for things the scale rates do not cover, but they should seldom be given for things which the rates are supposed to cover.

The nub of the problem is how to find ways of dealing humanely with the few cases where we must give extra help – despite the fact that the scale rates should meet the need – without allowing discretionary payments to proliferate all over the place, as they have done twice over since the war (once under the National Assistance Board, and now again under the SBC).

. . . Some people fear that a service with less discretion will be less concerned about people's welfare. But our responsibility for 'welfare' (written into the act) cannot be discharged by giving people small, semi-charitable hand-outs. It means that we must treat people courteously and efficiently, be alert to their needs, do our best to explain their rights to them, and never humiliate them. If the burden of discretionary payments can be reduced, there should be more time, not less, to devote to claimants' welfare.

A last-resort system of means-tested income maintenance will always have to retain some discretion: we can never shed all of it. (If your home is burnt to the ground tonight and you are left without money, possessions or family, you will need discretionary help, too.) But we should reduce the widespread and growing use of small discretionary payments and the stress they impose on frequently overworked staff. That will not be achieved unless people on both sides of the counter are convinced that the new system to be created is comprehensible, efficient, and at least in a rough and ready way, fair. Some claimants may be left a little worse off, but the majority must not suffer. Those who now get no discretionary benefits may be better off. Although such a reform will cost very little, it cannot be cost-free. For if large numbers of claimants previously regarded as needing special help are felt to be unfairly treated, they, their representatives and our staff will eventually find ways of ensuring that more money is spent on them. We are dealing with a 'culture' of social security which must be sympathetically understood. It cannot be legislated out of existence.

If these arguments are convincing now, why not in Richard Titmuss's day? Several things have changed since then. In the early days of the SBC, a massive reduction in discretionary payments was deliberately brought about. This was done to correct what was felt to be the excessive and degrading use of such payments into which our predecessors, the National Assistance Board, had with the best of intentions been led. In 1965, the NAB's last full year, discretionary additions to weekly benefits went to about 58 per cent of all claimants and to 73 per cent of retirement pensioners. Two years later, the numbers getting ECAs had been cut to 23 per cent of all claimants and by 1971, when Titmuss wrote his famous article on 'Welfare, "rights," law and discretion,'[2] they had fallen still further to 15 per cent. At that level the SBC was making sensible use of discretionary powers for giving help in what the law described as 'exceptional' circumstances. But since then our use of these powers has constantly increased, till by 1976 we were outdoing the NAB. It must be nonsense to treat two thirds of our pensioners as having 'exceptional' needs for heating – and to the extent of only 70 pence a week in most cases! It is more sensible and more efficient to give them all a little extra in their scale rates.

Throughout Titmuss's years on the commission, the staff administering the scheme were constantly growing in numbers. The 12,000 in local offices taken over from the NAB grew by 1975 to 30,000. The number of claimants grew too, but at nowhere near a comparable pace. The complexity of the work increased, and the quality of the service improved in many ways. There was more training, and the worst of the offices taken over from the NAB were abandoned or rebuilt. The scope for humane and flexible exercise of discretion in the smaller number of cases to which it was then applied must, for many of these years, have been growing. And, with new pension plans and other benefits under discussion, everyone expected the SBC's caseload to fall before long.

But the caseload has risen. And the present policy of severe restraint on staffing in all branches of the civil service has changed everything. Local offices are now having to cope with more discretionary decisions, more appeals, rising demands from the unemployed, one-parent families, students – all the shorter-term and more complicated kinds of claim – with no comparable increase in staff. Many offices will soon have to consider not *whether* to simplify rules and procedures and reduce discretionary decisions, but *how* to achieve these things. The new policies which we are formulating . . . are designed to bring about a constructive and orderly reorganisation before clumsier local improvisations are forced upon us.

Meanwhile, on another front altogether, changes are taking place which would in any case compel the SBC to think again about discretion. The tribunals are getting more carefully prepared evidence and giving more carefully reasoned decisions which are being more widely reported; more lawyers are being appointed to them, and their chairmen will soon be getting more training; appellants are more often and more effectively represented by advocates better prepared to quote the tribunals' previous decisions; and these decisions are being more frequently reviewed by the courts. In short, the tribunals are themselves becoming more like courts: they are being 'judicialised.' Kathleen Bell's report[3] hastened this development, but other forces were leading in the same direction.

The tribunals' decisions may increasingly acquire something like the authority of legal precedents. Recent decisions of the courts have

[2] [42 *Political Quarterly*, 113.]
[3] [*Research Study on Supplementary Benefit Appeals Tribunals*, p. 558 *infra*.]

already overturned a number of assumptions which we thought to be firmly established. If confusion is to be avoided, and staff and claimants are not to be left wondering whether to look to the commission or the tribunals for guidance to our policies, we must rely less on administrative discretion and more on law – on regulations approved by parliament.

In Titmuss's time it was natural to feel that the American welfare administration's 'pathology of legalism' owed a lot to the lawyers. But the American lawyers only gave their country's particular forms and tones to a development which is well under way here, too. Bring together three things – *first* a bureaucracy with a lot of discretion, *second* a demanding body of customers served by aggressive advocates, and *third* a government which wants to be fair, so makes increasingly elaborate rules to ensure that like cases are treated alike – and you will get increasingly detailed specification of entitlements, bewildering complexity, administrative rigidity and all the other things which Titmuss deplored, right down to his famous example of legal argument about the price of a claimant's toothbrush. The Americans were a bit ahead of us. But without much help from lawyers, who rarely appear before our tribunals, Britain is more than half way down the road to that toothbrush and its degrading implications. The pressure group which two years ago urged claimants to appeal to tribunals for ENPs to buy sanitary towels was trying to take us the rest of the way. It is time we stopped – before being a woman comes to be treated as an 'exceptional circumstance.'

. . . Finally, and most important of all, we face a change in the composition of our customers which no one foresaw in Titmuss's day. When the NAB closed down, at the end of the Butskellite[4] boom years, 71 per cent of its customers were old age pensioners and 6 per cent were unemployed. Most of the rest were sick and disabled. Since then the pensioners have declined proportionately, one-parent families are now the third largest group of claimants, and the unemployed have grown faster still to second place, where they constitute 22 per cent of claimants – about 700,000 people. That is almost the same number as the 720,000 unemployed people supported by the SBC's ancestor, the Unemployment Assistance Board, in 1935. And these numbers are still growing.

This change in the composition of our customers has profound implications for the whole supplementary benefit scheme. The legislation treats the unemployed less generously than other claimants. They get less generous insurance benefits than the sick and disabled. Unlike other claimants, when they turn to us they have to go to three different offices (to seek work, register as unemployed and claim supplementary benefit) in order to get their rights. They may suffer penal deductions of benefit if their need is thought to arise from their own action, and they do not qualify for the long-term scale rates which are about 20 per cent higher than the basic rates – although to give them these rates would cost less than 1½ per cent of the total spent on supplementary benefits.

4 [A reference to R. A. Butler (Conservative) and Hugh Gaitskell (Labour), used to describe the consensus politics of the 1950s.]

The unemployed are poorer than other claimants: they are less likely to have the full set of clothing listed in the SBC's B040 guidelines for the replacement of clothing; they are less likely to own domestic equipment such as vacuum cleaners and refrigerators, they are more likely to live in over-crowded houses, more likely to have debts, and less likely to have savings. A man's status in the labour market is fundamental to all his life chances. Unemployment without insurance benefits, more than other conditions which compel people to live on supplementary benefit, is concentrated among the least skilled, the least affluent and the least powerful: 60 per cent of unemployed claimants are drawn from the unskilled workers who form only 10 per cent of the whole labour force.

Yet, despite their greater hardships, the unemployed are less likely than other claimants to get ENPs or ECAs. And if they appeal against our decisions, they are less likely to win: 13 per cent of unemployed appellants get a more generous decision from the tribunals, compared with 26 per cent of other appellants under pension age.

What amounts, in effect, to discrimination against the unemployed may be due partly to a concern (usually misplaced) about their incentives to work – a concern which reimposes a concealed form of the old wage stop.[5] But the main reason for this discrimination, I believe, is that it is genuinely harder for the unemployed to demonstrate that they have 'exceptional' needs. The pensioners are old, or frail, or they live in houses which are hard to heat. Sickness, disability and lone parenthood are rife with 'exceptional' circumst-ances and special needs. But the needs of the unemployed differ little from those of millions of others in low-paid work – they are the circumstances of a whole class.

Discretionary powers, far from coming to the rescue of this most deprived group among the SBC's claimants, tend to load the scales even further against them. We must find other ways of helping the unemployed. The administra-tive procedures and philosophies of the 1960s – which relied on benign discretion and a lot of visiting, often among old ladies whom the staff got to know pretty well – will not do in the harsher world of the 1970s with its staff shortages, sharper class conflicts, a punitive scrounger-bashing press, and a range of customers for supplementary benefit who are growing more like those of the 1930s than anyone thought possible.

That is why we want to reduce the discretion in the supplementary benefit scheme. I think Richard Titmuss might have agreed with us.

Notes

1. The Social Security Act 1980 changed the supplementary benefit system radi-cally. Not only did it abolish the Supplementary Benefits Commission (s. 6 (2)) but it also sharply reduced the amount of discretion in the award of benefits, both standard rate and additional payments, such as the exceptional circumstances additions and the

---

[5] [Until abolished by s. 19 of the Child Benefit Act 1975, this prevented a claimant from receiving benefit in excess of 'what would be his net weekly earnings if he were engaged in full time work in his normal occupation'; para. 5(2) of Sch. 2 to the Supplementary Benefits Act 1966.]

exceptional needs payments (see generally Sch. 2, Part II to the 1980 Act). The statute and statutory instruments (see especially S.I. 1980 Nos. 985, 1300, 1642, and 1774) set out rules for determining an applicant's 'resources', 'requirements', and eligibility for a payment to meet an exceptional need. These matters had been in the discretion of the Supplementary Benefits Commission. See further pp. 557, 558, and 562 *infra* for other developments.

Ogus and Barendt state (*The Law of Social Security*, 2nd edn., p. 454) that 'statutory instruments are now the primary source of supplementary benefits law, whereas they had played a relatively small part in the system established in 1948 and 1966. Not only do they contain provisions previously set out in the primary Act, but they also regulate the award of benefit in areas which were subject to the discretion of the SBC.' In its final Annual Report, for 1979, the Supplementary Benefits Commission welcomed the changes and commented:

... [N]ot all discretion is being abolished under the new structure. Really exceptional circumstances will always call for wide discretionary powers. But the vast majority of cases are already handled under broad rules with a minimum of real discretion. . . . The new structure gives Ministers a better chance of permanently focusing the remaining discretion on the small minority of claimants with really exceptional problems' (paras. 16.8 and 16.10).

See also Donnison, *The Politics of Poverty*, pp. 89–100.

2. In *Shire of Swan Hill* v. *Bradbury* (1937) 56 C.L.R. 746 Dixon J. said (at p. 757):

In the course of the modern attempt by provisions of a legislative nature to reconcile the exercise and enjoyment of proprietary and other private rights with the conflicting considerations which are found to attend the pursuit of the common good, it has often been thought necessary to arm some public authority with a discretionary power to allow or disallow the action of the individual, notwithstanding that it has been found impossible to lay down for the guidance of the individual, or of the public authority itself, any definite rule for the exercise of the discretion. The reason for leaving the ambit of the discretion undefined may be that legislative foresight cannot trust itself to formulate in advance standards that will prove apt and sufficient in all the infinite variety of facts which may present themselves. On the other hand, it may be because no general principles or policy for governing the particular matter it is desired to control are discoverable, or, if discovered, command general agreement. Whatever may be the cause, the not infrequent result has been a general embargo or fetter upon the exercise of the individual's private or proprietary rights unless he obtains the sanction of the public authority. When a provision of this kind is made, it is incumbent upon the public authority in whom the discretion is vested not only to enter upon the consideration of applications for its exercise but to decide them bona fide and not with a view of achieving ends or objects outside the purpose for which the discretion is conferred. The duty may be enforced by mandamus. But courts of law have no source whence they may ascertain what is the purpose of the discretion except the terms and subject matter of the statutory instrument. They must, therefore, concede to the authority a discretion unlimited by anything but the scope and object of the instrument conferring it. This means that only a negative definition of the grounds governing the discretion may be given. It may be possible to say that this or that consideration is extraneous to the power, but it must always be practicable in such cases to make more than the most general positive statement of the permissible limits within which the discretion is exercisable and is beyond legal control.

BASIC PRINCIPLES OF JUDICIAL CONTROL

Associated Provincial Picture Houses Ltd., v. Wednesbury Corporation

[1948] 1 K.B. 223   Court of Appeal

The plaintiff applied for permission to give Sunday performances at its cinema. The local authority was empowered to allow cinemas to be open and used on Sundays 'subject to such conditions as the authority think fit to impose' (s. 2 (1) of the Sunday Entertainments Act 1932). The authority gave the plaintiff permission on the condition that no children under fifteen should be admitted to Sunday performances. The plaintiff sought a declaration that the condition was ultra vires.

LORD GREENE M.R.: . . . Mr. Gallop, for the plaintiffs, argued that it was not competent for the Wednesbury Corporation to impose any such condition and he said that if they were entitled to impose a condition prohibiting the admission of children, they should at least have limited it to cases where the children were not accompanied by their parents or a guardian or some adult. His argument was that the imposition of that condition was unreasonable and that in consequence it was ultra vires the corporation. The plaintiffs' contention is based, in my opinion, on a misconception as to the effect of this Act in granting this discretionary power to local authorities. The courts must always, I think, remember this: first, we are dealing with not a judicial act, but an executive act, secondly, the conditions which, under the exercise of that executive act, may be imposed are in terms, so far as language goes, put within the discretion of the local authority without limitation. Thirdly, the statute provides no appeal from the decision of the local authority.

What, then, is the power of the courts? They can only interfere with an act of executive authority if it be shown that the authority has contravened the law. It is for those who assert that the local authority has contravened the law to establish that proposition. On the face of it, a condition of the kind imposed in this case is perfectly lawful. It is not to be assumed prima facie that responsible bodies like the local authority in this case will exceed their powers; but the court, whenever it is alleged that the local authority have contravened the law, must not substitute itself for that authority. It is only concerned with seeing whether or not the proposition is made good. When an executive discretion is entrusted by Parliament to a body such as the local authority in this case, what appears to be an exercise of that discretion can only be challenged in the courts in a strictly limited class of case. As I have said, it must always be remembered that the court is not a court of appeal. When discretion of this kind is granted the law recognizes certain principles upon which that discretion must be exercised, but within the four corners of these principles the discretion, in my opinion, is an absolute one and cannot be questioned in any court of law. What then are those principles? They are well understood. They are principles which the court looks to in considering any question of discretion of this kind. The exercise of such a discretion must be a real exercise of the discretion. If, in the statute conferring the discretion, there is to be found expressly or by implication matters which the authority exercising the discretion ought to have regard to, then in exercising the discretion it must have regard to these matters. Conversely, if the nature of the subject-matter and the general interpretation of the Act makes it clear that certain matters would not be germane to the matter in question, the authority must disregard those irrelevant collateral matters. There have been in the cases expressions used relating to the sort of things that authorities must not do, not merely in cases under the Cinematograph Act but, generally speaking, under other cases where the powers of local authorities came to be considered. I am not sure myself whether the permissible grounds of attack cannot be defined under a single head. It has been perhaps a little bit confusing to find a series of grounds set out. Bad faith, dishonesty – those of course, stand by themselves – unreasonableness, attention given to extraneous circumstances, disregard of public policy and things like that have all been referred to, according to the facts of individual cases, as being matters which are relevant to the question. If they cannot all be confined under one head, they at any rate, I think, overlap to a very great extent. For instance, we have heard in this case a great deal about the meaning of the word 'unreasonable.'

It is true the discretion must be exercised reasonably. Now what does this mean? Lawyers familiar with the phraseology commonly used in relation to exercise of statutory discretions often use the word 'unreasonable' in a rather comprehensive sense. It has frequently been used and is frequently used as a general description of the things that must not be done. For instance, a person entrusted with a discretion must, so to speak, direct himself properly in law. He must call his own attention to the matters which he is bound to consider. He must exclude from his consideration matters which are irrelevant to what he has to consider. If he does not obey those rules, he may truly be said, and often is said, to be acting 'unreasonably.' Similarly, there may be something so absurd that no sensible person could ever dream that it lay within the powers of the authority. Warrington L.J. in *Short* v. *Poole Corporation*[6] gave the example of the red-haired teacher, dismissed because she had red hair. That is unreasonable in one sense. In another sense it is taking into consideration extraneous matters. It is so unreasonable that it might almost be described as being done in bad faith; and, in fact, all these things run into one another.

In the present case, it is said by Mr. Gallop that the authority acted unreasonably in imposing this condition. It appears to me quite clear that the matter dealt with by this condition was a matter which a reasonable authority would be justified in considering when they were making up their mind what condition should be attached to the grant of this licence. Nobody, at this time of day, could say that the well-being and the physical and moral health of children is not a matter which a local authority, in exercising their powers, can properly have in mind when those questions are germane to what they have to consider. Here Mr. Gallop did not, I think, suggest that the council were directing their mind to a purely extraneous and irrelevant matter, but he based his argument on the word 'unreasonable,' which he treated as an independent ground for attacking the decision of the authority; but once it is conceded, as it must be conceded in this case, that the particular subject-matter dealt with by this condition was one which it was competent for the authority to consider, there, in my opinion, is an end of the case. Once that is

6 [1926] Ch. 66, 90, 91.

granted, Mr. Gallop is bound to say that the decision of the authority is wrong because it is unreasonable, and in saying that he is really saying that the ultimate arbiter of what is and is not reasonable is the court and not the local authority. It is just there, it seems to me, that the argument breaks down. It is clear that the local authority are entrusted by Parliament with the decision in a matter which the knowledge and experience of that authority can best be trusted to deal with. The subject-matter with which the condition deals is one relevant for its consideration. They have considered it and come to a decision upon it. It is true to say that, if a decision on a competent matter is so unreasonable that no reasonable authority could ever have come to it, then the courts can interfere. That, I think, is quite right; but to prove a case of that kind would require something over-whelming, and, in this case, the facts do not come anywhere near anything of that kind. I think Mr. Gallop in the end agreed that his proposition that the decision of the local authority can be upset if it is proved to be unreasonable, really means that it must be proved to be unreasonable in the sense that the court considers it to be a decision that no reasonable body could have come to. It is not what the court considers unreasonable, a different thing altogether. If it is what the court considers unreasonable, the court may very well have different views to that of a local authority on matters of high public policy of this kind. Some courts might think that no children ought to be admitted on Sundays at all, some courts might think the reverse, and all over the country I have no doubt on a thing of that sort honest and sincere people hold different views. The effect of the legislation is not to set up the court as an arbiter of the correctness of one view over another. It is the local authority that are set in that position and provided they act, as they have acted, within the four corners of their jurisdiction, this court, in my opinion, cannot interfere.

[His Lordship then considered the authorities including *R.* v. *Burnley JJ.*[7] and *Ellis* v. *Dubowski*[8] and continued:] Those were cases where the illegal element which the authority had imported into the conditions imposed consisted of a delegation of their powers to some outside body. It was not that the delegation was a thing which no reasonable person could have thought was a sensible thing to do. It was outside their powers altogether to pass on this discretion which the legislature had confided to them to some outside body. . . .

In the result, this appeal must be dismissed. I do not wish to repeat myself but I will summarize once again the principle applicable. The court is entitled to investigate the action of the local authority with a view to seeing whether they have taken into account matters which they ought not to take into account, or, conversely, have refused to take into account or neglected to take into account matters which they ought to take into account. Once that question is answered in favour of the local authority, it may be still possible to say that, although the local authority have kept within the four corners of the matters which they ought to consider, they have nevertheless come to a

[7] (1916) 85 L.J. (K.B.) 1565.
[8] [1921] 3 K.B. 621.

conclusion so unreasonable that no reasonable authority could ever have come to it. In such a case, again, I think the court can interfere. The power of the court to interfere in each case is not as an appellate authority to override a decision of the local authority, but as a judicial authority which is concerned, and concerned only, to see whether the local authority have contravened the law by acting in excess of the powers which Parliament has confided in them. . . .

[SOMERVELL L.J. and SINGLETON J. agreed.]

Appeal dismissed.

Note

Lord Greene's statement of the basic principles of judicial review has been highly influential and should be considered again when the various grounds of review he lists are examined more fully. See in particular p. 164 *infra* (relevant and irrelevant considerations) and p. 182 *infra* (reasonableness). See also p. 130 *infra* (improper delegation) and p. 181 *infra* (good faith).

REVIEWABILITY OF DISCRETIONARY POWERS

Note

The limited nature of judicial review in such cases was mentioned in *Associated Provincial Picture Houses Ltd.* v. *Wednesbury Corporation* p. 118 *supra*, but in that case it was not necessary to consider whether all discretionary power is reviewable. Where a discretionary power is not subject to judicial review, this fact is sometimes explained in terms of the non-justiciability of the discretion. This may simply mean that legal procedures do not in fact exist to control the power. It can, however, also refer to the unsuitability of such procedures as a method of controlling a particular kind of discretion. There are many areas of discretion where there is, in fact, no close scrutiny by the courts, for instance government contracts (see p. 430 *infra*) and the machinery of extra-statutory concessions, although in others such as immigration and supplementary benefits (see p. 117 *supra* and p. 558 *infra*), recent years have seen a move towards more 'legalism' and intervention by virtue of the introduction of statutory rights of appeal: see Bradley, (1974) 13 J. S. P. T. L. (N. S.) 35. The question of 'suitability' is more difficult and cannot be discussed fully here. See Marshall in *Oxford Essays in Jurisprudence* (ed. Guest), Ch. 10; Jowell, [1973] P.L. 178. See also Sawer, (1963), 15 U.T.L.J. 49.

The other reasons given for non-reviewability are less satisfactory. As has been seen (p. 11 *supra*), the traditional view that the courts could never review the exercise of discretion under the Royal Prerogative is now under attack. It cannot therefore be said that the statutory or non-statutory basis of the power is a decisive factor, and the traditional judicial approach to exercises of prerogative discretion is explained by some commentators as turning on the non-justiciability of such questions. Furthermore, it can no longer be said in this context that the classification of a particular function as 'legislative', 'administrative', or 'judicial' is conclusive, although it is referred to in some cases (see pp. 12 and 119 *supra*; pp. 132 and174 *infra*). For a general discussion of the question of reviewability, see de Smith, p. 286.

Chandler v. Director of Public Prosecutions

[1964] A.C. 763   House of Lords

The appellants, who sought to further the aims of the Campaign for Nuclear Disarmament, wished to demonstrate on Wethersfield airfield, which was occupied by United States Air Force squadrons, and which was a 'prohibited place' within s. 3 of the Official Secrets Act 1911. Their aim was to immobilize the airfield and to prevent aircraft from taking off by sitting in front of them. They were prevented from entering the airfield but were charged with conspiracy to commit a breach of s. 1 of the 1911 Act, namely 'for any purposes prejudicial to the safety or interests of the State' to enter a 'prohibited place'. Evidence was given on behalf of the prosecution that interference with the ability of aircraft to take off was prejudicial to the interests of the State, but the appellants were not allowed to cross-examine or call evidence as to their beliefs that their acts would benefit the State and that their purpose was not in fact prejudicial to the interests of the State. They were convicted and appealed. The Court of Criminal Appeal dismissed the appeal but gave leave for a further appeal to the House of Lords. In the House of Lords it was argued that the cross-examination and evidence had been wrongly excluded.

LORD REID: . . . Next comes the question of what is meant by the safety or interests of the State. 'State' is not an easy word. It does not mean the Government or the Executive. 'L'Etat c'est moi' was a shrewd remark, but can hardly have been intended as a definition even in the France of the time. And I do not think that it means, as counsel argued, the individuals who inhabit these islands. . . . Perhaps the country or the realm are as good synonyms as one can find and I would be prepared to accept the organised community as coming as near to a definition as one can get.

Who, then, is to determine what is and what is not prejudicial to the safety and interests of the State? The question more frequently arises as to what is or what is not in the public interest. I do not subscribe to the view that the Government or a Minister must always or even as a general rule have the last word about that.

But here we are dealing with a very special matter – interfering with a prohibited place which Wethersfield was. The definition in section 3 shows that it must either be closely connected with the armed forces or be a place such that information regarding it or damage to it or interference with it would be useful to an enemy. It is in my opinion clear that the disposition and armament of the armed forces are and for centuries have been within the exclusive discretion of the Crown and that no one can seek a legal remedy on the ground that such discretion has been wrongly exercised. I need only refer to the numerous authorities gathered together in *China Navigation Co. Ltd.* v. *Attorney-General.*[9] Anyone is entitled, in or out of Parliament, to urge that

---

[9] [1932] 2 K.B. 197.

policy regarding the armed forces should be changed; but until it is changed, on a change of Government or otherwise, no one is entitled to challenge it in court. . . .

I am prepared to start from the position that, when an Act requires certain things to be established against an accused person to constitute an offence, all of those things must be proved by evidence which the jury accepts, unless Parliament has otherwise provided. But normally such things are facts and where questions of opinion arise they are on limited technical matters on which expert evidence can be called. Here the question whether it is beneficial to use the armed forces in a particular way or prejudicial to interfere with that use would be a political question – a question of opinion on which anyone actively interested in politics, including jurymen, might consider his own opinion as good as that of anyone else. Our criminal system is not devised to deal with issues of that kind. The question therefore is whether this Act can reasonably be read in such a way as to avoid the raising of such issues.

[LORD REID went on to find that it could and was therefore in favour of dismissing the appeal.]

LORD DEVLIN: . . . The effect of the authorities considered by the Court of Criminal Appeal and again in this House was summarised by the Lord Chief Justice as follows: 'A number of matters relating to the safety of the realm and the command of the royal forces are now regulated by statute. In so far, however, as this is not the case, the powers in that regard are at common law in the prerogative of the Crown acting on the advice of its servants. The powers so left to the unfettered control of the Crown include both in time of peace and war all matters related to the disposition and armament of the military, naval and air forces . . . In our opinion the manner of the exercise of such prerogative powers cannot be inquired into by the courts, whether in a civil or a criminal case . . . A similar principle underlies the powers of the executive, though pursuant to statute and not the prerogative, to requisition or to do other acts where in its discretion that is considered necessary in the national interest.'

My Lords, I do not question these passages as a general statement of the law, but there are three comments I wish to make by way of further clarification.

The first is to emphasise that the principle is not peculiar to the exercise of the prerogative power. It applies wherever discretionary powers of management and control are given by statute, whether to the Crown itself or to one of its Ministers or to any public body. In *Short* v. *Poole Corporation*[10] Warrington L.J. made the point just as forcibly to an education authority as in *In re A Petition of Right*[11] he did in relation to the Crown. In the former case[12] he said: 'With the question whether a particular policy is wise or foolish the court is not concerned; it can only interfere if to pursue it is beyond the powers of the authority.' When Lord Parker of Waddington in *The Zamora*[13]

---

[10] [1926] Ch. 66.   [11] [1915] 3 K.B. 649.
[12] [1926] Ch. 66, 91, 92.   [13] [1916] 2 A.C. 77, 107.

said that 'Those who are responsible for the national security must be the sole judges of what the national security requires,' he was not, I think, laying down any special constitutional doctrine about the powers of the Crown in relation to national security. He was simply stating the reason why the court should declare those powers to be discretionary. The cases cited by the Attorney-General are, I think, essentially decisions of the prerogative powers at common law in relation to the armed forces and the defence of the realm and show that, as is to be expected, those powers carry with them the same wide discretion as is now commonly conferred by statute.

The second comment is that inquiry is not altogether excluded. The courts will not review the proper exercise of discretionary power but they will intervene to correct excess or abuse. This is a familiar doctrine in connection with statutory powers. In relation to the prerogative, it was expressed by Warrington L.J. in *In re A Petition of Right*,[14] in the proviso which he made to his general statement of principle. Lord Parker of Waddington in the dictum to which I have referred accepted Warrington L.J.'s statement of principle and added his own qualification in the words 'as a rule.'[15] There is here no question of abuse of power so that I need not pursue this point further.

The third and most significant comment is as to the nature and effect of the principle. Where it operates, it limits the issue which the court has to determine; it does not exclude any evidence or argument relevant to the issue. Take the ordinary case, as exemplified in both *In re A Petition of Right*[16] and *The Zamora*,[17] where the Crown or a Minister has power to requisition goods or land as necessary for the defence of the realm. Once it is decided that that is a discretionary power, the question for the court is not whether the goods are in fact necessary, but whether the Minister thinks them to be. That is the only fact about which the court has to be satisfied. It is said that in such cases the Minister's statement is conclusive. Certainly: but conclusive of what? Conclusive, in the absence of any allegation of bad faith or abuse, that he does think what he says he thinks. The court refrains from any inquiry into the question whether the goods are in fact, necessary, not because it is bound to accept the statement of the Crown that they are, and to find accordingly, but because that is not the question which it has to decide.

What, then, in the present case, is the question which the jury had to decide? They were not inquiring into whether powers of requisition, management or control had been validly exercised. They were inquiring whether a fact, constituted by statute as an ingredient of a criminal offence, has been proved. The fact to be proved is the existence of a purpose prejudicial to the State – not a purpose which 'appears to the Crown' to be prejudicial to the State. Words of that sort could have been written into the statute. In emergency legislation they frequently are. In exceptional cases they can be implied: *Liversidge* v. *Anderson*.[18] But there has been no suggestion that they are to be implied into this statute. Their place cannot be filled by the common

[14] [1915] 3 K.B. 649, 666.
[16] [1915] 3 K.B. 649.
[18] [1942] A.C. 206.
[15] [1916] 2 A.C. 77, 106, 107.
[17] [1916] 2 A.C. 77.

law. There is no rule of common law that whenever questions of national security are being considered by any court for any purposes, it is what the Crown thinks to be necessary or expedient that counts, and not what is necessary or expedient in fact. If there were, the reasoning in *Liversidge* v. *Anderson*[19] would, in effect, be part of the common law instead of the exegesis of an emergency regulation.

Consequently, the Crown's opinion as to what is or what is not prejudicial in this case is just as inadmissible as the appellants'. The Crown's evidence about what its interests are is an entirely different matter. They can be proved by an officer of the Crown wherever it may be necessary to do so. In a case like the present, it may be presumed that it is contrary to the interests of the Crown to have one of its airfields immobilised just as it may be presumed that it is contrary to the interests of an industrialist to have his factory immobilised. The thing speaks for itself, as the Attorney-General submitted. But the presumption is not irrebuttable. Men can exaggerate the extent of their interests and so can the Crown. The servants of the Crown, like other men animated by the highest motives, are capable of formulating a policy ad hoc so as to prevent the citizen from doing something that the Crown does not want him to do. It is the duty of the courts to be as alert now as they have always been to prevent abuse of the prerogative. But in the present case there is nothing at all to suggest that the Crown's interest in the proper operation of its airfields is not what it may naturally be presumed to be or that it was exaggerating the perils of interference with their effectiveness.

I make no apology to your Lordships for having dealt at some length with the arguments put forward in this appeal. They have embraced big constitutional questions concerning the right to trial by jury and not by judge, and the extent to which the courts can question statements on political matters by the executive. All such questions which concern the liberty of the subject need great care in their consideration. . . . I can see no other conclusion than that the appellants have committed the offence of which they were accused and so I would dismiss this appeal.

[VISCOUNT RADCLIFFE, LORD HODSON, and LORD PEARCE delivered speeches in favour of dismissing the appeal.]

Appeal dismissed.

Note

An example of judicial unwillingness to consider such questions for the sort of reasons given by Lord Reid is provided by *Essex C.C.* v. *Minister of Housing and Local Government* (1967) 66 L.G.R. 23. In that case the Council sought a declaration that the Minister's decision, after an inquiry, to grant planning permission by a special development order to develop Stansted airport as the third London airport was void. The council contended *inter alia* that it had not been informed of changes in the development proposal and given a chance to make representations on questions of fact put before the Minister after the end of the inquiry. The Minister moved to have the claim struck out on the ground that it disclosed no reasonable cause of action. The case

[19] [1942] A.C. 206.

involved consideration of whether the Minister's power, under s. 14 of the Town and Country Planning Act 1962 (re-enacted as s. 24 of the 1971 Act), imposed a duty on the Minister to act judicially and to observe the rules of natural justice. Plowman J. rejected the Council's argument that it did. He appeared to accept the Minister's argument (at p. 28) 'that the whole question of whether and when and where there should be a third London airport is a question of national policy to be resolved in the political arena, and that the [Council] is trying to turn a political matter into a justiciable issue'. He said (at p. 26) that 'it is clear that the government's decision that Stansted should be developed as the third London Airport was a political decision, a matter of government policy, and, as such, it is unchallengeable in a court of law'. He concluded that 'the Minister's power to make a development order under section 14 is a purely administrative or legislative power fully exercisable discretionarily. He is responsible to nobody except Parliament, and that this should be so seems to me to be quite sensible in a case like the present where planning permission is required only as one aspect of the implementation of government policy.' How could a court adjudicate on the question of whether or not it was beneficial for the United Kingdom to have a nuclear deterrent or which, if any, of the various sites for the third London airport should be chosen?

Gouriet v. Union of Post Office Workers

[1978] A.C. 435   House of Lords

Gouriet applied to the Attorney-General for his consent to act as plaintiff in a relator action for an injunction against the Union, which was alleged to be about to call on its members not to handle mail between the United Kingdom and South Africa for a week beginning on Sunday, 16 January 1977. Such interference with postal communications constituted an offence under the Post Office Act 1953. The Attorney-General refused to give his consent and Gouriet then issued a writ in his own name. A judge in chambers refused the application on Friday, 14 January, but the Court of Appeal granted him an interim injunction the next day. At a later hearing Gouriet amended his pleadings by adding a claim for a declaration that the Attorney-General, by refusing his consent to the relator action, had wrongfully exercised his discretion. The majority of the Court of Appeal held that the courts had no jurisdiction to review the Attorney-General's decision and that Gouriet was not entitled to a permanent injunction. However, a majority also held that he could claim a declaration and that, pending a decision on this point, a court could grant an interim injunction. Both parties appealed to the House of Lords but Gouriet no longer claimed that the refusal of consent to the relator action was wrongful or reviewable. Only this aspect of the case is set out here; for other points see pp. 299 and 339 *infra*.

LORD WILBERFORCE: . . . There is now no longer a claim that the Attorney-General's refusal of consent to relator proceedings was improper or that it can be reviewed by the court. This issue, originally presented as one of great constitutional importance, has disappeared from the case. The importance remains, but the issue has vanished. The Attorney-General's decision is accepted as, in the courts, unassailable. The prerogatives of his office are no longer attacked. All that Mr. Gouriet now claims is that the refusal of the Attorney-General to act does not bar him from acting . . .

VISCOUNT DILHORNE: . . . The Attorney-General has many powers and duties. He may stop any prosecution on indictment by entering a nolle prosequi. He merely has to sign a piece of paper saying that he does not wish the prosecution to continue. He need not give any reasons. He can direct the institution of a prosecution and direct the Director of Public Prosecutions to take over the conduct of any criminal proceedings and he may tell him to offer no evidence. In the exercise of these powers he is not subject to direction by his ministerial colleagues or to control and supervision by the courts. If the court can review his refusal of consent to a relator action, it is an exception to the general rule. No authority was cited which supports the conclusion that the courts can do so. Indeed such authority as there is points strongly in the opposite direction. In 1902 in *London County Council* v. *Attorney-General* [1902] A.C. 165 Lord Halsbury L.C. said, at pp. 168–169:

> 'My Lords, one question has been raised, though I think not raised here – it appears to have emerged in the court below – which I confess I do not understand. I mean the suggestion that the courts have any power over the jurisdiction of the Attorney-General when he is suing on behalf of a relator in a matter in which he is the only person who has to decide those questions. It may well be that it is true that the Attorney-General ought not to put into operation the whole machinery of the first law officer of the Crown in order to bring into court some trifling matter. But if he did, it would not go to his jurisdiction; it would go I think, to the conduct of his office, and it might be made, perhaps in Parliament, the subject of adverse comment; but what right has a court of law to intervene? If there is excess of power claimed by a particular public body, and it is a matter that concerns the public, it seems to me that it is for the Attorney-General and not for the courts to determine whether he ought to initiate litigation in that respect or not . . . In a case where as a part of his public duty he has a right to intervene, that which the courts can decide is whether there is the excess of power which he, the Attorney-General, alleges. Those are the functions of the court; but the initiation of the litigation, and the determination of the question whether it is a proper case for the Attorney-General to proceed in, is a matter entirely beyond the jurisdiction of this or any other court. It is a question which the law of this country has made to reside exclusively in the Attorney-General. I make this observation upon it, though the thing has not been urged here at all, because it seems to be to be very undesirable to throw any doubt upon the jurisdiction, or the independent exercise of it by the first law officer of the Crown.'

In the same case Lord Macnaghten said, at p. 170, that he entirely concurred in these observations. Although obiter, they nevertheless have great authority and in my opinion the view that refusal of consent to a relator action is an exception to the general rule and is subject to review by the courts must be rejected. It is because I think it undesirable that any judicial observations suggesting that the exercise by the Attorney-General of these functions and duties is subject to control, supervision and review by the courts should be left unanswered that I have ventured to make these observations. . . .

[LORD DIPLOCK, LORD EDMUND-DAVIES, and LORD FRASER OF TULLY-BELTON delivered speeches in favour of dismissing the appeal on this point.]

Question

To what extent, if at all, were the views in *Chandler* v. *D.P.P., Essex C.C.* v. *Minister of Housing and Local Government*, and *Gouriet* v. *U.P.O.W.* influenced by (a) the source of the discretion (whether it was statutory or not), (b) the fact that major issues of national policy were involved, (c) the nature and range of the considerations which were relevant to the exercise of the discretion, (d) the fact that the power did not primarily affect individuals, or (e) the classification of the power in question as 'legislative', 'administrative', or 'judicial'.

Note

The references to the 'political' nature of the issue and the availability of Parliamentary control of the Minister (in *Essex C.C.* v. *Minister of Housing and Local Government* (1967) 66 L.G.R. 25, noted at p. 126 *supra*, and *Gouriet* v. *U.P.O.W.*, respectively) show how it is possible for the courts to take account of the availability and appropriateness of non-judicial methods of control in determining the scope of judicial review, and see *R.* v. *G.L.C., ex p. Royal Borough of Kensington and Chelsea*, The Times, 7 April 1982; *Walsh* v. *McCluskie*, The Times, 16 December 1982; and the Appendix. See also *Bushell* v. *Secretary of State for the Environment*, p. 606 *infra*, where a similar line of reasoning was used to justify limiting the protection afforded by the principles of natural justice. Although political control of the administration may be more appropriate in some situations where it is used, it is not always effective: see p. 525 *infra* (Parliamentary supervision of delegated legislation). Furthermore, its presence does not in general lead the courts to adopt a narrower scope of review: see e.g. *Padfield* v. *Minister of Agriculture, Fisheries and Food*, p. 164 *infra*.

5

RETENTION OF DISCRETION

DELEGATION

Inalienable discretionary power

Delegatus non potest Delegare

John Willis (1943) 21 Can. B. Rev. 257

When is delegation permissible? The answer to this question depends entirely on the interpretation of the statute which confers the discretion. A discretion conferred by statute is prima facie intended to be exercised by the authority on which the statute has conferred it and by no other authority, but this intention may be negatived by any contrary indications found in the language, scope or object of the statute; to put the matter in another way, the word 'personally' is to be read into the statute after the name of the authority on which the discretion is conferred unless the language, scope or object of the statute shows that the words 'or any person authorized by it' are to be read thereinto in its place. This prima facie rule of construction dealing with delegation is derived in part from the 'literal' rule of construction, in part from the political theory known as 'the rule of law,' and in part from the presumption that the naming of a person to exercise some discretion indicates that he was deliberately selected because of some aptitude peculiar to himself. The literal rule of construction prescribes that nothing is to be added to a statute unless there are adequate grounds to justify the inference that the legislature intended something which it omitted to express;[1] to read in the word 'personally' adds nothing to the statute, to read in the words 'or any person authorized by it' does. The 'rule of law' says that, since the common law recognizes no distinction between government officials and private citizens, all being equal before the law, no official can justify interference with the common law rights of the citizen unless he can point to some statutory provision which expressly or impliedly permits him to do so; to point to a provision justifying interference by A does not, of course, justify interference by B. The presumption that the person named was selected because of some aptitude peculiar to himself requires the authority named in the statute to use its own peculiar aptitude and forbids it to entrust its statutory discretion to

---

[1] See *Maxwell, Interpretation of Statutes*, 7th ed., 12 and such cases as *Ex p. Sharps* (1864), 5 R. & S. 322 (successor in office incapable of acting); *Peebles* v. *Oswaldtwistle Urban District Council*, [1897] 1 Q.B. 384 (statutory forum exclusive); *Liverpool Corporation* v. *Hope*, [1938] 1 K.B. 751 (statutory method of enforcement exclusive).

another who may be less apt than it, unless it is clear from the circumstances that some reason other than its aptitude dictated the naming of it to exercise the discretion. Because, however, the courts will readily mould the literal words of a statute to such a construction as will best achieve its object; because they will, recognizing the facts of modern government, readily imply in an authority such powers as it would normally be expected to possess; because the presumption of deliberate selection, strong when applied to the case of a principal who appoints an agent or a testator who selects a trustee, wears thin when applied to a statute which authorizes some governmental authority, sometimes with a fictitious name such as 'Governor-in-Council' or 'Minister of Justice', to exercise a discretion which everyone, even the legislature, knows will in fact be exercised by an unknown underling in the employ of the authority, the prima facie rule of *delegatus non potest delegare* will readily give way, like the principles on which it rests, to slight indications of a contrary intent.

What are these indications? The prima facie rule is displaced, of course, by a section in the statute which expressly permits the authority entrusted with a discretion to delegate it to another.[2] In the absence of such a provision, how does the court decide whether the rule is or is not intended to apply; how does it decide whether to read in the word 'personally' or the words 'or any person authorized by it'? The language of the statute does not, ex hypothesi, help it; it is driven therefore to the scope and object of the statute. Is there anything in the nature of the authority to which the discretion is entrusted, in the situation in which the discretion is to be exercised, in the object which its exercise is expected to achieve to suggest that the legislature did not intend to confine the authority to the personal exercise of its discretion? This question is answered in practice by comparing the prima facie rule with the known practices or the apprehended needs of the authority in doing its work; the court inquires whether the policy-scheme of the statute is such as could not easily be realized unless the policy which requires that a discretion be exercised by the authority named thereto be displaced; it weighs the presumed desire of the legislature for the judgment of the authority it has named against the presumed desire of the legislature that the process of government shall go on in its accustomed and most effective manner and where there is a conflict between the two policies it determines which, under all the circumstances, is the more important.

Barnard v. National Dock Labour Board

[1953] 2 Q.B. 18   Court of Appeal

The plaintiffs appealed from a decision of McNair J. ([1952] 2 All E.R. 424) dismissing the plaintiffs' claim for a declaration that they had been wrongfully suspended, and that, as their suspension had been carried out not by the local dock labour board but by the port manager, it was ultra vires.

---

[2] As in two well known English Acts, Education Act, 1921, sec. 4 (2) and Emergency Powers (Defence) Act, 1939, sec. 1 (3).

DENNING L.J.: . . . The second matter on which the men sought the ruling of the court was the question of procedure; whether they had been lawfully suspended; and this involved a consideration of the disciplinary powers of the board. Under the Dock Workers (Regulation of Employment) Scheme, 1947, the power to suspend a man is entrusted to the local dock labour board, which is composed of equal numbers of representatives of the workers and employers. In this case the board did not themselves suspend the men; the port manager did. The local board did not have anything to do with it; they did not see the report made by the employers; they did not investigate the matter; they did not make any decision upon it themselves; they left it all to the port manager. The suspension was not brought to their notice until after the appeal tribunal had given its decision.

It was urged on us that the local board had power to delegate their functions to the port manager on the ground that the power of suspension was an administrative and not a judicial function. It was suggested that the action of the local board in suspending a man was similar in character to the action of an employer in dismissing him. I do not accept this view. Under the provisions of the scheme, so far from the board being in the position of an employer, the board are put in a judicial position between the men and the employers; they are to receive reports from the employers and investigate them; they have to inquire whether the man has been guilty of misconduct, such as failing to comply with a lawful order, or failing to comply with the provisions of the scheme; and if they find against him they can suspend him without pay, or can even dismiss him summarily. In those circumstances they are exercising a judicial function just as much as the tribunals which were considered by this court in the cornporter's case, *Abbot* v. *Sullivan*,[3] and in *Lee* v. *Showmen's Guild of Great Britain*,[4] the only difference being that those were domestic tribunals, and this is a statutory one. The board, by their procedure, recognize that before they suspend a man they must give him notice of the charge and an opportunity of making an explanation. That is entirely consonant with the view that they exercise a judicial function and not an administrative one, and we should, I think, so hold.

While an administrative function can often be delegated, a judicial function rarely can be. No judicial tribunal can delegate its functions unless it is enabled to do so expressly or by necessary implication. In *Local Government Board* v. *Arlidge*,[5] the power to delegate was given by necessary implication; but there is nothing in this scheme authorizing the board to delegate this function, and it cannot be implied. It was suggested that it would be impracticable for the board to sit as a board to decide all these cases; but I see nothing impracticable at all; they have only to fix their quorum at two members and arrange for two members, one from each side, employers and workers, to be responsible for a week at a time: probably each pair would only have to sit on one day during their week.

³ [1952] 1 K.B. 189.
⁴ [1952] 2 Q.B. 329.
⁵ [1915] A.C. 120.

Next, it was suggested that even if the board could not delegate their functions, at any rate they could ratify the actions of the port manager; but if the board have no power to delegate their functions to the port manager, they can have no power to ratify what he has done. The effect of ratification is to make it equal to a prior command; but just as a prior command, in the shape of a delegation, would be useless, so also is a ratification.

[SINGLETON and ROMER L.JJ. delivered judgments in favour of allowing the appeal.]

Appeal allowed.

Questions

1. In what way, if any, does the approach of Lord Denning differ from that of Professor Willis? See Thorpe, (1972) Auck. U.L.J. 85.

2. Consider the case of *Lever Finance Ltd.* v. *Westminster L.B.C.,* p. 153 *infra*. What, if anything, was the legal basis for the Council's practice of delegating powers to settle whether modifications to an approved plan were 'material'?

Notes

1. Lord Denning's approach was adopted by the House of Lords in another disciplinary case, *Vine* v. *N.D.L.B.* [1957] A.C. 488. The rule against delegation has been applied less rigorously in cases involving licensing, dispensing, or investigatory powers, and particularly strictly in cases of legislative powers: see p. 494 *infra*; Wade, pp. 319–25; de Smith, p. 298.

Where delegation is permitted, it does not normally imply a denudation of powers which are subject to resumption (Wade, pp. 323–7; *Huth* v. *Clarke* (1890) 25 Q.B.D. 391). Some cases go further and appear to hold that 'delegate' means little more than agent (*Manton* v. *Brighton Corporation* [1951] 2 K.B. 393; *Huth* v. *Clarke* (1890) 25 Q.B.D. at p. 395, per Willes J.), while others assume that an authority can employ an agent but cannot delegate. De Smith, pp. 301–3, prefers the former view. Not all the attributes of agency are, however, relevant. In *Barnard*'s case a claim to ratify the invalid suspension was firmly rejected. This reflects the rule that 'where the Act allows proceedings to be instituted by an officer authorised by resolution, a later resolution cannot validly ratify action already taken (Wade, p. 324, citing *Bowyer Philpott & Payne Ltd.* v. *Mather* [1919] 1 K.B. 419). *Blackpool Corporation* v. *Locker*, p. 493 *infra*, in which it was suggested that a Minister who has validly delegated his powers has divested himself of those powers, should be treated with caution because the court held that the Minister did not try to exercise his powers for himself. The case is probably an example of the inability to ratify retrospectively. De Smith, p. 303 n. 44, states that this is the best explanation of the case. See also Wade, p. 324.

2. Many statutes grant express powers of delegation, especially in the areas of local government and planning (ss. 101 and 102 of the Local Government Act 1972; ss. 36, 88, 95, 97, and 103 and Sch. 2, 9, and 11, para. 8 of the Town and Country Planning Act 1971, but these will be strictly construed (see *General Medical Council* v. *U.K. Dental Board* [1936] Ch. 41 and Wade, pp. 325) and will probably not extend to sub-delegation.

3. Undue adherence to the *delegatus* maxim can disrupt efficient administration, and various devices have been used to reduce this danger. Delegation is the conferring

of authority and must be distinguished from getting assistance, which is permitted (*John Fowler & Co. Ltd.* v. *Duncan* [1941] Ch. 450, but see Note 1, p. 133 *supra*). The degree of control over the subordinate is an important factor in drawing the line: in general it must be close enough for a decision to be regarded as that of the proper authority (*Ex p. Forster, re University of Sydney* (1963) S.R. (N.S.W.) 723 at p. 733).

Ex p. Forster was concerned with the relationship between a body and a committee appointed by it, but it should be noted that, even where the degree of control is close enough for there to be no infringement of the *delegatus* maxim, the use of a committee system can lead to difficulties. In *Jeffs* v. *New Zealand Dairy Production and Marketing Board* [1967] 1 A.C. 551 a committee report on a re-zoning application was accepted by the Board with no change. It was held that the Board were in breach of the rules of natural justice in that they had not heard the parties. The reason for this was that the full Board had not seen the witnesses' statements and the report did not set out the evidence and the written submissions made before the committee. Secondly, although a body is not permitted to empower one of its number to execute a task granted to it (*Allingham* v. *Minister of Agriculture* [1948] 1 All E.R. 780), it may be able to achieve the same result by manipulating quorum requirements (see p. 132 *supra*). Thirdly, as *Re Golden Chemical Products Ltd.*, *infra*, shows, functions given to a government minister are normally exercisable by his departmental officials, but this is not regarded as delegation. This principle does not, however, permit another minister to act (*Lavender* v. *Minister of Housing and Local Government*, p. 138 *infra*), although where powers are conferred on 'the Secretary of State' they are exercisable by any Secretary of State (Sch. 1 to the Interpretation Act 1978). The principle has not been extended to all cases in which a function is entrusted to the head of a hierarchical body, but in which it is difficult or impossible for that person to act himself. Thus, in *Nelms* v. *Roe* [1970] 1 W.L.R. 4 it was held that subordinates could only exercise power given to a 'Chief Officer of Police' if he delegated it to them, whether expressly or impliedly.

Government departments

In Re Golden Chemical Products Ltd.

[1976] Ch. 300　　　　　　　　　　　　　　　　　　　　Chancery Division

Section 35 of the Companies Act 1967 empowered the Board of Trade, where it appeared expedient in the public interest, to present a petition for the winding up of a company. The functions of the Board were exercisable by the Secretary of State for Trade. Gill was a senior civil servant in the Department of Trade holding the office of Inspector of Companies. He presented a petition under s. 35. On a preliminary issue whether the power to present such a petition could be exercised by the Secretary of State acting through a departmental officer:

BRIGHTMAN J.: ... The practice, as a general rule, is that the Inspector of Companies decides ... whether under section 35 it is expedient in the public interest that a company shall be wound up and whether a petition ought to be presented. Mr. Gill's immediate superior, one of the under-secretaries, has a fairly close contact with Mr. Gill's work as Inspector of Companies and knows precisely what is going on. ... In a very important case Mr. Gill may decide to refer the matter to the under-secretary rather than deal with it himself. Exceptionally a decision may be taken by the Secretary of State himself. But normally it is Mr. Gill, as Inspector of Companies, who operates section 35. . . . The powers are exercised by Mr. Gill with the full knowledge of the under-secretary and have devolved on Mr. Gill because they are of the same character as other work which is done by him. To put the matter shortly, Mr. Gill exercises the powers given to the Secretary of State by section 35 because that is the departmental practice and not because they have been delegated to him by the Secretary of State or by any other superior. I find as a fact that Mr. Gill is an officer of the Department of Trade entrusted by the Secretary of State for Trade with the power to make decisions under section 35.

Mr. Chadwick, for the Secretary of State, has formulated five propositions. (1) As a general rule a Minister is not required to exercise personally every power and discretion conferred upon him by statute. It is otherwise if there is a context in the statute which shows that the power is entrusted to the Minister personally. (2) As a general rule it is for the Minister or his appropriate officials to decide which of his officers shall exercise a particular power. (3) Unless the level at which the power is to be exercised appears from the statute, it is not for the courts to examine the level or to inquire whether a particular official entrusted with the power is the appropriate person to exercise that power. (4) As a general rule officers of a government department exercise powers incidental and appropriate to their functions. In the absence of a statutory requirement it is neither necessary nor usual for specific authority to be given orally or in writing in relation to a specific power. (5) Constitutionally there is no delegation by a Minister to his officers. When an officer exercises a power or discretion entrusted to him, constitutionally and legally that exercise is the act of the Minister.

Mr. Chadwick relies upon four cases, the earliest of which is *Carltona Ltd. v. Commissioners of Works* [1943] 2 All E.R. 560. Regulation 51 (1) of the Defence (General) Regulations 1939, read with certain other enactments, provided that a competent authority, if it appeared to that authority necessary or expedient so to do, might requisition land. An assistant secretary of the Ministry of Works and Planning, which was the relevant department, signed a requisitioning notice. The notice was challenged by the proprietor of the land on the ground, among others, that the Commissioners of Works, wrongly assumed by the proprietor to be the competent authority, had not themselves personally brought their minds to bear on the exercise of the power. The argument, allowing for the necessary interpolation, was rejected. Lord Greene M.R. said, at p. 563:

'In the administration of government in this country the functions which are given to Ministers (and constitutionally properly given to Ministers because they are constitutionally responsible) are functions so multifarious that no Minister could ever personally attend to them. To take the example of the present case no doubt there have been thousands of requisitions in this country by individual ministries. It cannot be supposed that this regulation meant that, in each case, the Minister in person should direct his mind to the matter. The duties imposed upon Ministers and the powers given to Ministers are normally exercised under the authority of the Ministers by responsible officers of the department. Public business could not be carried on if that were not the case. Constitutionally, the decision of such an official is, of course, the decision of the Minister. The Minister is responsible. It is he who must answer before Parliament and for anything that his officials have done under his authority, and, if for an important matter he selected an official of such junior standing that he could not be expected competently to perform the work, the Minister would have to answer for that in Parliament. The whole system of departmental organisation and administration is based on the view that Ministers, being responsible to Parliament, will see that important duties are committed to experienced officials. If they do not do that, Parliament is the place where complaint must be made against them.

In the present case the assistant secretary, a high official of the Ministry, was the person entrusted with the work of looking after this particular matter and the question, therefore, is, relating those facts to the argument with which I am dealing, did he direct his mind to the matters to which he was bound to direct it in order to act properly under the regulation?'

The other members of the court agreed.

In the case before me, Mr. Gill, pursuant to the organisation of the Department of Trade, for which organisation the Secretary of State for Trade is responsible to Parliament, is the person who exercises the powers conferred on the Secretary of State by section 35 unless Mr. Gill decides to refer a particular matter to his superior. The *Carltona* case is authority that such a devolution of power – delegation is the wrong word – is lawful. At first blush the *Carltona* case, which has been applied in other cases, appears decisive of the preliminary issue.

[His Lordship then considered three other cases to the same effect (*Lewisham Metropolitan Borough* v. *Roberts* [1949] 2 K.B. 608; and *R.* v. *Skinner* [1968] 2 Q.B. 700; and *R.* v. *Holt* [1968] 1 W.L.R. 1942), and continued:]

Counsel for the company sought to breach this formidable line of authority by evolving certain counter-propositions which can be shortly paraphrased in this way. Where a power is conferred in a Minister to do an act if it appears to him expedient, the execution of that act, once it has appeared expedient to the Minister, can naturally be delegated within the department; for once the decision has been taken, the execution of the act is purely administrative. But, unless the statute conferring the power expressly or by implication otherwise provides, the initial decision-making process can be performed by someone other than the Minister if, but only if, it leads to no serious invasion of the freedom or property rights of the subject. There are, therefore, two categories of decision-making power, those which must, and those which need not, be

exercised by the Minister personally. I have not formulated these propositions exactly as originally presented but I have, I hope, accurately
paraphrased them so as to accord with the argument as it developed during
the course of Mr. Muir Hunter's submissions. The question therefore before
me, was whether the power in section 35 was such as to require the personal
attention of the Minister before being exercised. He referred me first to
Liversidge v. *Anderson* [1942] A.C. 206 and *Greene* v. *Secretary of State for
Home Affairs* [1942] A.C. 284. These were cases in which the appellant
sought to challenge a detention order made under the Defence (General)
Regulations 1939, regulation 18B. This regulation provided that if the Secretary of State had reasonable cause to believe a person to be of hostile origin
or associations, etc., he might make an order that the person be detained. It
was not suggested in those cases, submitted by Mr. Muir Hunter, that such a
power could be exercised by a mere official of the Home Office. The appeals
proceeded on the basis that the decision was taken, and was rightly taken, by
the Minister personally. Mr. Muir Hunter also referred me to a large number
of other cases where important issues were involved in the exercise of a
statutory decision-making power and the decision was taken by the Minister
personally. . . .

If there is a true distinction which must be drawn as a matter of law
between powers which the Minister must exercise personally and those which
can be exercised by an officer of his department, I might well come to the view
that the power given by section 35 is so potentially damaging that it falls into
the former category, however burdensome that may be to a Secretary of State
personally. But is such a distinction to be drawn? I find no warrant for it in the
authorities. In fact, the reverse. The accuracy of the breath test equipment
with which *Reg.* v. *Skinner* [1968] 2 Q.B. 700 was concerned was of vital
importance to every motorist as indeed the judgment of the Court of Appeal
recognised. . . . If a motorist fails the breath test he is arrested. So if the
equipment over-registers, an innocent subject is placed under arrest; if it
under-registers, a potentially lethal motorist is let loose on the highway. Yet
the Court of Appeal decided that although such a 'vitally important matter
might well have occupied the Minister's personal attention . . . there is in
principle no obligation upon the Minister to give it his personal attention':
p. 709. As Mr. Chadwick pointed out, there are important cases in which the
Minister will exercise a statutory discretion personally, not because it is a
legal necessity but because it is a political necessity. The regulation 18B cases
are examples.

I reach the conclusion that Mr. Muir Hunter's submissions have not started
to breach the formidable line of authority against which they were gallantly
ranged. Nor do I think that the principle which he advocates is of practical
application. A distinction between a case which involves a serious invasion of
the freedom or property rights of the subject, and a case which involves a
similar invasion that is not serious, seems to me to be impossibly vague. I am
aware that the absence of a precise demarcation line is not, as Mr. Muir
Hunter reminded me, a practical impediment to telling night from day. But if

Mr. Muir Hunter's principles were adopted, it seems to me that one would be groping in a perpetual twilight, except at the extremes of midnight and midday. . . .

Declaration accordingly.

Note

Institutional decision-making gives rise to several problems. On the issue dealt with in this case see further de Smith, pp. 299–300 and pp. 307–9. However, problems have also arisen in the context of the principles of natural justice, on which see *Bushell v. Secretary of State for the Environment*, p. 601 *infra*, and de Smith, p. 207 and pp. 254–6.

SURRENDER, ABDICATION, DICTATION

Power in the wrong hands

H. Lavender & Son Ltd. v. Minister of Housing and Local Government

[1970] 1 W.L.R. 1231   Queen's Bench Division

Lavender & Son Ltd. sought to use a farm belonging to them for gravel extraction. When permission was refused by the local authority they appealed to the Minister and an inquiry was held. The Minister stated that it was his policy to apply the recommendations of a report on gravel working on agricultural land which stated that such land should be protected against disturbance by gravel working, that he would not deviate from these 'unless the Minister of Agriculture is not opposed to working' and that as in this case the Minister of Agriculture had not consented, planning permisssion would not be granted. On a motion to quash the Minister's decision:

WILLIS J.: . . . Mr. Frank[6] . . . really puts his argument in two ways – (1) that the Minister has fettered his decision by a self created rule of policy, and (2) that the Minister, who has a duty to exercise his own discretion in determining an appeal, has in this case delegated that duty to the Minister of Agriculture, who has no such duty and is, statutorily, a stranger to any decision.

It is, of course, common ground between Mr. Frank and Mr. Slynn[7] that the Minister is entitled to have a policy and to decide an appeal in the context of that policy. . . .

The courts have no authority to interfere with the way in which the Minister carries out his planning policy: see *per* Lord Denning M.R. in *Luke v. Minister of Housing and Local Government* [1968] 1 Q.B. 172, 192. There is also no question but that the Minister, before making a decision whether or not to allow an appeal, may obtain the views of other government departments: *Darlassis v. Minister of Education* (1954) 52 L.G.R. 304, *per* Barry J. at p. 318.

[6] [Counsel for Lavender & Son Ltd.]
[7] [Counsel for the Minister.]

. . . Can there, nevertheless, come a point . . . when the court can interfere with a Ministerial decision which, ex facie, proceeds upon a consideration of the inspector's report and concludes by applying Ministerial policy?

Mr. Frank submits that such a point can be reached and has been reached in this case. It is reached, he says, adopting the words of Professor de Smith in his book, *Judicial Review of Administrative Action*, at p. 294, if a tribunal, entrusted with a discretion as the Minister was in the present case, disables itself from exercising that discretion in a particular case by the prior adoption of a general policy. In *Rex* v. *Port of London Authority, Ex parte Kynoch Ltd.* [1919] 1 K.B. 176, Bankes L.J. said, at p. 184:

'In the present case there is another matter to be borne in mind. There are on the one hand cases where a tribunal in the honest exercise of its discretion has adopted a policy, and, without refusing to hear an applicant, intimates to him what its policy is, that, after hearing him, it will in accordance with its policy decide against him, unless there is something exceptional in his case . . . On the other hand there are cases where a tribunal has passed a rule, or come to a determination not to hear an application of a particular character by whomsoever made.'

In another licensing case, *Reg.* v. *Flintshire County Council Licensing (Stage Plays) Committee, Ex parte Barrett* [1957] 1 Q.B. 350, where the decision was given in the interests of consistency, Jenkins L.J. said, at pp. 367, 368:

'Then they went on . . . to conclude . . . that the Queen's Theatre licence must follow the fate of the Pavilion Theatre licence, because it was essential that the same rule should be applied in all cases or, in other words, that the committee should be consistent. I cannot think that that method fulfils the requirement that the matter should be heard and determined according to law . . . It seems to me that it wrongly pursues consistency at the expense of the merit of individual cases.'

I have referred to those two cases since they were relied on by Mr. Frank, but I am inclined to agree with Mr. Slynn that the considerations applicable to licensing cases are not of much assistance when considering the scope of a Minister's duties within a statutory framework.

. . . It is, of course, clear that if the Minister has prejudged any genuine consideration of the matter before him, or has failed to give genuine consideration to, inter alia, the inspector's report, he has failed to carry out his statutory duties properly. *Franklin* v. *Minister of Town and Country Planning* [1948] A.C. 87.

In the present case, Mr. Frank does not shrink from submitting that the decision letter shows that no genuine consideration was given to the question whether planning permission could, in the circumstances, be granted. I have carefully considered the authorities cited by counsel, but I have not found any clear guide to what my decision should be in this case. I have said enough to make it clear that I recognise that in the field of policy, and in relation to ministerial decisions coloured or dictated by policy, the courts will interfere only within a strictly circumscribed field: see *per* Lord Greene M.R. in *Associated Provincial Picture Houses Ltd.* v. *Wednesbury Corporation* [1948] 1 K.B. 223, 228. It is also clear, and is conceded by Mr. Slynn, that where a Minister is entrusted by Parliament with the decision of any particular case he must keep that actual decision in the last resort in his own hands: see *Rex* v. *Minister of Transport, Ex parte Grey Coaches,* 'The Times,' March 19, 1933. I return, therefore, to the words used by the Minister. It seems to me that he has said in language which admits of no doubt that his decision to refuse permission was solely in pursuance of a policy not to permit minerals in the Waters agricultural reserve to be worked unless the Minister of Agriculture was not opposed to their working. . . . Everything else might point to the desirability of granting permission, but by applying and acting on his stated policy I think the Minister has fettered himself in such a way that in this case it was not he who made the decision for which Parliament made him responsible. It was the decision of the Minister of Agriculture not to waive his objection which was decisive in this case, and while that might properly prove to be the decisive factor for the Minister when taking into account all material considerations, it seems to me quite wrong for a policy to be applied which in reality eliminates all the material considerations save only the consideration, when that is the case, that the Minister of Agriculture objects. That means, as I think, that the Minister has by his stated policy delegated to the Minister of Agriculture the effective decision on any appeal within the agricultural reservations where the latter objects to the working. . . .

If the Minister was intending to follow his stated policy, I think it was very undesirable that it should not have been made known in advance. It is possible to imagine great hardship falling on appellants, who, all unawares, embark on an expensive appeal foredoomed to failure by reason of a strict though unannounced policy. However, I agree with Mr. Slynn that the failure to publicise the policy is not a ground for questioning the decision. . . .

> *Order to quash under s. 179 of the Town and Country Planning Act 1962 granted.*

Questions

1. How, if at all, does the rule applied in *Lavender*'s case differ from that applied in *Barnard* v. *N.D.L.B.,* p. 131 *supra*? Except in cases where the wrong person decides the question, is it possible to make a sensible distinction between failure to exercise a discretion and abuse of discretion?

2. How can one reconcile the need for 'fairness and consistency' with the need to exercise discretion in each case?

3. Should the failure to make the existence of a policy known in advance invalidate a decision made in reliance on the policy?

OVER-RIGID POLICIES

British Oxygen Co. Ltd. v. Minister of Technology

[1971] A.C. 610   House of Lords

Section 1 (1) of the Industrial Development Act 1966 provides that the Board of Trade 'may make to any person carrying on a business in Great Britain a grant towards approved capital expenditure incurred by that person in providing new machinery or plant'. The Board adopted a policy of denying grants for any item of plant costing less than £25 and, in pursuance of that policy, rejected an application for a grant in respect of gas cylinders costing just under £20 each. In proceedings for a declaration the court was asked, *inter alia*, to determine the extent of the Board's discretion.

LORD REID: ... There are two general grounds on which the exercise of an unqualified discretion can be attacked. It must not be exercised in bad faith, and it must not be so unreasonably exercised as to show that there cannot have been any real or genuine exercise of the discretion. But, apart from that, if the Minister thinks that policy or good administration requires the operation of some limiting rule, I find nothing to stop him.

It was argued on the authority of *Rex* v. *Port of London Authority Ex parte Kynoch Ltd.* [1919] 1 K.B. 176 that the Minister is not entitled to make a rule for himself as to how he will in future exercise his discretion. In that case Kynoch owned land adjoining the Thames and wished to construct a deep water wharf. For this they had to get the permission of the authority. Permission was refused on the ground that Parliament had charged the authority with the duty of providing such facilities. It appeared that before reaching their decision the authority had fully considered the case on its merits and in relation to the public interest. So their decision was upheld.

Bankes L.J. said, at p. 184:

'There are on the one hand cases where a tribunal in the honest exercise of its discretion has adopted a policy, and, without refusing to hear an applicant, intimates to him what its policy is, and that after hearing him it will in accordance with its policy decide against him, unless there is something exceptional in his case. I think counsel for the applicants would admit that, if the policy has been adopted for reasons which the tribunal may legitimately entertain, no objection could be taken to such a course. On the other hand there are cases where a tribunal has passed a rule, or come to a determination, not to hear any application of a particular character by whomsoever made. There is a wide distinction to be drawn between these two classes.'

I see nothing wrong with that. But the circumstances in which discretions are exercised vary enormously and that passage cannot be applied literally in every case. The general rule is that anyone who has to exercise a statutory discretion must not 'shut his ears to an application' (to adapt from Bankes

L.J. on p. 183). I do not think there is any great difference between a policy and a rule. There may be cases where an officer or authority ought to listen to a substantial argument reasonably presented urging a change of policy. What the authority must not do is to refuse to listen at all. But a Ministry or large authority may have had to deal already with a multitude of similar applications and then they will almost certainly have evolved a policy so precise that it could well be called a rule. There can be no objection to that, provided the authority is always willing to listen to anyone with something new to say – of course I do not mean to say that there need be an oral hearing. In the present case the respondent's officers have carefully considered all that the appellants have had to say and I have no doubt that they will continue to do so. . . .

VISCOUNT DILHORNE: . . . [T]he distinction between a policy decision and a rule may not be easy to draw. In this case it was not challenged that it was within the power of the Board to adopt a policy not to make a grant in respect of such an item. That policy might equally well be described as a rule. It was both reasonable and right that the Board should make known to those interested the policy it was going to follow. By doing so fruitless applications involving expense and expenditure of time might be avoided. The Board says that it has not refused to consider any application. It considered the appellants'. In these circumstances it is not necessary to decide in this case whether, if it had refused to consider an application on the ground that it related to an item costing less than £25, it would have acted wrongly.

I must confess that I feel some doubt whether the words used by Bankes L.J. in the passage cited above [see p. 141 *supra*] are really applicable to a case of this kind. It seems somewhat pointless and a waste of time that the Board should have to consider applications which are bound as a result of its policy decision to fail. Representations could of course be made that the policy should be changed. . . .

[LORD MORRIS OF BORTH-Y-GEST, LORD WILBERFORCE, and LORD DIPLOCK agreed with LORD REID.]

Notes

1. The *British Oxygen* case should be compared with *Merchandise Transport Ltd.* v. *British Transport Commission* [1962] 2 Q.B. 173 and *Sagnata Investments Ltd.* v. *Norwich Corporation* [1971] 2 Q.B. 614. In *Merchandise Transport* the Court of Appeal warned the Transport Tribunal against developing a rigid body of precedent. Devlin L.J. accepted that reasoned judgments disclosing the general principles upon which the tribunal proceeded were both inevitable and desirable but went on to say (at p. 193) that 'a tribunal must not pursue consistency at the expense of the merits of individual cases. If the discretion is to be narrowed, that must be done by statute; the tribunal has no power to give its decisions the force of statute.' The implication of the majority judgments in the *Sagnata* case is that policies should not carry any more weight than any other relevant factor in a given case. This has been persuasively criticized by Galligan, [1976] P.L. 332 and may need modification in the light of Lord Denning's judgment in *H.T.V. Ltd.* v. *Price Commission* [1976] I.C.R. 170, noted at p. 162 *infra*. Farmer states (*Tribunals and Government*, pp. 178–9) that tribunals

have, in fact, laid down 'general principles for application in subsequent cases while stopping short of developing these into hard and fast legal rules'. He concludes that 'theoretical differences between the operation of precedent in courts and tribunals have little practical significance [because of] what may be described as the first principle of justice – the basic premise upon which the whole of our law and of our legal system rests – namely the requirement of consistency, uniformity and equal treatment'. See also Wraith and Hutchinson, *Administrative Tribunals*, pp. 274–6.

2. In *R. v. Torquay Licensing J.J., ex p. Brockman* [1951] 2 K.B. 784 at p. 788, Lord Goddard C.J. said that if tribunals 'have decided upon a policy to guide them in considering applications it is only fair that they should make it public so that applicants may know what to expect', but there appears to be no effective method of ensuring that they do so: see *Lavender's* case, p. 140 *supra*. See also p. 175 *infra* on the status of statutory codes of practice and ministerial circulars. Again, where there is power to make rules, whether statutory instruments or by-laws, in individual cases there is no compulsion to make and enforce such rules rather than exercising a discretionary power. In *Ex p. Forster, Re University of Sydney* (1963) 63 S.R. (N.S.W.) 723 the fact that the University had power to make by-laws was held not to oust its discretionary power to adjudicate in individual cases provided that no by-law restricted the particular exercise of discretion. The University had formed a policy by a Senate resolution rather than a by-law and sought to apply it. The court did concede (at p. 731) that if the University intended to make 'a general rule which is to operate as such – as part of the "law" of the University – it must proceed under its by-law and regulation-making power', but also said that 'resolutions of the Senate have their place in the scheme of government of the University by the Senate under s. 14 (2) of the [University and University Colleges Act, 1902–1959].'

This is broadly in line with the position adopted by the Supreme Court of the United States (Schwartz and Wade, *Legal Control of Government*, pp. 93–6 and pp. 104–5), although Davis argues that more recent decisions are moving towards a requirement that the interstices of a statute must be filled, where possible, by rule-making: *Administrative Law of the Seventies*, § 6.132. See also *Discretionary Justice, A Preliminary Inquiry*, pp. 15–21, 42–4, and pp. 102–3, where Davis suggests that, where it is undesirable or impractical to make a rule, policy statements should be used. Despite the fundamentally different constitutional and statutory background (especially s. 4 of the U.S.A.'s Administrative Procedure Act 1946) recent statements in the Court of Appeal about the need for consistency may be a prelude to change: see *H.T.V. Ltd. v. Price Commission* [1976] I.C.R. 170, noted at p. 162 *infra*; *R. v. Preston S.B.A.T., ex p. Moore*, p. 79 *supra*; *Laker Airways Ltd. v. Department of Trade*, p. 15 *supra*; *Pearlman v. Harrow School*, p. 55 *supra*.

Asher v. Secretary of State for the Environment [1974] Ch. 208 does, however, show the limits of the consistency argument. The Secretary of State had to deal with a local council which was politically opposed to implementing a statutory housing policy calling for the increase of council house rents. He had power either to appoint a Housing Commissioner or to order an extraordinary audit. He chose the latter, which led to the imposition of a surcharge on the defaulting councillors for the deficit and their eventual disqualification from serving as councillors. They argued that the Secretary of State wished to punish them rather than to enforce the Act, stating that other councils which had refused to implement the policy had been treated differently. This was rejected by the court because there was no evidence that the appointment of a Housing Commissioner was 'established practice', and (at p. 226) '[b]alancing the advantages and disadvantages of one possible course of action against another and making a decision is what Secretaries of State have to do: it is the very stuff of government, and the courts should not interfere save for good reason, and disagreeing with the decision is not in itself a good reason.'

3. The application of a policy may lead to a breach of the rules of natural justice. This may either be because of bias (i.e. prejudgment) or due to a refusal to hear the other side. On bias, see pp. 203 and 207 *infra* and *Boyle* v. *Wilson* [1907] A.C. 45 at pp. 54 and 56–7. On the overlap with *audi alteram partem* see Galligan, op cit., pp. 345 and 355–6 and *R.* v. *Secretary of State for the Environment, ex p. Brent L.B.C.* [1982] 2 W.L.R. 693. In the latter the Divisional Court held that where the Secretary of State 'decided to turn a deaf ear to any and all representations to change the policy formulated by him' (p. 732) before deciding to reduce the rate support grant to certain local authorities, he was both unlawfully fettering his discretion and not properly discharging his duty of fairness as enunciated in *McInnes* v. *Onslow-Fane*, p. 265 *infra*. Both of these required that the Secretary of State should have been ready to hear anything new which might be said by the authorities. See further on this case Note 3, p. 240 *infra* and see Appendix.

4. Until 1979 the Department of Health and Social Security had broad discretionary powers (described at p. 113 *supra*) to make Exceptional Circumstances Allowances to cover, for instance, heating costs. Despite this discretion the Department standardized payments at three weekly levels determined by eight factors (such as age, chronic ill health, or the fact that the accommodation was exceptionally difficult to heat adequately: *Supplementary Benefits Handbook, A Guide to Claimants' Rights*, revised edn. 1977, para. 73). These criteria, which were described as 'guidelines', ignored actual expenditure on heating and other needs. A study by Lister in 1974 (*Justice for the Claimant*, C.P.A.G. Poverty Research Series No. 4), showed that tribunals tended to follow the rules established by the Commission: 'in some cases this was done to preserve uniformity and in an attempt to attain a balance between appellants and non-appellants but in many cases it was clearly believed that these rates established by the Commission had the same status as the basic scale rates established by Parliament'. This confirmed the earlier and more extensive study conducted by Herman, *Administrative Justice and Supplementary Benefits, Occasional Papers on Social Administration*, No. 47, pp. 53–4. Donnison, p. 112 *supra*, argued that it was impossible to deal with large numbers of cases by discretionary powers and the sharp reduction in the amount of discretion in the Department of Health and Social Security was welcomed by the Supplementary Benefits Commission in their Annual Report for 1979 (noted at p. 118 *supra*). On the general question of the relationship between tribunals and ministries, see Ch. 16 *infra*. See also White in *Social Needs and Legal Action* (eds. Morris, White, and Lewis), pp. 30–1. Compare the number of cases heard by S.B.A.T.s (45,471 in 1980) with the number heard by the Transport Tribunal on Road Traffic Act licensing matters (2,782 in 1980). Would this justify a different approach to the degree to which each tribunal might legitimately adopt rules?

5. For the legitimacy of policies in prosecutors' discretion, see *R.* v. *Metropolitan Police Commissioner, ex p. Blackburn* [1968] 2 Q.B. 1128; *Gouriet* v. *U.P.O.W.*, p. 127 *supra* and p. 339 *infra*; Williams in *Crime, Criminology and Public Policy* (ed. Hood), pp. 179–84; Wade, p. 359.

RESTRICTION BY CONTRACT OR GRANT

Ayr Harbour Trustees v. Oswald

(1883) 8 App. Cas. 623   House of Lords

The Harbour Trustees were given statutory powers compulsorily to purchase land for the management and improvement of a harbour. The Trustees
wished to acquire Oswald's land subject to an undertaking that they would
not use the land acquired in such a manner as to interfere with the access from
Oswald's remaining land to the harbour. The reason for this was to justify a
lower sum being paid to Oswald as compensation. Oswald brought an action
for a decree of declarator contending that the Trustees' decision (recorded in
a minute) was ultra vires and that the purchase should be made without the
undertaking and for payment of the larger sum. On appeal by the Trustees
from the Scottish Court of Session, which had granted the relief sought:

LORD BLACKBURN: . . . But in this case the trustees . . . endeavoured by a
minute to fix once for all the way in which they and their successors in office
would use their powers. And if they could at that time bind themselves by a
bargain with Mr. Oswald, if he had agreed to it, and that agreement would
prevent his land from being injuriously affected, I should be unwilling to hold
that he could, by refusing his assent to that agreement, get compensation for
the injury which he might have prevented. As Lord Shand says, 'he cannot
insist on being injured that he may get money.' There are great technical
difficulties in the way of working out this, but if I thought that his assent to the
minute would have made the minute effectual to prevent the trustees and their
successors from using their powers so as to injuriously affect the lands, I
should have tried to overcome them. But I do not think that if Mr. Oswald
had assented to the minute it would have bound the successors of the present
trustees.

I think that where the legislature confer powers on any body to take lands
compulsorily for a particular purpose, it is on the ground that the using of
that land for that purpose will be for the public good. Whether that body be
one which is seeking to make a profit for shareholders, or, as in the present
case, a body of trustees acting solely for the public good, I think in either case
the powers conferred on the body empowered to take the land compulsorily
are intrusted to them, and their successors, to be used for the furtherance of
that object which the legislature has thought sufficiently for the public good
to justify it in intrusting them with such powers; and, consequently, that a
contract purporting to bind them and their successors not to use those powers
is void. This is, I think, the principle on which this House acted in *Stafford-
shire Canal* v. *Birmingham Canal*[8] and on which the late Master of the Rolls
acted in *Mulliner* v. *Midland Ry. Co.*[9] In both these cases there were shareholders, but, said the Master of the Rolls, at p. 619, 'Now for what purpose is

[8] Law Rep. 1 H.L. 254.
[9] 11 Ch. D. 611.

the land to be used? It is to be used for the purposes of the Act, that is, for the general purposes of a railway. It is a public thoroughfare, subject to special rights on the part of the railway company working and using. But it is in fact a property devoted to public purposes as well as to private purposes; and the public have rights, no doubt, over the property of the railway company. It is property which is allowed to be acquired by the railway company solely for this purpose, and it is devoted to this purpose.'

This reasoning, which I think sound, is à fortiori applicable where there are no shareholders, and the purposes are all public. . . .

There is only, I think, one further point on which I think it necessary to remark. The trustees are under no obligation to make erections on any part of the land. If they in the bonâ fide exercise of their discretion think it best for the interest of the harbour to leave the portion of the land between Mr. Oswald's land and the quay wall open as a road of access and wharf, they may do so. If they think it best to make erections there not inconsistent with the main purpose of leaving a road of access from York Street to near the gates of the wet dock, though injuriously affecting the frontage of Mr. Oswald's remaining land, they may do so. And it was strongly argued that the trustees at the present time in the exercise of their general administrative powers may fix what is to be done now; and that if they do so they practically fix what will be done for all time to come; if the present trustees now lay out an open road thirty feet wide, along the inner side of the land, erecting what erections they think advisable on other parts of the wharf, their successors can hardly be supposed likely to change this plan.

I think that it is quite true that as to all such things as from their nature must be done once for all at the beginning of the trust, the present trustees must bind their successors. And if the Act had required the trustees to make and maintain a road thirty feet wide upon the land taken along the north quay, I am by no means prepared to say that their successors could have closed the road they laid out and made a new one; something would depend on the very terms of the enactment. But such is not the enactment in this Act. And though I think that the mode in which the trustees now lay out the road of access and wharf will probably have great influence on the exercise of the discretion of their successors, and is therefore an element which ought to be, and I do not doubt was, considered by the oversman in fixing the fair compensation for the probable injury to the frontage, it goes, I think, no further.

I come therefore to the conclusion that the interlocutor appealed against should be affirmed and the appeal dismissed with costs.

[LORD WATSON and LORD FITZGERALD delivered speeches in favour of dismissing the appeal.]

Appeal dismissed.

Questions

1. Is the *Ayr Harbour* case authority for the proposition that the holder of a discretionary power can never fetter his discretion by entering a contract. If not, does the case provide criteria for distinguishing permissible and impermissible fetters?

2. Is it correct to state that whenever a contract connected with discretionary power is valid the discretion is fettered? See Note 2 *infra*; p. 33 *supra* and p. 448 *infra*; Campbell, (1971) 45 A.L.J. 338; Mitchell, *The Contracts of Public Authorities*, pp. 57–65.

Notes

1. For the position of the Crown, see Ch. 14 *infra*.

2. It is important to separate the issue of the validity of the contract *ab initio* from the question whether, assuming the contract is valid, the public authority is thereafter under a duty to exercise its powers in a manner consistent with the contract. The cases have not always scrupulously done this. The second issue will be considered in Ch. 14 *infra*; this section is only concerned with the first, although see also p. 000 *infra*. An illustration of the problem is provided by *Dowty Boulton Paul Ltd. v. Wolverhampton Corporation* [1971] 1 W.L.R. 204. There Pennycuick V.-C. was dealing with a right of access to an airfield granted by the Corporation to the plaintiff in a conveyance of adjoining land. The *Ayr Harbour* case was inapplicable because it was accepted that the conveyance and the grant of the right of access were within the powers of the corporation. The judge said (at p. 210): 'The cases are not concerned with the position which arises after a statutory power has been validly exercised. Obviously, where a power is exercised in such a manner as to create a right extending over a term of years, the existence of that right *pro tanto* excludes the exercise of the statutory powers in respect of the same subject-matter, but there is no authority and I can see no principle on which that sort of exercise could be held to be invalid as a fetter on the future exercise of power.' This approach may appear to recognize the distinction between the initial validity of the contract and the legitimacy of any subsequent exercise of statutory powers. However, the fact that the answer to the second was solely determined by the answer to the first means that the distinction can only be a formal one without any dispositional importance. Doubt has been thrown on Pennycuick V.-C.'s approach by the judgments of the Court of Appeal in *Dowty Boulton Paul Ltd. v. Wolverhampton Corporation (No. 2)* [1976] Ch. 13. Although the court accepted that the right of access was validly created, it held that it was not a breach of the Corporation's contract to resolve to use the land for housing in pursuance of its power under s. 163 (1) of the Local Government Act 1933, although this would make the right of access meaningless. But see *Windsor and Maidenhead R.B.C. v. Brandrose Investments Ltd.* [1981] 1 W.L.R. 1083, in which Fox J. took the same approach as Pennycuick V.-C., although *Dowty Boulton Paul (No. 2)* was not cited.

3. In *Birkdale District Electricity Supply Co. v. Corporation of Southport* [1926] A.C. 355 at pp. 371–2 Lord Sumner distinguished the *Ayr Harbour* case as follows:

[I]t is plain that, in effect, the trustees did not merely propose to covenant in a manner that committed the business of the harbour to restricted lines in the future; they were to forbear, once and for all, to acquire all that the statute intended them to acquire, for, though technically they acquired the whole of the land, they were to sterilize part of their acquisition, so far as the statutory purpose of their undertaking was concerned. This is some distance from a mere contract entered into with regard to trading profits. The land itself was affected in favour of the former owner in the *Ayr* case just as a tow-path is affected in favour of the owner of a dominant tenement, if he is given a personal right of walking along it. If the Ayr trustees had reduced the acquisition price by covenanting with the respondent for a perpetual right to moor his barges, free of tolls, at any wharf they might construct on the water front of the land acquired, the decision might, and I think would, have been different.

There is, however, another aspect of the *Ayr Harbour* case which ought to be loyally recognized. It is certainly some ground for saying that there may be cases where the question of competence to contract does not depend on a proved incompatibility between the statutory purposes and the user, which is granted or renounced, but is established by the very nature of the grants or the contract itself. It was not proved in the *Ayr* case that there was any actual imcompatibility between the general purposes of the undertaking and the arrangement by which the particular proprietor was to be spared a particular interference with the amenities or the advantages of his back land. I think the case was supposed to speak for itself and that, in effect, the trustees were held to have renounced a part of their statutory birthright.'

See further Rogerson, [1971] P.L. 388.

ESTOPPEL – MISLEADING ADVICE

Robertson v. Minister of Pensions

[1949] 1 K.B. 227   King's Bench Division

The War Office originally had jurisdiction over all claims in respect of disability attributable to war service. By a Royal Warrant of 1940 the jurisdiction over claims in respect of service after 3 September 1939 was transferred to the Ministry of Pensions. In 1941, the appellant, a serving officer, wrote to the War Office regarding a disability of his which had resulted from an injury in December 1939. He received a reply stating: 'Your disability has been accepted as attributable to military service.' Relying on that assurance, he forbore to obtain an independent medical opinion on his own behalf. The Minister of Pensions later decided that the disability was not attributable to war service but to an injury sustained in 1927. On appeal from a pensions tribunal:

DENNING J.: . . . The assurance was given to the appellant in these explicit words: 'Your disability has been accepted as attributable to military service.' That was, on the face of it, an authoritative decision intended to be binding and intended to be acted on. Even if the appellant had studied the Royal Warrant in every detail there would have been nothing to lead him to suppose that the decision was not authoritative. He might well presume that the army medical board was recognized by the Minister of Pensions for the purpose of certifying his disability to be attributable to military service under the Royal Warrant of June, 1940: and that their certificate of attributability was sufficient for the purpose of the warrant.

What then is the result in law? If this was a question between subjects, a person who gave such an assurance as that contained in the War Office letter would be held bound by it unless he could show that it was made under the influence of a mistake or induced by a misrepresentation or the like. No such defence is made here. There are many cases in the books which establish that an unequivocal acceptance of liability will be enforced if it is intended to be binding, intended to be acted on, and is in fact acted on. . . .

The next question is whether the assurance in the War Office letter is binding on the Crown. The Crown cannot escape by saying that estoppels do not bind the Crown, for that doctrine has long been exploded. Nor can the Crown escape by praying in aid the doctrine of executive necessity, that is, the doctrine that the Crown cannot bind itself so as to fetter its future executive action. That doctrine was propounded by Rowlatt J. in *Rederiaktiebolaget Amphitrite* v. *The King*,[10] but it was unnecessary for the decision because the statement there was not a promise which was intended to be binding but only an expression of intention. Rowlatt J. seems to have been influenced by the cases on the right of the Crown to dismiss its servants at pleasure, but those cases must now all be read in the light of the judgment of Lord Atkin in *Reilly* v. *The King*.[11] That judgment shows that, in regard to contracts of service, the Crown is bound by its express promises as much as any subject. The cases where it has been held entitled to dismiss at pleasure are based on an implied term which cannot, of course, exist where there is an express term dealing with the matter. In my opinion the defence of executive necessity is of limited scope. It only avails the Crown where there is an implied term to that effect or that is the true meaning of the contract. It certainly has no application in this case. The War Office letter is clear and explicit and I see no room for implying a term that the Crown is to be at liberty to revoke the decision at its pleasure and without cause.

I come therefore to the most difficult question in the case. Is the Minister of Pensions bound by the War Office letter? I think he is. The appellant thought, no doubt, that, as he was serving in the army, his claim to attributability would be dealt with by or through the War Office. So he wrote to the War Office. The War Office did not refer him to the Minister of Pensions. They assumed authority over the matter and assured the appellant that his disability had been accepted as attributable to military service. He was entitled to assume that they had consulted any other departments that might be concerned, such as the Ministry of Pensions, before they gave him the assurance. He was entitled to assume that the board of medical officers who examined him were recognized by the Minister of Pensions for the purpose of giving certificates as to attributability. Can it be seriously suggested that, having got that assurance, he was not entitled to rely on it? In my opinion if a government department in its dealings with a subject takes it upon itself to assume authority upon a matter with which he is concerned, he is entitled to rely upon it having the authority which it assumes. He does not know, and cannot be expected to know, the limits of its authority. The department itself is clearly bound, and as it is but an agent for the Crown, it binds the Crown also; and as the Crown is bound, so are the other departments, for they also are but agents of the Crown. The War Office letter therefore binds the Crown, and, through the Crown, it binds the Minister of Pensions. The function of the Minister of Pensions is to administer the Royal Warrant issued by the Crown, and he must so administer it as to honour all assurances given by or on behalf of the Crown.

In my opinion therefore the finding of the tribunal that the disability was not attributable to war service must be set aside. . . .

Appeal allowed.

[10] [1921] 3 K.B. 500, 503, 504. [But see the actual words used by Rowlatt J. at p. 446 *infra*.]
[11] [1934] A.C. 176, 179. [But this point is controversial: see p. 456 *infra*.]

Questions

1. Is *Robertson* an example of estoppel of a public authority by an act outside its jurisdiction? Compare Fazal, [1972] P.L. 43 at pp. 46–7 and Ganz, [1965] P.L. 237 at pp. 244–5.

2. Can the application of ordinary principles of the law of agency justify the Crown, and through it, the Minister of Pensions being bound by the War Office's letters? For discussion of this question see pp. 155 and 450 *infra*. See further Treitel, [1957] P.L. 327.

Note

The precise relationship between estoppel in public law and in contract law is unclear. For instance, can a public law estoppel be raised by reprensentations of intention as well as representations of fact, i.e. does it include 'common law' and 'promissory' estoppel? If it does, then can it be said that the effect of an estoppel based on a representation of intention is only suspensory? See further Fazal, op cit., pp. 54–6; Alder, [1974] J.P.L. at pp. 450–1; and contrast Craig, (1977) 93 L.Q.R. 398 at p. 407 n. 44. The requirement of reliance was clearly satisfied in *Robertson*'s case but it should be noted that the question of what constitutes sufficient detriment to raise an estoppel has proved a difficult one in the law of contract; see Treitel, *The Law of Contract*, 5th edn., pp. 81–8 and pp. 93–6. For a case in which there was insufficient detriment, see *Norfolk C.C. v. Secretary of State for the Environment* [1973] 1 W.L.R. 1400.

Howell v. Falmouth Boat Construction Co. Ltd.

[1951] A.C. 837   House of Lords

The Restriction of Repairs of Ships Order 1940 (St. R.40, 1940, No. 142) prohibited 'repairs or alterations to or the drydocking of ships . . . except under the authority of a licence granted by the Admiralty'. In 1942 the Director of Merchant Shipping Repairs at the Admiralty directed licensing officers as to the policy to be followed, stating, *inter alia*, that '[w]hen you are dealing with reliable ship repairers and owners with a good record you ought not to delay the putting in hand of obvious repairs merely pending the actual issue of a licence.' Work was carried out on the appellant's vessel to adapt her for passenger carrying after inspection by and oral permission of the licensing officer. Later a written licence was issued for repairs 'set out in the . . . form of application'. The licence also stated that it should 'automatically determine if any unauthorised alterations or repairs are carried out'. The form of application applied for a licence 'to complete Board of Trade requirements'. Some of the work done, in particular a cocktail bar, was suitable for a passenger ship but not within the Board of Trade requirements. The licensing officer knew all that was done and said that none of it was unauthorized by him. The action was brought by the ship repairers to recover sums due for work done and materials supplied. The appellant (the original defendant) argued that work done before the written licence was granted was illegal and the sums claimed were irrecoverable and that, because of the unauthorized work, the licence automatically determined rendering all work done thereafter illegal.

These questions were treated as a preliminary issue. The Court of Appeal ([1950] 2 K.B. 16) held that oral permission was a sufficient 'licence' but Denning L.J. also stated that the work was not illegal because the public authority was estopped from asserting that it was.

The House of Lords held that 'licence' in the Order did mean 'licence in writing' but that the written licence could have retrospective as well as prospective effect, and that the work, which was authorized but not within the terms of the written licence, should not bar the ship repairers' contractual action on the grounds of illegality because the licensing officer had power to cure the defect.

LORD SIMMONDS: [Denning L.J., in the Court of Appeal,] described the principle that he invoked as of particular importance in these days when the officers of government departments are given much authority by Orders and circulars which are not available to the public. I will state this principle in his own words:[12] 'Whenever governmental officers, in their dealings with a subject, take on themselves to assume authority in a matter with which he is concerned, the subject is entitled to rely on their having the authority which they assume. He does not know and cannot be expected to know the limits of their authority, and he ought not to suffer if they exceed it. That was the principle which I applied in *Robertson* v. *Minister of Pensions*,[13] and it is applicable in this case also'. My Lords, I know of no such principle in our law nor was any authority for it cited. The illegality of an act is the same whether or not the actor has been misled by an assumption of authority on the part of a government officer however high or low in the hierarchy. I do not doubt that in criminal proceedings it would be a material factor that the actor had been thus misled if knowledge was a necessary element of the offence, and in any case it would have a bearing on the sentence to be imposed. But that is not the question. The question is whether the character of an act done in face of a statutory prohibition is affected by the fact that it has been induced by a misleading assumption of authority. In my opinion the answer is clearly No. Such an answer may make more difficult the task of the citizen who is anxious to walk in the narrow way, but that does not justify a different answer being given. . . .

[LORD NORMAND delivered a speech in favour of dismissing the appeal and LORD OAKSEY, LORD RADCLIFFE, and LORD TUCKER concurred.]

Appeal dismissed.

Southend-on-Sea Corporation v. Hodgson (Wickford) Ltd.

[1962] 1 Q.B. 416   Divisional Court of the Queen's Bench Division

A company, wishing to acquire premises for use as a builders' yard, wrote to the Borough Engineer stating that they understood that the premises had been used for this purpose for about twenty years and asked whether they

---

[12] [1950] 2 K.B. 16, 26.
[13] [1949] 1 K.B. 227.

could still be so used. He replied that 'the land you have shown on the plan accompanying your letter has an existing user right as a builders' yard and no planning permission is therefore necessary'. Relying on this, the company bought the premises and used them as a builders' yard. The planning authority was later presented with evidence showing that there was no existing user right as a builders' yard. The authority decided that the premises could not be so used without planning permission and that such use did not appear to be in keeping with the surrounding development. The company did not discontinue the use and was served with an enforcement notice under s. 23 of the Town and Country Planning Act 1947 [see now s. 87 of the 1971 Act] which made provision for such a notice if, *inter alia*, 'it appears to the local planning authority that any development of land has been carried out . . . without the grant of permission'. The company appealed and the justices held, *inter alia*, that the authority was estopped by the letter from contending that planning permission was required. The authority appealed.

LORD PARKER C.J.: . . . The broad submission made by Mr. Bridge on behalf of the appellants is that estoppel cannot operate to prevent or hinder the performance of a statutory duty or the exercise of a statutory discretion which is intended to be performed or exercised for the benefit of the public or a section of the public. It is further said that the discretion of a local planning authority to serve an enforcement notice under section 23 in respect of development in fact carried out without permission is a statutory discretion of a public character. It is perfectly clear that that proposition is sound, at any rate to this extent, that estoppel cannot operate to prevent or hinder the performance of a positive statutory duty. That, indeed, is admitted by Mr. Forbes on behalf of the respondents, but he maintains that it is limited to that and that it does not extend to an estoppel which might prevent or hinder the exercise of a statutory discretion. . . .

. . . I can see no logical distinction between a case such as that of an estoppel being sought to be raised to prevent the performance of a statutory duty and one where it is sought to be raised to hinder the exercise of a statutory discretion. After all, in a case of discretion there is a duty under the statute to exercise a free and unhindered discretion. There is a long line of cases to which we have not been specifically referred which lay down that a public authority cannot by contract fetter the exercise of its discretion. Similarly, as it seems to me, an estoppel cannot be raised to prevent or hinder the exercise of the discretion.

. . . [I]f the appellants are not allowed in this case to adduce evidence as to what the true position was in regard to existing user, they must be prevented from exercising their free discretion under [section 23]. It is true that it can be said, as in this case, that they have exercised their discretion. They have said that it appears to them that the development of land has been carried out without permission, and therefore to that extent the exercise of the discretion has not been hampered; but it seems to me quite idle to say that a local authority has in fact been able to exercise its discretion and issue an enforcement notice if by reason of estoppel it is prevented from proving and showing that it is a valid enforcement notice in that amongst other things planning permission was required. I have reluctantly come to the conclusion, accordingly, that the argument for the appellants is right, and that this appeal should succeed.

[WINN and WIDGERY JJ. agreed.]

Appeal allowed.

Question

Lord Parker C.J. placed great importance on the duty of an authority to exercise a 'free and unhindered discretion' and was influenced by the 'long line of cases which lay down that a public authority cannot by contract fetter the exercise of its discretion'. Is the prohibition in the contract cases really so absolute? (See Note 2 p. 147 *supra.*) If it is not, how should Lord Parker's judgment be modified to incorporate the analogy more precisely?

Lever Finance Ltd. v. Westminster (City) L.B.C.

[1971] 1 Q.B. 222   Court of Appeal

The plaintiff obtained planning permission from the defendant to build fourteen houses in accordance with a detailed plan. Later the plaintiff's architect, Rottenberg, (R.) prepared a larger plan showing small variations (including moving one house seventeen feet nearer to some existing houses) and sent it to Carpenter (C.) the defendant's planning officer. C., who had lost the relevant file, telephoned R. and told him that the alterations were not material and no further consent was necessary. The plaintiff proceeded with the building but the residents in the nearby houses objected to the fact that one house was so much nearer. Planning permission was then applied for and supported by the planning officer but the Planning Committee refused permission. An enforcement notice was to be issued and the plaintiff sought a declaration that it was entitled to complete the house in question by reason of the planning consent and the statement by C., and an injunction to restrain the defendant from seeking enforcement notices. Bridge J. granted this relief. He found that there was a practice to settle whether minor modifications to an approved plan were material with the planning officer and to go ahead without further permission if he did not think they were. The defendant appealed.

LORD DENNING M.R.: . . . In my opinion a planning permission covers work which is specified in the detailed plans and any immaterial variation therein. . . . It should not be necessary for the developers to go back to the planning committee for every immaterial variation. The permission covers any variation which is not material. But then the question arises: Who is to decide whether a variation is material or not? In practice it has been the planning officer. This is a sensible practice and I think we should affirm it. If the planning officer tells the developer that a proposed variation is not material, and the developer acts on it, then the planning authority cannot go back on it. I know that there are authorities which say that a public authority cannot be estopped by any representations made by its officers. It cannot be estopped from doing its public duty: see, for instance, the recent decision of the Divisional Court in *Southend-on-Sea Corporation* v. *Hodgson (Wickford) Ltd.* [1962] 1 Q.B. 416. But those statements must now be taken with considerable reserve. There are many matters which public authorities can now delegate to their officers. If an officer, acting within the scope of his ostensible authority, makes a representation on which another acts, then a public authority may be bound by it, just as much as a private concern would be. A good instance is the recent decision of this court in *Wells* v. *Minister of Housing and Local Government* [1967] 1 W.L.R. 1000. It was proved in that case that it was the practice of planning authorities, acting through their officers, to tell applicants whether or not planning permission was necessary. A letter was written by the council engineer telling the applicants that no permission was necessary. The applicants acted on it. It was held that the planning authority could not go back on it. I would like to quote what I then said, at p. 1007:

> 'It has been their practice to tell applicants that no planning permission is necessary. Are they now to be allowed to say that this practice was all wrong and their letters were of no effect? I do not think so. I take the law to be that a defect in procedure can be cured, and an irregularity can be waived, even by a public authority so as to render valid that which would otherwise be invalid.'[14]

So here it has been the practice of the local authority, and of many others to allow their planning officers to tell applicants whether a variation is material or not. Are they now to be allowed to say that that practice was all wrong? I do not think so. It was a matter within the ostensible authority of the planning officer; and, being acted on, it is binding on the council.

I would only add this: the conversation with Mr. Carpenter took place early in May, 1969. At that date there had been in force for one month at least, since April 1, 1969, the provisions of the Town and Country Planning Act, 1968. Section 64 enables a local authority as from April 1, 1969, to delegate to their officers many of their functions under the Planning Acts. An applicant cannot himself know, of course, whether such a delegation has taken place. That is a matter for the 'indoor managament' of the planning authority. It depends on the internal resolutions which they have made. Any person dealing with them is entitled to assume that all necessary resolutions have been passed. Just as he can in the case of a company: see *Royal British Bank* v. *Turquand* (1856) 6 E. & B. 327. It is true that section 64 (5) speaks of a notice in writing. But this does not alter the fact that much authority can now be delegated to planning officers.

I do not think this case can or should be decided on the new Act: for there

---

[14] [This is immediately followed by: 'Thus in *Robertson* v. *Minister of Pensions*, an assurance (that Colonel Robertson's disability was accepted as attributable to war service) was held binding on the Crown, even though it was given independently by the War Office instead of the Ministry of Pensions. And in *Howell* v. *Falmouth Boat Construction Co.*, a defect in the licence (about the cocktail bar) was disregarded by the House of Lords.']

was no notice in writing here. I think it should be decided on the practice proved in evidence. It was within the ostensible authority of Mr. Carpenter to tell Mr. Rottenberg that the variation was not material. Seeing that the developers acted on it by building the house, I do not think the council can throw over what has been done by their officer, Mr. Carpenter.

[SACHS L.J. delivered a judgment in favour of dismissing the appeal. MEGAW L.J. agreed with LORD DENNING M.R.]

Appeal dismissed.

Note

Two difficult questions arise when a public body makes a representation. The first, as such bodies have to act through agents, is whether the particular official acting on behalf of the body has authority (actual or ostensible) to make the representation. The second is whether the decision embodied in the representation is within the jurisdiction of the body for whom it is made. Unless both questions are answered affirmatively, an orthodox application of the ultra vires doctrine should mean that the decision will not bind the public body. Thus the representation must be within the ostensible authority of the official and the actual jurisdiction of the body itself if it is not to flout the 'jurisdictional principle'. The first question, involving the applicability of ordinary agency principles to the Crown and other public authorities, will be considered at p. 450 *infra*. See also *Robertson*'s case, p. 148 *supra*. At this stage suffice it to say that ostensible authority involves a representation by the principal – the public body – as to the authority of the agent – the official. Did the practice of delegation discussed in *Lever Finance* constitute such a representation? If, in that case, there was in fact no legal authority for the practice of delegation (see p. 154 *supra*), in what sense was the statement by the planning officer a statement *by the* local authority?

On the 'jurisdictional principle', Craig ((1977) 93 L.Q.R. 398 at p. 420) argues that:

When the application of [that] principle is examined it becomes more doubtful whether it can achieve a reconciliation of the cases. More important is that when the basis of the jurisdictional principle is scrutinised it is found to be wanting. The objective of preventing extension of power by public officials is obviously correct, but the operation of the doctrine in practice is misdirected. In the rare cases of intentional extension of power it strikes at the wrong person, the innocent representee, rather than the public official. In the more common case of careless, or inadvertent, extension of power any deterrent effect upon the public officer will be minimal. The unspoken hypothesis must be that whenever, *in fact*, the powers of the body are extended any hardship to the representee must be outweighed by the harm to the public, who are the beneficiaries of the *ultra vires* principle, were estoppel allowed to operate.

The argument put forward [is] that the complexity and diversity of situations in which representations occur does not permit of such a categorical answer. The balance of public and individual interest will produce different answers in areas as diverse as planning and licensing, social security and taxation, and even within each area. A doctrine with sufficient flexibility to recognise this diversity is needed. Whether it is introduced through the courts or through the legislature is a choice as to mechanism.

He finds such a doctrine in recent United States cases which weigh these interests against each other and allow an estoppel to be raised (even in the case of an ultra vires representation) where the balance comes down in favour of the individual; in such cases the harm to the public is likely to be spread in minute proportions through those who benefit from performance of the public duty – the public at large. While it is possible to see Lord Denning's judgment in *H.T.V. Ltd.* v. *Price Commission* [1976]

I.C.R. 170, noted at p. 162 *infra*, as an example of such an approach (and see also the *Laker Airways* case, p. 14 *supra*), the *Western Fish Products* case, p. 99 *infra*, suggests that it will not commend itself to an English court. Craig accepts that this approach is open to criticism as leaving too much discretion in the courts and consequent uncertainty as well as involving difficulties with the doctrine of Parliamentary Sovereignty. He nevertheless prefers it to the alternatives, which are:

(*a*) permitting a public body to be estopped if it acts 'in a proprietary rather than [a] governmental capacity';

(*b*) applying the company law 'indoor management' rule to permit estoppel where the representation is intra vires the body but not within the actual authority of the particular officer who makes it (see p. 154 *supra* and pp. 159 and 450 *infra* for further consideration of this); or

(*c*) compensating those who have relied on an ultra vires representation (see e.g. Gould, (1971) 87 L.Q.R. 15 at p. 18).

Craig criticizes (*a*) and (*b*) as merely narrowing the scope of the jurisdictional principle while accepting its rationale, and (*b*) as changing the result in a small number of cases. How, if at all, would the adoption of (*b*) have changed the result in *Lever Finance*? Is that case consistent with either (*a*) or (*b*)? On the question whether this is so and whether the representation in *Lever Finance* was intra vires, see Note 1, p. 161 *infra*, and Evans, (1971) 34 M.L.R. 335 at pp. 337–8. Craig criticizes (*c*) – compensation – because, in a case such as *Lever Finance*, refusing to grant the estoppel, i.e. requiring the house to be demolished *and* compensating the developer, would amount to a waste of resources. A further criticism is that, in the type of case exemplified by *Robertson* v. *Minister of Pensions*, p. 148 *supra*, there is no difference between permitting the estoppel and granting compensation.

Even if one accepts the balancing approach, however, it does not follow that there is no role for compensation. Where the detriment to the public interest by allowing an estoppel outweighs that to the individual by not allowing it, there may well be a justification for compensation. For instance, in the *Southend-on-Sea* case, p. 151 *supra*, the detriment to the surrounding property (i.e. loss of amenity) if the premises were used as a builders' yard may well have outweighed the detriment to the company which bought them relying on the Borough Engineer's letter. In such a case the public interest would be vindicated simply by ending the use and it is difficult to see why the individual who relied on the representation should not be compensated. A public authority that was tempted to avoid compensation by not vindicating the public interest (e.g. by ending the use) could be faced with an action for mandamus. On mandamus, see p. 402 *infra*. For the present possibilities of compensation see Ch. 13 *infra*.

One particular difficulty with the balancing approach advocated by Craig is referred to in the next case, *Western Fish Products*, where the court (p. 160 *infra*) noted the difficulty of adequately taking account of the interests of third parties who are not before the court.

Western Fish Products Ltd. v. Penwith D.C.

[1981] 2 All E.R. 204   Court of Appeal

The plaintiff bought a disused factory, which had been used for the production of fertilizer from fish, with the intention of manufacturing fish oil and fishmeal, and preparing and packing fresh fish for human consumption. Substantial alterations to the buildings were necessary. At a meeting the plaintiff asserted that no planning permission was needed by virtue of 'existing user rights' but Giddens, the representative of the local planning authority, asked for information in writing. This was done and, on 26 April 1976, Giddens replied accepting the description of the previous use of the site. The plaintiff started to carry out the work with the knowledge of the planning authority. Later it was asked to apply for planning permission and for an established use certificate (s. 94 of the Town and Country Planning Act 1971) and the Council resolved to refuse the applications. Enforcement notices were served. The plaintiff sought a declaration that, *inter alia*, the Council was estopped by Gidden's letter from disputing its existing user rights. Walton J. refused to grant the relief sought. The plaintiff appealed.

MEGAW L.J. delivered the judgment of the court (MEGAW, LAWTON and BROWNE L.JJ.):

[The court first considered whether the letter of 26 April was a representation and concluded:]

At the most the letter means that Mr Giddens on behalf of the defendant council was satisfied that the buildings on the site had been used previously for the purposes written on the plan and that the dimensions of the respective buildings used for those various purposes were correctly shown. If and in so far as it could be interpreted as confirming any use right, it was no more than a use right for the purposes for which the site had previously been used.

It follows that no relevant estoppel, 'proprietary' or otherwise, can be founded on any representation contained in that letter. . . .

Even if we had been satisfied that the defendant council through their officers had represented to the plaintiffs that all they wanted to do on the Stable Hobba site could be done because of the existing uses, planning permission being required only for new buildings and structures, and that they had acted to their detriment to the knowledge of the defendant council because of their representations, their claim would still have failed. There are two reasons for this: first, because they did not have the equitable right which has come to be called proprietary estoppel; and, second, because in law the defendant council could not be estopped from performing their statutory duties under the 1971 Act.

[MEGAW L.J. then considered the authorities on proprietary estoppel and continued:]

The second reason why the plaintiffs' own case cannot succeed is this. The defendant council's officers, even when acting within the apparent scope of their authority, could not do what the 1971 Act required the defendant council to do; and if their officers did or said anything which purported to determine in advance what the defendant council themselves would have to determine in pursuance of their statutory duties, they would not be inhibited from doing what they had to do. An estoppel cannot be raised to prevent the exercise of a statutory discretion or to prevent or excuse the performance of a statutory duty (see Spencer Bower and Turner on Estoppel by Representation (3rd Edn, 1977, p 141) and the cases there cited). The application of this principle can be illustrated on the facts of this case: under s 29 of the 1971 Act the defendant council as the planning authority had to determine applications for planning permission, and when doing so had to have regard to the provision of the development plan and 'to any other material considerations'. The plaintiffs made an application for planning permission to erect a tall chimney on the site. When considering this application the defendant council had to 'take into account any representations to that application' which were received by them following the publishing and posting of notices: see ss 26 and 29(2). This requirement was in the interests of the public generally. If any representations made by the defendant council's officers before the publication or posting of notices bound the council to act in a particular way, the statutory provision which gave the public opportunities of making representations would have been thwarted and the defendant council would have been dispensed from their statutory obligation of taking into account any representation made to them. The officers were appointed by the defendant council but the council's members were elected by their inhabitants of their area. Parliament by the 1971 Act entrusted the defendant council, acting through their elected members, not their officers, to perform various statutory duties. If their officers were allowed to determine that which Parliament had enacted the defendant council should determine there would be no need for elected members to consider planning applications. This cannot be. Under s 101(1) of the Local Government Act 1972 (which repealed s 4 of the 1971 Act, which re-enacted in an amended form s 64 of the Town and Country Planning Act 1968), a local authority may arrange for the discharge of any of their functions by an officer of the authority. This has to be done formally by the authority acting as such. In this case the defendant council issued standing orders authorising designated officers to perform specified functions including those arising under ss 53 and 94 of the 1971 Act.[15] Their officers had no authority to make any other determinations under the 1971 Act. We can see no reason why Mr de Savary, acting on behalf of the plaintiffs, and having available the advice of lawyers and architects, should have assumed, if he ever did, that Mr Giddens could bind the defendant council generally by anything he wrote or said.

Counsel for the plaintiffs submitted that, notwithstanding the general principle that a statutory body could not be estopped from performing its statutory duties, there are exceptions recognised by this court. This case, he asserted, came within the exceptions.

There seem to be two kinds of exceptions. If a planning authority, acting as such, delegates to its officers powers to determine specific questions, such as applications under ss 53 and 94 of the 1971 Act, any decisions they make cannot be revoked. This kind of estoppel, if it be estoppel at all, is akin to res judicata. Counsel for the Department of the Environment accepted that there was this exception, as did counsel for the defendant council in his final submissions. *Lever (Finance) Ltd v Westminster Corpn* . . . [1971] 1 QB 222

[15] [Determining whether operations on land required planning permission and certifying that there were existing user rights.]

can, we think, be considered as an application of this exception. The trial judge had found that it was a common practice amongst planning authorities, including the defendants, for planning officers to sanction immaterial modifications to plans sent with successful applications for planning permission. This is what one of the defendants' planning officers thought he was doing when he agreed with the plaintiffs' architect that they could make a modification to the plans of some houses which were being erected; but Lord Denning MR thought that what he had agreed to was not an immaterial modification: it was a material one. [After considering the judgments in the *Lever Finance* case, MEGAW L.J. continued:] This case, of course, binds us unless there is in the reasoning an element which can be said to be 'per incuriam'. In our judgment it is not an authority for the proposition that every representation made by a planning officer within his ostensible authority binds the planning authority which employs him. For an estoppel to arise there must be some evidence justifying the person dealing with the planning officer for thinking that what the officer said would bind the planning authority. Holding an office, however senior, cannot, in our judgment, be enough by itself. In the *Lever (Finance) Ltd* case there was evidence of a widespread practice amongst planning authorities of allowing their planning officers to make immaterial modifications to the plans produced when planning permission was given. Lever (Finance) Ltd's architect presumably knew of this practice and was entitled to assume that the practice had been authorised by the planning authorities in whose areas it was followed. The need for some evidence of delegation of authority can be illustrated in this way. Had Lever (Finance) Ltd's architect produced plans showing material and substantial modifications to the planning permission for a large development in Piccadilly Circus already granted, he could not sensibly have assumed that the planning officer with whom he was dealing had authority to approve the proposed modifications without putting them before the planning authority. Whether anyone dealing with a planning officer can safely assume that the officer can bind his authority by anything he says must depend on all the circumstances. In the *Lever (Finance) Ltd* case [1971] 1 QB 222 at 231 Lord Denning MR said: 'Any person dealing with them [ie officers of a planning authority] is entitled to assume that all necessary resolutions have been passed.' This statement was not necessary for the conclusion he had reached and purported to be an addendum. We consider it to be obiter; with all respect, it stated the law too widely.

In this case there was no evidence of any relevant delegations of authority save in relation to applications under ss 53 and 94. We deal later in this judgment with the plaintiffs' submissions about the operation of those sections.

We can deal with the second exception shortly. If a planning authority waives a procedural requirement relating to any application made to it for the exercise of its statutory powers, it may be estopped from relying on lack of formality. Much, however, will turn on the construction of any statutory provisions setting out what the procedure is to be. *Wells v Minister of*

Housing and Local Government [[1967] 1 W.L.R. 1000] is an example of the exception. . . . Save in relation to the plaintiffs' submissions as to the operation of ss 53 and 94 on the facts of this case, this exception cannot have any application to this case.

The extension of the concept of estoppel beyond these two exceptions, in our judgment, would not be justified. A further extension would erode the general principle as set out in a long line of cases of which the decision of the Privy Council in *Maritime Electric Co Ltd v General Dairies Ltd* . . . [1937] AC 610 and the judgment of the Divisional Court in *Southend-on-Sea Corpn v. Hodgson (Wickford) Ltd* . . . [1962] 1 QB 416 are notable examples. Parliament has given those who are aggrieved by refusals of planning permission or the serving of enforcement notices a right of appeal to the Secretary of State: see ss 36 and 88 of the 1971 Act. He can hear evidence as to the merits and take into account policy considerations. The courts can do neither. The application of the concept of estoppel because of what a planning officer had represented could result in a court adjudging that a planning authority was bound to allow a development which flouted its planning policy, with which the courts are not concerned.

There is another objection to any extension of the concept of estoppel which is illustrated by the facts of the *Lever (Finance) Ltd* case. If the modifications which were permitted by the planning officer in that case had been properly to be regarded as immaterial, no problem of general principle would arise. But the court regarded itself as competent to decide as to the materiality and, despite the submission to the contrary by the successful plaintiffs, held that the modifications were material. On what basis of evidence or judicial notice the court reached that conclusion, we need not stay to consider. We assume both that the court had jurisdiction to decide that question, and that, on the facts of that case, their decision as to materiality was right. But then comes the difficulty, and the real danger of injustice. To permit the estoppel no doubt avoided an injustice to the plaintiffs. But it also may fairly be regarded as having caused an injustice to one or more members of the public, the owners of adjacent houses who would be adversely affected by this wrong and careless decision of the planning officer that the modifications were not material. Yet they were not, and it would seem could not, be heard. How, in their absence, could the court balance the respective injustices according as the court did or did not hold that there was an estoppel in favour of the plaintiffs? What 'equity' is there in holding, if such be the effect of the decision, that the potential injustice to a third party, as a result of the granting of the estoppel is irrelevant? At least it can be said that the less frequently this situation arises the better for justice.

In *Brooks and Burton Ltd v Secretary of State for the Environment* (1976) 75 LGR 285 at 296 Lord Widgery CJ adverted to extending the concept of estoppel. He said:

> 'There has been some advance in recent years of this doctrine of estoppel as applied to local authorities through their officers, and the most advanced case is the one referred to by the inspector, namely *Lever Finance Ltd.* v.

Westminster (City) London Borough Council. I do not propose to read it. It no doubt is correct on its facts, but I would deprecate any attempt to expand this doctrine because it seems to me, as I said a few minutes ago, extremely important that local government officers should feel free to help applicants who come and ask them questions without all the time having the shadow of estoppel hanging over them and without the possibility of their immobilising their authorities by some careless remark which produces such an estoppel.'

We agree with what he said.

[MEGAW L.J. then turned to the statutory position under ss. 53 and 94 of the 1971 Act and held that the Council's letter did not constitute a determination that planning permission was not required or an established user certificate.]

Appeal dismissed.

Notes

1. The court's treatment of the first exception is not free from difficulty. Although the statement that the estoppel is 'akin to res judicata' suggests (and see the preceding sentence in the extract, p. 158 *supra*) that delegation and representation must be authorized, i.e. intra vires the public body, the importance given to the 'widespread practice' of delegation as explaining *Lever Finance* was surely only necessary if the delegation was improper. On the effect of *Western Fish Products* see further Williams, [1981] C.L.J. 198; Bradley, (1981) 34 C.L.P. 1 at p. 6.

2. *Wells* v. *Minister of Housing and Local Government* [1967] 1 W.L.R. 1000, which was considered in both *Lever Finance*, p. 154 *supra*, and *Western Fish Products*, stated that representations may cure 'defects in procedure' and prevent reliance on 'technicalities' but cannot stop an authority from doing its public duty. This is apparently a distinction between substance and procedure and, as *Western Fish Products* now shows, waiver of procedural requirements has been accepted as an exception though not a universal one, to the general no-estoppel rule. In *Wells* a letter in reply to an application for planning permission stated that the proposed structure was 'permitted development'. One question which arose was whether the statement constituted a 'determination' under s. 43 of the Town and Country Planning Act 1962 (now s. 53 of the 1971 Act) that planning permission was not needed. The Minister argued that it was not, because no written application had expressly been made for a s. 43 determination. This argument was rejected by a majority of the Court of Appeal. Lord Denning M.R..stated (at p. 1007):

If we were to require the applicant to go through such a formality, it would be a work of supererogation. Nay more, it would be a trap. Anyone receiving such a letter . . . would think that was enough. He would not dream of doing more. Nor should he be bound to do so.'

He then stated the words quoted at p. 154 *supra*, and continued:

[The] omission was a defect in procedure only. It did not prevent the planning authority from considering the matter if they thought fit. If they decided that it was unnecessary, they were entitled to tell the applicants so. Once the planning authority determined that no planning permission was necessary, and told the applicants so, that was a determination within section 43, even though there had been no formal application before them for that purpose.

Although the distinction between substance and procedure can work well in some cases (e.g. in *Re L(A.C.)* [1971] 3 All E.R. 743 at p. 752, where a notice of objection to local authority proceedings to vest parental rights over a child in care in the authority was not served in time because the mother's solicitor was told that an earlier notice was good), it can cause difficulties. In *Well*'s case Lord Denning cited *Robertson* v. *Minister of Pensions*, p. 148 *supra*, and *Howell* v. *Falmouth Boat Construction Co. Ltd.*, p. 150 *supra*, as having been decided on this ground. But in *Howell*'s case nothing was expressly said about substance and procedure. It seems clear that the defect there was disregarded because the licensing officer had power to cure it by issuing a retrospective licence and the evidence suggested that he was willing to do this (see Lord Normand, [1951] A.C. 837 at p. 848). Furthermore, if *Robertson*'s case concerned a procedural defect, it is difficult to see why all cases involving the authority of the agent to make the statement (see p. 155 *supra* and p. 450 *infra*) should not be decided in the same way.

It is, moreover, arguable that, despite the references to defects being 'cured' and 'irregularities waived', *Wells* itself did not infringe the jurisdictional principle and is an example of the *Re 56 Denton Road* principle, p. 31 *supra*. See especially Lord Denning's words quoted at p. 161 *supra*; but cf. Craig, op. cit., p. 407 and contrast Alder, [1974] J.P.L. 447 at p. 448. Alternatively, if, as is suggested in *Western Fish Products*, p. 159 *supra*, the availability of estoppel based on waiver of a procedural requirement depends on the construction of the relevant statute, might *Wells* be an example of a 'directory' statutory requirement? On mandatory and directory requirements see p. 17 *supra*.

In *Wells* Russell L.J. dissented on the ground that the planning authority was 'not a free agent to waive statutory requirements in favour of (so to speak) an adversary: it is the guardian of the planning system'. The Court of Appeal in *Western Fish Products* found his judgment 'very powerful': [1981] 2 All E.R. 204 at p. 223. See also Lord Denning in *Co-operative Retail Services Ltd.* v. *Taff-Ely B.C.* (1980) 39 P. & C.R. 223 at p. 238, quoted in Note 3, p. 163 *infra*.

3. In *H.T.V. Ltd.* v. *Price Commission* [1976] I.C.R. 170 the plaintiff television company provided television programmes and, under contracts with the broadcasting authority, made additional payments, called the Exchequer levy, which were passed to the Exchequer. From June 1974 this levy was calculated as a percentage of profits. In its returns of profit margin to the Price Commission under the Counter-Inflation Act 1973 H.T.V. had deducted the levy in order to arrive at its relevant profit and in 1973 the Commission had stated that it was 'of the opinion that the levy . . . should be treated as a cost for the purpose of determining the net profit margin'. In July 1975 H.T.V. notified the Commission that it intended to increase its advertising charges in accordance with the Counter-Inflation (Price-Code) Order 1974 so that its prices reflected the permitted margin over total costs per unit of output. H.T.V. included the levy in calculating such total costs, as it had done on two occasions in 1974. The Commission informed H.T.V. that the levy was not a cost for the purposes of the Order and H.T.V. successfully challenged this. In the Court of Appeal Lord Denning M.R. said (at p. 185):

> It is, in my opinion, the duty of the Price Commission to act with fairness and consistency in their dealings with manufacturers and traders. Allowing that it is primarily for them to interpret and apply the code, nevertheless if they regularly interpret the words of the code in a particular sense – or regularly apply the code in a particular way – they should continue to interpret it and apply it in the same way thereafter unless there is good cause for departing from it. At any rate they should not depart from it in any case where they have, by their conduct, led the manufacturer or trader to believe that he can safely act on that interpretation of the code or on

that method of applying it, and he does so act on it. It is not permissible for them to depart from their previous interpretation and application where it would not be fair or just to do so. It has been often said, I know, that a public body, which is entrusted by Parliament with the exercise of powers for the public good, cannot fetter itself in the exercise of them. It cannot be stopped from doing its public duty. But that is subject to the qualification that it must not misuse its powers: and it is a misuse of power for it to act unfairly or unjustly towards a private citizen when there is no overriding public interest to warrant it.

He then purported to justify *Robertson, Wells,* and *Lever Finance* on this principle. Can they be? Contrast *Co-operative Retail Services Ltd.* v. *Taff-Ely B.C.* (1980) 39 P. & C.R. 223 (affirmed by the House of Lords, (1981) 42 P. & C.R. 1), where the balancing approach was not adopted. There the issue was whether a grant of planning permission made without authority by the clerk to the District Council was valid. Lord Denning M.R. said (at p. 238) that a grant that has never been authorized is *'ultra vires and void and of no legal effect whatever'* and could not be relied on. 'A grant of planning permission is made in the public interest – so as to ensure that the amenities of our countryside are preserved for the good of all. The protection of the public interest is entrusted to the representative bodies and to the minister. It would be quite wrong that it should be preempted by a mistaken issue by a clerk of a written form – without any authority in that behalf.' How, if at all, can this be reconciled with *Lever Finance?*

In *R.* v. *Basildon D.C., ex p. Brown* (1981) 79 L.G.R. 655 Dunn L.J. said (at p. 674) that the *H.T.V.* case is 'no authority for the proposition that if a statutory body mistakenly holds itself out as having powers which it does not, and by law cannot have, then it is to be deemed not only to possess those powers but also the obligations that go with them'.

4. Consider *R.* v. *Liverpool Corporation, ex p. Liverpool Taxi Fleet Operators' Association* [1972] Q.B. 299, noted at p. 269 *infra.* Was that a case of 'procedural' estoppel? Is it analogous to the cases discussed in this section? See further Evans, (1973), 36 M.L.R. 93 at p. 96 and, on acting fairly, see p. 282 *infra* and *R.* v. *I.R.C., ex p. Parker,* noted in the Appendix.

6

ABUSE OF DISCRETION

NO UNFETTERED DISCRETION?

Associated Provincial Picture Houses Ltd. v. Wednesbury Corporation, p. 118 *supra*

Padfield v. Minister of Agriculture, Fisheries and Food, *infra*

Note

The question of the scope of review of discretionary powers has been discussed in Ch. 4 *supra*, in particular at pp. 111 and 122 ff., and see p. 17 *supra*. See further Wade, pp. 355–9.

RELEVANT AND IRRELEVANT CONSIDERATIONS

Associated Provincial Picture Houses Ltd. v. Wednesbury Corporation, p. 118 *supra*

Padfield v Minister of Agriculture, Fisheries and Food

[1968] A.C. 997   House of Lords

Section 19 (3) of the Agriculture Marketing Act 1958 provides that:

A committee of investigation shall . . . (*b*) be charged with the duty, if the Minister in any case so directs, of considering, and reporting to the Minister on . . . any . . . complaint made to the Minister as to the operation of any scheme which, in the opinion of the Minister, could not be considered by a Consumers' Committee. . . .

England and Wales were divided into eleven regions for the purpose of the Milk Marketing Board. Producers had to sell their milk to the Board at prices which differed from region to region to reflect the varying costs of transporting milk from the producers to the consumers. Transport costs had altered and the South-Eastern Region wished the differential to be altered. The constitution of the Board made it impossible for the South-Eastern producers to get a majority for their proposals and they asked the Minister to appoint a committee of investigation. When the Minister refused they applied for an order of mandamus directing him to refer the complaint to a committee of investigation or to deal with it on relevant considerations only, to the exclusion of irrelevant considerations. At first instance this was granted but the Court of Appeal allowed an appeal by the Minister and the producers appealed to the House of Lords. (A further extract, on the 'duty' to give reasons, is set out at p. 29 *supra*.)

LORD REID: . . . [The Minister] contends that his only duty [under s. 19 (3) (*b*)] is to consider a complaint fairly and that he is given an unfettered discretion with regard to every complaint either to refer it or not to refer it to the committee as he may think fit. The appellants contend that it is his duty to refer every genuine and substantial complaint, or alternatively that his discretion is not unfettered and that in this case he failed to exercise his discretion according to law because his refusal was caused or influenced by his having misdirected himself in law or by his having taken into account extraneous or irrelevant considerations.

In my view, the appellants' first contention goes too far. There are a number of reasons which would justify the Minister in refusing to refer a complaint. For example, he might consider it more suitable for arbitration, or he might consider that in an earlier case the committee of investigation had already rejected a substantially similar complaint, or he might think the complaint to be frivolous or vexatious. So he must have at least some measure of discretion. But is it unfettered?

It is implicit in the argument for the Minister that there are only two possible interpretations of this provision – either he must refer every complaint or he has an unfettered discretion to refuse to refer in any case. I do not think that is right. Parliament must have conferred the discretion with the intention that it should be used to promote the policy and objects of the Act; the policy and objects of the Act must be determined by construing the Act as a whole and construction is always a matter of law for the court. In a matter of this kind it is not possible to draw a hard and fast line, but if the Minister, by reason of his having misconstrued the Act or for any other reason, so uses his discretion as to thwart or run counter to the policy and objects of the Act, then our law would be very defective if persons aggrieved were not entitled to the protection of the court. So it is necessary first to construe the Act.

When these provisions were first enacted in 1931 it was unusual for Parliament to compel people to sell their commodities in a way to which they objected and it was easily foreseeable that any such scheme would cause loss to some producers. Moreover, if the operation of the scheme was put in the hands of the majority of the producers, it was obvious that they might use their power to the detriment of consumers, distributors or a minority of the producers. So it is not surprising that Parliament enacted safeguards.

The approval of Parliament shows that this scheme was thought to be in the public interest, and in so far as it necessarily involved detriment to some persons, it must have been thought to be in the public interest that they should suffer it. But in sections 19 and 20 Parliament drew a line. They provide machinery for investigating and determining whether the scheme is operating or the board is acting in a manner contrary to the public interest.

The effect of these sections is that if, but only if, the Minister and the committee of investigation concur in the view that something is being done contrary to the public interest the Minister can step in. Section 20 enables the

Minister to take the initiative. Section 19 deals with complaints by individuals who are aggrieved. I need not deal with the provisions which apply to consumers. We are concerned with other persons who may be distributors or producers. If the Minister directs that a complaint by any of them shall be referred to the committee of investigation, that committee will make a report which must be published. If they report that any provision of this scheme or any act or omission of the board is contrary to the interests of the complainers *and* is not in the public interest, then the Minister is empowered to take action, but not otherwise. He may disagree with the view of the committee as to public interest, and, if he thinks that there are other public interests which outweigh the public interest that justice should be done to the complainers, he would be not only entitled but bound to refuse to take action. Whether he takes action or not, he may be criticised and held accountable in Parliament but the court cannot interfere.

I must now examine the Minister's reasons for refusing to refer the appellants' complaint to the committee. . . .

The first reason which the Minister gave in his letter of March 23, 1965,[1] was that this complaint was unsuitable for investigation because it raised wide issues. Here it appears to me that the Minister has clearly misdirected himself. Section 19 (6)[2] contemplates the raising of issues so wide that it may be necessary for the Minister to amend a scheme or even to revoke it. Narrower issues may be suitable for arbitration but section 19 affords the only method of investigating wide issues. In my view it is plainly the intention of the Act that even the widest issues should be investigated if the complaint is genuine and substantial, as this complaint certainly is.

Then it is said that this issue should be 'resolved through the arrangements available to producers and the board within the framework of the scheme itself.' This re-states in a condensed form the reasons given in paragraph 4 of the letter of May 1, 1964, where it is said 'the Minister owes no duty to producers in any particular region,' and reference is made to the 'status of the Milk Marketing Scheme as an instrument for the self-government of the industry,' and to the Minister 'assuming an inappropriate degree of responsibility.' But, as I have already pointed out, the Act imposes on the Minister a responsibility whenever there is a relevant and substantial complaint that the board are acting in a manner inconsistent with the public interest, and that has been relevantly alleged in this case. I can find nothing in the Act to limit this responsibility or to justify the statement that the Minister owes no duty to producers in a particular region. The Minister is, I think, correct in saying that the board is an instrument for the self-government of the industry. So long as it does not act contrary to the public interest the Minister cannot

[1] [Notifying the producers of his decision not to refer the issue to a committee of investigation.]

[2] [This states: 'If a committee of investigation report to the Minister that any provision of a scheme or any act or omission of a board administering a scheme is contrary to the interests of consumers . . . or any persons affected by the scheme and is not in the public interest, the Minister, if he thinks fit so to do after considering the report,' may amend or revoke the scheme or direct the board to rectify the matter.]

interfere. But if it does act contrary to what both the committee of investigation and the Minister hold to be the public interest the Minister has a duty to act. And if a complaint relevantly alleges that the board has so acted, as this complaint does, then it appears to me that the Act does impose a duty on the Minister to have it investigated. If he does not do that he is rendering nugatory a safeguard provided by the Act and depriving complainers of a remedy which I am satisfied that Parliament intended them to have.

Paragraph 3 of the letter of May 1, 1964,[3] refers to the possibility that, if the complaint were referred and the committee were to uphold it, the Minister 'would be expected to make a statutory Order to give effect to the committee's recommendations.' If this means that he is entitled to refuse to refer a complaint because, if he did so, he might later find himself in an embarrassing situation, that would plainly be a bad reason. . . .

[After considering the Minister's reasons, in a passage set out at p. 29 *supra*, his Lordship turned to the argument that the discretion was unfettered, and said:] I have found no authority to support the unreasonable proposition that it must be all or nothing – either no discretion at all or an unfettered discretion. Here the words 'if the Minister in any case so directs' are sufficient to show that he has some discretion but they give no guide as to its nature or extent. That must be inferred from a construction of the Act read as a whole, and for the reasons I have given I would infer that the discretion is not unlimited, and that it has been used by the Minister in a manner which is not in accord with the intention or the statute which conferred it.

As the Minister's discretion has never been properly exercised according to law, I would allow this appeal. It appears to me that the case should now be remitted to the Queen's Bench Division with a direction to require the Minister to consider the complaint of the appellants according to law.

LORD UPJOHN: . . . The Minister in exercising his powers and duties, conferred upon him by statute, can only be controlled by a prerogative writ which will only issue if he acts unlawfully. Unlawful behaviour by the Minister may be stated with sufficient accuracy for the purposes of the present appeal (and here I adopt the classification of Lord Parker C.J., in the Divisional Court): (a) by an outright refusal to consider the relevant matter, or (b) by misdirecting himself in point of law, or (c) by taking into account some wholly irrelevant or extraneous consideration, or (d) by wholly omitting to take into account a relevant consideration.

There is ample authority for these propositions which were not challenged in argument. In practice they merge into one another and ultimately it becomes a question whether for one reason or another the Minister has acted unlawfully in the sense of misdirecting himself in law, that is, not merely in respect of some point of law but by failing to observe the other headings I have mentioned.

In the circumstances of this case, which I have sufficiently detailed for this

---

[3] [The letter written by the Ministry after the issue had first been raised by the producers. This explained the complaint procedure and set out the considerations that the Minister would take into account in deciding whether to refer the issue to a committee of investigation.]

purpose, it seems to me quite clear that prima facie there seems a case for investigation by the committee of investigation. As I have said already, it seems just the type of situation for which the machinery of section 19 was set up, but that is a matter for the Minister.

He may have good reasons for refusing an investigation, he may have, indeed, good policy reasons for refusing it, though that policy must not be based on political considerations which as Farwell L.J. said in *Rex* v. *Board of Education*[4] are pre-eminently extraneous. So I must examine the reasons given by the Minister, including any policy upon which they may be based, to see whether he has acted unlawfully and thereby overstepped the true limits of his discretion, or, as it is frequently said in the prerogative writ cases, exceeded his jurisdiction. Unless he has done so, the court has no jurisdiction to interfere. It is not a Court of Appeal and has no jurisdiction to correct the decision of the Minister acting lawfully within his discretion, however much the court may disagree with its exercise.

[His Lordship then considered the Minister's reasons. In dealing with the argument that the discretion was 'unfettered' he said:]

My Lords, I believe that the introduction of the adjective 'unfettered' and its reliance thereon as an answer to the appellants' claim is one of the fundamental matters confounding the Minister's attitude, bona fide though it be. First, the adjective nowhere appears in section 19, it is an unauthorised gloss by the Minister. Secondly, even if the section did contain that adjective I doubt if it would make any difference in law to his powers, save to emphasise what he has already, namely that acting lawfully he has a power of decision which cannot be controlled by the courts: it is unfettered. But the use of that adjective, even in an Act of Parliament, can do nothing to unfetter the control which the judiciary have over the executive, namely that in exercising their powers the latter must act lawfully and that is a matter to be determined by looking at the Act and its scope and object in conferring a discretion upon the Minister rather than by the use of adjectives.

[LORD HODSON and LORD PEARCE delivered speeches in favour of allowing the appeal. LORD MORRIS OF BORTH-Y-GEST delivered a speech in favour of dismissing the appeal.]

Appeal allowed.

Notes

1. As a result of the case the Minister referred the complaint to the Committee, which reported that the current prices were contrary to the interests of the South-Eastern region and the public interest. The Minister decided not to direct the Milk Marketing Board to implement the Committee's conclusions because this could eventually bring to an end the system for organized milk marketing, and as he had taken account of 'wider questions of agricultural, economic and social policy' which were beyond the scope of the Committee's inquiry (H.C. 423, Session 1967/8, p. 10; H.C. 445, Session 1968/9; 780 H.C. Deb., cols. 46–7). Harlow, [1976] P.L. 116 at

---

[4] [1910] 2 K.B. 165, 181.

p. 120 states that the judicial 'remedy had proved illusory; the same decision could be reached with only nominal deference to the court, and the waste of time and money entailed is a deterrent to future complainants'. Do you agree? If so, can the distinction between review and appeal be supported? If not, should judicial review be seen as a purely procedural phenomenon? (Cf. Garner, (1968) 31 M.L.R. 446).

2. Austin ((1975) 28 C.L.P. 150 at p. 169) has criticized Lord Reid's reasoning (at p. 165 *supra*). He argues that to say the Minister was under a duty to have complaints investigated but that he 'could refuse to carry out that duty if a complaint was vexatious or frivolous, or had already been investigated and rejected or (possibly) if he possessed sufficient information on the merits of the complaint to decide that whatever the Committee might recommend he would hold it to be contrary to the public interest to take any action' is inconsistent. 'If the Minister has a *duty* to refer complaints, he cannot at the same time possess a *discretion* not to refer.' Austin also states (at p. 172) that 'the court exercised [the Minister's] duty/discretion for him, a power which Lord Halsbury expressly denied to any court, in *Westminster Corporation* v. *London and N.W. Ry. Co.*' p. 178 *infra*. Do you agree? Is it possible to make as sharp a distinction between duty and discretion in any one statutory power as Austin suggests?

Roberts v. Hopwood

[1925] A.C. 578   House of Lords

At a time when both the cost of living and trade union scale wage rates had been falling for some time, Poplar Borough Council resolved not to reduce its employees' wages. The Council also continued to pay male and female employees at the same rate. Section 62 of the Metropolis Management Act 1855 gave the Council power to pay employees 'such . . . wages as . . .[the Council] may think fit'. Under s. 247 (7) of the Public Health Act 1875 the district auditor had power to 'disallow any item of account contrary to law, and surcharge the same on the person making or authorising the illegal payment'. He calculated the amount by which the pre-1914–18 war rate should have been increased in accordance with the rise in the cost of living, added a further £1 as a margin and, after hearing representations from the councillors, reduced the figure he had been minded to disallow by £12,000. He then disallowed the remaining excess (£5,000) and surcharged those responsible. The councillors applied for certiorari to quash this under s. 247 (8) of the Public Health Act 1875 (which permitted relief for errors of law and of fact: *R.* v. *Roberts* [1908] 1 K.B. 407). They failed in the Divisional Court ([1924] 1 K.B. 514) but succeeded in the Court of Appeal ([1924] 2 K.B. 695). The district auditor appealed.

LORD BUCKMASTER: . . . [T]he general rule applicable is that the council shall pay such wages as they may think fit, the discretion as to the reasonable nature of the wages being with them. The discretion thus imposed is a very wide one, and I agree with the principle enunciated by Lord Russell in the case of *Kruse* v *Johnson*,[5] that when such a discretion is conferred upon a local authority the Court ought to show great reluctance before they attempt to determine how, in their opinion, the discretion ought to be exercised.

    [5] [1898] 2 Q.B. 91, 99.

Turning to what the borough council have done, the reason for their action is to be found in the affidavit sworn by Mr. Scurr, Mr. Key, Mr. Lansbury and Mr. Sumner. In para. 6 of that affidavit they make the following statement: 'The council and its predecessors the district board of works have always paid such a minimum wage to its employees as they have believed to be fair and reasonable without being bound by any particular external method of fixing wages, whether ascertainable by Trade Union rate, cost of living, payments by other local or national authorities or otherwise.' And if the matter ended there it would be my opinion that a decision so reached could not be impeached until it were shown that it was not bona fide, and absence of bona fides is not alleged in the present proceedings. Para. 9, however, of the same affidavit puts the matter in a different form. It is there said: '9 . . . The Council did not and does not take the view that wages paid should be exclusively related to the cost of living. They have from time to time carefully considered the question of the wages and are of the opinion, as a matter of policy, that a public authority should be a model employer and that a minimum rate of 4*l.* is the least wage which ought to be paid to an adult having regard to the efficiency of their workpeople, the duty of a public authority both to the ratepayers and to its employees, the purchasing power of the wages and other considerations which are relevant to their decisions as to wages.'

Now it appears that on August 31, 1921, a resolution was passed by the borough council to the effect that no reduction of wage or bonus should be made during the ensuing four months, and this was acted upon for the following twelve months. It was, I think, well within their power to fix wages for a reasonable time in advance, and there are cogent reasons why this should be done, but that decision should be made in relation to existing facts, which they appear to have ignored. In August, 1921, the cost of living had been continuously falling since November of the previous year, and it continued to fall, so that it is difficult to understand how, if the cost of living was taken into account in fixing the wages for adult workers at a minimum basis of 4*l.*, the sharp decline in this important factor should have been wholly disregarded by the borough council. But the affidavit contains another statement, which I think is most serious for the council's case. It states that 4*l.* a week was to be the minimum wage for adult labour, that is without the least regard to what that labour might be. It standardised men and women not according to the duties they performed, but according to the fact that they were adults. It is this that leads me to think that their action cannot be supported, and that in fact they have not determined the payment as wages, for they have eliminated the consideration both of the work to be done and of the purchasing power of the sums paid, which they themselves appear to regard as a relevant though not the dominant factor. Had they stated that they determined as a borough council to pay the same wage for the same work without regard to the sex or condition of the person who performed it, I should have found it difficult to say that that was not a proper exercise of their discretion. It was indeed argued that that is what they did, but I find it impossible to extract that from the statement contained in the affidavit. It appears to me, for the reasons I have given, that they cannot have brought into account the considerations which they say influenced them, and that they did not base their decision upon the ground that the reward for work is the value of the work reasonably and even generously measured, but that they took an arbitrary principle and fixed an arbitrary sum, which was not a real exercise of the discretion imposed upon them by the statute....

LORD ATKINSON: ... The council would, in my view, fail in their duty if, in administering funds which did not belong to their members alone, they put aside all [the] aids to the ascertainment of what was just and reasonable remuneration to give for the services rendered to them, and allowed themselves to be guided in preference by some eccentric principles of socialistic philanthropy, or by a feminist ambition to secure the equality of the sexes in the matter of wages in the world of labour.

... It was strongly pressed in argument that the auditor believed the council acted bona fide; but what in this connection do the words 'bona fide' mean? Do they mean, as apparently this gentleman thought, that no matter how excessive or illegal their scale of wages might be, they were bound to put it into force because their constituents gave them a mandate so to do, or again, do the words mean that as the payment of wages was a subject with which they had legally power to deal, the amount of their funds which they devoted to that purpose was their own concern which no auditor had jurisdiction to revise, or in reference to which he could surcharge anything? The whole system of audit to which the Legislature has subjected every municipal corporation or council is a most emphatic protest against such opinions as these....

... [A]s wages are remuneration for services, the words 'think fit' [in section 62] must, I think, be construed to mean 'as the employer shall think fitting and proper' for the services rendered. It cannot, in my view, mean that the employer, especially an employer dealing with moneys not entirely his own, may pay to his employee wages of any amount he pleases. Still less does it mean that he can pay gratuities or gifts to his employees disguised under the name of wages....

What is a reasonable wage at any time must depend, of course, on the circumstances which then exist in the labour market. I do not say there must be any cheeseparing or that the datum line, as I have called it, must never be exceeded to any extent, or that employees may not be generously treated. But it does not appear to me that there is any rational proportion between the rates of wages at which the labour of these women is paid and the rates at which they would be reasonably remunerated for their services to the council.

LORD SUMNER: ... The respondents conceded that for wages fixed mala fide no exemption from review could be claimed and that the mere magnitude of the wages paid, relatively to the wages for which the same service was procurable, might be enough in itself to establish bad faith. This admission, I am sure, was rightly made, but it leads to two conclusions. Firstly, the final words of the section are not absolute, but are subject to an implied qualification of good faith – 'as the board may bona fide think fit.' Is the implication of good faith all? That is a qualification drawn from the general legal doctrine, that persons who hold public office have a legal responsibility towards those whom they represent – not merely towards those who vote for them – to the discharge of which they must honestly apply their minds. Bona fide here cannot simply mean that they are not making a profit out of their office or acting in it from private spite, nor is bona fide a short way of saying that the council has acted within the ambit of its powers and therefore not contrary to law. It must mean that they are giving their minds to the comprehension and their wills to the discharge of their duty towards that public, whose money and local business they administer.

The purpose, however, of the whole audit is to ensure wise and prudent administration and to recover for the council's funds money that should not have been taken out of them. If, having examined the expenditure and found clear proof of bad faith, which admittedly would open the account, the auditor further found that the councillors' evil minds had missed their mark, and the expenditure itself was right, then the expenditure itself would not be 'contrary to law' and could not be disallowed. Bad faith admittedly vitiates the council's purported exercise of its discretion, but the auditor is not confined to asking, if the discretion, such as it may be, has been honestly exercised. He has to restrain expenditure within proper limits. His mission is to inquire if there is any excess over what is reasonable. I do not find any words limiting his functions merely to the case of bad faith, or obliging him to leave the ratepayers unprotected from the effects on their pockets of honest stupidity or unpractical idealism. The breach in the words 'as they may think fit,' which the admitted implication as to bad faith makes, is wide enough to make the necessary implication one both of honesty and of reasonableness. . . .

Much was said at the Bar about the wide discretion conferred by the Local Government Acts on local authorities. In a sense this is true, but the meaning of the term needs careful examination. What has been said in cases, which lie outside the provisions as to audit altogether, is not necessarily applicable to matters, which are concerned with the expenditure of public money. There are many matters, which the Courts are indisposed to question. Though they are the ultimate judges of what is lawful and what is unlawful to borough councils, they often accept the decisions of the local authority simply because they are themselves ill equipped to weigh the merits of one solution of a practical question as against another. This, however, is not a recognition of the absolute character of the local authority's discretion, but of the limits within which it is practicable to question it. There is nothing about a borough council that corresponds to autonomy. It has great reponsibilities, but the limits of its powers and of its independence are such as the law, mostly statutory, may have laid down, and there is no presumption against the accountability of the authority. Everything depends on the construction of the sections applicable. In the present case, I think that the auditor was entitled to inquire into all the items of expenditure in question, to ask whether in incurring them the council had been guided by aims and objects not open to them or had disregarded considerations by which they should have been guided, and to the extent to which they had in consequence exceeded a reasonable expenditure, it was his duty to disallow the items.

[After considering the facts, his Lordship said:] I think it is plain that the respondents have deliberately decided not to be guided by ordinary economic (and economical) considerations. . . . I am . . . of opinion that on their own showing the respondents have exercised such discretion as the Metropolis Management Act gives to the council in the matter of wages upon principles which are not open to the council, and for objects which are beyond their powers. Their exercise of those powers was examinable by the auditor, and on the above grounds the excess expenditure was liable to be disallowed by him as contrary to law. . . .

[LORD WRENBURY and LORD CARSON delivered speeches in favour of allowing the appeal.]

Appeal allowed.

Notes

1. The powers of the district auditor are now substantially different and are governed by ss. 19 ff. of the Local Government 1982 on which see Jones, [1982] L.G.C. 886. The power to surcharge had been removed by s. 121 of the Local Government Act 1972 and replaced by a procedure involving a court order.

2. In *Prescott* v. *Birmingham Corporation* [1955] Ch. 210 the Corporation owned and operated a transport undertaking and had statutory power to charge fares (subject to prescribed maxima) for the conveyance of passengers. There was no express obligation to charge all passengers at the same rate and the Corporation decided to provide free travel for certain classes of old persons. This would have cost an estimated £90,000 per annum and a ratepayer successfully sought a declaration that the scheme was ultra vires. It was argued that age, means, and health were relevant factors in deciding whether any, and if so what, discrimination should be made in favour of certain classes of potential passengers. Jenkins L.J. (delivering the judgment of the Court of Appeal) said (at pp. 235–6):

[L]ocal authorities running an omnibus undertaking at the risk of their ratepayers, in the sense that any deficiencies must be met by an addition to the rates, are not, in our view, entitled, merely on the strength of a general power, to charge different fares to different passengers or classes of passengers, to make a gift to a particular class of persons of rights of free travel on their vehicles, simply because the local authority concerned are of opinion that the favoured class of persons ought, on benevolent or philanthropic grounds, to be accorded that benefit. In other words, they are not, in our view, entitled to use their discriminatory power as proprietors of the transport undertaking in order to confer out of rates a special benefit on some particular class of inhabitants whom they, as the local authority for the town or district in question, may think deserving of such assistance. In the absence of clear statutory authority for such a proceeding (which to our mind a mere general power to charge differential fares certainly is not) we would, for our part regard it as illegal. . . . We think it is clearly implicit in the legislation, that while it was left to the defendants to decide what fares should be charged within any prescribed statutory maxima for the time being in force, the undertaking was to be run as a business venture, or, in other words, that fares fixed by the defendants at their discretion, in accordance with ordinary business principles, were to be charged. That is not to say that in operating their transport undertaking the defendants should be guided by considerations of profit to the exclusion of all other considerations. They should, no doubt, aim at providing an efficient service of omnibuses at reasonable cost, and it may be that this objective is impossible of attainment without some degree of loss. But it by no means follows that they should go out of their way to make losses by giving away rights of free travel.

. . . In our opinion the scheme now in question goes beyond anything which can reasonably be regarded as authorized by the discretionary power of fixing fares and differentiation in the fares charged to different passengers or classes of passengers possessed by the defendants under the relevant legislation, and is, accordingly, ultra vires the defendants.

See also *Taylor* v. *Munrow* [1960] 1 W.L.R. 151, noted by Wade, [1960] C.L.J. 135, in which a council's decision not to use a power to raise rents and not to investigate the means of individual tenants because of opposition to the Rent Act 1957 and a dislike of means tests was held ultra vires. The particular scheme struck down in *Prescott's* case and other existing free travel schemes operated by local authorities were retrospectively validated by the Public Service Vehicles (Travel Concessions) Act 1955, but the court's approach to the exercise of general discretionary powers by local authorities remained valid. See Fox, (1956) 72 L.Q.R. 237. On the duties of municipal authorities to ratepayers, which were said in *Prescott's* case to be 'fiduciary' ([1955] Ch. 210 at p. 235), see further Wade, pp. 379–81, and *Arsenal F.C. Ltd.* v. *Ende* [1979] A.C. 1. The fiduciary nature of the duty was confirmed by the House of Lords in *Bromley L.B.C.* v. *G.L.C.* [1982] 2 W.L.R. 762. In that case Lord Wilberforce also said (at p. 94) that *Roberts* v. *Hopwood* 'remains authoritative as to principle although social considerations may have changed since 1925'.

3. In *R.* v. *Barnet and Camden Rent Tribunal, ex p. Frey Investments Ltd.* [1972] 2 Q.B. 342 it was suggested that the 'relevant considerations' test did not always apply. There the power of a local authority to refer furnished tenancies to a rent tribunal (see also p. 47 *supra*) was considered. The landlord contended that the reference was invalid because the authority had considered two irrelevant matters (representations by a local pressure group and the landlord's refusal to permit inspection of other premises belonging to it) and had failed to consider the tenants' views and whether a reference was likely to result in a reduction of rent. The Court of Appeal held that the reference was valid on the grounds, *inter alia*, that it was neither frivolous, capricious, nor vexatious, and that, as it did not affect the landlord's basic rights, the fact that the authority might have considered irrelevant factors or failed to consider relevant ones did not necessarily vitiate their decision. It should, however, be noted that neither Salmon L.J. nor Edmund Davies L.J. thought that the authority had in fact erred in this way. Stamp L.J. said (at p. 368) that the 'relevant considerations' test only applied where an authority '[has] to weigh, and [has] an obvious duty to weigh, one thing against the other and there is a body of legislation guiding [it] in the performance of [its] powers or duties', but he also agreed that it did not apply 'to a purely administrative decision not affecting rights'. Edmund Davies L.J. (at pp. 364–5) also mentioned the inability of the authority to compel information, and so it could not be blamed for failing to take account of a relevant matter. Are any of the restrictions suggested by the *Barnet and Camden* case sound? See Wade, p. 377.

De Smith has argued ((1972) 35 M.L.R. 415 at p. 416) that the *Barnet and Camden* case 'underline[s] the point that, as a general rule, the test of relevancy is material only in so far as the considerations taken (or not taken) into account actually affect or must be presumed to have affected the *quality* of the administrative decision'. Do you agree with this as a general proposition? See Appendix and consider also *Pickwell* v. *Camden L.B.C.*, [1983] 2 W.L.R. 583; *Chief Constable of North Wales Police* v. *Evans* [1982] 1 W.L.R. 1155 at p. 1175, noted at p. 283 *infra*.

4. In the *Barnet and Camden* case Lord Edmund-Davies said (at p. 367) that the question of whether an authority is entitled to allow their determination to be affected by a pressure group 'must depend on what the action group say and how they say it, and, in so far as their assertion could be tested, the extent to which it appeared to have some foundation. If it was manifestly baseless, if there were suspicion of some ulterior motive, be it financial or political or inspired solely by personal aggrandisement, then of course the Council should dismiss it from their minds. But if what was said by the action group provided food for thought, and if it appeared to have at least some reasonable degree of support, for my part I reject the idea that it would be improper to be influenced by what the action group said'. Why should the motives of such an outside body determine whether the actions of a public authority are intra vires? What dangers are there in being influenced by the opinions of pressure groups? (See p. 138 *supra.*)

5. The question of what will, in a particular case, be a relevant consideration has given rise to difficulty. In *Bristol D.C. v. Clark* [1975] 1 W.L.R. 1443 the question whether the Council, which sought to exercise a statutory power to evict a tenant in arrears, should take account of the guidance on alternative procedures to eviction given in circulars issued by the Department of Health and Social Security and the Department of the Environment, was answered affirmatively. Scarman L.J. said (at p. 1451) that it was not 'possible to rely on these circulars as imposing any direct statutory duty on a housing authority; but I think they are a good indication as to the purposes to be served by the Housing Acts and as to what are relevant matters within the language of Lord Greene M.R. in the *Wednesbury Corporation* case [1948] 1 K.B. 223, 233 to be taken into account by a local authority serving a notice to quit'. He went on to say that '[r]elevance and materiality will vary from case to case' and should not be determined by an examination of the statutory power which is divorced from the facts. The radically different context of *Congreve* v. *Home Office* [1976] Q.B. 629 may explain the apparently contradictory statement by Roskill L.J. (at p. 658) that the intention of Parliament (and therefore the relevance of a particular consideration) is, in the majority of cases, 'to be ascertained only from the relevant legislation, be it statute or delegated legislation. How the [government department] interpreted or sought to administer that legislation is irrelevant'. See also *Lewis Group* v. *Wiggins* [1973] I.C.R. 335 (statutory code of practice an important factor but not determinative; its significance varies according to the circumstances of each individual case).

Bristol D.C. v. *Clark* has been criticized for providing a means for central government to circumscribe the exercise of discretions given to local authorities (Buxton, (1976) 39 M.L.R. 470 at p. 473). In practice, will this be done to an unjustifiable extent? See p. 138 *supra* (rules against abdication and surrender of discretion and over-rigid policies) and *Secretary of State for Education and Science* v. *Tameside M.B.C.*, p. 182 *infra.*

6. There are examples of statutory prescription of relevant considerations. See, for instance, s. 25 (2) of the Consumer Credit Act 1974; s. 4 (1) of the Housing Act 1957; and s. 29 of the Town and Country Planning Act 1971. It is for the courts to determine whether the authority is bound to have regard to the listed circumstances. Although the formula 'may have regard' is normally construed as merely permissive (*Perry* v. *Wright* [1908] 1 K.B. 441 at p. 458; *R.* v. *Greater Birmingham Appeal Tribunal, ex p. Simper* [1974] Q.B. 543), this is not always the case (*Yorkshire Copper Works Ltd.* v. *Registrar of Trade Marks* [1954] 1 W.L.R. 554). For discussion of mandatory and permissive (or directory) requirements, see p. 17 *supra.*

EXPRESS AND IMPLIED STATUTORY PURPOSES:
MIXED MOTIVES

Municipal Council of Sydney v. Campbell

[1925] A.C. 339   Judicial Committee of the Privy Council

The facts are sufficiently stated in the judgment. For a fuller statement see (1924) 24 S.R. (N.S.W.) 179.

The judgment of their Lordships was delivered by MR JUSTICE DUFF. By s. 16 of the Sydney Corporation Amendment Act, 1905, the Municipal Council of Sydney is empowered from time to time, with the approval of the Governor, to purchase or 'resume' any land required for 'carrying out improvements in or remodelling any portion of the city.' . . . By s. 3 of an amending Act of 1906, the Council is authorized to purchase or 'resume' any lands required for the opening of new public ways or for widening, enlarging or extending any public ways in the city, as well as any lands of which those required for such purposes are a part.

On March 12, 1923, the Lord Mayor prepared a minute relating to the subject of the extension of Martin Place, an important thoroughfare in the centre of Sydney, and in this minute he recommended the extension of Martin Place to Macquarie Street, and the resumption of a considerable area, which embraced property belonging to the respondents. The proposals of the Lord Mayor's minute were adopted by a resolution of the Council on June 28, and the resumption provided for by the resolutiuon was approved by the Governor in Council.

On the application of the respondents, injunctions were granted by the Chief Judge in Equity, restraining the Council from proceeding under this resolution; and subsequently the Lord Mayor presented another minute, and on November 29 another resolution was passed by the Council, authorizing the resumption of the identical area affected by the former resolution. Again proceedings were taken before the Chief Judge in Equity, who granted injunctions restraining the Council from proceeding under the second resolution; and at the hearing of the actions these injunctions were made permanent. Admittedly, the Council had authority (under s. 3 of the amending Act of 1906) to 'resume' lands for the purpose of extending Martin Place. It is also undisputed that the lands of the respondents which the Council proposes to take are not within the limits of any area which could be required for that purpose. The right to resume them is based upon the assertion that they are 'required' for the purpose of remodelling and improving the city within the sense of s. 16 of the Sydney Corporation Amendment Act.

The learned Chief Judge in Equity held that in point of fact these lands were not really 'required' for any such purpose, but that, as in the case of the other parts of the area affected which were not necessary for the extension of the street, the resumption proceedings were taken with the object of enabling the Council to get the benefit of any increment in the value of them arising from the extension, and thus, in some degree at all events, recouping the municipality the cost of it; and that, since the resumption of lands for such a purpose alone was indisputably not within the ambit of the authority committed to the Council, the resolutions of June and November were both invalid. . . .

The legal principles governing the execution of such powers as that conferred by s. 16, in so far as presently relevant, are not at all in controversy. A body such as the Municipal Council of Sydney, authorized to take land compulsorily for specified purposes, will not be permitted to exercise its powers for different purposes, and if it attempts to do so, the Courts will interfere. As Lord Loreburn said, in *Marquess of Clanricarde* v. *Congested Districts Board:*[6] 'Whether it does so or not is a question of fact.' Where the proceedings of the Council are attacked upon this ground, the party impeaching those proceedings must, of course, prove that the Council, though professing to exercise its powers for that statutory purpose, is in fact employing them in furtherance of some ulterior object.

Their Lordships think that the conclusion of the learned Chief Judge in Equity upon this question of fact is fully sustained by the evidence. . . . [I]t is admitted that no plan of improvement or remodelling was at any time before the Council; and their Lordships think there is great force in the argument that the course of the oral discussion, as disclosed in the shorthand note produced, shows, when the events leading up to the second minute of the Lord Mayor are considered, that in November the Council was applying itself to the purpose of giving a new form to a transaction already decided upon, rather than to the consideration and determination of the question whether the lands to be taken were required for the purpose of remodelling or improvement. Their Lordships think the learned Chief Judge was right in his conclusion, that upon this question there was no real decision or determination by the Council.

Their Lordships accordingly will humbly advise His Majesty that this appeal should be dismissed with costs.

Appeal dismissed.

Notes

1. Many other examples of the same principle could be given. Thus, a power 'to carry out such coast protection work . . . as may appear to [a coast protection authority] to be necessary or expedient for the protection of any land in their area' and compulsorily to acquire land for this purpose could not be used to acquire land for a footpath as well as a sea-wall: *Webb* v. *Minister of Housing and Local Government* [1965] 1 W.L.R. 755. This case also illustrates the fact that judicial review will not be ousted by a subjectively worded statutory formula, on which see also p. 183 *infra*.

2. Establishing the purpose of an act is not always as easy as the judgment in *Municipal Council of Sydney* v. *Campbell, supra,* may suggest. In *R.* v. *Governor of Brixton Prison, ex p. Soblen* [1963] 2 Q.B. 243 at p. 308, Donovan L.J. stated that where the difficulty arises because of the withholding of evidence under a claim of Crown privilege (now called public interest immunity – see p. 461 *infra*) an applicant will seldom be able to do more than raise a *prima facie* case or sow such substantial and

[6] 79 J.P. 481.

disquieting doubts in the mind of the court about the bona fides of the order he is challenging that the court will consider that some answer is called for. 'If that answer is withheld, or . . . is found unsatisfactory, then, in my view, the order challenged ought not to be upheld, for otherwise there would be virtually no protection for the subject against some illegal order which had been clothed with the garments of legality simply for the sake of appearances and where discovery was resisted on the ground of privilege'. (See also p. 29 *supra* on the duty to give reasons.)

3. It is rare to find a statutory authorization to act for a single clear-cut purpose, and it is equally rare for an authority to have one exclusive purpose in mind when exercising its statutory powers. Often it will have several in mind, some legitimate and others not, and the question is whether the mere presence of an unauthorized purpose vitiates the exercise of the power. This is the concern of the next extract, but see also Note 1, p. 180 *infra*.

Westminster Corporation v. London and North Western Railway Co.

[1905] A.C. 426   House of Lords

The corporation had power to provide public conveniences and to construct these in, on, or under any road. It built an underground convenience in the middle of Parliament Street with access from the pavement on either side of the street. The appellant railway company owned premises opposite one of the entrances to the convenience and sought to have the conveniences removed. The company alleged that the Corporation wished to build a subway which it had no power to do. This extract is only concerned with the purposes for which the Corporation acted.

EARL OF HALSBURY L.C.: My Lords, it seems to me that the power of the local authority to erect certain public conveniences cannot be disputed. The shape, site, and extent of them are left to the discretion of the authority in question, and so far as regards the things themselves, which, under this discretion, have been erected, I do not understand that any objection can be made. The objections, so far as they assume the force of legal objections, refer to the access to them, and to the supported motives of the local authority in the selection of the site.

Assuming the thing done to be within the discretion of the local authority, no Court has power to interfere with the mode in which it has exercised it. . . .

It appears to me impossible to contend that these conveniences are not the things authorized by the Legislature. It seems to me that the provision of the statute itself contemplates that such conveniences should be made beneath public roads, and if beneath public roads some access underneath the road level must be provided; and if some access must be provided, it must be a measure simply of greater and less convenience, when the street is a wide one, whether an access should be provided at only one or at both sides of the street. That if the access is provided at both sides of the street, it is possible that people who have no desire or necessity to use the convenience will nevertheless pass through it to avoid the dangers of crossing the carriageway seems to me to form no objection to the provision itself; and I decline altogether to sit in judgment upon the discretion of the local authorities upon such materials as are before us.

I quite agree that if the power to make one kind of building was fraudulently used for the purpose of making another kind of building, the power given by the Legislature for one purpose could not be used for another . . .

LORD MACNAGHTEN: . . . It is not enough to shew that the corporation contemplated that the public might use the subway as a means of crossing the street. That was an obvious possibility. It cannot be otherwise if you have an entrance on each side and the communication is not interrupted by a wall or a barrier of some sort. In order to make out a case of bad faith it must be shewn that the corporation constructed this subway as a means of crossing the street under colour and pretence of providing public conveniences which were not really wanted at that particular place. . . .

LORD JAMES: . . . And so the question to be solved seems to be thus formulated. Was the so-called tunnel an approach to the convenience only, or was it something more? (1.) was it a subway distinct from the approach, or (2.) was it a subway in combination with the approach used for two distinct purposes?

In my judgment the construction in question comes within one or other of the two latter alternatives. Possibly within the first, certainly within the second.

If this finding on the facts be correct, the works, so far as they constitute the subway, are constructed without legal authority. The Legislature has not thought it right to confer on local bodies the power to compulsorily take land or impose rates for the purpose of constructing subways. . . .

Question

In what way does Lord James's approach in the *Westminster Corporation* case differ from the majority? See p. 180 *infra* and the decision in the court below: [1904] 1 Ch. 759.

Notes

1. The courts have also limited the ambit of apparently wide statutory discretions by reference to the implied purposes of the statute and Lord Diplock has stated ([1974] C.L.J. 233 at p,. 243) that the growing tendency to give statutes a purposive construction has led to the extension of the concept of error of law because it would be a misconstruction and hence an error of law to act for the wrong purpose. On review for error of law see pp. 53 and 57 *supra*. *Mixnams Properties Ltd.* v. *Chertsey U.D.C.* [1965] A.C. 735, noted at p. 9 *supra*, and *Padfield* v. *Minister of Agriculture, Fisheries and Food*, p. 164 *supra*, are examples of this. The courts will not, however, always subject a statute to a purposive interpretation. For instance, in *British Oxygen Co. Ltd.* v. *Minister of Technology*, p. 141 *supra*, the House of Lords refused to limit a discretionary power under the Industrial Development Act 1966 to make grants. It rejected the argument that the statutory object was to promote the modernization of machinery and plant and that, therefore, the Minister was bound to make grants to all who were eligible unless the expenditure would not promote the alleged object of the statute. The court did not attribute any other purpose to the statute: [1971] A.C. at p. 624 per Lord Reid. Similarly, in *R.* v. *Barnet and Camden Rent Tribunal, ex p. Frey*

Investments Ltd. [1972] 2 Q.B. 342, noted at p. 174 *supra*, the Court of Appeal, considering the power of a local authority to refer furnished tenancies to a rent tribunal, did not consider whether the power was to be used only for certain purposes and seemed to say that unless it was used in a frivolous or vexatious manner no interference was possible.

The question of when a court will use a purposive interpretation is a difficult one. It is linked with the question of whether review on the ground of abuse of discretion permits the indiscriminate selection of this technique for review or the alternative 'relevant considerations' or 'relevance' technique (on which see p. 164 *supra*) simply to suit the conclusion sought to be reached on the merits.

Taylor has argued ([1976] C.L.J. 272) that the proper ground of review is determined by the form of the empowering provision. Purposive interpretations should be used where an enabling statute does not enumerate reasons for action but gives an authority discretion as to its reasons. Where the statute does enumerate reasons the 'relevant considerations' technique should be used. This pattern does not, however, reflect the state of the authorities. It is equally possible to assert that a purposive interpretation, and hence wider review, is more likely to be adopted where the exercise of discretion can be categorized as having a direct impact on a person's rights. Compare the *Mixnam's Properties* case [1965] A.C. 735, noted at p. 9 *supra* (property rights and freedom of contract) and *Padfield*, p. 164 *supra* (freedom of contract) with the *British Oxygen* case, p. 141 *supra* (government grant), and the *Barnet and Camden Rent Tribunal* case (the reference to the tribunal would not automatically prejudice the landlords). Alternatively, it can be said to depend on the *nature* of the factors conditioning an exercise of discretionary power. If, as in *Asher* v. *Secretary of State for the Environment* [1974] Ch. 208, noted at p. 143 *supra*, and *Dowty Boulton Paul Ltd.* v. *Wolverhampton Corporation (No. 2)* [1976] Ch. 13, noted at p. 51 *supra*, they involve political considerations or questions of comparative needs upon which a minister or authority is best qualified to judge, it is unlikely that a purposive interpretation will be used. In the latter case the question was almost put in terms of justiciability. In *Bromley L.B.C.* v. *G.L.C.* [1982] 2 W.L.R. 62 Lord Diplock stated (at p. 100) that a court was less likely to imply purposes where the power was given to a government minister that where it was given to a local authority.

The relationship between the purposive technique and the 'relevance' technique also causes difficulties. The techniques are, as de Smith has pointed out (p. 332), intimately related and often analytically indistinguishable. In most cases the technique adopted will not affect the result of a case but three points should be noted. The 'relevance' technique lends itself to a more literal construction of the statute, while the purposive technique, which tends to invoke the 'golden' or 'mischief' rules of statutory interpretation, is likely to lead to a narrower range of permissible objects. Secondly, it has been suggested that the 'relevance' test does not apply in all cases (p. 174 *supra*), and it is just possible, though unlikely, that in such a situation review will be available by virtue of the statute being given a purposive interpretation. Finally, the 'relevance' technique may have one advantage. Where it applies, it will be seen that if an authority is influenced by an irrelevant factor, it will be held to act ultra vires even if this factor is not the dominant factor motivating it. Cf. Note 3 p. 178 *supra* and the Appendix.

2. Sometimes an authority will be able to choose the method by which it achieves its purpose. In *Westminster Bank Ltd.* v. *Minister of Housing and Local Government* [1971] A.C. 508 planning permission was refused because of an ill-defined road-widening scheme. This was done under discretionary power given to local authorities by the Town and Country Planning Act 1962, although there was also power, under

s. 72 of the Highways Act 1959, to reserve – and therefore prevent – the development of land required for road-widening on payment of compensation. No compensation was payable on a simple refusal of planning permission. The landowner sought to set aside the refusal of permission on the ground that the scope of the planning legislation was limited so as to exclude situations governed by the Highways Act. This was rejected, partly because s. 220 of the Town and Country Planning Act 1962 stated that the planning legislation was applicable despite the existence of any other statute providing for the regulation of development. Lord Reid said (at p. 530):

> Parliament has chosen to set up two different ways of preventing development which would interfere with schemes for street widening. It must have been aware that one involved paying compensation but the other did not. Nevertheless it expressed no preference, and imposed no limit on the use of either. No doubt there might be special circumstances which make it unreasonable or an abuse of power to use one of these methods but here there were none. Even if the appellants' view of the facts is right, the authority had to choose whether to leave the appellants without compensation or to impose a burden on its ratepayers.

See also *Asher* v. *Secretary of State for the Environment* [1974] Ch. 208, noted at p. 143 *supra; Hoveringham Gravels Ltd.* v. *Secretary of State for the Environment* [1974] Q.B. 754; Wade, p. 368; cf. *Hall & Co. Ltd.* v. *Shoreham U.D.C.* [1964] 1 W.L.R. 240.

In general, however, the courts will incline the view that if a public body has statutory powers which it may at will exercise in a manner hurtful to third parties' rights, or in a manner innocuous to those rights, the body is not entitled to choose the former mode unless, as in the *Westminster Bank* case, this is specifically authorized: *Lagan Navigation Co.* v. *Lambeg Bleaching, Dyeing and Finishing Co.* [1927] A.C. 226 at p. 243; *Robins* v. *Minister of Health* [1939] 1 K.B. 520 at p. 531.

3. Planning authorities may well try to evade judicial limitation of the purposes for which they can act or the conditions which they may impose. The use of agreements with developers to achieve the sort of result which has been struck down by courts is well documented: Jowell, [1977] J.P.L. 414; Grant, [1978] J.P.L. 8; Tucker, [1978] J.P.L. 806; Report of the Property Advisory Group, *Planning Gain*; Law Society's Observations on the Report of the Property Advisory Group, [1982] J.P.L. 346. The dangers in planning by agreements are that there are no procedural controls in the bargaining process to control corruption and abuse of discretion, to ensure even-handedness, and to prevent authorities from shifting their responsibilities on to the developer. The process also takes place in relative secrecy (cf. Loughlin, [1978] J.P.L. 290; (1981) 1 O.J.L.S. 61 at pp. 89 ff.).

GOOD FAITH

Westminster Corporation v. London and North Western Railway Co., p. 178 *supra*

Associated Provincial Picture Houses v. Wednesbury Corporation Ltd., p. 118 *supra*

Smith v. East Elloe Rural District Council, p. 380 *infra*

Note

In the context of judicial review bad faith has been seen as a wider concept than dishonesty (Wade, p. 391), including mistakes as to the extent of an authority's powers and other instances of ultra vires acts. In this sense it is rarely seen as an independent ground of review from extraneous considerations and unreasonableness: see for instance Lord Sumner in *Roberts* v. *Hopwood*, p. 172 *supra*. This has been criticized by the Court of Appeal in *Western Fish Products Ltd.* v. *Penwith D.C.* [1981] 2 All E.R. 204 at pp. 215–6 on the ground that '[i]t is not fair to a public authority or its members or its servants that the public, not versed in the technical jargon, should read that a court has held them to be guilty of "bad faith" when they have made an honest mistake. Nor is the use of the phrase in such a technical sense conducive to preserving the seriousness of a finding of bad faith where there has been dishonesty.' See further de Smith, pp. 324, 335–7, and 408–9; p. 120 *supra*; p. 424 *infra*.

SUBJECTIVE LANGUAGE

Padfield v. Minister of Agriculture, Fisheries and Food, p. 164 *supra*

Secretary of State for Education and Science v. Tameside Metropolitan Borough Council, *infra*

Note

See pp. 5 and 171 *supra* and pp. 190 and 512 *infra*. See further Wade, p. 393; de Smith, pp. 291–4.

REASONABLENESS

Roberts v. Hopwood, p. 169 *supra*

Associated Provincial Picture Houses Ltd. v. Wednesbury Corporation, p. 118 *supra*

Question

In what way, if any, is 'unreasonableness' an independent ground for judicial review of abuse of discretion? What is its relationship with the other grounds of review? See further Wade, pp. 348–50, 353–5, and pp. 372 ff.

Secretary of State for Education and Science v. Tameside Metropolitan Borough Council

[1977] A.C. 1014   House of Lords

A local education authority's scheme for introducing comprehensive education was approved by the Secretary of State in November 1975, and was due to be implemented at the beginning of the school year in September 1976. Control of the council and the education authority changed as a result of local elections in May 1976 and the new majority, which had promised to reconsider the question of comprehensive education in its election literature, proposed to postpone plans to convert a number of grammar schools. The authority informed the Secretary of State that the schools in the area were not ready for the changes which, if implemented then, would, in its view, gravely disrupt the children's education. It proposed to retain 240 selective places for eleven-year-olds and planned to select them by a combination of reports, records, and interviews. 783 applications (in response to letters sent to 3,200 parents) were made for these places. Section 68 of the Education Act 1944 gives the Secretary of State power to give such directions as to the exercise of any power or duty given to or imposed on any local education authority 'as appear to him to be expedient' provided that he 'is satisfied, either on complaint by any person or otherwise, that any local education authority . . . have acted or are proposing to act unreasonably with respect to the exercise of any power conferred or the performance of any duty imposed by or under this Act'. Acting under this section, he directed the authority to implement the scheme approved by him in 1975 including the arrangements previously made for the allocation of eleven-year-olds on a non-selective basis. He then applied for an order of mandamus to compel compliance with the direction. The Divisional Court made the order but their decision was reversed by the Court of Appeal. The Secretary of State appealed:

LORD WILBERFORCE: . . . [Section 68] does not say what the consequences of giving of directions are to be, but I accept, for the purposes of the appeal, that the consequences are to impose on the authority a statutory duty to comply with them which can be enforced by an order of mandamus.

Analysis of the section brings out three cardinal points.

(1) The matters with which the section is concerned are primarily matters of educational administration. The action which the Secretary of State is entitled to stop is unreasonable action with respect to the exercise of a power or the performance of a duty – the power and the duty of the authority are presupposed and cannot be interfered with. Local education authorities are entitled under the Act to have a policy, and this section does not enable the Secretary of State to require them to abandon or reverse a policy just because the Secretary of State disagrees with it. Specifically, the Secretary of State cannot use power under this section to impose a general policy of comprehensive education upon a local education authority which does not agree with the policy. He cannot direct them to bring in a scheme for total comprehensive education in their area, and if they have done so he cannot direct them to implement it. If he tries to use a direction under section 68 for this purpose, his direction would be clearly invalid. . . .

The critical question in this case, and it is not an easy one, is whether, on a matter which appears to be one of educational administration, namely whether the change of course proposed by the council in May 1976 would lead to educational chaos or undue disruption, the Secretary of State's judgment can be challenged.

(2) The section is framed in a 'subjective' form – if the Secretary of State 'is satisfied.' This form of section is quite well known, and at first sight might seem to exclude judicial review. Sections in this form may, no doubt, exclude judicial review on what is or has become a matter of pure judgment. But I do not think that they go further than that. If a judgment requires, before it can

be made, the existence of some facts, then, although the evaluation of those facts is for the Secretary of State alone, the court must inquire whether those facts exist, and have been taken into account, whether the judgment has been made upon a proper self-direction as to those facts, whether the judgment has not been made upon other facts which ought not to have been taken into account. If these requirements are not met, then the exercise of judgment, however bona fide it may be, becomes capable of challenge: see *Secretary of State for Employment* v. *ASLEF (No. 2)* [1972] 2 Q.B. 455, *per* Lord Denning M.R., at p. 493.

(3) The section has to be considered within the structure of the Act. In many statutes a minister or other authority is given a discretionary power and in these cases the court's power to review any exercise of the discretion, though still real, is limited. In these cases it is said that the courts cannot substitute their opinion for that of the minister: they can interfere on such grounds as that the minister has acted right outside his powers or outside the purpose of the Act, or unfairly, or upon an incorrect basis of fact. But there is no universal rule as to the principles on which the exercise of a discretion may be reviewed: each statute or type of statute must be individually looked at. This Act, of 1944, is quite different from those which simply create a ministerial discretion. The Secretary of State, under section 68, is not merely exercising a discretion: he is reviewing the action of another public body which itself has discretionary powers and duties. He, by contrast with the courts in the normal case, may substitute his opinion for that of the authority: this is what the section allows, but he must take account of what the authority, under the statute, is entitled to do. The authority – this is vital – is itself elected, and is given specific powers as to the kind of schools it wants in its area. Therefore two situations may arise. One is that there may be a difference of policy between the Secretary of State (under Parliament) and the local authority: the section gives no power to the Secretary of State to make his policy prevail. The other is that, owing to the democratic process involving periodic elections, abrupt reversals of policy may take place, particularly where there are only two parties and the winner takes all. Any reversal of policy if at all substantial must cause some administrative disruption – this was as true of the 1975 proposals as of those of the respondents. So the mere possibility, or probability of disruption cannot be a ground for issuing a direction to abandon the policy. What the Secretary of State is entitled, by a direction if necessary, to ensure is that such disruptions are not 'unreasonable,' i.e., greater than a body, elected to carry out a new programme, with which the Secretary of State may disagree, ought to impose upon those for whom it is responsible. After all, those who voted for the new programme, involving a change of course, must also be taken to have accepted some degree of disruption in implementing it.

The ultimate question in this case, in my opinion, is whether the Secretary of State has given sufficient, or any, weight to this particular factor in the exercise of his judgment.

I must now inquire what were the facts upon which the Secretary of State expressed himself as satisfied that the council were acting or proposing to act unreasonably. The Secretary of State did not give oral evidence in the courts, and the facts on which he acted must be taken from the department's letters at the relevant time – i.e., on or about June 11, 1976 – and from affidavits sworn by its officers. These documents are to be read fairly and in bonam partem. If reasons are given in general terms, the court should not exclude reasons which fairly fall within them: allowance must be fairly made for difficulties in expression. The Secretary of State must be given credit for having the background to this actual situation well in mind, and must be taken to be properly and professionally informed as to educational practices used in the area, and as to resources available to the local education authority. His opinion, based, as it must be, upon that of a strong and expert department, is not to be lightly overridden. . . .

On June 11, the direction under section 68 was given in a letter of that date. The letter stated that the Secretary of State was satisfied that the authority was proposing to act unreasonably according to the formula used in section 68 of the Act. A change of plan designed to come into effect in less than three months must, in the opinion of the Secretary of State, give rise to 'considerable difficulties.' It pointed out that over 3,000 pupils transferring from primary schools had already been allocated and allotted places. Then followed this paragraph (which I shall call 'paragraph A').

'The authority's revised proposals *confront* the parents of children due to transfer in September *with the dilemma* of either adhering to secondary school allocations for their children which they may no longer regard as appropriate, or else *submitting* to an improvised selection procedure (the precise form of which, the Secretary of State understands, has even now not been settled) carried out in circumstances and under a timetable which raise substantial doubts about its educational validity.' (My emphasis.)

A further objection was taken to the proposed possible reallocation during or after the first year. . . . The change of plan at this time in the educational year threatened to give rise to practical difficulties in relation to the appointments of staff already made and the construction of buildings for the new comprehensive schools and to create a degree of confusion and uncertainty which could impair the efficient working of the schools.

These arguments were restated and expended in the affidavit sworn on behalf of the · Secretary of State in support of the application for mandamus, . . . were dealt with fully by the authority and I need say no more about them than that they were completely exploded. . . .

Some attempt was made to rehabilitate these points in this House, but learned counsel decided, no doubt wisely, to concentrate on the allocation issue. But these three points cannot just be discarded as if they had never been made. They form part of a composite set of facts relied upon as showing unreasonable conduct, and I am not at all sure that the disappearance of so many planks does not fatally weaken the stability of the platform. At the least – and I will give the department the benefit of this assumption – the remaining factual basis would need to be strong and clear if it alone were to be the basis for the Secretary of State's 'satisfaction' as to unreasonable conduct.

So I come to the question of allocation, which was at the centre of the case as argued, and it can best be approached via 'paragraph A' above, a paragraph which I regard as revealing. It shows a very strange attitude toward the decision taken by the authority. After the electorate, including no doubt a large number of parents, had voted the new council into office on the platform that some selective basis would be preserved, to say that this created 'a dilemma' for the parents, with the undertone that this was something unreasonable, appears to me curious and paradoxical. Parents decided to have a chance of selective places. The new council was giving it to them. If they did not want selective places, they had no need and no obligation to apply for them. Unless the creation of freedom of choice, where no such freedom existed previously, is intrinsically an evil, it seems hard to understand how this so-called dilemma could be something unreasonably created. The impression which it gives of upsetting 3,000 places is entirely a false one since over 90 per cent of these would remain unaltered. Then, to refer to 'submitting to an improvised selection procedure' hardly does justice to the authority's plan. Some selection procedure was inherent in what the electorate had voted for, a choice which, if it meant anything, must involve some change in allocations for the forthcoming school year and, unless exactly 240 parents applied for the 240 places, some selection. It would seem likely that in voting for this change in May 1976 the electors must have accepted, if not favoured, some degree of improvisation. The whole paragraph forces the conclusion that the Secretary of State was operating under a misconception as to what would be reasonable for a newly elected council to do, and that he failed to take into account that it was entitled – indeed in a sense bound – to carry out the policy on which it was elected, and failed to give weight to the fact that the limited degree of selection (for 240 places out of some 3,000) which was involved, though less than perfect, was something which a reasonable authority might accept and which the parents concerned clearly did accept.

What the Secretary of State was entitled to do, under his residual powers, was to say something to the effect: 'the election has taken place; the new authority may be entitled to postpone the comprehensive scheme: this may involve some degree of selection and apparently the parents desire it. Nevertheless from an educational point of view, whatever some parents may think, I am satisfied that in the time available this, or some part of it, cannot be carried out, and that no reasonable authority would attempt to carry it out.' Let us judge him by this test – though I do not think that this was the test he himself applied. Was the procedure to be followed for choosing which of the applicants were to be allotted the 240 selective places such that no reasonable authority could adopt it? The authority's letter of June 7[7] said that selection would be by 'a combination of reports, records and interviews.'

---

[7] [To the Secretary of State.]

They had about three months in which to carry it out. The plan was lacking in specification, but it must have conveyed sufficient to the experts at the department to enable them to understand what was proposed. Selection by 11-plus examination was not the only selection procedure available. Lancashire, part of which was taken over by Tameside, had evolved and operated a method of selection by head teacher recommendation, ranking of pupils, reports and records and standardised verbal reasoning tests. The Tameside authority had set up in May a panel of selection to operate a procedure of this kind, the chairman of which was experienced in the Lancashire method. He, as he deposed in an affidavit before the Court of Appeal, was of opinion that even though a verbal reasoning test might not be practicable in the time there would be no difficulty in selecting the number of pupils required. There were other opinions, expressed with varying degrees of confidence by experts, and no doubt the procedure could not be said to be perfect, but I do not think that such defects as there were could possibly, in the circumstances, having regard to the comparatively small numnber of places involved, enable it to be said that the whole of the authority's programme of which this was a part was such that no reasonable authority would carry it out.

But there is a further complication. The authority's selection plans were opposed by a number of the teachers' unions, and there was the likelihood of non-cooperation by some of the head teachers in the primary schools in production of records and reports. The department letters and affidavits do not rely upon this matter, for understandable reasons, but they must be assumed to have had it in mind. Is this a fact upon which the Secretary of State might legitimately form the judgment that the authority was acting unreasonably?

To rephrase the question: on June 11, 1976 (this is the date of the direction, and we are not entitled to see what happened thereafter), could it be said that the authority was acting unreasonably in proceeding with a selection procedure which was otherwise workable in face of the possibility of persistent opposition by teachers' unions and individual teachers, or would *the only* (not 'the more') reasonable course have been for the authority to abandon its plans? This is, I think, the ultimate factual question in the case. And I think that it must be answered in the negative – i.e., that it could not be unreasonable, in June 1976, and assuming that the Secretary of State did not interfere, for the authority to put forward a plan to act on its approved procedure. The teachers, after all, are public servants, with responsibility for their pupils. They were under a duty to produce reports. These reports and the records in the primary schools are public property. I do not think that it could be unreasonable (not 'was unreasonable') for the authority to take the view that if the Secretary of State did not intervene under his statutory powers the teachers would cooperate in working the authority's procedure – a procedure which had, in similar form, been operated in part of this very area.

On the whole case, I come to the conclusion that the Secretary of State, real though his difficulties were, fundamentally misconceived and misdirected himself as to the proper manner in which to regard the proposed action of the Tameside authority after the local election of May 1976: that if he had exercised his judgment on the basis of the factual situation in which this newly elected authority was placed – with a policy approved by its electorate, and massively supported by the parents – there was no ground – however much he might disagree with the new policy, and regret such administrative dislocation as was brought about by the change – upon which he could find that the authority was acting or proposing to act unreasonably. In my opinion the judgments in the Court of Appeal were right and the appeal must be dismissed.

LORD DIPLOCK: ... My Lords, in public law 'unreasonable' as descriptive of the way in which a public authority has purported to exercise a discretion vested in it by statute has become a term of legal art. To fall within this expression it must be conduct which no sensible authority acting with due appreciation of its responsibilities would have decided to adopt.

The very concept of administrative discretion involves a right to choose between more than one possible course of action upon which there is room for reasonable people to hold differing opinions as to which is to be preferred. ... What [the Secretary of State] had to consider was whether the way in which they proposed to give effect to that preference would, in the light of the circumstances as they existed on June 11, 1976, involve such interference with the provision of efficient instruction and training in secondary schools in their area that no sensible authority acting with due appreciation of its responsibilities under the Act could have decided to adopt the course which the Tameside council were then proposing.

It was for the Secretary of State to decide that. It is not for any court of law to substitute its own opinion for his; but it is for a court of law to determine whether it has been established that in reaching his decision unfavourable to the council he had directed himself properly in law and had in consequence taken into consideration the matters which upon the true construction of the Act he ought to have considered and excluded from his consideration matters that were irrelevant to what he had to consider: see *Associated Provincial Picture Houses Ltd.* v. *Wednesbury Corporation* [1948] 1 K.B. 223, *per* Lord Greene M.R., at p. 229. Or, put more compendiously, the question for the court is, did the Secretary of State ask himself the right question and take reasonable steps to acquaint himself with the relevant information to enable him to answer it correctly?

There has never been the least suggestion in this case that the Secretary of State acted otherwise than in good faith.

... [T]he question that the Secretary of State had to ask himself was: in face of the trade unions' threat that their members would refuse to cooperate was the council on June 11 acting unreasonably in not having abandoned by that date all plans for reintroducing selective entry to grammar schools in their area?

The letter of June 11 contains no indication that the Secretary of State directed his mind to this question, let alone that he relied that it lay at the heart of what he had to decide.

Like all your Lordships, I would dismiss this appeal, although I prefer to put it on the ground that, in my view, the respondents have succeeded in establishing in these proceedings that the Secretary of State did not direct his mind to the right question; and so, since his good faith is not in question, he cannot have directed himself properly in law.

LORD SALMON: . . . In my opinion, section 68, on its true construction, means that before the Secretary of State can lawfully issue directions under it he must satisfy himself not only that he does not agree with the way in which the authority have acted or are proposing to act nor even that the authority is mistaken or wrong. The question he must ask himself is: 'Could any reasonable local authority act in the way in which this authority has acted or is proposing to act?' If, but only if, he is satisfied on any material capable of satisfying a reasonable man that the answer to the crucial question is "No," he may lawfully issue directions under section 68. I would adopt what Lord Hailsham of St. Marylebone L.C. said in *In re W. (An Infant)* [1971] A.C. 682, 700:

'Two reasonable [persons] can perfectly reasonably come to opposite conclusions on the same set of facts without forfeiting their title to be regarded as reasonable . . . Not every reasonable exercise of judgment is right, and not every mistaken exercise of judgment is unreasonable.'

. . . I find it impossible . . . to accept that any reasonable man could have been satisfied that no reasonable authority on the evidence could take the view that a satisfactory selection of candidates for the 240 places in the grammar schools could have been made between June 11 and September 1, 1976. Therefore either the Secretary of State must have erred in law by misconstruing section 68 and failing to ask himself the right question or he asked himself that question and answered it 'no' without any valid ground for doing so. . . .

I am convinced that there are no valid grounds for holding that the authority acted or were proposing to act unreasonably within the meaning of section 68. The directions given by the Secretary of State on June 11, 1976, were in my view unlawful. . . .

[VISCOUNT DILHORNE and LORD RUSSELL OF KILLOWEN delivered speeches in favour of dismissing the appeal.]

Appeal dismissed.

Questions

1. Section 1 of the Education Act 1944 imposes the duty to promote education and secure the efficient execution by local authorities of the national policy of the Secretary of State for Education. Does it follow that a Minister with primary responsibility for education should only be able to interfere with the decisions of local authorities in the same circumstances as members of the judiciary can review administrative action? Is the *Tameside* case authority for such an approach?

2. How, if at all, does judicial review in this case differ from judicial review in *Associated Provincial Picture Houses Ltd.* v. *Wednesbury Corporation*, p. 118 *supra?*

Notes

1. The requirement of 'reasonableness' is often expressly prescribed by statutes granting discretion: see Wade, pp. 404. In *Nakkuda Ali* v. *Jayaratne* [1951] A.C. 66 (on which see p. 221 *infra*) the Privy Council rejected the view that words such as 'where the Controller has reasonable grounds to believe' – always mean (as they had done in *Liversidge* v. *Anderson* [1942] A.C. 206) that, granted honesty and good faith, the donee of the discretion is the only judge of the conditions of his own jurisdiction. Such words must be intended to limit an otherwise arbitrary power and in many cases to permit judicial review only in cases of dishonesty is pointless and hardly more than a formality. In the context of the case (discretion to cancel a textile dealer's licence), the requirement was held to impose 'a condition that there must in fact exist such reasonable grounds, known to the [donee of the power] before he can readily exercise the power'. In *I.R.C.* v. *Rossminster Ltd.* [1980] A.C. 952 at pp. 1011 and 1025 the House of Lords went further and said that *Liversidge* v. *Anderson* was wrong. And see now *Khawaja's* case discussed in the Appendix where certain difficulties are discussed.

2. In *Luby* v. *Newcastle-under-Lyme Corporation* [1964] 2 Q.B. 64, affirmed [1965] 1 Q.B. 214, Diplock L.J. (at first instance) said (at p. 70) of a discretion to make 'reasonable charges' for council houses, that he 'doubt[ed] whether the addition of the adjective "reasonable" has the effect of narrowing the wide discretion which the local authority would have if that word were not present, since . . . where a local authority is exercising a discretion conferred upon it by Parliament it must in any event exercise it "reasonably" in the sense in which that ambiguous word was used by Lord Russell in the leading case of *Kruse* v. *Johnson*', p. 504 *infra*. He also cited the *Wednesbury Corporation* case, p. 118 *supra*. Wade, p. 405, explains the difference of approach on the ground that 'the degree of objectivity in the test of reasonableness can therefore vary widely with the statutory context and purpose' (see also de Smith, pp. 346–7). What is the point of expressly specifying a requirement of reasonableness if, in some statutory contexts, it makes no difference?

3. For the control of subordinate legislation on this ground see p. 503 *infra*.

4. The reasonableness of administrative action could be raised in a tort action, e.g. for negligence, against a public authority. See generally Ch. 13 *infra* and see de Smith, pp. 350–2, although note that, in that context, it may have a different meaning.

PART III
Natural Justice

7

THE RULE AGAINST BIAS

JUDICIAL AND ADMINISTRATIVE IMPARTIALITY

Dimes v. The Proprietors of the Grand Junction Canal

(1852) 3 H.L.C. 759   House of Lords

The respondent company had been involved in proceedings before Lord Cottenham L.C. and had been granted relief by him. Lord Cottenham, however, held shares in the company (partly on his own account and partly as a trustee for others), and the validity of his action was in issue in this case. The opinion of all the judges was sought, and extracts from this opinion on two particular points will be set out at pp. 194 and 208 *infra*. At this stage it is only necessary to consider one of the speeches in the House of Lords.

LORD CAMPBELL: . . . No one can suppose that Lord Cottenham could be, in the remotest degree, influenced by the interest that he had in this concern; but, my Lords, it is of the last importance that the maxim that no man is to be a judge in his own cause should be held sacred. And that is not to be confined to a cause in which he is a party, but applies to a cause in which he has an interest. Since I have had the honour to be Chief Justice of the Court of Queen's Bench, we have again and again set aside proceedings in inferior tribunals because an individual, who had an interest in a cause, took a part in the decision. And it will have a most salutary influence on these tribunals when it is known that this high Court of last resort, in a case in which the Lord Chancellor of England had an interest, considered that his decree was on that account a decree not according to law, and was set aside. This will be a lesson to all inferior tribunals to take care not only that in their decrees they are not influenced by their personal interest, but to avoid the appearance of labouring under such an influence. . . .

[The LORD CHANCELLOR (LORD ST. LEONARDS) and LORD BROUGHAM agreed that Lord Cottenham had been disqualified from acting as a judge in the proceedings in question on account of his interest.]

Questions

1. Do you think that the company could have successfully attacked an adverse decision by Lord Cottenham?

2. What would the position have been if the company had been granted relief by a court composed of several judges sitting with Lord Cottenham, and Lord Cottenham had dissented?

Notes

1. The *Dimes* case, of course, concerned a court of law, but the rule against bias (*nemo iudex in re sua*) extends beyond such bodies. An example, also in the context of pecuniary interest, is provided by *R. v. Hendon R.D.C., ex p. Chorley* [1933] 2 K.B. 696. In this case a councillor voted for a resolution granting permission to develop certain land which was subject to a provisional contract of sale; the contract was contingent on the granting of the Council's permission. The councillor was in fact the one and only member of the firm of estate agents acting for the vendor, and it was held that the Council's decision should be quashed because of the councillor's participation in the matter. Indeed, even if the councillor had not voted, it would seem that the decision would still have been quashed because of his presence at the meeting. See further de Smith, p. 273, who cites the case to support the view that the pecuniary interest of only one member will lead to the invalidity of proceedings of administrative or local government bodies exercising judicial functions. He suggests, however, that the fact of a member's likelihood of bias (see p. 195 *infra*), as opposed to his pecuniary interest, may not have the same effect. The proceedings of the bodies just mentioned may not be invalidated in this situation, unless the person 'plays a prominent part in the proceedings'. The size of the body involved is put forward as a possible 'material factor'. Compare the stricter position with tribunals as outlined by de Smith.

2. Whilst a pecuniary interest, however small it may be, is sufficient to disqualify a person from deciding a matter, nevertheless that interest must be a direct one. For an example of a possible indirect interest, see *Metropolitan Properties Co. (F.G.C. Ltd. v. Lannon*, p. 197 *infra*, per Lord Denning. In cases of pecuniary interest it has been said that the courts do not inquire into the likelihood of bias: 'the law raises a conclusive presumption of bias' (*R. v. Sunderland JJ.* [1901] 2 K.B. 357 at p. 371 per Vaughan Williams L.J.) but see de Smith, p. 260; Whitmore and Aronson, *Review of Administrative Action*, p. 124. In other cases, however, the question of the likelihood of bias can certainly arise, and this question will be considered at p. 195 *infra*.

Cases of necessity: statutory dispensation

Dimes v. The Proprietors of the Grand Junction Canal

(1852) 3 H.L.C. 759   House of Lords

For the facts and decision in this case, see p. 193 *supra*. This extract concerns the point that there could be no appeal to the House of Lords from the decision of the Vice-Chancellor (who had been involved in the proceedings in the case) without enrolment of the appeal, and this required the Lord Chancellor's signature. The House of Lords sought the opinion of all the judges. This opinion, which was delivered by Parke B., met with approval in the House of Lords.

PARKE B.: . . . [T]his is a case of necessity, and where that occurs the objection of interest cannot prevail. Of this the case in the Year Book[1] is an instance, where it was held that it was no objection to the jurisdiction of the Common Pleas that an action was brought against all the Judges of the Common Pleas, in a case in doubt which could only be brought in that Court. . . .

[1] Year Book, 8 Hen. VI. 19; 2 Roll. Abr. 93.

Question

Do you think the necessity doctrine could validate a decision in which the adjudicator was actually biased? (See Flick, *Natural Justice*, p. 141.)

Notes

1. The bias rule may also be modified or excluded by statute (see e.g. the situation in *Wilkinson* v *Barking Corporation* [1948] 1 K.B. 721); in particular, a statute might specifically state that an adjudicator is not disqualified by some interest which he possesses (e.g. s. 304 of the Public Health Act 1936), though on the interpretation of this sort of provision, see Wade, pp. 428–9.

The relationship between the statutory modification or exclusion of the rule against bias and the doctrine of necessity might be considered in the light of *Jeffs* v. *New Zealand Dairy Production and Marketing Board* [1967] 1 A.C. 551, noted on a different point at p. 134 *supra*. A dairy company had applied to the respondent Board for an order (a 'zoning order') whereby all the milk produced in a particular area would go to its factory. The company already possessed such an order in respect of the production of cream. A committee set up by the Board investigated the matter and recommended that, with the exception of one area from which the milk and cream would go to another company's factory, the company should also receive milk from that part of the country previously allocated to it for the supply of cream; in addition, it was proposed that these recommendations should be conditional on certain compensation being awarded to the company. These recommendations were approved by the Board, but the consequent zoning order made by the Board, which was owed money by the company, was attacked on the ground of the Board's pecuniary interest. Various sections of the statute under which the Board was acting gave it powers, the exercise of which could obviously create a financial link between the Board and a dairy company (e.g. those authorizing loans by the Board to dairy companies), and yet the statute did not establish any alternative body to the Board to decide zoning questions. In the Privy Council's opinion, the New Zealand Parliament had intended that the Board should decide these questions, despite the fact that it might possess a financial interest in the matter. No specific reference was made to the doctrine of necessity either in the Privy Council or in the New Zealand Court of Appeal [1966] N.Z.L.R. 73, but see the judgment at first instance [1965] N.Z.L.R. 522. Could the *Jeffs* case have been decided on this? On necessity, see generally Tracey, [1982] P.L. 628.

2. For the position where a statute lays down a disqualification for interest but also validates any action taken by the person in question, see Wade, pp. 429–30.

'Reasonable suspicion' versus 'real likelihood' of bias

R. v. Sussex Justices, ex parte McCarthy

[1924] 1 K.B. 256   Divisional Court of the King's Bench Division

Whitworth, the driver of a motorbike which was involved in a collision with McCarthy's motorbike, made a claim through his solicitors for damages from McCarthy. In addition, a criminal prosecution was brought for dangerous driving and McCarthy was convicted by a magistrates' court. The person who acted as the clerk to the justices on the day in question (the deputy clerk) was a partner in the firm of solicitors which was acting on Whitworth's behalf. He had retired with the justices, but, according to the justices' affidavit, he had not referred to the case during his retirement with them and he had not been consulted whilst the justices were coming to their decision. McCarthy's solicitor stated that he (the solicitor) had been unaware of the deputy clerk's interest in the case until the justices had retired; however, he brought the matter to their attention when they returned to court. McCarthy later sought certiorari to quash his conviction.

LORD HEWART C.J.: . . . It is clear that the deputy clerk was a member of the firm of solicitors engaged in the conduct of proceedings for damages against the applicant in respect of the same collision as that which gave rise to the charge that the justices were considering. It is said, and, no doubt, truly, that when that gentleman retired in the usual way with the justices, taking with him the notes of the evidence in case the justices might desire to consult him, the justices came to a conclusion without consulting him, and that he scrupulously abstained from referring to the case in any way. But while that is so, a long line of cases shows that it is not merely of some importance but is of fundamental importance that justice should not only be done, but should manifestly and undoubtedly be seen to be done. The question therefore is not whether in this case the deputy clerk made any observation or offered any criticism which he might not properly have made or offered; the question is whether he was so related to the case in its civil aspect as to be unfit to act as clerk to the justices in the criminal matter. The answer to that question depends not upon what actually was done but upon what might appear to be done. Nothing is to be done which creates even a suspicion that there has been an improper interference with the course of justice. Speaking for myself, I accept the statements contained in the justices' affidavit, but they show very clearly that the deputy clerk was connected with the case in a capacity which made it right that he should scrupulously abstain from referring to the matter in any way, although he retired with the justices; in other words, his one position was such that he could not, if he had been required to do so, discharge the duties which his other position involved. His twofold position was a manifest contradiction. In those circumstances I am satisfied that this conviction must be quashed, unless it can be shown that the applicant or his solicitor was aware of the point that might be taken, refrained from taking it, and took his chance of an acquittal on the facts, and then, on a conviction being recorded, decided to take the point. On the facts I am satisfied that there has been no waiver of the irregularity. . . .

[LUSH and SANKEY JJ. agreed.]

Conviction quashed.

Notes

1. In relation to the position of the deputy clerk, it might be noted that, at the time when this case was decided, McCarthy's conviction (even if it had not been quashed) would not apparently have been admissible in evidence to help Whitworth prove negligence in any civil proceedings which might have been brought. This view was certainly clearly taken in 1943 in *Hollington* v. *F. Hewthorn & Co. Ltd.* [1943] K.B. 587, but the position is different today: see s. 11 of the Civil Evidence Act 1968.

2. The question of waiver will be discussed in Note 2, p. 209 *infra*.

3. The test for disqualification which is to be found in *R. v. Sussex JJ., ex p. McCarthy* should be compared with the test which had been propounded in *R. v. Rand* (1866) L.R. 1 Q.B. 230 and approved in many cases. This requires 'a real likelihood of bias'. For further discussion of the appropriate test, see the next case.

Metropolitan Properties Co. (F.G.C.) Ltd. v. Lannon

[1969] 1 Q.B. 577   Court of Appeal

Lannon, a solicitor, lived with his father in a flat in Regency Lodge, the landlords of which were part of the Freshwater group of companies. Lannon's firm had acted for some tenants in Regency Lodge in their negotiations with this group and it was 'presumed' (per Lord Denning) that he had conducted these negotiations. In addition, in the cases of two of these tenants, the firm had made representations on their behalf to a rent officer. Lannon assisted his father in certain dealings with his landlords about the rent of his flat and, in particular, had helped in the writing of a letter to a rent officer in support of his father's case. This dispute was unresolved when Lannon sat as chairman of a rent assessment committee which fixed the rent of three flats in Oakwood Court at a figure lower even than that which had been offered by the tenants of those premises. Oakwood Court was owned by the appellant company, which was a member of the Freshwater group of companies, and the tenants in these cases were putting forward arguments which were similar to those advanced in Lannon's father's case. The Divisional Court ([1968] 1 W.L.R. 815) rejected the company's challenge to the decision of the rent assessment committee and the company appealed to the Court of Appeal.

LORD DENNING M.R.: . . . A man may be disqualified from sitting in a judicial capacity on one of two grounds. First a 'direct pecuniary interest' in the subject-matter. Second, 'bias' in favour of one side or against the other.

So far as 'pecuniary interest' is concerned, I agree with the Divisional Court that there is no evidence that Mr. John Lannon had any direct pecuniary interest in the suit. He had no interest in any of the flats in Oakwood Court. The only possible interest was his father's interest in having the rent of 55 Regency Lodge reduced. It was put in this way: if the committee reduced the rents of Oakwood Court, those rents would be used as 'comparable' for Regency Lodge, and might influence their being put lower than they otherwise would be. Even if we identify the son's interest with the father's, I think this is too remote. It is neither direct nor certain. It is indirect and uncertain.

So far as bias is concerned, it was acknowledged that there was no actual bias on the part of Mr. Lannon, and no want of good faith. But it was said that there was, albeit unconscious, a real likelihood of bias. This is a matter on which the law is not altogether clear: but I start with the oft-repeated saying of Lord Hewart C.J. in *Rex v. Sussex Justices, Ex parte McCarthy*.[2] 'It is not

---

[2] [1924] 1 K.B. 256, 259.

merely of some importance, but is of fundamental importance that justice should not only be done, but should manifestly and undoubtedly be seen to be done.'

In *Reg. v. Barnsley Licensing Justices, Ex parte Barnsley and District Licensed Victuallers' Association*,[3] Devlin J.[4] appears to have limited that principle considerably,[5] but I would stand by it. It brings home this point: in considering whether there was a real likelihood of bias, the court does not look at the mind of the justice himself or at the mind of the chairman of the tribunal, or whoever it may be, who sits in a judicial capacity. It does not look to see if there was a real likelihood that he would, or did, in fact favour one side at the expense of the other. The court looks at the impression which would be given to other people. Even if he was as impartial as could be, nevertheless if right-minded persons would think that, in the circumstances, there was a real likelihood of bias on his part, then he should not sit. And if he does sit, his decision cannot stand: see *Reg. v. Huggins;*[6] and *Rex. v. Sunderland Justices*,[7] *per* Vaughan Williams L.J.[8] Nevertheless there must appear to be a real likelihood of bias. Surmise or conjecture is not enough: see *Reg. v. Camborne Justices, Ex parte Pearce*,[9] and *Reg. v. Nailsworth Licensing Justices, Ex parte Bird.*[10] There must be circumstances from which a reasonable man would think it likely or probable that the justice, or chairman, as the case may be, would, or did, favour one side unfairly at the expense of the other. The court will not inquire whether he did, in fact, favour one side unfairly. Suffice is that reasonable people might think he did. The reason is plain enough. Justice must be rooted in confidence: and confidence is destroyed when right-minded people go away thinking: 'The judge was biased.'

Applying these principles, I ask myself: Ought Mr. John Lannon to have sat? I think not. If he was himself a tenant in difference with his landlord about the rent of his flat, he clearly ought not to sit on a case against the selfsame landlord, also about the rent of a flat, albeit another flat. In this case he was not a tenant, but the son of a tenant. But that makes no difference. No reasonable man would draw any distinction between him and his father, seeing he was living with him and assisting him with the case.

Test it quite simply: if Mr. John Lannon were to have asked any of his friends: 'I have been asked to preside in a case about the rents charged by the Freshwater Group of Companies at Oakwood Court. But I am already assisting my father in his case against them, about the rent of his flat in Regency Lodge, where I am living with him. Do you think I can properly sit?' The answer of any of his good friends would surely have been: 'No, you should not sit. You are already acting, or as good as acting, against them. You should not, at the same time, sit in judgment on them.'

---

[3] [1960] 2 Q.B. 167, 187.   [4] [This should be Devlin L.J.]
[5] [By requiring the court to be satisfied that there was a real likelihood of bias: see p. 199 *infra.*]   [6] [1895] 1 Q.B. 563.
[7] [1901] 2 K.B. 357, C.A.   [8] Ibid. 373.
[9] [1955] 1 Q.B. 41, 48–51.   [10] [1953] 1 W.L.R. 1046.

No man can be an advocate for or against a party in one proceeding, and at the same time sit as a judge of that party in another proceeding. Everyone would agree that a judge, or a barrister or solicitor (which he sits ad hoc as a member of a tribunal) should not sit on a case to which a near relative or a close friend is a party. So also a barrister or solicitor should not sit on a case to which one of his clients is a party. Nor on a case where he is already acting against one of the parties. Inevitably people would think he would be biased.

I hold, therefore, that Mr. John Lannon ought not to have sat on this rent assessment committee. The decision is voidable on that account and should be avoided.

Although we are differing from the Divisional Court,[11] I would like to say that we have had a good deal more information than that court had. In particular, we have seen the letter of January 13, 1967, and other things not before them when they gave their ruling. Otherwise I would not have thought it right to interfere.

I would allow the appeal and remit the case to another rent assessment committee. Let it be heard again as soon as may be.

EDMUND DAVIES L.J.: . . . [I]n *Reg.* v. *Barnsley Licensing Justices,*[12] referring to the dissenting judgment of Salmon J. in the Divisional Court,[13] Devlin L.J. said:[14]

'I am not quite sure what test Salmon J. applied. If he applied the test based on the principle that justice must not only be done but manifestly be seen to be done, I think he came to the right conclusion on that test. . . . But . . . it is *not* the test. *We have not to enquire what impression might be left on the minds of the present applicants or on the minds of the public generally.* We have to satisfy ourselves that there was a real likelihood of bias – *not* merely satisfy ourselves that that was the sort of impression that might reasonably get abroad. The term "real likelihood of bias" is not used, in my opinion, to import the principle in *Rex.* v. *Sussex Justices.*[15] . . . It is used to show that it is *not* necessary that actual bias should be proved. It is unnecessary . . . to investigate the state of mind of each individual justice. *"Real likelihood" depends on the impression which the court gets from the circumstances in which the justices were sitting.* Do they give rise to a real likelihood that the justices might be biased? The court might come to the conclusion that there was such a likelihood, without impugning the affidavit of a justice that he was not in fact biased. Bias is or may be an unconscious thing. . . . The matter must be determined upon the probabilities to be inferred from the circumstances in which the justices sat.'

With profound respect to those who have propounded the 'real likelihood' test, I take the view that the requirement that justice must manifestly be done operates with undiminished force in cases where bias is alleged and that any development of the law which appears to emasculate that requirement should

[11] [1968] 1 W.L.R. 815.　　[12] [1960] 2 Q.B. 167.
[13] [1959] 2 Q.B. 276.　　[14] [1960] 2 Q.B. 167, 187.
[15] [1924] 1 K.B. 256 [i.e. 'that justice should not only be done, but should manifestly and undoubtedly be seen to be done'.]

be strongly resisted. That the different tests, even when applied to the same facts, may lead to different results is illustrated by *Reg.* v. *Barnsley Licensing Justices*[16] itself, as Devlin L.J. made clear in the passage I have quoted.[17] But I cannot bring myself to hold that a decision may properly be allowed to stand even although there is *reasonable* suspicion of bias on the part of one or more members of the adjudicating body.

. . . It is conceivable that, although 'startling,' the decisions of the committee were nevertheless correct – that remains to be seen. But it is not manifest that they were just, and they therefore ought not to be allowed to stand. . . .

[DANCKWERTS L.J. delivered a judgment in favour of allowing the appeal.]

Appeal allowed.

Questions

1. Is there any difference between the test propounded by Lord Denning and that put forward by Edmund Davies L.J. (and see Note 2 *infra*)?

2. Lord Denning states that 'a barrister or solicitor should not sit on a case to which one of his clients is a party'. Do you think that a judge could sit in a case in which, before being elevated to the bench, he had acted as a barrister for one of the parties? (On this point, see *Thellusson* v. *Rendlesham* (1859) 7 H.L.C. 429, and on the question of a judge sitting on appeal from his own decision, see Note 1, p. 203 *infra*.)

3. Do you think the rule against bias has to be applied at all differently in cases concerned with professional associations or bodies such as trade unions? (See e.g. *Maclean* v. *The Workers' Union* [1929] 1 Ch. 602 at p. 626; *White* v. *Kuzych* [1951] A.C. 585; *Roebuck* v. *N.U.M. (Yorkshire Area) (No. 2)* [1977] I.C.R. 676 at p. 682; de Smith, p. 256.)

Notes

1. See p. 209 *infra* in relation to Lord Denning's opinion that the decision in this case was voidable.

2. It was not long before the Court of Appeal was again troubled with the question of the appropriate test for disqualification for likelihood of bias. In *Hannam* v. *Bradford Corporation* [1970] 1 W.L.R. 937 Sachs L.J. expressed a preference for the following test – whether 'a reasonable man would say that a real danger of bias existed' – rather than the 'real likelihood' test, but he doubted whether the application of one of these tests rather than the other would lead to any real differences in practice. Widgery L.J.'s opinion was that the plaintiff had established a real likelihood of bias and that he should succeed on the bias aspect of the case no matter which of the tests to be found in *Lannon*'s case was applicable. Cross L.J.'s judgment, however, merits fuller treatment. He thought that 'there really is little (if any) difference between the two tests which are propounded in the cases which have been cited to us', and continued by stating (at p. 949):

If a reasonable person who has no knowledge of the matter beyond knowledge of the relationship which subsists between some members of the tribunal and one of the parties would think that there might well be bias, then there is in his opinion a real likelihood of bias. Of course, someone else with inside knowledge of the characters of the members in question might say:

[16] [1960] 2 Q.B. 167.
[17] Ibid. 187.

'Although things don't look very well, in fact there is no real likelihood of bias'. That, however, would be beside the point, because the question is not whether the tribunal will in fact be biased, but whether a reasonable man with no inside knowledge might well think that it might be biased.

More recently, in R. v. Altrincham JJ., ex p. Pennington [1975] Q.B. 549, Lord Widgery had said that both the 'real likelihood' and 'reasonable suspicion' tests were appied in Lannon's case and that that decision did not make it clear which test should be applied in any particular case. In the light of this opinion, Lord Widgery's concept of the 'real likelihood' test must be contrasted with that of Devlin L.J. in R. v. Barnsley Licensing JJ., ex p. Barnsley and District Licensed Victuallers' Association [1960] 2 Q.B. 167 at p. 187, since the latter's view was disapproved in Lannon's case. For Lord Widgery it must mean whether the reasonable man would think there was a real likelihood of bias (though cf. [1975] Q.B. at p. 552). On the facts of the case Lord Widgery did not find it necessary to favour one test rather than the other (and see also R. v. Eastern Traffic Area Licensing Authority, ex p. J. Wyatt Jnr. (Haulage) Ltd. [1974] R.T.R. 480 at p. 487); indeed, he expressed the view that each may have its own appropriate sphere of operation. What do you think these spheres may be?

In R. v. Colchester Stipendiary Magistrate, ex p. Beck [1979] Q.B. 674 Lord Widgery, in rejecting any breach of the bias rule, applied the 'real likelihood' test to the case of a magistrate who, it was alleged, had been supplied by the prosecution with documents containing matter prejudicial to the accused before committal proceedings had begun. Note also the application of the 'real likelihood' test by Lawton L.J. in U.K.A.P.E. v. A.C.A.S. [1979] 1 W.L.R. 570 when that case was in the Court of Appeal. For general discussion see Rawlings, [1980] P.L. 122, where, relying on Anderton v. Auckland C.C. [1978] 1 N.Z.L.R. 657, a distinction is drawn between an allegation of an association between a party and the decision-making body (real likelihood) and an allegation concerning the way in which the proceedings were conducted (reasonable suspicion). As Rawlings points out, the application of the 'real likelihood' test by Lord Widgery in R. v. Colchester Stipendiary Magistrate, ex p. Beck and by Lawton L.J. in U.K.A.P.E. v. A.C.A.S. is consistent with this distinction; but there was no express support for it in the reasoning in these two judgments. For an article discussing the 'real likelihood' and 'reasonable suspicion' tests, see Alexis, [1979] P.L. 143. See further R. v. Liverpool City JJ., ex p. Topping [1983] 1 W.L.R. 119.

3. On the question of the knowledge with which the reasonable man is deemed to be invested, see, in addition to Lannon's case and the comments of Cross L.J. in Hannam v. Bradford Corporation supra; J.J. Steeples v. Derbyshire C.C. [1981] J.P.L. 581; R. v. West Yorkshire Coroner, ex p. Smith, The Times, 6 November 1982 (the reasonable man is to be taken to know everything in evidence before the reviewing court).

4. In some spheres neither test to be found in Lannon's case may be thought appropriate. R. v. Secretary of State for Trade, ex p. Perestrello [1981] Q.B. 19 furnishes an example. The case concerned s. 109 of the Companies Act 1967, which empowers the Board of Trade or its authorized officers to demand the production of certain papers from a company if it thinks there is good reason to do so. Woolf J. stated (at p. 35):

What is done under section 109 is to ascertain whether there is evidence to support a prima facie view of a possible undesirable situation in relation to a company, and that being so, the role of the Department is very much the role of the potential prosecutor. The person performing that role will of necessity be an inappropriate person to perform the function which was being considered in the *Lannon* case. So I regard the *Lannon* approach as not being applicable to these circumstances.

The function involved in the *Lannon* case was regarded as a 'judicial or quasi-judicial role; a situation where the person is making a determination'. See further p. 4 *supra*. Is this a case of implied exclusion by Parliament? The limits spelt out by the court (and this was said not to be an exhaustive list) were that the discretion under s. 109 should not be exceeded or abused or used for an ulterior purpose. Fairness required this much, but, of course, this could have been required by the ultra vires doctrine. On acting fairly, see further p. 282 *infra*.

CAUSES OF PREJUDICE

R. v. Sussex Justices, ex parte McCarthy, p. 195 *supra*

Metropolitan Properties Co. (F.G.C.) Ltd. v. Lannon, p. 197 *supra*

Notes

1. The cases *supra* provide examples of the sort of complaint that can be made. There are many others which can be found in the textbooks. For example, a person should not act as a prosecutor and judge: see e.g. *Taylor* v. *N.U.S.* [1967] 1 W.L.R. 532.

Hannam v. *Bradford Corporation* [1970] 1 W.L.R. 937, noted at p. 200 *supra*, provides an illustration of disqualification arising where a person sits as a member of one body which is considering the decision of another body of which he is also a member. The governors of a school decided to dismiss a schoolteacher, and gave him the appropriate period of notice. Some time later, the Council, affirming the decision of one of its committees, declined to exercise the power which it possessed to stop the dismissal. Three of the committee's ten members (including its chairman) were governors of the school and, although they had not been present at the meeting of the school governors at which the decision to dismiss had been taken, their attendance at the meeting of the committee was found by the Court of Appeal to be a breach of natural justice.

This case should be considered along with *Ward* v. *Bradford Corporation* (1972) 70 L.G.R. 27, in which the Court of Appeal has been said to have 'diminished the effect of its earlier decision in the *Hannam* case' (*Re Ringrose and College of Physicians & Surgeons of Alberta* (1975) 52 D.L.R. (3d) 584 at p. 594). In *Ward*'s case five women who lived in a college of education's hall of residence were found to have male visitors in their rooms in the early hours of the morning. The presence of these visitors was a breach of the terms on which the rooms were occupied. Only the College Principal had power to refer a case to the disciplinary committee and she did not wish to do so. The College's governing body amended the rules so as to enable it to refer cases to the committee, and then decided to refer the cases of these five women to that body. The committee was composed of nine members, three of whom, however, were members of the governing body, and its findings had to be approved by the governing body. The committee recommended that Miss Ward should be expelled from the college, and this was approved by the governing body.

The validity of this expulsion was questioned on several grounds, including one relevant to the issue in the *Hannam* case since it led the court to consider the role of the governing body. The Court of Appeal concluded that the governing body had acted fairly, and it was emphasized that it had not considered the merits of the cases before deciding to refer them to the committee. Phillimore L.J. also pointed out that none of the three members of the governing body who had been members of the disciplinary committee sat with the governing body when it approved the committee's recommendations. Do you agree with the view in the Canadian case which was quoted at the beginning of this paragraph? Note that in an interview published in The Guardian, 20 December 1978, Lord Denning said of *Ward*'s case that he would probably have interfered with the decision if he had thought it to be a wrong one (although which of the grounds of challenge he would have relied upon is not made clear).

For an example of a judge being involved in proceedings in which his earlier ruling was in question, see *Cooper* v. *Wandsworth Board of Works*, p. 211 *infra*. On the history of the position of judges of courts of law sitting on appeal from or review of their own decisions, see Marshall, *Natural Justice*, pp. 36–7, and note now s. 56 of the Supreme Court Act 1981. This prohibits any judge from sitting as a member of the civil or criminal division of the Court of Appeal when he has been involved in the proceedings from which the appeal is taken.

2. Preconceived opinions (even if openly expressed) will not *per se* disqualify, for the possession of such opinions by a person does not mean that he will not listen fairly to all the evidence (*R.* v. *L.C.C.; Re The Empire Theatre* (1894) 71 L.T. 638 at p. 639). (The problem to which such opinions give rise in the context of 'departmental bias' will be considered at p. 204 *infra*.)

An example of a case in which a preconceived opinion did disqualify is provided by *R.* v. *Bingham JJ., ex p. Jowitt*, The Times, 3 July 1974, where a particular opinion, which was held by the chairman of a bench of magistrates and which he expressed in court, did lead to the quashing of a conviction. The only evidence before the magistrates had come from a policeman and from Jowitt. The chairman of the bench stated that, in cases where there was a conflict of evidence between a policeman and a member of the public, his principle was to believe the former, and that therefore the magistrates found that the case against Jowitt had been established. On account of this bias, the Divisional Court quashed Jowitt's conviction for driving his car in excess of a 50 m.p.h. speed limit. Cf. *Ex p. Wilder* (1902) 66 J.P. 761, and on prejudgment and preconceived opinions see further, e.g., *R.* v. *Kent Police Authority, ex p. Godden* [1971] 2 Q.B. 662 (doctor who had previously expressed an opinion about Godden's mental state disqualified from later deciding whether he was likely to be 'permanently disabled' which could lead to his compulsory retirement from the police).

A certain similarity with the rule against fettering the exercise of discretion by over-rigid policy rules (p. 144 *supra*) might be noticed. Nevertheless, the similarity only goes so far. In *Hamilton City* v. *Electricity Distribution Commission* [1972] N.Z.L.R. 605 at p. 638, Richmond J. stated:

> In the . . . case [of bias by predetermination], the question generally is as to whether the members of the tribunal have so conducted themselves as to lead other persons to believe that there is a real possibility of the tribunal having pre-determined matters in issue before it. The requirement of justice not only being done but appearing to be done is important in the context of bias. When it comes to questions of fettering a discretion, however, I believe that the Court is concerned to ascertain the reality of the position rather than the inference which people could reasonably draw from the conduct of members of a tribunal.

Cf. *Stringer* v. *Minister of Housing and Local Government* [1970] 1 W.L.R. 1281, noted at p. 208 *infra*.

Departmental or administrative bias

Franklin v. Minister of Town and Country Planning

[1948] A.C. 87   House of Lords

After objections had been received to the draft Stevenage New Town
(Designation) Order 1946, which had been prepared by the respondent
Minister under the New Towns Act 1946, a public local inquiry was held by
Morris, an inspector of the Ministry of Town and Country Planning. The
inspector reported to the Minister, who, having considered the report, confirmed the draft Order. The appellants, owners and occupiers of premises at
Stevenage, applied to the court under s. 16 of the Town and Country Plan-
ning Act 1944 for the order to be quashed. One ground of attack was that the
Minister was biased. The appellants placed particular reliance on comments
he had made at a public meeting in Stevenage, sufficient details of which
appear in the extract from Lord Thankerton's speech. The Minister's speech
had been made in May 1946, two days before the empowering legislation (the
New Towns Act 1946) had received its second reading in the House of
Commons. Henn Collins J. ((1947) 176 L.T. 200) was in favour of quashing
the order on the ground that the Minister had not had an open mind when
making his decision. He rejected the view that the Minister was acting purely
administratively when making the order and accepted that he was acting
judicially or quasi-judicially in this situation. In the Court of Appeal (ibid.
312) it was assumed that *at the time of making the speech* the Minister had
prejudged issues which might be raised by objectors. Nevertheless, the
Minister's appeal was allowed because, in the Court of Appeal's view, the
evidence did not show that the Minister had been biased when he had made
the order. There was a further appeal to the House of Lords.

LORD THANKERTON: . . . My Lords, I agree with the decision of the Court
of Appeal, but I am of opinion that an incorrect view of the law applicable in
this case was taken by the learned judge, and I feel bound, despite the
assumption of its correctness by the Court of Appeal, to examine the correctness of the learned judge's view as to the proper inference[18] from the respondent's speech of May 6, 1946. While the fact that the speech was made just
before the second reading of the Bill, and some months before the statutory
duties as to designation of new towns was imposed on the respondent has
some bearing on the fair construction of the speech, I am prepared to assume
in favour of the appellants that, under the Bill as introduced it was proposed
to impose these duties on the respondent, as Minister of Town and Country
Planning, and that these duties presented no material difference from those
contained in the Bill when passed into law. It could hardly be suggested that,
prior to its enactment, he was subject to any higher duty than is to be found in
the statute. In my opinion, no judicial, or quasi-judicial, duty was imposed on
the respondent, and any reference to judicial duty, or bias, is irrelevant in the

[18] [See p. 205 *infra.*]

present case. The respondent's duties under s. 1 of the Act and sch. 1 thereto are, in my opinion, purely administrative, but the Act prescribes certain methods of or steps in, discharge of that duty. It is obvious that, before making the draft order, which must contain a definite proposal to designate the area concerned as the site of a new town, the respondent must have made elaborate inquiry into the matter and have consulted any local authorities who appear to him to be concerned, and obviously other departments of the Government, such as the Ministry of Health, would naturally require to be consulted. It would seem, accordingly, that the respondent was required to satisfy himself that it was a sound scheme before he took the serious step of issuing a draft order. It seems clear also, that the purpose of inviting objections, and, where they are not withdrawn, of having a public inquiry, to be held by someone other than the respondent, to whom that person reports, was for the further information of the respondent, in order to the final consideration of the soundness of the scheme of the designation; and it is important to note that the development of the site, after the order is made, is primarily the duty of the development corporation established under s. 2 of the Act. I am of opinion that no judicial duty is laid on the respondent in discharge of these statutory duties, and that the only question is whether he has complied with the statutory directions to appoint a person to hold the public inquiry, and to consider that person's report. On this contention of the appellants no suggestion is made that the public inquiry was not properly conducted, nor is there any criticism of the report by Mr. Morris. In such a case the only ground of challenge must be either that the respondent did not in fact consider the report and the objections, of which there is here no evidence, or that his mind was so foreclosed that he have no genuine consideration to them, which is the case made by the appellants. . . .

My Lords, I could wish that the use of the word 'bias' should be confined to its proper sphere. Its proper significance, in my opinion, is to denote a departure from the standard of even-handed justice which the law requires from those who occupy judicial office, or those who are commonly regarded as holding a quasi-judicial office, such as an arbitrator. The reason for this clearly is that, having to adjudicate as between two or more parties, he must come to his adjudication with an independent mind, without any inclination or bias towards one side or other in the dispute. . . .[I]n the present case, the respondent having no judicial duty, the only question is what the respondent actually did, that is, whether in fact he did genuinely consider the report and the objections.

Coming now to the inference of the learned judge from the respondent's speech on May 6, that he had not then a mind open to conviction, the learned judge states it thus:[19] 'If I am to judge by what he said at the public meeting which was held very shortly before the Bill, then published, became an Act of Parliament, I could have no doubt but that any issue raised by objectors was forejudged. The Minister's language leaves no doubt about that. He was not only saying there must and shall be satellite towns, but he was saying that

[19] 176 L.T. 200, 203.

Stevenage was to be the first of them.' It seems probable that the learned judge's mind was influenced by his having already held that the respondent's function was quasi-judicial, which would raise the question of bias, but, in any view, I am clearly of opinion that nothing said by the respondent was inconsistent with the discharge of his statutory duty, when subsequently objections were lodged, and the local public inquiry took place, followed by the report of that inquiry, genuinely to consider the report and the objections. The only passages in the speech quoted in the appellants' case are contained in the third quotation I have made from the speech, and are as follows: 'I want to carry out in Stevenage a daring exercise in town planning (*jeers*). It is no good your jeering: it is going to be done. . . . After all this new town is to be built in order to provide for the happiness and welfare of some sixty thousand men, women and children. . . . The project will go forward, because it must go forward. It will do so more surely and more smoothly and more successfully with your help and co-operation. Stevenage will in a short time become world famous. People from all over the world will come to Stevenage to see how we here in this country are building for the new way of life.' The only two additional passages founded on by the appellants' counsel at the hearing before this House were the sentence in my first quotation, 'In anticipation of the passage of the Bill – and I have no doubt that it will go through,' and, in my fourth quotation, But we have a duty to perform, and I am not going to be deterred from that duty. While I will consult as far as possible all the local authorities, at the end, if people become fractious and unreasonable I shall have to carry out my duty – (*Voice*: Gestapo!).' My Lords, these passages in a speech, which was of a political nature, and of the kind familiar in a speech on second reading, demonstrate (1.) the speaker's view that the Bill would become law, that Stevenage was a most suitable site and should be the first scheme in the operation, and that the Stevenage project would go forward, and (2.) the speaker's reaction to the hostile interruptions of a section of the audience. In my opinion, these passages are not inconsistent with an intention to carry out any statutory duty imposed on him by Parliament, although he intended to press for the enactment of the Bill, and thereafter to carry out the duties thereby involved, including the consideration of objections which were neither fractious nor unreasonable. I am, therefore of opinion that the . . . contention of the appellants fails, in that they had not established either that in the respondent's speech he had forejudged any genuine consideration of the objections or that he had not genuinely considered the objections at the later stage when they were submitted to him. . . .

[LORD PORTER, LORD UTHWATT, LORD DU PARCQ, and LORD NORMAND concurred.]

Appeal dismissed.

Notes

1. On the topic of statutory inquiries, see further Ch. 17 *infra*.

2. On the classification of functions, see further ׀p. 4 *supra*. The decision of the House of Lords in *Franklin* has been the object of severe criticism in relation to its

approach to the classification of functions by Wade, pp. 437–8. As will be seen in the next chapter, a more flexible approach has prevailed since *Franklin* in the sphere of natural justice, both as to what is classified as judicial and indeed as to the need for such classification (and, in the context of the bias rule, see *R. v. Secretary of State for Trade, ex p. Perestrello* [1981] Q.B. 19, noted at p. 201 *supra*).

To what extent, it may be asked, could the rules of natural justice reasonably apply in a situation like that in *Franklin*'s case, a case which provides a prime example of what has been termed 'departmental bias'? It seems obvious that a minister, who has made a draft proposal which will doubtless reflect the policy of his department, is bound to have a predisposition in favour of it, and yet Parliament has imposed on him the task of deciding whether to confirm it. The law must, as Wade states (p. 437), 'allow for the departmental bias which he is expected and indeed required to have', but this does not necessarily lead to the conclusion that the rule against bias can have no application. The content of the rules of natural justice is flexible and it is possible to cater for the realities of the situation without denying the applicability of the rule against bias.

Support for this sort of approach can be found (in a slightly different context) in *Lower Hutt C.C. v. Bank* [1974] 1 N.Z.L.R. 545. It was held that the rules of natural justice were applicable, but that the position in which the Council had been placed by the legislature – that of considering objections to proposals it had put forward – had to be taken into account. The court said (at p. 550):

> We think that the state of impartiality which is required is the capacity in a council to preserve a freedom, notwithstanding earlier investigations and decisions, to approach their duty of inquiring into and disposing of the objections without a closed mind, so that if considerations advanced by objectors bring them to a different frame of mind they can, and will go back on their proposals.

(The court's judgment then went on to emphasize that it was the appearance of this impartiality which was all-important.)

Does this test differ from the requirement that a minister must genuinely consider the objections, the test adopted in *Franklin*'s case, where the applicability of the rule against bias was denied? See further *CREEDNZ Inc. v. Governor-General* [1981] 1 N.Z.L.R. 172, in which Richardson J. in the New Zealand Court of Appeal answered the question just posed in the negative. In *R. v. City of London Corporation, ex p. Allan* (1981) 79 L.G.R. 223, Woolf J. accepted counsel's description of *Franklin*'s case as the 'low-water mark of administrative law'. He also accepted the proposition (based on *Franklin*'s case and *Bushell v. Secretary of State for the Environment*, p. 601 *infra*) that a local planning authority which had to hold a public local inquiry into objections to a proposal in its draft local plan must, in relation to the inquiry, deal with the objections fairly; and in relation to prejudgment he adopted a similar requirement to that to be found in the cases *supra*, i.e. a willingness to consider objections and the report of the person who held the inquiry with an open mind. On policy and the bias rule, see further *R. v. Commonwealth Conciliation and Arbitration Commission, ex p. Angliss* (1969) 122 C.L.R. 546.

For a defence of Lord Thankerton's views in *Franklin*'s case concerning the non-applicability of the bias rule, see Davis, [1962] P.L. 139 at p. 155. Note further his discussion of the American authorities in this area (*Administrative Law Text*, pp. 245–9). At p. 247 he argues that the 'theoretically ideal administrator is one whose broad point of view is in general agreement with the policies he administers but who maintains sufficient balance to perceive and to avoid the degree of zeal which substantially impairs fair-mindedness'.

3. For the position of the minister who is not the initiating authority, see *Stringer* v. *Minister of Housing and Local Government* [1970] 1 W.L.R. 1281, in which the rules of natural justice were applied to a minister deciding an appeal from a refusal of planning permission by a local planning authority. He was entitled to have a general policy so long as it did not 'preclude him from fairly judging all the issues which are relevant to each individual case as it comes up for decision' (p. 1298).

EFFECTS OF PREJUDICE

Void or voidable?

Dimes v. The Proprietors of the Grand Junction Canal

(1852) 3 H.L.C. 759   House of Lords

For the facts of this case, see p. 193 *supra*.

BARON PARKE [having referred to *Brookes* v. *Earl of Rivers*[20] and *The Company of Mercers and Ironmongers of Chester* v. *Bowker*,[21] both of which deal with disqualification for interest:]

. . . In neither of these cases was the judgment held to be absolutely void. Till prohibition had been granted in one case, or judgment reversed in the other, we think that the proceedings were valid, and the persons acting under the authority of the Court would not be liable to be treated as trespassers.

The many cases in which the Court of King's Bench has interfered (and may have gone to a great length), where interested parties have acted as magistrates, and quashed the orders made by the Court of which they formed part, afford an analogy.

None of these orders is absolutely void; it would create great confusion and inconvenience if it was. The objection might be one of which the parties acting under these orders might be totally ignorant till the moment of the trial of an action of trespass for the act done; but these orders may be quashed after being removed by *certiorari*, and the Court shall do complete justice in that respect.

We think that the order of the Chancellor is not void; but we are of opinion, that as he had such an interest which would have disqualified a witness under the old law, he was disqualified as a Judge; that it was a voidable order, and might be questioned and set aside by appeal or some application to the Court of Chancery, if a prohibition would not lie. . . .

THE LORD CHANCELLOR [LORD ST. LEONARDS] said. — In reference to the question upon which her Majesty's Judges, a few days since, gave their opinion, at the desire of this House, the effect of that opinion, in which I for one entirely concur, is, that having regard to the interest which the late Lord Chancellor had in the Grand Junction Canal Company, his decision must be deemed to be voidable and that an appeal to this House must be considered,

---

[20] Hardres, 503.
[21] 1 Strange, 639.

as a proceeding in the Court of Equity, the proper step to be taken to avoid such a decree. . . .

[LORD BROUGHAM and LORD CAMPBELL delivered speeches in which they agreed with the advice given by the judges.]

Notes

1. The *Dimes* case has been influential in promoting the view that a breach of the bias rule renders a decision voidable. However, Wade, p. 438, argues that too wide a view should not be taken of the case. As Lord Cottenham's judgment was given in a *superior* court of law, Wade states that 'it would be naturally valid unless and until reversed on appeal'. Furthermore, he is critical of Parke B.'s treatment of *Brookes v. Earl of Rivers* (1668) Hardres 503 and *The Company of Mercers and Ironmongers of Chester v. Bowker* (1726) 1 Str. 639: see Wade, (1968) 84 L.Q.R. 95 at p. 108. There is, indeed, authority to support the view that a breach of the bias rule makes a decision void, rather than voidable (e.g. *Cooper v. Wilson* [1937] 2 K.B. 309). Some cases talk broadly of a decision in breach of natural justice being void: see e.g. *Ridge v. Baldwin*, p. 225 *infra*; *Hibernian Property Co. Ltd. v. Secretary of State for the Environment* (1973) 27 P. & C.R. 197. As Browne J. points out in this latter decision, *Anisminic Ltd. v. Foreign Compensation Commission* [1969] 2 A.C. 147 supports the view that a decision in breach of natural justice is a nullity: see [1969] 2 A.C. at p. 171 per Lord Reid, p. 195 per Lord Pearce, and pp. 207–8 per Lord Wilberforce. The use of the word nullity in fact caused Lord Wilberforce some misgiving, but in Browne J.'s view this was 'a matter of words and not of substance' ((1973) 27 P. & C.R. at p. 216). More recently the Privy Council has affirmed that a breach of natural justice is a jurisdictional defect (*Attorney-General v. Ryan* [1980] A.C. 718; *South East Asia Fire Bricks Sdn. Bhd. v. Non-Metallic Mineral Products Manufacturing Employees Union* [1981] A.C. 363 and the comment in Note 3, p. 377 *infra*); see also *Calvin v. Carr* [1980] A.C. 574, noted at p. 230 *infra*, and *Dunlop v. Woollahra M.C.*, p. 421 *infra*. Note also that Lord Denning, at one time a member of the 'voidable' school – see *Metropolitan Properties (F.G.C.) Ltd. v. Lannon*, p. 199 *supra*, and *R. v. Secretary of State for the Environment, ex p. Ostler*, p. 385 *infra* – has changed his mind: he has stated that a breach of natural justice renders a decision void (*Firman v. Ellis* [1978] Q.B. 886, although see the view quoted in Note 2, p. 107 *supra*). Several of the cases cited *supra* were in fact concerned with the other limb of natural justice (the *audi alteram partem* rule), but the comments contained in them were not expressly so restricted and therefore have been cited here. Thus the 'voidable' view seem not to hold sway today in Administrative Law; and see now *O'Reilly v. Mackman*, p. 326 *infra*.

For other authorities and arguments in favour of the view that a breach of the bias rule renders a decision void, see Wade, pp. 438–40 and (1968) 84 L.Q.R. at pp. 104–106, but see Jackson, *Natural Justice*, 2nd edn., pp. 187–94. For discussion of the problem, see also Akehurst, (1968) 31 M.L.R. 2 and 138. (Both this article and the discussion by Jackson cover the *audi alteram partem* aspect of natural justice as well, on which see p. 225 *infra*.) The points made in Note 2 *infra* are also relevant to that aspect of natural justice. Both this Note and Note 2 should be seen as part of a more general problem which has been discussed in Ch. 3 *supra*. For example, we have been using the terms 'void' and 'voidable' here, but it should be remembered that these terms have not always met with judicial approval recently: see Note 2, p. 107 *supra*.

2. There is a common law rule that a body with a jurisdiction laid down by statute cannot have its jurisdiction increased by the consent of the parties: *Farquharson v.*

Morgan [1894] 1 Q.B. 552; *Essex C.C.* v. *Essex Incorporated Congregational Church Union*, p. 33 *supra*. However, there are many cases where a person has waived objection to or acquiesced in the participation in a decision by an interested person and, as a consequence, the decision has been upheld. The efficacy of waiver in this situation could be used to support the view that breach of the bias rule merely renders a decision voidable. On the other hand, various explanations can be put forward to show that the operation of the doctrine of waiver is not inconsistent with the view that such a breach is a jurisdictional error, rendering a decision void.

(a) A court may refuse a *remedy* on account of waiver by the applicant, but this is not to deny that the impugned decision is void: see Wade, (1968) 84 L.Q.R. 95 at pp. 109–10, citing *R.* v. *Williams, ex p. Phillips* [1914] 1 K.B. 608.

(b) Alternatively, where an objection to the participation of a biased person is waived, it has been argued that there is in fact no breach of natural justice. This is on the basis that the term requiring natural justice which is implied in the statute should be so defined as to exclude cases of waiver: see Wade, (1968) 84 L.Q.R. at p. 109. (A similar argument can be made in relation to the *audi alteram partem* rule.)

(c) Akehurst, (1968) 31 M.L.R. 138 at pp. 144–49 would argue that the common law rule as set out *supra* is stated too widely and that *certain* defects, which would otherwise go to jurisdiction, can be cured by consent or waiver. This leads him to reject the view that a breach of natural justice must necessarily be regarded as a non-jurisdictional defect merely because waiver is effective in natural justice cases.

The preceding discussion has assumed that waiver can always operate in some way in natural justice cases, but for an inconsistent view see *Mayes* v. *Mayes* [1971] 1 W.L.R. 679 at p. 684 per Sir Jocelyn Simon P. For two recent decisions touching on waiver and natural justice see *Walsh* v. *McCluskie*, The Times, 16 December 1982; *R.* v. *B.B.C., ex p. Lavelle* [1983] 1 W.L.R. 23 at p. 39: both in fact concerned the *audi alteram partem* rule.

8

THE RIGHT TO A FAIR HEARING

ADMINISTRATIVE CASES

Cooper v. The Board of Works for the Wandsworth District

(1863) 14 C.B.N.S. 180   Court of Common Pleas

The plaintiff brought an action in trespass for the demolition of a house which was in the course of erection. Willes J. directed a verdict to be entered for the plaintiff, leave being reserved to the defendants to move to enter the verdict for them, or a nonsuit if the court should be of the opinion that the action was not maintainable. A rule nisi was accordingly obtained.

ERLE C.J.: I am of opinion that this rule ought to be discharged. This was an action of trespass by the plaintiff against the Wandsworth district board, for pulling down and demolishing his house; and the ground of defence that has been put forward by the defendants has been under the 76th section of the Metropolis Local Management Act, 18 & 19 Vict. c. 120. By the part of that section which applies to this case, it is enacted, that, before any person shall begin to build a new house, he shall give seven days' notice to the district board of his intention to build; and it provides at the end, that, in default of such notice it shall be lawful for the district board to demolish the house. The district board here say, that no notice was given by the plaintiff of his intention to build the house in question, wherefore they demolished it. The contention on the part of the plaintiff has been, that, although the words of the statute, taken in their literal sense, without any qualification at all, would create a justification for the act which the district board has done, the powers granted by that statute are subject to a qualification which has been repeatedly recognized, that no man is to be deprived of his property without his having an opportunity of being heard. The evidence here shews that the plaintiff and the district board had not been quite on amicable terms. Be that as it may, the district board say that no notice was given, and that consequently they had a right to proceed to demolish the house without delay, and without notice to the party whose house was to be pulled down, and without giving him an opportunity of shewing any reason why the board should delay. I think that the power which is granted by the 76th section is subject to the qualification suggested. It is a power carrying with it enormous consequences. The house in question was built only to a certain extent. But the power claimed would apply to a complete house. It would apply to a house of any value, and completed to any extent; and it seems to me to be a power which may be exercised most perniciously, and that the limitation which we are going to put upon it is one which ought, according to the decided cases, to be put upon it, and one which is required by a due consideration for the public interest. I think the board ought to have given notice to the plaintiff, and to have allowed him to be heard. The default in sending notice to the board of the intention to build, is a default which may be explained. There may be a great many excuses for the apparent default. The party may have intended to conform to the law. He may have actually conformed to all the regulations which they would wish to impose, though by accident his notice may have miscarried; and, under those circumstances, if he explained how it stood, the proceeding to demolish, merely because they had ill-will against the party, is a power that the legislature never intended to confer. I cannot conceive any harm that could happen to the district board from hearing the party before they subjected him to a loss so serious as the demolition of his house; but I can conceive a great many advantages which might arise in the way of public order, in the way of doing substantial justice, and in the way of fulfilling the purposes of the statute, by the restriction which we put upon them, that they should hear the party before they inflict upon him such a heavy loss. I fully agree that the legislature intended to give the district board very large powers indeed: but the qualification I speak of is one which has been recognised to the full extent. It has been said that the principle that no man shall be deprived of his property without an opportunity of being heard, is limited to a judicial proceeding, and that a district board ordering a house to be pulled down cannot be said to be doing a judicial act. I do not quite agree with that; neither do I undertake to rest my judgment solely upon the ground that the district board is a court exercising judicial discretion upon the point: but the law, I think, has been applied to many exercises of power which in common understanding would not be at all more a judicial proceeding than would be the act of the district board in ordering a house to be pulled down. . . .

WILLES J.: . . . I apprehend that a tribunal which is by law invested with power to affect the property of one of Her Majesty's subjects, is bound to give such subjects an opportunity of being heard before it proceeds: and that that rule is of universal application, and founded upon the plainest principles of justice. Now, is the board in the present case such a tribunal? I apprehend it clearly is, whether we consider it with reference to the discretion which is vested in it, or whether we look at the analogy which exists between it and other recognised tribunals (and no one ever doubted that such tribunals are bound by the rules which a court of justice is bound by), or whether you look at it with reference to the estimation in which it is held by the legislature, as appears from the language used in the statute. . . .

BYLES J.: . . . This is a case in which the Wandsworth district board have taken upon themselves to pull down a house, and to saddle the owner with the expenses of demolition, without notice of any sort. . . . It seems to me that the board are wrong whether they acted judicially or ministerially. I conceive they acted judicially, because they had to determine the offence, and they had to apportion the punishment as well as the remedy. That being so, a long course of decisions, beginning with *Dr. Bentley's Case*,[1] and ending with some very recent cases, establish, that, although there are no positive words in a statute requiring that the party shall be heard, yet the justice of the common law will supply the omission of the legislature. The judgment of Mr. Justice Fortescue, in *Dr. Bentley's Case*,[1] is somewhat quaint, but it is very applicable, and has been the law from that time to the present. He says, 'The objection for want of notice can never be got over. The laws of God and man both give the party an opportunity to make his defence, if he has any. I remember to have heard it observed by a very learned man, upon such an occasion, that even God himself did not pass sentence upon Adam before he was called upon to make his defence. "Adam" (says God), "where art thou? Hast thou not eaten of the tree whereof I commanded thee that thou shouldest not eat?" And the same question was put to Eve also.' If, therefore, the board acted judicially, although there are no words in the statute to that effect, it is plain they acted wrongly. . . .

[KEATING J. delivered a judgment in favour of discharging the rule.]

Rule discharged.

Question

Given that to require a hearing will slow down the decision-making process, can it nevertheless be argued that such a requirement will make the process more efficient?

Notes

1. The right to a fair hearing is, it should be noted, often termed *audi alteram partem*.

2. Those interested in the events in the Garden of Eden should consult Taylor, *Evidence*, 12th ed., p. 1181 which discusses the biblical precedent cited by Fortescue J. in *Dr. Bentley's* case (1723) 1 Str. 557 and which considers the position of the serpent.

3. It might have been noticed by the student that Willes J. was a member of the Court of Common Pleas which was dealing with a case in which his earlier ruling was under consideration. On this point see Note 1, p. 203 *supra*.

4. *Cooper's* case concerned a public body exercising a statutory power. In other natural justice cases the source of the power has been contractual (and note the extension of control in *McInnes* v. *Onslow-Fane*, p. 262 *infra*.). This difference should be borne in mind, but the importance of natural justice in the sphere where people's livelihood is governed by a private body (e.g. a trade union) is sufficiently important for it to receive some attention in this chapter in particular. Furthermore, cases on natural justice from that sphere are cited in cases concerned with public bodies exercising statutory powers (and *vice versa*).

5. Another point to notice about *Cooper's* case is that it is an example of the *audi alteram partem* principle being applied to the activities of an administrative body. See

[1] *The King* v. *The Chancellor & c. of Cambridge*, 1 Stra, 557, 2 Ld. Raym. 1334, 8 Mod. 148, Fortesque, 202.

also the oft-cited view of Lord Loreburn L.C. in *Board of Education v. Rice* [1911] A.C. 179 at p. 182, quoted by Wade, p. 451, but note *Local Government Board v. Arlidge* [1915] A.C. 120. In the latter case an inspector had held a public local inquiry into a particular matter at which Arlidge's case was put forward; the inspector made a report to the Board which then made its decision. The House of Lords held that it was not a breach of natural justice for the Board to refuse to disclose the report (though see now p. 614 *infra*); nor did the deciding officer have to give Arlidge a further hearing after the inquiry. Viscount Haldane thought that the Board was similar to a government department in that it was 'an organisation with executive functions'. He continued by saying that where 'Parliament entrusts it with judicial duties, Parliament must be taken, in the absence of any declaration to the contrary, to have intended it to follow the procedure which is its own, and is necessary if it is to be capable of doing its work efficiently' (p. 132).

For an explanation of the reasons for the approach in this case, see Abel-Smith and Stevens, *Lawyers and the Courts*, p. 115. *Arlidge*'s case has been seen as the forerunner of an era in which the courts showed undue restraint in imposing procedural protection: see further the next but one section.

STATUTORY HEARINGS

Errington v. Minister of Health, p. 581 *infra*

Franklin v. Minister of Town and Country Planning, p. 204 *supra*

Note

On this topic see *Arlidge*'s case [1915] A.C. 120, noted *supra*, and see generally Wade, p. 452 where he traces the development of the relationship of natural justice to the statutory procedures involving the public local inquiry: see especially Wade, pp. 457–8 in relation to the *Franklin* case, which, of course, directly concerned the rule against bias. The position today will be considered to some extent in Ch. 17 *infra*.

THE RETREAT FROM NATURAL JUSTICE

Franklin v. Minister of Town and Country Planning, p. 204 *supra*

Note

For comment on other relevant cases, especially *Nakkuda Ali v. Jayaratne* [1951] A.C. 66, which is discussed in the case *infra*, see Wade, p. 458; de Smith, p. 164.

THE RIGHT TO BE HEARD REINSTATED

Ridge v. Baldwin

[1964] A.C. 40   House of Lords

Ridge, the Chief Constable of Brighton, was suspended from duty after he had been arrested and charged with conspiracy to obstruct the course of justice. At his trial Ridge was acquitted. However, when sentencing two police officers from his force who were charged with him (but who were convicted), the trial judge (Donovan J.) was critical of Ridge's leadership of his force. At a later date, when a corruption charge was brought against Ridge, the prosecution offered no evidence. Donovan J. directed Ridge's acquittal, but made another comment concerning the leadership of the force.

The watch committee met the next day (7 March 1958) and decided that Ridge should be dismissed. Section 191 (4) of the Municipal Corporations Act 1882 provided that a watch committee could dismiss 'any borough constable whom they think negligent in the discharge of his duty, or otherwise unfit for the same'. Ridge was not asked to attend the meeting, but was later told that he had been summarily dismissed and was also told of certain resolutions passed at the meeting. At the request of Ridge's solicitor, the watch committee reconvened some days later (18 March 1958). Having received representations from Ridge's solicitor, the watch committee decided not to change the original decision. Before this second meeting Ridge gave formal notice of appeal against the original decision to the Home Secretary under the Police (Appeals) Act 1927. However, he also stated that this was without prejudice to his right to argue that the procedure adopted by the watch committee had been in breach of the relevant statutory provisions and in breach of natural justice, and therefore invalid. The Home Secretary dismissed the appeal and Ridge resorted to the courts. Part of the relief sought was a declaration that the purported termination of his appointment was illegal, ultra vires, and void, and that he was still the Chief Constable of Brighton.

After his action had failed before Streatfield J. and his appeal had been dismissed by the Court of Appeal ([1963] 1 Q.B. 539), Ridge appealed to the House of Lords. The extracts *infra* are concerned with the question whether Ridge's dismissal contravened the rules of natural justice. Apart from this question, however, it should be noted that a majority of the House of Lords (Lord Reid, Lord Morris, Lord Hodson, and Lord Devlin, Lord Evershed dissenting) decided that the dismissal was invalid on the ground that there had been a breach of the statutory regulations governing police discipline. For consideration of (*a*) the argument that nothing that Ridge could have said would have made any difference to the decision, and (*b*) the status of a decision reached in breach of natural justice, see pp. 234 and 225 *infra* respectively.

LORD REID: . . . The appellant's case is that in proceeding under the Act of 1882 the watch committee were bound to observe what are commonly called the principles of natural justice. Before attempting to reach any decision they were bound to inform him of the grounds on which they proposed to act and give him a fair opportunity of being heard in his own defence. The authorities on the applicability of the principles of natural justice are in some confusion, and so I find it necessary to examine this matter in some detail. The principle audi alteram partem goes back many centuries in our law and appears in a multitude of judgments of judges of the highest authority. In modern times opinions have sometimes been expressed to the effect that natural justice is so vague as to be practically meaningless. But I would regard these as tainted by the perennial fallacy that because something cannot be cut and dried or nicely weighed or measured therefore it does not exist. . . . It appears to me that one reason why the authorities on natural justice have been found difficult to reconcile is that insufficient attention has been paid to the great difference between various kinds of cases in which it has been sought to apply the principle. What a minister ought to do in considering objections to a scheme may be very different from what a watch committee ought to do in considering whether to dismiss a chief constable. So I shall deal first with cases of dismissal. These appear to fall into three classes: dismissal of a servant by his master, dismissal from an office held during pleasure, and dismissal from an office where there must be something against a man to warrant his dismissal.

The law regarding master and servant is not in doubt. There cannot be specific performance of a contract of service, and the master can terminate the contract with his servant at any time and for any reason or for none. But if he does so in a manner not warranted by the contract he must pay damages for breach of contract. So the question in a pure case of master and servant does not at all depend on whether the master has heard the servant in his own defence: it depends on whether the facts emerging at the trial prove breach of contract. But this kind of case can resemble dismissal from an office where the body employing the man is under some statutory or other restriction as to the kind of contract which it can make with its servants, or the grounds on which it can dismiss them. The present case does not fall within this class because a chief constable is not the servant of the watch committee or indeed of anyone else.

Then there are many cases where a man holds an office at pleasure. Apart from judges and others whose tenure of office is governed by statute, all servants and officers of the Crown hold office at pleasure, and this has been held even to apply to a colonial judge (*Terrell* v. *Secretary of State for the Colonies*[2]). It has always been held, I think rightly, that such an officer has no right to be heard before he is dismissed, and the reason is clear. As the person having the power of dismissal need not have anything against the officer, he need not give any reason. That was stated as long ago as 1670 in *Rex* v. *Stratford-on-Avon Corporation*[3]. . . . I fully accept that where an office is simply held at pleasure the person having power of dismissal cannot be bound to disclose his reasons. No doubt he would in many cases tell the officer and hear his explanation before deciding to dismiss him. But if he is not bound to disclose his reason and does not do so, then, if the court cannot require him to do so, it cannot determine whether it would be fair to hear the officer's case before taking action. But again that is not the case. In this case the Act of 1882 only permits the watch committee to take action on the grounds of negligence or unfitness. Let me illustrate the difference by supposing that a watch committee who had no complaint against their present chief constable heard of a man with quite outstanding qualifications who would like to be

[2] [1953] 2 Q.B. 482.
[3] (1809) 11 East 176.

appointed. They might think it in the public interest to make the change, but they would have no right to do it. But there could be no legal objection to dismissal of an officer holding office at pleasure in order to put a better man in his place.

So I come to the third class, which includes the present case. There I find an unbroken line of authority to the effect that an officer cannot lawfully be dismissed without first telling him what is alleged against him and hearing his defence or explanation. . . .

[Having cited *Bagg's Case*;[4] *R. v. Gaskin*;[5] *R. v. Smith*;[6] *Ex p. Ramshay*;[7] *Osgood v. Nelson*;[8] *Fisher v. Jackson*;[9] *Cooper v. Wilson*;[10] and *Hogg v. Scott*;[11] his Lordship continued:]

Stopping there, I would think that authority was wholly in favour of the appellant, but the respondent's argument was mainly based on what has been said in a number of fairly recent cases dealing with different subject-matter. Those cases deal with decisions by ministers, officials and bodies of various kinds which adversely affected property rights or privileges of persons who had had no opportunity or no proper opportunity of presenting their cases before the decisions were given. And it is necessary to examine those cases for another reason. The question which was or ought to have been considered by the watch committee on March 7, 1958, was not a simple question whether or not the appellant should be dismissed. There were three possible courses open to the watch committee – reinstating the appellant as chief constable, dismissing him, or requiring him to resign. The difference between the latter two is that dismissal involved forfeiture of pension rights, whereas requiring him to resign did not. Indeed, it is now clear that the appellant's real interest in this appeal is to try to save his pension rights. . . .

I would start an examination of the authorities dealing with property rights and privileges with *Cooper v. Wandsworth Board of Works*.[12] Where an owner had failed to give proper notice to the Board they had under an Act of 1855 authority to demolish any building he had erected and recover the cost from him. This action was brought against the board because they had used that power without giving the owner an opportunity of being heard. The board maintained that their discretion to order demolition was not a judicial discretion and that any appeal should have been to the Metropolitan Board of Works. But the court decided unanimously in favour of the owner. . . .

[LORD REID also referred to *Hopkins v. Smethwick Local Board of Health*;[13] *Smith v. R*;[14] *De Verteuil v. Knaggs*;[15] and *Spackman v. Plumstead District Board of Works*,[16] and continued:]

[4] (1615) 11 Co. Rep 93b. [5] (1799) 8 Term Rep. 209.
[6] (1844) 5 Q.B. 614. [7] (1852) 18 Q.B. 173.
[8] (1872) L.R. 5 H.L. 636 H.L.
[9] [1891] 2 Ch. 84. [10] [1937] 2 K.B. 309.
[11] [1947] K.B. 759. [12] (1863) 14 C.B.N.S. 180.
[13] (1890) 24 Q.B.D. 712.
[14] (1878) L.R. 3 App. Cas. 614, P.C.
[15] [1918] A.C. 557. [16] (1885) 10 App. Cas. 229.

I shall now turn to a different class of case – deprivation of membership of a professional or social body. In *Wood* v. *Woad*[17] the committee purported to expel a member of a mutual insurance society without hearing him, and it was held that their action was void, and so he was still a member. Kelly C.B. said of audi alteram partem:[18] 'This rule is not confined to the conduct of strictly legal tribunals, but is applicable to every tribunal or body of persons invested with authority to adjudicate upon matters involving civil consequences to individuals.' This was expressly approved by Lord Macnaghten giving the judgment of the Board in *Lapointe* v. *L'Association de Bienfaisance et de Retraite de la Police de Montréal.*[19] . . .

Then there are the club cases, *Fisher* v. *Keane*[20] and *Dawkins* v. *Antrobus.*[21] In the former, Jessel M.R. said of the committee:[22] 'They ought not, as I understand it, according to the ordinary rules by which justice should be administered by committee of clubs, or by any other body of persons who decide upon the conduct of others, to blast a man's reputation for ever – perhaps to ruin his prospects for life, without giving him an opportunity of either defending or palliating his conduct.' In the latter case it was held that nothing had been done contrary to natural justice. . . .

. . . It appears to me that if the present case had arisen thirty or forty years ago the courts would have had no difficulty in deciding this issue in favour of the appellant on these authorities which I have cited. So far as I am aware none of these authorities has ever been disapproved or even doubted. Yet the Court of Appeal have decided this issue against the appellant on more recent authorities which apparently justify that result. How has this come about?

At least three things appear to me to have contributed. In the first place there have been many cases where it has been sought to apply the principles of natural justice to the wider duties imposed on Ministers and other organs of government by modern legislation. For reasons which I shall attempt to state in a moment, it has been held that those principles have a limited application in such cases and those limitations have tended to be reflected in other decisions on matters to which in principle they do not appear to me to apply. Secondly, again for reasons which I shall attempt to state, those principles have been held to have a limited application in cases arising out of war-time legislation; and again such limitations have tended to be reflected in other cases. And, thirdly, there has, I think, been a misunderstanding of the judgment of Atkin L.J. in *Rex* v. *Electricity Commissioners, Ex parte London Electricity Joint Committee Co.*[23]

In cases of the kind I have been dealing with the Board of Works or the Governor or the club committee was dealing with a single isolated case. It was not deciding, like a judge in a lawsuit, what were the rights of the person before it. But it was deciding how he should be treated – something analogous to a judge's duty in imposing a penalty. No doubt policy would play some

---

[17] (1874) L.R. 9 Ex. 190.
[18] Ibid. 196.
[19] [1906] A.C. 535.
[20] (1878) 11 Ch. D. 353.
[21] (1879) 17 Ch. D. 615 C.A.
[22] 11 Ch. D. 353, 362–363.
[23] [1924] 1 K.B. 171.

part in the decision – but so it might when a judge is imposing a sentence. So it was easy to say that such a body is performing a quasi-judicial task in considering and deciding such a matter, and to require it to observe the essentials of all proceedings of a judicial character – the principles of natural justice.

Sometimes the functions of a minister or department may also be of that character, and then the rules of natural justice can apply in much the same way. But more often their functions are of a very different character. If a minister is considering whether to make a scheme for, say, an important new road, his primary concern will not be with the damage which its construction will do to the rights of individual owners of land. He will have to consider all manner of questions of public interest and, it may be, a number of alternative schemes. He cannot be prevented from attaching more importance to the fulfilment of his policy than to the fate of individual objectors, and it would be quite wrong for the courts to say that the minister should or could act in the same kind of way as a board of works deciding whether a house should be pulled down. And there is another important difference. As explained in *Local Government Board* v. *Arlidge*[24] a minister cannot do everything himself. His officers will have to gather and sift all the facts, including objections by individuals, and no individual can complain if the ordinary accepted methods of carrying on public business do not give him as good protection as would be given by the principles of natural justice in a different kind of case.

We do not have a developed system of administrative law – perhaps because until fairly recently we did not need it. So it is not surprising that in dealing with new types of cases the courts have had to grope for solutions, and have found that old powers, rules and procedure are largely inapplicable to cases which they were never designed or intended to deal with. But I see nothing in that to justify our thinking that our old methods are any less applicable today than ever they were to the older types of case. And if there are any dicta in modern authorities which point in that direction, then, in my judgment, they should not be followed.

And now I must say something regarding war-time legislation. The older authorities clearly show how the courts engrafted the principles of natural justice on to a host of provisions authorising administrative interference with private rights. Parliament knew quite well that the courts had an inveterate habit of doing that and must therefore be held to have authorised them to do it unless a particular Act showed a contrary intention. And such an intention could appear as a reasonable inference as well as from express words. It seems to me to be a reasonable and almost an inevitable inference from the circumstances in which Defence Regulations were made and from their subject-matter that, at least in many cases, the intention must have been to exclude the principles of natural justice. . . . I would not think that any decision that the rules of natural justice were excluded from war-time legislation should be regarded as of any great weight in dealing with a case such as this case, which is of the older type, and which involves the interpretation of an Act passed

[24] [1915] A.C. 120.

long before modern modifications of the principles of natural justice became necessary, and at a time when, as Parliament was well aware, the courts habitually applied the principles of natural justice to provisions like section 191 (4) of the Act of 1882.

The matter has been further complicated by what I believe to be a misunderstanding of a much-quoted passage in the judgment of Atkin L.J. in *Rex v. Electricity Commissioners, Ex parte London Electricity Joint Committee Co.*[25] He said: '. . . the operation of the writs [of prohibition and certiorari] has extended to control the proceedings of bodies which do not claim to be, and would not be recognised as courts of justice. Wherever any body of persons having legal authority to determine questions affecting the rights of subjects, and having the duty to act judicially, act in excess of their legal authority, they are subject to the controlling jurisdiction of the King's Bench Division exercises in these writs.'

A gloss was put on this by Lord Hewart C.J. in *Rex v. Legislative Committee of the Church Assembly, Ex parte Haynes-Smith.*[26] . . . Lord Hewart said,[27] having quoted the passage from Atkin L.J.'s judgment: . . . It is to be observed that in the last sentence which I have quoted . . . the word is not "or", but "and". . . . In order that a body may satisfy the required test it is not enough that it should have legal authority to determine questions affecting the rights of subjects; there must be superadded to that characteristic the further characteristic that the body has the duty to act judicially. The duty to act judicially is an ingredient which, if the test is to be satisfied, must be present. As these writs in the earlier days were issued only to bodies which without any harshness of construction could be called, and naturally would be called courts, so also today these writs do not issue except to bodies which act or are under the duty to act in a judicial capacity.'

. . . [T]his passage . . . is typical of what has been said in several subsequent cases. If Lord Hewart meant that it is never enough that a body simply has a duty to determine what the rights of an individual should be, but that there must always be something more to impose on it a duty to act judicially before it can be found to observe the principles of natural justice, then that appears to me impossible to reconcile with the earlier authorities. . . . And, as I shall try to show, it cannot be what Atkin L.J. meant.

In *Rex v. Electricity Commissioners, Ex parte London Electricity Joint Committee Co.*[28] . . . . Bankes L.J. . . . . inferred the judicial element from the nature of the power. And I think that Atkin L.J. did the same. . . .

There is not a word in Atkin L.J.'s judgment to suggest disapproval of the earlier line of authority which I have cited. On the contrary, he goes further than those authorities. I have already stated my view that it is more difficult for the courts to control an exercise of power on a large scale where the treatment to be meted out to a particular individual is only one of many matters to be considered. This was a case of that kind, and, if Atkin L.J. was prepared to infer a judicial element from the nature of the power in this case,

[25] [1924] 1 K.B. 171, 205.   [26] [1928] 1 K.B. 411.
[27] Ibid. 415.   [28] [1924] 1 K.B. 171.

he could hardly disapprove such an inference when the power relates solely to the treatment of a particular individual.

The authority chiefly relied on by the Court of Appeal [in the present case] in holding that the watch committee were not bound to observe the principles of natural justice was *Nakkuda Ali v. Jayaratne.*[29] In that case the Controller of Textiles in Ceylon made an order cancelling the appellant's licence to act as a dealer, and the appellant sought to have that order quashed. The controller acted under a Defence Regulation which empowered him to cancel a licence 'where the controller has reasonable grounds to believe that any dealer is unfit to be allowed to continue as a dealer.'

The Privy Council regarded that[30] as 'imposing a condition that there must in fact exist such reasonable grounds, known to the controller, before he can validly exercise the power of cancellation.' But according to their judgment certiorari did not lie, and no other means was suggested whereby the appellant or anyone else in his position could obtain redress even if the controller acted without a shred of evidence. It is quite true that the judgment went on, admittedly unnecessarily, to find that the controller had reasonable grounds and did observe the principles of natural justice, but the result would have been just the same if he had not. This House is not bound by decisions of the Privy Council, and for my own part nothing short of a decision of this House directly in point would induce me to accept the position that, although an enactment expressly requires an official to have reasonable grounds for his decision, our law is so defective that a subject cannot bring up such a decision for review however seriously he may be affected and however obvious it may be that the official acted in breach of his statutory obligation.

... [T]he crucial passage[31] [is]: 'But the basis of the jurisdiction of the courts by way of certiorari has been so exhaustively analysed in recent years that individual instances are now only of importance as illustrating a general principle that is beyond dispute. That principle is most precisely stated in the words of Atkin L.J. in *Rex v. Electricity Commissioners, Ex parte London Electricity Joint Committee Co.*'[32] – and then follows the passage with which I have already dealt at length. And then there follows the quotation from Lord Hewart, which I have already commented on, ending with the words – 'there must be superadded to that characteristic the further characteristic that the body has the duty to act judicially.' And then it is pointed out:[33] 'It is that characteristic that the controller lacks in acting under regulation 62.'

Of course, if it were right to say that Lord Hewart's gloss on Atkin L.J. stated 'a general principle that is beyond dispute,' the rest would follow. But I have given my reasons for holding that it does no such thing, and in my judgment the older cases certainly do not 'illustrate' any such general principle – they contradict it. No case older than 1911 was cited in *Nakkuda's* case[34] on this question, and this question was only one of several difficult questions which were argued and decided. So I am forced to the conclusion

[29] [1951] A.C. 66.   [30] [1951] A.C. 66, 77, P.C.
[31] [1951] A.C. 66, 78.   [32] [1924] 1 K.B. 171, 205.
[33] [1951] A.C. 66, 78.   [34] [1951] A.C. 66.

that this part of the judgment in *Nakkuda's* case[35] was given under a serious misapprehension of the effect of the older authorities and therefore cannot be regarded as authoritative.

I would sum up my opinion in this way. Between 1882 and the making of police regulations in 1920 section 191(4) had to be applied to every kind of case. The respondents' contention is that, even where there was a doubtful question whether a constable was guilty of a particular act of misconduct, the watch committee were under no obligation to hear his defence before dismissing him. In my judgment it is abundantly clear from the authorities I have quoted that at that time the courts would have rejected any such contention. In later cases dealing with different subject-matter, opinions have been expressed in wide terms so as to appear to conflict with those earlier authorities. But learned judges who expressed those opinions generally had no power to overrule those authorities, and in any event it is a salutary rule that a judge is not to be assumed to have intended to overrule or disapprove of an authority which has not been cited to him and which he does not even mention. So I would hold that the power of dismissal in the Act of 1882 could not then have been exercised and cannot now be exercised until the watch committee have informed the constable of the grounds on which they propose to proceed and have given him a proper opportunity to present his case in defence.

Next comes the question whether the respondents' failure to follow the rules of natural justice on March 7 was made good by the meeting on March 18. I do not doubt that if an officer or body realises that it has acted hastily and reconsiders the whole matter afresh, after affording to the person affected a proper opportunity to present his case, then its later decision will be valid. An example is *De Verteuil's* case.[36] But here the appellant's solicitor was not fully informed of the charges against the appellant and the watch committee did not annul the decision which they had already published and proceed to make a new decision. In my judgment, what was done on that day was a very inadequate substitute for a full rehearing. Even so, three members of the committee changed their minds, and it is impossible to say what the decision of the committee would have been if there had been a full hearing after disclosure to the appellant of the whole case against him. I agree with those of your Lordships[37] who hold that this meeting of March 18 cannot affect the result of this appeal. . . .

. . . [I]n my judgment, this appeal must be allowed. . . . I do not think that this House should do more than declare that the dismissal of the appellant is null and void and remit the case to the Queen's Bench Division for further procedure. But it is right to put on record that the appellant does not seek to be reinstated as chief constable: his whole concern is to avoid the serious financial consequences involved in dismissal as against being required or allowed to resign.

[35] [1951] A.C. 66.
[36] [1918] A.C. 557.
[37] [Lord Morris and Lord Hodson.]

LORD MORRIS OF BORTH-Y-GEST: . . . Being of the view that . . . a decision to dismiss the appellant for neglect of duty ought only to have been taken in the exercise of a quasi-judicial function which demanded an observance of the rules of natural justice – I entertain no doubt that such rules were not observed. Before March 7 there was neither notice of what was alleged nor opportunity to deal with what was alleged. . . .

LORD HODSON: My Lords, I have reached the conclusion . . . that this appeal should succeed upon the ground that the appellant was entitled to and did not receive natural justice at the hands of the watch committee of Brighton when he was dismissed on March 7, 1958. . . .

I should not delay further before referring to the terms of the statute of 1882 itself, for it is upon the construction of that statute that the answer to the question posed before your Lordships depends.

It is quite true that upon its terms there is a power to dismiss any borough constable (and this applies to the appellant) whom they think negligent in the discharge of his duty or otherwise unfit for the same. I entirely accept the reasoning underlying the judgments of the Lords Justices[38] that if a statute gives an unfettered power to dismiss at pleasure without more that is an end of the matter.

The topic is, however, not as simple as would seem. A large number of authorities were cited to your Lordships beginning with *Bagg's Case*[39] and extending to the present day. I will not travel over the field of the authorities, which I am bound to say are not easy to reconcile with one another, for if I did, I should surely omit some which might be thought to be of equal or greater importance than those I mentioned, but certain matters seem to me clearly to emerge. One is that the absence of a lis or dispute between opposing parties is not a decisive feature although, no doubt, the presence of a lis would involve the necessity for the applications of the principles of natural justice. Secondly, the answer in a given case is not provided by the statement that the giver of the decision is acting in an executive or administrative capacity as if that was the antithesis of a judicial capacity. The cases seem to me to show that persons acting in a capacity which is not on the face of it judicial but rather executive or administrative have been held by the courts to be subject to the principles of natural justice. . . .

The matter which, to my mind, is relevant in this case is that where the power to be exercised involves a charge made against the person who is dismissed, by that I mean a charge of misconduct, the principles of natural justice have to be observed before the power is exercised.

. . . No one, I think, disputes that three features of natural justice stand out – (1) the right to be heard by an unbiased tribunal; (2) the right to have notice of charges of misconduct; (3) the right to be heard in answer to those charges. The first does not arise in the case before your Lordships, but the two last most certainly do, and the proceedings before the watch committee, therefore, in my opinion, cannot be allowed to stand. . . .

[38] [[1963] 1 Q.B. 539.]
[39] 11 Co. Rep. 93b.

[LORD EVERSHED delivered a speech in favour of dismissing the appeal.
LORD DEVLIN delivered a speech in favour allowing the appeal.]

Appeal allowed.

Questions

1. If the matter had gone back to the watch committee for redetermination (on which see Note 2 *infra*), might the argument that the committee would be biased because of its earlier decision have succeeded?

2. Did Lord Reid deny the need for there to be any 'judicial element' in a case before the rules of natural justice could apply?

Notes

1. Lord Devlin based his decision on the regulations governing police discipline and did not find it necessary to decide whether the rules of natural justice were applicable. Compare Lord Evershed's speech. On the assumption that the rules of natural justice were applicable and that initially there had been a breach of natural justice, Lord Evershed decided that the breach had been remedied at the second meeting of the watch committee.

2. After the House of Lords had reached its decision, the appellant gave notice of resignation. The proceedings were stayed on terms which included the payment to the appellant of £6,424. 6s. 8d. as a settlement of his claim for arrears of salary and an undertaking that the appellant would receive a pension, the amount being such as would have been appropriate if he had been compulsorily retired on the date when the watch committee purported to dismiss him (*Ridge* v. *Baldwin*, The Times, 30 July 1963). On the consequences of a declaration that dismissal was invalid, see Note 5, p. 297 *infra*.

3. For comment on *Ridge* v. *Baldwin*, see de Smith, (1963) 26 M.L.R. 543; Goodhart, (1964) 80 L.Q.R. 105; Bradley, [1964] C.L.J. 83. The unsatisfactory state of the law before this decision will not be set out in detail here (see p. 4 *supra*). Suffice it to say that *Ridge* v. *Baldwin* helped to free the rules of natural justice from the unduly restrictive limitations imposed by earlier decisions. In particular, Lord Reid's rejection of the need for a court to find a duty to act judicially on the part of the body involved *in addition* to the possession by that body of a power to determine questions affecting the rights of subjects, rendered the 'judicial requirement' much less of an obstacle, and, as will be seen, later cases have taken the matter further: see p. 282 *infra*.

4. On the traditional approach, both the availability of the remedies of certiorari and prohibition and the applicability of the rules of natural justice depend on the body concerned being under a duty to act judicially or exercising judicial or quasi-judicial functions. It will, therefore, be appreciated that Lord Reid's speech (in particular) in *Ridge* v. *Baldwin* is also of relevance to these remedies. The interrelationship between natural justice and these remedies is evidenced by the fact that an important part of Lord Reid's speech is concerned with the interpretation of a passage in Atkin L.J.'s judgment in *R.* v. *Electricity Commissioners, ex p. London Electricity Joint Committee Co.*, p. 308 *infra*, a passage which deals with the availability of certiorari and prohibition. Yet *Ridge* v. *Baldwin* did not involve an application for certiorari or prohibition and *R.* v. *Electricity Commissioners* was not concerned with natural justice. On the question of the need for a 'judicial element' before certiorari or

prohibition will be available, see further Note 1, p. 310 *infra*, and on the classification of functions more generally, see p. 4 *supra*.

5. The applicability of natural justice to cases of dismissal from employment is discussed more fully at p. 270 *infra*.

Rights, liberties, and expectations

Schmidt v. Secretary of State for Home Affairs, p. 280 *infra*

Cinnamond v. British Airports Authority, p. 236 *infra*

McInnes v. Onslow-Fane, p. 262 *infra*

Notes

1. Consider Lord Denning's shift in *Cinnamond* from the phrase 'some legitimate expectation of which it would not be fair to deprive him without hearing what he has to say' (quoting from his judgment in *Schmidt*'s case) to 'a legitimate expectation of being heard'. How much guidance does the latter phrase give? And see Appendix.

2. For further discussion in Australian case law, see *Salemi v. MacKellar (No. 2)* (1977) 137 C.L.R. 396; *Heatley v. Tasmanian Racing and Gaming Commission* ibid. 487; *Forbes v. N.S.W. Trotting Club Ltd.* (1978–79) 143 C.L.R. 242; Cane, (1980) 54 A.L.J. 546; Churches, [1980] P.L. 397 at pp. 407–13.

Void or voidable?

Ridge v. Baldwin

[1964] A.C. 40   House of Lords

For the facts of and decision in this case, see p. 214 *supra*.

LORD REID: ... Time and again in the cases I have cited it has been stated that a decision given without regard to the principles of natural justice is void, and that was expressly decided in *Wood* v. *Woad*.[40] I see no reason to doubt these authorities. The body with the power to decide cannot lawfully proceed to make a decision until it has afforded to the person affected a proper opportunity to state his case. ...

LORD MORRIS OF BORTH-Y-GEST: ... [T]here was an abnegation of the quasi-judicial duties involved in the function of the watch committee, with the result that their decision must be regarded as of no effect and invalid, and so can be declared by the court to be void. (See *Bagg's Case*,[41] *R.* v. *University of Cambridge*,[43] *Wood* v. *Woad*,[43] *Fisher* v. *Keane*.[44])

It was submitted that the decision of the watch committee was voidable but not void. But this involves the inquiry as to the sense in which the word 'voidable,' a word deriving from the law of contract, is in this connection

[40] L.R. 9 Ex. 190.
[41] 11 Co. Rep. 93b.   [42] 1 Stra. 557.
[43] L.R. 9 Ex. 190.   [44] 11 Ch. D. 353.

used. If the appellant had bowed to the decision of the watch committee and had not asserted that it was void, then no occasion to use either word would have arisen. When the appellant in fact at once repudiated and challenged the decision, so claiming that it was invalid, and when in fact the watch committee adhered to their decision, so claiming that it was valid, only the court could decide who was right. If in that situation it was said that the decision was voidable, that was only to say that the decision of the court was awaited. But if and when the court decides that the appellant was right, the court is deciding that the decision of the watch committee was invalid and of no effect and null and void. The word 'voidable' is therefore apposite in the sense that it became necessary for the appellant to take his stand: he was obliged to take action, for unless he did, the view of the watch committee, who were in authority, would prevail. In that sense the decision of the watch committee could be said to be voidable. The appellant could, I think, have applied for an order of certiorari: he was not saying that those who purported to dismiss him were not the watch committee; he was recognising that they had a power and jurisdiction to dismiss, but he was saying that whether the regulations applied or whether they did not, the committee could only exercise their power and jurisdiction after hearing his reply to what was said against him. In these circumstances he could, I think, have applied for an order of certiorari (though considerations of convenience would probably have pointed against pursuing such a course) or he could have asked for a declaration. . . .

LORD HODSON: . . . In all the cases where the courts have held that the principles of natural justice have been flouted, I can find none where the language does not indicate the opinion held that the decision impugned was void. It is true that the distinction between void and voidable is not drawn explicitly in the cases, but the language used shows that where there is a want of jurisdiction as opposed to a failure to follow a procedural requirement the result is a nullity. This was, indeed, decided by the Court of Exchequer in *Wood* v. *Woad*[45] where, as here, there was a failure to give a hearing.

In *Spackman* v. *Plumstead District Board of Works*,[46] referring to another statement, Lord Selborne said. 'There would be no decision within the meaning of the statute if there were anything of that sort done contrary to the essence of justice.' . . .

Note

For the views of Lord Evershed and Lord Devlin on this question, see the extract from the next case.

Durayappah v. Fernando

[1967] 2 A.C. 337   Judicial Committee of the Privy Council

This was an appeal from the Supreme Court of Ceylon. Section 277 (1) of the Municipal Councils Ordinance (c. 252), as amended, provided:

[45] L.R. 9 Ex. 190.
[46] L.R. 10 App. Cas. 229, 240.

If at any time, upon representation made or otherwise, it appears to the Minister [of Local Government] that a municipal council is not competent to perform, or persistently makes default in the performance of, any duty or duties, imposed upon it, or persistently refuses or neglects to comply with any provision of law, the Minister may, by Order published in the Gazette, direct that the council shall be dissolved and superseded, and thereupon such council shall . . . be dissolved, and cease to have, exercise, perform and discharge any of the rights, privileges, powers, duties, and functions conferred or imposed upon it, or vested in it. . . .

The Minister had received a number of complaints about the Jaffna Municipal Council. The Commissioner of Local Government, who was sent to investigate these matters, reported to the Minister, who, acting under s. 277, dissolved the Council on the ground that it appeared to him that the Council was not competent to perform its duties: see further p. 230 *infra*, where it will be seen that the Privy Council decided the Minister had acted in breach of natural justice. This extract is concerned with the status of the Minister's order dissolving the Council of which the appellant had been the Mayor at the time of its dissolution.

LORD UPJOHN [delivering the judgment of their Lordships]: . . . [D]uring the hearing of the appeal, their Lordships raised the question, not taken in the court below, whether the appellant was entitled to maintain this action and appeal. The question is of some general importance. The answer must depend essentially upon whether the order of the Minister was a complete nullity or whether it was an order voidable only at the election of the council. If the former it must follow that the council is still in office and that, if any councillor, ratepayer or other person having a legitimate interest in the conduct of the council likes to take the point, they are entitled to ask the court to declare that the council is still the duly elected council with all the powers conferred upon it by the Municipal Ordinance.

Apart altogether from authority their Lordships would be of opinion that this was a case where the Minister's order was voidable and not a nullity. Though the council should have been given the opportunity of being heard in its defence, if it deliberately chooses not to complain and takes no step to protest against its dissolution, there seems no reason why any other person should have the right to interfere. . . . Their Lordships deprecate the use of the word void in distinction to the word voidable in the field of law with which their Lordships are concerned because, as Lord Evershed pointed out in *Ridge v. Baldwin*,[47] quoting from Sir Frederick Pollock, the words void and voidable are imprecise and apt to mislead. These words have well-understood meanings when dealing with questions of proprietary or contractual rights. It is better, in the field where the subject matter of the discussion is whether some order which has been made or whether some step in some litigation or quasi-litigation is effective or not, to employ the verbal distinction between whether it is truly a 'nullity,' that is to all intents and purposes, of which any

[47] [1964] A.C. 40, 92.

person having a legitimate interest in the matter can take advantage or whether it is 'voidable' only at the instance of the party affected. On the other hand the word 'nullity' would be quite inappropriate in questions of proprietary or contractual rights; such transactions may frequently be void but the result can seldom be described as a nullity.

. . . Their Lordships understand Lord Reid [in *Ridge* v. *Baldwin*[48]] to have used the word 'void' in the sense of being a nullity. . . . Lord Hodson[49] took the view that the decision of the watch committee was a nullity. On the other hand Lord Evershed,[50] though he differed on the main question as to whether the principle audi alteram partem applied, devoted a considerable part of his judgment to the question whether the decision was voidable or a nullity and with this part of his judgment Lord Devlin expressly stated his agreement. Lord Evershed[50] examined the case of *Wood* v. *Woad*[51] in some detail and he reached the conclusion that in *Wood* v. *Woad*[51] the question whether the purported exclusion from the association by the committee was void or voidable was not essential or indeed material to the claim made in the action by the plaintiffs for damages against the members of the committee. He continued,[52] speaking of that case

'Certainly in my judgment it cannot be asserted that the judgments in the case cited or indeed any of them support or involve the proposition that where a body such as the watch committee in the present case, is invested by the express terms of a statute with a power of expulsion of any member of the police force and purports in good faith to exercise such power, a failure on their part to observe the principle of natural justice, audi alteram partem, has the result that the decision is not merely voidable by the court but is wholly void and a nullity.'

Lord Morris of Borth-y-Gest[53] also considered this question and reached the conclusion that the order of the watch committee was voidable and not a nullity. He examined the question as to the nature of the relief that the party aggrieved (Ridge) would apply for, which would be that the decision was invalid and of no effect and null and void. Their Lordships entirely agree with that and with the conclusions which he drew from it, namely, that if the decision is challenged by the person aggrieved on the grounds that the principle has not been obeyed, he is entitled to claim that as against him it is void ab initio and has never been of any effect. But it cannot possibly be right in the type of case which their Lordships are considering to suppose that if challenged successfully by the person entitled to avoid the order yet nevertheless it has some limited effect even against him until set aside by a court of competent jurisdiction. While in this case their Lordships have no doubt that in an action by the council the court should have held that the order was void ab initio and never had any effect, that is quite a different matter from saying

[48] [[1964] A.C. 40.]
[49] [1964] A.C. 40, 135.
[50] Ibid. 88–90.
[51] (1874) L.R. 9 Ex. 190.
[52] [1964] A.C. 40, 90.
[53] [1964] A.C. 119.

that the order was a nullity of which advantage could be taken by any other person having a legitimate interest in the matter.

Their Lordships therefore are clearly of opinion that the order of the Minister on May 29, 1966, was voidable and not a nullity. Being voidable it was voidable only at the instance of the person against whom the order was made, that is the council. But the council have not conplained. The appellant was no doubt mayor at the time of its dissolution but that does not give him any right to complain independently of the council. . . .

Appeal dismissed.

Questions

1. Was the majority view in *Ridge* v. *Baldwin* that the watch committee's decision was void or voidable?

2. Do you think the Privy Council was using the word 'voidable' in the same sense as that in which it is sometimes used to describe the status of a decision flawed by an error of law on the face of the record?

3. If the Privy Council was relying on Lord Evershed's views in *Ridge* v. *Baldwin*, should it not have been said that the decision was voidable even in relation to the Council? (See Wade, (1967), 83 L.Q.R. 499 at p. 506.)

Notes

1. For general discussion of this area of the law, see Wade, (1967) 83 L.Q.R. 499 and (1968) 84 L.Q.R. 95; Akehurst, (1968) 31 M.L.R. 2 and 138; Jackson, *Natural Justice*, 2nd edn., pp. 187–94; de Smith, p. 240.

2. Lord Evershed's speech in *Ridge* v. *Baldwin*, which favoured the view that a decision reached in breach of natural justice was voidable, was relied on in *Durayappah* v. *Fernando*. Lord Evershed suggested that a court should only upset such a decision if there was a 'real substantial miscarriage of justice'. This brings in a discretionary element, on which see Note 3, p. 108 *supra*, and p. 239 *infra*. Compare *Stevenson* v. *U.R.T.U.* [1977] I.C.R. 893 in which it was the view of the Court of Appeal (at p. 906) that where a dismissal from employment had been in breach of natural justice, 'any distinction between such a decision being "voidable" and it being "void" (i.e. a nullity) can only reside in the degree of freedom which the court may feel itself entitled to enjoy in the exercise of its discretion; but it appears to us that the difference must be one of approach rather than one of substance'. The discretion referred to related to the granting of the remedy on which see Wade's comment quoted in Note 3, p. 108 *supra*, though cf. *Glynn* v. *Keele University* [1971] 1 W.L.R. 487, noted at p. 239 *infra*.

3. Generally on the question of invalidity, see Ch. 3 *supra* and p. 209 *supra*. Lord Morris's speech in *Ridge* v. *Baldwin* underlines Wade's view quoted in Note 1, p. 107 *supra*, and see also *Hounslow L.B.C.* v. *Twickenham Garden Developments Ltd.* [1971] Ch. 233, where Megarry J. warns that to use the word 'voidable' in relation to a decision to cover the situation where the only person or persons who can challenge it choose not to do so is 'liable to mislead'. On the problem of waiver, note that some of the comments in Note 2, p. 209 *supra*, relate to the *audi alteram partem* rule.

4. Although the approach in *Durayappah* v. *Fernando* was adopted in *Fullbrook* v. *Berkshire Magistrates' Courts Committee* (1971) 69 L.G.R. 75, the *Hounslow* case

provides authority for the view that a breach of natural justice makes a decision void, as do several of the authorities cited in the context of the bias rule. They will not be repeated here: see Note 1, p. 209 *supra*. Note in particular though the recent support in *O'Reilly* v. *Mackman*, p. 326 *infra*, for the view that a breach of the *audi alteram partem* rule by a statutory tribunal renders its decision null and void. For a later interpretation of *Durayappah* v. *Fernando* see the Note at p. 241 *infra*.

5. *London & Clydeside Estates Ltd.* v. *Aberdeen D.C.*, p. 104 *supra*, supports the view that there can be an appeal from a decision which is liable to be declared invalid. In the context of natural justice the same point was made by the Privy Council in *Calvin* v. *Carr* [1980] A.C. 574, in which one question was whether a committee of the Australian Jockey Club was entitled to hear an appeal from a decision made by certain stewards to disqualify the plaintiff for one year. The facts are more fully set out at p. 254 *infra*; at this stage it should merely be noted that, for the purposes of argument, the Privy Council assumed that there had been a breach of natural justice (the *audi alteram partem* rule) by the stewards. Lord Wilberforce stated (at pp. 589–90):

> A condition precedent, it was said, of an appeal was the existence of a real, even though voidable, decision. This argument led necessarily into the difficult area of what is void and what is voidable, as to which some confusion exists in the authorities. Their Lordships' opinion would be, if it became necessary to fix upon one or other of these expressions, that a decision made contrary to natural justice is void, but that, until it is so declared by a competent body or court, it may have some effect, or existence, in law. This condition might be better expressed by saying that the decision is invalid or vitiated. In the present context, where the question is whether an appeal lies, the impugned decision cannot be considered as totally void, in the sense of being legally non-existent. So to hold would be wholly unreal. The decision of the stewards resulted in disqualification, an effect with immediate and serious consequences for the plaintiff. This was a fact: the plaintiff's horses could not run in, or be entered for, any race; the plaintiff lost his membership of the Australian Jockey Club and could be excluded from their premises. These consequences remained in effect unless and until the stewards' decision was challenged and, if so, had sufficient existence in law to justify an appeal.

FAIR HEARINGS – GENERAL ASPECTS

Scope and limits of the principle: supplementation of statutory procedures

Durayappah v. Fernando

[1967] 2 A.C. 337   Judicial Committee of the Privy Council

For the facts of this case, see p. 226 *supra*.

LORD UPJOHN [delivering the judgment of their Lordships]: . . . [I]t is not in doubt that if [the Minister] was bound to observe the principle audi alteram partem he failed to do so. . . .

Upon the question of audi alteram partem the Supreme Court [of Ceylon] followed and agreed with the earlier decision of *Sugathadasa* v. *Jayasinghe*,[54] a decision of three judges of the Supreme Court upon the same section and upon the same issue, namely, whether a council was not competent to perform its duties. That decision laid down[55]

---

[54] (1958) 59 N.L.R. 457.
[55] Ibid. 471.

'as a general rule that words such as "where it appears to . . ." or "if it appears to the satisfaction of . . ." or "if the . . . considers it expedient that . . ." or "if the . . . is satisfied that . . ." standing by themselves without other words or circumstances of qualification, exclude a duty to act judicially.'

Their Lordships disagree with this approach. These various formulae are introductory of the matter to be considered and [give] little guidance upon the question of audi alteram partem. The statute can make itself clear upon this point and if it does cadit quaestio. If it does not then the principle stated by Byles J. in *Cooper v. Wandsworth Board of Works*[56] must be applied. He said:

> 'A long course of decisions, beginning with *Dr. Bentley's* case,[57] and ending with some very recent cases, establish, that, although there are no positive words in the statute requiring that the party shall be heard, yet the justice of the common law will supply the omission of the legislature.'

. . . The solution to this case is not to be found merely upon a consideration of the opening words of section 277. A deeper investigation is necessary. Their Lordships were of course referred to the recent case of *Ridge v. Baldwin*[58] where this principle was very closely and carefully examined. In that case no attempt was made to give an exhaustive classification of the cases where the principle audi alteram partem should be applied. In their Lordships' opinion it would be wrong to do so. Outside well-known cases such as dismissal from office, deprivation of property and expulsion from clubs, there is a vast area where the principle can only be applied upon most general considerations. For example, as Lord Reid[59] when examining *Rex v. Electricity Commissioners*[60] pointed out, Bankes L.J.[61] inferred the judicial element from the nature of the power and Atkin L.J.[62] did the same. Pausing there, however, it should not be assumed that their Lordships necessarily agree with Lord Reid's analysis of that case or with his criticism of *Nakuda Ali v. Jayaratne*.[63] Outside the well-known classes of cases, no general rule can be laid down as to the application of the general principle in addition to the language of the provision. In their Lordships' opinion there are three matters which must always be borne in mind when considering whether the principle should be applied or not. These three matters are: first, what is the nature of the property, the office held, status enjoyed or services to be performed by the complainant of injustice. Secondly, in what circumstances or upon what occasions is the person claiming to be entitled to exercise the measure of control entitled to intervene. Thirdly, when a right to intervene is proved, what sanctions in fact is the latter entitled to impose upon the other. It is only upon a consideration of all these matters that the question of the

---

56 (1863) 14 C.B.N.S. 180, 194.   57 (1723) 1 Stra. 557.
58 [1964] A.C. 40.   59 [1964] A.C. 40, 76.
60 [1924] 1 K.B. 171.   61 [1924] 1 K.B. 171, 198.
62 Ibid. 206–207.   63 [1951] A.C. 66.

application of the principle can properly be determined. Their Lordships therefore proceed to examine the facts of this case upon these considerations.

As to the first matter it cannot be doubted that the Council of Jaffna was by statute a public corporation entrusted like all other municipal councils with the administration of a large area and the discharge of important duties. No one would consider that its activities should be lightly intefered with. . . . The legislature has enacted a statute setting up municipal authorities with a considerable measure of independence from the central government within defined local areas and fields of government. No Minister should have the right to dissolve such an authority without allowing it the right to be heard upon that matter unless the statute is so clear that it is plain it has no right of self-defence. However, this consideration is perhaps one of approach only. The second and third matters are decisive.

Upon the second matter it is clear that the Minister can dissolve the council on one of three grounds: that it (a) is not competent to perform any duty or duties imposed upon it (for brevity their Lordships will refer to this head as incompetence); or (b) persistently makes default in the performance of any duty or duties imposed upon it; or (c) persistently refuses or neglects to comply with any provisions of law. . . .

While their Lordships are only concerned with the question of incompetence, the true construction of the section must be considered as a whole and its necessary intendment in the light of the common law principles already stated. It seems clear to their Lordships that it is a most serious charge to allege that the council, entrusted with these very important duties, persistently makes default in the performance of any duty or duties imposed upon it. No authority is required to support the view that in such circumstances it is plain and obvious that the principle audi alteram partem must apply.

Equally it is clear that if a council is alleged persistently to refuse or neglect to comply with a provision of law it must be entitled (as a matter of the most elementary justice) to be heard in its defence. Again this proposition requires no authority to support it. If, therefore, it is clear that in two of the three cases, the Minister must act judicially, then it seems to their Lordships, looking at the section as a whole, that it is not possible to single out for different treatment the third case, namely incompetence. Grammatically, too, any differentiation is impossible. Section 277 confers upon the Minister a single power to act in the event of one or more closely allied failures and he can only do so after observing the principle audi alteram partem. Had the Minister been empowered to dissolve the council only for incompetence and on no other ground it might have been argued that as 'incompetence' is very vague and difficult to define Parliament did not intend that the principle audi alteram partem to apply, in the circumstances, but their Lordships would point out that charges of inefficiency or failing to be diligent or to set a good example have been held subject to the principle: see *Fisher* v. *Jackson*.[64]

The third matter can be dealt with quite shortly. The sanction which the

---

[64] [1891] 2 Ch. 84.

Minister can impose and indeed, if he is satisfied of the necessary premise, must impose upon the erring council is as complete as could be imagined; it involves the dissolution of the council and therefore the confiscation of all its properties. . . . The council owned large areas of land, had a municipal fund and was empowered to levy rates from its inhabitants though it was bound to apply them in accordance with its constitution. In their Lordships' opinion this case falls within the principle of Cooper v. Wandsworth Board of Works[65] where it was held that no man is to be deprived of his property without having an opportunity of being heard. For the purposes of the application of the principle it seems to their Lordships that this must apply equally to a statutory body having statutory powers, authorities and duties just as it does to an individual. Accordingly on this ground too the Minister should have observed the principle.

For these reasons their Lordships have no doubt that in the circumstances of this case the Minister should have observed the principle audi alteram partem. Sugathadasa v. Jayasinghe[66] was wrongly decided. . . .

[The appeal was in fact dismissed on a ground which has been dealt with at p. 226 supra.]

Note

This case underlines the fact that, where statutory powers are concerned, the courts are involved in a process of statutory interpretation. In relation to this, Byles J.'s view in Cooper v. Wandsworth Board of Works, p. 213 supra (quoted in Durayappah v. Fernando) that 'the justice of the common law will supply the omission of the legislature' is important. Nevertheless, it must be kept in proper perspective, for the role of the judge in supplementing a legislative provision and filling in the gaps in the procedural protection (if any) provided for a person adversely affected by the exercise of power has its limits (though note O'Reilly v. Mackman, p. 326 infra). In Wiseman v. Borneman [1971] A.C. 297 at p. 308 Lord Reid said that 'before this unusual kind of power is exercised it must be clear that the statutory procedure is insufficient to achieve justice and that to require additional steps would not frustrate the apparent purpose of the legislation'; cf. Lord Wilberforce at p. 317. The proper conclusion may be that the omission was deliberate, and in that case 'the justice of the common law' must remain in abeyance. (For the position where a contractual, as opposed to a statutory, provision deliberately fails to provide what natural justice would require, see Enderby Town F.C. Ltd. v. F.A. Ltd., p. 246 infra; de Smith, p. 183) For an example of what was thought to be a deliberate omission by Parliament, see Pearlberg v. Varty [1972] 1 W.L.R. 534. Indeed, if some procedural protection has been provided, then it could be argued that this supports the view that no other protection was intended (see Bates v. Lord Hailsham of St. Marylebone [1972] 1 W.L.R. 1373 at p. 1378). The more comprehensive this express protection is, then the stronger this argument becomes; cf. de Smith, p. 165; Nicholson v. Haldimand–Norfolk Regional Board of Commissioners of Police [1979] 1 S.C.R. 311 and note Evans' comment ((1973) 36 M.L.R. 439 at p. 441) that on occasions 'express provisions establishing some elements of "judicial procedure" [have been used] as a springboard for implying more.'

In Furnell v. Whangarei High Schools Board [1973] A.C. 660 the Privy Council was

[65] (1863) 14 C.B.N.S. 180.
[66] (1958) 59 N.L.R. 457.

concerned with a procedural code set out in regulations made by the Governor-General of New Zealand on the advice of the appropriate Minister and on the joint recommendation of two organizations which were particularly concerned in the matter. In such a situation the Privy Council stated that it was 'not lightly to be affirmed' that such a regulation was unfair. (For criticism of this view, see Evans, op. cit., but for an approach reminiscent of that adopted in the *Furnell* case, see *Lake District Special Planning Board* v. *Secretary of State for the Environment* [1975] J.P.L. 220, noted at p. 595 *infra*. The Privy Council in the *Furnell* case denied that the court should redraft the code, and approved the view of Barwick C.J. in *Brettingham-Moore* v. *Municipality of St. Leonards* (1969) 121 C.L.R. 509 at p. 524 that the 'legislature has addressed itself to the very question and it is not for the Court to amend the statute by engrafting upon it some provision which the Court might think more consonant with a complete opportunity for an aggrieved person to prevent his views and to support them by evidentiary materials'.

However, the *Furnell* case (and the *Lake District* case), as opposed to the *Brettingham-Moore* case, concerned subordinate legislation. Is Barwick C.J.'s view appropriate in this context? In the case of subordinate legislation, should not attention be paid not only to the intention of the law-maker but also to the terms of the enabling power so as to see whether it gives sufficient authority to enable a person to exclude what a court might otherwise think fairness requires?

Where a fair hearing 'would make no difference'

Ridge v. Baldwin

[1964] A.C. 40   House of Lords

For the facts and decision in this case, see p. 214 *supra*.

LORD REID: . . . It may be convenient at this point to deal with an argument that, even if as a general rule a watch committee must hear a constable in his own defence before dismissing him, this case was so clear that nothing that the appellant could have said could have made any difference. It is at least very doubtful whether that could be accepted as an excuse. But, even if it could, the respondents would, in my view, fail on the facts. It may well be that no reasonable body of men could have reinstated the appellant. But as between the other two courses open to the watch committee the case is not so clear. Certainly on the facts, as we know them, the watch committee could reasonably have decided to forfeit the appellant's pension rights, but I could not hold that they would have acted wrongly or wholly unreasonably if they had in the exercise of their discretion decided to take a more lenient course. . . .

LORD MORRIS OF BORTH-Y-GEST: . . . My Lords, it was submitted to your Lordships that the decision of the watch committee should be upheld as having been the only reasonable decision. I consider this to be an entirely erroneous submission. Since no charges have been formulated it is impossible to assess their weight or the weight of the answering evidence of the appellant and others. When the appellant was in the witness-box in the present action he was questioned as to what witnesses he would have wished to call in order to deal with [two particular] matters. As charges in respect of those matters were not formulated, I cannot think that it was appropriate to elicit the names of certain witnesses whom the appellant might have decided to call, and then without hearing or being able to hear such witnesses to seek to discount their value and effectiveness, and then to seek to draw a vague and artificial conclusion that if matters had been regularly done, and if the appellant had been heard, and if his witnesses had been heard, a result adverse to him would have followed. All the defects and all the unfairness of the original irregularity are inherent in any such approach. The suggested conclusion must fail because it is based upon a perpetuation of the very defects which vitiate the dismissal of the appellant, and also because the process involves endowing the court with a function that belongs elsewhere. . . .

LORD HODSON: . . . [I]n my opinion, it will not do to say that the case was so plain there was no need for the appellant to be heard and, therefore, the claims of natural justice were satisfied. . . .

Malloch v. Aberdeen Corporation

[1971] 1 W.L.R. 1578   House of Lords

The facts are set out more fully at p. 270 *infra*, where a more substantial extract from the case is to be found. The case concerned the procedure surrounding the dismissal of the appellant, a schoolteacher, and one argument raised was that even if he had a right to be heard, the education authority was legally bound to dismiss him and that any hearing would have been a useless formality. The relevant regulations, as amended, provided that 'every teacher employed by an education authority shall be a registered teacher', and the appellant had not registered.

LORD REID: . . . Then it was argued that to have afforded a hearing to the appellant before dismissing him would have been a useless formality because whatever he might have said could have made no difference. If that could be clearly demonstrated it might be a good answer. But I need not decide that because there was here, I think, a substantial possibility that a sufficient number of the committee might have been persuaded not to vote for the appellant's dismissal. The motion for dismissal had to be carried by a two-thirds majority of those present, and at the previous meeting of the committee there was not a sufficient majority to carry a similar motion. Between these meetings the committee had received a strong letter from the Secretary of State urging them to dismiss the teachers who refused to register. And it appears that they had received some advice which might have been taken by them to mean that those who failed to vote for dismissal might incur personal liability. The appellant might have been able to persuade them that they need not have any such fear.

Then the appellant might have argued that on their true construction the regulations did not require the committee to dismiss him and that, if they did require that, they were ultra vires. . . .

LORD WILBERFORCE: . . . The appellant has first to show that his position was such that he had, in principle a right to make representations before a decision against him was taken. But to show this is not necessarily enough, unless he can also show that if admitted to state his case he had a case of substance to make. A breach of procedure, whether called a failure of natural justice, or an essential administrative fault, cannot give him a remedy in the courts, unless behind it there is something of substance which has been lost by the failure. The court does not act in vain. . . .

Questions

1. Has Lord Reid changed his mind since *Ridge* v. *Baldwin*?

2. Clark, [1975] P.L. 27 at p. 48 interprets Lord Wilberforce in *Malloch* as 'arguing that an "insubstantial" breach of *audi alteram partem* is, *as a matter of substantive law*, not recognised as having any effect on the validity of the resultant decision'. Do you agree?

Cinnamond v. British Airports Authority

[1980] 1 W.L.R. 582   Court of Appeal

It was alleged that the six minicab drivers involved in this case had hung around the airport and touted for custom. They were prosecuted by the Airports Authority on many occasions for breach of two by-laws applying to the airport. One by-law prohibited remaining on the airport without reasonable cause and the other prohibited the offering of services without the Authority's permission. Breach of either by-law involved a maximum fine of £100 and in the case of the six drivers there was an amount of money which each had been fined but which had not been paid.

The proceedings in this case were in fact concerned with a different by-law to which the Airports Authority resorted. By-law 5 (59) provided that no one 'shall enter the aerodrome, except as a bona fide airline passenger, whilst having been prohibited from entering by an authorized officer of the authority', and each of the drivers received a notice banning them from entering Heathrow (except as a passenger). In an action brought by the drivers, Mocatta J. ordered that the question whether the Authority was empowered to impose this ban should be tried as a preliminary issue, but at the hearing before Forbes J. ((1979) 77 L.G.R. 730) the parties requested that he should deal with all the issues as the final trial of the action. Several points were raised in the action, which was unsuccessful before Forbes J. There was an appeal to the Court of Appeal. This extract deals only with the question of natural justice.

LORD DENNING M.R.: ... What does natural justice demand in such a case as this? Mr Macdonald[67] said, quite rightly, that nowadays the rules of natural justice apply not only to people doing a judicial act: they often apply to people exercising an administrative power. I should like to say that it depends upon the nature of the administrative power which is being exercised. In *Schmidt* v. *Secretary of State for Home Affairs* [1969] 2 Ch. 149, 170, I said:

'... an administrative body may, in a proper case, be bound to give a person who is affected by their decision an opportunity of making representations. It all depends on whether he has some right or interest, or, I would add, some legitimate expectation of which it would not be fair to deprive him without hearing what he has to say.'

That is the sort of administrative power upon which a person should be entitled to make representations.

Mr. Macdonald urged us to say that this was such a case: that there ought to have been an opportunity to give these six car-hire drivers so that they could be heard. They might give reasons on which the prohibition order might be modified; or they might be given a little time; or they might be ready to give an undertaking which might be acceptable – to behave properly in future. When it was said that a fair hearing would make no difference, Mr. Macdonald cited a passage from Professor Wade's book *Administrative Law*, 4th ed. (1977), p. 455:

'. . . in the case of a discretionary administrative decision, such as the dismissal of a teacher or the expulsion of a student, hearing his case will often soften the heart of the authority and alter their decision, even though it is clear from the outset that punitive action would be justified.'

I can see the force of that argument. But it only applies where there is a legitimate expectation of being heard. In cases where there is no legitimate expectation, there is no call for a hearing. We have given some illustrations in earlier cases. I ventured to give two in *Reg.* v. *Gaming Board for Great Britain, Ex parte Benaim and Khaida* [1970] 2 Q.B. 417, 430. I instanced the Board of Trade when they granted industrial development certificates,[68] or the television authorities when they awarded television programme contracts. In administrative decisions of that kind, a hearing does not have to be given to those who may be disappointed. Only recently in *Norwest Holst Ltd.* v. *Secretary of State for Trade* [1978] Ch. 201, 224 I gave the instance of a police officer who is suspended for misconduct. Pending investigations, he is suspended on full pay. He is not given any notice of the charge at that stage, nor any opportunity of being heard. Likewise the Stock Exchange may suspend dealings in a broker's shares. In none of these cases is it necessary to have a hearing.

Applying those principles: suppose that these car-hire drivers were of good

---

[67] [Counsel for the plaintiffs.]
[68] [Now discontinued: see Wade, p. 497, n. 17.]

character and had for years been coming into the airport under an implied licence to do so. If in that case there was suddenly a prohibition order preventing them from entering, then it would seem only fair that they should be given a hearing and a chance to put their case. But that is not this case. These men have a long record of convictions. They have large fines outstanding. They are continuing to engage in conduct which they must know is unlawful and contrary to the by-laws. When they were summonsed for past offences, they put their case, no doubt, to the justices and to the Crown Court. Now when the patience of the authority is exhausted, it seems to me that the authority can properly suspend them until further notice – just like the police officer I mentioned. In the circumstances they had no legitimate expectation of being heard. It is not a necessary preliminary that they should have a hearing or be given a further chance to explain. Remembering always this: that it must have been apparent to them why the prohibition was ordered: and equally apparent that, if they had a change of heart and were ready to comply with the rules, no doubt the prohibition would be withdrawn. They could have made representations immediately, if they wished, in answer to the prohibition order. That they did not do.

The simple duty of the airport authority was to act fairly and reasonably. It seems to me that they have acted fairly and reasonably. I find nothing wrong in the course which they have taken. I find myself in substantial agreement with the judge, and I would dismiss the appeal.

SHAW L.J.: . . . As to the suggestion of unfairness in that the drivers were not given an opportunity of making representations, it is clear on the history of this matter that the drivers put themselves so far outside the limits of tolerable conduct as to disentitle themselves to expect that any further representations on their part could have any influence or relevance. The long history of contraventions, of flouting the regulations, and of totally disregarding the penalties demonstrate that in this particular case there was no effective deterrent. The only way of dealing with the situation was by excluding them altogether.

It does not follow that the attitude of the authority may not change if they can be persuaded by representations on behalf of the drivers that they are minded in future to comply with the regulations. . . .

BRANDON L.J.: . . . So far as [natural justice] is concerned, I agree with what has been said by Lord Denning M.R. and Shaw L.J. I do not think that in the circumstances of this case there was any need to give these minicab drivers an opportunity to make representations to the authority before they issued the ban. The reason for the ban must have been well known when the letters were received. Any representations which were desired to be made could have been made immediately by letter. None were. The truth is that no representations other than representations which included satisfactory undertakings about future behaviour would have been of the slightest use.

If I am wrong in thinking that some opportunity should have been given, then it seems to me that no prejudice was suffered by the minicab drivers as a result of not being given that opportunity. It is quite evident that they were not prepared then, and are not even prepared now, to give any satisfactory undertakings about their future conduct. Only if they were would representations be of any use. I would rely on what was said in *Malloch* v. *Aberdeen Corporation* [1971] 1 W.L.R. 1578, first *per* Lord Reid at p. 1582 and secondly *per* Lord Wilberforce at p. 1595. The effect of what Lord Wilberforce said is that no one can complain of not being given an opportunity to make representations if such an opportunity would have availed him nothing. . . .

Appeal dismissed.

Questions

1. Explain how Lord Denning's reasons for deciding that there was no right to be heard differ from the grounds on which it could have been argued that a fair hearing would have made no difference in this case.

2. Is Brandon L.J. saying that if a hearing should have been given then there was no *breach* of natural justice?

Notes

1. The extracts in this section are concerned with a problem that has been raised in the courts on several occasions in recent years. For discussion of the case law see Clark, [1975] P.L. 27; for later material in addition to *Cinnamond* see e.g. *Lake District Special Planning Board* v. *Secretary of State for the Environment* [1975] J.P.L. 220, noted by Jaconelli and Sauvain, (1977) 40 M.L.R. 87; *George* v. *Secretary of State for the Environment* (1979) 39 P. & C.R. 609; but see *Performance Cars Ltd.* v. *Secretary of State for the Environment* (1977) 34 P. & C.R. 92. Two later cases will also be referred to in the Notes *infra*, and see *R.* v. *Blundeston Prison Board of Visitors, ex p. Fox-Taylor* [1982] 1 All E.R. 646. See further *Calvin* v. *Carr*, p. 260 *infra*, on the question of the relevance of a fair result, but it should also be noted that Lord Morris's views in *Ridge* v. *Baldwin* were quoted with apparent approval in *R.* v. *Board of Visitors of Hull Prison, ex p. St. Germain (No. 2)* [1979] 1 W.L.R. 1401. Consider, in addition, the speeches of Lord Edmund-Davies and Lord Lane in *Bushell* v. *Secretary of State for the Environment*, pp. 611–12 *infra*, though on the relevance of the remedy sought in that case see Note 1, p. 612 *infra*. See also the view of Lord Denning noted at p. 203 *supra* and for a recent House of Lords decision, see Appendix.

2. The contention that the complainant has suffered no injustice by the lack of a hearing has been used as an argument against the grant of discretionary relief. In *Glynn* v. *Keele University* [1971] 1 W.L.R. 487, a case in which the plaintiff had been fined and excluded from residence on the campus for a particular period, Pennycuick V.-C. found that there had been a breach of natural justice; nevertheless, he refused to grant an injunction since he thought that all that had been lost was the chance to make a plea in mitigation and that that was not a sufficient reason to set aside a decision which he believed to be perfectly proper. See further *R.* v. *Aston University Senate, ex p. Roffey* [1969] 2 Q.B. 538 at pp. 554 and 559, but see p. 557; *R.* v. *Board of Visitors of Hull Prison, ex p. St. Germain* [1979] Q.B. 425 at pp. 450–1 and 456. As Clark points out, op. cit., p. 48, the approach in *Glynn* v. *Keele University* and that of Lord Wilberforce in *Malloch* v. *Aberdeen Corporation*, as interpreted by Clark (see Question 2, p. 236 *supra*), would produce different results in a case of collateral challenge. (On the extent

to which a breach of natural justice can be raised collaterally, see Wade, p. 299, and Note 4, p. 90 *supra*.)

In contrast to *Glynn* v. *Keele University*, attention might be drawn to *R.* v. *Thames Magistrates' Court, ex p. Polemis* [1974] 1 W.L.R. 1371, in which it was held that the applicant had not been given a reasonable opportunity to prepare his case. In the course of considering the court's discretion whether or not to grant certiorari, Lord Widgery stated (at pp. 1375–6):

> It is ... absolutely basic to our system that justice must not only be done but must manifestly be seen to be done. If justice was so clearly not seen to be done, as on the afternoon in question here, it seems to me that it is no answer to the applicant to say: 'Well, even if the case had been properly conducted, the result would have been the same'. This is mixing up doing justice with seeing that justice is done, so I reject that argument.

The idea that justice must manifestly be seen to be done is, of course, one that is raised particularly in cases dealing with the rule against bias, where, it might be noted, the courts do not inquire whether an adjudicator was in fact biased and therefore whether a person was prejudiced. See further Jaconelli and Sauvain, op. cit., p. 91.

3. Clark's article (mentioned in Note 1 *supra*) repays study. The author is critical of the discounting by a reviewing court of the fact that procedural fair play was not observed in reaching a decision because on the substantive merits of the case, the complainant is not thought to have been prejudiced: see generally pp. 43–60. At p. 60 he argues:

> The essential mission of the law in this field is to win acceptance by administrators of the principle that to hear a man before he is penalised is an integral part of the decision-making process. A measure of the importance of resisting the incipient abnegation by the courts of the firm rule that breach of *audi alteram partem* invalidates, is that if it gains ground the mission of the law is doomed to fail to the detriment of all.

Note also the following view expressed by Megarry J. in *John* v. *Rees* [1970] Ch. 345 at p. 402:

> It may be that there are some who would decry the importance which the courts attach to the observance of the rules of natural justice. 'When something is obvious,' they may say, 'why force everybody to go through the tiresome waste of time involved in framing charges and giving an opportunity to be heard? The result is obvious from the start.' Those who take this view do not, I think, do themselves justice. As everybody who has anything to do with the law well knows, the path of the law is strewn with examples of open and shut cases which, somehow, were not; of unanswerable charges which, in the event, were completely answered; of inexplicable conduct which was fully explained; of fixed and unalterable determinations that, by discussion, suffered a change. Nor are those with any knowledge of human nature who pause to think for a moment likely to underestimate the feelings of resentment of those who find that a decision against them has been made without their being afforded any opportunity to influence the course of events.

Part of this passage was quoted with approval in *R.* v. *Secretary of State for the Environment, ex p. Brent L.B.C.* [1982] 2 W.L.R. 693, the facts of which have been noted at p. 144 *supra*. The court thought it would 'be wrong to speculate as to how the Secretary of State would have exercised his discretion if he had heard the representations' (p. 734); and on the facts the court was not convinced that any hearing would have been a useless formality (although seemingly accepting the argument if the point could have been established). Interestingly, representations made by the boroughs concerned did lead the Secretary of State to make certain modifications which, it was thought, might help the boroughs (18 H.C. Deb., col. 155), although for later developments see *R.* v. *Secretary of State for the Environment, ex p. Hackney L.B.C.* [1983] 1 W.L.R. 524.

Who is entitled to sue?

Durayappah v. Fernando, p. 226 *supra*

Note

In *F. Hoffmann-La Roche & Co. A.G.* v. *Secretary of State for Trade and Industry* both Lord Wilberforce at p. 97 *supra* and Lord Diplock at p. 100 *supra* explain *Durayappah* v. *Fernando* as turning on the question of locus standi, a topic which will be dealt with at p. 338 *infra*. This explanation may seem a little surprising in view of the fairly liberal standing requirement for certiorari, one of the remedies sought in the case: the appellant was the Mayor of the Council although he was not suing on its behalf. However, it is possible that the standing requirement is strict where a breach of the *audi alteram partem* rule is alleged and compare the position with the bias rule (Wade, pp. 478–9 – note also the alternative explanation set out there).

The right to know the opposing case

Errington v. Minister of Health, p. 581 *infra*

Note

Generally see Wade, p. 479.

Limits to the right to see adverse evidence

R. v. Gaming Board for Great Britain, ex parte Benaim and Khaida

[1970] 2 Q.B. 417   Court of Appeal

Under the Gaming Act 1968 a person wishing to apply to a licensing authority for a gaming licence must first apply to the Gaming Board for a certificate consenting to such an application. The applicants in this case, who sought a gaming licence in respect of Crockford's, were given a hearing but consent was refused. The Gaming Board stated that it was not obliged to give reasons for its decisions, and would not specify on which of the matters that had been discussed at the hearing it remained unsatisfied. The applicants sought certiorari to quash the refusal and mandamus to compel the Board to give sufficient information to the applicants so as to enable them to deal with the case against them.

LORD DENNING M.R.: . . . To what extent are the board bound by the rules of natural justice? That is the root question before us. Their jurisdiction is countrywide. They have to keep under review the extent and character of gaming in Great Britain: see s. 10 (3) [of the Gaming Act 1968]. Their particular task in regard to Crockford's is to see if the applicants are fit to run a gaming club: and if so, to give a certificate of consent.
Their duty is set out in Schedule 2, para. 4 (5) and (6):

'. . . (5) . . . the board shall have regard only to the question whether, in their opinion, the applicant is likely to be capable of, and diligent in, securing that the provisions of this Act and of any regulations made under it will be complied with, that gaming on those premises will be fairly and properly conducted, and that the premises will be conducted without disorder or disturbance.

(6) For the purposes of sub-paragraph (5) . . . the board shall in particular take into consideration the character, reputation and financial standing – (a) of the applicant, and (b) of any person (other than the applicant) by whom . . . the club . . . would be managed, or for whose benefit . . . that club would be carried on, but may also take into consideration any other circumstances appearing to them to be relevant in determining whether the applicant is likely to be capable of, and diligent in, securing the matters mentioned in that sub-paragraph.

Note also that Schedule 1, paragraph 7, gives the board power to regulate their own procedure. Accordingly the board have laid down an outline procedure which they put before us. It is too long to read in full. So I will just summarise it. It says that the board will give the applicant an opportunity of making representations to the board, and will give him the best indications possible of the matters that are troubling them. Then there are these two important sentences:

'In cases where the *source* or *content* of this *information* is *confidential*, the board accept that they are obliged to withhold particulars the disclosure of which would be a breach of confidence inconsistent with their statutory duty and the public interest. . . .'

'In the course of the interview the applicant will be made aware, to the greatest extent to which this is consistent with the board's statutory duty and the public interest, of the matters that are troubling the board.'

Mr. Quintin Hogg[69] criticised that outline procedure severely. He spoke as if Crockford's were being deprived of a right of property or of a right to make a living. He read his client's affidavit saying that 'Crockford's has been established for over a century and is a gaming club with a worldwide reputation for integrity and respectability,' with assets and goodwill valued at £185,000. He said that they ought not to be deprived of this business without knowing the case they had to meet. He criticised especially the way in which the board proposed to keep that confidential information. He relied on some words of mine in *Kanda* v. *Government of Malaya* [1962] A.C. 322, 337, when I said 'that the judge or whoever has to adjudicate must not hear evidence or receive representations from one side behind the back of the other.'

Mr. Hogg put his case, I think, too high. It is an error to regard Crockford's as having any right of which they are being deprived. They have not had in the past, and they have not now, any right to play these games of chance – roulette, chemin-de-fer, baccarat and the like – for their own profit. What they are really seeking is a privilege – almost, I might say, a franchise – to carry on gaming for profit, a thing never hitherto allowed in this country. It is for them to show that they are fit to be trusted with it.

[69] [Counsel for the applicants.]

If Mr. Hogg went too far on his side, I think Mr. Kidwell went too far on the other. He submitted that the Gaming Board are free to grant or refuse a certificate as they please. They are not bound, he says, to obey the rules of natural justice any more than any other executive body, such as, I suppose, the Board of Trade, which grants industrial development certificates,[70] or the Television Authority, which awards television programme contracts. I cannot accept this view. I think the Gaming Board are bound to observe the rules of natural justice. The question is: What are those rules?

It is not possible to lay down rigid rules as to when the principles of natural justice are to apply: nor as to their scope and extent. Everything depends on the subject-matter: see what Tucker L.J. said in *Russell* v. *Norfolk (Duke of)* [1949] 1 All E.R. 109, 118 and Lord Upjohn in *Durayappah* v. *Fernando* [1967] 2 A.C. 337, 349. At one time it was said that the principles only apply to judicial proceedings and not to administrative proceedings. That heresy was scotched in *Ridge* v. *Baldwin* [1964] A.C. 40. At another time it was said that the principles do not apply to the grant of revocation of licences. That too is wrong. *Reg.* v. *Metropolitan Police Commissioner, Ex parte Parker* [1953] 1 W.L.R. 1150 and *Nakkuda Ali* v. *Jayaratne* [1951] A.C. 66 are no longer authority for any such proposition. See what Lord Reid and Lord Hodson said about them in *Ridge* v. *Baldwin* [1964] A.C. 40, 77–79, 133.

So let us sheer away from those distinctions and consider the task of this Gaming Board and what they should do. The best guidance is, I think, to be found by reference to the cases of immigrants. They have no right to come in, but they have a right to be heard. The principle in that regard was well laid down by Lord Parker C.J. in *In re H.K. (An Infant)* [1967] 2 Q.B. 617. He said, at p. 630:

'. . . even if an immigration officer is not in a judicial or quasi-judicial capacity, he must at any rate give the immigrant an opportunity of satisfying him of the matters in the subsection, and for that purpose let the immigrant know what his immediate impression is so that the immigrant can disabuse him. That is not, as I see it, a question of acting or being required to act judicially, but of being required to act fairly.'

Those words seem to me to apply to the Gaming Board. The statute says in terms that in determining whether to grant a certificate, the board 'shall have regard only' to the matters specified. It follows, I think, that the board shall have a duty to act fairly. They must give the applicant an opportunity of satisfying them of the matters specified in the sub-section. They must let him know what their impressions are so that he can disabuse them. But I do not think that they need quote chapter and verse against him as if they were dismissing him from an office, as in *Ridge* v. *Baldwin* [1964] A.C. 40; or depriving him of his property, as in *Cooper* v. *Wandsworth Board of Works* (1863) 14 C.B.N.S. 180. After all, they are not charging him with doing anything wrong. They are simply inquiring as to his capability and diligence and are having regard to his character, reputation and financial standing.

---

[70] [Now discontinued: see Wade, p. 497, n. 17.]

They are there to protect the public interest, to see that persons running the gaming clubs are fit to be trusted.

Seeing the evils that have led to this legislation, the board can and should investigate the credentials of those who make application to them. They can and should receive information from the police in this country or abroad who know something of them. They can, and should, receive information from any other reliable source. Much of it will be confidential. But that does not mean that the applicants are not to be given a chance of answering it. They must be given the chance, subject to this qualification: I do not think they need tell the applicant the source of their information, if that would put their informant in peril or otherwise be contrary to the public interest. . . .

. . . [The] board was set up by Parliament to cope with disreputable gaming clubs and to bring them under control. By bitter experience it was learned that these clubs had a close connection with organised crime, often violent crime, with protection rackets and with strong-arm methods. If the Gaming Board were bound to disclose their sources of information, no one would 'tell' on those clubs, for fear of reprisals. Likewise with the details of the information. If the board were bound to disclose every detail, that might itself give the informer away and put him in peril. But, without disclosing every detail, I should have thought that the board ought in every case to be able to give to the applicant sufficient indication of the objections raised against him such as to enable him to answer them. That is only fair. And the board must at all costs be fair. If they are not, these courts will not hesitate to interfere.

Accepting that the board ought to do all this when they come to give their decision, the question arises, are they bound to give their reasons? I think not. Magistrates are not bound to give reasons for their decisions: see *Rex* v. *Northumberland Compensation Appeal Tribunal, Ex parte Shaw* [1952] 1 K.B. 338, at p. 352. Nor should the Gaming Board be bound. After all, the only thing that they have to give is their *opinion* as to the capability and diligence of the applicant. If they were asked by the applicant to give their reasons, they could answer quite sufficiently: 'In our opinion, you are not likely to be capable of or diligent in the respects required of you.' Their opinion would be an end of the matter.

Tested by those rules, applying them to this case, I think that the Gaming Board acted with complete fairness. They put before the applicants all the information which led them to doubt their suitability. They kept the sources secret, but disclosed all the information. Sir Stanley Raymond[71] said so in his affidavit: and it was not challenged to any effect. The board gave the applicants full opportunity to deal with the information. And they came to their decision. There was nothing whatever at fault with their decision of January 9, 1970. They did not give their reasons. But they were not bound to do so.

But then complaint is made as to what happened afterwards. It was said that the board did not pin-point the matters on which they thought the

[71] [The Chairman of the Gaming Board.]

explanations were not satisfactory. They did not say which of the matters [discussed at the hearing] they were not satisfied about. But I do not see anything unfair in that respect. It is not as if they were making any charges against the applicants. They were only saying they were not satisfied. They were not bound to give any reasons for their misgivings. And when they did give some reasons, they were not bound to submit to cross-examination on them. . . .

[LORD WILBERFORCE and PHILLIMORE L.J. agreed.]

Appeal dismissed.

Notes

1. On the relevance of the confidentiality of information and the need to protect its sources, see further *Re Pergamon Press Ltd.*, p. 276 *infra* and consider *R. v. Secretary of State for the Home Department, ex p. Hosenball* [1977] 1 W.L.R. 766, noted at p. 282 *infra*.

2. The development of the duty to act fairly has been one of the important features of Administrative Law in recent years, and the passage from Lord Parker's judgment in *Re H.K. (An Infant)* [1967] 2 Q.B. 617 (set out by Lord Denning in the extract *supra*) seems to have been very influential. The student will find the duty to act fairly referred to in several of the ensuing cases, and it is treated more fully at p. 282 *infra*.

Procedure generally

Russell v. Duke of Norfolk

[1949] 1 All E.R. 109   Court of Appeal

TUCKER L. J.: . . . There are, in my view, no words which are of universal application to every kind of inquiry and every kind of domestic tribunal. The requirements of natural justice must depend on the circumstances of the case, the nature of the inquiry, the rules under which the tribunal is acting, the subject-matter that is being dealt with, and so forth. Accordingly, I do not derive much assistance from the definitions of natural justice which have been from time to time used, but, whatever standard is adopted, one essential is that the person concerned should have a reasonable opportunity of presenting his case. . . .

Note

Generally see Wade, p. 482; de Smith, p. 195. See further Note 3, p. 85 *supra*, where it is pointed out that administrative bodies and tribunals do not have to comply with the rules of evidence, though on the use of hearsay evidence note *R. v. Board of Visitors of Hull Prison, ex p. St. Germain (No. 2)* [1979] 1 W.L.R. 1401. Another issue is, for example, whether an oral hearing must be given or whether a restriction to written representations will suffice. Note also the unsuccessful arguments in relation to cross-examination in the situations involved in *Re Pergamon Press Ltd.*, p. 276 *infra*, and *Bushell* v. *Secretary of State for the Environment*, p. 601 *infra*. On the question whether or not natural justice requires that cross-examination be allowed, see Wade, pp. 403–4. Compare, for example, the *Hull Prison* case, which has just been mentioned, with *R. v. Commission for Racial Equality, ex p. Cottrell & Rothon* [1980] 1 W.L.R. 1580. The rest of this section will select one particular topic – the question of legal representation – and deal with it in some detail.

Enderby Town Football Club Ltd. v. Football Association Ltd.

[1971] Ch. 591   Court of Appeal

The club wished to be legally represented at the hearing of its appeal to the Football Association after a commission, which had investigated certain charges against the club, had fined it and severely censured the club and its directors. The club sought an interim injunction to stop the hearing of the appeal if it was not permitted to have legal representation. Foster J. refused to grant the injunction and there was an appeal to the Court of Appeal. The relevant rule of the Football Association was construed as excluding legal representation on the appeal to the Association, and the validity of this rule was in question in the case.

LORD DENNING M.R.: . . . Is a party who is charged before a domestic tribunal entitled *as of right* to be legally represented? Much depends on what the rules say about it. When the rules say nothing, then the party has no absolute right to be legally represented. It is a matter for the *discretion* of the tribunal. They are masters of their own procedure: and, if they, in the proper exercise of their discretion, decline to allow legal representation, the courts will not interfere. Such was held in the old days in a case about magistrates: see *Collier v. Hicks* (1831) 2 B. & Ad. 663. It is the position today in the tribunals under the Tribunals and Inquiries Act, 1921. I think the same should apply to domestic tribunals, and for this reason: In many cases it may be a good thing for the proceedings of a domestic tribunal to be conducted informally without legal representation. Justice can often be done in them better by a good layman than by a bad lawyer. This is especially so in activities like football and other sports, where no points of law are likely to arise, and it is all part of the proper regulation of the game. But I would emphasise that the discretion must be properly exercised. The tribunal must not fetter its discretion by rigid bonds. A domestic tribunal is not at liberty to lay down an absolute rule: 'We will *never* allow anyone to have a lawyer to appear for him.' The tribunal must be ready, in a proper case, to allow it. That applies to anyone in authority who is entrusted with a discretion. He must not fetter his discretion by making an absolute rule from which he will never depart. . . . That is the reason why this court intervened in *Pett v. Greyhound Racing Association Ltd.* [1969] 1 Q.B. 125. Mr. Pett was charged with doping a dog – a most serious offence carrying severe penalties. He was to be tried by a domestic tribunal. There was nothing in the rules to exclude legal representation, but the tribunal refused to allow it. Their reason was because they never did allow it. This court thought that that was not a proper exercise of their discretion. Natural justice required that Mr. Pett should be defended, if he so wished, by counsel or solicitor. So we intervened and granted an injunction. Subsequently Lyell J. thought we were wrong. He held that Mr. Pett had no right to legal representation: see *Pett* v. *Greyhound Racing Association (No. 2)* [1970] 1 Q.B. 46. But I think we were right. Maybe Mr. Pett had no positive right, but it was a case where the tribunal in their discretion ought to have allowed it. And on appeal the parties themselves agreed it. They came to an arrangement which permitted the plaintiff to be legally represented at the inquiry: see [1970] 1 Q.B. 67. The long and short of it is that if the court sees that a domestic tribunal is proposing to proceed in a manner contrary to natural justice, it can intervene to stop it. The court is not bound to wait until after it has happened: see *Dickson* v. *Pharmaceutical Society of Great Britain* [1970] A.C. 403, 433, *per* Lord Upjohn.

The present case differs from *Pett's* case [1969] 1 Q.B. 125; [1970] 1 Q.B. 46 in that here there is a rule which says that legal representation is not allowed. The question is whether the rule is valid.

A preliminary point arises here: Has the court any power to go behind the wording of the rule and consider its validity? On this point Sir Elwyn Jones made an important concession. He agreed that if the rule was contrary to natural justice, it would be invalid. I think this concession was rightly made and I desire to emphasise it. The rules of a body like this are often said to be a contract. So they are in legal theory. But it is a fiction – a fiction created by the lawyers so as to give the courts jurisdiction. This is no new thing. There are many precedents for it from the time of John Doe onwards. Putting the fiction aside, the truth is that the rules are nothing more nor less than a legislative code – a set of regulations laid down by the governing body to be observed by all who are, or become, members of the association. Such regulations, though said to be a contract, are subject to the control of the courts. If they are in unreasonable restraint of trade, they are invalid: see *Dickson* v. *Pharmaceutical Society of Great Britain* [1967] Ch. 708; [1970] A.C. 403. If they seek to oust the jurisdiction of the court, they are invalid: see *Scott* v. *Avery* (1865) 5 H.L. Cas. 811. If they unreasonably shut out a man from his right to work, they are invalid: see *Nagle* v. *Feilden* [1966] 2 Q.B. 633; *Edwards* v. *Society of Graphical and Allied Trades* [1971] Ch. 354. If they lay down a procedure which is contrary to the principles of natural justice, they are invalid: see *Faramus* v. *Film Artistes' Association* [1964] A.C. 925, 947, *per* Lord Pearce. All these are cases where the judges have decided, avowedly or not, according to what is best for the public good. I know that over 300 years ago Hobart C.J. said the 'Public policy is an unruly horse.' It has often been repeated since. So unruly is the horse, it is said [*per* Burrough J. in *Richardson* v. *Mellish* (1824) 2 Bing. 229, 252], that no judge should ever try to mount it lest it run away with him. I disagree. With a good man in the saddle, the unruly horse can be kept in control. It can jump over obstacles. It can leap the fences put up by fictions and come down on the side of justice, as indeed was done in *Nagle* v. *Feilden* [1966] 2 Q.B. 633. It can hold a rule to be invalid even though it is contained in a contract. . . .

Seeing that the courts can inquire into the validity of the rule, I turn to the next question: Is it lawful for a body to stipulate in its rules that its domestic tribunal shall not permit legal representation? Such a stipulation is, I think, clearly valid so long as it is construed as directory and not imperative: for that leaves it open to the tribunal to permit legal representation in an exceptional case when the justice of the case so requires. But I have some doubt whether it is legitimate to make a rule which is so imperative in its terms as to exclude legal representation altogether, without giving the tribunal any discretion to admit it, even when the justice of the case requires it. Suppose a case should arise when both the parties and the tribunal felt that it was essential in the interests of justice that the parties should be legally represented, and that the tribunal should have the assistance of a lawyer. Would not the tribunal be able to allow it, or, at any rate, to allow the rule to be waived? I do not find it necessary to express any opinion on this point. I will know how to decide it when it arises. But in this case, no matter whether the rule is construed as directory or imperative, I am of opinion that the court should not insist on legal representation before the tribunal of the F.A. The points which the club wishes to raise are points of law which should be decided by the courts and not by the tribunal. The club is at liberty to bring these points before the courts at once and have them decided with the aid of skilled advocates. If they choose not to bring them before the courts, but prefer to put them before a lay tribunal, they must put up with the imperfections of that tribunal and must abide by their ruling that there be no legal representation. On this ground I would dismiss the appeal.

FENTON ATKINSON L.J.: . . . [Counsel for the club] says that an opportunity to state one's case means a fair opportunity, and that now and again a case may raise legal problems of such complexity and difficulty that no layman could be expected to put his case intelligibly and no lay tribunal could hope to understand and adjudicate correctly upon the points raised without the assistance of counsel. The present case, he contends, is such a one. No doubt it is true that questions of construction such as will arise on this appeal are more likely to be answered correctly, by a court of law with the assistance of counsel on both sides than by a lay tribunal however conscientious and fair minded after hearing the points put to them by laymen. . . .

On the other hand, the rule against legal representation applies to both parties to this dispute, in that the local association who appear in the role of prosecutors cannot appear by counsel or solicitor, and the case will be heard by men no doubt of fairness and integrity and with a great fund of common sense and experience of football and the rules in question.

The rule enables a decision to be given speedily without either party to the dispute being at risk of having to pay a heavy bill for costs, and there is always the right of either party to challenge a decision in the courts if the lay tribunal go wrong in law (e.g., in adopting a mistaken view on the construction of the rules). Further if a decision of a local association appears to have been reached contrary to the true legal construction of the rules, and difficult questions of law arise, a club can go direct to the courts instead of appealing to the F.A.

For my part, I can see nothing unfair in this rule – certainly nothing so unfair as to offend against the rules of natural justice. A similar rule is laid down by Parliament for a number of domestic tribunals. One notes especially that any police officer below the rank of chief constable may not be legally represented at a disciplinary inquiry even though his whole future is at stake (vide Police Disciplinary Regulations, 1965).

The F.A. have been dealing with appeals by clubs or players for years past without legal representation. Similarly, many other domestic tribunals have been discharging their particular responsibilities without hearing lawyers. So far as counsel have been able to discover, this is the first case where it has been suggested that the rules of natural justice demand a right to legal representation before such a tribunal. If such a rule is indeed contrary to natural justice, a very large number of persons, including our legislators, must have been very insensitive over a long period of years to what natural justice requires.

I would dismiss this appeal.

CAIRNS L.J.: I agree with both judgments that have been delivered, save that, as at present advised, I am of the opinion that it is open to an organisation to make an absolute rule that a tribunal set up by it is not to hear legal representatives.

I would add a few words in reference to [the] contention [of counsel for the club] that to deny representation to his clients is to allow administrative convenience to override the claims of justice. I am satisfied that this is not so. It is in the interest of justice and not only of administrative convenience that a decision should be arrived at quickly and cheaply. Where the tribunal is composed of intelligent laymen who have a great knowledge of the sport of business concerned, I think that the employment of lawyers is likely to lengthen proceedings and certainly greatly to increase the expense of them without any certainty of bringing about a fairer decision. I therefore consider that those responsible for drafting rules for such a tribunal are entitled to take the view that justice as well as convenience is served by a rule barring legal representation. There is no need to make any exceptions. In the very rare cases (of which the instant case may well be an example) where difficult points of law arise, it is far better for the points of law to be dealt with by resort to the court.

Appeal dismissed.

Notes

1. Compare with the views expressed in the *Enderby Town* case the following passage from the judgment of Lord Denning in *Pett* v. *Greyhound Racing Association Ltd.* [1969] 1 Q.B. 125 at p. 132:

It is not every man who has the ability to defend himself on his own. He cannot bring out the points in his own favour or the weaknesses in the other side. He may be tongue-tied or nervous, confused or wanting in intelligence. He cannot examine or cross-examine witnesses. We see it every day. A magistrate says to a man: 'You can ask any questions you like'; whereupon the man immediately starts to make a speech. If justice is to be done, he ought to have the help of someone to speak for him. And who better than a lawyer who has been trained for the task? I should have thought, therefore, that when a man's reputation or livelihood is at stake, he not only has a right to speak by his own mouth. He also has a right to speak by counsel or solicitor.

The case concerned the alleged drugging of a greyhound entered for a race by the plaintiff, a greyhound trainer. On the facts two of the members of the Court of Appeal held that a prima facie case had been made out that the plaintiff was entitled, on the basis of natural justice, to have legal representation at the inquiry. (The other member of the court based his judgment on agency, on which see Note 2 *infra*.) For the later history of the case, see Lord Denning's judgment in the *Enderby Town* case *supra*.

2. For a valuable discussion of the question of representation before tribunals, in relation to which the law is in a rather uncertain state, see Alder, [1972] P.L. 278.

Apart from the argument based (as in the *Enderby Town* case) on natural justice – that legal representation should be allowed if a person is to have a *fair* chance to be heard – a person with a right to appear before a tribunal might also argue (though with no certainty of success) that he has a right to appoint an agent to act on his behalf. This agent, the argument continues, could be a lawyer, a view supported by the *Pett* case in 1969; cf. *Re Mackey* (1972) 23 N.I.L.Q. 113, though see de Smith, ibid. 331.

The question of agency cannot be further pursued here. If natural justice, as opposed to agency, can be relied upon, then there is the advantage, as Alder points out, that a court may not allow it to be restricted by a contractual rule of a domestic body. Lord Denning in particular has spoken of the inability of certain bodies to oust natural justice by contractual rules: see e.g. the *Enderby Town* case *supra* and *Edwards* v. *S.O.G.A.T.* [1971] Ch. 354, where Sachs L.J. supported him. However, compare the following comment of Lord Denning in *Maynard* v. *Osmond* [1977] Q.B. 240 at p. 252. Having expressed the opinion that a tribunal should have a discretion to permit legal representation, his Lordship later stated that 'it is permissible for [a domestic body] to decree otherwise . . .', and see also the judgment of Cairns L.J. in the *Enderby Town* case *supra*.

3. Various decisions since the *Enderby Town* case was decided should be mentioned. *Fraser* v. *Mudge* [1975] 1 W.L.R. 1132 will be discussed *infra*, but note also *R.* v. *Race Relations Board, ex p. Selvarajan* [1975] 1 W.L.R. 1686, where at pp. 1693–4 Lord Denning talked of bodies which had to make an investigation and form an opinion, examples being the Gaming Board (and see the case at p. 241 *supra*) and inspectors under the Companies Act (and see the case at p. 276 *infra*). Such bodies in Lord Denning's opinion need not allow legal representation. Lord Denning was also a member of the Court of Appeal when it decided *Maynard* v. *Osmond* in which the Police (Discipline) Regulations 1965 (now the Police (Discipline) Regulations 1977) were construed (in accordance with Fenton Atkinson L.J.'s view in the *Enderby Town* case) as excluding any right to legal representation; cf Alder, op. cit., p. 294. It was also held that there was no discretion to allow legal representation and further that the regulations were intra vires. Lord Denning stated that a person charged before a tribunal with a disciplinary offence, at any rate one which could 'result in his dismissal from the force or other body to which he belongs', or 'the loss of his livelihood' or which could 'ruin his character for ever', 'should . . . be entitled to have a lawyer if he wants one'. His Lordship continued: 'But, even if he should not be entitled *as of right*, I should have thought that as a general rule the tribunal should have a *discretion* in the matter' ([1977] Q.B. at p. 252). Note also that Orr L.J. lent some support to the view of Cairns L.J. in the *Enderby Town* case that an organization could have an absolute

rule barring legal representation. For further comment on the case, see Matthews, (1977) 6 I.L.J. 248; McKean, [1977] C.L.J. 205.

Fraser v. Mudge

[1975] 1 W.L.R. 1132   Court of Appeal

LORD DENNING M.R.: This is an unusual application on behalf of the plaintiff, Mr. Francis Davidson Fraser. He is at present serving a long sentence of imprisonment and is detained in Her Majesty's Prison at Bristol. It is said that last weekend he assaulted a police officer. He is charged with an offence against police discipline. It is to be heard by an adjudication committee of the board of visitors at 2.15 today at Bristol Prison. Now he or someone on his behalf has instructed lawyers. They wish to represent him at the hearing by the board of visitors. They sent a telegram to the governor of the prison:

'Re our client Fraser No. 536648 we are instructed to represent him at adjudication by board of visitors. Request adjudication delayed until we are able to visit to take further instructions. . . .'

They have had no reply to that telegram. They have spoken by telephone to the clerk to the board of visitors. He said he would not advise the board either to allow legal representation or to adjourn the inquiry. Whereupon a writ has been issued today against the three named members of the board of inquiry seeking a declaration that he is entitled to be represented by solicitor and counsel and an injunction restraining the board from inquiring into the charge until he has had an opportunity of appearing by lawyers. Chapman J. has refused. Now Mr. Sedley applies to this court.

The Prison Act 1952 says that rules are to be made for ensuring that a prisoner who is charged with any offence under the rules shall be given a proper opportunity of presenting his case. Rule 49 (2) of the Prison Rules 1964 (S.I. 1964 No. 388) is in virtually the same words. It says:

'At any inquiry into a charge against a prisoner he shall be given a full opportunity of hearing what is alleged against him and of presenting his own case.'

The rule applies not only to a charge before the board of visitors, but also to an inquiry made by the governor, and also in addition to an inquiry by an officer appointed by the Secretary of State: see rules 49–52. The point is one, therefore, of very considerable importance.

Mr. Sedley has referred us to *Pett* v. *Greyhound Racing Association Ltd.* [1969] 1 Q.B. 125, where a charge was made before the Greyhound Racing Association that dogs had been doped. We indicated that it might well be proper that a legal representation should be allowed. But it seems to me that disciplinary cases fall into a very different category. We all know that, when a man is brought up before his commanding officer for a breach of discipline, whether in the armed forces or in ships at sea, it never has been the practice to allow legal representation. It is of the first importance that the cases should be decided quickly. If legal representation were allowed, it would mean considerable delay. So also with breaches of prison discipline. They must be heard and decided speedily. Those who hear the cases must, of course, act fairly. They must let the man know the charge and give him a proper opportunity of presenting his case. But that can be done and is done without the matter being held up for legal representation. I do not think we ought to alter the existing practice. We ought not to create a precedent such as to suggest that an individual is entitled to legal representation. There is no real arguable case in support of this application and I would reject it.

ROSKILL L.J.: I entirely agree with the refusal of Chapman J. to grant this ex parte injunction and with what Lord Denning M.R. has said. In so far as reliance is placed upon *Pett* v. *Greyhound Racing Association Ltd.* [1969] 1 Q.B. 125, that case is clearly distinguishable, because there was there a contractual or quasi-contractual relationship between the plaintiff and defendant, since the plaintiff held a licence from the defendants which the defendants were intending to revoke. The present case arises under the Prison Rules 1964 made under the Prison Act 1952.

. . . [I]f the argument in relation to rule 49 (2) of the Prison Rules 1964 were well founded, it would equally apply to complaints heard by the governor to which the same language applies, a proposition which I think it also untenable. One looks to see what are the broad principles underlying these rules. They are to [maintain] discipline in prison by proper, swift and speedy decisions, whether by the governor or the visitors; and it seems to me that the requirements of natural justice do not make it necessary that a person against whom disciplinary proceedings are pending should as of right be entitled to be represented by solicitors or counsel or both.

I also agree that this application should be refused.

ORMROD L.J.: I agree. In my view it is for Parliament to make rules as they think fit. I agree that this application should be refused.

Application refused.

Questions

1. What is the relevance of the distinction which Roskill L.J. draws between *Fraser* v. *Mudge* and *Pett* v. *Greyhound Racing Assocation Ltd.*?

2. How is Ormrod L.J.'s view to be reconciled with the view that 'the justice of the common law will supply the omission of the legislature' (per Byles J. in *Cooper* v. *Wandsworth Board of Works*, p. 213 *supra*)?

Notes

1. Under the Prison Rules 1964 the board of visitors are likely to deal with more serious matters and can impose more severe punishments than the governor. In the light of this, might not 'a full opportunity of hearing what is alleged against him and of presenting his own case' (r. 49 (2) of the Prison Rules) quite properly involve legal representation in some cases but quite properly not do so in other less serious cases? Compare the view of Roskill L.J. in *Fraser* v. *Mudge supra*.

2. In the Home Office's *Report of the Working Party on Adjudication Procedures in Prisons* in 1975 the majority opinion was that 'it should remain the task of the prisoner to present his defence himself' (para. 63), which 'underlines the obligation of those conducting adjudications to take all the action necessary to ensure that the prisoner's side of the case is fully developed' (para. 64). It was suggested however, that there should be an experiment to gauge the effect (in cases which were destined for a board of visitors) of allowing a prison officer or assistant governor to help the prisoner prepare his case; this did not include presenting the case (paras. 65–6); cf. the Note of Dissent by Harris, pp. 42–3. For later developments, see Zellick, [1981] P.L. 435 at pp. 438–40 who comments on the Home Office Research Unit Paper 3. The main conclusion from the Paper was 'that prisoners do seem to require some form of assistance before and perhaps during the hearing'. Note also the view in 1979 in the *Report of the Royal Commission on Legal Services*, Cmnd. 7648, vol. 1, para 9.29, that (in general) loss of remission, if more than seven days, should not be imposed on a prisoner unless he has been given the chance of being legally represented in the proceedings.

3. At one time there was a view favouring non-intervention in disciplinary cases (see Wade, p. 460), but the law has moved away from that position and the Court of Appeal in *Fraser* v. *Mudge* was not returning to the old view. Lord Denning emphasized the need for speedy decisions in the sort of disciplinary matter dealt with in that case, and saw legal representation as compromising this goal (though see Mosonyi, (1976) 39 M.L.R. 210 at p. 213). Nevertheless, he did acknowledge that those people who hear the cases must act fairly, which carries the implication that the courts will control them if they do not. A contrary view, however, was taken by the Divisional Court in *R.* v. *Board of Visitors of Hull Prison, ex p. St. Germain* [1978] Q.B. 678, where it was held that certiorari – and it would seem any other judicial remedy – would not lie against a board of visitors acting in disciplinary matters, but this decision was reversed by the Court of Appeal, [1979] Q.B. 425. Whether the courts would control the prison governor's disciplinary functions was the subject of a difference of opinion.

4. In practice many tribunals will allow legal representation, although some trade unions have rules forbidding it in disciplinary proceedings (Gennard, Gregory, and Dunn, *Employment Gazette*, 1980, p. 591). However, the drawback that legal aid is not available in the case of the great majority of tribunals should be borne in mind. On natural justice and legal aid, see the cases cited by Jackson, *Natural Justice*, 2nd edn., p. 10 and p. 214; cf. *R.* v. *Ealing JJ., ex p. Coatsworth* (1980) 78 L.G.R. 439. On the advantages and disadvantages of legal representation, see further p. 563 *infra*.

Reasons for decisions

R. v. Gaming Board for Great Britain, ex parte Benaim and Khaida, p. 241 *supra*

McInnes v. Onslow-Fane, p. 262 *infra*

Question

Should the giving of reasons be comprised within the *audi alteram partem* principle? In what way, if at all, would it help a person in a particular case?

Note

These cases stand as authorities for the proposition that natural justice does not require that reasons be given for a decision. See further *Payne* v. *Lord Harris of Greenwich* [1981] 1 W.L.R. 754; cf. Lord Denning's judgment in *Breen* v. *A.E.U.* [1971] 2 Q.B. at pp. 190–1; Bridge in *Fundamental Duties* (eds. Lasok *et al.*), Ch. VII. Consider also Wade, p. 487. De Smith, p. 149, argues that a 'person prejudicially affected by a decision must be adequately notified of the case he has to meet in order to exercise any right he may have to make further representations or effectively to exercise a right of appeal'; cf. *Payne* v. *Lord Harris*. Compare the *Report of the Committee on Ministers' Powers*, Cmd. 4060, p. 80, where in 1932 the Committee stated the opinion 'that there are some cases when the refusal to give grounds for a decision may be plainly unfair; and this may be so, even when the decision is final and no further proceedings are open to the disappointed party by way of appeal or otherwise'. Natural justice does not seem to have gone this far, however. The question of the giving of reasons for a decision arises in other parts of Administrative Law and has been dealt with elsewhere: see p. 22 *supra*. Note, in particular, *R.* v. *Knightsbridge Crown Court, ex p. International Sporting Club (London) Ltd.*, p. 75 *supra*, in relation to Lord Denning's view *supra* that magistrates are not bound to give reasons for their decision. The *Knightsbridge* case suggests that a court could order a professional judge to give reasons (although this is not apparently based on natural justice), and thus the position of stipendiary magistrates may differ from that of lay magistrates.

Appeals

Calvin v. Carr

[1980] A.C. 574   Judicial Committee of the Privy Council

The plaintiff was part owner of a horse which, though starting at short odds, only finished fourth in a race. The stewards held an inquiry and, as a result, decided to bring charges under r. 135 of the Rules of Racing. The jockey was found guilty of a breach of r. 135 (*a*), which requires every horse to be run on its merits. It was also found that the plaintiff was a party to the breach and a disqualification of one year was imposed on him; this meant that for the year in question he could not enter any horses in races and that he temporarily ceased to be a member of the Australian Jockey Club. There was an appeal to the committee of the Australian Jockey Club by the jockey and the plaintiff, which was unsuccessful. In the appeal proceedings the plaintiff was legally represented and his counsel made submissions; he also gave evidence and was cross-examined (as was the jockey). The transcript of the proceedings before the stewards was put before the committee, and film of the race and of the horse's prior performance was shown with the parties present. Evidence was given by all the stewards (bar one) and all those whose evidence had been received by the stewards were present and could have been cross-examined.
   The plaintiff challenged the validity of the disqualification and the dismissal of the appeal in an action in which he sought both declaratory and injunctive relief. Rath J. in the Equity Division of the New South Wales

Supreme Court ([1977] 2 N.S.W.L.R. 308) found that natural justice had been breached by the stewards but that this had been cured by the proceedings before the committee. There was an appeal to the Judicial Committee of the Privy Council. On the first point raised in this appeal see Note 5, p. 230 *supra*, where the Privy Council's opinion that the committee had jurisdiction to hear the appeal is dealt with. This extract is concerned with the plaintiff's second argument.

LORD WILBERFORCE [delivering their Lordship's judgment]: . . . [Their Lordships] will deal . . . with the appeal upon the assumed basis that the judge was correct in deciding that there had been a failure to observe natural justice in the proceedings before the stewards. They wish, however, to make it clear that, while they accept that the principles of natural justice ought to have been observed by the stewards, yet, having read the transcript of those proceedings, and the judge's careful judgment on this point, they appreciate that a substantial argument could be put forward that there was no failure of natural justice at all. . . .

[Having referred to relevant provisions in the Australian Rules of Racing, the Local Rules of the Australian Jockey Club, and the Australian Jockey Club Act 1873, LORD WILBERFORCE continued:] Although these rules and statutory provisions contain a good deal of repetition and circularity it is clear that they provide a comprehensive scheme or code for the administration of racing and for the exercise of discipline through domestic bodies whose jurisdiction, though reinforced by statute, is founded on consensual acceptance by those engaged in the various activities connected with horse racing. Under this scheme the committee has general control and powers of supervision. It may exercise disciplinary powers itself, including the power to punish for breach of the rules, or disciplinary powers, including the power to punish, may be exercised by the stewards. In the latter event, there is an appeal to the committee, such appeal being in the nature of a rehearing, and on such appeal the committee may remit the case to the stewards, or may make such order as ought to have been made by the stewards. The committee has a wide discretion as to the admission of evidence in the appeal, not being limited to the evidence heard by the stewards. . . .

The plaintiff's second argument can be stated, for purposes of description, as being that such defects of natural justice as may have existed as regards the proceedings before the stewards, were not capable of being cured by the appeal proceedings before the committee, even though, as was not contested before this Board, these were correctly and fairly conducted. The defendants contend the contrary. This part of the argument involved consideration of a wide range of authorities of this Board, and in Australia, Canada, England and New Zealand. As regards decisions of this Board a conflict was said to exist between *Annamunthodo v. Oilfields Workers' Trade Union* [1961] A.C. 945 and *Pillai v. Singapore City Council* [1968] 1 W.L.R. 1278, each of which has been followed by other decisions. . . . Other individual decisions were cited which it appears difficult to reconcile.

Although, as will appear, some of the suggested inconsistencies of decisions disappear, or at least diminish, on analysis, their Lordships recognise and indeed assert that no clear and absolute rule can be laid down on the question whether defects in natural justice appearing at an original hearing, whether administrative or quasi-judicial, can be 'cured' through appeal proceedings. The situations in which this issue arises are too diverse, and the rules by which they are governed so various, that this must be so. There are, however, a number of typical situations as to which some general principle can be stated. First there are cases where the rules provide for a rehearing by the original body, or some fuller or enlarged form of it. This situation may be found in relation to social clubs. It is not difficult in such cases to reach the conclusion that the first hearing is superseded by the second, or, putting it in contractual terms, the parties are taken to have agreed to accept the decision of the hearing body, whether original or adjourned. Examples of this are *De Verteuil* v. *Knaggs* [1918] A.C. 557, 563; *Posluns* v. *Toronto Stock Exchange and Gardiner* (1965) 53 D.L.R. (2d) 193; *In re Clark and Ontario Securities Commission* (1966) 56 D.L.R. (2d) 585; *In re Chromex Nickel Mines Ltd.* (1970) 16 D.L.R. (3d) 273; and see also *Ridge* v. *Baldwin* [1964] A.C. 40, 79, per Lord Reid.

At the other extreme are cases, where, after examination of the whole hearing structure, in the context of the particular activity to which it relates (trade union membership, planning, employment, etc.) the conclusion is reached that a complainant has the right to nothing less than a fair hearing both at the original and at the appeal stage. This was the result reached by Megarry J. in *Leary* v. *National Union of Vehicle Builders* [1971] Ch. 34. In his judgment in that case the judge seems to have elevated the conclusion thought proper in that case into a rule of general application. In an eloquent passage he said, at p. 49:

'If the rules and the law combine to give the member the right to a fair trial and the right of appeal, why should he be told that he ought to be satisfied with an unjust trial and a fair appeal? . . . As a general rule . . . I hold that a failure of natural justice in the trial body cannot be cured by a sufficiency of natural justice in an appellate body.'

In their Lordships' opinion this is too broadly stated. It affirms a principle which may be found correct in a category of cases: these may very well include trade union cases, where movement solidarity and dislike of the rebel, or renegade, may make it difficult for appeals to be conducted in an atmosphere of detached impartiality and so make a fair trial at the first — probably branch — level an essential condition of justice. But to seek to apply it generally overlooks, in their Lordships' respectful opinion, both the existence of the first category, and the possibility that, intermediately, the conclusion to be reached, on the rules and on the contractual context, is that those who have joined in an organisation, or contract, should be taken to have agreed to accept what in the end is a fair decision, notwithstanding some initial defect.

In their Lordships' judgment such intermediate cases exist. In them it is for the court, in the light of the agreements made, and in addition having regard to the course of proceedings, to decide whether, at the end of the day, there has been a fair result, reached by fair methods, such as the parties should fairly be taken to have accepted when they joined the association. Naturally there may be instances when the defect is so flagrant, the consequences so severe, that the most perfect of appeals or re-hearings will not be sufficient to produce a just result. Many rules (including those now in question) anticipate that such a situation may arise by giving power to remit for a new hearing. There may also be cases when the appeal process is itself less than perfect: it may be vitiated by the same defect as the original proceedings: or short of that there may be doubts whether the appeal body embarked on its task without predisposition or whether it had the means to make a fair and full inquiry, for example where it has no material but a transcript of what was before the original body. In such cases it would no doubt be right to quash the original decision. These are all matters (and no doubt there are others) which the court must consider. Whether these intermediate cases are to be regarded as exceptions from a general rule, as stated by Megarry J., or as a parallel category covered by a rule of equal status, is not in their Lordships' judgment necessary to state, or indeed a matter of great importance. What is important is the recognition that such cases exist, and that it is undesirable in many cases of domestic disputes, particularly in which an inquiry and appeal process has been established, to introduce too great a measure of formal judicialisation. While flagrant cases of injustice, including corruption or bias, must always be firmly dealt with by the courts, the tendency in their Lordships' opinion in matters of domestic disputes should be to leave these to be settled by the agreed methods without requiring the formalities of judicial processes to be introduced.

Their Lordships now comment on the principal authorities. *Annamunthodo* v. *Oilfields Workers' Trade Union* [1961] A.C. 945 was a trade union case. It is not, in their Lordships' judgment, a case of 'curing the defect' at all. The general council had acted invalidly in expelling the appellant through a rule (11 (7)) under which he had not been charged. It would seem clear that the annual conference which had appellate functions, had no more power to use the rule in order to expel him. Thus the same defect existed at both instances (*cf. Fagan* v. *National Coursing Association* (1974) 8 S.A.S.R. 546 for another example). The argument in the case turned only on whether rule 11 (7) created merely a penalty or a fresh charge, and on whether the appellant having appealed to the annual conference had lost his right to go to the court. It does not support a general proposition that defects at first instance cannot be 'cured' on appeal. *Pillai* v. *Singapore City Council* [1968] 1 W.L.R. 1278 was a case of administrative bodies concerned with the dismissal of an employee. The decision of the Board against the employee was put on cumulative grounds: first that the employee was not entitled to require that the rules of natural justice should be observed in proceedings leading to his dismissal; secondly that the rules of natural justice, if applicable, had not been breached thirdly, that if the rules of natural justice had been breached at first instance, the defect was cured on appeal. There had been a rehearing by way of evidence de novo which cured the initial defect. Their Lordships regard this as a decision that in the context, namely one of regulations concerning establishments procedures, justice can be held to be done if, after all these procedures had been gone through, the dismissed person has had a fair hearing and put his case. It is thus an authority in favouring the existence of the intermediate category but not necessarily one in favour of a general rule that first instance defects are cured by an appeal. Their Lordships are also of opinion that the phrase 'hearing of evidence de novo,' though useful in that case, does not provide a universal solvent. What is required is examination of the hearing process, original and appeal as a whole, and a decision on the question whether after it has been gone through the complainant has had a fair deal of the kind that he bargained for. From this analysis it appears that there is no real conflict between the cases of *Annamunthodo* and *Pillai*. The situations to which they applied are different: neither lays down a rule contradicted by the other.

[Having considered various Australian and Canadian authorities, he continued:]

Finally, there are cases in New Zealand. *Denton* v. *Auckland City* [1969] N.Z.L.R. 256 . . . was reviewed together with other New Zealand cases by the Court of Appeal in *Reid* v. *Rowley* [1977] 2 N.Z.L.R. 472 – a case concerned with trotting. The decision was that an appeal to a domestic or administrative tribunal does not normally cure a breach of natural justice by a tribunal of first instance *so as to oust the jurisdiction* of the courts to redress such breaches, but that the exercise of such a right of appeal is a matter that may be taken into account by the courts in considering the grant of discretionary remedies. This decision was reached, as the judgment of Cooke J. shows, after examination of *Annamuthodo* v. *Oilfields Workers' Trade Union* [1961] A.C. 945 and *Pillai* v. *Singapore City Council* [1968] 1 W.L.R. 1278, and other relevant English and Canadian cases. In general their Lordships find that the approach of that case is in line with that sought to be made in this judgment. It may be that the court adopted a more reserved attitude as regards the effect after a denial or breach of natural justice at first instance, of a full examination on appeal. Cooke J. said at p. 482:

'. . . the conferment of wide powers on a domestic or statutory appeal tribunal, including power to rehear the evidence orally, is not enough to insulate the appellate jurisdiction automatically from the effects of a failure of natural justice at first instance.'

Their Lordships agree, and have given their reasons for concluding that in this field there is no automatic rule. But they do not understand the Court of Appeal to be subscribing to a view that cases of 'insulation' or 'curing,' after a full hearing by an appellate body, may not exist: on the contrary, Cooke J. expresses the opinion that the court in the exercise of its discretion, when reviewing the domestic or statutory decision, should take into account all the proceedings which led to it, the conduct of the complaining party and the gravity of any breach of natural justice which may have occurred. This, though perhaps with some difference in emphasis, is their Lordships approach.

It remains to apply the principles above stated to the facts of the present case. In the first place, their Lordships are clearly of the view that the proceedings before the committee were in the nature of an appeal, not by way of an invocation, or use, of whatever original jurisdiction the committee may have had. The nature of the appeal is laid down by section 32 of the Australian Jockey Club Act 1873, and by the rules. Under the Act, the appeal is to be in the nature of a rehearing – a technical expression which does little more than entitle the committee to review the facts as at the date when the appeal is heard (see *Builders Licensing Board (N.S.W.)* v. *Sperway Constructions (Sydney) Pty. Ltd.* (1977) 51 A.L.J.R. 260, 261, *per* Mason J.) not one which automatically insulates their findings from those of the stewards. The decision is to be 'upon the real merits and justice of the case' – an injunction to avoid technicalities and the slavish following of precedents but not one which entitles the committee to brush aside defective or improper proceedings before the stewards. The section is then required to be construed as supplemental to and not in derogation of or limited by the Rules of Racing. This brings the matter of disputes and discipline clearly into the consensual field. The Rules of Racing (Local Rules 70 to 74) allow the committee to take account of evidence already taken and of additional evidence, and confer wide powers as to the disposal of appeals.

In addition to these formal requirements, a reviewing court must take account of the reality behind them. Races are run at short intervals; bets must be disposed of according to the result. Stewards are there in order to take rapid decisions as to such matters as the running of horses, being entitled to use the evidence of their eyes and their experience. As well as acting inquisitorially at the stage of deciding the result of a race, they may have to consider disciplinary action: at this point rules of natural justice become relevant. These require, at the least, that persons should be formally charged, heard in their own defence, and know the evidence against them. These essentials must always be observed but it is inevitable, and must be taken to be accepted, that there may not be time for procedural refinements. It is in order to enable decisions reached in this way to be reviewed at leisure that the appeal procedure exists. Those concerned know that they are entitled to a full hearing with opportunities to bring evidence and have it heard. But they know also that this appeal hearing is governed by the Rules of Racing, and that it remains an essentially domestic proceeding, in which experience and opinions as to what is in the interest of racing as a whole play a large part, and in which the standards of those which have come to be accepted over the history of this sporting activity. All those who partake in it have accepted the Rules of Racing, and the standards which lie behind them: they must also have accepted to be bound by the decisions of the bodies set up under those rules so long as when the process of reaching these decisions has been terminated, they can be said, by an objective observer, to have had fair treatment and consideration of their case on its merits.

In their Lordships' opinion precisely this can, indeed must, be said of the present case. The plaintiff's case has received, overall, full and fair consideration, and a decision, possibly a hard one, reached against him. There is no basis on which the court ought to interfere, and his appeal must fail.

The defendants took other points against the plaintiff, notably that, having elected to take his case to the committee on appeal, he had lost his right of resort to the court. Their Lordships need say no more of this argument than that it appears to present difficulties both on the authorities and in principle. But they need come to no conclusion upon it.

They will humbly advise Her Majesty that the appeal be dismissed. . . .

Questions

1. How much guidance does this Privy Council opinion give for a case where bodies exercising statutory powers are involved? (See Elliott, (1980) 43 M.L.R. 66; R. v. Oxfordshire Local Valuation Panel, ex p. Oxford C.C. (1981) 79 L.G.R. 432; R. v. Greater Manchester Valuation Panel, ex p. Shell Chemicals U.K. Ltd. [1982] Q.B. 255 at p. 263; cf Wade, p. 488.)

2. Would the decision have been the same if the right of appeal had not been exercised? (See the Oxfordshire Local Valuation Panel case.)

3. Does this Privy Council opinion bring into consideration the merits of the decision as well as the procedures by which it was reached? If so, should it?

Notes

1. Natural justice does not require that there be an appeal against a decision (Ward v. Bradford Corporation (1972) 70 L.G.R. 27, noted at p. 202 supra), but the fact that there is such an appeal may be relevant in several respects to a case in which it is alleged that the original decision was reached in breach of natural justice:

(a) The fact that there is some later hearing may lead to the inference that no hearing was intended at the initial stage. See Pearlberg v. Varty [1972] 1 W.L.R. 534; Twist v. Randwick M.C. (1976) 136 C.L.R. 106 per Barwick C.J. See further p. 233 supra and p. 278 infra. On the other hand, the existence of an appeal could be used to support the argument for a hearing at an earlier stage since 'cases which lend themselves to ultimate judicial determination are those which require for their satisfactory resolution a hearing or at least a consideration of the contentions of the opposing parties' (Twist v. Randwick M.C. (1976) 136 C.L.R. at p. 114 per Mason J., referring to the case of an appeal to a court or judge). The judgment of Willes J. in particular in Cooper v. Wandsworth Board of Works (1863) 14 C.B. (N.S.) 180 at p. 193 was cited in support (although that case concerned an appeal to a metropolitan board).

(b) It could be argued that a statutory right of appeal is the exclusive remedy for challenging a decision allegedly made in breach of natural justice: see Twist v. Randwick M.C. per Mason J.. Cf. Ch. 11 infra.

(c) It might be argued that the appellate proceedings have cured any breach of natural justice there may have been in the way in which the original decision was reached. This was the point raised in *Calvin v. Carr.*

(*d*) A fourth argument could be that the fact that a right of appeal has been exercised should lead a court to refuse to grant a discretionary remedy. For further consideration see *Wislang v. Medical Practitioners Disciplinary Committee* [1974] 1 N.Z.L.R. 29 and *Reid v. Rowley* [1977] 2 N.Z.L.R. 472 (the approach in the latter case being thought in *Calvin v. Carr* to be broadly in line with that of their Lordships, though 'with some difference of emphasis'). On this approach, however, some difficulty might arise in the case of, for example, an action for damages (which is not a discretionary remedy). The problem is going to arise generally in cases of collateral challenge, on which see Wade, p. 299; Note 4, p. 90 *supra*, and *Reid v. Rowley* [1977] 2 N.Z.L.R. at p. 483. Note further that the exercise of a right of appeal is not in general regarded as a waiver of the right to seek judicial review: see *Ridge v. Baldwin* [1964] A.C. 40 at p. 81.

The discretionary nature of Administrative Law remedies means that it is possible that a right of appeal which has not been exercised (i.e. a potentially curative appeal) might also operate so as to defeat a complainant. (See *R. v. Oxfordshire Local Valuation Panel, ex p. Oxford C.C.* (1981) 79 L.G.R. 432.) Note, however, that the courts do not necessarily require prior exhaustion of internal appeals, even where a peron is contractually bound by the rules of a body to exhaust them before having resort to the courts: *Leigh v. N.U.R.* [1970] Ch. 326; cf. *White v. Kuzych* [1951] A.C. 585. On appeals and judicial review, see further p. 366 *infra.*

2. Although *Leary v. N.U.V.B.* [1971] Ch. 34 came in for criticism in *Calvin v. Carr*, it might be worth underlining the point made by Megarry J., that a person loses a right of appeal from the effective decision if appellate proceedings are regarded as curing the original breach of natural justice.

3. Do you think that *Calvin v. Carr* gives sufficient guidance on the question of curative appeals? Note Elliott's comments on the case, op. cit. He writes (at p. 67, footnote omitted):

. . . [T]he Privy Council has stated that, in natural justice, transaction-typing and a contextual policy analysis has ousted abstract principles. This line of development makes it very hard to maintain – as the standard books tend to – that the rules of natural justice are merely applied in marginally different fashions in changing transaction types; on the contrary, the view of the Privy Council must mean that, in different circumstances 'natural justice' *means different things. . . .*

At a later point he continues:

. . . [T]here is now a substantial body of evidence to the effect that the judges are so conscious of the need to apply natural justice flexibly that, if they do not follow the contextual analysis of *Calvin v. Carr*, they will discover and exercise a discretion at the remedial stage of an inquiry. . . .

It is arguable, then, that the problem of the flexibility of natural justice resolves itself into choosing the least painful way of skinning a cat: either by asserting binding 'rules' and derogating from them at the remedial stage, or by asserting different rules for different contexts. Both methods have support from authority. It is submitted that the clear preference shown in *Calvin v. Carr* for the second approach is to be welcomed . . . always given that rules are consistently applied in specific subject areas.

FAIR HEARINGS – PARTICULAR SITUATIONS

Licensing and commercial regulation

R. v. Gaming Board of Great Britain, ex parte Benaim and Khaida, p. 241 *supra*

McInnes v. Onslow-Fane

[1978] 1 W.L.R. 1520   Chancery Division

In May 1976 the plaintiff unsuccessfully applied to the western area council of the British Boxing Board of Control for a boxing manager's licence.

MEGARRY V.C.: . . . On November 29, 1976, the originating summons was issued. The only parts of it with which I am concerned seek a declaration and a mandatory order. The declaration is to the effect that in refusing the plaintiff's application of May 28, 1976, the board acted in breach of natural justice and/or unfairly in that they failed to comply with the plaintiff's request in his application: (i) to be informed of the case against him so that he could answer it before the board considered his application, and/or (ii) to be granted an oral hearing. The mandatory order is much to the same effect: and Mr. Beloff, who appeared for the plaintiff, readily accepted that he did not really need the order, since the declaration would suffice him. Mr. Moses, who appeared for the board, accepted that there was jurisdiction to grant a declaration.

I have set out something of the history of the dealings between the plaintiff and the board and councils,[72] but I should emphasise that all that is before me for decision is what for brevity I may call the 1976 application for a manager's licence, and the refusal of this. The plaintiff had held a promoter's licence for about a year in 1954 and 1955, a trainer's licence granted in 1971, and a master of ceremonies' licence granted in 1973: but in May 1973 all licences had been withdrawn. Before the 1976 application in issue before me, the plaintiff had made five applications for a manager's licence during the years 1972 to 1975, and all had failed: he has never had a manager's licence. The originating summons includes a claim for a declaration relating to the 1976 application and the last four previous applications for such a licence, as well as a claim for a mandatory order requiring the board to grant the plaintiff a manager's licence; but by a consent order made last June, these matters were excluded from the present hearing. Whether they proceed hereafter depends, at least to some extent, on the outcome of the present hearing. What I am concerned with is, in essence, the procedural aspects of the 1976 application and refusal. The board admittedly did not inform the

---

[72] [This has been omitted for the reason set out in the rest of the sentence.]

plaintiff of 'the case against him,' nor did the board agree to give him an oral hearing. In so doing, did the board act either in breach of natural justice, or unfairly? That was the question which was argued for most of three days, with the citation of over a dozen authorities. . . .

It was common ground between Mr. Beloff and Mr. Moses that the point before me was the subject of no direct authority: although expulsion from clubs and other bodies is the subject of an ample range of authorities, the refusal of applications for membership is much less richly endowed. It was also accepted that the point is of considerable importance. There are many bodies which, though not established or operating under the authority of statute, exercise control, often on a national scale, over many activities which are important to many people, both as providing a means of livelihood and for other reasons. Sometimes that control is exercised, as by the board, by means of a system of granting or refusing licences, and sometimes it is operated by means of accepting or rejecting applications for membership. One particular aspect of this is membership of a trade union, without which it is impossible to obtain many important forms of work. In such cases it is plainly important, both to the body and the applicant, for them to know whether, before the application is rejected, the applicant is entitled to prior notice of any case against granting him a licence or admitting him to membership, and whether he is entitled to an oral hearing.

I think that I should take the matter by stages. First, there is the question of whether the grant or refusal of a licence by the board is subject to any requirements of natural justice or fairness which will be enforced by the courts. The question is not one that is governed by statute or contract, with questions of their true construction or the implication of terms; for there is no statute, and there is no contract between the plaintiff and the board. Nevertheless, in recent years there has been a marked expansion of the ambit of the requirements of natural justice and fairness, reaching beyond statute and contract. A striking example is *Nagle* v. *Feilden* [1966] 2 Q.B. 633. There, a woman sought a declaration and injunctions against the Jockey Club to enforce her claim that she ought not to be refused a trainer's licence for horse-racing merely because she was a woman. . . . Lord Denning M.R. accepted that social clubs could refuse to admit an application for membership as they wished; but the Jockey Club exercised 'a virtual monopoly in an important field of human activity,' and what gave the courts jurisdiction was 'a man's right to work': see pp. 644, 646. . . .

. . . I observe that Salmon L.J. put it, rather differently, as being a man's 'right not to be capriciously and unreasonably prevented from earning his living as he wills': see p. 653. Furthermore in *Reg.* v. *Gaming Board for Great Britain Ex parte Benaim and Khaida* [1970] 2 Q.B. 417, 429, Lord Denning M.R. himself rejected 'right' in favour of 'privilege' for a particular claim of this sort. Alternatively the term 'liberty' may be used, as it was by Lord Lindley in *Quinn* v. *Leathem* [1901] A.C. 495, 534, when he referred to the plaintiff's liberty to earn his living in his own way. One difficulty, of course, is that the 'right to work' is a familiar phrase that trips easily off the tongue, whereas 'privilege to work' sounds strange. Perhaps 'liberty to work' would be more successful. . . .

The decision in *Nagle* v. *Feilden* [1966] 2 Q.B. 633 was, of course, merely a decision that the plaintiff's claim should not be struck out, since it was capable of succeeding. It was not a decision that the plaintiff's claim should in fact succeed. However, in *Enderby Town Football Club Ltd.* v. *Football Association Ltd.* [1971] Ch. 591, 606, 607, Lord Denning M.R. adhered to his views in reaching a substantive decision. It seems to me that the case before me is one in which the court is entitled to intervene in order to enforce the appropriate requirements of natural justice and fairness, and that Mr. Moses was right to accept that the case fell within this category.

Second, where the court is entitled to intervene, I think it must be considered what type of decision is in question. I do not suggest that there is any clear or exhaustive classification; but I think that at least three categories may be discerned. First, there are what may be called the forfeiture cases. In these, there is a decision which takes away some existing right or position, as where a member of an organisation is expelled or a licence is revoked. Second, at the other extreme there are what may be called the application cases. These are cases where the decision merely refuses to grant the applicant the right or position that he seeks, such as membership of the organisation, or a licence to do certain acts. Third, there is an intermediate category, which may be called the expectation cases, which differ from the application cases only in that the applicant has some legitimate expectation from what has already happened that his application will be granted. This head includes cases where an existing licence-holder applies for a renewal of his licence, or a person already elected or appointed to some position seeks confirmation from some confirming authority: see, for instance, *Weinberger* v. *Inglis* [1919] A.C. 606; *Breen* v. *Amalgamated Engineering Union* [1971] 2 Q.B. 175; and see *Schmidt* v. *Secretary of State for Home Affairs* [1969] 2 Ch. 149, 170, 173 and *Reg.* v. *Barnsley Metropolitan Borough Council, Ex parte Hook* [1976] 1 W.L.R. 1052, 1058.

It seems plain that there is a substantial distinction between the forfeiture cases and the application cases. In the forfeiture cases, there is a threat to take something away for some reason: and in such cases, the right to an unbiased tribunal, the right to notice of the charges and the right to be heard in answer to the charges (which in *Ridge* v. *Baldwin* [1964] A.C. 40, 132, Lord Hodson said were three features of natural justice which stood out) are plainly apt. In the application cases, on the other hand, nothing is being taken away, and in all normal circumstances there are no charges, and so no requirement of an opportunity of being heard in answer to the charges. Instead, there is the far wider and less defined question of the general suitability of the applicant for membership or a licence. The distinction is well-recognised, for in general it is clear that the courts will require natural justice to be observed for expulsion from a social club, but not on an application for admission to it. The intermediate category, that of the expectation cases, may at least in some respects be regarded as being more akin to the forfeiture cases than the application cases; for although in form there is no forfeiture but merely an attempt at acquisition that fails, the legitimate expectation of a renewal of the licence or confirmation of the membership is one which raises the question of what it is that has happened to make the applicant unsuitable for the membership or licence for which he was previously thought suitable.

I pause there. I do not think that I need pursue the expectation cases, for in the present case I can see nothing that would bring the plaintiff within them. Although he has at different times held a promoter's licence, a trainer's licence and a master of ceremonies' licence, he has never held a manager's licence. His 1976 application for a manager's licence has to be viewed in the light of the five unsuccessful applications for a manager's licence that he made during the years 1972 to 1975. I can see nothing that could fairly be called a legitimate expectation that his 1976 application would succeed. Mr. Beloff relied on the other types of licence that had been granted to the plaintiff; but I do not think that these help him. The functions of a promoter, a trainer or a master of ceremonies are not the same as those of a manager, and in May 1973 all his licences had been withdrawn. When he made the 1976 application he was someone who had held no licence for three years, and had had five applications for a manager's licence refused over the previous four years. In my judgment, the case is plainly an application case in which the plaintiff is seeking to obtain a licence that he has never held and had no legitimate expectation of holding; he had only the hope (which may be confident or faint or anything between) which any applicant for anything may always have.

Third, there is the question of the requirements of natural justice or fairness that have to be applied in an application case such as this. What are the requirements where there are no provisions of any statute or contract either conferring a right to the licence in certain circumstances, or laying down the procedure to be observed, and the applicant is seeking from an unofficial body the grant of a type of licence that he has never held before, and, though hoping to obtain it, has no legitimate expectation of receiving?

I do not think that much help is to be obtained from discussing whether 'natural justice' or 'fairness' is the more appropriate term. If one accepts that 'natural justice' is a flexible term which imposes different requirements in different cases, it is capable of applying appropriately to the whole range of situations indicated by terms such as 'judicial,' 'quasi-judicial' and 'administrative.' Nevertheless, the further the situation is away from anything that resembles a judicial or quasi-judicial situation, and the further the question is removed from what may reasonably be called a justiciable question, the more appropriate it is to reject an expression which includes the word 'justice' and to use instead terms such as 'fairness' or 'the duty to act fairly': see *In re H.K. (An Infant)* [1967] 2 Q.B. 617, 630, *per* Lord Parker C.J.; *In re Pergamon Press Ltd.* [1971] Ch. 388, 399, *per* Lord Denning M.R.; *Breen's* case [1971] 2 Q.B. 175, 195, *per* Edmund Davies L.J. ('fairly exercised'); *Pearlberg* v. *Varty* [1972] 1 W.L.R. 534, 545, *per* Viscount Dilhorne, and at p. 547, *per* Lord Pearson. The suitability of the term 'fairness' in such cases is increased by the curiosities of the expression 'natural justice.' Justice is far from being a 'natural' concept. The closer one goes to a state of nature, the less justice does one find. . . . However, be that as it may, the question before me is that of the content of 'the duty to act fairly' (or of 'natural justice') in this particular case. What does it entail? In particular, does it require the board to afford the plaintiff not only information of the 'case against him' but also an oral hearing?

Before I turn to these heads, I should say that at the outset of his submission Mr. Moses accepted, and asserted, that the board were under a duty to reach an honest conclusion, without bias, and not in pursuance of any capricious policy. To this extent the board were under a duty to act fairly. But that duty, he said, did not require the board either to inform the plaintiff of 'the case against him' or to give him an oral hearing. Mr. Beloff, on the other hand, contended that both of these requirements were constituent elements of 'fairness' in cases of this kind. He disclaimed any submission that the board were required to give any reasons for their past rejection of applications, or that, once the decision was made, there was any obligation to give reasons in order to enable the plaintiff to apply to the courts to set it aside. He also made no positive attack on the substance of the board's decision, as distinct from the procedure adopted.

I therefore take as the fourth point the alleged obligation of the board to give the plaintiff information as to the case against him, or, as it was sometimes put during argument, information about what was troubling them. . . .

I think it is clear that there is no general obligation to give reasons for a decision. Certainly in an application case, where there are no statutory or contractual requirements but a simple discretion in the licensing body, there is no obligation on that body to give their reasons. . . .

[MEGARRY V.-C. referred in particular to R. v. *Gaming Board for Great Britain, ex p. Benaim and Khaida,* p. 241 *supra,* and continued:]

Mr. Beloff, of course, relied on this decision. He also relied on *In re H.K. (An Infant)* [1967] 2 Q.B. 617. There the question was whether an immigrant was under 16 years old, and so, as the son of a Commonwealth citizen ordinarily resident in the United Kingdom, had a statutory right of entry into the United Kingdom. Lord Parker C.J. held that the immigration officer was under a duty to give the immigrant an opportunity of satisfying him of the matters in the relevant subsection, and for that purpose to let him know what his immediate impression was so that the immigrant could disabuse him. On the facts, it was held that this duty had been discharged.

These cases seem to me to be very different from the case before me. In each there was a statute which conferred the power and the duty to decide upon some defined issue. Here there is no statute and no defined issue but merely a general discretion. In the *Gaming Board* [1970] 2 Q.B. 417, the character, reputation and financial standing of the applicants were in issue, so that the refusal of the certificate of fitness would be a slur on the applicants. In *In re H.K. (An Infant)* [1967] 2 Q.B. 617, the question was whether or not the immigrant had a statutory right of entry. Here, there is no statutory or, indeed, any other true right; and certainly the refusal of a licence by no means necessarily puts any slur on the plaintiff's character. There are many reasons why a licence might be refused to an applicant of complete integrity, high repute and financial stability. Some may be wholly unconnected with the applicant, as where there are already too many licensees for the good of boxing under existing conditions. Others will relate to the applicant. They may be discreditable to him, as where he is dishonest or a drunkard; or they may be free from discredit, as where he suffers from physical or mental ill-health, or is too young, or too inexperienced, or too old, or simply lacks the personality or strength of character required for what no doubt may be an exacting occupation. There may be no 'case against him' at all, in the sense of something warranting forfeiture or expulsion; instead, there may simply be the absence of enough in favour of granting the licence. Indeed, in most cases the more demanding and responsible the occupation for which the licence is required, the greater will be the part likely to be played by considerations of the general suitability of the applicant, as distinct from the mere absence of moral or other blemishes. The more important these general considerations are, the less appropriate does it appear to be to require the licensing body to indicate to the applicant the nature of the 'case against him.' I think that this applies in the present case.

Let the distinctions between this case and the authorities that I have mentioned be accepted. There still remains the question whether in this case the board's procedure was fair. . . .

. . . [A]ssume a board acting honestly and without bias or caprice: why should a duty to act fairly require them to tell an applicant the gist of the reasons (which may vary from member to member) why they think he ought not to be given a licence? Is a college or university, when selecting candidates for admission or awarding scholarships, or a charity when making grants to the needy, acting 'unfairly' when it gives no reason to the unsuccessful? Are editors and publishers 'unfair' when they send out unreasoned rejection slips? Assume that they are under no enforceable duty to act fairly, and it may still be a matter of concern to them if they are to be told that they are acting 'unfairly' in not giving the gist of their reasons to the rejected. Again, do judges act unfairly when, without any indication of their reasons, they refuse leave to appeal, or decide questions of costs? . . .

Looking at the case as whole, in my judgment there is no obligation on the board to give the plaintiff even the gist of the reasons why they refused his application, or proposed to do so. This is not a case in which there has been any suggestion of the board considering any alleged dishonesty or morally culpable conduct of the plaintiff. A man free from any moral blemish may nevertheless be wholly unsuitable for a particular type of work. The refusal of the plaintiff's application by no means necessarily puts any slur on his character, nor does it deprive him of any statutory right. There is no mere narrow issue as to his character, but the wide and general issue whether it is right to grant this licence to this applicant. In such circumstances, in the absence of anything to suggest that the board have been affected by dishonesty or bias or caprice, or that there is any other impropriety, I think that the board are fully entitled to give no reasons for their decision, and to decide the application without any preliminary indication to the plaintiff of those reasons. The board are the best judges of the desirability of granting the licence, and in the absence of any impropriety the court ought not to interfere.

There is a more general consideration. I think that the courts must be slow to allow any implied obligation to be fair to be used as a means of bringing before the courts for review honest decisions of bodies exercising jurisdiction over sporting and other activities which those bodies are far better fitted to judge than the courts. This is so even where those bodies are concerned with the means of livelihood of those who take part in those activities. The concepts of natural justice and the duty to be fair must not be allowed to discredit themselves by making unreasonable requirements and imposing undue burdens. Bodies such as the board which promote a public interest by seeking to maintain high standards in a field of activity which otherwise might easily become degraded and corrupt ought not to be hampered in their work without good cause. Such bodies should not be tempted or coerced into granting licences that otherwise they would refuse by reason of the courts having imposed on them a procedure for refusal which facilitates litigation against them. . . . The individual must indeed be protected against impropriety; but any claim of his for anything more must be balanced against what the public interest requires.

That brings me to the fifth point, the contention that the board are obliged to afford the plaintiff a hearing. This, I think, has in large part been disposed of by what I have said in rejecting the contention that the plaintiff has a right to be told the gist of the reasons for proposing to reject his application. The contention that the plaintiff ought to be given a hearing seems to have been put forward mainly as an ancillary to the alleged obligation to inform him of the gist of the reasons for provisionally deciding not to grant him the licence, and so as to enable him to meet what is said. However, if one treats the right to a hearing as an independent requirement, I would say that I cannot see how the obligation to be fair can be said in a case of this type to require a hearing. I do not see why the board should not be fully capable of dealing fairly with the plaintiff's application without any hearing. The case is not an expulsion case where natural justice confers the right to know the charge and to have an opportunity of meeting it at a hearing. I cannot think that there is or should be any rule that an application for a licence of this sort cannot properly be refused without giving the applicant the opportunity of a hearing, however hopeless the application, and whether it is the first or the fifth or the fiftieth application that he has made. . . .

Summons dismissed.

Notes

1. Megarry V.-C.'s decision that he could intervene to see if natural justice or fairness were complied with in the absence of any contract with the plaintiff or the

exercise of any statutory power is quite significant. For the earlier case law, see Jackson, *Natural Justice*, 2nd edn., pp. 121–3, and see in particular *Stininato v. Auckland Boxing Association (Inc.)* [1978] 1 N.Z.L.R. 1. One obvious area of application is in relation to trade unions operating closed shops. Would natural justice or fairness require some form of hearing for an applicant to such a union? Cf. *Faramus v. Film Artistes' Association* [1964] A.C. 925 at pp. 941 and 947. Union rules do not in fact expressly provide for a hearing, although some union rules require reasons to be given for rejection and some give an appeal against refusal of admission (Gennard, Gregory, and Dunn, *Employment Gazette*, 1980, p. 591). To what extent would the requirement of a hearing depend on the criteria for admission and the reasons for rejection? See further Campbell and Bowyer, *Trade Unions and the Individual*, para. 1.25. Gennard, Gregory and Dunn, op. cit., pp. 593–4, reporting on a survey of the rule books of all major trade unions, state that all these unions (cf. Campbell and Bowyer, op. cit., para. 1.56) have rules allowing refusal of admission for reasons other than lack of basic occupational entry qualifications: an example is the possession of a criminal record.

For further discussion of *McInnes v. Onslow-Fane*, see Elias, (1979) 8 I.L.J. 111, who, *inter alia*, comments on the substantive principles which it was thought the duty to act fairly encompassed – see the concession of counsel, p. 266 *supra*, and see generally p. 283 *infra*. On the position of the union member and natural justice, see Rideout, *Principles of Labour Law*, 3rd edn., pp. 275–80, and note that the courts can strike down union rules that contravene natural justice.

It should also be realized that the position of the union applicant or member has been affected by legislation. See now ss. 4–5 of the Employment Act 1980 and para. 51 of the *Code of Practice on Closed Shop Agreements and Arrangements*. Note further the possibility of redress by the T.U.C.'s Independent Review Committee on which see Ewing and Rees, (1981) 10 I.L.J. 84. Generally see Hepple and O'Higgins, *Encyclopedia of Labour Relations Law*, paras. 2-2054–7, who, *inter alia*, point to the suggestion by Gennard, Gregory, and Dunn (op. cit.) that 'there are probably few instances of injustice to individual members' of unions.

2. Many trades and activities are regulated by licensing, and therefore the grant, renewal, or revocation of a licence are all matters of extreme importance to a person who wishes to participate in such a regulated trade or activity.

Note the old approach in *Nakkuda Ali v. Jayaratne* [1951] A.C. 66, summarized in *Ridge v. Baldwin*, p. 221 *supra*, and *R. v. Metropolitan Police Commissioner, ex p. Parker* [1953] 1 W.L.R. 1150; but, as Lord Denning observed in *R. v. Gaming Board for Great Britain, ex p. Benaim and Khaida*, p. 243 *supra*, *Nakkuda Ali v. Jayaratne* was subject to criticism in *Ridge v. Baldwin*. See further *Banks v. Transport Regulation Board (Vic.)* (1968) 119 C.L.R. 222, and for a recent case concerning the revocation of a licence to which natural justice applied, see *R. v. Barnsley M.B.C., ex p. Hook* [1976] 1 W.L.R. 1052; cf. *R. v. Basildon R.D.C., ex p. Brown* (1981) 79 L.G.R. 655. Indeed, as the *Gaming Board* case indicates, procedural protection can be accorded in the case of an application for a licence, but the *Gaming Board* case must be compared with the case which has just been set out (*McInnes v. Onslow-Fane*), in which it was distinguished. For criticism of the latter case, see Wade, p. 496, n. 10.

3. The discussion so far has been concerned with action in individual cases, but of course an increase in the overall number of licences may adversely affect the existing licence holders. In *R. v. Liverpool Corporation, ex p. Liverpool Taxi Fleet Operators' Association* [1972] 2 Q.B. 299 the Court of Appeal required the Corporation to give a

hearing to the taxicab owners association before it increased the number of taxicab licences. The Corporation was in fact proposing to act contrary to an undertaking that no such increase would take place before legislation controlling private hire cabs was in force, and two of the judges in the Court of Appeal (Roskill L.J. and Sir Gordon Willmer) did not decide what the position would have been in the absence of the undertaking. See Evans, (1973) 36 M.L.R. 93 at pp. 94–5 and note the other possibly influential factors he mentions. However, as Evans points out, Lord Denning would have required a hearing in any event. For comment on the case, see Evans, op. cit.; Ganz, *Administrative Procedures*, pp. 101–2. Having referred to the fact that it was the undertaking which gave rise to the duty to give a hearing, Ganz argues that although 'this may be an admirable decision from the point of political morality it is questionable whether the courts are the right place to enforce such conduct'.

In the *Liverpool* case the function in question was regarded as an administrative one, to which the duty to act fairly was applicable: cf. Ganz, op. cit. If the function is a legislative one, then there is no implied right to be heard: p. 516 *infra*, though see Note 1, p. 518 *infra*.

Offices and employments

Ridge v. Baldwin, p. 214 *supra*

Malloch v. Aberdeen Corporation

[1971] 1 W.L.R. 1578　　　　　　　　　　　　　　　　　　House of Lords

Malloch had been employed as a school teacher in Scotland. The Schools (Scotland) Code 1956, S.I. 1956 No. 894 (s. 40), as amended in 1967, provided that 'every teacher employed by an education authority shall be a registered teacher holding the qualifications required by [the Code] for the post in which he is employed'. Malloch objected to applying for registration and declined to do so. A resolution was passed by the education committee of Aberdeen Corporation to dismiss Malloch (along with another thirty-seven teachers) 'on the grounds that they are unregistered and that their continued employment is no longer lawful by virtue of the . . . Code'. As provided by statute, he had been given notice of the motion for his dismissal at least three weeks before the relevant meeting, but was not allowed to make written representations or to be heard before the passing of the resolution. Malloch, who was dismissible at pleasure, unsuccessfully attacked the resolution and the notice of dismissal before the Lord Ordinary and the Second Division of the Court of Session (1970 S.L.T. 369), and he appealed to the House of Lords.

LORD REID: . . . At common law a master is not bound to hear his servant before he dismisses him. He can act unreasonably or capriciously if he so chooses but the dismissal is valid. The servant has no remedy unless the dismissal is in breach of contract and then the servant's only remedy is damages for breach of contract.

In my opinion, that is not the present status of teachers employed by Scottish education authorities. . . .

. . . In the Public Schools (Scotland) Teachers Act 1882 certificated teachers are said by section 3 to 'hold office' under school boards and their dismissal without 'due deliberation' is forbidden. In particular it is enacted that no dismissal shall be valid unless three weeks' notice of a meeting to consider a motion for dismissal is given both to every member of the board and to the teacher. I can see no possible reason for requiring notice to the teacher other than to give him an opportunity to prepare his defence, and it appears to me to be implicit in this requirement that the teacher shall be entitled to submit his defence to the board. Moreover, a school board refusing to hear the teacher whom it proposed to dismiss could hardly be said to proceed with due deliberation. It was said that this three weeks' notice may have been intended to give the teacher extra time to find new employment. I cannot accept that because until the motion for dismissal is put to the vote he does not know whether it will be carried – that required an absolute majority – and it would be premature for him to look for other employment: indeed if the board knew he was already looking for other employment that might affect the voting.

Then it was said that there was no obligation to give notice of any reason why it was proposed to dismiss him – so how could he prepare his defence? That appears to me quite unrealistic. It is extremely unlikely that such a motion could be put to a body of elected members representing a small area without the teacher getting to know its cause. A private employer may act in secret but a responsible elected public body can hardly do so.

Then it was said that it is inconsistent that a body should be entitled to act at pleasure but nevertheless bound to hear the teacher before acting. I can see no inconsistency. Acting at pleasure means that there is no obligation to formulate reasons. Formal reasons might lead to legal difficulties. But it seems to me perfectly sensible for Parliament to say to a public body: you need not give formal reasons but you must hear the man before you dismiss him. In my view, that is what Parliament did say in the 1882 Act.

Then by the Education (Scotland) Act 1908, section 21, a teacher could petition the Education Department for an enquiry into the reasons for his dismissal. If the department were of opinion that the dismissal was not reasonably justifiable they could give the school board an opportunity of reconsidering the matter and on refusal could award to the teacher up to a year's salary to be paid by the board. So there was not thought to be any difficulty in practice in discovering why the board had dismissed the teacher.

An elected public body is in a very different position from a private employer. Many of its servants in the lower grades are in the same position as servants of a private employer. But many in higher grades or 'offices' are given special statutory status or protection. The right of a man to be heard in his own defence is the most elementary protection of all and, where a statutory form of protection would be less effective if it did not carry with it a right to be heard, I would not find it difficult to imply this right. Here it appears to me that there is a plain implication to that effect in the 1882 Act. The terms of the Act have been altered by later legislation, but I can find nothing in any later Act which can reasonably be interpreted as taking away that elementary right. . . .

LORD WILBERFORCE: . . . The argument that, once it is shown that the relevant relationship is that of master and servant, this is sufficient to exclude the requirements of natural justice is often found, in one form or another, in reported cases. There are two reasons behind it. The first is that, in master and servant cases, one is normally in the field of the common law of contract inter partes, so that principles of administrative law, including those of natural justice, have no part to play. The second relates to the remedy: it is that in pure master and servant cases, the most that can be obtained is damages, if the dismissal is wrongful: no order for reinstatement can be made, so no room exists for such remedies as administrative law may grant, such as a declaration that the dismissal is void. I think there is validity in both of these arguments, but they, particularly the first, must be carefully used. It involves the risk of a compartmental approach which, though convenient as a solvent, may lead to narrower distinctions than are appropriate to the broader issues of administrative law. A comparative list of situations in which persons have been held entitled or not entitled to a hearing, or to observation of rules of natural justice, according to the master and servant test, looks illogical and even bizarre. A specialist surgeon is denied protection which is given to a hospital doctor; a University professor, as a servant, has been denied the right to be heard, a dock labourer and an undergraduate have been granted it; examples can be multiplied (see *Barber* v. *Manchester Regional Hospital Board* [1958] 1 W.L.R. 181, *Palmer* v. *Inverness Hospitals Board of Management*, 1963 S.C. 311, *Vidyodaya University Council* v. *Silva* [1965] 1 W.L.R. 77, *Vine* v. *National Dock Labour Board* [1957] A.C. 488, *Glynn* v. *Keele University* [1971] 1 W.L.R. 487). One may accept that if there are relationships in which all requirements of the observance of rules of natural justice are excluded (and I do not wish to assume that this is inevitably so), these must be confined to what have been called 'pure master and servant cases,' which I take to mean cases in which there is no element of public employment or service, no support by statute, nothing in the nature of an office or a status which is capable of protection. If any of these elements exist, then, in my opinion, whatever the terminology used, and even though in some inter partes aspects the relationship may be called that of master and servant, there may be essential procedural requirements to be observed, and failure to observe them may result in a dismissal being declared to be void.

This distinction was, I think, clearly perceived in two cases in this House. In *Vine* v. *National Dock Labour Board* [1957] A.C. 488, 500, dealing with a registered dock labourer, Vicount Kilmuir, L.C., said that the situation was entirely different from the ordinary master and servant case and referred to his status as a registered worker which he was entitled to have secured. And Lord Keith said, at p. 507: 'This is not a straightforward relationship of master and servant.' The dock labour scheme gave the dock worker a status, supported by statute (l.c. pp. 500, 508–9).

[LORD WILBERFORCE then considered Lord Reid's speech in *Ridge* v. *Baldwin*, p. 216 *supra*, and continued:]

On the other hand, there are some cases where the distinction has been lost sight of, and where the mere allocation of the label – master and servant – has been thought decisive against an administrative law remedy.

One such, which I refer to because it may be thought to have some relevance here, is *Vidyodaya University Council* v. *Silva* [1965] 1 W.L.R. 77, concerned with a university professor, who was dismissed without a hearing. He succeeded before the Supreme Court of Ceylon in obtaining an order for certiorari to quash the decision of the University, but that judgment was set aside by the Privy Council on the ground that the relation was that of master and servant to which the remedy of certiorari had no application. It would not be necessary or appropriate to disagree with the procedural or even the factual basis on which this decision rests: but I must confess that I could not follow it in this country in so far as it involves a denial of any remedy of administrative law to analogous employments. Statutory provisions similar to those on which the employment rested would tend to show, to my mind, in England or in Scotland, that it was one of a sufficiently public character, or one partaking sufficiently of the nature of an office, to attract appropriate remedies of administrative law.

I come now to the present case. Its difficulty lies in the fact that Mr. Malloch's appointment was held during pleasure, so that he could be dismissed without any reason being assigned. There is little authority on the question whether such persons have a right to be heard before dismissal, either generally, or at least in a case where a reason is in fact given. The case of *Reg.* v. *Darlington School Governors* (1844) 6 Q.B. 682 was one where by charter the governors had complete discretion to dismiss without hearing, so complete that they were held not entitled to fetter it by by-law. It hardly affords a basis for modern application any more than the more recent case of *Tucker* v. *British Museum Trustees* decided on an Act of 1753 – The Times, December 8, 1967.

In *Ridge* v. *Baldwin* my noble and learned friend, Lord Reid, said [1964] A.C. 40, 65: 'It has always been held, I think rightly, that such an officer' (sc. one holding at pleasure) 'has no right to be heard before being dismissed.' As a general principle, I respectfully agree: and I think it important not to weaken a principle which, for reasons of public policy, applies, at least as a starting point, to so wide a range of the public service. The difficulty arises when, as here, there are other incidents of the employment laid down by statute, or regulations, or code of employment, or agreement. The rigour of the principle is often, in modern practice mitigated for it has come to be perceived that the very possibility of dismissal without reason being given – action which may vitally affect a man's career or his pension – makes it all the more important for him, in suitable circumstances, to be able to state his case and, if denied the right to do so, to be able to have his dismissal declared void. So, while the courts will necessarily respect the right, for good reasons of public policy, to dismiss without assigned reasons, this should not, in my opinion, prevent them from examining the framework and context of the employment to see whether elementary rights are conferred upon him expressly or by necessary implication, and how far these extend. The present case is, in my opinion, just such a case where there are strong indications that a right to be heard, in appropriate circumstances, should not be denied.

My noble and learned friend, Lord Reid, has traced the history of legislation in Scotland down to 1908. In my opinion, this shows very clearly that concurrently with the change from an officer ad vitam aut culpam to an officer holding at pleasure, the legislature intended to preserve the status of the teacher as one holding a public office, only to be dismissed after due process, in 1882 described as due deliberation by a body of elected members. If it is pointed out that the words 'holding office' (which were in section 3 of the Public Schools (Scotland) Teachers Act 1882) were dropped in the Education Act of 1946, I can only reply that it would seem to me pitiful if this had the effect, by mere withdrawal of a label, of totally altering the teacher's status and his remedy. Equally I can draw no conclusion from the use of the words 'master and servant' in certain passages in the judgments in *Morrison v. Abernethy School Board* (1876) 3 R. 945. I do not think that the Second Division were intending to do more than point out, as the opinions justly do, the ordinary consequence of holding at pleasure, that is, that no reasons need be given for dismissal, while at the same time indicating that the schoolmaster was entitled to reasonable notice or compensation in lieu. The legislature, in 1882, repeated the words 'holding office,' thus endorsing, or restoring, the position as it existed before *Morrison's* case.

The significant section now is section 85 (1) of the Education (Scotland) Act 1962 which reads:

> 'No resolution of an education authority for the dismissal from their service of a certificated teacher other than a teacher who has completed forty-five years of first class service or of first class service and second class service within the meaning of the Teachers (Superannuation) Regulations shall be valid unless − (*a*) written notice of the motion for his dismissal shall, not less than three weeks before the meeting at which the resolution is adopted, have been sent to the teacher and to each member of the education authority; and (*b*) not less than one half of the members of the education authority are present at the meeting; and (*c*) the resolution is agreed to by two-thirds of the members so present.'

I ask what purpose the imposition of these requirements could serve, if the teacher had no right in any circumstances to state his case? Why give him three weeks' notice of the motion, to be put to elected members, of which a two-thirds majority is required, if he can do nothing during the three weeks except wait for the announcement of his fate? How could any responsible body of men reach a fair decision without hearing him? I find the right to be heard in an appropriate situation clearly given by implication.

It is said that this implication is inconsistent with, or negatived by, the teacher's right, by way of appeal, to petition the Secretary of State for an enquiry into the reason for his dismissal (see section 85 (3) of the Act of 1962). This at least indicates that the teacher was considered entitled to protection against unreasoned dismissal but I do not find that it supports an argument against a right to be heard. The reasons for dismissal may be known – they are known in the present case ('on the ground that his continued employment is no longer lawful by virtue of the Schools (Scotland) Code 1956 as amended'). What the teacher needs is an opportunity to show that the assigned reason is invalid; it is to be noted that even if he takes the case to the Secretary of State (which he can only do *after* dismissal) the latter can only refer the matter back again to the education authority – it is there that the power of decision ultimately rests. A limited right of appeal on the merits affords no argument against the existence of a right to a precedent hearing, and, if that is denied, to have the decision declared void. . . .

[LORD SIMON OF GLAISDALE delivered a speech in favour of allowing the appeal. LORD MORRIS OF BORTH-Y-GEST and LORD GUEST delivered speeches in favour of dismissing the appeal.]

Appeal allowed.

Question

Could the House of Lords have required the education committee to give Malloch notice of the charge as well as a chance to be heard? Can notice of the charge and a chance to present one's case be separated? (See Clark, [1975] P.L. 27 at pp. 36–43.)

Notes

1. For further proceedings by Malloch (though not on the natural justice point), see *Malloch* v. *Aberdeen Corporation* 1974 S.L.T. 253. See also the Education (Scotland) Act 1973. The *Malloch* litigation and its aftermath are mentioned by Harlow, [1976] P.L. 116 at pp. 120–1 (although the article ranges much more widely).

2. The courts will not normally specifically enforce a contract of service. As Lord Reid points out in *Ridge* v. *Baldwin*, p. 216 *supra*, in the case of a mere servant a dismissal is effective even if wrongful and the servant has no right to be heard (though see now Note 4 *infra* and note the approach of Lord Wilberforce in *Malloch*). Nevertheless, *Ridge* v. *Baldwin* and *Malloch* show that not all people complaining about their dismissal are precluded from obtaining certiorari or a declaration of its invalidity. However, exactly what will suffice to permit the courts to quash or declare invalid any dismissal effected without a hearing has proved to be a matter of some difficulty: see Lord Wilberforce's speech in *Malloch*; Wade, p. 497; de Smith, p. 227; Freedland, *The Contract of Employment*, pp. 278–90.

Recently, in *Stevenson* v. *United Road Transport Union* [1977] I.C.R. 893, the Court of Appeal, in a movement away from the orthodox approach, did not think it profitable to categorize the plaintiff as a servant or an officer. This was a case in which the purported dismissal of the plaintiff from office in the union was by the union's executive committee (the union being the actual employer). Under the union rules (as interpreted by the court) the committee could dismiss a union officer if it was decided that his performance of his job as an officer had been unsatisfactory. The Court of Appeal held that the committee must give an officer a fair hearing and that they had not done so on the facts of this case. In the course of the judgment, which was delivered by Buckley L.J., the following test was set out (at p. 902):

Where one party has a discretionary power to terminate the tenure or enjoyment by another of an employment or an office or a post or a privilege, is that power conditional upon the party invested with the power being first satisfied upon a particular point which involves investigating some matter upon which the other party ought in fairness to be heard or to be allowed to give his explanation or put his case? If the answer to the question is 'Yes', then unless, before the power purports to have been exercised, the condition has been satisfied after the other party has been given a fair opportunity of being heard or of giving his explanation or putting his case, the power will not have been well exercised.

For comment on this case, see de Smith, pp. 229–30, and see further Note 5, p. 297 *infra*. Note that the decision was based on the law of contract rather than on 'more general grounds of administrative law': [1977] I.C.R. at p. 903. Consider further *R.* v. *B.B.C., ex p. Lavelle* [1983] 1 W.L.R. 23, noted (1983) 12 I.L.J. 43, where the servant had a right to be heard under the contract and where there was a restriction, though largely procedural, on the circumstances for dismissal.

3. The view that an office-holder who is dismissible at pleasure has no right to a hearing before dismissal (see Lord Reid's speech in *Ridge* v. *Baldwin*, p. 000 *supra*) has been criticized by writers (Wade, pp. 500–1; de Smith, p. 228; Ganz, (1967) 30 M.L.R. 288 at pp. 292–4) and by the majority of the Supreme Court of Canada, who approved de Smith's criticism in *Nicholson* v. *Haldimand-Norfolk Regional Board of Commissioners of Police* [1979] 1 S.C.R. 311 at p. 323. This view was, however, accepted in *Malloch* and it was only the process of implication from the statutory framework that led to Malloch's entitlement to a hearing. Nevertheless, do you think that Lord Reid's comments on this matter are totally consistent with his discussion of the point in *Ridge* v. *Baldwin*?

4. As a result of legislation in recent years, the position of the mere servant today is a little different from that existing when *Ridge* v. *Baldwin* was decided. Under the provisions of the Employment Protection (Consolidation) Act 1978, as amended, a person may recover compensation or secure an order for re-engagement or reinstatement from an industrial tribunal if he has been unfairly dismissed, and the concept of unfair dismissal can include procedural unfairness. See Hepple and O'Higgins, *Encyclopedia of Labour Relations Law*, para. 1-391/1; Elias, (1981) 10 I.L.J. 201 at pp. 213–17. This legislation does, however, presuppose an effective dismissal (*Earl* v. *Slater & Wheeler (Airlyne) Ltd.* [1973] 1 W.L.R. 51 (decided under the now repealed Industrial Relations Act 1971)); compare the position in *Ridge* v. *Baldwin* and *Malloch*. Consider further *Chief Constable of the North Wales Police* v. *Evans* [1982] 1 W.L.R. 1155, noted at p. 283 *infra*.

Preliminary and advisory acts, investigations and reports

In Re Pergamon Press Ltd.

[1971] Ch. 388   Court of Appeal

The Board of Trade appointed inspectors under s. 165 (*b*) of the Companies Act 1948 to investigate and report on the affairs of Pergamon Press Ltd., and in this case, which was an appeal from the judgment of Plowman J. ([1970] 1 W.L.R. 1075), the Court of Appeal was concerned with the procedures before the inspectors.

LORD DENNING M.R.: . . . It is true, of course, that the inspectors are not a court of law. Their proceedings are not judicial proceedings: see *In re Grosvenor & West-End Railway Terminus Hotel Co. Ltd.* (1897) 76 L.T. 337. They are not even quasi-judicial, for they decide nothing; they determine nothing. They only investigate and report. They sit in private and are not entitled to admit the public to their meetings: see *Hearts of Oak Assurance Co. Ltd.* v. *Attorney-General* [1932] A.C. 392. They do not even decide whether there is a prima facie case, as was done in *Wiseman v. Borneman* [1971] A.C. 297.

But this should not lead us to minimise the significance of their task. They have to make a report which may have wide repercussions. They may, if they think fit, make findings of fact which are very damaging to those whom they name. They may accuse some; they may condemn others; they may ruin reputations or careers. Their report may lead to judicial proceedings. It may expose persons to criminal prosecutions or to civil actions. It may bring about the winding up of the company, and be used itself as material for the winding up: see *In re S.B.A. Properties Ltd.* [1967] W.L.R. 799. Even before the inspectors make their report, they may inform the Board of Trade of facts which tend to show that an offence has been committed: see section 41 of the [Companies] Act 1967. When they do make their report, the Board are bound to send a copy of it to the company; and the board may, in their discretion, publish it, if they think fit, to the public at large.

Seeing that their work and their report may lead to such consequences, I am clearly of the opinion that the inspectors must act fairly. This is a duty which rests on them, as on many other bodies, even though they are not judicial, or quasi-judicial, but only administrative: see *Reg.* v. *Gaming Board for Great Britain, Ex parte Benaim and Khaida* [1970] 2 Q.B. 417. The inspectors can obtain information in any way they think best, but before they condemn or criticise a man, they must give him a fair opportunity for correcting or contradicting what is said against him. They need not quote chapter and verse. An outline of the charge will usually suffice.

This is what the inspectors here propose to do, but the directors of the company want more. They want to see the transcripts of the witnesses who speak adversely of them, and to see any documents which may be used against them. They, or some of them, even claim to cross-examine the witnesses.

In all this the directors go too far. This investigation is ordered in the public interest. It should not be impeded by measures of this kind. Witnesses should be encouraged to come forward and not hold back. Remember, this not being a judicial proceeding, the witnesses are not protected by an absolute privilege, but only by a qualified privilege: see *O'Connor* v. *Waldron* [1935] A.C. 76. It is easy to imagine a situation in which, if the name of a witness were disclosed, he might have an action brought against him, and this might deter him from telling all he knew. No one likes to have an action brought against him, however unfounded. Every witness must, therefore, be protected. He must be encouraged to be frank. This is done by giving every witness an assurance that his evidence will be regarded as confidential and will not be used except for the purpose of the report. This assurance must be honoured. It does not mean that his name and his evidence will *never* be disclosed to anyone. It will often *have* to be used for the purpose of the report, not only in the report itself, but also by putting it in general terms to other witnesses for their comments. But it *does* mean that the inspectors will exercise a wide discretion in the use of it so as to safeguard the witness himself and any others affected by it. His evidence may sometimes, though rarely, be so confidential that it cannot be put to those affected by it, even in general terms. If so, it should be ignored so far as they are concerned. For I take it to be axiomatic that the inspectors must not use the evidence of a witness so as to make it the basis of an adverse finding unless they give the party affected sufficient information to enable him to deal with it. . . .

Notes

1. For later related proceedings, see *Maxwell* v. *Department of Trade and Industry* [1974] Q.B. 523. A limit to the imposition of any procedural requirements in the context of Board of Trade inquiries was revealed in *Norwest Holst Ltd.* v. *Secretary of State for Trade* [1978] Ch. 201 where inspectors had been appointed under s. 165 (*b*) (ii) of the Companies Act 1948 to investigate the plaintiff company's affairs. The Court of Appeal denied that the relevant Minister had any obligation to hear the company before making the appointment. Despite this limit, however, *Re Pergamon Press Ltd.* shows that natural justice or fairness can be required even when no decision directly affecting rights is made.

A few years before the decision in *Re Pergamon Press Ltd.*, the House of Lords had decided that natural justice could apply where a decision was made as to whether there was a prima facie case (*Wiseman* v. *Borneman* [1971] A.C. 297). Nevertheless, in *Pearlberg* v. *Varty* [1972] 1 W.L.R. 534, Viscount Dilhorne expressed the opinion that although 'it cannot be said that the rules of natural justice do not apply to a judicial determination of the question where there is a prima facie case. . . . I do not think they apply with the same force or as much force as they do to decisions which determine the rights of persons' (p. 546). Thus the fact that only a prima facie decision is being reached is still a relevant factor and in *Pearlberg* v. *Varty* was one factor leading to the decision that the plaintiff in that case had no right to be heard at the stage of the prima facie decision. In line with this approach, attention might also be paid to the following passage, which appears in Lord Reid's speech in *Wiseman* v. *Borneman* [1971] A.C. at p. 308:

It is, I think, not entirely irrelevant to have in mind that it is very unusual for there to be a judicial determination of the question whether there is a prima facie case. Every public officer who has to decide whether to prosecute or raise proceedings ought first to decide whether there is a prima facie case, but no one supposes that justice requires that he should first seek the comments of the accused or the defendant on the material before him.

For further discussion see *Furnell* v. *Whangarei High Schools Board* [1973] A.C. 660; *R.* v. *Race Relations Board, ex p. Selvarajan* [1975] 1 W.L.R. 1686; *Moran* v. *Lloyd's* [1981] 1 Lloyd's Rep. 423.

It should not be forgotten, however, that preliminary decisions can clearly affect a person adversely, and, as mentioned *supra*, some procedural safeguards may be required by the courts. In particular, as Whitmore and Aronson, *Review of Administrative Action*, point out (at p. 81), it 'should always be remembered that there is some danger that a preliminary or prima facie decision will tend to persist, especially when the power to make the final decision is given to a body other than a court'. The weight of the preliminary decision in the consideration of the final decision should obviously be of importance: for example, is the onus of proof now on the person adversely affected by it to reverse the recommendation or will it be reconsidered *de novo*? Cf. *Herring* v. *Templeman* [1973] 3 All E.R. 569. Contrast the case where a preliminary decision, which is merely part of a wider decision, may itself not be open to question in later proceedings. Here the argument for procedural protection would seem to be strengthened: see e.g. *R.* v. *Kent Police Authority, ex p. Godden* [1971] 2 Q.B. 662.

2. What if, at an early stage of an inquiry, a person is actually suspended? Lord Denning in *Lewis* v. *Heffer* [1978] 1 W.L.R. 1061 – and see also *Norwest Holst Ltd.* v. *Secretary of State for Trade* [1978] Ch. 201 at p. 224 and *Cinnamond* v. *B.A.A.*, p. 237 *supra* – expressed the following opinion (at p. 1073):

> Very often irregularities are disclosed in a government department or in a business house: and a man may be suspended on full pay pending enquiries. Suspicion may rest on him: and so he is suspended until he is cleared of it. No one, so far as I know, has ever questioned such a suspension on the ground that it could not be done unless he is given notice of the charge and an opportunity of defending himself and so forth. The suspension in such a case is merely done by way of good administration. A situation has arisen in which something must be done at once. The work of the department or the office is being affected by rumours and suspicions. The others will not trust the man. In order to get back to proper work, the man is suspended. At that stage the rules of natural justice do not apply: see *Furnell* v. *Whangarei High Schools Board* [1973] A.C. 660.

For criticism, however, of the *Furnell* case, see Evans, (1973) 36 M.L.R. 439.

Note that Lord Denning distinguished punitive suspension (e.g. suspension of a solicitor from practice) from the sort of suspensions *supra* which were a 'holding operation, pending inquiries'. Consider *ex p. Posgate*, The Times, 12 January 1983.

3. For the opposite situation to that being considered here (i.e. 'deciding without hearing' rather than 'hearing without deciding' – de Smith, pp. 219 and 233), see *Jeffs* v. *New Zealand Dairy Production and Marketing Board* [1967] 1 A.C. 551, noted at p. 134 *supra*; cf. *R.* v. *Race Relations Board, ex p. Selvarajan* [1975] 1 W.L.R. 1686. See further *Chief Constable of the North Wales Police* v. *Evans* [1982] 1 W.L.R. 1155.

EXCEPTIONS

Legislation

Bates v. Lord Hailsham of St. Marylebone, p. 516 *infra*

Notes

1. The distinction between administrative and legislative functions can be very difficult to draw. On this distinction, see Note 1, p. 493 and Note 3, p. 495 *infra*.

2. Legislation may *expressly* require consultation with some particular body before it is made (as in the *Bates* case): see p. 517 *infra*.

3. Note, alongside the *Bates* case, the recent decision in *R.* v. *G.L.C., ex p. The Rank Organisation Ltd.*, The Times, 19 February 1982, in which it was stated that the right to be heard for a person affected prior to a decision being made 'did not extend to a decision which was universal in its application . . .'. Compare, however, with the

Bates case the Commonwealth cases mentioned in Note 1, p. 518 *infra* and see further that Note generally.

4. Although this section has been headed 'Exceptions', the earlier material in the chapter will, of course, reveal other situations in which the right to be heard does not exist. Note further *Essex C.C.* v. *Minister of Housing and Local Government* (1967) 66 L.G.R. 23, noted at p. 126 *supra*, and see Wade, p. 507.

Aliens

Schmidt v. Secretary of State for Home Affairs

[1969] 2 Ch. 149   Court of Appeal

Two Scientology students who were citizens of the U.S.A. had been admitted to the United Kingdom for a limited period. On the expiry of that period, the Secretary of State refused them an extension of time, and one complaint was that he had made this decision without giving the students a hearing. Ungoed-Thomas J. ordered that the statement of claim be struck out as an abuse of the process of court and that the action be dismissed. There was an appeal to the Court of Appeal.

LORD DENNING M.R.: ... Mr. Quintin Hogg[73] submitted that the Minister ought to have given the students a hearing before he refused to extend their stay in this country. I see no basis for this suggestion. I quite agree, of course, that where a public officer has power to deprive a person of his liberty or his property, the general principle is that it is not to be done without his being given an opportunity of being heard and of making representations on his own behalf. But in the case of aliens, it is rather different: for they have no right to be here except by licence of the Crown. And it has been held that the Home Secretary is not bound to hear representations on their behalf, even in the case of a deportation order, though, in practice he usually does so. It was so held in *Rex* v. *Leman Street Police Station Inspector and Secretary of State for Home Affairs, Ex parte Venicoff* [1920] 3 K.B. 72, which was followed by this court in *Soblen's* case [1963] 2 Q.B. 243.[74] Some of the judgments in those cases were based on the fact that the Home Secretary was exercising an administrative power and not doing a judicial act. But that distinction is no longer valid. The speeches in *Ridge* v. *Baldwin* [1964] A.C. 40 show that an administrative body may, in a proper case, be bound to give a person who is affected by their decision an opportunity of making representations. It all depends on whether he has some right or interest, or, I would add, some legitimate expectation, of which it would not be fair to deprive him without hearing what he has to say. Thus in *re H.K. (An Infant)* [1967] 2 Q.B. 617 a Commonwealth citizen had a right to be admitted to this country if he was (as he claimed to be) under the age of 16. The immigration officers were not satisfied that he was under 16 and refused him admission. Lord Parker C.J., at

---

[73] [Counsel for the students.]

[74] [In both cases deportation was ordered on the ground that the Home Secretary deemed 'it to be conducive to the public good': see now s. 3 (5) of the Immigration Act 1971.]

p. 630, held that, even if they were acting in an administrative capacity, they were under a duty to act fairly – and that meant that they should give the immigrant an opportunity of satisfying them that he was under 16. By contrast in the later case of *Reg.* v. *Secretary of State for the Home Department, Ex parte Avtar Singh* (Divisional Court, July 25, 1967, unreported) a Commonwealth citizen said he wanted to come in so as to marry a girl here. He had no right at all to be admitted. The statute gave the immigration officers a complete discretion to refuse. Lord Parker C.J. held that they were under no duty to tell him why he was refused admission and were not bound to give him an opportunity of making representations. If such be the law for a commonwealth immigrant, it is all the more so for a foreign alien. He has no right to enter this country except by leave: and, if he is given leave to come for a limited period, he has no right to stay for a day longer than the permitted time. If his permit is revoked *before* the time limit expires, he ought, I think, to be given an opportunity of making representations: for he would have a legitimate expectation of being allowed to stay for the permitted time. Except in such a case, a foreign alien has no right – and, I would add, no legitimate expectation – of being allowed to stay. He can be refused without reasons given and without a hearing. Once his time has expired, he has to go. In point of practice, however, I am glad to say that the Home Secretary does not act arbitrarily. He is always ready to consider any representations that are put before him: as indeed, we are told he is ready to do in these very cases. . . .

WIDGERY L.J.: I agree with the judgment which has been delivered by the Master of the Rolls and accordingly I also would dismiss this appeal. . . .

. . . I see no reason whatever in the Aliens Order to suggest that an alien possessing a permit for a limited period of residence has any kind of right to a renewal; and accordingly when he asks for renewal, there is no obligation upon the Secretary of State to give reasons which are consistent with the legislation or to act fairly or to do any of the other things for which Mr. Hogg has contended in this case. Of course, very different considerations may arise on the making of a deportation order. An alien in this country is entitled to the protection of the law as is a native, and a deportation order which involves an interference with his person or property may raise quite different considerations; but a deportation order is not the matter with which we are concerned and I forbear to say more about it. . . .

[RUSSELL L.J. delivered a judgment in favour of allowing the appeal.]

Appeal dismissed.

Notes

1. Since the decision in *Schmidt*'s case, legislation has provided various rights of appeal to an adjudicator and then to the Immigration Appeal Tribunal (and on occasions to this latter body initially) in immigration and deportation cases: see now the Immigration Act 1971. What effect, if any, will this have on the position concerning natural justice (and see Evans's comment in Note 2 *infra*)?

2. Widgery L.J.'s judgment in *Schmidt*'s case shows that the old position in relation to natural justice and deportation (the old cases are referred to in Lord

Denning's judgment in *Schmidt*'s case) was beginning to change. See also Lord Denning's judgment on the position where the permit has not expired and note his earlier judgment in *Soblen*'s case [1963] 2 Q.B. 243 at pp. 298–9; see further *Daganayasi* v. *Minister of Immigration* [1980] 2 N.Z.L.R. 130; cf. *Salemi* v. *MacKellar (No. 2)* (1977) 137 C.L.R. 396; *R.* v. *MacKellar, ex p. Ratu* ibid. 461. Section 15 of the Immigration Act 1971 now provides a right of appeal against certain deportation orders. Do you agree with Evans (*Immigration Law*, p. 111) that the existence of an appeal against many deportation decisions 'strengthens the argument for procedural fairness at the level of the original decision'? The right of appeal does not exist in every case. For example, s. 15 (3) excludes an appeal by anyone 'if the ground of decision was that his deportation is conducive to the public good as being in the interests of national security or of the relations between the United Kingdom and any other country or for other reasons of a political nature'. In this situation, as an administrative concession representations can be made to a body known as the Three Advisers, who may give non-binding advice to the Home Secretary. The procedure is now to be found in r. 150 of the Immigration Rules. (For the position concerning appeals and E.E.C. nationals, see Hartley, *EEC Immigration Law*, pp. 235–41; cf. Grant and Martin, *Immigration Law and Practice*, pp. 255–7.)

In relation to natural justice the problem with this procedure is that the Home Secretary might not feel able on security grounds to divulge that amount of information which natural justice would normally require for the proposed deportee to have a fair hearing before the Advisers. Could a deportation order in such a case be attacked for a breach of natural justice? The Court of Appeal thought not in *R.* v. *Secretary of State for the Home Department, ex p. Hosenball* [1977] 1 W.L.R. 766, noted at p. 495 *infra*. The clash between national security and natural justice had to be resolved in favour of the former. Lord Denning did, however, suggest that the court might interfere if the Advisers refused to hear any representations.

3. There is no appeal under the Immigration Act 1971 against a deportation order resulting from a court recommendation. On the relevance of natural justice when the Home Secretary decides whether or not to implement the recommendation, see *R.* v. *Secretary of State for the Home Department, ex p. Santillo* [1981] Q.B. 778.

ACTING FAIRLY

Schmidt v. Secretary of State for Home Affairs, p. 280 *supra*

R. v. Gaming Board for Great Britain, ex parte Benaim and Khaida, p. 241 *supra*

In Re Pergamon Press Ltd., p. 276 *supra*

McInnes v. Onslow-Fane, p. 262 *supra*

Cinnamond v. British Airports Authority, p. 236 *supra*

Note

It has been argued that the tendency to look at the merits of a decision in natural justice cases in a manner adverse to the complainant (see p. 234 *supra*) will be encouraged by the use of duty to act fairly (de Smith, p. 240). Nevertheless, it should be remembered that *Glynn* v. *Keele University* [1971] 1 W.L.R. 487, noted at p. 239 *supra*, was decided on the traditional natural justice approach.

This raises the more general problem as to the extent to which the duty to act fairly is confined to matters of procedure or covers matters of substantive fairness as well. In *Uppal* v. *Home Office*, The Times, 21 October 1978, Megarry V.-C. limited it to the former category; cf. Lord Denning in *Machin* v. *F.A.*, The Times, 21 July 1973. As de Smith acknowledges (p. 346), the duty to act fairly has in recent cases been primarily concerned with matters of procedural fairness, but it does also exist, in de Smith's words, as a 'substantive principle', involving, for example, a duty not to discriminate on unacceptable grounds, and this aspect of the duty is discussed in de Smith under the heading 'Excess or Abuse of Discretionary Power': see further the concession of counsel in *McInnes* v. *Onslow-Fane*, p. 266 *supra*; *R.* v. *Secretary of State for Trade, ex p. Perestrello* [1981] Q.B. 19, noted at p. 201 *supra*; *R.* v. *Secretary of State for the Home Department, ex p. Santillo* [1981] Q.B. 778 at p. 795; *Williams* v. *Home Office (No. 2)* [1981] 1 All E.R. 1211 at p. 1247; *Daganayasi* v. *Minister of Immigration* [1980] 2 N.Z.L.R. 130 at p. 149; *Re Erebus (No. 2)* [1981] 1 N.Z.L.R. 618 at p. 629 Mullan, (1975) 25 U.T.L.J. 281 at p. 283; (1982) 27 McGill L.J. 250, and note his comment here on *R.* v. *Barnsley M.B.C., ex p. Hook* [1976] 1 W.L.R. 1052.

It may be that this 'substantive' aspect of the duty to act fairly explains why, in *H.T.V. Ltd.* v. *Price Commission* [1976] I.C.R. 170, noted at p. 162 *supra*, Scarman L.J. was prepared to review the activities of the Price Commission on the basis that the Commission had acted inconsistently and unfairly. His Lordship did, however, rely on de Smith for the view that the duty to act fairly began to be used in *Re H.K. (An Infant)* [1967] 2 Q.B. 617, and it should not be forgotten that that case was concerned with procedural fairness. It would seem from the authority Goff L.J. cited in support (*General Electric Co. Ltd.* v. *Price Commission* [1975] I.C.R. 1 at pp. 12 and 14) that he was also willing to secure consistency by virtue of the duty to act fairly; cf. the approach of Lord Denning, noted at p. 162 *supra*.

The development of the duty to act fairly must now be considered in the light of the recent House of Lords case of *Chief Constable of the North Wales Police* v. *Evans* [1982] 1 W.L.R. 1155, in which it was held that a probationer police constable, who was given the chance to resign as an alternative to dismissal, had not received a fair hearing. In the course of his speech Lord Brightman (with the agreement of three of the other four members of the House) stated (at pp. 1174–5):

> There is . . . a wider point than the injustice of the decision-making process of the chief constable. With profound respect to the Court of Appeal, I dissent from the view that 'Not only must [the probationer constable] be given a fair hearing, but the decision itself must be fair and reasonable.' If that statement of the law passed into authority without comment, it would in my opinion transform, and wrongly transform, the remedy of judicial review. Judicial review, as the words imply, is not an appeal from a decision, but a review of the manner in which the decision was made. The statement of law which I have quoted implies that the court sits in judgment not only on the correctness of the decision-making process but also on the correctness of the decision itself. In his printed case counsel for the appellant made this submission:
>
> '. . . Where Parliament has entrusted to an administrative authority the duty of making a decision which affects the rights of an individual, the court's supervisory function on a judicial review of that decision is limited. The court cannot be expected to possess knowledge of the reasons of policy which lie behind the administrative decision nor is it desirable that evidence should be called before the court of the implications of such policy. It follows that the court ought not to attempt to weigh the merits of the particular decision but should confine its function to a consideration of the manner in which the decision was reached.'
>
> When the sole issue raised on an application for judicial review is whether the rules of natural justice have been observed, these propositions are unexceptionable. Other considerations arise

when an administrative decision is attacked on the ground that it is vitiated by self-misdirection, by taking account of irrelevant or neglecting to take account of relevant factors, or is so manifestly unreasonable that no reasonable authority, entrusted with the power in question, could reasonably have made such a decision; see the well known judgment of Lord Greene M.R. in *Associated Provincial Picture Houses Ltd.* v. *Wednesbury Corporation* [1948] 1 K.B. 223.

Fairness: The New Natural Justice?

D. J. Mullan, (1975) 25 U.T.L.J. 281 at p. 300

It is the ultimate thrust of this article that the development of the doctrine of procedural fairness is a most desirable advance in the common law relating to judicial review of administrative action. It is desirable primarily because it allows the courts to ask what kind of procedural protections are necessary for a particular decision-making process unburdened by the traditional classification process.[75] In other words, it enables the asking of the real questions which the classification process has hidden artificially for many years. It recognizes that there is a very broad spectrum of decision-making functions for which varying procedural requirements are necessary and rejects the notion that such functions can be categorized satisfactorily into either one of two categories. The classification process was essentially accepted at a time when the administrative process was far less sophisticated. Its deceptive simplicity was perhaps adequate initially but it rapidly ceased to be realistic. If 'fairness' enables the courts to move away from this approach much will have been achieved in that an effective functional approach will have been substituted for a superficially attractive but actually inappropriate functional approach.

Notes

1. The development of the duty to act fairly, which has allowed courts to require procedural fairness in cases where administrative functions are involved, has raised the question of the precise relationship between natural justice and the duty to act fairly. (A particular aspect of this problem was considered in the Note at p. 283 *supra*). One approach is to deny any difference between the two, either by regarding the duty to act fairly as applicable to both administrative and judicial functions, or by regarding natural justice as applicable to administrative functions as well as judicial ones, or by using the phrases interchangeably. Compare the view of Lord Parker in *Re H.K. (An Infant)* [1967] 2 Q.B. 617 at p. 630, set out at p. 243 *supra*. An alternative approach has been to make a clear division between the duty to act fairly and natural justice. Thus, in *Pearlberg* v. *Varty* [1972] 1 W.L.R. 534 Lord Pearson stated (at p. 547):

A tribunal to whom judicial or quasi-judicial functions are entrusted is held to be required to apply [natural justice] in performing those functions unless there is a provision to the contrary. But where some person or body is entrusted by Parliament with administrative or executive functions there is no presumption that compliance with the principles of natural justice is required, although, as 'Parliament is not to be presumed to act unfairly', the courts may be able in suitable cases (perhaps always) to imply an obligation to act with fairness. Fairness, however,

---

[75] [i.e. classifying a function as judicial or quasi-judicial before any procedural fairness was involved.]

does not necessarily require a plurality of hearings or representations and counter-represen-
tations.

The words 'perhaps always' cause some uncertainty as to the scope of the duty to act
fairly, but more importantly the contrast between the duty to act fairly and natural
justice suggests a difference between them. Yet, as natural justice is concerned with
procedural fairness, and as it varies in content from case to case, should this distinction
be maintained?

If we abandon Lord Pearson's approach, nevertheless the fact that a court is
concerned with an administrative function will make it possible that a hearing will not
be required (e.g. *Pearlberg v. Varty*); the factors which could lead to that classification
(e.g. lack of immediate impact on rights) may militate against the provision of a
hearing. On the classification of functions, see *Ridge v. Baldwin*, p. 220 *supra*, and
more generally, p. 4 *supra*.

On the relationship between the duty to act fairly and natural justice, see further the
view expressed in *McInnes v. Onslow-Fane*, p. 268 *supra*, per Megarry V.-C. (who in
Bates v. Lord Hailsham of St. Marylebone, p. 516 *infra*, had set out a view similar to
that of Lord Pearson); *Bushell v. Secretary of State for the Environment*, p. 601 *infra*,
per Lord Diplock; *O'Reilly v. Mackman*, p. 324 *infra*. See in addition the article by
Mullan from which an extract was set out *supra*; Taylor, (1977) 3 Mon. L.R. 191;
Salemi v. MacKellar (No. 2) (1977) 137 C.L.R. 396 at p. 418; cf. *Nicholson v.
Haldimand–Norfolk Regional Board of Commissioners of Police* [1979] 1 S.C.R. 311
at p. 324 but see *Martineau v. Matsqui Institution Disciplinary Board* [1980] 1 S.C.R.
602 at p. 630–1. Contrast in particular with Lord Pearson's approach *supra* that of
Lord Diplock (in a speech with which his brethren agreed) in *R. v. Commission for
Racial Equality, ex p. Hillingdon L.B.C.* [1982] 3 W.L.R. 159 at p. 165. He rejected
the application of the label 'quasi-judicial' as at all significant and stated that where 'an
Act of Parliament confers upon an administrative body functions which involve its
making decisions which affect to their detriment the rights of other persons or curtail
their liberty to do as they please, there is a presumption that Parliament intended that
the administrative body should act fairly towards those persons who will be affected
by their decisions'.

2. One feature of the duty to act fairly, is that it can apply and yet not involve a
hearing. In the past, if natural justice applied, it always involved *some* sort of hearing
(*Russell v. Duke of Norfolk*, p. 245 *supra*). But in so far as the duty applies to areas
which the rules of natural justice would not previously have encompassed, then there
may well be cases where it is quite fair to act without a hearing; cf. *Cinnamond v.
B.A.A.*, p. 236 *supra*. A danger is perhaps that the courts will become accustomed to
deciding that the duty to act fairly will involve very little or nothing, and that this might
then adversely affect cases to which in the past natural justice would have applied and
hence have involved some sort of hearing: see *Dunlop v. Woollahra M.C.* [1975] 2
N.S.W.L.R. 446 at pp. 467–71, referring to cases suggesting that natural justice does
not always involve a hearing, and see Clark, [1975] P.L. 27 at pp. 28–36. (On the
Dunlop case, see Taylor, op. cit.; Sykes, Lanham, and Tracey, *General Principles of
Administrative Law*, Ch. 18; *Salemi v. MacKellar (No. 2)* (1977) 137 C.L.R. 396.)
This argument, if accepted, would suggest that there is an advantage in Lord Pearson's
approach in *Pearlberg v. Varty*. A further argument about the notion of the duty to act
fairly is that it has been utilised to decrease the amount of procedural protection that
might otherwise be thought to have flowed from the wide application of *natural justice*
by virtue of *Ridge v. Baldwin*, p. 214 *supra*, coupled with the adoption of a broad view
of the idea of 'rights' (see Lord Reid's speech in that case at p. 218 *supra*).

3. Mullan, op. cit., sets out — and then proceeds to answer — three criticisms of the duty to act fairly which are to be found in New Zealand academic literature. These are:

(a) that different judges see the duty to act fairly as meaning different things and that the boundaries of the duty to act fairly are unclear;

(b) that the concept of the duty to act fairly is so unpredictable that, as opposed to the question of the content of natural justice, lawyers cannot tell the relevant parties what it involves; and

(c) that it will impose 'entirely inappropriate procedural requirements' on statutory bodies which will in turn have an adverse effect on the efficiency and effectiveness of the decision-making process.

In the light of the relevant materials in this chapter, what is your opinion of these criticisms? For further discussion of the duty to act fairly, see Loughlin, (1978) 28 U.T.L.J. 215.

4. The two traditional limbs of natural justice have been set out in the last two chapters. Note that it has been said that natural justice requires the decision-maker to act on evidence of some probative value (R. v. *Deputy Industrial Injuries Commissioner, ex p. Moore* [1965] 1 Q.B. 456 and see further *Ong Ah Chuan* v. *Public Prosecutor* [1981] A.C. 648). Can this be regarded as part of the *audi alteram partem* principle or is it another limb of natural justice? For further aspects of natural justice, see the argument of Jackson, [1976] P.L. 1; *Natural Justice*, 2nd edn., Ch. 4 and see the Note at p. 253 *supra*.

PART IV

Remedies and Liability

9

ORDINARY REMEDIES

ACTIONS FOR DAMAGES

Note
  See Ch. 13 *infra*.

INJUNCTIONS

Bradbury v. Enfield London Borough Council

[1967] 1 W.L.R. 1311   Court of Appeal

The Council proposed to reorganize secondary education in its area. Under s. 13 of the Education Act 1944 (as amended) – see now s. 12 of the Education Act 1980 – a local education authority which was intending either to establish a particular type of school or cease to maintain certain types of school was required to submit proposals to the Minister of Education; thereafter, it had to give public notice of the proposals, and certain people specified in s. 13 were allowed to make objections to the Minister. The Council's proposals were in fact approved by the Minister, and the reorganization was due to come into effect in September 1967. However, no public notice had been given in relation to eight particular schools. The plaintiffs, nine in all, had issued a writ in June 1967, and in the case we are considering here were seeking an interim injunction temporarily to stop the Council from implementing the proposals. The plaintiffs included six parents, a foundation governor of a boys' grammar school, and a parent of a child receiving private education: these eight were all ratepayers. Goff J. refused interim relief as he though it would cause chaos. On appeal to the Court of Appeal, it was held that the failure to give public notice constituted a breach of s. 13.

LORD DENNING M.R.: . . . Ought an injunction to be granted against the council? It has been suggested by the chief education officer that, if an injunction is granted, chaos will supervene. All the arrangements have been made for the next term, the teachers appointed to the new comprehensive schools, the pupils allotted their places, and so forth. It would be next to impossible, he says, to reverse all these arrangements without complete chaos and damage to teachers, pupils and the public.

I must say this: If a local authority does not fulfil the requirements of the law, this court will see that it does fulfil them. It will not listen readily to suggestions of 'chaos'. The Department of Education and the local education authority are subject to the rule of law and must comply with it, just like everybody else. Even if chaos should result, still the law must be obeyed. But I do not think that chaos will result. . . .

[DANCKWERTS L.J. delivered a judgment in which he expressly agreed with LORD DENNING's judgment. DIPLOCK L.J. delivered a judgment in favour of allowing the appeal.]

Appeal allowed.

Notes

1. In relation to the avoidance of chaos, see *R.* v. *Paddington Valuation Officer, ex p. Peachey Property Corporation Ltd.*, p. 103 *supra*. However, see now s. 31(6) of the Supreme Court Act 1981, p. 316 *infra*, which, in the light of the development mentioned in Note 4 *infra*, is likely to govern such cases in the future.

2. The *Bradbury* case is given as an example of the use of the injunction – here an interim injunction – as an Administrative Law remedy. In the area unaffected by s. 21 of the Crown Proceedings Act 1947, *infra*, an interim or interlocutory injunction is particularly useful because of the courts' refusal to grant interim declarations (see p. 291 *infra*); a request for an interim or interlocutory injunction can be made in a case where a declaration is sought.

3. The status of the plaintiffs in the *Bradbury* case was mentioned in the statement of facts *supra*. Whether they had sufficient locus standi to obtain an injunction was not expressly discussed in the case. The question of locus standi will be considered at p. 338 *infra*.

4. An injunction and a declaration can be obtained in an action begun by writ or originating summons. As a result of a reform introduced in 1977, it has become possible to obtain these remedies in what is known as an application for judicial review, on which see p. 315 *infra*. Furthermore, it has been held by the House of Lords in *O'Reilly* v. *Mackman*, p. 324 *infra*, that, as a general rule, in Administrative Law cases these remedies must be obtained by such an application.

The Crown and its servants

Crown Proceedings Act 1947

21. – (1) In any civil proceedings by or against the Crown the court shall, subject to the provisions of this Act, have power to make all such orders as it has power to make in proceedings between subjects, and otherwise to give such appropriate relief as the case may require:

Provided that:-

    (*a*) where in any proceedings against the Crown any such relief is sought as might in proceedings between subjects be granted by way of injunction or specific performance, the court shall not grant an injunction or make an order for specific performance, but may in lieu thereof make an order declaratory of the rights of the parties; and

(b) in any proceedings against the Crown for the recovery of land or other property the court shall not make an order for the recovery of the land or the delivery of the property, but may in lieu thereof make an order declaring that the plaintiff is entitled as against the Crown to the land or property or to the possession thereof.

(2) The court shall not in any civil proceedings grant any injunction or make any order against an officer[1] of the Crown if the effect of granting the injunction or making the order would be to give any relief against the Crown which could not have been obtained in proceedings against the Crown.

Questions

Why might it be thought necessary to protect the Crown against the grant of an injunction? Note that not all jurisdictions do protect the government against injunctive relief – see e.g. the position of the federal government and all the state governments (except Tasmania) in Australia; Hogg, *Liability of the Crown*, p. 22.

International General Electric Company of New York Ltd. v. Commissioners of Customs and Excise

[1962] Ch. 784   Court of Appeal

The defendants (a department of the Crown) stopped the importation of certain goods into this country by the plaintiff, an importation which they believed contravened the Merchandise Marks Acts 1887–1953. The plaintiff *ex parte* sought temporary relief in the form of interim declarations from Plowman J., but was unsuccessful. There was an appeal to the Court of Appeal.

UPJOHN L.J.: ... Plowman J., in a very short judgment, followed a decision of Romer J. as a judge of first instance in *Underhill* v. *Ministry of Food*,[2] where he said:[3] '[The Minister of Food] says that when the Crown Proceedings Act, 1947, s. 21, refers to the court making a declaration, it refers to a final declaration and it is an unheard-of suggestion that an interlocutory declaration should be made which might be in precisely the opposite sense of the final declaration made at the trial. He says, and I think rightly says, that what is usually done on the hearing of an interlocutory application is to grant some form of temporary remedy which will keep matters in statu quo until the rights of the parties are ultimately found and declared, and that, accordingly, the reference to making a declaration of rights means a declaration at the trial as distinct from a declaration on some interlocutory application.'

That seems to me, subject possibly only to one point which I will mention, entirely correct. The court has to approach the matter in this way. Having regard to section 21, in order to see what powers the court has to make orders

---

[1] [See s. 38(2) of the Act, p. 438 *infra*.]
[2] [1950] 1 All E.R. 591.
[3] [1950] 1 All E.R. 591, 593.

in actions between the subject and the Crown, one has to ascertain what powers it has to make orders between subjects. . . . As between subjects it cannot be doubted that some form of interlocutory relief can properly be sought and might be granted; but I say no more about that. It is, however, perfectly plain that the court in proceedings between subjects could not grant some form of interlocutory relief in the sense of some interim declaration. When you read on in the proviso, you find, however, that as against the Crown an injunction cannot be granted but an order may be made declaratory of the rights of the parties. But, as Romer J. pointed out, an order declaring the rights of the parties must in its nature be a final order after a hearing when the court is in a position to declare what the rights of the parties are, and such an order must necessarily then be res judicata and bind the parties for ever, subject only, of course, to a right of appeal. It may be – and this is the only reservation I make upon the observations of Romer J. – that in certain cases it is proper on a motion or on a summons under Order 25, r. 2, to make some declaration of rights upon some interlocutory proceeding. That, however, is infrequent and should only sparingly be exercised, but the point is that if it is determined on some interlocutory proceeding, it finally determines and declares the rights of the parties: it is not open to further review except on appeal. In this case, as in the case before Romer J., that is not sought. It is said that some form of interim declaration should be made merely to preserve the status quo and, therefore, this order we are being asked to make today ex parte, without hearing the defendants, is not apparently to be finally binding on the parties; it is something which later can be re-examined and some other form of declaration substituted if it is found to be appropriate after a full hearing when the matter comes on for trial.

Speaking for my part I simply do not understand how there can be such an animal, as I ventured to call it in argument, as an interim declaratory order which does not finally declare the rights of the parties. It seems to me quite clear that in proceedings against the Crown it is impossible to get anything which corresponds to an interim injunction. When you come to the question of a final injunction, no doubt a declaratory order may be made in lieu thereof, for that finally determines the rights of the parties. But it seems to me quite impossible to invent some form of declaration which does not determine the rights of the parties but is only meant to preserve the status quo.

For these reasons I entirely agree with the judgment of Plowman J. and I would dismiss this appeal.

DIPLOCK L.J.: I agree. In 1950 Romer J. was able to say that it was an unheard-of suggestion that an interim declaration should be made; because it might be in the precisely opposite sense to the final declaration made at the trial. It is no longer possible to say it is an unheard-of suggestion, but I have no doubt, for the reasons given by my Lord, that this court was given no jurisdiction under the Crown Proceedings Act, 1947, to make such an order, which in my view would be a contradiction in terms.

Appeal dismissed.

Note

To fill the lacuna in the remedies against the Crown evidenced by the case *supra*, in 1976 the Law Commission in its *Report on Remedies in Administrative Law*, Law Com. No. 73, Cmnd. 6407, recommended (at para. 51):

[S]ection 21 of the Crown Proceedings Act 1947 should be amended to provide that, in addition to the power there given to make a declaratory order in proceedings against the Crown, there is also power to declare the terms of an interim injunction which would have been granted between subjects.

The Law Commission envisaged that a lot of the proposals – and there were many others – in the Report would be brought into being by statute. In fact the reform that has occurred was brought about originally by a change in the Rules of the Supreme Court (i.e. by subordinate legislation), although it is now partly in statutory form (see p. 315 *infra*); but nothing has happened in relation to the proposal set out *supra* which would have required primary legislation for its implementation. This was regretted by Lord Diplock in *Inland Revenue Commissioners* v. *Rossminster Ltd.* [1980] A.C. 952, a case in which the House of Lords confirmed the decision in the *International General Electric Co.* case. Lord Diplock hoped that the Law Commission's recommendation 'will not continue to fall upon deaf parliamentary ears' (p. 1015), but he was alone in this respect in the House of Lords. See the different view of Lord Wilberforce at p. 1001, Viscount Dilhorne at p. 1007, and Lord Scarman, who stated (at p. 1027):

I gravely doubt the wisdom of interim relief against the Crown. The state's decisions must be respected unless and until they are shown to be wrong. Judges neither govern nor administer the state: they adjudicate when required to do so. The value of judicial review, which is high, should not be allowed to obscure the fundamental limits of the judicial function. And, if interim relief against the Crown be acceptable, the interlocutory declaration is not the way to provide it. For myself, I find absurd the posture of a court declaring one day in interlocutory proceedings that an applicant has certain rights and upon a later day that he has not. Something less risible must be devised.

Do you agree with Lord Scarman that an interlocutory declaration would be absurd (and see Zamir, [1977] C.L.P. 43 at p. 52)? Note that this passage of Lord Scarman's seems to use the presumption of validity, which was referred to in *F. Hoffmann-La Roche & Co. A.G.* v. *Secretary of State for Trade and Industry*, p. 100 *supra*, and *Lovelock* v. *Minister of Transport* (1980) 40 P. & C.R. 336, noted at p. 101 *supra*, to support the case against interim relief. Compare its use, equally to defeat an opponent, when a Minister was seeking interim relief in the *Hoffmann-La Roche* case.

Merricks v. Heathcoat-Amory and the Minister of Agriculture, Fisheries and Food

[1955] Ch. 567   Chancery Division

In this action a mandatory injunction was sought by the plaintiff against (*a*) Mr. Heathcoat-Amory, who was the Minister of Agriculture but who was sued personally; and (*b*) the Minister of Agriculture, who by virtue of s. 1 (2) of the Ministry of Agriculture and Fisheries Act 1919 was a corporation sole. The plaintiff alleged that a scheme for the marketing of potatoes, a draft of which had been laid before both Houses of Parliament by the Minister acting under s. 1 of the Agricultural Marketing Act 1931, was ultra vires. He wanted the defendants to be ordered (*a*) to withdraw the draft scheme, and (*b*) not to seek approval of the scheme.

UPJOHN J.: . . . I have heard full arguments from Mr. Walker-Smith[4] and from the Attorney-General, and I think in those circumstances that I can properly express my own views as to the capacity in which the Minister acts in carrying out or proposing to carry out the relevant functions under section 1 of the Agricultural Marketing Act, 1931. It seems to me clear that in carrying out his functions under that section he is acting as a representative or as an officer of the Crown. He is the Minister of Agriculture, who is responsible for the conduct of agricultural matters in this country; as part of his general responsibility, he was the person who would naturally be designated in the Agricultural Marketing Act as the person to carry out the functions, purposes and policy of that Act. It was no doubt for that reason that it was the Minister who was to approve any scheme under section 1 (1). It was his duty, not merely as a delegated person but as a person acting in his capacity as Minister of Agriculture, to consider the scheme, to hear objections and representations, and to hold inquiries, and he had the power and duty of making such modifications as he thought fit.

It was his duty in his capacity as Minister of Agriculture and not merely as a delegated person, if he was satisfied – with the satisfaction which he had to feel in his capacity as Minister of Agriculture and an official of the Crown – that the scheme would conduce to the more efficient production and marketing of the regulated product, to lay a draft scheme before the Houses of Parliament, and ultimately in the same capacity to make an order bringing the scheme into effect.

It seems to me that from start to finish he was acting in his capacity as an officer representing the Crown. That being so, it is conceded that no injunction can be obtained against him, and therefore the motion fails in limine.

I am not satisfied that it is possible to have the three categories which were suggested. Of course there can be an official representing the Crown, that is plainly this case. But if he were not, it was said that he was a person designated in an official capacity but not representing the Crown. The third suggestion was that his capacity was purely that of an individual. I understand the conception of the first and the third categories, but I confess to finding it difficult to see how the second category can fit into any ordinary scheme. It is possible that there may be special Acts where named persons have special duties to perform which would not be duties normally fulfilled by them in their official capacity; but in the normal case where the relevant or appropriate Minister is directed to carry out some function or policy of some Act, he is either acting in his capacity as a Minister of the Crown representing the Crown, or is acting in his personal capacity, usually the former. I find it very difficult to conceive of a middle classification. . . .

Motion dismissed.

[4] [Counsel for the plaintiff.]

Notes

1. Compare the position where mandamus is sought against a minister (p. 405 *infra*), and for the view that the decision in *Merricks* v. *Heathcoat-Amory* is 'anomalous', see Wade, p. 519.

2. The judgment of Roxburgh J. on the application *ex parte* for an interim injunction in *Harper* v. *Home Secretary*, The Times, 18 December 1954, provides support for the middle classification mentioned by Upjohn J., but see the note of caution expressed when the case reached the Court of Appeal,[1955] Ch. 238 at p. 254.

3. Hogg, op. cit., pp. 25–6, submits that s. 21 (2) does not affect the courts' ability to issue an injunction to stop a Crown servant committing an unauthorized act. He continues by stating that 'such an injunction is directed against the servant in his personal capacity, not in his capacity as a Crown servant; and its effect is to give relief against the individual and not the Crown'. What meaning can be given to s. 21 (2) on this view? If the argument is that because the Crown servant is doing something unauthorized, he cannot be acting as a Crown servant, then note that a servant commiting a tort is often held to have been acting in the course of his employment for the purposes of the vicarious liability of his employer, and this can be so even if the act is criminal as well as tortious. Furthermore, *Underhill* v. *Ministry of Food* [1950] 1 All E.R. 591 and (by implication) *Merricks* v. *Heathcoat-Amory* seem to go against Hogg's view (see Strayer, (1964) 42 Can. Bar. Rev. 1 at pp. 36–8), though see Hogg, op. cit., p. 26 n. 80.

4. In *Merricks* v. *Heathcoat-Amory* the court touched on but did not answer the question whether an injunction (or indeed any remedy) can be granted in relation to matters connected with the Parliamentary process. On this problem, see Wade, p. 519; de Smith, pp. 465–9; and the Appendix.

DECLARATIONS

Declarations against public authorities

Dyson v..Attorney-General

[1911] 1 K.B. 410   Court of Appeal

The statement of claim alleged that the Commissioners of Inland Revenue had served a notice on the plaintiff, who was thereby obliged to make certain returns within a fixed period, that there was a penalty for non-compliance, and that the Commissioners threatened to enforce this. The plaintiff disputed the validity of the notice and sought declaratory relief against the Attorney-General, in particular a declaration that he was not obliged to comply with the notice. The Attorney-General then successfully applied to a Master to have the plaintiff's statement of claim struck out as disclosing no reasonable cause of action, and Lush J. upheld the decision. The plaintiff appealed.

COZENS-HARDY M.R.: ... But then it is urged that in the present action no relief is sought except by declaration, and that no such relief ought to be granted against the Crown, there being no precedent for any such action. The absence of any precedent does not trouble me. The power to make declaratory decrees was first granted to the Court of Chancery in 1852 by s. 50 of 15 & 16 Vict. c. 86, under which it was held that a declaratory decree could only be granted in cases in which there was some equitable relief which might be granted if the plaintiff chose to ask for it: see *Rooke* v. *Lord Kensington*.[5] The jurisdiction is, however, now enlarged, for by Order xxv., r. 5,[6] 'no action or proceeding shall be open to objection on the ground that a merely declaratory judgment, or order, is sought thereby, and the Court may make binding declarations of right whether any consequential relief is or could be claimed or not.' I can see no reason why this section should not apply to an action in which the Attorney-General, as representing the Crown, is a party. The Court is not bound to make a mere declaratory judgment, and in the exercise of its discretion will have regard to all the circumstances of the case. I can, however, conceive many cases in which a declaratory judgment may be highly convenient, and I am disposed to think, if all other objections are removed, this is a case to which r. 5 might with advantage be applied. But I desire to guard myself against the supposition that I hold that a person who expects to be made defendant, and who prefers to be plaintiff can, as a matter of right, attain his object by commencing an action to obtain a declaration that his opponent has no good cause of action against him. The Court may well say 'Wait until you are attacked and then raise your defence,' and may dismiss the action with costs. This may be the result in the present case. That, however, is not a matter to be dealt with on an interlocutory application. It is pre-eminently a matter for the trial. . . .

FARWELL L.J.: . . . The next argument on the Attorney-General's behalf was 'ab inconvenienti'; it was said that if an action of this sort would lie there would be an innumerable actions for declarations as to the meaning of numerous Acts, adding greatly to the labours of the law officers. But the Court is not bound to make declaratory orders and would refuse to do so unless in proper cases, and would punish with costs persons who might bring unnecessary actions: there is no substance in the apprehension, but if inconvenience is a legitimate consideration at all, the convenience in the public interest is all in favour of providing a speedy and easy access to the Courts for any of His Majesty's subjects who have any real cause of complaint against the exercise of statutory powers by Government departments and Government officials. . . .

[FLETCHER MOULTON L.J. delivered a judgment in favour of allowing the appeal.]

Appeal allowed.

Question

Cozens-Hardy M.R. mentioned that in some cases a court would refuse a declaration and tell the plaintiff 'Wait until you are attacked and then raise your defence.' Why should a court take this line?

[5] (1856) 2 K. & J. 753.
[6] [Of the Rules of the Supreme Court: see now Ord. 15, r. 16.]

Notes

1. At the hearing of the action, the plaintiff succeeded before Horridge J. and an appeal from that decision was rejected by the Court of Appeal, [1912] 1 Ch. 158. Fletcher Moulton L.J. took the opportunity to remark on the convenience in this case of the procedure invoked by the plaintiff.

2. The defendant in *Dyson's* case was the Attorney-General, but a declaration may well be sought against a particular government department rather than the Attorney-General today: see s. 17 (3) of the Crown Proceedings Act 1947, p. 458 *infra*.

3. The extract *supra* from the judgment of Cozens-Hardy M.R. refers to the Court of Chancery granting declarations. For discussion of whether or not the declaration is an equitable remedy, see Wade, pp. 522–3; de Smith, pp. 517–8; Zamir, *The Declaratory Judgment*, pp. 187–91.

4. *Dyson's* case concerned the power of the High Court to make declaratory judgments in actions commenced by writ or originating summons. It is now also possible to seek declaratory relief by an application for judicial review, on which see p. 315 *infra*. The declaration has been an important remedy in Administrative Law, especially in the light of s. 21 of the Crown Proceedings Act 1947, p. 290 *supra*, and we have already seen several cases in which it was sought, e.g. *Anisminic Ltd.* v. *Foreign Compensation Commission*, p. 38 *supra*; *Associated Provincial Picture Houses Ltd.* v. *Wednesbury Corporation*, p. 118 *supra*; *Barnard* v. *N.D.L.B.*, p. 131 *supra*; *Ridge* v. *Baldwin*, p. 214 *supra*. These cases provide examples of its scope and utility in the past. Its future must now be seen in the light of *O'Reilly* v. *Mackman*, p. 324 *infra*.

5. In relation to the question of declaratory relief where there has been an improper dismissal, note, along with *Ridge* v. *Baldwin*, the extract from *Malloch* v. *Aberdeen Corporation*, p. 272 *supra*, per Lord Wilberforce. Of the cases cited by Lord Wilberforce in this passage, declarations were sought in *Barber* v. *Manchester Regional Hospital Board* [1958] 1 W.L.R. 181 and *Vine* v. *N.D.L.B.* [1957] A.C. 488. See further Note 2, p. 275 *supra*; Zamir, op. cit., pp. 140–8; Ganz, (1967) 30 M.L.R. 288 at pp. 297–300. The earlier discussion occurred in the context of natural justice, but the declaration can be used in cases where for some other reason a dismissal was invalid, e,g, *Vine* v. *N.D.L.B.*

Despite some judicial opinion to the contrary, a declaration of invalidity of dismissal should not necessarily be taken to involve an entitlement to wages for the employee as if the dismissal had not taken place: see Ganz, [1964] P.L. 367 at pp. 381–3 and (1967) 30 M.L.R. 288 at pp. 299–300; Freedland, *The Contract of Employment*, pp. 290–2. This point arose in *Stevenson* v. *United Road Transport Union* [1977] I.C.R. 893, noted in the context of natural justice at p. 275 *supra*, in which a declaration was granted that the plaintiff's dismissal from a union office by an executive committee of the union was in breach of the union rules, in breach of natural justice, ultra vires, null and void. The Court of Appeal stated that the fact that the plaintiff had been employed by others since the time of the purported dismissal could affect the declaration's financial consequences and pointed out that the declaration did not 'quantify the union's financial obligations to the plaintiff.' More generally the court seemed concerned to divorce the precise declaration granted from what might be thought to be its natural consequence – that the plaintiff was still employed as an officer of the union: compare the approach of the judge in the court below, [1976] 3

All E.R. 29 at pp. 42–5. The Court of Appeal stressed that the declaration did not specifically enforce the contract of employment and did not declare that such contract still existed or had existed for any specific length of time. This was presumably to allow for events occurring after the time of the purported dismissal. For example, there had been a later purported dismissal of the plaintiff, the effect of which was not being considered by the court in the case in hand.

This view that the contract of employment was not being specifically enforced should be contrasted with the statement in Wade, p. 528, that 'a dismissed employee cannot obtain a declaration that his dismissal was a nullity, for in that case his employment would still continue and the court would be enforcing the contract of employment specifically', something which, as was mentioned at p. 275 supra, a court will not normally do. Are these two views inconsistent?

For further discussion see Chief Constable of the North Wales Police v. Evans [1982] 1 W.L.R. 1155, briefly noted at p. 283 supra, in which the probationer constable wished to be re-instated. The Court of Appeal had granted a declaration that the decision requiring him to resign or be dismissed was void. In the House of Lords, however, it was thought that the consequences of such a declaration were unclear and there was substituted a declaration that 'by reason of his lawfully induced resignation, the [probationer constable] had thereby become entitled to [the] same rights and remedies, not including reinstatement, as he would have had if [the Chief Constable] had unlawfully dispensed with his services under [the relevant regulation].'

In the case just mentioned, the declaration was granted under an application for judicial review. O'Reilly v. Mackman, p. 324 infra, decided that, as a general rule, Administrative Law cases must be brought by such an application and not by writ or originating summons. It may, however, be (see pp. 330 and 334 infra) that declarations relating to contracts of employment will be exceptions to that rule even though statutory powers are involved. Consider further R. v. B.B.C., ex p. Lavelle [1983] 1 W.L.R. 23, noted (1983) 12 I.L.J. 43.

Limits of the declaration

Barraclough v. Brown, p. 366 infra

Pyx Granite Co. Ltd. v. Ministry of Housing and Local Government, p. 368 infra

Note

These cases concern the question whether a statutory remedy excludes the availability of a declaration which will be discussed at p. 366 infra. A further restriction on the availability of a declaration which has been raised in the past concerns errors of law on the face of the record. It has been said, relying in particular on Punton v. Ministry of Pensions and National Insurance (No. 2) [1964] 1 W.L.R. 226, that a declaration cannot be granted in relation to such an error, although the precise extent of this limitation on the remedy was controversial: see e.g. Zamir, op. cit., pp. 151–66; Nettheim, (1968–71) 6 Sydney L.R. 184 at p. 190; Cane, (1980) 43 M.L.R. 266; cf. Alder, (1980) 43 M.L.R. 670 at p. 674 n. 25.

However, whatever the extent of the limitation, subsequent developments mean that it is unlikely to be of any practical importance today. First, it has been seen at p. 58 supra that there has been a great expansion in the concept of jurisdictional error of law; indeed, in the case of administrative bodies (as opposed to inferior courts of law), note the view that all errors of laws are jurisdictional. Secondly, the decision in *O'Reilly* v. *Mackman*, p. 324 *infra*, states that, as a general rule, declarations in Administrative Law cases *must* be obtained by an application for judicial review rather than in an action begun by writ or, as in *Punton (No. 2)*, by originating summons. As, under an application for judicial review, a declaration and certiorari can be sought in the alternative, the limit in *Punton (No. 2)* is avoided (other than at the theoretical level) because certiorari is, of course, available in respect of errors of law on the face of the record. Consider further *Re Tillmire Common, Heslington* [1982] 2 All E.R. 615, though note the suggestion in that case concerning expertise which is mentioned in Note 4, p. 336 *infra*. See further, Appendix.

RELATOR ACTIONS

Gouriet v. Union of Post Office Workers

[1978] A.C. 435   House of Lords

For the facts of this case, see p. 127 *supra*.

LORD WILBERFORCE: . . . A relator action – a type of action which has existed from the earliest times – is one in which the Attorney-General, on the relation of individuals (who may include local authorities or companies) brings an action to assert a public right. It can properly be said to be a fundamental principle of English law that private rights can be asserted by individuals, but that public rights can only be asserted by the Attorney-General as representing the public. In terms of constitutional law, the rights of the public are vested in the Crown, and the Attorney-General enforces them as an officer of the Crown. And just as the Attorney-General has in general no power to interfere with the assertion of private rights, so in general no private person has the right of representing the public in the assertion of public rights. If he tries to do so his action can be struck out.

. . . [T]he Attorney-General's role has never been fictional. His position in relator actions is the same as it is in actions brought without a relator (with the sole exception that the relator is liable for costs: see *Attorney-General* v. *Cockermouth Local Board* (1874) L.R. 18 Eq. 172, 176, *per* Jessel M.R.). He is entitled to see and approve the statement of claim and any amendment in the pleadings, he is entitled to be consulted on discovery, the suit cannot be compromised without his approval: if the relator dies, the suit does not abate. For the proposition that his only concern is to 'filter out' vexatious and frivolous proceedings, there is no authority – indeed, there is no need for the Attorney-General to do what is well within the power of the court. On the contrary he has the right, and the duty, to consider the public interest generally and widely.

It was this consideration which led to the well known pronouncement of the Earl of Halsbury L.C. in 1902, for the suggestion was being made that the court could inquire whether, when the Attorney-General had consented to relator proceedings, the public had a material interest in the subject matter of the suit:

'. . . the initiation of the litigation, and the determination of the question whether it is a proper case for the Attorney-General to proceed in, is a matter entirely beyond the jurisdiction of this or any other court. It is a question which the law of this country has made to reside exclusively in the Attorney-General': see *London County Council* v. *Attorney-General* [1902] A.C. 165, *per* Earl of Halsbury L.C. at p. 169 and *per* Lord Macnaghten at p. 170.

To limit this passage to a case where the Attorney-General has given his consent (as opposed to a case where he refuses consent) goes beyond legitimate distinction: it ignores the force of the words 'whether he ought to initiate litigation . . . or not': see p. 168. . . .

That it is the exclusive right of the Attorney-General to represent the public interest – even where individuals might be interested in a larger view of the matter – is not technical, not procedural, not fictional. It is constitutional. . . [I]t is also wise.

From this general consideration of the nature of relator actions, I pass to the special type of relator action with which this appeal is concerned. It is of very special character, and it is one in which the predominant position of the Attorney-General is a fortiori the general case.

This is a right, of comparatively modern use, of the Attorney-General to invoke the assistance of *civil courts* in aid of the *criminal law*. It is an exceptional power confined, in practice, to cases where an offence is frequently repeated in disregard of a, usually, inadequate penalty – see *Attorney-General* v. *Harris* [1961] 1 Q.B. 74; or to cases of emergency – see *Attorney-General* v. *Chaudry* [1971] 1 W.L.R. 1614. It is one not without its difficulties and thse may call for consideration in the future.

If Parliament has imposed a sanction (e.g., a fine of £1), without an increase in severity for repeated offences, it may seem wrong that the courts – civil courts – should think fit, by granting injunctions, breaches of which may attract unlimited sanctions, including imprisonment, to do what Parliament has not done. Moreover, where Parliament has (as here in the Post Office Act 1953) provided for trial of offences by indictment before a jury, it may seem wrong that the courts, applying a civil standard of proof, should in effect convict a subject without the prescribed trial. What would happen if, after punishment for contempt, the same man were to be prosecuted in a criminal court? That Lord Eldon L.C. was much oppressed by these difficulties is shown by the discussions in *Attorney-General* v. *Cleaver* (1811) 18 Ves. Jun. 210.

These and other examples which can be given show that this jurisdiction – though proved useful on occasions – is one of great delicacy and is one to be used with caution. Further, to apply to the court for an injunction at all against the threat of a criminal offence, may involve a decision of policy with which conflicting considerations may enter. Will the law best be served by preventive action? Will the grant of an injunction exacerbate the situation? (Very relevant this in industrial disputes.) Is the injunction likely to be effective or may it be futile? Will it be better to make it clear that the law will be enforced by prosecution and to appeal to the law-abiding instinct, negotiations, and moderate leadership, rather than provoke people along the road to martyrdom? All these matters – to which Devlin J. justly drew attention in *Attorney-General* v. *Bastow* [1957] 1 Q.B. 514, 519, and the exceptional nature of this *civil* remedy, point the matter as one essentially for the Attorney-General's preliminary discretion. Every known case, so far, has been so dealt with: in no case hitherto has it ever been suggested that an individual can act, though relator actions for public nuisance which may also involve a criminal offence, have been known for 200 years.

There are two arguments put forward for permitting individual citizens to take this action.

The first points to the private prosecution. All citizens have sufficient interest in the enforcement of the law to entitle them to take this step. Why then should this same interest not be sufficient to support preventive action by way of injunction – subject it may be, to ultimate control by the Attorney-General? At one time I was attracted by this argument. But I have reached the conclusion that I cannot accept it.

The Attorney-General's right to seek, in the civil courts, anticipatory prevention of a breach of the law, is a part or aspect of his general power to enforce, in the public interest, public rights. The distinction between public rights, which the Attorney-General can and the individual (absent special interest) cannot seek to enforce, and private rights, is fundamental in our law. To break it, as the plaintiff's counsel frankly invited us to do, is not a development of the law, but a destruction of one of its pillars. Nor, in my opinion, at least in this particular field, would removal of the distinction be desirable. More than in any other field of public rights, the decision to be taken before embarking on a claim for injunctive relief, involving as it does the interests of the public over a broad horizon, is a decision which the Attorney-General alone is suited to make: see *Attorney-General* v. *Bastow* [1957] 1 Q.B. 514.

This brings me to the *second* argument. Surely, it is said, since the whole matter is discretionary it can be left to the court. The court can prevent vexatious or frivolous, or multiple actions: the court is not obliged to grant an injunction: leave it in the court's hands. I cannot accept this either. The decisions to be made as to the public interest are not such as courts are fitted or equipped to make. The very fact, that, as the present case very well shows, decisions are of the type to atract political criticism and controversy, shows that they are outside the range of discretionary problems which the courts can resolve. Judges are equipped to find legal rights and administer, on well-known principles, discretionary remedies. These matters are widely outside those areas. . . .

VISCOUNT DILHORNE [having delivered that part of his speech which is to be found at p. 128 *supra*, continued:] Mr. Gouriet's contention now is that the Attorney-General can only refuse his consent to the institution of a relator action if it is frivolous, vexatious or oppressive and that as the action for which he sought the Attorney-General's consent did not fall under any of these heads, the Attorney-General had acted improperly. The ancient cases to which we were referred show that there was a time when Attorneys-General freely gave their consent to such actions but since the days of Lord Eldon, Attorneys-General have exercised considerable control. The figures with which we were supplied show that over the last 25 years or so the number of applications for the Attorney-General's consent has increased, and while a good percentage of them are refused, the number of such actions has also increased. A relator action is not something to be regarded as archaic and obsolete. The courts have power to dismiss an action which is frivolous, vexatious or oppressive. If indeed the only purpose of requiring an application for the Attorney-General's consent was to give him the opportunity of saying in advance of the courts that an action was frivolous, vexatious or oppressive, this function of his would serve little useful purpose. Again in my opinion this contention for which no authority was cited must be rejected. The Attorney-General did not in my opinion act improperly as now suggested on behalf of Mr. Gouriet.

> 'there is no greater nonsense talked about the Attorney-General's duty,' said Sir John Simon in 1925, 'than the suggestion that in all cases the Attorney-General ought to decide to prosecute merely because he thinks there is what the lawyers call "a case." It is not true, and no one who has held that office supposes it is.' (See *Edwards, the Law Officers of the Crown*, p. 222.)

However clear it appears to be that an offence has been committed, it is, as Sir Hartley Shawcross then Attorney-General said in 1951, the Attorney-General's duty

> 'in deciding whether or not to authorise the prosecution, to acquaint himself with all the relevant facts, including, for instance, the effect which the prosecution, successful or unsuccessful as the case may be, would have upon public morale and order.' (See *Edwards*, p. 223).

This approach which the Attorney-General should make when considering whether a prosecution should be started, is in my opinion the kind of approach he should have made to the question of giving his consent to Mr. Gouriet's application.

In deciding whether or not to prosecute 'there is only one consideration which is altogether excluded,' Sir Hartley Shawcross said, 'and that is the repercussion of a given decision upon my personal or my party's or the Government's political fortunes.' (See *Edwards*, pp. 222–223.) In the discharge of any of the duties to which I have referred, it is, of course, always possible that an Attorney-General may act for reasons of this kind and may abuse his powers. One does not know the reasons for the Attorney-General's refusal in this case but it should not be inferred from his refusal to disclose them that he acted wrongly. For all one knows he may have attached considerable importance to the fact that the injunction sought did no more than repeat the language of the sections of the Post Office Act 1953. On the Friday he may indeed have thought that to start proceedings so speedily for an injunction which did no more than that was not likely to serve any useful purpose and might indeed exacerbate the situation. Instances of applications by Attorneys-General to the civil courts for aid in enforcing the criminal law are few in number and exceptional in character. In the Court of Appeal a number of observations were made as to the inability of the courts to 'enforce the law' if the Attorney-General refused his consent to an application for such an injunction. A breach of the law was impending according to Lord Denning M.R. 'Are the courts to stand idly by?' was the question he posed on the Saturday. On January 27 he said [1977] Q.B. 729, 761:

> 'If he' (the Attorney-General) 'does not act himself – or refuses to give his consent to his name being used – then the law will not be enforced. If one Attorney-General after another does this, if each in his turn declines to take action against those who break the law – then the law becomes a dead letter.'

With great respect the criminal law does not become a dead letter if proceedings for injunctions to restrain the commission of offences or for declarations that certain conduct is unlawful are not brought. The criminal law is enforced in the criminal courts by the conviction and punishment of offenders, not in the civil courts. The jurisdiction of the civil courts is mainly as to the determination of disputes and claims. They are not charged with responsibility for the administration of the criminal courts. The question 'Are the courts to stand idly by?' might be supposed to some to suggest that the civil courts have some executive authority in relation to the criminal law. The line between the functions of the executive and the judiciary should not be blurred.

There are a number of statutory offences for the prosecution of which the consent of the Attorney-General or of the Director of Public Prosecutions is required but apart from these offences, anyone can if he wishes start a prosecution without obtaining anyone's consent. The enforcement of the criminal law does not rest with the civil courts or depend on the Attorney-General alone.

An enactment by Parliament defining and creating a criminal offence amounts to an injunction by Parliament restraining the commission of the acts made criminal. If the injunction in the Act is not obeyed – and in these days it frequently is not – the statute normally states the maximum punishment that can be awarded on conviction. If in addition to the enactment, an injunction is granted in the civil courts to restrain persons from doing the acts already made criminal by Parliament, an injunction which does no more than embody the language of the statute, has that any greater potency than the injunction by Parliament contained in the Act? An injunction in the terms sought when the application in this case was made to the Attorney-General does not appear to me to be one that can with any accuracy of language be regarded as 'enforcing the law.' Repetition is not enforcement. The granting of such an injunction merely imposes a liability to fine or imprisonment for contempt additional to the maximum Parliament has thought fit to prescribe for the same conduct.

Great difficulties may arise if 'enforcement' of the criminal law by injunction became a regular practice. A person charged, for instance, with an offence under section 58 or 69 of the Post Office Act 1953 has the right of trial by jury. If, before he commits the offence, an injunction is granted restraining him from committing an offence under those sections and he is brought before the civil courts for contempt, his guilt will be decided not by a jury but by a judge or judges. If he is subsequently tried for the ciminal offence, might not the finding of guilt by a judge or judges prejudice his trial? This question is not to my mind satisfactorily answered by saying that juries can be told to ignore certain matters. It was suggested that this difficulty might be overcome by adjourning the proceedings for contempt until after the conclusion of the criminal trial. If that was done, the question might arise then as to the propriety of imposing a punishment in the contempt proceedings additional to that imposed on conviction for the same conduct in the criminal court.

Such considerations may have been present to the mind of the Attorney-General when he considered Mr. Gouriet's application on the Friday and may have provided valid grounds for his refusal of consent. Whether they did so or not, one does not know but I have mentioned them as they seem me to suffice to show that even if good legal reasons for his decision were not immediately apparent, the inference that he abused or misused his powers is not one that should be drawn.

An Attorney-General is not subject to restrictions as to the applications he makes, either ex officio or in relator actions, to the courts. In every case it will be for the court to decide whether it has jurisdiction to grant the application and whether in the exercise of its discretion it should do so. It has been and in my opinion should continue to be exceptional for the aid of the civil courts to be invoked in support of the criminal law and no wise Attorney-General will make such an application or agree to one being made in his name unless it appears to him that the case is exceptional.

One category of cases in which the Attorney-General has successfully sought an injunction to restrain the commission of criminal acts is where the penalties imposed for the offence have proved wholly inadequate to deter its commission: see *Attorney-General* v. *Sharp* [1931] 1 Ch. 121; *Attorney-General* v. *Premier Line Ltd.* [1932] 1 Ch. 303; *Attorney-General* v. *Bastow* [1957] 1 Q.B. 514 and *Attorney-General* v. *Harris* [1961] 1 Q.B. 74 where the defendant had been convicted on no less than 142 occasions of breaches of the Manchester Police Regulation Act 1844.

In *Attorney-General* v. *Chaudry* [1971] 1 W.L.R. 1614 an injunction was granted at the instance of the Attorney-General in a relator action to restrain the defendant from using a building as a hotel without a certificate under the London Building Acts. There was a serious fire risk and it was not possible to secure the early hearing of a summons charging the defendant with a criminal offence in so using the building without a certificate. In those circumstances an interlocutory injunction was granted prohibiting the use of the building as a hotel until the necessary certificate was granted.

I do not wish to suggest that the cases to which I have referred are the only types of cases in which the civil courts can and should come to the aid of the criminal law by granting injunctions at the instance of the Attorney-General but they, I think, serve to show that the exercise of that jurisdiction at the instance of the Attorney-General is exceptional. . . .

[LORD DIPLOCK, LORD EDMUND-DAVIES, and LORD FRASER OF TULLY-BELTON delivered speeches in favour of dismissing the appeal.]

Appeal dismissed.

Notes

1. The question of when a person has sufficient interest to obtain a declaration or injunction without seeking the help of the Attorney-General will be discussed in particular in Ch. 11 *infra*.

2. For general discussion of relator actions (before *Gouriet*), see Edwards, *The Law Officers of the Crown*, pp. 186–95; Thio, *Locus Standi and Judicial Review*, pp. 133–60; and for critical discussion of *Gouriet*, see Feldman, (1979) 42 M.L.R. 369; Mercer, [1979] P.L. 214.

3. The relator action will, of course, involve a discretionary remedy. Although the courts have disavowed any intention to control the Attorney-General's decision whether or not to consent to a relator action, there is still a discretion to refuse him relief. On the extent to which this discretion is affected by the fact that the Attorney-General is involved, see Edwards, op. cit., pp. 290–3; Thio, op. cit., pp. 146–55; Feldman, op. cit., p. 376.

4. A few years before *Gouriet*, the case of *Attorney-General (ex rel. McWhirter)* v. *I.B.A.* [1973] Q.B. 629, which involved an attempt to stop a particular programme being shown on television, had brought relator actions to the public's attention. The Attorney-General did in fact consent to a relator action and in any event no breach of duty was found, but in the course of his judgment Lord Denning propounded the following principle (at p. 649):

. . . I am of opinion that, in the last resort, if the Attorney-General refuses leave in a proper case, or improperly or unreasonably delays in giving leave, or his machinery works too slowly, then a member of the public who has a sufficient interest can himself apply to the court itself. He can apply for a declaration and, in a proper case, for an injunction, joining the Attorney-General, if need be, as defendant. . . . I would not restrict the circumstances in which an individual may be held to have a sufficient interest.

This principle was repeated by Lord Denning when *Gouriet* was decided by the Court of Appeal [1977] Q.B. 729 at p. 759; and see further *R. v. G.L.C., ex p. Blackburn* [1976] 1 W.L.R. 550 at p. 559 (quoted by Lord Diplock in the *Self-Employed* case, p. 353 *infra*). Lord Denning's principle was, however, disapproved in the House of Lords in *Gouriet*. This disapproval helped to support the view that *Gouriet* and its comments on the exclusive role of the Attorney-General in relation to the public interest could not be confined to cases in which an injunction was sought to stop an alleged crime (Wade, (1978) 94 L.Q.R. 4 at p. 8 and see Williams, [1977] C.L.J. 201 at p. 204, but see Wade, pp. 535–6).

Note now that declarations and injunctions are obtainable in an application for judicial review, on which see p. 315 *infra*. In such an application the locus standi requirement can be more liberal than in an action begun by writ or originating summons, which was the only way by which these remedies could be obtained at the time of *Gouriet*. Furthermore, according to *O'Reilly* v. *Mackman*, p. 324 *infra*, declarations and injunctions in Administrative Law cases must, as a general rule, be obtained under such an application. Whether Lord Denning's principle, especially as expounded in the *Blackburn* case, is valid in the case of an application for judicial review must be considered later: see p. 346 *infra*. More generally, see also the next Note.

5. One criticism that has been levelled at the part played by the Attorney-General in this area of the law is that he never seems to act against central government departments. Assuming that he does not, will invalid or unlawful acts of such departments go unchallenged? If no crime is involved, there can be no criminal prosecution to vindicate the rule of law, and where there is a criminal prosecution on indictment, the Attorney-General can direct the entry of a *nolle prosequi*.

In the light of *O'Reilly* v. *Mackman*, p. 324 *infra*, it seems unlikely that a declaration could be obtained in an action begun by writ or originating summons, but there is, of course, the possibility of an application for judicial review. However, this may not be without its difficulties. Delay may be a hurdle in those proceedings (see Note 7, p. 319 *infra*). Secondly, locus standi (discussed at p. 346 *infra*) may on occasions still pose a problem, although this depends upon whether the courts have accepted or will come to accept the broad view espoused by Lord Denning, on which see p. 353 *infra*. Thirdly, if the validity of delegated legislation is involved, there has been doubt whether the application for judicial review is available (although recent cases have *assumed* that a declaration could be obtained under that procedure): see Note 2, p. 323 *infra* and consider the approach in *O'Reilly* v. *Mackman*, p. 333 *infra*.

6. Viscount Dilhorne was not alone in *Gouriet* in pointing to the dangers posed by the use of an injunction in aid of the criminal law. Indeed, apart from cases of public nuisance, Lord Diplock would wish to restrict its use to enforcing obedience to statutes which were intended to safeguard public health, safety, or welfare; furthermore, within this category, he would want to restrict it to cases where the penalty laid down had been shown to be inadequate to stop repetition of the offence, or where contravention, even if only on one occasion, would produce serious and irreparable harm. Lord Wilberforce thought that in practice its use was confined to these two types of case. Cf. Viscount Dilhorne's view at p. 305 *supra*; de Smith, p. 457 n. 91. For further discussion of this use of the injunction, see Feldman, op cit., pp. 370–2; Wade, p. 536; de Smith, p. 457.

Local authorities

Local Government Act 1972

222.– (1) Where a local authority consider it expedient for the promotion or protection of the interests of the inhabitants of their area –

   (*a*) they may prosecute or defend or appear in any legal proceedings and, in the case of civil proceedings, may institute them in their own name. . . .

Note

On the interpretation of this section, see Wade, p. 534.

10

PREROGATIVE REMEDIES

HABEAS CORPUS

Note

For a brief description of this remedy and the reason for its exclusion from the book, see p. 6 *supra*.

CERTIORARI AND PROHIBITION

R. v. Electricity Commissioners, ex parte London Electricity Joint Committee Co. (1920) Ltd.

[1924] 1 K.B. 171   Court of Appeal

The Electricity Commissioners, a body established by the Electricity (Supply) Act 1919, had made a draft order 'constituting the London and Home Counties Electricity District and establishing and incorporating the London and Home Counties Joint Electricity Authority'. At the time of the application in this case a public local inquiry concerning the draft order was being conducted. Any order made thereafter by the Electricity Commissioners needed to be confirmed by the Minister of Transport and then laid before and approved by each House of Parliament. Various electricity companies sought a rule nisi for prohibition and a rule nisi for certiorari, contending that the scheme which was incorporated in the draft order was ultra vires. The applicants were unsuccessful in the Divisional Court, but appealed to the Court of Appeal, which held that the scheme was ultra vires.

BANKES L.J. [having discussed certain cases]: . . . These authorities are, I think, conclusive to show that the Court will issue the writ to a body exercising judicial functions, though that body cannot be described as being in any ordinary sense a Court. There are, I think, three dicta of learned judges which may usefully be borne in mind in approaching an examination of the decisions which bear most closely upon the present case. There is the dictum of Brett L.J., as he then was in *Reg.* v. *Local Government Board*[1] where he says: 'My view of the power of prohibition at the present day is that the Court should not be chary of exercising it, and that wherever the Legislature entrusts to any body of persons other than to the superior Courts the power of

---

[1] 10 Q.B.D. 309, 321.

imposing an obligation upon individuals, the Courts ought to exercise as widely as they can the power of controlling those bodies of persons if those persons admittedly attempt to exercise powers beyond the powers given to them by Act of Parliament.' There is the dictum of Lord Sumner in *In re Clifford and O'Sullivan,*[2] where he says: 'It is agreed also that, old as the procedure by writ of prohibition is, and few are older, there is not to be found in all the very numerous instances of the exercise of this jurisdiction any case in which prohibition has gone to a body which possessed no legal jurisdiction at all.' Lastly there is the dictum of Fletcher Moulton L.J. in *Rex* v. *Woodhouse,*[3] where he is discussing what, in his opinion, constitutes a judicial act. He there says: 'Other instances could be given, but these suffice to show that the procedure of certiorari applies in many cases in which the body whose acts are criticized would not ordinarily be called a Court, nor would its acts be ordinarily termed "judicial acts." The true view of the limitation would seem to be that the term "judicial act" is used in contrast with purely ministerial acts. To these latter the process of certiorari does not apply, as for instance to the issue of a warrant to enforce a rate, even though the rate is one which could itself be questioned by certiorari. In short, there must be the exercise of some right or duty to decide in order to provide scope for a writ of certiorari at common law.' In that case the Lord Justice was dealing with an application for a writ of certiorari, but his observations here quoted apply in my opinion equally to prohibition. . . .

ATKIN L.J.: . . . The question now arises whether the persons interested are entitled to the remedy which they now claim in order to put a stop to the unauthorized proceedings of the Commissioners. The matter comes before us upon rules for writs of prohibition and certiorari which have been discharged by the Divisional Court. Both writs are of great antiquity, forming part of the process by which the King's Courts restrained courts of inferior jurisdiction from exceeding their powers. Prohibition restrains the tribunal from proceeding further in excess of jurisdiction; certiorari requires the record or the order of the court to be sent up to the King's Bench Division, to have its legality inquired into, and, if necessary, to have the order quashed. It is to be noted that both writs deal with questions of excessive jurisdiction, and doubtless in their origin dealt almost exclusively with the jurisdiction of what is described in ordinary parlance as a Court of Justice. But the operation of the writs has extended to control the proceedings of bodies which do not claim to be, and would not be recognized as, Courts of Justice. Wherever any body of persons having legal authority to determine questions affecting the rights of subjects, and having the duty to act judicially, act in excess of their legal authority they are subject to the controlling jurisdiction of the King's Bench Division exercised in these writs. . . . I can see no difference in principle between certiorari and prohibition, except that the latter may be invoked at an earlier stage. If the proceedings establish that the body complained of its exceeding its jurisdiction by entertaining matters which would result in its final decision

---

[2] [1921] 2 A.C. 570, 589.
[3] [1906] 2 K.B. 501, 535.

being subject to being brought up and quashed on certiorari, I think that prohibition will lie to restrain it from so exceeding its jurisdiction. . . .

In the present case the Electricity Commissioners have to decide whether they will constitute a joint authority in a district in accordance with law, and with what powers they will invest that body. The question necessarily involves the withdrawal from existing bodies of undertakers of some of their existing rights, and imposing upon them of new duties, including their subjection to the control of the new body, and new financial obligations. It also provides in the new body a person to whom may be transferred rights of purchase which at present are vested in another authority. The Commissioners are proposing to create such a new body in violation of the Act of Parliament, and are proposing to hold a possibly long and expensive inquiry into the expediency of such a scheme, in respect of which they have the power to compel representatives of the prosecutors to attend and produce papers. I think that in deciding upon the scheme, and in holding the inquiry, they are acting judicially in the sense of the authorities I have cited,[4] and that as they are proposing to act in excess of their jurisdiction they are liable to have the writ of prohibition issued against them.

It is necessary, however, to deal with what I think was the main objection of the Attorney-General.[5] In this case he said the Commissioners come to no decision at all. They act merely as advisers. They recommend an order embodying a scheme to the Minister of Transport, who may confirm it with or without modifications. Similarly the Miniter of Transport comes to no decision. He submits the order to the Houses of Parliament, who may approve it with or without modifications. The Houses of Parliament may put anything into the order they please, whether consistent with the Act of 1919, or not. Until they have approved, nothing is decided, and in truth the whole procedure, draft scheme, inquiry, order, confirmation, approval, is only part of a process by which Parliament is expressing its will, and at no stage is subject to any control by the Courts. . . . In the provision that the final decision of the Commissioners is not to be operative until it has been approved by the two Houses of Parliament I find nothing inconsistent with the view that in arriving at that decision the Commissioners themselves are to act judicially and within the limits prescribed by Act of Parliament, and that the Courts have power to keep them within those limits. It is to be noted that it is the order of the Commissioners that eventually takes effect; neither the Minister of Transport who confirms, nor the Houses of Parliament who approve, can under the statute make an order which in respect of the matters in question has any operation. I know of no authority which compels me to hold that a proceeding cannot be a judicial proceeding subject to prohibition or certiorari because it is subject to confirmation or approval, even where the approval has to be that of the Houses of Parliament. The authorities are to the contrary. . . .

. . . I think . . . that the appeal should be allowed, so far as the writ of

----

[4] [These have been omitted.]
[5] [Appearing on behalf of the Electricity Commissioners.]

prohibition is concerned, and that the rule for the issue of the writ should be made absolute.

So far as the writ of certiorari is concerned, the matter becomes unimportant. I have considerable doubt whether there is any such definite order as could be made the subject of certiorari, and in this respect I think that the appeal should be dismissed without costs.

[YOUNGER L.J. delivered a judgment in favour of allowing the appeal in respect of the writ of prohibition but dismissing it in respect of the writ of certiorari.]

Appeal allowed.

Notes

1. The famous phrase of Atkin L.J. at p. 308 *supra* concerning the availability of certiorari and prohibition contains the requirement that the body against which relief is sought be under a duty to act judicially. (On the classification of functions see further p. 4 *supra*.) This requirement did in the past produce an unduly restrictive attitude towards the availability of the orders, just as it had with the rules of natural justice, the applicability of which was similarly limited. We have seen that *Ridge* v. *Baldwin*, p. 220 *supra*, and the later case law produced a more satisfactory position in the sphere of natural justice, and Lord Reid's interpretation (in *Ridge* v. *Baldwin*) of Atkin L.J.'s speech in the *Electricity Commissioners* case must be borne in mind in this context as well (and see further *O'Reilly* v. *Mackman*, p. 328 *infra*).

Lord Reid, it will be remembered, thought that Atkin L.J. (and indeed Bankes L.J.) inferred the judicial element from the nature of the power. Note also *R.* v. *Hillingdon L.B.C., ex p. Royco Homes Ltd.* [1974] Q.B. 720, where Lord Widgery C.J. underlined the point that Lord Reid had got rid of the need for any requirement of a duty to act judicially in addition to the power to determine questions affecting people's rights (though on this case see de Smith, p. 394). Some judges have gone so far as to abandon the use of the word 'judicial' altogether (e.g. Roskill L.J. in *R.* v. *Liverpool Corporation, ex p. Liverpool Taxi Fleet Operators' Association* [1972] 2 Q.B. 299 at p. 310; Lord Denning in *R.* v. *Barnsley M.B.C., ex p. Hook* [1976] 1 W.L.R. 1052 at p. 1058; cf. Scarman L.J. at p. 1060; *Jayawardane* v. *Silva* [1970] 1 W.L.R. 1365, noted *infra*). The approach which favours discontinuing the use of the word 'judicial' can now derive support from *O'Reilly* v. *Mackman*, p. 328 *infra*. Nevertheless, Lord Widgery C.J. perhaps spoke for many judges when he said: 'One knows nowadays that it is not necessary to show a judicial act in order to get certiorari, but if the order is a judicial act it makes it that much easier to justify the making of the order' (*R.* v. *Board of Visitors of Hull Prison, ex p. St. Germain* [1978] Q.B. 678 at p. 689); cf. the views expressed in the Court of Appeal, [1979] Q.B. 425 at pp. 445, 448, and 465). One category of case in which it seems certiorari will issue in the absence of any 'judicial' element is where there has been a breach of the duty to act fairly. (The cases on procedural fairness have established that the duty to act fairly applies to administrative decisions even though there is no duty to act judicially.) For example, in *R.* v. *Birmingham City Justice, ex p. Chris Foreign Foods (Wholesalers) Ltd.* [1970] 1 W.L.R. 1428 Lord Parker C.J. granted certiorari to quash a decision for a breach of the duty to act fairly without concerning himself with the question whether the function in question was judicial or administrative. Might certiorari for breach of the duty to act fairly be available in wider circumstances than those outlined in *O'Reilly* v. *Mackman*, p. 328 *infra*?

Whatever the approach to the judicial/administrative dichotomy in this context today, legislative matters may still have to be distinguished. Certiorari and prohibition were held not to lie against the Church Assembly (or its Legislative Committee), which had the power to initiate legislation that, after receiving Parliamentary approval and the Royal Assent, would become a statute: *R*. v. *Legislative Committee of the Church Assembly, ex p. Haynes-Smith* [1928] 1 K.B. 411. The position in general is not as clear as it might be (on which see further Wade, pp. 560–1; de Smith, p. 395; and consider *Minister of Health* v. *The King (on the prosecution of Yaffe)* [1931] A.C. 494), but the traditional view seems to have been that certiorari or prohibition are not available in a case where subordinate legislation is challenged. Commentators have questioned whether the exercise of a legislative function can be said to involve the determination of a question within Atkin L.J.'s formulation in the *Electricity Commissioners* case (and see *R*. v. *Wright, ex p. Waterside Workers' Federation of Australia* (1955) 93 C.L.R. 528 at p. 542). The declaration and, if not prohibited by s. 21 of the Crown Proceedings Act 1947, p. 290 *supra*, the injunction have been regarded as the weapons with which to attack subordinate legislation. Note that the borderline between legislative and administrative acts can be very fine: see Note 1, p. 493 and Note 3, p. 495 *infra*; de Smith, pp. 71–6; *R*. v. *Liverpool Corporation, ex p. Liverpool Taxi Fleet Operators' Association* [1972] 2 Q.B. 299, noted at p. 269 *supra*. A particular problem raised by the point discussed in this paragraph will be considered in Note 2, p. 323 *infra*.

2. Although the application for prohibition was successful in the *Electricity Commissioners* case, the application for certiorari was premature. If the court had been concerned with an order made after the inquiry by the Commissioners, then it would seem that it could have been quashed by certiorari despite the need for further approval before it could come into effect. Contrast with this situation the case where one body merely makes some recommendation to another body. See *R*. v. *St. Lawrence's Hospital Statutory Visitors, ex p. Pritchard* [1953] 1 W.L.R. 1158, but see further Wade, pp. 558–60; de Smith, pp. 489–90.

It should not, however, be assumed that all preliminary decisions are reviewable by certiorari. A court may think that the impact on an individual's rights is too slight. *Jayawardane* v. *Silva* [1970] 1 W.L.R. 1365 provides an example. An assistant collector of customs in Ceylon had power, once he had decided that a breach of a Customs Ordinance had taken place, to impose a forfeiture of three times the value of the goods involved or a fixed penalty of 1,000 rupees. In the case of the applicant for certiorari in *Jayawardane* v. *Silva*, he chose the former, which in fact amounted to approximately 5,000,000 rupees. Although the district court would later determine whether or not a breach had occurred if proceedings were brought to obtain the money, the court had no power to alter the amount to be forfeited. However, the collector himself could exercise a power of mitigation, a power which at the time of this application for certiorari could still be exercised. The Privy Council in rejecting the application held that the applicant's rights were 'adequately preserved' and that no quasi-judicial decision had yet been made. If the power of mitigation had ceased to be available, the decision would probably have been different.

3. At one time there was a particular problem with intervention by certiorari (or indeed any remedy) in disciplinary proceedings (and see Note 3, p. 253 *supra*). For a more modern approach see *R*. v. *Board of Visitors of Hull Prison, ex p. St. Germain* [1979] Q.B. 425, noted at p. 253 *supra*.

4. Certiorari and prohibition are discretionary remedies, on which see further p. 364 *infra*.

Non-statutory decisions: 'questions affecting the rights of subjects'

R. v. Criminal Injuries Compensation Board, ex parte Lain

[1967] 2 Q.B. 864   Divisional Court of the Queen's Bench Division

For the facts of this case and other extracts from the judgments, see p. 11 *supra*. These extracts should be read before the extracts *infra*.

DIPLOCK L.J.: . . . True it is that a determination of the board that a particular sum by way of ex gratia payment of compensation should be offered to an applicant does not give the applicant any right to sue either the board or the Crown for that sum. But it does not follow that a determination of the board in favour of an applicant is without any legal effect upon the rights of the applicant to whom it relates. It makes lawful a payment to an applicant which would otherwise be unlawful. The moneys which the board is authorised to distribute are held by the board in a fiduciary capacity and 'The Scheme' defines and limits the board's authority to make any payment out of them to anyone. It makes a determination by the board, in the exercise of its judicial functions, that an offer of a particular sum to a particular applicant is justified, a condition precedent to the board's authority in the exercise of its administrative functions to make any payment to that applicant. Any payment made by the board to any person contrary to those instructions, that is, without a prior determination that an offer of that sum to the payee is justified in accordance with the principles laid down in 'The Scheme,' would constitute a breach of duty by the board as agents of the Crown and could be recovered by the Crown from the recipient as money had and received – at any rate if he had notice of the breach. . . .

I do not find it necessary for the purposes of this case to express any view as to whether certiorari would lie in respect of a determination which was incapable of having any effect upon legal rights in any circumstances. It is, however, in my opinion quite sufficient to attract the supervisory jurisdiction of the High Court to quash by certiorari a determination of an inferior tribunal made in the exercise of its quasi-judicial powers, that such determination should have the effect of rendering lawful and irrecoverable a payment to a subject which would otherwise be unlawful and recoverable. I would therefore hold that we have jurisdiction to entertain the present application for an order of certiorari against the Criminal Injuries Compensation Board. . . .

ASHWORTH J.: . . . In the familiar passage from the judgment of Atkin L.J. in *Rex* v. *Electricity Commissioners, Ex parte London Electricity Joint Committee Co. (1920) Ltd.*[6] there are included the words: 'affecting the rights of subjects' and Mr. Bridge[7] contended that they constitute an insuperable obstacle to any relief by way of certiorari, because nobody has any legal right to compensation. He argued with force that the payment of compensation is expressly declared to be ex gratia: it is bounty and nothing else. For my

6 [1924] 1 K.B. 171, 205.   7 [Counsel for the Board.]

part I doubt whether Atkin L.J. was propounding an all-embracing definition of the circumstances in which relief by way of certiorari would lie. In my judgment the words in question read in the context of what precedes and follows them, would be of no less value if they were altered by omitting 'the rights of' so as to become 'affecting subjects.' . . .

Note

For another situation in which there has been control by prerogative order of rules which have been held not to be of statutory force, see *R. v. Chief Immigration Officer, Gatwick Airport, ex p. Kharrazi* [1980] 1 W.L.R. 1396, in which, as Wade points out (p. 562), the Court of Appeal intervened by certiorari when an immigration officer misinterpreted the Immigration Rules. Contrast *R. v. Secretary of State for Home Affairs, ex p. Hosenball* [1977] 1 W.L.R. 766 (a natural justice case), noted at p. 282 *supra* and p. 495 *infra*. In the situation involved in that case it was held, distinguishing *ex p. Lain,* that the court could review for unfairness, but that this was not necessarily constituted by a breach of the Immigration Rules. Generally see further Note 3, p. 495 *infra*.

Domestic tribunals. Contractual jurisdiction

R. v. Post Office, ex parte Byrne

[1975] I.C.R. 221   Divisional Court of the Queen's Bench Division

BRIDGE J.: . . . [T]he first question which has to be considered and decided before we could properly pronounce upon the merits of any of [the] matters of complaint is whether the remedy of certiorari lies to quash such a decision as the decision given here: a disciplinary decision in respect of a Post Office employee made by a superior officer of that employee in the Post Office.

Almost inevitably any consideration of the ambit of the prerogative orders in the modern law starts from the much quoted statement of general principle to be found in the judgment of Atkin L.J. in *Rex v. Electricity Commissioners, Ex parte London Electricity Joint Committee Co. (1920) Ltd.* [1924] 1 K.B. 171, 205. . . .

[Having quoted this passage from the *Electricity Commissioners* case and also passages from *R. v. Criminal Injuries Compensation Board, ex p. Lain* [1967] 2 Q.B. 864 at pp. 882 and 890, he continued:]

Both those passages[8] echo the decision of this court to which reference should also be made in *Reg. v. National Joint Council for the Craft of Dental Technicians (Disputes Committee), Ex parte Neate* [1953] 1 Q.B. 704 that certiorari would not lie to a private arbitrator. It is unnecessary to refer at length to the judgments in that case, but it is to be observed that Lord Goddard C.J. says, at p. 708:

'There is no instance of which I know in the books where certiorari or prohibition has gone to any arbitrator except a statutory arbitrator, and a statutory arbitrator is a person to whom by statute the parties must resort. . . .'

[8] [From *ex p. Lain.*]

Our attention has also been drawn to *Reg.* v. *Aston University Senate, Ex parte Roffey* [1969] 2 Q.B. 538, where it appears to have been assumed, though clearly not decided, since the point was not canvassed in argument, that certiorari would lie to the decision of a university senate excluding a student member of the university senate from continuing his studies. The university was one established by Royal Charter and its constitution appears to have derived from ordinances and regulations made by the senate of the university under powers derived from its charter.

But that case has attracted criticism in the Court of Appeal subsequently. Russell L.J. pointed out in *Herring* v. *Templeman* [1973] 3 All E.R. 569, 585 that the majority judgments of Donaldson J. and Blain J. in the *Aston University Senate* case have been the subject of criticism by Professor Wade in an article in the *Law Quarterly Review*, (1969) 85 L.Q.R. 468, not least by reason of the fact that it does not appear to have been appreciated that the relationship between the applicants and the university was one of contract. Russell L.J. continues, at p. 585:

'Professor Wade points out, inter alia, that certiorari would – to say the least – be an unusual remedy for breach of contract. Yet no one appears to have examined what the precise contractual relationship between the applicants and the university was. . . .

In the light of both that criticism and the fact that the question whether the senate was a public or private tribunal was never considered in the *Aston University* case, I do not for my part think that that is an authority which throws any light on the issue which we have to decide today.

[His Lordship then considered Sch. 1 to the Post Office Act 1969 and continued:]

. . . [I]t seems to me quite inescapable that the only legal authority which any Post Office employee superior in rank to the present applicant exercises, or can exercise, in relation to the applicant is an authority which derives exclusively from the contract with the applicant has made with the Post Office, namely, his contract of employment.

Again reverting to Atkin L.J.'s classic dictum in *Rex* v. *Electricity Commissioners, Ex parte London Electricity Joint Committee Co. (1920) Ltd.* [1924] 1 K.B. 171, 205 and applying the language of first principle, the legal authority of a superior officer of the Post Office pronouncing a disciplinary sentence against the applicant is not an authority which affects the applicant's rights qua subject; it affects the applicant's rights qua Post Office employee. The worst sentence that could be pronounced against him under the disciplinary code would be sentence of dismissal, in other words termination of the contract.

For those reasons I have reached the clear conclusion that certiorari does not lie in this case. . . .

[LORD WIDGERY C.J. and ASHWORTH J. agreed.]

Application dismissed.

Note

On domestic tribunals, see also *R.* v. *B.B.C., ex p. Lavelle* [1983] 1 W.L.R. 23, noted in the Appendix. On the *Aston University* case, which was criticized in *R.* v. *Post Office, ex p. Byrne,* see further Wade, (1969) 85 L.Q.R. 468; Garner, (1974) 90 L.Q.R. 6; Wade, (1974) 90 L.Q.R. 157; cf. *O'Reilly* v. *Mackman* [1982] 3 W.L.R. 604 at p. 620 (per Lord Denning). More generally, see *R.* v. *Barnsley M.B.C., ex p. Hook* [1976] 1 W.L.R. 1052; *R.* v. *Basildon B.C., ex p. Brown* (1981) 79 L.G.R. 655, and Ward, (1982) 45 M.L.R. 588.

APPLICATION FOR JUDICIAL REVIEW

Supreme Court Act 1981

31. – (1) An application to the High Court for one or more of the following forms of relief, namely –

(*a*) an order of mandamus, prohibition or certiorari;

(*b*) a declaration or injunction under subsection (2); . . .

shall be made in accordance with rules of court by a procedure to be known as an application for judicial review.

(2) A declaration may be made or an injunction granted under this subsection in any case where an application for judicial review, seeking that relief, has been made and the High Court considers that, having regard to –

(*a*) the nature of the matters in respect of which relief may be granted by orders of mandamus, prohibition or certiorari;

(*b*) the nature of the persons and bodies against whom relief may be granted by such orders; and

(*c*) all the circumstances of the case,

it would be just and convenient for the declaration to be made or the injunction to be granted, as the case may be.

(3) No application for judicial review shall be made unless the leave of the High Court has been obtained in accordance with rules of court; and the court shall not grant leave to make such an application unless it considers that the applicant has a sufficient interest in the matter to which the application relates.

(4) On an application for judicial review the High Court may award damages to the applicant if –

(*a*) he has joined with his application a claim for damages arising from any matter to which the application relates; and

(*b*) the court is satisfied that, if the claim had been made in an action begun by the applicant at the time of making his application, he would have been awarded damages.

(5) If, on an application for judicial review seeking an order of certiorari, the High Court quashes the decision to which the application relates, the

High Court may remit the matter to the court, tribunal or authority concerned, with a direction to reconsider it and reach a decision in accordance with the findings of the High Court.

(6) Where the High Court considers that there has been undue delay in making an application for judicial review, the court may refuse to grant –

(*a*) leave for the making of the application; or

(*b*) any relief sought on the application,

if it considers that the granting of the relief sought would be likely to cause substantial hardship to, or substantially prejudice the rights of, any person or would be detrimental to good administration.

(7) Subsection (6) is without prejudice to any enactment or rule of court which has the effect of limiting the time within which an application for judicial review may be made.

Rules of the Supreme Court

Order 53

APPLICATIONS FOR JUDICIAL REVIEW

Joinder of claims for relief

2. On an application for judicial review any relief mentioned in rule 1(1) or (2)[9] may be claimed as an alternative or in addition to any other relief so mentioned if it arises out of or relates to or is connected with the same matter.

Grant of leave to apply for judicial review

3. . . .

(2) An application for leave must be made *ex parte* to a judge by filing in the Crown Office –

(*a*) a notice in Form No. 86A containing a statement of

(i)   the name and description of the applicant,

(ii) the relief sought and the grounds upon which it is sought,

(iii) the name and address of the applicant's solicitors (if any), and

(iv) the applicant's address for service; and

(*b*) an affidavit verifying the facts relied on.

(3) The judge may determine the application without a hearing, unless a hearing is requested in the notice of application, and need not sit in open court; in any case, the Crown Office shall serve a copy of the judge's order on the applicant.

(4) Where the application for leave is refused by the judge, or is granted on terms, the applicant may renew it by applying –

(*a*) in any criminal cause or matter, to a Divisional Court of the Queen's Bench Division;

---

[9] [Similar provisions to these are to be found in s. 31 (1) and (2) of the Supreme Court Act 1981, *supra* but see Note 7, p. 337 *infra*.]

(b) in any other case, to a single judge sitting in open court or, if the Court so directs, to a Divisional Court of the Queen's Bench Division;

Provided that no application for leave may be renewed in any non-criminal cause or matter in which the judge has refused leave under paragraph (3) after a hearing.

(10) Where leave to apply for judicial review is granted, then –

(a) if the relief sought is an order of prohibition of certiorari and the Court so directs, the grant shall operate as a stay of the proceedings to which the application relates until the determination of the application or until the Court otherwise orders;

(b) if any other relief is sought, the Court may at any time grant in the proceedings such interim relief as could be granted in an action begun by writ.

Delay in applying for relief

4. – (1) An application for judicial review shall be made promptly and in any event within three months from the date when grounds for the application first arose unless the Court considers that there is good reason for extending the period within which the application shall be made.

(2) Where the relief sought is an order of certiorari in respect of any judgment, order, conviction or other proceeding, the date when grounds for the application first arose shall be taken to be the date of that judgment, order, conviction or proceeding.

(3) Paragraph (1) is without prejudice to any statutory provision which has the effect of limiting the time within which an application for judicial review may be made.

Mode of applying for judicial review

5. – (1) In any criminal cause or matter where leave has been granted to make an application for judicial review, the application shall be made by originating motion to a Divisional Court of the Queen's Bench Division.

(2) In any other such cause or matter, the application shall be made by originating motion to a judge sitting in open court, unless the Court directs that it shall be made –

(a) by originating summons to a judge in chambers; or

(b) by orginating motion to a Divisional Court of the Queen's Bench Division. . . .

(7) If on the hearing of the motion or summons the Court is of opinion that any person who ought, whether under this rule or otherwise, to have been served has not been served, the Court may adjourn the hearing on such terms (if any) as it may direct in order that the notice or summons may be served on that person.

Application for discovery interrogatories, cross-examination, etc.

8. – (1) Unless the Court otherwise directs, any interlocutory application in proceedings on an application for judicial review may be made to any judge or a master of the Queen's Bench Division, notwithstanding that the application for judicial review has been made by motion and is to be heard by a Divisional Court. . . .

(3) This rule is without prejudice to any statutory provision or rule of law restricting the making of an order against the Crown.

Hearing of application for judicial review

9. – (1) On the hearing of any motion or summons under rule 5, any person who desires to be heard in opposition to the motion or summons, and appears to the Court to be a proper person to be heard, shall be heard, notwithstanding that he has not been served with notice of the motion or the summons.

(5) Where the relief sought is a declaration, an injunction or damages and the Court considers that it should not be granted on an application for judicial review but might have been granted if it had been sought in an action begun by writ by the applicant at the time of making his application, the Court may, instead of refusing the application, order the proceedings to continue as if they had been begun by writ; . . .

Notes

1. Section 31 of the Supreme Court Act 1981 reproduces (though not always in absolutely identical language) certain provisions that appear in Ord. 53. Those parts of Ord. 53 have therefore been omitted.

2. The provisions set out *supra* owe much to the work of the Law Commission. In 1969 the Law Commission had unsuccessfully urged the establishment of a wide-ranging inquiry into Administrative Law (Law Com. No. 20, Cmnd. 4059), but the Commission was merely requested 'to review the existing remedies for the judicial control of administrative acts or omissions with a view to evolving a simpler and more effective procedure'. The result of this review was the *Report of Remedies in Administrative Law*, Law Com. No. 73, Cmnd. 6407. It was assumed that the implementation of a lot of the recommendations contained in the Report would be by legislation; indeed, the Law Commission's Report contained a Draft Procedure for Judicial Review Bill. However, the bulk of the proposals were in fact brought into being by an amendment in 1977 to Ord. 53 of the Rules of the Supreme Court, this amendment coming into force in 1978 (S.I. 1977 No. 1955). (The Law Commission's proposal on interim relief against the Crown where a declaration is being sought would have needed legislation for its implementation and was not included in this reform: see the Note, p. 293 *supra*.) Some of the provisions laid down in Ord. 53 by S.I. 1977 No. 1955 were themselves amended by S.I. 1980 No. 2000, and now the Supreme Court Act 1981 sets out part of the rules governing the application for judicial review. Although s. 31 of the 1981 Act is primarily codificatory, it should be noted that s. 31 (6) differs both from the provision on time limits laid down by S.I. 1977 No. 1955 and also from the amended provision introduced by S.I. 1980 No. 2000: see Note 7 *infra*.

3. For consideration of the availability of a declaration or injunction under s. 31 (2) of the 1981 Act, see Note 2, p. 322 *infra*. For discussion of the question of the effect on the availability of a declaration or injunction in an action begun by writ or originating summons of the provision now contained in s. 31 (2), see p. 324 *infra*.

4. The question of locus standi, which is mentioned in s. 31 (3) of the 1981 Act, is discussed at p. 338 *infra*.

5. Procedure at first sight seems to be distinct from the substantive law, but the following three Notes should reveal the influence it may have on it.

6. Section 31 (4) of the 1981 Act does not appear to attempt to change the substantive law of damages against public authorities (though see Jacob, [1981] P.L. 452 at pp. 457–8; cf. Dobson, [1982] P.L. 34 at pp. 36–7). The present position will be discussed in Ch. 13 *infra*. Before the recent procedural reforms, damages could not be obtained along with a prerogative order: two separate sets of proceedings were required. The fact that a person can now claim damages in an application for judicial review without going to the trouble (and expense, if unsuccessful) of bringing a separate action may well make such claims more frequent and thereby make judges address their minds to this difficult area of the law to a greater extent.

7. Prior to the coming into force of S.I. 1977 No. 1955, mandamus (with one exception), prohibition, the declaration, and the injunction were subject to no specific time limit but to the discretion of the court. Prohibition indeed, by its very nature, contains its own time limit. In the case of certiorari there was a six-month time limit within which to seek the order. It would be a rare case in which an applicant would be refused the order within the six months; on the other hand, it seems that the courts would not readily grant certiorari after the six-month period had elapsed: see Beatson and Matthews, (1978) 41 M.L.R. 419 at pp. 442–3. The problem revealed by *Punton v. Ministry of Pensions and National Insurance (No. 2)*, [1964] 1 W.L.R. 226, on which see the Note at p. 298 *supra* could in practice have been ameliorated by a longer time limit for certiorari.

The position on time limits was altered by S.I. 1977 No. 1955 (on which see Beatson and Matthews, op. cit., pp. 441–4), but this time limit provision was in turn amended by S.I. 1980 No. 2000. However, s. 31 (6) also deals with time limits and the conditional clause in the latter part of s. 31 (6) repeats a provision that used to be contained in Ord. 53 by virtue of S.I. 1977 No. 1955, but which had been deleted by S.I. 1980 No. 2000. In relation to the 'detrimental to good administration' provision, contrast *Bradbury v. Enfield L.B.C.*, p. 290 *supra*; *R. v. Paddington Valuation Officer, ex p. Peachey Property Corporation Ltd.* [1966] 1 Q.B. 380 at pp. 418 and 419; cf. [1964] 1 W.L.R. 1186; [1966] 1 Q.B. at p. 402. Note also that s. 31 (6) and Ord. 53 r. 4 (as amended by S.I. 1980 No. 2000) exist alongside each other. It seems a little odd that there should be two differently worded provisions governing the same matter. Are there situations in which an applicant will fall foul of one of these provisions but not the other? When do the grounds for the application arise? Is it the time when the error actually occurred, the time when the decision was made, or the time when the applicant knew or should have known of the error? Is it possible to say whether the applicant for certiorari is in a better position today than in 1977? See further *R. v. Merseyside C.C., ex p. Great Universal Stores Ltd.* (1982) 80 L.G.R. 639.

8. Although the Law Commission suggested that discovery of documents and interrogatories were available in theory in prerogative order proceedings before the coming into force of S.I. 1977 No. 1955, no case was found in which either was

ordered. In relation to cross-examination on affidavits, note the exceptional case of *R. v. Stokesley, Yorkshire, JJ., ex p. Bartram* [1956] 1 W.L.R. 254 where it was ordered. The fact that reference is now made to all three in Ord. 53, r. 8, might be thought to be likely to lead to their more frequent use. The importance of discovery, for example, was shown in *Barnard* v. *N.D.L.B.*, p. 131 *supra,* where it was only through discovery of documents more than six months after the relevant date that the plaintiffs found out the ground on which they succeeded in that case. At one time, however, the case law after the introduction of Ord. 53, r. 8 suggested for the most part that there would not be a great change in practice: see e.g. the comment of Lord Scarman in *I.R.C.* v. *Rossminster Ltd.* [1980] A.C. 952 at p. 1027, noted at p. 52 *supra; George* v. *Secretary of State for the Environment* (1979) 38 P. & C.R. 609 at pp. 615 and 618; *R.* v. *Board of Visitors, Nottingham Prison, ex p. Moseley,* The Times, 23 January 1981; *O'Reilly* v. *Mackman* [1982] 3 W.L.R. 604 at p. 621 and pp. 620–7; but see *U.K.A.P.E.* v. *A.C.A.S.* [1979] 1 W.L.R. 570 at p. 576; *Irlam Brick Co. Ltd.* v. *Warrington B.C.,* The Times, 5 February 1982.

Consider now *O'Reilly* v. *Mackman,* p. 332 *infra.* In relation to cross-examination on affidavits Lord Diplock argued that in an application for judicial review factual disputes will only arise in limited situations and that widespread cross-examination might tempt a reviewing court to usurp the fact-finding jurisdiction of the administrative body. On the other hand, *O'Reilly* v. *Mackman* states that cross-examination on affidavits, interrogatories and discovery of documents will be available in an application for judicial review whenever the justice of the case requires it. How much guidance does this give? Is it consistent with a view such as that of Lord Scarman referred to *supra*? Consider further *Khawaja's* case in the Appendix.

9. On mandamus, which is covered by s. 31 of the Supreme Court Act 1981 and Ord. 53, see Ch. 14 *infra.*

The New Face of Judicial Review: Administrative Changes in Order 53

Louis Blom-Cooper, [1982] P.L. 250 at pp. 259–60

The amendment[10] of January 1981 to Order 53 under which judicial review cases (other than criminal) are to be heard by a single judge of the Queen's Bench Division is in effect a creation of an administrative list, based on the model of the Commercial List (now officially called the Commercial Court).[11] Judges with specialist knowledge of commercial law have, since the beginning of the century, been regularly assigned to hear cases listed in the Commercial Court. So, too, a cadre of Queen's Bench judges known for their expertise in some aspect of administrative law has been nominated by the Lord Chief Justice to operate the new Order 53.[12]

But judicial adroitness in completing the process of a list into which *all* administrative cases would be put was not yet complete.

---

[10] [S.I. No. 2000 of 1980.]
[11] Supreme Court Act 1981, s. 6 (1) (*b*).
[12] The judges are Forbes, Phillips, Hodgson, Comyn, McNeill, Woolf, Webster, Glidewell and McCullough JJ.

Following the coming into force of the 1980 amendment and the nomination of the judges to try cases in the Divisional Court List, an attempt was made to identify those other cases which might also be concerned with aspects of administrative law and might be suitable for hearing before the same court. The results of this exercise are to be found in the Directions for London issued by the Lord Chief Justice in July 1981.[13] Paragraph 1 of those Directions establishes the Crown Office List, which encompasses the Order 53 cases. But there was an important departure. Provision is made for non-jury actions having an administrative flavour to be transferred into the Crown Office List from the ordinary non-jury list. The wording is wide enough to bring in administrative cases even from the Chancery Division. The Directions achieve the aim of bringing all administrative cases before the same tribunal. Further provisions bring in appeals to the High Court from tribunals and the like – Order 55; appeals under the Town and Country Planning Acts – Order 94; appeals under the Social Security Act 1975 – Order 111. The rest is finally something of a catch-all provision to include cases emanating from VAT tribunals and other like bodies.

The Divisional Court, as we know it, has disappeared in everything but name when dealing with judicial review of administrative actions involving civil disputes. The new framework has been constructed in which a new jurisprudence on administrative law can flourish. A specialised administrative court – albeit one which lacks the distinctiveness and constitutional status of a body like the French *Conseil d'Etat* – has been established, even if it has been achieved by administrative stealth rather than by the democratic process of legislation.

Note

See further Blom-Cooper, op. cit., pp. 260–1, for the role of Lord Lane, the Lord Chief Justice, in this area of the law, and see [1982] P.L. 353.

Inland Revenue Commissioners v. National Federation of Self-Employed and Small Businesses, Ltd.

[1982] A.C. 617   House of Lords

For the facts of this case, see p. 346 *infra*.

LORD WILBERFORCE: . . . The proceedings have been brought by the procedure now called 'judicial review.' There are two claims, the first for a declaration that the Board of Inland Revenue 'acted unlawfully' in granting an amnesty to [certain] casual workers; the second, for an order of mandamus to assess and collect income tax from the casual workers according to the law. These two claims rest, for present purposes, upon the same basis, since a declaration is merely an alternative kind of relief which can only be given if, apart from convenience, the case would have been one for mandamus. . . .

---

[13] [1981] 1 W.L.R. 1296. Practice Direction (Trials in London).

LORD DIPLOCK: . . . [J]udicial review is a remedy that lies exclusively in public law. In my view the language of rules 1 (2)[14] and rule 3[15] of the new Order 53 shows an intention that upon an application for judicial review the court should have jurisdiction to grant a declaration or an injunction as an alternative to making one of the prerogative orders, whenever in its discretion it thinks that it is just and convenient to do so; and that this jurisdiction should be exercisable in any case in which the applicant would previously have had locus standi to apply for any of the prerogative orders. The matters specified in paragraphs (a) and (b) of rule 1 (2) as matters to which the court must have regard, make this plain. So if, before the new Order 53 came into force, the court would have had jurisdiction to grant to the applicant any of the prerogative orders it may now grant him a declaration or injunction instead, notwithstanding that the applicant would have no locus standi to claim the declaration or injunction under private law in a civil action against the respondent to the application. . . .

LORD SCARMAN: . . . The new procedure is more flexible than that which it supersedes. An applicant for relief will no longer be defeated merely because he has chosen to apply for the wrong remedy. Not only has the court a complete discretion to select and grant the appropriate remedy: but it now may grant remedies which were not previously available. Rule 1 (2)[16] enables the court to grant a declaration or injunction instead of, or in addition to, a prerogative order, where to do so would be just and convenient. This is a procedural innovation of great consequence: but it neither extends nor diminishes the substantive law. For the two remedies (borrowed from the private law) are put in harness with the prerogative remedies. They may be granted only in circumstances in which one or other of the prerogative orders can issue. I so interpret R.S.C., Ord 53, r. 1 (2) because to do otherwise would be to condemn the rule as ultra vires.

. . . The new Order has made the declaration available as an alternative, or an addition, to a prerogative order. Its availability has, therefore, been extended, but only in the field of public law where a prerogative order may be granted. . . .

O'Reilly v. Mackman, p. 323 *infra*

Notes

1. For discussion of locus standi, which is mentioned in the extract from the *Self-Employed* case and on which it is a leading authority, see p. 338 *infra*.

2. Prior to the coming into force of S.I. 1977 No. 1955, a declaration or injunction could not be obtained alongside a prerogative order (or vice versa). The fact that this position was changed and that a declaration or injunction can now be obtained in addition to a prerogative order or even on its own in an application for judicial review was perhaps the most important of the recent procedural reforms.

[14] [See now s. 31 (2) of the Supreme Court Act 1981, p. 315 *supra.*]
[15] [See now s. 31 (3) of the Supreme Court Act 1981, p. 315 *supra.*]
[16] [*Supra* note 14.]

The object of the provision which is now to be found in s. 31 (2) was to ensure that the new procedure should only be available for cases 'in the public law field' (Law Commission, *Report on Remedies in Administrative Law,* para. 45), but on the crucial question of what weight is to be afforded to the factors set out in s. 31 (2) (*a*) and (*b*), the section is not particularly helpful. The extracts *supra* from the *Self-Employed* case can be taken to suggest a rigid test – that a court must be satisfied a prerogative order could have been granted before a declaration or injunction can be awarded under this procedure: see Cane, [1981] P.L. 322 at pp. 323–9; cf. Griffiths, [1982] C.L.J. 6 at p. 11. Lord Scarman is perhaps the clearest on the point, but his view is expressly based on the fact that only practice or procedure could be changed by the new Ord. 53. Section 31 (2) of the Supreme Court Act 1981, being part of a statute, could, of course, change the substantive law. However, given its origin in Ord. 53, r. 1 (2), it can be argued that it should be interpreted in a similar way (though Lord Denning would not agree with this argument – see O'Reilly v. *Mackman* [1982] 3 W.L.R. 604 at p. 620).

A less strict approach (and, it seems, the one that will prevail) is to regard the non-availability of a prerogative order as relevant but capable of being overridden in what was thought to be a suitable case for the grant of a declaration or injunction. This more liberal approach can derive support from the speech of Lord Diplock in *O'Reilly* v. *Mackman* (referred to *supra*) which states that 'all remedies for infringements of rights protected by public law can be obtained upon an application for judicial review'. See further the judgment of Lord Denning in the Court of Appeal in *O'Reilly* v. *Mackman* [1982] 3 W.L.R. 604 at p. 620; *Re Islam (Tafazzul)* [1981] 3 W.L.R. 942 at p. 954; *R.* v. *B.B.C., ex p. Lavelle* [1983] 1 W.L.R. 23. Consider also the cases mentioned in (*c*) *infra*. On this view the limitations on the prerogative orders would not be a rigid bar but on the former view they would be. The student should particularly bear in mind:

(*a*) cases such as *R.* v. *Post Office, ex p. Byrne,* p. 313 *supra* and *R.* v. *B.B.C., ex p. Lavelle* on which see Appendix;

(*b*) the judicial element, *if* it is still required to any extent before certiorari or prohibition will issue (on which see Note 1, p. 310 *supra*); and

(*c*) the traditional view, mentioned in Note 1, p. 311 *supra*, that certiorari and prohibition cannot be used to challenge the validity of delegated legislation. Note, however, *R.* v. *London Committee of Deputies of British Jews, ex p. Helmcourt Ltd.,* The Times, 2 May 1981, where in an application for judicial review a declaration was granted that a provision in a statutory instrument was invalid. The report in The Times does not indicate that the question of the suitability of this procedure was discussed by the judge. On appeal (The Times, 16 July 1981) the provision was held to be valid, but this report of the judgment does not contain any expression of opinion on the suitability of the choice of procedure either. Similarly the Divisional Court's judgment in *R.* v. *Secretary of State for the Environment, ex p. Brent L.B.C.* [1982] 2 W.L.R. 693, noted at p. 518 *infra*, does not contain any discussion of this point in the course of upholding the validity of a statutory instrument which was sought to be challenged by a declaration in an application for judicial review. Note also the view of Lord Denning in Note 5, p. 337 *infra*. See further *O'Reilly* v. *Mackman,* p. 334 *infra*, which implies that declarations will be available under an application for judicial review in relation to delegated legislation.

If an applicant is ruled out by any of these limitations, then his mistake can be rectified, without too much trouble, by the 'safety net' to be found in Ord. 53, r. 9 (5): see *R.* v. *B.B.C., ex p. Lavelle.* Indeed, the existence of r. 9 (5) might encourage boldness on the part of applicants in seeking a declaration or injunction under s. 31.

Generally on this problem, see Cane, op. cit., who points to another restriction on the prerogative orders as opposed to the declaration; this is that the former will not lie against the Crown. However, certiorari and prohibition have in the past been issued against government departments and ministers when exercising powers conferred upon them: see Wade, p. 564; de Smith, pp. 384–5. There does not, therefore, appear to be any major problem on this point, whichever of the views mentioned *supra* as to the availability of declarations is adopted. Compare Cane, op. cit., p. 326, esp. n. 18, where he refers to *Town Investments Ltd.* v. *Secretary of State for the Environment* [1978] A.C. 359, noted at p. 435 *infra*; but it is submitted that the wide view of 'the Crown' to be found in that case is unlikely to cause problems in this context.

An exclusive procedure?

O'Reilly v. Mackman

[1982] 3 W.L.R. 1096   House of Lords

The appellants, who were all prisoners at the Hull Prison, wished to challenge decisions reached by the Prison's Board of Visitors in relation to allegations that the appellants had committed breaches of the Prison Rules 1964. It was argued that the rules of natural justice had not been complied with by the Board and the appellants sought declarations that the findings and consequent penalties were null and void. They did not make use of Ord. 53; rather the proceedings were begun by writ (or, in one of the four cases involved, by originating summons) and an application was made to strike out the statments of claim (and the originating summons) on the ground that they were an abuse of the process of the court. The application was refused by Peter Pain J. at first instance but the Court of Appeal allowed an appeal by the Board ([1982] 3 W.L.R. 604). An appeal from that decision was made to the House of Lords.

LORD DIPLOCK: . . . My Lords, it is not contested that if the allegations set out in the orginating summons or statements of claim are true each of the appellants would have had a remedy obtainable by the procedure of an application for judicial review under R.S.C., Ord. 53; but to obtain that remedy, whether it took the form of an order of certiorari to quash the board's award or a declaration of its nullity, would have required the leave of the court under R.S.C., Ord. 53, r. 3. That judicial review lies against an award of the board of visitors of a prison made in the exercise of their disciplinary functions was established by the judgment of the Court of Appeal (overruling a Divisional Court) in *Reg.* v. *Board of Visitors of Hull Prison, Ex parte St. Germain* [1979] Q.B. 425: a decision that was, in my view, clearly right and has not been challenged in the instant appeals by the respondents.

In the *St. Germain* case, the only remedy that had been sought was certiorari to quash the decision of the board of visitors; but the alternative remedy of a declaration of nullity if the court considered it to be just and convenient would also have been available upon an application for judicial review under R.S.C., Ord. 53 after the replacement of the old rule by the new rule in 1977. In the instant cases, which were commenced after the new rule came into effect (but before the coming into force of section 31 of the Supreme Court Act 1981), certiorari would unquestionably have been the more appropriate remedy, since rule 5 (4) of the Prison Rules 1964, which provides for remission of sentence up to a maximum of one-third, stipulates that the 'rule shall have effect subject to any disciplinary award of forfeiture. . . .' Prison rule 56, however, expressly empowers the Secretary of State to remit a disciplinary award and, since he would presumably do so in the case of a disciplinary award that had been declared by the High Court to be a nullity, such a declaration would achieve, though less directly, the same result in practice as quashing the award by certiorari.

So no question arises as to the 'jurisdiction' of the High Court to grant to each of the appellants relief by way of a declaration in the terms sought, if they succeeded in establishing the facts alleged in their respective statements of claim or originating summons and the court considered a declaration to be an appropriate remedy. All that is at issue in the instant appeal is the procedure by which such relief ought to be sought. Put in a single sentence the question for your Lordships is: whether in 1980 after R.S.C., Ord. 53 in its new form, adopted in 1977, had come into operation it was an abuse of the process of the court to apply for such declarations by using the procedure laid down in the Rules for proceedings begun by writ or by originating summons instead of using the procedure laid down by Ord. 53 for an application for judicial review of the awards of forfeiture of remission of sentence made against them by the board which the appellants are seeking to impugn?

In their respective actions, the appellants claim only declaratory relief. . . . So the first thing to be noted is that the relief sought in the action is discretionary only.

It is not, and it could not be, contended that the decision of the board awarding him forfeiture of remission had infringed or threatened to infringe any right of the appellant derived from private law, whether a common law right or one created by a statute. Under the Prison Rules remission of sentence is not a matter of right but of indulgence. So far as private law is concerned all that each appellant had was a legitimate expectation, based upon his knowledge of what is the general practice, that he would be granted the maximum remission, permitted by rule 5 (2) of the Prison Rules, of one third of his sentence if by that time no disciplinary award of forfeiture of remission had been made against him. So the second thing to be noted is that none of the appellants had any remedy in private law.

In public law, as distinguished from private law, however, such legitimate expectation gave to each appellant a sufficient interest to challenge the legality of the adverse disciplinary award made against him by the board on the ground that in one way or another the board in reaching its decision had acted outwith the powers conferred upon it by the legislation under which it was acting; and such grounds would include the board's failure to observe the rules of natural justice: which means no more than to act fairly towards him in carrying out their decision-making process, and I prefer so to put it.

. . . In exercising their functions under [the Prison Rules] members of the board are acting as a statutory tribunal, as contrasted with a domestic tribunal upon which powers are conferred by contract between those who agree to submit to its jurisdiction. Where the legislation which confers upon a statutory tribunal its decision-making powers also provides expressly for the procedure it shall follow in the course of reaching its decision, it is a question of construction of the relevant legislation, to be decided by the court in which the decision is challenged, whether a particular procedural provision is mandatory, so that its non-observance in the process of reaching the decision makes the decision itself a nullity, or whether it is merely directory, so that the statutory tribunal has a discretion not to comply with it if, in its opinion, the exceptional circumstances of a particular case justify departing from it. But the requirement that a person who is charged with having done something which, if proved to the satisfaction of a statutory tribunal, has consequences that will, or may, affect him adversely, should be given a fair opportunity of hearing what is alleged against him and of presenting his own case, is so fundamental to any civilised legal system that it is to be presumed that Parliament intended that a failure to observe it should render null and void any decision reached in breach of this requirement. What is alleged by the appellants other than the Millbanks would amount to an infringement of the express rule 49; but even if there were no such express provision a requirement to observe it would be a necessary implication from the nature of the disciplinary functions of the board. In the absence of express provision to the contrary Parliament, whenever it provides for the creation of a statutory tribunal, must be presumed not to have intended that the tribunal should be authorised to act in contravention of one of the fundamental rules of natural justice or fairness: audi alteram partem.

In the Millbanks's case, there is no express provision in the Prison Rules that the members of the board who inquire into a disciplinary offence under rule 51 must be free from personal bias against the prisoner. It is another fundamental rule of natural justice or fairness, too obvious to call for express statement of it, that a tribunal exercising functions such as those exercised by the board in the case of Millbanks should be constituted of persons who enter upon the inquiry without any pre-conceived personal bias against the prisoner. Failure to comply with this implied requirement would likewise render the decision of the tribunal a nullity. So the third thing to be noted is that each of the appellants, if he established the facts alleged in his action, was entitled to a remedy in public law which would have the effect of preventing the decision of the board from having any adverse consequences upon him.

My Lords, the power of the High Court to make declaratory judgments is conferred by what is now R.S.C., Ord. 15, r. 16. The language of the rule which was first made in 1883 has never been altered. . . .

'No action or other proceeding shall be open to objection on the ground that a merely declaratory judgment or order is sought thereby, and the court may make binding declarations of right whether or not any consequential relief is or could be claimed.'

This rule . . . has been very liberally interpreted in the course of its long history, wherever it appeared to the court that the justice of the case required the grant of declaratory relief in the particular action before it. . . . [Ord. 15, r. 16 does not] draw any distinction between declarations that relate to rights and obligations under private law and those that relate to rights and obligations under public law. Indeed the appreciation of the distinction in substantive law between what is private law and what is public law has itself been a latecomer to the English legal system. It is a consequence of the development that has taken place in the last 30 years of the procedures available for judicial control of administrative action. This development started with the expansion of the grounds upon which orders of certiorari could be obtained as a result of the decision of the Court of Appeal in *Rex.* v. *Northumberland Compensation Appeal Tribunal, Ex parte Shaw* [1952] 1 K.B. 338; it was accelerated by the passing of the Tribunals and Inquiries Act 1958, and culminated in the substitution in 1977 of the new form of R.S.C., Ord. 53 which has since been given statutory confirmation in section 31 of the Supreme Court Act 1981.

[His Lordship then considered R. v. *Northumberland Compensation Appeal Tribunal, ex p. Shaw,* the Tribunals and Inquiries Acts 1958 and 1971, and in particular s. 14 (1) of the 1971 Act, p. 379 *infra,* and continued:]

. . . [Section 14 (1) provides] as follows:

'As respects England and Wales . . . any provision in an Act passed before [the commencement of this Act] that any order or determination shall not be called into question in any court, or any provision in such an Act which by similar words excludes any of the powers of the High Court, shall not have effect so as to prevent the removal of proceedings into the High Court by order of certiorari or to prejudice the powers of the High Court to make orders of mandamus: . . .'

The subsection, it is to be observed, says nothing about any right to bring civil actions for declarations of nullity of orders or determinations of statutory bodies where an earlier Act of Parliament contains a provision that such order or determination 'shall not be called into question in any court.' Since actions begun by writ seeking such declarations were already coming into common use in the High Court so as to provide an alternative remedy to orders of certiorari, the section suggests a parliamentary preference in favour of making the latter remedy available rather than the former. I will defer consideration of the reasons for this preference until later.

. . . It was [the exclusion of the Foreign Compensation Commission from the predecessor to s. 14 of the Tribunals and Inquiries Act 1971 (s. 11 of the 1958 Act) and the ouster clause in s. 4 (4) of the Foreign Compensation Act 1950, on which see p. 374 *infra*] that provided the occasion for the landmark decision of this House in *Anisminic Ltd.* v. *Foreign Compensation Commission* [1969] 2 A.C. 147, and particularly the leading speech of Lord Reid, which has liberated English public law from the fetters that the courts had theretofore imposed upon themselves so far as determinations of inferior courts and statutory tribunals were concerned, by drawing esoteric distinctions between errors of law committed by such tribunals that went to their jurisdiction, and errors of law committed by them within their jurisdiction. The breakthrough that the *Anisminic* case made was the recognition by the majority of this House that if a tribunal whose jurisdiction was limited by statute or subordinate legislation mistook the law applicable to the facts as it had found them, it must have asked itself the wrong question, i.e., one into which it was not empowered to inquire and so had no jurisdiction to determine. Its purported 'determination' not being a "determination" within the meaning of the empowering legislation, was accordingly a nullity.

Anisminic Ltd. v. *Foreign Compensation Commission* was an action commenced by writ for a declaration, in which a minute of the commission's reasons for their determination adverse to the plaintiff company did not appear upon the face of their determination, and had in fact been obtained only upon discovery. . . . In the House of Lords the question of the propriety of suing by writ for a declaration instead of applying for certiorari and mandamus played no part in the main argument for the commission. . . .

My Lords, *Anisminic Ltd.* v. *Foreign Compensation Commission* [1969] 2 A.C. 147 was decided by this House before the alteration was made R.S.C., Ord. 53 in 1977. . . . The pre-1977 Order 53, like its predecessors, placed under considerable procedural disadvantage applicants who wished to challenge the lawfulness of a determination of a statutory tribunal or any other body of persons having legal authority to determine questions affecting the common law or statutory rights or obligations of other persons as individuals. It will be noted that I have broadened the much-cited description by Atkin L.J. in *Rex.* v. *Electricity Commissioners, Ex parte London Electricity Joint Committee Co. (1920) Ltd.* [1924] 1 K.B. 171, 205 of bodies of persons subject to the supervisory jurisdiction of the High Court by prerogative remedies (which in 1924 then took the form of prerogative writs of mandamus, prohibition, certiorari, and quo warranto) by excluding Atkin L.J.'s limitation of the bodies of persons to whom the prerogative writs might issue, to those 'having the duty to act judicially.' For the next 40 years this phrase gave rise to many attempts, with varying success, to draw subtle distinctions between decisions that were quasi-judicial and those that were administrative only. But the relevance of arguments of this kind was destroyed by the decision of this House in *Ridge* v. *Baldwin* [1964] A.C. 40, where again the leading speech was given by Lord Reid. Wherever any person or body of persons has authority conferred by legislation to make decisions of the kind I have described, it is amenable to the remedy of an order to quash its decision either for error of law in reaching it or for failure to act fairly towards the person who will be adversely affected by the decision by failing to observe either one or other of the two fundamental rights accorded to him by the rules of natural justice or fairness. . . . In *Ridge* v. *Baldwin* it is interesting to observe that Lord Reid said at p. 72 'We do not have a developed system of administrative law – perhaps because until fairly recently we did not need it.' By 1977 the need had continued to grow apace and this reproach to English law had been removed. We did have by then a developed system of administrative law, to the development of which Lord Reid himself, by his speeches in cases which reached this House, had made an outstanding contribution. To the landmark cases of *Ridge* v. *Baldwin* and *Anisminic Ltd.* v. *Foreign Compensation Commission* [1969] 2 A.C. 147 I would add a third, *Padfield* v. *Minister of Agriculture, Fisheries and Food* [1968] A.C. 997, another case[17] in which a too-timid judgment of my own in the Court of Appeal was (fortunately) overruled.

Although the availability of the remedy of orders to quash a decision by certiorari had in theory been widely extended by these developments, the procedural disadvantages under which applicants for this remedy laboured remained substantially unchanged until the alteration of Order 53 in 1977. Foremost among these was the absence of any provision for discovery. In the case of a decision which did not state the reasons for it, it was not possible to challenge its validity for error of law in the reasoning by which the decision had been reached. If it had been an application for certiorari those who were the plaintiffs in the *Anisminic* case would have failed; it was only because by pursuing an action by writ for a declaration of nullity that the plaintiffs were entitled to the discovery by which the minute of the commission's reasons which showed that they had asked themselves the wrong question, was obtained. Again under Order 53 evidence was required to be on affidavit. This in itself is not an unjust disadvantage; it is a common feature of many forms of procedure in the High Court, including originating summonses; but in the absence of any express provision for cross-examination of deponents, as your Lordships who are familiar with the pre-1977 procedure will be aware, even *applications* for leave to cross-examine were virtually unknown – let alone the grant of leave itself – save in very exceptional cases of which I believe none of your Lordships has ever had actual experience. Lord Goddard C.J., whose experience was at that time unrivalled, had so stated in *Reg.* v. *Stokesley, Yorkshire, Justices, Ex parte Bartram* [1956] 1 W.L.R. 254, 257.

On the other hand as compared with an action for a declaration commenced by writ or originating summons, the procedure under Order 53 both before and after 1977 provided for the respondent decision-making statutory tribunal or public authority against which the remedy of certiorari was sought protection against claims which it was not in the public interest for courts of justice to entertain.

First, leave to apply for the order was required. The application for leave which was ex parte but could be, and in practice often was, adjourned in order to enable the proposed respondent to be represented, had to be supported by a statement setting out, inter alia, the grounds on which the relief was sought and by affidavits verifying the facts relied on: so that a knowingly false statement of fact would amount to the criminal offence of perjury. Such affidavit was also required to satisfy the requirement of uberrima fides, with the consequence that failure to make on oath a full and candid disclosure of

[17] [The first, mentioned in a passage not extracted, was his judgment in *Anisminic* itself: [1968] 2 Q.B. 862.]

material facts was of itself a ground for refusing the relief sought in the substantive application for which leave had been obtained on the strength of the affidavit. This was an important safeguard, which is preserved in the new Order 53 of 1977. The public interest in good administration requires that public authorities and third parties should not be kept in suspense as to the legal validity of a decision the authority has reached in purported exercise of decision-making powers for any longer period than is absolutely necessary in fairness to the person affected by the decision. In contrast, allegations made in a statement of claim or an indorsement of an originating summons are not on oath, so the requirement of a prior application for leave to be supported by full and candid affidavits verifying the facts relied on is an important safeguard against groundless or unmeritorious claims that a particular decision is a nullity. There was also power in the court on granting leave to impose terms as to costs or security.

Furthermore, as Order 53 was applied in practice, as soon as the application for leave had been made it provided a very speedy means, available in urgent cases within a matter of days rather than months, for determining whether a disputed decision was valid in law or not. A reduction of the period of suspense was also effected by the requirement that leave to apply for certiorari to quash a decision must be made within a limited period after the impugned decision was made, unless delay beyond that limited period was accounted for to the satisfaction of the judge. The period was six months under the pre-1977 Order 53; under the current Order 53 it is further reduced to three months.

My Lords, the exclusion of all right to discovery in application for certiorari under Order 53, particularly before the passing of the Tribunal and Inquiries Act 1958, was calculated to cause injustice to persons who had no means, if they adopted that procedure, of ascertaining whether a public body, which had made a decision adversely affecting them, had done so for reasons which were wrong in law and rendered their decision invalid. It will be within the knowledge of all of your Lordships that, at any rate from the 1950s onwards, actions for declarations of nullity of decisions affecting the rights of individuals under public law were widely entertained, in parallel to applications for certiorari to quash, as means of obtaining an effective alternative remedy. I will not weary your Lordships by reciting examples of cases where this practice received the express approval of the Court of Appeal, though I should point out that of those cases in this House in which this practice was approved, *Vine* v. *National Dock Labour Board* [1957] A.C. 488 and *Ridge* v. *Baldwin* [1964] A.C. 40 involved, as well as questions of public law, contracts of employment which gave rise to rights under private law. In *Anisminic Ltd.* v. *Foreign Compensation Commission* [1969] 2 A.C. 147 the procedural question was not seriously argued, while *Pyx Granite Ltd.* v. *Ministry of Housing and Local Government* [1960] A.C. 260, which is referred to in the notes to Order 19 appearing in the *Supreme Court Practice* (1982) as an instance of the approval by this House of the practice of suing for a declaration instead of applying for an order of certiorari, appears on analysis to have been concerned with declaring that the plaintiffs had a legal right to do what they were seeking to do without the need to obtain any decision from the Minister. Nevertheless I accept that having regard to disadvantages, particularly in relation to the absolute bar upon compelling discovery of documents by the respondent public authority to an applicant for an order of certiorari, and the almost invariable practice of refusing leave to allow cross-examination of deponents to affidavits lodged on its behalf, it could not be regarded as an abuse of the process of the court, before the amendments made to Order 53 in 1977, to proceed against the authority by an action for a declaration of nullity of the impugned decision with an injunction to prevent the authority from acting on it, instead of applying for an order of certiorari; and this despite the fact that, by adopting this course, the plaintiff evaded the safeguards imposed in the public interest against groundless, unmeritorious or tardy attacks upon the validity of decisions made by public authorities in the field of public law.

Those disadvantages, which formerly might have resulted in an applicant's being unable to obtain justice in an application for certiorari under Order 53, have all been removed by the new Order introduced in 1977. There is express provision in the new rule 8 for interlocutory applications for discovery of documents, the administration of interrogatories and the cross-examination of deponents to affidavits. Discovery of documents (which may often be a time-consuming process) is not automatic as in an action begun by writ, but otherwise Order 24 applies to it and discovery is obtainable upon application whenever, and to the extent that, the justice of the case requires; similarly Order 26 applies to applications for interrogatories; and to applications for cross-examination of deponents to affidavits Ord. 28, r. 2 (3) applies. This is the rule that deals with evidence in actions begun by originating summons and permits oral cross-examination on affidavit evidence wherever the justice of the case requires. It may well be that for the reasons given by Lord Denning M.R. in *George* v. *Secretary of State for the Environment* (1979) 77 L.G.R. 689, it will only be upon rare occasions that the interests of justice will require that leave be given for cross-examination of deponents on their affidavits in applications for judicial review. This is because of the nature of the issues that normally arise upon judicial review. The facts, except where the claim that a decision was invalid on the ground that the statutory tribunal or public authority that made the decision failed to comply with the procedure pre-scribed by the legislation under which it was acting or failed to observe the fundamental rules of natural justice or fairness, can seldom be a matter of relevant dispute upon an application for judicial review, since the tribunal or authority's findings of fact, as distinguished from the legal consequences of the facts that they have found, are not open to review by the court in the exercise of its supervisory powers except on the principles laid down in *Edwards* v. *Bairstow* [1956] A.C. 14, 36: and to allow cross-examination presents the court with a temptation, not always easily resisted, to substitute its own view of the facts for that of the decision-making body upon whom the exclusive jurisdiction to determine fcts had been conferred by Parliament.

Nevertheless having regard to a possible misunderstanding of what was said by Geoffrey Lane L.J. in *Reg.* v. *Board of Visitors of Hull Prison, Ex parte St. Germain (No. 2)* [1979] 1 W.L.R. 1401, 1410 your Lordships may think this an appropriate occasion on which to emphasise that whatever may have been the position before the rule was altered in 1977 in all proceedings for judicial review that have been started since that date the grant of leave to cross-examine deponents upon applications for judicial review is governed by the same principles as it is in actions begun by originating summons; it should be allowed whenever the justice of the particular case so requires.

Another handicap under which an applicant for a prerogative order under Order 53 formerly laboured (though it would not have affected the appellants in the instant cases even if they had brought their actions before the 1977 alteration to Order 53) was that a claim for damages for breach of a right in private law of the applicant resulting from an invalid decision of a public authority could not be made in an application under Order 53. Damages could only be claimed in a separate action begun by writ; whereas in an action so begun they could be claimed as additional relief as well as a declaration of nullity of the decision from which the damage claimed had flowed. Rule 7 of the new Order 53 permits the applicant for judicial review to include in the statement in support of his application for leave a claim for damages and empowers the court to award damages on the hearing of the application if satisfied that such damages could have been awarded to him in an action begun by him by writ at the time of the making of an application.

Finally rule 1 of the new Order 53 enables an application for a declaration or an injunction to be included in an application for judicial review. This was not previously the case; only prerogative orders could be obtained in proceedings under Order 53. Declarations or injunctions were obtainable only in actions begun by writ or originating summons. So a person seeking to challenge a decision had to make a choice of the remedy that he sought at the outset of the proceedings, although when the matter was examined more closely in the course of the proceedings it might appear that he was not entitled to that remedy but would have been entitled to some other remedy available only in the other kind of proceeding.

This reform may have lost some of its importance since there have come to be realised that the full consequences of the *Anisminic* case, in introducing the concept that if a statutory decision-making authority asks itself the wrong question it acts without jurisdiction, have been virtually to abolish the distinction between errors within jurisdiction that rendered voidable a decision that remained valid until quashed, and errors that went to jurisdiction and rendered a decision void ab initio provided that its validity was challenged timeously in the High Court by an appropriate procedure. Failing such challenge within the applicable time limit, public policy, expressed in the maxim omnia praesumuntur rite esse acta, requires that after the expiry of the time limit it should be given all the effects in law of a valid decision.

Nevertheless, there may still be cases where it turns out in the course of proceedings to challenge a decision of a statutory authority that a declaration of rights rather than certiorari is the appropriate remedy. *Pyx Granite Co. Ltd.* v. *Ministry of Housing and Local Government* [1960] A.C. 260 provides an example of such a case.

So Order 53 since 1977 has provided a procedure by which every type of remedy for infringement of the rights of individuals that are entitled to protection in public law can be obtained in one and the same proceeding by way of an application for judicial review, and whichever remedy is found to be the most appropriate in the light of what has emerged upon the hearing of the application, can be granted to him. If what should emerge is that his complaint is not of an infringement of any of his rights that are entitled to protection in public law, but may be an infringement of his rights in private law and thus not a proper subject for judicial review, the court has power under rule 9 (5), instead of refusing the application, to order the proceedings to continue as if they had begun by writ. There is no such converse power under the R.S.C. to permit an action begun by writ to continue as if it were an application for judicial review; . . . nor do I see the need to amend the rules in order to create one.

My Lords, at the outset of this speech, I drew attention to the fact that the remedy by way of declaration of nullity of the decisions of the board was discretionary – as are all the remedies available upon judicial review. Counsel for the plaintiffs accordingly conceded that the fact that by adopting the procedure of an action begun by writ or by originating summons instead of an application for judicial review under Order 53 (from which there have now been removed all those disadvantages to applicants that had previously led the courts to countenance actions for declarations and injunctions as an alternative procedure for obtaining a remedy for infringement of the rights of the individual that are entitled to protection in public law only) the plaintiff had thereby been able to evade those protections against groundless, un-meritorious or tardy harassment that were afforded to statutory tribunals or decision-making public authorities by Order 53, and which might have resulted in the summary, and would in any event have resulted in the speedy disposition of the application, is among the matters fit to be taken into consideration by the judge in deciding whether to exercise his discretion by refusing to grant a declaration; but, it was contended, this he may only do at the conclusion of the trial.

So to delay the judge's decision as to how to exercise his discretion would defeat the public policy that underlies the grant of those protections: viz., the need, in the interests of good administration and of third parties who may be indirectly affected by the decision, for speedy certainty as to whether it has the effect of a decision that is valid in public law. An action for a declaration or injunction need not be commenced until the very end of the limitation period; if begun by writ, discovery and interlocutory proceedings may be prolonged and the plaintiffs are not required to support their allegations by evidence on oath until the actual trial. The period of uncertainty as to the validity of a decision that has been challenged upon allegations that may eventually turn out to be baseless and unsupported by evidence on oath, may thus be strung out for a very lengthy period, as the actions of the first three appellants in the instant appeals show. Unless such an action can be struck out summarily at the outset as an abuse of the process of the court the whole purpose of the public policy to which the change in Order 53 was directed would be defeated.

My Lords, Order 53 does not expressly provide that procedure by application for judicial review shall be the exclusive procedure available by which the remedy of a declaration or injunction may be obtained for infringement of rights that are entitled to protection under public law; nor does section 31 of the Supreme Court Act 1981. There is great variation between individual cases that fall within Order 53 and the Rules Committee and subsequently the legislature were, I think, for this reason content to rely upon the express and the inherent power of the High Court, exercised upon a case to case basis, to prevent abuse of its process whatever might be the form taken by that abuse. Accordingly, I do not think that your Lordships would be wise to use this as an occasion to lay down categories of cases in which it would necessarily always be an abuse to seek in an action begun by writ or originating summons a remedy against infringement of rights of the individual that are entitled to protection in public law.

The position of applicants for judicial review has been drastically ameliorated by the new Order 53. It has removed all those disadvantages, particularly in relation to discovery, that were manifestly unfair to them and had, in many cases, made applications for prerogative orders an inadequate remedy if justice was to be done. . . .

Now that those disadvantages to applicants have been removed and all remedies for infringements of rights protected by public law can be obtained upon an application for judicial review, as can also remedies for infringements of rights under private law if such infringements should also be involved, it would in my view as a general rule be contrary to public policy, and as such an abuse of the process of the court, to permit a person seeking to establish that a decision of a public authority infringed rights to which he was entitled to protection under public law to proceed by way of an ordinary action and by this means to evade the provisions of Order 53 for the protection of such authorities.

My Lords, I have described this as a general rule; for though it may normally be appropriate to apply it by the summary process of striking out the action, there may be exceptions, particularly where the invalidity of the decision arises as a collateral issue in a claim for infringement of a right of the plaintiff arising under private law, or where none of the parties objects to the adoption of the procedure by writ or originating summons. Whether there should be other exceptions should, in my view, at this stage in the development of procedural public law, be left to be decided on a case to case basis – a process that your Lordships will be continuing in the next case in which judgment is to be delivered to-day [*Cocks* v. *Thanet District Council*[18]].

---

[18] [[1982] 3 W.L.R. 1121.]

In the instant cases where the only relief sought is a declaration of nullity of the decisions of a statutory tribunal, the Board of Visitors of Hull Prison, as in any other case in which a similar declaration of nullity in public law is the only relief claimed, I have no hesitation, in agreement with the Court of Appeal, in holding that to allow the actions to proceed would be an abuse of the process of the court. They are blatant attempts to avoid the protections for the defendants for which Order 53 provides.

I would dismiss these appeals.

[LORD FRASER OF TULLYBELTON, LORD KEITH OF KINKEL, LORD BRIDGE OF HARWICH and LORD BRIGHTMAN agreed with LORD DIPLOCK.]

Appeal dismissed.

Notes

1. The Law Commission's *Report on Administrative Law Remedies,* Law Com. No. 73, Cmnd. 6407, on which see Note 2, p. 318 *supra,* stated in para. 34, which was headed 'Ordinary actions raising public law issues to remain unaffected', that, 'we are clearly of the opinion that the new procedure we envisage in respect of applications to the Divisional Court should not be exclusive in the sense that it would become the only way by which issues relating to the acts or omissions of public authorities should come before the courts'. The context makes it clear that the Commisison intended to give a choice of procedure in Administrative Law cases and that there should be a less restrictive approach than is evidenced in *O'Reilly* v. *Mackman.* Do the reasons given by Lord Diplock and in the following Notes for the exclusivity of Ord. 53 justify this departure from the scheme envisaged by the Law Commission? Contrast Lord Scarman in *I.R.C.* v. *Rossminster Ltd.* [1980] A.C. 952 at pp. 1052–3; Ackner and O'Connor L.JJ. in the Court of Appeal in *O'Reilly* v. *Mackman* [1982] 3 W.L.R. 604 at pp. 627–8 and 630.

2. Earlier cases permitting a choice of proceedings (*U.K.A.P.E* v. *A.C.A.S.* [1979] 1 W.L.R. 570; *De Falco* v. *Crawley B.C.* [1980] Q.B. 460) must now be read subject to *O'Reilly* v. *Mackman* (and *Cocks* v. *Thanet D.C.* [1982] 3 W.L.R. 1121, on which see Note 3 *infra*). There had also been various cases before *O'Reilly* v. *Mackman* in which it had been thought that the Ord. 53 procedure would have been more appropriate (although on occasions the court was still willing to consider the case despite that procedure not having been used): see *Uppal* v. *Home Office,* The Times, 11 November 1978; *Heywood* v. *Board of Visitors of Hull Prison* [1980] 1 W.L.R. 1386; *Royal College of Nursing of the U.K.* v. *D.H.S.S.* [1981] 1 All E.R. 545; *Payne* v. *Lord Harris of Greenwich* [1981] 1 W.L.R. 754; *Irlam Brick Co. Ltd.* v. *Warrington B.C.,* The Times, 5 February 1982; *Lambert* v. *Ealing L.B.C.* [1982] 1 W.L.R. 550; *Re Tillmire Common, Heslington* [1982] 2 All E.R. 615. Note also the opinion of Forbes J. in *Price Bros. (Rode Heath) Ltd.* v. *Department of the Environment* (1979) 38 P. & C.R. 579 at p. 586 concerning the action for a declaration which is equivalent in nature to an application for mandamus.

The requirement of leave and the safeguard it provides has often been mentioned in these cases – and see *O'Reilly* v. *Mackman* – as a factor in favour of the use of the Ord. 53 procedure. Other factors pointing in this direction which can be found in the case law include:

(*a*) the greater speed of the Ord. 53 procedure;
(*b*) the availability of the power provided by s. 31 (5), p. 316 *supra*; and

(c) the experience and expertise of the judge who will hear the application for judicial review: see further Blom-Cooper, p. 320 *supra*, and Note 4 *infra*).

The position regarding cross-examination on affidavits, interrogatories and discovery of documents was not regarded as a disadvantage of the Ord. 53 procedure in *O'Reilly* v. *Mackman* because of the limited scope of judicial review and the existence of Ord. 53, r. 8, p. 318 *supra* and see Note 8, p. 319 *supra*. Compare *I.R.C.* v. *Rossminster Ltd.* [1980] A.C. 952, the facts of which have been given at p. 91 *supra*. In this case, given the state of the affidavit evidence, the House of Lords took the view that a declaration should not have been granted: the full High Court trial process was thought to be necessary. Is this decision consistent with *O'Reilly* v. *Mackman*?

Precisely what the case by case approach will reveal as exceptions to the exclusive nature of the Ord. 53 procedure is, of course, a particular problem thrown up by *O'Reilly* v. *Mackman*. See, for example, the suggestion in Note 4 *infra*. At one time it might have been thought that if a restrictive approach were adopted to Ord. 53, r. 8, one exception to any ruling favouring the exclusive nature of the Ord. 53 procedure would be cases in which the determination of facts was relevant and in dispute: see the examples given by Lord Diplock in *O'Reilly* v. *Mackman* and note that he did not mention jurisdictional facts, on which see p. 52 *supra*. However, does *O'Reilly* v. *Mackman* suggest that this exception exists? And see Appendix.

3. In *Cocks* v. *Thanet D.C.* [1982] 3 W.L.R. 1121, referred to by Lord Diplock in *O'Reilly* v. *Mackman,* p. 334 *supra*, Lord Bridge applied the principles in *O'Reilly* v. *Mackman* and stated that an application challenging a housing authority's decision that the applicant had become homeless 'intentionally' could only be made by an application for judicial review. This was so even though the housing authority's decision prevented the applicant establishing a necessary condition precedent to the statutory private law right to be accommodated under the Housing (Homeless Persons) Act 1977. One reason for this appears to be that an application for judicial review would underline the limited scope of review of the housing authority's decision. See also on this point *Lambert* v. *Ealing L.B.C.* [1982] 1 W.L.R. 550 at pp. 557 and 559. Contrast, however, one of the exceptions to the general rule in *O'Reilly* v. *Mackman* which was collateral attack on the validity of a decision in a case involving private rights. This should be distinguished from *Cocks* v. *Thanet D.C.* and see further Question 3, p. 419 *infra* in relation to damages.

4. As was mentioned in Note 2 *supra,* the experience and expertise of the judges who hear applications for judicial review has been seen as a reason for regarding the Ord. 53 procedure as the most appropriate one. Interestingly enough, this factor was not mentioned by Lord Diplock in *O'Reilly* v. *Mackman*. Some cases have referred to the expertise of the Divisional Court, but note the changes to Ord. 53 coming into force in 1981 which are mentioned by Blom-Cooper, p. 321 *supra*. The point about expertise is an important one. The more Administrative Law questions are channelled to one particular group of judges with expertise in the subject, then the more this should develop a coherent and consistent body of case law.

Are there any cases in which greater expertise may not reside in the judges who would decide an application for judicial review? If so, might these constitute exceptions to the exclusive nature of the Ord. 53 procedure? (For one suggestion, see *Price Bros. (Rode Heath) Ltd.* v. *Department of the Environment* (1979) 38 P. & C.R. 579 (legality of the Secretary of State's decisions in planning matters), but this is now out of date in the light of the developments mentioned by Blom-Cooper, p. 321 *supra*.) Consider further *Re Tillmire Common, Heslington* [1982] 2 All E.R. 615, a case which was concerned with an alleged error of law on the face of the record. Although it was decided that, as a general rule, an application for judicial review should be used in such a case, it was hinted (at p. 622) that if the error alleged raised questions of law within the expertise of Chancery Division judges, then the position might be different. Note, however, that this case was decided before *O'Reilly* v. *Mackman*.

5. Questions concerning the validity of some particular action can arise in appeals to the courts from tribunals. In *Henry Moss of London Ltd.* v. *Customs and Excise Commissioners* [1981] 2 All E.R. 86 in which the validity of conditions laid down by the Commissioners was questioned, Lord Denning stated that this point could not be raised 'on an appeal properly so called'. An application for judicial review should have been brought, this being 'the proper way of challenging the validity of regulations and conditions' (p. 90). This view could no doubt be restricted to the case of appeals; for criticism of it, even in this limited sphere, see Bradley, [1981] P.L. 476 at p. 477. For other authorities, see Wade, pp. 822–3. Furthermore, an appeal in this sort of case today would fall into one of the categories of proceedings assigned by the *Practice Direction* [1981] 1 W.L.R. 1296 to the Crown Office list which is in any event to be heard by the group of judges referred to at p. 320 *supra*. Thus, the 'expertise argument', as opposed to others in favour of the exclusive use of Ord. 53, seems not to be applicable.

6. For Lord Diplock's view concerning the availability of a declaration under the Ord. 53 procedure even when certiorari is available, see p. 324 *supra*, commenting on *R.* v. *Board of Visitors of Hull Prison, ex p. St. Germain* [1979] Q.B. 425. Contrast the view of Lord Bridge in *Cocks* v. *Thanet D.C.* [1982] 3 W.L.R. 1121 (on which see Note 3 *supra*). Lord Bridge stated (at p. 1128):

Now that all public law remedies are available to be sought by the unified and simplified procedure of an application for judicial review, there could be no reason, where the quashing of a decision was the sole remedy sought, why it should be sought otherwise than by certiorari.

This suggests that a declaration would not be available in this situation under Ord. 53. If so, would it matter?

7. There is some difference in wording between s. 31(1) and (2) of the Supreme Court Act 1981, p. 315 *supra*, and Ord. 53, r. 1(1) and (2) which might have affected the 'exclusivity' argument: see Wade, p. 576. Nevertheless the provisions were described in *R.* v. *B.B.C., ex p. Lavelle* [1983] 1 W.L.R. 23 at p. 30 as 'almost identical', and see *O'Reilly* v. *Mackman*, p. 334 *supra*: 'exclusivity' has been achieved without reliance on the statute. Consider also *Tozer* v. *National Greyhound Racing Club Ltd.*, The Times, 16 May 1983.

8. On the distinction between public law and private law, see the Appendix.

11

RESTRICTION OF REMEDIES

LOCUS STANDI

Injunction and declaration

Boyce v. Paddington Borough Council

[1903] 1 Ch. 109   Chancery Division

The plaintiff sought an injunction to stop the defendant erecting a screen which would obstruct the light to the windows of blocks of flats he had built on some land he owned. The case in fact went to the Court of Appeal ([1903] 2 Ch. 556) and then to the House of Lords ([1906] A.C. 1), but it is an oft-quoted passage in the judgment of Buckley J. that is of relevence here.

BUCKLEY J.: . . . A plaintiff can sue without the Attorney-General in two cases: first, where the interference with the public right is such as that some private right of his is at the same time interfered with (e.g., where an obstruction is so placed in a highway that the owner of premises abutting upon the highway is specially affected by reason that the obstruction interferes with his private right to access from and to his premises to and from the highway); and, secondly, where no private right is interfered with, but the plaintiff, in respect of his public right, suffers special damage peculiar to himself from the interference with the public right. . . .

Bradbury v. Enfield London Borough Council, p. 289 *supra*

Notes

1. This section is primarily concerned with locus standi for the injunction and declaration in an action begun by writ or originating summons. In view of the decision in *O'Reilly* v. *Mackman*, p. 324 *supra*, that, as a general rule, Administrative Law cases should proceed by an application for judicial review, it might be thought somewhat academic. However, it may be that in applications for judicial review the courts will still look at the earlier case law on standing for declarations and injunctions. Furthermore, note that in *O'Reilly* v. *Mackman* Lord Diplock acknowledged that there might be exceptions to the exclusive nature of the application for judicial review. For locus standi under the application for judicial review, see p. 346 *infra*.

2. For a general survey of locus standi for the injunction before *Gouriet* v. *U.P.O.W.*, p. 339 *infra*, see Thio, *Locus Standi and Judicial Review*, Ch. 7. The case law has not been consistent. A restrictive approach can be found in, for example, *Thorne* v. *B.B.C.* [1967] 1 W.L.R. 1104 (legal right required) but *Bradbury* v. *Enfield*

L.B.C. reveals a more liberal view although the point was not expressly discussed; cf. *Lee* v. *Enfield L.B.C.* (1967) 66 L.G.R. 195. Indeed, in *R.* v. *G.L.C., ex p. Blackburn* [1976] 1 W.L.R. 550 at p. 559 Lord Denning, relying on *Bradbury* v. *Enfield L.B.C.,* went so far as to say that the court could in its discretion grant the remedy to anyone, although a 'busybody' would be turned away. Between the two extremes just mentioned lies the well-known proposition in *Boyce* v. *Paddington B.C. supra.* There was, therefore, a certain amount of disagreement to be found in the case law prior to *Gouriet.*

3. A survey of locus standi for the declaration prior to *Gouriet* would have revealed that consistency was also lacking in respect of that remedy. In one case (*Gregory* v. *Camden L.B.C.* [1966] 1 W.L.R. 899) the plaintiffs were held to lack standing for a declaration that two grants of planning permission were ultra vires, even though they were owners of adjoining land. This was on the ground that they had no legal rights in the matter. (On the interpretation of this case, however, see Wade, p. 581; Zamir, (1977) 30 C.L.P. 30 at pp. 45–6.) This approach could have been contrasted in particular with a case such as *Prescott* v. *Birmingham Corporation* [1955] Ch. 210, noted at p. 273 *supra* and with the views of Lord Denning in, for example, *Blackburn* v. *Attorney-General* [1971] 1 W.L.R. 1037. In *Prescott* v. *Birmingham Corporation,* it will be remembered, the plaintiff, a ratepayer, successfully sought a declaration that the local authority's scheme allowing free bus travel for certain classes of old people was ultra vires, but the locus standi of the plaintiff was not discussed, thereby weakening its authority on this point, on which see *Barrs* v. *Bethell* [1982] Ch. 294 at p. 308. In *Blackburn* v. *Attorney-General,* in which the plaintiff sought a declaration that it would be a breach of the law for Her Majesty's Government to sign the Treaty of Rome, Lord Denning was not prepared to rule out the action on the ground of locus standi, and see further his views in *R.* v. *G.L.C., ex p. Blackburn* [1976] 1 W.L.R. 550 at p. 559, noted *supra,* which also covered the declaration.

Again, as in the case of the injunction, somewhere between these two positions can be found the view expressed in *Boyce* v. *Paddington B.C. supra.* Although that case concerned a claim for an injunction, it was treated (obiter) as relevant to the declaration as well in *London Passenger Transport Board* v. *Moscrop* [1942] A.C. 332 at p. 345 per Viscount Maugham, with whose speech Lord Wright agreed.

For another view, which does not seem to fit any of the formulations just mentioned, see *Thorne R.D.C.* v. *Bunting* [1972] Ch. 470, and for general discussion see Zamir, *The Declaratory Judgment,* Ch. 7; (1977) 30 C.L.P. 30 at pp. 47–8; Thio, op. cit. Ch. 7; Heydon in *Locus Standi* (ed. Stein), pp. 40–55. On challenges to delegated legislation see Note 3, p. 343 *infra.*

Gouriet v. Union of Post Office Workers

[1978] A.C. 435 House of Lords

For the facts and decision in this case, see p. 127 *supra.*

LORD WILBERFORCE: ... Since, as I understand, others of your Lordships intend to deal fully ... with the authorities, I shall content myself with saying that, in my opinion, there is no support in authority for the proposition that declaratory relief can be granted unless the plaintiff, in proper proceedings, in which there is a dispute between the plaintiff and the defendant concerning their legal respective rights or liabilities either asserts a legal right which is denied or threatened, or claims immunity from some claim of the defendant against him or claims that the defendant is infringing or threatens to infringe some public right so as to inflict special damage on the plaintiff. The present proceedings do not possess the required characteristic. The case on which so much reliance was placed by the plaintiff – *Dyson v. Attorney-General* [1912] 1 Ch. 158, was one where a person was affected in his private rights: if the issue of the form had been proceeded with, and a penalty levied, the levy would have been wrongful and Mr. Dyson would have had a right to recover it. A right is none the less a right, or a wrong any the less a wrong, because millions of people have a similar right or may suffer a similar wrong. On the other hand, the case in this House of *London Passenger Transport Board v. Moscrop* [1942] A.C. 332 is clear and strong authority that where there is no interference with a private right and no personal damage, a declaratory relief cannot be sought without joining the Attorney-General as a party (s.c. as relator) – see pp. 344–345 *per* Viscount Maugham. . . .

VICOUNT DILHORNE: . . . Mr. Gouriet does not . . . assert a private right of any kind. . . .

The conclusion to which I have come in the light of the many authorities to which we were referred is that it is the law, and long established law, that save and in so far as the Local Government Act 1972, section 222,[1] gives local authorities a limited power so to do, only the Attorney-General can sue on behalf of the public for the purpose of preventing public wrongs and that a private individual cannot do so on behalf of the public though he may be able to do so if he will sustain injury as a result of a public wrong. In my opinion the cases establish that the courts have no jurisdiction to entertain such claims by a private individual who has not suffered and will not suffer damage. . . .

The majority of the Court of Appeal thought that the court had jurisdiction to make the declarations sought by virtue of R.S.C., Ord. 15, r. 16 which is in the same terms as Ord. 25, r. 5 made in 1883. It reads as follows:

'No action or other proceeding shall be open to objection on the ground that a merely declaratory judgment or order is sought thereby, and the court may make binding declarations of right whether or not any consequential relief is or could be claimed.'

It does not provide that an action will lie whenever a declaration is sought. It does not enlarge the jurisdiction of the court. It merely provides that no objection can be made on the ground only that a declaration is sought. In my opinion it provides no ground for saying that since 1883 the courts have had jurisdiction to entertain an action instituted by a person other than the Attorney-General who does not claim that any personal right or interest will be affected and who is seeking just to protect public rights. . . .

LORD DIPLOCK: . . . [T]hat there are limits to the jurisdiction [to grant declarations] is inherent in the nature of the relief: a declaration of rights. . . .

The early controversies as to whether a party applying for declaratory relief must have a subsisting cause of action or a right to some other relief as well

[1] [Set out at p. 306 *supra*.]

can now be forgotten. It is clearly established that he need not. Relief in the form of a declaration of right is generally superfluous for a plaintiff who has a subsisting cause of action. It is when an infringement of the plaintiff's rights in the future is threatened or when, unaccompanied by threats, there is a dispute between parties as to what their respective rights will be if something happens in the future, that the jurisdiction to make declarations of right can be most usefully invoked. But the jurisdiction of the court is not to declare the law generally or to give advisory opinions; it is confined to declaring contested legal rights, subsisting or future, of the parties represented in the litigation before it and not those of anyone else. . . .

LORD EDMUND-DAVIES: . . . The .point of cardinal importance that nevertheless remains is: assuming that the Attorney-General was entitled to decide as he did, does that preclude others who take a different view from seeking relief in the courts? For this purpose, we have to suppose that Mr. Gouriet's private legal rights have not been threatened or breached, and that although a public right is involved he has not suffered, and does not apprehend, any special damage over and above that sustained by the public at large. (If the circumstances are other than those predicated, a private citizen can sue in his own name and needs no consent from anyone before doing so: *Springhead Spinning Co.* v. *Riley*, L.R. 6 Eq. 551.)

[Having referred to the fact that the Court of Appeal had granted Gouriet certain declarations, he continued:]

But the primary question is: Had the court jurisdiction to make them? The answer given by the Attorney-General may be simply stated and has a familiar ring: Whenever public rights are in issue, the general rule is that relief may be sought only by, and granted solely at the request of, the Attorney-General. There are certain exceptions to the general rule, but none of them applies here. For example, there are statutory exceptions, such as section 222 of the Local Government Act 1972 which enables a local authority to institute civil proceedings for the promotion or protection of the interests of the inhabitants of their area: see *Solihull Metropolitan Borough Council* v. *Maxfern Ltd.* [1977] 1 W.L.R. 127. And there are the familiar common law exceptions to the general rule, dealt with by Buckley J. in *Boyce* v. *Paddington Borough Council* [1903] 1 Ch. 109, 114, where a private right has also been invaded or special damage suffered.

For the plaintiff, it is urged that the power of the court to grant declaratory relief is extremely wide. . . .

London Passenger Transport Board v. *Moscrop* [1942] A.C. 332 is a conclusive authority against Mr. Gouriet's entitlement to declaratory relief. Mr. Moscrop, an employee of the London Passenger Transport Board, sought a declaration that certain conditions of his employment were unlawful. Rejecting that claim, Viscount Maugham said, at pp. 344–345:

'My Lords, I cannot call to mind any action for a declaration in which (as in this case) the plaintiff claims no right for himself, but seeks to deprive others of a right which does not interfere with his liberty or his private rights. . . . We are not here concerned with anything but his civil right, if any, under the section. I think it plain that there has been no interference with any private right of his, nor has he suffered special damage peculiar to himself from the alleged breach . . .'

. . . [I]n my judgment the ratio decidendi of *Moscrop* applies in full force to this case. . . .

Conclusion

The plaintiff is confronted by insurmountable difficulties. For *either* (a) he is asserting a public right, which (since no private rights were invaded and he neither feared nor suffered any special damage in consequence) he cannot do without the concurrence of the Attorney-General in a relator action; or (b) he is asserting a private right by means of an action in tort, and that is barred against the defendant by section 14 of the Trade Union and Labour Relations Act 1974 and section 29 of the Post Office Act 1969. . . .

LORD FRASER OF TULLYBELTON: . . . The general rule is that a private person is only entitled to sue in respect of interference with a public right if either there is also interference with a private right of his or the interference with the public right will inflict special damage on him – *Boyce* v. *Paddington Borough Council* [1903] 1 Ch. 109. . . .

Notes

1. How does *Gouriet* tie in with the previous case law set out in Notes 2 and 3, p. 338 *supra*, concerning locus standi for the declaration and the injunction in an action begun by writ or originating summons? This question is of much less importance in Administrative Law today in the light of *O'Reilly* v. *Mackman*, p. 324 *supra*, and therefore the matter will not be discussed in any great detail here. It will merely be submitted that *Gouriet* supports the *Boyce* v. *Paddington B.C.* 'special damage' test, p. 338 *supra*; cf. Wade, p. 580. From the subsequent case law attention should perhaps be drawn to *Barrs* v. *Bethell* [1982] Ch. 294, on which see further Note 4 *infra*. Here Warner J., rejecting broader views on locus standi, accepted the 'special damage' test in a case which involved three ratepayers seeking, *inter alia*, declaratory relief in an action begun by writ against certain councillors and a local authority. (As to whether this sort of relief would have to be sought by an application for judicial review, see *O'Reilly* v. *Mackman*.)

Precisely what constitutes special damage for these purposes is not free from difficulty. It can at least be said that the damage suffered by the plaintiff must be greater than that suffered by the public in general, but this only takes us so far; for further discussion see Zamir, *The Declaratory Judgment*, pp. 270–2; Thio, op. cit., pp. 171–203; Cane, [1980] P.L. 303 at pp. 312–4.

2. Lord Diplock was the most restrictive of their Lordships in *Gouriet* on the question of locus standi for the declaration. See further his earlier views in *Anisminic Ltd.* v. *Foreign Compensation Commission* [1968] 2 Q.B. 862 at p. 910, but for a broad approach to rights see *J.J. Steeples* v. *Derbyshire C.C.* [1981] J.P.L. 581 at p. 588. Note also that in *I.R.C.* v. *National Federation of Self-Employed and Small Businesses Ltd.* [1982] A.C. 617 at p. 639 Lord Diplock interpreted *Gouriet* as accepting the 'special damage' test, though cf. p. 357 *infra*. In the *Self-Employed* case, p. 352 *infra*, his Lordship argued for wide access to the courts so as to preserve the

integrity of the rule of law and adopted a liberal view on standing for the declaration under an application for judicial review. *Gouriet* was explained as a case in which 'the defendant trade union . . . was not exercising any governmental powers; it was acting as a private citizen and could only be sued as such in a civil action under private law [and] was not amenable to any remedy in public law' ([1982] A.C. at p. 639). How do you think Lord Diplock would approach the question of locus standi for a declaration in a case that he sees as a public law one, but which falls within one of the exceptions to the general rule favouring the exclusivity of the Ord. 53 procedure which, according to *O'Reilly* v. *Mackman*, p. 334 *supra*, are to be revealed by the case by case approach? Might he wish to apply a more liberal test than that of 'special damage'? Cf. *Barrs* v. *Bethell* [1982] Ch. 294, noted *supra*.

3. The standing required on the part of a plaintiff challenging delegated legislation in an action for a declaration begun by writ or originating summons has been disputed: see Zamir, *The Declaratory Judgment*, pp. 276–81 rejecting the 'special damage' requirement, but see Thio, op. cit., pp. 183–9. *Gouriet* now seems to support the 'special damage' requirement, but, of course, it did not directly concern the validity of delegated legislation. (Nevertheless, see the comments on *London Association of Shipowners and Brokers* v. *London and India Docks Joint Committee* [1892] 3 Ch. 242 (which did concern delegated legislation) in *Gouriet* [1978] A.C. at pp. 480, 493 and 523). Consider further Wade, p. 581; cf. de Smith, p. 485. A challenge to the validity of delegated legislation is one of the situations in relation to which it has been questioned whether an application for judicial review would be available: see Note 2, p. 323 *supra*, but see the cases cited there.

4. It was suggested in Note 1, p. 338 *supra*, that cases dealing with locus standi for the declaration or injunction when the action had been begun by writ or originating summons might still be referred to when these remedies are sought by an application for judicial review. Nevertheless, the different nature of the proceedings has been seen as a reason for adopting different locus standi requirements. In *Barrs* v. *Bethell* [1982] Ch. 294 Warner J., disagreeing with some comments of Webster J. in *J.J. Steeples* v. *Derbyshire C.C.* [1981] J.P.L. 581, stated (at p. 313):

To my mind the crucial difference between an action [begun by writ] and an application for judicial review is that the former can be brought as of right whereas the latter requires the leave of the court. It appears to me, with respect, illogical to say that, because a person has a 'sufficient interest' [see s. 31 (3) of the Supreme Court Act 1981, p. 315 *supra*] to apply for a declaration or an injunction in proceedings for judicial review, he has a sufficient right to apply for the same relief in an action brought, without leave, in his own name. Nor do I think that the substantial difference between the two kinds of proceedings can be disregarded on the ground that at the end of the day the court has a discretion as to the relief to be given. As it was put by Woolf J. in *Covent Garden Community Association Ltd.* v. *Greater London Council* [[1981] J.P.L. 183]:

The fact that leave is required in judicial review proceedings and was required before prerogative orders prior to the new rule, is a significant factor to be taken into account in the approach to locus standi, since the requirement of leave provides a necessary filter to prevent frivolous actions by persons who have no sufficient interest in the result of the proceeding.

. . . [I]n *Reg* v. *Inland Revenue Commissioners, Ex parte Natiional Federation of Self-Employed and Small Businesses Ltd.* [1982] A.C. 617, 630, Lord Wilberforce observed that the right for the court to refuse a person, at the threshold, leave to apply for judicial review '. . . is an important safeguard against the courts being flooded and public bodies harassed by irresponsible applications.' The Court's discretion as to the relief to be given does not afford a prospective defendant the same kind of protection. It does not protect him from the burden of being subjected to litigation or from the risk of having to bear all or part of the costs of it – because the plaintiff may not be good for them and because, in any case, only party and party costs will normally be recoverable from him.

This passage suggests one of the functions of locus standi. What other functions might it perform? See Cane, [1980] P.L. 303; Thio, op. cit., Ch. 1.

Certiorari and prohibition

R. v. Thames Magistrates' Court, ex parte Greenbaum

(1957) 55 L.G.R. 129   Court of Appeal

Mr. Gritzman (G1) and Mr. Greenbaum (G2), who were street traders, both wanted a particular pitch in a street. The relevant Borough Council decided in G2's favour, but G1 appealed to the Metropolitan Magistrate against the refusal to grant a licence for the pitch to him. G2 gave evidence in the appeal proceedings but was not a party to them. The Magistrate decided in G1's favour and the Borough Council complied with this ruling. G2 successfully applied to the Divisional Court for certiorari, the court holding that the Magistrate had lacked jurisdiction to hear G1's appeal. On appeal to the Court of Appeal.

DENNING L.J.: [having held that the Magistrate had had no jurisdiction to hear G2's appeal, continued:] It was said that Mr. Greenbaum had no *locus standi* to come before the Court of Queen's Bench because (it was said) he was not a party to the proceedings before the magistrate: that the only people before the magistrate were Mr. Gritzman and the borough council, and, therefore, Mr. Greenbaum had no place from which to come before the Court and ask for a *certiorari* to quash the magistrate's decision. Upon that matter I would say that the remedy by *certiorari* is not confined to the parties before the lower court. It extends to any person aggrieved, and, furthermore, to any stranger. The Court of Queen's Bench, by virtue of its inherent jurisdiction over inferior tribunals, has always the right to interfere if it sees that the lower tribunal is going or has gone beyond its jurisdiction, or has acted in a way contrary to law, or appears from the record to have fallen into error in point of law: and it can so interfere, not only at the instance of a party or a person aggrieved but also at the instance of a stranger if it thinks proper. When application is made to it by a party or a person aggrieved, it will intervene (as it is said) *ex debito justitiae*, in justice to the applicant. When application is made by a stranger it considers whether the public interest demands its intervention. In either case it is a matter which rests ultimately in the discretion of the Court. In this regard I would refer to *Reg. v. Justices of Surrey* (1870) L.R. 5 Q.B. 466.

I should have thought that in this case Mr. Greenbaum was certainly a person aggrieved; and not a stranger. He was affected by the magistrate's order because the magistrate ordered another person to be put on his pitch. It is a proper case for the intervention of the Court by means of *certiorari*. . . .

PARKER L.J.: . . . [T]he remedy by way of *certiorari* is a discretionary remedy. Anybody can apply for it – a member of the public who has been inconvenienced, or a particular party or a person who has a particular grievance of his own. If the application is made by what for convenience one may call a stranger, the remedy is purely discretionary. Where, however, it is made by a person who has a particular grievance of his own, whether as a party or otherwise, then the remedy lies *ex debito justitiae*, and that, I think, has always been the position from 1869 (cf. *Reg.* v. *Surrey Justices (supra)* and *Reg.* v. *Manchester Legal Aid Committee, ex parte R. A. Brand and Co., Ltd.* [1952] 2 Q.B. 413). The remedy will be granted whenever the applicant has shown a particular grievance of his own beyond some inconvenience suffered by the general public.

Applying those tests, I should have thought that in this case it was clear beyond doubt that Mr. Greenbaum was a person with a particular grievance of his own. . . .

[ROMER L.J. delivered a judgment in favour of dismissing the appeal.]

Appeal dismissed.

Question

Durayappah v. *Fernando*, pp. 226 and 230 *supra*, was explained in *F. Hoffmann-La Roche & Co. A.G.* v. *Secretary of State for Trade and Industry*, p. 94 *supra*, as a decision on locus standi. If so, should the appellant, who sought certiorari amongst other remedies have been refused relief? (See the Note at p. 241 *supra*.)

Notes

1. If the application is by a person aggrieved, it is said that certiorari will be granted *ex debito justitiae*; but, as Lord Denning acknowledged in *Greenbaum*'s case, the court does retain a discretion to refuse the remedy to such a person if his conduct merits it (though see Note 2 *infra*).

2. *Greenbaum*'s case concerned the remedy of certiorari but locus standi for prohibition has been said to be 'very analogous' (*R.* v. *Surrey JJ.* (1870) L.R. 5 Q.B. 466 at p. 472) and will not be discussed separately here. One possible difference should be mentioned, however. There is authority for the view that where a lack of jurisdiction is apparent on the face of the proceedings, prohibition *must* be granted even to a complete stranger; but see Note 3, p. 365 *infra*, where it is pointed out that (*a*) the existence of this rule today has been doubted and (*b*) if it exists today the rule *may* also apply to certiorari.

3. There has been some dispute on the question whether any member of the public can apply for certiorari or prohibition. *Greenbaum*'s case represents one side of the argument; for discussion of the competing authorities, see Thio, op. cit., Ch. 4 and pp. 91–102. Thio favours the view that only a person aggrieved may seek either remedy: for the contrary view see Wade, p. 583; de Smith, p. 418 (on certiorari; cf. pp. 416–8 for his views on prohibition). This difference of opinion can be illustrated by some of Lord Denning's pronouncements over the years. His views in *Greenbaum*'s case should be contrasted with his statements in *R.* v. *Paddington Valuation Officer, ex p. Peachey Property Corporation Ltd.* [1966] 1 Q.B. 380, where (with the concurrence of the other members of the Court of Appeal) he seems to be suggesting that only a person aggrieved can apply (and see also *R.* v. *Liverpool Corporation, ex p. Liverpool Taxi Fleet Operators' Association* [1972] 2 Q.B. 299). On the other hand, in *R.* v. *G.L.C., ex p. Blackburn* [1976] 1 W.L.R. 550, in a passage of which part is set out at p. 353 *infra*, the Master of the Rolls reverts to the view he had expressed in

Greenbaum's case that any member of the public can apply. Nevertheless, in the *Blackburn* case (as on previous occasions) it is pointed out that the 'busybody who is interfering in things that do not concern him' will be refused relief. Since Lord Denning, in the *Liverpool Taxi* case for example, has taken a broad view of the meaning of the phrase 'person aggrieved' – anyone 'whose interests may be prejudicially affected by what is taking place' [1972] 2 Q.B. at pp. 308–9 – the difference between his statements in these cases may not be as great as might first appear. On the *Blackburn* case, which concerned prohibition and which adopted a liberal approach to locus standi, see p. 353 *infra* where it is summarised by Lord Diplock in his speech in the *Self-Employed* case.

4. Who is a 'person aggrieved'? Compare with Parker L.J.'s definition of such a person the broader view of Lord Denning referred to in Note 3 *supra*. For example, in the *Paddington Valuation Officer* case the ratepayer company in its challenge to the rating valuation list was held to be a 'person aggrieved'. Could a ratepayer fit within Parker L.J.'s definition? See further *R. v. Hendon R.D.C., ex p. Chorley* [1933] 2 K.B. 696, but this case is difficult to classify as the court, although granting the remedy, did not expressly discuss locus standi; and for comment on that decision, see *R. v. Bradford-on-Avon U.D.C., ex p. Boulton* [1964] 1 W.L.R. 1136 at p. 1145. In the *Blackburn* case, summarised at p. 353 *infra*, the fact that Mrs. Blackburn was a ratepayer was an additional reason (per Stephenson L.J.) and the reason (per Bridge L.J.) why she had locus standi, but the 'person aggrieved' terminology was not used.

5. For locus standi in relation to mandamus, see the cases mentioned in *I.R.C. v. National Federation of Self-Employed and Small Businesses Ltd.*, *infra*, and see further p. 403 *infra*, where some of the case law is discussed.

6. The phrase 'person aggrieved' appears in various statutes as a description of those people who may appeal from a particular decision made under that statute. See Note 3, p. 394 *infra*.

The new law of standing

Supreme Court Act 1981, Section 31 (3), p. 315 *supra*

Inland Revenue Commissioners v. National Federation of Self-Employed and Small Businesses Ltd.

[1982] A.C. 617   House of Lords

Section 31 (3) of the Supreme Court Act 1981 repeats the provision that is contained in R.S.C. Ord. 53, r. 3 (5). It is this latter provision which is discussed in these extracts.

LORD WILBERFORCE: My Lords, the respondent federation, whose name sufficiently describes its nature, is asking for an order upon the Inland Revenue Commissioners to assess and collect arrears of income said to be due by a number of people compendiously described as 'Fleet Street casuals.' These are workers in the printing industry who, under a practice sanctioned apparently by their unions and their employers, have for some years been engaged in a process of depriving the Inland Revenue of tax due in respect of their casual earnings. This they appear to have done by filling in false or imaginary names on the call slips presented on collecting their pay. The sums involved were very considerable. The Inland Revenue, having become aware of this, made an arrangement ... under which these workers are to register in respect of their casual employment, so that in the future tax can be collected in the normal way. Further, arrears of tax from 1977–1978 are to be paid and current investigations are to proceed, but investigations as to tax lost in earlier years are not to be made. This arrangement, described inaccurately as an 'amnesty,' the federation wishes to attack. It asserts that the revenue acted unlawfully in not pursuing the claim for the full amount of tax due. It claims that the board exceeded its powers in granting the 'amnesty;' alternatively that if it had power to grant it, reasons should be given and that those given cannot be sustained; that the board took into account matters to which it was not entitled to have regard; that the board ought to act fairly as between taxpayers[2] and has not done so; and that the board is under a duty to see that income tax is duly assessed, charged, and collected.

The proceedings have been brought by the procedure now called 'judicial review.' There are two claims, the first for a declaration that the Board of Inland Revenue 'acted unlawfully' in granting an amnesty to the casual workers; the second, for an order of mandamus to assess and collect income tax from the casual workers according to the law. These two claims rest, for present purposes, upon the same basis, since a declaration is merely an alternative kind of relief which can only be given if, apart from convenience, the case would have been one for mandamus.

In the Order which introduced the simplified remedies by way of judicial review (R.S.C., Ord. 53, dating from 1977), it is laid down (r. 3.(5)) that: 'The court shall not grant leave unless it considers that the applicant has a sufficient interest in the matter to which the application relates.' The issue which comes before us is presented as one related solely to the question whether the federation has the 'sufficient interest' required.

In the Divisional Court, when the motion for judicial review came before it, the point as to locus standi was treated as a preliminary point. 'Before we embark on the case itself,' said Lord Widgery C.J., 'we have to decide whether the federation has power to bring it at all.' After hearing argument, the court decided that it had not. The matter went to the Court of Appeal [1980] Q.B. 407, and again argument was concentrated on the preliminary point, though it, and the judgments, did range over the merits. The Court of Appeal by majority reversed the Divisional Court and made a declaration that the applicants have a sufficient interest to apply for judicial review. On final appeal to this House, the two sides concurred in stating that the only ground for decision was whether the applicants have such sufficient interest.

I think it is unfortunate that this course has been taken. There may be simple cases in which it can be seen at the earliest stage that the person applying for judicial review has no interest at all, or no sufficient interest to

---

[2] [Lord Wilberforce later referred to the allegation, on behalf of the Federation, of 'the very different attitude, viz. one of strictness and even severity, taken by the revenue as regards persons represented by the federation' ([1982] A.C. at p. 633).]

support the application: then it would be quite correct at the threshold to refuse him leave to apply. The right to do so is an important safeguard against the courts being flooded and public bodies harassed by irresponsible applications. But in other cases this will not be so. In these it will be necessary to consider the powers or the duties in law of those against whom the relief is asked, the position of the applicant in relation to those powers or duties, and to the breach of those said to have been committed. In other words, the question of sufficient interest can not, in such cases, be considered in the abstract, or as an isolated point: it must be taken together with the legal and factual context. The rule requires sufficient interest *in the matter to which the application relates*. This, in the present case, necessarily involves the whole question of the duties of the Inland Revenue and the breaches or failure of those duties of which the respondents complain.

Before proceeding to consideration of these matters, something more needs to be said about the threshold requirement of 'sufficient interest.' The courts in exercising the power to grant prerogative writs, or, since 1938, prerogative orders, have always reserved the right to be satisfied that the applicant had some genuine locus standi to appear before it. This they expressed in different ways. Sometimes it was said, usually in relation to certiorari, that the applicant must be a person aggrieved; or having a particular grievance (*Reg.* v. *Thames Magistrates' Court, Ex parte Greenbaum* (1957) 55 L.G.R. 129); usually in relation to mandamus, that he must have a specific legal right (*Reg.* v. *Lewisham Union Guardians* [1897] 1 Q.B. 498 and *Reg.* v. *Russell, Ex parte Beaverbrook Newspapers Ltd.* [1969] 1 Q.B. 342); sometimes that he must have a sufficient interest (*Reg.* v. *Cotham* [1898] 1 Q.B. 802, 804 (mandamus), *Ex parte Stott* [1916] 1 K.B. 7 (certiorari)). By 1977, when R.S.C., Ord. 53 was introduced, the courts, guided by Lord Parker C.J., in cases where mandamus was sought, were moving away from the *Lewisham Union* test of specific legal right, to one of sufficient interest. In *Reg.* v. *Russell* Lord Parker had tentatively adhered to the test of legal specific right but in *Reg.* v. *Customs and Excise Commissioners, Ex parte Cook* [1970] 1 W.L.R. 450 he had moved to sufficient interest. Shortly afterwards the new rule (R.S.C., Ord. 53, r. 3) was drafted with these words.

R.S.C., Ord. 53 was, it is well known, introduced to simplify the procedure of applying for the relief formerly given by prerogative writ or order – so the old technical rules no longer apply. So far as the substantive law is concerned, this remained unchanged: the Administration of Justice (Miscellaneous Provisions) Act 1938 preserved the jurisdiction existing before the Act, and the same preservation is contemplated by legislation now pending.[3] The Order, furthermore, did not remove the requirement to show locus standi. On the contrary, in rule 3, it stated this in the form of a threshold requirement to be found by the court. For all cases the text is expressed as one of sufficient interest in the matter to which the application relates. As to this I would state two negative propositions. First, it does not remove the whole – and vitally

---

[3] [The Supreme Court Act 1981.]

important – question of locus standi into the realm of pure discretion. The matter is one for decision, a mixed decision of fact and law, which the court must decide on legal principles. Secondly, the fact that the same words are used to cover all the forms of remedy allowed by the rule does not mean that the test is the same in all cases. When Lord Parker C.J. said that in cases of mandamus the test may well be stricter (sc. than in certiorari) – the *Beaverbrook Newspapers* case [1969] 1 Q.B. 342 and in *Cook's* case [1970] 1 W.L.R. 450, 455F, 'on a very strict basis,' he was not stating a technical rule – which can now be discarded – but a rule of common sense, reflecting the different character of the relief asked for. It would seem obvious enough that the interest of a person seeking to compel an authority to carry out a duty is different from that of a person complaining that a judicial or administrative body has, to his detriment, exceeded its powers. Whether one calls for a stricter rule than the other may be a linguistic point: they are certainly different and we should be unwise in our enthusiasm for liberation from procedural fetters to discard reasoned authorities which illustrate this. It is hardly necessary to add that recognition of the value of guiding authorities does not mean that the process of judicial review must stand still.

In the present case we are in the area of mandamus – an alleged failure to perform a duty. It was submitted by the Lord Advocate that in such cases we should be guided by the definition of the duty – in this case statutory – and inquire whether expressly, or by implication, this definition indicates – or the contrary – that the complaining applicant is within the scope or ambit of the duty. I think that this is at least a good working rule though perhaps not an exhaustive one.

The Inland Revenue Commissioners are a statutory body. Their duties are, relevantly, defined in the Inland Revenue Regulation Act 1890 and the Taxes Management Act 1970. Section 1 of the Act of 1890 authorises the appointment of commissioners 'for the collection and management of inland revenue' and confers on the commissioners 'all necessary powers for carrying into execution every Act of Parliament relating to inland revenue.' By section 13 the commissioners must 'collect and cause to be collected every part of inland revenue and all money under their care and management and keep distinct accounts thereof.'

Section 1 of the Act of 1970 provides that 'Income tax . . . shall be under the care and management of the commissioners.' This Act contains the very wide powers of the board and of inspectors of taxes to make assessments upon persons designated by Parliament as liable to pay income tax. With regard to casual employment, there is a procedure laid down by statutory instrument (the Income Tax (Employments) Regulations 1973 (S.I. 1973 No. 334)) by which inspectors of taxes may proceed by way of direct assessment or in accordance with any special arrangements which the Commissioners of Inland Revenue may make for the collection of the tax. . . . [I]t was a 'special arrangement' that the commissioners set out to make in the present case.

From this summary analysis it is clear that the Inland Revenue Commissioners are not immune from the process of judicial review. They are an administrative body with statutory duties, which the courts, in principle, can supervise. They have indeed done so – see *Reg.* v. *Income Tax Special Commissioners* (1881) 21 Q.B.D. 313 (mandamus) and *Income Tax Special Commissioners* v. *Linsleys (Established 1894) Ltd.* [1958] A.C. 569, where it was not doubted that a mandamus could be issued if the facts had been right. It must follow from these cases and from principle that a taxpayer would not be excluded from seeking judicial review if he could show that the revenue had either failed in its statutory duty toward him or had been guilty of some action which was an abuse of their powers or outside their powers altogether. Such a collateral attack – as contrasted with a direct appeal on law to the courts – would no doubt be rare, but the possibility certainly exists.

The position of other taxpayers – other than the taxpayers whose assessment is in question – and their right to challenge the revenue's assessment or non-assessment of that taxpayer, must be judged according to whether, consistently with the legislation, they can be considered as having sufficient interest to complain of what has been done or omitted. I proceed thereto to examine the revenue's duties in that light.

These duties are expressed in very general terms and it is necessary to take account also of the framework of the income tax legislation. This establishes that the commissioners must assess each individual taxpayer in relation to his circumstances. Such assessments and all information regarding taxpayers' affairs are strictly confidential. There is no list or record of assessments which can be inspected by other taxpayers. Nor is there any common fund of the produce of income tax in which income taxpayers as a whole can be said to have any interest. The produce of income tax, together with that of other inland revenue taxes, is paid into the consolidated fund which is at the disposal of Parliament for any purposes that Parliament thinks fit.

The position of taxpayers is therefore very different from that of ratepayers. As explained in *Arsenal Football Club Ltd.* v. *Ende* [1979] A.C. 1, the amount of rates assessed upon ratepayers is ascertainable by the public through the valuation list. The produce of rates goes into a common fund applicable for the benefit of the ratepayers. Thus any ratepayer has an interest, direct and sufficient, in the rates levied upon other ratepayers; for this reason, his right as a 'person aggrieved' to challenge assessments upon them has long been recognised and is so now in section 69 of the General Rate Act 1967. This right was given effect to in the *Arsenal* case.

The structure of the legislation relating to income tax, on the other hand, makes clear that no corresponding right is intended to be conferred upon taxpayers. Not only is there no express or implied provision in the legislation upon which such a right could be claimed, but to allow it would be subversive of the whole system, which involves that the commissioners' duties are to the Crown, and that matters relating to income tax are between the commissioners and the taxpayer concerned. No other person is given any right to make proposals about the tax payable by any individual: he cannot even inquire as to such tax. The total confidentiality of assessments and of negotiations between individuals and the revenue is a vital element in the working of the system. As a matter of general principle I would hold that one taxpayer has no sufficient interest in asking the court to investigate the tax affairs of another taxpayer or to complain that the latter has been under-assessed or over-assessed; indeed, there is a strong public interest that he should not. And this principle applies equally to groups of taxpayers: an aggregate of individuals each of whom has no interest cannot of itself have an interest.

That a case can never arise in which the acts or abstentions of the revenue can be brought before the court I am certainly not prepared to assert, nor that, in a case of sufficient gravity, the court might not be able to hold that another taxpayer or other taxpayers could challenge them. Whether this situation has been reached or not must depend upon an examination, upon evidence, of what breach of duty or illegality is alleged. Upon this, and relating it to the position of the complainant, the court has to make its decision.

[His Lordship then discussed the evidence in detail, in the course of which he said: '. . . a sense of fairness as between one taxpayer or group of taxpayers and another is an important objective, so that a sense of unfairness may be the beginning of a recognisable grievance. I say the beginning, because the income tax legislation contains a large number of anomalies which are naturally not thought to be fair to those disadvantaged.' After his review of the evidence, he continued:]

On the evidence as a whole, I fail to see how any court considering it as such and not confining its attention to an abstract question of locus standi could avoid reaching the conclusion that the Inland Revenue . . . were acting in this matter genuinely in the care and management of the taxes, under the powers entrusted to them. This has no resemblance to any kind of case where the court ought, at the instance of a taxpayer, to intervene. To do so would involve permitting a taxpayer or a group of taxpayers to call in question the exercise of management powers and involve the court itself in a management exercise. Judicial review under any of its headings does not extend into this area. Finally, if as I think, the case against the revenue does not, on the evidence, leave the ground, no court, in my opinion, would consider ordering discovery against the revenue in the hope of eliciting some impropriety. Looking at the matter as a whole, I am of opinion that the Divisional Court, while justified on the ex parte application in granting leave, ought, having regard to the nature of 'the matter' raised, to have held that the federation had shown no sufficient interest in that matter to justify its application for relief. I would therefore allow the appeal and order that the originating motion be dismissed.

LORD DIPLOCK: . . . I agree with my noble and learned friend that no court considering [the] evidence could avoid reaching the conclusion that the board and its inspector were acting solely for 'good management' reasons and in the lawful exercise of the discretion which the statutes confer on them.

For my part, I should prefer to allow the appeal and dismiss the federation's application under R.S.C., Ord. 53, not upon the specific ground of no sufficient interest but upon the more general ground that it has not been

shown that in the matter of which complaint was made, the treatment of the
tax liabilities of the Fleet Street casuals, the board did anything that was ultra
vires or unlawful. They acted in the bona fide exercise of the wide managerial
discretion conferred on them by statute. Since judicial review is available only
as a remedy for conduct of a public officer, or authority which is ultra vires or
unlawful, but not for acts done lawfully in the exercise of an administrative
discretion which are complained of only as being unfair or unwise, there is a
sense in which it may be said that the federation had not a sufficient interest in
the matter to which their application related; but this is not a helpful statement; it would be equally true of anyone, including the Attorney-General,
who sought to complain.

[Nevertheless, his Lordship went on to consider the question of the Federation's locus standi.]

Your Lordships can take judicial notice of the fact that the main purpose of
the new Order 53 was to sweep away [the] procedural differences [between
the declaration and the injunction on the one hand and the prerogative orders
on the other, and also between the prerogative orders themselves] including,
in particular, differences as to locus standi; to substitute for them a single
simplified procedure for obtaining all forms of relief, and to leave to the court
a wide discretion as to what interlocutory directions, including orders for
discovery, were appropriate to the particular case.

[Having discussed *Gouriet* v. *U.P.O.W.* pp. 127, 299 and 339 *supra*, he
distinguished it on the ground that the union 'was not exercising any governmental powers' and 'was not amenable to any remedy in public law'. LORD
DIPLOCK then set out the passage to be found at p. 322 *supra* and continued:]

... I turn first to consider what constituted locus standi to apply for one or
other of the prerogative orders immediately before the new Order 53 came
into force. ...

The rules as to 'standing' for the purpose of applying for prerogative
orders, like most of English public law, are not to be found in any statute.
They were made by judges, by judges they can be changed; and so they have
been over the years to meet the need to preserve the integrity of the rule of law
despite changes in the social structure, methods of government and the extent
to which the activities of private citizens are controlled by governmental
authorities, that have been taking place continuously, sometimes slowly,
sometimes swiftly, since the rules were originally propounded. Those changes
have been particularly rapid since World War II. Any judicial statements on
matters of public law if made before 1950 are likely to be a misleading guide
to what the law is today.

In 1951, the decision of the Divisional Court in *Reg.* v. *Northumberland
Compensation Appeal Tribunal, Ex parte Shaw* [1951] 1 Q.B. 711 resur-
rected error of law upon the face of the record as a ground for granting
certiorari. Parliament by the Tribunals and Inquiries Act 1958 followed this
up by requiring reasons to be given for many administrative decisions that had

previously been cloaked in silence; and the years that followed between then and 1977 witnessed a dramatic liberalisation of access to the courts for the purpose of obtaining prerogative orders against persons and authorities exercising governmental powers. This involved a virtual abandonment of the former restrictive rules as to the locus standi of persons seeking such orders. The process of liberalisation of access to the courts and the progressive discarding of technical limitations upon locus standi is too well known to call for detailed citation of the cases by which it may be demonstrated. They are referred to and discussed in *Wade, Administrative Law*, 4th ed. (1977), pp. 543–546 (prohibition and certiorari) and pp. 610–612 (mandamus). The author points out there that although lip-service continued to be paid to a difference in standing required to entitle an applicant to mandamus on the one hand and prohibition or certiorari on the other, in practice the courts found some way of treating the locus standi for all three remedies as being the same. A striking example of this is to be found in *Reg. v. Hereford Corporation, Ex parte Harrower* [1970] 1 W.L.R. 1424, where the applicants were treated as having locus standi in their capacity as ratepayers though their real interest in the matter was as electrical contractors only. For my part I need only refer to *Reg. v. Greater London Council, Ex parte Blackburn* [1976] 1 W.L.R. 550. In that case Mr. Blackburn who lived in London with his wife who was a ratepayer, applied successfully for an order of prohibition against the council to stop them acting in breach of their statutory duty to prevent the exhibition of pornographic films within their administrative area. Mrs. Blackburn was also a party to the application. Lord Denning M.R. and Stephenson L.J. were of opinion that both Mr. and Mrs. Blackburn had locus standi to make the application: Mr. Blackburn because he lived within the administrative area of the council and had children who might be harmed by seeing pornographic films and Mrs. Blackburn not only as a parent but also on the additional ground that she was a ratepayer. Bridge L.J. relied only on Mrs. Blackburn's status as a ratepayer; a class of persons to whom for historical reasons the court of King's Bench afforded generous access to control ultra vires activities of the public bodies to whose expenses they contributed. But now that local government franchise is not limited to ratepayers, this distinction between the two applicants strikes me as carrying technicality to the limits of absurdity having regard to the subject matter of the application in the *Blackburn* case. I agree in substance with what Lord Denning M.R. said, at p. 559, though in language more eloquent than it would be my normal style to use:

'I regard it as a matter of high constitutional principle that if there is good ground for supposing that a government department or a public authority is transgressing the law, or is about to transgress it, in a way which offends or injures thousands of Her Majesty's subjects, then any one of those offended or injured can draw it to the attention of the courts of law and seek to have the law enforced, and the courts *in their discretion* can grant whatever remedy is appropriate.' (The italics in this quotation are my own).

The reference here is to flagrant and serious breaches of the law by persons and authorities exercising governmental functions which are continuing unchecked. To revert to technical restrictions on locus standi to prevent this that were current 30 years or more would be to reverse that progress towards a comprehensive system of administrative law that I regard as having been the greatest achievement of the English courts in my judicial lifetime.

. . . The expression that [the draftsman] used in rule 3 (5) had cropped up sporadically in judgments relating to prerogative writs and orders and consisted of ordinary English words which, on the face of them, leave the court an unfettered discretion to decide what in its own good judgment it considers to be 'a sufficient interest' on the part of an applicant in the particular circumstances of the case before it. For my part I would not strain to give them any narrower meaning.

The procedure under the new Order 53 involves two stages: (1) the application for leave to apply for judicial review, and (2) if leave is granted, the hearing of the application itself. The former, or 'threshold,' stage is regulated by rule 3. The application for leave to apply for judicial review is made initially ex parte, but may be adjourned for the persons or bodies against whom relief is sought to be represented. This did not happen in the instant case. Rule 3 (5) specifically requires the court to consider at this stage whether 'it considers that the applicant has a sufficient interest in the matter to which the application relates.' So this is a 'threshold' question in the sense that the court must direct its mind to it and form a prima facie view about it upon the material that is available at the first stage. The prima facie view so formed, if favourable to the applicant, may alter on further consideration in the light of further evidence that may be before the court at the second stage, the hearing of the application for judicial review itself.

The need for leave to start proceedings for remedies in public law is not new. It applied previously to applications for prerogative orders, though not to civil actions for injunctions or declarations. Its purpose is to prevent the time of the court being wasted by busybodies with misguided or trivial complaints of administrative error, and to remove the uncertainty in which public officers and authorities might be left as to whether they could safely proceed with administrative action while proceedings for judicial review of it were actually pending even though misconceived. . . .

My Lords, at the threshold stage, for the federation to make out a prima facie case of reasonable suspicion that the board in showing a discriminatory leniency to a substantial class of taxpayers had done so for ulterior reasons extraneous to good management, and thereby deprived the national exchequer of considerable sums of money, constituted what was in my view reason enough for the Divisional Court to consider that the federation or, for that matter, any taxpayer, had a sufficient interest to apply to have the question whether the board was acting ultra vires reviewed by the court. The whole purpose of requiring that leave should first be obtained to make the application for judicial review would be defeated if the court were to go into the matter in any depth at that stage. If, on a quick perusal of the material then

available, the court thinks that it discloses what might on further consideration turn out to be an arguable case in favour of granting to the applicant the
relief claimed, it ought, in the exercise of a judicial discretion, to give him
leave to apply for that relief. The discretion that the court is exercising at this
stage is not the same as that which it is called upon to exercise when all the
evidence is in and the matter has been fully argued at the hearing of the
application. . . .

It would, in my view, be a grave lacuna in our system of public law if a
pressure group, like the federation, or even a single public-spirited taxpayer,
were prevented by outdated technical rules of locus standi from bringing the
matter to the attention of the court to vindicate the rule of law and get the
unlawful conduct stopped. The Attorney-General, although he occasionally
applies for prerogative orders against public authorities that do not form part
of central government, in practice never does so against government departments. It is not, in my view, a sufficient answer to say that judicial review of
the actions of officers or departments of central government is unnecessary
because they are accountable to Parliament for the way in which they carry
out their functions. They are accountable to Parliament for what they do so
far as regards efficiency and policy, and of that Parliament is the only judge;
they are responsible to a court of justice for the lawfulness of what they do,
and of that the court is the only judge. . . .

LORD FRASER OF TULLYBELTON: My Lords, I agree with all my noble
and learned friends that this appeal should be allowed. I agree with the
reasoning of Lord Wilberforce and Lord Roskill but I wish to explain my
reasons in my own words.

. . . [T]he question whether the respondents have a sufficient interest to
make the application at all is a separate, and logically prior, question which
has to be answered affirmatively before any question on the merits arises.
Refusal of the application on its merits therefore implies that the prior
question has been answered affirmatively. I recognise that in some cases,
perhaps in many, it may be impracticable to decide whether an applicant has
a sufficient interest or not, without having evidence from both parties as to
the matter to which the application relates, and that, in such cases, the court
before whom the matter comes in the first instance cannot refuse leave to the
applicant at the ex parte stage, under rule 3 (5). The court which grants leave
at that stage will do so on the footing that it makes a provisional finding of
sufficient interest, subject to revisal later on, and it is therefore not necessarily
to be criticised merely because the final decision is that the applicant did not
have sufficient interest. But where, after seeing the evidence of both parties,
the proper conclusion is that the applicant did not have a sufficient interest to
make the application, the decision ought to be made on that ground. The
present appeal is, in my view, such a case and I would therefore dismiss
the appeal on that ground. When it is also shown, as in this case, that the
application would fail on its merits, it is desirable for that to be stated by
the court which first considers the matter in order to avoid unnecessary
appeals on the preliminary point.

... [W]hile the standard of sufficiency has been relaxed in recent years, the need to have an interest has remained and the fact that R.S.C., Ord. 53, r. 3 requires a sufficient interest undoubtedly shows that not every applicant is entitled to judicial review of right.

The new Order 53, introduced in 1977, no doubt had the effect of removing technical and procedural differences between the prerogative orders, and of introducing a remedy by way of declaration or injunction in suitable cases, but I do not think it can have had the effect of throwing over all the older law and of leaving the grant of judicial review in the uncontrolled discretion of the court. On what principle, then, is the sufficiency of interest to be judged? All are agreed that a direct financial or legal interest is not now required, and that the requirement of a legal specific interest laid down in *Reg. v. Lewisham Union Guardians* [1897] 1 Q.B. 488 is no longer applicable. There is also general agreement that a mere busybody does not have a sufficient interest. The difficulty is, in between those extremes, to distinguish between the desire of the busybody to interfere in other people's affairs and the interest of the person affected by or having a reasonable concern with the matter to which the application relates. In the present case that matter is an alleged failure by the appellants to perform the duty imposed upon them by statute.

The correct approach in such a case is, in my opinion, to look at the statute under which the duty arises, and to see whether it gives any express or implied right to persons in the position of the applicant to complain of the alleged unlawful act or omission. . . .

The respondents are a body with some 50,000 members, but their counsel conceded, rightly in my opinion, that if they had a sufficient interest to obtain judicial review, then any individual taxpayer, or at least any payer of income tax, must also have such an interest. . . . [I]f the class of persons with a sufficient interest is to include all taxpayers it must include practically every individual in the country who has his own income, because there must be few individuals, however frugal their requirements, who do not pay some indirect taxes including V.A.T. It would, I think, be extravagant to suggest that every taxpayer who believes that the Inland Revenue or the Customs and Excise Commissioners are giving an unlawful preference to another taxpayer, and who feels aggrieved thereby, has a sufficient interest to obtain judicial review under R.S.C., Ord. 53. It may be that, if he was relying upon some exceptionally grave or widespread illegality, he could succeed in establishing a sufficient interest, but such cases would be very rare indeed and this is not one of them.

For these reasons I would allow the appeal on the ground that the respondents have no sufficient interest in the matters complained of.

LORD SCARMAN: . . . The application for judicial review was introduced by rule of court in 1977. The new R.S.C., Ord. 53 is a procedural reform of great importance in the field of public law, but it does not – indeed, cannot – either extend or diminish the substantive law. Its function is limited to ensuring 'ubi jus, ibi remedium.'

[He then set out the passage to be found at p. 322 *supra* and continued:]

The appeal is said by both parties to turn on the meaning to be attributed to R.S.C., Ord. 53, r. 3 (5), which has been described as the heart of the Order. It is in these terms: 'The court shall not grant leave unless it considers that the applicant has a sufficient interest in the matter to which the application relates.' There is, my Lords, no harm in so describing the issue, so long as it is remembered that the right to apply for a prerogative order is a matter of law, not to be modified or abridged by rule of court. The right has always been, and remains today, available only at the discretion of the High Court, which has to be exercised upon the facts of the particular case and according to principles developed by the judges. The case law, as it has developed and continues to develop in the hands of the judges, determines the nature of the interest an applicant must show to obtain leave to apply. The rule, however, presents no problems of construction. Its terms are wide enough to reflect the modern law without distorting or abridging the discretion of the judges: and it draws attention to a feature of the law, which has been overlooked in the present case. The sufficiency of the applicant's interests has to be judged in relation to the subject matter of his application. This relationship has always been of importance in the law. It is well illustrated by the history of the development of the prerogative writs, notably the difference of approach to mandamus and certiorari and it remains a factor of importance in the exercise of the discretion today.

. . . [The Lord Advocate] submitted that, notwithstanding the language of R.S.C., Ord. 53, r. 1 (2) the court has no jurisdiction to grant to a private citizen a declaration save in respect of a private right or wrong: and he relied on the House's decision in *Gouriet* v. *Union of Post Office Workers* [1978] A.C. 435. Declaration is, of course, a remedy developed by the judges in the field of private law. *Gouriet's* case is authority for the proposition that a citizen may not issue a writ claiming a declaration or other relief against another for the redress of a public wrong unless he can persuade the Attorney-General, on his 'relation,' to bring the action. The case has nothing to do with the prerogative jurisdiction of the High Court; and it was decided before the introduction of the new Order 53, at a time when a declaration could not be obtained by a private citizen unless he could show (as in a claim for injunction) that a private right of his was threatened or infringed.[4] The new Order[5] has made the remedy available as an alternative, or an addition, to a prerogative order. Its availability has, therefore, been extended, but only in the field of public law where a prerogative order may be granted. I have already given my reasons for the view that this extension is purely a matter of procedural law, and so within the rule-making powers of the Rules Committee. I therefore reject this submission of the Lord Advocate. . . .

The interest

. . . My Lords, I will not weary the House with citation of many authorities. Suffice it to refer to the judgment of Lord Parker C.J. in *Reg.* v. *Thames*

---

[4] [But note the submission at p. 342 *supra* that special damage will also be sufficient.]
[5] [See also s. 31(2) of the Supreme Court Act 1981, p. 315 *supra.*]

Magistrates' Court, Ex parte Greenbaum, 55 L.G.R. 129, a case of certiorari; and to words of Lord Wilberforce in *Gouriet* v. *Union of Post Office Workers* [1978] A.C. 435, 482, where he stated the modern position in relation to prerogative orders: 'These are often applied for by individuals and the courts have allowed them liberal access under a generous conception of locus standi.' The one legal principle, which is implicit in the case law and accurately reflected in the rule of court, is that in determining the sufficiency of an applicant's interest it is necessary to consider the matter to which the application relates. It is wrong in law, as I understand the cases, for the court to attempt an assessment of the sufficiency of an applicant's interest without regard to the matter of his complaint. If he fails to show, when he applies for leave, a prima facie case, or reasonable grounds for believing that there has been a failure of public duty, the court would be in error if it granted leave. The curb represented by the need for an applicant to show, when he seeks leave to apply, that he has such a case is an essential protection against abuse of legal process. It enables the court to prevent abuse by busybodies, cranks, and other mischief-makers. I do not see any further purpose served by the requirement for leave.

But, that being said, the discretion belongs to the court; and, as my noble and learned friend Lord Diplock has already made clear, it is the function of the judges to determine the way in which it is to be exercised. Accordingly I think that the Divisional Court was right to grant leave ex parte. [The Vice-President of the Federation's] affidavit of March 20, 1979, revealed a prima facie case of failure by the Inland Revenue to discharge its duty to act fairly between taxpayer and taxpayer. But by the time the application reached the Divisional Court for a hearing, inter partes, of the preliminary issue, two very full affidavits had been filed by the revenue explaining the 'management' reasons for the decision not to seek to collect the unpaid tax from the Fleet Street casuals. At this stage the matters of fact and degree upon which depends the exercise of the discretion whether to allow the application to proceed or not became clear. It was now possible to form a view as to the existence or otherwise of a case meriting examination by the court. And it was abundantly plain upon the evidence that the applicant could show no such case. But the Court of Appeal, misled into thinking that, at that stage and notwithstanding the evidence available, locus standi was to be dealt with as a preliminary issue, assumed illegality (where in my judgment none was shown) and, upon that assumption, held that the applicant had sufficient interest. Were the assumption justified, which on the evidence it was not, I would agree with the reasoning of Lord Denning M.R. and Ackner L.J. I think the majority of the Court of Appeal, in formulating a test of genuine grievance reasonably asserted, were doing no more than giving effect to the general principle which Lord Mansfield C.J.[6] had stated in the early days on the remedy. Any more stringent test would, as *Wade, Administrative Law*, 4th ed., p. 612 observes, open up 'a serious gap in the system of public law.' . . .

---

[6] [In *R.* v. *Barker* (1762) 3 Burr. 1265, 1267.]

The federation, having failed to show any grounds for believing that the revenue has failed to do its statutory duty, have not, in my view, shown an interest sufficient in law to justify any further proceedings by the court on its application. Had they shown reasonable grounds for believing that the failure to collect tax from the Fleet Street casuals was an abuse of the revenue's managerial discretion or that there was a case to that effect which merited investigation and examination by the court, I would have agreed with the Court of Appeal that they had shown a sufficient interest for the grant of leave to proceed further with their application. I would, therefore, allow the appeal.

LORD ROSKILL: . . . My Lords, much time was spent in the courts below and in argument before your Lordships' House with citation of well-known cases, some of now respectable antiquity in which prerogative orders or formerly prerogative writs have been allowed to issue or have been refused. With all respect to the authority of the judges by whom those cases were decided, such decisions are today of little assistance for two reasons. First, in the last 30 years – no doubt because of the growth of central and local government intervention in the affairs of the ordinary citizen since the second World War, and the consequent increase in the number of administrative bodies charged by Parliament with the performance of public duties – the use of prerogative orders to check usurpation of power by such bodies to the disadvantage of the ordinary citizen, or to insist upon due performance by such bodies of their statutory duties and to maintain due adherence to the laws enacted by Parliament, has greatly increased. The former and stricter rules determining when such orders, or formerly the prerogative writs, might or might not issue, have been greatly relaxed. It is unnecessary in the present appeal to trace through a whole series of decisions which demonstrates that change in legal policy. The change is well known as are the decisions.

Secondly, since those cases were decided and following the change in legal policy to which I have just referred, Order 53 was introduced into the Rules of the Supreme Court in 1977. . . .

. . . Order 53 took effect on January 11, 1978, some six months after the decision of your Lordships' House in *Gouriet* v. *Union of Post Office Workers* [1978] A.C. 435, on July 26, 1977, an authority much relied upon by the learned Lord Advocate on behalf of the appellants in support of his submissions regarding the circumstances in which declarations might be granted. But *Gouriet's* case was a relator action and was not concerned with prerogative orders or judicial review, and the relevant observations of your Lordships must be read in the light of that fact and of the subsequent enactment of Order 53.

. . . [T]he court is enjoined by rule 3 (5) not to grant leave unless the applicant has a 'sufficient interest' in the matter to which the application relates, plain words of limitation upon an applicant's right to relief.

In my opinion it is now clear that the solution to the present appeal must lie in the proper application of the principles now enshrined in Order 53, in the light of modern judicial policy to which I have already referred, to the facts of the present case without excessive regard to the fetters seemingly previously imposed by judicial decisions in earlier times and long before that modern policy was evolved or Order 53 was enacted.

My Lords, the all important phrase in rule 3 (5) is 'sufficient interest.' Learned counsel were agreed that this phrase had not been used in any previous relevant enactment. My Lords, careful review of the earlier authorities in which learned counsel for both parties engaged, reveals that many different phrases have been used in different cases to describe the required standing of a particular applicant for what is now described as judicial review before the courts would entertain his application. He might be 'a party' to the relevant proceedings. He might be 'a person aggrieved.' He might be 'a person with a particular grievance.' He might be a 'stranger.' All those, and some other phrases, will be found in the cases. None is exhaustive or indeed definitive and indeed in this field it would be, I think, impossible to find a phrase which was exhaustive or definitive of the class of person entitled to apply for judicial review. No doubt it was for this reason that the Rules Committee of the Supreme Court in 1977 selected the phrase 'sufficient interest' as one which could sufficiently embrace all classes of those who might apply, and yet permit sufficient flexibility in any particular case to determine whether or not 'sufficient interest' was in fact shown. . . .

Your Lordships' attention was drawn to note 14/21 to Order 53 of *The Supreme Court Practice* (1979), which your Lordships were told bore the authority of Master Sir Jack Jacob, Q.C. The learned editor stated that that which was a 'sufficient interest'

'. . . appears to be a mixed question of fact and law; a question of fact and degree and the relationship between the applicant and the matter to which the application relates, having regard to all the circumstances of the case.'

With this admirably concise statement, I respectfully agree. . . .

Mr. Harvey, for the respondents, contended that not only was there jurisdiction to grant the relief sought but that his clients had a 'sufficient interest' to be granted that relief because once it was accepted that the appellants were a statutory body charged with the performance of a public duty, any member of the public had a right to come to the court and complain that that duty had not been performed in some relevant respect, and that this right of that member of the public did not depend upon the precise nature of the obligation cast by the statute upon the appellants. More narrowly, Mr. Harvey argued that an individual taxpayer had as much interest in the performance by the appellants of their statutory duty as the ratepayer in [*Arsenal F.C. Ltd.* v. *Ende* [1979] A.C. 1] and was not too remote from the appellants in seeking to insist upon performance of their duty in accordance with the law, a submission which found favour in the Court of Appeal with Ackner L.J. . . .

My Lords, the learned Lord Denning M.R. was willing to accept the wider of these propositions founded upon what he had previously said in *Attorney-*

General ex rel. McWhirter v. *Independent Broadcasting Authority* [1973] Q.B. 629, 646, and again in a revised form in *Blackburn's* case [1976] 1 W.L.R. 550, 559. He accepted that my noble and learned friend, Lord Wilberforce, had expressly disapproved the former passage in his speech in *Gouriet's* case [1978] A.C. 435, 483 but claimed that that disapproval was limited to relator actions such as *Gouriet's* case was. My Lords, with profound respect, I cannot agree. Though my noble and learned friend's disapproval was, of course, made in the context of a relator action, the view of the learned Lord Denning M.R., if applied to all applications for judicial review, would extend the individual's right of application for that relief far beyond any acceptable limit, and would give a meaning so wide to a 'sufficient interest' in R.S.C., Ord. 53, r. 3 (5) that they would in practice cease to be, as they were clearly intended to be, words of limitation upon that right of application.

. . . I . . . think that the majority of the Court of Appeal was wrong in granting the relief claimed either on the wider ground the learned Lord Denning M.R. preferred or on the narrower ground which appealed to Ackner L.J.

My Lords, I hope I yield to no one in stressing the importance that relief by way of judicial review should be freely available in whatever form may be appropriate in a particular case, and it is today especially important not to cut down by judicial decision the scope of Order 53 in creating modern procedure for applications for judicial review. I emphasise in particular that relief by way of declaration is expressly made a form of judicial review additional to or alternative to relief by way of prerogative order or injunction. The court has a general discretion which, if any, relief shall be granted and many of the old decisions restricting the circumstances in which declarations may be granted to establish legal rights seem to me to be no longer in point. On the other hand, it is equally important that the courts do not by use or misuse of the weapon of judicial review cross that clear boundary between what is administration, whether it be good or bad administration, and what is an unlawful performance of the statutory duty by a body charged with the performance of that duty. . . . [T]he arguments that [the Lord Advocate] advanced on jurisdiction which I have rejected[7] become highly relevant when the question of 'sufficient interest' arises. The first question must be to inquire what is the relevant duty of the statutory body against which the order is sought, of the performance or non-performance of which complaint is sought to be made. . . .

The next matter is to consider the complaint made and the relief sought. It is clear that the respondents are seeking to intervene in the affairs of individual taxpayers, the Fleet Street casual workers, and to require the appellants to assess and collect tax from them which the appellants have clearly agreed not to do. Theoretically, but one trusts only theoretically, it is possible to envisage a case when because of some grossly improper pressure or motive the appellants have failed to perform their statutory duty as respects a

---

[7] [In a passage that has been omitted.]

particular taxpayer or class of taxpayer. In such a case, which emphatically is not the present, judicial review might be available to other taxpayers. But it would require to be a most extreme case for I am clearly of the view, having regard to the nature of the appellant's statutory duty and the degree of confidentiality enjoined by statute which attaches to their performance, that in general it is not open to individual taxpayers or to a group of taxpayers to seek to interfere between the appellants and other taxpayers, whether those other taxpayers are honest or dishonest men, and that the court should, by refusing relief by way of judicial review, firmly discourage such attempted interference by other taxpayers. It follows that, in my view, taking all those matters into account, it cannot be said that the respondents had a 'sufficient interest' to justify their seeking the relief claimed by way of judicial review....

My Lords, since preparing this speech, I have had the advantage of reading in draft the speeches of my noble and learned friends, Lord Wilberforce and Lord Fraser of Tullybelton. I am in full agreement with what both my noble and learned friends have said.

Appeal allowed.

Questions

1. Is it logical for locus standi to be more liberal if the illegality is very grave?

2. Assuming that a mere stranger could in the past have applied for certiorari or prohibition (on which see Note 3, p. 345 *supra*), is this still the position in the light of Ord. 53, r. 3 (5) (and s. 31 (3) of the Supreme Court Act 1981)? (See de Smith, pp. 416 n. 45 and 418 n. 62 and especially Lord Fraser's comment at p. 356 *supra* and Lord Roskill's comment at p. 359 *supra*.)

3. In *R. v. Horsham JJ., ex p. Farquharson* [1982] 2 W.L.R. 430 at p. 446 Lord Denning noted that Lord Diplock (at pp. 353 and 355 *supra*) had endorsed his view in *R. v. G.L.C., ex p. Blackburn*, p. 353 *supra*, in favour of what has been termed a 'citizen's action'. To what extent do the other speeches lend support to Lord Denning's view?

4. What different view of the function of Administrative Law remedies do the speeches of Lord Wilberforce and Lord Diplock reveal? Which do you prefer? (See Feldman, (1982) 45 M.L.R. 92 at pp. 94–5.)

Notes

1. As has been mentioned, s. 31 (3) re-enacts a provision that used to be contained in Ord. 53, r. 3 (5), the latter being the subject of discussion in the extracts *supra*. In the light of this, the interpretation of r. 3 (5) is obviously relevant to the way in which s. 31 (3) should be interpreted. On the question of the interpretation of r. 3 (5) (before the *Self-Employed* case), see Beatson and Matthews, (1978), 41 M.L.R. 437 at p. 440, referring, *inter alia*, to the problem as to whether any change in locus standi would have been ultra vires. Now the position is governed by statute, any difficulty that might have arisen on the point has been avoided (and see further *O'Reilly v. Mackman* [1982] 3 W.L.R. 604 at p. 620).

2. Both s. 31 (3) of the 1981 Act and Ord. 53, r. 3 (5) only refer to the question of standing being raised at the stage of the application for leave; compare the provisions

concerning the effect of delay (s. 31 (6) of the 1981 Act, p. 316 *supra*, and Ord. 53, r. 4, p. 317 *supra*). The *Self-Employed* case supports the view that s. 31 (3) and r. 3 (5) operate in particular at the stage of the full hearing; cf. Wade, pp. 588–9.

3. According to Lord Wilberforce in the *Self-Employed* case, p. 349 *supra*, (and note generally the agreement with Lord Wilberforce expressed by Lord Fraser and Lord Roskill), the case law prior to the introduction of the application for judicial review remains relevant. Should one distinguish the earlier case law dealing with the declaration and injunction from that concerned with the prerogative orders?

Some of the earlier cases of mandamus will be set out atp. 403 *infra*. Note, however, at this stage Lord Wilberforce's view that the locus standi required for mandamus will be different from that required for certiorari. Some of the earlier case law in relation to certiorari and prohibition was set out at p. 344 *supra*, and should be borne in mind here. See further *Covent Garden Community Association Ltd.* v. *G.L.C.* [1981] J.P.L. 183 and Comment, [1981] J.P.L. 187. (This case was decided after the introduction of the 'sufficient interest' requirement by r. 3 (5), but before the *Self-Employed* case reached the House of Lords, and, as will be seen in Note 4 *infra*, locus standi and the merits might not be kept so distinct today.)

4. The relationship forged between the merits of the case and the question of locus standi is one of the prime features of the *Self-Employed* case. A distinction should, perhaps, be drawn here between the nature of the illegality alleged and the question of whether the illegality has been established. The former was, it was submitted at p. 241 *supra*, particularly important in *Durayappah* v. *Fernando*, p. 226 *supra*, and obviously in a mandamus case the nature of the duty which the applicant alleges has been broken must be considered in order fully to assess his interest in the matter. Do the references in the *Self-Employed* case to greater liberality in standing where there is a grave illegality fall into this category? See further Cane, [1980] P.L. 303 at pp. 322–3. The more closely the question of the nature of the illegality is tied to the facts of the case, of course, then the more difficult it becomes to predict the degree of interest that will be required in advance of the court's decision (and see generally Cane, [1981] P.L. at pp. 334–7).

It seems, however, that Lord Scarman at p. 359 *supra* and also Lord Wilberforce at the end of his speech in the *Self-Employed* case were looking at whether the alleged illegality had been established. Lord Roskill agreed with Lord Wilberforce's speech, and Lord Fraser agreed with Lord Wilberforce's reasoning, but do their speeches expressly agree with him on this point? What role, if any, is left for locus standi on this approach, once the sifting out of the obviously hopeless case has been carried out at the leave stage?

See further *R.* v. *Hammersmith and Fulham L.B.C., ex p. People Before Profit Ltd.* (1982) 80 L.G.R. 322, where Comyn J. held, when leave was sought to apply, *inter alia*, for certiorari, that the applicant company had 'technical locus standi', but that in law the company had no reasonable case to put forward. This latter point was accepted as 'an essential part of deciding the question of locus standi' (p. 326). It seems, therefore, that on this basis the application for leave was rejected on the ground of locus standi, despite the view that the applicant had 'technical locus standi'. Should the law adopt this position? Compare, however, the way the issue is phrased by Comyn J. at pp. 335–6. Note also that Comyn J.'s decision was made at the leave stage: cf. the *Self-Employed* case and see Comment, [1981] J.P.L. 873–4.

DISCRETION, IMPLIED EXCLUSION

Discretion

R. v. Hillingdon London Borough Council, ex parte Royco Homes Ltd.

[1974] Q.B. 720   Divisional Court of the Queen's Bench Division

This was a successful application for certiorari to quash a purported grant of planning permission by the Hillingdon London Borough Council.

LORD WIDGERY C.J.: . . . [I]t has always been a principle that certiorari will go only where there is no other equally effective and convenient remedy. In the planning field there are very often, if not in an almost overwhelming number of cases, equally effective and convenient remedies. As is well known, there is now under the Town and Country Planning Act 1971 a comprehensive system of appeals from decisions of local planning authorities. In the instant case the applicants could, had they wished, have gone to the Secretary of State for the Environment in the form of a statutory appeal under the Act of 1971 instead of coming to this court. There would, if they had taken that course, have been open to them a further appeal to this court on a point of law following on the decision of the Secretary of State.

It seems to me that in a very large number of instances it will be found that the statutory system of appeals is more effective and more convenient than an application for certiorari, and the principal reason why it may prove itself to be more convenient and more effective is that an appeal to the Secretary of State on all issues arising between the parties can be disposed of at one hearing. Whether the issue between them is a matter of law or fact, or policy or opinion, or a combination of some or all of these, one hearing before the Secretary of State has jurisdiction to deal with them all, whereas of course an application for certiorari is limited to cases where the issue is a matter of law and then only when it is a matter of law appearing on the face of the order.

Furthermore, of course, there are in some instances reasons for saying that an action for a declaration[8] is more appropriate and more convenient than an order of certiorari, and in cases where such an argument can be used certiorari should not in my opinion go because to allow it to go would be contrary to the necessary restrictions on its use. An application for certiorari has, however, this advantage: that it is speedier and cheaper than the other methods, and in a proper case, therefore, it may well be right to allow it to be used in preference to them. I would, however, define a proper case as being one where the decision in question is liable to be upset as a matter of law because on its face it is clearly made without jurisdiction or in consequence of an error of law. . . .

---

[8] [This judgment was given before there was the possibility of a declaration being available in an application for judicial review which, according to *O'Reilly* v. *Mackman*, p. 324 *supra*, will, as a general rule, be an exclusive procedure in Administrative Law cases.]

[MELFORD STEVENSON J. agreed. BRIDGE J. delivered a judgment in which he agreed with LORD WIDGERY C.J.]

Question

1. Do you agree with Lord Widgery that 'an application for certiorari is limited to cases where the issue is a matter of law and then only when it is a matter of law appearing on the face of the order'? If these are not limitations, is there any other reason why Lord Widgery (in the last sentence of the extract *supra*) might require the error to appear on the face of the decision if the case is to be a 'proper' one for certiorari?

Notes

1. Certiorari is a discretionary remedy, as are prohibition (though see Note 4 *infra*), mandamus, the declaration, and the injunction, and the existence of an alternative remedy is one factor – but only one factor – that may lead a court to refuse to grant one of these remedies. On the discretionary nature of these remedies generally, see de Smith, pp. 422–8, 437–42, and 512–17.

2. The *Hillingdon* case is concerned with the sphere of planning, and in other contexts Lord Widgery's requirement that the error appear on the face of the decision will not be found. For other recent statements of the position in relation to certiorari, see e.g. *R. v. Peterkin (Adjudicator), ex p. Soni* [1972] Imm. A.R. 253; *R. v. Chief Immigration Officer, Gatwick Airport, ex p. Kharrazi* [1980] 1 W.L.R. 1396; *R. v. Oxfordshire Local Valuation Panel, ex p. Oxford C.C.* (1981) 79 L.G.R. 432. If an appeal has actually been set in motion, then this may render it more likely that the court will deline to grant the remedy (*R. v. Peterkin (Adjudicator), ex p. Soni* [1972] Imm. A.R. at p. 257). Furthermore, in this connection note R.S.C. Ord. 53, r. 3 (6), which provides that where certiorari is sought to quash proceedings from which an appeal can be taken within a limited time, then the application for leave to seek certiorari may be adjourned until the appeal has been decided or the time limit for appealing has expired.

Out of the many cases dealing with certiorari and appeals reference might also be made to one other recent case – *R. v. Crown Court at Ipswich, ex p. Baldwin* [1981] 1 All E.R. 596. In this case, appeal by case stated was thought to be more appropriate than judicial review if factual difficulties are involved, on which see Note 8, p. 319 *supra*.

3. It has already been mentioned that in the *Hillingdon* case emphasis was placed on the error appearing on the face of the decision. There is authority that there is no discretion to refuse an application for prohibition if a jurisdictional error is apparent on the face of the proceedings (e.g. *R. v. Comptroller-General of Patents and Designs, ex p. Parke, Davis, & Co.* [1953] 2 W.L.R. 760 at p. 764), but the survival of the rule today has been questioned (de Smith, p. 418). It has also been said to be uncertain whether the rule, if it survives, applies to certiorari (ibid. 419). The case law concerning the relevance of an alternative remedy in those cases where the grant of prohibition is discretionary does not present a particularly clear picture. Attention might be paid, however, to *R. v. North, ex p. Oakey* [1927] 1 Q.B. 491, where it was said that an appeal would not bar prohibition if the error alleged constituted the breach of 'a fundamental principle of justice' (per Atkin and Scrutton L.JJ.) or was 'contrary to the general law of the land' (per Scrutton L.J.).

4. As will have been seen from the *Hillingdon* case, the availability of an action for a declaration did not necessarily preclude the issue of certiorari. The converse has also been said to be true (*Pyx Granite Co. Ltd.* v. *Ministry of Housing and Local Government* [1960] A.C. 260 at p. 290. Today the availability of the application for judicial review will generally preclude the granting of a declaration in Administrative Law cases other than by such an application: see *O'Reilly* v. *Mackman*, p. 324 *supra*. On the question whether a declaration will be available even in an application for judicial review if certiorari would lie, see Note 6, p. 337 *supra*. On the declaration and alternative remedies, see de Smith, pp. 514–17; Zamir, *The Declaratory Judgment*, pp. 225–44, and on mandamus and alternative remedies, see p. 397 *infra*.

5. The relevance of an appeal to the exercise of the courts' discretionary power to grant a remedy has been discussed at p. 258 *supra* in the context of natural justice. That discussion – and indeed the other ways in which an appeal might affect a natural justice case – should be borne in mind here, and note in particular the following points made at p. 261 *supra*:

(*a*) the exercise of a right of appeal is not regarded as a waiver of the right to seek judicial review of the decision;

(*b*) the courts may refuse to enforce even a contractual obligation to exhaust internal remedies before having resort to the courts.

The discussion in this section has been concerned with the effect of an appeal on the courts' discretion in granting a remedy, but compare *R.* v. *Surrey Coroner, ex p. Campbell* [1982] 2 W.L.R. 626, noted at p. 61 *supra*, in which the existence of a right of appeal was regarded as affecting the scope of review.

6. Whereas we have been considering the question how the courts' *discretion* to grant a remedy is affected by the availability of an alternative remedy, there is an additional question to be considered: this is whether the existence of the alternative remedy in fact takes away the courts' *jurisdiction* to grant a remedy. Both issues, for example, were mentioned by Megaw L.J. in *R.* v. *Board of Visitors of Hull Prison, ex p. St. Germain* [1979] Q.B. 425 at pp. 448–9; cf. Shaw L.J. at p. 456. The effect of an alternative remedy on the courts' jurisdiction is the concern of the next section.

Does a statutory remedy exclude ordinary remedies?

Barraclough v. Brown

[1897] A.C. 615   House of Lords

A vessel, the *J.M. Lennard,* sank in the River Ouse at a time when it was owned by the respondents. The appropriate statutory undertakers, whose secretary was the appellant here, were empowered in the circumstances of this case by s. 47 of the Aire and Calder Navigation Act 1889 to remove the vessel. They incurred expenses in exercising this power, and by virtue of s. 47 were authorized, *inter alia*, to recover the expenses from the vessel's owner in an action in a court of summary jurisdiction. However, the present action to recover these expenses was brought in the Queen's Bench Division of the High Court, and it was unsuccessful before Mathew J. An appeal to the Court of Appeal was also unsuccessful, and there was a further appeal to the House of Lords.

LORD HERSCHELL: . . . Unwilling as I am to determine the appeal otherwise than on the merits of the case, I feel bound to hold that it was not competent for the appellant to recover the expenses, even if the respondents were liable for them, by action in the High Court. The respondents were under no liability to pay these expenses at common law. The liability, if it exists, is created by the enactment I have quoted.[9] No words are to be found in that enactment constituting the expenses incurred a debt due from the owners of the vessel. The only right conferred is 'to recover such expenses from the owner of such vessel in a court of summary jurisdiction.' I do not think the appellant can claim to recover by virtue of the statute, and at the same time insist upon doing so by means other than those prescribed by the statute which alone confers the right.

It was argued for the appellant that, even if not entitled to recover the expenses by action in the High Court, he was, at all events, entitled to come to that court for a declaration that on the true interpretation of the statute he had a right to recover them. It might be enough to say that no such case was made by the appellant's claim. But, apart from this, I think it would be very mischievous to hold that when a party is compelled by statute to resort to an inferior court he can come first to the High Court to have his right to recover – the very matter relegated to the inferior court – determined. Such a proposition was not supported by authority, and is, I think, unsound in principle. . . .

LORD WATSON: . . . I am of opinion that the claim founded upon s. 47 of the Act of 1889 was not competently brought before the Court in this suit. The only right which the undertakers have to recover from an owner is conferred by these words: 'Or the undertakers may, if they think fit, recover such expenses from the owner of such boat, barge, or vessel in a court of summary jurisdiction.' The right and the remedy are given uno flatu, and the one cannot be dissociated from the other. By these words the Legislature has, in my opinion, committed to the summary court exclusive jurisdiction, not merely to assess the amount of expenses to be repaid to the undertaker, but to determine by whom the amount is payable; and has therefore, by plain implication, enacted that no other court has any authority to entertain or decide these matters. . . .

The appellant's counsel maintained that your Lordships ought to substitute for a debt decree, which is the only remedy claimed under s. 47, a declaration that, under that clause, he has a right to recover from the respondents, who were admittedly the owners of the *J. M. Lennard* at the time when she sank. It is possible that your Lordships might accede to such a suggestion, if it were necessary, in order to do justice. But apart from the circumstances that such a declaration would not be in accordance with law, the substance of it is one of those matters exclusively committed to the jurisdiction of the summary court. In the absence of authority, I am not prepared to hold that the High Court of Justice has any power to make declarations of right with respect to any matter from which its jurisdiction is

[9] [Section 47 of the Aire and Calder Navigation Act 1889.]

excluded by an Act of the Legislature; and were such an authority produced, I should be inclined to overrule it. The declaration which we were invited to make could be of no practical utility, and it would be an interference by a court having no jurisdiction in the matter with the plenary jurisdiction conferred by the Legislature upon another tribunal. . . .

[LORD SHAND agreed with LORD WATSON. LORD DAVEY delivered a speech in favour of dismissing the appeal.]

Appeal dismissed.

Question

If the suit had been brought in court of summary jurisdiction, and that court had dismissed the suit without giving the appellant a fair hearing, does *Barraclough* v. *Brown* suggest that the decision of the court of summary jurisdiction could not be reviewed? (See de Smith, p. 360.)

Pyx Granite Co. Ltd. v. Ministry of Housing and Local Government

[1960] A.C. 260   House of Lords

Pyx Granite Co. Ltd. claimed that it had unconditional planning permission to carry out quarrying operations on certain land. The Minister of Housing and Local Government disagreed and only granted permission to quarry in a particular part of the land, and he made that permission subject to certain conditions. The company sought several declarations, including one stating that it had unconditional planning permission in relation to quarrying and another to the effect that the Minister's decision was of no effect and invalid. The Court of Appeal ([1958] 1 Q.B. 554) reversed the decision of Lloyd-Jacob J. in the company's favour, but a majority of the Court of Appeal did think that there was jurisdiction to grant the declarations sought. The company appealed to the House of Lords which, disagreeing with the Court of Appeal's decision on the substantive matters involved, allowed the appeal. On the question of jurisdiction:

VISCOUNT SIMONDS: . . . It was submitted by the respondents that the court had no jurisdiction to entertain the action. It was urged that section 17 of the Act[10] supplied the only procedure by which the subject could ascertain whether permission is necessary for the development of his land. That section enacts that if any person who proposes to carry out 'any operations on land . . . wishes to have it determined . . . whether an application for permission in respect thereof is required under this Part of this Act having regard to the provisions of the development order, he may . . . apply to the local planning authority to determine that question.' . . . The question is whether the statutory remedy is the only remedy and the right of the subject to have recourse to the courts of law is excluded. Obviously it cannot altogether be excluded; for, as Lord Denning has pointed out,[11] if the subject does what he

---

[10] [The Town and Country Planning Act 1947 – see now s. 53 of the Town and Country Planning Act 1971.]
[11] [1958] 1 Q.B. 554, 566, 567.

has not permission to do and so-called enforcement proceedings are taken against him, he can apply to the court of summary jurisdiction under . . . the Act and ask for the enforcement notice to be quashed, and he can thence go to the High Court upon case stated. But I agree with Lord Denning and Morris L.J. in thinking that this circuity is not necessary. It is a principle not by any means to be whittled down that the subject's recourse to Her Majesty's courts for the determination of his rights is not to be excluded except by clear words. That is, as McNair J. called it in *Francis* v. *Yiewsley and West Drayton Urban District Council*,[12] a 'fundamental rule' from which I would not for my part sanction any departure. It must be asked, then, what is there in the Act of 1947 which bars such recourse. The answer is that there is nothing except the fact that the Act provides him with another remedy. Is it, then, an alternative or an exclusive remedy? There is nothing in the Act to suggest that, while a new remedy, perhaps cheap and expeditious, is given, the old and, as we like to call it, the inalienable remedy of Her Majesty's subjects to seek redress in her courts is taken away. And it appears to me that the case would be unarguable but for the fact that in *Barraclough* v. *Brown*[13] upon a consideration of the statute there under review it was held that the new statutory remedy was exclusive. But that case differs vitally from the present case. There the statute gave to an aggrieved person the right in certain circumstances to recover certain costs and the expenses from a third party who was not otherwise liable in a court of summary jurisdiction. It was held that that was the only remedy open to the aggrieved person and that he could not recover such costs and expenses in the High Court. . . . The circumstances here are far different. The appellant company are given no new right of quarrying by the Act of 1947. Their right is a common law right and the only question is how far it has been taken away. They do not uno flato claim under the Act and seek a remedy elsewhere. On the contrary, they deny that they come within its purview and seek a declaration to that effect. There is, in my opinion, nothing in *Barraclough* v. *Brown*[14] which denies them that remedy, if it is otherwise appropriate. . . .

LORD JENKINS: . . . The section is permissive and not imperative. That in itself is not a circumstance of any positive weight (see the permissive language of the section in *Barraclough* v. *Brown*[15]); but the fact remains that it is not in terms made obligatory to apply under section 17, which is at least consistent with the company's contention. . . .

[LORD GODDARD, with whom LORD OAKSEY agreed, and LORD KEITH OF AVONHOLM delivered speeches in favour of allowing the appeal.]

Appeal allowed.

Notes

1. The question of exclusion of jurisdiction by the availability of a statutory remedy has been of importance in the area of ministerial 'default powers' and will be dealt with at p. 395 *infra*.

[12] [1957] 2 Q.B. 136, 148.   [13] [1897] A.C. 615.
[14] [1897] A.C. 615.   [15] [1897] A.C. 615.

2. The appellant in *Barraclough* v. *Brown*, p. 366 *supra*, was attempting to invoke the court's original jurisdiction — 'the determination of disputes at first instance' (Zamir, op. cit., p. 69) — rather than its supervisory jurisdiction. In *Pyx Granite* the declarations sought involved both original and supervisory jurisdiction, although on the facts of the case the supervisory declaration — that the Minister's decision was of no effect and invalid — might well be thought to have flowed by necessary implication from the declaration granted in the court's original jurisdiction. If original jurisdiction is not excluded, then *a fortiori* it would seem that supervisory jurisdiction remains intact. This is not to say, however, that there is no authority that supervisory jurisdiction cannot be impliedly excluded. For example, see *R.* v. *Paddington Valuation Officer, ex p. Peachy Property Corporation Ltd.* [1966] 1 Q.B. 380, where it seemed to be accepted that jurisdiction to grant certiorari or mandamus could be excluded by a statutory remedy. On the facts, however, it was not so excluded, since the statutory remedy was not 'so convenient, beneficial and effectual' as these prerogative orders. Nevertheless, recent authority on default powers (see p. 397 *infra*) supports the view that control over ultra vires errors is not excluded by such powers.

3. If a matter has already been decided by the authority to which it is entrusted under the relevant statute or statutory regulations, and the plaintiff seeks a declaration relating to the matter, a court may, in refusing to deal with the case, take the view that it is being asked to exercise appellate rather than original jurisdiction. See *Healey* v. *Minister of Health*, p. 6 *supra*, but note that it can be argued — although without necessarily questioning the actual decision in the case — that the plaintiff there was really attempting to invoke the court's original jurisdiction (Zamir, op. cit., pp. 71–2). More generally, see also *General Electric Co. Ltd.* v. *Price Commission* [1975] I.C.R. 1, though see the comments in de Smith, p. 360, n. 19. As Zamir points out, if the court's supervisory jurisdiction had been invoked in *Healey* v. *Minister of Health*, then the question of jurisdiction to grant a remedy could have been decided differently. (See further *Fullbrook* v. *Berkshire Magistrates' Courts Committee* (1971) 69 L.G.R. 75 at pp. 88–9.

4. Note now the comments on *Pyx Granite* in *O'Reilly* v. *Mackman*, pp. 330 and 332 *supra*. To what extent does *O'Reilly* v. *Mackman* require recourse to an application for judicial review when a declaration of rights is sought?

PROTECTIVE AND PRECLUSIVE CLAUSES

Finality clauses

R. v. Medical Appeal Tribunal, ex parte Gilmore

[1957] 1 Q.B. 574   Court of Appeal

For the facts and decision in this case, see p. 70 *supra*. The point at issue in these extracts concerns s. 36 (3) of the National Insurance (Industrial Injuries) Act 1946, which has now been repealed, but which provided that any decision of a medical appeal tribunal 'shall be final'.

DENNING L.J.: ... The second point is the effect of section 36 (3) of the Act of 1946. . . . Do those words preclude the Court of Queen's Bench from issuing a certiorari to bring up the decision?

This is a question which we did not discuss in *Rex v. Northumberland Compensation Appeal Tribunal, Ex parte Shaw*,[16] because it did not there arise. It does arise here, and on looking again into the old books I find it very well settled that the remedy by certiorari is never to be taken away by any statute except by the most clear and explicit words. The word 'final' is not enough. That only means 'without appeal.' It does not mean 'without recourse to certiorari.' It makes the decision final on the facts, but not final on the law. Notwithstanding that the decision is by a statute made 'final,' certiorari can still issue for excess of jurisdiction or for error of law on the face of the record. . . .

[Having discussed several authorities, he continued:] I venture therefore to use in this case the words I used in the recent case of *Taylor (formerly Kraupl) v. National Assistance Board*[17] (about declarations) with suitable variations for certiorari: 'The remedy is not excluded by the fact that the determination of the board is by statute made "final." Parliament only gives the impress of finality to the decisions of the tribunal on the condition that they are reached in accordance with the law.'

In my opinion, therefore, notwithstanding the fact that the statute says that the decision of the medical appeal tribunal is to be final, it is open to this court to issue a certiorari to quash it for error of law on the face of the record. . . .

PARKER L.J.: . . . One thing is clear beyond doubt. The ordinary remedy by way of certiorari for lack of jurisdiction is not ousted by a statutory provision that the decision sought to be quashed is final. Indeed, that must be so, since a decision arrived at without jurisdiction is in effect a nullity. This, however, is not so where the remedy is invoked for error of law on the face of the decision. In such a case it cannot be said that the decision is a nullity. The error, 'however grave, is a wrong exercise of a jurisdiction which he has, and not a usurpation of a jurisdiction which he has not': see *per* Lord Sumner in *Rex v. Nat Bell Liquors Ltd.*[18] But is the statement that the decision shall be final sufficient to oust the remedy? There are many instances where a statute provides that a decision shall be 'final.' Sometimes, as here, the statute provides that subject to a specific right of appeal the decision shall be final. In such a case it may be said that the expression 'shall be final' is merely a pointer to the fact that there is no further appeal, and the remedy by way of certiorari is not by way of appeal. Since, however, appeal is the creature of statute the expression is strictly unnecessary. In other cases the expression is used in the statutes when no rights of appeal are provided. In such a case it could be said that the expression was of no effect unless it was intended to oust the remedy by way of certiorari. Be that as it may, I am satisfied that such an expression is not sufficient to oust this important and well-established jurisdiction of the courts.

Not only is there no authority to the contrary, but Parliament has, I think, long recognized that the expression does not have that effect. As Lord Sumner points out in *Rex v. Nat Bell Liquors Ltd.*:[19] 'Long before Jervis's Acts

---

[16] [1952] 1 K.B. 338.   [17] [1957] P. 101.
[18] [1922] 2 A.C. 128, 151–152.   [19] Ibid. 159–160.

statutes had been passed which created an inferior court, and declared its decisions to be "final" and "without appeal," and again and again the Court of King's Bench had held that language of this kind did not restrict or take away the right of the court to bring the proceedings before itself by certiorari. There is no need to regard this as a conflict between the court and Parliament; on the contrary, the latter, by continuing to use the same language in subsequent enactments, accepted this interpretation, which is now clearly established. . . .

[ROMER L.J. delivered a judgment in which he agreed with DENNING and PARKER L.JJ.'s comments on finality clauses.]

Question

The finality clause involved in this case has now been repealed. Today there can be an appeal on a point of law from a medical appeal tribunal to a Social Security Commissioner (s. 112 of the Social Security Act 1975) and a further appeal to the Court of Appeal (s. 14 of the Social Security Act 1980). In the light of this, would certiorari still be available? (See p. 366 *supra*.)

Notes

1. *Gilmore*'s case was concerned with certiorari, but it should be noted that a finality clause will not exclude judicial review whatever the remedy sought.

2. It has been suggested recently that a finality clause may only bar some but not all appeals. In *Pearlman* v. *Harrow School* [1979] Q.B. 56 at p. 71 Lord Denning M.R. (obiter), with whom Eveleigh L.J. was inclined to agree on this point, regarded the finality clause involved in that case as only applicable to (i.e. only excluding) an appeal on the facts and not an appeal on a point of law. Geoffrey Lane L.J. took a different view, and in *Re Racal Communications Ltd.* [1981] A.C. 374 at p. 382 Lord Diplock, with whose speech Lord Keith agreed, thought that Lord Denning's view was wrong. On the relationship of appeals and finality clauses, see further *Tehrani* v. *Rostron* [1972] 1 Q.B. 182, on which see Wade, p. 599; de Smith, p. 366 n. 68.

3. In relation to the finality clause governing medical appeal tribunals, Lord Denning has been reported as saying (in a discussion at a meeting of the Medico-Legal Society – (1977) 45 Medico-Legal J. 49 at p. 56):

> We managed to get around that all right (*Laughter*) We said that it [the decision of a medical appeal tribunal] might be final on questions of fact, but if it was a question of law and we could see on the face of the record that it was wrong, it was not final for us; and we have often managed to turn a question of fact into a question of law! (*Laughter*) We managed to get that one all right. It was about a man getting some compensation.

In some contexts, however, judicial restraint can be found. Although not concerned with a finality clause, note the view of Roskill L.J. in *R.* v. *National Insurance Commissioner, ex p. Michael* [1977] 1 W.L.R. 109, in which he discussed the question of judicial review of decisions of the Commissioners. He said (at p. 116):

> The courts must not be astute to convert questions of fact or of mixed fact and law into questions of law so as to justify interference by prerogative order in cases where no right of appeal has been given by statute.

On law and fact see generally p. 71 *supra*.

'No certiorari' clauses

R. v. Medical Appeal Tribunal, ex parte Gilmore

[1957] 1 Q.B. 574   Court of Appeal

For the facts and decision in this case, see p. 70 *supra*.

DENNING L.J.: . . . In contrast to the word 'final' I would like to say a word about the old statutes which used in express words to take away the remedy by certiorari by saying that the decision of the tribunal 'shall not be removed by certiorari.' Those statutes were passed chiefly between 1680 and 1848, in the days when the courts used certiorari too freely and quashed decisions for technical defects of form. In stopping this abuse the statutes proved very beneficial, but the court never allowed those statutes to be used as a cover for wrongdoing by tribunals. If tribunals were to be at liberty to exceed their jurisdiction without any check by the courts, the rule of law would be at an end. Despite express words taking away certiorari, therefore, it was held that certiorari would still lie if some of the members of the tribunal were disqualified from acting: see *Reg. v. Cheltenham Commissioners*,[20] where Lord Denman C.J. said:[21] 'The statute cannot affect our right and duty to see justice executed.' So, also, if the tribunal exceeded its jurisdiction: see *Ex parte Bradlaugh*,[22] or if its decision was obtained by fraud: see *Reg v. Gillyard*,[23] the courts would still grant certiorari. . . .

Note

As will have been seen, a 'no certiorari' clause will not stop a court issuing certiorari if a jurisdictional defect can be established. However, it is important to realize that such a clause – in contrast to a finality clause – will stop a court issuing certiorari in a case of error of law on the face of the record. This is why it was so important for the applicant in *Pearlman* v. *Harrow School*, p. 53 *supra*, to establish that the error of law in question was a jurisdictional one. Of course, the developments in relation to jurisdictional error discussed at p. 58 *supra* should be borne in mind, as should the fact that 'no certiorari' clauses are in little use today (de Smith, p. 368). *Pearlman*, however, provided an example. Note also s. 14 of the Tribunals and Inquiries Act 1971, p. 379 *infra*, but see s. 14 (3).

'As if enacted' clauses

Minister of Health v. The King (on the prosecution of Yaffe), p. 509 *infra*

Note

For a comment on s. 14 of the Tribunals and Inquiries Act 1971 and this type of clause, see Note 4, p. 380 *infra*.

---

[20] (1841) 1 Q.B. 467.
[21] Ibid. 474.
[22] (1878) 3 Q.B.D. 509.
[23] (1848) 12 Q.B. 527.

'Shall not be questioned' clauses

Anisminic Ltd. v. Foreign Compensation Commission

[1969] 2 A.C. 147   House of Lords

For the facts and discussion of the nature of the error made by the Commission, see p. 38 *supra*. These extracts are concerned with the ouster clause which was then to be found in the Foreign Compensation Act 1950. Section 4 (4) of the 1950 Act provided that any determination by the Commission of an application 'shall not be called in question in any court of law'.

LORD REID: . . . The next argument was that, by reason of the provisions of section 4 (4) of the 1950 Act, the courts are precluded from considering whether the respondent's determination was a nullity, and therefore it must be treated as valid whether or not inquiry would disclose that it was a nullity. . . .

The respondent maintains that these are plain words only capable of having one meaning. Here is a determination which is apparently valid: there is nothing on the face of the document to cast any doubt on its validity. If it is a nullity, that could only be established by raising some kind of proceedings in court. But that would be calling the determination in question, and that is expressly prohibited by statute. The appellants maintain that that is not the meaning of the words of this provision. They say that 'determination' means a real determination and does not include an apparent or purported determination which in the eyes of the law has no existence because it is a nullity. Or, putting it in another way, if you seek to show that a determination is a nullity you are not questioning the purported determination – you are maintaining that it does not exist as a determination. It is one thing to question a determination which does exist: it is quite another thing to say that there is nothing to be questioned.

Let me illustrate the matter by supposing a simple case. A statute provides that a certain order may be made by a person who holds a specified qualification or appointment, and it contains a provision, similar to section 4 (4), that such an order made by such a person shall not be called in question in any court of law. A person aggrieved by an order alleges that it is a forgery or that the person who made the order did not hold that qualification or appointment. Does such a provision require the court to treat that order as a valid order? It is a well established principle that a provision ousting the ordinary jurisdiction of the court must be construed strictly – meaning, I think, that, if such a provision is reasonably capable of having two meanings, that meaning shall be taken which preserves the ordinary jurisdiction of the court.

Statutory provisions which seek to limit the ordinary jurisdiction of the court have a long history. No case has been cited in which any other form of words limiting the jurisdiction of the court has been held to protect a nullity. If the draftsman or Parliament had intended to introduce a new kind of ouster clause so as to prevent any inquiry even as to whether the document relied on was a forgery, I would have expected to find something much more specific than the bald statement that a determination shall not be called in question in any court of law. Undoubtedly such a provision protects every determination which is not a nullity. But I do not think that it is necessary or even reasonable to construe the word 'determination' as including everything which purports to be a determination but which is in fact no determination at all. And there are no degrees of nullity. There are a number of reasons why the law will hold a purported decision to be a nullity. I do not see how it could be said that such a provision protects some kinds of nullity but not others: if that were intended it would be easy to say so.

The case which gives most difficulty is *Smith* v. *East Elloe Rural District Council* [1956] A.C. 736 where the form of ouster clause was similar to that in the present case. But I cannot regard it as a very satisfactory case. The plaintiff was aggrieved by a compulsory purchase order. After two unsuccessful actions she tried[24] again after six years. As this case never reached the stage of a statement of claim we do not know whether her case was that the clerk of the council had fraudulently misled the council and the Ministry, or whether it was that the council and the Ministry were parties to the fraud. The result would be quite different, in my view, for it is only if the authority which made the order had itself acted in mala fide that the order would be a nullity. I think that the case which it was intended to present must have been that the fraud was only the fraud of the clerk because almost the whole of the argument was on the question whether a time limit in the Act applied where fraud was alleged; there was no citation of the authorities on the question whether a clause ousting the jurisdiction of the court applied when nullity was in question, and there was little about this matter in the speeches. I do not therefore regard this case as a binding authority on this question. . . . I have come without hesitation to the conclusion that in this case we are not prevented from inquiring whether the order of the commission was a nullity. . . .

LORD PEARCE: . . . It has been argued that your Lordships should construe 'determination' as meaning anything which is on its face a determination of the commission including even a purported determination which has no jurisdiction. It would seem that on such an argument the court must accept and could not even inquire whether a purported determination was a forged or inaccurate order which did not represent that which the commission had really decided. Moreover, it would mean that however far the commission ranged outside its jurisdiction or that which it was required to do, or however far it departed from natural justice its determination could not be questioned. A more reasonable and logical construction is that by 'determination' Parliament meant a real determination, not a purported determination. On the assumption, however, that either meaning is a possible construction and that therefore the word 'determination' is ambiguous, the latter meaning would accord with a long-established line of cases which adopted that construction. . . .

In my opinion, the subsequent case of *Smith* v. *East Elloe Rural District*

---

[24] [Unsuccessfully – see p. 381 *infra*.]

Council [1956] A.C. 736 does not compel your Lordships to decide otherwise. If it seemed to do so, I would think it necessary to reconsider the case in the light of the powerful dissenting opinions of my noble and learned friends, Lord Reid and Lord Somervell. It might possibly be said that it related to an administrative or executive decision, not a judicial decision, and somewhat different considerations might have applied; certainly none of the authorities relating to absence or excess of jurisdiction were cited to the House. I agree with Browne J.[25] that it is not a compelling authority in the present case. . . .

LORD WILBERFORCE: . . . The question, what is the tribunal's proper area, is one which it has always been permissible to ask and to answer, and it must follow that examination of its extent is not precluded by a clause conferring conclusiveness, finality, or unquestionability upon its decisions. These clauses in their nature can only relate to decisions given within the field of operation entrusted to the tribunal. They may, according to the width and emphasis of their formulation, help to ascertain the extent of that field, to narrow it or to enlarge it, but, unless one is to deny the statutory origin of the tribunal and of its power, they cannot preclude examination of its extent.

It is sometimes said, the argument was presented in these terms, that the preclusive clause does not operate on decisions outside the permitted field because they are a nullity. There are dangers in the use of this word if it draws with it the difficult distinction between what is void and what is voidable, and I certainly do not wish to be taken to recognise that this distinction exists or to analyse it if it does. But it may be convenient so long as it is used to describe a decision made outside the permitted field, in other words, as a word of description rather than as in itself a touchstone.

The courts, when they decide that a 'decision' is a 'nullity,' are not disregarding the preclusive clause. For, just as it is their duty to attribute autonomy of decision of action to the tribunal within the designated area, so, as the counterpart of this autonomy, they must ensure that the limits of that area which have been laid down are observed (see the formulation of Lord Sumner in *Rex* v. *Nat Bell Liquors Ltd.* [1922] 2 A.C. 128, 156). In each task they are carrying out the intention of the legislature, and it would be misdescription to state it in terms of a struggle between the courts and the executive. What would be the purpose of defining by statute the limit of a tribunal's powers if, by means of a clause inserted in the instrument of definition, those limits could safely be passed?

. . . I find myself obliged to state that I cannot regard *Smith* v. *East Elloe Rural District Council* [1956] A.C. 736 as a reliable solvent of this appeal, or of any case where similar questions arise. The preclusive clause was indeed very similar to the present but, however inevitable the particular decision may have been, it was given on too narrow a basis to assist us here. I agree with my noble and learned friends, Lord Reid and Lord Pearce, on this matter. . . .

[LORD MORRIS OF BORTH-Y-GEST and LORD PEARSON delivered speeches

[25] [At first instance in this case: see [1969] 2 A.C. 223.]

in which they agreed that the ouster clause would not protect a decision if a jurisdictional error could be established.]

Notes

1. The fact that the error of law in this case was regarded as a jurisdictional error by a majority of the House of Lords, thereby taking it beyond the protection of the ouster clause, was a particularly significant feature of the decision. (See p. 54 *supra*, and generally see Wade, (1969) 85 L.Q.R. 198 for discussion of this aspect of the case, as well as its treatment of ouster clauses.) If it becomes accepted that all errors of law are jurisdictional either in general or in relation to certain bodies (see p. 58 *supra*), then – to take up a point made by Wade, (1979) 95 L.Q.R. 163 at p. 166 and Griffiths, [1979] C.L.J. 11 at p. 14 – this may pose problems for judicial review in the face of an ouster clause. If the category of error of law on the face of the record is redundant, it is surely more difficult to give to the ouster clause a meaning (and a sphere of operation) which allows the court to say that it does not cover jurisdictional errors and thereby avoid an overt clash with Parliamentary intention. Yet if the choice is between this confrontation and a denial of judicial review, then under the doctrine of Parliamentary sovereignty the latter alternative should be chosen; but in the prevailing judicial climate it is submitted that the judges are unlikely to do so (and see the approach of Parker L.J. in *R. v. Medical Appeal Tribunal, ex p. Gilmore*, p. 372 *supra*). See further Wade, pp. 605–6.

2. In *R. v. Hickman, ex p. Fox and Clinton* (1945) 70 C.L.R. 598 Dixon J., referring to this type of 'shall not be questioned' clause, said (at p. 615):

> Such a clause is interpreted as meaning that no decision which is in fact given by the body concerned shall be invalidated on the ground that it has not conformed to the requirements governing its proceedings or the exercise of its authority or has not confined its acts within the limits laid down by the instrument giving it authority, provided always that its decision is a bona fide attempt to exercise its power, that it relates to the subject matter of the legislation, and that it is reasonably capable of reference to the power given to the body.

Without going into detail as to any other limitation on the operation of an ouster clause which must be read into this passage – see Whitmore and Aronson, *Review of Administrative Action*, pp. 505–6 and Sykes, Lanham, and Tracey, *General Principles of Administrative Law*, para. 2913 – do you think that its approach is more in tune with Parliament's intention concerning the scope of s. 4 (4) of the Foreign Compensation Act 1950 than the approach in the speeches in *Anisminic*?

3. *Anisminic*, p. 38 *supra*, supports the view that a breach of natural justice is a jurisdictional defect, and see pp. 42 and 43 *supra*. It is clear from the speeches in *Anisminic* that if the Foreign Compensation Commission had committed such a breach, then the ouster clause would have been equally ineffective, and this view has been confirmed by a recent Privy Council decision, albeit one concerned with a differently worded clause. In *Attorney-General v. Ryan* [1980] A.C. 718 a clause protecting the decision in question from 'appeal or review in any court' was held to be inapplicable in a case of breach of natural justice, which, it was reaffirmed, was a jurisdictional error. A passage in *South East Asia Fire Bricks Sdn. Bhd. v. Non-Metallic Mineral Products Manufacturing Employees Union* [1981] A.C. 363 might seem to conflict with this view. It was stated (at p. 370):

> But if the interior tribunal has merely made an error of law which does not affect its jurisdiction, and if its decision is not a nullity for some reason such as breach of the rules of natural justice, then the ouster will be effective.

Griffiths, [1980] C.L.J. 232 at pp. 236–7 has argued that this passage denies that a breach of natural justice renders a decision a nullity. Although the passage is not unambiguous, it is suggested that on its true interpretation it is in fact stating the opposite, i.e. a breach of natural justice is being given as an example of an error that *would* make a decision a nullity.

4. *Smith* v. *East Elloe R.D.C.*, p. 380 *infra*, was referred to in the extracts *supra* from *Anisminic*. After the former case has been set out, the relationship between the two decisions will be considered.

Foreign Compensation Act 1969

3. – (1) The Foreign Compensation Commission shall have power to determine any question as to the construction or interpretation of any provision of an Order in Council under section 3 of the Foreign Compensation Act 1950 with respect to claims falling to be determined by them.

(2) . . . the Commission shall, if so required by a person mentioned in subsection (6) below who is aggrieved by any determination of the Commission on any question of law relating to the jurisdiction of the Commission or on any question mentioned in subsection (1) above, state and sign a case for the decision of the Court of Appeal.

(3) In this section 'determination' includes a determination which under rules under section 4 (2) of the Foreign Compensation Act 1950 (rules of procedure) is a provisional determination, and anything which purports to be a determination. . . .

(6) The persons who may make . . . a requirement under subsection (2) above in relation to any claim are the claimant and any person appointed by the Commission to represent the interests of any fund out of which the claim would, if allowed, be met. . . .

(8) Notwithstanding anything in section 3 of the Appellate Jurisdiction Act 1876 (right of appeal to the House of Lords from decisions of the Court of Appeal), no appeal shall lie to the House of Lords from a decision of the Court of Appeal on an appeal under this section.

(9) Except as provided by subsection (2) above and subsection (10) below, no determination by the Commission on any claim made to them under the Foreign Compensation Act 1950 shall be called in question in any court of law.

(10) Subsection (9) above shall not affect any right of any person to bring proceedings questioning any determination of the Commission on the ground that it is contrary to natural justice. . . .

Questions

1. If the Foreign Compensation Act 1969 had been in force at the time of the *Anisminic* case, do you think the House of Lords would have decided that there was jurisdiction to grant the declaration sought?

2. If a person today wishes to challenge a determination of the Foreign Compensation Commission on the ground of a breach of natural justice, could he avail himself of s. 3 (2)? (See Wade p. 606, n. 76.) If so, why should a person alleging a breach of natural justice be in the special position established by s. 3 (10)?

3. Why should there be no appeal from the Court of Appeal to the House of Lords under the s. 3 (2) procedure, bearing in mind that by virtue of s. 3 (10) a natural justice case could reach the House of Lords?

Note

For the legislative history of s. 3, see Wade, 606.

Statutory reform

Tribunals and Inquiries Act 1971

14. – (1) As respects England and Wales[26] . . . any provision in an Act passed before 1st August 1958 that any order or determination shall not be called into question in any court, or any provision in such an Act which by similar words excludes any of the powers of the High Court, shall not have effect so as to prevent the removal of the proceedings into the High Court by order of certiorari or to prejudice the powers of the High Court to make orders of mandamus: . . .

(2) As respects Scotland, any provision in an Act passed before 1st August 1958 that any order or determination shall not be called into question in any court, or any provision in such an Act which by similar words excludes any jurisdiction which the Court of Session would otherwise have to entertain an application for reduction or suspension of any order or determination, or otherwise to consider the validity of any order or determination, shall not have effect so as to prevent the exercise of any such jurisdiction.

(3)[27] Nothing in this section shall apply to any order or determination of a court of law or where an Act makes special provision for application to the High Court or the Court of Session within a time limited by the Act.

Question

When, if at all, could a person challenging a decision, but faced with an ouster clause, rely on (a) both s. 14 and the '*Anisminic* doctrine', (b) only s. 14, or (c) only the '*Anisminic* doctrine' to get round the ouster clause?

Notes

1. This provision, the origin of which lies in the Franks Committee's *Report on Administrative Tribunals and Enquiries*, Cmnd. 218, para. 117, was formerly to be found in s. 11 of the Tribunals and Inquiries Act 1958, and this explains the reference to 1 August 1958 in s. 14 (1) *supra*. In this earlier statutory existence, sub-s. 3 additionally covered any order or determination of the Foreign Compensation Commission, but in *Anisminic* Lord Pearce stated that this had no bearing on the

---

[26] [For the position in Northern Ireland, see s. 22 of the Judicature (Northern Ireland) Act 1978.]   [27] [As amended by the British Nationality Act 1981.]

question of construction which the House of Lords was considering. See now the
Foreign Compensation Act 1969, p. 378 *supra*.

2. In *R.* v. *Preston S.B.A.T., ex p. Moore*, p. 77 *supra*, Lord Denning stated that
the determinations of these appeal tribunals, which by virtue of the Supplementary
Benefit Act 1966 were 'conclusive for all purposes', were subject to control by
certiorari, and s. 14 was cited in support. However, as the Supplementary Benefit Act
was passed in 1966, it is difficult to see the relevance of s. 14. Wade, p. 607, suggests
one possible answer, when he writes that a 'post-1958 clause which substantially
re-enacts a pre-1958 clause [as the Supplementary Benefit Act 1966 did] will be treated
as pre-1958 for the purpose'.

The fact that Lord Denning referred to s. 14 in *ex p. Moore* might be thought to
suggest that in the absence of s. 14 certiorari would not have been available. Yet this
should not be assumed, for the type of clause in *ex p. Moore* might be treated like a
finality clause (Wade, p. 607), and other writers (de Smith, p. 366; Whitmore and
Aronson, op. cit., p. 492) take the view that a clause stating that a decision shall be
'final and conclusive' will not affect the availability of judicial review. Cf. however,
Zamir, op. cit., pp. 116–17, and see *South East Asia Fire Bricks Sdn. Bhd.* v.
Non-Metallic Mineral Products Manufacturing Employees Union [1981] A.C. 363 at
p. 370.

3. Section 14 (1) does not mention the remedies of prohibition, declaration or
injunction. Note the use made by Lord Diplock in *O'Reilly* v. *Mackman*, p. 327 *supra*,
of the omission of the declaration from s. 14 (1). Do you agree with the inference he
drew? Could s. 14 (1) in fact be construed so as to cover the declaration? (Consider
Ridge v. *Baldwin* [1964] A.C. 40 at pp. 120–1.) In any event does it matter that the
three remedies mentioned *supra* are not covered by s. 14 (1)?

4. It is not clear whether an 'as if enacted' clause (see p. 509 *infra*) is caught by s. 14.
If it is, but if the provision to which the clause relates is classified by a court as
legislative, then on the traditional view certiorari is not available (see Note 1, p. 311
supra), and the obvious remedy is the declaration (for s. 21 of the Crown Proceedings
Act 1947, p. 290 *supra*, poses a problem in relation to the injunction, which in any
event is not mentioned in s. 14 (1)). Thus in this situation we return to the problem,
raised in Note 3 *supra*, that the declaration is not mentioned in s. 14 (1). How
important this is depends, of course, on the effectiveness of 'as if enacted' clauses to
preclude judicial review, on which see p. 509 *infra*. Note also that this sort of clause is
not used today.

EXCLUSIVE STATUTORY REMEDIES

Statutory review provisions: effect of expiry of the six weeks

Smith v. East Elloe Rural District Council

[1956] A.C. 736   House of Lords

On 26 August 1948 the Council made a compulsory purchase order
(confirmed later that year by the Minister of Health) in relation to some land
belonging to the appellant. The Council caused a house on this land to be
demolished and new houses to be built by a firm of builders. A writ was issued

by the appellant on 6 July 1954. Her action involved claims for damages for trespass against the Council, a declaration that the compulsory purchase order was wrongfully made and in bad faith, and a similar declaration in respect of its confirmation. In addition the appellant sought a declaration that Pywell (the clerk to the Council) 'knowingly acted wrongfully and in bad faith in procuring the [compulsory purchase] order and confirmation of the same', and she also claimed damages. The writ and later proceedings were set aside by Master Clayton because of the terms of para. 16 of Part IV of Sch. 1 to the Acquisition of Land (Authorisation Procedure) Act 1946, which is set out, along with para. 15, at the beginning of the extract *infra* from Viscount Simonds's speech. This decision was upheld by Havers J.and the Court of Appeal. On appeal to the House of Lords:

VISCOUNT SIMONDS: ... '15. (1) If any person aggrieved by a compulsory purchase order desires to question the validity thereof, or of any provision contained therein, on the ground that the authorization of a compulsory purchase thereby granted is not empowered to be granted under this Act or any such enactment as is mentioned in subsection (1) of section 1 of this Act, or if any person aggrieved by a compulsory purchase order or a certificate under Part III of this Schedule desires to question the validity thereof on the ground that any requirement of this Act or of any regulation made thereunder has not been complied with in relation to the order or certificate, he may, within six weeks from the date on which notice of the confirmation or making of the order or of the giving of the certificate is first published in accordance with the provisions of this Schedule in that behalf, make an application to the High Court, and on any such application the court – (a) may by interim order suspend the operation of the compulsory purchase order or any provision contained therein, or of the certificate, either generally or in so far as it affects any property of the applicant, until the final determination of the proceedings; (b) if satisfied that the authorization granted by the compulsory purchase order is not empowered to be granted as aforesaid, or that the interests of the applicant have been substantially prejudiced by any requirement of this Schedule or of any regulation made thereunder not having been complied with, may quash the compulsory purchase order or any provision contained therein, or the certificate, either generally or in so far as it affects any property of the applicant.

'16. Subject to the provisions of the last foregoing paragraph, a compulsory purchase order or a certificate under Part III of this Schedule shall not, either before or after it has been confirmed, made or given, be questioned in any legal proceedings whatsoever, and shall become operative on the date on which notice is first published as mentioned in the last foregoing paragraph.'

... It was [argued] that, as the compulsory purchase order was challenged on the ground that it had been made and confirmed 'wrongfully' and 'in bad faith,' paragraph 16 had no application. It was said that that paragraph, however general its language, must be construed so as not to oust the jurisdiction of the court where the good faith of the local authority or the Ministry was impugned and put in issue. ...

My Lords, I think that anyone bred in the tradition of the law is likely to regard with little sympathy legislative provisions for ousting the jurisdiction of the court, whether in order that the subject may be deprived altogether of remedy or in order that his grievance may be remitted to some other tribunal. But it is our plain duty to give the words of an Act their proper meaning and, for my part, I find it quite impossible to qualify the words of the paragraph in the manner suggested. . . . What is abundantly clear is that words are used which are wide enough to cover any kind of challenge which any aggrieved person may think fit to make. I cannot think of any wider words. . . .

. . . I am . . . reluctant to express a final opinion upon a matter much agitated at your Lordships' bar, whether the words 'is not empowered' [in para. 15] were apt to include a challenge not only on the ground of vires but also on the ground of bad faith or any other ground which would justify the court in setting aside a purported exercise of a statutory power. The inclination of my opinion is that they are, but I would prefer to keep the question open until it arises in a case where the answer will be decisive, as it is not here.

. . . [T]he appellant by her writ claims against the personal defendant a declaration that he knowingly acted wrongfully and in bad faith in procuring the order and its confirmation, and damages, and that is a claim which the court clearly has jurisdiction to entertain. I am far from saying that the claim has any merit. Of that I know nothing. But because the court can entertain it, I think that the Court of Appeal, to whose attention this particular aspect of the case appears not to have been called, were wrong in striking out the whole writ and I propose that their order should be varied by striking out the defendants other than Mr. Pywell. . . . Against Mr. Pywell the action may proceed but upon the footing that the validity of the order cannot be questioned. . . .

LORD MORTON OF HENRYTON: . . . Mr. Roy Wilson, for the appellant, puts forward propositions which I summarize as follows: (1) Paragraph 15 gives no opportunity to a person aggrieved to question the validity of a compulsory purchase order on the ground that it was made or confirmed in bad faith. (2) Although, prima facie, paragraph 16 excludes the jurisdiction of the court in all cases, subject only to the provision of paragraph 15, it is inconceivable that the legislature can have intended wholly to exclude all courts from hearing and determining an allegation that such an order was made in bad faith. (3) Therefore, paragraph 16 should be read as applying only to an order or a certificate made in good faith. . . .

My Lords, I accept Mr. Wilson's first proposition. I cannot construe paragraph 15 as covering a case in which all the requirements expressly laid down by statute have been observed, but the person aggrieved has discovered that in carrying out the steps laid down by statute the authority has been actuated by improper motives. . . .

My Lords, having accepted Mr. Wilson's first proposition . . . I reject his second and third propositions, on the short and simple ground that the words of paragraph 16 are clear, and deprive all courts of any jurisdiction to try the issues raised by [certain] paragraphs . . . of the writ, whereby the appellant undoubtedly seeks to question the validity of the order of August 26, 1948. . . .

I would allow the writ in this action to stand only in so far as it claims relief against the respondent Pywell. . . . The writ should, in my view, be set aside for want of jurisdiction in so far as it claims relief against the other respondents. The appeal should, therefore, be allowed to the extent just mentioned.

LORD REID: . . . [I]n order to determine how far the 1946 Act has limited the jurisdiction of the courts I must see what were the grounds on which the court could give relief under the ordinary law. . . . It seems to me that there were four grounds on which the courts could give relief. First, informality of procedure; where, for example, some essential step in procedure has been omitted. Secondly, ultra vires in the sense that what was authorized by the order went beyond what was authorized by the Act under which it was made. Thirdly, misuse of power in bona fide. And, fourthly, misuse of power in mala fide. In the last two classes the order is intra vires in the sense that what it authorizes to be done is within the scope of the Act under which it is made, and every essential step in procedure may have been taken: what is challenged is something which lies behind the making of the order. I separate these two classes for this reason. There have been few cases where actual bad faith has even been alleged, but in the numerous cases where misuse of power has been alleged judges have been careful to point out that no question of bad faith was involved and that bad faith stands in a class by itself.

Misuse of power covers a wide variety of cases, and I am relieved from considering at length what amounts to misuse of power in bona fide because I agree with the analysis made by Lord Greene M.R. in *Associated Provincial Picture Houses Ltd.* v. *Wednesbury Corporation.*[28] . . .

[Having quoted the passages in this case to be found at pp. 119, 121–2 *supra*, he continued:]

I can draw no other conclusion from the form in which paragraph 15 is now enacted than that Parliament intended to exclude from the scope of this paragraph the whole class of cases referred to in the passages which I quoted. No doubt in one sense it might be said that in none of these cases is authority 'empowered to be granted,' but that would be a strained and unnatural reading of these words only to be accepted if there were in the Act some clear indication requiring it. But, to my mind, all the indications are the other way, and this part of the paragraph only refers to cases of ultra vires in the narrow sense in which I have used it.

If other cases of misuse of power in bona fide are excluded, can a distinction be made when male fides is in question? As I shall explain when I come to paragraph 16, I am of opinion that cases involving mala fides are in a special position in that mere general words will not deprive the court of jurisdiction to deal with them, and, if that is so, then no question would arise under paragraph 15. But, if I am wrong about cases of mala fides being in this special position, I do not see how there can be a distinction under paragraph 15

[28] [1948] 1 K.B. 223.

between cases of bona fide and mala fide misuse of power. I can see nothing to indicate any intention to that effect, and if Parliament intended to treat bad faith as a special case it would be very strange to introduce the exception here. The time limit under paragraph 15 is six weeks, which is appropriate for grounds which appear from the terms of the order but not appropriate for grounds based on facts lying behind the order which may not be discoverable for some time after it is confirmed. . . .

In my view, the question whether authority is empowered to be granted is intended to be capable of immediate answer: if it can depend on facts lying behind the order, then neither the Minister nor the owner could know for certain at the time of confirmation whether any order is empowered to be granted or not, because facts showing misuse of power might subsequently emerge. Accordingly, in my opinion, the appellant could not have brought her case within paragraph 15, even if she had raised it immediately after the order was confirmed.

I turn to paragraph 16. . . . In my judgment, paragraph 16 is clearly intended to exclude, and does exclude entirely, all cases of misuse of power in bona fide. But does it also exclude the small minority of cases where deliberate dishonesty, corruption or malice is involved? . . . I think that . . . the general words in this case must be limited so as to accord with the principle, of which Parliament cannot have been ignorant, that a wrongdoer cannot rely on general words to avoid the consequences of his own dishonesty. . . .

LORD RADCLIFFE: My Lords, I think that this appeal must fail except so far as the action against the defendant Pywell is concerned. . . .

. . . I should myself read the words of paragraph 15 (1), 'on the ground that the authorization of a compulsory purchase thereby granted is not empowered to be granted under this Act,' as covering any case in which the complainant sought to say that the order in question did not carry the statutory authority which it purported to. In other words, I should regard a challenge to the order on the ground that it had not been made in good faith as within the purview of paragraph 15. . . . I do not see any need to pick and choose among the different reasons which may support the plea that the authorization ostensibly granted does not carry the powers of the Act. But, even if I did not think that an order could be questioned under paragraph 15 on the ground that it had been exercised in bad faith, and I thought, therefore, that the statutory code did not allow for an order being questioned on this ground at all, I should still think that paragraph 16 concluded the matter, and that it did not leave to the courts any surviving jurisdiction. . . .

At one time the argument was shaped into the form of saying that an order made in bad faith was in law a nullity and that, consequently, all references to compulsory purchase orders in paragraphs 15 and 16 must be treated as references to such orders only as had been made in good faith. But this argument is in reality a play on the meaning of the word nullity. An order, even if not made in good faith, is still an act capable of legal consequences. It bears no brand of invalidity upon its forehead. Unless the necessary proceedings are taken at law to establish the cause of invalidity and to get it quashed or otherwise upset, it will remain as affective for its ostensible purpose as the most impeccable of orders. . . .

LORD SOMERVELL OF HARROW: . . . The words of paragraph 15 are plainly appropriate to ultra vires in the ordinary sense. They do not in their ordinary meaning, in my opinion, cover orders which 'on the face of it' are proper and within the powers of the Act, but which are challengeable on the ground of bad faith. . . .

The limited right under paragraph 15, therefore, does not apply to applications based on bad faith. Pausing there, the victim of mala fides would have his ordinary right of resort to the courts. It is said, however, that paragraph 16 takes away this right. In other words, Parliament, without ever using words which would suggest that fraud was being dealt with has deprived a victim of fraud of all right of resort to the courts, while leaving the victim of a bona fide breach of a regulation with such a right. If Parliament has done this it could only be by inadvertence. The two paragraphs fall to be construed together. Mala fides being, in my opnion, clearly excluded from paragraph 15, it should not, I think, be regarded as within the general words of paragraph 16. . . .

Appeal allowed in part.

Notes

1. The question of the scope of review under a statutory application to quash will be considered at p. 393 *infra*.

2. For later unsuccessful proceedings against Pywell, see the Note, p. 424 *infra*.

3. The Acquisition of Land (Authorisation Procedure) Act 1946 was repealed and replaced by the Acquisition of Land Act 1981, a point that should be borne in mind throughout the rest of this chapter. For provisions corresponding to paras. 15 and 16 of Part IV of Sch. 1 to the 1946 Act, see ss. 23–5 of the 1981 Act.

4. Various statutes contain an ouster clause similar to that which was in issue in *Smith* v. *E. Elloe R.D.C.* See, e.g. the Highways Act 1981, the predecessor of which was involved in the case *infra*.

R. v. Secretary of State for the Environment, ex parte Ostler

[1977] Q.B. 122   Court of Appeal

In September 1973 a public inquiry was held to consider objections to two proposed orders relating to a new trunk road. Thereafter the orders were confirmed by the Minister: one (under the Highways Act 1959) was for the stopping-up of highways and the construction of new ones, and the other was for the compulsory acquisition of the necessary land. Up to this time, Ostler had not made any objection, but he did make an objection to a later supplementary compulsory purchase order which was proposed so as to enable the local authority to widen a particular lane (Craythorne Lane). He thought it would adversely affect his pemises. At the public inquiry held to consider objections to the supplementary order Ostler's evidence was restricted to the Craythorne Lane scheme, and he was not allowed to pursue the point that he would have objected at the first stage if he had realized that his property was going to be affected. In July 1975 the supplementary order was confirmed by the Minister.

This case concerned an application for certiorari to quash the two earlier orders. Ostler alleged that, two or three months after the confirmation of the supplementary order, he learnt of a secret assurance given before the first public inquiry by a Department of the Environment official to a particular firm. It was said that this firm was assured of the widening of Craythorne Lane, in consequence of which assurance it withdrew its objection at the first inquiry.

LORD DENNING M.R. We are here presented with a nice question. Is *Smith* v. *East Elloe Rural District Council* [1956] A.C. 736 a good authority or has it been overruled by *Anisminic* v. *Foreign Compensation Commission* [1969] 2 A.C. 147?

. . . [Mr. Ostler's] case is that there was a want of natural justice and, further, that there was a want of good faith because of the secret agreement.

The Divisional Court thought that the authority of *Smith* v. *East Elloe Rural District Council* [1956] A.C. 736 might have been shaken by the *Anisminic* case [1969] 2 A.C. 147. So they thought that there should be further evidence before them, such as evidence about the secret agreement and evidence as to whether or no there had been any lack of good faith or any want of natural justice. The department feel that this taking of evidence would involve delay and hold up the work. So Mr. Woolf has come to this court by way of appeal.

The earlier orders were made in March and May 1974. Much work has been done in pursuance of them. We are told that 80 per cent. of the land has been acquired and 90 per cent. of the buildings demolished. Nevertheless, Mr. Ostler seeks to say that now, nearly two years later, those orders should be upset and declared to be null and void or set aside.

Now it is quite clear that if Mr. Ostler had come within six weeks, his complaint could and would have been considered by the court. The relevant provision is contained in Schedule 2 to the Highways Act 1959.[29] Paragraph 2 says:

'If a person aggrieved by a scheme or order to which this Schedule applies desires to question the validity thereof, or of any provision contained therein, on the ground that it is not within the powers of this Act or on the ground that any requirement of this Act or of regulations made thereunder has not been complied with in relation thereto, he may, within six weeks from the date on which the notice required by the foregoing paragraph is first published, make an application for the purpose to the High Court.'

[29] [See now para. 2 of Sch. 2 to the Highways Act 1981.]

That is a familiar clause which appears in many statutes or schedules to them. Although the words appear to restrict the clause to cases of ultra vires or non-compliance with regulations, nevertheless the courts have interpreted them so as to cover cases of bad faith. On this point the view of Lord Radcliffe has been accepted (which he expressed in *Smith* v. *East Elloe Rural District Council* [1956] A.C. 736, 769). In addition this court has held that under this clause a person aggrieved – who comes within six weeks – can upset a scheme or order if the Minister has taken into account considerations which he ought not to have done, or has failed to take into account considerations which he ought to have done, or has come to his decision without any evidence to support it, or has made a decision which no reasonable person could make. It was so held in *Ashbridge Investments Ltd.* v. *Minister of Housing and Local Government* [1965] 1 W.L.R. 1320, and the Minister did not dispute it. It has been repeatedly followed in this court ever since and never disputed by any Minister. So it is the accepted interpretation. But the person aggrieved must come within six weeks. That time limit has always been applied.

That paragraph is succeeded by . . . paragraph 4 . . .:

'Subject to the provisions of the last foregoing paragraph, a scheme or order to which this Schedule applies shall not, either before or after it has been made or confirmed, be questioned in any legal proceedings whatever, and shall become operative on the date on which the notice required by paragraph 1 of this Schedule is first published, or on such later date, if any, as may be specified in the scheme or order.'

So those are the strong words, 'shall not . . . be questioned in any legal proceedings whatever.' They were considered by the House of Lords in *Smith* v. *East Elloe Rural District Council* [1956] A.C. 736. . . .

Thirteen years later the House had to consider the *Anisminic* case [1969] 2 A.C. 147. . . .

Some of their Lordships seem to have thrown doubt on *Smith* v. *East Elloe Rural District Council* [1956] A.C. 736: see what Lord Reid said at [1969] 2 A.C. 147, 170–171. But others thought it could be explained on the ground on which Browne J. explained it. Lord Pearce said, at p. 201: 'I agree with Browne J. that it is not a compelling authority in the present case'; and Lord Wilberforce said, at p. 208: 'After the admirable analysis of the authorities made by Browne J. . . . no elaborate discussion of authority is needed.'

I turn therefore to the judgment of Browne J. His judgment is appended as a note to the case at p. 223 et seq. He put *Smith* v. *East Elloe Rural District Council*, at p. [244], as one of the 'cases in which the inferior tribunal has been guilty of bias, or has acted in bad faith, or has disregarded the principles of natural justice.' He said of those cases:

'It is not necessary to decide it for the purposes of this case, but I am inclined to think that such decisions are not nullities but are good until quashed (cf. the decision of the majority of the House of Lords in *Smith* v. *East Elloe Rural District Council* [1956] A.C. 736, that a decision made in bad faith cannot be challenged on the ground that it was made beyond powers and Lord Radcliffe's dissenting speech. . . .).'

In these circumstances, I think that *Smith v. East Elloe Rural District Council* must still be regarded as good and binding on this court. It is readily to be distinguished from the *Anisminic* case [1969] 2 A.C. 147. The points of difference are these:

First, in the *Anisminic* case the Act ousted the jurisdiction of the court altogether. It precluded the court from entertaining any complaint at any time about the determination. Whereas in the *East Elloe* case the statutory provision has given the court jurisdiction to inquire into complaints so long as the applicant comes within six weeks. The provision is more in the nature of a limitation period than of a complete ouster. That distinction is drawn by Professor Wade, *Administrative Law*, 3rd ed. (1971), pp. 152–153, and by the late Professor S. A. de Smith in the latest edition of *Halsbury's Laws of England*, 4th ed., vol. 1 (1973), para. 22, note 14.

Second, in the *Anisminic* case, the House was considering a determination by a truly judicial body, the Foreign Compensation Tribunal, whereas in the *East Elloe* case the House was considering an order which was very much in the nature of an administrative decision. That is a distinction which Lord Reid himself drew in *Ridge v. Baldwin* [1964] A.C. 40, 72. There is a great difference between the two. In making a judicial decision, the tribunal considers the rights of the parties without regard to the public interest. But in an administrative decision (such as a compulsory purchase order) the public interest plays an important part. The question is, to what extent are private interests to be subordinated to the public interest.

Third, in the *Anisminic* case the House had to consider the actual determination of the tribunal, whereas in the *Smith v. East Elloe* case the House had to consider the validity of the process by which the decision was reached.

So *Smith v. East Elloe Rural District Council* [1956] A.C. 736 must still be regarded as the law in regard to this provision we have to consider here. I would add this: if this order were to be upset for want of good faith or for lack of natural justice, it would not to my mind be a nullity or void from the beginning. It would only be voidable. And as such, if it should be challenged promptly before much has been done under it, as Lord Radcliffe put it forcibly in *Smith v. East Elloe Rural District Council*, [1956] A.C. 736, 769–770:

> 'But this argument is in reality a play on the meaning of the word nullity. An order,' – and he is speaking of an order such as we have got here – 'even if not made in good faith, is still an act capable of legal consequences. It bears no brand of invalidity upon its forehead. Unless the necessary proceedings are taken at law to establish the cause of invalidity and to get it quashed or otherwise upset, it will remain as effective for its ostensible purpose as the most impeccable of orders. And that brings us back to the question that determines this case: Has Parliament allowed the necessary proceedings to be taken?'

The answer which he gave was 'No.' That answer binds us in this court today. . . .

Looking at it broadly, it seems to me that the policy underlying the statute is that when a compulsory purchase order has been made, then if it has been wrongly obtained or made, a person aggrieved should have a remedy. But he must come promptly. He must come within six weeks. If he does so, the court can and will entertain his complaint. But if the six weeks expire without any application being made, the court cannot entertain it afterwards. The reason is because, as soon as that time has elapsed, the authority will take steps to acquire property, demolish it and so forth. The public interest demands that they should be safe in doing so. Take this very case. The inquiry was held in 1973. The orders made early in 1974. Much work has already been done under them. It would be contrary to the public interest that the demolition should be held up or delayed by further evidence or inquiries. I think we are bound by *Smith* v. *East Elloe Rural District Council* [1956] A.C. 736 to hold that Mr. Ostler is barred by the statute from now questioning these orders. He ought to be stopped at this moment. I would allow the appeal accordingly.

GOFF L.J.: . . . [T]he provisions considered in *Smith* v. *East Elloe Rural District Council* [1956] A.C. 736 are identical for all practical purposes with those in the Highways Act of 1959.

In my judgment, in *Smith* v. *East Elloe Rural District Council* the majority did definitely decide that those statutory provisions preclude the order from being challenged after the statutory period allowed, then by paragraph 15, and now by paragraph 2 [of Sch. 2 to the Highways Act 1959] and we are bound by that unless *Anisminic Ltd.* v. *Foreign Compensation Commission* [1969] 2 A.C. 147 has [so] cut across it that we are relieved from the duty of following *Smith* v. *East Elloe Rural District Council* and, indeed, bound not to follow it.

That raises a number of problems. With all respect to Lord Denning M.R. and Professor Wade, I do myself find difficulty in distinguishing *Anisminic* on the ground that in that case there was an absolute prohibition against recourse to the court, whereas in the present case there is a qualified power for a limited period, because the majority in the *Smith* case said either that fraud did not come within paragraph 15, so that, in effect, it was an absolute ouster, or that it made no difference to the construction if it did.

Nevertheless, it seems to me that the *Anisminic* case is distinguishable on two grounds. First, the suggestion made by Lord Pearce [1969] 2 A.C. 147, 201, that *Anisminic* dealt with a judicial decision, and an administrative or executive decision might be different. I think it is. It is true that the Minister has been said to be acting in a quasi judicial capacity, but he is nevertheless conducting an administrative or executive matter, where questions of policy enter into and must influence his decision.

I would refer in support of that to a passage from the speech of Lord Reid in the well-known case of *Ridge* v. *Baldwin* [1964] A.C. 40, 72. I need not read it. It sets out what I have been saying.

Where one is dealing with a matter of that character and where, as Lord Denning M.R. has pointed out, the order is one which must be acted upon promptly, it is, I think, easier for the courts to construe Parliament as meaning exactly what it said – that the matter cannot be questioned in any court, subject to the right given by paragraph 2, where applicable, and where application is made in due time – than where, as in *Anisminic*, one is dealing with a statute setting up a judicial tribunal and defining its powers and the question is whether it has acted within them. I think that is supported by the passage in the speech of Lord Reid in the *Anisminic* case [1969] 2 A.C. 147, 170. . . .

The second ground of distinction is that the ratio in the *Anisminic* case was that the House was dealing simply with a question of jurisdiction, and not a case where the order is made within jurisdiction, but it is attacked on the ground of fraud or mala fides. There are, I am fully conscious, difficulties in the way of that distinction, because Lord Somervell of Harrow in *Smith* v. *East Elloe Rural District Council* [1956] A.C. 736, 771, in his dissenting speech, said that fraud does not make the order voidable but a nullity. Lord Reid said the same in the *Anisminic* case [1969] 2 A.C. 147, 170; and at p. 199 Lord Pearce equated want of natural justice with lack of jurisdiction.

Nevertheless, despite those difficulties, I think there is a real distinction between the case with which the House was dealing in *Anisminic* and the case of *Smith* v. *East Elloe Rural District Council* on that ground, that in the one case the determination was a purported determination only, because the tribunal, however eminent, having misconceived the effect of the statute, acted outside its jurisdiction, and indeed without any jurisdiction at all, whereas here one is dealing with an actual decision made within jurisdiction though sought to be challenged.

It cannot be gainsaid that some of the speeches in *Anisminic* do appear to cast doubts upon the correctness of the decision in *Smith* v. *East Elloe Rural District Council*, but it certainly was not expressly overruled, nor did any of their lordships, as I see it, say that it was wrong. There are substantial differences, such as Lord Denning M.R. and I have indicated, between the two cases, and it seems to me that *Smith* v. *East Elloe Rural District Council* stands, is binding on this court, and is a decision directly in point.

I would therefore allow the appeal on that ground. . . .

SHAW L.J.: I agree that this appeal should succeed, and I would respectfully adopt the reasons given by Lord Denning M.R. The present case falls fairly and squarely within the decision determined by the majority opinion of the House of Lords in *Smith* v. *East Elloe Rural District Council* [1956] A.C. 736. . . .

It seems to me that *Anisminic* v. *Foreign Compensation Commission* [1969] 2 A.C. 147 can be distinguished on two or perhaps three grounds: first, that the statutory order considered in that case, namely the Foreign Compensation Order, prescribed the basis on which the Foreign Compensation Commission were to found a determination as to whether the substance of a claim was to be treated as established. This rendered the question of whether or not there had been a valid determination at all open to review in circumstances where it could be shown that the commission proceeded on a wrong view of the law.

Secondly, the determination considered in *Anisminic* could not in any circumstances have been a valid determination so that it was void ab initio, while the order in the present case, as in *East Elloe*, was one which *could* be arrived at as a proper order.

Lastly, in the *East Elloe* case it was the validity of the compulsory purchase order that was in question and not any ultimate question of payment of compensation, which, in the last resort, remains as a means of affording redress to a person who has been dispossessed against his will. . . .

Appeal allowed.
Application for certiorari dismissed.

Questions

1. Goff L.J. said that in *Anisminic* the tribunal acted without jurisdiction 'whereas here one is dealing with an actual decision made within jurisdiction though sought to be challenged'. Is this consistent with your understanding of the position where a decision is challenged for breach of natural justice or fraud? If, adopting this distinction for the moment, the alleged error had involved the former of Goff L.J.'s two categories, would the decision in this case have been any different? (See Whomersley, [1977] C.L.J. 4 at p. 6.)

2. Shaw L.J. agreed with Lord Denning's judgment, but is his last point of distinction between *Anisminic* and *Smith* v. *E. Elloe R.D.C.* consistent with Lord Denning's third ground of distinction? Furthermore, in relation to this third ground, could it be said that in *Anisminic* the House of Lords 'had to consider the validity of the process by which the decision was reached'?

3. Is the time limit of six weeks for the statutory challenge an adequate one? (Compare the time limit provisions under the application for judicial review, on which see Note 7, p. 319 *supra*.)

Notes

1. The decision in this case that *Smith* v. *E. Elloe R.D.C.* was still authoritative after *Anisminic* on the question of exclusion of review had already been reached in two other decisions: *Routh* v. *Reading Corporation* (1971) 217 E.G. 1337; *Hamilton* v. *Secretary of State for Scotland* 1972 S.L.T. 233; consider further *Jeary* v. *Chailey R.D.C.* (1973) 26 P & C.R. 280, and contrast its treatment by Wade, p. 614, and Purdue, (1974) 37 M.L.R. 222. It might be argued that, in relation to *Routh* v. *Reading Corporation*, this statement is too bold, for *Anisminic* was not mentioned in the judgments in the Court of Appeal in that case. However, in *Ostler* Goff L.J. stated that although this omission should make 'one . . . proceed with a little caution . . . it is difficult to imagine that their lordships were unaware of it or overlooked it.' *Anisminic* certainly was mentioned in *Ostler*, and that decision – and in particular the distinctions drawn between *Anisminic* and *Smith* v. *E. Elloe R.D.C.* – has provoked much discussion: see the Notes *infra* and also Wade, (1977) 93 L.Q.R. 8; Whomersley, op. cit.; Harlow, [1976] P.L. 304; Alder, [1976] J.P.L. 270; Gravells, (1978) 41 M.L.R. 383; cf. Alder, (1980) 43 M.L.R. 670. See further Gravells, (1980) 43 M.L.R. 173; Leigh, [1980] P.L. 34.

2. Lord Denning's first distinction between *Anisminic* and *Smith* v. *E. Elloe R.D.C.* finds support, as the Master of the Rolls acknowledged, in a previous edition of Wade – see now pp. 613–14 of the fifth edition. But note Goff L.J.'s point at p. 389 *supra*

that, according to *Smith* v. *E. Elloe R.D.C.*, fraud was not a ground of challenge under para. 15 of Part IV of Sch. 1 to the Acquisition of Land (Authorisation Procedure) Act 1946 (and the grounds of challenge under the Highways Act 1959 were similarly worded). Lord Denning, however, would not accept this exclusion, as his judgment in *Ostler* makes clear: he would allow fraud to be raised under one of these statutory challenges. See further Note 1, p. 393 *infra*. Thus this objection can be met. Nevertheless, there is a more practical problem. As has been pointed out – Gravells, (1978) 41 M.L.R. at p. 389 – a person wishing to challenge a decision may not discover and may have no means of discovering the grounds of challenge until the time limit for the statutory challenge has expired; indeed, on the facts alleged, Ostler was in this position.

3. The Court of Appeal in *Ostler* drew a distinction between judicial and administrative decisions. This is a distinction which has appeared in other areas of Administrative Law, where it has caused problems, and its use in *Ostler* has not been welcomed by commentators. Note, however, that Lord Pearce did refer to such a distinction in this context in *Anisminic*. See further p. 4 *supra*, but it is perhaps worth underlining here that although the Minister's decision was not judicial for the purposes of the distinction drawn in *Ostler*, 'the Minister has been said to be acting in a quasi judicial capacity' (per Goff L.J. in *Ostler*, p. 389 *supra*). In relation to the view expressed in *Ostler* that the Foreign Compensation Commission was a 'truly judicial' body, compare the approach of Lord Diplock in *Re Racal Communications Ltd.*, p. 58 *supra*.

4. We have seen the distinctions drawn in *Ostler* between *Anisminic* and *Smith* v. *E. Elloe R.D.C.*, but it might be questioned whether the Court of Appeal needed to go to all that trouble. The basis of *Anisminic* was that as a matter of statutory construction the word 'determination' in the ouster clause did not include a 'purported' (i.e. ultra vires) determination, but this sort of construction cannot be so easily adopted with the type of ouster clause to be found in *Smith* v. *E. Elloe R.D.C.* Let us take the 1946 Act which was involved in that case as an example. It is surely rather difficult to argue that the phrase 'compulsory purchase order' in para. 16 of Part IV of Sch. 1 to the 1946 Act was not intended to include orders that are ultra vires, when in the preceding paragraph, to which there is a reference back at the beginning of para. 16, the phrase has been used in a way which clearly encompasses such orders, since that paragraph sets out the grounds of challenge to orders and these grounds include ultra vires. The same argument can be applied to ss. 23–5 of the Acquisition of Land Act 1981, which replaces these provisions, or adapted appropriately to other similar legislation. See Alder, (1975) 38 M.L.R. 274 at pp. 284–5; cf. *Hamilton* v. *Secretary of State for Scotland* 1972 S.L.T. 233. In this way the policy behind upholding the ouster clause (see the end of Lord Denning's judgment in *Ostler*) can be achieved without the problems posed by the distinctions drawn in *Ostler* between *Anisminic* and *Smith* v. *E. Elloe R.D.C.* For criticism of this approach, however, see Gravells, (1978) 41 M.L.R. 383; cf. Alder, (1980) 43 M.L.R. 670.

5. After being unsuccessful in the Court of Appeal, Ostler made a complaint to the Parliamentary Commissioner for Administration, who conducted an investigation: see Case C.236/K in the Third Report from the Parliamentary Commissioner for Administration, H.C. 223, Session 1976–7. As a result of the Parliamentary Commissioner's investigation, the Department of the Environment made an *ex gratia* payment to Ostler to cover the reasonable costs he incurred in seeking a remedy in the courts. On the Parliamentary Commissioner generally, see Ch. 18 *infra*.

6. For the possibilities of resisting a compulsory acquisition without the compulsory purchase order itself being challenged, see Oliver, [1980] J.P.L. 236.

7. Someone in Ostler's position might wish to try to claim damages (in addition to any statutory compensation he would get), and on the question of damages see Ch. 13 *infra*.

8. In his book, *The Discipline of Law*, pp. 108–9, Lord Denning mentions the *Ostler* decision, in which he confesses he had made some 'unguarded' statements. He now states that if there had been a breach of natural justice or bad faith, then the Minister's decision would have been a nullity; see also *Firman v. Ellis* [1978] Q.B. 886 and pp. 209 and 229 *supra*, but cf. Lord Denning's view in *Lovelock v. Minister of Transport* (1980) 40 P. & C.R. 336, noted at p. 101 *supra*. The Master of the Rolls wishes that the decision in *Ostler* had rested on what he stated in the last paragraph of his judgment in that case. See further Gravells, (1980) 43 M.L.R. 173, though in relation to his discussion of *Pearlman v. Harrow School*, p. 53 *supra*, see now p. 373 *supra*.

Scope of review: standing

Smith v. East Elloe Rural District Council, p. 380 *supra*

Coleen Properties Ltd. v. Minister of Housing and Local Government, p. 81 *supra*

R. v. Secretary of State for the Environment, ex parte Ostler, p. 385 *supra*

Notes

1. The difference of opinion in *Smith* v. *E. Elloe R.D.C.* concerning the scope of the grounds of review permitted within the six weeks was such as to lead Lord Denning in *Webb* v. *Minister of Housing and Local Government* [1965] 1 W.L.R. 755 to the assertion that it gave no binding ruling. In fact, the Master of the Rolls has adopted a wide view of the scope of these statutory challenges: see the *Coleen Properties* case, p. 82 *supra*, quoting from *Ashbridge Investments Ltd.* v. *Minister of Housing and Local Government* [1965] 1 W.L.R. 1320, and the *Ostler* decision, p. 387 *supra* (though see Wade, p. 615, n. 52). Note that a breach of natural justice can come under either limb of the statutory formula (*Fairmount Investments Ltd.* v. *Secretary of State for the Environment* [1976] 1 W.L.R. 1255, and see further *George* v. *Secretary of State for the Environment* (1979) 38 P. & C.R. 609). Cf. *Errington* v. *Minister of Health*, p. 581 *infra*; *Bushell* v. *Secretary of State for the Environment*, p. 601 *infra*, but see Note 4, p. 584 *infra*.

On the interpretation favoured by Lord Denning – and this interpretation has been adopted in other cases (e.g. *British Dredging (Services) Ltd.* v. *Secretary of State for Wales and Monmouthshire* [1975] 1 W.L.R. 687) – the statutory challenge is apparently wider than judicial review. It would seem to cover all errors of law, whether on the face of the record or not (although Wade, p. 619, suggests that it may be restricted to those found on the face of the record). On the other hand, if non-jurisdictional errors of law come under the second limb of the statutory formula, substantial prejudice is expressly required (but see Note 2 *infra*). For support for the view that all non-jurisdictional errors of law come under the second limb of the statutory formula, see Alder, (1975) 38 M.L.R. 274 at pp. 279–81. Wade, p. 618, seems to disagree and see Leigh, [1980] P.L. 34 at p. 43 n. 41; furthermore, whilst Lord Denning has acknowledged that his interpretation of the statutory challenge does not distinguish between the two limbs (*Gordondale Investments Ltd.* v. *Secretary of State for the Environment* (1971) 23 P. & C.R. 335 at p. 340), in the course of commenting on the *Ashbridge* case in *The Discipline of Law*, pp. 106–8, he does refer to the Minister going beyond his powers if he goes wrong in law. This discussion becomes irrelevant, of course, if Lord Diplock's views in *Re Racal Communications Ltd.*, p. 58 *supra*, concerning jurisdictional errors of law are accepted. Note the repetition of his opinion in *O'Reilly* v. *Mackman*, p. 328 *supra*, in a speech concurred in by the other members of the House, but see Note 6, p. 62 *supra*.

On review for 'no evidence', which is covered by the broad interpretation of the statutory formula, see p. 80 *supra*, and for discussion of the scope of the statutory formula, see Alder, op. cit., pp. 279–84; Leigh, op. cit., pp. 41–3; Wade, pp. 615–9. Consider also the restriction laid down in *Lovelock* v. *Minister of Transport* (1980) 40 P. & C.R. 336, noted at p. 101 *supra*.

2. The court has a discretion whether or not to quash a decision under one of these statutory challenges, and if the applicant has not suffered any prejudice or the point is a purely technical one, may exercise it against him (*Miller* v. *Weymouth and Melcombe Regis Corporation* (1974) 27 P. & C.R. 468, criticized by Alder, (1975) 91 L.Q.R. 10; *Peak Park Joint Planning Board* v. *Secretary of State for the Environment* (1979) 39 P. & C.R. 361; and note that substantial prejudice is specifically required as part of the ground of challenge in the second limb of the statutory formula).

3. The cases cited at the beginning of this section did not expressly raise any problem of standing, though see Whomersley, [1977] C.L.J. at p. 7; nevertheless a brief comment on the statutory requirement that the applicant be a 'person aggrieved' is perhaps called for. This phrase appears in many statutes and at times has received a restrictive interpretation. *Buxton* v. *Minister of Housing and Local Government* [1961] 1 Q.B. 278 provides an example from the area we are currently considering. Here it was held that the words 'person aggrieved' in s. 31 of the Town and Country Planning Act 1959 (see now s. 245 of the Town and Country Planning Act 1971) meant someone whose legal rights had been infringed. For general discussion, see Thio, *Locus Standi and Judicial Review*, Ch. 8; Bayne in *Locus Standi* (ed. Stein), pp. 100–7.

In recent years the *Buxton* case has not found support. In *Turner* v. *Secretary of State for the Environment* (1973) 28 P. & C.R. 123, which concerned the Town and Country Planning Act 1971, Ackner J. was prepared not to follow *Buxton* in the light of *Maurice* v. *L.C.C.* [1964] 2 Q.B. 362, in which it had been criticized. See further *Attorney-General of the Gambia* v. *N'Jie* [1961] A.C. 617, and for a recent interpretation of the phrase 'person aggrieved' in the context of rating, see *Arsenal F.C. Ltd.* v. *Ende* [1979] A.C. 1. Here it was held that a ratepayer was a 'person aggrieved' under s. 69 (1) of the General Rate Act 1967, so as to be able to challenge the valuation of another property in the rating area, even if there was no demonstrable effect on his pocket from the alleged undervaluation. A mere taxpayer, whose taxes help to pay the rate support grant, would not be a 'person aggrieved' under the section. Note that this case was mentioned in the *Self-Employed* case, pp. 350 and 360 *supra*. It would seem that, subject to precedent, a fairly liberal approach is likely to prevail in relation to the phrase 'person aggrieved'. As Wade (p. 621) points out, relying on statements in the *Maurice* and *N'Jie* cases, the phrase 'person aggrieved' is 'likely to cover any person who has a genuine grievance of whatever kind'.

12

REMEDIES FOR ENFORCING
PUBLIC DUTIES

DEFAULT POWERS

Default powers: exclusive effect

Pasmore v. The Oswaldtwistle Urban District Council
[1898] A.C. 387   House of Lords

EARL OF HALSBURY L.C.: My Lords, the question on this appeal is whether a mandamus which was ordered to issue by Charles J.[1] can be supported. According to that learned judge's view it was a mandamus 'commanding the defendants to cause to be made such sewers as may be necessary for effectually draining their district under the Public Health Act 1875 and in particular the plaintiff's premises.' My Lords, I think it right to call attention to the language the learned judge uses, because I am of opinion that it is the key to what I consider to be the error which the learned judge committed in the course of the judgment he delivered in this case. Your Lordships will observe that the first part of that mandamus 'for effectually draining their district under the Public Health Act 1875' follows the language of the statute.[2] Then he has put in this in addition – 'and in particular the plaintiff's premises.' In the view I take of the statute that was a provision which there was no authority to add to the mandamus at all. There is no such provision in the statute, and it appears to me that the whole purview, object and purpose of the statute is one which would not justify such an addition to the language of the mandamus. The principle that where a specific remedy is given by a statute, it thereby deprives the person who insists upon a remedy of any other form of remedy than that given by the statute, is one which is very familiar and which runs through the law. I think Lord Tenterden accurately states that principle in the case of *Doe* v. *Bridges*.[3] He says: 'where an Act creates an obligation and enforces the performance in a specified manner, we take it to be a general rule that performance cannot be enforced in any other manner.'

---

[1] [[1897] 1 Q.B. 384. This was reversed by the Court of Appeal ([1897] 1 Q.B. 625) from which decision this appeal was taken.]

[2] [Section 15 required the local authority to cause to be made such sewers as may be necessary for effectually draining their district.]

[3] (1831) 1 B. & Ad. 847, 859.

The words which the learned judge, Lord Tenterden, uses there appear to be strictly applicable to this case. The obligation which is created by this statute is an obligation which is created by the statute and by the statute alone. It is nothing to the purpose to say that there were other statutes which created similar obligations, because all those statutes are repealed; you must take your stand upon the statute in question, and the statute which creates the obligation is the statute to which one must look to see if there is a specified remedy contained in it. There is a specified remedy contained in it, which is an application to the proper Government department.[4]

My Lords, it seems to me that if it were possible to conceive a case in which it would be extremely inconvenient that each suitor in turn should be permitted to apply for a specific remedy against the body charged with the care of the health of the inhabitants of the district in respect of drainage, it is such a case as this; and it is illustrated by the form of the mandamus. When I called the attention of the learned counsel to the form of the mandamus, he treated the observation as if it were a question of some mistake made in the pleadings which would be remedied as a matter of course in these days. But that was not the object of the observation, nor is it the importance of the observation. It is that the obligation itself is such that the form of the mandamus becomes of the substance of the argument. You cannot get out of the form of the mandamus. I know no other form which could be adopted than that which has been adopted. But then that shews how important it is that the particular jurisdiction to call upon the whole district to reform their mode of dealing with sewage and drainage should not be in the hands, and should not be open to the litigation, of any particular individual, but should be committed to a Government department.

My Lords, it appears to me that that is enough to dispose of this appeal, because I entirely concur in the judgment of the Court of Appeal, in which it is pointed out that this comes within the very familiar principle of law to which I have called attention. . . .

LORD MACNAGHTEN: My Lords, I am of the same opinion.

Assuming the appellants to have a just cause of complaint against the Oswaldtwistle Urban District Council, founded on the 15th section of the Public Health Act of 1875, it seems to me to be plain that they can have no remedy outside that Act.

The law is stated nowhere more clearly or, I think, more accurately, than by Lord Tenterden in the passage cited by my noble and learned friend on the woolsack. Whether the general rule is to prevail, or an exception to the general rule is to be admitted, must depend on the scope and language of the Act which creates the obligation and on considerations of policy and convenience. It would be difficult to conceive any case in which there could be less reason for departing from the general rule than one like the present. . . .

[LORD MORRIS and LORD JAMES OF HEREFORD concurred.]

Appeal dismissed.

---

[4] [Section 299 of the Public Health Act 1875 provided that on complaint, the Local Government Board might order a defaulting authority to perform its duty.]

Notes

1. Compare the cases set out at p. 366 *supra*, where the question whether the courts' jurisdiction to grant a declaration had been excluded by a statutory remedy was under consideration. In that context a distinction was drawn between original and supervisory jurisdiction. Would you classify *Pasmore* v. *Oswaldtwistle U.D.C.* under one of these heads rather than the other?

2. Lord Macnaghten's comments about the enforcement of the 'general rule' were interpreted by Scrutton L.J. in *R.* v. *Poplar M.B.C., ex p. L.C.C. (No. 1)* [1922] 1 K.B. 72 at p. 94. In his view Lord Macnaghten 'meant that, where the performance of the statutory obligation will not be ensured by the statutory remedy, the importance from a view of policy of securing the performance of the statutory obligation may lead the Court to grant other remedies than the statutory one'. The *Poplar* case also underlines two other points. First, the rule in *Doe* v. *Bridges* (1831) 1 B. & Ad. 847, which was followed in *Pasmore* v. *Oswaldtwistle U.D.C.*, only applies where it is the same statute that establishes both the duty and the remedy. (This is, of course, something which is stated in the rule, but which deserves to be emphasized.) Secondly, if there is some other remedy, but one which does not fall within the rule in *Doe* v. *Bridges,* then the existence of the remedy could lead the court in its discretion to refuse mandamus. The alternative remedy must, however, be equally convenient, beneficial and effectual, as it must be if the courts' jurisdiction is to be excluded (*R.* v. *Paddington Valuation Officer, ex p. Peachey Property Corporation Ltd.* [1966] 1 Q.B. 380).

Default powers: non-exclusive effect

Meade v. Haringey London Borough Council

[1979] 1 W.L.R. 637   Court of Appeal

The Council closed more than 100 schools because its caretakers were on strike. Section 8 of the Education Act 1944 imposed a duty on the Council to provide sufficient schools in their area, and a complaint about the closure of the schools was made under s. 99 of the 1944 Act to the Secretary of State for Education. Section 99 provides a mechanism whereby the Secretary of State may compel performance of a duty imposed under the 1944 Act if satisfied that an authority has failed to discharge any such duty. However, in this case the Secretary of State decided that there had been no failure of duty. The Council's position was that it had good reason for the closures, since, in its view, to open the schools would have caused or increased industrial strife. In an action brought by Meade (on his own behalf and on behalf of (amongst others) all the parents of the affected children), Goulding J. rejected the claim for interlocutory relief, and there was an appeal to the Court of Appeal. In fact, on the day of the hearing in the Court of Appeal, the schools reopened fully as the strike had by that time ended. In the course of dismissing the appeal, the Court of Appeal commented on the question whether s. 99 barred any other remedy.

LORD DENNING M.R.: The point of law which arises is this: if the local education authority have failed to perform their duty (to keep open the schools), have the parents any remedy in the courts of law? There is a remedy given by the statute itself. It is to complain to the Secretary of State under section 99 of the Act. But that remedy has proved to be of no use to the parents. Can they now come to the courts? This depends on the true construction of the statute. Lord Simonds put it thus in *Cutler* v. *Wandsworth Stadium Ltd.* [1949] A.C. 398, 407:

> 'It is . . . often a difficult question whether, where a statutory obligation is placed on A., B. who conceives himself to be damnified by A.'s breach of it has a right of action against him . . . the answer must depend on a consideration of the whole Act and the circumstances, including the pre-existing law, in which it was enacted.'

[Having set out s. 99 of the Education Act 1944, he continued:]

Now although that section does give a remedy – by complaint to a Minister – it does not exclude any other remedy. To my mind it leaves open all the established remedies which the law provides in cases where a public authority fails to perform its statutory duty either by an act of commission or omission. Thus when a local education authority were put by the statute under a duty to secure that school premises were up to prescribed standards, and they failed in that duty by letting them fall into disrepair – as a result of which a child was injured – it was held that there was a remedy by action in the courts for any person who was particularly damaged by the breach: see *Ching* v. *Surrey County Council* [1910] 1 K.B. 736 and *Reffell* v. *Surrey County Council* [1964] 1 W.L.R. 358. Again when a local education authority were under a duty to provide education free of charge and then they sought to exclude some children from that benefit, the parents were held entitled to sue for damages and if need be, an injunction: see *Gateshead Union* v. *Durham County Council* [1918] 1 Ch. 146, where Scrutton L.J. said, at p. 167:

> 'A parent is a person specially injured by any unauthorised exclusion of his child from the free education to which he is entitled, and therefore a person entitled to sue for such a breach of statutory obligation.'. . .

So reviewing all the cases afresh, they seem to me to bear out the principle which I stated in *Cumings* v. *Birkenhead Corporation* [1972] Ch. 12, 36, that the local education authority are liable when

> 'They are acting beyond their powers, or, in Latin, ultra vires. If that were the case, then this court would interfere. The courts will always interfere if a Minister or local authority or any other body is acting beyond the powers conferred on it by the law.'

That view was accepted by Brightman J. in *Herring* v. *Templeman* [1973] 2 All E.R. 581. Conversely, when the local education authority is acting within its powers, there is no recourse to the courts: see *Watt* v. *Kesteven County Council* [1955] 1 Q.B. 408 and *Smith* v. *Inner London Education Authority* [1978] 1 All E.R. 411.

This principle has received powerful support from the House of Lords. If a statute imposes a duty on a public authority – or entrusts it with a power – to do this or that in the public interest, but expresses it in general terms so that it leaves it open to the public authority to do it in one of several ways or by one of several means, then it is for the public authority to determine the particular way or the particular means by which the performance of the statute can best be fulfilled. If it honestly so determines – by a decision which is not entirely unreasonable – its action is then intra vires and the courts will not interfere with it: see especially by Lord Diplock in *Dorset Yacht Co. Ltd.* v. *Home Office* [1970] A.C. 1004, 1067–1068. But if the public authority flies in the face of the statute, by doing something which the statute expressly prohibits, or by failing to do something which the statute expressly enjoins, or otherwise so conducts itself – by omission or commission – as to frustrate or hinder the policy and objects of the Act, then it is doing what it ought not to do – it is going outside its jurisdiction – it is acting ultra vires. Any person who is particularly damnified thereby can bring an action in the courts for damages or an injunction, whichever be the most appropriate.

[Having cited several House of Lords cases in support of his view, he continued:]

This case

Applying these principles, I am clearly of opinion that if the borough council of Haringey, of their own free will, deliberately closed one school in their borough for one week – without just cause or excuse – it would be ultra vires: and each of the parents whose child suffered thereby would have an action for damages. All the more so if they closed it for five weeks or more. Or for all schools. No one can suppose that Parliament authorised the borough council to renounce their duties to such an extent as deliberately to close the schools without just cause or excuse. To use Lord Reid's words, it was their duty 'not to act so as to frustrate the policy and objects of the Act'; *Padfield* v. *Minister of Agriculture, Fisheries and Food* [1968] A.C. 997. 1032–1033.

Just cause or excuse

Now comes the great question in this case: had the borough council any just cause or excuse for closing the schools as they did? . . .

[LORD DENNING went on to express the opinion that, on the evidence then before the court, the Council had no just cause or excuse for closing the schools, but decided that, as the strike had ended, no relief should be granted.]

EVELEIGH L.J.: . . . It has been argued by the [Council] that the plaintiff has no right to sue. If there is a single failure to comply with the duty under section 8, I could accept the argument in an appropriate case. Section 99 provides a procedure by complaint to the Minister. However, whether the conduct of the council is justifiable or not in this case, it is not a simple failure. We have a situation where educational facilities exist and are being used by all concerned when the council take a decision positively to stop production, as it were. Teachers who are in receipt of their salaries and under a duty to teach are discouraged from doing so.[5] This is positive conduct bringing the system to a halt. I therefore do not think that section 99 can apply. . . .

SIR STANLEY REES: . . . Then the question arises as to whether the plaintiff has a right of action in the courts having regard to the fact that the Education Act contains provisions for the enforcement of the duties imposed by the statute upon local education authorities. Most important for the present purpose is section 99. . . .

There is of course a well established general principle that where a statute expressly provides machinery for the enforcement of its provisions that is the only remedy. There are to be found dicta applying that principle to a failure to carry out the duty imposed by section 8 of the Education Act by Denning L.J. and by Parker L.J. in *Watt* v. *Kesteven County Council* [1955] 1 Q.B. 408 and by Lord Denning M.R. in *Bradbury* v. *Enfield London Borough Council* [1967] 1 W.L.R. 1311. . . . To that general principle there are well established exceptions which enable an aggrieved person who has suffered damage as a result of a breach of statutory duty to seek a remedy in the courts notwithstanding that the relevant statute contains provisions for enforcement.

The first exception applies if it be established that the act complained of constitutes malfeasance and not mere nonfeasance. In this context Diplock L.J. said in *Bradbury* v. *Enfield London Borough Council* [1967] 1 W.L.R. 1311, 1326 these words:

'That section' – he is referring to section 99 of the Education Act, which is relevant in this case – 'follows closely the wording of section 299 of the Public Health Act 1875 which was considered by the House of Lords in *Pasmore* v. *Oswaldtwistle Urban Council* [1898] A.C. 387, where it was held that the effect of that section, in the case of nonfeasance by a local authority, was to deprive the subject aggrieved by that nonfeasance of a remedy in the courts by mandatory injunction and to substitute therefor as the sole remedy the exercise by the Minister of the powers given in cases of default. That, however, is confined to acts of nonfeasance – failure to perform a duty which is imposed upon the local education authority by the Act. It does not, in my view, and in the view of the judge [Goff J.], exclude a remedy by injunction at the suit of a person aggrieved where there is a direct prohibition in the Act of certain acts by a local education authority.'

There are, of course, inescapable practical difficulties in distinguishing between an act which may be misfeasance or malfeasance from one which is mere nonfeasance. The difficulty of making the distinction between nonfeasance and misfeasance in the instant case is especially acute because the case against the defendants is that they did not comply with their statutory duty under section 8 to open the schools.

The second exception applies if it be established that the defendants have acted outside their powers or ultra vires. Again this exception presents difficulties of interpretation in the instant case. . . .

[5] [This seems to be a reference to a communication from the Council's chief education officer to headteachers: see [1969] 1 W.L.R. at p. 643.]

The argument in the present case . . . is that the defendants acted ultra vires because their decision not to open the schools was (a) governed by political sympathy with the strikers' cause or (b) because they submitted to intimidation from the strikers or (c) because they entered into an unlawful agreement with the strikers not to open the schools. . . .

[*Padfield* v. *Minister of Agriculture, Fisheries and Food* [1968] A.C. 997] in my judgment, supports the view that, if in the instant case it were established by the evidence that the decision of the defendants was based wholly or partly upon any of the motives alleged, then their failure to take action to comply with their statutory duty to make schools available under section 8 would be enforceable in the courts at the suit of a person who had suffered damage. . . .

Question

Do you agree with Sir Stanley Rees that to base the decision *partly* on any of the motives alleged would render the defendant's action ultra vires? (See p. 424 *supra* and Griffiths, [1979] C.L.J. 228 at p. 232.)

Notes

1. On the question of actions for damages against public authorities for breach of statutory duty, see p. 000 *infra*.

2. The Master of the Rolls has developed his views in this area. In *Watt* v. *Kesteven C.C.* [1955] 1 Q.B. 408, to which reference was made in *Meade* v. *Haringey L.B.C.*, Lord Denning stated (obiter) 'that the duty under section 8 (to make schools available) can only be enforced by the Minister under section 99 of the Act and not by action at law' ([1955] 1 Q.B. at p. 425, and see Parker L.J. ibid. at p. 430). Note also that the idea of a remedy from the courts not being excluded by a statutory remedy if the body in question has acted ultra vires has not always been mentioned, even in some recent cases: see e.g. *Southwark L.B.C.* v. *Williams* [1971] Ch. 734 (in which Lord Denning was a member of the court); *R.* v. *Kensington and Chelsea (Royal) L.B.C., ex p. Birdwood* (1976) 74 L.G.R. 424.
   If the term ultra vires is translated, we find that it is concerned with powers, yet in *Meade* v. *Haringey L.B.C.* reference can be found to ultra vires, as opposed to intra vires, breaches of *duty*. Does it make sense to talk of an ultra vires breach of duty? This issue is the concern of the next extract which discusses *Meade* v. *Haringey L.B.C.*, as well as two other cases concerning s. 8 of the Education Act 1944 in which the idea of an ultra vires breach of duty has been involved (*Cumings* v. *Birkenhead Corporation* [1972] Ch. 12 and *Smith* v. *I.L.E.A.* [1978]1 All E.R. 411).

Ultra Vires Breach of Statutory Duty

Peter Cane, [1981] P.L. 11 at pp. 17–19.

. . . [T]he notion of *ultra vires* breach of duty involves applying a doctrine relevant to the control of discretions to a duty. Alternatively if *'ultra vires'* is translated loosely as 'illegal,' the notion involves the paradox that some breaches of legal duty are not illegal acts.
   . . . It is suggested that what the courts have done is to [construe s. 8 of the Education Act 1944] as imposing a duty to provide a minimum level of

schooling coupled with a discretion to determine, consistently with the fulfilment of that duty and in accordance with the statutory guidelines, what the requirement of sufficient schools entails. The reason why I suggest that the section has been interpreted as imposing a duty coupled with a power, rather than just a power to provide such schooling as is sufficient to the needs of the children of the area, is that it is really only at the margins that the discretion operates. Authorities clearly have no discretion to provide no schools, nor even, for example, schools enough on any view for only 75 per cent. of the child population of school age. But authorities do have a discretion whether to go comprehensive, or whether to consider children from Roman Catholic primary schools for admission to non-Roman Catholic secondary schools, or whether to close schools because of a strike.

It is, therefore, tempting to argue that these cases did not concern breach of statutory duty at all, but rather the control of discretionary powers. This would not be impossible in relation to *Cumings* and *Smith*, since both involved only a claim for an injunction. . . . But in *Meade*, specific reference was made to cases on breach of statutory duty, and both Lord Denning M.R.[6] and Sir Stanley Rees[7] seem to have contemplated the possibility of an action for damages. It is submitted that this line of reasoning is confused, and that in *Meade*, as well as in *Cumings* and *Smith*, the court was really concerned with a power and not a duty. . . .

. . . [B]y developing the notion of *ultra vires* breach of duty, the courts have given themselves a degree of flexibility and power in the enforcement (or non-enforcement) of the duties of public authorities which has hitherto existed only in relation to the control of powers and discretions. This may or may not be thought to be a good thing, but it is at least worth noting.

MANDAMUS

Padfield v. Minister of Agriculture, Fisheries and Food, p. 164 *supra*

Notes

1. This case is given as an example of mandamus. Note that the Minister was not required to refer the complaint to the committee but to consider the complaint according to law. The case shows that mandamus can lie even though a discretionary power is involved if the person invested with the discretion has abused it. Other than by identifying what constituted the abuse, which must now, of course, be corrected, and by directing that the case be considered according to law, the court in issuing mandamus will not tell the respondent how to exercise his discretion. On the aftermath of this case, see Note 1, p. 168 *supra*.

2. Compare *Re Fletcher's Application* [1970] 2 All E.R. 527 with *Padfield*: see Note 3, p. 652 *infra*, and consider the question raised there.

---

[6] [1979] 2 All E.R. 1016, at p. 1023 [p. 398 *supra*].
[7] Ibid. at pp. 1033–1034 p. 401 *supra*].

Mandamus and certiorari

R. v. Paddington Valuation Officer, ex parte Peachey Property Corporation Ltd., p. 102 *supra*

Note

See the comments on this case at p. 104 *supra*, and contrast with Lord Denning's judgment the following view which he expressed in *Baldwin & Francis Ltd.* v. *Patents Appeal Tribunal* [1959] A.C. 663 at pp. 693–4:

> There are many cases in the books which show that if a tribunal bases its decision on extraneous considerations which it ought not to have taken into account, or fails to take into account a vital consideration which it ought to have taken into account, then its decision may be quashed on certiorari and a mandamus issued for it to hear the case afresh. The cases on mandamus are clear enough: and if mandamus will go to a tribunal for such a cause, then it must follow that certiorari will go also: for when a mandamus is issued to the tribunal, it must hear and determine the case afresh, and it cannot well do this if its previous order is still standing. The previous order must either be quashed on certiorari or ignored: and it is better for it to be quashed.

See also Salmon L.J.'s judgment in the *Paddington Valuation Officer* case. *Padfield* v. *Minister of Agriculture, Fisheries and Food*, p. 164 *supra*, to which we have just referred, provides an example of mandamus being issued without certiorari. The requirement that the Minister determine the complaint according to law had the same effect as if his earlier decision to refuse to refer the complaint to the committee had been quashed.

Standing

Inland Revenue Commissioners v. National Federation of Self-Employed and Small Businesses Ltd, p. 346 *supra*

Notes

1. For comment on this decision in relation to locus standi in general, see pp. 362–4 *supra*.

2. The decision in the *Self-Employed* case provides one example where locus standi for mandamus was lacking; on the other hand, it clearly states that the old 'specific legal right' test is too strict. Thereafter, however, it becomes more difficult to know precisely what will or will not constitute sufficient locus standi for the remedy. Lord Wilberforce's speech (and note the agreement expressed by Lord Fraser at p. 355 *supra* and Lord Roskill at p. 362 *supra*) asserts that authorities before the introduction of the new Ord. 53 in 1977 are still relevant, and for discussion of these authorities, see Wade, pp. 640–3; de Smith, pp. 550–3; Thio, *Locus Standi and Judicial Review*, Ch. 6. The development in locus standi for mandamus noted by Lord Wilberforce suggests that the more recent authorities will be safer guides and some of these decisions are set out briefly *infra*:

(*a*) In *R. v. Paddington Valuation Officer, ex p. Peachey Property Corporation Ltd.*, p. 102 *supra*, mandamus was sought to compel the Valuation Officer to perform his statutory duties in preparing the valuation list in accordance with s. 1 (2) of the Rating and Valuation (Miscellaneous Provisions) Act 1955. Although the application failed on the merits, it was decided that the applicant, a company which was a ratepayer, did have locus standi, even though it appeared that, if successful, the company would gain little, if any, financial benefit.

(*b*) In R. v. *Commissioner of Police of the Metropolis, ex p. Blackburn* [1968] 2 Q.B. 118 and ibid. (*No. 3*) [1973] Q.B. 241 the applicant sought mandamus to compel the Commissioner in the former case to reverse a policy decision concerning the prosecution of gaming clubs, in the latter case to enforce the law against those illegally publishing and selling pornography. Mandamus was not granted in either case, but neither decision rested on the question of standing. In the 1968 case the applicant's standing was left open by Lord Denning and doubted by Salmon and Edmund Davies L.JJ., and in the 1973 case the issue of standing was not mentioned at all. It was argued by Wade, (1973) 89 L.Q.R. 329 at p. 331 that by these two decisions the courts 'have . . . thrown open mandamus to the public-spirited citizen' (and see Wade, p. 643). Indeed, Lord Denning has subsequently asserted that Blackburn had locus standi in both cases (*Attorney-General, ex rel. McWhirter v. I.B.A.* [1973] Q.B. 629 at p. 649). See further R. v. *Metropolitan Police Commissioner, ex p. Blackburn*, The Times, 7 March 1980, in which the applicant was held to have locus standi to seek an order of mandamus similar to that sought in the 1973 case. The application failed on the merits. Note, however, that the case was decided before the Court of Appeal's decision in the *Self-Employed* case had been reversed by the House of Lords.

(*c*) R. v. *Commissioners of Customs and Excise, ex p. Cook* [1970] 1 W.L.R. 450 concerned the Finance Act 1969, which imposed a tax on bookmakers' off-course betting premises, to be paid either for a whole or half a year in advance. Non-payment meant that a person could not have a betting premises licence. As a result of representations to the Chancellor of the Exchequer, a system was evolved whereby, despite the statutory provision, payment could be made monthly by one cheque and eleven post-dated cheques. Two bookmakers who had paid the tax applied for mandamus to compel the Commissioners to collect the tax in accordance with the Act. The applicants did not have a specific legal right within the terms of R. v. *Lewisham Union Guardians* [1897] 1 Q.B. 498 (now discredited, of course, by the *Self-Employed* case); but Lord Parker C.J. expressed the view ([1970] 1 W.L.R. at p. 455) that 'it might be sufficient if they were able to show that they had some interest, although not a direct personal interest, over and above the interests of the community as a whole'. To get the applicants within this category, their counsel argued that Parliament, by this tax, intended to cut down on the number of betting premises, and he pointed out that the easing of the payment of the tax meant that the applicants had a larger number of competitors. However, the application failed because the closing of betting premises was not felt to be the purpose of the Finance Act and, secondly, because the motive behind the application (that of closing other premises) was an ulterior motive. Should commercial rivalry be treated more sympathetically by the courts? Cf. R. v. *Thames Magistrates' Court, ex p. Greenbaum*, p. 344 *supra*.

(*d*) In 1970 electrical contractors who were on the Hereford Council's approved list sought mandamus in effect to force the Council to comply with two of its standing orders in connection with a proposed installation of heating equipment in some flats (R. v. *Hereford Corporation, ex p. Harrower* [1970] 1 W.L.R. 1424). These standing orders, which by statute had to be complied with, related to public notice before the placing of, and the invitation of tenders for, contracts of particular values. The applicants' interest as electrical contractors was held not to be sufficient, but what turned the scales in their favour so as to give them locus standi was that they, or a certain number of them, were also ratepayers.

The 'specific legal right' test was in fact employed in the case noted at (*d*) *supra*. As has been mentioned, this was disapproved in the *Self-Employed* case, but decisions in which this test was adopted and held to be satisfied can be used as examples of cases in which, presumably *a fortiori*, applicants would have locus standi for mandamus today.

In the *Paddington Valuation Officer* case, noted at (*a*) *supra*, the Court of Appeal seemed to equate the standing required for mandamus with that required for certiorari, and this approach later found favour again with Lord Denning in *R. v. G.L.C., ex p. Blackburn* [1976] 1 W.L.R. 550 at p. 559. Compare with this view the opinion expressed in, for example, the *Hereford Corporation* case that greater interest was required for mandamus, but this was a case in which the 'specific legal right' test was being used. Nevertheless, Lord Wilberforce in the *Self-Employed* case would not seem to agree with Lord Denning.

Does the *Self-Employed* case cast any doubt on (*a*) the decision in *R. v. Commissioners of Customs and Excise, ex p. Cook* or (*b*) Lord Denning's view that Blackburn had locus standi in his applications against the Metropolitan Police Commissioner in the 1968 and 1973 cases?

Effect of alternative remedies

Pasmore v. The Oswaldtwistle Urban District Council, p. 395 *supra*

Note

See especially Note 2, p. 397 *supra*, pointing out that even if a case does not fall within the *Pasmore* decision, the court in its discretion can refuse to grant mandamus because of an alternative remedy.

Statutory protection

Tribunals and Inquiries Act 1971, Section 14, p. 379 *supra*

The Crown and its servants

R. v. The Secretary of State for War

[1891] 2 Q.B. 326   Divisional Court of the Queen's Bench Division

This case in fact went to the Court of Appeal, but it is a passage from the Divisional Court's judgment which can more usefully be set out here.

CHARLES J. [delivering the judgment of the court (CAVE and CHARLES JJ.)]: . . . Now there are no doubt cases where servants of the Crown have been constituted by statute agents to do particular acts, and in those cases a mandamus would lie against them as individuals designated to do those acts. But it is also beyond question that a mandamus cannot be directed to the Crown or to any servant of the Crown simply acting in his capacity of servant. 'With reference to that jurisdiction,' says Cockburn, C.J., in *Reg. v. Lords of the Treasury*,[8] 'we must start with this unquestionable principle – that when a duty has to be performed (if I may use that expression) by the Crown, this Court cannot claim even in appearance to have any power to command the

---

[8] Law Rep. 7 Q.B. 387, at p. 394.

Crown. The thing is out of the question. Over the Sovereign we can have no power. In like manner where the parties are acting as servants of the Crown and are amenable to the Crown, whose servants they are, they are not emenable to us in the exercise of our prerogative jurisdiction.'

Padfield v. Minister of Agriculture, Fisheries and Food, p. 164 *supra*

Note

Padfield, in which mandamus did issue against a Minister of the Crown, must be taken to fit into Charles J.'s first category (sometimes referred to as the *persona designata* rule), although the point was not discussed in *Padfield.* The difficulty, of course, is to decide into which category a particular case falls. Williams, *Crown Proceedings,* p. 150, in referring to the fact that mandamus will lie if a duty is imposed directly on the servant, argues: 'What this generally means is that mandamus will issue if the servant happens to be named in the statute imposing the duty', and de Smith writes (at pp. 554–5):

> Where . . . a duty has been directly imposed by statute for the benefit of the subject upon a Crown servant as *persona designata,* and the duty is to be wholly discharged by him in his own official capacity, as distinct from his capacity as an advisor to or instrument of the Crown, the courts have shown readiness to grant applications for mandamus by persons who have a direct and substantial interest in securing the performance of the duty.

For further explanation of the position, see Street, *Governmental Liability,* pp. 137–40; Hogg, *Liability of the Crown,* pp. 12–15; Whitmore and Aronson, *Review of Administrative Action,* pp. 362–8. Cf. *Teh Cheng Poh* v. *Public Prosecutor, Malaysia* [1980] A.C. 458 at pp. 473–4. The Crown Proceedings Act 1947 did not alter the position. Should it have done so? See Wade, p. 646. See also Wade, p. 50, n. 2 for comment on the implications in this area of *Town Investments Ltd.* v. *Department of the Environment* [1978] A.C. 359, noted at p. 435 *infra.*

Procedure

Supreme Court Act 1981, Section 31, p. 315 *supra*

Rules of the Supreme Court, Order 53, p. 316 *supra*

13

LIABILITY OF PUBLIC AUTHORITIES

LIABILITY IN TORT IN GENERAL

Cooper v. The Board of Works for The Wandsworth District, p. 211 *supra*

Crown Proceedings Act 1947, Section 2, p. 435 *infra*

Note

The position regarding the award of exemplary damages was authoritatively laid down by Lord Devlin in *Rookes* v. *Barnard* [1964] A.C. 1129 at p. 1226, where he identified three categories of case in which such an award of damages was permissible. His first category is of interest here.

The first category is oppressive, arbitrary or unconstitutional action by the servants of the government. I should not extend this category . . . to oppressive action by private corporations or individuals. Where one man is more powerful than another it is inevitable that he will try to use his power to gain his ends; and if his power is much greater than the other's, he might, perhaps, be said to be using it oppressively. If he uses his power illegally, he must of course pay for his illegality in the ordinary way; but he is not to be punished simply because he is the more powerful. In the case of the government it is different, for the servants of the government are also the servants of the people and the use of their power must always be subordinate to their duty of service.

Lord Devlin saw the award of exemplary damages in this category as 'restraining the arbitrary and outrageous use of executive power' (p. 1223) and, more generally, as serving 'a useful purpose in vindicating the strength of the law' (p. 1226). For an example of exemplary damages being awarded against a government servant, see *Wilkes* v. *Wood* (1763) Lofft. 1, and see McBride, [1979] C.L.J. 323 at pp. 340–1. Lord Devlin's ruling was followed by the House of Lords when it returned to the question in *Cassell & Co. Ltd.* v. *Broome* [1972] A.C. 1027, but compare Lord Reid's view (at p. 1088) that the reason for the distinction between government servants and others was merely the established pattern of the pre-existing case law. Note also the support in *Cassell & Co. Ltd.* v. *Broome* for the idea that this category is to be interpreted liberally so as to include local government, the police, and all those 'exercising functions of a governmental character' (pp. 1077–8, 1087–8, 1130, and 1134).

On Lord Devlin's reasoning, should the government be vicariously liable for exemplary damages? Whether it is or not is a matter of some conjecture: see Atiyah, *Vicarious Liability in the Law of Torts*, p. 435.

Inevitable injury

Managers of the Metropolitan Asylum District v. Frederick Hill, William Lund and Alfred Fripp

(1881) 6 App. Cas. 193   House of Lords

The respondents brought an action alleging that the appellants had caused a nuisance by building and operating near the respondents' properties a hospital for people suffering from smallpox and other infectious and contagious diseases. At the trial of the action the jury found that the hospital did constitute a nuisance and the respondents obtained judgment in their favour. In these appeal proceedings the question was whether the appellants, who had acted in accordance with the directions of the Poor Law Board (later the Local Government Board), could successfully raise the defence of statutory authority (the Metropolitan Poor Act 1867). This Act authorized the Board to provide hospital facilities and to direct the appellants to build them. For the purposes of the appeal it was assumed that the maintenance of this hospital, irrespective of how it was run, must necessarily constitute a nuisance.

LORD BLACKBURN: . . . I think that the case of *The Hammersmith Railway* v. *Brand*,[1] in your Lordship's House, settles, beyond controversy, that where the Legislature directs that a thing shall at all events be done, the doing of which, if not authorized by the Legislature, would entitle any one to an action, the right of action is taken away. It is enough to say that such was the unanimous decision of this House; but the reason briefly given by Lord *Cairns*[2] seems indisputable. 'It is a *reductio ad absurdum*' to suppose it left in the power of the person who had the cause of complaint, to obtain an injunction, and so prevent the doing of that which the Legislature intended to be done at all events. The Legislature has very often interfered with the rights of private persons, but in modern times it has generally given compensation to those injured; and if no compensation is given it affords a reason, though not a conclusive one, for thinking that the intention of the Legislature was, not that the thing should be done at all events, but only that it should be done, if it could be done, without injury to others. What was the intention of the Legislature in any particular Act is a question of the construction of the Act. . . .

It is clear that the burthen lies on those who seek to establish that the Legislature intended to take away the private rights of individuals, to shew that by express words, or by necessary implication, such an intention appears. There are no express words in this Act, and I think the weight of argument is rather against than in favour of such an implication. . . .

LORD WATSON: . . . The judgment of this House in *The Hammersmith Railway Company* v. *Brand*[3] determines that where Parliament has given express powers to construct certain buildings or works according to plans

[1] Law Rep. 4 H.L. 171.
[2] Law Rep. 4 H.L. at p. 215.
[3] Law Rep. 4 H.L. 171.

and specifications, upon a particular site, and for a specific purpose, the use of these works or buildings, in the manner contemplated and sanctioned by the Act, cannot, except in so far as negligent, be restrained by injunction, although such use may constitute a nuisance at common law; and that no compensation is due in respect of injury to private rights, unless the Act provides for such compensation being made. Accordingly the Respondents did not dispute that if the Appellants or the Local Government Board had been, by the *Metropolitan Poor Act, 1867,* expressly empowered to build the identical hospital which they have erected at *Hampstead,* upon the very site which it now occupies, and that with a view to its being used for the treatment of patients suffering from small-pox, the Respondents would not be entitled to the judgment which they have obtained. The Appellants do not assert that express power or authority to that effect has been given by the Act either to themselves or to the Board; but they contend that, having regard to the nature of the public duties laid upon them, and the necessities of the case, it must, on a fair construction of the Act, be held that the Legislature did intend them to exercise, and authorize them to exercise, such power and authority under the direction and control of the Poor Law Board.

I see no reason to doubt that, wherever it can be shewn to be matter of plain and necessary implication from the language of a statute, that the Legislature did intend to confer the specific powers above referred to, the result in law will be precisely the same as if these powers had been given in express terms. And I am disposed to hold that if the Legislature, without specifying either plan or site, were to prescribe by statute that a public body shall, within certain defined limits, provide hospital accommodation for a class or classes of persons labouring under infectious disease, no injunction could issue against the use of an hospital established in pursuance of the Act, provided that it were either apparent or proved to the satisfaction of the Court that the directions of the Act could not be complied with at all, without creating a nuisance. In that case, the necessary result of that which they have directed to be done must presumably have been in the view of the Legislature at the time when the Act was passed.

On the other hand, I do not think that the Legislature can be held to have sanctioned that which is a nuisance at common law, except in the case where it has authorized a certain use of a specific building in a specified position, which cannot be so used without occasioning nuisance, or in the case where the particular plan or locality not being prescribed, it has imperatively directed that a building shall be provided within a certain area and so used, it being an obvious or established fact that nuisance must be the result. In the latter case the onus of proving that the creation of a nuisance will be the inevitable result of carrying out the directions of the Legislature, lies upon the persons seeking to justify the nuisance. Their justification depends upon their making good these two propositions – in the first place, that such are the imperative orders of the Legislature; and in the second place, that they cannot possibly obey those orders without infringing private rights. If the order of the Legislature can be implemented without nuisance, they cannot, in my opinion, plead the protection of the statute; and, on the other hand, it is insufficient for their protection that what is contemplated by the statute cannot be done without nuisance, unless they are also able to shew that the Legislature has directed it to be done. Where the terms of the statute are not imperative, but permissive, when it is left to the discretion of the persons empowered to determine whether the general powers committed to them shall be put into execution or not, I think the fair inference is that the Legislature intended that discretion to be exercised in strict conformity with private rights, and did not intend to confer license to commit nuisance in any place which might be selected for the purpose.

[His Lordship went on to dismiss the appeal. After analysing the statutory powers he rejected the defence of statutory authority, pointing out that the powers were permissive, not imperative.]

[LORD SELBORNE L.C. delivered a speech in favour of dismissing the appeal.]

Appeal dismissed.

Marriage v. East Norfolk Rivers Catchment Board

[1950] 1 K.B. 284   Court of Appeal

JENKINS L.J.: . . . There is, I think an important distinction for this purpose between (A) statutory powers to execute some particular work or carry on some particular undertaking for example, . . . the provision of hospitals, in *Metropolitan Asylum District Managers* v. *Hill*[4] . . .; and (B) statutory powers to execute a variety of works of specified descriptions in a given area (the works in question being of such a kind as necessarily to involve some degree of interference with the rights of others) as and when the body invested with the powers deems it necessary or expedient to do so in furtherance of a general duty imposed on it by the Act. . . .

In cases of the former class, the powers are, in the absence of clear provision to the contrary in the Act, limited to the doing of particular things authorized without infringement of the rights of others, except in so far as any such infringement may be a demonstrably necessary consequence of doing what is authorized to be done. . . . In cases of the latter class . . . it is obvious that, if the powers are subjected to an implied limitation to the effect that they are not to be exercised so as to cause any avoidable infringement of the rights of others, the powers will in great measure be nullified and the manifest object of the Act will be largely frustrated. . . . The injury, or apprehended injury, would, moreover, always be avoidable by abandonment of the particular project, . . . and the board would therefore never be able to defeat the complainant on the ground that the injury or apprehended injury was an unavoidable consequence of the exercise of their statutory powers. . . .

---

[4] 6 App. Cas. 193.

Notes

1. Jenkins L.J.'s suggested distinction should not perhaps be taken too far. In applying it to the case in hand, it was the existence of a statutory provision for compensation that proved decisive, even though the case fell into his second category. See Wade, p. 653.

2. This defence is likely to be raised by public authorities, but on occasions it will also apply to private bodies with statutory powers and duties. For an example see the recent House of Lords decision in *Allen* v. *Gulf Oil Refining Ltd.* [1981] A.C. 1001.

3. The defence will fail if the plaintiff's damage was caused by the defendant's lack of reasonable care, for obviously the injury is not inevitable in this case and Parliament cannot have intended to authorize it. See generally *Manchester Corporation* v. *Farnworth* [1930] A.C. 171, and note Viscount Dunedin's view (at p. 183) that 'the criterion of inevitability is not what is theoretically possible but what is possible according to the state of scientific knowledge at the time, having also in view a certain common sense appreciation, which cannot be rigidly defined, of practical feasibility in view of situation and of expense'. Compare the opinion of Lord Edmund-Davies in *Allen* v. *Gulf Oil Refining Ltd.* [1981] A.C. at p. 1015, but see Murdoch, (1981) 97 L.Q.R. 203 at p. 205. And see Appendix.

4. The time at which the question of inevitability is to be judged is the time of the passing of the Act in question: see *Pride of Derby and Derbyshire Angling Association* v. *British Celanese Ltd.* [1953] Ch. 149, in which one of the defendants to a nuisance claim was Derby Corporation. The complaint concerned river pollution, in part from the Corporation's sewage disposal works, which they were under a duty to provide and which were described in some detail by the Derby Corporation Act 1901: the pollution arose from an increase in population after the works, which were originally adequate, had been built. One reason given by Romer L.J. for the rejection of the defence of statutory authority was that it was not inevitable that the authorized works would cause a nuisance, since, when the relevant Act was passed, an increase in population so as to exceed the capacity of the works was not inevitable and Parliament had not envisaged that it might take place. The case also stands for the proposition that a local authority as a defendant is not in any better position than a private person in relation to the grant of an injunction (although on the suspension of the operation of injunctions (which happened in the *Pride of Derby* case) see [1953] Ch. at p. 181).

5. Are the courts reading too much into the words used by Parliament? With Lord Watson's speech, p. 410 *supra,* in particular in mind, Craig argues ((1980) 96 L.Q.R. 413 at p. 415) that a lot of modern legislation is 'framed in permissive form for administrative reasons and contain[s] no indication of site or method because the matter is too complex or best decided upon by the public body; this tells us nothing about whether a private law action should be sustainable or not'. (See further Friedmann, (1944) 8 M.L.R. 31 at pp. 35–7.) See also Craig, op. cit., pp. 414–5 for difficulties in the case law.

6. When *Allen* v. *Gulf Oil Refining Ltd.* was before the Court of Appeal, [1980] Q.B. 156, Lord Denning put forward a radical suggestion: this was that in any case in which 'private undertakers seek statutory authority to construct and operate an installation which may cause damage to people living in the neighbourhood, it should not be assumed that Parliament intended that damage should be done to innocent

people without redress' (pp. 168–9). In Lord Denning's opinion compensation should be paid whether or not there has been negligence: 'they ought not to be allowed – for their own profit – to damage innocent people or property without compensation'. It might be thought that there is also a case for this suggestion to apply if a public body is the defendant, but note the Land Compensation Act 1973. Section 1 of this Act provides a right to compensation when public works cause the value of an interest in land (see s. 2) to be depreciated by physical factors (defined by s. 1 (2) so as to include, *inter alia*, noise, vibration, smell, and fumes). With one exception, this only applies where there is statutory immunity from liability in nuisance. See Wade, p. 691.

NEGLIGENCE

Anns v. Merton London Borough Council

[1978] A.C. 728   House of Lords

The plaintiffs were lessees of flats in a block which had been built under plans passed by the Mitcham Borough Council, to the duties and liabilities of which the defendant Council had succeeded. The plaintiffs claimed that there had been structural movements in the block of flats because it had been erected on inadequate foundations which did not comply with the plans. The negligence alleged in the claim against the Council related to approving the foundations and/or failing to inspect them. A question arose as to whether the limitation period had expired; this was tried and answered in the affirmative by Judge Edgar Fay, but reversed by the Court of Appeal. We shall not concern ourselves with this point, but when the case came before the House of Lords leave was given for the Council to argue that it owed no duty of care to the plaintiffs. The Court of Appeal in *Dutton* v. *Bognor Regis U.D.C.* [1972] 1 Q.B. 373 had previously decided that a council could be liable if there had been negligent approval of foundations.

LORD WILBERFORCE: . . . Through the trilogy of cases in this House – *Donoghue* v. *Stevenson* [1932] A.C. 562, *Hedley Byrne & Co. Ltd.* v. *Heller & Partners Ltd.* [1964] A.C. 465, and *Dorset Yacht Co. Ltd.* v. *Home Office* [1970] A.C. 1004, the position has now been reached that in order to establish that a duty of care arises in a particular situation, it is not necessary to bring the facts of that situation within those of previous situations in which a duty of care has been held to exist. Rather the question has to be approached in two stages. First one has to ask whether, as between the alleged wrongdoer and the person who has suffered damage there is a sufficient relationship of proximity or neighbourhood such that, in the reasonable contemplation of the former, carelessness on his part may be likely to cause damage to the latter – in which case a prima facie duty of care arises. Secondly, if the first question is answered affirmatively, it is necessary to consider whether there are any considerations which ought to negative, or to reduce or limit the scope of the duty or the class of person to whom it is owed or the damages to which a breach of it may give rise: see *Dorset Yacht* case [1970] A.C. 1004, *per* Lord Reid at p. 1027. Examples of this are *Hedley Byrne's* case [1964] A.C. 465 where the class of potential plaintiffs was reduced to those shown to have relied upon the correctness of statements made, and *Weller & Co.* v. *Foot and Mouth Disease Research Institute* [1966] 1 Q.B. 569; and (I cite these merely as illustrations, without discussion) cases about 'economic loss' where, a duty having been held to exist, the nature of the recoverable damages was limited: see *S.C.M. (United Kingdom) Ltd.* v. *W. J. Whittall & Son Ltd.* [1971] 1 Q.B. 337 and *Spartan Steel & Alloys Ltd.* v. *Martin & Co. (Contractors) Ltd.* [1973] Q.B. 27.

The factual relationship between the council and owners and occupiers of new dwellings constructed in their area must be considered in the relevant statutory setting – under which the council acts. That was the Public Health Act 1936. . . .

To summarise the statutory position. The Public Health Act 1936, in particular Part II, was enacted in order to provide for the health and safety of owners and occupiers of buildings, including dwelling houses, by inter alia setting standards to be complied with in construction, and by enabling local authorities, through building byelaws, to supervise and control the operations of builders. One of the particular matters within the area of local authority supervision is the foundations of buildings – clearly a matter of vital importance, particularly because this part of the building comes to be covered up as building proceeds. Thus any weakness or inadequacy will create a hidden defect which whoever acquires the building has no means of discovering: in legal parlance there is no opportunity for intermediate inspection. So, by the byelaws, a definite standard is set for foundation work (see byelaw 18 (1) (b)[5] . . .: the builder is under a statutory (sc. byelaw) duty to notify the local authority before covering up the foundations: the local authority has at this stage the right to inspect and to insist on any correction necessary to bring the work into conformity with the byelaws. It must be in the reasonable contemplation not only of the builder but also of the local authority that failure to comply with the byelaws' requirement as to foundations may give rise to a hidden defect which in the future may cause damage to the building affecting the safety and health of owners and occupiers. And as the building is intended to last, the class of owners and occupiers likely to be affected cannot be limited to those who go in immediately after construction.

What then is the extent of the local authority's duty towards these persons? Although, as I have suggested, a situation of 'proximity' existed between the council and owners and occupiers of the houses, I do not think that a description of the council's duty can be based upon the 'neighbourhood' principle alone or upon merely any such factual relationship as 'control' as suggested by the Court of Appeal.[6] So to base it would be to neglect an essential factor which is that the local authority is a public body, discharging functions under statute: its powers and duties are definable in terms of public not private law. The problem which this type of action creates, is to define the circumstances in which the law should impose, over and above, or perhaps alongside, these public law powers and duties, a duty in private law towards individuals such that they may sue for damages in a civil court. It is in this

[5] [It is concerned to ensure that the foundations shall be such as to stop damage to the building from swelling or shrinking of the subsoil.]
[6] [In *Dutton* v. *Bognor Regis U.D.C.* [1972] 1 Q.B. 373.]

context that the distinction sought to be drawn between duties and mere powers has to be examined.

Most, indeed probably all, statutes relating to public authorities or public bodies, contain in them a large area of policy. The courts call this 'discretion' meaning that the decision is one for the authority or body to make, and not for the courts. Many statutes also prescribe or at least presuppose the practical execution of policy decisions: a convenient description of this is to say that in addition to the area of policy or discretion, there is an operational area. Although this distinction between the policy area and the operational area is convenient, and illuminating, it is probably a distinction of degree; many 'operational' powers or duties have in them some element of 'discretion.' It can safely be said that the more 'operational' a power or duty may be, the easier it is to superimpose upon it a common law duty of care.

I do not think that it is right to limit this to a duty to avoid causing extra or additional damage beyond what must be expected to arise from the exercise of the power or duty. That may be correct when the act done under the statute *inherently* must adversely *affect* the interest of individuals. But many other acts can be done without causing any harm to anyone — indeed may be directed to preventing harm from occurring. In these cases the duty is the normal one of taking care to avoid harm to those likely to be affected.

Let us examine the Public Health Act 1936 in the light of this. Undoubtedly it lays out a wide area of policy. It is for the local authority, a public and elected body, to decide upon the scale of resources which it can make available in order to carry out its functions under Part II of the Act — how many inspectors, with what expert qualifications, it should recruit, how often inspections are to be made, what tests are to be carried out, must be for its decision. It is no accident that the Act is drafted in terms of functions and powers rather than in terms of positive duty. As was well said, public authorities have to strike a balance between the claims of efficiency and thrift (du Parcq L.J. in *Kent* v. *East Suffolk Rivers Catchment Board* [1940] 1 K.B. 319, 338): whether they get the balance right can only be decided through the ballot box, not in the courts. It is said — there are reflections of this in the judgments in *Dutton* v. *Bognor Regis Urban District Council* [1972] 1 Q.B. 373 — that the local authority is under no duty to inspect, and this is used as the foundation for an argument, also found in some of the cases, that if it need not inspect at all, it cannot be liable for negligent inspection: if it were to be held so liable, so it is said, councils would simply decide against inspection. I think that this is too crude an argument. It overlooks the fact that local authorities are public bodies operating under statute with a clear responsibility for public health in their area. They must, and in fact do, make their discretionary decisions responsibly and for reasons which accord with the statutory purpose; see *Ayr Harbour Trustees* v. *Oswald* (1883) 8 App. Cas. 623, 639, *per* Lord Watson: . . . If they do not exercise their discretion in this way they can be challenged in the courts. Thus, to say that councils are under no duty to inspect, is not a sufficient statement of the position. They are under a duty to give proper consideration to the question whether they should inspect or not. Their immunity from attack, in the event of failure to inspect, in other words, though great is not absolute. And because it is not absolute, the necessary premise for the proposition 'if no duty to inspect, then no duty to take care in inspection' vanishes.

Passing then to the duty as regards inspection, if made. On principle there must surely be a duty to exercise reasonable care. The standard of care must be related to the duty to be performed – namely to ensure compliance with the byelaws. It must be related to the fact that the person responsible for construction in accordance with the byelaws is the builder, and that the inspector's function is supervisory. It must be related to the fact that once the inspector has passed the foundations they will be covered up, with no subsequent opportunity for inspection. But this duty, heavily operational though it may be, is still a duty arising under the statute. There may be a discretionary element in its exercise – discretionary as to the time and manner of inspection, and the techniques to be used. A plaintiff complaining of negligence must prove, the burden being on him, that action taken was not within the limits of a discretion bona fide exercised, before he can begin to rely upon a common law duty of care. But if he can do this, he should, in principle, be able to sue.

Is there, then, authority against the existence of any such duty or any reason to restrict it? It is said there is an absolute distinction in the law between statutory duty and statutory power – the former giving rise to possible liability, the latter not, or at least not doing so unless the exercise of the power involves some positive act creating some fresh or additional damage.

My Lords, I do not believe that any such absolute rule exists: or perhaps, more accurately, that such rules as exist in relation to powers and duties existing under particular statutes, provide sufficient definition of the rights of individuals affected by their exercise, or indeed their non-exercise, unless they take account of the possibility that, parallel with public law duties there may coexist those duties which persons – private or public – are under at common law to avoid causing damage to others in sufficient proximity to them. This is, I think, the key to understanding of the main authority relied upon by the appellants – *East Suffolk Rivers Catchment Board* v. *Kent* [1941] A.C. 74.

The statutory provisions in that case were contained in the Land Drainage Act 1930 and were in the form of a power to repair drainage works including walls or banks. The facts are well known: there was a very high tide which burst the banks protecting the respondent's land. The Catchment Board, requested to take action, did so with an allocation of manpower and resources (graphically described by MacKinnon L.J. [1940] 1 K.B. 319, 330) which was hopelessly inadequate and which resulted in the respondent's land being flooded for much longer than it need have been. There was a considerable difference of judicial opinion. Hilbery J. [1939] 2 All E.R. 207 who tried the case, held the board liable for the damage caused by the extended flooding and his decision was upheld by a majority of the Court of Appeal [1940] 1 K.B. 319. This House, by majority of four to one, reached the opposite conclusion [1941] A.C. 74. The speeches of their Lordships contain discussion of earlier authorities, which well illustrate the different types of statutory enactment under which these cases may arise. There are private Acts conferring powers – necessarily – to interfere with the rights of individuals: in such cases, an action in respect of damage caused by the exercise of the powers generally does not lie, but it may do so 'for doing that which the legislature has authorised, if it be done negligently': see *Geddis* v. *Bann Reservoir Proprietors* (1878) 3 App.Cas. 430, 456, *per* Lord Blackburn. Then there are cases where a statutory power is conferred, but the scale on which it is exercised is left to a local authority: *Sheppard* v. *Glossop Corporation* [1921] 3 K.B. 132. That concerned a power to light streets and the corporation decided, for economy reasons, to extinguish the lighting on Christmas night. Clearly this was within the discretion of the authority but Scrutton L.J. in the Court of Appeal, at p. 146, contrasted this situation with one where 'an option is given by statute to an authority to do or not to do a thing and it elects to do the thing that does it negligently.' (Compare *Indian Towing Co. Inc.* v. *United States* (1955) 350 U.S. 61, which makes just this distinction between a discretion to provide a lighthouse, and at operational level, a duty, if one is provided, to use due care to keep the light in working order.) Other illustrations are given.

My Lords, a number of reasons were suggested for distinguishing the *East Suffolk* case [1941] A.C. 74 – apart from the relevant fact that it was concerned with a different Act, indeed type of Act. It was said to be a decision on causation: I think that this is true of at least two of their Lordships (Viscount Simon L.C. and Lord Thankerton). It was said that the damage was already there before the board came on the scene: so it was but the board's action or inaction undoubtedly prolonged it, and the action was in respect of the prolongation. I should not think it right to put the case aside on such arguments. To me the two significant points about the case are, first, that it is an example, and a good one, where operational activity – at the breach in the wall – was still well within a discretionary area, so that the plaintiff's task in contending for a duty of care was a difficult one. This is clearly the basis on which Lord Romer, whose speech is often quoted as a proposition of law, proceeded. Secondly, although the case was decided in 1940, only one of their Lordships considered it in relation to a duty of care at common law. It need cause no surprise that this was Lord Atkin. . . . My Lords, I believe that the conception of a general duty of care, not limited to particular accepted situations, but extending generally over all relations of sufficient proximity, and even pervading the sphere of statutory functions of public bodies, had not at that time become fully recognised. Indeed it may well be that full recognition of the impact of *Donoghue* v. *Stevenson* in the latter sphere only came with the decision of this House in *Dorset Yacht Co. Ltd.* v. *Home Office* [1970] A.C. 1004.

In that case the Borstal officers, for whose actions the Home Office was vicariously responsible, were acting, in their control of the boys, under statutory powers. But it was held that, nevertheless they were under a duty of care as regards persons who might suffer damage as the result of their carelessness – see *per* Lord Reid, at pp. 1030–1031, Lord Morris of Borth-y-Gest, at p. 1036, Lord Pearson, at p. 1055: 'The existence of the statutory duties does not exclude liability at common law for negligence in the performance of the statutory duties.' Lord Diplock in his speech gives this topic extended consideration with a view to relating the officers' responsibility under public law to their liability in damages to members of the public under private, civil law: see pp. 1064 et seq. My noble and learned friend points out that the accepted principles which are applicable to powers conferred by a private Act of Parliament, as laid down in *Geddis* v. *Bann Reservoir Proprietors,* 3 App.Cas. 430, cannot automatically be applied to public statutes which confer a large measure of discretion upon public authorities. As regards the latter, for a civil action based on negligence at common law to succeed, there must be acts or omissions taken outside the limits of the delegated discretion: in such a case 'Its actionability falls to be determined by the civil law principles of negligence': see [1970] A.C. 1004, 1068.

It is for this reason that the law, as stated in some of the speeches in *East Suffolk Rivers Catchment Board* v. *Kent* [1941] A.C. 74, but not in those of Lord Atkin or Lord Thankerton, requires at the present time to be understood and applied with the recognition that, quite apart from such consequences as may flow from an examination of the duties laid down by the particular statute, there may be room, once one is outside the area of legitimate discretion or policy, for a duty of care at common law. It is irrelevant to the existence of this duty of care whether what is created by the statute is a duty or a power: the duty of care may exist in either case. The difference between the two lies in this, that, in the case of a power, liability cannot exist unless the act complained of lies outside the ambit of the power. In *Dorset Yacht Co. Ltd.* v. *Home Office* [1970] A.C. 1004 the officers may (on the assumed facts) have acted outside any discretion delegated to them and having disregarded their instructions as to the precautions which they should take to prevent the trainees from escaping: see *per* Lord Diplock, at p. 1069. So in the present case, the allegations made are consistent with the council or its inspector having acted outside any delegated discretion either as to the making of an inspection, or as to the manner in which an inspection was made. Whether they did so must be determined at the trial. In the event of a positive determination, and only so, can a duty of care arise. . . .

To whom the duty is owed. There is, in my opinion, no difficulty about this. A reasonable man in the position of the inspector must realise that if the foundations are covered in without adequate depth or strength as required by the byelaws, injury to safety or health may be suffered by owners or occupiers of the house. The duty is owed to them – not of course to a negligent building owner, the source of his own loss. I would leave open the case of users, who might themselves have a remedy against the occupier under the Occupiers' Liability Act 1957. A right of action can only be conferred upon an owner or occupier, who is such when the damage occurs (see below). This disposes of the possible objection that an endless, indeterminate class of potential plaintiffs may be called into existence.

The nature of the duty. This must be related closely to the purpose for which powers of inspection are granted, namely, to secure compliance with the byelaws. The duty is to take reasonable care, no more, no less, to secure that the builder does not cover in foundations which do not comply with byelaw requirements. The allegations in the statements of claim, in so far as they are based upon non-compliance with the plans, are misconceived. . . .

Nature of the damages recoverable. . . . The damages recoverable include all those which foreseeably arise from the breach of the duty of care which, as regards the council, I have held to be a duty to take reasonable care to secure compliance with the byelaws. Subject always to adequate proof of causation, these damages may include damages for personal injury and damage to property. In my opinion they may also include damage to the dwelling house itself; for the whole purpose of the byelaws in requiring foundations to be of a certain standard is to prevent damage arising from weakness of the foundations which is certain to endanger the health or safety of occupants.

To allow recovery for such damage to the house follows, in my opinion, from normal principle. If classification is required, the relevant damage is in my opinion material, physical damage, and what is recoverable is the amount of expenditure necessary to restore the dwelling to a condition in which it is no longer a danger to the health or safety of persons occupying and possibly (depending on the circumstances) expenses arising from necessary displacement. . . .

Conclusion. I would hold:

1. that *Dutton* v. *Bognor Regis Urban District Council* [1972] 1 Q.B. 373 was in the result rightly decided. The correct legal basis for the decision must be taken to be that established by your Lordships in this appeal;

2. that the question whether the defendant council by itself or its officers came under a duty of care toward the plaintiffs must be considered in relation to the powers, duties and discretions arising under the Public Health Act 1936;

3. that the defendant council would not be guilty of a breach of duty in not carrying out inspection of the foundations of the block unless it were shown (*a*) not properly to have exercised its discretion as to the making of inspections, and (*b*) to have failed to exercise reasonable care in its acts or omissions to secure that the byelaws applicable to the foundations of the block were complied with;

4. that the defendant council would be liable to the respondents for breach of duty if it were proved that its inspector, having assumed the duty of inspecting the foundations, and acting otherwise than in the bona fide exercise of any discretion under the statute, did not exercise reasonable care to ensure that the byelaws applicable to the foundations were complied with; . . .

And consequently that the appeal should be dismissed with costs.

[LORD DIPLOCK, LORD SIMON OF GLAISDALE, and LORD RUSSELL OF KILLOWEN agreed with LORD WILBERFORCE. LORD SALMON delivered a speech in favour of dismissing the appeal.]

Appeal dismissed.

Questions

1. Is the reason for requiring a finding of ultra vires as a precondition of liability in negligence that to do otherwise would be to take away decisions from public bodies which had been entrusted to them by Parliament; or is it because the courts are not suitable bodies to decide on the competing claims to what may be scarce resources; or is it both?

2. Should the ultra vires precondition to liability also apply in the case of the tort of nuisance? (Consider *Page Motors Ltd.* v. *Epsom and Ewell B.C.* (1982) 80 L.G.R. 337 on this point and more generally on the position of public authorities as defendants in nuisance actions. See further Appendix.)

3. Could *Anns* today be regarded as falling within the decision in *Cocks* v. *Thanet D.C.,* [1982] 3 W.L.R. 1121, on which see Note 3, p. 336 *supra,* or is it encompassed by Lord Diplock's comments on collateral attack in *O'Reilly* v. *Mackman,* p. 334 *supra?* And see further, Appendix.

Notes

1. As the student will no doubt be aware, *Anns* is of great importance to the tort of negligence in general, something that cannot be pursued here: on this point the student should consult textbooks on Tort. We shall concentrate upon its importance in relation to cases where a public, as opposed to a private body, is the defendant.

2. What is the position where the court is concerned with a duty rather than a power? There may, of course, be an action for breach of statutory duty, but can there in any event be an action for negligence? Lord Wilberforce in *Anns* clearly indicates that there can, and note Lord Pearson's comment in *Home Office* v. *Dorset Yacht Co. Ltd.* [1970] A.C. 1004 at p. 1055 that the existence of certain statutory duties owed to the Crown by Borstal officers 'does not exclude liability at common law for negligence in the performance of the statutory duties'. Some difficulty seems to be caused at first sight, however, by the later decision in *Haydon* v. *Kent C.C.* [1978] Q.B. 343. Lord Denning distinguished *Anns,* on which the plaintiff relied, as being concerned with powers as opposed to duties. In this case the duty of the authority was prescribed by statute 'and the only task of the courts is to define the scope of the statutory duty'. For Goff L.J. the alleged duty at common law fell within and could not exceed a particular statutory duty involved in the case (s. 44 of the Highways Act 1959) and he did not think the plaintiff had established any breach of that section.

It is submitted that this should be seen as a case where on the facts a statutory duty impliedly excluded any, or any greater, common law duty and that *Anns* can apply where statutory duties are involved. See further Oliver, (1980) 33 C.L.P. 269 at pp. 276–7.

3. Lord Wilberforce in *Anns* requires, as a precondition to liability in negligence, that even at the operational level the act or failure to act in question should be in excess or abuse of power. There is a danger that this would give public authorities an unjustified immunity, but, it is submitted, the best solution is to be found by regarding negligence as constituting an excess or abuse of power at this level: see Craig, (1978) 94 L.Q.R. 428 at pp. 452–4. On the other hand, at the policy level, differences between negligence and excess or abuse of power will certainly occur. The fact that an authority has exceeded or abused its powers may often not in itself be negligent: see Craig, op. cit., pp. 447–52. Thus the problem arises that the courts may still be faced with a claim which would require them to re-determine questions concerning the use of resources: the ultra vires hurdle, which will often protect them from this sort of question, would have failed to serve that purpose. *Anns* does not specifically deal with this problem. How do you think the courts will answer it? Consider further *Dunlop* v. *Woollahra M.C.,* p. 421 *infra.*

4. The distinction between the operational and the policy or discretionary area is obviously an important one and deserves some attention: see Craig, op. cit., pp.

442–7 for relevant American authorities. See further *Haydon* v. *Kent C.C.* [1978] Q.B. 343, where Goff L.J. regarded a decision to give priority to the gritting of roads rather than footpaths in wintry conditions as within the discretionary area, and see also the judgment of Lord Denning.

In *Bird* v. *Pearce* [1978] R.T.R. 290 a highway authority had, in the course of road re-surfacing, obliterated some double dotted white lines on the minor road at a crossing; the white lines were not replaced until some days after an accident had occurred at the crossing and no temporary warning sign had been in position in the meantime. Wood J. classified the re-surfacing work as something done at the operational level. He also referred to the highway authority's traffic system and to its decision to maintain that system (which involved warning users of the minor roads to give way) in that the system was reinstated once the re-surfacing was completed; the authority had 'exercised a discretion as to the siting, type and existence of the necessary road signs at this particular road junction' (p. 298). Wood J. then applied normal negligence principles in holding the authority liable, thereby (perhaps) impliedly supporting the argument *supra* that negligence will be regarded as ultra vires at the operational level. It had been argued by counsel for the authority that the decision not to put a warning sign was a policy decision, but this seems to have been overridden by Wood J. by virtue of the classification he adopted. For the decision of the Court of Appeal, see the Note following the next extract.

5. For further discussion of *Anns,* see *Takaro Properties Ltd.* v. *Rowling* [1978] 2 N.Z.L.R. 314. One of several interesting points in this case is that it concerned pure financial loss; note also Woodhouse J.'s view that only time will tell whether the ultra vires precondition of liability in negligence will apply to all statutory contexts (and see *Bird* v. *Pearce* [1979] R.T.R. 369, noted *infra*).

Liability of the Crown

Peter W. Hogg, p. 89

. . . [T]he line which separates the planning from the operational [a line which Hogg sees as separating liability from non-liability; cf. *Anns*] is crossed when a public body embarks on activity which creates *new* sources of danger to the public. Even then the taking of precautions may involve difficult questions of priority between competing demands for limited resources, but at the point where new dangers are created the proper judicial reluctance to interfere with administrative discretion is outweighed by the countervailing concern that members of the public should not be exposed to unreasonable risks – even from public bodies.

Note

Hogg, basing his argument on *East Suffolk Rivers Catchment Board* v. *Kent* [1941] A.C. 74, was writing before the decision in *Anns,* which should be compared with the first sentence of the extract. Nevertheless, Hogg's view should be considered along with the decision of the Court of Appeal in *Bird* v. *Pearce* [1979] R.T.R. 369. For the facts of that case, see Note 4 *supra*. The Court of Appeal did not specifically mention the operational/policy distinction, but emphasized the establishment of the traffic system (giving priority to the main road), which would be relied on by drivers. On this basis Eveleigh L.J. found that the authority came under a duty of care not to allow the system to get into such a condition that it constituted a danger (which had happened here). Megaw L.J. thought the authority had a duty to consider whether it was reasonable and practicable to establish temporary warning signs. In his opinion it was, and the authority, which was therefore under a duty to provide such a sign, was in breach of duty by not doing so.

But what about the authority's argument on policy (see Note 4, p. 420 *supra*)? Does *Bird* v. *Pearce* reveal some area to which *Anns* is inapplicable? See Oliver, op. cit., pp. 269–76, esp. at pp. 274–5, where the suggested rationalization of the decision is that 'if by the prior exercise of some function, whether discretionary or compulsory, a public authority creates a danger, then in the absence of some statutory provision to the contrary, whether express or implied, a duty of care arises; in such a case it is of no account that the actions involved in discharging the duty of care might, were it not for the existence of the duty of care, be "discretionary" '.

In *Anns* the power was to be exercised so as to *avoid* a danger created by another. Do you think a distinction should be taken between powers concerning the avoidance of danger created by the authority and those concerning its avoidance when created by another, in which the 'policy protection' of *Anns* would only be relevant to the latter? Does this reintroduce the sort of distinction which was put forward in argument in *Anns* about the *East Suffolk* case (see p. 416 *supra*), and which Lord Wilberforce was concerned to avoid? Is it consistent with *Home Office* v. *Dorset Yacht Co. Ltd.* [1970] A.C. 1004, referred to at p. 417 *supra*?

Dunlop v. Woollahra Municipal Council

[1982] A.C. 158   Judicial Committee of the Privy Council

The appellant claimed damages under various heads, including (*a*) negligence, and (*b*) abuse of public office. This extract concerns (*a*), but see p. 427 *infra* in relation to (*b*).

The judgment of their Lordships was delivered by LORD DIPLOCK.

The action in which this appeal to Her Majesty in Council is brought by the unsuccessful plaintiff, Dr. Dunlop, is the sequel to the previous action between the self-same parties tried before Wootten J. in which the plaintiff was successful: *Dunlop* v. *Woollahra Municipal Council* [1975] 2 N.S.W.L.R. 446. From that judgment the defendant, the council, did not appeal. Both that action and the present action arose out of two resolutions which the council passed on June 10, 1974, in purported exercise of their powers under section 308 and section 309 respectively in Part XI of the Local Government Act 1919, to fix a building line for the plaintiff's property at no. 8, Wentworth Street, Point Piper, and to regulate the number of storeys which might be contained in any residential flat building erected on that property.

In the first action the plaintiff sought and obtained from Wootten J. on September 26, 1975, declarations that each of the resolutions was invalid and void: the resolution fixing a building line because a procedural requirement as to giving notice to the plaintiff had not been satisfied, the resolution regulating the number of storeys because it was ultra vires. The judge expressly rejected the plaintiff's allegation that in passing the resolutions the council were not acting bona fide. In the instant case, which was tried by Yeldham J., the plaintiff claimed to recover from the council damages which he alleged he had sustained as a result of the invalid resolutions during the period from the passing of the resolutions on June 10, 1974, to October 25, 1975, this being the last day on which the council might have appealed against the judgment of Wootten J. . . . .

The basis of the plaintiff's allegation of negligence by the council in passing the resolution regulating the number of storeys that might be contained in any flat building on [no. 8] Wentworth Street at not more than three, was that they owed him a duty to take reasonable care to ascertain whether such a resolution was within their statutory powers. The breach of this duty of care that was alleged was the council's failure to seek proper detailed legal advice.

After discussing a number of Australian, English and Canadian cases Yeldham J. felt considerable doubt, which their Lordships share, as to the existence of any such duty of care owed to the plaintiff, but he found it unnecessary to go into this interesting jurisprudential problem since he was clear that even assuming the existence of such a duty no breach of it had been proved. The council's resolution of June 10, 1974, limiting the number of storeys was passed on the initiative and advice of their solicitors, as a lawful means of preventing the erection of residential flat buildings of more than three storeys on the properties in question if they were satisfied that this was desirable on planning grounds. What more could the council be reasonably expected to do than to obtain the advice of qualified solicitors whose competence they had no reason to doubt? It is true that Wootten J. held the legal advice which the council had received from their solicitors had been wrong; but it is only fair to the reputation of the solicitors, who gave it, to add that until that judgment made the matter res judicata between the parties, the question of law, which turned on the construction to be placed on two clauses in the planning scheme and in particular on whether or not a restriction upon the maximum number of storeys in residential flat buildings was inconsistent with a restriction upon the maximum height above sea level of all buildings, was an evenly balanced one and, in their Lordship' view, to answer it either way at any time before that judgment, could not have amounted to negligence on the part of a solicitor whose advice was sought upon the matter.

As respects the resolution which purported to fix the building lines the only ground on which Wootten J. held this to be void was because the council had failed to give the plaintiff the kind of hearing to which he was entitled before they passed it, and, in particular, because he should have been specifically informed, but was not, that the council were contemplating exercising their powers under section 308 to fix building lines. This question too was not an easy one, as is shown by the fact that it took Wootten J. 20 closely reasoned pages of his judgment and the citation of some two score of authorities to reach the conclusion that he did. Yeldham J. held that failure by a public authority to give a person an adequate hearing before deciding to exercise a statutory power in a manner which will affect him or his property, cannot by itself amount to a breach of a duty of care sounding in damages. Their Lordships agree. The effect of the failure is to render the exercise of the power void and the person complaining of the failure is in as good a position as the public authority to know that that is so. He can ignore the purported exercise of the power. It is incapable of affecting his legal rights. In agreement with Yeldham J. their Lordships are of opinion that the claim in negligence fails. . . .

Question

Do you agree that, in this sort of case (or more generally), a person may ignore a purported exercise of power? (See further Note 2 *infra*.)

Notes

1. On the relationship of natural justice and negligence, see also *Welbridge Holdings Ltd.* v. *Metropolitan Corporation of Greater Winnipeg* [1971] S.C.R. 957. In this case Laskin J., delivering the judgment of the Supreme Court of Canada, denied that a statutory body which was under an obligation to hold a public hearing owed a duty of care to see that natural justice was complied with in the hearing. More generally, the judgment goes against the imposition of a duty of care to keep within their powers on legislative bodies or statutory bodies exercising quasi-judicial functions; and see Wade, pp. 674–6 on judicial immunity. Does *Anns*, p. 412 *supra*, affect this (see Dugdale and Stanton, *Professional Negligence*, para. 5.14)? On the other hand, according to the *Welbridge* case, negligence could operate in relation to an authority's business powers (its administrative or ministerial powers). See further *Anns*, and on the relationship of business powers to the policy/operational distinction in *Anns*, see *Takaro Properties Ltd.* v. *Rowling* [1978] 2 N.Z.L.R. 314 at pp. 334–5. Procedural fairness can now, of course, be required in relation to administrative functions, a point also accepted in Canada. Do you think that a duty of care to comply with procedural fairness would be required in such a case?

2. For an example of causation problems that can arise in the application of the tort of negligence to public authorities, see Craig, (1978) 94 L.Q.R. 428 at p. 451. A causation issue is raised in particular by the Privy Council's opinion in the *Dunlop* case that a person can ignore a purported exercise of power. On this point see p. 94 *supra*. There has, however, been support for this approach in English law, for discussion of which see Rubinstein, *Jurisdiction and Illegality*, pp. 131–3; McBride, [1979] C.L.J. 323 at pp. 337–40, but compare the other authorities discussed there.

3. The well-known decision in *Hedley Byrne & Co. Ltd.* v. *Heller & Partners Ltd.* [1964] A.C. 465 has been applied to public authorities. Note the use of it in *Ministry of Housing and Local Government* v. *Sharp* [1970] 2 Q.B. 223.

4. Liability in negligence, of course, requires proof of fault. Other torts may involve strict liability, e.g. breach of statutory duty, *infra*, and *Rylands* v. *Fletcher* (1866) L.R. 1 Ex. 265; (1868) L.R. 3 H.L. 330. For discussion of the difficulties of the latter tort in this context, in particular the defence of statutory authority (which has been considered at p. 408 *supra*), see Craig, (1980) 96 L.Q.R. 413 at pp. 419–22; Wade, p. 664; and see especially *Dunne* v. *N. W. Gas Board* [1964] 2 Q.B. 806.

BREACH OF DUTY AND MISFEASANCE

Breach of statutory duty

Meade v. Haringey London Borough Council, p. 397 *supra*

Note

The action for damages for breach of statutory duty, which is quite frequently also brought against private bodies, is a well-recognized tort, but the question whether a particular breach of duty does give rise to a civil action is, in the absence of some express provision by the legislator, no easy one. See Winfield and Jolowicz on *Tort*, 11th edn., pp. 155–9. In *Meade* v. *Haringey L.B.C.* Lord Denning, citing Lord Simonds in *Cutler* v. *Wandsworth Stadium Ltd.* [1949] A.C. 398 at p. 407, referred to the question of actionability as being a question of construction of the statute; but his later comments in that case suggest a wide scope for the action for damages even where there is a default power so long as there has been an 'ultra vires breach of duty', on which see p. 401 *supra*. Is Lord Denning here going too far? Note Street's view (*The Law of Torts*, 7th edn., p. 278) that 'the courts will not readily allow an action in tort where public bodies have violated their general statutory duties'. On the basis of cases such as *Ferguson* v. *Earl of Kinnoull* (1842) 9 Cl. & Fin. 251, however, it can be said that where there is a public duty of a *ministerial* character (i.e. one involving no discretion or choice), then an action will lie and the court is not concerned with statutory interpretation: see Wade, p. 666; Rubinstein, op. cit., pp. 135–9. Nevertheless, the principle does not seem to have been put to use in recent times in actions for damages for breach of statutory duty, when the search for the legislator's intention has been paramount (Hogg, op. cit., p. 99; Craig, (1980) 96 L.Q.R. at pp. 422–3); nor do Lord Denning's later comments in *Meade* v. *Haringey L.B.C.* support the principle.

Misfeasance in public office

Smith v. East Elloe Rural District Council, p. 380 *supra*

Note

The point to pay attention to here is that the House of Lords thought that the action against the clerk should go to trial. For later unsuccessful proceedings against the clerk, see *Smith* v. *Pywell*, The Times, 29 April 1959. Diplock J. found that the purpose of the clerk was to further the interests of Council rather than injure the plaintiff, and that bad faith had not been established.

David v. Abdul Cader

[1963] 1 W.L.R. 834   Judicial Committee of the Privy Council

The appellant alleged that the respondent had wrongfully and maliciously refused to grant him a licence for his cinema even though he had paid the fee and satisfied the necessary conditions. The respondent put in an answer to the allegations, but a preliminary issue was tried as to whether the complaint disclosed a cause of action. The Supreme Court of Ceylon, following *Davis* v. *Bromley Corporation* [1908] 1 K.B. 170, answered the question in the negative. There was an appeal to the Judicial Committee of the Privy Council.

The judgment of their Lordships was delivered by VISCOUNT RADCLIFFE.

. . . The [Supreme Court's] judgment adopts the view that for an action in delict to succeed and afford a right to damages there must have been an infringement of an antecedent legal right of the person injured. The appellant, it appeared to the court, had no such right, since under the governing statute he was not entitled to exhibit cinematographs in his building without the licence of the local authority, and it had been left to the discretion of the chairman of the local council to decide whether to grant or to withhold the necessary licence.

If they were to regard this as a proposition equally valid for the English law of tort as for the Roman-Dutch law of delict (and the Supreme Court judgment relies exclusively on the authority of decisions in the English courts), their Lordships would have great difficulty in upholding it in so general a form. It does not appear to them that a right to damages is excluded by the mere circumstance that the appellant could not lawfully operate his cinema without a licence. Plainly the law forbade his doing so. But the question to be determined is not what rights he had without a licence but rather what rights were created between these two parties by the relationship under which one wished to operate a cinema and had applied for a licence to do so and the other had the statutory responsibility for deciding how to deal with that application. Whatever the limits of the range of the latter's discretion in carrying out that responsibility, a separate question which would need careful consideration if the action came to be tried, the appellant has at any rate pleaded that he had done everything required to qualify him for the grant of a licence and that he was entitled to have one issued. Given that relationship and the assumption of that state of facts, it seems to their Lordships impossible to say that the respondent did not owe some duty to the appellant with regard to the execution of his statutory power; and if, as pleaded, he had been malicious in refusing or neglecting to grant the licence, it is equally impossible to say without investigation of the facts that there cannot have been a breach of duty giving rise to a claim for damages.

The Supreme Court's opinion was based on the decision of the English Court of Appeal in *Davis* v. *Bromley Corporation*,[7] a decision which they presumably regarded as satisfactorily illustrative of the principles of the Roman-Dutch law of delict. The facts, indeed, of the *Davis* case[7] were closely similar to those pleaded here. There, too, a licence or statutory approval had been sought from and refused by a local authority, and the applicant issued a writ alleging that the authority had not acted bona fide in rejecting his plans but from motives of spite and claiming a declaration that he was entitled to

[7] [1908] 1 K.B. 170.

carry out his proposed works and damages for the refusal. The judgment of the court, which is shortly expressed, is to the effect that no action would lie in these circumstances; that the possible indirect motives attributed to the defendants could not render the exercise of their statutory discretion the more susceptible to judicial review than it would be otherwise; and that the plaintiff's only remedy, if the defendants had really made no true or bona fide exercise of their authority, was to apply for a mandamus to have his application properly heard and determined.

Davis's case[7] was decided in the year 1907. Since then the English courts have had to give much consideration to the general question of the rights of the individual dependent upon the exercise of statutory powers by a public authority, and the decision of that case would now have to be seen in the context of a very great number of later decisions that have dealt with the question at more length and with more elaboration. In their Lordships' opinion it would not be correct today to treat it as establishing any wide general principle in this field; certainly it would not be correct to treat it as sufficient to found the proposition, as asserted here, that an applicant for a statutory licence can in no circumstances have a right to damages if there has been a malicious misuse of the statutory power to grant the licence. Much must turn in such cases on what may prove to be the facts of the alleged misuse and in what the malice is found to consist. The presence of spite or ill-will may be insufficient in itself to render actionable a decision which has been based on unexceptionable grounds of consideration and has not been vitiated by the badness of the motive. But a 'malicious' misuse of authority, such as is pleaded by the appellant in his plaint, may cover a set of circumstances which go beyond the mere presence of ill-will, and in their Lordships' view it is only after the facts of malice relied upon by a plaintiff have been properly ascertained that it is possible to say in a case of this sort whether or not there has been any actionable breach of duty. . . .

[The Judicial Committee of the Privy Council's advice was that the appeal should be allowed. At one point it was said that the issue was 'a question of liability dependent directly upon the Roman–Dutch law of delict and only indirectly and by way of analogy and illustration upon the English law of torts'.]

Notes

1. Although the Privy Council was technically concerned with Roman–Dutch law in this case, it is submitted that the tenor of the judgment is such that it is also relevant to English law (and see *Campbell* v. *Ramsay* (1968) 70 S.R. (N.S.W.) 327 at pp. 332–3). A 'foreign element' was also present in another case which ought to be noted in relation to the misfeasance tort. This is the decision of the Supreme Court of Canada, on appeal from Quebec, in *Roncarelli* v. *Duplessis* [1959] S.C.R. 121. The Prime Minister of that Province had directed the cancellation of the plaintiff's restaurant's liquor licence by the Quebec Liquor Commission. He had no power over the Commission and his motive was (in part) to punish the plaintiff for having given security for bail for certain Jehovah's Witnesses, of which sect the plaintiff was a

member. The Prime Minister was held liable in damages, but the complication arising from the 'foreign element' concerns the extent to which the decision was based on Art. 1053 of the Quebec Civil Code, and hence how much guidance it gives to English law. See Rubinstein, op. cit., pp. 129–30.

2. The tort of misfeasance in public office has been the subject of a good deal of academic discussion in recent years: see e.g. Rubinstein, op. cit., pp. 128–33; Hogg, op. cit., pp. 81–5; Gould, (1972) 5 N.Z.U.L.R. 105; McBride, [1979] C.L.J. 323; Craig, (1980) 96 L.Q.R. 413 at pp. 426–8. Although the precise limits of the tort may be uncertain, it will be seen that the tort itself was described by the Privy Council in *Dunlop* v. *Woollahra M.C., infra*, as 'well-established'. Indeed it can be traced back to the famous decision of *Ashby* v. *White* (1703) 2 Ld. Raym. 938, 3 Ld. Raym. 320.

3. Causation can pose a particular problem with this tort. For example, where the plaintiff requires some positive exercise of power in his favour (e.g. the grant of a licence), then it may well not be clear that the wrongful denial of the licence has caused him any loss. The court may be unable to say what the result of an exercise of the power without the improper factor would have been. Note that in *David* v. *Abdul Cader* the appellant alleged that he had done everything necessary to entitle him to a licence, a point underlined in *Campbell* v. *Ramsay* (1968) 70 S.R. (N.S.W.) 327. (This latter case, in fact, suggests that the appellant in *David* v. *Abdul Cader* was issued with a licence but one which contained allegedly unlawful conditions: thus in the case there was an allegation of a refusal of a licence.) For further difficulty with causation, see *Dunlop* v. *Woollahra M.C.*, p. 421 *supra*, and Note 2, p. 423 *supra*.

Dunlop v. Woollahra Municipal Council

[1982] A.C. 158   Judicial Committee of the Privy Council

For the facts of this case, see p. 421 *supra*.

LORD DIPLOCK [delivering their Lordships' judgment]: . . . In pleading . . . that the council abused their public office and public duty the plaintiff was reying upon the well-established tort of misfeasance by a public officer in the discharge of his public duties. Yeldham J. rightly accepted that the council as a statutory corporation exercising local governmental functions was a public officer for the purposes of this tort. He cited a number of authorities upon the nature of this tort, to which their Lordships do not find it necessary to refer, for they agree with his conclusion that, in the absence of malice, passing without knowledge of its invalidity a resolution which is devoid of any legal effect is not conduct that of itself is capable of amounting to such 'misfeasance' as is a necessary element in this tort. So, in their Lordships' view, the claim . . . fails.

Their Lordships will humbly advise Her Majesty that this appeal should be dismissed. . . .

Notes

1. Prior to *Dunlop* v. *Woollahra M.C.* the mental element required for this tort had received particular attention in *Farrington* v. *Thomson and Bridgland* [1959] V.R.

286, a case in which the defendants had purported to give a binding order to the plaintiff to close his hotel for the sale of drink even though they knew they possesed no such power. Having surveyed earlier authorities, Smith J. rejected any requirement of an intent to injure and concluded (at p. 297):

> In my view . . . the rule should be taken to go this far at least, that if a public officer does an act which, to his knowledge, amounts to an abuse of his office, and he thereby causes damage to another person, then an action in tort for misfeasance in a public office will lie against him at the suit of that person.

Do you think that this test encompasses the ruling in *David* v. *Abdul Cader* that a malicious exercise of power could lead to liability? Does the latter cover any cases not caught by the former?

Smith J. did not go so far as to suggest any *general* rule that the mere abuse of office without malice or knowledge is actionable. Although there is authority against it, some cases seem to go this far: see *Brayser* v. *Maclean* (1875) L.R. 6 P.C. 398 (but see Wade, p. 672 n. 59); *McGillivray* v. *Kimber* (1915) 52 S.C.R. 146, on which see McBride, op. cit., pp. 329–31; *Wood* v. *Blair and Helmsley R.D.C.*, The Times, 5 July 1957. In this last-mentioned case the plaintiff, a dairy farmer, was prohibited from selling milk unless it was pasteurized. The notices prohibiting the sale of milk were held to be invalid by Hallett J. It was also held that, despite the defendants having acted from the best of motives, the plaintiff could have recovered damages for misfeasance from the Council if he had shown any damage (which in Hallett J.'s view he had not done). Note that, as commentators have pointed out, knowledge of the invalidity on the part of the defendants does not seem to have been established. An appeal was allowed by the Court of Appeal on the question whether any damage resulted, but the authority of the case is weakened by the fact that the defendants' counsel conceded in argument in the Court of Appeal that there was liability for misfeasance: see *Takaro Properties Ltd.* v. *Rowling* [1978] 2 N.Z.L.R. 314 at p. 340.

As has been mentioned, there is authority against so wide a liability, in particular in the recent case law. In addition to *Dunlop* v. *Woollahra M.C.*, *supra*, see *Takaro Properties Ltd.* v. *Rowling* and *Western Fish Products Ltd.* v. *Penwith D.C.* [1981] 2 All E.R. 204 at p. 226. In relation to a claim for damages based on an unsuccessful allegation of abuse of power in the *Western Fish* case, the Court of Appeal was in any event unconvinced that such an action could lie in the absence of fraud or malice. But what constitutes malice? Obviously it includes spite and ill-will, but note that in *Roncarelli* v. *Duplessis* Rand J. defined malice in this context as 'simply acting for a reason and purpose knowingly foreign to the administration' ([1959] S.C.R. at p. 141). Is the view in the *Western Fish* case consistent with the view of Smith J., *supra*, and of the Privy Council in the *Dunlop* case?

2. The limitations on this tort, and on the liability of public authorities in tort in general, have led many people to the view that this is an area of the law that is ripe for reform (and see further the comments of Lord Wilberforce in *F. Hoffmann-La Roche & Co. A.G.* v. *Secretary of State for Trade and Industry*, p. 98 *supra*). Consideration of this question was not within the terms of reference of the Law Commission in its review of remedies (Working Paper No. 40, paras. 145–8, though note the comments there; *Report on Remedies in Administrative Law*, Law Com. No. 73, Cmnd. 6407, para. 9). Nevertheless, a procedural reform did occur as a result of the Law Commission's deliberations, on which see Note 6, p. 319 *supra*. The judiciary may now in practice have more opportunity to develop the law. On the question of reform, note

further JUSTICE's proposal for a right to damages (*Administration under Law*, para. 73); Craig, op. cit., pp. 435–55; Fourteenth Report of the New Zealand Public and Administrative Law Reform Committee (*Damages in Administrative Law*).

JUDICIAL IMMUNITY

Sirros v. Moore

[1975] Q.B. 118   Court of Appeal

LORD DENNING M.R.: ... In the old days ... there was a sharp distinction between the inferior courts and the superior courts. Whatever may have been the reason for this distinction, it is no longer valid. There has been no case on the subject for the last one hundred years at least. And during this time our judicial system has changed out of all knowledge. So great is this change that it is now appropriate for us to reconsider the principles which should be applied to judicial acts. In this new age I would take my stand on this: as a matter of principle the judges of superior courts have no greater claim to immunity than the judges of the lower courts. Every judge of the courts of this land – from the highest to the lowest – should be protected to the same degree, and liable to the same degree. If the reason underlying this immunity is to ensure 'that they may be free in thought and independent in judgment,' it applies to every judge, whatever his rank. Each should be protected from liability to damages when he is acting judicially. Each should be able to do his work in complete independence and free from fear. He should not have to turn the pages of his books with trembling fingers, asking himself: 'If I do this, shall I be liable in damages?' So long as he does his work in the honest belief that it is within his jurisdiction, then he is not liable to an action. He may be mistaken in fact. He may be ignorant in law. What he does may be outside his jurisdiction – in fact or in law – but so long as he honestly believes it to be within his jurisdiction, he should not be liable. Once he honestly entertains his belief, nothing else will make him liable. He is not to be plagued with allegations of malice or ill-will or bias or anything of the kind. Actions based on such allegations have been struck out and will continue to be struck out. Nothing will make him liable except it be shown that he was not acting judicially, knowing that he had no jurisdiction to do it.

This principle should cover the justices of the peace, also. ... Aided by their clerks, they do their work with the highest degree of responsibility and competence – to the satisfaction of the entire community. They should have the same protection as the other judges. ...

Question

Should immunity extend to a judge who is carrying out essentially administrative functions, e.g. a magistrate in relation to licensing?

Note

For the relevance of the distinction between inferior and superior courts which has been drawn in this context, but which Lord Denning is rejecting, see Wade, pp. 674–5. In *Sirros* v. *Moore,* which in fact concerned a circuit judge sitting in the Crown Court, Ormrod L.J. agreed with Lord Denning's approach (although he also dealt with the case on the alternative basis that the old rules applied unmodified). On the difficulties of *Sirros* v. *Moore,* see further Brazier, [1976] P.L. 397. Lord Denning in essence repeated his views, but applied them more broadly, in the Court of Appeal in *O'Reilly* v. *Mackman* [1982] 3 W.L.R. 604. (The judgment in the House of Lords, p. 324 *supra,* did not refer to this point.) In *O'Reilly* v. *Mackman* Lord Denning, while accepting that certiorari might have been available, equated the position of a prison board of visitors with that of magistrates, and used judicial immunity to justify the refusal of declaratory relief in an action begun by writ or originating summons. Do the reasons for judicial immunity in *Sirros* v. *Moore* support this?

On the question of how far judicial immunity extends beyond courts of law, see, in addition to Lord Denning's views in *O'Reilly* v. *Mackman,* Wade, p. 676; Brazier, op. cit., pp. 409–18.

LIABILITY IN CONTRACT

Ayr Harbour Trustees v. Oswald, p. 145 *supra*

Rederiaktiebolaget Amphitrite v. The King, p. 446 *infra*

Note

There is no special body of law governing the contracts of public authorities, although they are subject to the doctrine of ultra vires, which limits their contractual capacity. See pp. 147 and 155 *supra*; Wade, p. 678. For the position of the Crown, which is somewhat different, see p. 438 *infra.*

Another aspect of government contracting is the use of the contracting power as an instrument of policy: see Turpin, *Government Contracts,* Ch. 9; Wade, p. 679. This may occur in the allocation of contracts, for example to support certain home industries (e.g. computer manufacturers), to support certain underdeveloped regions by preferring tenders from companies operating in those regions, and to encourage the reorganization of an industry (e.g. aircraft manufacturing) by the selective allocation of contracts. It may also occur where the government insists on the inclusion of certain terms in contracts. Thus the Fair Wages Resolution of the House of Commons (first introduced in 1891) is invariably incorporated in government contracts. *Inter alia,* this requires those who contract with the goverment to pay their employees wages that are not less favourable than those established for the relevant industry in the district where the work is to be carried out and to refrain from unlawful discrimination in employment. The government has, however, announced its intention to rescind the current resolution which dates from 1946 (28 H.C. Deb., col. 597).

The most notable recent example of the use of the contracting power to implement policy has been the government's attempt, between 1975 and 1978, to ensure that various non-statutory wages policies set out in 'guidelines' issued by the government were adhered to. Terms were inserted in government contracts requiring the contractor to adhere to the policies and to require a similar undertaking from any sub-contractor. Companies that broke the pay policy were placed on a 'blacklist' and were not awarded contracts thereafter. The government also sought to withhold assistance and grants under the Export Credit Guarantee scheme and the Industry Act 1972; see further Ganz, [1978] P.L. 333; Daintith, (1979) 32 C.L.P. 41; Wade, *Constitutional Fundamentals,* p. 55. The absence of any special law of government contracts means that the government appears to have the same freedom in deciding with whom to contract as the private citizen, subject only to the fact that contracts made in pursuance of statutory powers will be subject to the ultra vires doctrine and any restrictions imposed by virtue of the U.K.'s membership of the European Economic Community. The potential of the ultra vires doctrine as a control is as yet untested, although see the arguments advanced in *British Oxygen Co. Ltd.* v. *Minister of Technology,* p. 141 *supra,* but cf. *Wilson, Walton International Ltd.* v. *Tees and Hartlepools Port Authority* [1969] 1 Lloyd's Rep. 120. For general consideration of this issue, see Ganz, op. cit.; Daintith, op. cit., Detailed consideration of the obligations imposed on members of the European Economic Community is not possible here, but Community directives prohibiting certain forms of discrimination and co-ordinating contracting procedures in tender have been issued: see Turpin, (1972) 9 C.M.L.R. 411; and more recetly Daintith, op. cit., and Directive 80/767, O.J. 1980, L. 215. Practices such as 'blacklisting' and the removal of names from departmental lists of 'approved contractors' which do not appear to be subject to judicial control under domestic English law, even for breach of natural justice (see e.g. Turpin, *Government Contracts,* pp. 140–3), may now be reviewed by reference to the law of the European Community; Daintith, op. cit. Consider further p. 633 *infra.*

LIABILITY TO MAKE RESTITUTION

William Whiteley Ltd. v. The King

(1909) 101 L.T. 741 King's Bench Division

William Whiteley Ltd. brought a petition of right to recover fees paid to the Inland Revenue for licences in respect of certain of its employees who were said to be 'male servants' for the purposes of the relevant statute. The servants in question were employed to prepare and serve meals to other employees. William Whiteley Ltd. claimed that these servants were not 'male servants' under the Act and, having taken out licences and paid the fees under protest for a number of years, then declined to apply for licences and withheld payment. The company was later summonsed for employing those servants without having the appropriate licences for them. However, the Divisional Court held (*Whiteley* v. *Burns* [1908] 1 K.B. 705) that the servants were not 'male servants' for the purposes of the relevant statute, and that the company was not liable to take out or pay for licences for them. Thereafter the proceedings in this case were brought.

WATSON J.: . . . Undoubtedly the moneys were paid under a mistaken belief on the part of Messrs. Whiteley Limited that they were bound to pay them; but there is no general rule that if duties are paid to the Inland Revenue by mistake as to liability – by mistake as to law – they can be recovered back. In fact the general rule is the other way – namely, that if they have been voluntarily paid under a mistake, a mistake not of fact but a mistake of law, then they cannot be recovered back. . . .

. . . There is no doubt as to the general rule . . . what money paid voluntarily – that is to say, without compulsion or extortion or undue influence, and, of course, I may add without any fraud on the part of the person to whom it is paid, and with knowledge of all the facts, though paid without any consideration, or in discharge of a claim not due, or a claim which might have been successfully resisted, cannot be recovered back. There is no doubt, and no question raised, that that is an accurate statement of the general rule. But, on the other hand, if the payment is not voluntary a different rule applies which may be stated, perhaps, as it is stated in Leake on Contracts, (5th edit., p. 61), that money extorted by a person for doing what he is legally bound to do without payment, or for a duty which he fails to perform, may be recovered back; as in the cases of illegal or excessive fees and payments extorted in the discharge of an office; and money paid under duress either of the person or of goods may be recovered back (pp. 58, 59). In all those cases the payment is not voluntary. The question which I have to decide here is whether the payments made . . . were or were not voluntary payments. Was there any duress here? I cannot find any evidence of duress or compulsion beyond this, that the supervisor, the officer of Inland Revenue, told Messrs. Whiteley Limited that in the opinion of the Commissioners of Inland Revenue these duties were payable, and that if they were not paid proceedings would be taken for penalties. That is the only evidence of anything which could be called duress or compulsion. The suppliants knew all the facts. They had present to their minds plainly, when these payments were made, that there was a question as to whether upon such servants as those in question duty was payable. They themselves raised that question and they paid the duties. . . . They knew that the Commissioners of Inland Revenue could not determine whether the duties were payable or not. They could take no action if the duties were not paid except by legal proceedings. . . . In these circumstances I have come to the conclusion that there was nothing in this case which amounted to compulsion. But it was suggested that the case came within that class of cases in which money has been held to be recoverable back if it has been paid in discharge of a demand illegally made under colour of an office. . . . In all those cases in order to have that done which the person making the payment was entitled to have done without a payment, he had to make the payment, and someone who was bound to do something which the person paying the money desired to have done, refused to do his duty unless he was paid the money. If in those circumstances money is paid, then it can be recovered back. There is there an element of duress. . . . I am satisfied that this case does not fall within that class of cases, and that neither on that ground nor on the ground that this was a compulsory payment are the suppliants entitled to recover back the moneys which they paid. . . .

Judgment for the Crown.

Notes

1. This case appears to assume that restitutionary claims against public bodies rest on the same rules of law that govern claims against individuals and non-public bodies. See also *Twyford v. Manchester Corporation* [1946] Ch. 236 and *F. Hoffmann-La Roche & Co. A.G. v. Secretary of State for Trade and Industry* per Lord Reid at p. 95 *supra*. It has, however, been criticized for this reason. See especially Birks, (1980) 33 C.L.P. 191 at p. 194, a most valuable article to which this discussion is much indebted. See also Goff and Jones, *The Law of Restitution*, 2nd edn., p. 173; Beatson, [1974] C.L.J. 97 at pp. 110–12; Marsh, (1946) 62 L.Q.R. 333. There is, moreover, authority which supports recovery on a broader basis. Subject to a limit (on which see Note 3 *infra*), this would allow recovery where a public body receives payment in response to an ultra vires demand in a situation in which the public body has power to withhold something which it is under a statutory duty to provide at no cost or for less than is demanded. This is the case whether or not there was duress in the sense of an actual or threatened withholding of the subject-matter of the duty. Thus, in *Steele v. Williams* (1853) 8 Ex. 625, a person who wished to take extracts from a parish register and did this after the parish clerk had asserted that a certain charge would be due, recovered the sum paid. It appears that the payment was made after the extracts were taken and that the plaintiff had not been told that he could not search if he did not pay. Platt B. said (at p. 631) that the parish clerk took the money at his peril: 'he was a public officer, and ought to have been careful that the sum demanded did not exceed the legal fee'. For other cases, see Birks, op. cit., Birks also argues (at p. 203) that constitutional principle requires that money levied without parliamentary consent should not be kept by a public body.

2. Another criticism of the assimilation of the rules governing payments to public bodies and those governing payments to private individuals is that it is not uniformly applied. Thus, where an ultra vires payment is made *by* a public body it would seem that the recipient will find it more difficult to establish a defence (such as estoppel) than if the payment had been made by a private individual. See *Commonwealth of Australia v. Burns* [1971] V.R. 825 at pp. 827–8 and *Auckland Harbour Board v. The King* [1924] A.C. 318 at p. 327. In the latter case the Privy Council stated that any 'payment . . . made without Parliamentary authority is simply illegal and ultra vires, and may be recovered by the Government if it can . . . be traced. . . . [T]o invoke analogies of what might be held in a question between subject and subject is hardly relevant.'

3. Even if the distinction between payments to public bodies and payments to others is rejected, the scope of the 'mistake of law' doctrine applied in *William Whiteley Ltd. v. The King* is open to criticism. Goff and Jones, *op. cit.*, p. 91, argue that money paid under such a mistake should only be irrecoverable if it was paid in settlement of an honest claim. On the other hand, although this may not seem conclusive when weighed against the requirements of the ultra vires doctrine and constitutional principle, the broad principle enunciated in Note 1 *supra* needs to be limited to protect the stability of public funds. To require repayment of all sums collected, perhaps over a period of years, once litigation has established that the payments were not authorized could cause chaos. For example, in *Daymond v. South West Water Authority* [1976] A.C. 609 it was declared that the collection of sewerage charges from individuals whose houses were not connected to the public sewers was ultra vires. The plaintiff's own charge was £4.89 but the total annual sum collected from such charges was £33,000,000. See further Birks, op. cit., pp. 204–5.

4. In the case of overpayment of taxes, s. 33 (1) of the Taxes Management Act 1970 provides for repayment where the assessment was excessive by reason of some error or mistake in the return made by the taxpayer. Goff and Jones, op. cit., p. 104, state that relief may be given where the taxpayer's mistake is one of law, but not where the return is made on the basis of Revenue practice which has subsequently been shown to be wrong in law (s. 33 (2)).

LIABILITY TO PAY COMPENSATION

Note

See Wade, p. 685.

14

CROWN PROCEEDINGS

THE CROWN IN LITIGATION

Notes

1. See Wade, p. 697, especially on the position of the Crown prior to the passing of the Crown Proceedings Act 1947.

2. For a recent comment on the use of the term 'the Crown', see *Town Investments Ltd. v. Department of the Environment* [1978] A.C. 359. Lord Diplock, with the agreement of Lord Simon, Lord Kilbrandon, and Lord Edmund-Davies, stated (at pp. 380–1):

> . . . [T]o continue nowadays to speak of 'the Crown' as doing legislative or executive acts of government, which, in reality as distinct from legal fiction, are decided on and done by human beings other than the Queen herself, involves risk of confusion. . . . Where . . . we are concerned with the legal nature of the exercise of executive powers of government, I believe that some of the more Athanasian-like features of the debate in your Lordships' House could have been eliminated if instead of speaking of 'the Crown' we were to speak of 'the government' – a term appropriate to embrace both collectively and individually all of the ministers of the Crown and parliamentary secretaries under whose direction the administrative work of government is carried on by the civil servants employed in the various government departments. It is through them that the executive powers of Her Majesty's government in the United Kingdom are exercised, sometimes in the more important administrative matters in Her Majesty's name, but most often under their own official designation. Executive acts of government that are done by any of them are acts done by 'the Crown' in the fictional sense in which that expression is now used in English public law.

For comment see Wade, p. 50 n. 2 who states that 'the case did not concern statutory powers and it should presumably not be taken to alter the rule that powers conferred upon ministers belong to them personally and not to the Crown'; as Wade points out, if it did there would be an adverse impact on remedies, on which see pp. 324 and 405–6 *supra*.

LIABILITY IN TORT

Crown Proceedings Act 1947

2. – (1) Subject to the provisions of this Act, the Crown shall be subject to all those liabilities in tort to which, if it were a private person of full age and capacity, it would be subject: –

(*a*) in respect of torts committed by its servants or agents;

(*b*) in respect of any breach of those duties which a person owes to his servants or agents at common law by reason of being their employer; and

(*c*) in respect of any breach of the duties attaching at common law to the ownership, occupation, possession or control of property:

Provided that no proceedings shall lie against the Crown by virtue of paragraph (*a*) of this subsection in respect of any act or omission of a servant or agent of the Crown unless the act or omission would apart from the provisions of this Act have given rise to a cause of action in tort against that servant or agent or his estate.

(2) Where the Crown is bound by a statutory duty which is binding also upon persons other than the Crown and its officers, then, subject to the provisions of this Act, the Crown shall, in respect of a failure to comply with that duty, be subject to all those liabilities in tort (if any) to which it would be so subject if it were a private person of full age and capacity.

(3) Where any functions are conferred or imposed upon an officer of the Crown as such either by any rule of the common law or by statute, and that officer commits a tort while performing or purporting to perform those functions, the liabilities of the Crown in respect of the tort shall be such as they would have been if those functions had been conferred or imposed solely by virtue of instructions lawfully given by the Crown.

(4) Any enactment which negatives or limits the amount of the liability of any Government department or officer of the Crown in respect of any tort committed by that department or officer shall, in the case of proceedings against the Crown under this section in respect of a tort committed by that department or officer, apply in relation to the Crown as it would have applied in relation to that department or officer if the proceedings against the Crown had been proceedings against that department or officer.

(5) No proceedings shall lie against the Crown by virtue of this section in respect of anything done or omitted to be done by any person while discharging or purporting to discharge any responsibilities of a judicial nature vested in him, or any responsibilities which he has in connection with the execution of judicial process.

(6)[1] No proceedings shall lie against the Crown by virtue of this section in respect of any act, neglect or default of any officer of the Crown, unless that officer has been directly or indirectly appointed by the Crown and was at the material time paid in respect of his duties as an officer of the Crown wholly out of the Consolidated Fund of the United Kingdom, moneys provided by Parliament, or any other Fund certified by the Treasury for the purposes of this subsection or was at the material time holding an office in respect of which the Treasury certify that the holder thereof would normally be so paid.

10. – (1) Nothing done or omitted to be done by a member of the armed

---

[1] [As amended by the Statute Law (Repeals) Act 1981.]

forces of the Crown while on duty as such shall subject either him or the Crown to liability in tort for causing the death of another person, or for causing personal injury to another person, in so far as the death or personal injury is due to anything suffered by that other person while he is a member of the armed forces of the Crown if –

(a) at the time when that thing is suffered by that other person, he is either on duty as a member of the armed forces of the Crown or is, though not on duty as such, on any land, premises, ship, aircraft or vehicle for the time being used for the purposes of the armed forces of the Crown; and

(b) the [Secretary of State][2] certifies that his suffering that thing has been or will be treated as attributable to service for the purposes of entitlement to an award under the Royal Warrant, Order in Council or Order of His Majesty relating to the disablement or death of members of the force of which he is a member:

Provided that this subsection shall not exempt a member of the said forces from liability in tort in any case in which the court is satisfied that the act or omission was not connected with the execution of his duties as a member of those forces.

(2) No proceedings in tort shall lie against the Crown for death of personal injury due to anything suffered by a member of the armed forces of the Crown if –

(a) that thing is suffered by him in consequence of the nature or condition of any such land, premises, ship, aircraft or vehicle as aforesaid, or in consequence of the nature or condition of any equipment or supplies used for the purposes of those forces; and

(b) the [Secretary of State][2] certifies as mentioned in the preceding subsection;

nor shall any act or omission of an officer of the Crown subject him to liability in tort for death or personal injury, in so far as the death or personal injury is due to anything suffered by a member of the armed forces of the Crown being a thing as to which the conditions aforesaid are satisfied.

(3)[3] A Secretary of State, if satisfied that it is the fact: –

(a) that a person was or was not on any particular occasion on duty as a member of the armed forces of the Crown; or

(b) that at any particular time any land, premises, ship, aircraft, vehicle, equipment or supplies was or was not, or were or were not, used for the purposes of the said forces;

may issue a certificate certifying that to be the fact; and any such certificate shall, for the purposes of this section, be conclusive as to the fact which it certifies.

[2] [Substituted by S.I. 1968 No. 1699.]
[3] [As amended by S.I. 1964 No. 488.]

38. (2) In this Act, except in so far as the context otherwise requires or it is otherwise expressly provided, the following expressions have the meanings hereby respectively assigned to them, that is to say:–

'Agent', when used in relation to the Crown, includes an independent contractor employed by the Crown; . . .

'Officer', in relation to the Crown, includes any servant of His Majesty, and accordingly (but without prejudice to the generality of the foregoing provision) includes a Minister of the Crown; . . .

40. – (1) Nothing in this Act shall apply to proceedings by or against, or authorise proceedings in tort to be brought against, His Majesty in His private capacity. . . .

Note

For general discussion of these provisions, see in particular Wade, p. 703; Williams, *Crown Proceedings,* Ch. 2; Street, *Governmental Liability,* pp. 25–50. These passages discuss, *inter alia,* who is a Crown servant or agent for this purpose, on which see also Treitel, [1957] P.L. 321 at pp. 326–35. The question of the liability in tort of public authorities was discussed in Ch. 13 *supra,* and that discussion is, of course, relevant to this section as well.

LIABILITY IN CONTRACT

General principles

Crown Proceedings Act 1947

1. Where any person has a claim against the Crown after the commencement of this Act, and, if this Act had not been passed, the claim might have been enforced, subject to the grant of His Majesty's fiat, by petition of right, or might have been enforced by a proceeding provided by any statutory provision repealed by this Act, then, subject to the provisions of this Act, the claim may be enforced as of right, and without the fiat of His Majesty, by proceedings taken against the Crown for that purpose in accordance with the provisions of this Act.

Notes

1. Until the Crown Proceedings Act, it was recognized that the Crown could be liable for breach of contract, but the only remedy was a petition of right. As a result of the Act proceedings against the Crown in contract are, for the most part, governed by the same rules as proceedings between subjects (see Wade, pp. 678–81 and 708–12. There are, however, significant differences. As has been seen (p. 290 *supra*), no injunctive or specific relief may be given against the Crown. Other differences will be explored in this chapter. Note further s. 40 of the 1947 Act, *supra,* and Sch. 1 to the Act, p. 460 *infra,* on the position of Her Majesty in her personal capacity: see Wade, p. 710.

2. The Crown has the power to contract without the need for any specific statutory authority since, as a non-statutory Corporation sole, its contractual capacity does not appear to be limited. It has been suggested, however, that this may only be the case for

contracts which are incidental to the ordinary and well-recognized functions of government (*New South Wales* v. *Bardolph* (1934) 52 C.L.R. 455 at pp. 474–75, 496, 502–3, and 508) but there appears to be no reason in principle for such a limitation (*Verrault & Fils Ltée* v. *Attorney General of the Province of Quebec* [1977] 1 S.C.R. 41; Turpin, *Government Contracts*, p. 19. In certain cases the powers of individual ministers have been defined by statute (e.g. s. 1 of the Supply Powers Act 1975) or by statutory instruments made under the Ministers of the Crown Act 1975. These may limit the capacity of the Crown itself (*Cugden Rutile (No. 2) Ltd.* v. *Chalk* [1975] A.C. 520) or the scope of the authority possessed by ministers and Crown agents (p. 450 *infra*).

The State of New South Wales v. Bardolph

(1934) 52 C.L.R. 455   High Court of Australia

Acting on the authority of the State Premier, and 'as a matter of Government policy', the New South Wales Tourist Bureau contracted for the insertion of advertisements in the plaintiff's newspaper, *Labor Weekly*, for a period of twelve months in the financial years 1931–2 and 1932–3. Shortly after the making of the contract there was a change of government and the new administration refused to use or to pay for any further advertising space in the newspaper. The plaintiff (Bardolph) continued to insert the advertisements for the remainder of the contract period and claimed £1,114. 10s., the amount outstanding on the contract. The contract had not been expressly authorized by the State legislature or by any Order in Council or executive minute. The Supply and Appropriation Acts for the relevant years included the provision of sums for 'Government advertising'. This provision was for sums much larger than the amount involved in the contract.

EVATT J.: . . . The suggested defence that the contract was not authorized by the Government completely fails. It is only right to add that, although raised in the pleadings, this defence was not seriously pressed at the hearing.

The main, indeed the only real defence relied upon by the State of New South Wales, was that Parliament did not make public moneys available for the express purpose of paying the plaintiff for his advertising services. The defence is, of course, quite unmeritorious, and its success might tend to establish a dangerous precedent in the future. But it raises an interesting question of law, the examination of which shows that the repudiation of subsisting agreements by a new administration can seldom be ventured upon with success. . . .

[He then considered the facts in relation to the relevant grants of public money by Parliament for the period ending 30 June 1932, and concluded:] The net result is that the total supply which Parliament made available during the year for Government advertising can be reckoned as amounting to eleven-twelfths of £6,600, plus one-twelfth of £9,900, that is, £6,875 in all.

It appears from the statement prepared by Mr. Kelly, Chief Accountant at the Treasury, that if payment had been made to the plaintiff in respect of the advertisements inserted before the end of the financial year, 30th June, 1932, but not paid for, the total expenditure for the service would only have amounted to £4,595 18s., a figure considerably lower than the assumed minimum supply voted by Parliament, that is, £6,875....

Before referring to what took place in the financial year 1932–1933, it is convenient to consider the legal position as it existed on and in respect of 30th June, 1932. It was argued for the State that it was a condition of the contracts with the plaintiff that all payments of money thereunder should be authorized by Act of Parliament, and it was said that no person can successfully sue the State of New South Wales in the absence of a precise or specific Parliamentary allocation of public moneys for the purpose of making payments under the contracts. It was further contended that, even in an Appropriation Act, the constitutional condition of such contracts is not fulfilled unless it can be shown that Parliament's intention was directed to the particular payment to the particular contractor....

In the well-known case of *Churchward* v. *The Queen*,[4] *Shee* J., in a passage often cited, adopted the principle that, in the case of a contract by a subject with the Crown, there should be implied a condition that the providing of funds by Parliament is a condition precedent to the Crown's liability to pay moneys which would otherwise be payable under the contract. In that case the actual promise was to pay a sum 'out of the moneys to be provided by Parliament' (see *Churchward* v. *The Queen*[5]); so that the judgment of *Shee* J. went beyond the actual point necessary to determine the case. *Churchward's Case*[6] was decided upon demurrer, the third plea alleging that 'no moneys were ever provided by Parliament for the payment to the suppliant for, *or out of which the suppliant could be paid* for the performance of the said contract, for any part of the said period subsequent to the 20th June, 1863, or for the payment to the suppliant for, and in respect of, or *out of which the suppliant could be paid or compensated for,* in respect of any damages sustained by the suppliant by reason of any of the breaches of the said contract committed subsequent to the said 20th of June, 1863'.[7] (I italicize certain words.)

Further, the *Appropriation Acts* referred to in that case expressly provided that Churchward's claim was to be excluded from the large sum of money (£950,000) thereby voted for the general purposes of providing and maintaining the Post Office Packet Service.

The judgment of *Shee* J. has always been accepted as determining the general constitutional principle. But it should be added that *Cockburn* C.J. said:[8]

> 'I agree that, if there had been no question as to the fund being supplied by Parliament, if the condition to pay had been absolute, or if there had been a fund applicable to the purpose, and this difficulty did not stand in the petitioner's way, and he had been throughout ready and willing to

---

[4] (1865) L.R. 1 Q.B. 173, at pp. 209, 210.
[5] (1865) L.R. 1 Q.B., at p. 174.
[6] (1865) L.R. 1 Q.B. 173.
[7] (1865) L.R. 1 Q.B. at p. 183.
[8] (1865) L.R. 1 Q.B., at p. 201.

perform this contract, and had been prevented and hindered from rendering these services by the default of the Lords of the Admiralty, then he would have been in a position to enforce his right to remuneration.'

It appears clear that the first part of this passage has not been acted upon by the Courts in the cases subsequently determined, and that, even where the contract to pay is in terms 'absolute' and the contract fails to state that the fund has to be 'supplied by Parliament,' the Crown is still entitled to rely upon the implied condition mentioned by *Shee* J.

The second part of *Cockburn's* C.J. statement, that, if there is fund 'applicable to the purpose' of meeting claims under the contract, the contractor may enforce his right to remuneration, has never, so far as I know, been questioned. Moreover, its correctness was assumed by the terms of the Crown's third plea in *Churchward's Case*[9] which denies that moneys were ever provided by Parliament 'out of which the suppliant could be paid for the performance of the said contract.' . . .

In *Commercial Cable Co.* v. *Government of Newfoundland*[10] Viscount *Haldane* said:

'For all grants of public money, either direct or by way of prospective remission of duties imposed by statute, must be in the discretion of the Legislature, and where the system is that of responsible government, there is no contract unless that discretion can be taken to have been exercised in some sufficient fashion.'

This general principle adopts the main principle of *Churchward* v. *The Queen*,[11] though expressing it somewhat differently. However, the statement affords no guidance as to what will, under any particular circumstances, constitute a 'sufficient' expression of the exercise of the Legislature's discretion to grant or withhold public moneys.

[He then considered *Auckland Harbour Board* v. *R*.[12] and continued:] It is abundantly clear, I think, that the *Auckland Harbour Board Case*[12] does not justify the theory that, where there is nothing unlawful in a contract entered into by the Crown, and that contract is authorized by responsible Ministers, and made by them in the ordinary course of administering the affairs of Government, a detailed reference to the particular contract must be found in the statutory grant in order to satisfy the constitutional condition laid down in *Churchward's Case*.[13] . . .

It has been the practice of the Government to enter into advertising contracts, the performance of which extends or may extend into more than one financial year, apart altogether from the innumerable contracts for single insertion advertisements in newspapers and periodicals. For instance, on 1st June, 1932, the Government entered into a contract with the proprietor of the

[9] (1865) L.R. 1 Q.B. 173.
[10] (1916) 2 A.C. 610, at p. 617.
[11] (1865) L.R. 1 Q.B. 173.
[12] (1924) A.C. 318.
[13] (1865) L.R. 1 Q.B. 173.

Sydney Morning Herald, and accepted a heavy liability for advertisements covering the month of June in the financial year 1931–1932, and eleven months during the following financial year. Payments were made to the proprietor from time to time in accordance with the contract. But no reference whatever was made to this particular contract in any Act of Parliament. If the argument for the State is right, this money is recoverable back from the proprietor, although the contract has been fully performed on the part of the newspaper. Contracts of a like character were admitted in evidence in order to show the practice of the Government in relation to the Government advertising business of the State and in order to measure the precise surplus or deficiency in the Parliamentary grants for advertising. But the contracts also show that it has never been the practice for Parliament itself to consider with particularity that large number of contracts, payments under all of which are made in reliance upon the general Parliamentary grant for Government advertising. . . .

[He then considered the views of Durell, *Parliamentary Grants,* pp. 21, 296, and 297, and Maitland, *Constitutional History of England,* pp. 445–6, and concluded:] . . . [I]n the absence of some controlling statutory provision, contracts are enforceable against the Crown if (*a*) the contract is entered into in the ordinary or necessary course of Government administration, (*b*) it is authorized by the responsible Ministers of the Crown, and (*c*) the payments which the contractor is seeking to recover are covered by or referable to a parliamentary grant for the class of service to which the contract relates. In my opinion, moreover, the failure of the plaintiff to prove (*c*) does not affect the validity of the contract in the sense that the Crown is regarded as stripped of its authority or capacity to enter into the contract. Under a constitution like that of New South Wales where the legislative and executive authority is not limited by reference to subject matter, the general capacity of the Crown to enter into a contract should be regarded from the same point of view as the capacity of the King would be by the Courts of common law. No doubt the King had special powers, privileges, immunities and prerogatives. But he never seems to have been regarded as being less powerful to enter into contracts than one of his subjects. The enforcement of such contracts is to be distinguished from their inherent validity. . . .

In the present case, the position as it existed on 30th June, 1932, was that (*a*) the Crown had made contracts with the plaintiff, and (*b*) moneys had been made legally available by the Supply Acts, including that of June, 1932. It is admitted that the advertising service vote, if otherwise sufficient to satisfy the rule in *Churchward's Case,*[14] covered the service called for by the contracts with the plaintiff. On 30th June, therefore, there was (*a*) an existing contract, (*b*) a sufficient compliance with the rule in *Churchward's Case*[14], (*c*) a proved performance by the plaintiff of the contract on his part, (*d*) proved non-payment for this service for five weeks at £29 12s. 6d. per week, that is, £148. 2s. 6d. in all.

[14] (1865) L.R. 1 Q.B. 173.

It cannot be too strongly emphasized at all points of this case that the plaintiff's contracts were not with the Ministers individually or collectively, but with the Crown. . . .

. . . The honour of the Crown demands that, subject to Parliament's having made one or more funds available, all contracts for the Crown's departments and services should be honoured. The position on 30th June, 1932, having been examined, what was the position existing on 1st July, 1932, the first day of the financial year 1932–1933? In my opinion, it was plainly this, that the plaintiff's contract with the Crown was still on foot. . . .The condition that payments thereunder depended upon moneys being made legally available by Parliament still subsisted, but the contract was not inchoate or suspended but existing. . . .

The only question therefore, is whether in respect to the year 1932–1933 also the condition of *Churchward's Case*[14a] was satisfied. . . .

In order to secure a judgment declaring the Crown's liability, a person who has a subsisting contract with the Crown satisfies the constitutional doctrine laid down in *Churchward's Case*[14a] in respect of payments accruing during the financial year when he completes the performance of his contract if, at the time of such completion, there exists in respect of such financial year sufficient moneys in the vote for the relevant service to enable the payments in question to be lawfully made. I also think that the plaintiff is entitled to say that the constitutional doctrine was satisfied in respect of all payments falling due between 1st July, 1932, and the date of his completing his contract if, at the date of the passing of the *Appropriation Act* (8th November, 1932), enough moneys to pay him in full could have been lawfully paid or set aside to pay him from moneys then remaining from the parliamentary grant in respect of advertising. From a close consideration of the figures and evidence, I draw the inferences of fact that (*a*) on 8th November, 1932, sufficient moneys were available to pay him what was then owing to him in respect of services rendered in the year 1932–1933, and (*b*) sufficient moneys from the same grant were also available to pay him in full on 31st March, when he finally completed the performance of his contracts. . . .

The above reasoning shows that the plaintiff is entitled to succeed in the argument based on *Churchward's Case*.[14a]

Judgment for the plaintiff.

[The State appealed to the Full Court.]

DIXON J.: . . . It remains to deal with the contention that the contract is unenforceable because no sufficient appropriation of moneys has been made by Parliament to answer the contract. 'The general doctrine is that all obligations to pay money undertaken by the Crown are subject to the implied condition that the funds necessary to satisfy the obligation shall be appropriated by Parliament' (*New South Wales* v. *The Commonwealth* [No. 1]).[15]

[14a] (1865) L.R. 1 Q.B. 173.
[15] (1930) 44 C.L.R., at p. 353.

But, in my opinion, that general doctrine does not mean that no contract exposes the Crown to a liability to suit . . . unless and until an appropriation of funds to answer the contract has been made by the Parliament concerned, or unless some statutory authorization or recognition of the contract can be found.

. . . The principles of responsible government impose upon the administration a responsibility to Parliament, or rather to the House which deals with finance, for what the Administration has done. It is a function of the Executive, not of Parliament, to make contracts on behalf of the Crown. The Crown's advisers are answerable politically to Parliament for their acts in making contracts. Parliament is considered to retain the power of enforcing the responsibility of the Administration by means of its control over the expenditure of public moneys. But the principles of responsible government do not disable the Executive from acting without the prior approval of Parliament, nor from contracting for the expenditure of moneys conditionally upon appropriation by Parliament and doing so before funds to answer the expenditure have actually been made legally available. Some confusion has been occasioned by the terms in which the conditional nature of the contracts of the Crown from time to time has been described, terms chosen rather for the sake of emphasis than of technical accuracy. But, in my opinion, the manner in which the doctrine was enunciated by *Isaacs* C.J., when he last had occasion to state it, gives a correct as well as a clear exposition of it. In *Australian Railways Union* v. *Victorian Railways Commissioners*,[16] he said: 'It is true that every contract with any responsible government of His Majesty, whether it be one of a mercantile character or one of service, is subject to the condition that before payment is made out of the Public Consolidated Fund Parliament must appropriate the necessary sum. But subject to that condition, unless some competent statute properly construed makes the appropriation a condition precedent, a contract by the Government otherwise within its authority is binding.' Notwithstanding expressions capable of a contrary interpretation which have occasionally been used, the prior provision of funds by Parliament is not a condition preliminary to the obligation of the contract. If it were so, performance on the part of the subject could not be exacted nor could he, if he did perform, establish a disputed claim to an amount of money under his contract until actual disbursement of the money in dispute was authorized by Parliament.

[He then considered the authorities, including *Churchward* v. *R.*,[17] and continued:]

[The true position there was that] the provision of funds by Parliament [was] simply . . . a contractual condition and . . . a condition which must be fulfilled before actual payment by the Crown, but not . . . a matter going to the formation, legality, or validity of the contract, and not . . . a condition precedent to suit. . . .

[16] (1932) 46 C.L.R., at p. 176.
[17] (1865) L.R. 1 Q.B. 173.

In my opinion, it is not an answer to a suit against a State . . . upon a contract, that the moneys necessary to answer the liability have not up to the time of the suit been provided by Parliament. This does not mean that, if Parliament has by an expression of its will in a form which the Court is bound to notice, refused to provide funds for the purposes of the contract, it remains actionable. . . . That question does not arise in the present case. Indeed a ground upon which the judgment of *Evatt* J. is based is that moneys were provided by Parliament out of which the liability to the plaintiff might lawfully be discharged. I do not in any way disagree with this view, but, as I have formed a definite opinion that the contention of the Crown misconceives the doctrine upon which it is founded, I have thought it desirable to place my judgment upon the grounds I have given.

In my opinion the judgment of *Evatt* J. is right and should be affirmed.

[GAVAN DUFFY C.J. agreed with DIXON J. RICH, STARKE, and McTIERNAN JJ. delivered judgments in favour of dismissing the appeal.]

Appeal dismissed.

Question

If the *dictum* of Shee J. in *Churchward*'s case represented the law, what would the effect be on government contracting? (See Turpin, *Government Contracts*, pp. 25–7.)

Notes

1. The Full Court differed from Evatt J. on the effect of a failure to appropriate. Evatt J. held (pp. 441 and 443 *supra*) that failure to appropriate relieved the Crown from its obligation to make payments under the contract because its obligation to make such payments depended upon moneys being made legally available by Parliament. In the Full Court Dixon J.'s view that failure to appropriate the necessary money would not excuse the Crown from performance and would lead to a breach of contract by the Crown was shared by a majority of the Court (see Rich and Starke JJ. at pp. 497–8 and 503 respectively). See further Hogg, *Liability of the Crown*, pp. 122–3. Hogg states that Evatt J.'s view is 'unacceptable on principle'. Do you agree? What is the relevant principle?

2. Street, *Governmental Liability*, pp. 91–2, argues that without the necessary Parliamentary appropriation the contract, although valid, is 'unenforceable' in the sense in which that word is used for contracts which do not comply with formal requirements, such as the requirement of writing formerly specified in the Statute of Frauds (see now, for example, s. 40 of the Law of Property Act 1925). Compare Turpin, op. cit., p. 27, who points out that even if there has been no appropriation, there is no reason in principle why a contractor should not be able to sue the Crown and obtain judgment. Turpin does concede that Parliament may frustrate the *implementation* of a judgment by not providing money, since payment in satisfaction can only be made out of appropriate funds, and furthermore that Parliament may even set aside the judgment by retrospective legislation. However, he argues that 'these remote eventualities do not render the original contract either invalid or, in any usual sense, "unenforceable" '. See also Hogg, op. cit., p. 124.

Rederiaktiebolaget Amphitrite v. The King

[1921] 3 K.B. 500   King's Bench Division

During World War I the British Government operated a 'ship for ship' policy whereby neutral ships in British ports should be allowed to leave only if they were replaced by other ships of the same tonnage. The applicants, the Swedish owners of the *Amphitrite,* wrote to the British Legation in Stockholm stating that they would send the vessel to England if they were guaranteed that it would not be detained. After consulting the proper authorities, on 18 March 1918 the Legation replied: 'I am instructed to say that the S.S. *Amphitrite* will earn her own release and be given a coal cargo if she proceed to the United Kingdom with a full cargo consisting of at least 60% approved goods.' The vessel completed a round trip to Hull and the owners asked that the undertaking be renewed for another voyage. This was done, but on the second voyage she was detained and told that clearance would only be granted if the application was made through a body known as the Swedish Shipping Committee. As a result of former dealings they had had with the Germans, the applicants were disqualified from applying through the Committee and, eventually, they sold the vessel. After the war they presented a petition of right claiming damages for breach of the contract contained in the two letters.

ROWLATT J.: . . . I have not to consider whether there was anything of which complaint might be made outside a Court, whether that is to say what the Government did was morally wrong or arbitrary; that would be altogether outside my province. All I have got to say is whether there was an enforceable contract, and I am of opinion that there was not. No doubt the Government can bind itself through its officers by a commercial contract, and if it does so it must perform it like anybody else or pay damages for the breach. But this was not a commercial contract; it was an arrangement whereby the Government purported to give an assurance as to what its executive action would be in the future in relation to a particular ship in the event of her coming to this country with a particular kind of cargo. And that is, to my mind, not a contract for the breach of which damages can be sued for in a Court of law. It was merely an expression of intention to act in a particular way in a certain event. My main reason for so thinking is that it is not competent for the Government to fetter its future executive action, which must necessarily be determined by the needs of the community when the question arises. It cannot by contract hamper its freedom of action in matters which concern the welfare of the State. Thus in the case of the employment of public servants, which is a less strong case than the present, it has been laid down that, except under an Act of Parliament, no one acting on behalf of the Crown has authority to employ any person except upon the terms that he is dismissible at the Crown's pleasure; the reason being that it is in the interests of the community that the ministers for the time being advising the Crown should be able to dispense with the services of its employees if they think it desirable. Again suppose that a man accepts an office which he is perfectly at liberty to refuse, and does so on the express terms that he is to have certain leave of absence, and what when the time arrives the leave is refused in circumstances of the greatest hardship to his family or business, as the case may be. Can it be conceived that a petition of right would lie for damages? I should think not. I am of opinion that this petition must fail and there must be judgment for the Crown.

Judgment for the Crown.

Questions

1. Is the ratio of this case that (*a*) on the facts there was no intention to contract (see *Robertson* v. *Minister of Pensions* p. 148 *supra*), (*b*) the Crown can only make contracts of a commercial nature, or (*c*) a contract that purports to fetter the Crown's freedom of executive action is invalid? If your answer is (*c*), how, if at all, is the authority of the case affected by the fact that the cases on public authorities (p. 145 *supra*) were not considered? Furthermore, if Rowlatt J. had held that there was a contract, what real fetter would there have been on the Crown in view of the immunity of the Crown from specific performance and injunctive relief (see p. 290 *supra*)?

2. Could the decision be justified on the ground that the defence of Act of State might have been available? (It was not until after *Johnstone* v. *Pedlar* [1921] 2 A.C. 262 that it was settled that the defence could not be invoked against a friendly alien visitor to the United Kingdom in respect of governmental action within the United Kingdom. See further *Commercial & Estates Co. Ltd. of Egypt* v. *Board of Trade* [1925] 1 K.B. 271.)

Notes

1. As has been said at pp. 147 and 155 *supra,* the question of the validity of the contract is separate from the question whether the Crown is under a duty to exercise its powers consistently with the provisions of an admittedly valid contract, but as the cases, including *The Amphitrite,* have not always taken the distinction, both can conveniently be considered together. For discussion of the first in relation to public authorities other than the Crown, see p. 145 *supra*. As far as initial validity is concerned, Rowlatt J.'s distinction between commercial and non-commercial contracts has been criticized (Holdsworth, (1929) 45 L.Q.R. 166; Mitchell, *The Contracts of Public Authorities,* p. 62; *Ansett Transport Industries (Operations) Pty. Ltd.* v. *Commonwealth of Australia* (1977) 17 A.L.R. 513 at p. 562), and it is difficult to see how, for instance, procurement contracts involving large capital expenditure are to be classified (see Turpin, op. cit., p. 21). It may, however, be possible to explain Rowlatt J.'s view that there was no contract on the ground that the only consideration moving from the Crown was the undertaking to exercise its discretion in a particular way. Even on this approach the applicability of the 'incompatibility' test used in the cases on public authorities (p. 147 *supra*) might have saved the contract. What reasons would justify treating the Crown differently from other public authorities in this respect?

For a possible example of an agreement limiting executive power which would not be an improper fetter, see the *Ansett Transport* case. There it was argued by the airline that an agreement with the government to ensure that only two airlines operated on any one route impliedly prohibited the government from permitting other airlines to import aircraft into Australia and that the government had broken this term. Although the High Court of Australia held that there had been no breach, a majority went on to say that, had there been a breach, the agreement would not have been regarded as an invalid fetter on the discretion conferred on the government by the regulations governing import controls. The main reason for this was that the agreement had been authorized by statute, although neither Barwick C.J. nor Aickin J. thought that this was the only reason for its validity. Even if the agreement had not been authorized by statute they thought that it would have been valid ((1977) 17 A.L.R. at pp. 519 and 562). Compare *Cudgen Rutile (No. 2) Ltd.* v. *Chalk* [1975] A.C. 520 at pp. 533–4, where it was said that 'when a statute regulating the disposal of Crown lands . . . prescribes a mode of exercise of the statutory power, that mode must be followed and observed: and if it contemplates the . . . use of discretions at particular stages of the statutory process, those . . . discretions [must be] used, at the stages laid down. From this in turn it must follow that the freedom of the Minister or officer of the Crown responsible for implementing the statute to . . . use his discretions cannot validly be fettered by anticipatory action; and if the Minister or officer purports to do this, by contractually fettering himself in advance, his action in doing so exceeds his statutory powers', and (at p. 535) '[n]o purported agreement could give rise to any contractual obligation enforceable in the courts.'

Turpin, op. cit., p. 24, states that '[t]he practical importance of the [*Amphitrite*] rule in the context of procurement is not great. If the government decides that the public interest requires a procurement contract to be brought to an end, it is most unlikely to contend that the contract was void from the beginning on the ground of this rule; in practice it will exercise its right of determining the contract under the standard contractual "break" clause, which makes due provision for the compensation of the contractor.'

2. On the doctrine of 'executive necessity', see further p. 147 *supra*; Mitchell, op. cit., pp. 27–32 and 57–65; Hogg, op. cit., pp. 129–40. Hogg argues (at p. 139) that the advantages enjoyed by the government in setting the terms suggest that there is no need for the further advantage of *The Amphitrite* rule, and that so long as the remedies of specific performance and injunction are withheld, as they are by statute in the United Kingdom (p. 290 *supra*), the ordinary law would adjust the conflict between public purposes and private interests quite satisfactorily by an award of damages. This would prevent the government reallocating the risks of the contract while preserving its freedom of action. Hogg recognizes that the burden of damages might itself fetter governmental action, but argues that such situations would be unusual and could be dealt with by retrospective legislation. But cf. Craig, (1977) 93 L.Q.R. 398 at pp. 418–20, noted at p. 155 *supra*.

3. For examples of governmental use of the contracting power see the references at p. 430 *supra*.

4. Where the Crown has made a valid contract it is necessary to consider the extent of its obligations under the contract. The question whether it is ever justifiable for the Crown to escape from an otherwise enforceable contract in the public interest is considered in the next extract.

Commissioners of Crown Lands v. Page

[1960] 2 Q.B. 274   Court of Appeal

The Crown had leased premises for twenty-five years, but eight years later, acting under the Defence (General) Regulations 1939, the Minister of Works, on behalf of the Crown, requisitioned the premises. There was no express covenant for quiet enjoyment in the lease and it was held that the implied covenant could not have been intended to 'extend to prevent the future exercise by the Crown of powers and duties imposed upon it by statute' ([1960] 2 Q.B. at p. 287). The majority of the Court of Appeal reserved their opinion on what the position would have been had the covenant been express and unqualified but Devlin L.J. went further.

DEVLIN L.J.: . . . When the Crown, or any other person, is entrusted, whether by virtue of the prerogative or by statute, with discretionary powers to be exercised for the public good, it does not, when making a private contract in general terms, undertake (and it may be that it could not even with the use of specific language validly undertake) to fetter itself in the use of those powers, and in the exercise of its discretion. This principle has been accepted in a number of authorities; it is sufficient to mention *Ayr Harbour Trustees* v. *Oswald*;[18] *Rederiaktiebolaget Amphitrite* v. *The King*;[19] *Board of Trade* v. *Temperley Steam Shipping Co. Ltd.*[20] and *William Cory & Sons Ltd.* v. *City of London Corporation.*[21]

The covenant for quiet enjoyment in the present case is implied, and is not dissimilar to the contractual provision considered in the two cases last cited, which were both concerned with the implied obligation on one party to a contract not to interfere with the performance by the other party of his obligations under it. In *Board of Trade* v. *Temperley Steam Shipping Co. Ltd.*,[22] the Board were the charterers of the defendant's ship, and it was contended that they had prevented the defendants from making their ship efficient for her service under the charterparty because one of the Board's surveyors had refused a licence to do certain repairs. In *William Cory & Sons Ltd.* v. *City of London Corporation*,[23] the city corporation had a contract with the plaintiffs whereunder the plaintiffs undertook to remove refuse by means of lighters and barges. Some time later the city corporation passed a by-law concerning the fitment of vessels transporting refuse which it was agreed was such as to make the performance of the contract impossible. It was held by the Court of Appeal that the corporation was not in breach of the implied term.

I do not, however, rest my decision in the present case simply on the fact that the covenant for quiet enjoyment has to be implied. For reasons which I think will appear sufficiently in the next paragraph, I should reach the same conclusion if the ordinary covenant was expressed.

In some of the cases in which public authorities have been defendants, the judgments have been put on the ground that it would be ultra vires for them to bind themselves not to exercise their powers; and it has also been said that a promise to do so would be contrary to public policy. It may perhaps be

---

[18] (1883) 8 App.Cas. 623, H.L.
[19] [1921] 3 K.B. 500
[20] (1926) 26 Ll.L.R. 76; affirmed (1927) 27 Ll.L.R. 230, C.A.
[21] [1951] 2 K.B. 476, C.A.
[22] 26 Ll.L.R. 76.
[23] [1951] 2 K.B. 476, C.A.

difficult to apply this reasoning to the Crown, but it seems to me to be unnecessary to delve into the constitutional position. When the Crown, in dealing with one of its subjects, is dealing as if it too were a private person, and is granting leases or buying and selling as ordinary persons do, it is absurd to suppose that it is making any promise about the way in which it will conduct the afairs of the nation. No one can imagine, for example, that when the Crown makes a contract which could not be fulfilled in time of war, it is pledging itself not to declare war for so long as the contract lasts. Even if, therefore, there was an express covenant for quiet enjoyment, or an express promise by the Crown that it would not do any act which might hinder the other party to the contract in the performance of his obligations, the covenant or promise must by necessary implication be read to exclude those measures affecting the nation as a whole which the Crown takes for the public good.

 . . . I need not examine the question whether, if the Crown sought to fetter its future action in express and specific terms, it could effectively do so. It is most unlikely that in a contract with the subject, it would ever make the attempt. For the purpose of this case it is unnecessary to go further than to say that in making a lease or other contract with its subjects, the Crown does not (at least in the absence of specific words) promise to refrain from exercising its general powers under a statute or under the prerogative, or to exercise them in any particular way. That does not mean that the Crown can escape from any contract which it finds disadvantageous by saying that it never promised to act otherwise than for the public good. . . . Here we are dealing with an act done for a general executive purpose, and not an act done for the purpose of achieving a particular result under the contract in question. . . .

Agents in contract

Attorney-General for Ceylon v. A. D. Silva

[1953] A.C. 461   Judicial Committee of the Privy Council

The Principal Collector of Customs of Ceylon, in the mistaken belief that certain steel plates belonging to the Crown which were on customs premises were unclaimed goods, obtained the permission of the Chief Secretary of Ceylon to sell them by public auction in accordance with the provisions of the Ceylon Customs Ordinance (p. 451 *infra*). The plaintiff, Silva, purchased the steel plates at the auction on 4 March 1947, but when the Collector refused to deliver them Silva brought an action for damages for breach of contract against the Attorney-General as the representative of the Crown. The Collector had refused to make delivery to Silva when he learned of a prior authorized sale of the steel plates to another purchaser. On 23 January 1947, the Services Disposal Board of Ceylon, which had been appointed by the Ministry of Supply in England to dispose of the steel plates, had contracted to sell them to a firm in Ceylon. The Supreme Court of Ceylon held that there had been a valid contract to sell to the plaintiff and awarded him substantial damages. On appeal by the Attorney-General:

The judgment of their Lordships was delivered by MR. L. M. D. DE SILVA:

. . . The precise question which arises for their Lordships' decision is whether the Principal Collector of Customs had authority to enter into a contract binding on the Crown for the sale of the goods in question to the plaintiff. This question can conveniently be dealt with under two heads: had the Principal Collector actual authority to enter into a contract; if not, did he have ostensible authority to do so?

It is argued that the Principal Collector had actual authority to enter into the contract by reason of the provisions of sections 17 and 108 of the Customs Ordinance (chapter 185, Legislative Enactments of Ceylon). Section 17 makes warehouse rent payable in respect of goods left in customs warehouses. . . .

. . . Section 108 authorizes the sale of goods left for more than three months in customs warehouses 'to answer' the charges due thereon.

It is claimed by the plaintiff that the Customs Ordinance was binding on the Crown, that warehouse rent was due under section 17 of the Ordinance on the goods in question, and that as they had been left on the customs premises for a period longer than three months, they were liable to be sold after public advertisement under section 108. This was in fact the basis on which the Principal Collector held the sale, and it would without doubt have been a sound basis if the property had all the time been private property. But it is argued by the Crown that, no matter what the Principal Collector thought or did, the Customs Ordinance was not binding on the Crown; that it, or at any rate the provisions in it relevant to this case, were inapplicable to property belonging to the Crown and that therefore the plaintiff's contention fails.

The first matter which arises for consideration is whether the Ordinance binds the Crown. . . .

[Their Lordships, having considered the relevant legislation, concluded that the Ordinance did not bind the Crown and continued:]

It has been argued that apart from the Ordinance the Principal Collector has actual authority to do what he did, and that this authority was reinforced by the letter written to him by the Chief Secretary. It is a simple and clear proposition that a public officer has not by reason of the fact that he is in the service of the Crown the right to act for and on behalf of the Crown in all matters which concern the Crown. The right to act for the Crown in any particular matter must be established by reference to statute or otherwise. It has not been shown that the Principal Collector had any authority to sell property of the Crown or to enter into a contract on its behalf for its sale: nor has it been shown that the Chief Secretary, who authorized the sale, had any such authority. His functions were defined by the Ceylon (State Council) Order in Council, 1931, and under this Order the most that can be said is that he was authorized to deal with certain Crown property under the direct administration of the Government of Ceylon. It is therefore clear that the Principal Collector of Customs had no actual authority to enter into a contract for the sale of the goods which are the subject-matter of this action.

Next comes the question whether the Principal Collector of Customs had ostensible authority, such as would bind the Crown, to enter into the contract sued on. All 'ostensible' authority involves a representation by the principal as to the extent of the agent's authority. No representation by the agent as to the extent of his authority can amount to a 'holding out' by the principal. No public officer, unless he possesses some special power, can hold out on behalf of the Crown that he or some other public officer has the right to enter into a contract in respect of the property of the Crown when in fact no such right exists. Their Lordships think, therefore, that nothing done by the Principal Collector or the Chief Secretary amounted to a holding out by the Crown that the Principal Collector had the right to enter into a contract to sell the goods which are the subject-matter of this action. . . .

In advertising the goods for sale the Principal Collector no doubt represented to the public that the goods were saleable. But the question is whether this act of the Principal Collector can be said to be an act of the Crown. Their Lordships have considered whether by reason of the fact that the Principal Collector had been appointed to his office under the Customs Ordinance, and was the proper officer to administer it, he must be regarded as having had ostensible authority on behalf of the Crown to represent to the public that goods advertised for sale under the Customs Ordinance were in fact saleable under that Ordinance. It is argued that, if so, although the goods were in fact not saleable under the Ordinance because they were Crown property, or property to which the sections of the Ordinance authorizing sale were not applicable, or for some other reason, the contract would be binding on the Crown and the Crown would be liable in damages as it could not fulfil it.

Their Lordships think that the Principal Collector cannot be regarded as having any such authority. He had, no doubt, authority to do acts of a particular class, namely, to enter on behalf of the Crown into sales of certain goods. But that authority was limited because it arose under certain sections of the Ordinance and only when those sections were applicable. It was said by Lord Atkinson in *Russo-Chinese Bank* v. *Li Yau Sam*:[24] 'If the agent be held out as having only a limited 'authority to do on behalf of his principal acts of a particular class, then the principal is not bound by an act done outside that authority, even though it be an act of that particular class, because, the authority being thus represented to be limited, the party prejudiced has notice, and should ascertain whether or not the act is authorized.' With that view their Lordships respectfully agree. In that case the authority did not arise under a statute, but in their Lordships' view this fact makes no difference. If there is a difference at all it would lie in the circumstance that in a statute the limits of the authority conferred are fixed rigidly and no recourse to evidence is necessary to ascertain them. The Ordinance could no doubt have made the representation by the Principal Collector binding on the Crown, but it has not done so, and to read into any such provision would be unduly to extend its meaning.

[24] [1910] A.C. 174, 184.

It may be said that it causes hardship to a purchaser at a sale under the Customs Ordinance if the burden of ascertaining whether or not the Principal Collector has authority to enter into the sale is placed upon him. This undoubtedly is true. But where, as in the case of the Customs Ordinance, the Ordinance does not dispense with that necessity, to hold otherwise would be to hold that public officers had dispensing powers because they then could by unauthorized acts nullify or extend the provisions of the Ordinance. Of the two evils this would be the greater one. . . .

. . . Their Lordships will therefore humbly advise Her Majesty that the appeal be allowed. . . .

Notes

1. It has been argued that *Silva*'s case failed to take account of 'usual authority' as a distinct method of rendering a principal liable for the unauthorized acts of his agent (Treitel, [1957] P.L. 321 at pp. 337 ff.). But (*a*) note the section of the opinion at p. 452 *supra*, and (*b*) see *Bowstead on Agency*, 14th edn., pp. 71–4, for doubts as to whether usual authority is independent of implied and ostensible authority: see Craig, (1977) 93 L.Q.R. 398 at p. 401 n. 13. Cautious support for an independent doctrine of usual authority can be found in *Meates* v. *Attorney-General* [1979] 1 N.Z.L.R. 415 at p. 462, where Davison C.J., while noting the criticisms, appeared to recognize its applicability to statements made by a Prime Minister. But cf. the curious use made of the concept of ostensible authority in *Western Fish Products Ltd.* v. *Penwith D.C.*, p. 159 *supra*. See further Turpin, op. cit., pp. 33–6.

2. The position of a person who deals with a Crown agent acting outside the scope of his authority is exacerbated by the fact that the agent will not be personally liable on the contract (*MacBeath* v. *Haldimand* (1786) 1 T.R. 172) or, as other agents are, for breach of an implied waranty of authority (*Dunn* v. *MacDonald* [1897] 1 Q.B. 401 and 555; *The Prometheus* (1949) 82 Ll. L.R. 859). The doctrine of implied warranty of authority was said not to be applicable to Crown agents for reasons of public policy, viz. that if they were not free of personal liability 'no man would accept any office of trust under Government' (per Ashhurst J. in *MacBeath* v. *Haldimand* at p. 181, adopted by Charles J. in *Dunn* v. *MacDonald* at p. 405). For criticism see Wade, p. 711; Street, *Governmental Liability*, p. 93.

3. The jurisdictional principle means that the authority of an agent cannot extend to a contract that is ultra vires the agent or *a fortiori* his department. Thus, in *Silva*'s case, quite apart from the ordinary principles of agency, it is difficult to see how the Crown could have been bound by the contract in view of the provisions of the Customs Ordinance (p. 452 *supra*). For further discussion of the relationship between ultra vires and agency, see Craig, op. cit., pp. 398–404. See also p. 155 *supra* for the similar problems that arise from ultra vires statements by public officials.

The law of Crown service

Dunn v. The Queen

[1896] 1 Q.B. 116   Court of Appeal

The petitioner was appointed consular agent in the Niger Protectorate for a period of three years by Sir Claude McDonald, Her Majesty's Commissioner and Consul-General for the Protectorate. Before the end of that time the Crown dismissed him. He brought a petition of right claiming that the Crown had no right to do this and that he was therefore entitled to damages.

LORD ESHER M.R.: In this case the petitioner was employed as a civil servant of the Crown in the public service at a certain salary, and the question has arisen with relation to his service which, in the case of *De Dohsé* v. *Reg.*,[25] I foresaw might arise . . . I said, in giving judgment in that case: 'It is said that it was lawful to make such an engagement with him (the suppliant) for seven years, because the engagement offered and proposed was not an engagement of military service, it being admitted in argument that, if the engagement was for military service as a soldier, whether as officer or private, it is contrary to public policy that any such contract should be made. Now, whether that doctrine with regard to the Crown is confined to military service or not need not be decided to-day, but I do not at all accept the suggestion that it is so confined. All service under the Crown itself is public service, and to my mind it is most likely that the doctrine which is said to be confined to military service applies to all public service under the Crown, because all public service under the Crown is for the public benefit.' That case came before the House of Lords; and it seems to me that Lord Watson in his judgment almost in terms decides that what I thought would probably turn out to be the right view on the subject is correct. He says: 'In the first place it appears to me that no concluded contract is disclosed in the statements contained in this petition of right; and in the second place I am of opinion that such a concluded contract, if it had been made, must have been held to have imported into it the condition that the Crown has the power to dismiss. Further, I am of opinion that, if any authority representing the Crown were to exclude such a power by express stipulation, that would be a violation of the public policy of the country and could not derogate from the power of the Crown.' Anything more distinct and general than that there could not be. It seems to me that the rule, as laid down by the House of Lords, is in consonance with what I suggested to be the true rule in the Court of Appeal. . . . It seems to me that both on authority and on principle it is clear that the petitioner is not entitled to succeed. . . .

LORD HERSCHELL: . . . I take it that persons employed as the petitioner was in the service of the Crown, except in cases where there is some statutory provision for a higher tenure of office, are ordinarily engaged on the understanding that they hold their employment at the pleasure of the Crown. So I think that there must be imported into the contract for the employment of the petitioner the term which is applicable to civil servants in general, namely, that the Crown may put an end to the employment at its pleasure. In this case there is not a tittle of evidence that, supposing it were possible, Sir Claude McDonald had any authority to employ the petitioner on any other terms

---

[25] [Unreported. Decided in the Court of Appeal, 2 June 1885, by Brett M.R., Baggallay and Bowen L.JJ.; and in the House of Lords, 25 November 1886, by Lord Halsbury L.C. and Lords Blackburn, Watson, and Fitzgerald.]

than those which are applicable to the civil service generally. It seems to me that it is the public interest which has led to the term which I have mentioned being imported into contracts for employment in the service of the Crown. The cases cited shew that, such employment being for the good of the public, it is essential for the public good that it should be capable of being determined at the pleasure of the Crown, except in certain exceptional cases where it has been deemed to be more for the public good that some restriction should be imposed on the power of the Crown to dismiss its servants. . . .

[KAY L.J. delivered a judgment in favour of dismissing the application.]

Application dismissed.

Note

Does this case decide that the common law rule that Crown servants are dismissible at pleasure (*a*) can only be excluded by statute, or (*b*), as Nettheim suggests ([1975] C.L.J. 253 at p. 271), that the common law rule is not impliedly excluded by a contractual stipulation of a fixed term of employment with nothing more because that is not inconsistent with retention of power to dismiss at pleasure? See further Nettheim, op. cit., but note Lord Esher's approval of Lord Watson's speech (p. 454 *supra*). If (*b*) is correct, would a requirement of cause for dismissal exclude the rule, or would it be necessary to stipulate both a fixed period and provision for dismissal for cause? On procedural protection in cases of dismissal at pleasure, note the comments at pp. 216 and 276 *supra*, from which it would appear that the civil servant is not even entitled to a hearing in such cases. In *Reilly* v. *The King* [1934] A.C. 176 at p. 179 Lord Atkin said obiter:

If the terms of the appointment definitely prescribe a term and expressly provide for a power to determine 'for cause' it appears necessarily to follow that any implication of a power to dismiss at pleasure is excluded.

But note that the terms of the appointment there were specified by statute and it is possible that Lord Atkin's reference to 'terms' should be limited to that context. If this is so, Lord Atkin's statement is not inconsistent with (*a*), although for a wider interpretation of its effect see *Robertson* v. *Minister of Pensions*, p. 149 *supra*. See further the next extract.

Terrell v. Secretary of State for the Colonies

[1953] 2 Q.B. 482   Queen's Bench Division

A colonial judge, who had been appointed after correspondence in which the Secretary of State indicated that the retiring age was sixty-two, was dismissed after the occupation of Malaya by the Japanese in 1942, seventeen months before his sixty-second birthday. Lord Goddard C.J. held that the security of tenure enjoyed by English High Court judges by virtue of the Act of Settlement 1700 did not extend to colonial judges, and that there was no good reason why a judge appointed during pleasure should be in any different position from this point of view from any other person in the service of the Crown. This extract is only concerned with the alleged contract to employ until the judge's sixty-second birthday.

LORD GODDARD C.J.: . . . I have difficulty . . . in seeing how the Secretary of State, on whose behalf the letters were written, would have authority to bind the Crown even if he had purported to do so. So to do would appear to me clearly to constitute a clog on the Crown's right to dismiss at pleasure. I regard this right as a rule of law firmly established by the decisions (for instance, *Dunn* v. *The Queen*,[26] *Shenton* v. *Smith*[27] and *Rodwell* v. *Thomas*[28]), and once it is established that the Crown has power to dismiss at pleasure that right cannot be taken away by any contractual arrangement made by an executive officer or department of State. . . .

. . . [E]ven if the Secretary of State purported to contract with the claimant he could not in my opinion limit the power of the Crown to dismiss at pleasure. He might have advised the withdrawal of the Letters Patent of February, 1911,[29] and the issue of others giving the Governor directions to appoint judges during good behaviour, or he might have advised a Royal Warrant to be issued . . . authorizing the Governor in a particular case to appoint not at pleasure, but during good behaviour, and then the appointment would be by the Crown, and I have no doubt that if His late Majesty had chosen to appoint a judge on those terms the appointment would have been perfectly valid. But having appointed the claimant to hold office during pleasure, in my opinion no correspondence which took place before or after the appointment could affect the terms of appointment.

. . . I think that the correspondence referred to does no more than inform the claimant of the general conditions applicable to the office. It tells him that at the age of 62 he will have to retire and might expect to receive a pension; it does not amount to an agreement that he is to be appointed for a definite period and not at the pleasure of the Crown.

[Counsel for the plaintiff] placed great reliance on *Reilly* v. *The King*,[30] but I do not read that case as going anything like the length for which he contends. The actual point material to this case which the Judicial Committee decided was that if the terms of an appointment definitely prescribe a term and expressly provide for a power to determine 'for cause' that excludes an implication that the appointment is at pleasure. The case also shows that there may be contractual rights existing before determination of a contract at will which are not inconsistent with a power to determine. . . . Since that case I think it may very well be that if the Crown appoints to an office on the terms that it is to be held during good behaviour or that the holder is only to be removed 'for cause' – which is really the same thing – he would be entitled formerly to present a Petition of Right and now to bring an action if he were removed without cause. . . .

Were I to accede to the argument that these letters amount to a contract I should he holding, in effect, that every person entering the service of the

---

[26] [1896] 1 Q.B. 116.
[27] [1895] A.C. 229.   [28] [1944] K.B. 596.
[29] [This contained the Governor's authority from the Crown to appoint judges 'all of whom, unless otherwise provided by law, shall hold their offices during our pleasure' (art. 14).]
[30] [1934] A.C. 176.

Crown who is told before he enters that his retiring age will be so and so could say that he had a contractual right to remain in the service till that age, and this would in effect override all the cases which have decided that a servant of the Crown holds office at pleasure, at least unless his appointment definitely prescribes a term or expressly provides for a power to determine only 'for cause.' That seems to have been exactly the argument put forward in *Shenton* v. *Smith*[31] and rejected by the Judicial Committee. . . .

Questions

1. In *Terrell*'s case does Lord Goddard accept that the Crown itself can exclude dismissal at pleasure? If so, would it follow that the Crown could delegate such power to an agent (p. 450 *supra*)?

2. Is the first paragraph of the extract consistent with the penultimate one? See Nettheim, op. cit., pp. 276–7. Is Lord Goddard's view that an appointment until a fixed retiring age 'constitutes a clog on the Crown's right to dismiss at pleasure', which was therefore presumed to be unauthorized, consistent with Lord Herschell's speech in *Dunn* v. *The Queen*, p. 454 *supra*? See Nettheim, op. cit., pp. 267 and 274–8.

Notes

1. *Terrell*'s case supports the dictum of Lord Atkin in *Reilly* v. *The King* [1934] A.C. 176 at p. 179, noted at p. 455 *supra*, but compare *Thomas* v. *Attorney-General of Trinidad and Tobago* [1981] 3 W.L.R. 601 at p. 610 for a strong affirmation by the Privy Council (albeit obiter) of the traditional view that the Crown itself cannot exclude dismissal at pleasure. Are the policy arguments in favour of the legal insecurity of Crown service compelling in view of the fact that, quite apart from the general immunity of the Crown from specific relief (p. 290 *supra*), there can be no specific relief in contracts of employment?

2. An analogy with the armed forces was made in *Dunn* v. *The Queen*, p. 454 *supra*, by Lord Esher. Members of the armed forces have been held to be unable to sue for arrears of pay (*Leaman* v. *The King* [1920] 3 K.B. 663) and this has influenced the position of civil servants on this point: see e.g. *Lucas* v. *Lucas* [1943] P. 68, criticized by Logan, (1945) 61 L.Q.R. 240. Cf. *I.R.C.* v. *Hambrook* [1956] 2 Q.B. 641 at p. 654 (where a claim in restitution was said to be available). The analogy should not, however, be taken too far and the better view is that arrears of pay are recoverable. In *Kodeeswaran* v. *Attorney-General of Ceylon* [1970] A.C. 1111 at p. 1123 Lord Diplock, delivering the opinion of the Privy Council, said in criticism of the argument that it was an 'ineluctable consequence' of the power of the Crown to dismiss at pleasure that a civil servant had no claim to arrears of salary accrued due before his dismissal:

> . . . [T]his is a non sequitur. A right to terminate a contract of service at will coupled with a right to enter into a fresh contract of service may in effect enable the Crown to change the terms of employment in futuro if the true inference to be drawn from the communication of the intended change to the servant and his continuing to serve thereafter is that his existing contract has been terminated by the Crown and a fresh contract entered into on the revised terms. But this cannot affect any right to salary already earned under the terms of his existing contract before its termination.

[31] [1895] A.C. 229.

See further Wade, pp. 65–67 (especially on *Sutton v. Attorney-General* (1923) 39 T.L.R. 294); *Chitty on Contracts*, 25th edn., para. 692.

3. As Wade points out (p. 62), there is a sharp contrast between the theoretical position and reality, for Crown service has been one of the most secure types of employment, with an extremely low rate of dismissal for misconduct or inefficiency (20–25 a year between 1963 and 1967: Fulton Committee, Cmnd. 3638, para. 123). Furthermore, the position of a person dismissed without cause has been ameliorated by statute. The remedies available to employees for unfair dismissal are, for the most part, available to civil servants: s. 138 of the Employment Protection (Consolidation) Act 1978. In effect, the power of the Crown to dismiss at pleasure without paying compensation is now substantially limited by this statute, but it should be noted that the statute does not deal with the contractual position. Not all the statutory rights relating to employment are, however, extended to Crown servants. In particular they are not entitled to a written statement of their terms of employment, to minimum periods of notice, or to redundancy payments. Is there a justification for the discrepancy between the actual position of civil servants and the legal rules governing their relationship with the Crown?

REMEDIES AND PROCEDURE

The statutory procedure

Crown Proceedings Act 1947

4. – (1) Where the Crown is subject to any liability by virtue of this Part of this Act, the law relating to indemnity and contribution shall be enforceable by or against the Crown in respect of the liability to which it is so subject as if the Crown were a private person of full age and capacity.

(3) Without prejudice to the general effect of section one of this Act, the Law Reform (Contributory Negligence) Act, 1945 (which amends the law relating to contributory negligence) shall bind the Crown.

17. – (1) [The Minister for the Civil Service][32] shall publish a list specifying the several Government departments which are authorised departments for the purposes of this Act . . . and may from time to time amend or vary the said list. . . .

(2) Civil proceedings by the Crown may be instituted either by an authorised Government department in its own name, whether that department was or was not at the commencement of this Act authorised to sue, or by the Attorney General.

(3) Civil proceedings against the Crown shall be instituted against the appropriate authorised Government department, or, if none of the authorised Government departments is appropriate or the person instituting the proceedings has any reasonable doubt whether any and if so which of those departments is appropriate, against the Attorney General. . . .

[32] [Substituted by S.I. 1968 No. 1656.]

25. – (1) Where in any civil proceedings by or against the Crown, or in any proceedings on the Crown side of the King's Bench Division, or in connection with any arbitration to which the Crown is a party, any order (including an order for costs) is made by any court in favour of any person against the Crown or against a Government department or against an officer of the Crown as such, the proper officer of the court shall, on an application in that behalf made by or on behalf of that person at any time after the expiration of twenty-one days from the date of the order or, in case the order provides for the payment of costs and the costs require to be taxed, at any time after the costs have been taxed, whichever is the later, issue to that person a certificate in the prescribed form containing particulars of the order:

Provided that, if the court so directs, a separate certificate shall be issued with respect to the costs (if any) ordered to be paid to the applicant.

(2) A copy of any certificate issued under this section may be served by the person in whose favour the order is made upon the person for the time being named in the record as the solicitor, or as the person acting as solicitor, for the Crown or for the Government department or officer concerned.

(3) If the order provides for the payment of any money by way of damages or otherwise, or of any costs, the certificate shall state the amount so payable, and the appropriate Government department shall, subject as hereinafter provided, pay to the person entitled or to his solicitor the amount appearing by the certificate to be due to him together with the interest, if any, lawfully due thereon:

Provided that the court by which any such order as aforesaid is made or any court to which an appeal against the order lies may direct that, pending an appeal or otherwise, payment of the whole of any amount so payable, or any part thereof, shall be suspended, and if the certificate has not been issued may order any such directions to be inserted therein.

(4) Save as aforesaid no execution or attachment or process in the nature thereof shall be issued out of any court for enforcing payment by the Crown of any such money or costs as aforesaid, and no person shall be individually liable under any order for the payment by the Crown, or any Government department, or any officer of the Crown as such, of any such money or costs.

. . .

26. – (1) Subject to the provisions of this Act, any order made in favour of the Crown against any person in any civil proceedings to which the Crown is a party may be enforced in the same manner as an order made in an action between subjects, and not otherwise. . . .

PART IV

MISCELLANEOUS AND SUPPLEMENTAL

Miscellaneous

28. – (1) Subject to and in accordance with rules of court and county court rules:–

(*a*) in any civil proceedings in the High Court or a county court to which the Crown is a party, the Crown may be required by the court to make discovery of documents and produce documents for inspection; and

(*b*) in any such proceedings as aforesaid, the Crown may be required by the court to answer interrogatories:

Provided that this section shall be without prejudice to any rule of law which authorises or requires the withholding of any document or the refusal to answer any question on the ground that the disclosure of the document or the answering of the question would be injurious to the public interest.

Any order of the court made under the powers conferred by paragraph (*b*) of this subsection shall direct by what officer of the Crown the interrogatories are to be answered.

(2) Without prejudice to the proviso to the preceding subsection, any rules made for the purposes of this section shall be such as to secure that the existence of a document will not be disclosed if, in the opinion of a Minister of the Crown, it would be injurious to the public interest to disclose the existence thereof.

38. – (2) In this Act, except in so far as the context otherwise requires or it is otherwise expressly provided, the following expressions have the meanings hereby respectively assigned to them, that is to say: –...

'Civil proceedings' includes proceedings in the High Court or the county court for the recovery of fines or penalties, but does not include proceedings on the Crown side of the King's Bench Division. . . .

SCHEDULES

FIRST SCHEDULE

PROCEEDINGS ABOLISHED BY THIS ACT

2. – (1) Proceedings against His Majesty by way of petition of right. . . .

Note

For general discussion of this topic see Wade, p. 712. See further p. 290 *supra*, where s. 21 is set out. In relation to s. 4, see further the Civil Liability (Contribution) Act 1978 (which expressly states that it binds the Crown), and on s. 28 see further Note 3, p. 490 *infra*.

STATUTES AFFECTING THE CROWN

Note

On this topic see in particular Wade, p. 715; Treitel, [1957] P.L. 321 at pp. 322–6; Hogg, op cit., Ch. 7.

LIMITATIONS OF STATE LIABILITY

Political action: tort

Note

The Crown and its servants may be able to plead the defence of Act of State in respect of action performed abroad. The exact scope of the defence is somewhat uncertain; in particular it is not clear whether it can be invoked against a British subject. See Wade, p. 717; E.C.S. Wade, (1934) 15 B.Y.B.I.L. 98; *Nissan v. Attorney-General* [1970] A.C. 179. See further Collier, [1968] C.L.J. 102; Cane, (1980) 29 I.C.L.Q. 681. This topic is usually treated as part of Constitutional Law. See de Smith, *Constitutional and Administrative Law*, 4th edn., p. 152; Wade and Phillips, *Constitutional and Administrative Law*, 9th edn., p. 299.

Political action: contract

Rederiaktiebolaget Amphitrite v. The King, p. 446 *supra*

Note

This topic is discussed by Wade, p. 719. Consider also the analogous situation in *Laker Airways Ltd.* v. *Department of Trade*, p. 14 *supra*, where, however, there was no contract between the government and the subject. See also p. 430 *supra*, where the use of contracting power as an instrument of policy is discussed.

SUPPRESSION OF EVIDENCE IN THE PUBLIC INTEREST

Crown privilege: public interest immunity

Conway v. Rimmer

[1968] A.C. 910   House of Lords

The appellant, a probationary police constable who had been acquitted on a larceny charge, brought an action for malicious prosecution against the respondent, who had been instrumental in the charge being brought. When discovery of documents was sought, immunity from production was claimed for five documents on the ground of Crown privilege, four of the five documents in question being reports on the appellant. The affidavit sworn by the Home Secretary, in which he asserted that production would harm the public interest, stated that these four documents 'fell within a class of documents comprising confidential reports by police officers to chief officers of police relating to the conduct, efficiency and fitness for employment of individual police officers under their command'. The remaining document was said to fall 'within a class of documents comprising reports by police officers to their superiors concerning investigations into the commission of crime'. The documents, Lord Reid thought, 'may be of crucial importance' to the action. In this type of claim the argument is that the authors of a particular class of documents will be less candid than they would otherwise have been, if they know the document may be disclosed at a later stage: thus the public interest is adversely affected.

A District Registrar's order in favour of production of the documents was reversed by Browne J. (in chambers) in a decision upheld by the Court of Appeal ([1967] 1 W.L.R. 1031). There was a further appeal to the House of Lords.

LORD REID [having set out the Home Secretary's affidavit]: . . . The question whether such a statement by a Minister of the Crown should be accepted as conclusively preventing any court from ordering production of any of the documents to which it applies is one of very great importance in the administration of justice. If the commonly accepted interpretation of the decision of this House in *Duncan* v. *Cammell, Laird & Co. Ltd.*[33] is to remain authoritative the question admits of only one answer – the Minister's statement is final and conclusive. Normally I would be very slow to question the authority of a unanimous decision of this House only 25 years old which was carefully considered and obviously intended to lay down a general rule. But this decision has several abnormal features.

Lord Simon thought that on this matter the law in Scotland was the same as the law in England and he clearly intended to lay down a rule applicable to the whole of the United Kingdom. But in *Glasgow Corporation* v. *Central Land Board*[34] this House held that that was not so, with the result that today on this question the law is different in the two countries. There are many chapters of the law where for historical and other reasons it is quite proper that the law should be different in the two countries. But here we are dealing purely with public policy – with the proper relation between the powers of the executive and the powers of the courts – and I can see no rational justification for the law on this matter being different in the two countries.

Secondly, events have proved that the rule supposed to have been laid down in *Duncan's* case[35] is far from satisfactory. In the large number of cases in England and elsewhere which have been cited in argument much dissatisfaction has been expressed and I have not observed even one expression of whole-hearted approval. Moreover a statement made by the Lord Chancellor in 1956 on behalf of the Government . . . makes it clear that that Government did not regard it as consonant with public policy to maintain the rule to the full extent which existing authorities had held to be justifiable.

I have no doubt that the case of *Duncan* v. *Cammell, Laird & Co. Ltd.*[36] was rightly decided. The plaintiff sought discovery of documents relating to the submarine *Thetis* including a contract for the hull and machinery and plans and specifications. The First Lord of the Admiralty had stated that 'it would be injurious to the public interest that any of the said documents should be disclosed to any person.' Any of these documents might well have given valuable information, or at least clues, to the skilled eye of an agent of a foreign power. But Lord Simon L.C. took the opportunity to deal with the

---

[33] [1942] A.C. 624.   [34] 1956 H.L.(S.C.) 1.
[35] [1942] A.C. 624.   [36] Ibid.

whole question of the right of the Crown to prevent production of documents in a litigation. Yet a study of his speech leaves me with the strong impression that throughout he had primarily in mind cases where discovery or disclosure would involve a danger of real prejudice to the national interest. I find it difficult to believe that his speech would have been the same if the case had related, as the present case does, to discovery of routine reports on a probationer constable. . . .

It is universally recognised that here there are two kinds of public interest which may clash. There is the public interest that harm shall not be done to the nation or the public service by disclosure of certain documents, and there is the public interest that the administration of justice shall not be frustrated by the withholding of documents which must be produced if justice is to be done. There are many cases where the nature of the injury which would or might be done to the nation or the public service is of so grave a character that no other interest, public or private, can be allowed to prevail over it. With regard to such cases it would be proper to say, as Lord Simon did, that to order production of the document in question would put the interest of the state in jeopardy. But there are many other cases where the possible injury to the public service is much less and there one would think that it would be proper to balance the public interests involved. . . .

It is to be observed that [in *Duncan* v. *Cammell, Laird & Co. Ltd.*[37]] Lord Simon referred to the practice of keeping a class of documents secret being '*necessary* [my italics] for the proper functioning of the public interest.' But the certificate of the Home Secretary in the present case does not go nearly so far as that. It merely says that the production of a document of the classes to which it refers would be 'injurious to the public interest': it does not say what degree of injury is to be apprehended. It may be advantageous to the functioning of the public service that reports of this kind should be kept secret – that is the view of the Home Secretary – but I would be very surprised if anyone said that that is necessary.

There are now many large public bodies, such as British Railways and the National Coal Board, the proper and efficient functioning of which is very necessary for many reasons including the safety of the public. The Attorney-General made it clear that Crown privilege is not and cannot be invoked to prevent disclosure of similar documents made by them or their servants even if it were said that this is required for the proper and efficient functioning of that public service. I find it difficult to see why it should be *necessary* to withhold whole classes of routine 'communications with or within a public department' but quite unnecessary to withhold similar communications with or within a public corporation. There the safety of the public may well depend on the candour and completeness of reports made by subordinates whose duty it is to draw attention to defects. But, so far as I know, no one has ever suggested that public safety has been endangered by the candour or completeness of such reports having been inhibited by the fact that they may have to be

[37] [1942] A.C. 624, 642.]

produced if the interests of the due administration of justice should ever require production at any time.

[His Lordship then referred again to the Lord Chancellor's 1956 statement, which with one exception excluded from the protection of Crown privilege documents that were relevant to a defence in criminal proceedings. He continued:] That is a very wide ranging exception, for the Attorney-General stated that it applied at least to all manner of routine communications and even to prosecutions for minor offences. Thus it can no longer be said that the writer of such communications has any 'certainty at the time of writing that the document would not be disclosed.' So we have the curious result that 'freedom and candour of communication' is supposed not to be inhibited by knowledge of the writer that his report may be disclosed in a criminal case, but would still be supposed to be inhibited if he thought that his report might be disclosed in a civil case.

The Attorney-General did not deny that, even where the full contents of a report have already been made public in a criminal case, Crown privilege is still claimed for that report in a later civil case. And he was quite candid about the reason for that. Crown privilege is claimed in the civil case not to protect the document – its contents are already public property – but to protect the writer from civil liability should he be sued for libel or other tort. No doubt the Government have weighed the danger that knowledge of such protection might encourage malicious writers against the advantage that honest reporters shall not be subjected to vexatious actions, and have come to the conclusion that it is an advantage to the public service to afford this protection. But that seems very far removed from the original purpose of Crown privilege.

And the statement, as it has been explained to us, makes clear another point. The Minister who withholds production of a 'class' document has no duty to consider the degree of public interest involved in a particular case by frustrating in that way the due administration of justice. If it is in the public interest in his view to withhold documents of that class, then it matters not whether the result of withholding a document is merely to deprive a litigant of some evidence on a minor issue in a case of little importance or, on the other hand, is to make it impossible to do justice at all in a case of the greatest importance. I cannot think that it is satisfactory that there should be no means at all of weighing, in any civil case, the public interest involved in withholding the document against the public interest that it should be produced.

So it appears to me that the present position is so unsatisfactory that this House must re-examine the whole question in light of all the authorities.

Two questions will arise: first, whether the court is to have any right to question the finality of a Minister's certificate and, secondly, if it has such a right, how and in what circumstances that right is to be exercised and made effective.

A Minister's certificate may be given on one or other of two grounds: either because it would be against the public interest to disclose the contents of the particular document or documents in question,[38] or because the document belongs to a class of documents which ought to be withheld, whether or not there is anything in the particular document in question disclosure of which would be against the public interest.[39] It does not appear that any serious difficulties have arisen or are likely to arise with regard to the first class. However wide the power of the court may be held to be, cases would be very rare in which it could be proper to question the view of the responsible Minister that it would be contrary to the public interest to make public the contents of a particular document. A question might arise whether it would be possible to separate those parts of a document of which disclosure would be innocuous from those parts which ought not to be made public, but I need not pursue that question now. In the present case your Lordships are directly concerned with the second class of documents. . . .

[Having surveyed the relevant authorities, he continued:] I would . . . propose that the House ought now to decide that courts have and are entitled to exercise a power and duty to hold a balance between the public interest, as expressed by a Minister, to withhold certain documents or other evidence, and the public interest in ensuring the proper administration of justice. That does not mean that a court would reject a Minister's view: full weight must be given to it in every case, and if the Minister's reasons are of a character which judicial experience is not competent to weigh, then the Minister's view must prevail. But experience has shown that reasons given for withholding whole classes of documents are often not of that character. For example a court is perfectly well able to assess the likelihood that, if the writer of a certain class of document knew that there was a chance that his report might be produced in legal proceedings, he would make a less full and candid report than he would otherwise have done.

I do not doubt that there are certain classes of documents which ought not to be disclosed whatever their content may be. Virtually everyone agrees that Cabinet minutes and the like ought not to be disclosed until such time as they are only of historical interest. But I do not think that many people would give as the reason that premature disclosure would prevent candour in the Cabinet. To my mind the most important reason is that such disclosure would create or fan ill-informed or captious public or political criticism. The business of government is difficult enough as it is, and no government could contemplate with equanimity the inner workings of the government machine being exposed to the gaze of those ready to criticise without adequate knowledge of the background and perhaps with some axe to grind. And that must, in my view, also apply to all documents concerned with policy making within departments including, it may be, minutes and the like by quite junior officials and correspondence with outside bodies. Further it may be that deliberations about a particular case require protection as much as deliberations about policy. I do not think that it is possible to limit such documents by any

[38] [This is known as a 'contents claim'.]
[39] [This is known as a 'class claim'.]

definition. But there seems to me to be a wide difference between such documents and routine reports. There may be special reasons for withholding some kinds of routine documents, but I think that the proper test to be applied is to ask, in the language of Lord Simon in *Duncan's* case,[40] whether the withholding of a document because it belongs to a particular class is really 'necessary for the proper functioning of the public service.'

It appears to me that, if the Minister's reasons are such that a judge can properly weigh them, he must, on the other hand, consider what is the probable importance in the case before him of the documents or other evidence sought to be withheld. If he decides that on balance the documents probably ought to be produced, I think that it would generally be best that he should see them before ordering production and if he thinks that the Minister's reasons are not clearly expressed he will have to see the documents before ordering production. I can see nothing wrong in the judge seeing documents without their being shown to the parties. Lord Simon said (in *Duncan's* case[41]) that 'where the Crown is a party . . . this would amount to communicating with one party to the exclusion of the other.' I do not agree. The parties see the Minister's reasons. Where a document has not been prepared for the information of the judge, it seems to me a misuse of language to say that the judge 'communicates with' the holder of the document by reading it. If on reading the document he still thinks that it ought to be produced he will order its production.

But it is important that the Minister should have a right to appeal before the document is produced. . . .

The documents in this case are in the possession of a police force. The position of the police is peculiar. They are not servants of the Crown and they do not take orders from the Government. But they are carrying out an essential function of Government, and various Crown rights, privileges and exemptions have been held to apply to them. Their position was explained in *Coomber* v. *Berkshire Justices*[42] and cases there cited. It has never been denied that they are entitled to Crown privilege with regard to documents, and it is essential that they should have it.

The police are carrying on an unending war with criminals many of whom are today highly intelligent. So it is essential that there should be no disclosure of anything which might give any useful information to those who organise criminal activities. And it would generally be wrong to require disclosure in a civil case of anything which might be material in a pending prosecution: but after a verdict has been given or it has been decided to take no proceedings there is not the same need for secrecy. With regard to other documents there seems to be no greater need for protection than in the case of departments of Government.

It appears to me to be most improbable that any harm would be done by disclosure of the probationary reports on the appellant or of the report from

----

[40] [1942] A.C. 624, 642.
[41] [1942] A.C. 624, 640.
[42] (1883) 9 App.Cas. 61, H.L.

the police training centre. With regard to the report which the respondent made to his chief constable with a view to the prosecution of the appellant there could be more doubt, although no suggestion was made in argument that disclosure of its contents would be harmful now that the appellant has been acquitted. And . . . these documents may prove to be of vital importance in this litigation.

In my judgment, this appeal should be allowed and these documents ought now to be required to be produced for inspection. . . .

LORD MORRIS OF BORTH-Y-GEST: . . . I have come to the conclusion that it is now right to depart from the decision in *Duncan's* case.[43] . . .

In my view, it should now be made clear that whenever an objection is made to the production of a relevant document it is for the court to decide whether or not to uphold the objection. The inherent power of the court must include a power to ask for a clarification or an amplification of an objection to production though the court will be careful not to impose a requirement which could only be met by divulging the very matters to which the objection related. The power of the court must also include a power to examine documents privately, a power, I think, which in practice should be sparingly exercised but one which could operate as a safeguard for the executive in cases where a court is inclined to make an order for production, though an objection is being pressed. I see no difference in principle between the consideration of what have been called the contents cases and the class cases. The principle which the courts will follow is that relevant documents normally liable to production will be withheld if the public interest requires that they should be withheld. In many cases it will be plain that documents are within a class of documents which by their very nature ought not to be disclosed. Indeed, in the majority of cases I apprehend that a decision as to an objection will present no difficulty. The cases of difficulty will be those in which it will appear that if there is non-disclosure some injustice may result and that if there is disclosure the public interest may to some extent be affected prejudicially. The courts can and will recognise that a view honestly put forward by a Minister as to the public interest will be based upon special knowledge and will be put forward by one who is charged with a special responsibility. As Lord Radcliffe said in the *Glasgow Corporation* case,[44] the courts will not seek on a matter which is within the sphere and knowledge of a Minister to displace his view by their own. But where there is more than one aspect of the public interest to be considered it seems to me that a court, in reference to litigation pending before it, will be in the best position to decide where the weight of public interest predominates. I am convinced that the courts, with the independence which is their strength, can safely be entrusted with the duty of weighing all aspects of public interests and of private interests and of giving protection where it is found to be due. . . .

LORD PEARCE. My Lords, I agree with the opinion of my noble and learned friend, Lord Reid.

[43] [1942] A.C. 624.   [44] 1956 S.C.(H.L.) 1.

There is not and never has been any doubt that the High Court will not order the production of any document where this would imperil the state or harm the public interest as a whole. It has normally accepted the Minister's word on such a point. For he is cognisant of the contents of the document and the background which makes its production harmful. Nevertheless, the final responsibility lies on the High Court itself with its inherent power to decide what evidence it shall demand in the fulfilment of its public duty to administer justice. . . .

LORD UPJOHN: . . . On the one side there is the public interest to be protected; on the other side of the scales is the interest of the subject who legitimately wants production of some documents which he believes will support his own or defeat his adversary's case. Both are matters of public interest, for it is also in the public interest that justice should be done between litigating parties by production of all documents which are relevant and for which privilege cannot be claimed under the ordinary rules. They must be weighed in the balance one against the other.

Your Lordships have reviewed the earlier authorities which are many and are not easy to reconcile and I shall not discuss them again, but it seems to me that there is sufficient authority to support the view held by all of your Lordships that the claim of privilege by the Crown, while entitled to the greatest weight, is only a claim and the decision whether the court should accede to the claim lies within the discretion of the judge; and it is real discretion. . . . First, with regard to the 'contents' cases there is, I think, no dispute and it does not strictly arise in this case. A claim made by a Minister on the basis that the disclosure of the contents would be prejudicial to the public interest must receive the greatest weight; but even here I am of opinion that the Minister should go as far as he properly can without prejudicing the public interest in saying why the contents require protection. In such cases it would be rare indeed for the court to overrule the Minister but it has the legal power to do so, first inspecting the document itself and then, if he thinks proper to do so, ordering its production.

Secondly, the 'class' cases. . . .

No doubt there are many cases in which documents by their very nature fall in a class which require protection such as, only by way of example, Cabinet papers, Foreign Office dispatches, the security of the state, high level inter-departmental minutes and correspondence and documents pertaining to the general administration of the naval, military and air force services. Nearly always such documents would be the subject of privilege by reason of their contents but by their 'class' in any event they qualify for privilege. So, too, high level inter-departmental communications, to take, only as an example upon establishment matters, the promotion or transfer of reasonably high level personnel in the service of the Crown. But no catalogue can reasonably be compiled. The reason for this privilege is that it would be quite wrong and entirely inimical to the proper functioning of the public service if the public were to learn of these high level communications, however innocent of prejudice to the state the actual contents of any particular document might be; that is obvious. But it has nothing whatever to do with candour or uninhibited freedom of expression; I cannot believe that any Minister or any high level military or civil servant would feel in the least degree inhibited in expressing his honest views in the course of his duty on some subject, such as even the personal qualifications and delinquencies of some colleague, by the thought that his observations might one day see the light of day. His worst fear might be libel and there he has the defence of qualified privilege like everyone else in every walk of professional, industrial and commercial life who every day has to express views on topics indistinguishable in substance from those of the servants of the Crown.

So this plea of the necessity for the protection of documents written by junior servants of the Crown must depend soley on the necessity for candour.

. . .

. . . The tests to be applied to claims for Crown privilege in class cases I think should be as follows:

There are some documents which, apart altogether with the alleged necessity for candour, fall within the claim of protection; and probably at the same time, though not necessarily, within the 'contents' class. I have already given some examples and do not repeat them; the judge still has, though I should be surprised if it were ever necessary to exercise it, the rights I have mentioned in the 'contents' cases.

Then within the 'class' cases we come to the 'candour' cases pure and simple. For my part I find it difficult to justify this when those in other walks of life which give rise to equally important matters of confidence in relation to security and personnel matters as in the public service can claim no such privilege. . . .

[LORD HODSON delivered a speech in favour of allowing the appeal.]

Appeal allowed.

Questions

1. Are the courts in a better position than a minister to balance the competing public interests? (See de Smith, *Constitutional and Administrative Law*, 4th edn., p. 621.)

2. Is the candour argument such a bad one? (See de Smith, op. cit., pp. 621–2; Evans, (1980) 50 Can. Bar. Rev. 360 at pp. 368–72; and see further *Burmah Oil Co. Ltd.* v. *Bank of England,* p. 472 *infra,* and Note 3, p. 483 *infra.*)

3. Is the case of a person who is seeking discovery of documents which he requires for his defence in criminal proceedings any stronger than that of a person who requires the documents so as to prosecute another?

Notes

1. The five documents in question in this case were examined. Their disclosure, it was thought, would not be contrary to the public interest and consequently the District Registrar's order in favour of production was restored.

2. For discussion of the law prior to the House of Lords decision in *Conway* v.

Rimmer, see Clark, (1967) 30 M.L.R. 489, and for analysis of *Conway* v. *Rimmer* in the House of Lords, see Clark, (1969) 32 M.L.R. 142.

3. The argument that s. 28 of the Crown Proceedings Act 1947, p. 459 *supra*, had given 'statutory confirmation' to *Duncan* v. *Cammell Laird* was rejected in *Conway* v. *Rimmer*. 'It merely preserves in the operation of the section whatever may from time to time be the courts' rule of law for the withholding of documents' [1968] A.C. at pp. 983–4 per Lord Pearce.

Rogers v. Home Secretary

[1973] A.C. 388   House of Lords

It is sufficient for the purposes of this extract to note that this case concerned a successful claim to immunity from production for a letter sent by an assistant chief constable to the Gaming Board. The Gaming Board was established by the Gaming Act 1968 to 'keep under review the extent, character and location of gaming facilities'. It is not a government department.

LORD REID: . . . The ground put forward has been said to be Crown privilege. I think that that expression is wrong and may be misleading. There is no question of any privilege in the ordinary sense of the word. The real question is whether the public interest requires that the letter shall not be produced and whether that public interest is so strong as to override the ordinary right and interest of a litigant that he shall be able to lay before a court of justice all relevant evidence. A Minister of the Crown is always an appropriate and often the most appropriate person to assert this public interest, and the evidence or advice which he gives to the court is always valuable and may sometimes be indispensable. But, in my view, it must always be open to any person interested to raise the question and there may be cases where the trial judge should himself raise the question if no one else has done so. In the present case the question of public interest was raised by both the Attorney-General and the Gaming Board. In my judgment both were entitled to raise the matter. Indeed I think that in the circumstances it was the duty of the board to do as they have done. . . .

Notes

1. The use of the term 'Crown privilege' also came in for criticism from Lord Pearson [1973] A.C. at p. 406, Lord Simon at pp. 406–7, and Lord Salmon at p. 412 (though compare the view of Lord Scarman in *Science Research Council* v. *Nassé* [1980] A.C. 1028 at p. 1087). The preferred term is now 'public interest immunity'.

2. Related to the point in the extract *supra* is the rejection by the House of Lords in *D.* v. *N.S.P.C.C.* [1978] A.C. 171 of the idea that this immunity from production should be confined to the operations of central government departments or organs. This case concerned a civil action brought against the N.S.P.C.C., which is, of course, concerned with the welfare of children and which in particular is the only body (apart from the police and a local authority) authorized to bring care proceedings under s. 1 of the Children and Young Persons Act 1969. It was held that the N.S.P.C.C. could withhold the identity of a person who had made a particular allegation to them. The

House of Lords did, however, proceed with some caution; an important factor in favour of the claim was the similarity of the position of the informant to that of a police informer, whose identity receives some protection from the law (though see Tapper, (1978) 41 M.L.R. 192). Lord Hailsham approached the case with a certain 'willingness to extend established principles by analogy and legitimate extrapolation' ([1978] A.C. at p. 226), an attitude which seems to be a fair reflection of the general line adopted in the House of Lords. On the protection of sources of information, see further *Rogers v. Home Secretary* [1973] A.C. 388 at pp. 401, 407, 412–3.

It would seem, therefore, that the scope of a potential claim to immunity has increased over the years; contrast the change in attitude to claims by local authorities in *Blackpool Corporation v. Locker* [1948] 1 K.B. 349 at p. 380 with *Re D. (Infants)* [1970] 1 W.L.R. 599. However, one stopping point was reached in *Science Research Council v. Nassé* [1980] A.C. 1028, which involved two actions by employees alleging unlawful discrimination by their employers. The employers involved in the two cases (the S.R.C. and British Leyland) refused to disclose, in one case some confidential reports on, in the second case some confidential records of, other employees (along with certain additional material); but the House of Lords rejected the claim of public interest immunity which was raised by British Leyland. (Without going into detail, the argument against disclosure related to securing efficiency in industry and avoiding industrial unrest.) One reason for the rejection of the claim was the lack of any suitable analogy with an already accepted category.

The view to be found in Lord Reid's speech in *Conway v. Rimmer*, p. 463 *supra*, in relation to nationalized industries (e.g. the National Coal Board) and Crown privilege, should be considered in the light of the developments since that case. Do you think that a claim of public interest immunity could be made by such a body?

3. In *Alfred Crompton Amusement Machines Ltd.* v. *Customs and Excise Commissioners (No. 2)* [1974] A.C. 405 immunity from production was successfully sought for documents containing certain information given in confidence by third parties to the Commissioners. (Cf. *Norwich Pharmacal Co.* v. *Customs and Excise Commissioners* [1974] A.C. 133.) Confidentiality, it was held, did not of itself give rise to immunity, but it was a factor to consider. It was argued in *Alfred Crompton* that those who supplied the information in confidence would resent its potential disclosure to others who might in fact be their rivals in trade. This, it was said, could lead to the consequence that in future cases these people might feel tempted not to provide the information (even though there was a statutory provision requiring it to be given), and also that their relationship with the Commissioners would be prejudiced: in this way the public interest would be jeopardized. The case indeed raises the question of providing a limit on the scope of government invasion of privacy, on which see Zuckerman in *Crime, Proof and Punishment* (ed. Tapper), pp. 279–80.

A particular passage in the speech of Lord Cross (with whom on this point all the other Law Lords agreed) has caused some debate. He stated (at p. 434) that the claim to immunity had been made 'in the interests of the third parties concerned as much as in the interests of the commissioners and if any of them is in fact willing to give evidence, privilege in respect of any documents or information obtained from him will be waived'. Tapper, (1974) 37 M.L.R. 92 at p. 93 concludes from this passage that 'secondary evidence could be given, use of the material could not be restrained in the hands of third parties, and the privilege could be waived', all of which would be different under the traditional notion of Crown privilege (though see Zuckerman, op. cit., p. 289). How far does Lord Cross's view really go? On the facts of *Alfred Crompton*, if the third parties did not object to disclosure, would the public interest have been prejudiced? Do his comments suggest that waiver can operate in all cases of public interest immunity? Is waiver an appropriate term in this area? See generally on these questions Zuckerman, op. cit., pp. 289–92.

The idea that public interest immunity cannot be waived was, it should be noted, mentioned in the House of Lords in *Science Research Council* v. *Nassé* [1980] A.C. 1020, but see *Hehir* v. *Commissioner of Police of the Metropolis* [1982] 1 W.L.R. 715, which, while rejecting the possibility of waiver of immunity in general, left open the question of waiver by the maker of the statement in question: see especially the judgment of Brightman L.J. at p. 723. See also the views of Lord Denning in *Campbell* v. *Tameside M.B.C.* [1982] 3 W.L.R. 74 at pp. 79–80, although he refers to waiver in some cases by the maker *and* recipient of a document; cf. the *Hehir* case. Compare Lord Denning's earlier views in *Burmah Oil Co. Ltd.* v. *Bank of England* [1979] 1 W.L.R. 473 at pp. 487–8, and see *Neilson* v. *Laugharne* [1981] Q.B. 736 at pp. 746–7. It should be borne in mind, of course, that if the Crown does not object to production, then this will have an important evidential influence.

Burmah Oil Co. Ltd. v. Governor and Company of the Bank of England

[1980] A.C. 1090   House of Lords

LORD WILBERFORCE. My Lords, in this action the appellant the Burmah Oil Co. Ltd. ('Burmah') is suing the Governor and Company of the Bank of England ('the bank') for relief in respect of the sale to the bank of Burmah in 1975 of 77,817,507 ordinary stock units of £1 each of the British Petroleum Co. Ltd. ('B.P.') at a price of approximately £179 million. Burmah claims, in brief, that this price represented a substantial undervalue of the stock and that the bargain was unconscionable, inequitable and unreasonable. It is important to understand that this action, and these issues, arise exclusively between Burmah and the bank.

The present appeal arises out of an application by Burmah for production of 62 documents[45] listed in the list of documents served by the bank. The bank on the instructions of the Crown have objected to produce these on the ground that they belong to classes of documents production of which would be injurious to the public interest. They have put forward a certificate dated October 18, 1977, signed by the Chief Secretary to the Treasury supporting this objection. On the interlocutory hearing of the objection in the High Court Her Majesty's Attorney-General intervened in order to argue the case in support of it, and it was upheld by Foster J. On appeal by Burmah to the Court of Appeal [1979] 1 W.L.R. 473, the Attorney-General took a similar course, and that court, by majority, affirmed the judge. On a further appeal to this House, the Attorney-General was joined as a respondent and as such argued the case against production; the bank, as in the High Court of Appeal, took no part in the argument. But, I repeat, the only defendant in the action is the bank. . . .

The starting point in the discussion must be the certificate of the Chief Secretary. . . .

Omitting some passages, the certificate is as follows:

[45] [The House of Lords was in fact only concerned with ten documents.]

'3. I have personally read and carefully considered all the documents listed in the schedule and I have formed the opinion that their production would be injurious to the public interest for the reasons hereinafter set out. 4. The documents listed in the schedule fall within three categories described below. There is or are shown in the schedule against each document listed the appropriate category of, where a document falls within more than one category, the appropriate categories. The three catgories are as follows:–

'Category A

'These consist of communications between, to and from ministers (including ministers' personal secretaries acting on behalf of ministers) and minutes and briefs for ministers and memoranda of meetings attended by ministers. All such documents relate to the formulation of the policy of the government – (a) in face of the financial difficulties of the Burmah Oil Co. Ltd. (hereinafter called "Burmah") in December 1974 and January 1975, and having regard especially to: – (i) the likely effect of the default of Burmah in respect of large dollar loan upon: – (a) The £ sterling, (b) Other British companies with large overseas borrowings; (ii) the possible effect of a financial collapse by Burmah upon the government's North Sea oil policy and upon the future production of North Sea oil; (iii) the expectations which would be aroused on the part of other private borrowers defaulting on dollar debts if Burmah were to receive assistance; (b) in consequence of the measures taken in response to Burmah's said financial difficulties and in particular as to what was to be done with the B.P. stock sold by Burmah to the bank in January 1975 having regard especially to the international consequences of a sale by the bank of that stock; (c) in connection with the giving of further support to Burmah after January 1975, having regard particularly to the international consequences of a financial collapse by Burmah and the effect of such a collapse on the government's North Sea oil policy.

'Category B

'These consist of communications between, to and from senior officials of the Department of Energy, of the Treasury and of the bank including memoranda of meetings of and discussions between such officials, and drafts prepared by such officials (including drafts of minutes and briefs comprised in category A), all such communications and drafts relating to the formulation of one or more aspects of the policy described in category A.

[His Lordship said that the category C documents did not call for separate consideration.] . . .

'6. It is, in my opinion, necessary for the proper functioning of the public service that the documents in category A and category B should be withheld from production. They are all documents falling within the class of documents relating to the formulation of government policy. Such policy was decided at a very high level, involving as it did matters of major economic importance to the United Kingdom. The documents in question cannot properly be described as routine documents. Those in category A are all documents passing at a very high level, including communications intended for the guidance and recording the views of the Prime Minister or recording discussions at a very high level. The documents in category B though passing at a lower level or recording discussions at a lower level, nevertheless all relate to the policy decisions to be taken at a higher level. . . . [I]t would, in my view, be against the public interest that documents revealing the process of providing for ministers honest and candid advice on matters of high level policy should be subject to disclosure. In this connection, I would respectfully agree with the reasoning of Lord Reid in *Conway* v. *Rimmer* [1968] A.C. 910, 952, to whose remarks . . . my attention has been drawn, as regards the effect on the inner workings of the government machine of the public disclosure of documents concerned with policy. . . .'

[One] argument [by Burmah] is . . . that, whatever may have been the need to protect governmental policy from disclosure at the time (1975) all is now past history: the decision has been made; the sale has gone through; Burmah has been saved from collapse. So what is the public interest in keeping up the protective screen?

I think that there are several answers to this. The first (and easiest) is that all is not past history – at least we do not know that it is. Government policy as to supporting private firms in danger of collapse: as to ownership of B.P. stock: as to the development of North Sea oil is ongoing policy; the documents are not yet for the Record Office. They are not, to use a phrase picked out of Lord Reid's speech in *Conway* v. *Rimmer* [1968] A.C. 910, 952, of purely historical interest. Secondly the grounds on which public interest immunity is claimed for this class of document are, no doubt within limits, independent of time. One such ground is the need for candour in communication between those concerned with policy making. It seems now rather fashionable to decry this, but if as a ground it may at one time have been exaggerated, it has now, in my opinion, received an excessive dose of cold water. I am certainly not prepared – against the view of the minister – to discount the need, in the formation of such very controversial policy as that with which we are here involved, for frank and uninhibited advice from the bank to the government, from and between civil servants and between ministers. It does not require much imagination to suppose that some of those concerned took different views as to the right policy and expressed them. The documents indeed show that they did. To remove protection from revelation in court in this case at least could well deter frank and full expression in similar cases in the future.

Another such ground is to protect from inspection by possible critics the inner working of government while forming important governmental policy. I do not believe that scepticism has invaded this, or that it is for the courts to assume the role of advocates for open government. If, as I believe, this is a valid ground for protection, it must continue to operate beyond the time span of a particular episode. Concretely, to reveal what advice was *then* sought and given and the mechanism for seeking and considering such advice, might well make the process of government more difficult *now*. On this point too I am certainly not prepared to be wiser than the minister. So I think that the 'time factor' argument must fail.

The basis for an immunity claim, then, having been laid, it is next necessary to consider whether there is any other element of public interest telling in favour of production. The interest of the proper and fair administration of justice falls under this description. It is hardly necessary to state that the mere fact that the documents are or may be 'relevant' to the issues, within the extended meaning of relevance in relation to dicovery, is not material. The question of privilege or immunity only arises in relation to 'relevant' documents and itself depends on other considerations, viz., whether production of these documents (admittedly relevant) is necessary for the due administration of justice. In considering how these two elements are to be weighed one against the other, the proper starting point must be the decision of this House in *Conway* v. *Rimmer* [1968] A.C. 910. . . . Of course *Conway* v. *Rimmer,* as the speeches of their Lordships show, does not profess to cover every case, nor has it frozen the law, but it does provide a solid basis for progress as regards the point now under discussion.

It may well be arguable whether, when one is faced with a claim for immunity from production on 'public interest' grounds, and when the relevant public interest is shown to be of a high, or the highest, level of importance, that fact is of itself conclusive, and nothing which relates to the interest in the administration of justice can prevail against it. As Lord Pearce said in *Conway* v. *Rimmer* [1968] A.C. 910, 987: 'Obviously production would never be ordered of fairly wide classes of documents at a high level' and see *Reg.* v. *Lewes Justices, Ex parte Secretary of State for the Home Department* [1973] A.C. 388, 412 *per* Lord Salmon. In the words of May J. in *Barty-King* v. *Ministry of Defence* (unreported), October 10, 1978 (concerned with internal thinking and policy at a high civil service level), it is not even necessary to bring out the scales. Mr. Silkin for the Attorney-General did not contend for any such rigorous proposition, i.e. that a high level public interest can never, in any circumstances, be outweighed. In this I think that he was in line with the middle of the road position taken by Lord Reid in *Conway* v. *Rimmer* and also with the median views of the members of the High Court of Australia in *Sankey* v. *Whitlam,* 53 A.L.J.R. 11 – see particularly the judgment of Gibbs A.C.J. I am therefore quite prepared to deal with this case on the basis that the courts may, in a suitable case, decide that a high level governmental public interest must give way to the interests of the administration of justice.

But it must be clear what this involves. A claim for public interest immunity having been made, on manifestly solid grounds, it is necessary for those who seek to overcome it to demonstrate the existence of a counteracting interest calling for disclosure of particular documents. When this is demonstrated, but only then, may the court proceed to a balancing process. . . . [In] the present case . . . [t]here is not, and I firmly assert this, the slightest ground, apart from pure speculation, for supposing that there is any document in existence, among those which it is sought to withhold, or anything in a document which could outweigh the public interest claim for immunity. . . .

[Having stated his reasons for this opinion more fully, he continued:]

This brings me to the issue of inspection. For now it is said, 'Well, let us look at the documents and see – to do so cannot do any harm. If there is nothing there no damage will be done: if there is, we can weigh its importance.' As presented (and to be fair to Burmah's very able counsel, such a submission occupied a far from prominent place in their argument) this may appear to have some attraction. But with all respect to those who think otherwise, I am firmly of opinion that we should not yield to this siren song. The existing state of the authorities is against it: and no good case can be made for changing the law. Indeed, to do so would not in my opinion be progress.

As to authority . . . [in] *Conway* v. *Rimmer* [1968] A.C. 910 itself, it was said that the power should be exercised 'sparingly' (*per* Lord Morris of Borth-y-Gest, p. 971), and then only if there are reasons to doubt the accuracy of the certificate or the cogency of the minister's reasons. Inspection should be by way of final check. Or, as Lord Upjohn put it, inspection should be made if the judge 'feels any doubt about the reason for [the document's] inclusion as a class document' (p. 995). In *Alfred Crompton Amusement Machines Ltd.* v. *Customs and Excise Commissioners (No. 2)* [1974] A.C. 405 this House upheld the claim to public interest immunity without inspecting the documents, although that course had been taken by the Court of Appeal. In first instance cases, the judges have treated the power to inspect as an exceptional one, to be rarely used: in two instances they sought and obtained the Crown's consent to inspect selected documents: *Tito* v. *Waddell* (unreported), March 3, 1975, and *Barty-King* v. *Ministry of Defence* (unreported), October 10, 1978. This is inconsistent with the recognition of a general right or duty to inspect.

As to principle, I cannot think that it is desirable that the courts should assume the task of inspection except in rare instances where a strong positive case is made out, certainly not upon a bare unsupported assertion by the party seeking production that something to help him may be found, or upon some unsupported – viz., speculative – hunch of its own. In the first place it is necessary to draw a reasonably clear line between the responsibility of ministers on the one hand, and those of the courts on the other. Each has its proper contribution to make towards solution of the problem where the public interest lies – judicial review is not a 'bonum in se' it is a part – and a valuable one – of democratic government in which other responsibilities coexist. Existing cases, from *Conway* v. *Rimmer* onwards, have drawn this line carefully and suitably. It is for the minister to define the public interest and the grounds on which he considers that production would affect it. Similarly, the court, responsible for the administration of justice, should, before it decides that the minister's view must give way, have something positive or identifiable to put into the scales. . . . Secondly, decisions on grounds of public interest privilege fall to be made at first instance, by judges or masters in chambers. They should be able to make these decisions according to simple rules: these are provided by the law as it stands. To invite a general procedure of inspection is to embark the courts on a dangerous course: they have not in general the time nor the experience, to carry out in every case a careful inspection of documents and thereafter a weighing process. The results of such a process may, indeed are likely, to be variable from court to court and from case to case. This case provides an example of opposite conclusions come to upon identical materials: see [1979] 1 W.L.R. 473. This inevitable uncertainty is not likely to do credit to the administration of justice and is bound to encourage appeals.

In the end, I regard this as a plain case: of public interest immunity properly claimed on grounds of high policy on the one hand in terms which cannot be called in question; of nothing on any substance to put in the scale on the other. I return to the point that both courts below have refused to exercise a discretionary power to order production of these documents, or to inspect them. Their decision can only be reversed if they erred in law. To say that they erred in law in not inspecting the documents involves the proposition that there is a duty, either in all cases or at least in such a case as this, to inspect. In my opinion it is not the law, and ought not to be the law, that there is any such duty. In saying this and in the previous discussion I have done no more than adopt, with greater prolixity, the completely convincing judgment of Bridge L.J. (with whom in substance Foster J. and Templeman L.J. agreed) in the Court of Appeal.

I would dismiss the appeal.

LORD EDMUND-DAVIES: . . . In the face of the bank's umbrella denial of any inequality of bargaining power, the sale of B.P. stock at an undervalue, and all other forms of unconscionable conduct on their part, it could, as I think, prove a valuable reinforcement of Burmah's case if they could establish by means of some of the withheld documents that the bank had itself committed themselves to the view that the terms finally presented to Burmah were tainted by those unconscionable features of which Burmah complained.

What are the probabilities of such documentary support being in existence? Is it merely pure conjecture? If so, applying the plaintiffs' own test, production should be refused. But in my judgment, there is more to it than that. . . . [I]n my judgment the existence of such documentary material is likely. And that, in my judgment, is sufficient. . . .

[Having therefore moved on to consider the 'balancing exercise', he continued:] . . . [S]ince not only justice itself but also the *appearance* of justice is of considerable importance, the balancing exercise is bound to be affected to some degree where the party objecting to discovery is not a wholly detached observer of events in which it was in no way involved. It cannot realistically be thought that the government is wholly devoid of interest in the outcome of these proceedings. . . .

[LORD EDMUND-DAVIES then went on to decide that in the light of the material before the court, and especially his view (*supra*) concerning the likelihood of documentary support for Burmah, the documents should be inspected.]

LORD KEITH OF KINKEL: . . . [I]n my opinion no definitive body of binding rules universally applicable to future cases in the field is to be gathered from the speeches delivered [in *Conway* v. *Rimmer* [1968] A.C. 910] and the sound development of the law now requires that it be examined afresh. . . .

Lord Hodson in [*Conway* v. *Rimmer*] at p. 979 said that he did not regard the classification which places all documents under the heading either of contents or class as being wholly satisfactory. I agree with him. What really matters is the specific ground of public interest upon which the ministerial objection is based, and it scarcely needs to be said that the more clearly this ground is stated the easier will be the task of the court in weighing it against the public interest in the administration of justice. The weight of a contents claim is capable of being very readily measured. Obvious instances are documents relating to defence of the realm or relations with other states. It might be said that such documents constitute a class defined by reference to the nature of their contents. But I would prefer to regard the claim in regard to such a document as being in substance a contents claim. . . .

[Having quoted a passage from Lord Upjohn's speech in *Conway* v. *Rimmer* set out at p. 468 *supra*, he continued:]

Claims to immunity on class grounds stand in a different category because the reasons of public interest upon which they are based may appear to some minds debatable or even nebulous. In *Duncan* v. *Cammell, Laird & Co. Ltd.* [1942] A.C. 624, Viscount Simon L.C. at p. 642 referred to cases 'where the practice of keeping a class of documents secret is necessary for the proper functioning of the public service.' These words have been seized on as convenient for inclusion in many a ministerial certificate, including the one under consideration in the present case. But they inevitably stimulate the query 'why is the concealment necessary for that purpose?' and unless it is answered there is nothing tangible to put in the balance against the public interest in the proper administration of justice.

Over a considerable period it was maintained, not without success, that the prospect of the disclosure in litigation of correspondence or other communications within government departments would inhibit a desirable degree of candour in the making of such documents, with results detrimental to the proper functioning of the public service. . . . This contention must now be treated as having little weight, if any. In *Conway* v. *Rimmer* [1968] A.C. 910, Lord Morris of Borth-y-Gest, at p. 957, referred to it as being of doubtful validity. Lord Hodson, at p. 976, thought it impossible at the present day to justify the doctrine in its widest term. Lord Pearce, at p. 986, considered that a general blanket protection of wide classes led to a complete lack of common sense. Lord Upjohn, at p. 995, expressed himself as finding it difficult to justify the doctrine 'when those in other walks of life which give rise to equally important matters of confidence in relation to security and personnel matters as in the public service can claim no such privilege.' The notion that any competent and conscientious public servant would be inhibited at all in the candour of his writings by consideration of the off-chance that they might have to be produced in a litigation is in my opinion grotesque. To represent that the possibility of it might significantly impair the public service is even more so. Nowadays the state in multifarious manifestations impinges closely upon the lives and activities of individual citizens. Where this has involved a citizen in litigation with the state or one of its agencies, the candour argument is an utterly insubstantial ground for denying him access to relevant documents. I would add that the candour doctrine stands in a different category from that aspect of public interest which in appropriate circumstances may require that the sources and nature of information confidentially tendered should be withheld from disclosure. *Reg.* v. *Lewes Justices, Ex parte Secretary of State for the Home Department* [1973] A.C. 388 and *D.* v. *National Society for the Prevention of Cruelty to Children* [1978] A.C. 171 are cases in point on that matter.

I turn to what was clearly regarded in *Conway* v. *Rimmer* [1968] A.C. 910 as the really important reason for protecting from disclosure certain categories of documents on a class basis. It was thus expressed by Lord Reid. . . .

[Having quoted a passage from Lord Reid's speech set out at p. 465 *supra*, he continued:]

Lord Hodson at p. 973 referred to classes of documents which from their very character ought to be withheld from production, such as Cabinet minutes, dispatches from ambassadors abroad and minutes of discussions between heads of departments. Lord Pearce at p. 987 said that obviously production would never be considered of fairly wide classes of documents at a high level such as Cabinet correspondence, letters or reports on appointments to office of importance and the like. Lord Upjohn spoke to similar effect at p. 993, saying that the reason for the privilege was that it would be wrong and entirely inimical to the proper functioning of the public service if the public were to learn of these high level communications, however innocent of prejudice to the state the actual contents of any particular document might be, and that this was obvious.

In my opinion, it would be going too far to lay down that no document in any particular one of the categories mentioned should never in any circumstances be ordered to be produced, and indeed I did not understand counsel for the Attorney-General to pitch his submission that high before this House. Something must turn upon the nature of the subject matter, the persons who dealt with it, and the manner in which they did so. In so far as matter of government policy is concerned, it may be relevant to know the extent to which the policy remains unfulfilled, so that its success might be prejudiced by disclosure of the considerations which led to it. In that context the time element enters into the equation. Details of an affair which is stale and no longer of topical significance might be capable of disclosure without risk of damage to the public interest. The ministerial certificate should offer all practicable assistance on these aspects. But the nature of the litigation and the apparent importance to it of the documents in question may in extreme cases demand production even of the most sensitive communications at the highest level. Such a case might fortunately be unlikely to arise in this country, but in circumstances such as those of *Sankey* v. *Whitlam*, 53 A.L.J.R. 11[46] . . . I do not doubt that the principles there expounded would fall to be applied. There can be discerned in modern times a trend towards more open governmental methods than were prevalent in the past. No doubt it is for Parliament and not for courts of law to say how far that trend should go. The courts are, however, concerned with the consideration that it is in the public interest that justice should be done and should be publicly recognised as having been done. This may demand, though no doubt only in a very limited number of cases, that the inner workings of government should be exposed to public gaze, and there may be some who would regard this as likely to lead, not to captious or ill-informed criticism, but to criticism calculated to improve the nature of that working as affecting the individual citizen. . . .

There are cases where consideration of the terms of the ministerial certificate and of the nature of the issues in the case before it as revealed by the pleadings, taken with the description of the document sought to be recovered, will make it clear to the court that the balance of public interest lies against disclosure. In other cases the position will be the reverse. But there may be situations where grave doubt arises, and the court feels that it cannot properly decide upon which side the balance falls without privately inspecting the documents. In my opinion the present is such a case. . . . Having carefully considered all the circumstances, I have come to the conclusion that a reasonable probability exists of finding the documents in question to contain a record of the views of the responsible officials of the Bank of England expressed in such terms as to lend substantial support to the contention that the bargain eventually concluded with the appellants was unconscionable. . . . There can be no doubt that the court has power to inspect the documents privately. This was clearly laid down in *Conway* v. *Rimmer* [1968] A.C. 910. I do not consider that exercise of such power, in cases responsibly regarded by the court as doubtful, can be treated as itself detrimental to the public interest. Indeed, I am of opinion that it is calculated to promote the public interest, by adding to public confidence in the administration of justice. . . . Apprehension has on occasion been expressed lest the power of inspection might be irresponsibly exercised, perhaps by one of the lower courts. As a safeguard against this, an appeal should always be available, as indicated in *Conway* v. *Rimmer* [1968] A.C. 910, *per* Lord Reid at p. 953.

For these reasons I am in agreement with the majority of your Lordships that this is a proper case for the court to require the 10 documents in question to be made available for private inspection. I do not consider that the

---

[46] [See Note 1, p. 483 *infra.*]

discretion to order or refuse production of the documents was capable of being exercised soundly and with due regard to principle in the absence of such inspection. Accordingly I see no difficulty in differing from Foster J. and the majority of the Court of Appeal.

Having inspected the documents, I agree with the majority of your Lordships, though with some hesitation, that none of them contains matter of such evidential value as to make an order for their disclosure, in all the circumstances, necessary for disposing fairly of the case.

It follows that I would dismiss the appeal.

LORD SCARMAN: . . . I do not . . . accept that there are any classes of document which, however harmless their contents and however strong the requirement of justice, may never be disclosed until they are only of historical interest. In this respect I think there may well be a difference between a 'class' objection and a 'contents' objection – though the residual power to inspect and to order disclosure must remain in both instances. A Cabinet minute, it is said, must be withheld from production. Documents relating to the formulation of policy at a high level are also to be withheld. But is the secrecy of the 'inner workings of the government machine' so vital a public interest that it must prevail over even the most imperative demands of justice? If the contents of a document concern the national safety, affect diplomatic relations or relate to some state secret of high importance, I can understand an affirmative answer. But if they do not (and it is not claimed in this case that they do), what is so important about secret government that it must be protected even at the price of injustice in our courts?

The reasons given for protecting the secrecy of government at the level of policy-making are two. The first is the need for candour in the advice offered to ministers: the second is that disclosure 'would create or fan ill-informed or captious public or political criticism.' Lord Reid in *Conway* v. *Rimmer* [1968] A.C. 910, 952, thought the second 'the most important reason.' Indeed, he was inclined to discount the candour argument.

I think both reasons are factors legitimately to be put into the balance which has to be struck between the public interest in the proper functioning of the public service (i.e., the executive arm of government) and the public interest in the administration of justice. Sometimes the public service reasons will be decisive of the issue: but they should never prevent the court from weighing them against the injury which would be suffered in the administration of justice if the document was not to be disclosed. And the likely injury to the cause of justice must also be assessed and weighed. Its weight will vary according to the nature of the proceedings in which disclosure is sought, the relevance of the documents, and the degree of likelihood that the document will be of importance in the litigation. In striking the balance, the court may always, if it thinks it necessary, itself inspect the documents.

Inspection by the court is, I accept, a power to be exercised only if the court is in doubt, after considering the certificate, the issues in the case and the relevance of the documents whose disclosure is sought. Where documents are relevant (as in this case they are), I would think a pure 'class' objection would by itself seldom quieten judicial doubts – particularly if, as here, a substantial case can be made out for saying that disclosure is needed in the interest of justice. . . .

[LORD SALMON delivered a speech in which he favoured inspecting the documents, but, having inspected, his Lordship was in favour of dismissing the appeal.]

Appeal dismissed.

Question

What, if any, difference in judicial philosophy is there between Lord Wilberforce and Lord Keith? (See Williams, [1980] C.L.J. 1.)

Notes

1. In the subsequent civil action before Walton J., Burmah were unsuccessful: *Burmah Oil Co. Ltd.* v. *The Governor of the Bank of England*, The Times, 4 July 1981.

2. *Burmah Oil* involved a claim for immunity in relation to documents concerned with policy decided at a high level. As has been pointed out by Williams, op. cit., until *Burmah Oil* the cases following *Conway* v. *Rimmer* [1968] A.C. 910 had, with one exception (*F. Hoffman La Roche & Co.* v. *Department of Trade and Industry*, The Times, 19 April 1975), arisen 'in contexts, such as police or customs and excise, falling outside the inner machinery of central government'. (This was not true of the position in the Commonwealth: see, e.g., *Lanyon Pty. Ltd.* v. *The Commonwealth* (1974) 129 C.L.R. 650 and *Sankey* v. *Whitlam*, p. 483 *infra* and Note 1, p. 483 *infra*, and for the position in the U.S.A. see *Nixon* v. *U.S.* 418 U.S. 683 (1974), which was referred to in *Burmah Oil.*) For a more recent English case in which documents concerned with the formulation of government policy were ordered to be produced, see *Williams* v. *Home Office* [1981] 1 All E.R. 1151, but see *Air Canada* v. *Secretary of State for Trade* (No. 2) noted in the Appendix.

3. On the 'candour argument', see further *Campbell* v. *Tameside M.B.C.* [1982] 3 W.L.R. 74, where Ackner L.J. took the view that recent dicta in the House of Lords (in *Science Research Council* v. *Nassé* [1980] A.C. 1028) had led to its 'quietus', and O'Connor L.J. thought that it had not survived *Conway* v. *Rimmer* [1968] A.C. 610. Cf. Lord Denning, [1892] 3 W.L.R. at p. 79 and see *Gaskin* v. *Liverpool C.C.* [1980] 1 W.L.R. 1549; *Neilson* v. *Laugharne* [1981] Q.B. 736 at p. 748; *R.* v. *Birmingham C.C., ex p. O* [1982] 1 W.L.R. 679 at p. 694. Note also that the candour doctrine was distinguished by Lord Keith in *Burmah Oil*, p. 479 *supra,* from cases in which the source or nature of confidential information may need protection, e.g. information given to the Gaming Board or the N.S.P.C.C. (see pp. 470–1 *supra*).

4. In *Alfred Crompton Amusement Machines Ltd.* v. *Customs and Excise Commissioners (No. 2)* [1974] A.C. 405 Lord Cross, with the agreement of all of their Lordships in the case on this point, stated (at p. 434) that 'where the considerations for and against disclosure appear to be fairly evenly balanced the courts should I think uphold a claim to privilege on the ground of public interest and trust to the head of the department concerned to do whatever he can to mitigate the ill-effects of non-disclosure'.

Compare, for example, the opinion expressed in *Burmah Oil* by Lord Edmund-Davies (which was quoted with apparent approval by McNeill J. recently in *Williams*

v. *Home Office*) that a 'party to litigation who seeks, as here, to withhold from disclosure to the other party documents which being included in their list or affidavit of documents are ex concessis relevant to the litigation has . . . a heavy burden of proof' [1980] A.C. at pp. 1124–5. See also his Lordship's similar opinion in *D.* v. *N.S.P.C.C.* [1978] A.C. 171 at p. 242 and Lord Reid's view in *Rogers* v. *Home Secretary* [1973] A.C. 388 at p. 400 to the effect that on the authority of *Conway* v. *Rimmer* [1968] A.C. 910 a heavy burden of proof is imposed on a person presenting a 'class claim' (though see his views in *Conway* v. *Rimmer* at p. 465 *supra* concerning 'policy' documents). Are these statments inconsistent with Lord Cross's opinion? If so, which do you prefer? See further Tapper, (1974) 37 M.L.R. at pp. 94–5; Zuckerman in *Crime, Proof and Punishment* (ed. Tapper), p. 279, both of whom are critical of Lord Cross's approach.

Zuckerman op. cit., pp. 274–5, is also critical of the burden Lord Edmund-Davies and Lord Keith place on a person seeking disclosure of documents before the court will even *inspect* the documents. Compare, however, the approach of Lord Denning in *Neilson* v. *Laugharne* [1981] Q.B. 736 at p. 749 that in 'class' cases 'the court should rarely inspect the documents themselves' and see *Gaskin* v. *Liverpool C.C.* [1980] 1 W.L.R. 1549 at p. 1555 per Megaw L.J. And see Appendix.

Sankey v. Whitlam

(1978) 142 C.L.R. 1   Full Court of the High Court of Australia

GIBBS A.C.J.: . . . Although the statement that cabinet documents and other papers concerned with policy decisions at a high level ('state papers', as I shall henceforth call them) are immune from disclosure was repeated in *Conway* v. *Rimmer,*[47] it accords ill with the principles affirmed in that case. The fundamental principle is that documents may be withheld from disclosure only if, and to the extent, that the public interest renders it necessary. That principle in my opinion must also apply to state papers. It is impossible to accept that the public interest requires that all state papers should be kept secret for ever, or until they are only of historical interest. In some cases the legitimate need for secrecy will have ceased to exist after a short time has elapsed; this will be so, to take Lord Widgery's example, [in *Attorney-General* v. *Jonathan Cape Ltd.*[48]] when new taxation proposals have passed into legislation. In other cases it may be necessary to maintain secrecy for many years. This may be so where the documents concern national security or diplomatic relations, to give two obvious examples. In other words state papers do not form a homogeneous class, all the members of which must be treated alike. The subject matter with which the papers deal will be of great importance, but all the circumstances have to be considered in deciding whether the papers in question are entitled to be withheld from production, no matter what they individually contain. . . .

Notes

1. In *Sankey* v. *Whitlam* two informations had been laid by a private citizen alleging criminal conspiracy against a former Prime Minister, two former Ministers, and a

---

[47] [1968] A.C. 910.
[48] [[1976] Q.B. 752, at p. 770.]

former Attorney-General. The Australian High Court, having examined the competing public interests, decided to order production of documents, some of which were Cabinet documents or were close to that status. It should be noted that the documents related to a proposal which was no longer of any importance to the national interest (but not, it would seem, 'only of historical interest', and see Mason J., (1978) 142 C.L.R. at p. 98). Furthermore, the legal proceedings for which production was sought were an attempt to prosecute former Ministers for conduct related to their office, and the court was concerned that, if any crime had been committed, the Ministers should not be protected from the consequences by public interest immunity (though cf. Mason J., (1978) 142 C.L.R. at p. 100). The prosecution was in fact unsuccessful. See Eagles, [1980] P.L. 263 for general discussion of *Sankey* v. *Whitlam*.

2. The extract *supra* relates to the problem whether there are any cases in which the Minister's objection is *de facto* conclusive. In relation to English authorities, note that certain passages in the speeches in *Conway* v. *Rimmer* suggest that this is so: see e.g. Lord Reid's speech at p. 465 *supra*, although the protection he gives to 'Cabinet minutes and the like' is restricted to those that are not of purely historical interest. See also *Attorney-General* v. *Jonathan Cape Ltd.* [1976] Q.B. 752 in which Lord Widgery C.J. stated (at p. 764) that 'no court will compel production of Cabinet papers in the course of discovery in an action'. Nevertheless, note that in that case the court, on the facts, refused to issue injunctions stopping publication of all or part of volume 1 of the Crossman Diaries, which recorded Cabinet discussions. The volume was to be published almost ten years after the events in question, but it is by no means certain that this would place it in Lord Reid's 'only of historical interest' category.

As will have been seen, the whole problem – and it is not confined merely to Cabinet papers – was further considered in *Burmah Oil*. The flexible approach which can be found in Lord Keith's speech at p. 479 *supra* (and see Lord Edmund-Davies, [1980] A.C. at p. 1127; cf. the speech of Lord Wilberforce at p. 475 *supra*) is similar to that to be found in *Sankey* v. *Whitlam*. Where does Lord Scarman stand on this issue? See also *Environmental Defence Society Inc.* v. *South Pacific Aluminium Ltd.* [1981] 1 N.Z.L.R. 153, noted by Eagles, [1982] C.L.J. 11; Hannan, (1982) 45 M.L.R. 471. In this case the New Zealand Court of Appeal, relying on *Burmah Oil* and *Sankey* v. *Whitlam*, accepted that Cabinet documents are not absolutely immune from production. The position in relation to documents concerning diplomatic relations, national security or defence seems rather more uncertain. For a recent English contribution to the topic, note *Williams* v. *Home Office* [1981] 1 All E.R. 1151. Here McNeill J. ordered the production of a number of documents for which public interest immunity had been claimed, but, in so doing, he stressed that he was not dealing with a 'claim for immunity . . . based on matters of state policy such as foreign affairs, defence or the like, what was conveniently in argument referred to as "high policy", where it might well be that the certificate would be accepted without more' (p. 1154). Even if the certificate is accepted 'without more', it is, of course, the *court*'s decision that it should be so accepted. See further the *Air Canada* case noted in the Appendix.

3. For the position of the Parliamentary Commissioner for Administration (the Ombudsman) in relation to Cabinet papers, and indeed to claims for immunity from production of documents or the giving of evidence in general, see pp. 625–6 *infra*.

PART V

Legislative and Adjudicative Procedures

15

DELEGATED LEGISLATION

LEGAL FORMS AND CHARACTERISTICS

Note

In terms of volume, most legislation is not made by Parliament but by government departments, local authorities, and other public bodies, such as nationalized industries and professional bodies. This 'delegated', 'subordinate', or 'administrative' legislation is normally made in pursuance of a statutory power and, like all subordinate functions, is subject to the ultra vires doctrine. Such legislation has existed since Tudor times (see Allen, *Law and Orders*, 3rd edn., Ch. 2, hereafter Allen; Wade, p. 735) but only since the late nineteenth century has there been widespread delegation of legislative power.

Delegated legislation may take several forms and be described by a variety of terms: rules, Orders in Council, by-laws, circulars, and codes of practice (see pp. 490 and 494 *infra*; Allen, pp. 90–103; Wade, pp. 741–7). Many of these fall within the definition of 'statutory instrument' in s. 1 of the Statutory Instruments Act 1946, p. 512 *infra*. Allen, p. 101, states that the general effect of this statute and the regulations (S.I. 1948 No. 1) made under it is 'that the term "statutory instrument" apparently covers every known form of delegated legislation, provided that (if the tautology may be pardoned) it is legislative and not executive, and that it is not expressly excluded from the operation of the Act'. But, as will be seen, the definition is primarily a mechanical one. It does, however, have important consequences because only statutory instruments are subject to a general requirement of registration and publication (see pp. 439 and 490 *infra*).

There has always been hostility to delegated legislation on the grounds that it constitutes an infringement of the doctrines of the rule of law and of the separation of powers, that it undermines Parliamentary sovereignty, and that it gives large powers to the bureaucracy without an effective system of control (Allen, pp. 33–42; Wade, pp. 733–6). The acceptance, by all governments, of the welfare state has meant that the widespread existence of subordinate law-making power is no longer an issue. The important question now is how to subject this power to an adequate system of control. This chapter will consider three methods of control: judicial review, pre-promulgation consultation, and parliamentary supervision. For further details, see Allen, *passim*; Carr, *Delegated Legislation*; Griffith and Street, *Principles of Administrative Law*, 5th edn., Chs. 2–3 (hereafter Griffith and Street); Wade, Ch. 22; Wade and Phillips, *Constitutional and Administrative Law*, 9th edn., Ch. 33.

Blackpool Corporation v. Locker

[1948] 1 K.B. 349   Court of Appeal

Regulation 51 of the Defence (General) Regulations 1939 stated:

(1) A competent authority, if it appears to that authority to be necessary or expedient so to do for any of the purposes specified in sub-s. 1

of s. 1 of the Supplies and Services (Transitional Provisions) Act, 1945 [which included the provision of housing for the inadequately housed] may take possession of any land, and may give such directions as appear to the authority to be necessary or expedient in connexion with the taking of possession of the land. . . .

(5) A competent authority may, to such extent and subject to such restrictions as it thinks proper, delegate all or any of its functions under paras. (1) to (3) of this regulation to any specified persons or class of persons.

The Minister of Health, who was a 'competent authority' for the purposes of this regulation, delegated his powers to requisition houses to certain local authorities or their clerks by ministerial circulars. Circular 2845 of 4 August 1943, *inter alia*, provided in para. 9:

When . . . requisitioning is being considered in relation to a particular property the intention of the owner or tenant should be ascertained and he should be afforded a reasonable opportunity for letting or re-occupation, as the case may be, before requisitioning is applied,

and in para. 5:

The delegation is subject to the conditions set out in the appendix to this circular, which also indicates the procedure to be adopted in the exercise of these powers.

The first part of the appendix stated:

1. The requisitioning power is limited to the taking possession of (a) unoccupied houses or other residential buildings whether furnished or not; (b) unoccupied non-residential buildings . . .

3. No chattels contained in any house of which possession is taken may be requisitioned, and the requisition notice shall contain a direction to the owner requiring him to remove the chattels.

Part III, para. 3, of Circular 138 of 20 July 1945 stated that no house was to be taken into occupation until fourteen days after notices were on the premises and served on the owner or his agent. It continued:

[W]here, within this [fourteen-day] period the owner notifies his intention to occupy the house by himself or his family, the Authority shall not proceed further in the matter.

Blackpool Corporation or their town clerk, purporting to act under these regulations, took possession of an unoccupied dwelling house by serving the required notices (on 20 June 1946) and obtaining the keys (on 21 June 1946) from the owner's agent under threat of putting a new lock on the door. The notices made no reference to the furniture on the premises, despite the provision in para. 3 of the Appendix *supra*. The Corporation did not give up possession on being informed (on 27 June 1946) that the owner wanted the house for his own occupation and refused to inform the owner of the actual terms of the ministerial circulars. The Minister purported to ratify the acts of the Corporation by various letters written between 20 August and 28 November 1946. The owner had entered the house and the Corporation sought an injunction to restrain him from continuing to occupy it and damages for trespass. The county court judge found that the owner had the bona fide intention of occupying the house as his home, that the original requisition was invalid, but that the Minister had independently requisitioned the house and/or ratified the acts of his agents. On appeal:

SCOTT L.J.: This appeal raises several important questions about the delegated legislation enacted by the Ministry of Health under reg. 51 of the Defence (General) Regulations, 1939, during the war and since the enactment of the Supplies and Services (Transitional Provisions) Act, 1945, in connexion with the requisitioning of houses; there is one quite general question affecting all such sub-delegated legislation, and of supreme importance to the continuance of the rule of law under the British constitution, namely, the right of the public affected to know what that law is. That right was denied to the defendant in the present case. The maxim that ignorance of the law does not excuse any subject represents the working hypothesis on which the rule of law rests in British democracy. That maxim applies in legal theory just as much to written as to unwritten law, i.e., to statute law as much as to common law or equity. But the very justification for that basic maxim is that the whole of our law, written or unwritten, is accessible to the public – in the sense, of course, that, at any rate, its legal advisers have access to it, at any moment, as of right. When a government bill is brought before Parliament in a form which, even in regard to merely executive or administrative matters, gives a wide and unlimited discretion to a minister, and objection is made, the answer is sometimes given that the minister may be trusted by the House to use his powers with a wise and reasonable discretion. The answer may be perfectly bona fide; but tempora mutantur, and another minister or another government may use the unlimited powers indiscreetly or oppressively. If that happens, the only remedy practically open to the aggrieved citizen is action in Parliament to which alone the minister is responsible. But the Act when passed may contain delegated powers to a minister of the Crown to legislate, and the minister may within his powers make rules or orders which constitute binding legislation. Again, the aggrieved citizen has no legal remedy against the legislative act of the minister; he is bound by the terms of the delegated legislation. But in both types of legislation, Parliamentary and delegated, the aggrieved citizen at least knows, or his lawyers can tell him, just what his rights and duties and restrictions are under the new law: because each kind of statutory law is at once published by the King's Printer – whether as Acts of Parliament or as statutory instruments. On the other hand, if the power delegated to the minister is to make sub-delegated legislation and he exercises it, there is no duty on him, either by statute or at common law, to publish his sub-delegated legislation: and John Citizen may remain in complete ignorance of what rights over him and his property have been secretly conferred by the minister on some authority or other, and what residual rights have been left to himself. For practical purposes, the rule of law, of which the nation is so justly proud, breaks down because the aggrieved subject's legal remedy is gravely impaired. When executive or administrative directions falling short of legislation accompany the sub-delegated legislation, as they may often do, the omission to publish such directions raises no legal issue, or at any rate none relevant to the present appeal: but such cases as the present do appear to me ex debito ju[s]titiae to demonstrate the crying need of immediate publication of all matter that is truly legislative. That might mean, I think, an amendment of the Statutory Instruments Act, 1946.[1] . . .

The delegation of powers, both executive and legislative, was effected by what the Minister of Health styled 'circulars.' The instruments of delegation were justly entitled to that name as they were on their face addressed to all councils with powers of local government above the level of parish councils. . . . [T]he delegation of power was in reality to the corporation. The series of delegations which finally came before the learned judge and on appeal before us, was progressive, in the sense that, as the housing need increased, the scope was from time to time extended and more and more houses brought within the compulsory powers. . . .

Before I approach the history of the ways in which in the present case the corporation, on the one hand, and the Ministry, on the other, sought to use or misuse the provisions of the circulars, it is necessary to consider their true legal effect. As I have already indicated, they seem to me to have been well drafted for the purpose of effecting a considerate and fair adjustment between the public duty of housing the homeless, and the private rights of the individual householder in possession, carefully differentiating between the occupied and the unoccupied, the furnished and the unfurnished house, and between a passing interruption of occupation and a continuing state of unoccupation with no present prospect of its termination. The startling feature of the whole story before the court is that both the corporation and the officers of the Ministry of Health, when writing the letters in the correspondence and taking the views and actions therein appearing, radically misunderstood their own legal rights and duties, and appear to have been oblivious of the rights of the private house-owner affected. That the Minister's 'circulars' were not mere executive directions but delegated legislation with statutory force, conferring powers on the corporation which they would not otherwise have possessed and imposing on them duties for the reasonable protection of the individual house-owner, does not seem to have entered the minds of either the corporation or the Ministry of Health. And yet the nature of delegated legislation is quite plain; and the senior officials of the Ministry had no excuse for ignorance. The report of the Ministers' Powers Committee (Cmd. 4060 of 1932), which led to the appointment by the House of Commons of the present Select Committee on Delegated Legislation and the passing of the Statutory Instruments Act, 1946, explains the whole

---

[1] [At the date of the decision, 18 December 1947, this Act had not come into effect. The Rules Publication Act 1893, which was in force, did not provide for publication of such delegated legislation.]

subject quite clearly. I was chairman of the committee at the time we had to consider our report . . . and I still think the committee's description and analysis of delegated legislation is correct. It is shortly stated in para. 2 in page 15 of the report: 'The word "legislation" has grammatically two meanings – the operation or function of legislating: and the laws which result therefrom. So too "delegated legislation" may mean either exercise by a subordinate authority, such as a minister, of the legislative power delegated to him by Parliament; or the subsidiary laws themselves, passed by ministers in the shape of departmental regulations and other statutory rules and orders.' . . . In this appeal the court is concerned with both meanings of the phrase, logically in the first instance with the former, namely, the law-making function entrusted by reg. 51, para. (5.) to the Minister of Health; and only in the second instance with his 'circulars' – the name he gave to his sub-delegated output of 'laws.' As the committee point out on page 19 of the report the content of any given instrument issued by a minister in exercise of a power of delegated legislation may include administrative or executive instructions and directions and other matter not legislative in character, which (to use the committee's own phrase on page 19) 'might equally well be expressed in a circular letter.' I am tempted to wonder whether someone in the Ministry of Health thought the name 'circulars' would save them from recognition as delegated legislation! As the Ministers' Powers Committee itself pointed out, it is the substance and not the form, or the name, that matters. In the delegated legislation, law-making is the essential feature, and law-making (except in the case of mere codification) means altering the existing law – whether written or unwritten – and, therefore, means interfering with existing rights vested in persons affected. The committee in para. 3 (pp. 20–1) discuss 'the essentially subordinate character of 'delegated legislation.' After pointing out the unlimited power of Parliament (under our English constitution) to legislate, the committee go on to refer to the two fundamental principles of our constitution (p. 21): 'It is a principle of our constitution that whatever laws are passed by Parliament are binding, as the law of the land, on everybody. But it is also a principle of our constitution that no one may be deprived of his liberty or of his rights except in due course of law – that is, unless he has done something which the law says specifically shall have that effect. In the absence of a common law or a statutory authority, "A" cannot be deprived of rights by an executive act of a minister; and if the minister claims to have made a regulation entitling him to interfere with "A" 's rights, the court will interfere to stop the minister unless he can show by what authority, statutory or otherwise, he has made the regulation in question. It follows, therefore, that to safeguard the second of the two principles just mentioned the precise limits of the law-making power, which Parliament intends to confer on a minister, should always be defined in clear language by the statute which confers it.'

It is just in that protection for the liberty of the subject that sub-delegated legislation such as that authorized by reg. 51, para. (5.) is so dangerously lacking. Paragraph 1 of the regulation gives the Minister powers which are as unlimited as they are undefined. . . . Fortunately, successive ministers exercised their power with great care for the protection of the individual when they handed over their powers by their circulars: but I cannot help thinking that much of the legal misconceptions in the minds both of the Ministry of Health and of the corporation about the extent and scope of powers remaining vested in the Minister, after he had delegated almost all of them to the corporation, was due to the mistaken belief that he was under para. (1.) still retaining a general power of supervision. . . .

The Rules Publication Act, 1893, and the Statutory Instruments Act, 1946, which repealed the former and re-enacted an amended edition of it, had publicity as well as control by Parliament as a main object; but both have what seems to me the grave defect of not being applicable to any but primary delegated legislation. They are both expressly limited to such delegated legislation as is made under powers conferred by Act of Parliament, whether on H.M. in Council or on a Minister of the Crown. Such primary delegated legislation has now (and had under the Act of 1893) to be printed forthwith by the King's Printer and published as a statutory rule or order, etc.: but for delegated legislation made under powers conferred *by a regulation or other legislative instrument not being itself an Act of Parliament*, there is no general statutory requirement of publicity in force to-day. Of such secondary or 'sub-delegated' legislation, as I call it for clarity, neither the general public, of which the defendant in this case is typical, nor the legal adviser of an affected member of the public, however directly he may be affected, has any source of information about his rights, to which he can turn as of right and automatically. The modern extent of sub-delegated legislation is almost boundless: and it seems to me vital to the whole English theory of the liberty of the subject, that the affected person should be able at any time to ascertain what legislation affecting his rights has been passed under sub-delegated powers. So far as I know, this is the first case where that aspect of delegated legislation has come before the courts for direct consideration. . . .

The present case is a glaring illustration of the danger of th[e] denial [of the protection afforded by automatic publication]. The defendants' solicitor had the greatest difficulty in ascertaining from either the corporation or the Ministry what his client's rights were. . . .

[His Lordship considered the facts, and continued:] The object of the letter of the twenty-eighth [August from the Ministry of Health] is self-evident – it was an eleventh-hour attempt retrospectively, after action brought, to strengthen a legal position open to serious attack, and as such I cannot conceive how the Ministry could have thought it consistent with justice to the defendant. On it was founded the argument addressed below and to us, that the town clerk was a mere agent for the Minister, that the act of requisition on June 20 had been performed by him as agent: and that, therefore, the Minister as principal could ratify. In my opinion that view of the legal relationship between them is radically mistaken. As I have already said, the circulars contained (together with much explanatory matter) ministerial legislation with statutory force, transferring to the local authorities concerned the

Minister's legal power to override the common law rights of individual members of the public, for the purposes defined in the circulars, and limited by their conditions. In any area of local government, where the Minister had by his legislation transferred such powers to the local authority, he, for the time being, divested himself of those powers, and, out of the extremely wide executive powers, which the primary delegated legislation contained in reg. 51, para. 1 had conferred on him to be exercised at his discretion, retained only those powers, which in his sub-delegated legislation he had expressly or impliedly reserved for himself. The constitutional justification for the delegation permitted by para. 5 was obviously that local needs and opportunities relevant to the housing problem would necessarily be infinitely more within the local knowledge of the local authorities than in the Ministry whether central or regional. The letter . . . was, in my opinion, ultra vires the Minister, and legally a nullity.

My conclusions on the whole case are as follows: (1.) The original attempt at requisition on June 20, was inoperative for these reasons: (*a*) because the notice purported to requisition the house and its contents, whereas the corporation was by the terms of the sub-delegated legislation forbidden to requisition furniture (see Circular No. 2845, para. 9); (*b*) because a similar illegal usurpation of power was attempted in the corporation's omission to have the furniture contents put into a separate room at the time of requisition, or immediately after it. Thus, the notice, combined with the taking of the keys colore officii, involved an actual taking possession of both house and furniture, which in law was a trespass by the corporation. (2.) On the notification by the defendant on June 22 and again on June 27, of his intention himself to occupy, the corporation ought to have taken their hands right off ('shall not proceed further in the matter'). The house was never in fact 'occupied' by the corporation and when the defendant entered, he occupied an unoccupied house, of which the corporation never had any such possession in law as would make him then or thereafter a trespasser. . . . The view of the learned judge that by the letters of July 29[2] and August 20, the Minister of Health himself requisitioned and thereby came into possession is wrong: on the grounds: (*a*) that he had not in his sub-delegated legislation reserved power so to act; (*b*) that neither the corporation nor its town clerk was acting as his agent; and (*c*) that he did not in fact then requisition, or take possession. . . . The argument that by any of his letters to the town clerk or the defendant the Minister ratified the inoperative requisition by the corporation on June 20, is, for the reasons I have already stated, wholly misconceived.

[ASQUITH L.J. agreed with SCOTT L.J. EVERSHED L.J. delivered a judgment in favour of allowing the appeal.]

Appeal allowed.

Notes

1. Did Scott L.J. consider that the circulars were legislative, administrative, or a

___

[2] [This was in fact from the town clerk who, however, purported to act on behalf of the Minister.]

mixture of the two? *Blackpool Corporation* v. *Locker* should be contrasted with *Lewisham M.B.C.* v. *Roberts* [1949] 2 K.B. 608, another requisitioning case. There the ground floor of a house had been de-requisitioned and occupied by the owner, who, however, refused to allow access to the upper, requisitioned floor. The town clerk applied to the Minister of Health to re-requisition the whole house so that the owner might be permitted to occupy the ground floor as a licensee. A Ministry official replied that 'in the circumstances [the Minister] hereby delegates to you . . . his functions under reg. 51 of the Defence (General) Regulations, 1939, for the purpose of requisitioning the whole of the . . . premises . . . and consent is hereby given to such requisitioning'. The necessary notices were served but the owner continued to refuse access to the upper floor, and the town clerk successfully claimed possession of the house in the county court. On appeal it was contended that the delegation which purported to have been effected was a legislative act which could only be validly done by the Minister personally. The Court of Appeal held that the Minister was entitled to act by an authorized official (see p. 134 *supra*) and that the delegation was an administrative and not a legislative act. Denning L.J. said obiter (at p. 621):

> Now I take it to be quite plain that when a minister is entrusted with administrative, as distinct from legislative, functions he is entitled to act by any authorized official of his department. The minister is not bound to give his mind to the matter personally. It is sufficient if one of the officials of that department brings his mind to bear on the propriety of it. When the government department delegates its functions to a town clerk under reg. 51 (5), it is really only putting someone in its place to do the acts which it is authorized to do. The town clerk is, so to speak, an agent of the department, and a sub-agent of the Crown. The delegation to the town clerk is simply administrative machinery so as to enable the administrative function of requisitioning to operate smoothly and efficiently; and, like all administrative functions, the act of delegating can be exercised by any authorized official of the government department. The delegation, whether general or specific, is not a legislative act, but an administrative one . . . and it does not divest the government department of its powers. . . . I cannot agree with the observations of Scott L.J. to the contrary in *Blackpool Corporation* v. *Locker* [p. 493 *supra*]. They were, I think, unnecessary for the decision, which turned on the fact that the town clerk there acted outside his actual authority and his action could not be ratified.

Compare the approach of Jenkins J., who said (at p. 630):

> I do not . . . agree that the delegation here in question was a legislative act. It related simply and solely to the requisitioning of one particular house and delegated nothing more than the power required for that specific purpose. There is, so far as I can see, nothing in the nature of legislation in that. Reference was made to the case of *Blackpool Corporation* v. *Locker*, but the court had there to consider the effect of a general delegation to local authorities of the minister's power of requisitioning effected by circulars which laid down what amounted to a code of regulations and restrictions governing the exercise of the delegated powers. I do not think it follows from that case that every delegation of power to requisition, however specific and in particular that even a delegation of power to requisition one particular house, is a legislative act.

For the status of ministerial circulars, see further *Bristol D.C.* v. *Clark* [1975] 1 W.L.R. 1443, noted at p. 175 *supra*, and *Coleshill & District Investment Co. Ltd.* v. *Minister of Housing and Local Government* [1969] 1 W.L.R. 746 at p. 765, where Lord Wilberforce stated that although a planning circular concerning development may have no legal status when issued, it may acquire 'vitality and strength when, through the years, it passed . . . into planning practice and text books, was acted on . . . in planning decisions, and when [a later] Act . . . maintained the same definition of "development" under which it was issued'. On generality see also *F. Hoffmann-La Roche & Co. A.G.* v. *Secretary of State for Trade and Industry*, p. 94 *supra*, noted at p. 520 *infra*, in which a statutory instrument (S.I. 1973 No. 1093) specifying the maximum prices to be charged for librium and valium was assumed by the court to be legislative despite the fact that it only applied to the Roche group of companies. Cf. *Hoffmann-La Roche Inc.* v. *Kleindienst* 478 F 2d 1 at pp. 12–13 (1973), where a different view was taken. On the facts of the British *Hoffmann-La Roche* case nothing turned on the distinction but, as the *Blackpool* and *Lewisham* cases show, it can be important.

2. The classification of a function as 'legislative' has several practical consequences apart from the one that emerges from Note 1 *supra*, viz. that the rule prohibiting the sub-delegation of powers is applied more strictly if the power in question is a legislative one (and cf. *Barnard* v. *N.D.L.B.*, p. 132 *supra*). Thus, r. 2 of S.I. 1948 No. 1, made under s. 1 (2) of the Statutory Instruments Act 1946, exempts rules of an executive character from the statutory publication requirement (on which see p. 512 *infra*). Again, the scope of judicial review may be narrower where the power is legislative (p. 513 *infra*, 'unreasonableness', and p. 516 *infra*, natural justice) and certiorari and prohibition have been assumed to be unavailable in relation to legislative orders (p. 308 *supra*), but see Note 1, p. 311 *supra* and Note 2, p. 323 *supra*. Finally, the Parliamentary Commissioner for Administration has interpreted his terms of reference so as to prevent him from investigating procedures in connection with the making of a statutory instrument (see s. 5 (1) of the Parliamentary Commissioner Act 1967, p. 623 *infra*). See further de Smith, pp. 71–6.

3. One of the hallmarks of legislation is that it establishes a binding norm which is finally determinative of any questions to which it is addressed. This was an important point in *R.* v. *Secretary of State for Home Affairs, ex p. Hosenball* [1977] 1 W.L.R. 766, in which the Court of Appeal considered the Statement of Immigration Rules for Control after Entry: EEC and Other Non-Commonwealth Nationals, H.C. 81, Session 1972/3 (see now H.C. 169, Session 1982/83). Geoffrey Lane L.J. said (at p. 785):

> There have been dicta to the effect that these rules have the force of statute. In particular the judgment of Roskill L.J. in *Reg.* v. *Chief Immigration Officer, Heathrow Airport, Ex parte Bibi* [1976] 1 W.L.R. 979, 985, where he said:
>
>> These rules are just as much delegated legislation as any other form of rule-making activity or delegated legislation which is empowered by Act of Parliament.
>
> I entertain a respectful doubt as to whether that is the case. These rules are very difficult to categorise or classify. They are in a class of their own. They are certainly a practical guide for the immigration officers at the various ports and airports of the country, who have the everyday task of trying to administer the Immigration Act 1971 of Parliament. Indeed they are, as to large parts, if one reads them, little more than explanatory notes of the Act itself.

The other two members of the court made it clear that the rules did not have legislative force and were rules of practice rather than rules of law: [1977] 1 W.L.R. 766 at pp. 780 and 788. See also *Zamir* v. *Secretary of State for the Home Department* [1980] A.C. 934 at p. 947 but note that despite their status, prerogative relief has been granted where the rules are misinterpreted by the immigration authorities: *R.* v. *Chief Immigration Officer, Gatwick Airport, ex p. Kharrazi* [1980] 1 W.L.R. 1396, noted at p. 313 *supra*.

Hosenball's case should be compared with *Vestey* v. *I.R.C. (No. 2)* [1979] Ch. 198, in which it was argued by the Crown that it was free to choose to apply the same extra-statutory concession differently in different cases. Such concessions are an established part of our tax system and a list of them is published by the Inland Revenue. Walton J. (at p. 203) doubted the constitutionality of extra-statutory concessions, but also said:

[E]ven if, contrary to my views, extra-statutory concessions are permissible and do form part of our tax code, nevertheless they do represent a published code, which applies indifferently to all those who fall, or who can bring themselves within, its scope.

They would therefore constitute a binding norm and could not be applied in a discriminatory manner by the Crown. See also *R.* v. *Criminal Injuries Compensation Board, ex p. Lain*, p. 11 *supra*. To what extent, if at all, were the provisions of the compensation scheme legislative? If they were not, how could the court justify intervention? See Wade, p. 561. Walton J.'s decision in *Vestey* v. *I.R.C.* was affirmed on other grounds by the House of Lords ([1980] A.C. 1148), but his views on the legal basis of extra-statutory concessions appeared to be shared by Lord Wilberforce and Lord Edmund-Davies at p. 1173 and pp. 1194–5 respectively. On such concessions see further Megarry, (1944) 60 L.Q.R. 125 and 218; Williams, [1979] B.T.R. 137; Sumption, [1980] B.T.R. 4 and 61.

JUDICIAL CONTROL

Control by the courts

Hotel and Catering Industry Training Board v. Automobile Proprietary Ltd.

[1969] 1 W.L.R. 697   House of Lords

Section 1 (1) of the Industrial Training Act 1964 authorized the Minister of Labour to establish, by order, training boards for 'the purpose of making better provision for the training of persons . . . for employment in any activities of industry or commerce specifying "those activities" to be covered in any particular case'. The Minister established the appellant board by an order (S.I. 1966 No. 1347) made under the Act in respect of, *inter alia*, 'the supply in the course of any business of food or drink to persons for immediate consumption' (para. 1 (*a*) of Sch. 1 to the Order). 'Business' was defined as including the management of a club, but 'club' did not include a members' club unless the main activities of the club included habitually providing main meals or board and lodgings for reward. Section 4 of the 1964 Act authorized the imposition of training levies upon 'employers in the industry'. The respondents were a members' club which habitually provided main meals but which objected to the imposition of a training levy. They contended that it was ultra vires to include members' clubs in the Order and the appellant sought a declaration that, *inter alia*, the Order was validly made pursuant to the powers conferred by s. 1 (1) of the 1964 Act. Bridge J. granted the declaration sought but his decision was reversed by the Court of Appeal ([1968] 1 W.L.R. 1526), which decided that the Order was invalidly made in so far as it purported to extend to members' clubs, and issued a declaration to this effect. On appeal by the board:

LORD REID: The crucial words [in s. 1 (1) of the Industrial Training Act 1964] are 'any activities of industry or commerce' and 'those activities.' If the activities of members' clubs in supplying food or drink for immediate consumption are activities of industry or commerce, then the inclusion of members' clubs in the Order was admittedly intra vires: if they are not, then the inclusion of members' clubs in the Order was admittedly ultra vires. It is admitted that members' clubs (including the respondents) are not engaged in industry or commerce in supplying food or drink or in any other way. So the respondents contend that their activities cannot be activities of industry or commerce. But the appellants contend that 'activities of industry or commerce' means activities of a kind which are carried on in industry or commerce, or, as Winn L.J. put it [1968] 1 W.L.R. 1526, 1533, that that expression includes any 'activity of which it can be postulated: this is an activity which belong to, in the sense that it occurs in, industry or commerce.' Putting the matter in concrete terms the appellants say that cooking meals is part of the trade of a hotel keeper or caterer, therefore it is an activity of industry or commerce, and therefore the Minister has power to bring within the scope of an Order under the Act all private householders who employ cooks, so as to make them liable to pay a levy. Counsel did not attempt to argue that there is any relevant distinction between members' clubs and private householders, or that the Minister has power to specify the activities of members' clubs but no power to bring in such private householders as may employ cooks or other domestic staff. He maintained that, whenever the Minister specifies in an Order activities which are carried on in industry or commerce, every person who employs anyone to carry on activities of that kind will be subjected to a levy unless exempted under the Order. . . .

It will be observed that levies can only be made on 'employers in the industry.' But the appellants argue that every householder who employs a cook is an 'employer in the industry.' They contend that this strange misuse of language is justified by the terms of the definition of 'the industry' in section 1 (2): ' "the industry", in relation to an industrial training board, means the activities in relation to which it exercises functions; . . .' . . .

. . . [T]he crucial question is the same – what is meant by 'activities of industry or commerce.' One first looks for the ordinary or natural meaning of the phrase. I do not think that anyone would say that the activities of a cook in private employment or of her employer are activities of industry or of the catering industry. At most he would say that they are similar to or of the same kind as the activities of the catering industry. It appears to me that the natural meaning of activities of industry or commerce is industrial or commercial activities or activities carried on in industry or commerce. But I would not deny that the words in the Act are capable of having the meaning for which the appellants contend, if the context clearly indicates that that meaning was intended.

One first looks for the general purpose of the Act in so far as it can be inferred from reading the Act as a whole. I think that it is to assist employers engaged in industry or commerce to increase production by increasing the number of persons having the skills necessary for employment by them in skilled work, and to assist persons seeking better positions by equipping them for skilled work in industry and commerce. I see no sign of any purpose of assisting private employers not engaged in industry or commerce or of assisting employees to obtain work with such employers. . . .

Then one must look at the particular provisions of the Act to see whether any of them throw any light on the matter.

[His Lordship then examined various sections of the Act, and concluded:]

None of these particular provisions in the 1964 Act is at all conclusive but they are more consistent with the respondents' contention than with the appellants'. So, in my opinion, the context in which the crucial phrase 'activities of industry or commerce' occurs in no way requires this phrase to be given the meaning for which the appellants contend: on the contrary it tends to confirm my view that this phrase must be given its ordinary or natural meaning. I would therefore dismiss this appeal.

[LORD PEARCE, LORD UPJOHN, and LORD PEARSON agreed with LORD REID. LORD DONOVAN delivered a speech in favour of dismissing the appeal.]

Appeal dismissed.

Note

This case is an example of judicial technique used when reviewing delegated legislation. This tends to be technical and closely related to the wording of the enabling (or primary) legislation. On the form of the declaration given, see further *Dunkley* v. *Evans*, p. 508 *infra*. The *Hotel and Catering Industry T.B.* case should be compared with the next extract.

McEldowney v. Forde

[1971] A.C. 632   House of Lords

LORD HODSON: My Lords, the question for determination on this appeal is whether the resident magistrates sitting as a Magistrates' Court for the Petty Sessions District of Magherafelt on June 12, 1968, were right in law in dismissing a complaint against the present appellant. He was charged in these words:

'You the said defendant were and remained a member of an unlawful association, namely, a republican club, contrary to regulation 24A of the regulations made under the Civil Authorities (Special Powers) Acts (Northern Ireland) 1922–1943.'

The Act of 1922, which I will call 'the Act,' was enacted, as the title shows, to empower certain authorities of the Government of Northern Ireland to take steps for preserving the peace and maintaining order in Northern Ireland and for purposes connected therewith. Section 1 provides:

'1. (1) the civil authority shall have power, in respect of persons, matters and things within the jurisdiction of the Government of Northern Ireland, to take all such steps and issue all such orders as may be necessary for preserving the peace and maintaining order, according to and in the execution of this Act and the regulations contained in the Schedule thereto, or such regulations as may be made in accordance with the provisions of this Act (which regulations, whether contained in the said Schedule or made as aforesaid, are in this Act referred to as "the regulations"): Provided that the ordinary course of law and avocations of life and the enjoyment of property shall be interfered with as little as may be permitted by the exigencies of the steps required to be taken under this Act. (2) For the purposes of this Act the civil authority shall be the Minister of Home Affairs for Northern Ireland. . . . (3) The Minister of Home Affairs shall have power to make regulations – (a) for making further provision for the preservation of the peace and maintenance of order, and (b) for varying or revoking any provision of the regulations, and any regulations made as aforesaid shall, subject to the provisions of this Act, have effect and be enforced in like manner as regulations contained in the Schedule to this Act. . . .

On May 22, 1922, the then Minister of Home Affairs made a further regulation under the powers conferred by section 1 (3) of the Act. This was regulation 24A and reads:

'Any person who becomes or remains a member of an unlawful association or who does any act with a view to promoting or calculated to promote the objects of an unlawful association or seditious conspiracy shall be guilty of an offence against these regulations. . . .

The following organisations shall for the purposes of this regulation be deemed to be unlawful associations:

The Irish Republican Brotherhood,
The Irish Republican Army,
The Irish Volunteers,
The Cumann na m'Ban,
The Fianna na h'Eireann.'

These named organisations were specific existing organisations of a militant type and it was conceded before your Lordships, as it was before the Court of Appeal in Northern Ireland, that they were in fact unlawful organisations.

On March 7, 1967, the present Minister of Home Affairs purporting to act under section 1 (3) of the Act made a further regulation by way of addition to the list of organisations deemed to be unlawful associations. This, which is the impugned regulation, recites that it is expedient that further provision for the preservation of the peace and maintenance of order should be made, and runs:

'1. Regulation 24A of the principal regulations shall have effect as if the following organisations were added to the list of organisations which for the purpose of that regulation are deemed to be unlawful associations:

"The organisations at the date of this regulation or at any time thereafter describing themselves as 'republican clubs' or any like organisation howsoever described." '

The appellant was found by the magistrates to have been on the date stated in the charge and thereafter a member of the Slaughtneil Republican Club. They also found that no evidence was given that he

'or the said club was at any time a threat to peace law and order but it was conceded by witnesses for the complainant in cross-examination that in so far as the police were aware there was nothing seditious in its pursuits or those of its members.'

In dismissing the complaint the magistrates . . . came to the conclusion that the only reasonable interpretation to be given to the words 'organisations . . . describing themselves as "republican clubs" ' is 'clubs which have as their object the absorption of Northern Ireland in the Republic of Ireland the activities of whose members in seeking to further that object constitute a threat to peace and order in Northern Ireland – or any like organisation howsoever described.'

The magistrates accordingly found that the complainant had not proved that the Slaughtneil Republican Club was an unlawful association within the meaning of regulation 24A and dismissed the complaint.

The Court of Appeal in Northern Ireland by a majority allowed the appeal . . . and [t]he appellant obtained leave to appeal to this House but in argument has not sought to sustain the opinion expressed by the magistrates or the reasons given by them for their decision in his favour. . . .

The arguments directed to the Court of Appeal and to your Lordships have been directed solely to the question whether or not the impugned regulation is ultra vires the Act.

The majority of the Court of Appeal held that it was for the Minister to decide whether a particular association should be deemed to be unlawful and the court could not question what he had done. The Lord Chief Justice, on the other hand, held that the 1967 regulation was far too vague and wide to come within even the extensive powers conferred by section 1 of the Act. It was not, to apply the language contained in the judgement of the Privy Council in *Attorney-General for Canada* v. *Hallet & Carey Ltd.* [1952] A.C. 427, 450, '. . . capable of being related to one of the prescribed purposes.' The Lord Chief Justice attached importance to the use of the words 'any like organisation howsoever described' as making the regulation even more vague than it would otherwise be and taking it even further out of the scope and meaning of the Act.

The question may be put in this way – is the whole regulation too vague and so arbitrary as to be wholly unreasonable as if, to take an example from one of the cases, a person were to be proscribed because he had red hair; or is the regulation, as the majority of the court held, a legitimate and valid exercise of the Minister's power confirmed on him by statute? . . .

There was a difference of opinion in the Court of Appeal as to the effect of the words . . . contained in subsection (1) of Section 1 of the Act. [Subsection (1) contains the] proviso that the ordinary course of law and avocations of life and the enjoyment of property should be interfered with as little as may be permitted by the exigencies of the steps required to be taken under [the] Act. I cannot, however, accept the argument that regulations made under subsection (3) are invalid unless it is proved that they are made for the preservation of peace and good order or that the word 'necessary' limits the power to be exercised within the confines of that word.

In my view section 1 (1) is directed to the enforcement of regulations not to the making of them. . . .

In my opinion there is a distinction between the powers given by section 1 subsection (1) and those given by subsection (3) of the same section, in that the former are executive and the latter legislative powers. The Minister is not restricted by the language relating to his executive powers when executing his legislative powers, though no doubt he will not be unmindful on the language of Parliament in the whole Act.

The vexed question remains whether the impugned regulation is capable of being related to the prescribed purpose, that is to say, the preservation of the peace and the maintenance of order. The authorities show that where, as here, there is no question of bad faith the courts will be slow to interfere with the exercise of wide powers to make regulations.

There is, on the face of the impugned regulation, no apparent misconstruction of the enabling Act or failure to comply with any conditions prescribed by the Act for the exercise of its powers.

The proscription of present and future 'republican clubs' including 'any like organisations howsoever described' is said to be something outside the scope and meaning of the Act and so incapable of being related to the prescribed purposes of the Act. Accepting that the word 'republican' is an innocent word and need not connote anything contrary to law, I cannot escape the conclusion that in its context, added to the list of admittedly unlawful organisations of a militant type, the word 'republican' is capable of fitting the description of a club which in the opinion of the Minister should be proscribed as a subversive organisation of a type akin to those previously named in the list of admittedly unlawful organisations. The context in which the word is used shows the type of club which the Minister had in mind and there is no doubt that the mischief aimed at is an association which had subversive objects. On this matter, in my opinion, the court should not substitute its judgment for that of the Minister, on the ground that the banning of 'republican clubs' is too remote. I agree that the use of the words 'any like organisation howsoever described' lends some support to the contention that the regulation is vague and for that reason invalid, but on consideration I do not accept the argument based on vagueness. It is not difficult to see why the Minister, in order to avoid subterfuge, was not anxious to restrict himself to the description 'republican' seeing that there might be similar clubs which he might seek to proscribe whatever they called themselves. If and when any case based on the words 'any like organisation' arises it will have to be decided, but I do not, by reason of the use of those words, condemn the regulation as being too vague or uncertain to be supported. I would dismiss the appeal.

LORD PEARCE: . . . I can find no reality in the argument that whereas Parliament was [in section 1 (1)] carefully and somewhat apprehensively restricting any repressive *steps* and *orders* to the minimum demanded by the crises, it was giving a free run to the making of repressive *regulations* [under section 1 (3)]. Such a refinement could not, I feel sure, have occurred to any of the Members of Parliament who voted for the Act. . . .

. . . In my opinion the normal ordinary meaning which this statute would bear is that the Minister, whether making orders or regulations or enforcing the statute, must confine himself to that which any crisis made necessary, and which caused the minimum disruption of the citizen's rights. It is within that limited area that his discretion was confined.

Does the 1967 regulation come within the power thus given? In my opinion it does not. I agree with the judgment of the learned Lord Chief Justice. . . .

It is argued that it is for the Minister alone to decide how he should use his power and that the court should not interfere, however wrong it thinks that decision, unless there is some element of bad faith. But in my opinion the duty of surveillance entrusted to the courts for the protection of the citizen goes deeper than that. It cannot take the easy course of 'passing by on the other side' when it seems clear to it that the Minister is using a power in a way which Parliament, who gave him that power, did not intend. When there is doubt, of course the courts will not interfere. But if it seems clear on the grounds of rationality and common sense that he was exceeding the power with which Parliament was intending to clothe him to further the purposes of the Act, the courts have a duty to interfere. The fact that this is not an easy line to draw is no reason why the courts should give up the task and abandon their duty to protect the citizen.

I accept the observations of the Lord Chief Justice as to the regulation being 'too sweeping and too remote on any rational view.' 'It is not,' he said, 'to use the words of Lord Radcliffe,[3] "capable of being related to"

> these proscribed purposes. An association may call itself a Republican Club without exhibiting any evidence that its objects or activities are in any sense seditious or otherwise unlawful. . . . If this regulation is good where must the Minister stop? Will "Irish Clubs" or "Ulster Clubs" or "Green Clubs" or "Orange Clubs" or "Gaelic Clubs" or "Friends of the Republic" or "Friends of the North" or "Catholic Clubs" or "Protestant Clubs" all have to be deemed unlawful associations if similar regulations are made regarding such titles? Mr. Gibson had to concede that if the Minister thought fit he could in the exercise of his discretion make any club with any name in effect an unlawful association. I do not think that width of power lies within the Act of 1922.'

Further, the 1967 regulation is too vague and ambiguous. A man must not be put in peril on an ambiguity under the criminal law. When the 1967 regulation was issued the citizen ought to have been able to know whether he

---

[3] [In *Attorney-General for Canada* v. *Hallet & Carey Ltd.* [1982] A.C. 427 at p. 450.]

could or could not remain a member of his club without being subject to a criminal prosecution. Yet I doubt if one could have said with certainty that any man or women was safe in remaining a member of any club in Northern Ireland, however named or whatever its activities or objects. . . .

I would therefore allow the appeal.

[LORD GUEST and LORD PEARSON delivered speeches in favour of dismissing the appeal. LORD DIPLOCK delivered a speech in favour of allowing the appeal.]

Appeal dismissed.

Notes

1. For criticism of this case see MacCormick, (1970) 86 L.Q.R. 171. Does it suggest that the scope of review of legislative acts is narrower than the scope of review of administrative acts? Does the *Hotel and Catering Industry T.B.* case suggest this? See further pp. 506, 518 and 522 *infra*. To what extent, if at all, was the court influenced by the political situation in Northern Ireland? Is this a legitimate consideration?

2. There are certain constitutional principles which would make a court more likely to intervene. On these, see Wade, p. 749; *Attorney General* v. *Wilts United Dairies Ltd.* (1921) 37 T.L.R. 884, affirmed (1922) 38 T.L.R. 781 (judicial refusal to interpret statute giving a general power to control trade as authorizing the imposition of taxation); *Commissioners of Customs and Excise* v. *Cure & Deeley Ltd.* [1962] 1 Q.B. 340, noted at p. 511 *infra* (maintaining access to the courts in the face of an ouster clause).

Unreasonableness

Kruse v. Johnson

[1898] 2 Q.B. 91   Divisional Court of the Queen's Bench Division

The court considered the validity of a by-law made by a county council prohibiting the playing of music or singing in a public place within fifty yards of any dwelling house.

LORD RUSSELL OF KILLOWEN C.J.: . . . Parliament has thought fit to delegate to representative public bodies in town and cities, and also in counties, the power of exercising their own judgment as to what are the by-laws which to them seem proper to be made for good rule and government in their own localities. But that power is accompanied by certain safeguards. There must be antecedent publication of the by-law with a view, I presume, of eliciting the public opinion of the locality upon it, and such by-laws shall have no force until after they have been forwarded to the Secretary of State. . . . I agree that the presence of these safeguards in no way relieves the Court of the responsibility of inquiring into the validity of by-laws where they are brought in question, or in any way affects the authority of the Court in the determination of their validity or invalidity. . . . [T]he great majority of the cases in which the question of by-laws has been discussed are not cases of by-laws of bodies of a public representative character entrusted by Parliament with delegated authority, but are for the most part cases of railway companies, dock companies, or other like companies, which carry on their business for their own profit, although incidentally for the advantage of the public. In this class of case it is right that the Courts should jealously watch the exercise of these powers, and guard against their unnecessary or unreasonable exercise to the public disadvantage. But, when the Court is called upon to consider the by-laws of public representative bodies clothed with the ample authority . . . and exercising that authority accompanied by . . . checks and safeguards . . ., I think the consideration of such by-laws ought to be approached from a different standpoint. They ought to be supported if possible. They ought to be, as has been said, 'benevolently' interpreted, and credit ought to be given to those who have to administer them that they will be reasonably administered. . . . I think courts of justice ought to be slow to condemn as invalid any by-law, so made under such conditions, on the ground of supposed unreasonableness. Notwithstanding what Cockburn C.J. said in *Bailey* v. *Williamson*,[4] an analogous case, I do not mean to say that there may not be cases in which it would be the duty of the Court to condemn by-laws, made under such authority as these were made, as invalid because unreasonable. But unreasonable in what sense? If, for instance, they were found to be partial and unequal in their operation as between different classes; if they were manifestly unjust; if they disclosed bad faith; if they involved such oppressive or gratuitous interference with the rights of those subject to them as could find no justification in the minds of reasonable men, the Court might well say, 'Parliament never intended to give authority to make such rules; they are unreasonable and ultra vires.' But it is in this sense, and in this sense only, as I conceive, that the question of unreasonableness can properly be regarded. A by-law is not unreasonable merely because particular judges may think that it goes further than is prudent or necessary or convenient, or because it is not accompanied by a qualification or an exception which some judges may think ought to be there. Surely it is not too much to say that in matters which directly and mainly concern the people of the county, who have the right to choose those whom they think best fitted to represent them in their local government bodies, such representatives may be trusted to understand their own requirements better than judges. Indeed, if the question of the validity of by-laws were to be determined by the opinion of judges as to what was reasonable in the narrow sense of that word, the cases in the books on this subject are no guide; for they reveal, as indeed one would expect, a wide diversity of judicial opinion, and they lay down no principle or definite standard by which reasonableness or unreasonableness may be tested. . . .

[His Lordship went on to find that the by-law before the court was reasonable.]

[CHITTY L.J., WRIGHT, DARLING, and CHANNELL JJ. agreed with LORD RUSSELL OF KILLOWEN C.J. SIR F. H. JEUNE delivered a judgment upholding the validity of the by-law and MATHEW J. delivered a dissenting judgment.]

---

[4] (1873) L.R. 8 Q.B. 118, at p. 124.

Notes

1. The question whether the same doctrine applies to a legislative power exercised by a minister is not altogether clear. In *Sparks* v. *Edward Ash Ltd.* [1943] 2 K.B. 223 Scott L.J. said (at p. 229):

> If it is the duty of the courts to recognize and trust the discretion of local authorities, much more must it be so in the case of a minister directly responsible to Parliament and entrusted by the constitution with the function of administering the department to which the relevant field of natural activity is remitted. Over and above these grounds for trusting to that minister's constitutional discretion is the further consideration that these regulations have to be laid on the table of both Houses [of Parliament], . . . and can be annulled in the usual way.
>
> For the above reasons, this court has, in my opinion, no power to declare these two regulations invalid for unreasonableness, certainly not on any ground submitted in argument before us. The duty of compliance may, even in broad daylight, put on motor traffic a considerable burden of inconvenience, but it is for the minister, and, ultimately, for Parliament, to consider and weigh that drawback, and, if necessary, to amend the regulations under the procedure of the Act. As the regulations stand, they seem to me to rest on the vital importance of safeguarding life and limb, and it is not for the court to do anything but construe their language and apply their provisions, so far as that is in a practical sense possible, without straining their language in order to prevent inconvenience to motor traffic.

See also *Taylor* v. *Brighton B.C.* [1947] K.B. 736 at p. 748 (per Lord Greene M.R.). In the quotation *supra*, do you think that Scott L.J. was totally excluding judicial review on this ground? (See Griffith and Street, p. 111 n. 4.) There is, in any event, authority for a less restrictive approach. In *Maynard* v. *Osmond* [1977] Q.B. 240 the reasonableness of regulations made by a minister was considered and *Kruse* v. *Johnson* was cited as the leading authority by Griffiths J. at first instance ([1977] 1 All E.R. 64 at pp. 75–6) in a judgment that met with approval in the Court of Appeal ([1977] Q.B. 240 at pp. 254 and 256). Furthermore, there are dicta, for example in *McEldowney* v. *Forde*, p. 500 *supra*, which, as Wharam has pointed out ((1973) 36 M.L.R. 611 at p. 622), support the proposition that even a statutory instrument otherwise intra vires can be invalidated if it is unreasonable. See further Wharam, op. cit.; Garner, *Administrative Law*, 5th edn., p. 85; Wade, p. 753–4; *R.* v. *Essex Appeal Tribunal, ex p. Pikesley* (1917) 117 L.T. 773.

2. The bulk of the litigation on local government by-laws took place in the nineteenth century and there have been few cases in recent years. One reason for this is the control exercised by the confirmation procedure, under which central government departments must confirm or refuse to confirm a by-law (s. 236 of the Local Government Act 1972). Another, and perhaps more important, reason is the practice of central departments drawing up and issuing sets of model by-laws to local authorities. Adherence to the model both assures confirmation and minimizes the risk of judicial interference on the ground of unreasonableness. See further *Hart's Introduction to the Law of Local Government and Administration*, 9th edn., pp. 233–4.

Wrong purposes and bad faith

In re Toohey; ex parte Northern Land Council

(1981) 38 A.L.R. 439   Full Court of the High Court of Australia

The case concerned an application to the Aboriginal Land Commissioner by the Northern Land Council claiming that Aboriginals were the traditional owners of certain land, including part of the Cox Peninsula, an undeveloped and sparsely populated area about six kilometres from Darwin by sea, but considerably more remote from it by land. The Commissioner was empowered by statute to entertain such claims in relation to *inter alia*, 'unalienated Crown land', which was defined as not to include land in a town. 'Town' in turn was defined to take its meaning from the law of town planning. The Planning Act 1979 (Northern Territory) defined town to include land specified by regulation to be treated as such, and a regulation was made so specifying an area including the Cox Peninsula. The Northern Land Council contended, *inter alia*, that the regulation made under the 1979 Act was invalid because it was not made for any relevant purposes under the Act but simply for the purpose of defeating the land claim. The Commissioner had held that since the regulation had been made by the representative of the Crown no inquiry could be made into the motives in making it. The judgments of the High Court dealt at length with this point, which was rejected. They also considered the scope of review of delegated legislation in general, and it is with this that these extracts are primarily concerned.

MASON J.: . . . There is no rational basis for drawing a distinction in the application of the rule that the acts of the Crown representative cannot be impugned – by conceding its application to the exercise of legislative powers and denying its application to the exercise of adjudicative powers. Such a startling difference in approach is not justified by the difference in character of the two functions, especially when we recall that the modern view, now received doctrine, is that the classification of powers is not a sound criterion for the operation of precise rules of law.

The general principles which guide judicial review of legislative and adjudicative powers do not suggest such a difference in approach. There is much common ground between the process by which a court arrives at the conclusion that a legislative act is *ultra vires* and that by which a court decides that the exercise of a statutory power is void or voidable. A legislative power which is purpor[s]ive is, like any other statutory discretion, open to attack for purpose.

A more complex question is the extent to which, if at all, the distinction expressed by Latham C.J. in *Arthur Yates* (72 C.L.R. at 68) still holds good. There his Honour said: 'But the purpose of *legislation* is to be ascertained by considering the true nature and operation of the law and the facts with which it deals, and . . . not by examining the motives of the legislative authority. . . . No such limitation applies in the case of administrative acts (see also pp. 64–5, per Latham C.J. and pp. 82–3, per Dixon J.).

It is incontestable that the courts will not examine the motives which inspire members of Parliament to enact laws. No doubt the courts will continue to adopt a similar approach to the exercise by a subordinate law-making body of legislative powers which are not purposive and are not conditioned on the opinion of the body as to the existence of a state of facts. But when the legislative power is purposive or conditioned on such an opinion the objection to an examination of the motives of the members of the legislative body lies not so much in the character of the function as in the relationship or lack of relationship between the motives of the individual members on the one hand and the extraneous purpose or the want of a *bona fide* opinion on the other hand. The problem is partly a practical problem of proof. In one case there is the difficulty of translating individual motives into objective purpose. In the other case there is the difficulty of deducing from individual motives the conclusion that a collective opinion was not a *bona fide* held opinion. . . .

AICKIN J.: . . . Delegated legislative power may be conferred in respect of a subject matter rather than a purpose, though the two ideas overlap, as some cases concerning municipal by-laws demonstrate. However, for present purposes there is no distinction between legislative and administrative acts; each may be attacked in the courts. . . .

Notes

1. Gibbs C.J., Stephen and Wilson JJ., were in agreement with Mason and Aickin JJ. on this point.

2. See also *Municipal Council of Sydney* v. *Campbell*, p. 176 *supra* (evidence admissible to show the invalidity of by-laws: [1925] A.C. 338 at p. 343); *Westminster Corporation* v. *L.N.W. Railway Co.*, p. 178 *supra*.

Natural justice

Bates v. Lord Hailsham of St. Marylebone, p. 516 *infra*

Sub-delegation

Blackpool Corporation v. Locker, p. 487 *supra*

Partial invalidity

Dunkley v. Evans

[1981] 1 W.L.R. 1522   Divisional Court of the Queen's Bench Division

The defendants were charged with fishing in a prohibited area contrary to the West Coast Herring (Prohibition of Fishing) Order 1978 (S.I. 1978 No. 930) made under s. 5 (2) of the Sea Fish (Conservation) Act 1967. They admitted fishing in an area over which an order could have been made but contended that the Order of 1978 was ultra vires because, contrary to s. 23 (1) of the 1967 Act, it purported to include Northern Irish waters within the prohibited area. The magistrate dismissed the case. On appeal by the prosecutor:

ORMROD L.J. delivered the judgment of the court (ORMROD L.J. and WEBSTER J.):

. . . The prosecutor submits that the fact that this Order is ultra vires in so far as this area off the coast of Northern Ireland is concerned, does not render the whole Order ultra vires. For the defence Mr. Phillips contended that the whole Order is rendered invalid by including this area of the sea. The offending area represents 0·8 per cent. of the area covered by the Order. The only question, therefore, is whether it is possible to sever the invalid part from the valid part of the Order, or whether the whole Order is invalidated by the inclusion of this small area.

The general principle is stated in *Halsbury's Laws of England*, 4th ed., vol. 1 (1973), para. 26:

'Unless the invalid part is inextricably interconnected with the valid, a court is entitled to set aside or disregard the invalid part, leaving the rest intact.'

The principle is more fully formulated in the judgment of Cussen J. sitting in the Supreme Court of Victoria in *Olsen* v. *City of Camberwell* [1926] V.L.R. 58, 68, where he said:

'If the enactment, with the invalid portion omitted, is so radically or substantially different a law as to the subject-matter dealt with by what remains from what it would be with the omitted portions forming part of it as to warrant a belief that the legislative body intended it as a whole only, or, in other words, to warrant a belief that if all could not be carried into effect the legislative body would not have enacted the remainder independently, then the whole must fail.'

We respectfully agree with and adopt this statement of the law. It would be difficult to imagine a clearer example than the present case of a law which the legislative body would have enacted independently of the offending portion and which is so little affected by eliminating the invalid portion. This is clearly, therefore, an order which the court should not strive officiously to kill to any greater extent than it is compelled to do. . . .

[The defendants' main point] was that the court could not sever the invalid portion of this Order from the remainder because it was not possible to excise from the text of the Order the words which rendered part of it invalid. This is the so-called 'blue pencil test.' This test has been elaborated mainly in connection with covenants in restraint of trade. . . .

We can see no reason why the powers of the court to sever the invalid portion of a piece of subordinate legislation from the valid should be restricted to cases where the text of the legislation lends itself to judicial surgery, or textual emendation by excision. It would have been competent for the court in an action for a declaration that the provisions of the Order in this case did not apply to the area of the sea off Northern Ireland reserved by section 23 (1) of the Act of 1967, as amended, to make the declaration sought, without in any way affecting the validity of the Order in relation to the remaining 99·2 per cent. of the area referred to in the Schedule to the Order. Such an order was made, in effect, by the House of Lords in *Hotel and Catering Industry Training Board* v. *Automobile Proprietary Ltd.* [1969] 1 W.L.R. 697, and by Donaldson J. in *Agricultural, Horticultural and Forestry Industry Training Board* v. *Aylesbury Mushrooms Ltd.* [1972] 1 W.L.R. 190.

Accordingly we hold that the West Coast Herring (Prohibition of Fishing) Order 1978 is not ultra vires the minister who made the order, save in so far as it affects the area of the sea reserved by section 23 (1) of the Sea Fish (Conservation) Act 1967. . . .

Appeal allowed.

Notes

1. The approach in *Olsen* v. *City of Camberwell* should be contrasted with that in *Bank of New South Wales* v. *Commonwealth* (1948) 76 C.L.R. 1, where Dixon J. said (at p. 730):

It was not to be assumed that connected or associated provisions were enacted as separate expressions of the will of the legislature. No severance can be effected unless an inference that the provisions are not to be interdependent can be positively drawn from the nature of the provisions, from the manner in which they are expressed or from the fact that they independently affect the persons or things within power in some way and with the same results as if the full intended operation of the legislation had been valid.

Pearce, *Delegated Legislation in Australia and New Zealand*, p. 616, states that the former case 'seeks to preserve the legislation if at all possible while the [latter] contemplates severance in only the exceptional case'. Would this difference of approach have affected the result in *Dunkley* v. *Evans*? The approach of the court in *Dunkley* v. *Evans* is consistent with that taken in *Hinds* v. *The Queen* [1977] A.C. 195 in the context of a partially invalid Jamaican statute. There the Privy Council was of the opinion (at p. 230) that '[t]his may be only half the loaf that Parliament believed it was getting when it passed the [legislation], but their Lordships do not doubt that Parliament would have preferred it to no bread.' It should, however, be noted that it was possible to apply the 'blue pencil' test in that case (p. 229).

2. The practical advantages of a wide power of severance are clear (see Wade, p. 758), but it might be said that it constitutes a judicial power to amend delegated legislation, a power which Parliament does not have and which (see p. 529 *infra*) it does not appear to want. Do the reasons for rejecting a Parliamentary power of amendment apply to a judicial power? Are there other, for instance constitutional, objections to such judicial power?

Statutory restriction of judicial control

Minister of Health v. The King (on the prosecution of Yaffe)

[1931] A.C. 494   House of Lords

Section 40 of the Housing Act 1925, which empowered the Minister to make an order confirming, with or without modifications, an improvement scheme made under the Act, also provided by s. 40 (5), that 'the order of the minister when made shall have effect as if enacted in this Act'. Liverpool Corporation submitted an improvement scheme and the Minister, after holding a local inquiry, made an order confirming it with modifications. The owner of two houses which were to be compulsorily purchased sought to quash the Minister's order as being ultra vires. The Minister contended that once a scheme had been confirmed by him it was in the same position as an Act of Parliament in the sense that it could not be reviewed by the courts. This argument was accepted by the Divisional Court but rejected by the Court of Appeal ([1930] 2 K.B. 98). On appeal:

VISCOUNT DUNEDIN: . . . The first question, and it is a very important and far-reaching one, is, therefore, as to the effect of s. 40, sub-s. 5. Has it the effect of preventing any inquiry by way of certiorari proceeding of a scheme confirmed by the Minister? It is evident that it is inconceivable that the protection should extend without limit. If the Minister went out of his province altogether, if, for example, he proposed to confirm a scheme which said that all proprietors in a scheduled area should make a per capita contribution of 5*l.* to the municipal authority to be applied by them for the building of a hall, it is repugnant to common sense that the order would be protected, although, if there were an Act of Parliament to that effect, it could not be touched. Now, the high water mark of inviolablity of a confirmed order is to be found in a case in this House which necessarily binds your Lordships. It is the case of the *Institute of Patent Agents* v. *Lockwood.*[5] That case arose under the Patents, Designs, and Trade Marks Act. By that Act the Board of Trade was empowered to pass such general rules as they thought expedient for the purposes of the Act. Such rules were, 'subject as hereinafter prescribed,' to be of the same effect as if they were contained in the Act, and were to be judicially noticed. The 'as hereinafter prescribed' was that the rules were to be laid before Parliament for forty days, and if, within forty days, either House disapproved of any rule, it was to be of no effect. The Board of Trade made rules as to the register of patent agents, which were laid before Parliament for forty days and were not objected to. The rules provided that an annual subscription should be paid by all registered patent agents, and prescribed a penalty for any one calling himself a patent agent who was not on the register. The respondent in the case, who was duly registered, refused to pay the subscription and was put off the register. He continued to practise and call himself a patent agent. The Institute of Patent Agents raised an action for a declaration and an injunction. In defence, the respondent pleaded that the rule was ultra vires of the Board of Trade. The House of Lords held that the provision as to the rules being of like effect as if they had been enacted in the Act, precluded inquiry as to whether the rules were ultra vires or not.

Now, there is an obvious distinction between that case and this, because there Parliament itself was in control of the rules for forty days after they were passed, and could have annulled them if motion were made to that effect, whereas here there is no Parliamentary manner of dealing with the confirmation of the scheme by the Minister of Health. Yet, I do not think that that distinction, obvious as it is, would avail to prevent the sanction given being an untouchable sanction. I think the real clue to the solution of the problem is to be found in the opinion of Herschell L.C., who says this:[6] 'No doubt there might be some conflict between a rule and a provision of the Act. Well, there is a conflict sometimes between two sections to be found in the same Act. You have to try and reconcile them as best you may. If you cannot, you have to

[5] [1894] A.C. 347.
[6] [1894] A.C. 360.

determine which is the leading provision and which the subordinate provision, and which must give way to the other. That would be so with regard to the enactment, and with regard to rules which are to be treated as if within the enactment. In that case, probably the enactment itself would be treated as the governing consideration and the rule as subordinate to it.'

What that comes to is this: The confirmation makes the scheme speak as if it was contained in an Act of Parliament, but the Act of Parliament in which it is contained is the Act which provides for the framing of the scheme, not a subsequent Act. If therefore the scheme, as made, conflicts with the Act, it will have to give way to the Act. The mere confirmation will not save it. It would be otherwise if the scheme had been, per se, embodied in a subsequent Act, for then the maxim to be applied would have been 'Posteriora derogant prioribus.' But as it is, if one can find that the scheme is inconsistent with the provisions of the Act which authorizes the scheme, the scheme will be bad, and that only can be gone into by way of proceedings in certiorari.

[He then went on to consider whether the scheme, and consequently the order, were ultra vires and, reversing the Court of Appeal, held that they were not. He concluded:] [T]he scheme, as confirmed, is a good scheme, and . . . this appeal should be allowed, and . . . the judgment of the Divisional Court, although on very different grounds, should be restored.

[LORD WARRINGTON OF CLYFFE, LORD TOMLIN, and LORD THANKERTON delivered speeches in favour of allowing the appeal. LORD RUSSELL OF KILLOWEN delivered a speech in favour of dismissing the appeal.]

Appeal allowed.

Question

Can *Institute of Patent Agents* v. *Lockwood* [1894] A.C. 347 be distinguished on the ground that, in that case, the court was considering 'general rules' which had been laid before Parliament and were subject to the negative procedure, whereas in *Minister of Health* v. *The King* the official act was not legislative?

Notes

1. On the effect of s. 14 of the Tribunals and Inquiries Act 1971 on 'as if enacted' clauses, see Note 4, p. 380 *supra*, where it is also pointed out that these clauses are not used by Parliament today.

2. The hostility of the courts to ouster clauses (see Ch. 11 *supra*) is equally strong where the power exercised is legislative. In *Commissioners of Customs and Excise* v. *Cure & Deeley Ltd.* [1962] 1 Q.B. 340 Sachs J. considered a legislative power granted by the Finance Act (No. 2) 1940. The Commissioners were empowered to make regulations 'for any matter for which provision appears to them to be necessary' for the administration of purchase tax. A regulation was made which stated that if a person failed to furnish a tax return, or furnished an incomplete return, the Commissioners had power to determine the amount of tax appearing to them to be due and to demand payment of that amount. The regulation also provided that the amount so determined should be deemed to be the proper tax due unless the contrary was shown

within seven days. It was held that the regulation was ultra vires as the Finance Act (No. 2) 1940 did nothing to deny a taxpayer his 'vital right to have the independent decision of the courts on the question of whether or not tax is due' (p. 351). In the absence of clear words in the enabling statute the presumption that statutes do not oust the jurisdiction of the courts applied. Sachs J. rejected the argument that the subjective wording of the enabling statute made the Commissioners the sole judges of the extent of their powers and the way they exercised them, although he recognized that in some cases this might be the consequence.

3. For a possible half-way house between the widest interpretation of the dicta in *Institute of Patent Agents* v. *Lockwood* [1894] A.C. 347 and *Minister of Health* v. *The King*, see *Foster* v. *Aloni* [1951] V.L.R. 481; Whitmore and Aronson, *Review of Administrative Action*, pp. 510–11.

PUBLICATION

Arrangements for publication

Blackpool Corporation v. Locker, p. 487 *supra*

Statutory Instruments Act 1946

1. – (1) Where by this Act or any Act passed after the commencement of this Act power to make, confirm or approve orders, rules, regulations or other subordinate legislation is conferred on His Majesty in Council or on any Minister of the Crown then, if the power is expressed –

(a) in the case of a power conferred on His Majesty, to be exercisable by Order in Council;

(b) in the case of a power conferred in a Minister of the Crown, to be exercisable by statutory instrument,

any document by which that power is exercised shall be known as a 'statutory instrument' and the provisions of this Act shall apply thereto accordingly....

2. – (1) Immediately after the making of any statutory instrument, it shall be sent to the King's printer of Acts of Parliament and numbered in accordance with regulations made under this Act, and except in such cases as may be provided by any Act passed after the commencement of this Act or prescribed by regulations made under this Act, copies thereof shall as soon as possible be printed and sold by the King's printer of Acts of Parliament....

3. – (1) Regulations made for the purposes of this Act shall make provision for the publication by His Majesty's Stationery Office of lists showing the date upon which every statutory instrument printed and sold by the King's printer of Acts of Parliament was first issued by that office; and in any legal proceedings a copy of any list so published purporting to bear the imprint of the King's printer shall be received in evidence as a true copy, and an entry

therein shall be conclusive evidence of the date on which any statutory instrument was first issued by His Majesty's Stationery Office.

(2) In any proceedings against any person for an offence consisting of a contravention of any such statutory instrument, it shall be a defence to prove that the instrument had not been issued by His Majesty's Stationery Office at the date of the alleged contravention unless it is proved that at that date reasonable steps had been taken for the purpose of bringing the purport of the instrument to the notice of the public, or of persons likely to be affected by it, or of the person charged.

(3) Save as therein otherwise expressly provided, nothing in this section shall affect any enactment or rule of law relating to the time at which any statutory instrument comes into operation.

8. − (1) The Treasury may, with the concurrence of the Lord Chancellor and the Speaker of the House of Commons, by statutory instrument make regulations for the purposes of this Act, and such regulations may, in particular: − . . .

(c) provide with respect to any classes or descriptions of statutory instrument that they shall be exempt, either altogether or to such extent as may be determined by or under the regulations, from the requirement of being printed and of being sold by the King's printer of Acts of Parliament, or from either of those requirements: . . .

Note

The Statutory Instruments Regulations 1947 (S.I. 1948 No. 1) exempt the following regulations from the publication requirements of the 1946 Act: local instruments and instruments otherwise regularly published (r. 5); temporary instruments (r. 6); schedules to rules if they are too bulky and other steps to bring their substance to the notice of the public have been taken (r. 7); and cases in which publication before the coming into operation of a rule would be contrary to the public interest (r. 8). In the cases covered by rr. 6−8 the minister who makes the regulation must certify that the relevant conditions for the exception to operate are fulfilled.

Effect of non-publication on validity

R. v. Sheer Metalcraft Ltd.

[1954] 1 Q.B. 586   Kingston-upon Thames Assizes

STREATFIELD J.: This matter comes before the court in the form of an objection to the admissibility in evidence of a statutory instrument known as the Iron and Steel Prices Order, 1951. It appears that part and parcel of that instrument consisted of certain deposited schedules in which maximum prices for different commodities of steel were set out. The instrument is said to have been made by the Minister of Supply on February 16, 1951; laid before Parliament on February 20, 1951; and to have come into operation on

February 21, 1951. It is under that statutory instrument that the present charges are made against the two defendants in this case.

The point which has been taken is that by reason of the deposited schedules not having been printed and not having been certified by the Minister as being exempt from printing, the instrument is not a valid instrument under the Statutory Instruments Act, 1946. . . . The point arises in this way: under regulation 55 AB of the Defence (General) Regulations, 1939, as amended, a competent authority, which in this case is the Minister of Supply, may by statutory instrument provide for controlling the prices to be charged for goods of any description or the charges to be made for services of any description, and for any incidental and supplementary matters for which the competent authority thinks it expedient for the purposes of the instrument to provide. It is said in the statutory instrument here that it was made in exercise of the powers conferred upon the Minister by regulations 55 AB and 98 of the Defence (General) Regulations, and other statutory authorities.

The contention is that the making of that instrument is governed by the provisions of the Statutory Instruments Act, 1946, which repeals and simplifies the more cumbrous procedure under the Rules Publication Act, 1893.

[His Lordship read sections 1 and 2 of the Act of 1946 and regulation 7 of the Statutory Instruments Regulations, 1947,[7] and continued:] Section 1 visualizes the making of what is called a statutory instrument by a Minister of the Crown; section 2 visualizes that after the making of a statutory instrument it shall be sent to the King's Printer to be printed, except in so far as under regulations made under the Act it may be unnecessary to have it printed. It is said here that the Minister did not certify that the printing of these very bulky deposited schedules was unnecessary within the meaning of regulation 7. It is contended, therefore, that as he did not so certify it, it became an obligation under the Act that the deposited schedules as well as the instrument itself should be printed under section 2 of the Act of 1946, and in the absence of their having been printed as part of the instrument, the instrument cannot be regarded as being validly made.

To test that matter it is necessary to examine section 3 of the Act of 1946. [He read s. 3 (1), p. 512 *supra*, and continued:] There does not appear to be any definition of what is meant by 'issue,' but presumably it does mean some act by the Queen's Printer of Acts of Parliament which follows the printing of the instrument. That section, therefore, requires that the Queen's Printer shall keep lists showing the date upon which statutory instruments are printed and issued.

---

[7] [This provides: 'If the responsible authority considers that the printing and sale in accordance with the requirements of subsection (1) of section 2 of the [Statutory Instruments Act 1946] of any Schedule or other document which is identified by or referred to in a statutory instrument and would, but for the priovisions of this regulation, be required to be included in the instrument as so printed and sold, is unnecessary or undesirable having regard to the nature or bulk of the document and to any other steps taken or to be taken for bringing its substance to the notice of the public, he may, on sending it to the King's printer of Acts of Parliament, certify accordingly; and any instrument so certified shall . . . be exempt from the requirements aforesaid.']

[He then read s. 3 (2), p. 513 *supra*, and continued:] It seems to follow from the wording of this subsection that the making of an instrument is one thing and the issue of it is another. If it is made it can be contravened; if it has not been issued then that provides a defence to a person charged with its contravention. It is then upon the Crown to prove that, although it has not been issued, reasonable steps have been taken for the purpose of bringing the instrument to the notice of the public or persons likely to be affected by it.

I do not think that it can be said that to make a valid statutory instrument it is required that all of these stages should be gone through; namely, the making, the laying before Parliament, the printing and the certification of that part of it which it might be unnecessary to have printed. In my judgment the making of an instrument is complete when it is first of all made by the Minister concerned and after it has been laid before Parliament. When that has been done it then becomes a valid statutory instrument, totally made under the provisions of the Act.

The remaining provisions to which my attention has been drawn, in my view, are purely procedure for the issue of an instrument validly made – namely, that in the first instance it must be printed by the Queen's Printer unless it is certified to be unnecessary to print it; it must then be included in a list published by Her Majesty's Stationery Office showing the dates when it is issued and it may be issued by the Queen's Printer of Acts of Parliament. Those matters, in my judgment, are matters of procedure. If they were not and if they were stages in the perfection of a valid statutory instrument, I cannot see that section 3 (2) would be necessary, because if each one of those stages were necessary to make a statutory instrument valid, it would follow that there could be no infringement of an unissued instrument and therefore it would be quite unnecessary to provide a defence to a contravention of any such instrument. In my view the very fact that subsection (2) of section 3 refers to a defence that the instrument has not been issued postulates that the instrument must have been validly made in the first place otherwise it could never have been contravened.

In those circumstances I hold that this instrument was validly made and approved and that it was made by or signed on behalf of the Minister on its being laid before Parliament; that so appears on the face of the instrument itself. In my view, the fact that the Minister failed to certify under regulation 7 does not invalidate the instrument as an instrument but lays the burden upon the Crown to prove that at the date of the alleged contraventions reasonable steps had been taken for bringing the instrument to the notice of the public or persons likely to be affected by it. I, therefore, rule that this is admissible.

[When evidence of the steps taken to bring the instrument to the notice of the public and of the contravention of it by the accused had been given, His Lordship summed up and the jury, after a retirement of two minutes, found both the accused guilty on all counts.]

Verdict: Guilty on all counts.

Note

For a detailed analysis of s. 3 of the Statutory Instruments Act 1946 and the *Sheer Metalcraft* case, see Lanham, (1974) 37 M.L.R. 510. He rejects the idea that at common law delegated legislation comes into affect when made and that s. 3 (2) is an exception to that rule. He argues that at common law delegated legislation does not come into effect until it is published and that s. 3 (2) is therfore 'a rather limited statutory declaration of that rule'. Reliance is placed on *Johnson* v. *Sargant* [1918] 1 K.B. 101. In that case Bailhache J. considered an Order requiring certain food importers to hold all stocks at the disposal of the food controller unless they had been sold and paid for. The Order was made on 16 May 1917 but was not published until 17 May. The defendants paid for a consignment of beans on 16 May but the plaintiff refused to deliver, relying on the Order. The judge said:

> While I agree that the rule is that a statute takes effect on the earliest moment of the day on which it is passed or on which it is declared to come into operation, there is about statutes a publicity even before they come into operation which is absent in the case of many Orders such as that with which we are now dealing; indeed, if certain Orders are to be effective at all, it is essential that they should not be known until they are actually published. In the absence of authority upon the point I am unable to hold that this Order came into operation before it was known, and . . . it was not known until the morning of May 17.

He therefore gave judgment for the defendants. This case has been questioned by Allen, pp. 112–15, and de Smith, pp. 147–8. Is it authority for the view that delegated legislation does not come into force until published or until actually known? See Griffith and Street p. 104; Lanham, op. cit., pp. 510–16. Cf. Wade, pp. 764; *Jones* v. *Robson* [1901] 1 Q.B. 673. Is *Sheer Metalcraft* distinguishable on the ground that the instrument there specified the date on which it was to come into effect (see s. 3 (3) of the Statutory Instruments Act 1946, p. 513 *supra*)? Does r. 8 of the Statutory Instruments Regulations 1947 (S.I. 1948 No. 1, noted at p. 513 *supra*) support Lanham's view of the effect of s. 3 (2)? The Joint Committee on Statutory Instruments does not appear to share Lanham's view. It has criticized the practice of laying instruments before Parliament in manuscript form because they may become 'the law of the land' before they are printed and available to the public (H.C. 169, Session 1977/8), para. 17; and see Note 2, p. 530 *infra*). The different views as to the common law rule have important practical consequences in cases in which s. 3 (2) has no application. On these, see Lanham, op. cit., p. 523, but, briefly, they are said to include civil proceedings, cases of sub-delegated legislation (possibly – see Wade, p. 764), and cases where the legislation in question is not a statutory instrument.

PRELIMINARY CONSULTATION

Bates v. Lord Hailsham of St. Marylebone

[1972] 1 W.L.R. 1373   Chancery Division

Section 56 of the Solicitors Act 1957 gives power to a committee consisting of the Lord Chancellor, the Lord Chief Justice, the Master of the Rolls, the President of the Law Society, the Chief Land Registrar and the President of a local Law Society to make orders prescribing solicitors' remuneration in respect of non-contentious business. By s. 56 (3):

Before any such order is made, the Lord Chancellor shall cause a draft to be sent to the council [of the Law Society], and the Committee shall, before making the order, consider any observations in writing submitted to them by the council within one month of the sending to them of the draft, and may then make the order. . . .

The committee proposed to abolish scale fees for conveyancing and substitute a *quantum meruit* system. A draft order was sent to the Law Society. The plaintiff was a member of the British Legal Association. This body, which had 2,900 members, objected to the proposals and sought to delay the making of the order to allow further consultation with the profession. The plaintiff sought a declaration that any order made would be ultra vires unless, *inter alia*, before making the order the committee gave the British Legal Association a reasonable opportunity to make representations as to its terms.

MEGARRY J.: . . . Mr. Nicholls[8] relied on *Reg. v. Liverpool Corporation, Ex parte Liverpool Taxi Fleet Operators' Association* [1972] 2 Q.B. 299; and he read me some passages from the judgments of Lord Denning M.R. and Roskill L.J. It cannot often happen that words uttered by a judge in his judicial capacity will, within six months, be cited against him in his personal capacity as defendant; yet that is the position here. The case was far removed from the present case. It concerned the exercise by a city council of its powers to licence hackney carriages, and a public undertaking given by the chairman of the relevant committee which the council soon proceeded to ignore. The case supports propositions relating to the duty of a body to act fairly when exercising administrative functions under a statutory power: see at pp. 307, 308 and 310. Accordingly, in deciding the policy to be applied as to the number of licences to grant, there was a duty to hear those who would be likely to be affected. It is plain that no legislation was involved: the question was one of the policy to be adopted in the exercise of a statutory power to grant licences.

In the present case, the committee in question has an entirely different function: it is legislative rather than administrative or executive. The function of the committee is to make or refuse to make a legislative instrument under delegated powers. The order, when made, will lay down the remuneration for solicitors generally; and the terms of the order will have to be considered and construed and applied in numberless cases in the future. Let me accept that in the sphere of the so-called quasi-judicial the rules of natural justice run, and that in the administrative or executive field there is a general duty of fairness.[9] Nevertheless, these considerations do not seem to me to affect the process of legislation, whether primary or delegated. Many of those affected by delegated legislation, and affected very substantially, are never consulted in the process of enacting that legislation: and yet they have no remedy. Of course, the informal consultation of representative bodies by the legislative

---

[8] [Counsel for the plaintiff.]

[9] [But cf. his views in *McInnes v. Onslow-Fane*, p. 265 *supra*.]

authority is a commonplace; but although a few statutes have specifically provided for a general process of publishing draft delegated legislation and considering objections (see, for example, the Factories Act 1961, Schedule 4), I do not know of any implied right to be consulted or make objections, or any principle upon which the courts may enjoin the legislative process at the suit of those who contend that insufficient time for consultation and consideration has been given. I accept that the fact that the order will take the form of a statutory instrument does not per se make it immune from attack, whether by injunction or otherwise; but what is important is not its form but its nature, which is plainly legislative. . . .

Order accordingly.

Notes

1. In *CREEDNZ Inc.* v. *Governor General* [1981] 1 N.Z.L.R. 172 at p. 189 Richardson J. appeared to take a different view on natural justice and legislative functions. He said that 'the dividing line between "adjudication" (or "administration") on the one hand and "legislation" on the other is not easy to draw and the attempt may be an arid exercise for in the twilight area the conceptual foundations for a distinction are not self-evident'. See also to the same effect, *Bread Manufacturers of New South Wales* v. *Evans* (1982) 38 A.L.R. 93 at pp. 103 and 116–7. Is it true, as Megarry J. suggests in the *Bates* case, that the policy underlying the *audi alteram partem* doctrine has no application to legislative functions? Should any distinction between 'legislative' and 'administrative' turn on the impracticability of imposing a general duty to hear all those affected by legislation rather than the formal classification of functions? See further Note 3 *infra*. See also *R.* v. *G.L.C., ex p. The Rank Organisation*, The Times, 19 February 1982, noted at p. 279 *supra*. The fineness of the distinction between 'legislation' and 'administration' is, however, illustrated by *R.* v. *Secretary of State for the Environment, ex p. Brent L.B.C.* [1982] 2 W.L.R. 693, noted at pp. 144 and 323 *supra*. In that case the Minister was held to be under a duty to receive representations from those affected before *exercising* a power given to him under subordinate legislation, even though it was clear that the legislation in question had been passed to enable him to do what he had done (reduce the rate support grant payable to certain local authorities).

2. Section 56 (3) of the Solicitors Act 1957 did refer to consultation, but only with the Law Society. Is the *Bates* case better seen as an example of the *expressio unius exclusio alterius* canon of statutory interpretation, on which Megarry J. also relied? See further p. 233 *supra* for the application of *audi alteram partem* in cases in which the procedure is governed by a code.

3. See generally on consultation Garner [1964] P.L. 105; Griffith and Street, pp. 123–33; Jergson, [1978] P.L. 291; Wade, p. 766. Compare the position in the U.S.A., where s. 4 of the Administrative Procedure Act 1946 (5 U.S.C. para. 553) requires that administrative legislation be undertaken only after notice and an opportunity for the public to comment on a proposed rule. See Davis, *Administrative Law Text*, 3rd edn., Ch. 6. The Rules Publication Act 1893 imposed a limited duty to consider objections, but it did not apply to all rules and its requirements could be avoided (*Report of the Committee on Ministers' Powers*, Cmd. 4060, pp. 44–8 and 66). It was repealed by the Statutory Instruments Act 1946. The undoubted practical difficulties that would result from the imposition of a general 'duty to consult' appear

to be avoided if the more limited 'notice and opportunity to comment' approach is adopted.

4. *Agricultural, Horticultural, and Forestry Industry T.B.* v. *Aylesbury Mushrooms Ltd.* [1972] 1 W.L.R. 190, noted by Foulkes, (1972) 35 M.L.R. 647, suggests that a statutory duty to consult will be classified as 'mandatory'. On 'mandatory' and 'directory' requirements see further p. 17 *supra*.

PARLIAMENTARY SUPERVISION

Laying before Parliament

First Report from the Select Committee on Procedure

H.C. 588, Session 1977/8

3. DELEGATED LEGISLATION

3.1. 'Delegated Legislation' is a wide term covering 'every exercise of a power to legislate conferred by or under an Act of Parliament or which is given the force of law by virtue of an Act of Parliament'.[10] . . . We have confined our consideration only to those general statutory instruments which are subject to some form of parliamentary scrutiny or control. Certain of our observations and recommendations concerning delegated legislation apply also to the consideration of European Communities Legislation. . . .

3.2. Parliament faces a dilemma in relation to delegated legislation which cannot easily be resolved. Indeed, the very concept of delegated legislative powers, some of which are subject to parliamentary procedure, involves an uneasy confusion between executive and legislative authority. On the one hand, the Executive is given statutory powers, within varying degrees of limitation, to exercise the legislative authority of Parliament. On the other hand, the Legislature retains, within varying limits, the freedom to scrutinise the exercise by the Executive of the legislative authority so delegated, and in certain cases either to withhold consent to a particular use of delegated powers or to prevent its continuation in force. Whereas in some countries it is possible to distinguish with reasonable clarity between the field of exclusive authority and the field of legislative authority,[11] the absence of a written constitution in the United Kingdom leaves the determination of the boundaries between the two fields to Parliament (in each separate decision to delegate legislative authority) and to the courts (whenever the exercise of delegated authority is contested).

---

[10] Report from the Joint Committee on Delegated Legislation, Session 1971–72 (H.C. 475 H.L. 184) para. 6 (Evidence by Speaker's Counsel.)

[11] The Constitution of the Fifth French Republic, for instance, lays down quite clear boundaries between the 'domain of law' within which alone Parliament can legislate and where normally the Government cannot: and the 'domain of regulations' where the Government can make rules with which Parliament cannot interfere: the boundaries being subject to the adjudication of the Constitutional Council and *Conseil d'Etat*.

3.3. The general reasons for the delegation by Parliament of its legislative powers may be summarised briefly as (i) the desire to avoid excessive detail in primary legislation, particularly in fields where frequent or sudden changes may be required; and (ii) the need to give the Executive the freedom to vary the effect of legislation in the face of changing circumstances or in its application to particular fields. The Executive is thereby freed from the necessity of introducing legislative proposals subject to the full parliamentary process; and Parliament is likewise freed from the obligation to subject such proposals to detailed scrutiny. Although it may be argued that the greater gain lies with the Executive, the advantages to Parliament – in terms of facilitating the continuity of administrative action as well as in terms of saving the time of Members – should not be underestimated.

3.4. Whatever arrangements the House, or the two Houses together may make for the consideration of the exercise of delegated powers, a balance must be struck between the desirability of effective parliamentary scrutiny, where there is statutory provision for it, and the Executive's need to exercise the legislative authority delegated to it. Having in many cases imposed statutory constraints on the exercise of delegated powers, Parliament must ensure that they can be applied. Equally, having decided that legislative authority should be delegated, Parliament should not by procedural means so circumscribe the exercise of that authority as to frustrate the intentions of the enabling act. It is in our view unsatisfactory that the ability of Members to propose that the House should exercise its statutory right to 'pray' against certain categories of statutory instruments should be restricted by the Executive's control of the business of the House. It would be equally unsatisfactory if the House were to subject statutory instruments to scrutiny in the same detail and at the same length as primary legislation.

Categories of parliamentary control

3.5. Delegated legislation may be divided into categories according to the kind of Parliamentary control which is applied to it. The category into which an instrument falls is determined by its parent Act. The Act may provide that:

(i) the instrument shall expire or shall not come into effect unless it, or a draft of it, is approved by a resolution of both Houses of Parliament (or in certain cases, usually if finance is involved, of the House of Commons only) (the affirmative procedure);

(ii) the instrument shall come into effect automatically but shall be subject to annulment in pursuance of a resolution of either House of Parliament (or the House of Commons only); or shall come into effect only if no annulling resolution is passed while it is laid in draft; a motion to annul such an instrument is referred to as a 'prayer' (the negative procedure);

(iii) the instrument shall be laid before both Houses of Parliament (or the House of Commons only) with no provision for Parliament to take any action upon it;

(iv) the instrument shall be a statutory instrument, with no provision that it shall be laid before either House. . . .

Statutory Instruments Act 1946

4. − (1) Where by this Act or any Act passed after the commencement of this Act any statutory instrument is required to be laid before Parliament after being made, a copy of the instrument shall be laid before each House of Parliament and, subject as hereinafter provided, shall be so laid before the instrument comes into operation:

Provided that if it is essential that any such instrument should come into operation before copies thereof can be so laid as aforesaid, the instrument may be made so as to come into operation before it has been so laid; and where any statutory instrument comes into operation before it is laid before Parliament, notification shall forthwith be sent to the Lord Chancellor and to the Speaker of the House of Commons drawing attention to the fact that copies of the instrument have yet to be laid before Parliament and explaining why such copies were not so laid before the instrument came into operation. . . .

5. − (1) Where by this Act or any Act passed after the commencement of this Act, it is provided that any statutory instrument shall be subject to annulment in pursuance of resolution of either House of Parliament, the instrument shall be laid before Parliament after being made and the provisions of the last foregoing section shall apply thereto accordingly, and if either House, within the period of forty days beginning with the day on which a copy thereof is laid before it, resolves that an Address be presented to His Majesty praying that the instrument be annulled, no further proceedings shall be taken thereunder after the date of the resolution, and His Majesty may by Order in Council revoke the instrument, so, however, that any such resolution and revocation shall be without prejudice to the validity of anything previously done under the instrument or to the making of a new statutory instrument. . . .

6. − (1) Where by this Act or any Act passed after the commencement of this Act it is provided that a draft of any statutory instrument shall be laid before Parliament, but the Act does not prohibit the making of the instrument without the approval of Parliament, then, in the case of an Order in Council the draft shall not be submitted to His Majesty in Council, and in any other case the statutory instrument shall not be made, until after the expiration of a period of forty days beginning with the day on which a copy of the draft is laid before each House of Parliament, or, if such copies are laid on different days, with the later of the two days, and if within that period either House resolves that the draft be not submitted to His Majesty or that the statutory instrument be not made, as the case may be, no further proceedings shall be taken thereon, but without prejudice to the laying before Parliament of a new draft. . . .

7. – (1) In reckoning for the purposes of either of the last two foregoing sections any period of forty days, no account shall be taken of any time during which Parliament is dissolved or prorogued or during which both Houses are adjourned for more than four days.

(2) In relation to any instrument required by any Act, whether passed before or after the commencement of this Act, to be laid before the House of Commons only, the provisions of the last three foregoing sections shall have effect as if references to that House were therein substituted for references to Parliament and for references to either House and each House thereof.

(3) The provisions of sections four and five of this Act shall not apply to any statutory instrument being an order which is subject to special Parliamentary procedure, or to any other instrument which is required to be laid before Parliament, or before the House of Commons, for any period before it comes into operation.

Notes

1. Sections 4 (2), 5 (2), and 6 (2) made similar provision for laying requirements in legislation passed before the commencement of the Statutory Instruments Act.

2. In *F. Hoffmann-La Roche & Co. A.G.* v. *Secretary of State for Trade and Industry*, p. 94 *supra*, the House of Lords considered an instrument which was subject to the affirmative procedure. In the Court of Appeal it was suggested that once the necessary resolutions were passed the instrument 'was a valid and effective legislative act as binding as an Act of Parliament' (Buckley L.J. [1975] A.C. at p. 322). Lord Denning M.R. said that the instrument became the law of the land and (at p. 322) '[w]hen the courts are asked to enforce it they must do so'. In the House of Lords it was made clear that this did not preclude the courts from declaring the making of the order ultra vires the statutory power from which it purported to derive its validity. Lord Wilberforce said (at p. 354):

> That an attack can be made on a statutory instrument for want of power needs no demonstration, and I agree with your Lordships that it makes no difference, for this purpose, that the instrument has been laid before and approved by the two Houses of Parliament.

The dicta in the Court of Appeal show that the very existence of legislative scrutiny could inhibit other, potentially more effective, methods of control such as judicial review. See Wallington, [1974] 33 C.L.J. 26 at pp. 30–1; Wade, (1974) 90 L.Q.R. 436 at p. 439; *Sparks* v. *Edward Ash Ltd.* [1943] K.B. 223 at p. 229, noted at p. 505 *supra*. See also *McEldowney* v. *Forde* [1971] A.C. 632 at pp. 648–9 per Lord Guest, critically noted by MacCormick, (1970) 86 L.Q.R. 171.

3. Legislative scrutiny does, however, have several advantages when compared with judicial review. It is systematic and it is not subject to the limits of the doctrine of ultra vires or to the need for a person with standing to be willing to litigate. Furthermore, as legislation has normative effects, a method of control, such as judicial review, that may occur long after the promulgation of a rule may lead to difficulties. See, for instance, the 'void or voidable' issue discussed in Ch. 3 *supra*, and in particular *F. Hoffmann-La Roche & Co. A.G.* v. *Secretary of State for Trade and Industry*, p. 94 *supra*. See also the consequence of the decision in *Agricultural, Horticultural, and Forestry T.B.* v. *Aylesbury Mushrooms Ltd.* [1972] 1 W.L.R. 190, where a rule

that was otherwise valid did not bind one group of farmers. But see the explanation of this in *Dunkley* v. *Evans*, p. 508 *supra*. When reading the material in the following extracts, consider whether the system of legislative control that has been adopted does in fact have these advantages.

Legislative Control of Administrative Rulemaking: Lessons from the British Experience?

Jack Beatson

(1979) 11 Cornell Int. L.J. 199

2. *Choosing Among Methods of Control*[12]

Despite the availability of several types of control procedure, Parliament has failed to develop any rational criteria for determining which procedure is appropriate in making a particular delegation of rulemaking power. This is particularly true in choosing between the negative procedure and the 'laying only' procedure. The failure to develop criteria has been justified on the ground that '[r]ules for the settlement of questions such as this, which must arise in circumstances of infinite variety, are nothing but an embarrassment, tending to encumber the task of arriving at the right answer in any particular case.' On the other hand, the absence of criteria means that when granting rulemaking power, Parliament is hindered from making a considered choice of the means by which it is to exercise control over such power in any given situation. Consequently, the political judgment of the minister whose rules are to be scrutinized tends to prevail.

The Joint Committee on Delegated Legislation has recently recommended that the affirmative procedure should normally be employed for rules that substantially affect the provisions of primary legislation, impose or increase taxation, or involve considerations of special importance – such as the creation of new varieties of criminal offences. The committee recommended use of the negative procedure for other cases in which Parliament wishes to retain some control. It rejected the argument that 'skeleton' powers, which are broad delegations of power by Parliament leaving broad discretion in formulating administrative rules, should always be controlled by the affirmative procedure.

The Scrutiny Committee and the Joint Committee

Report from the Joint Committee on Delegated Legislation

H.C. 475, Session 1971/2

Distinction between technical scrutiny and consideration of merits

28. The essentially subordinate character of delegated legislation causes it to differ fundamentally from the primary legislation on which it depends. . . .

29. It follows that in controlling delegated legislation it is necessary to ensure that an instrument does no more than it is authorised to do by the

---

[12] [Footnotes omitted.]

parent Act, and does it only in the manner and subject to the conditions authorised. Parliament therefore in controlling delegated legislation needs to carry out an examination not only of its political content (consideration of merits), but also of its drafting, scope and effects in relation to the powers given by its parent Act (technical scrutiny).

30. It has been the settled practice of both Houses to keep this consideration of merits and technical scrutiny quite separate. The Officers of both Houses in their memoranda of evidence emphasised to Your Committee the importance of this practice. The Second Clerk Assistant of the House of Commons, Mr. Barlas, in his memorandum[13] summarises the reasons for the distinction as follows:

'It is important to stress the need to keep the two functions of control separate: viz. control of technique and control over merits. . . . [I]n the debate in 1944 which led to the establishment of the Statutory Instruments Committee much emphasis was laid both by backbenchers and by the House Secretary of the day (Mr. Herbert Morrison) on the importance of the proposed Committee working in a judicial spirit.'

Your Committee agree that this practice is right and should be rigidly maintained.

Note

The distinction between technical scrutiny and scrutiny of the merits has been criticized on the ground that, although it is not rigidly adhered to, M.P.'s, who generally wish to debate merits and politically important issues, do not have a report on the very issues that interest them: Beatson, (1979) 11 Cornell Int. L.J. 199 at pp. 218 and 220. See further, para. 3.8 of the next extract. Sir Cecil Carr admitted that the House of Commons scrutiny committee sometimes 'peep[ed] at the merits' ((1955) 30 N.Y.U.L. Rev. 1045 at p. 1055), and this is still the case. The tendency to blur the distinction is increased by the committee's custom of taking evidence from outside bodies and its practice of giving reasons for reporting an instrument. The distinction is also breaking down in the context of the control of European Community rules. The House of Lords Select Committee on the European Communities considers the policy of a rule and whether its strategy can be improved (Bates, (1976) 1 Eur. L. Rev. 22 at p. 26), and, although the House of Commons Committee on European Secondary Legislation is only supposed to identify matters of legal or political importance and not to consider merits, the criteria of 'importance' have been flexible enough to include indirect consideration of merits (Bates, op. cit., pp. 27–8 and 35–6). On the scrutiny of E.E.C. legislation see further Bates, op. cit., *passim*; First Report from the Select Committee on Procedure for the Session 1977/8, H.C. 588, vol. i, Ch. 4 and vol. iii, Appendix 25 to Minutes of Evidence; Sixth Report from the Joint Committee on Statutory Instruments for the Session 1981/2, H.C. 15–viii, paras. 5, 6 and 19; Government Response to the Sixth Report of the Joint Committee on Statutory Instruments, Cmnd. 8600, paras. 4–5; Wade and Philips, *Constitutional and Administrative Law*, 9th edn., pp. 120–2 and 130–3.

The precise meaning of 'merits' is not altogether clear, but the term certainly includes political content. In 1946 a suggestion by the Clerk of the House of Commons

---

[13]   p. 42.

that the scrutiny committee should consider the 'merits of an instrument *as an exercise of the power delegated*' (Third Report from the Select Committee on Procedure for the Session 1945/6, H.C. 189–I, Minutes of Evidence, p. 353, para. 39) was rejected. Although this might draw the committee into controversy, such power is vital, and indeed now probably falls within the heading 'unusual or unexpected use of power' in the committee's present terms of reference, which are set out in para. 3.7 of the next extract.

First Report from the Select Committee on Procedure

H.C. 588, Session 1977/8

Existing provisions for the technical scrutiny of delegated legislation

3.6. The House has devised separate procedures for the technical scrutiny of delegated legislation and the consideration of its merits. Between 1944 and 1973 the technical scrutiny of statutory instruments was undertaken on behalf of the House by a Select Committee on Statutory Instruments.[14] As a result of the recommendations of the Joint Committee on Delegated Legislation in session 1971–72,[15] a Joint Committee on Statutory Instruments was appointed in 1973. The Committee absorbed the work of the Select Committee in relation to statutory instruments laid before both Houses as well as that of the House of Lords Special Orders Committee (first established in 1924) which had scrutinised instruments subject to affirmative procedure only. For the purpose of scrutinising instruments laid before the House of Commons and not before the House of Lords the Commons Members of the Joint Committee meet on their own as a Select Committee. The Joint Committee is chaired by a Member of the House of Commons.

3.7. The Joint Committee is required to consider every statutory instrument laid before Parliament (excluding instruments made under paragraph 1 of Schedule 1 to the Northern Ireland Act 1974) together with every general statutory instrument not required by statute to be laid before Parliament. It is required to determine whether the special attention of the House should be drawn to it on specific grounds, such as: that it imposes a charge on the public revenues; that it purports to have retrospective effect where the parent statute confers no express authority so to provide; that there appears to have been unjustifiable delay in publication or laying; that there appears to be doubt whether it is *intra vires*; that it appears to make unusual or unexpected use of the powers conferred by statute; that its drafting appears to be defective; or on any other grounds not impinging on its merits or the policy behind it. . . . An indication of the volume of the work undertaken by the Statutory Instruments Committee is given in Table I. Table II[16] shows the total number of general statutory instruments made in the period 1948–1977, and indicates that while the numbers fell between the end of the Second World War and the mid-1960s, they appear now to have reached a plateau of between 1,100 and

[14] Originally called the Select Committee on Statutory Rules and Orders, etc.
[15] Op. cit. paras. 55–84.
[16] [Omitted.]

TABLE 1

STATUTORY INSTRUMENTS CONSIDERED BY THE JOINT AND SELECT
COMMITTEES ON STATUTORY INSTRUMENTS, 1972–1977

Session	Affirmative Procedure	Negative Procedure	General (Laid)	General (Unlaid)	Total
1972–73	94	368	22	156	640
1973–74	40	396	29	189	654
1974	75	433	25	174	707
1974–75	147	1,039	90	380	1,656
1975–76	158	906	66	261	1,391
1976–77	127	669	37	197	1,030

NOTES: (a) The great majority of instruments subject to affirmative or negative procedure are general S.I.s. Those listed as 'General (Laid)' are general S.I.s required by the enabling Act to be laid before Parliament but subject to no parliamentary procedure. Those listed as 'General (Unlaid)' are general S.I.s not required to be laid and subject to no parliamentary procedure.

(b) When compared with the figures in Table II those figures indicate the growing proportion of general statutory instruments subject, under the provisions of the enabling Acts, to one or other form of parliamentary procedure.

1,300 per year. On the other hand, the length of instruments has markedly increased: in 1955 the total length of all statutory instruments was 3,240 pages, in 1965 it had grown to 6,435 pages, and in 1974 to 8,667 pages.[17] ...

3.8. Little formal notice is taken of the work of the Joint Committee in the House. There is no procedure to ensure that its views on an instrument are taken into consideration before a substantive decision on the instrument is taken by the House, save that if the Committee has drawn the special attention of the House to an instrument, or has not considered, or completed consideration, of an instrument, an italicised note to that effect is printed on the Order Paper. An adverse report by the Committee has no effect on the manner in which an instrument is considered, and there is no procedure to prevent a substantive decision before the Committee has completed its consideration. In Session 1976–77 this happened in the case of 15 instruments debated on the Floor of the House and nine instruments debated in a Standing Committee.[18] This is in contrast with the House of Lords, whose Standing Order No. 68 prevents an instrument subject to the affirmative procedure being brought before the House for approval until the Joint Committee have reported on it.

[17] Appendix 1, part 1, para. 21.

[18] The Chairman of the Joint Committee told us that in the Commons 'It quite commonly happens that instruments, negative and affirmative, are brought on for debate before the Joint Committee's scrutiny is complete and, indeed, often at a time when the Department concerned is well aware ... that the Committee has queries on the instrument'. Appendix 22.

Existing provisions for the consideration of the merits of statutory instruments

3.9. Consideration of the merits of statutory instruments now takes place either on the Floor of the House, normally after 10.00 p.m. and subject to a time limit of, at the most, one-and-a-half hours, or in a standing committee, with a similar limit on the time of the debate.[19] A time-limit on debates on instruments subject to negative procedure taken after 10.00 p.m. was first introduced in 1954, and on debates on those subject to affirmative procedure in 1967,[20] although the Government occasionally find time for debates on contentious instruments before 10.00 p.m. The reference of statutory instruments to Standing Committees was introduced in 1973, following another recommendation from the Joint Committee on Delegated Legislation, which was primarily concerned to ensure the more adequate consideration of prayers against negative instruments.[21] . . .

3.10 .The present system for the reference of statutory instruments to standing committees[22] has contributed to the alleviation of the pressure of business on the Floor of the House and has provided for the consideration of more, but not all, prayers. It has, however, been subject to criticism, and service on such committees is not universally popular amongst Members. The most obvious drawbacks are (i) that the reference of instruments to a standing committee can only be proposed by a Minister, thus militating against backbench Members who have tabled prayers; (ii) that the procedure may be used indiscriminately by the Government business managers as a means of unloading business from the Floor of the House which would, if taken on the Floor, take little or no time, thus wasting the time of the Members called to serve on the committees; (iii) that, in line with the recommendations of the Joint Committee in session 1971–72, the committees are required to consider instruments on a neutral motion ('That they have considered' the instrument), and are unable to report any kind of recommendation to the House, thus lessening interest in their proceedings; (iv) that the subsequent effective motion in the House can be brought on by the Government for decision without debate at any time, and usually late at night, whatever the committee's decision on the neutral motion put before them; and (v) that in the case of instruments subject to negative procedure the subsequent prayers are rarely brought to the Floor of the House at all. The Chairman of the Joint Committee on Statutory Instruments described the system as 'an unsatisfactory procedural device which has failed to meet the real needs of the

[19] Standing committees dealing with Northern Ireland statutory instruments may sit for up to two-and-a-half hours.

[20] Debates on prayers may not be entered upon or proceeded with after 11.30 p.m., with the proviso that Mr Speaker may adjourn the debate without putting the Question if he is of the opinion that the time for debate has been inadequate (S.O. No. 4). Debates on affirmative instruments must conclude at 11.30 p.m. or 1½ hours after they have begun, whichever is the later, with a similar proviso (S.O. No. 3).

[21] [H.C. 475, Session 1971/2], paras. 110–128.

[22] S.O. No. 73A.

House'.[23] We believe that the system provides only vestigial parliamentary control of statutory instruments – particularly in the case of negative procedure instruments – and is in need of comprehensive reform.

Technical scrutiny

3.12. The Chairman of the Joint Committee on Statutory Instruments told us that in his view 'there would be many difficulties and disadvantages in transferring the functions of the Joint Committee on Statutory Instruments to subject committees with wide-ranging terms of reference'. He drew attention to the advantages of the separate consideration of the form of an instrument and its merits, and found it 'difficult to believe that subject committees would be capable of exercising the same degree of effective vigilance in this technical and specialised field'.[24] We agree with this view, and recommend no change in the powers or composition of the Joint Committee.

3.13. To give greater effect to the work of the Joint Committee, however, we recommend the adoption by the House of a standing order, similar to Standing Order No. 68 of the House of Lords, which would provide that a statutory instrument should not be brought before the House or before a standing committee until the Joint Committee on Statutory Instruments (or the Select Committee, as the case may be) has completed consideration of the instrument. The House of Lords standing order applies only to instruments subject to affirmative procedure. The Joint Committee has recently suggested that the House of Commons, in adopting such a provision, should consider extending it to prayers against instruments subject to the negative procedure.[25] The Committee's Chairman has urged that it should be extended in this way, arguing that 'if reasonable notice is given to the Joint Committee of the proposed timing of a debate, arrangements can nearly always be made to ensure that consideration of an instrument is completed in time.'[26] We believe that the provision should apply to all debates on statutory instruments, subject to either procedure, but in order to avoid unnecessary delays we recommend that it should be possible for the House to refer instruments to standing committees before the Joint Committee's consideration is complete, thus allowing the committees to be summoned, with the proviso that a committee should not complete its work until the Joint Committee has reported.

3.14. Two other suggestions have been made to reinforce the work of the Joint and Select Committees on Statutory Instruments in relation to negative instruments, both of which would require amendments to the Statutory Instruments Act 1946. The Select Committee on Delegated Legislation in session 1952–53 recommended that where the Select Committee on Statutory Instruments had drawn the particular attention of the House to an instrument subject to negative procedure, the period of praying time should be altered to 10 days from the date of the Committee's Report, if that period

---

[23] Appendix 22.   [24] Appendix 22.
[25] First Special Report from the Joint Committee on Statutory Instruments, Session 1977–78 (H.L. 51, H.C. 169), para. 22.   [26] Appendix 22.

would be longer than the 40 days provided under the 1946 Act.[27] We recommend that this proposal be adopted. A second proposal made in evidence to us by the present Chairman of the Joint and Select Committees on Statutory Instruments was that where the Joint or Select Committees have drawn the special attention of the House to such an instrument, the instrument should automatically become subject to the affirmative procedure. This proposal is more far-reaching, in that in would alter the intention of Parliament with respect to the nature of the procedure governing statutory instruments made under numerous previous enabling Acts. It would, however, encourage more care in the preparation of statutory instruments and ensure that all instruments which have been drawn to the special attention of the House by the Joint or Select Committees would be debated. We recommend that consideration be given to this proposal as an alternative to our proposal above for the extension of the praying time.

Consideration of merits

3.15. Our main pre-occupation has been to ensure that the procedure for referring statutory instruments to standing committees should operate in such a way as to ensure the effective expression of opinion on the merits of statutory instruments by Members, either in a Committee or in the House, without needless use of the time of the House. . . . The main effect of our recommendations . . . should be to allow the reference of a larger number of statutory instruments to a committee (or the reference of more contentious statutory instruments) but to ensure that the committees should be able to make specific recommendations to the House and that the House should, in certain defined circumstances, be able to debate those recommendations.

Amendment of statutory instruments

3.19. We have also considered the possibility of procedural and statutory changes to enable the House to propose amendments to statutory instruments. The Chairman of the Joint Committee on Statutory Instruments drew our attention to the practical problems which would be involved, including: the need for agreement between the two Houses, the congestion of parliamentary business and the likely need to relax the existing time limits for debates on statutory instruments. He also emphasised the 'confusion and uncertainty' which would be introduced into the system of delegated legislation including the possibility that Parliament might seek to go beyond the boundaries of delegated authority imposed on the responsible Minister by the enabling statute.[29] Moreover it must be borne in mind that, if statutory instruments were to become subject to amendment by Parliament, Governments might eventually seek to avoid the need for them by writing more detail into bills, and the advantage of flexibility given by statutory instruments could thus be lost.

[27] Report from the Select Committee on Delegated Legislation, Session 1952–53 (H.C. 310), para. 98.
[29] Appendix 22.

3.20. We have concluded that the power to amend statutory instruments would be likely to exacerbate the existing difficulties relating to delegated legislation and to undermine the advantages of the system of delegation. . . .

Notes

1. The Committee's detailed proposals for reform have not been set out because it seems unlikely that they will be implemented. Indeed the recommendation that a statutory instrument should not be brought before the House of Commons until the Joint Committee on Statutory Instruments has completed its deliberations has been rejected. The government has said that 'occasions sometimes arise when the pressure of Parliamentary business, or the need for immediate administrative action prevent debates not taking place before scrutiny. Ministers will, however, do all they can to reduce these instances to the minimum' (see Second Special Report from the Joint Committee on Statutory Instruments for the Session 1977/8, H.C. 579, p. 11) and the situation has improved. In 1980–1 only two instruments were debated in the House of Commons before scrutiny as compared with twenty-four (including those debated in the merits committee) in 1976–7: see Sixth Report from the Joint Committee on Statutory Instruments for the Session 1981/2, H.C. 15–viii.

2. The Joint Committee has also criticized the 'recurring tendency of Departments to seek to by-pass Parliament' by omitting necessary details from instruments, thus conferring upon themselves wide discretion to vary or add to the provisions of an instrument instead of making a new instrument that would itself be subject to Parliamentary control (First Special Report for the Session 1977/8, H.C. 169, paras. 9–12). While recognizing that the need for executive flexibility is one of the justifications for granted delegated powers in the first place, the committee stated that the corollary of this 'must be that the delegated legislation itself should be detailed, specific and self-explanatory and should not depend on the exercise of ministerial or departmental discretion unless provision to that effect is expressly contained in the enabling Statute' (para. 12). The committee felt that rules should not be made by departmental circular when Parliament had enacted a statute providing that they were to be made by statutory instrument subject to further Parliamentary scrutiny. Note also that legislation by circular would avoid the statutory requirements of publication, on which see p. 489 *supra*, but would still be subject to judicial review, on which see Notes 1 and 3, pp. 501 and 522 *supra*. In the same report the Joint Committee also commented that it was disturbed 'by what appears to be an astonishingly casual attitude on the part of the Executive' to the practice of laying instruments before Parliament in manuscript form without a printed version appearing until well after the instrument has become law. This was said to amount 'on the face of it to a cynical disregard of the rights of the subject' to know the law (H.C. 169, Session 1977/8, paras. 17–18).

16

STATUTORY TRIBUNALS

THE TRIBUNAL SYSTEM

Note

The proliferation of statutory tribunals with specialist jurisdictions has been well documented: see Street, *Justice in the Welfare State*, 2nd edn.; Wraith and Hutchesson, *Administrative Tribunals* (hereafter Wraith and Hutchesson); Farmer, *Tribunals and Government*; as well as Wade, Ch. 23. The variety of tribunals, ranging from the highly judicial Lands Tribunal and Social Security Commissioners to those which are more closely involved with the development of policy, makes it very difficult to describe them generically. It also makes it difficult to set out critieria for determining when a dispute should be decided by such a body as opposed to a court or some form of purely administrative process such as a discretionary decision by a minister. See Wraith and Hutchesson, Chs. 9 and 10; Farmer, op. cit., Chs. 1, 7, and 8. One thing that is clear is that, despite the preference for adjudication by the courts expressed by both the Donoughmore Committee in the *Report on Ministers' Powers*, Cmd. 4060, and the Franks Committee (p. 537 *infra*), the number of tribunals has continued to grow. The reasons for this include cheapness, speed, informality, and specialized expertise (p. 537 *infra*). This chapter will consider their constitution and procedures, and the methods by which they are controlled. The starting point will be the *Report of the Committee on Administrative Tribunals and Enquiries*, Cmnd. 218, hereafter the Franks Report, which, reporting in 1957, made a full review of the system and led to the important reforms in the Tribunals and Inquiries Act 1958 (see now the Act of 1971). As there have, since then, been several studies of social welfare tribunals, particular attention will be paid to those tribunals.

As far as the structure of the system is concerned, Wraith and Hutchesson, Ch. 3, distinguish national, regional, and local tribunals. Examples of the first type are the National Insurance Commissioners (now the Social Security Commissioners), who hear appeals from National Insurance Local Tribunals, and the Civil Aviation Authority, the adjudicatory functions of which in relation to disputes concerning the licensing of, for instance, operators or pilots, are only part of a wider jurisdiction. An example of the second type is the Rent Assessment Committee, which sits in sixteen 'Panel Areas', and which is organized with a 'presidential system' (see p. 539 *infra*). National Insurance Local Tribunals and Supplementary Benefit Appeal Tribunals are examples of the third type of tribunal. In some contexts, such as national insurance supplementary benefits and immigration, there is an appellate tribunal (the Social Security Commissioners and the Immigration Appeal Tribunal respectively), in others there is provision for an appeal on a point of law to the Divisional Court under s. 13 of the Tribunals and Inquiries Act 1971 (e.g. Rent Tribunals), while in others (e.g. the National Health Service Tribunal) the only way to question a decision is by seeking judicial review. The increasing willingness of the court to regard questions, particularly questions of law, as going to jurisdiction, and the rediscovery in 1952 of the doctrine of error of law on the face of the record (see p. 62 *supra*; Wraith and Hutchesson, pp. 157–61; Wade, pp. 791 and 822–3), have sometimes been used as arguments for not providing any form of appeal (Annual Report of the Council on Tribunals for 1972/3, p. 16). Do you think this is a sound approach? It should be noted that judicial action has not affected all areas equally. Social security, for instance, is an area in which there has been judicial restraint. See *R. v. Preston S.B.A.T., ex p. Moore* p. 77 *supra*; Williams in *Welfare Law and Policy* (eds. Partington and Jowell) p. 101. There may, however, now be an appeal in such cases: see p. 568 *infra*.

The Council on Tribunals, established as a consequence of the Franks Report, albeit in a very modified form (see p. 568 *infra*), has been concerned with the need to avoid an undue proliferation of tribunals. The Annual Report for 1969/70 stated (at para. 45):

> The fundamental difficulty is that each government department frames its own proposals for tribunals, usually as part of a scheme of important legislation in which the tribunal machinery attracts little public and parliamentary attention. There is usually a tight time-table and a strong reluctance to disturb existing arrangements. In the result, legislation about tribunals tends to be shaped by the short term exigencies of political and administrative convenience rather than by any coherent long term policy. In particular, it may tend to produce relatively weak tribunals with awkward divisions of jurisdiction between them.

It appears from the Annual Reports for 1970/1 (Part II) and 1972/3 (para. 18) that little has been done to improve matters.

Report of The Committee on Administrative Tribunals and Enquiries

Cmnd. 218 (1957)

PART I

CHAPTER 2

THE SCOPE AND NATURE OF OUR ENQUIRY

5. Our terms of reference involve the consideration of an important part of the relationship between the individual and authority. At different times in the history of this country it has been necessary to adjust this relationship and to seek a new balance between private right and public advantage, between fair play for the individual and efficiency of administration. The balance found has varied with different governmental systems and different social patterns. Since the war the British electorate has chosen Governments which accepted general responsibilities for the provision of extended social services and for the broad management of the economy. It has consequently become desirable to consider afresh the procedures by which the rights of individual citizens can be harmonised with wider public interests.

Disputes between the individual and authority

7. How do disputes between the individual and authority arise in this country at the present time? In general the starting point is the enactment of legislation by Parliament. Many statutes apply detailed schemes to the whole or to large classes of the community (for example national insurance) or lay on a Minister and other authorities a general duty to provide a service (for

example education or health). Such legislation is rarely sufficient in itself to achieve all its objects, and a series of decisions by administrative bodies, such as Government Departments and local authorities is often required. For example, in a national insurance scheme decisions have to be given on claims to benefit, and in providing an educational service decisions have to be taken on the siting of new schools. Many of these decisions affect the rights of individual citizens, who may then object.

8. Once objection has been raised, a further decision becomes inevitable. This further decision is of a different kind: whether to confirm, cancel or vary the original decision. In reaching it account must be taken not only of the original decision but also of the objection.

The resolution of these disputes

9. These further decisions are made in various ways. Some are made in courts of law and therefore by the procedure of a court of law. For example, an order made by a local authority for the demolition of an insanitary house may be appealed against to the County Court. Frequently the statutes lay down that these further decisions are to be made by a special tribunal or a Minister. For example, a contested claim to national insurance benefit has to be determined by a special tribunal, and the decision whether or not to confirm an opposed scheme for the compulsory acquisition of land by a local authority must be made by the Minister concerned. In these cases the procedure to be followed in dealing with objections to the first decision and in arriving at the further decision is laid down in the statute or in regulations made thereunder.

10. But over most of the field of public administration no formal procedure is provided for objecting or deciding on objections. For example, when foreign currency or a scarce commodity such as petrol or coal is rationed or allocated, there is no other body to which an individual applicant can appeal if the responsible administrative authority decides to allow him less than he has requested. Of course the aggrieved individual can always complain to the appropriate administrative authority, to his Member of Parliament, to a representative organisation or to the press. But there is no formal procedure on which he can insist.

11. There are therefore two broad distinctions to be made among these further decisions which we have been discussing. The first is between those decisions which follow a statutory procedure and those which do not. The second distinction is within the group of decisions subject to a statutory procedure. Some of these decisions are taken in the ordinary courts and some are taken by tribunals or by Ministers after a special procedure.[1]

12. These two distinctions are essential for understanding our terms of reference. We are not instructed to consider those many cases in which no formal procedure has been prescribed. Nor are we instructed to consider

[1] [Decisions taken by a minister after a special procedure has been followed are considered in Ch. 17 *infra.*]

decisions made in the ordinary courts. What we are instructed to consider are the cases in which the decision on objections, the further decision as we have called it, is taken by a tribunal or by a Minister after a special procedure has been followed.

13. At this stage two comments may be added. First, although the foregoing broad analysis holds good over nearly all the field covered by our terms of reference, there are a few tribunals (for example Rent Tribunals) which determine disputes not between the individual and authority but between citizen and citizen, . . . [The second is omitted.]

Developments since the Donoughmore Report[2] . . .

17. At the time when the Donoughmore Committee was appointed there already existed a number of tribunals, almost entirely in the field of unemployment insurance and contributory and war pensions; and local authorities already possessed considerable powers to acquire or restrict the use of private land. Since then the expansion of governmental activities and responsibilities has led to corresponding developments and innovations in our field on a large scale. Old tribunals have been adapted to wider purposes, and new tribunals have been established.[3] . . .

CHAPTER 3

20. It is noteworthy that Parliament, having decided that the decisions with which we are concerned should not be remitted to the ordinary courts, should also have decided that they should not be left to be reached in the normal course of administration. Parliament has considered it essential to lay down special procedures for them.

Good administration

21. This must have been to promote good administration. Administration must not only be efficient in the sense that the objectives of policy are securely attained without delay. It must also satisfy the general body of citizens that it is proceeding with reasonable regard to the balance between the public interest which it promotes and the private interest which it disturbs. Parliament has, we infer, intended in relation to the subject-matter of our terms of reference that the further decisions or, as they may rightly be termed in this context, adjudications must be acceptable as having been properly made.

22. It is natural that Parliament should have taken this view of what constitutes good administration. In this country government rests fundamentally upon the consent of the governed. The general acceptability of these adjudications is one of the vital elements in sustaining that consent.

Openness, fairness and impartiality

23. When we regard our subject in this light, it is clear that there are

[2] [*Report of the Committee on Ministers' Powers*, Cmd. 4060.]
[3] [For the general impact of decisions by tribunals see the table in Wade, p. 824, of the numbers of cases heard.]

certain general and closely linked characteristics which should mark these special procedures. We call these characteristics openness, fairness and impartiality.

24. Here we need only give brief examples of their application. Take openness. If these procedures were wholly secret, the basis of confidence and acceptability would be lacking. Next take fairness. If the objector were not allowed to state his case, there would be nothing to stop oppression. Thirdly, there is impartiality. How can the citizen be satisfied unless he feels that those who decide his case come to their decision with open minds?

25. To assert that openness, fairness and impartiality are essential characteristics of our subject-matter is not to say that they must be present in the same way and to the same extent in all its parts. Difference in the nature of the issue for adjudication may give good reasons for difference in the degree to which the three general characteristics should be developed and applied. Again, the method by which a Minister arrives at a decision after a hearing or enquiry cannot be the same as that by which a tribunal arrives at a decision. . . . For the moment it is sufficient to point out that when Parliament sets up a tribunal to decide cases, the adjudication is placed outside the Department concerned. The members of the tribunal are neutral and impartial in relation to the policy of the Minister, except in so far as that policy is contained in the rules which the tribunal has been set up to apply. . . .

The allocation of decisions to tribunals and Ministers

26. At this stage another question naturally arises. On what principle has it been decided that some adjudications should be made by tribunals and some by Ministers? If from a study of the history of the subject we could discover such a principle, we should have a criterion which would be a guide for any future allocation of these decisions between tribunals and Ministers.

27. The search for this principle has usually involved the application of one or both of two notions, each with its antithesis. Both notions are famous and have long histories. They are the notion of what is judicial, its antithesis being what is administrative, and the notion of what is according to the rule of law, its antithesis being what is arbitrary.

29. The rule of law stands for the view that decisions should be made by the application of known principles or laws. In general such decisions will be predictable, and the citizen will know where he is. On the other hand there is what is arbitrary. A decision may be made without principle, without any rules. It is therefore unpredictable, the antithesis of a decision taken in accordance with the rule of law.

30. Nothing that we say diminishes the importance of these pairs of antitheses. But it must be confessed that neither pair yields a valid principle on which one can decide whether the duty of making a certain decision should be laid upon a tribunal or upon a Minister or whether the existing allocation of decisions between tribunals and Ministers is appropriate. But even if there is

no such principle and we cannot explain the facts, we can at least start with them. An empirical approach may be the most useful.

31.   Starting with the facts, we observe that the methods of adjudication by tribunals are in general not the same as those of adjudication by Ministers. All or nearly all tribunals apply rules. . . . Many matters remitted to tribunals and Ministers appear to have, as it were, a natural affinity with one or other method of adjudication. Sometimes the policy of the legislation can be embodied in a system of detailed regulations. Particular decisions cannot, single case by single case, alter the Minister's policy. Where this is so, it is natural to entrust the decisions to a tribunal, if not to the courts. On the other hand it is sometimes desirable to preserve flexibility of decision in the pursuance of public policy. Then a wise expediency is the proper basis of right adjudication, and the decision must be left with a Minister.

32.   But in other instances there seems to be no such natural affinity. For example, there seems to be no natural affinity which makes it clearly appropriate for appeals in goods vehicle licence cases to be decided by the Transport Tribunal when appeals in a number of road passenger cases are decided by the Minister.

33.   We shall therefore respect this factual difference between tribunals and Ministers and deal separately with the two parts of the subject. When considering tribunals we shall see how far the three characteristics of openness, fairness and impartiality can be developed and applied in general and how far their development and application must be adapted to the circumstances of particular tribunals. . . .

TRIBUNALS IN GENERAL

CHAPTER 4

INTRODUCTORY

The development of tribunals . . .

36.   Tribunals today vary widely in constitution, function and procedure. Appointments of chairmen and members are usually made by the Minister responsible for the legislation under which they operate, but some are made by the Crown and some by the Lord Chancellor, even though he may have no direct responsibility for the subject-matter of their work. Most tribunals deal with cases in which an individual citizen is at issue with a Government Department or other public body concerning his rights or obligations under a statutory scheme. But a few (for example Rent Tribunals) are concerned with disputes between citizens. Still others (for example the Licensing Authorities for Public Service and Goods Vehicles) have regulatory functions and are therefore just as much administrative bodies as they are adjudicating tribunals. Some tribunals, like the courts, have a detailed code of procedure, with testimony on oath and strict rules of evidence. Most have a simple

procedure, usually without the oath. . . . Finally, there are differences regarding appeals. Sometimes there is no appeal, and further redress can only be had by seeking a court order to set aside the decision. But in most cases there is an appeal – either to an appellate tribunal, a Minister or the courts.

37. Reflection on the general social and economic changes of recent decades convinces us that tribunals as a system for adjudication have come to stay. The tendency for issues arising from legislative schemes to be referred to special tribunals is likely to grow rather than to diminish. . . .

The choice between tribunals and courts of law

38. We agree with the Donoughmore Committee that tribunals have certain characteristics which often given them advantages over the courts. These are cheapness, accessibility, freedom from technicality, expedition and expert knowledge of their particular subject. . . . But as a matter of general principle we are firmly of the opinion that a decision should be entrusted to a court rather than to a tribunal in the absence of special considerations which make a tribunal more suitable.

39. . . . [I]f all decisions arising from new legislation were automatically vested in the ordinary courts the judiciary would by now have been grossly overburdened. . . . We agree with the Permanent Secretary to the Lord Chancellor[4] that any wholesale transfer to the courts of the work of tribunals would be undesirable. . . .

Tribunals as machinery for adjudication

40. Tribunals are not ordinary courts, but neither are they appendages of Government Departments. Much of the official evidence, including that of the Joint Permanent Secretary to the Treasury, appeared to reflect the view that tribunals should properly be regarded as part of the machinery of administration, for which the Government must retain a close and continuing responsibility. Thus, for example, tribunals in the social service field would be regarded as adjuncts to the administration of the services themselves. We do not accept this view. We consider that tribunals should properly be regarded as machinery provided by Parliament for adjudication rather than as part of the machinery of administration. The essential point is that in all these cases Parliament has deliberately provided for a decision outside and independent of the Department concerned, either at first instance (for example in the case of Rent Tribunals and the Licensing Authorities for Public Service and Goods Vehicles) or on appeal from a decision of a Minister or of an official in a special statutory position (for example a valuation officer or an insurance officer). Although the relevant statutes do not in all cases expressly enact that tribunals are to consist entirely of persons outside the Government service, the use of the term 'tribunal' in legislation undoubtedly bears this connotation, and the intention of Parliament to provide for the independence of tribunals is clear and unmistakable.

---

[4] [In his written evidence to the Committee; days 6–7, pp. 191–2.]

The application of the principles of openness, fairness and impartiality

41. We have already expressed our belief, in Part I, that Parliament in deciding that certain decisions should be reached only after a special procedure must have intended that they should manifest three basic characteristics: openness, fairness and impartiality. The choice of a tribunal rather than a Minister as the deciding authority is itself a considerable step towards the realisation of these objectives, particularly the third. But in some cases the statutory provisions and the regulations thereunder fall short of what is required to secure these objectives. . . .

42. In the field of tribunals openness appears to us to require the publicity of proceedings and knowledge of the essential reasoning underlying the decisions; fairness to require the adoption of a clear procedure which enables parties to know their rights, to present their case fully and to know the case which they have to meet; and impartiality to require the freedom of tribunals from the influence, real or apparent, of Departments concerned with the subject-matter of their decisions.

The proposed Councils on Tribunals

43. These general statements give expression, in the field of tribunals, to that fair play for the citizen which it is both the citizen's right to expect and the duty of good administration to provide. We shall now attempt to work out in some detail the proper application of these principles. Our most important recommendation in this Part of the Report is that two standing councils, one for England and Wales and one for Scotland, should be set up to keep the constitution and working of tribunals under continuous review. . . .

Notes

1. Many of the recommendations of the Franks Report were implemented by the Tribunals and Inquiries Act 1958 (re-enacted with amendments in 1971). Although the proposal for a Council on Tribunals was only partially implemented (see p. 568 *infra*), the Council now exists to keep under review the constitution and working of the tribunals specified in Sch. 1 to the 1971 Act. This in fact includes nearly all statutory tribunals. The Council supervises most central government tribunals; for a list, together with relevant rights of appeal, see Wade, p. 824. See also Wade, p. 798, for those tribunals which are not subject to the Council's control.

2. See Farmer, *Tribunals and Government*, pp. 182–97, for a different approach. Farmer argues that the Franks Report with its basic characteristics of openness, fairness, and impartiality is 'unduly restrictive and serves to exclude certain tribunals which have an indistinguishable constitutional purpose from *some* of those which are included'. He adopts a distinction between 'court-substitute' and 'policy-orientated' tribunals (see Abel Smith and Stevens, *In Search of Justice*, pp. 220–1). In the latter, but not the former, the minister often retains the power to issue directions on procedure or even policy (e.g. s. 58 (6) of the Transport Act 1962; s. 59 (2) of the Transport Act 1968; s. 3 (2) of the Civil Aviation Act 1971). These differences in classification may be important in the context of judicial review. Compare the distinction made in *Re Racal Communications Ltd.*, p. 58 *supra*, between 'courts of law' and 'administrative tribunals or authorities'.

3. One structural method that has been used to ensure that tribunals are part of the machinery of adjudication rather than the machinery of administration is to develop the 'presidential system' for certain tribunals. Under this a full time national or regional officer, usually with legal qualifications, is appointed by the Lord Chancellor to be responsible for co-ordinating the administration and practice of the tribunals in question. Examples include the Pensions Appeal Tribunals (President), the Lands Tribunal (President) and Supplementary Benefit Appeal Tribunals (Senior Chairmen). See further Robson, (1979) 32 C.L.P. 107 at p. 113; pp. 544 and 572 *infra*; and the next extract. The alternative is to have a number of separate and independent tribunals or a number of separate panels of one tribunal sitting in different parts of the country.

Administrative Tribunals

R. E. Wraith and P. G. Hutchesson

pp. 84 and 90–2

THE PRESIDENTIAL SYSTEM

Certainly the most interesting development from the structural point of view has been the recent application of the presidential idea to tribunals which meet locally in a great many different places.

The Advantages of the Presidential System . . .

There is *first* the question of manifest independence from a parent department, emphasized by the fact that presidential tribunals have their own independent premises, on whose notice-boards and stationery the name of a government department does not appear. There is no evidence that tribunals which are served by departmental staff, or even held on departmental premises, are less impartial or independent than others, but their public appearance is obviously open to criticism. One might in theory suppose that it was more urgent to have a presidential system for tribunals where the issue was between citizen and state rather than between citizen and citizen, but neither rent assessment panels nor (in much of their jurisdiction) industrial tribunals quite bear this out. Manifest independence is important whatever the nature of the issue.

Second, there is a group of considerations which could be brought together under the general head of 'communication'. One aspect of this is communication between a department and a tribunal, which ought occasionally to take place but which is open to the criticism of interference with independent adjudication if a department communicates directly with, say, a local tribunal chairman. If there is a national or regional president who stands above the battle such communication is eased. Similarly there are matters on which it is easier for the Council on Tribunals to communicate with a president than with either a department or a local tribunal chairman.[5]

[5] See Annual Report 1969–70 para. 50. 'Where tribunals are organized under a President with some administrative responsibility for their working we find that our task of keeping a general oversight . . . is very much less difficult.'

Another aspect of communication is the passing, up and down the line, of information and ideas. For example, the bi-annual meetings of rent assessment panel presidents under the aegis of the London President have served the dual purpose of advising the Department and of keeping their own panels in touch with current legislation, recent court decisions and the practice of panels in other parts of the country. Some presidents have devised check lists of points to be accounted for at hearings, of basic questions to which answers must always be sought, or of criteria which should be applied in particular situations, and have circulated these as *aides-mémoire* to tribunal members. Visits by a national President to the regions, by regional presidents to local tribunals, or occasional conferences of them all foster team spirit and a sense of purpose which is none the less important for being somewhat elusive to define. In the light of hindsight it is evident, for example, that the rent tribunals' deficiencies in the 1950s and early 1960s need not have developed if they had been supported by such a system.

Third, presidents, and particularly regional presidents, play an important part in public relations. The public becomes aware not of an amorphous department but of a prominent local figure, inevitably known for other public activities. . . .

Fourth, although primarily the head of a team of adjudicators a president is also head of an office administered by a seconded civil servant, whom he is able to advise and support more easily and appropriately than could the Department.

Fifth, and less visible on the surface, national presidents exercise a considerable influence over the development of tribunal case law through their function of selecting cases to be reported.

Sixth, the presidential system promotes consistency, not only of practice and procedure but of decisions, the converse of which was to be seen in the rent tribunals of the 1950s.

The advantage of flexibility which is claimed for the presidential system is perhaps over-stated, for government departments can be equally flexible. For example officials of the DHSS are quick to adjust supply to demand by asking tribunal members to cross their normal frontiers should occasion arise, by establishing tribunals in new places or closing them down should they become redundant. On the other hand, presidents can stimulate, inform or broaden the experience of members, and ascertain that all are carrying a fair share of duty, more effectively than a regional office of the Department. . . .

Question

Is the presidential system equally useful for policy-orientated tribunals and court-substitutes? What are its disadvantages?

Note

See also p. 572 *infra* for the views of the Council on Tribunals on the presidential system.

Independence. Membership

Report of the Committee on Administrative Tribunals and Enquiries

Cmnd. 218 (1957)

The appointment of chairmen and members[6]

45. We have already said that it is important to secure the independence of the personnel of tribunals from the Departments concerned with the subject-matter of their decisions. This is particularly so when a Government Department is a frequent party to proceedings before a tribunal. We wish to make it clear that we have received no significant evidence that any influence is in fact exerted upon members of tribunals by Government Departments. But present practice can give no guarantee for the future. It appears to us undesirable in principle that the appointment of so many chairmen and members of tribunals should rest solely with the Ministers concerned, and we have received some evidence that this method of appointment can lead to misunderstanding.

46. A substantial volume of the evidence has advocated the appointment of all chairmen and members of tribunals by the Lord Chancellor. There is no doubt that such a change would serve to stress the independence of tribunals; it might also, by reason of the esteem in which the office of Lord Chancellor is held, enhance their status. The change would not involve any new principle, since the Lord Chancellor is already responsible for the appointment not only of a number of chairmen of tribunals but in some cases for the appointment of members also.

47. On the other hand some evidence placed before us, particularly by the Permanent Secretary to the Lord Chancellor, while accepting as reasonable that the Lord Chancellor should appoint all chairmen whether legally qualified or not, opposed the suggestion that the Lord Chancellor should appoint all members of tribunals. . . . [I]t was argued that responsibility for all appointments to tribunals would involve duplication of work with those Departments which already have, in their own regional or local organisations or in local advisory committees, adequate facilities for scrutinising nominations for such appointments. It was also urged upon us that to require the Lord Chancellor to exercise patronage in cases so numerous that it would be obvious that he could not give personal consideration to the choice of the candidates would be to weaken his authority as an instrument of judicial patronage.

48. We appreciate the force of the contention that all appointments to tribunals should be made by the Lord Chancellor so as to demonstrate clearly the intention that tribunals should be wholly independent of departmental influence. But we feel that the best practical course would be for the responsi-

---

[6] [The Committee recommended that the arrangements for considering the reappointment should be the same as those for considering new appointments. (para. 51).]

bility of the Lord Chancellor for such appointments not to be extended beyond the chairman, though we consider that he should retain his present responsibility for appointing members of certain tribunals and that there may be scope for extending this responsibility to a few other tribunals.

49. Although we are unable to recommend that all members of tribunals should be appointed by the Lord Chancellor we are satisfied that their appointment should not rest with the Ministers concerned with the subject-matter of the adjudications. In order to enhance the independence of tribunals, both in appearance and in fact, we consider that the Council on Tribunals should make these appointments. We see no need for the Council to review any existing appointments.

The qualifications of chairmen and members

55. There has been substantial agreement among witnesses that at any rate the majority of chairmen of tribunals should have legal qualifications. We attach great importance to the quality of chairmanship. Objectivity in the treatment of cases and the proper sifting of facts are most often best secured by having a legally qualified chairman, though we recognise that suitable chairmen can be drawn from fields other than the law. We therefore recommend that chairmen of tribunals should ordinarily have legal qualifications but that the appointment of persons without legal qualifications should not be ruled out when they are particularly suitable.

56. It is impossible, we think, to lay down any such general desideratum in the case of members because of the wide variety of experience which has to be drawn on for the different tribunals. Such evidence as we have received indicates that the quality of members is on the whole satisfactory, and we have ourselves no general proposals to make with regard to their qualifications. The new arrangements which we have recommended for the appointment of members will maintain and may well improve their quality.

The chairmen and members of appellate tribunals

58. Everything we have said so far in this Chapter applies also to tribunals which hear appeals from tribunals of first instance, except that all chairmen of appellate tribunals should have legal qualifications. Also the quality of membership should be higher than that in tribunals of first instance.

Clerks

59. The practice whereby the majority of clerks of tribunals are provided by the Government Departments concerned from their local and regional staffs seems partly to be responsible for the feeling in the minds of some people that tribunals are dependent upon and influenced by those Departments. Not only for this reason but also becasuse there would appear to be advantages in improving the general quality of tribunal clerks we have considered the possibility of establishing under the Lord Chancellor's Department a central corps of clerks from which a service could be provided for all tribunals.

60. Though this idea has many attractions we have, after careful consideration, rejected it. It would have the advantage of further enhancing

the independence of tribunals, and it would be more appropriate for independent clerks to advise and help applicants than for departmental clerks to do so. The main objection is that it is difficult to see how any reasonable prospects of a career could be held out to the members of such a general service. It would also be difficult to arrange sittings for the various tribunals in one area in such a way that the clerks were fully occupied and the tribunals could meet when most convenient to the members. Finally, it would no longer be possible for the social service Departments to give some members of their staff a period of service as clerks of tribunals which is doubtless valuable in developing the outlook appropriate to the administration of a social service.

61. We therefore consider that the present arrangements for providing clerks of tribunals should continue. In order, however, to ensure that departmental clerks cannot exercise a departmental influence upon tribunals, we regard it as essential that their duties and conduct should be regulated on the advice of the Council on Tribunals. The general principles to be followed are that the duties of a clerk should be confined to secretarial work, the taking of such notes of evidence as may be required and the tendering of advice, when requested, on points connected with the tribunal's functions. Like a magistrates' clerk he should be debarred from retiring with the tribunal when they consider their decision, unless he is sent for to advise on a specific point.

Note

The recommendation that the Council on Tribunals should appoint the members of tribunals was not implemented. The Council is, in fact, a purely advisory body: see s. 5 of the Tribunals and Inquiries Act 1971, which provides that the Council may make 'general recommendations' to the appropriate Minister as to the making of appointments to membership of the specified tribunals (pp. 545 and 569 *infra*) and that the Minister shall have regard to such recommendations.

Tribunals and Inquiries Act 1971

7. – (1) The chairman, or any person appointed to act as chairman, of any of the tribunals to which this subsection applies shall (without prejudice to any statutory provisions as to qualifications) be selected by the appropriate authority from a panel of persons appointed by the Lord Chancellor.

(2) Members of panels constituted under this section shall hold and vacate office under the terms of the instruments under which they are appointed, but may resign office by notice in writing to the Lord Chancellor; and any such member who ceases to hold office shall be eligible for re-appointment.

(4) The person or persons constituting any such tribunal as is specified in paragraph 16 of Schedule 1[7] to this Act shall be appointed by the Lord Chancellor, and where such a tribunal consists of more than one person the Lord Chancellor shall designate which of them is to be the chairman.

(5) In this section 'the appropriate authority' means the Minister who apart from this Act would be empowered to appoint or select the chairman, person to act as chairman, members or member of the tribunal in question. . . .

---

[7] [Mines and Quarries Tribunals.]

8. – (1) Subject to subsection (2) of this section, no power of a Minister other than the Lord Chancellor to terminate a person's membership of any such tribunal as is specified in Schedule 1 to this Act, or of a panel constituted for the purposes of any such tribunal, shall be exercisable except with the consent of

(a) the Lord Chancellor, the Lord President of the Court of Session and the Lord Chief Justice of Northern Ireland, if the tribunal sits in all parts of the United Kingdom;

(b) the Lord Chancellor and the Lord President of the Court of Session, if the tribunal sits in all parts of Great Britain;

(c) the Lord Chancellor and the Lord Chief Justice of Northern Ireland, if the tribunal sits both in England and Wales and in Northern Ireland;

(d) the Lord Chancellor, if the tribunal does not sit outside England and Wales;

(e) The Lord President of the Court of Session, if the tribunal sits only in Scotland;

(f) the Lord Chief Justice of Northern Ireland, if the tribunal sits only in Northern Ireland. . . .

Notes

1. See Wade, p. 824, for the tribunals specified in Sch. 1 and see *infra*.

2. The Council on Tribunals has recommended that chairmen of tribunals should normally be legally qualified, stating (Annual Report for 1959, para. 29) that its experience showed that proceedings did not tend to become more formal with a legally qualified chairman. See also Annual Report for 1964, paras. 53–5; Bell, pp. 554 and 556 *infra*. Cf. p. 565 *infra*.

3. On the need for independent clerks, see Bell, p. 550 *infra*; pp. 563 and 573 *infra*; Annual Report of the Council on Tribunals for 1973/4, paras. 77–8.

4. In the Introduction to the 1970 edition of the Supplementary Benefits Handbook, Lord Collison, then Chairman of the Supplementary Benefits Commission, said:

An exclusively legal approach to a non-contributory benefits scheme can only lead to a narrower not a broader scheme of the 'rights' of claimants, since those rights are or should be social as well as legal.

Compare this with the approach of Donnison, the last Chairman (p. 112 *supra*). How would these different approaches affect the arguments for and against requiring chairmen of S.B.A.T.s to be legally qualified? See also the Social Security Act 1979, Sch. 2, § 11 (provision for the appointment of legally qualified Senior Chairmen of S.B.A.T.s to oversee the workings of tribunals, hear complaints about the conduct of hearings, and participate in the selection of chairmen and clerks).

Representation and Administrative Tribunals

A. Frost and C. Howard

pp. 22 and 44

[This reports on a series of studies of National Insurance Local Tribunals, Supplementary Benefits Appeal Tribunals, and Rent Tribunals in two

D.H.S.S. administrative regions, London South and North-west Merseyside, during the period 1971–4.]

TABLE 2.8 Age of the respondents*

Age	Chairmen and members %	Appellants %	Representatives %
Under 35	1·7	34·0	40·5
35–under 60	44·3	46·3	39·6
60 or over	53·9	19·9	10·9
Total	100 (N = 115)	100 (N = 229)	100 (N = 101)

* Totals may not agree with sample size as cases where there is no information are excluded.

TABLE 4.1 The process by which tribunal chairmen and members were selected*

Process	%
Through trade union	33·3
Through local/regional office of DHSS/Department of Employment	16·7
Through personal contact with tribunal or DHSS	8·8
Through place of employment	7
Through Home Office or Lord Chancellor's Office	6·1
Through self-nomination	3·5
Through Chamber of Commerce or employers' association	3·5
Through the Law Society	1·8
Other (including combination of above)	11·4
Did not know	7·9
Total	100 (N = 114)

* Total does not agree with sample size because one case where there is no information is excluded.

Notes

1. On the membership of tribunals, see further Bell, p. 546 *infra*; Wraith and Hutchesson, Ch. 4; Cavenagh and Newton, [1971] *Public Administration* 218; Lister, *Justice for the Claimant*, C.P.A.G. Poverty Research Series No. 4, pp. 4–8; Flockhart, Ch. 8 in *Justice, Discretion and Poverty* (eds. Adler and Bradley).

A common pattern is to have an independent chairman and two unpaid lay members representing different interest groups – such as employers and employees or property owners and tenants. The chairman may or may not be legally qualified. In some cases where a particular expertise is required membership may be drawn from a particular profession such as surveyors for the Lands Tribunal or doctors for Medical Appeal Tribunals. An attempt is made to ensure that representatives of all sorts of groups serve on tribunals. For instance, the Council on Tribunals has commented on the 'remarkably low' proportion of women serving on tribunals (Annual Reports for

1971/2, para. 87, 1972/3, paras. 74–6, and 1974/5, paras. 82–3. Wraith and Hutchesson point out (at p. 113) that 'it is a matter of common observation, and not infrequently of complaint, that the average age of tribunal members is high and that tribunals have become too much the province of the retired'.

2. On the presidential system see pp. 539 and 540 *supra* and p. 572 *infra*.

A Case Study

Department of Health and Social Security Research Study on Supplementary Benefits Appeal Tribunals, Review of main findings; Conclusions; Recommendations

Kathleen Bell

Adjudication in Supplementary Benefits – the statutory framework

In Britain, appeal tribunals for settling disputes about entitlement to and amount of benefit have from the beginning been a feature of centrally administered non-contributory benefit schemes.

The National Assistance Act 1948 reconstituted the previously existing tribunals and gave legislative expression to procedures which had been developing since 1934. Under that Act national assistance appeal tribunals became responsible for hearing and deciding appeals against determinations of the National Assistance Board. Further developments were embodied in the Ministry of Social Security Act 1966.[8] This abolished the National Assistance Board and set up the Supplementary Benefits Commission (S.B.C.)[9] to administer the new scheme of supplementary benefits. Thus it again became necessary to reconstitute the appeal tribunals. Schedule 3 of the 1966 Act (as amended) requires that each S.B.A.T. shall consist of a chairman and two other members appointed by the Secretary of State, one of whom shall be appointed from among persons appearing to the Secretary of State to represent workpeople. In practice this member is appointed from a panel nominated by the local Trades Council Federation. The second member is appointed from a panel of persons selected by the Secretary of State. Qualifications for the 'other member' are not statutorily prescribed but the broad aim is to appoint people with relevant knowledge and appropriate ability. Chairmen are selected by the Secretary of State from a panel appointed by the Lord Chancellor . . . in accordance with section 7 of the Tribunals and Inquiries Act 1971. Each tribunal has jurisdiction over an area assigned to it by the Secretary of State. There is no requirement that chairmen be legally qualified and in practice they have often served previously as members. Chairmen but not members are paid fees.

[8] [See now the Supplementary Benefits Act 1976, the Social Security Act 1979, and the Social Security Act 1980.]

[9] [Abolished by s. 6 (2) of the Social Security Act 1980. Decisions on entitlement to benefit will be the responsibility of benefit officers. Matters of policy will be determined by ministers aided by the Social Security Advisory Committee (s. 9).]

S.B.A.Ts. are appellate authorities for determining appeals from decisions under the Family Income Supplements Act 1970 but, in fact, their case loads consist mainly of supplementary benefit appeals. Under the 1966 Act a claimant of supplementary benefit has the right of appeal against the Commission if dissatisfied with decision on his or her claim, with a refusal to review an award or with a condition attaching to an award of benefit. The tribunal is empowered either to confirm the disputed decision or substitute for it any other which the Commission could have made. In law it is bound only by the relevant statutes and regulations and therefore within that framework possesses wide jurisdiction and discretionary power. . . .

Procedure is governed by statutory rules made by the Secretary of State under Schedule 3 of the 1966 Act.[10] These provide a general framework within which chairmen have a good deal of freedom in the actual conduct of hearings. Informality is the keynote and evidence is not taken on oath. Legal aid is not available but legal advice may be obtained under the provision of the Legal Aid Act 1974. From an appellant's point of view the main features of the procedural rules are:

1. Appeals must be made in writing, normally within 21[11] days of notification of the decision.
2. Reasonable notice of the time and place of the hearing must be given together with copies of the documents supplied to the tribunal for the purpose of the appeal.
3. Provided the appellant does not object, the hearing may proceed in the absence of any one member of the tribunal other than the chairman.
4. The tribunal may hear and decide an appeal in the absence of the appellant provided that due notice of the hearing has been given and documents have been provided.
5. The tribunal may adjourn a hearing if it sees fit and an appellant may ask for an adjournment.
6. The appellant and any other interested party (e.g. the Commission) is entitled to attend the hearing, to be heard, to be accompanied or represented, legally or otherwise, normally by not more than 2 persons, and to call witnesses. The right to representation is not affected by absence of the appellant.
7. Hearings are private. The public and press are not admitted.
8. The tribunal is required to record and give a written statement of the reasons for its decision.[12] Copies of this must be sent to the appellant and any other interested party as soon as possible.
9. Provision is made for payment of travelling expenses and compensation for loss of remunerative time.

[10] The Supplementary Benefit (Appeal Tribunal) Rules 1971 (S.I. 1971 No. 680) and The Family Income Supplements (Appeal Tribunal) Rules 1971 (S.I. 1971 No. 622). [Now superseded by the Supplementary Benefit and Family Income Supplements (Appeal) Rules 1980 (S.I. 1980 No. 1605).]

[11] [Now twenty-eight days (S.I. 1980 No. 1605, r. 4).]

[12] [By S.I. 1980 No. 1605, r. 7 (2), the tribunal is now legally obliged to record its findings of fact and to indicate whether and, if so, why one of its members dissents.]

General Review of Findings

The research was designed as a study of the working of the supplementary benefit appeal system looking particularly at its independence, impartiality, consistency and general quality. It was hoped that some light might be shed on the experiences of ordinary people using the machinery, on any difficulties they may encounter in exercising their rights of appeal effectively and on the kinds of assistance likely to be most helpful to them. . . .

1. *The Tribunals*

Undoubtedly chairmen and members were well disposed and well mentioned. But the degree of commitment to the work varied – especially amongst members. In my view there were too many occasions when a member was missing, thus necessitating a two-person tribunal. One session had to be cancelled as neither of the members turned up.

Chairmen varied widely –

(a) in the scope, manner and effectiveness of their introduction before each hearing and in their ability to make clear to appellants the essential facts about the tribunal and its procedure.

(b) in the order in which they conducted hearings.

(c) in their knowledge and understanding of the law relating to supplementary benefits.

(d) in their knowledge and understanding of the jurisdiction of S.B.A.Ts.

(e) in their ability to understand and differentiate law and policy.

(f) in their understanding of the tribunal's use of discretionary powers in the legislation and their ability to maintain reasonable consistency in its exercise.

(g) in their ability to control the proceedings during the hearing, by allowing both parties a full hearing, moving logically, step by step, from testing the evidence to establishment of the facts and the application of the law to the facts as found.

(h) in their ability to recognise situations in which an adjournment is indicated.

(i) in their ability to recognise cases in which their own value judgements about the 'deserving' and 'undeserving' may influence their conduct of some hearings and deliberations.

(j) in their ability to lead the tribunal during its deliberation; by summarising the evidence, initiating discussion on areas of doubt, clarifying the law, indicating possible exercise of discretionary power, and eventually guiding the tribunal to a reasoned decision.

(k) in their ability to articulate a reasoned decision and ensure that this is properly and adequately recorded either by completing the Record of Proceedings themselves or ensuring that the clerk does so under instruction.

Looking at the quality of chairmen's work on the basis of these criteria it was clear that some of them maintained high standards, some had potential if this could be realised by adequate training and some were weak. The superior quality of the legal chairmen stood out from amongst their colleagues when judged on these criteria. Because chairmen were, on the whole, isolated from each other (there had been one Regional Conference), and had received little or no formal training, it is hardly surprising that, generally speaking, they did not fully comprehend the complexities of the work. Their level of commitment and good will was high but they tended to regard the job as much more straightforward than in reality it is. The result was that too often proceedings were unsystematic, inconsistent and over-influenced by sympathy or otherwise. Separate deliberations were frequently non-existent when the appellant was absent, and in other instances were quite often somewhat rambling and of rather poor quality. We examined a large number of official Reports of Proceedings the majority of which did not adequately record a reasoned decision.

Members also varied in quality. Some of them appeared to concern themselves with wider welfare issues relating to the general problems of appellants. The extent of their participation in the proceedings varied during both hearing and deliberation. Some made a most valuable contribution but many were rather passive and some hearings were marked by lack of involvement on the part of both members. It was only in a minority of hearings that both members played an active role. We thought at one stage that inactivity might be closely related to infrequency of sitting, but in fact our data does not support this hypothesis. What did emerge was evidence of some confusion and lack of definition of the proper role of panel members which could leave them in a kind of 'no man's land'. Some chairmen tended to dominate the proceedings and did not create opportunities for the two others to make a significant contribution. However, we became convinced that members can and should play an active part. There are clear indications in our records of how much a tribunal is strengthened by having good panel members. Moreover, the appellants' survey produced abundant evidence that respondents regarded them as an essential component of the tribunal and were critical of their degree of involvement. I shall return to this point later.

Training

Chairmen and members were asked a series of questions about training. On the issue of training for newly appointed chairmen, there were differences of opinion; 2 had not thought they had needed it for themselves, 4 thought it unnecessary for those promoted from the ranks of members, 2 considered it depended on existing qualifications and experience, and 9 supported the idea, making a variety of suggestions as to the form it might take – from 'sitting in' to conferences extending over several days.

As regards serving chairmen, there was overwhelming support for Chairmen's Conferences.[13] Thirteen out of 17 thought regular conferences

[13] Since the fieldwork was completed a second conference for chairmen has taken place in the Northern Region and they are now a regular feature in all regions.

could be of real value and mention was made of feelings of isolation and 'being out on a limb'. . . .

Legally Qualified Chairmen[14]

Three of the chairmen were legally qualified. All respondents were asked to comment on the suggestion that it would be an improvement if all chairmen were legally qualified. Overall 21% agreed and 75% disagreed. Chairmen were divided in their views but the general impression was a lack of real enthusiasm for the proposal. As regards members, 25% were in favour whilst 72% were on the whole against lawyers as chairmen and 33% of these were distinctly negative to the suggestion. The latter, in fact, were mainly those without any experience of sitting with a legal chairman. Of those who had sat, only 3 out of 25 thought legal chairmen would be a disadvantage. . . .

2. The Clerk

There has been some controversy about the role of clerks. It was, therefore, part of the research task to examine what they actually did, shed light on the problems involved and examine the attitudes of chairmen, members and appellants.

Schedule 3 of the 1966 Act provides for a clerk to be assigned to each S.B.A.T. by the Secretary of State and the procedural rules require him to be present at all its sittings. In practice they are officers of the Department but while acting as clerks are servants of the tribunals. They normally work on a full-time basis while doing this job and in the Northern Region were based on Regional Office, serving all the tribunals in the Region. In this connection they arranged sittings, distributed appeal documents before hearings, notified decisions and dealt with any correspondence. There was nothing controversial about these aspects of the work and they carried out these duties efficiently.

The controversy centres round the role of the clerk during tribunal sittings and some critics have questioned his independence. In 1971, following a review of the situation and after consultation between D.H.S.S. and the Council on Tribunals, revised official instructions were issued which somewhat curtailed the clerk's previous role in connection with the part he should play in hearings and deliberations. They were designed to re-emphasise that the tribunal's proceedings are entirely a matter for the tribunal. Accordingly, the instructions laid down that the clerk should not take an active part in the hearing, nor prompt, nor ask questions other than those relating to his secretarial work for the tribunal. It was made clear that if he were asked questions about tribunal procedure or the case being heard he should direct them to the presenting officer or appellant. He was allowed to assist the

[14] [There is now provision for the appointment of legally qualified Senior Chairmen to oversee the working of tribunals in the areas to which they are assigned: Social Security Act 1979, Sch. 2, para. 11; Note 4, p. 544 *supra*.]

tribunal by turning up legislation which had already been referred to but was not to intervene by stating which parts of the law he thought applicable to the case. He was instructed to take notes during the hearing so as to be in a position, if necessary, to assist the tribunal refresh its memory on salient points during its subsequent deliberation. It was emphasised that the clerk was not to take part in the deliberation or try to influence the decision. In cases where a tribunal, in some doubt about an issue or the law, asked the clerk for advice he was informed that he should not give it but should suggest recalling the parties so that further evidence might resolve the areas of doubt. In a situation where the tribunal was still unable to reach a decision itself and again asked the clerk for advice the instructions allowed him to suggest an adjournment so that further evidence or argument might clarify the issues.

The part actually played by the clerk varied with different tribunals and was related to the strength or weakness of the chairman, but on the whole, the clerks we observed and talked to did not confine themselves strictly to the instructions. For the most part the clerk played a minor role in the hearing, although there is evidence of occasions when he prompted a tribunal in danger of becoming entangled in irrelevant issues or ignoring important aspects of a case. Their role was more crucial during the deliberation and with a weak tribunal a conscientious clerk found it difficult to confine himself strictly to the instructions. These tribunals continued to rely on him for advice, not only for factual information about the law but also about 'what they could do'. He exercised some influence during the deliberation in quite a number of appeals and our evidence reveals a few examples of what we would regard as intervention in the decision-making. It was not the research team's view that the permanent clerk's action and attitudes were disadvantageous to appellants – rather the reverse. His interventions were usually promoted by a desire to achieve a fair decision, to exclude irrelevant considerations and to maintain reasonable consistency between similar appeals. Generally the clerk fills in the Record of Proceedings and in theory this should be mainly a clerical exercise after the tribunal has reached a reasoned decision. But, here again, the clerk found it difficult to confine himself in this way with a weak tribunal. There were situations in which, in order to complete the Record, he had to 'press' the tribunal to produce clearer reasons for what it had decided to do. Sometimes when the tribunal was 'woolly' in its thinking, he articulated the reasons himself. Occasionally he 'found' reasons for what the tribunal wished to do by the way he wrote up the findings and reasons.

In sum, we felt that the clerk was in a difficult position. It is certainly not the intention to suggest that the permanent clerk abused his position by acting as a second advocate for the Commission. On occasions, however, temporary replacements were used and were clearly not as good. They appeared less independent and more inclined to be sympathetic towards Commission decisions. There would, therefore, be some danger in the present situation if clerks were less permanent, not so experienced and of poorer calibre. I hold strongly the view that the role is a difficult and demanding one where tribunals tend to be weak and until they can be strengthened would consider it unwise to attempt further restrictions. Problems connected with the clerk cannot be permanently solved without improving the quality of the tribunals.[15] . . .

Chairmen and members were asked a series of questions about the clerk. A large majority expressed general satisfaction with his work and contribution. . . . But it would appear that most tribunals have not noticed any significant changes in the way the clerk conducts himself since the 1971 instructions were issued.[16] . . .

3. *Presenting Officer*

A number of presenting officers were operating in the Region during the research. They were not individually assigned to any particular tribunal so that we saw them in different situations.

Firstly, we wish to make it clear that there was no evidence of the overbearing rather intimidating manner and attitude which has been referred to in some publications on S.B.A.Ts. The common style was rather low key – courteous and reasonable. We saw few examples of hostility towards appellants although there were one or two instances where a presenting officer found it difficult to suppress his feelings. . . .

The presenting officer's duty, as presently defined, is to familiarise himself with the details in the documents, attend the hearing, explain the Commission's decision, elaborate upon the material in the official form if necessary, and answer any questions from the tribunal, appellant or representative. He is a specialist officer engaged full-time in this work. Official instructions emphasise that he is not a prosecution attorney for the Commission but rather an unbiased presenter of all the facts, both favourable and unfavourable to the appellant. In effect, this means that if necessary he must be prepared to help an appellant by bringing out facts or pointing to the significance of them which the appellant himself may have overlooked. There are examples in our evidence of presenting officers putting points favourable to appellants. But this role is difficult and demanding. As the research proceeded, we were driven to ask ourselves whether it is a realistic one and whether these officers are placed in an almost impossible dilemma.

More than half the hearings are unattended and in these the presenting officer is virtually responsible for presenting the appellant's case as well as the Commission's. Frequently, with sparse information in the documents and no-one to amplify it, we found there was little he could do. But there were cases when we felt he might have raised the issue of hardship for the appellant or the question of discretionary power. Although we had not seen the local

---

[15] Since the research was completed, amended instructions have been issued to clerks after discussion with the Council on Tribunals. These should help to resolve some of the immediate difficulties. [See further p. 573 *infra.*]

[16] [See Appendix 1 to the D.H.S.S. publication, Supplementary Benefit Appeal Tribunals: A guide to procedure.]

office papers[17] which the presenting officer had access to, we felt there were occasions when he might have placed fuller information before the tribunal.

... The majority of chairmen and members had little criticism of presenting officers but many did not fully understand the complexities and contradictions of their position. Almost a quarter of respondents, including 3 chairmen, were not even aware that the presenting officer had the responsibility of presenting facts on both sides.

... One of the problems at present is that if the presenting officer is not responsible for putting the facts for the appellant there is frequently nobody else to do it, and given the present weakness of many tribunals, together with low attendance and representation rates, there is no way of ensuring that all the relevant facts are brought out. Our view is that the long term solution lies not so much in making further (rather desperate) attempts to purge presenting officers of any bias but to strengthen the tribunals so that they perform what we consider to be their essential function – namely to ensure that the appellant's case is fully examined. To this end we also advocate measures to secure improved attendance rates and facilities for advice and representation.

6. *Special Problems Encountered by S.B.A.Ts.*

On the basis of substantial evidence arising from the research, I summarise here the special problems encountered by S.B.A.Ts.:

(*a*) confusion about the jurisdiction of S.B.A.Ts. particularly in appeals involving legal aspects of national insurance.

(*b*) ... Overall, the tribunals had not evolved a disciplined and systematic approach to the exercise of discretion. I appreciate the problems and accept that two equally experienced tribunals might examine the same case and arrive at a different decision. But, at present, some of them do not fully understand the difficulties involved in the exercise of their wide discretionary powers[18] and that it requires a systematic and consistent framework of inquiry which first seeks to establish the facts and then proceeds to the application of recognised principles.

(*c*) problems connected with advice and representation for appellants....

7. *The Appellants* ...

We asked unrepresented respondents whether they would have liked to have a representative. Just over half would have welcomed this – the rest did not feel the need for it. Analysis of the 1973 Northern Region statistics showed that there was representation in about 17% of S.B.A.T. appeals as compared with about 20% in N.I.L.Ts ([National Insurance Local Tribunals]. But the *pattern* was very different. In S.B.A.Ts. representation was as follows:

12·8% by relatives and friends
2·3% by claimants' unions

[17] I had access to the tribunal papers, having previously established in each case, following an explanatory letter, that the appellant had no objection to participating in the research.
[18] [This has now been sharply reduced: see p. 117 *supra*.]

1·4%   by social workers
0·5%   by trade unions
0·2%   by lawyers

For N.I.L.Ts., about 16% were represented by trade unions, 3% by relatives, 1% by friends and 1% by lawyers. . . .

Low attendance rates are a feature of S.B.A.T. appeals despite the fact that the whole system is based on the principle of an oral hearing. In the 1973 S.B.A.T. Northern Region data 43% attended. In the N.I.L.T. study the figure was about 50%. In both we show that the percentage of allowed appeals was much higher where the appellant attended and his appearance is frequently a crucial factor in determining success. In N.I.L.Ts. the success rate was 35% where the appellant appeared and 8% where he did not. In the S.B.A.T. data it was 34·6% and 6·9%.

It was a major objective of the research to isolate the factors determining attendance and non-attendance. We found little evidence of what might be termed irresponsibility in this matter. What the interviews revealed was a decision-making process on the part of the appellants which, generally speaking, was not irrational but was frequently not in their best interest. Over 80% of non-attenders had practical reasons for not turning up at the hearing. These were connected with job commitments, family circumstances, health reasons, shortage of money or suitable clothes in which to appear, and travel problems. Almost a third mentioned factors related to their perception of what would happen at the hearing – many of these had more or less abandoned hope after seeing the tribunal papers. In other words, non-attendance resulted from a combination of pessimism about the outcome and practical difficulties. There are a number of problems which our findings indicate need further examination by D.H.S.S. – for example, the proportion who for health reasons are not really fit to attend, the proportion who found the day and time inconvenient but did not realise they could have requested an adjournment, those who had serious problems connected with travelling to the tribunal, the influence of time lag, the combined effects of misunderstanding the appeal documents and confusion about the tribunal's constitution and procedure.

Attenders were asked a series of questions about their experience of the hearing, their perception of the roles of chairmen and members and their level of satisfaction with the hearing and decision. . . . Inevitably these were coloured by the decision, but it was by no means a 'win or lose' divide. For example, 60% of attenders whose appeals had failed judged the tribunal to be independent, 56% of losers said the chairman had a favourable or at least neutral attitude towards them, and 66% of those who felt they had had a fair hearing had lost their appeal.

Asked what they thought of the way the chairman handled their case, 53% gave favourable comments and 36% were critical. The rest were either ambivalent or gave answers which could not be classified. Although there was no widespread general mistrust of the chairman's attitude (70% said it was either favourable or neutral towards them) their criticisms are very revealing of appellants' expectations and indicate the serious consequences of inadequacies [in chairmen]. . . . Although appellants were not able to make the same technical criticisms we made they were not unaware of deficiencies.

Compared with chairmen, members were the subject of much more widespread and deep seated criticisms by appellants. Thirty-one per cent of attenders made favourable comments [but] about 59% made comments which referred in one way or another to their lack of involvement. . . . Their comments, some of which were undoubtedly hostile, show clearly both what appellants expected of members and what they found lacking. Members were expected to be interested, alert, knowledgeable, active, questioning and *helpful*.

Turning to the appellants' own part in the hearing, 21% said they had had difficulty in following the proceedings and 78% that they had not. The majority also said they thought they had been given adequate opportunity to put their case. . . .

After reviewing all these aspects we asked attenders to try to sum up their experience. All in all, did they think they had had a fair hearing? Almost two-thirds felt their hearing was fair. Moreover, there was relatively little difference between the successful and unsuccessful – 74% and 62%. These answers contrast rather starkly with those given in reply to a final question which asked all respondents (attenders and non-attenders) whether on the whole they were satisfied with the decision. Overall only 19% were satisfied. Attendance at the hearing is clearly a significant factor influencing satisfaction with the decision, whichever way it goes. I suggest this is an important finding and one which is parallelled in the N.I.L.T. study.[19] Face-to-face discussions of grievances in which they participate are important to people.

In conclusion, we tried to discover what sort of body appellants would regard as appropriate for hearing appeals like theirs. A court model did not emerge. Rather it was a body with a competent professional chairman (legal qualifications were frequently referred to) balanced by active lay members. Our people felt more deeply about lay members than about any other single aspect of their experience. In attaching importance to lay membership they had definite views about their role as well as expectations about their performance. As seen by respondents, members should play an active and *enabling* role towards the appellant by showing sympathetic understanding of his problem, by listening, asking relevant questions, drawing him out and generally helping him sort out his case. They were able to distinguish this enabling role from that of an advocate. Moreover, they clearly wanted ordinary people as panel members – particularly people with first-hand knowledge and experience of the kinds of problems and conditions experienced by supplementary benefit claimants. Sadly, they frequently had not even been able to identify the workpeople's representative and generally felt that the tribunal was remote from their world. . . .

[19] [Bell *et al.*, (1974/5) Journal of Social Policy vol. 3, pt. 4; vol. 4, pt. 1.]

Conclusions and Recommendations

No comprehensive review of the adjudication system in supplementary benefits or, for that matter in the national assistance scheme which preceded it, has ever been undertaken. This is, of course, not to say that changes have not been made. But, on the whole, these have been *ad hoc* adjustments to pressures generated in the post-Franks era.

Franks accepted that the (then) national assistance appeal tribunals were working satisfactorily. However, the Committee's statement about their constitutional position was somewhat ambiguous:

'Although in form these Tribunals hear and determine appeals against decisions of local officers of the National Assistance Board and therefore, exercise adjudicating functions, in practice their task much resembles that of an assessment committee, taking a further look at the facts and in some cases arriving at a fresh decision on the extent of need.'[20]

This reads, to some extent, as if the Committee regarded these tribunals as rather different from others they had examined. Be that as it may, in the period since publication of the Report it has become increasingly clear that they cannot be isolated from general trends and must be subject to the same constitutional principles which, since Franks, have gradually been applied in the tribunal world. During this period, movement has been towards further judicialisation of tribunals – by ensuring their independence of Departments; by procedural rules which require them to follow a judicial process; by appointing lawyers as chairmen; by requiring tribunals to give reasoned decisions; by embodying constitutional rights of appellants in statutory rules (including the right to legal representation); and by granting rights of appeal from tribunals of first instance, frequently to a second-tier body and, generally, to the courts on a point of law. S.B.A.Ts. have not stood entirely outside these trends. Their national assistance predecessors were immediately subject to certain reforms embodied in the Tribunals and Inquiries Act 1958. Moreover, changes in their statutory rules have tightened up procedure, and either widened appellants' rights or produced more precise definition of them. Additionally, frequent official discussion of the roles of clerk and presenting officer have resulted in various adjustments and changes. And a more or less continuous dialogue between D.H.S.S. and the Council on Tribunals about both constitutional issues and practical arrangements for these appeals has been a feature of the period. The Council on Tribunals took the unusual step in 1972 of issuing a letter of guidance to all S.B.A.T. chairmen on recording reasons for decisions.

Despite all this, S.B.A.Ts. have increasingly been the subject of criticism and complaint. Caught up in a developing citizens' rights movement which emphasises legal rights in welfare, social security tribunals are now recognized as key institutions of the Welfare State. An increasing number of people have become aware of their rights of appeal and are exericising them.

[20] Franks Report, H.M.S.O. Cmnd. 218, 1957, para. 182.

Moreover, concern about tribunals is not longer centred on somewhat abstract constitutional questions but on whether, and to what extent, rights of appeal enshrined in statute law can be exercised effectively by ordinary people. S.B.A.Ts., heavily under fire from lawyers and others, have been criticised on many grounds but the nub of it is that in failing to follow a consistent and clear judicial process in their decision-making they are not acting as judicial bodies. And, as the research clearly shows, they are in a particularly difficult position in this respect. The law they have to administer leaves them with wide, problematic and in some areas ambiguous discretionary powers. Each tribunal is isolated from the rest, there is no second-tier appeal structure[21] and thus no body of decisions which can be referred to. Furthermore, although there are some lawyer chairmen, the practice on the whole has been to appoint laymen to this position.[22] One of the objectives of this report is to draw attention to the difficulties and problems they encounter through no fault of their own.

. . . S.B.A.Ts. are not composed of mean-minded, punitive people bent on grinding the face of the poor. On the contrary, for the most part, they are anxious to be helpful. At times they feel frustrated by the desperate plight of some individuals appearing before them and the tribunal's inability to do much about it. On the whole they behave in a courteous and sympathetic manner, although this has to be qualified as we encountered some exceptions in cases which presented as 'most undeserving'. What we found, in other words, were S.B.A.Ts. behaving very much like case committees of the kind described by Franks. They have to a considerable extent, retained their original pattern despite all attempts to change it. They are not yet full, independent adjudicating bodies following a clear judicial process – which in the post-Franks era has come to be accepted and expected as the essential hall-mark of a tribunal. To transform them so that they measure up to this standard will mean finding solutions to some extremely difficult problems and will require a major overhaul of the system.

Note

See further Herman, *Administrative Justice and Supplementary Benefits* (Occasional Papers in Social Administration); *Justice Discretion and Poverty* (edd. Adler and Bradley); Ogus and Barendt, *The Law of Social Security*, 2nd edn., pp. 605–17.

Bell's study was highly influential. The report and the work of Council on Tribunals have led to important reforms in the administration of social security. In particular, the amount of administrative discretion has been sharply reduced (see p. 118 *supra*), rights of appeal have been granted (see p. 558 *infra*) and provision has been made for the appointment of legally qualified Senior Chairmen for Supplementary Benefits Appeal Tribunals (see p. 544 *supra*). Although Bell's study may therefore be thought in part to be of only historical interest, it is nevertheless relevant as showing the problems which may arise in a highly informal tribunal and more general issues that arise when decisions are remitted to tribunals (e.g. the role of the clerk, the importance of representation).

[21] [See now p. 558 *infra*.]
[22] [But see p. 544 *supra* for the provision of legally qualified Senior Chairmen.]

RIGHTS OF APPEAL

Report of the Committee on Administrative Tribunals and Enquiries, p. 62 *supra*

Tribunals and Inquiries Act 1971, section 13, p. 64 *supra*

Notes

1. From what has been said about the structure of tribunals it should come as no surprise that there is no consistent pattern of rights of appeal. In some areas, such as national insurance social security, and the national health service, there are appellate tribunals, but in other appeals go to the relevant minister (e.g. from the Traffic Commissioners). As will have been seen in the extracts at p. 62 *supra* the principle that there should be a right of appeal on a point of law to the ordinary courts is generally accepted. Section 13 of the Tribunals and Inquiries Act 1971 confers a right of appeal to the High Court on a point of law from many tribunals, on which see Note 1, p. 64 *supra*. Other rights of appeal are given by specific statutes, on which see the references in Note 2, p. 64 *supra*.

2. It should not be assumed that appeals to the ordinary courts are always most appropriate. First, there is the point, made in the Franks Report at p. 62 *supra*, that appeals to the courts on fact would constitute an appeal from an expert to a relatively inexpert body. Furthermore, an appeal on a point of law, while theoretically valuable, may be irrelevant in practice. In 1978 a right of appeal on a point of law from Supplementary Benefits Appeal Tribunals (hereafter S.B.A.T.s) to the High Court was introduced (S.I. 1977 No. 1735). The expense of a High Court hearing in relation to the sort of sum at issue in most S.B.A.T. cases (see e.g. *R. v. Preston S.B.A.T., ex p. Moore*, p. 77 *supra*) made this an inappropriate solution and it was abolished by s. 6 of the Social Security Act 1979. The 1979 Act implemented the suggestion in the Bell study, p. 557 *supra*, that appeal should lie to a second-tier tribunal (the National Insurance (now Social Security) Commissioner). For discussion of these appeals see Loosemore, (1982) 132 N.L.J. 115, 143, 165 and 199. Section 14 of the Social Security Act 1980 provides for a further appeal on a point of law to the Court of Appeal. See p. 71 *supra* for discussion of what constitutes a question of 'law'.

3. On the question of judicial review of the decisions of tribunals, see Chs. 1 and 2 *supra*. Note, in particular, the duty to give reasons imposed by s. 12 of the Tribunals and Inquiries Act 1971, p. 22 *supra*, and the fact that they then form part of the record and can be reviewed for error of law on the face of the record, on which see p. 64 *supra*. This means that the absence of a right of appeal on a point of law is often of little importance because the distinction between such an appeal and this non-jurisdictional form of review is wafer-thin.

4. For a suggested limitation on the type of question that can be raised in an appeal from a tribunal, see *Henry Moss of London Ltd.* v. *Customs and Excise Commissioners* [1981] 2 All E.R. 86, noted at p. 337 *supra*, and see Wade, pp. 822–3.

5. The importance of administrative review of decisions should be noted. Coleman has said (*Supplementary Benefits and the Administrative Review of Administrative Action*, C.P.A.G. Poverty Pamphlet No. 7) that 'from the point of view of the citizen

who is aggrieved by a decision of a public authority, the administrative processing of his complaint may be as important as any actual hearing before a quasi-judicial body'. His study showed that, in the year ending 31 October 1969, 23·2% of the decisions in which the claimant had indicated a desire to appeal were altered by administrative review before the appeal was taken, almost always to the claimant's advantage. Only 12·8% were resolved by an S.B.A.T. revising the initial decision. See also the Annual Report of the Council on Tribunals for 1977/8, para, 5·38; the Annual Report of the Supplementary Benefits Commission for 1979, para. 13·6. In 1978 there were 115,467 appeals to S.B.A.T.s. Of these, 21,079 were withdrawn or not admitted as being time-barred or outside the tribunals' jurisdiction. A further 32,080 were dealt with administratively and not heard by a tribunal, while 62,308 were heard by tribunals. Of these 49,782 decisions were confirmed by the tribunals while 12,526 were revised. Of the revised decisions, 66 were revised in a manner that was unfavourable to the claimants. Coleman's conclusions would appear to remain valid.

THE FRANKS COMMITTEE: THE REFORMS OF 1958

Note

The report of the Franks Committee and the Tribunals and Inquiries Act 1958 have been and will be referred to at various points. On the Council on Tribunals see p. 568 *infra*.

PROCEDURE OF TRIBUNALS

Procedural rules

Report of The Committee on Administrative Tribunals and Enquiries

Cmnd. 218 (1957)

62. Most of the evidence we have received concerning tribunals has placed great emphasis upon procedure, not only at the hearing itself but also before and after it. There has been general agreement on the broad essentials which the procedure, in this wider sense, should contain, for example provision for notice of the right to apply to a tribunal, notice of the case which the applicant has to meet, a reasoned decision by the tribunal and notice of any further right of appeal. Some witnesses have suggested that a standard code of procedure should be devised which would be applicable to all tribunals, and others have suggested that some four or five different codes should be formulated, from which Parliament would designate the particular code appropriate to each tribunal.

63. We agree that procedure is of the greatest importance and that it should be clearly laid down in a statute or statutory instrument. Because of the great variety of the purposes for which tribunals are established, however, we do not think it would be appropriate to rely upon either a single code or a small number of codes. We think that there is a case for greater procedural differentiation and prefer that the detailed procedure for each type of tribunal should be designed to meet its particular circumstances.

64. There has been considerable emphasis, in much of the evidence we have received, upon the importance of preserving informality of atmosphere in hearings before tribunals, though it is generally conceded that in some tribunals, for example the Lands Tribunal, informality is not an overriding necessity. We endorse this view, but we are convinced that the attempt which has been made to secure informality in the general run of tribunals has in some instances been at the expense of an orderly procedure. Informality without rules of procedure may be positively inimical to right adjudication, since the proceedings may well assume an unordered character which makes it difficult, if not impossible, for the tribunal properly to sift the facts and weigh the evidence. It should here be remembered that by their very nature tribunals may well be less skilled in adjudication than courts of law. None of our witnesses would seek to make tribunals in all respects like courts of law, but there is a wide measure of agreement that in many instances their procedure could be made more orderly without impairing the desired informality of atmosphere. The object to be aimed at in most tribunals is the combination of a formal procedure with an informal atmosphere. We see no reason why this cannot be achieved. On the one hand it means a manifestly sympathetic attitude on the part of the tribunal and the absence of the trappings of a court, but on the other hand such prescription of procedure as makes the proceedings clear and orderly.

Tribunals and Inquiries Act 1971

10. (1) No power of a Minister, the Lord President of the Court of Session or the Commissioners of Inland Revenue to make, approve, confirm or concur in procedural rules for any such tribunal as is specified in Schedule 1 to this Act shall be exercisable except after consultation with the Council [on Tribunals]. . . .

(3) In this section 'procedural rules' includes any statutory provision relating to the procedure of the tribunal in question.

Notes

1. On Sch. 1 see Note 1, p. 544 *supra*.

2. Most of the tribunals subject to the supervision of the Council on Tribunals now have statutory rules of procedure (see e.g. Annual Reports for 1964, paras. 23–30, 1973/4, paras. 59–63, and 1975/6, paras. 18–22, p. 569 *infra*). The Council has given attention to a large number of points, including (*a*) the circumstances in which a hearing may be held in private and confidential information can be considered but not disclosed; (*b*) restricting the right of representation to lawyers (as was attempted for the Scottish Betting Levy Appeal Tribunal); (*c*) whether and, if so, when evidence which would not have been admissible in a court should be considered (the Council's experience suggested that fairness would not be imperilled by hearing such evidence); (*d*) reasons for decisions (see p. 22 *supra* and p. 567 *infra*); and (*e*) time limits within which notice of the time and place of a hearing must be given or an application be made.

See p. 547 *supra* for the main features of the procedure for S.B.A.T.s. See further Wraith and Hutchesson, pp. 152–3, for a description of the different procedural types recommended by the Franks Report.

Knowledge of the case to be met

Report of the Committee on Administrative Tribunals and Enquiries

Cmnd. 218 (1957)

71. The second most important requirement before the hearing is that citizens should know in good time the case which they will have to meet, whether the issue to be heard by the tribunal is one between citizen and administration or between citizen and citizen. This constituent of fairness is one to which much of the evidence we have received has rightly drawn attention. We are satisfied that the requirement is generally met, but in some cases, most clearly in the case of some hearings before County Agricultural Executive Committees, we are not satisfied.

72. We do not suggest that the procedure should be formalised to the extent of requiring documents in the nature of legal pleadings. What is needed is that the citizen should receive in good time beforehand a document setting out the main points of the opposing case. It should not be necessary, and indeed in view of the type of persons frequently appearing before tribunals it would in many cases be positively undesirable, to require the parties to adhere rigidly to the case previously set out, provided always that the interests of another party are not prejudiced by such flexibility.

Note

See further Bell, p. 547 *supra*; Wraith and Hutchesson, pp. 193–40; Ch. 8 *supra* (*audi alteram partem* principle of natural justice).

Hearings. Evidence. Precedent

Report of The Committee on Administrative Tribunals and Enquiries

Cmnd. 218 (1957)

Public hearings

76. We have already said that we regard openness as one of the three essential features of the satisfactory working of tribunals. Openness includes the promulgation of reasoned decisions, but its most important constituent is that the proceedings should be in public. The consensus of opinion in the evidence received is that hearings before tribunals should take place in public except in special circumstances. . . .

77. We are in no doubt that if adjudicating bodies, whether courts or tribunals, are to inspire that confidence in the administration of justice which is a condition of civil liberty they should, in general, sit in public. But just as on occasion the courts are prepared to try certain types of case wholly or partly *in camera* so, in the wide field covered by tribunals, there are occasions

on which we think that justice may be better done, and the interests of the citizen better served, by privacy.

78. The first type of case is where considerations of public security are involved. Such cases are not often likely to arise before tribunals, but provision should be included in the codes of procedure for enabling a tribunal to sit in private on this type of case.

79. The more frequent type of case in which privacy is desirable is that in which intimate personal or financial circumstances have to be disclosed. Few people would doubt the wisdom of the practice whereby hearings before the General and Special Commissioners of Income Tax are held in private in order that details of taxpayers' affairs shall not become public knowledge. In the case of National Assistance Appeal Tribunals[23] the issue is the relief of need. The arguments against the disclosure of need and the disclosure of taxable capacity seem to have equal validity. Indeed in the case of national assistance there is a danger that public proceedings would so deter applicants that the purpose of the legislation would be frustrated. Another case in which the privacy of proceedings is justified is the hearing at which a medical examination of the applicant may take place.

80. A third type of case in which privacy is on balance desirable is that involving professional capacity and reputation where the machinery includes provision for a preliminary and largely informal hearing before any decision is made to institute formal proceedings which may involve penalties. Thus we consider . . . that hearings by Service Committees under the National Health Service Acts of complaints against practitioners should continue to be held in private, though we think that some of the subsequent proceedings should in future be held in public.

81. Accordingly we recommend that where a tribunal is of a class which has to deal almost exclusively with any of these three types of case the hearing should continue to be in private. In the case of all other classes of tribunal, however, the hearing should be in public, subject to a discretionary power in the chairman to exclude the public should he think that a particular case involves any of these considerations.

Notes

1. See further Bell, p. 547 *supra*; Wade, p. 805; Wraith and Hutchesson, pp. 140–8.

2. The hearings of S.B.A.T.s are not held in public (S.I. 1980 No. 1605, r. 6 (4), and see p. 547 *supra*), but there is discretion (r. 6 (7)) for the chairman to permit 'a person who is genuinely engaged in research connected with appeals to tribunals or has other good and sufficient reasons for being present' to attend the hearing. The principles of natural justice provide a broad framework with which to ensure procedural fairness (see Ch. 8 *supra*), although they do not themselves require a hearing to be in public: *R. v. Denbigh JJ., ex p. Williams* [1974] Q.B. 759 at p. 764 (referring to a court, but tribunals are surely *a fortiori*). See further Jackson, *Natural Justice*, 2nd edn., p. 93; de Smith, p. 201).

[23] [Now Supplementary Benefit Appeal Tribunals.]

Most tribunals give oral hearings but some (e.g. the Social Security Commissioner) may dispose of appeals 'on the papers'. The Council on Tribunals tries to ensure that rules of procedure provide for an oral hearing, although sometimes all this means is that the chairman of the tribunal has discretion to permit such a hearing (e.g. Civil Aviation Authority and Immigration Appeal Tribunal: see Annual Report of the Council on Tribunals for 1971/2, paras. 51–3 and 65).

3. As has been noted at p. 85 *supra* tribunals, 'are entitled to act on any material which is logically probative, even though it is not evidence in a court of law' (Lord Denning in *T. A. Miller Ltd.* v. *Minister of Housing and Local Government* [1968] 1 W.L.R. 992 at p. 995). The Franks Report recommended (recommendation No. 18) that tribunals should be given power to subpoena witnesses to give evidence or produce documents to enable the procedure to be conducted in an inquisitional manner. The Council on Tribunals initially thought (Annual Report for 1960, paras. 76–85) that this was not a problem but later revised its opinion. In its Annual Report for 1964 (para. 28 (8)) it reported that it was less easy to obtain High Court subpoenas than it had been led to believe and decided that the question should be reviewed. Many tribunals in fact have these powers (e.g. Civil Aviation Authority, Pensions Appeal Tribunals, and the Lands Tribunal), but the extent to which they are exercised to promote an inquisitorial procedure varies greatly. For instance, Wraith and Hutchesson, p. 147, note that, despite wide powers to inspect land and to call for documents, the Lands Tribunal 'remains firmly committed to the adversarial method of obtaining evidence'. The need for an inquisitorial procedure is particularly strong in cases where one party is unrepresented or absent.

4. The role of departmental officers (clerks and presenting officers) at the hearing has led to complaints (see p. 542 *supra*), some of which are set out in Bell's study, p. 550 *supra*. Lister (*Justice for the Claimant*, C.P.A.G. Poverty Research Series No. 4) appears to be more critical than Bell of the role of departmental officers in S.B.A.T.s. In 1974 (in relation to clerks, for example) she said (at p. 16) that 'the tribunal's dependence on the clerk for guidance in dealing with cases that come before it clearly represents a grave threat to its independence'. The nub of the problem is that clerks fill a gap in expertise which should be filled by tribunal chairmen.

Legal Representation. Legal Aid. Costs

Recommendations of the Lord Chancellor's Advisory Committee on Legal Aid, 1973/4 (Twenty-fourth report)

H.C. 20, Session 1974/5

31. . . . In our opinion it is essential for applicants[24] to have access to competent advice at as early a stage as possible. Many of those who should consider appealing to a tribunal are confused about what is involved and in need of advice and help. They are far from clear about the provisions governing the subject matter with which they are dealing, whether this be the premises in which they are living, their entitlement to a social security benefit or their right to remain in this country. They frequently believe that the official with whom they are dealing has wider discretionary powers than in

[24] We use this term throughout our Report to describe persons concerned in proceedings before tribunals, including appellants, claimants and, where appropriate, respondents.

fact he possesses and they may often feel helpless before officialdom. When told that they possess a right of appeal against a decision they frequently have only a limited understanding of the nature of that right and do not comprehend that, by lodging an appeal, they are setting in motion a system of adjudication which is independent of the officer who took the decision. Very few understand how a tribunal will be composed and the roles which will be played by the clerk to the tribunal and by any officer who may be presenting the case on behalf of the Government Department concerned. To meet their needs and those of the tribunal, what is required is a reliable system to ensure that a person in this position will receive

(a) preliminary advice as to his rights, as to the advisability of appealing and as to the consequences which will follow if he decides to do so;

(b) guidance as to how the tribunal will be constituted, the powers it will be entitled to exercise and the procedure which will apply at the hearing;

(c) frequently, assistance in gathering information and preparing his case;

(d) in many cases, preparation of a written statement for the tribunal, clearly setting out the relevant facts and any law which may be applicable; and

(e) in a limited number of cases, representation at the hearing and advice thereafter.

32. Much of this assistance can already be made available under the new legal advice and assistance scheme which was introduced by the Legal Advice and Assistance Act 1972. Such evidence as we have so far received suggests ... that the extent to which use has been made of the scheme for tribunal work has been disappointing. We are keeping this matter under review.

Assistance and representation by lay organisations

33. A large body of assistance in tribunal cases is provided by lay organisations. In particular, there are the services of trades unions, ex-service organisations, Citizens' Advice Bureaux and other bodies. There are many types of case which are too complex for a lay client to handle but in which these organisations have built up their own skills and expertise. At the same time, most of these organisations would recognise that there are some cases where a lawyer is essential. There is a wide spectrum of need on the part of tribunal applicants, ranging from moral support and encouragement at one extreme to experienced legal advocacy on difficult issues of law at the other. . . .

Legal aid for representation

35. Whatever arrangements are made for lay representation and assistance, there remains the question whether legal aid should be extended to cover representation by a solicitor or, where necessary, counsel in tribunal matters. We set out the arguments on either side.

36. *The arguments for extension.* The basic arguments for extending legal aid to tribunals are that many of those appearing before them are at a

disadvantage in that they lack confidence and skill to make the best of their case, and because they find it hard to deal with the complex issues which can arise to a greater or less degree in all tribunals. This point was repeatedly made in evidence to us and in our view there can be no doubt of its validity. A more difficult question is to determine the form which the assistance should take and the machinery for selecting those cases where legally aided representation is needed.

37. *The arguments against extension.* The arguments which we received against extending legal aid to tribunals fell broadly into two categories. The first comprised ones which suggested that legal aid was unnecessary, the second were ones maintaining that it would be positively undesirable. We need not take up much time in considering the first, since, once it is assumed that there will be effective selection machinery, few of the arguments appeared to us to raise any issues of difficulty. . . . The only argument in this category which appeared to us to be of consequence was the suggestion that tribunals can be relied on to look after applicants' interests and to see that relevant facts are brought out. We know that many tribunal chairmen are experienced and conscientious in acting in this way but we do not consider that it is a satisfactory substitute for effective representation, particularly in cases where the other side is represented.

38. The arguments suggesting that it would be undesirable to extend legal aid to tribunals seemed to raise more serious issues of principle. The first, which was put forward by a number of witnesses, was that legal aid would lead to proceedings being formalised and the benefits of informality being lost. . . . We agree there is a danger that some informality may be lost if, through the introduction of legal aid, representation by legally qualified persons becomes more common in tribunals, but we do not consider it would justify a refusal to extend legal aid.[25] This would amount, in effect, to saying that representation is permissible provided it is restricted to those who are able to afford it. In our view, if legal aid has the effect suggested, the Government will have to consider whether the advantages of informality outweigh those of representation. If they do, the right course, we suggest, will be to ban legal representation altogether; what cannot be justifiable is to restrict its benefits to those wealthy enough to afford it for themselves.

39. Another objection put forward is that legal aid would lead to proceedings being lengthened and would cause delay. We think there is force in this. We have received evidence that solicitors and counsel find it difficult, because of their other commitments, to match the need for expedition to which many tribunals attach importance. Moreover, some of them tend to conduct the preliminary stages of proceedings before a tribunal in the same way as those before a court. They are likely, for example, to seek further and better particulars and to take other interlocutory steps which are not well suited for

[25] Moreover, it needs to be borne in mind that the presenting officer who regularly appears for a Government Department before a particular type of tribunal can acquire comparable expertise to a lawyer and can be intimidating to an applicant.

the type of work with which tribunals normally deal. . . . It may be, however, that as solicitors become more accustomed to tribunal work, they will cease to take steps which are rarely suited to the type of case dealt with by tribunals.

40. The other main objection is that members of the legal profession are inexpert in tribunal work and are too hard-pressed to be able to deal with it. We think that the first part of this objection may often be valid; the work of some tribunals tends to be specialised and to need considerable expertise. . . .

Our conclusion

41. Having taken all the evidence into account, we are satisfied that legal aid should be extended to all statutory tribunals at present within the supervision of the Council on Tribunals[26] in which representation is permitted. . . . We do not suggest any order of priority as between different tribunals since we consider that such an approach would be unsound. . . .

Notes

1. The Committee also considered machinery for determining those cases where assistance is required. It stated that the best and most economical way of proceeding would be by an extension of the green form advice and assistance scheme under ss. 1–5 of the Legal Aid Act 1974 (see *infra*). The Committee's recommendations were supported by the Council on Tribunals (Annual Report for 1974/5, paras. 84–9), but constraints on public expenditure and the urgent need to improve legal services generally mean that they have still not been implemented. The only tribunals to which legal aid has so far been extended are the Lands Tribunal, the Commons Commissioners, and the Employment Appeal Tribunal. The Legal Aid Act 1979 has, however, (by s. 1) made provision for the extension of the green form scheme by the provision of 'assistance by way of representation' in inferior courts and tribunals prescribed by regulations. The only tribunals covered so far are mental health review tribunals: S.I. 1982 No. 1592. The Council on Tribunals (Annual Report for 1974/5) also said:

85. . . . We believe that, in addition to applicants who would benefit from the provision of legal aid, there is a substantial number of applicants for whom non-legal advice or representation is required and is indeed the more appropriate form of aid. There is a danger, in our view, that if there can be no assurance of non-legal advice and representation being available on an aided basis in appropriate cases there will be unnecessary recourse to legal aid.

86. While we support the need for both legal and non-legal aid for certain applicants, we wish to make it clear that in our view it is the essence of the tribunal system that many if not most applicants should be able to present their cases satisfactorily without recourse to either form of assistance. The availability of such assistance should not lead to any slackening of the efforts of Departments to simplify the processes of appeal to tribunals and of tribunals to regulate their proceedings in such a way as to help the unrepresented applicant.

For a more recent statement of the Council's views see p. 576 *infra*. See also Whitmore, (1970) 33 M.L.R. 481 at pp. 484–9.

The *Report of the Royal Commission on Legal Services* (the Benson Report) took a similar approach to the question of representation. It stated (para. 15.11) that it 'is desirable that every applicant before any tribunal should either be able adequately to present his case in person or to obtain representation. For this purpose, three separate but linked policies will be needed. These are the simplification of tribunal procedures, the development of lay advice and representation and the extension of legal aid to

[26] [See p. 544 *supra*.]

tribunals.' On the first, the Commission doubted that simplification of procedure would be possible unless the relevant law is first made less complex, but recommended a review of tribunal procedures by the Council on Tribunals. On the second, it recommended that public funds should be made available to support approved agencies (such as the Free Representation Unit in London, the Child Poverty Action Group, and the United Kingdom Immigration Advisory Service) that provide lay representation to the public at large. On the third, it recommended that in some tribunal cases legal representation is necessary and should be available. The Commission recommended the adoption of criteria proposed by the Council on Tribunals to identify these cases. These included cases (a) where a significant point of law arises; (b) where evidence is likely to be too complex or specialized for the average layman to assemble, evaluate, and test; (c) where deprivation of liberty or the ability of an individual to follow his occupation is at stake; (d) where the amount at stake, although low, is significant in relation to the financial circumstances of the applicant, and (d) where suitable lay representation is not available.

2. For the question whether representation can be required by the rules of natural justice see p. 246 *supra*. On representation in general see further Bell, p. 553 *supra*; Wade, p. 810; Wraith and Hutchesson, pp. 176–81 and 263–5. Since the implementation of the Franks Report's recommendation (paras. 83–8) that, where they existed, bans on legal representation should be removed, as a general rule a party may be represented by a lawyer or anyone else. (Bans are most frequent in domestic tribunals: see *Enderby Town F.C. Ltd.* v. *F.A. Ltd.*, p. 246 *supra*). In many tribunals legal representation is still uncommon (see p. 554 *supra*). The reasons for this include the fact that (a) legal aid is not normally available in tribunal proceedings although this was recommended by the Franks Report, and see now p. 566 *supra*; (b) costs are not normally awarded (but see s. 3 (5) of the Lands Tribunal Act 1949; and (c) representatives from trade unions and pressure groups have often been more successful: see Milton in *Justice, Discretion and Poverty* (edd. Alder and and Bradley), p. 139 for a survey which suggested that, in S.B.A.T.s, voluntary representatives were more effective than solicitors, and social workers were more effective than both. See also the *Report of the Royal Commission on Legal Services*, vol. 2, Tables 4.5 and 4.9, which confirm Milton's results. Legal advice under the Legal Advice and Assistance Act 1972 is, however, available. Both the Council on Tribunals and the Royal Commission on Legal Services (Note 1 *supra*) have emphasized the need to tap the skills of laymen if an adequate scheme of representation. is to be provided. See also Lawrence, *Tribunal Representation, The Role of Advice and Advocacy Services*.

Reasons for decisions

Tribunals and Inquiries Act 1971, Section 12, p. 22 *supra*

Crake v. Supplementary Benefits Commission, p. 25 *supra*

Note

For consideration of whether the statutory duty is mandatory or directory, see p. 26 *supra*; Wraith and Hutchesson, pp. 149–52. The Council on Tribunals has, over the years, drawn attention to a number of ways in which this obligation was not being observed, for instance by the use of standard formulae (see Annual Reports for 1961, paras. 43–5; 1962, para. 44; 1963, paras. 29 and 31; 1966, para. 69; and 1972/3, paras. 70–3). Particular concern was expressed about reasons given by

S.B.A.T.s and in 1972 the Council asked the Department of Health and Social Security to send a letter, containing the Council's views, to all S.B.A.T. chairmen (this is set out as Appendix B to the Annual Report for 1972/3). It stated, *inter alia*:

3. The Council fully endorse the views expressed by the Franks Committee (paragraph 98 of the Report) that a decision is apt to be better if reasons for it have to be set out in writing because the reasons are then more likely to have been properly thought out. . . .

4. Rulings of the courts in recent years have indicated that reasons for tribunal decisions will not be regarded as adequate unless they deal with the substantial points in the case and are in themselves clear and intelligible so that a party affected by the decision can tell what the reasons for it were. The Council would regard the need to ensure that decisions were intelligible as of scarcely lesser importance than the need to ensure that they were right.

5. In all cases coming before tribunals it should be possible to record the salient facts – they will rarely be many – which the tribunal has found to be established. The tribunal's findings on the facts shown in the appeal documents, and on any written or oral evidence submitted, should therefore be specific and not merely referred to obliquely. . . .

6. The reasons which, on the facts established, led the tribunal to their decision should, in the Council's view, be clearly identified however briefly they may be expressed. Formulas such as –

'The tribunal was satisfied after due consideration that on all the evidence the Appellant and Mr. X were considered to be living as man and wife.'

disclose no reasons whatever for the decision: it is impossible to identify any particular consideration that may have weighed with the tribunal and the person adversely affected by such a finding would have no means of knowing on what evidence the finding rested. . . .

This advice is repeated in the official guide to the procedure of S.B.A.T.s (Appendix 4).

APPEALS ON QUESTIONS OF LAW AND DISCRETION

Note

See Wade, p. 814. This topic has been dealt with at pp. 62, 64, 364, and 558 *supra*.

THE COUNCIL ON TRIBUNALS

The Functions of the Council on Tribunals

Cmnd. 7805 (1980)

THE FRANKS COMMITTEE AND SUBSEQUENT LEGISLATION

2.4. The Committee recommended[27] that two Councils on Tribunals, one for England and Wales and the other for Scotland, should be set up to supervise tribunal and inquiry procedures. The report stressed[28] the importance of continuous supervision: the supervising bodies would be consulted whenever it was proposed to establish a new type of tribunal, and would also keep under review the constitution and working of existing tribunals. The Council for England and Wales would be appointed by and report to the Lord Chancellor. . . .

[27] 1957, Cmnd. 218 (Chapter 4). [See p. 538 *supra*.]
[28] *ibid.* (Chapter 11).

2.5. As proposed by the Franks Committee, the Council on Tribunals would have had important executive powers as well as advisory ones. For example, they would have been empowered to appoint the members (as distinct from the chairmen) of tribunals; to review the remuneration of tribunal appointments; to give advice on the basis of which the duties and conduct of tribunal clerks would be regulated; and to formulate procedural rules for tribunals, in the light of the general principles enunciated by the Committee.

2.6. The main powers which were in fact conferred on us and on the Scottish Committee on the Council by the Tribunals and Inquiries Act of 1958 were subsequently embodied in the Act of 1971.[29] They may be paraphrased as follows:

(a) to keep under review the constitution and working of the tribunals specified in Schedule 1 to the Act;

(b) to consider and report on particular matters referred to the Council by the Lord Chancellor and the Lord Advocate[30] with respect to any tribunal other than an ordinary court of law, whether or not specified in Schedule 1; and

(c) to consider and report on such matters as may be so referred, or as the Council may consider to be of special importance, with respect to administrative procedures which may involve the holding by or on behalf of a Minister of a statutory inquiry.

2.7 Our powers are thus consultative and advisory, not executive; and in certain respects they are more limited than the Franks Committee recommended. We have no function with regard to the remuneration or conditions of service of tribunal chairmen, members or staff: and no power to make appointments or to formulate rules.

2.8 However, we must be consulted by the appropriate rule-making authority before procedural rules are made for any tribunal specified in Schedule 1 to the 1971 Act[31] and on procedural rules made by the Lord Chancellor in connection with statutory inquiries.[32] We must be consulted before any scheduled tribunal can be exempted from the requirement under Section 12 of the Act to give reasons for its decisions upon request. The same situation applies to Ministerial decisions taken after a statutory inquiry. We may make general recommendations to appropriate Ministers about tribunal membership.[33] We are required to make an Annual Report to the Lord Chancellor and the Lord Advocate, which must be laid by them before Parliament with such comments, if any, as they think fit.[34]

2.9 It is clear from this summary that our powers in relation to tribunals are differently expressed from those in relation to inquiries. We have a duty

---

[29] Tribunals and Inquiries Act 1971, s. 1(1)(a), (b) & (c).
[30] S. 4; and Transfer of Functions (Secretary of State and Lord Advocate) Order 1972, S.I. 1972 no. 2002.   [31] S. 10 [See Wade, p. 824, for this list.]
[32] S. 11.   [33] S. 5.
[34] S. 4; and S.I. 1972 no. 2002.

'to keep under review the constitution and working' of the tribunals listed in Schedule 1, but no corresponding duty with respect to procedures involving statutory inquiries.[35] On the other hand, the wording of the Act relating to our power to consider and report on particular matters concerning tribunals is more restrictive than it is in relation to inquiries. In the case of tribunals, our powers are limited to such matters as are referred to the Council, whereas in the case of statutory inquiries, we have an additional power to report on any matter we may ourselves think to be of 'special importance'. . . .

THE CONSTITUTION, STAFFING AND OPERATION OF THE COUNCIL

3.1 Under the Tribunals and Inquiries Act 1971 we are to have not more than fifteen nor less than ten members appointed by the Lord Chancellor and the Lord Advocate. . . .

3.3 Appointments to the Council have generally been for terms of three years. Most members have been appointed for a second term and some for several terms. The appointments of the Chairman and members are all part-time ones. . . .

3.4 [I]n making appointments the practice has been to strike a balance between legal and other skills and experience. At present there are four practising lawyers, one academic lawyer and one qualified but non-practising barrister serving on the Council. Thus there is a preponderance of non-lawyers. One member is an academic with special experience of research in the field of social administration. Other members have a background of trade unionism, social work, consumer protection, public administration, business and agriculture.

3.5 The full Council meet once a month, except during August, and major issues are dealt with at these meetings. A good deal of preparatory and routine work is entrusted to committees.[36] . . .

3.6 Our work at any given time is difficult to classify. The consideration of draft procedural rules for tribunals and inquiries continues to form an important part of it, but we often have on hand the consideration of several Bills currently before Parliament, proposals for legislation and problems relating to inquiries.

3.7 Our members visit tribunals and inquiries to observe the operation in practice of the procedures which we have helped to settle. Visiting members take the opportunity, before or after a tribunal hearing, to discuss the work of the tribunal with the chairman and to have a look at the premises. Members always report in writing to the Council on their visits, and these reports are considered in confidence at Council meetings.

3.8 The visiting of tribunals and inquiries is carried out under our general supervisory powers.[37] Doubts have been raised from time to time about our

---

[35] Act of 1971, ss. 1(1)(*a*) & 1(1)(*c*). The expression 'to keep under review' is vague, and its scope is difficult to interpret.   [36] See Appendix 5 to this report.
[37] See chapter 2 of this report.

entitlement to attend hearings held in private, and to remain at the 'deliberation stage' after public or private hearings. For certain tribunals the position has been clarified to some extent by rules,[38] but it would be more satisfactory if our members were empowered to visit the private hearings of all tribunals under our supervision, and to attend the deliberation stage of the proceedings of those tribunals. We attach a good deal of importance to visiting, and the strengthening of our powers in this way would add to our influence and authority.

3.9 We frequently have discussions with representatives of Government departments, and occasionally with Ministers. In addition, we have to deal with a considerable volume of complaints, representations and general correspondence from people or organisations concerned with tribunal or inquiry procedures. . . .

3.10 Our secretariat is very small. In addition to the Secretary, the staff of the Council consists of one Principal, two Senior Legal Assistants, one Higher Executive Officer, three Executive Officers and clerical staff. For operational purposes our organisation is regarded as part of the Lord Chancellor's Department; we rely on that department to authorise our expenditure and we have no independent budget.

SOME PROBLEMS

5.4 Under the heading of matters requiring statutory attention, our committee considered [*inter alia*] the absence of any requirement that we be consulted on proposed primary legislation affecting tribunals or inquiries, and of any power to require our views (expressed in response to statutorily prescribed consultation) to be made public.

5.5 The last mentioned point is of particular importance. From time to time we have been consulted by a Minister and our views have not been accepted. Ministers are, of course, fully entitled to disregard our recommendations, but a statement in Parliament or in regulations that action has been taken after consultation with us is then – although strictly correct – misleading because it gives the impression that we agreed with the course adopted. . . .

SOME FEATURES OF THE COUNCIL'S WORK

6.3 Our most important contribution over the years has, we believe, been our constant effort to translate the general ideals of the Franks Committee into workable codes of principles and practice, accepted and followed by all those who are responsible for setting up administrative tribunals, devising their manner of operation and, indeed, serving upon them as chairmen and members.

6.4 So we operate at several different levels. In the first place we seek to influence the shape of prospective legislation which may establish new tribunals or inquiry procedures, or may affect existing tribunals or inquiries;

[38] e.g. Immigration Appeals (Procedure) Rules 1972 (S.I. 1972 no. 1684) rules 32(4); Mental Health Review Tribunal Rules 1960 (S.I. 1960 no. 1139) rule 24(5).

or – equally important – which may fail to provide such procedures in circumstances in which we believe that the citizen needs their protection. Thus we welcome, and indeed have come to expect, consultation by Government departments while new procedures are still in the formative stage, and before officials or Ministers are firmly committed to their design and scope. Our interest naturally continues while those procedures are being developed and (where necessary) passing through Parliament, and covers the detailed provisions of the regulations which govern their operation. As already mentioned, our consideration of draft primary legislation is carried out without any specific authority and we should be considerably strengthened in this part of our work if consultation with us on such legislation were clearly provided for by statute. . . .

6.7 The points with which we are particularly concerned at the formative stage are all directed to improving the ability of citizens to challenge administrative decisions affecting their interests. For example, we are vigilant in seeking to ensure that people are given a hearing as of right in suitable cases, and are not denied one if they request it; that rights of appeal are granted whenever appropriate and not eroded where they already exist; and that parties to tribunal proceedings are treated equitably, neither side being given an unfair advantage.

6.8 In relation to the constitution of tribunals we have (following a recommendation of the Franks Committee[39]) advocated that chairmen should, in most cases, be legally qualified: and we have lost no opportunity of recommending the 'presidential' system of organisation under which a particular class of tribunal has a national president or chairman and, where the number of tribunals in that class justifies it, regional chairmen as well.[40] This form of organisation facilitates the training of chairmen and members, fosters a desirable spirit of independence and properly emphasises a feeling of separation between the tribunals and the administration of the responsible Government department. It also provides us with an excellent channel of communication. We have had many valuable meetings with national presidents and chairmen.

6.9 Some of the safeguards which we are anxious to secure are best embodied in primary legislation or procedural rules. This applies, for example, to provisions governing time-limits within which rights of appeal must be exercised and various procedural steps taken. Another example is the giving of properly reasoned decisions by tribunals. In relation to this matter we are fortified by a statutory provision,[41] but it is also necessary for us to monitor the observance of this practice so far as we are able to do so. For instance, we found it necessary to issue detailed advice to Supplementary Benefit Appeal Tribunals as to how they should interpret and implement the duty to give

---

[39] (1957) Cmnd. 218: rec. (4).
[40] For example, Industrial Tribunals.
[41] Tribunals and Inquiries Act 1971, section 12.

reasons which is placed upon them by the relevant rules.[42] This advice is repeated in the official guide to the procedure of these tribunals.[43]

6.10 Our interest is not, however, limited to matters which figure in Acts of Parliament or procedural rules. For example, we are particularly concerned that tribunals should be able to cope effectively with the volume of business coming before them, and the appearance of a substantial back-log of cases awaiting decision has caused us to intervene on several occasions.[44] We take constant interest in the fitness and accessibility of the premises in which tribunal hearings are held, and make representations if premises appear to be unsuitable – for example, because of their lack of provision for disabled people,[45] or because of their location in relation to the offices of the responsible Government department.[46]

6.11 We have repeatedly stressed the importance of proper training for chairmen and members of tribunals, to cover not only the particular subject of a tribunal's work but also – even more important – the general principles of fair adjudication. We have frequently taken part in training conferences and have attended many meetings of chairmen at which training and other subjects of common interest have been discussed. . . .

6.13 Finally, we have always been concerned that clerks to tribunals should be independent of the departments concerned and be regarded as working solely for those tribunals during their period of service. They should play an important but at the same time a defined and limited part in tribunal proceedings. This implies that they, rather than representatives of the department concerned, should serve all notices of hearings and notifications of decisions:[47] and that they should not appear in any way to be associated with a 'sponsoring' department. Our detailed advice on the duties of clerks to Supplementary Benefit Appeal Tribunals has been reprinted in the procedural guide.[48]

6.14 In all our work in connection with tribunals we have to bear in mind that they do not represent a single homogeneous group but vary widely in their constitution, membership, functions and organisation. . . .

COMPLAINTS

7.3 We have no statutory jurisdiction in relation to complaints, but during the Parliamentary proceedings which led to the enactment of the Tribunals and Inquiries Act 1958 it was indicated by a Government spokesman[49] that we would be able to deal with complaints. In our early years the handling of

---

[42] AR 1972/73 (HC 82) Appendix B.
[43] ISBN 0 11 760642 1, Appendix 4.
[44] e.g. AR 1975/76 (HC 236) para. 70 (Immigration Appeals).
[45] e.g. AR 1977/78 (HC 74) paras. 6.1 & 6.2.
[46] e.g. AR 1976/77 (HC 108) para. 6.3.
[47] e.g. AR 1977/78 (HC 74) paras. 6.30 & 6.31 (General Commissioners of Income Tax).
[48] ISBN 0 11 760642 1, Appendix 1.
[49] Official Report, Standing Committee B, 10 July 1958, col. 28.

complaints – in the absence of any other machinery for dealing with them – bulked quite large in our work. For some years our Annual Reports provided details of the more important investigations we carried out.

7.5 We can usefully consider complaints drawing attention to some procedural difficulty which points to the need for an amendment of rules or an alteration of administrative practice. Even in relation to complaints of this type, however, we are conscious that we can very rarely give any direct satisfaction to an individual who has complained.

7.7 The Parliamentary Commissioner[50] cannot consider the substance of any matter which has been referred to a tribunal or public inquiry, but he can investigate a department's administrative handling of its own procedures before and after a tribunal or inquiry hearing. He can also investigate the way in which public local inquiries are conducted. In relation to tribunals, the actual proceedings and decisions are outside the jurisdiction of the Parliamentary Commissioner.

7.10 This leaves us with the problem of deciding how best to deal with the residual body of complaints arising from the hearings of tribunals. We see no difficulty in continuing to handle those representations which can be satisfactorily answered without carrying out an investigation. The main difficulty for us lies in those cases where there is a suggestion of procedural deficiencies but conflicting accounts are given of the same events, because we have no means of getting at the truth by interviewing people or calling for files and other papers. After making whatever enquiries are possible in the circumstances we frequently have to say that there is a conflict of evidence which cannot be resolved. Inevitably, time is taken up by these enquiries, and this may increase the disappointment felt by some complainants with the results of our investigations.

7.17 To give us a wide statutory power for the handling of complaints would almost inevitably have certain consequences. The work-load would increase, with heavier pressure on the members; and there would be repercussions on staffing and accommodation. Although unlikely, it is also possible that our present relationship with Government departments might be endangered, and the chairmen and members of tribunals and inspectors at statutory inquiries might become less co-operative than they now are. In the long run, the balance of our work might be significantly changed, with the focus shifting to our rôle as ombudsman for tribunals and inquiries, in priority over our existing statutory functions. This in our view would be undesirable.

7.18 On balance, therefore, although we propose that we should be given specific responsibility for complaints in relation to our field of work, it is important that the extent of our jurisdiction be clearly defined. The power could be on the following lines:

(*a*) a member of the public alleging a procedural irregularity in a hearing

[50] [See Ch. 18 *infra.*]

before a tribunal or statutory inquiry would be entitled to make a formal complaint to us;

(b) we would then have to consider whether the complaint *prima facie* raised a substantial point of principle relating to procedure;

(c) if we came to that conclusion, we would be empowered to obtain papers and other information from the relevant tribunal or inquiry and from the Government department concerned, to question the complainant and any other person involved, and to submit a report to the complainant, the department and, at our discretion, to anyone else . . .

(d) if we decided that the complaint did not *prima facie* raise a substantial point of principle we would refer the matter without comment to the department concerned, who would be required to report to us the outcome of their own enquiries.

7.19 In addition to this action on complaints from members of the public, we would be empowered at our discretion to conduct an investigation into an alleged procedural irregularity referred to us by the department concerned. We would not, however, at any time investigate a complaint relating to the merits of a decision or recommendation; or concerning the conduct of chairmen or members; or which fell within the competence of the Parliamentary Commissioner; or which could reasonably form the basis for an appeal or some other proceeding in a court of law. . . .

7.20 This solution would not remove the slight overlap of functions between the Parliamentary Commissioner and ourselves, which already exists. The Parliamentary Commissioner would retain his jurisdiction to investigate complaints of maladministration against Government departments in relation to procedures which included public inquiries, and in relation to the pre-hearing and post-decision administrative handling by departments of matters referred to tribunals. Our jurisdiction would be limited to the form and operation of procedures, but within that limitation it would extend to events which took place within the doors of the tribunal or inquiry.

INFORMATION, ANALYSIS AND RESEARCH

8.4 The essential point is that our activity in relation to tribunals and inquiries must be founded on detailed knowledge. At present there is no other statutory body to collect information, on a methodical basis, about the operation of the tribunal and inquiry system. Departments do, of course, provide us with some statistics on tribunals and inquiries with which they are concerned, but the overall coverage is incomplete, unco-ordinated and rather superficial. We ourselves do not have the resources to produce what is needed.

8.5 Such a stock of information is a necessary foundation for the tasks of evaluation which must be undertaken if we are to do our job properly. Our problem-solving would become better, faster and more reliable. At present, our staff are fully stretched in coping with day-to-day work connected mainly with matters of immediate concern, and have little time to undertake systematic studies.

WHAT IS NEEDED – A GENERAL PERSPECTIVE

9.2 The case for a statutory advisory body with . . . [a] . . . general oversight appears to us to be even stronger now than at the time of the Franks Committee. Since then the tendency for issues arising out of legislative schemes to be referred to tribunals has continued unabated, in a largely piecemeal manner. Not only has there been considerable growth in the number of tribunals, they are operating increasingly in difficult and sensitive areas – for example, immigration,[51] compulsory detention under mental health legislation,[52] misuse of drugs,[53] equal pay,[54] redundancy,[55] unfair dismissal from employment,[56] and supplementary benefits.[57]

9.4 Moreover, the changed situation since 1957 is not confined to tribunals. Statutory inquiries have assumed an increasingly controversial rôle. Planning, redevelopment, land usage, highway policy, siting of major airports, development of natural resources and exploitation of new sources of energy are raising issues of a greater order of magnitude than those current at the time of the Franks Committee. Our position as an independent statutory advisory body with the broadest range of knowledge in this field is being recognised by Ministers, Government departments and other organisations.

9.5 Since we were set up, significant changes have also taken place in the general constitutional and administrative climate. There is, for example, a movement towards greater formalism in procedures for settling disputes. The process started with reforms following the Franks Report which, in general, made tribunals more like courts. It had to be demonstrated that tribunals were not adjuncts of Government departments and that in their decision-making they followed a judicial process. Since then the trend towards judicialisation has gathered momentum with the result that tribunals are becoming more formal, expensive and procedurally complex. Consequently they tend to become more difficult for an ordinary citizen to comprehend and cope with on his own. There is, we believe, an urgent need to keep the whole of this movement under the closest scrutiny. We believe that we are in a position to play a key rôle in the achievement of a right balance.

9.6 There is also a constant need, as was emphasised in discussion with our Committee, for an independent body able to offer advice to Government on what kinds of dispute are appropriate or inappropriate for adjudication by

[51] Immigration Act 1971, s. 12.
[53] Mental Health Act 1959, s. 3.
[53] Misuse of Drugs Act 1971, Schedule 3.
[54] Equal Pay Act 1970.
[55] Redundancy Payments Act 1965 and subsequent legislation.
[56] Trade Union and Labour Relations Act 1974 Schedule 1, as amended, and Employment Protection (Consolidation) Act 1978.
[57] Supplementary Benefits Act 1976, Schedule 4.

tribunals. We believe that we can exercise this function, and can develop criteria indicating the kinds of decision which, if disputed, should be subject to review by processes external to the departments concerned; the most appropriate form of review; the degree of formality required, according to the type of decision; and whether a proposed tribunal should come under our supervision.

9.8 Finally, we draw attention to particular problems running across the whole field which need co-ordinated rather than piecemeal approach: for example, a much wider system for recruitment of tribunal members, including more women; arrangements for training of both chairmen and members; the presidential system; conferences and seminars; the publication of explanatory leaflets; and the clarification and simplification of official forms.

9.10 . . . At present, we are perhaps in a better position than any other official body to appreciate the wider implications of the particular matters referred to us, and to consider the important issues relating to the system as a whole to which they give rise. We therefore recommend strongly that the statutory power of the Council to act as a *general* advisory body in the field of administrative adjudication be placed beyond doubt.

Notes

1. It is unlikely that any major changes will result from this report. The Lord Chancellor has said (419 H.L. Deb., col. 1118) that 'the case has not been made out for any substantial widening of [the Council's] powers or functions on the lines proposed in the report's principal recommendations, particularly as this would create additional demands on resources'. However, he went on to say that the Government accepted that it would be desirable for the Council's entitlement to be consulted about procedural rules for tribunals and inquiries to be restated in clearer and more general terms. In the Annual Report for 1980/1 the Council regretted that its major recommendations had not been accepted but welcomed the recognition that the Council's entitlement to be consulted needed restatement. To this end it drafted guidelines for the consultations (para. 2.8).

2. The report also concerns statutory inquiries, on which see the next chapter.

17

STATUTORY INQUIRIES

THE SYSTEM OF INQUIRIES

An administrative technique

Note

The second head of the Franks Committee's terms of reference was 'the working of such administrative procedures as include the holding of an enquiry or hearing by or on behalf of a Minister' (see p. 533 *supra*). Inquiries are often used to hear objections and fully to inform the Minister before a decision is made on some question of government policy. The bulk of the evidence before the Franks Committee concerned inquiries relating to land such as those preceding compulsory purchase orders and housing and highway development, but many other administrative functions also use the inquiry as a procedural mechanism. See Wade, Ch. 24, and, for a more detailed study, Wraith and Lamb, *Public Inquiries as an Instrument of Government* (hereafter Wraith and Lamb); see also Ganz, *Administrative Procedures*, Ch. 4–6. Examples include discretionary inquiries (Wade, p. 860; Wraith and Lamb, pp. 157–9), accident inquiries into, for instance, railway accidents (Wade, p. 870; Wraith and Lamb, pp. 146–53), and Tribunals of Inquiry under the Tribunals of Inquiry (Evidence) Act 1921 on issues such as the unauthorized disclosure of budget secrets, the Aberfan disaster, and accusations of brutality against the police (Wade, p. 872; Wraith and Lamb, pp. 214–17). More recently two public local inquiries, into the proposals to build a plant to reprocess nuclear fuel waste at Windscale and to develop a major new coalfield in the Vale of Belvoir, were used as a forum for wide-ranging investigations into the manner in which competing interests for the utilization of energy resources and the protection of the environment were to be accommodated. On such inquiries see The Outer Circle Policy Unit, *The Big Public Inquiry*, noted at [1979] J.P.L. 501; Beatson, (1981) 55 Tulane L. Rev. 435 at pp. 453–7. For a useful general study of public local inquiries, see Williams, (1980) 29 I.C.L.Q. 701.

The person appointed by the Minister (in many cases the Secretary of State for the Environment) to conduct the inquiry may either be a full-time salaried departmental inspector or a part time fee-paid independent inspector. In planning cases a departmental inspector will normally be used where the department is, in effect, adjudicating between a local authority and a citizen, but if the department itself initiates the proposals it is more usual to have an independent inspector. In major inquiries the inspector may be a Queen's Counsel or even, as in the Windscale Inquiry, a High Court judge. The traditional position is that the inspector reports to the relevant Minister, who makes the decision, but, as will be seen, the number of cases in which the Minister differs from the inspector is very small. Moreover, centralized decision-making led to delays and since 1968 inspectors have been authorized to determine certain classes of case (see p. 581 *infra*). By 1972 eighty per cent of planning appeals had been transferred to inspectors for decision and the Department of the Environment has proposed that nearly all (ninty-five per cent) appeals should be so transferred. The Secretary of State would only decide a case where the scale of the development, the complexity of the issue, or other policy considerations warrant it (Justice–All Souls, *Review of Administrative Law in the United Kingdom, Discussion Paper*, p. 29).

There have been many changes, particularly in town and country planning, since the Franks Report. For details see Wade, pp. 157–82, and specialist books on planning law, e.g. Heap, *An Outline of Planning Law*, 7th edn.; McAuslan, *Land, Law and Planning*; *The Ideologies of Planning Law*; Blundell and Dobry's, *Planning Appeals and Inquiries*, 3rd edn., ed. Carnwath. For present purposes it is sufficient to give an outline of them:

(a) *Compulsory Purchase*, governed by the Acquisition of Land Act 1981 and similar procedures under other statutes, e.g. the Housing Act 1957 and *Coleen Properties Ltd.* v. *Minister of Housing and Local Government*, p. 81 *supra*. The acquiring authority must advertise a compulsory purchase order in the local press, describing the land, giving particulars of the purpose of the acquisition and of the procedure by which objections may be made. Similar notice must also be served on all owners, lessees, and occupiers. If there are objections, the Minister must arrange for a hearing at which all interested parties may be heard unless the objections relate solely to compensation, in which case they are dealt with by a tribunal (see Wade, pp. 685–90). Before confirming a compulsory purchase order the Minister must consider the objections and the inspector's report of the hearing and recommendations. If there are no objections, the Minister may confirm (or modify) the order without a hearing. On the extent to which judicial review is available, see *Smith* v. *East Elloe R.D.C.*, p. 380 *supra*; *R.* v. *Secretary of State for the Environment, ex. p. Ostler*, p. 385 *supra*; and see p. 393 *supra*.

(b) *Development Control* is primarily governed by the Town and Country Planning Act 1971 (hereafter T. & C.P. Act 1971). The existing system of planning controls dates from 1947. The basis of the system is that each local planning authority is required to prepare a detailed development plan for its area and that all development requires permission. Compensation is not payable where permission is refused.

(i) *The formation of development plans*: Before 1968 all authorities had to submit development plans and all plans had to be reviewed every five years. Both the initial plan and any revisions were subject to Ministerial approval. If there were any objections the Minister was obliged to hold an inquiry. The large number of plans, their constant tendency towards detail and precision, the length of the public inquiries to which they gave rise, and the generally cumbersome nature of the procedure caused great administrative inconvenience (*The Future of Development Plans: Report of the Planning Advisory Group*). In 1968 the development plan was replaced by a two-tier system of structure plans and local plans: structure plans to deal with broad issues of planning policy, and local plans to deal with details. Local plans do not normally need affirmative Ministerial approval. Structure plans are prepared by county councils, after consulting district councils, and show general planning proposals. They are publicized (s. 8 of the T. & C.P. Act 1971) and at least six weeks must be allowed for members of the public to make representations to the planning authority (T. & C.P. (Structure and Local Plans) Regulations S.I. 1974 No. 1486, para. 5). The old-style public inquiry is replaced by an 'examination in public' to consider 'such matters affecting his consideration of the plan as [the Secretary of State] considers ought to be so examined' (s. 9 (3) (*b*) of the T. &

C.P. Act 1971, as amended by s. 3 of the T. & C.P. (Amendment) Act 1972). The examination in public is not regulated by statutory rules but by a code of practice. This makes it clear that the primary purpose of the examination is to provide the Secretary of State with the information he needs, with which, together with the material submitted with the plan and any objections, he can reach a decision on the structure plan. The examination is to be seen as only a part, though a very important part, in the process by which this decision is made (*Structure Plans: The Examination in Public*, paras. 3.1 and 3.3). Section 3 (5) of the T. & C.P. (Amendment) Act 1972 provides that no one (including a local planning authority) shall have a *right* to be heard and that only those whom the Secretary of State invites may take part in the examination. This is an attempt to limit the issues and reduce the delays, and ensure that matters on which the Secretary of State needs to be more informed are investigated in depth (paras. 3.12 and 3.47). Matters which need to be examined are likely to arise, for instance, from clashes between the plan and national or regional policies or from issues involving substantial controversy which has not been resolved (para. 3.13). The intention was to open the examination, in a normal case, about six to eight months after the submission of the plan and for it to take from between three to six weeks (para. 3.41). 'The essential feature [was to] be a probing discussion, led by the Chairman and other members of the panel, with the local planning authority and the other participants' (para. 3.45). There was to be less formality than in a traditional local inquiry. The Secretary of State may approve (with or without reservations), modify, or reject the plan after the examination in public and is not required to give reasons for his decisions. Greater use has been made of the power to modify than of the power to express reservations on particular issues. The whole procedure is subject to the supervision of the Council on Tribunals.

The legal validity of structure plans and local plans may be questioned by a statutory application to quash within six weeks of publication of approval or adoption (ss. 242 and 244 of the T. & C.P. Act 1971; on the exclusion of review and the scope of review see pp. 380 and 393 *supra*).

(ii) *Planning Permission* is granted by local planning authorities and is required for all development (see further Wade, pp. 169–74 and 365–8. See also pp. 138 and 368 *supra* for cases involving points on planning permission). The sanction for breach of this part of the system of development control is the enforcement notice, requiring the discontinuance of a use or the demolition of a building (ss. 87–9 of the T. & C.P. Act 1971). Development is defined (s. 22 of the T. & C.P. Act 1971) as 'the carrying out of building, engineering, mining or other operations in, on, over or under land' or 'the making of any material change in the use' of the buildings or land. Application may be made to the relevant planning authority to determine whether a proposed change of use is 'material', and therefore needs permission (see *Wells* v. *Minister of Housing and Local Government* [1976] 1 W.L.R. 1000, noted at p. 161 *supra*; *Western Fish Products Ltd.* v. *Penwith D.C.*, p. 156 *supra*).

Applications for planning permission must be advertised on the site and in the local press. Normally no hearings are held before permission is refused although written representations by the landowner and objectors are often considered. There is a right of appeal to the Secretary of State on all these questions. The Secretary of State is obliged to hold a hearing, which generally takes the form of a public local inquiry before an inspector, unless the appellant elects to proceed by way of written representations (s. 36 of the T. & C.P. Act 1971). Most appeals (about seventy per cent), normally involving smaller developments, may be determined by the inspector (Sch. 9 to the T. & C.P. Act 1971; S.I. 1972 No. 1652; S.I. 1977 No. 1939) but otherwise the final decision is made by the Secretary of State. The number of cases in which the Secretary of State differs from the inspector is very small (two to three per cent, according to Payne, (1971) *Journal of the Royal Town Planning Institute*, 114).

Local plans are prepared and publicized in the same way as structure plans except that they are much more detailed. Where there are objections, a local inquiry will be held before a departmental inspector and the local authority may adopt, modify, or reject the plan. Although, before adopting a plan, a local authority must give notice to objectors and to the Secretary of State (who may direct that it shall not have effect: ss. 14 (3) and 35 of the T. & C.P. Act 1971), the fact that, in practice, it is the ultimate judge of its own proposals (even where the inspector has disagreed with them) has been criticized as incompatible with the rules of natural justice (see further p. 584 *infra*; Ch. 7 *supra*, especially *Franklin v. Minister of Town and Country Planning*, p. 204 *supra*. Cf. *R. v. Hammersmith and Fulham L.B.C., ex p. People Before Profit Ltd.* (1982) 80 L.G.R. 322). Another way in which the Secretary of State may control the local planning authority is by the 'call-in' procedure under s. 35 of the T. & C.P. Act 1971, which allows him to determine any planning application himself. This is normally used for particularly large or sensitive developments such as those at Windscale and the Vale of Belvoir (p. 578 *supra*). See further Wraith and Lamb, p. 61.

The decision of the Secretary of State is subject to judicial review (for the extent of which see pp. 138 and 393 *supra*; Wade, pp. 609–19) on much the same lines as in compulsory purchase cases. There is also an appeal to the High Court on a point of law from the Secretary of State's decision on the question of whether planning permission is needed and also against a local authority's enforcement order (ss. 246 and 247 of the T. & C.P. Act 1971).

Statutory inquiries and natural justice

Franklin v. Minister of Town and Country Planning, p. 204 *supra*

Errington v. Minister of Health

[1935] 1 K.B. 249   Court of Appeal

Jarrow Corporation made a clearance order under s. 1 of the Housing Act 1930 and submitted it to the Minister for confirmation. The appellants, who owned property in the area, objected and a public inquiry was held. When the inspector had reported, the Ministry suggested that the Corporation accept a less expensive scheme, but the Corporation disagreed and wanted to send a deputation to the Ministry in London to make its case. The Minister refused to meet representatives of only one side because of his 'quasi-judicial' function. A few days later, the Minister notified the Corporation that two senior officials and the inspector who had held the inquiry would visit Jarrow and could discuss the matter with local councillors and officials. This was done and, afterwards, the Corporation submitted evidence from the borough engineer. The Minister confirmed the order and the appellants sought to have it quashed on the grounds, *inter alia*, that consultation with the Corporation after the inquiry without notice to the appellants or an opportunity for them to attend and reply was a breach of the requirements of the Housing Act and also a breach of the rules of natural justice. (On statutory applications to quash see p. 380 *supra* and Note 4, p. 584 *infra*). Swift J. dismissed the application. On appeal:

GREER L.J.: . . . The powers of the Minister are contained in the Act . . . and under those powers he could, if no objection be taken on behalf of the persons interested in the property, make an Order confirming the order made by the local authority; and in so far as the Minister deals with the matter of the confirmation of a closing order in the absence of objection by the owners it is clear to me . . . that he would be acting in a ministerial or administrative capacity, and would be entitled to make such inquiries as he thought neces-sary to enable him to make up his mind whether it was in the public interest that the Order should be made. But the position, in my judgment, is different where objections are taken by those interested in the properties which will be affected by the order if confirmed and carried out. It seems to me that in deciding whether a closing order should be made in spite of the objections which have been raised by the owners the Minister should be regarded as exercising quasi-judicial functions. The effect of the closing order if con-firmed would be to diminish greatly the value of the property owned by the objecting parties, and the decision of the Minister is a decision relating to the rights of the objecting parties and, in my view, it is a decision in respect of which he is exercising quasi-judicial functions. . . .

. . . [After the inquiry] the Council maintained their view that the only right way of dealing with the situation was to have their clearance order confirmed, and they passed resolutions to that effect and communicated those resolu-tions to the Minister in London. So far as my view of this case goes I am satisfied that there was nothing wrong in the Minister receiving those com-munications from the Council. It was a matter on which the Council were entitled to stress the view that was already implied in the clearance order that they had made in the first instance, but I think it would have been a wise precaution on the part of the Minister when he received those further com-munications from the Council pressing for the confirmation of the order to communicate those letters or verbal persuasions to the other side, the objectors, and ask whether they had anything further to say on the matter. Still, I doubt very much whether, if the position had remained there, any real objection could be taken to the conduct of the Minister in confirming the order. But it did not rest there. . . .

. . . It seems to me that if it was improper . . . to meet in London, it was equally improper . . . to meet in Jarrow in the absence of the representatives of the owners of the property in Jarrow, whom they could easily have obtained.

. . . [I]f, as I think, the Ministry were acting in a quasi-judicial capacity they were doing what a semi-judicial body cannot do, namely, hearing evidence from one side in the absence of the other side, and viewing the property and forming their own views about the property without giving the owners of the property the opportunity of arguing that the views which the Ministry were inclined to take were such as could be readily dealt with by means of repairs and alterations to the buildings. Whether the surveyor was one of the officials, or whether the borough engineer was one of the officials, we do not know; but we do know this, that by a letter of February 24, 1934, which was sent by the Town Clerk to the Ministry of Health, the views of the borough engineer were put before the Minister before the Minister gave his decision. The borough engineer had not been called at the public inquiry. Those who represented the owners had not had the opportunity of cross-examining him, testing the value of his opinion, and representing to the Minister through the Inspector that no weight should be attached to his view. The view of the borough engineer . . . is hardly consistent with the view which had been expressed on behalf of the Borough Council . . . at the inquiry. It is an additional reason being urged by the Council . . . in order to put pressure upon the Ministry to confirm the order which had been made by them.

Now I think it quite clear on the authorities that if this were a case not affected by the special legislation contained in s. 11 of the Act of 1930, certiorari would have been granted to quash the confirming Order. I take that to be the law as laid down by Viscount Haldane L.C. and Lord Parmoor in *Local Government Board* v. *Arlidge.*[1]

[After considering that case and other authorities, he said: Para. 4 of Sch. 1 to the Housing Act 1930 provides that, where there are objections to a clearance order, the Minister] '. . . shall, before confirming the order, cause a public local inquiry to be held and shall consider any objection not withdrawn and the report of the person who held the inquiry, and may then confirm the order, either with or without modification.' It seems to me that that involves the proposition that the matters there mentioned are the only matters which he is entitled to consider, and that if, instead of directing his mind solely to those matters, he takes into consideration evidence which might have been, but was not, given at the public inquiry, but was given ex parte afterwards without the owners having any opportunity whatever to deal with that evidence, then it seems to me that the confirming Order was not within the powers of the Act. . . . [A] quasi-judicial officer in exercising his powers must do it in accordance with the rules of natural justice, that is to say, he must hear both sides and must not hear one side in the absence of the other.
. . .

MAUGHAM L.J.: . . . [H]ad it been intended by the legislature to authorise the Minister after having caused a public inquiry to be held and after having received the report, then to hold a private inquiry of his own – with regard to something which was the subject of an objection which was being considered before the Inspector, I should have expected the legislature to say so in plain terms. My conclusion is, that on the fair construction of the clause he has no right to do anything of the kind. That is not to say that there may not be

[1] [1915] A. C. 120.

matters which were not in dispute at all at the inquiry, and which were not the subject of anything dealt with at the inquiry, with regard to which he might, if he thought fit, inform himself. . . .

[ROCHE L.J. delivered a judgment in favour of allowing the appeal.]

Appeal allowed,
Order quashed.

Notes

1. *Errington's* case has been set out as an example of the application of natural justice to the statutory inquiry procedure. See further *Bushell* v. *Secretary for the Environment,* p. 601 *infra*; Ch. 8 *supra* (natural justice in general). For the application of natural justice in this area and the limitations on it see Wade, pp. 452 and 837; de Smith, pp. 208–11. Note, for example, *Lake District Special Planning Board* v. *Secretary of State for the Environment* [1975] J.P.L. 220 in which it was said that receiving representations from one side after the inquiry and not communicating them to others will not necessarily be a breach of natural justice: the reasonable man knowing all the facts must think there was a risk of injustice having resulted. See Jaconelli and Sauvain, (1977) 40 M.L.R. 87, and, more generally on the question of the risk of injustice, see p. 234 *supra*.

2. The presence of a *lis inter partes* may be less important than it was in the light of recent developments in the rules of natural justice: see Ch. 8 *supra*. The influence of the *lis* has been uneven: see Wade, p. 455. Although it justified the imposition of certain procedural safeguards, it also led to rather artificial distinctions between different stages of the inquiry (which are still influential: see p. 607 *infra*). It also led to the distinction, which is still made, between inquiries into schemes initiated by the Minister (such as in *Franklin's* case, p. 204 *supra*, and *Bushell's* case, p. 608 *infra*) and those in which the Minister's role is to confirm a scheme made by another, for instance, a local authority (such as in *Errington's* case). The Franks Committee (para. 267, p. 586 *infra*) thought that such distinctions were not useful when considering the general nature of the various types of inquiry and in *Bushell's* case Lord Diplock did not think that the analogy of a *lis* was useful (see p. 608 *infra*).

3. Such inquiries are now governed by procedural rules, on which see Note 2, p. 595 *infra*, and p. 598 *infra*.

4. *Errington's* case involved a statutory application to quash, hence Greer L.J.'s reference (p. 583 *supra*) to the fact that the order was 'not within the powers of the Act'. The statute, in common with others, empowered the court to quash an order on this ground or on the ground that the interests of the applicants had been substantially prejudiced by failure to comply with any statutory requirement. At one time there was doubt as to whether, as Greer L.J. thought, breach of natural justice fell under the former or the latter limb of the statutory formula (Maugham and Roche L.JJ. differed from Greer L.J.: see [1935] K.B. 249 at pp. 279 and 282). The better view is that it falls under both: see *Fairmount Investments Ltd.* v. *Secretary of State for the Environment* [1976] 1 W.L.R. 1255; *George* v. *Secretary of State for the Environment* (1979) 38 P. & C.R. 609 (but note the view here on the need for prejudice in a natural justice case even under the first limb, and see more generally p. 234 *supra*). Cf. Lord Edmund-Davies and Lord Lane in *Bushell* v. *Secretary of State for the Environment,* pp. 611–12 *infra*. For an example (now repealed but replaced) of this type of statutory formula, see *Smith* v. *East Elloe R.D.C.,* p. 380 *supra*.

REFORMS

Report of The Committee on Administrative Tribunals and Enquiries
Cmnd 218 (1957)

The general nature and purpose of . . . procedures [involving an enquiry or hearing]

262. Two strongly opposed views may be held about these procedures. They may be termed the 'administrative' and the 'judicial' views, and we state them, for convenience and simplicity, at their extremes. We then set out some considerations which have led us to take a different view.

263. According to the first view the entire procedure must be regarded as administrative, in the sense that: – (i) the decisions taken at its culmination have as their purpose the furtherance of the positive processes of government; (ii) provided that the deciding Minister does not overstep the legal limits of his powers, his discretion whether to decide positively or negatively in a particular case and, if positively, whether or not to modify the original proposals, is wholly unfettered; (iii) the Minister is responsible only to Parliament for the decision taken; and finally (iv) in the nature of the subject-matter it is impossible to formulate rules to govern the decision and wholly inappropriate to base it upon precedent.

264. According to the other view the procedure possesses several essential elements of a judicial process, inasmuch as: – (i) special arrangements are provided by statute for the lodging and consideration of objections – a feature not to be found in the general course of administrative activity; and (ii) at the hearing or enquiry two or more parties, taking opposing views of what should be done, dispute the matter before a specially appointed person who, though he does not decide it himself, nevertheless plays an important part in the process of decision. Thus regarded, the enquiry appears to take on something of the nature of a trial and the inspector to assume the guise of a judge. It is further argued that, because of the 'judicial' nature of the enquiry, the ensuing decision is or should be 'judicial' in the sense that it should be based wholly and directly upon the evidence presented at the enquiry.

265. The administrative procedures relating to land may be classified in various ways. The courts, for example, have drawn a broad distinction between cases in which a Minister has the function of confirming the proposals of a local or other authority and cases in which the Minister is himself the initiator. On the statutes relevant to the former cases they have held that once objection has been lodged to the proposals, a *quasi-lis* (that is, something in the nature of a dispute between parties) comes into existence, and the Minister must from that moment until he has taken the decision act in a judicial manner. For example, he may not in that situation receive evidence from one party behind the back of the other party. When, however, the Minister is himself the initiating authority, the courts have not on the statutes relevant to such cases been able to introduce this conception.

266. Alternatively, the procedures might be divided into three categories: — (i) cases in which a Minister has to decide between a local authority and objectors concerning proposals initiated by the local authority (for example, in the acquisition of land by local authorities and the making of development plans); (ii) cases in which the Minister, as in (i), has to decide between a local authority and objectors, but in which the proposals at issue are initiated by the objectors, who in most cases would be private individuals (for example, in an appeal against a refusal of planning permission by a local planning authority); and (iii) cases in which the proposal is initiated by a Minister, whether a general scheme (for example, the designation of a new town site) or a proposal for the actual acquisition of land (for example, for an aerodrome or trunk road).

267. These and other possible distinctions are useful in considering detailed aspects of the various procedures, but they are misleading when what has to be considered is their general nature. Not only is the impact of these various procedures the same so far as the individual citizen is concerned, for he is at issue with a public authority in all of them, but they also have basic common features of importance when regarded from a wider point of view. All involve the weighing of proposals or decisions, or provisional proposals or decisions, made by a public authority on the one hand against the views and interests of individuals affected by them on the other. All culminate in a ministerial decision, in the making of which there is a wide discretion and which is final. Because of the importance of these common features it is reasonable to consider the various procedures together when formulating a broad approach to them.

269. The intention of the legislature in providing for an enquiry or hearing in certain circumstances appears to have been twofold: to ensure that the interest of the citizens closely affected should be protected by the grant to them of a statutory right to be heard in support of their objections, and to ensure that thereby the Minister should be better informed of the facts of the case.

270. In practice third parties are generally permitted to take part in public local enquiries, but in an acquisition case the Minister is only bound to hold a hearing or enquiry when objections are sustained by persons directly interested in the land affected by the proposals. He is not bound to do so if either no objections are raised or the objections raised come from parties without a direct interest in the land or they relate solely to compensation.

271. Although the statutory requirements are merely to hear and consider objections, it must surely be true that an objection cannot reasonably be considered as a thing in itself, in isolation from what is objected to. The consideration of objections thus involves the testing of an issue, though it must be remembered that it may be only a part of the issue which the Minister will ultimately have to determine. If so, then the case against which objections are raised should be presented and developed with sufficient detail and argument to permit the proper weighing of the one against the other.

272. Our general conclusion is that these procedures cannot be classified as purely administrative or purely judicial. They are not purely administrative because of the provision for a special procedure preliminary to the decision – a feature not to be found in the ordinary course of administration – and because this procedure, as we have shown, involves the testing of an issue, often partly in public. They are not on the other hand purely judicial, because the final decision cannot be reached by the application of rules and must allow the exercise of a wide discretion in the balancing of public and private interest. Neither view at its extreme is tenable, nor should either be emphasised at the expense of the other.

273. If the administrative view is dominant the public enquiry cannot play its full part in the total process, and there is a danger that the rights and interests of the individual citizens affected will not be sufficiently protected. In these cases it is idle to argue that Parliament can be relied upon to protect the citizen, save exceptionally. We agree with the following views expressed in the pamphlet entitled *Rule of Law*: 'Whatever the theoretical validity of this argument, those of us who are Members of Parliament have no hesitation in saying that it bears little relation to reality. Parliament has neither the time nor the knowledge to supervise the Minister and call him to account for his administrative decisions.'[2]

274. If the judicial view is dominant there is a danger that people will regard the person before whom they state their case as a kind of judge provisionally deciding the matter, subject to an appeal to the Minister. This view overlooks the true nature of the proceeding, the form of which is necessitated by the fact that the Minister himself, who is responsible to Parliament for the ultimate decision, cannot conduct the enquiry in person.

275. Most of the evidence which we have received, other than the evidence from Government Departments, has placed greater emphasis on judicial aspects of the procedure. The view is that present procedure, either in regard to actual law or to practice, do not sufficiently reflect the essentially adjudicative nature of the process. From the point of view the citizen what begins in many ways like an action at law, with two or more parties appearing before a judge-like inspector and stating their case to him, usually in public, is thereafter suddenly removed from public gaze until the ministerial decision is made. Often the main factors at the enquiry seem to have counted for little in the final decision. New factors – they may have been considerations of broad policy – have come in so that the final decision does not seem to flow from the proceedings at the enquiry.

... We shall ... address ourselves to the task of finding a reasonable balance between the conflicting interests. On the one hand there are Ministers and other administrative authorities enjoined by legislation to carry out certain duties. On the other hand there are the rights and feelings of individual citizens who find their possessions or plans interfered with by the administration. There is also the public interest, which requires both that Ministers and other admini-

---

[2] p. 20.

strative authorities should not be frustrated in carrying out their duties and also that their decisions should be subject to effective checks or controls, and these, as we have pointed out, can no longer be applied by Parliament in the general run of cases.

277. It is with these considerations in mind that we shall seek to apply the three principles of openness, fairness and impartiality – to which we have referred in Part I[3] – to the second part of our terms of reference, but we must recall that the third of these three principles, impartiality, cannot be applied here without qualification.

Tribunals and Inquiries Act 1971

11. – (1) The Lord Chancellor, after consultation with the Council [on Tribunals], may make rules regulating the procedure to be followed in connection with statutory inquiries held by or on behalf of Ministers; and different provision may be made by any such rules in relation to different classes of such inquiries.

(2) Any rules made by the Lord Chancellor under this section shall have effect, in relation to any statutory inquiry, subject to the provisions of the enactment under which the inquiry is held, and of any rules or regulations made under that enactment.

(3) Subject to subsection (2) of this section, rules made under this section may regulate procedure in connection with matters preparatory to such statutory inquiries as are mentioned in subsection (1) of this section, and in connection with matters subsequent to such inquiries, as well as in connection with the conduct of proceedings at such inquiries.

19. – (1) In this Act, except where the context otherwise requires –

... 'statutory inquiry' means –
    (*a*) an inquiry or hearing held or to be held in pursuance of a duty imposed by any statutory provision; or
    (*b*) an inquiry or hearing, or an inquiry or hearing of a class, designated for the purposes of this section by an order under subsection (2) of this section;
  'statutory provision' means a provision contained in, or having effect under, any enactment.

(2) The Lord Chancellor and the Secretary of State may by order designate for the purposes of this section any inquiry or hearing held or to be held in pursuance of a power conferred by any statutory provision specified or described in the order, or any class of such inquiries of hearings.[4] ...

---

[3] [See p. 534 *supra*.]
[4] [See S.I. 1975 No. 1375.]

Annual Report of The Council on Tribunals for 1963, Appendix A

ACTION TAKEN ON THE RECOMMENDATIONS OF THE
FRANKS COMMITTEE

Administrative Proceedings involving an Inquiry or Hearing

19. *General Questions*

The specific recommendations of the Franks Committee under this heading were confined to procedures relating to land, but the Committee made a general recommendation (No. 66) that the broad principles enunciated in relation to such procedures should ordinarily be applied to other procedures clearly within the second part of the Committee's terms of reference.[5] ...

All these procedures are subject to the Council's jurisdiction under section 1(1)(c) of the Tribunals and Inquiries Act [1971]. Sections [11] and [12] of the Act likewise provide generally for rules of procedure and reasons for decisions. An anomaly is that inquiries held at discretion are not caught by the Act (see paragraph 10 of our Report for 1962). Administratively, this recommendation is generally accepted.

20. *Procedure before the Inquiry or Hearing*

Recommendations: 67. An acquiring or planning authority should be required to make available, in good time before the inquiry, a written statement giving full particulars of its case.

68. The deciding Minister should, whenever possible, make available before the inquiry a statement of the policy relevant to the particular case, but should be free to direct that the statement be wholly or partly excluded from discussion at the inquiry.

69. If the policy changes after the inquiry the letter conveying the Minister's decision should explain the change and its relation to the decision.

Action taken: Present practice largely follows recommendations Nos. 67 and 69.

Recommendation No. 67 has also been given the force of law by the rules of procedure for inquiries into planning appeals and compulsory purchase orders by local authorities. Recommendation No. 68 was rejected by the Government, but since the Franks Committee reported the Ministry of Housing and Local Government have issued a large amount of material designed to clarify the general policy of the Minister in planning matters. The rules of procedure for planning appeal and compulsory purchase inquiries enable Inspectors to disallow questions directed to the merits of Government policy.

[5] [See p. 578 *supra*.]

21. *Inspectors*

Recommendation: 70. The main body of inspectors in England and Wales should be placed under the control of the Lord Chancellor, but inspectors may be kept in contact with policy developments in the Departments responsible for inquiries. The preference of certain Departments for independent inspectors appointed *ad hoc* need not be disturbed. If a corps of inspectors is established for Scotland, the Lord Advocate should assume responsibility for it.

Action taken: The Government rejected the first part of this recommendation. In practice, planning inspectors in England and Wales are now appointed after consultation with the Lord Chancellor's Office and are not dismissed without the Lord Chancellor's consent. The use of independent inspectors by certain Departments and in Scotland continues as before. In Scotland, the reporters are appointed by the Secretary of State.

22. *Procedure at the Inquiry*

Recommendations: 71. The initiating authority, whether a Minister or a local or other authority, should be required at the inquiry to explain its proposals fully and support them by oral evidence.

72. The code or codes of procedure for inquiries should be formulated by the Council on Tribunals and made statutory; the procedure should be simple and inexpensive but orderly.

73. In connection with the compulsory acquisition of land (and schemes which imply later acquisition), development plans, planning appeals and clearance schemes, a public inquiry should be held in preference to a private hearing unless for special reasons the Minister otherwise decides.

74. The proceedings should be opened by the initiating party. Strict rules of evidence are not required, but the inspector should have power to administer the oath and subpoena witnesses. He should have a wide discretion in controlling the proceedings and should give rulings on the scope of the proposed ministerial policy statements.

75. Officials of the Department of the deciding Minister should be required to give evidence if the inquiry is into a proposal initiated by that Minister, but not otherwise. Officials of other Departments should, if required, give factual evidence in support of the views of their Department if these views are referred to by a

public authority in its explanatory written statement (see recommendation 67) or in its evidence at the inquiry.

Action taken: Recommendations Nos. 71, 74 and 75 have been implemented administratively for inquiries generally, and legally by the statutory rules of procedure for planning appeals and local authorities' compulsory purchase orders. The Council are examining some aspects of the procedure followed by the Ministry of Agriculture as regards evidence at inquiries. The Council do not formulate rules of procedure for inquiries (recommendation No. 72), but section [11] of the Tribunals and Inquiries Act [1971] . . . requires the Lord Chancellor and the Lord President of the Court of Session to consult the Council before making rules of procedure for inquiries. Recommendation No. 73 is observed in practice.

23. *Costs*

Recommendations: 76. In compulsory acquisition cases and clearance schemes reasonable costs should generally be awarded to successful objectors directly interested in the land; they should only be awarded to unsuccessful objectors if the initiating authority has acted unreasonably. Costs should only be awarded against an unsuccessful objector if he has acted frivolously or vexatiously.

77. In planning appeals reasonable costs should generally be awarded to owner appellants if their appeals succeed or if the local planning authority has acted unreasonably. Costs should exceptionally be awarded to other successful appellants.

78. Any award of costs should be made by the Minister. The Inspector should hear submissions by the parties on costs and, where appropriate, make recommendations in his report.

79. The Council on Tribunals should consider the basis on which 'reasonable costs' should be assessed and keep under review the arrangements regarding the award of costs.

Action taken: The Council were asked by the Lord Chancellor and the Secretary of State for Scotland to submit a special report on the award of costs at statutory inquiries. When this was presented to Parliament in September 1964, the Government announced its acceptance of two of the Council's principal recommendations.[6]

24. *Inspector's Reports*

Recommendations: 80. Reports should be divided into two parts: (i) summary of evidence, findings of fact and inferences of

---

[6] [Ministry of Housing and Local Government Circular 73/65. See Wade, p. 860.]

fact; and (ii) reasoning from facts, including application of policy, and (normally) recommendations.

81. The complete text of the report should accompany the Minister's letter of decision and also be available on request centrally and locally.

82. Additionally, if any of the following parties desires an opportunity to propose corrections of fact, the first part of the report should, as soon as possible after the inquiry, be sent to: (i) the promoting authority (or local planning authority) and any other authority which gave evidence; and (ii) all persons who lodged written objections (in planning appeals the applicants). Recipients should be allowed 14 days in which to propose corrections. The inspector should decide whether to accept any proposed correction.

Action taken: Recommendations Nos. 80 and 81 have been implemented both by administrative action and by the new rules of procedure for planning appeal and compulsory purchase order inquiries. But over a third of planning appeals are in practice decided, with the appellants' consent, on written representations, to which these principles have not been applied.

Recommendation No. 82 was reserved by the Government for further consideration. In Scotland, where most inquiries are conducted by independent reporters, it is the practice already to make available (on request) the factual part of the report for comment by the parties to the inquiry and this is embodied in the relevant Scottish regulations. In England and Wales a somewhat similar practice is followed by some Departments but not by the Ministry of Housing and Local Government which holds by far the largest number of inquiries. The Ministry of Housing and Local Government have resisted this practie on the score of delay. Since delay in the handling of appeals is at present so serious a matter, the Council have not sought to press this question further. It will, however, be kept under review.

25. The Minister's Decision

Recommendations: 83. The deciding Minister should be required to submit to the parties concerned for their observations any factual evidence, including expert evidence, obtained after the inquiry.

84. The Minister's letter of decision should set out in full his findings and inferences of fact and the reasons for the decision.

Action taken: Recommendation No. 83 was described as being 'wholly or partly acceptable to the Government' and the fact that its acceptance was subject to an important reservation as regards evidence supplied to the Minister by Government Departments after an inquiry only emerged in the Chalkpit case (see paragraph 58 of our Report for 1961). The recommendation has now been satisfactorily implemented by the new rules of procedure for planning appeal and compulsory order inquiries. Recommendation No. 84 has been fully accepted.

Note

Recommendation 73 has now in effect been implemented by the Planning Inquiries (Attendance of Public) Act 1982, which provides that, as a general rule, at any planning inquiry oral evidence shall be heard in public and documentary evidence shall be open to public inspection. The Act provides that this requirement of publicity shall not apply if the Secretary of State is satisfied that issues of national security or measures taken to ensure the security of any premises or property will arise or that it would otherwise be contrary to the national interest for the inquiry to be public.

LAW AND PRACTICE TODAY

The right to know the opposing case

Town and Country Planning (Inquiries Procedure) Rules 1974

S.I. 1974 No. 419

Preliminary information to be supplied by local planning authority

4. – (1) The local planning authority, on being notified of the Secretary of State's intention to proceed with the consideration of an application or appeal to which these Rules apply and of the name and address of any person who, pursuant to the provisions of section 29 of the Act,[7] has made representations to the Secretary of State shall forthwith inform the applicant in writing of the name and address of every section 29 party and the Secretary of State of all such persons who have made representations to the local planning authority. . . .

Notification of inquiry

5. – (1) A date, time and place for the holding of the inquiry shall be fixed and may be varied by the Secretary of State who shall give not less than 42 days' notice in writing of such date, time and place to the applicant and to the local planning authority and to all section 29 parties at the address furnished by them:

Provided that –

    (i) with the consent of the applicant and of the local planning authority, the Secretary of State may give such lesser period of notice as shall be agreed with the applicant and the local planning authority;
    . . .

    (ii) where it becomes necessary or advisable to vary the time or place fixed for the inquiry, the Secretary of State shall give such notice of

---

[7] [Section 29 of the T. & C.P. Act 1971 requires the local planning authority to take into account any representations relating to the application which are received.]

the variation as may appear to him to be reasonable in the circumstances.

(2) Without prejudice to the foregoing provisions of this rule, the Secretary of State may require the local planning authority to take one or more of the following steps –

(a) to publish in one or more newspapers circulating in the locality in which land is situated such notices of the inquiry as he may direct;

(b) to serve notice of the inquiry in such form and on such persons or classes of persons as he may specify;

(c) to post such notices of the inquiry as he may direct in a conspicuous place or places near to the land;

but the requirements as to the period of notice contained in paragraph (1) of this rule shall not apply to any such notices.

(3) Where the land is under the control of the applicant, he shall, if so required by the Secretary of State, affix firmly to some object on the land, in such a manner as to be readily visible to and legible by the public, such notice of the inquiry as the Secretary of State may specify, and thereafter for such period before the inquiry as the Secretary of State may specify, the applicant shall not remove the notice, or cause or permit it to be removed.

Statements to be served before inquiry

6. – (1) In the case of a referred application, the Secretary of State shall . . . not later than 28 days before the date of the inquiry . . . serve or cause to be served on the applicant, on the local planning authority and on the section 29 parties a written statement of the reasons for his direction that the application be referred to him and of any points which seem to him to be likely to be relevant to his consideration of the application; and where a government department has expressed in writing to the Secretary of State the view that the application should not be granted either wholly or in part, or should be granted only subject to conditions, . . . the Secretary of State shall include this expression of view in his statement and shall supply a copy of the statement to the government department concerned.

(2) Not later than 28 days before the date of the inquiry . . . the local planning authority shall –

(a) serve on the applicant and on the section 29 parties a written statement of any submission which the local planning authority propose to put forward at the inquiry, and

(b) supply a copy of the statement to the Secretary of State.

(3) Where the Secretary of State or a local authority has given a direction restricting the grant of permission for the development for which application was made or a direction as to how the application was to be determined, the local planning authority shall mention this in their statement and shall include in the statement a copy of the direction and the reasons given for it and shall, within the period specified in paragraph (2) above, supply a copy of

the statement to the Secretary of State or local authority concerned; and where a government department or a local authority has expressed in writing to the local planning authority the view that the application should not be granted either wholly or in part, or should be granted only subject to conditions, . . . and the local planning authority propose to rely on such expression of view in their submissions at the inquiry, they shall include it in their statement and shall, within the period specified in paragraph (2) above, supply a copy of the statement to the government department or local authority concerned.

(4) Where the local planning authority intend to refer to, or put in evidence, at the inquiry documents (including maps and plans), the authority's statement shall be accompanied by a list of such documents, together with a notice stating the times and place at which the documents may be inspected by the applicant and the section 29 parties; and the local planning authority shall afford them a reasonable opportunity to inspect and, where practicable, to take copies of the documents.

(5) The local planning authority shall afford any other person interested a reasonable opportunity to inspect and, where practicable, to take copies of any statement served by the Secretary of State under paragraph (1) or by the authority under paragraph (2) and of the other documents referred to in paragraph (4) as well as any statement served on the authority by the applicant under paragraph (6) of this rule.

(6) The applicant shall, if so required by the Secretary of State, serve on the local planning authority, on the section 29 parties and on the Secretary of State, within such time before the inquiry as the Secretary of State may specify, a written statement of the submissions which he proposes to put forward at the inquiry; and such statement shall be accompanied by a list of any documents (including maps and plans) which the applicant intends to refer to or put in evidence at the inquiry, and he shall, if so required by the Secretary of State, afford the local planning authority and the section 29 parties a reasonable opportunity to inspect and, where practicable, to take copies of such documents.

Notes

1. These rules, which are fairly typical of those made in other classes of case, e.g. compulsory purchase (S.I. 1976 No. 746) and trunk roads (S.I. 1976 No. 721), will be used as the example in this section. As will be seen, from *Bushell's* case, p. 602 *infra*, where no rules have been made ministers often voluntarily follow them by analogy. See further Wade, p. 857.

2. It should, of course, be remembered that questions of natural justice can be raised in relation to the way the inquiry procedure has operated and this should be borne in mind when considering the ensuing material. Note, however, *Lake District Special Planning Board* v. *Secretary of State for the Environment* [1975] J.P.L. 220. In this case Kerr J. said that a litigant 'faces a heavy burden in seeking to establish a breach of the rules of natural justice when the allegation in question relates to something which is comprised within the scope of a statutory procedure . . . which is itself

designed to lay down the requirements which must be complied with to ensure that justice is done, but when no breach of this procedure has been established' (see the fuller report of the case in Purdue, *Cases and Materials on Planning Law*, p. 211). On procedural codes and natural justice, see further p. 230 *supra*.

3. On pre-inquiry procedure and publicity see further *Structure Plans: The Examination in Public*; Wraith and Lamb, pp. 163–4, 172–3, 295–301, and 309–13; Wade, p. 845; Annual Reports of the Council on Tribunals for 1960, para. 120; 1968, paras. 61–9; 1969/70, para. 68; and 1971/2, paras. 88–92. The main complaints have been of cases in which short notice of the inquiry has been given or where the statement of departmental policy has been unclear. As the forty-two-day period specified in r. 5 (1) of the 1974 Inquiries Procedure Rules can be waived by agreement between the Secretary of State, the local planning authority, and the applicant, the position of third parties can be materially affected. When the Council on Tribunals took up this matter, they were told that a very small percentage of inquiries (well under one per cent for the relevant period) were held with less than the forty-two days' notice: Annual Report for 1968, para. 65. An example of the second type of complaint was provided in the same year, where a local planning authority supported its refusal to permit land to be used for the extraction of sand and gravel, *inter alia*, because it had agreed with the Ministry of Housing and Local Government as a matter of policy that other land in the area should be used for this purpose. It did, however, refuse to identify the land and, at the inquiry, the Inspector declined to direct it to do so. The Council on Tribunals said that 'it was most undesirable in general for an authority to rely on a statement of fact which they were unwilling to substantiate in evidence'. In fact, this ground, which was included in the statement of submissions required by the provision now replaced by r. 6 of the 1974 Inquiries Procedure Rules, was inaccurate as well. This point was also criticized by the Council on Tribunals.

The right to participate

Errington v. Minister of Health, p. 581 *supra*

Note

For the present position on site inspections see r. 11 of the Town and Country Planning (Inquiries Procedure) Rules 1974, set out in the next extract.

Town and Country Planning (Inquiries Procedure) Rules 1974

S.I. 1974 No. 419

Appearances at inquiry

7. – (1) The persons entitled to appear at the inquiry shall be –

(*a*) the applicant;

(*b*) the local planning authority;

(*c*) where the land is not in Greater London, the council of the administrative county in which the land is situated, if not the local planning authority;

(*d*) where the land is not in Greater London, the council of the district in which the land is situated . . . if not the local planning authority;

(*e*) where the land is in a National Park, the National Park Committee (if any), if not the local planning authority;

(*f*) any joint planning board constituted under section 1 of the Act[8] (or any joint planning board or special planning board reconstituted under Part I of Schedule 17 to the Act of 1972),[9] where that board is not the local planning authority;

(*g*) where the land is in an area designated as the site of a new town, the development corporation of the new town;

(*h*) section 29 parties;

(*i*) that council of the parish or community in which the land is situated, if that council has made representations to the local planning authority in respect of the application in pursuance of a provision of a development order made under section 24 of the Act;

(*j*) any persons on whom the Secretary of State has required notice to be served under rule 5 (2) (*b*).

(2) Any other person may appear at the inquiry at the discretion of the appointed person.

(3) A local authority may appear by their clerk or by any other officer appointed for the purpose by the local authority, or by counsel or solicitor; and any other person may appear on his own behalf or be represented by counsel, solicitor or any other person. . . .

Representatives of government departments at inquiry

8. – (1) Where either –

(*a*) the Secretary of State has given a direction restricting the grant of permission for the development for which application was made, or

(*b*) a government department has expressed in writing the view that the application should not be granted either wholly or in part or should be granted only subject to conditions . . . and the Secretary of State or the local planning authority have included this view in their statement as required by paragraph (1) or (3) of rule 6,

the applicant may, not later than 14 days before the date of the inquiry apply in writing to the Secretary of State for a representative of his department or of the other government department concerned to be made available at the inquiry.

(2) Where an application is made to the Secretary of State under the last foregoing paragraph he shall make a representative of his department available to attend the inquiry or, as the case may be, transmit the application to the other government department concerned, who shall make a representative of that department available to attend the inquiry.

---

[8] [The T. & C.P. Act 1971.]
[9] [The Local Government Act 1972.]

(3) A representative of a government department who, in pursuance of this rule, attends an inquiry into a referred application shall state the reasons for the Secretary of State's direction restricting the grant of permission or, as the case may be, the reasons for the view expressed by his department . . . and shall give evidence and be subject to cross-examination to the same extent as any other witness.

(4) A representative of a government department who, in pursuance of this rule, attends an inquiry on an appeal, shall be called as a witness by the local planning authority and shall state the reasons for the Secretary of State's direction or, as the case may be, the reasons for the view expressed by his department . . . and shall give evidence and be subject to cross-examination to the same extent as any other witness.

(5) Nothing in either of the last two foregoing paragraphs shall require a representative of a government department to answer any question which in the opinion of the appointed person is directed to the merits of government policy and the appointed person shall disallow any such question.

Representatives of local authorities at inquiry

9. – (1) Where any local authority has –

(a) given to the local planning authority a direction restricting the grant of planning permission or a direction as to how an application for planning permission was to be determined; or

(b) expressed in writing the view that an application for planning permission should not be granted wholly or in part or should be granted only subject to conditions, and the local planning authority have included this view in their statement, as required under rule 6 (3),

the applicant may, not later than 14 days before the date of the inquiry, apply in writing to the Secretary of State for a representative of the authority concerned to be made available to attend the inquiry.

(2) Where an application is made to the Secretary of State under the last foregoing paragraph he shall transmit the application to the authority concerned, who shall make a representative of the authority available to attend the inquiry.

(3) A representative of a local authority who, in pursuance of this rule, attends an inquiry shall be called as a witness by the local planning authority and shall state the reasons for the authority's direction or, as the case may be, the reasons for the view expressed by them . . . and shall give evidence and be subject to cross-examination to the same extent as any other witness.

Procedure at inquiry

10. – (1) Except as otherwise provided in these Rules, the procedure at the inquiry shall be such as the appointed person shall in his discretion determine.

(2) Unless in any particular case the appointed person with the consent of the applicant otherwise determines, the applicant shall begin and shall have

the right of final reply; and the other persons entitled or permitted to appear shall be heard in such order as the appointed person may determine.

(3) The applicant, the local planning authority and the section 29 parties shall be entitled to call evidence and cross-examine persons giving evidence, but any other person appearing at the inquiry may do so only to the extent permitted by the appointed person.

(4) The appointed person shall not require or permit the giving or production of any evidence, whether written or oral, which would be contrary to the public interest; but save as aforesaid and without prejudice to the provisions of rule 8 (5) any evidence may be admitted at the discretion of the appointed person, who may direct that documents tendered in evidence may be inspected by any person entitled or permitted to appear at the inquiry and that facilities be afforded him to take or obtain copies thereof.

(5) The appointed person may allow the local planning authority or the applicant, or both of them, to alter or add to the submissions contained in any statement served under paragraph (2) or (6) of rule 6, or to any list of documents which accompanied such statement, so far as may be necessary for the purpose of determining the questions in controversy between the parties, but shall (if necessary by adjourning the inquiry) give the applicant or the local planning authority, as the case may be, and the section 29 parties an adequate opportunity of considering any such fresh submission or document; and the appointed person may make in his report a recommendation as to the payment of any additional costs occasioned by any such adjournment.

(7) The appointed person shall be entitled (subject to disclosure thereof at the inquiry) to take into account any written representations or statements received by him before the inquiry from any person. . . .

Site inspections

11. – (1) The appointed person may make an unaccompanied inspection of the land before or during the inquiry without giving notice of his intenion to the persons entitled to appear at the inquiry.

(2) The appointed person may, and shall if so requested by the applicant or the local planning authority before or during the inquiry, inspect the land after the close of the inquiry and shall, in all cases where he intends to make such an inspection, announce during the inquiry the date and time at which he proposes to do so.

(3) The applicant, the local planning authority and the section 29 parties shall be entitled to accompany the appointed person on any inspection after the close of the inquiry; but the appointed person shall not be bound to defer his inspection if any person entitled to accompany him is not present at the time appointed.

Notes

1. Rules 7 (2) and 10 (2) and (3) show that the issue of natural justice which arose in *Errington*'s case, p. 581 *supra*, can be closely linked to the issue of standing: see

Nicholson v. *Secretary of State for Energy* (1977) 76 L.G.R. 692; Wade, p. 848; Wraith and Lamb, pp. 253–65. On standing, see also *R.* v. *Hammersmith and Fulham L.B.C., ex p. People Before Profit Ltd.* (1982) 80 L.G.R. 322, noted at p. 363 *supra.* The Council on Tribunals has considered the position of third parties and the extent to which they are allowed to appear and to cross-examine witnesses. The Council reported (Annual Report for 1964, para. 85) that it had been suggested that 'in some cases Inspectors were not exercising their discretion at all, but always allowed cross-examination by third parties'. The Council continued:

The Ministry informed us that they had shown the correspondence to the Chief Inspector, who would take what action he thought necessary. In the following year, however, a member of the Bar drew our attention to what appeared to be a new practice which went to the other extreme: several members of the Bar had found when appearing for third parties that they were not allowed to cross-examine witnesses at the inquiry unless they were calling evidence on behalf of their own clients. It seemed to us that the question whether a third party proposed to call evidence in support of the case put in cross-examination was totally irrelevant to the question whether or not cross-examination should be allowed. One purpose of cross-examination is to try to obtain admissions from a witness which it might not be possible to put in evidence in any other way. It was recognised that there were bound to be occasions when cross-examination must be vetoed by an Inspector: but we ask that it should be made clear to Inspectors that there was no principle in law which excluded a party who did not propose to give evidence or to call evidence from cross-examining, and that his right to cross-examine should depend upon whether this was likely to elicit useful information.

2. In its Annual Report for 1966 the Council considered the position of third parties where, as is common, the appellant and the planning authority agree that the appeal be decided on the basis of written representations:

89. ... [W]e received an approach from a Rural Community Council about the absence of any provision in the written representations procedure for interested parties, other than the appellant and the local planning authority, to be informed by the publication of newspaper advertisements or the display of notices on public notice boards or on the appeal site that an appeal is pending so that they may make representations about it.

90. From what we were told by the Ministry of Housing and Local Government, who were invited to comment on the matter, it appears that the written representations procedure is only used when there seems no need to give third parties an opportunity of expressing their views on an appeal: when third parties enter into written representations, as happens occasionally, it is apt to lead to the proceedings being so long drawn out as to frustrate the main object of using the written representations procedure, namely to get a quick decision. If third party representations are received which develop into something highly important, then arrangements have to be made for the holding of an inquiry after all (as the Minister has power to do even if the appellant and local planning authority do not want it), but usually the third party concerned is asked whether he is agreeable to his representations being sent to the parties for their comments and, if he is, the Ministry then send his representations to the parties. Unless, however, there is some flagrant contradiction which needs clearing up, the comments of the parties on the representations are not referred back to the person making them.

91. We think it is reasonable that the use of the written representations procedure should be encouraged so far as possible at the present time, as it has the great advantage of being simpler and cheaper for the appellant than the statutory procedure and is of general benefit in that it relieves some of the very heavy pressure on the limited number of Inspectors who are available to conduct public inquiries. We did not feel that the Ministry's reply completely answered the point raised by the Rural Community Council but in the absence of any specific complaint that the written representations procedure had been used as a means of avoiding publicity for undesirable development, we considered that we would not be justified in pressing for any alterations in the existing arrangements and we so informed the Rural Community Council.

Scope of inquiries: the problem of policy

Town and Country Planning (Inquiries Procedure) Rules 1974, Rule 8 (5), p. 598 *supra*

Bushell v. Secretary of State for the Environment

[1981] A.C. 75   House of Lords

A public local inquiry was held to investigate objections to two draft motorway schemes initiated by the Secretary of State under s. 11 of the Highways Act 1959. The respondent objectors challenged the need for the motorways and sought to cross-examine a department witness as to the reliability of the department's method of forecasting traffic volume on the roads the motorways would be relieving. The inspector, who recommended that the schemes be made, had refused to allow this cross-examination but had permitted the objectors to call their own evidence as to the need for the motorways and the reliability of the method of forecasting.

After the inquiry had closed, the department revised its method of calculation, discovered that the capacity of existing roads was much larger than had been thought, and accordingly revised its method of forecasting. The objectors applied to have the inquiry reopened to investigate the revised method of forecasting. The Secretary of State refused this application, saying that he would consider any further representations as to need as part of the continuous consideration of any of the department's proposals and that, if the new information led him to disagree with the inspector's recommendations, the objectors would be given an opportunity to comment on it. In his decision he said that he had taken account of the general changes in design flow standards and traffic forecasts since the inquiry and was satisfied that they did not materially affect the evidence which was the basis of the inspector's recommendation. He accepted the recommendation and made the schemes.

The objectors applied for the schemes to be quashed on the ground that the inspector was wrong to disallow the cross-examination and the Secretary of State was wrong to take account of the undisclosed information. The application was a statutory application to quash under para. 2 of Sch. 2 to the Highways Act 1959[19]. Para. 3 of Sch. 2 provides:

> On any such application as aforesaid, the court − . . . (b) if satisfied that the scheme or order, or any provision contained therein, is not within the powers of this Act or that the interests of the applicant have been substantially prejudiced by failure to comply with any such requirement as aforesaid, may quash the scheme or order or any provision contained therein, either generally or in so far as it affects any property of the applicant.

The judge at first instance dismissed the application ((1977) 76 L.G.R.

[10] [See now the Highways Act 1981.]

460), but the Court of Appeal by a majority alllowed an appeal and quashed the schemes ((1979) 78 L.G.R. 10). On appeal by the Secretary of State:

LORD DIPLOCK: . . . The procedure to be followed by the minister in making schemes under section 11 of the Act is to be found in Part II of Schedule 1. It is not necessary to set it out in detail; it suffices to say that paragraph 9 provides for the lodging of objections by persons appearing to the minister to be affected by the proposed scheme and goes on to provide that if any such objection is not withdrawn 'the minister shall cause a local inquiry to be held.' . . .

The Act itself says nothing more than this about the scope of the inquiry or the procedure to be followed at or after it, save that paragraph 10 of Schedule 1 provides:

'After considering any objections to the proposed scheme which are not withdrawn, and, where a local inquiry is held, the report of the person who held the inquiry, the minister may make or confirm the scheme either without modification or subject to such modifications as he thinks fit.'

So before reaching his decision the minister must consider the objections, so far as not withdrawn, and the report of the inspector who held the local inquiry, before he makes up his mind whether to exercise his administrative discretion in favour of making the scheme either in its original form or with modifications or not making it at all; and section 12 of the Tribunals and Inquiries Act 1971 requires him to give reasons for his decision. At the time of the inquiry in the instant case no rules regulating the procedure to be followed at the inquiry had been made under section 11 of the latter Act. The Highways (Inquiries Procedure) Rules 1976 did not come into force until long after the inquiry in the instant case had closed. The minister had, however, announced his willingness at local inquiries into proposed schemes for motorways to comply with those rules that were already applicable in case of compulsory acquisition of land by ministers – the Compulsory Purchase by Ministers (Inquiries Procedure) Rules 1967. These are in substantially the same terms as the subsequent rules of 1976,[11] but with one difference to which I shall be referring later. . . .

The provision and improvement of a national system of routes for through traffic for which a government department and not a local authority should be the highway authority has formed a part of national transport policy since the passing of the Trunk Roads Act in 1936. . . . The construction of motorways is a lengthy and expensive process and it has been the policy of successive governments . . . to construct the network by stages. The order in which the various portions of the network are to be constructed thus becomes as much a matter of government transport policy as the total extent and configuration of the motorway network itself. It also has the consequence that schemes . . . which the minister proposes to make under section 11 of the Highways Act 1959 deal with comparatively short stretches in a particular

[11] [S.I. 1976 No. 721.]

locality of what, when the other stretches are completed, will be integral parts of the national network. It follows, therefore, that there will be a whole series of schemes relating to successive stretches of the national network of motorways each of which may be the subject of separate local inquiries under Schedule 1, paragraph 9, to the Act.

A scheme made by the minister under section 11 does no more than authorise the construction of the stretch of motorway to which it relates. . . . Before construction can start however it will be necessary to make compulsory purchase orders in respect of the lands required for the motorway and its approach roads and these in turn are likely to be the subject of further local inquiries. So from the publication of the draft scheme to the actual construction of the stretch of motorway which is authorised the process is necessarily a long one in the course of which circumstances may alter and even government policy may change.

. . . The essential characteristics of a 'local inquiry,' an expression which when appearing in a statute has by now acquired a special meaning as a term of legal art, are that it is held in public in the locality in which the works that are the subject of the proposed scheme are situated by a person appointed by the minister upon whom the statute has conferred the power in his administrative discretion to decide whether to confirm the scheme. The subject matter of the inquiry is the objections to the proposed scheme that have been received by the minister from local authorities and from private persons in the vicinity of the proposed stretch of motorway whose interests may be adversely affected, and in consequence of which he is required by Schedule 1, paragraph 9, to hold the inquiry. The purpose of the inquiry is to provide the minister with as much information about those objections as will ensure that in reaching his decision he will have weighed the harm to local interests and private persons who may be adversely affected by the scheme against the public benefit which the scheme is likely to achieve and will not have failed to take into consideration any matters which he ought to have taken into consideration.

Where rules regulating the procedure to be followed at a local inquiry held pursuant to a particular statutory provision have been made by the Lord Chancellor under section 11 of the Tribunals and Inquiries Act 1971, the minister and the inspector appointed to hold the inquiry must observe those rules; but no such rules were applicable in the instant case – they had not yet been made. The Highways Act 1959 being itself silent as to the procedure to be followed at the inquiry, that procedure, within such limits as are necessarily imposed by its qualifying for the description 'local inquiry,' must necessarily be left to the discretion of the minister or the inspector appointed by him to hold the inquiry on his behalf, or partly to one and partly to the other. In exercising that discretion, as in exercising any other administrative function, they owe a constitutional duty to perform it fairly and honestly and to the best of their ability, as Lord Greene M.R. pointed out in his neglected but luminous analysis of the quasi-judicial and administrative functions of a minister as confirming authority of a compulsory purchase order made by a local authority, which is to be found in B. *Johnson & Co. (Builders) Ltd.* v. *Minister of Health* [1947] 2 All E.R. 395, 399–400. That judgment contains a salutary warning against applying to procedures involved in the making of administrative decisions concepts that are appropriate to the conduct of ordinary civil litigation between private parties. So rather than use such phrases as 'natural justice' which may suggest that the prototype is only to be found in procedures followed by English courts of law, I prefer to put it that in the absence of any rules made under the Tribunals and Inquiries Act 1971, the only requirement of the Highways Act 1959, as to the procedure to be followed at a local inquiry held pursuant to Schedule 1, paragraph 9, is that it must be fair to all those who have an interest in the decision that will follow it whether they have been represented at the inquiry or not. What is a fair procedure to be adopted at a particular inquiry will depend upon the nature of its subject matter.

What is fair procedure is to be judged not in the light of constitutional fictions as to the relationship between the minister and the other servants of the Crown to serve in the government department of which he is the head, but in the light of the practical realities as to the way in which administrative decisions involving forming judgments based on technical considerations are reached. To treat the minister in his decision-making capacity as someone separate and distinct from the department of government of which he is the political head and for whose actions he alone in constitutional theory is accountable to Parliament is to ignore not only practical realities but also Parliament's intention. . . . Discretion in making administrative decisions is conferred upon a minister not as an individual but as the holder of an office in which he will have available to him in arriving at his decision the collective knowledge, experience and expertise of all those who serve the Crown in the department of which, for the time being, he is the political head. The collective knowledge, technical as well as factual, of the civil servants in the department and their collective expertise is to be treated as the minister's own knowledge, his own expertise. . . . This is an integral part of the decision-making process itself; it is not to be equiparated with the minister receiving evidence, expert opinion or advice from sources outside the department after the local inquiry has been closed.

. . . If the minister is to give proper consideration to objections to the scheme by persons in the vicinity of the proposed stretch of motorway, as he is required to do by Schedule 1, paragraph 10, fairness requires that the objectors should have an opportunity of communicating to the minister the reasons for their objections to the scheme and the facts on which they are based. The Highways Act 1959 requires that the form in which that opportunity is to be afforded to them is at a local inquiry. Fairness, as it seems to me, also requires that the objectors should be given sufficient information about the reasons relied on by the department as justifying the draft scheme to enable them to challenge the accuracy of any facts and the validity of any arguments upon which the departmental reasons are based. . . .

In the instant case the public inquiries into the two schemes which were for two adjoining stretches of the national motorway network were held together. There were 170 objections to the schemes which had not been withdrawn when the combined inquiry began. There were about 100 different parties who took part in it and made representations to the inspector orally or in writing in objection to or in support of the schemes. Many of these called witnesses in support of their representations. The hearing of the inquiry by the inspector took 100 working days between June 1973 and January 1974. He made his report to the minister on June 12, 1975.

It is evident that an inquiry of this kind and magnitude is quite unlike any civil litigation and that the inspector conducting it must have a wide discretion as to the procedure to be followed in order to achieve its objectives. These are to enable him to ascertain the facts that are relevant to each of the objections, to understand the arguments for and against them and, if he feels qualified to do so, to weigh their respective merits, so that he may provide the minister with a fair, accurate and adequate report on these matters.

Proceedings at a local inquiry at which many parties wish to make representations without incurring the expense of legal representation and cannot attend the inquiry throughout its length ought to be as informal as is consistent with achieving those objectives. To 'over-judicialise' the inquiry by insisting on observance of the procedures of a court of justice which professional lawyers alone are competent to operate effectively in the interests of their clients would not be fair. It would, in my view, be quite fallacious to suppose that at an inquiry of this kind the only fair way of ascertaining matters of fact and expert opinion is by the oral testimony of witnesses who are subjected to cross-examination on behalf of parties who disagree with what they have said. Such procedure is peculiar to litigation conducted in courts that follow the common law system of procedure; it plays no part in the procedure of courts of justice under legal systems based upon the civil law, including the majority of our fellow member states of the European Community; even in our own Admiralty Court it is not availed of for the purpose of ascertaining expert opinion on questions of navigation. . . . So refusal by an inspector to allow a party to cross-examine orally at a local inquiry a person who has made statements of facts or has expressed expert opinions is not unfair per se.

Whether fairness requires an inspector to permit a person . . . to be cross-examined by a party to the inquiry who wishes to dispute a particular statement must depend on all the circumstances. In the instant case, the question arises in connection with expert opinion upon a technical matter. Here the relevant circumstances in considering whether fairness requires that cross-examination should be allowed include the nature of the topic upon which the opinion is expressed, the qualifications of the maker of the statement to deal with that topic, the forensic competence of the proposed cross-examiner, and, most important, the inspector's own views as to whether the likelihood that cross-examination will enable him to make a report which will be more useful to the minister in reaching his decision than it otherwise would be is sufficient to justify any expense and inconvenience to other parties to the inquiry which would be caused by any resulting prolongation of it.

The circumstances in which the question of cross-examination arose in the instant case were the following. Before the inquiry opened each objector had received a document containing a statement of the minister's reasons for proposing the draft scheme. . . . The second paragraph of the minister's statement of reasons said: 'The government's policy to build these new motorways' (sc. for which the two schemes provided) 'will not be open to debate at the forthcoming inquiries [sic]: the Secretary of State is answerable to Parliament for this policy.'

'Policy' as descriptive of departmental decisions to pursue a particular course of conduct is a protean word and much confusion in the instant case has, in my view, been caused by a failure to define the sense in which it can properly be used to describe a topic which is unsuitable to be the subject of an investigation as to its merits at an inquiry at which only persons with local interests affected by the scheme are entitled to be represented. A decision to construct a nationwide network of motorways is clearly one of government policy in the widest sense of the term. Any proposal to alter it is appropriate to be the subject of debate in Parliament, not of separate investigations in each of scores of local inquiries before individual inspectors up and down the country upon whatever material happens to be presented to them at the particular inquiry over which they preside. So much the respondents readily concede.

At the other extreme the selection of the exact line to be followed through a particular locality by a motorway designed to carry traffic between the destinations that it is intended to serve would not be described as involving government policy in the ordinary sense of that term. It affects particular local interests only and normally does not affect the interests of any wider section of the public. . . . It is an appropriate subject for full investigation at a local inquiry and is one on which the inspector by whom the investigation is to be conducted can form a judgment on which to base a recommendation which deserves to carry weight with the minister in reaching a final decision as to the line the motorway should follow.

Between the black and white of these two extremes, however, there is what my noble and learned friend, Lord Lane, in the course of the hearing described as a 'grey area.' Because of the time that must elapse between the preparation of any scheme and the completion of the stretch of motorway that it authorises, the department, in deciding in what order new stretches of the national network ought to be constructed, has adopted a uniform practice throughout the country of making a major factor in its decision the likelihood that there will be a traffic need for that particular stretch of motorway in 15 years from the date when the scheme was prepared. This is known as the 'design year' of the scheme. Priorities as between one stretch of motorway and another have got to be determined somehow. Semasiologists may argue whether the adoption by the department of a uniform practice for doing this is most appropriately described as government policy or as something else.

But the propriety of adopting it is clearly a matter fit to be debated in a wider forum and with the assistance of a wider range of relevant material than any investigation at an individual local inquiry is likely to provide; and in that sense at least, which is the relevant sense for present purposes, its adoption forms part of government policy.

. . . [I]f a decision to determine priorities in the construction of future stretches of the national network of motorways by reference to their respective traffic needs in a design year 15 years ahead can properly be described as government policy, as I think it can, the definition of 'traffic needs' to be used for the purposes of applying the policy, viz. traffic needs as assessed by methods described in the Red Book [*Traffic Prediction for Rural Roads (Advisory Manual On)*] and the departmental publication on the capacity of rural roads, may well be regarded as an essential element in the policy. But whether the uniform adoption of particular methods of assessment is described as policy or methodology, the merits of the methods adopted are, in my view, clearly not appropriate for investigation at individual local inquiries by an inspector whose consideration of the matter is necessarily limited by the material which happens to be presented to him at the particular inquiry which he is holding. It would be a rash inspector who based on that kind of material a positive recommendation to the minister that the method of predicting traffic needs throughout the country should be changed and it would be an unwise minister who acted in reliance on it.

. . . In the result – and when one is considering natural justice it is the result that matters – the objectors were allowed to voice their criticisms of the methods used to predict traffic needs for the purposes of the two schemes and to call such expert evidence as they wanted to in support of their criticisms. What they were not allowed to do was to cross-examine the department's representatives upon the reliability and statistical validity of the methods of traffic prediction described in the Red Book and applied by the department. . . .

Was this unfair to the objectors? For the reasons I have already given and in full agreement with the minority judgment of Templeman L.J. in the Court of Appeal, I do not think it was. . . .

. . . The respondents [also] claim that it was a denial of natural justice to them on the minister's part not to reopen the local inquiry so as to give to objectors an opportunity of criticising [the] revised methods of assessment, cross-examining the department's representatives about them and advancing arguments as to the strength they added to the objectors' case. . . .

My Lords, in the analysis by Lord Greene M.R. in *B. Johnson & Co. (Builders) Ltd.* v. *Minister of Health* [1947] 2 All E.R. 395, 399–400 of the common case in which a minister's functions are to confirm, modify or reject a scheme prepared and promoted by a local authority, it is pointed out that the minister's ultimate decision is a purely administrative one. It is only at one stage in the course of arriving at his decision that there is imposed on his administrative character a character loosely described as being quasi-judicial; and that is: when he is considering the respective representations of the promoting authority and of the objectors made at the local inquiry and the report of the inspector upon them. In doing this he must act fairly as between the promoting authority and the objectors; after the inquiry has closed he must not hear one side without letting the other know; he must not accept from third parties fresh evidence which supports one side's case without giving the other side an opportunity to answer it. But when he comes to reach his decision, what he does bears little resemblance to adjudicating on a lis between the parties represented at the inquiry. Upon the substantive matter, viz., whether the scheme should be confirmed or not, there is a third party who was not represented at the inquiry, the general public as a whole whose interests it is the minister's duty to treat as paramount. No one could reasonably suggest that as part of the decision-making process after receipt of the report the minister ought not to consult with the officials of his department and obtain from them the best informed advice he can to enable him to form a balanced judgment on the strength of the objections and merits of the scheme in the interests of the public as a whole, or that he was bound to communicate the departmental advice that he received to the promoting authority and the objectors.

If the analogy of a lis inter partes be a false analogy even where the scheme which is the subject of the local inquiry is not a departmental scheme but one of which a public authority other than the minister is the originator, the analogy is even farther from reflecting the essentially administrative nature of the minister's functions when, having considered in the light of the advice of his department the objections which have been the subject of a local inquiry and the report of the inspector, he makes his decision in a case where the scheme is one that has been prepared by his own department itself and which it is for him in his capacity as head of that department to decide whether it is in the general public interest that it should be made or not. Once he has reached his decision he must be prepared to disclose his reasons for it, because the Tribunals and Inquiries Act 1971 so requires; but he is, in my view, under no obligation to disclose to objectors and give them an opportunity of commenting on advice, expert or otherwise, which he receives from his department in the course of making up his mind. If he thinks that to do so will be helpful to him in reaching the right decision in the public interest he may, of course, do so; but if he does not think it will be helpful – and this is for him to decide – failure to do so cannot in my view be treated as a denial of natural justice to the objectors.

In the instant case the respondents were in fact aware of the advice the minister had received from his department upon two matters after the local inquiry had closed and before he made his decision. . . .

. . . [W]hat the respondents really wanted to do in seeking the reopening of the local inquiry was to hold up authorisation of the construction . . . until the revised methods adopted by the department for estimating the comparative traffic needs for stretches of the national network of motorways which have not yet been constructed had been the subject of investigation at the reopened inquiry. For reasons that I have already elaborated, a local inquiry does not provide a suitable forum in which to debate what is in the relevant sense a matter of government policy. So the minister was in my view fully justified in refusing to reopen the local inquiry. . . . So the second ground on which the respondents claim they have suffered a denial of natural justice in my view also fails.

The schemes were, in my view, validly made by the minister . . . and I would allow the appeal. . . .

LORD EDMUND-DAVIES: . . . At the outset, objection was taken by learned counsel for the M42 Action Committee[12] to [the paragraph in the appellant's statement of case that is set out at p. 606 *supra*].Counsel for the objectors stated that he wished to call evidence that there was no need for the M42 scheme and also wished to cross-examine the department's witnesses on that topic. . . . The inspector's ruling [was]:

> . . . [I]n applying my decision as to what was relevant, I would not seek to be restrictive and that, in particular, I would admit any evidence or submission which was aimed at rebutting the department's case on the question of the need for the motorway. Nevertheless I could not allow the inquiry to be made into an inquiry into the government's general transport policy; such matters were for Parliament to decide and they could not properly or usefully be discussed at a local public inquiry. . . .

The ruling rendered this inquiry unique of its kind, and that fact may go a long way towards explaining the unexpected difficulty by which the inspector found himself confronted and of which, as I hold, he fell foul. For, seemingly unlike in all previous inquiries, it followed from his ruling that a cardinal question in this particular inquiry was whether there existed a *need* for the contested sections of the new motorways. That topic constantly recurred during the 100 working days it lasted. . . .

The key witness for the department in this respect was Mr. J. A. Brooks, a traffic engineer who very favourably impressed the inspector. A proof of his evidence was produced to the Court of Appeal, and three comments may fairly be made about it. (1) It recognised the fundamental importance of establishing the *need* for the proposed schemes. (2) It accepted that need depended to a great extent upon traffic projections, thus foreshadowing the view of the Leitch committee (*Report of the Advisory Committee on Trunk Road Assessment*, 1977, para. 19.1) that 'Traffic forecasts are of central importance in the decision to build roads.' (3) For Mr. Brooks the proper starting-point for such projections was . . . 'the Red Book.' Lord Denning M.R. was, with respect, clearly right in observing, 78 L.G.R. 10, 16 that, with certain modifications which the department accepted: 'The Red Book was the sheet-anchor of the department at the inquiry'. . . .

The respondents sought to challenge those methods at the outset by cross-examination. They wanted an opportunity to demonstrate out of the mouths of the department witnesses themselves that the Red Book methodology was neither accurate nor reliable. But the department resisted their application to

---

[12] [The respondent objectors were members of this Committee.]

do so, submitting that the procedures adopted in the Red Book were 'government policy' and so within the inspector's classification of 'irrelevant matter.' Most regrettably, the inspector upheld that submission and ruled that no such cross-examination could be permitted. . . .

Before your Lordships . . . Mr. Rippon Q.C., for the department, manifested difficulty in maintaining that the Red Book could itself be regarded as embodying government policy. . . . Rightly agreeing, as I think, with the learned trial judge on this point, Lord Denning M.R. said of the Red Book, 78 L.G.R. 10, 16:

'. . . I do not regard these traffic forecasts as government policy at all. They are the predictions by the department's experts about the future. They are just as much matters of fact as the evidence of a medical man as to the prognosis of a disease.'

. . . It is beyond doubt that the inspector could – and should – disallow questions relating to the merits of government policy. But matters of policy are matters which involve the exercise of political judgment, and matters of fact and expertise do not become 'policy' merely because a department of government relies on them. And, as the Franks committee had put it in 1957: 'We see no reason why the factual basis for a departmental view should not be explained and its validity tested in cross-examination.' (*Report of the Committee on Administrative Tribunals and Inquiries* (Cmnd. 218), para. 316.)

Then, if the Red Book is not 'government policy,' on what basis can the cross-examination of departmental witnesses relying on its methodology be properly refused? . . .

. . . The general law may, I think, be summarised in this way: (a) In holding an administrative inquiry (such as that presently being considered), the inspector was performing quasi-judicial duties. (b) He must therefore discharge them in accordance with the rules of natural justice. (c) Natural justice requires that objectors (no less than departmental representatives) be allowed to cross-examine witnesses called for the other side on all relevant matters, be they matters of fact or matters of expert opinion. (d) In the exercise of jurisdiction outside the field of criminal law, the only restrictions on cross-examination are those general and well-defined exclusionary rules which govern the admissibility of relevant evidence (as to which reference may conveniently be had to *Cross on Evidence*, 5th ed. (1979), p. 17); beyond those restrictions there is *no* discretion on the civil side to exclude cross-examination on relevant matters.

There is ample authority for the view that, as Professor H. W. R. Wade Q.C. puts it (*Administrative Law*, 4th ed. (1977), p. 418): '. . . it is once again quite clear that the principles of natural justice apply to administrative acts generally.' And there is a massive body of accepted decisions establishing that natural justice requires that a party be given an opportunity of challenging by cross-examination witnesses called by another party on relevant issues; see, for example, *Marriott* v. *Minister of Health* (1935) 52 T.L.R. 63, *per* Swift J., at p. 67 – compulsory purchase orders inquiry; *Errington* v. *Minister of*

Health [1935] 1 K.B. 249, *per* Maugham L.J., at p. 272 – clearance order; *Reg.* v. *Deputy Industrial Injuries Commissioner, Ex parte Moore* [1965] 1 Q.B. 465, *per* Diplock L.J., at pp. 488A, 490E–G; and *Wednesbury Corporation* v. *Ministry of Housing and Local Government (No. 2)* [1966] 2 Q.B. 275, *per* Diplock L.J., at pp. 302G–303A – local government inquiry.

Then is there any reason why those general rules should have been departed from in the present case? . . . [W]hile I am alive to the inconvenience of different inspectors arriving at different conclusions regarding different sections of a proposed trunk road, the risk of that happening cannot, in my judgment, have any bearing upon the question whether justice was done at this particular inquiry, which I have already explained was, in an important respect, unique of its kind.

. . . I find myself driven to the conclusion that the refusal in the instant case to permit cross-examination on what, by common agreement, was evidence of cardinal importance was indefensible and unfair and, as such, a denial of natural justice. But, even so, can it be said that no prejudice to the respondents resulted? It was urged for the appellant that, by allowing objectors to call witnesses to attack the Red Book methodology and including their proofs among the papers submitted to the Secretary of State by the inspector when he reported, the inspector had, in effect, put the objectors in as good a position as if he had indeed permitted cross-examination on the Red Book. But that cannot be so. The inspector was no mere messenger charged simply to convey to the minister the views of those appearing before him. His duty was to make recommendations, and these he arrived at by treating as 'irrelevant' material evidence for the objectors and by intimating to the department's counsel that they need not cross-examine upon it. That evidence therefore manifestly played no part in the formation of the inspector's conclusions.

That the objectors were in truth prejudiced is, in my judgment, clear. Professor Wade has warned (*Administrative Law*, 4th ed., p. 454): '. . . in principle it is vital that the procedure and the merits should be kept strictly apart, since otherwise the merits may be prejudged unfairly' . . . [I]n *Annamunthodo* v. *Oilfields Workers' Trade Union* [1961] A.C. 945 Lord Denning, delivering the judgment of their Lordships, said, at p. 956:

'If a domestic tribunal fails to act in accordance with natural justice, the person affected by their decision can always seek redress in the courts. It is prejudice to any man to be denied justice. He will not, of course, be entitled to damages if he suffered none. But he can always ask for the decision against him to be set aside.'

The Act of 1959 expressly provides that the court may quash a scheme or order if it is satisfied that the interests of an applicant have been substantially prejudiced. In *Miller* v. *Weymouth and Melcombe Regis Corporation* (1974) 27 P. & C.R. 468 Kerr J. rightly said, at p. 476:

'If there is a possibility that the applicants' interests *may* have been prejudiced, as in the line of cases in which ministers received evidence from improper souces or applicants were deprived of an opportunity to make representations, then the court will in general readily accept that they have satisfied this requirement because they can show that they have lost a chance: . . .'

My Lords, I consider that such test has here been abundantly satisfied, for the most effective 'representations' can and often are made in the process of cross-examination. . . .

Had the inspector not ruled as he did, I hold that there was a very real possibility that cross-examination of the department witnesses on the lines projected might have created serious doubts in his mind, regarding [the] traffic forecasts and therefore as to whether need for the motorways had been established. . . .

. . . I would therefore dismiss this appeal.

LORD LANE: . . . There can be no doubt that the obligation to hold an inquiry comprises the requirement that the inquiry should be fair. If the inquiry is not fair then there has been a 'failure to comply' within the terms of paragraph 3 of Schedule 2 to the Act of 1959. If that failure has resulted in the objectors' interests being substantially prejudiced, then the court may quash the order. . . .

The inspector's report contains more than 450 pages, and deals in detail with the contentions advanced by the objectors and their witnesses. . . .

It is clear that all the material was before the Secretary of State and his staff. The only things missing were the replies which Mr. Brooks might have made to questions put to him by the objectors and their representatives. I find it difficult to see how in the circumstances the inability to cross-examine can be described as unfair. . . .

[VISCOUNT DILHORNE delivered a speech in favour of allowing the appeal. LORD FRASER OF TULLYBELTON agreed with the speeches of the majority.]

Appeal allowed.

Question

Is *Bushell* v. *Secretary of State for the Environment* consistent with the general developments in the law on natural justice since *Ridge* v. *Baldwin*, p. 214 *supra*, and the recommendations of the Franks Committee and the Council of Tribunals set out at p. 590 and 592 *supra*?

Notes

1. The emphasis in Lord Lane's speech on substantive fairness must be seen in the light of the statutory provision which only empowered the court to quash where the interests of the applicant were 'substantially prejudiced' (p. 601 *supra*, a typical statutory formula); but see Note 4, p. 584 *supra*. Consider also Lord Edmund-Davies's speech at p. 611 *supra*. On natural justice and the need for prejudice, see p. 234 *supra*.

2. *Bushell*'s case has been said to be possibly the most important case arising from a formal administrative procedure since the Second World War (Williams, (1980) 29 I.C.L.Q. 701 at p. 715). What accounts for the difference between Lord Diplock's speech and that of Lord Edmund-Davies? Is it that they have different perceptions of the function of a public inquiry? Lord Diplock emphasized the advancement of public

welfare as the primary goal and, in effect, recognized only as much 'fairness' as is possible in the light of that primary goal (p. 603 *supra*). Lord Edmund-Davies appeared to take the view that, once participation is conceded, the rules of natural justice assure one of a basic minimum of procedural safeguards stemming from the nature of the individual interests that are affected. The first can be called a 'public interest' approach and the second an 'individual rights' approach; see McAuslan, *The Ideologies of Planning Law*, pp. 59 and 64; Comment, [1980] J.P.L. 461. Alternatively, Lord Edmund-Davies's view can be explained by the fact that he regarded *this* inquiry as 'unique of its kind' (p. 609 *supra*). The majority appeared to discount the fact that the inspector had broadened the scope of the inquiry; on their view whatever the inspector did was irrelevant to the nature of the inquiry, which was determined by the statute.

3. Lord Diplock, p. 603 *supra*, approved of Lord Greene M.R.'s 'luminous analysis' in *B. Johnson & Co. (Builders) Ltd.* v. *Minister of Health* [1947] 2 All E.R. 395, but it should be noted that *Johnson*'s case was decided during a period in which the rules of natural justice had been narrowed almost to vanishing point (p. 218 *supra*; Wade, p. 458). It is arguable that Lord Greene M.R.'s highly conceptual approach requires reconsideration in the light of modern developments: see pp. 224 and 243 *supra*. It should also be noted that in that case no inquiry had actually been held because the Minister had been relieved of the duty to hold one by s. 2 of the Housing (Temporary Provisions) Act 1944. See also de Smith, pp. 208–9, for criticism of *Johnson*'s case.

4. In the Court of Appeal Lord Denning's judgment in favour of the objectors was influenced by the need to restore confidence in the inquiry system. He said, (1980) 78 L.G.R. 10 at p. 14:

> There has been a deplorable loss of confidence in these inquiries. It is thought that those in the Department come to them with their minds made up and that they are determined to build the roads, no matter how strong or convincing the arguments against them. The inspector is regarded as the stooge of the Department. He is just there to rubber-stamp the decision already made. . . .

Is the solution to judicialize such inquiries?

5. In view of the length of this inquiry and the number of objectors one must sympathize with the attempt to keep procedures informal and the rejection of the view that the adversary process is the only 'fair' procedure (p. 605 *supra*), especially in relation to what has been termed a 'polycentric' problem (see e.g. Fuller, (1978) 92 Harv. L. Rev. 383 at pp. 384–405). Lord Diplock tried to show how legal control over the bureaucracy fits together with political control; hence his statement that the decision to construct and to alter a nationwide network of motorways 'is appropriate to be the subject of debate in Parliament, not of separate investigations in each of scores of local inquiries . . . up and down the country' (p. 606 *supra*). In fact, until the disruption of the inquiries at the Aire Valley and Winchester (Williams, op. cit., pp. 708–9), Parliament had not debated the policy for a considerable time (Sharman, [1977] J.P.L. 293), and it can be argued that to justify the refusal to exercise effective legal control by reference to the existence of a theoretical possibility of political control is to avoid the issue. In 1978 in the White Paper, *Report of the Review of Highway Inquiry Procedures*, Cmnd. 7133, it was proposed to meet the criticisms of existing procedures by improving public consultation and allowing as wide a hearing as possible. As a result of this a Standing Advisory Committee was established for such

inquiries. Although the absence of effective Parliamentary accountability has been a major reason for the continued demands for expansion of the scope of highway inquiries, the proposed solution seeks to institutionalize the abdication of political control in favour of wider inquiries despite the increased costs of delay, the marginal utility of the adversarial model for determining broad, polycentric questions, and the detraction from administrative responsibility that will result.

Inspectors' reports

Town and Country Planning (Inquiries Procedure) Rules 1974

S.I. 1974 No. 419

Procedure after inquiry

12. – (1) The appointed person shall after the close of the inquiry make a report in writing to the Secretary of State which shall include the appointed person's findings of fact and his recommendations, if any, or his reason for not making any recommendations. . . .

Notification of decision

13. – (1) The Secretary of State shall notify his decision, and his reasons therefor, in writing to the applicant, the local planning authority and the section 29 parties and to any person who, having appeared at the inquiry, has asked to be notified of the decision.

(2) Where a copy of the appointed person's report is not sent with the notification of the decision, the notification shall be accompanied by a summary of the appointed person's conclusions and recommendations; and if any person entitled to be notified of the Secretary of State's decision under the last foregoing paragraph has not received a copy of the appointed person's report, he shall be supplied with a copy thereof on written application made to the Secretary of State within one month from the date of his decision.

(3) For the purpose of this rule 'report' does not include documents, photographs or plans appended to the report but any person entitled to be supplied with a copy of the report under paragraph (2) of this rule may apply to the Secretary of State in writing within six weeks of the notification to him of the decision or the supply to him of the report, whichever is the later, for an opportunity of inspecting such documents, photographs and plans and the Secretary of State shall afford him an opportunity accordingly.

Extrinsic evidence

Errington v. Minister of Health, p. 581 *supra*

Town and Country Planning (Inquiries Procedure) Rules 1974

S.I. 1974 No. 419

12. (2) Where the Secretary of State –

(*a*) differs from the appointed person on a finding of fact, or

(b) after the close of the inquiry takes into consideration any new evidence (including expert opinion on a matter of fact) or any new issue of fact (not being a matter of government policy) which was not raised at the inquiry,

and by reason thereof is disposed to disagree with a recommendation made by the appointed person, he shall not come to a decision which is at variance with any such recommendation without first notifying the applicant, the local planning authority and any section 29 party who appeared at the inquiry of his disagreement and the reasons for it and affording them an opportunity of making representations in writing within 21 days or (if the Secretary of State has taken into consideration any new evidence or any new issue of fact, not being a matter of government policy) of asking within 21 days for the re-opening of the inquiry.

(3) The Secretary of State may in any case if he thinks fit cause the inquiry to be re-opened, and shall cause it to be re-opened if asked to do so in accordance with the last foregoing paragraph. . . .

Lord Luke of Pavenham v. Minister of Housing and Local Government

[1968] 1 Q.B. 172   Court of Appeal

LORD DENNING M.R.: . . . There is a small village in Bedfordshire called Pavenham. There used to be a mansion house there, but it has been demolished and is being replaced by other houses. On the other side of the road there is an old walled garden. It used to be the kitchen garden of the mansion house. It is about one acre in extent. It is owned by the applicant, Lord Luke, and he seeks permission to build a house there. The local planning authority refused permission for this reason:

'The proposal would constitute an undesirable form of isolated and sporadic development outside the limits of the village of Pavenham in an area where no further development should be permitted other than that which is essential for agricultural purposes.' . . .

Lord Luke appealed to the Minister under section 23 of the Town and Country Planning Act, 1962. The Minister appointed an inspector to hold an inquiry. It was held. The inspector made his report. He recommended that permission be granted. The Minister, however, disagreed with the inspector's recommendation. The Minister thought that Lord Luke's proposal was undesirable. He, therefore, confirmed the decision of the local planning authority and dismissed the appeal.

Prima facie the decision of the Minister was final: see section 23 (5) of the Act of 1962. But it was open to Lord Luke to question the Minister's decision if he could show that any of the relevant requirements [of the Act] had not been complied with: see section 179 (1) of the Act of 1962.

Lord Luke did question the validity of the Minister's decision. He said that the relevant requirements had not been complied with in that the Minister had differed from the inspector on findings of fact, and that the Minister ought to have notified him (Lord Luke) of the difference and given him an opportunity of making representations to him: and had not done so. Lawton J.[13] upheld this contention and quashed the Minister's decision. The Minister appeals to this court.

[He then referred to r. 12 (2) of the Town and Country Planning (Inquiries Procedure) Rules 1965, which is identical in all material respects to r. 12 (2) of the 1974 Inquiries Procedure Rules, p. 614 *supra*. He also referred to the inspector's report and Minister's letter of decision and continued:]

Did the Minister differ from the inspector on a finding of fact? In answering this question it is essential to draw a distinction between findings of fact by the inspector and an expression of opinion by him on the planning merits. If the Minister differs from the inspector on a finding of fact, he must notify the applicant, in accordance with the rules, before coming to his decision. But if the Minister differs from the inspector on the planning merits, he can announce his decision straight away without notifying the applicant beforehand.

In the present case the inspector has divided his report into sections headed: 'Findings of fact,' 'Inspector's conclusions' and 'Recommendations.' But I do not think this division is sacrosanct. We must look into them and see which of his findings are truly findings of fact and which are expressions of opinion on planning merits. All the findings which are headed 'Findings of fact' numbered (1) to (12) are undoubtedly findings of fact. So also the finding (13), which states the intention of the planning authority. The inspector's 'Conclusions' in paragraph (39) are partly findings of fact and partly expressions of opinion. The inspector stated a *finding of fact* when he said:

'The site is exceptional in that it is clearly defined by a tall and fine-looking wall and forms part of a long-established group of buildings which contribute to the attractive character of the village independent of distance.'

The inspector expressed his *opinion on planning merits* when he said:

'A well-designed house within the walled garden would, far from harming the countryside, add to the existing charm of its setting and could not be said to create a precedent for allowing development on farmland to the north or south.'

Now turning to the Minister's decision letter, the question is whether he differed from the inspector on a finding of fact. The decision letter is not happily expressed. The Minister said that he was unable to agree with the 'conclusions' drawn by the inspector. . . . I think the Minister's difference was only on the second sentence that 'a well-designed house would,' etc. He was

---

[13] [[1968] 1 Q.B. at p. 184 C–D.]

differing from that expression of opinion by the inspector. The Minister took the view that a house would be 'sporadic development' which would harm the countryside. That was a difference of opinion on a planning matter. The Minister was entitled to come to a different conclusion on such a matter without the necessity of notifying Lord Luke, or giving him an opportunity of making representations.

I must say that I have considerable sympathy with Lord Luke. The inspector's report was very much in his favour. But it must be remembered that the Minister has the responsibility for planning policy. In order to preserve our countryside he has adopted a policy of setting out an 'envelope' for each village. Development is permitted within the 'envelope' and not outside it. If one person is allowed to build outside, it will be difficult to refuse his neighbour. So the Minister must be strict. This is planning policy, and nothing else. The courts have no authority to interfere with the way the Minister carries it out.

I do not think the Minister was in breach of the relevant requirements. I would, therefore, allow this appeal and restore the Minister's decision.

[DAVIES and RUSSELL L.JJ. delivered judgments in favour of allowing the appeal.]

Appeal allowed.

Notes

1. Compare *Lord Luke of Pavenham*'s case with *Coleen Properties Ltd.* v. *Minister of Housing and Local Government*, p. 81 *supra*, especially p. 83 *supra*, where the question of whether the acquisition of a particular building was 'reasonably necessary' for the satisfactory development of a clearance area was held to be a question of fact upon which the Minister could not overrule the inspector.

2. On extrinsic evidence note *Darlassis* v. *Minister of Education* (1954) 52 L.G.R. 304, on which see p. 138 *supra*, and see further Wade, pp. 853–6. The present procedural rules are largely the result of the criticism by the Council on Tribunals (see p. 592 *supra*) of the *Chalkpit* inquiry of 1961 (see *Buxton* v. *Minister of Housing and Local Government* [1961] 1 Q.B. 278). In that inquiry the inspector had recommended the dismissal of an appeal against a refusal of planning permission, but the Minister allowed the appeal. The inspector's recommendation was based on a risk of injury to adjoining land and livestock from the proposed use (quarrying for chalk). The Minister's decision took account of evidence from another government department, which suggested ways of minimizing the risk but which had not been before the inquiry and upon which the objectors had had no opportunity of commenting.

The effect of *Bushell*'s case (p. 604 *supra*) on factual information that comes to light after an inquiry is difficult to forecast. Lord Diplock's view that new information derived from the collective expertise of a department (unlike expert evidence from outside the department) does not have to be communicated to the objectors could undermine the progress made by the Council on Tribunals after the *Chalkpit* case, p. 592 *supra*, unless a narrow view of 'advice' (p. 608 *supra*) is taken. The authority of the case on this point is unclear because the objectors in fact had a chance to comment on the new material and Viscount Dilhorne and Lord Lane appeared to base their conclusion on this aspect of the case on this point.

Reasons for decisions

Tribunals and Inquiries Act 1971, Section 12, p. 22 *supra*

Note

For consideration of the nature and extent of this statutory duty, see p. 23 *supra*. See also p. 567 *supra* in the context of statutory tribunals, and see further Wade, p. 847. For an example of this issue arising in the context of a statutory inquiry, see *Givaudan & Co. Ltd.* v. *Minister of Housing and Local Government* [1967] 1 W.L.R. 250.

Inspectors generally

Report of The Committee on Administrative Tribunals and Enquiries

Cmnd. 218 (1957)

INSPECTORS

292. The question whether inspectors should or should not be independent of the Departments concerned is controversial, and we have considered very carefully the substantial volume of evidence which we have received bearing upon it. We wish to make it clear at the outset that we have received virtually no criticism of the qualifications of inspectors or of the manner in which they conduct enquiries.

The case for departmental inspectors

293. The main arguments in favour of departmental inspectors are as follows. First, and most important, it is argued that a Minister is responsible for the final decision and that that decision must often be influenced by considerations of Government policy. The ideal would be for the Minister himself to hold the enquiry and thus hear the evidence at first hand, but since this is clearly out of the question the next best course is for one of his own officers, who can be kept in touch with developments in policy, to perform this function. It is further contended that it may be difficult for the Minister to accept full responsibility for a decision taken in his name if the report on the enquiry, which is an important and sometimes vital part of the advice on which the decision is based, is not made by someone within his Department.

294. The second argument is that, particularly in the case of the Ministry of Housing and Local Government, the number of enquiries is sufficient to justify, and indeed on practical grounds to make essential, a corps of full-time inspectors, if enquiries are to be arranged and completed with reasonable promptitude.

295. Third, it is argued that highly technical considerations frequently arise, particularly in planning enquiries, which make it advisable for the inspector to be a person constantly engaged in this kind of work and therefore a member of the Department concerned.

296. Lastly, it is argued that the establishment of a corps of independent inspectors, particularly if responsibility for it were given to the Lord

Chancellor – as has frequently been suggested – would foster the impression that the process was judicial. It might thus increase rather than decrease public dissatisfaction, the public being the more likely to expect the final decision to be based solely upon the evidence at the enquiry and the report following the enquiry or indeed to expect the inspector to act as a judge and give a decision himself. If, as an alternative to a corps of inspectors under the Lord Chancellor, independent persons were appointed *ad hoc* for each enquiry the whole process might be lengthened because of their unfamiliarity with the conduct of enquiries and their inability, through lack of knowledge of departmental policy, to give the Minister the kind of advice which he most needs.

The case for independent inspectors . . .

298. The main arguments advanced in favour of independent inspectors are as follows. First, it is argued that public confidence in the procedure, especially at the enquiry stage, would be increased and that the change would help to remove the feeling that the scales are weighted against the individual, particularly where the proposals have been initiated by the very Minister whose inspector is conducting the enquiry.

299. Second, it is argued that the need for the inspector to be conversant with departmental policy has been exaggerated and that it would be equally satisfactory if the considerations of policy thought to be relevant were placed before the inspector in departmental evidence given at the enquiry. As the Minister would continue to make the final decision, policy would, where necessary, prevail.

300. Third, it is pointed out that several Departments employ independent inspectors and find this arrangement satisfactory.

301. Fourth, it is argued that it would be less embarrassing for Departments to give oral evidence before an independent inspector than before a departmental inspector.

302. Finally, it is said that it would be less difficult to publish the report of an independent inspector than of a departmental inspector, since as an independent person he could more freely comment upon the evidence given, and that it would not be so embarrassing for the Minister to give a decision differing from any published recommendations. It is pointed out in this connection that the Ministry of Education, the only Department which invariably publishes inspectors' reports, employs independent inspectors.

Our recommendations

303. We recommend that inspectors be placed under the control of a Minister not directly concerned with the subject-matter of their work. This would most appropriately be the Lord Chancellor in England and Wales. Some may say that this would be a change in name only, but we feel no need to argue the point because we are convinced that here the appearance is what matters. This change, by no longer identifying the inspector in the minds of the objectors with the Department of the deciding Minister, would emphasise

impartiality at an important stage of the adjudication and thus do much to allay public misgiving. We see in this no obstacle to the inspectors being kept in close contact with developments of policy in the Departments responsible for the subject-matter of the enquiries. . . .

Note

For action taken in relation to this recommendation see p. 590 *supra*, and on the publication of inspectors' reports see pp. 592 and 614 *supra*.

Annual Report of the Council on Tribunals for 1972/3

Planning Inspectors: Use and Deployment

94. It has previously been reported[14] that we were examining the possibility of establishing principles which might serve as a guide on the appointment of inspectors and assessors for statutory inquiries into many different kinds of proposals affecting land, and that our consideration of this matter was being deferred pending administrative reorganization within the Department of the Environment which would extend to the inspectorates of the former Ministries of Housing and Local Government and of Transport.

95. . . . The [reorganized] inspectorate [of the Department of the Environment] (which also serves the Welsh Office) . . . consists . . . of the salaried inspectors of the former Ministry of Housing and Local Government and a panel of fee-paid inspectors, the nucleus of which has been formed from the former Ministry of Transport panel.

96. The proposals of the Department of the Environment and the Welsh Office for the use and deployment of the inspectors in connection with the many and various inquiries held by them . . . were of particular interest to us. Members of the inspectorate, both salaried and fee-paid, would now be available to take inquiries over the whole range of planning, transport and land-use matters. The general principle on which it was proposed that inspectors should be allocated to inquiries turned on the nature and degree of the Secretary of State's interest or prior involvement in the matter subject to inquiry. In the great majority of inquiries, where the matter at issue is between a local authority and the public and the Secretary of State, as appellate or confirming authority, is in the role of referee or arbiter, the appointment of a salaried inspector would normally be considered suitable. But where the Secretary of State himself had initiated the proposals giving rise to an inquiry, it was considered that the appointment of an inspector from the fee-paid panel would be more appropriate. It was accordingly proposed that salaried inspectors would normally continue to take planning appeals and development plan inquiries[15] and inquiries into compulsory purchase orders for housing and planning purposes. They would also in future take inquiries into compulsory purchase orders for local authority roads which were formerly

---

[14] See paras. 81–82 of our Annual Report for 1970/71.

[15] [Now replaced by a two-tier system of structure plans and local plans: see p. 579 *supra*.]

taken by fee-paid inspectors. Fee-paid inspectors would always take inquiries into orders concerning trunk road schemes and into objections to new town designation orders, since such schemes and orders originate in the Department; and they would take any inquiries into other plans for development by the Department, e.g. new government office buildings and motorway service areas.

97. We considered the principle on which it was proposed to allocate salaried and fee-paid inspectors to hold inquiries – and the indications given as to how those principles would be applied in practice – to be generally acceptable. There will, of course, be a 'grey area' in which it will be difficult to quantify and assess the extent of ministerial interest and involvement. But we consider that the broad principle which the Director of Planning Inspectorates will be seeking to apply is a sound one.

Notes

1. See further pp. 581 *supra* (decision by inspector, 618 *supra* (independence), 591 *supra* (report), 590, 600, and 605 *supra* (conduct of inquiry); Wade, p. 845 and pp. 863–6; Wraith and Lamb, pp. 180–97, 336–7; Annual Reports of the Council on Tribunals for 1961 (paras. 63–6); 1964 (para. 86); 1966 (para. 100); 1967 (para. 100); 1968 (para. 75); 1975/6 (para. 92); 1976/7 (para. 7.13 ff.).

2. The distinction between salaried departmental inspectors and fee-paid independent inspectors has been mentioned. However, Levin has pointed out ([1979] *Public Administration* 21) that objectors are unlikely to be confident of the independence of the latter in view of the fact that the panel is managed by the Department of the Environment and that inspectors are appointed to individual inquiries by the Secretary of State. Furthermore, many of those on the panel are former civil servants or local government officers. Although it has been claimed (*Report on the Review of Highway Inquiry Procedures*, Cmnd. 7133) that independence is assured by the fact that serving on the panel is not a career, Levin points out that, for instance, between 1970 and 1979 one inspector accepted more than one hundred appointments, was employed virtually full time on this work and derived a substantial income from it. 'But being employed anew for each inquiry he has no security of employment, and is consequently dependent on the goodwill of the departments for the continuation of this income.' In the case of highway inquiries appointments to individual inquiries are now made by the Lord Chancellor and the first two appointments to major inquiries were not members of the panel at all but members of the Bar who specialized in planning matters.

The Council on Tribunals

Tribunals and Inquiries Act 1971, Section 11, p. 588 *supra*

The Functions of The Council on Tribunals, p. 568*supra*

OTHER INQUIRY PROCEDURES

Note

These are briefly outlined at the beginning of this chapter, p. 578 *supra*. For fuller discussion see Wade, p. 867.

THE PARLIAMENTARY COMMISSIONER FOR ADMINISTRATION

THE STATUTORY PROVISIONS

Note

For the history of the introduction of the Parliamentary Commissioner for Administration (hereafter P.C.A.) – popularly known as the Ombudsman – see Wade, p. 75, and (in more detail) Stacey, *The British Ombudsman*. For other books discussing the P.C.A., see Stacey, *Ombudsmen Compared*, Ch. VII; Wheare, *Maladministration and its Remedies*, Chs. 5–6; Gregory and Hutchesson, *The Parliamentary Ombudsman*; Williams, *Maladministration. Remedies for Injustice*, Chs. 1–5.

Parliamentary Commissioner Act 1967

The Parliamentary Commissioner for Administration

1. – (1) For the purpose of conducting investigations in accordance with the following provisions of this Act there shall be appointed a Commissioner, to be known as the Parliamentary Commissioner for Administration.

(2) Her Majesty may by Letters Patent from time to time appoint a person to be the Commissioner, and any person so appointed shall (subject to subsection (3) of this section) hold office during good behaviour.

(3) A person appointed to be the Commissioner may be relieved of office by Her Majesty at his own request, or may be removed from office by Her Majesty in consequence of Addresses from both Houses of Parliament, and shall in any case vacate office on completing the year of service in which he attains the age of sixty-five years.

3. – (1) The Commissioner may appoint such officers as he may determine with the approval of the Treasury as to numbers and conditions of service.

(2) Any function of the Commissioner under this Act may be performed by any officer of the Commissioner authorised for that purpose by the Commissioner.

(3) The expenses of the Commissioner under this Act, to such amount as may be sanctioned by the Treasury, shall be defrayed out of moneys provided by Parliament.

Investigation by the Commissioner

4. – (1) Subject to the provisions of this section and to the notes contained

in Schedule 2 to this Act, this Act applies to the government departments and other authorities listed in that Schedule.

(2) Her Majesty may by Order in Council amend the said Schedule 2 by the alteration of any entry or note, the removal of any entry or note or the insertion of any additional entry or note; but nothing in this subsection authorises the inclusion in that Schedule of any body or authority not being a department or other body or authority whose functions are exercised on behalf of the Crown.

(4) Any reference in this Act to a government department or other authority to which this Act applies includes a reference to the Ministers, members or officers of that department or authority.

5. – (1) Subject to the provisions of this section, the Commissioner may investigate any action taken by or on behalf of a government department or other authority to which this Act applies, being action taken in the exercise of administrative functions of that department or authority, in any case where –

(a) a written complaint is duly made to a member of the House of Commons by a member of the public who claims to have sustained injustice in consequence of maladministration in connection with the action so taken; and

(b) the complaint is referred to the Commissioner, with the consent of the person who made it, by a member of that House with a request to conduct an investigation thereon.

(2) Except as hereinafter provided, the Commissioner shall not conduct an investigation under this Act in respect of any of the following matters, that is to say –

(a) any action in respect of which the person aggrieved has or had a right of appeal, reference or review to or before a tribunal constituted by or under any enactment or by virtue of Her Majesty's prerogative;

(b) any action in respect of which the person aggrieved has or had a remedy by way of proceedings in any court of law:

Provided that the Commissioner may conduct an investigation notwithstanding that the person aggrieved has or had such a right or remedy if satisfied that in the particular circumstances it is not reasonable to expect him to resort or have resorted to it.

(3) Without prejudice to subsection (2) of this section, the Commissioner shall not conduct an investigation under this Act in respect of any such action or matter as is described in Schedule 3 to this Act.

(4) Her Majesty may by Order in Council amend the said Schedule 3 so as to exclude from the provisions of that Schedule such actions or matters as may be described in the Order; and any statutory instrument made by virtue of this subsection shall be subject to annulment in pursuance of a resolution of either House of Parliament.

(5) In determining whether to initiate, continue or discontinue an investigation under this Act, the Commissioner shall, subject to the foregoing

provisions of this section, act in accordance with his own discretion; and any question whether a complaint is duly made under this Act shall be determined by the Commissioner.

6. – (1) A complaint under this Act may be made by any individual, or by any body of persons whether incorporated or not, not being –

(a) a local authority or other authority or body constituted for purposes of the public service or of local government or for the purposes of carrying on under national ownership any industry or undertaking or part of an industry or undertaking;

(b) any other authority or body whose members are appointed by Her Majesty or any Minister of the Crown or government department, or whose revenues consist wholly or mainly of moneys provided by Parliament.

(2) Where the person by whom a complaint might have been made under the foregoing provisions of this Act has died or is for any reason unable to act for himself, the complaint may be made by his personal representative or by a member of his family or other individual suitable to represent him; but except as aforesaid a complaint shall not be entertained under this Act unless made by the person aggrieved himself.

(3) A complaint shall not be entertained under this Act unless it is made to a member of the House of Commons not later than twelve months from the day on which the person aggrieved first had notice of the matters alleged in the complaint; but the Commissioner may conduct an investigation pursuant to a complaint not made within that period if he considers that there are special circumstances which make it proper to do so.

(4) [Except as provided in subsection (5) below][1] a complaint shall not be entertained under this Act unless the person aggrieved is resident in the United Kingdom (or, if he is dead, was so resident at the time of his death) or the complaint relates to action taken in relation to him while he was present in the United Kingdom or on an installation in a designated area within the meaning of the Continental Shelf Act 1964 or on a ship registered in the United Kingdom or an aircraft so registered, or in relation to rights or obligations which accrued or arose in the United Kingdom or on such an installation, ship or aircraft.

[(5) A complaint may be entertained under this Act in circumstances not falling within subsection (4) above where –

(a) the complaint relates to action taken in any country or territory outside the United Kingdom by an officer (not being an honorary consular officer) in the exercise of a consular function on behalf of the Government of the United Kingdom; and

(b) the person aggrieved is a citizen of the United Kingdom and Colonies who, under section 2 of the Immigration Act 1971, has the right of abode in the United Kingdom.][1a]

[1] [Added by the Parliamentary Commissioner (Consular Complaints) Act 1981.]
[1a] [See n. 1 *supra* and see ss. 39 and 51(3) of the British Nationality Act 1981.]

7. – (1) Where the Commissioner proposes to conduct an investigation pursuant to a complaint under this Act, he shall afford to the principal officer of the department or authority concerned, and to any other person who is alleged in the complaint to have taken or authorised the action complained of, an opportunity to comment on any allegations contained in the complaint.

(2) Every such investigation shall be conducted in private, but except as aforesaid the procedure for conducting an investigation shall be such as the Commissioner considers appropriate in the circumstances of the case; and without prejudice to the generality of the foregoing provision the Commissioner may obtain information from such persons and in such manner, and make such inquiries, as he thinks fit, and may determine whether any person may be represented, by counsel or solicitor or otherwise, in the investigation.

(3) The Commissioner may, if he thinks fit, pay to the person by whom the complaint was made and to any other person who attends or furnishes information for the purposes of an investigation under this Act –

(a) sums in respect of expenses properly incurred by them;
(b) allowances by way of compensation for the loss of their time,

in accordance with such scales and subject to such conditions as may be determined by the Treasury.

(4) The conduct of an investigation under this Act shall not affect any action taken by the department or authority concerned, or any power or duty of that department or authority to take further action with respect to any matters subject to the investigation; but where the person aggrieved has been removed from the United Kingdom under any Order in force under the Aliens Restriction Acts 1914 and 1919 or under the Commonwealth Immigrants Act 1962,[1b] he shall, if the Commissioner so directs, be permitted to re-enter and remain in the United Kingdom, subject to such conditions as the Secretary of State may direct, for the purposes of the investigation.

8. – (1) For the purposes of an investigation under this Act the Commissioner may require any Minister, officer or member of the department or authority concerned or any other person who in his opinion is able to furnish information or produce documents relevant to the investigation to furnish any such information or produce any such document.

(2) For the purposes of any such investigation the Commissioner shall have the same powers as the Court in respect of the attendance and examination of witnesses (including the administration of oaths or affirmations and the examination of witnesses abroad) and in respect of the production of documents.

(3) No obligation to maintain secrecy or other restriction upon the disclosure of information obtained by or furnished to persons in Her Majesty's service, whether imposed by any enactment or by any rule of law, shall apply

[1b][See Immigration Act 1971: s. 17(2)(a) of the Interpretation Act 1978.]

to the disclosure of information for the purposes of an investigation under this Act; and the Crown shall not be entitled in relation to any such investigation to any such privilege in respect of the production of documents or the giving of evidence as is allowed by law in legal proceedings.

(4) No person shall be required or authorised by virtue of this Act to furnish any information or answer any question relating to proceedings of the Cabinet or of any committee of the Cabinet or to produce so much of any document as relates to such proceedings; and for the purposes of this subsection a certificate issued by the Secretary of the Cabinet with the approval of the Prime Minister and certifying that any information, question, document or part of a document so relates shall be conclusive.

(5) Subject to subsection (3) of this section, no person shall be compelled for the purposes of an investigation under this Act to give any evidence or produce any document which he could not be compelled to give or produce in [civil]² proceedings before the Court.

9. – (1) If any person without lawful excuse obstructs the Commissioner or any officer of the Commissioner in the performance of his functions under this Act, or is guilty of any act or omission in relation to an investigation under this Act which, if that investigation were a proceeding in the Court, would constitute contempt of court, the Commissioner may certify the offence to the Court. . . .

10. – (1) In any case where the Commissioner conducts an investigation under this Act or decides not to conduct such an investigation, he shall send to the member of the House of Commons by whom the request for investigation was made (or if he is no longer a member of that House, to such member of that House as the Commissioner thinks appropriate) a report of the results of the investigation or, as the case may be, a statement of his reasons for not conducting an investigation.

(2) In any case where the Commissioner conducts an investigation under this Act, he shall also send a report of the results of the investigation to the principal officer of the department or authority concerned and to any other person who is alleged in the relevant complaint to have taken or authorised the action complained of.

(3) If, after conducting an investigation under this Act, it appears to the Commissioner that injustice has been caused to the person aggrieved in consequence of maladministration and that the injustice has not been, or will not be, remedied, he may, if he thinks fit, lay before each House of Parliament a special report upon the case.

(4) The Commissioner shall annually lay before each House of Parliament a general report on the performance of his functions under this Act and may from time to time lay before each House of Parliament such other reports with respect to those functions as he thinks fit.

² [Inserted by s. 17 (1) (b) of the Civil Evidence Act 1968.]

(5) For the purposes of the law of defamation, any such publication as is hereinafter mentioned shall be absolutely privileged, that is to say –

(a) the publication of any matter by the Commissioner in making a report to either House of Parliament for the purposes of this Act;

(b) the publication of any matter by a member of the House of Commons in communicating with the Commissioner or his officers for those purposes or by the Commissioner or his officers in communicating with such a member for those purposes;

(c) the publication by such a member to the person by whom a complaint was made under this Act of a report or statement sent to the member in respect of the complaint in pursuance of subsection (1) of this section;

(d) the publication by the Commissioner to such a person as is mentioned in subsection (2) of this section of a report sent to that person in pursuance of that subsection.

11. – (1) It is hereby declared that the Commissioner and his officers hold office under Her Majesty within the meaning of the Official Secrets Act 1911.

(2) Information obtained by the Commissioner or his officers in the course of or for the purposes of an investigation under this Act shall not be disclosed except –

(a) for the purposes of the investigation and of any report to be made thereon under this Act;

(b) for the purposes of any proceedings for an offence under the Official Secrets Acts 1911 to 1939 alleged to have been committed in respect of information obtained by the Commissioner or any of his officers by virtue of this Act or for an offence of perjury alleged to have been committed in the course of an investigation under this Act or for the purposes of an inquiry with a view to the taking of such proceedings; or

(c) for the purposes of any proceedings under section 9 of this Act;

and the Commissioner and his officers shall not be called upon to give evidence in any proceedings (other than such proceedings as aforesaid) of matters coming to his or their knowledge in the course of an investigation under this Act.

(3) A Minister of the Crown may give notice in writing to the Commissioner, with respect to any document or information specified in the notice, or any class of documents or information so specified, that in the opinion of the Minister the disclosure of that document or information, or of documents or information of that class, would be prejudicial to the safety of the State or otherwise contrary to the public interest; and where such a notice is given nothing in this Act shall be construed as authorising or requiring the Commissioner or any officer of the Commissioner to communicate to any person or for any purpose any document or information specified in the notice, or any document or information of a class so specified.

(4) The references in this section to a Minister of the Crown include references to the Commissioners of Customs and Excise and the Commissioners of Inland Revenue.

Supplemental

12. – (1) In this Act the following expressions have the meanings hereby respectively assigned to them, that is to say –

'action' includes failure to act, and other expressions connoting action shall be construed accordingly;

'the Commissioner' means the Parliamentary Commissioner for Administration;

'the Court' means, in relation to England and Wales the High Court, in relation to Scotland the Court of Session, and in relation to Northern Ireland the High Court of Northern Ireland;

'enactment' includes an enactment of the Parliament of Northern Ireland, and any instrument made by virtue of an enactment;

'officer' includes employee;

'person aggrieved' means the person who claims or is alleged to have sustained such injustice as is mentioned in section 5(1)(a) of this Act;

'tribunal' includes the person constituting a tribunal consisting of one person.

(3) It is hereby declared that nothing in this Act authorises or requires the Commissioner to question the merits of a decision taken without maladministration by a government department or other authority in the exercise of a discretion vested in that department or authority. . . .

SCHEDULE 2[3]

DEPARTMENTS AND AUTHORITIES SUBJECT TO INVESTIGATION

Advisory, Conciliation and Arbitration Service
Ministry of Agriculture, Fisheries and Food
Certification Officer
Charity Commission
Civil Service Commission
Crown Estate Office
Customs and Excise
Ministry of Defence
Department of Education and Science
Department of Employment
Department of Energy
Department of the Environment
Export Credits Guarantee Department
Office of the Director General of Fair Trading

---

[3] [As amended by various Acts and statutory instruments.]

Foreign and Commonwealth Office
Forestry Commission
Health and Safety Commission
Health and Safety Executive
Department of Health and Social Security
Home Office
Department of Industry
Central Office of Information
Inland Revenue
Intervention Board for Agricultural Produce
Land Registry
Lord Chancellor's Department
Lord President of the Council's Office
Management and Personnel Office
Manpower Services Commission
National Debt Office
Department for National Savings
Northern Ireland Court Service
Northern Ireland Office
Office of Population Censuses and Surveys
Public Record Office
Public Trustee
Department of the Registers of Scotland
General Register Office, Scotland
Registry of Friendly Societies
Royal Mint
Scottish Courts Administration
Scottish Office
Scottish Record Office
Stationery Office
Board of Trade
Department of Trade
Department of Transport
Treasury
Treasury Solicitor
Welsh Office

NOTES...

6. The references to the Management and Personnel Office and the Treasury do not include the Cabinet Office. . . .

SCHEDULE 3

MATTERS NOT SUBJECT TO INVESTIGATION

1. Action taken in matters certified by a Secretary of State or other Minister of the Crown to affect relations or dealings between the Govern-

ment of the United Kingdom and any other Government or any international organisation of States or Governments.

2. Action taken, in any country or territory outside the United Kingdom, by or on behalf of any officer representing or acting under the authority of Her Majesty in respect of the United Kingdom, or any other officer of the Government of the United Kingdom [other than action which is taken by an officer (not being an honorary consular officer) in the exercise of a consular function on behalf of the Government of the United Kingdom and which is so taken in relation to a citizen of the United Kingdom and Colonies who has the right of abode in the United Kingdom].[4]

3. Action taken in connection with the administration of the government of any country or territory outside the United Kingdom which forms part of Her Majesty's dominions or in which Her Majesty has jurisdiction.

4. Action taken by the Secretary of State under the Extradition Act 1870 or the Fugitive Offenders Act 1881.

5. Action taken by or with the authority of the Secretary of State for the purposes of investigating crime or of protecting the security of the State, including action so taken with respect to passports.

6. The commencement or conduct of civil or criminal proceedings before any court of law in the United Kingdom, of proceedings at any place under the Naval Discipline Act 1957, the Army Act 1955 or the Air Force Act 1955, or of proceedings before any international court or tribunal.

7. Any exercise of the prerogative of mercy or of the power of a Secretary of State to make a reference in respect of any person to the Court of Appeal, the High Court of Justiciary or the Courts-Martial Appeal Court.

8. Action taken on behalf of the Minister of Health or the Secretary of State by a [Regional Health Authority, an Area Health Authority, a District Health Authority, a special health authority except the Rampton Hospital Review Board, a Family Practitioner Committee, a Health Board or the Common Services Agency for the Scottish Health Service][5], or by the Public Health Laboratory Service Board.

9. Action taken in matters relating to contractual or other commercial transactions, whether within the United Kingdom or elsewhere, being transactions of a government department or authority to which this Act applies or of any such authority or body as is mentioned in paragraph (a) or (b) of subsection (1) of section 6 of this Act and not being transactions for or relating to –

   (a) the acquisition of land compulsorily or in circumstances in which it could be acquired compulsorily;
   (b) the disposal as surplus of land acquired compulsorily or in such circumstances as aforesaid.

---

[4] [Added by S.I. 1979 No. 915 and see s. 51(3) of the British Nationality Act 1981.]

[5] [Amended by the National Health Service Reorganisation Act 1973, the Health Services Act 1980, and S.I. 1981 No. 736.]

10. Action taken in respect of appointments or removals, pay, discipline, superannuation or other personnel matters, in relation to –

(a) service in any of the armed forces of the Crown, including reserve and auxiliary and cadet forces;

(b) service in any office or employment under the Crown or under any authority listed in Schedule 2 to this Act; or

(c) service in any office or employment, or under any contract for services, in respect of which power to take action, or to determine or approve the action to be taken, in such matters is vested in Her Majesty, any Minister of the Crown or any such authority as aforesaid.

11. The grant of honours, awards or privileges within the gift of the Crown, including the grant of Royal Charters.

Notes

1. There has been a proliferation of Ombudsmen within the United Kingdom since 1967. In 1969 we were presented with the P.C.A. for Northern Ireland and the Commissioner for Complaints for Northern Ireland: both offices are held by one man, and on the latter Ombudsman see Poole, [1972] P.L. 131. This was followed some time later by the establishment of the Health Service Commissioners for England, Wales, and Scotland – see Wade, p. 90 – all three posts being at present held by the person who is the P.C.A., and in 1974 the Local Commissioners came into existence. These latter Commissioners, as their name implies, are concerned with maladministration in local government: see Wade, p. 123. The extent to which all these Commissioners 'provide a comprehensive, accessible and effective Ombudsman service' was examined by the Select Committee on the P.C.A. in 1980: see the Second Report for the Session 1979/80, H.C. 254, part of which will be referred to at p.652 *infra*. See further the views expressed by the P.C.A. in para. 55 of the Annual Report for 1975, H.C. 141, Session 1975/6.

2. The introduction of an Ombudsman into this country was not favoured by all. Mitchell argued that we needed a reform of the *law*, rather than an Ombudsman, which he saw as a dangerous 'half-measure': it was dangerous, in his opinion, since it might provide an excuse for not bringing about other changes. See especially [1962] P.L. 24, but note that various developments in the judicial control of administrative action have occurred since that article was written. The effect of the P.C.A. on ministerial responsibility, a doctrine with which we assume the student is familiar, was also a matter of concern. On this topic, see Wade, p. 75, who argues that in fact the introduction of the P.C.A. has helped the doctrine to work more successfully. See further the Second Report from the Select Committee on the P.C.A. for the Session 1967/8, H.C. 350, paras. 24–30, and Fry, [1970] P.L. 336 at pp. 345–57.

Another problem was the delay the P.C.A. might cause. Although costing nothing to the complainant (a major advantage over the courts, of course), there will be a cost, not only in respect of his salary and that of his officers, but also in particular in terms of the time devoted by civil servants to a matter which the P.C.A. is investigating (as well as possibly some slowing down of the administrative process because of his very existence). However, the Select Committee on the P.C.A. received evidence in 1971 (confirming its earlier view) that the P.C.A. was not proving unduly burdensome or causing any significant delay to Government departments: see the Second Report from the Select Committee on the P.C.A. for the Session 1971/2, H.C. 334, paras. 13–16. Whilst discussing delay and costs, it might further be noted that in 1978 the cost of an investigation of a complaint could, it was said, amount to £2,000 (Harlow, (1978) 41 M.L.R. 446 at p. 451).

3. The P.C.A. reports to each House of Parliament, and his reports to the House of Commons are considered by the Select Committee on the P.C.A. The materials in this chapter should show the importance of that Committee, and see further Gregory, [1982] P.L. 49.

4. The prohibition on the P.C.A. being at the same time an M.P. was originally contained in s. 1 (4) of the Act. The House of Commons Disqualification Act 1975 repealed that subsection, but the ban remains: see Part III of Sch. 1 to the 1975 Act.

5. The P.C.A. is *ex officio* a member of the Council on Tribunals and its Scottish Committee, on which see p. 568 *supra*. This was initially enacted by s. 1 (5) of the 1967 Act, but is now to be found in s. 2 (3) of the Tribunals and Inquiries Act 1971. See further Wade, p. 90.

6. The first three appointments to the office of P.C.A. were ex-civil servants, but in January 1979 Sir Cecil Clothier, a Queen's Counsel, became the P.C.A. There are no other lawyers on his staff, however, although they did make a temporary appearance during the tenure of office of the previous P.C.A. (Yardley, *Principles of Administrative Law*, p. 214). Legal advice has, in the past, been obtained from the Treasury Solicitor and occasionally from outside sources. Can you see any objection to legal advice being given by the Treasury Solicitor?

7. At one time all the P.C.A.'s staff were civil servants. JUSTICE in their 1977 report, *Our Fettered Ombudsman*, suggested that his staff should include people with 'varied backgrounds', and the employment of non-civil service staff has begun: see para. 7 of the Annual Report for 1978, H.C. 205, Session 1978/9. (They also recommended that the P.C.A. should have his own legal adviser, but this recommendation was made, of course, before the appointment of Sir Cecil Clothier.)

Matters excluded

Parliamentary Commissioner Act 1967, Section 5 (3) and (4), p. 623 *supra*, and Schedule 3, p. 629 *supra*

Fourth Report from The Select Committee on The Parliamentary Commissioner For Administration. The Jurisdiction of The Parliamentary Commissioner

H.C. 593, Session 1979/80

2. We have . . . considered the Government's observations[6] on the Review of Access and Jurisdiction carried out by the Select Committee in 1978.[7] The Government accepted some of the Select Committee's conclusions but rejected their recommendations that the Parliamentary Commissioner should be able to investigate complaints about matters relating to contractual or

[6] Cmnd. 7449 of January 1979.
[7] Fourth Report for 1977–78 (H.C. 615 and 444 (1977–78)).

other commercial transactions and about certain public service personnel matters. . . .

Contractual and commercial matters

3. In its observations the Government said that it believed that the Parliamentary Commissioner system should operate in the field of the relations between the executive and those whom it governs, and that it would not be in the general interest to extend it to commercial transactions. It did not consider that the commercial activities of Government Departments should be open to examination while other contracting parties were free from such investigation. In the area of assistance to industry, the Government acknowledged that the dividing line between transactions that were within jurisdiction and those which were not was a difficult one, but it took the view that the use of statutory powers involving a wide measure of commercial discretion should not be subject to review by the Commissioner.[8]

8. We do not accept the Government's contention that only those activities which are unique to the function of government should be subject to review by the Parliamentary Commissioner; rather we believe that in principle all areas of Government administration should be investigable by him unless in particular cases a compelling argument can be made out for their exclusion. Accordingly the claim that the Government's commercial activities should be exempt from examination because private contractors are exempt is in our view beside the point. The Government has a duty to administer its purchasing policies fairly and equitably, and if those policies are the subject of complaint then the complaints should be investigated; this is particularly important if any future Government were again to use the award of contracts as a political weapon. Section 12 (3) of the Act would prevent the Commissioner from questioning a *bona fide* commercial decision to purchase goods or services from one firm rather than another, or the legitimate exercise of a Department's discretion to give selective assistance to one firm or one industry rather than another, but if decisions of this kind are taken with maladministration then it is right that they should be reviewed. It was suggested in evidence that the Commissioner would not be able to decide whether maladministration had been committed, but we note the Commissioner's view that that is the kind of judgment that he and his officers are making 'every day of the week.'[9] In any case, a belief that the Commissioner might have difficulty in making such a decision may be thought to be poor ground for refusing him the right to try. It is true that any commercial maladministration by a Department can be investigated by the Exchequer and Audit Department and censured by the Public Accounts Committee, but neither of these bodies is primarily concerned, as the Parliamentary Commissioner is, with any injustice a complainant might have suffered as a result. . . . We are satisfied that sections 5 and 12 (3) of the Parliamentary Com-

---

[8] Cmnd. 7449, paragraphs 23–4.
[9] Q104.

missioner Act are sufficient on their own and that the further exemption from investigation conferred by paragraph 9 of Schedule 3 is not justified.

Public service personnel matters

9. In 1978 the Select Committee again recommended that complaints about public service personnel matters, except complaints from serving civil servants and members of the armed forces about discipline, establishment questions and terms of service, should be investigable by the Parliamentary Commissioner. The Government rejected their recommendation, as it had a similar recommendation by the Select Committee[10] in 1977, on the ground that there was no evidence that grievance machinery available to intending, present or former Crown servants was inferior to that available to workers generally. The Government also noted that the Parliamentary Commissioner had not been established to deal with relations between the State as employer and its employees.[11]

11. The Commissioner told us that in his view the remedies for grievances about personnel matters which the Government had described to the Select Committee in 1977 were quite illusory. . . .

15. As we have said earlier in this Report, we do not accept the view that the role of the Parliamentary Commissioner should be restricted to those activities which are unique to the function of government, and so we reject the contention that because not every employee can call upon the Commissioner to enquire into grievances about personnel matters the State's employees should not be able to do so. We accept, as the Commissioner does and as the Committee did in 1978, that the exclusion of complaints from serving public employees about matters of discipline, promotion, rates of pay and terms of service is justified, but we do not consider that any evidence has been produced to show that bringing within jurisdiction other purely administrative acts of Government Departments in their capacity as employers would cause any harm to anyone: . . . There has always been evidence of a demand for the Commissioner's services in this area, and the argument that if they were available a great number of extra complaints might have to be investigated comes perilously close to saying that one ought not to have an Ombudsman at all lest people should complain to him.

Fourth Report from The Select Committee on The Parliamentary Commissioner for Administration, Session 1979/80. Observations by The Government

Cmnd. 8274 (1981)

Contractual and Commercial Matters . . .

3. The Government have given very careful consideration to the Committee's observations but have concluded that for . . . reasons previously given

---

[10] Second Report for 1976–77 (H.C. 524 (1976–77)).

[11] Cmnd. 7098, paras. 4–5.

. . . Parliament's decision to exclude this area of administration from the Commissioner's jurisdiction remains sound.

Recruitment [of Public Service Personnel]

8. The Government have . . . considered very carefully the proposal that the Commissioner should be empowered to investigate complaints about recruitment to the Home Civil Service and the Diplomatic Service.

9. The Civil Service Commissioners are responsible for the selection on merit by fair and open competition of all candidates for posts in the Civil and Diplomatic Services. The Commissioners are appointed by Order in Council to ensure their independence of Ministers, Parliament or anyone else. Recruitment is, therefore, already subject to rigorous scrutiny by an independent body. The Government are not persuaded of the justification for subjecting the activity of one independent body to oversight by another. Moreover, they believe that it would be inequitable to give applicants for jobs in the Civil Service a channel for the investigation of complaints not available to those who seek employment elsewhere. For these reasons, the Government are unable to agree with the Committee that the Commissioner's jurisdiction should be extended to include complaints about recruitment.

Superannuation

10. The Government have given equally thorough consideration to the Select Committee's view that complaints from former public servants about their superannuation should be open to investigation by the Commissioner.

11. Public service pensioners already have the advantage that their grievances may be raised in either House of Parliament. If the Commissioner's terms of reference were extended as recommended by the Committee, former public servants would be granted a further preferential means of redress which is not available to other occupational pensioners. In addition, a serious inequity would be created between retired public servants and those who are still in service. Since the decisions or actions complained of are as likely to arise during a person's service as after it, no valid distinction can be drawn between pensioners and those who are still serving. It would be highly anomalous if public service pensioners had access to the Commissioner, while serving officers wishing to raise similar or even identical complaints had not.

12. The Government share the view of successive Administrations that the Commissioner was not established to investigate relations between the State as employer and its employees. They also believe it would be wrong in principle to confer on public service pensioners a right, not available to others in similar circumstances, to seek the assistance of the Commissioner. The Government regret that they are unable to agree with the Select Committee on this point. They consider, however, that these arguments of principle together constitute a compelling reason not to extend the Parliamentary Commissioner's terms of reference to include matters raised by public service pensioners.

Notes

1. In relation to para. 8 of Sch. 3 to the 1967 Act, note that Health Service Commissioners for England and Wales were established in 1973 (in the case of Scotland the office was established in 1972): see now ss. 106–20 and Sch. 13 to the National Health Service Act 1977, and Wade, p. 90. In relation to local authorities, which are excluded by virtue of not being included in Sch. 2, note the establishment of the Local Commissioners by the Local Government Act 1974, and see Wade, p. 123.

2. As indicated in the extract *supra*, the question of the P.C.A.'s jurisdiction was discussed by the Select Committee in an earlier session (Fourth Report for the Session 1977/8, H.C. 615 and 444) and, prior to that, JUSTICE had also considered the matter. This latter body recommended several changes (*Our Fettered Ombudsman*, paras. 34–7). They wanted to remove paras. 4, 8, 9, and 10 from Sch. 3; to take action in relation to para. 3 so as to give some form of Ombudsman protection to citizens of British colonies and dependencies (this could be provided either by the P.C.A. or in the case of larger territories (e.g. Hong Kong) by an Ombudsman in the territory concerned); to amend para. 5 so as to delete the restriction on the P.C.A.'s power to investigate questions concerning passports; and to alter para. 6 so as to allow the P.C.A. to investigate the commencement or conduct of proceedings by the central administration (though not if it concerned a matter over which the court had control).

3. The Select Committee in its Fourth Report for the Session 1977/8 was less radical than JUSTICE, but in part, it seems, too radical for the Government. It was, however, successful in respect of para. 2 (and note s. 6 (5) of the Act as well): see S.I. 1979 No. 915, p. 630 *supra*, and the Parliamentary Commissioner (Consular Complaints) Act 1981, p. 624 *supra*. The Select Committee's views on paras. 9 and 10, and the Government's unsympathetic reaction to them, are revealed in the extracts *supra*. The Select Committee in para. 31 of its Second Report for the Session 1980/1, H.C. 243, expressed disappointment with the Government's reaction, and this disappointment was echoed by the P.C.A. in para. 12 of his Annual Report for 1981, H.C. 258, Session 1981/2. In relation to recruitment, the Select Committee castigated the Government's argument (in para. 9 of the extract *supra*) concerning lack of equity as a 'red herring' since the administrative staff of the Civil Service Commission are civil servants paid out of money provided by Parliament, whereas recruitment outside the civil service will not normally be carried out by civil servants. In addition to this point, the Committee thought that the Government should be prepared to adopt higher standards than those that prevail elsewhere. The battle is likely to continue but the eventual victor remains uncertain. For the history of the conflict, see Gregory, [1982] P.L. 49 at pp. 73–6.

The Committee in its Fourth Report for the Session 1977/8 made no other recommendations for change in Sch. 3. (For JUSTICE's views on the Select Committee's report in relation to Sch. 3, see p. 39 of the Select Committee's Fourth Report for the Session 1979/80, H.C. 593 and more generally see pp. 39–42 for their views on other matters dealt with in the earlier Report.)

Have the courts been particularly active in the sorts of subject matter contained in Sch. 3? (See, for example, in relation to para. 7, *Hanratty* v. *Lord Butler of Saffron Walden*, The Times, 13 May 1971: no tort action allowed against the Home Secretary for alleged negligence in respect of the way he exercised his duty to advise the Crown on the prerogative of mercy.) If not, does this indicate that the P.C.A. should be restricted in his investigation of these matters, does it perhaps indicate the opposite, or is it irrelevant?

THE OPERATION OF THE INSTITUTION

Statistics and inferences

Parliamentary Commissioner for Administration. Annual Report for 1980

H.C. 148, Session 1980/1

120. The number of complaints received through Members in 1980 has risen by 36 per cent over the numbers received in 1979. Apart from the exceptionally high number of 1259 in 1978, this year's total is the highest since 1968 and the fourth highest since the office was opened. The following table shows the number of complaints referred by Members each year since then:

1967	1069 (April to December)
1968	1120
1969	761
1970	645
1971	548
1972	573
1973	571
1974	704
1975	928
1976	815
1977	901
1978	1259
1979	758
1980	1031

The number of Members referring complaints during the year was 401 compared with 368 in 1979. (I also received 42 written enquiries from Members, usually for advice about the extent of my jurisdiction). 454 Members of the present Parliament had referred at least one complaint to me by the end of the year, over 70 per cent of the total possible compared with nearly 90 per cent by the end of the previous Parliament in April 1979.

Parliamentary Commissioner for Administration. Annual Report for 1981

H.C. 258, Session 1981/2

54. During 1981 I received 917 complaints (1031 in 1980) from a total of 387 Members, and 253 cases were carried forward from 1980. Of the total of 1170 complaints, 929 were disposed of during the year, 694 being rejected, 228 full investigations completed and the results reported to Members, and 7 investigations discontinued before completion. 241 cases were carried forward into 1982. 164 of these were under investigation and the remainder at some preliminary stage of consideration. . . .

55. During the year nearly 24 per cent of the complaints examined for

jurisdiction (including those received in 1980 on which a decision was taken in 1981) were accepted for investigation. . . . The main reasons [why complaints were not accepted or not investigated to a conclusion] and relevant proportions of all complaints rejected or investigations discontinued were:

		per cent of total 1981	1980
Section 5 (1)	– Not properly referred; not about administrative actions	41	(34)
Section 4 (1)	– Authorities outside scope	23	(26)
Section 5 (2) (a)	– Right of appeal to tribunals	13	(15)
Schedule 3 (10)	– Public service personnel matters	10	(12)
Section 5 (5)	– Parliamentary Commissioner's discretion	9	(9)

As in the last few years about a quarter of the complaints received were rejected because they were directed against authorities outside my scope (i.e. not listed in Schedule 2 to the Act). Of that quarter about 25 per cent were directed against local authorities and another 25 per cent against the police, solicitors or the courts.

56 . . . Of the 228 cases in which investigations were completed and the results reported to Members during 1981, I upheld 104 (46 per cent) and in 41 (18 per cent) I did not, but I criticised departmental actions.

57. The list of departments each with 20 or more complaints directed against them in 1981 is as follows:

	No. of complaints	Percentage of total referrals	No. accepted for investigation
Department of Health and Social Security	260	28%	86
Inland Revenue	148	16%	45
Department of the Environment	57	6%	8
Home Office	39	4%	11
Department of Transport	33	3½%	11
Department of Employment	32	3½%	17
Ministry of Defence	28	3%	3

The order of departments and the share they hold of complaints has remained remarkably consistent over the last few years; but the number of complaints against the Department of Education and Science has dropped from 31 last year to 18 and so they are not now included in the list. As before, DHSS and Inland Revenue account for nearly half the complaints (and over half the complaints that can even be considered – as 18 per cent of complaints are about authorities outside the scope of the Act).

58. The number of written communications received direct from the public during the year was 870. About two-thirds of these were clearly or probably about matters outside my jurisdiction. Of the remainder, some 13

per cent were either simply requests for information or were not specific enough to enable me to say whether I could help, but in some 19 per cent of cases my staff were able to make helpful suggestions, including that the writers would be well advised to approach their Members of Parliament. Seven letters were clearly about matters which I could investigate and I offered to forward their letters to Members so that they could be referred formally to me if the Members so wished.[12] All the writers took up my offer and their cases were referred by Members and accepted for investigation. In addition to letters, my staff also dealt with a substantial number of enquiries from the public: 1920 by telephone (a considerably higher number than in previous years) and 26 in person. As usual, there was a fairly busy interchange of misdirected complaints between my office and those of the Commissioners for Local Administration.

Question

In the light of the number of cases the P.C.A. investigated in 1981, do you think he is having any real impact? Is his importance to be judged in terms other than the mere number of cases he investigates?

Notes

1. For further statistics, see Wade, p. 80.

2. The fact that a large percentage of cases is not accepted for investigation each year despite the operation of what is known as the 'M.P. filter' (the requirement that a complaint can only be referred to the P.C.A. by an M.P.) suggests that the filter is not working as well as it might *as a filter*. There are, however, other arguments for its existence, on which see p. 646 *infra*. Furthermore, one point to be borne in mind is that the percentage of rejections includes those that are rejected after the P.C.A. has exercised a discretion whether or not to investigate the case, in addition to those cases where there is a rigid bar on his jurisdiction.

3. The percentage of cases in which maladministration has been found has increased since the institution of the office of the P.C.A. In 1967 it was ten per cent, which should be compared with the figure for 1981. However, as the next section will indicate, what constitutes maladministration may change, a point that must be remembered when this statistic is considered.

Maladministration: discretionary decisions and rules

Parliamentary Commissioner Act 1967, Section 5 (1) (a), p. 623 *supra*, and Section 12 (3), p. 628 *supra*

R. v. Local Commissioner for Administration for The North and East Area of England, ex parte Bradford Metropolitan City Council

[1979] Q.B. 287   Court of Appeal

This case concerned a Local Commissioner and not the P.C.A. The details of the case need not be explored here, but in the course of their judgments the members of the Court of Appeal expressed opinions about the concept of

[12] [On this procedure see further pp. 647 and 651 *infra*.]

maladministration which is to be found in s. 26 of the Local Government Act 1974. These comments are also of interest in relation to the P.C.A. Section 34 (3) of the Local Government Act 1974, which is discussed in the judgments, finds its counterpart in s. 12 (3) of the Parliamentary Commissioner Act 1967, p. 628 *supra*.

LORD DENNING M.R.:

The meaning of maladministration

. . . This brings me to the substantial point in this case. Has there been a sufficient claim of maladministration such as to justify investigation by the commissioner? The governing words of each statute[13] are the same. There must be a written complaint made by or on behalf of a member of the public 'who claims to have suffered injustice in consequence of maladministration.'

But Parliament did not define 'maladministration.' It deliberately left it to the ombudsman himself to interpret the word as best he could: and to do it by building up a body of case law on the subject. Now the Parliamentary ombudsman, Sir Edmund Compton,[14] has acknowledged openly that he himself gained assistance by looking at the debates in Parliament on the subject. He looked at Hansard and, in particular, at a list of instances of maladministration given by Mr. Crossman, the Lord President of the Council. It is called the 'Crossman Catalogue': and is used by the ombudsman and his advisers as a guide to the interpretation of the word. Now the question at once arises: Are we the judges to look at Hansard when we have the self-same task? When we have ourselves to interpret the word 'maladministration.' The construction of that word is beyond doubt a question of law. According to the recent pronouncement of the House of Lords in *Davis* v. *Johnson* [1978] 2 W.L.R. 553, we ought to regard Hansard as a closed book to which we as judges must not refer at all, not even as an aid to the construction of statutes.

By good fortune, however, we have been given a way of overcoming that obstacle. For the ombudsman himself in a public address to the Society of Public Teachers of Law quoted the relevant passages of Hansard (734 H.C. Deb., col. 51 (October 18, 1966)) as part of his address: and Professor Wade has quoted the very words in his latest book on *Administrative Law*, 4th ed. (1977), p. 82. And we have not yet been told that we may not look at the writings of the teachers of law. Lord Simonds was as strict upon these matters as any judge ever has been but he confessed his indebtedness to their writings, even very recent ones: see *Jacobs* v. *London County Council* [1950] A.C. 361, 374. So have other great judges. I hope therefore that our teachers will go on quoting Hansard so that a judge may in this way have the same help as others have in interpreting a statute.

So this is the guide suggested to the meaning of the word 'maladministration.' It will cover 'bias, neglect, inattention, delay, incompetence, ineptitude, perversity, turpitude, arbitrariness and so on.' It 'would be a long and

---

[13] [i.e. the Parliamentary Commissioner Act 1967 and the Local Government Act 1974.]
[14] [Sir Edmund was the first P.C.A.]

interesting list,' clearly open-ended, covering the *manner* in which a decision is reached or discretion is exercised; but excluding the *merits* of the decision itself or of the discretion itself. It follows that 'discretionary decision, properly exercised, which the complainant dislikes but cannot fault the manner in which it was taken, is excluded': see Hansard, 734 H.C. Deb., col. 51.

In other words, if there is no maladministration, the ombudsman may not question any decision taken by the authorities. He must not go into the merits of it or intimate any view as to whether it was right or wrong. This is explicitly declared in section 34 (3) of the Act of 1974.[15] He can inquire whether there was maladministration or not. If he finds none, he must go no further. If he finds it, he can go on and inquire whether any person has suffered injustice thereby. . . .

EVELEIGH L.J.: . . . Maladministration according to the *Shorter Oxford English Dictionary* means 'faulty administration' or 'inefficient or improper management of affairs, esp. public affairs.' . . .

Section 34 (3) of the Act reads:

'It is hereby declared that nothing in this part of this Act authorises or requires the Local Commissioner to question the merits of a decision taken without maladministration by an authority in the exercise of a discretion vested in that authority.'

[Counsel for the Council] says that the matters complained of were the result of decisions arrived at with authority and that the complaint in effect seeks to question the merits of the decision or decisions. . . .

Action that is taken may or may not be the result of a particular administrative decision. If it is an act that is complained of I do not think that the commissioner can be denied the right to investigate merely by contending that the act is the result of a decision. When the party alleges injustice as a result of administrative action which the party claims is faulty the commissioner may investigate. In the course of that investigation he may come across a number of decisions that have been taken. Section 34 does not say that he may not *investigate* those decisions. It says that he may not *question* the merits of a decision taken without maladministration. It will often not be possible to say if a decision was taken with or without maladministration until it has been investigated. That is the whole purpose of the role of a commissioner. It is to investigate what has gone on in administrative quarters so that members of the public can be satisfied that public affairs are properly conducted. I therefore do not think that section 34 provides any obstacle. If the commissioner carries out his investigation and in the course of it comes personally to the conclusion that a decision was wrongly taken, but is unable to point to any maladministration other than the decision itself, he is prevented by section 34 (3) from questioning the decision. Consequently his investigations into the complaint in whatever direction his inquiries might lead will have to be conducted upon the basis that the decision in question was validly taken. Administrative action therefore which is based upon or dictated by that

---

[15] [Set out *infra*.]

decision will not amount to maladministration simply because someone in the exercise of his discretion has come to a wrong decision. If the decision itself is affected by maladministration, different consequences will follow.

[In response to certain further argument of counsel, EVELEIGH L.J. continued:] . . . [T]he taking of a decision is action taken in the exercise of administrative function. A faulty decision may amount to maladministration. Consequently it may be investigated. The only limit imposed upon the commissioner is that he may not arrive at a conclusion hostile to the local authority based upon a finding that there was a faulty or wrong decision unless the decision was linked to some other act of maladministration. . . .

SIR DAVID CAIRNS: . . . I think a sufficient indication of what [maladministration] is intended to mean is given by section 34 (3) of the Act of 1974. I express no opinion as to whether we are entitled to obtain assistance from a passage in Hansard which happens to have been quoted in a text book or in an address. . . .

Notes

1. In addition to its consideration by the Court of Appeal in the *Bradford* case, the concept of maladministration has been subject to interpretation by the P.C.A. and the Select Committee. See generally Gregory and Hutchesson, op. cit., Ch. 8, and Marshall, [1973] P.L. 32. At an early stage the P.C.A. fought shy of the merits of decisions, restricting himself to procedural matters, but was soon encouraged by the Select Committee to be more aggressive. In its Second Report for the Session 1967/8, H.C. 350, the Committee suggested (at para. 14) that if the P.C.A. 'finds a decision which, judged by its effect upon the aggrieved person, appears to him to be thoroughly bad in quality, he might infer from the quality of the decision itself that there had been an element of maladministration in the taking of it and ask for its review' (the 'Bad Decision'). Marshall writes of this development that 'the stuffing is knocked out of section 12 of the 1967 Act, as it always deserved to be' (*The Commons in Transition* (eds. Hanson and Crick), p. 123, quoted in Wheare, op cit., p. 122). Do you agree with the second part of Marshall's statement? Is the 'Bad Decision' ruling consistent with the approach in the *Bradford* case? Note further the Committee's later hope, expressed in para. 20 of its Second Report for the Session 1970/1, H.C. 513, that the P.C.A. will use the 'Bad Decision' rule 'when he finds borderline cases where in his judgment clearly wrong decisions have been taken'.

The Select Committee, in its Second Report for the Session 1967/8, also commented on what is described as the 'Bad Rule', where an administrative rule, despite being applied properly, has caused hardship and injustice. Here the P.C.A. was urged (para. 17):

. . . to enquire whether, given the effect of the rule in the case under his investigation, the Department had taken any action to review the rule. If found defective and revised, what action had been taken to remedy the hardship sustained by the complainant? If not revised, whether there had been due consideration by the Department of the grounds for maintaining the rule?

Failure to review the rule or an inadequate review could constitute maladministration. (For the P.C.A.'s power in relation to statutory instruments and statutory orders, see Gregory and Hutchesson, op. cit., pp. 193–7; Marshall, [1973] P.L. at pp. 41–3.) The P.C.A. has accepted the suggestions concerning both the 'Bad Decision' and the 'Bad Rule' (although for their limited effect, see Gregory, [1982] P.L. 49 at pp. 67 and 69), and his approach to the concept of maladministration today is, it seems, a fairly wide-ranging one.

In 1977 JUSTICE wanted to break away from the concept altogether. In their discussion of this point in *Our Fettered Ombudsman*, Ch. VII, they suggested that, following the position in New Zealand, the P.C.A. should be allowed to investigate action which is 'unreasonable, unjust or oppressive . . . instead of "maladministration" '. The P.C.A. responded to this suggestion in his Annual Report for 1977, H.C. 157, Session 1977/8, as follows:

20. I believe in fact that I already have the power to investigate complaints that actions by Government departments are unjust or oppressive. An 'unreasonable' action is perhaps more difficult to define but I believe that I should find no difficulty in investigating a complaint on these grounds.

21. What the Act certainly does exclude from my jurisdiction are complaints about discretionary decisions taken 'without maladministration'. I believe this to be right. It is no part of my function to substitute my judgment for that of a Minister or one of his officials if I see no evidence of 'maladministration' either in the way the decision was taken or in the nature of the decision itself.

22. I believe therefore that the difficulty which has been detected in the limitation of my investigating powers to cases of 'maladministration' is more theoretical than practical. But if there is thought to be some semantic difficulty which confuses members of the public or Members of Parliament then I should see no objection to seeing my powers redefined in the sort of language suggested by JUSTICE. I think that in practice it would make very little difference.

Bearing in mind para. 21 *supra*, does the P.C.A. go as far as JUSTICE wanted? Did JUSTICE contemplate unreasonable decisions merely being investigated or being the subject of a recommendation for remedial action? If the two positions are not the same, can they be reconciled by (*a*) regarding JUSTICE's 'unreasonable' decision as within the 'Bad Decision' category, or (*b*), irrespective of (*a*), regarding an 'unreasonable' decision as maladministration *per se*? Perhaps we need not worry too much about this point, as JUSTICE now think that the concept of maladministration 'is not a source of difficulty', a point mentioned by the Select Committee in its Fourth Report for the Session 1977/8, H.C. 615 and 444, in the course of noting the broad approach to maladministration under the 'Crossman catalogue' (see the *Bradford* case, p. 640 *supra*) and the 'Bad Decision' ruling. The Government later agreed with the Select Committee that the reference in the 1967 Act to 'maladministration' should be left alone (Cmnd. 7449, para. 16).

2. Leaving aside s. 5 (2) (*b*) of the 1967 Act for the moment, how does maladministration relate to ultra vires? Clearly not all maladministration constitutes ultra vires action, but is all ultra vires action maladministration? What about action that is ultra vires because it is totally unreasonable under the principles in *Associated Provincial Picture Houses Ltd.* v. *Wednesbury Corporation*, p. 118 *supra*? What about action taken in breach of natural justice? See generally Bradley, [1980] C.L.J. 304 at pp. 324–9.

Cases where there are legal remedies

Parliamentary Commissioner Act 1967, Section 5 (2), p. 623 *supra*

Parliamentary Commissioner for Administration. Annual Report for 1980

H.C. 148, Session 1980/1

. . . The borderline between my Office and the courts was clearly perceived and provided for by those who framed the Parliamentary Commissioner Act

1967. It was decided that Section 5 (2) should do no more than lay down a basis for a practical and discretionary approach to the problem which arises when the citizen's complaint, if true, would be both an instance of mal-administration and a civil wrong actionable at law. The Act permits me to investigate such a complaint if the citizen has not yet taken it to the courts and I in my discretion think it is not reasonable to expect him to do so. As a matter of practice, where there appears on the face of things to have been a sub-stantial legal wrong for which, if proved, there is a substantial legal remedy, I expect the citizen to seek it in the courts and I tell him so. But where there is doubt about the availability of a legal remedy or where the process of law seems too cumbersome, slow and expensive for the objective to be gained, I exercise my discretion to investigate the complaint myself. For example, I may receive a complaint that a particular tax office has been dilatory and inattentive in issuing an amended assessment of liability to tax. The taxpayer may say that he is worried and anxious about how he stands and that it affects his business. But would it be reasonable for him to take the Inland Revenue to court to obtain an injunction commanding them forthwith to perform their statutory duty, a theoretically available remedy? Surely not. This approach derives validity from the fact that very few people whose complaints have been investigated by my Office have later gone on to seek a legal remedy in the courts. So the boundary is reasonably clear and well-observed.

Question

Would you expect it to be more difficult to persuade the P.C.A. to exercise his discretion in a case caught by s. 5 (2) (*a*) than in one covered by s. 5 (2) (*b*)?

Notes

1. For a discussion of the approach to s. 5 (2), see Foulkes, (1971) 34 M.L.R. 377 at pp. 377–84; Gregory and Hutchesson, op. cit., pp. 230–41. We have touched on the relationship of maladministration and ultra vires at p. 643 *supra*.

2. Probably the best known case in which both the powers of the P.C.A. and the courts were involved concerned television licences. Prior to a rise in licence fees, some people took out a new licence at the old rate during the currency of the old licence. The difference between the old and new fees was greater than the loss caused by the double payment due to the overlapping of the licences. Thereafter these people were asked to pay the difference in fees, in which event their new licence would be made to run for twelve months from the expiry of the old licence. As an alternative the Home Office said that it would revoke the new licence, thereby leaving the old licence to be renewed from the time it expired, which obviously would now have to be done at the new rate. At a later date a concession was introduced: if the holder so wished, the new licence would only be revoked after the holder had held it for that proportion of the year which the fee they had paid would entitle them to at the new rate.

A number of complaints were received by the P.C.A. and the results of his investiga-tion were reported to the appropriate M.P.s, but, because of the great interest in the matter, the P.C.A. also laid the report before Parliament (Seventh Report for the Session 1974/5, H.C. 680), as he is entitled to do under s. 10 (4) of the 1967 Act, p. 626 *supra*. The Home Office's legal advice was that it was lawfully entitled to act in the manner proposed, and the P.C.A. did not think that to act on this advice could be maladministration *per se*. He continued (at para. 30):

My consideration has therefore been directed essentially to the question whether, within the framework of their view of the law, the Home Office's actions have been administratively sound and reasonable. My conclusion is that they have acted with both inefficiency and lack of foresight.

Nevertheless, no remedy was recommended by the P.C.A. and the threat to revoke remained. But the story does not end here. One of the holders of an overlapping licence obtained a declaration that revocation of his licence would be unlawful (*Congreve* v. *Home Office* [1976] Q.B. 629) and those who had paid the additional money received a refund. (For another example of an interplay between the courts and the P.C.A., see *R.* v. *Secretary of State for the Environment, ex p. Ostler,* p. 385 *supra*, and Note 5, p. 392 *supra*).

Could the P.C.A. have sought a declaration from the courts as to whether the Home Office's action was ultra vires? Consider Bradley, op. cit., pp. 322–3. Seeking a declaration when he was in dispute with a government department on a jurisdictional question is something the P.C.A. has contemplated (Annual Report for 1980, H.C. 148, Session 1980/1, para. 107), but Bradley, op. cit., p. 322 mentions the power to refer to the courts to resolve a point of law as a procedural *reform*. If the P.C.A. had been able to obtain a ruling to a similar effect to that in *Congreve* v. *Home Office*, could he have continued with the investigation? Would he have needed to?

3. A particular area where the jurisdiction of the courts and the P.C.A. may overlap concerns cases in which the complainant alleges that he has been misled by advice given by a goverment department. This is the sort of case in which the P.C.A. has successfully recommended *ex gratia* compensation, but the possibilities of an action under *Hedley Byrne & Co. Ltd.* v. *Heller & Partners Ltd.* [1964] A.C. 465 should be borne in mind (although note Wade's point (p. 85) that the P.C.A.'s policy seems to be to disregard this possibility). Another legal remedy in this situation might be an estoppel, on which see p. 148 *supra*.

Complaints

Parliamentary Commissioner Act 1967, Sections 5 (1) and (5), and 6, pp. 623 and 624 *supra*

Fourth Report from The Select Committee on The Parliamentary Commissioner for Administration. Parliamentary Commissioner for Administration (Review of Access and Jurisdiction)

H.C. 615 and 444, Session 1977/8

ACCESS . . .

6. The 'MP filter' is the most important distinguishing feature of the British Ombudsman system. It is meant to ensure that the Commissioner receives those cases which are appropriate for an independent investigation, in which the files are examined and the officials concerned with a decision are interviewed, and that problems which do not require such thorough scrutiny are dealt with by the Member himself. . . . At its best, the filter works to the advantage of

(a) the complainant, because his problem can often be resolved quickly through the intervention of a Member;

(b) the Member, because he is kept in touch with the problems which his constituents are facing in their daily contact with the machinery of the State; and

(c) the Commissioner, because he is normally asked to investigate only complaints that the Member has been, or knows that he will be, unable to resolve himself.

7. . . . Calculated on the same basis as New Zealand, whose Chief Ombudsman said in evidence before Your Committee in London that he received 2,000 complaints each year, half of which were outside his jurisdiction, from a population of three million,[16] the Parliamentary Commissioner, who in 1977 received fewer than a thousand complaints from Members of Parliament,[17] could expect to receive about 40,000 complaints if there were direct access, which is less than half the number that Members of Parliament are dealing with now.

9. Your Committee consider that if a system of direct access were adopted it is unavoidable that many of the problems which are now resolved relatively quickly by Members of Parliament would be sent straight to the Commissioner. In an attempt to overcome this objection Professor Gregory[18] has suggested a way in which the Commissioner might deal with some complaints without having to start a full-scale investigation. Professor Gregory proposes that the Commissioner would explain to the complainant the possible advantages of having his case taken up by a Member, but if the complainant would not agree to that the Commissioner would refer the complaint to the department, inviting it to consider whether it could offer a remedy without further intervention by the Commissioner; only if the complainant was still dissatisfied would the Commissioner carry out a full investigation.[19] Your Committee accept that were there to be direct access some such system would have to be devised if the Commissioner's office were not to be transformed into an impersonal Complaints Department, and that Professor Gregory's scheme (which is the only practical suggestion for coping with this problem which has been made to Your Committee) is probably as good as any other. They consider however that any system of this kind would inevitably be slow and bureaucratic and would lose the flexibility of the present system.

10. Your Committee believe that the principle on which the 1965 White Paper[20] was founded – that the primary responsibility for defending the citizen against the executive rests with the Member of Parliament – is still valid, and they would be reluctant to endorse any change which might weaken it. Your Committee nevertheless accept that the original interpreta-

---

[16] Qs. 179, 193–4 and 197.
[17] Annual Report for 1977, para. 2.
[18] [In his evidence to the Select Committee.]
[19] [Minutes of] Evidence p. 101.
[20] [The Parliamentary Commissioner for Administration, Cmnd. 2767.]

tion of the requirement that complaints must be submitted through a Member of Parliament meant that those who sent their complaint direct to the Commissioner, simply because they did not understand the requirement or did not know who their Member of Parliament was or how to get in touch with him, had to be turned away. Only a small proportion of the complaints received in this way were ever re-submitted through a Member.[21] In his Annual Report [for 1977] the Commissioner said:

'I receive broadly as many complaints direct as I do through Members, though a smaller proportion proves to be *prima facie* investigable. At present I can only send such complainants back to square one by advising them to approach their Member of Parliament. My proposal would be to facilitate the progress of the complaint by myself offering to send it and any accompanying documents to the constituent's Member of Parliament saying that I am prepared to start an investigation should the Member wish me to do so. This would still leave the member of the public concerned free to decide whether or not to proceed. But if he had no objection to this he would be spared the need to start the process of complaining again from scratch, while the Member of Parliament would have the opportunity either to discuss the matter with the constituent or to consent to my starting an investigation. I believe that this would help to save people some trouble and lessen the risk of confusion about my ability to help them. It would help remove a practical difficulty which I think has some inhibiting effect on the way members of the public make use of this office.'[22]

In their Second Special Report Your Committee welcomed the Commissioner's proposal, and this system has accordingly been in operation since Easter [1978]. The Commissioner told Your Committee that up to 16th June he had received 1,066 written communications direct from the public, compared with 443 during the same period last year, but that in no more than 5 per cent of the cases received since the new procedure came into force had he concluded that there was something he could usefully look into if requested to do so by a Member.[23] This suggests that a system of direct access would not be of great benefit to the public. . . . Your Committee believe that this new procedure will meet most of the criticisms of the rules for access to the Commissioner, but they acknowledge that in two types of case it is possible that the Commissioner could be prevented from taking up an investigable complaint. However, for the reasons given below, they believe the danger of this to be slight.

11. The first of these types of case is where the complainant does not wish his Member of Parliament to be involved in the investigation of his complaint. Your Committee emphasise that Members are not concerned about, and usually do not know, the political allegiance of those who ask for their help or advice, and in any case are anxious to do what they can for their constituents irrespective of party, but Your Committee recognise that for one reason or

---

[21] Q. 275. [22] Para. 17.
[23] [Minutes of] Evidence p. 145.

another a Member may be unacceptable to at least some of his constituents for the purpose of forwarding a complaint to the Commissioner. This difficulty may arise in a small number of cases, not because of the wording of the 1967 Act, which allows any Member of Parliament to refer any complaint to the Commissioner, but because of the parliamentary convention which in general inhibits Members from taking up their colleagues' constituency cases. Your Committee believe that where the reference of cases to the Parliamentary Commissioner is concerned this convention needs to be operated flexibly. If a member of the public asks a Member for a different constituency to take up his case with the Commissioner, saying that he does not wish his own Member to do so, Your Committee trust that the Members involved will, as they usually do at present, agree to respect the complainant's wishes. As there are 635 Members in the House Your Committee think it unlikely that a complainant will be debarred from access to the Commissioner because there is no Member to whom he is prepared to take his complaint. Nor should difficulties arise if the complainant's Member happens to be a Minister, for Ministers can and do refer cases to the Commissioner, including complaints made against their own department which they might find difficult to deal with themselves in their capacity as constituency Members.

12. The second type of case is where a Member neither refers a *prima facie* investigable case to the Parliamentary Commissioner nor resolves it himself to the satisfaction of his constituent. The Commissioner said in evidence to Your Committee on 28 July [1978] that in the present Parliament 63 Members had never referred a case to him or to his predecessor, although 13 of that number had referred cases to him in his capacity as Health Service Commissioner.[24] It may be that all these Members have dealt with their constituency cases so effectively that there has been no need for them to refer anything to the Commissioner; it is possible, however, that at least some of them have not fully appreciated the role the Commissioner can play. Your Committee note that since the new procedure for access was introduced in March, at the same time as the Parliamentary Commissioner's widely publicised report on a war pensions case,[25] not only did members of the public respond by sending more complaints to the Commissioner in both his parliamentary and health service capacities, but the rate of referrals by Members of Parliament also increased and by 16 June it had reached a weekly figure about double the average for 1977.[26] Your Committee consider that there is a need for the Parliamentary Commissioner's work to be brought more forcefully to the attention not only of the general public but also of Members of Parliament.

Note

The Government in its Observations (Cmnd. 7449) was in agreement with this part of the Select Committee's report, and the P.C.A. regards the matter as closed for the

[24] Q. 472.

[25] Fourth Report of the Parliamentary Commissioner for Administration for 1977–78. *A War Pensions Injustice Remedied*, H.C. 312.

[26] [Minutes of] Evidence p. 146; Qs. 461–71.

moment (Annual Report for 1978, H.C. 205, Session 1978/9, para. 11 though note his view in para. 12). However, as the next extract will show, the Select Committee failed to convince JUSTICE, who had earlier recommended (*Our Fettered Ombudsman*, Ch. V) that there should be direct access to the P.C.A. as an alternative to access through an M.P. (Indeed, JUSTICE's report in 1961 (the Whyatt Report), which was influential in the establishment of the P.C.A., had envisaged the eventual disappearance of any filter.)

Fourth Report from The Select Committee on The Parliamentary Commissioner for Administration. The Jurisdiction of The Parliamentary Commissioner

H.C. 593, Session 1979/80

APPENDIX TO THE MINUTES OF EVIDENCE: ANNEX TO THE COMMENTS OF JUSTICE ON THE FOURTH REPORT OF THE SELECT COMMITTEE ON THE PARLIAMENTARY COMMISSIONER FOR ADMINISTRATION, SESSION 1977/8

Direct access to the Parliamentary Commissioner

1. The Select Committee advance two main arguments against direct access to the Ombudsman:

(i) that in a country as large as the UK the Ombudsman would be overwhelmed by the volume of complaints, and

(ii) that in any case it is the role of MPs to deal with complaints from their constituents, and direct access would undermine this part of their work; as the Select Committee put it, 'Each MP is an Ombudsman for his own constituents'.

Volume of complaints

2. This argument was referred to by the Government when the legislation was going through as 'a very subsidiary argument'. JUSTICE takes the view that if there is administrative injustice it should be remedied, whatever the volume.

3. There is no real reason to think that the Ombudsman would be flooded by direct access. When the office was set up, a case-load of 6,000–7,000 was anticipated. In the event, the case-load has only been about one-sixth of that. The Select Committee's calculation that, based on the New Zealand figure for complaints, a pro rata figure for the UK would be 40,000 a year is incorrect. The New Zealand Commissioner's figures given in evidence to the Select Committee included his local government functions. If the New Zealand figures are limited to central government, and to complaints within jurisdiction, the pro rata UK figure is about 15,000, not 40,000.

4. Whatever the volume of complaints, steps can be taken to deal with it. The Parliamentary Commissioner is at the moment a part-time appointment; he can be made full-time (ie, by hiving off the Health Services Commissioner

functions). Some of his investigations could be conducted with less intensity, and if necessary, further Ombudsmen could be appointed.

Role of MPs

5. The role of MPs as Ombudsmen suffers from two major defects when looked at from the citizen's point of view. First, it operates very unevenly, and second, it cannot be separated from the MPs political functions.

Unevenness

6. MPs vary greatly in the performance of their constituency functions; they perform their functions 'in roughly 600 different ways' (Mr Michael Foot, MP). Not all of them are interested in acting as Ombudsmen for their constituents. This unevenness is reflected in the way MPs have operated the Ombudsman 'filter'. Between 1970 and 1974, 25 per cent of MPs did not submit any complaints to the Ombudsman. From 1974 to 1975, some 12 per cent submitted no complaints. In 1975, only 381 MPs submitted complaints. Forty per cent submitted no complaints. . . . Of those who do send complaints, the number sent in any year varies between 1 and 12. The result is that the ordinary citizen, who is the touchstone, gets from MPs an Ombudsman service varying in effectiveness according to where he, the citizen, happens to live.

Politics

7. The Select Committee point out, and JUSTICE of course accepts, that 'Members are not concerned about, and usually do not know, the political allegiance of those who ask for their help, or advice, and in any case are anxious to do what they can for their constituents irrespective of party . . .' But some citizens do not see it like this, and have difficulty in separating the complaints function of their MP from his political function. The proposal of the Select Committee for a relaxation of the convention that a MP, who receives a complaint, always refers it to the constituency MP would help to meet this difficulty; but there would remain the case of the complainant with confidential matter, such as tax, health or domestic affairs, who does not want to involve any MP in it at all.

Conclusion

8. JUSTICE takes the view that with direct access the citizen would have an Ombudsman service which operates evenly throughout the country and which no citizen would hesitate to use. JUSTICE does not think that the complaints function of MPs would be weakened. It is not that the Parliamentary Commissioner has taken over any part of the functions of MPs; he has opened up an entirely new field of control over the administration which did not exist before. A large part of MPs' complaints work is concerned with the merits of administrative decisions, which are quite outside the Ombudsman's purview.

9. Finally, it may be useful to list the main consequences which flow from restricted access:

(i) The Ombudsman is restricted in the extent to which he can publicise his office. He must be careful not to present himself to the public as available to deal with their complaints, because he is not so available.

(ii) He cannot be permitted to investigate complaints on his own initiative, unlike most other Ombudsmen, because to do so would be to admit direct access by the back door (see paragraph 31 of the Select Committee Report).

(iii) He is limited to investigating bodies for which Ministers are answerable in Parliament (see paragraph 33 of Select Committee Report).[27] If other bodies require Ombudsmen, they will have to have separate ones.

(iv) He cannot report direct to the complainant. Not all complainants find this easy to understand.

(v) Limitations of access prevent Ombudsmen from transferring complaints one to another. If a Local Commissioner gets a complaint against a Government Department, for instance, he cannot send it on to the Parliamentary Commissioner.

10. The 'half-way house' procedure introduced at Easter 1978, whereby if the Parliamentary Commissioner receives a direct complaint he refers it to the constituency MP, asking whether the MP wishes the PC to deal with it, is a useful step but does not meet all the points listed above, or provide a fully effective and adequate Ombudsman system from the citizen's point of view.

Notes

1. The method discussed in the extract *supra* of offering to refer to M.P.s complaints received by the P.C.A. directly from members of the public (the 'half-way house') obviously weakens the case for direct access, but in JUSTICE's opinion does not destroy it. An important question is whether, despite the operation of the 'half-way house', any or many *prima facie* investigable complaints, which in a system of direct access would have been investigated further by the P.C.A., fall by the wayside. The statistics since the 'half-way house' has been operating are set out at p. 652 *infra* (and see further the Appendix). Two features of these statistics might be noted:

(*a*) The number of cases in which the P.C.A. thought it worthwhile to offer to pass the matter on to an M.P. has been a very small percentage of the number of direct written communications. This is surprising in the light of the view expressed in the Annual Report for 1977, H.C. 157, Session 1977/8 (before the 'half-way house' was operating) that 25% of the communications received directly from the public seemed to be *prima facie* investigable complaints.

(*b*) The figures for 1978 and 1980 show that some *prima facie* investigable cases are not being investigated by the P.C.A. In those years 15·52% and 18% respectively of those people with such complaints refused the P.C.A.'s offer to send the matter on to their M.P. We do not, of course, know the reason for this – and there could be several – but the presence of the 'M.P. filter' means that (though numerically small) a not insubstantial percentage of such complaints were not investigated in 1978 and 1980.

[27] [The Select Committee thought this was 'fundamental to the Parliamentary nature of his work'.]

	1978	1979	1980	1981
Number of direct written communications	1,777	822	1,194	870
Number of cases in which the offer was made to refer the matter to that person's M.P.	58	14	50	7
Number of cases so referred in which the M.P. referred the matter back to the P.C.A.	37	9	29*	7
Number of people who did not take up the offer	9	1†	9	–
Number of cases in which the M.P. decided to try to deal with it himself	12	–	7	–
Number of cases in which replies were awaited from M.P.s	–	3	5	–

* (+ 2 from 1979)   † (1 reply awaited)

2. The Select Committee in the extract at p. 645 *supra* referred to the 'M.P. filter' as a 'distinguishing feature' of the P.C.A. Apart from the case of the French Médiateur, it would seem that no other country has adopted any such device (see JUSTICE, *Our Fettered Ombudsman*, para. 40); nor is the use of a filter a general practice in the case of other Ombudsmen in the United Kingdom. A filter does exist in the case of the Northern Ireland P.C.A., but the Health Services Commissioners can receive complaints directly from the public, as can the Northern Ireland Commissioner for Complaints. The Local Commissioners are in a position somewhere between these two extremes. Section 26 (2) of the Local Government Act 1974 provides that a complaint must reach a Local Commissioner through a member of a local authority, but the Commissioner is also given a discretion to investigate a complaint received directly from a member of the public if he is satisfied that a member of an authority has failed to comply with a request to refer a complaint to him; for an example see *R.* v. *Local Commissioner for Administration for the North and East Area of England, ex p. Bradford M.C.C.* [1979] Q.B. 287.

The question of access to Ombudsmen in this country arose in a later Select Committee report (Second Report for the Session 1979/80, H.C. 254) in the context of a more general consideration of the system of Ombudsmen in the United Kingdom. The Committee discussed the possibility of a common system of access to all Ombudsmen. Perhaps the most obvious answer would have been to establish direct access in all cases, but the Committee thought that it was precluded from suggesting this solution because of the rejection of direct access to the P.C.A. in its earlier report. A different solution whereby, in addition to existing arrangements, M.P.s could refer complaints to any Ombudsman met with opposition and was also rejected. The Committee was left, however, with the feeling that the arrangements for access did perhaps leave something to be desired. See further the P.C.A.'s view in para. 13 of his Annual Report for 1978, H.C. 205, Session 1978/9.

3. Once a complaint has been passed on to the P.C.A. by an M.P., he may in his discretion refuse to carry out an investigation (s. 5 (1) and (5) of the 1967 Act, p. 623 *supra*), and the courts will not compel him to act: *Re Fletcher's Application* [1970] 2 All E.R. 527. Cf. *Padfield* v. *Minister of Agriculture, Fisheries and Food,* p. 164 *supra*. But suppose the P.C.A. were to refuse to investigate a complaint because he (erroneously) believed the action in question was not the responsibility of a depart-

ment listed in Sch. 2. Would a court refuse mandamus if it was limited to making him consider whether to investigate the complaint, as opposed to ordering him actually to investigate it (and see Jackson, [1971] P.L. 39 at p. 46)?

4. This section has been headed 'Complaints', but one question to consider is the extent to which the P.C.A. should have power to go beyond the redress of an individual complaint of maladministration. His mere existence – the possibility of an investigation – might be thought to make civil servants more careful and obviously a particular report, by virtue of criticizing some administrative practice, is likely to lead to an abandonment of that practice, a review of similar cases, and perhaps even to an internal review of some area of administration: for an example of this last result, see para. 15 of the Annual Report for 1979, H.C. 402, Session 1979/80. (For the role of the Select Committee in relation to improving administrative systems, see Gregory, [1982] P.L. 49 at pp. 63–6.) In these ways the general public is helped and Harlow, (1978) 41 M.L.R. 446 at p. 452 argues that 'his *primary* role should be that of an independent and unattached investigator, with a mandate to identify maladministration, recommend improved procedures and negotiate their implementation'. Harlow accordingly submits that any alteration in the P.C.A.'s jurisdiction or procedures should only be made if it serves that goal, rather than the objective of redressing individual grievances. Do you agree? Note also in this general context Bradley's suggestion ([1980] C.L.J. at p. 311) that since the P.C.A.'s case-work (in which, it seems, an informal precedent system has developed) will reveal what he considers to be good administration, 'new rights to the maintenance of a certain quality of administration' may be thought to have emerged from it.

But should the P.C.A.'s powers go further? Should he, like the New Zealand Ombudsman, be able to investigate something in the absence of a complaint, a position favoured by JUSTICE (*Our Fettered Ombudsman*, para. 67)? The Select Committee in paras. 30 and 31 of its Fourth Report for the Session 1977/8, H.C. 615 and 444, considered the question raised at the beginning of this Note and its two recommendations appear in a summarized form in the next extract.

Fourth Report from The Select Committee on The Parliamentary Commissioner for Administration (Review of Access and Jurisdiction) Session 1977/8. Observations by The Government

Cmnd. 7449 (1979)

(k) *The Commissioner should draw Parliament's attention to any unforeseen injustices resulting from legislation (paragraph 30)*

17. The Government believe that where the Commissioner finds a complaint to relate to the content of legislation, rather than to maladministration, he is already free to say so. However, as the Select Committee make clear, it is important to avoid any suggestion that 'the Commissioner might act as a constitutional court attempting to override Parliament's decisions'. It is for Parliament to consider whether legislation requires amendment, and it is open to Parliament, if it so wishes, to take note of any relevant findings of the Commissioner based on his examination of complaints from members of the public which he has investigated.

> (*l*) *The Commissioner should be able, subject to Your Committee's approval, to carry out inspections of branches or establishments of bodies within his jurisdiction (paragraph 31)*

18. The Government note the Select Committee's rejection of investigation by the Commissioner in the absence of direct evidence of possible maladministration; but that the Committee suggest that he should be able to extend the scope of his enquiries 'if, for example on the basis of complaints which he had investigated and upheld, the Commissioner had reason to believe that a particular branch or establishment . . . was not dealing efficiently with its business . . .'. The Committee think the Commissioner should be able, subject to their approval, 'to carry out a systematic investigation of all aspects of the work of the branch or establishment in question, with a view to identifying the cause of the problem and making recommendations for putting it right'.

19. This would represent a significant change in the nature of the Commissioner's role which the Government believe would be both unnecessary and undesirable. It would place a heavy burden on the Commissioner if he were required in effect to 'audit' the administrative competence of government departments and would distract him and his staff from their central purpose of investigating individual complaints. However, where the Commissioner investigates a series of complaints relating to a particular area of administration, he is, as a result of his normal investigations, able to form a clear view of the procedures in force there and to make any recommendations which he sees fit in consequence. Any lessons to be drawn from investigations by the Commissioner are already studied by departments and acted upon. In the nature of the present system of access to the Commissioner, the complaints which he investigates tend to be substantial ones. Section 10 (2) of the Act provides that in all cases the Commissioner shall send a report of the results of his investigation to the Principal Officer of the department concerned. The department is thus in a position to consider whether the act of maladministration was an isolated one, or whether it discloses wider deficiencies. The Government believe that it should be for Ministers and their departments to decide what action is necessary to prevent further maladministration by a particular branch or establishment, and to be answerable, as may be necessary, to Parliament for the adequacy of the action which has been taken to this end.

Note

The P.C.A. in para. 13 of his Annual Report for 1978, H.C. 205, Session 1978/9, commented that he regarded these two suggestions of the Select Committee as the most important of its proposals concerned with the extension of his jurisdiction. The views of JUSTICE, who support both recommendations, are also worthy of note, and are set out at p. 39 of the Fourth Report from the Select Committee on the P.C.A. for the Session 1979/80, H.C. 593. In relation to the 'unforeseen injustice' point, they would follow their earlier view expressed in *Our Fettered Ombudsmen*, para. 67, and go so far as to allow the P.C.A. to suggest changes both in the law and in departmental rules. In relation to the 'inspectorial power', they recorded that, when asking for such a power to be specifically granted in the 1967 Act, they received an assurance that it was implicit. Compare the view of the Government *supra*.

Investigation, reports, and remedies

Parliamentary Commissioner Act 1967, Sections 7–11, pp. 625–7 *supra*

Notes

1. Is the P.C.A. at an advantage compared with the courts in relation to claims for public interest immunity from the production of documents or the giving of evidence (see p. 461 *supra*); or does s. 8 (4) show that he can be at a disadvantage?

The Select Committee on the P.C.A. in its Fourth Report for the Session 1977/8, H.C. 615 and 444, suggested (at para. 34) that the P.C.A. should be allowed access to 'Cabinet or Cabinet committee papers in the very rare cases where he considered it necessary, except where the Attorney-General certified that such access would itself be "prejudicial to the safety of the State or otherwise contrary to the public interest".' The Government did not agree. In its observations on the Select Committee's report (Cmnd. 7449) the Government took the view (at para. 22) that there was no evidence indicating the current position posed any problems for the P.C.A. It was also stated that 'in more than eleven years since the Act came into force there has been no case in which the [P.C.A.] has indicated that any of his investigations were less than complete because of the relevant provision in the Act'. In so far as this was presented as an argument against any change, was it a good one? If the courts can look at and order disclosure of Cabinet papers (see Note 2, p. 484 *supra*), is there any reason why the P.C.A. should not be able to look at them? Note that the Parliamentary Commissioner Act was passed in 1967, shortly before the decision in *Conway* v. *Rimmer*, p. 461 *supra*.

2. The P.C.A., who, of course, has the Select Committee standing behind him, has not experienced much difficulty in practice in getting his recommendations followed, despite having no coercive powers. (For the role of the Select Committee in relation to remedies, see Gregory, [1982] P.L. 49 at pp. 55–63.) Furthermore, the P.C.A. has the power under s. 10 (3) of the Act to lay a special report before Parliament in this type of case. (Bear in mind also that certain coercive judicial remedies will not lie against the Government: see s. 21 of the Crown Proceedings Act 1947, p. 290 *supra*.) For a good example of compliance with a report from the P.C.A., see the Sachsenhausen case, H.C. 54, Session 1967/8. The relevant Minister (the Foreign Secretary) was prepared to change his decision even though he thought that the P.C.A. was wrong; compare the Government's reaction to the P.C.A.'s report on Court Line, H.C. 498, Session 1974/5, as evidenced in the debate on the report (897 H.C. Deb., cols. 532–86). See Wade, p. 78, and note, as he points out, that these two reports concerned decisions taken by Ministers: their actions can be investigated as well as those of their departments.

3. A comment by the then Foreign Secretary in the debate on the Sachsenhausen case can perhaps be used as a postscript to this chapter on the P.C.A. He said (758 H.C. Deb., col. 115):

When the Ombudsman has made enough decisions, perhaps we shall have an Ombudsman to look at the Ombudsman's decisions, and if he gets 100 per cent right, I shall be surprised.

APPENDIX

pp. 5, 315, 323, 327 and 419
Public law and private law

One result of the decision in *O'Reilly* v. *Mackman*, p. 324 *supra*, that a litigant who seeks a remedy for infringement of a right in public law, must, as a general rule, proceed by an application for judicial review (p. 315 *supra*), is that an important distinction is now made between public and private law. Dicey's argument in *The Law of the Constitution*, 10th edn., pp. 336 and 339, that the distinction between 'ordinary law' and 'administrative law' is alien to England can no longer be correct, if it ever was. Henceforth it will be vital to know whether one is dealing with a public or a private body and whether one is vindicating a public law or a private law right. The important procedural consequences of this, in particular the requirement of leave and the short time limit in public law cases which are designed to protect public authorities from harrassment and uncertainty, are discussed at pp. 315–20, 329–32 and 335–7 *supra*.

The Law Commission argued (see Note 1, p. 335 *supra*) that the application for judicial review should not be the exclusive way of impeaching the acts and omissions of public authorities, partly because of uncertainty as to what constituted 'public law' (*Report on Remedies in Administrative Law*, Law. Com. No. 73, Cmnd. 6407, para. 45); and for the difficulties of the distinction in French law, see Harlow, (1980) 43 M.L.R. 241. The uncertainty has not been resolved by *O'Reilly* v. *Mackman* or *Cocks* v. *Thanet D.C.* [1982] 3 W.L.R. 1121, noted at p. 336 *supra*, because in neither case was an attempt made to define 'public law' and 'private law' and rights 'protected by' or 'derived from' each category. The subsequent cases take matters a little further but the law is still at an early stage of development. In particular, it is not clear whether the distinction is to be drawn at the level of principles of substantive law (on which see *infra*) or only at the remedial level. However, it might be helpful to identify four possible methods of determining whether a court is concerned with a 'public law' issue.

First, the court may have regard to the source of the authority of the body in question. For instance, it could be argued that only the decisions of bodies whose power is derived from statute or prerogative (on which see p. 10 *supra*) can generate a public law issue. However, this test is not altogether satisfactory. Not only would it bring into public law the activities of any private company whose activities are to some extent regulated by statute (see for instance *Allen* v. *Gulf Oil Refining Ltd* [1981] A.C. 1001, noted at p. 411 *supra*), but it also fails to recognise that not all the activities of public authorities raise public law issues. Thus, although a local authority's powers in general are derived from statute, it may be treated as in the same position as a private person in respect of many of its activities: see the *Pride of Derby* case [1953] Ch. 149, noted at p. 411 *supra*, and *Page Motors Ltd.* v. *Epsom & Ewell B.C.* (1982) 80 L.G.R. 337. In the latter case it was said that the question whether the occupation of council land by gypsies constituted a nuisance by the Council did not raise questions of public law since the duty of the Council arose in its capacity as an occupier of land and the nuisance had not arisen out of the exercise of a statutory power. The substantive law principle that gives a public authority immunity from attack for breach of duty provided it is acting intra vires, i.e. the public law immunity from suit that was established by *Anns* v. *Merton L.B.C.*, p. 412 *supra*, did not therefore apply in the circumstances of *Page Motors*.

However, asking whether the issue arose out of the *exercise* of a statutory power does not obviate the difficulties. Thus, the exercise of functions under the Housing (Homeless Persons) Act 1977 was held, in *Cocks* v. *Thanet D.C.* [1982] 3 W.L.R. 1121, noted at p. 336 *supra*, to involve both public and private law issues. The public law issue concerned the Council's discretionary 'decision-making' functions as to whether the matters giving rise to a duty to re-house were established. Once the Council had decided that these matters were established, it had further 'executive functions' since rights and obligations were immediately created in private law. The Council's decision on the public law issue could only be challenged on limited grounds and by an application for judicial review, but the private law duties were enforceable by injunction and damages. Furthermore, in *Page Motors* itself, although the court held the Council's duty to abate the nuisance to be a matter of private law, it took account of the fact that it was a public authority in deciding whether the delay in abating it was reasonable.

Another difficulty with the 'source of power' approach is that substantive principles typically associated with 'public law', for instance natural justice and arguably the principles governing the exercise of discretionary powers, have been applied to bodies deriving their authority from contract: *Enderby Town F.C. Ltd.* v. *F.A. Ltd.*, p. 246 *supra*; *R.* v. *B.B.C., ex p. Lavelle* [1983] 1 W.L.R. 23, noted at (1983) 12 I.L.J. 43, and see *infra*.

A second approach is to ask whether the body in question exercises governmental powers (see, in a different context, the words from *Cassell & Co. Ltd.* v. *Broome* [1972] A.C. 1027, quoted at p. 407 *supra*). This is subject to some of the disadvantages of the 'source of power' approach. For instance, it does not adequately explain the applicability of the rules of natural justice to trade unions and domestic tribunals. The basis of this is an implied term in the contract between individuals or that between individuals and the body, but arguably one reason for the implication is that the courts have been influenced by the de facto power exercised by such bodies, and considered that this power imposes certain public responsibilities on them. It will also still be necessary to ask whether a particular power is exercised *qua* government or in some other capacity such as landowner or employer. Furthermore, difficult questions would arise in relation to what have been termed 'quangos' (such as the University Grants Committee or the Commission for Racial Equality which enjoy a certain measure of independence from government) and in relation to other emanations of government (such as Regional Health Authorities). Consider also the passage quoted in Note 2, p. 435 *supra*.

The third approach in determining whether an issue is a part of public law is to take account of the scope of the prerogative remedies. In the context of determining the ambit of the application for judicial review the courts have clearly been influenced by this, on which see s. 31(2)(*a*) of the Supreme Court Act 1981, p. 315 *supra*, Note 2, p. 322 *supra* and Lord Diplock's formulation at p. 328 *supra*. Thus, in *R.* v. *B.B.C., ex p. Lavelle* [1981] 1 W.L.R. 23 at p. 31 it was held that because a disciplinary appeal procedure set up by the B.B.C. depended purely upon the contract of employment between the applicant and the B.B.C., it was of a purely private or domestic character. It was not therefore sufficiently 'public' to permit proceedings by an application for judicial review.

Regard was also had to the scope of the prerogative orders in *Tozer* v. *National Greyhound Racing Club Ltd.*, The Times, 16 May 1983, which involved a club that was in practice the governing body of the sport. There it was said, *inter alia*, that the club had no relationship with members of the public other than those who chose to enter into contractual relations with it. Even though the club controlled most of the greyhound racing in this country and could, by suspending members, deprive them of their livelihood as greyhound trainers, its activities did not involve any element of public law so as to justify the mandatory use of the application for judicial review. To determine the limits of 'public law' today by reference to the availability in the past of the prerogative remedies is not attractive. Where one is dealing with the governing body of a trade or profession, why should the 'public' or 'private' nature of that body depend on the historical accident of whether the body is regulated by statute, charter, or contract especially in view of the important procedural consequences that might flow from this. Compare *R.* v. *The Committee of Lloyd's, ex p. Posgate*, The Times, 12 January 1983, where an application for judicial review was available against Lloyd's which has statutory regulatory powers. In any event, the limitations on prerogative relief are not to be a rigid bar (see s. 31(2) of the Supreme Court Act 1981, p. 315 *supra*, and Note 2, p. 322 *supra*) and as the unavailability of an application for judicial review does not necessarily rule out the application of public law principles at the level of substantive law (see *R.* v. *B.B.C., ex p. Lavelle*), this approach is unlikely to be of assistance in marginal cases.

Another approach in the cases is to ask whether the issue involves challenging a power which has been committed to the jurisdiction of the authority in question. This was the approach taken in *Cocks* v. *Thanet D.C.* where the 'decision-making' functions raised questions of public law because the Council's discretion in relation to them could only be challenged on limited grounds, while the 'executive functions' were not seen as raising any issue as to the Council's jurisdiction. The need to underline the limited scope of judicial review of decisions committed to the jurisdiction of an authority was an important reason for requiring the proceedings to be brought by the 'public law' procedure of an application for judicial review, on which see Note 3, p. 336 *supra*.

One difficulty with this approach is that it ultimately boils down to whether a statute imposes a duty to the public in general or to individuals, a difficult and often speculative question of interpretation on which see p. 424 *supra*; Wade, p. 665; Winfield and Jolowicz on *Tort*, 11th edn., pp. 155–9. Furthermore, the policy factors favouring the protection of public authorities from harrassment and uncertainty are not obviously inapplicable when private law rights are asserted against a public authority, except on the basis that 'public' rights are less deserving of protection than 'private' rights. Finally, this approach does not comfortably accommodate those situations in which the duty is held to be owed to individuals but nevertheless depends on an 'ultra vires breach of duty', on which see *Meade* v. *Haringey L.B.C.*, p. 397 *supra*: see also p. 424 *supra*, and for comment see p. 401 *supra*.

On this approach, cases in which it is a precondition to a claim for damages for negligence or breach of statutory duty that a public body's acts or omissions are ultra vires could be regarded, at the level of substantive principle, as 'public law' cases (see *Anns* v. *Merton L.B.C.*, p. 412 *supra*). It is therefore arguable that they should also be treated as such at the remedial level, i.e. subject exclusively to the procedure by application for judicial review: see Question 3, p. 419 *supra*.

The Court of Appeal's decision in *Davy* v. *Spelthorne B.C.*, The Times, 10 February 1983, in which it was held that in certain circumstances a claim founded on a private law right might raise a question of public law, is of interest in this context. The plaintiff sought an injunction to prevent the implementation of an enforcement notice requiring the discontinuance of the use of premises as a concrete works, and damages arising from the loss of the right to appeal against the notice. The basis of the claim for an injunction was an agreement by the local authority not to enforce the notice for three years provided the plaintiff did not appeal against it and the basis of the claim for damages was an allegation that the failure to appeal was the result of negligent advice by the defendant local authority.

It was accepted that all the causes of action were founded on private law rights. It was nevertheless held that any injunction would in substance attack the validity of the enforcement notice, 'a perfectly valid statutory order made for public purposes' (protection of the amenity of the locality). The remedy would therefore operate in the field of public law and for this reason the application for judicial review was the appropriate route for relief. It was also argued that the claim for damages, which, unlike the first claim, depended upon the notice being held valid, should also be brought by an application for judicial review since the risk of heavy damages was likely to deflect the local authority from the disinterested discharge of its public duties. The court, however, declined to compel the plaintiff to proceed by an application for judicial review with its requirement of leave and short time limit unless he successfully applied for leave to seek judicial review in respect of his claim for an injunction. In this event, because it was thought desirable that all the proceedings should be determined by the same court, the damages claim would have to continue as part of the application for judicial review. Might this pose a dilemma for the litigant in this type of situation?

The result of *Davy* v. *Spelthorne B.C.* is that even where rights in private law are asserted against a public authority, the case will be regarded as a public law case if the *necessary effect* of the relief sought is to prevent a valid statutory order having any adverse consequences on an individual, i.e. in substance having the same effect as a successful application for certiorari or a declaration. Is this consistent with *O'Reilly* v. *Mackman*? It will not, however, be regarded as a public law case merely because a remedy might *in practice* influence the authority in discharging its public law duties. Although it is difficult to see why the *effect* of a remedy necessarily justifies the exclusivity of the application for judicial review (see, for instance, the exception stated by Lord Diplock in *O'Reilly* v. *Mackman*, p. 334 *supra*, for matters arising as a collateral issue), the result in *Davy*'s case can be justified on the basis that the plaintiff could only have established his private law right by showing that the agreement did not constitute an improper fetter on the statutory duties of the local authority; on this point see further p. 147 *supra* and *R.* v. *I.R.C., ex p. Preston* [1983] 2 All E.R. 300, noted *infra*.

pp. 51, 85, 190, 320 and 336.

In *R.* v. *Secretary of State for the Home Department, ex p. Khawaja* [1983] 2 W.L.R. 321 the House of Lords held that an immigration officer is only entitled to order the detention and removal of a person who has entered the country by virtue of an ex facie valid permission if that person *is in fact* an illegal entrant, i.e. that this is a 'precedent' fact to the officer's jurisdiction. The reason for so holding was that any exercise of this draconian power would inevitably involve infringing the liberty of those subjected to it, a consideration that outweighed any difficulties in the administration of immigration control which might result from the redetermination of facts by a reviewing court: see [1983] 2 W.L.R. 321 at pp. 330, 338, 342, 352, 354 and 359. Although the decision was unanimous, Lord Wilberforce did point out (at pp. 334 and 337–8) that, while the procedural means exist to review facts by affidavit evidence and cross-examination (on which see Note 8, p. 319 *supra*), the court's investigation of facts is of a supervisory character and not by way of appeal. The limits of the court's power, he said, are dictated by the fact that they cannot repeat the extensive fact finding operations of the immigration officers. The court should therefore appraise the quality of the evidence and decide whether it justifies the conclusion reached. If the court is not satisfied as to the evidence, it may remit the matter for reconsideration or itself receive further evidence, and should quash the order where the evidence was not such as the authority should have relied upon, where it does not justify the decision or where there has been a serious procedural irregularity. See also Lord Templeman at pp. 359–60; the other members of the court do not expressly comment on this point. Compare *ex p. Zerek*, p. 51 *supra*.

pp. 62 and 77

R. v. Knightsbridge Crown Court, ex p. International Sporting Club (London) Ltd., p. 73 *supra*, was referred to in *R. v. Knightsbridge Crown Court, ex p. The Aspinall Curzon Ltd.*, The Times, 16 December 1982. In this case Woolf J. stated that a court could look at affidavit evidence that was not technically part of the record to find an error of law. He regarded the restriction on certiorari – that the error of law appear on the face of the record – as largely a result of the procedural history of the remedy, and thought that his approach was justified by the introduction of s. 31 of the Supreme Court Act 1981, p. 315 *supra*, and the different procedure now to be found in the new Ord. 53, especially r. 8, p. 318 *supra*.

It is only if the error of law is non-jurisdictional that it must appear on the face of the record, and so Woolf J. must have been concerned with such an error or he need not have troubled himself with the question of the record. However, if affidavit evidence is available to reveal a non-jurisdictional error of law, which can then be quashed, the difficult question concerning the extent to which all errors of law are jurisdictional (see p. 53 *supra*) becomes in practice irrelevant for the purpose of the amenability of an error to review. Is this consistent with the views expressed on errors of law in *Re Racal Communications Ltd.*, p. 59 *supra*, and *O'Reilly v. Mackman*, p. 328 *supra*? On *ex p. The Aspinall Curzon Ltd.* see also *R. v. South Western JJ., ex p. Wandsworth L.B.C.*, The Times, 20 January 1983.

pp. 129 and 295

In *R. v. Boundary Commission, ex p. Foot* [1983] 2 W.L.R. 458 it was stated by the Court of Appeal that, although it is no part of the function or duty of the courts to review or intervene in any matter which pertains to Parliament itself, it can ensure that the instructions of Parliament to an independent advisory body, the Boundary Commission, are carried out. Thus, the fact that the Commission's task was ancilliary to something which was exclusively the responsibility of Parliament, namely the final decision on parliamentary representation and constituency boundaries, did not preclude judicial review, although it might well make the court 'more slow to intervene' than it would be in relation to the activities of many other public authorities: see [1983] 2 W.L.R. 458 at pp. 465, 474–5 and 483.

p. 144

In *R. v. Police Complaints Board, ex p. Madden* [1983] 1 W.L.R. 447 McNeill J. said (at p. 470) that this 'fettered discretion' rule 'is strictly only a label for one aspect of natural justice'. Do you agree? Cf. Note 2, p. 203 *supra*.

p. 163

See also *Attorney-General of Hong Kong v. Ng Yuen Shiu* [1983] 2 W.L.R. 735, noted *infra*, and *R. v. I.R.C., ex p. Preston* [1983] 2 All E.R. 300. In *ex p. Preston* Woolf J. held that discretion in the I.R.C. was limited by, *inter alia*, a duty to treat taxpayers fairly. It was 'incumbent on the individual or individuals exercising the discretion to have regard to the fairness or otherwise of what they are doing' (p. 306). In this case the power could not be exercised without regard to an earlier agreement by the I.R.C. not to inquire further into the tax affairs of the taxpayer in return for certain undertakings by him. This would seem to be a substantive concept of fairness. See also p. 143 *supra* on consistency and p. 283 *supra* on 'acting fairly'.

pp. 174 and 180

In *R. v. Rochdale M.B.C., ex p. Cromer Ring Mill Ltd.* [1982] 3 All E.R. 761, Forbes J. (at p. 770) approved of the statement in de Smith (p. 340) that, if 'the influence of irrelevant factors is established, it does not appear to be necessary to prove that they were the sole or even the dominant influence; it seems to be enough to prove that their influence was substantial'. He also appears to agree with de Smith's view that 'it is immaterial that an authority may have considered irrelevant matters in arriving at its decision if it has not allowed itself to be influenced by those matters', on which see Note 3, p. 174 *supra*.

p. 225

In *Attorney-General of Hong Kong v. Ng Yuen Shiu* [1983] 2 W.L.R. 735 the Privy Council held that a member of a class of illegal immigrants in respect of which the authorities had stated that 'each case will be treated on its merits' had, by virtue of this statement, a 'legitimate expectation' of being accorded a hearing. The concept was said to include expectations which go beyond enforceable legal rights provided they have some reasonable basis, and an undertaking by a public authority as to the procedure it would follow bound it, provided the undertaking did not conflict with its statutory duty. Cf. *R. v. Haringey L.B. Leader's Investigative Panel, ex p. Edwards*, The Times, 22 March 1983, where it was held that leave to cross-examine did not found a legitimate expectation from which the panel could not resile since the applicant was not prejudiced by the withdrawal of leave. On the question of prejudice see Note 3, p. 240 *supra*.

p. 240

In *Cheall* v. *A.P.E.X.* [1983] 2 W.L.R. 679 one issue was whether the plaintiff had a right to be heard by the executive council of the defendant union before his membership of the union was terminated (so as to comply with a decision of a Disputes Committee of the T.U.C.). The House of Lords held that the plaintiff had no such right since the decision was inevitable and agreed with the view of the trial judge ([1982] I.C.R. 231 at p. 250) that to have given a hearing 'where nothing he said could affect the outcome would . . . have been a cruel deception'. See generally [1982] I.C.R. at pp. 249–50. The trial judge (Bingham J.) did say that the position might have been different if misconduct had been alleged. Do you think that the position would have been different if an allegation of misconduct had in fact been made, even though dismissal was inevitable for a reason unconnected with that misconduct? More generally, should a court be concerned with whether it was in fact inevitable that a particular decision would be reached or whether it would appear to the person affected or to the public that it was inevitable? Consider the judgment of Donaldson L.J. when *Cheall* v. *A.P.E.X.* was before the Court of Appeal: [1983] Q.B. 126 at p. 144, and see Note 3, p. 240 *supra*; cf. the judgment of Bingham J. and the House of Lords in that case. *Cheall* v. *A.P.E.X.* involved a claim for a declaration in an action begun by writ, as opposed to an application for judicial review. Might the type of procedure by which relief is sought (e.g. in relation to the method by which facts are proved) be at all relevant to the problem under consideration here?

p. 299

Consider *Tozer* v. *National Greyhound Racing Club Ltd.*, discussed in the Note on public and private law *supra*. Would the restriction on the availability of a declaration in *Punton* v. *Minister of Pensions and National Insurance (No. 2)* [1964] 1 W.L.R. 26 limit the utility of a declaration against a body such as the Greyhound Racing Club (i.e. one not 'public' for the purposes of Ord. 53)?

p. 411

Two recent cases dealing with the defence of statutory authority to an action in nuisance (*Department of Transport* v. *N.W. Water Authority* [1983] 1 All E.R. 892; *Tate & Lyle Industries Ltd.* v. *G.L.C.* [1983] 2 W.L.R. 649 have, *inter alia*, highlighted the view of Lord Wilberforce in *Allen* v. *Gulf Oil Refining Ltd.* [1981] A.C. 1001 concerning the role of negligence in this field (and see p. 409 *supra*). Lord Wilberforce referred to the requirement that, to secure immunity from suit, statutory powers must be exercised without negligence. He stated (at p. 1011) that the word 'negligence' is used here 'in a special sense so as to require the undertaker, as a condition of obtaining immunity from action, to carry out the work and conduct the operation with all reasonable regard and care for the interests of other persons'. How does this differ from the normal meaning of negligence? Consider Buckley, *The Law of Nuisance*, p. 21 and pp. 87–8.

p. 482

In *Air Canada* v. *Secretary of State for Trade* (No. 2) [1983] 2 W.L.R. 494 the House of Lords considered the circumstances in which documents, the subject of a 'class' claim for public interest immunity, should be inspected by the court. Although the 'reasonable probability' or 'likely' test that was applied by the majority in the *Burmah Oil* case (but cf. Lord Wilberforce's more rigid requirement of 'a strong positive case', p. 476 *supra*) was applied, a majority of their Lordships held that the criterion for determining whether to inspect or not is whether the party seeking production can establish that it is likely that the documents will assist his case or damage that of his opponent. Lord Scarman and Lord Templeman took a different view and stated that the criterion should be whether it is likely that the documents are necessary for the fair disposition of the case. In the *Burmah Oil* case, although it had been argued that the documents would support Burmah's case, this precise point had not been in issue. The view that prevailed in the *Air Canada* case reflects the formulations of Lord Edmund-Davies and Lord Keith in the *Burmah Oil* case (pp. 477 and 480 *supra*), but note that, in *Burmah Oil*, the formulations of Lord Salmon ([1980] A.C. 1090 at p. 1145) and Lord Scarman (p. 482 *supra*) were in terms of the 'fair disposition of the case'. The majority view in the *Air Canada* case will prevent a party from discovering timeously a document fatal to his case and thereby saving all parties the heavy costs of litigation ([1983] 2 W.L.R. 494 at p. 535). How would a person set about proving what is in documents the contents of which have not been disclosed? Can it be argued that the practical effect of the *Air Canada* case is to resurrect Lord Wilberforce's minority view in *Burmah Oil*?

p. 484

In relation to Cabinet papers, in the *Air Canada* case Lord Fraser, with whose speech Lord Edmund-Davies concurred, said ([1983] 2 W.L.R. 494 at p. 523) that 'I do not think that even Cabinet minutes are completely immune from disclosure in a case where, for example, the issue in a litigation involves serious misconduct by a Cabinet Minister. . . . But while Cabinet documents do not have a complete immunity, they are entitled to a high degree of protection against disclosure.' Note further Lord Scarman's view ([1983] 2 W.L.R. at p. 534) that if 'it is a "contents claim"', e.g., a specific national security matter, the court will *ordinarily* accept the judgment of the minister' (emphasis added).

p. 652

In 1982 the Parliamentary Commissioner for Administration received 1,002 letters from the public. In eight cases he offered to refer the matter to the person's M.P. with a view to a referral back to him, and in five cases the offer was accepted. In four of these five cases the M.P. asked the P.C.A. to carry out an investigation, and in one case the M.P. preferred to take action himself. See the Parliamentary Commissioner for Administration's Annual Report for 1982, H.C. 257, Session 1982/3, para. 63.

INDEX